Business Policy

Text and Cases

Business Policy

Text and Cases

C. ROLAND CHRISTENSEN, D.C.S.
Robert Walmsley University Professor

KENNETH R. ANDREWS, PH.D.
Donald Kirk David Professor of
Business Administration

JOSEPH L. BOWER, D.B.A.
Professor of Business Administration

RICHARD G. HAMERMESH, PH.D.
Associate Professor of
Business Administration

MICHAEL E. PORTER, PH.D.
Professor of Business Administration

*All of the Graduate School of
Business Administration
Harvard University*

Sixth Edition   1987

Homewood, Illinois   60430

© RICHARD D. IRWIN, INC., 1965, 1969, 1973, 1978, 1982, and 1987

ISBN 0-256-03358-7

Library of Congress Catalog Card No. 86–82216

Printed in the United States of America

1 2 3 4 5 6 7 8 9 0 K 4 3 2 1 0 9 8 7

To
Edmund P. Learned
For reasons he knows well

Preface

This sixth edition of *Business Policy: Text and Cases* provides educational concepts, text, and cases for a course in Business Policy and/or Corporate Strategy. Building on previous editions, the authors have again incorporated a number of changes in both text and case material; we hope that modifications will increase the usefulness of this edition for all concerned.

In the development of this edition we have retained those cases which our users have found most helpful in accomplishing the objectives of their seminar or course. Many of our holdover cases are listed as all-time classic "best sellers" by the Harvard Business School Publishing Division. They provide, as many of you know, challenging and "fun" discussion vehicles for education in the policy process.

In this sixth edition, as in preceding efforts, we have emphasized four basic educational themes. First, this material focuses on the tasks of general management in leading the overall enterprise, in contrast to the tasks of a specialist manager whose responsibilities are limited to a subdepartment of the total organization. Second, our text and cases highlight strategic management as a key function and responsibility of the line general manager, not as a staff planning activity. Third, critical to the success of any firm is the general manager's ability to manage the *process* by which an organization both formulates and implements its strategy. These case histories encourage apprentice managers to practice vicariously the organizational process of goal definition and accomplishment. Finally, a study of this material emphasizes the importance of general management practice as a professional activity. The general manager is responsible to multiple constituencies with conflicting needs and goals. He or she must manage that organization so as to achieve both economic and social-ethical goals.

The text and cases in this edition expand the attention given to the interdependence of strategy formulation and implementation. We have always viewed achieving commitment to purpose as essential to superior accomplishment, but now participation in the process of setting and amending goals is more explicitly emphasized as essential to commitment. The kind of corporation implied by our approach is now more clearly than ever the responsive, innovative, informal, and flexible corporation that builds on the strengths and traditions of its past while adapting to and bringing about changes in the marketplaces. In an increasingly egalitarian world, the general manager who leads a traditional pyramidal organization faces a major question as to his or her authority and administrative practices. We believe that leadership of the kind of corporation most likely to thrive in the early 21st century makes itself influential in stimulating continuous consideration of strategic alternatives by everyone whose cooperation is essential to the success of the chosen purpose.

The evolution of this book has been encouraged by many individuals—both business managers and academic instructors and students—who have taken the time and effort to send us suggestions for improvements. We are in their debt. Their continuing interest has helped us to develop a Policy course which can be taught effectively at the undergraduate, graduate, and executive seminar levels.

All students of Business Policy participate in a long-term, evolving intellectual adventure. The basic administrative processes and problems with which Business Policy is concerned have been part of organizational life for centuries, but the history of Business Policy as an academic field dates back less than seven decades.

This edition builds on substantial contributions made by former and present Policy colleagues; it carries their efforts further along the way to better understanding and greater applicability. The specific core ideas—the concept of corporate strategy and the organizational plan used in this book—were developed at the Harvard Business School in the early 1960s under the leadership of Kenneth R. Andrews, C. Roland Christensen, and now Professor Emeritus Edmund P. Learned. While course concepts, material, and organization have undergone steady modification, course objectives have been maintained. In the hands of many colleagues developing cases, doing research in general management, and teaching in both years of the MBA Program and executive programs, the emphasis on elements of the concept of corporate strategy has changed. The first half of the MBA Business Policy course, now taught in the first year, expands the study of the company in its industry environment, with strong emphasis on competitive analysis and economic strategy. Part I of this book addresses economic strategy as a combination of market opportunity and resources that properly positions the company in its industry.

Our emphasis on the subjective elements essential to the embodiment of economic strategy into the broader corporate strategy has moved to a new second part of the Business Policy course, now required in the second year. An experimental capstone course, primarily concerned with leadership of the formulation and implementation processes, combines the substance of a formerly separate course in Organizational Behavior with a traditional Business Policy concern for the organized accomplishment of purpose. We are not sure how this experiment will turn out, but nothing in the new course format invalidates the structure we provide here for the inquiry into the work of general management.

The concept of corporate strategy articulated in this book has been derived from the careful study in hundreds of company situations of the uniformities that constitute the way decisions about corporate strategy are made and carried out. Distinguishing more from less successful experience has led to a theory about how the formulation and execution of corporate purpose can be more effective against all the economic, organizational, and social tests that are properly applied to it. The idea of corporate strategy is a simple practitioner's theory. It is a kind of Everyman's conceptual scheme made for use in real life in unstructured, complex, and unique situations. Brought to its full power in intelligent use, it is capable of including the most extensive combination of interrelated variables involved in the most important of all business decisions.

The first function of the general manager, as we say again later, is leadership of the continuous process of determining the nature of the enterprise and setting, revising, and attempting to achieve its goals. Corporate strategy, as a concept, defines the manager's central function, whether he or she is a staff specialist contributing in depth and detail to the identification of alternatives, or the senior executive who must finally sign off on the decision and submit it to the board of directors.

Our modest characterization of this conceptual scheme as finding its power only in its application to the unique situation (that is, history, organization, present strengths, and future opportunity) of a particular company should not mislead you. It has been derived, not from theoretical modeling or laboratory inquiries and simulations of management science, but from experience. The authors, besides being familiar with the literature of strategic management and organizational behavior, have been teaching and doing research in Business Policy for a combined total of 130 years. They have written or supervised the preparation of more than 400 case studies of domestic, foreign, and multinational companies. They each have prepared or studied for class from 200 to 400 cases written by others. They have served as consultants to about 200 companies on strategy problems. They either now serve or have served on 30 different corporate boards of directors. Apart from case collections, they have authored 15 books, mostly research based.

We conclude from this varied experience that no more comprehensive or useful theory of general management is currently possible. The combination of objective and subjective elements, of economic and personal purposes, and of complex ethical and social responsibilities makes automatic outcomes impossible. Close competitive analysis may point to a generic economic or business strategy. A unique corporate strategy, however, will reflect judgment, aspiration, desire, and determination in ways which no theoretical model can prescribe. All-purpose management formulas are transparent fantasies. We cannot tell you from our conceptual scheme what the strategy should be in any one company we do not know; this book will help you find out, in a company you do know, how to approach your own conclusion.

How is this conceptual scheme translated into effective management practice? What is the relationship of strategy to the education of general managers? We would summarize our answers to these problems as follows:

The uniqueness of a good general manager lies in one's ability to lead effectively organizations whose complexities he or she can never fully understand, where a capacity to control directly the human and physical forces comprising that organization is severely limited, and where he or she must make or review and assume ultimate responsibility for present decisions which commit concretely major resources for a fluid and unknown future.

These circumstances—lack of knowledge, lack of an ability to control directly, and a mixture of past, present, and *future* time dimensions in every decision—make the concept of strategy so important for the generalist, senior manager. For strategy gives a manager reasonably clear indications of what one should try to know and understand in order to direct an organization's efforts. It counsels on what to decide, what to review, and what to ignore. It gives guidelines as to which critical, central activities and processes one should attempt to influence or, on rare occasions, attempt to control. It encourages a general manager to view every event and question from multiple time dimensions.

Chester Barnard said that the highest managerial traits are essentially intuitive, "being so complex and so rapid, often approaching the instantaneous, that they could not be analyzed by the person within whose brain they take place." If Barnard is correct, and we think that he is, how do those of us interested in management education strive to contribute to the development of future general managers? We do this first by disciplined classroom drill with the concept of strategy. Drill in the formal and analytic—what is the current strategy of the firm? What are its strengths and weaknesses? Where, in the firm's perceived industry, are profit and service opportunities? And how can those corporate capacities and industry opportunities be effectively related? This framework of questions helps to give order to the familiar chaos of complex organizations. It provides the manager with a map relating past, present and future, industry and company, and specific decisions to wider corporate strategy.

Moreover, this analytic classroom process focuses attention on a key administrative skill—the process of selecting and ordering data so that management asks the critical questions appropriate to a particular situation. Here the choice of abstraction level is key, for the question has to be stated in a way that avoids the specific that has no meaning and the general that has no content.

We seek also, via the classroom case discussion process, to educate in the nonlogical—that mixture of feelings and sentiment, comment and commitment, certainty and uncertainty—which goes into every decision and judgment. Such directed group discussions force attention to the human dimensions through which the analytic framework is filtered in real life. It serves further to emphasize the ongoing or process nature of the general manager's world.

It is a combination of these two forces—the analytic framework of strategic planning and the process framework emphasizing human interaction, the complexities of persons, and the difficulty of communication and persuasion—that make up our Business Policy educational fare. It is the discipline of practicing these two processes via a case discussion countless times that helps us to contribute to education for the future generalist.

The Business Policy subject area continues to evolve and develop. The need for professionally trained generalists—the men and women who make our organized society's critical decisions—is great. We continue to believe that this challenge will be met, at least in part, by all of us who work in the Policy area, both in academic and practical pursuits, throughout this country and the world. And we hope this book will be of some help in meeting that challenge.

C. Roland Christensen

Acknowledgments

The history of the Business Policy course at the Harvard Business School began in 1911, when a small group of instructors first developed a course outline and materials for a pioneering venture in education for general management. Those of us who currently teach and do research in the Business Policy area are in debt to those pioneers who provided the academic platform on which current efforts rest. We wish to especially recognize and thank the pioneering efforts of A. W. Shaw, the first Policy professor at the Harvard Business School, and M. T. Copeland, George Albert Smith, Jr., and Edmund P. Learned, who provided almost 60 years of dedicated leadership to course ideals and development. We are in their debt, as we are to those colleagues who worked under their leadership and who assisted in past course development.

Many members of the Harvard Business School faculty have contributed to the constant development of our field. We appreciate the help of the present members of the Business Policy teaching group: Francis J. Aguilar, Joseph L. Badaracco, Christopher A. Bartlett, Norman A. Berg, J. Ronald Fox, Kenneth E. Goodpaster, James L. Heskett, John B. Matthews, Andrall E. Pearson, Malcolm S. Salter, Howard H. Stevenson, Philip A. Wellons, John R. Wells, David B. Yoffie, and Michael Y. Yoshino.

Our sincere appreciation goes to the supervisors and authors of the cases included in this edition. To the following our thanks: Francis J. Aguilar for General Electric: Strategic Position—1981 and (assisted by Robert E. Swensk) for Introductory Note to DAAG Europe and DAAG Europe (A); Melvin Anshen for Consolidated Petroleum Corporation;

Joseph L. Badaracco for Allied Chemical Corporation (A) and Southern Packaging (A); Alexander Bergmann for Air, Inc.; E. Tatum Christiansen for her cases, International Harvester (A), Mitek Corporation, and Schlumberger, Ltd.: Jean Riboud Excerpts from "A Certain Poetry"; Nass Dossabhoy for Cleveland Twist Drill (A), Note on the Major Home Appliance Industry—1984 (Condensed), and the Competitive Positioning in the Dishwasher Industry series; Karen D. Gordon and John P. Reed for Crown Cork & Seal Company, Inc., a revised case based on an earlier document written by James Garrison and William D. Guth; Christine Harris and Mark B. Fuller for Marks and Spencer, Ltd.; Pierre Goetschin for Noble Objectives—False Means?; John W. Hennessey for The Viking Air Compressor, Inc.; and Edward J. Hoff for The Soft Drink Industry in 1985 and The Seven-Up Company, Division of Philip Morris Incorporated.

We are also indebted to Edmund P. Learned for his development of The Rose Company case; Laura Nash for Peter Green's First Day; Elizabeth Lyman Rachel for the BIC Pen Corporation (A) and (B) cases; David C. Rikert and Michael J. Roberts for the NIKE series; and John W. Rosenblum for the Basic Industries and Industrial Products, Inc. cases.

We would also like to thank Thomas W. Shreeve for Marshall-Bartlett, Incorporated (A); Hirotaka Takeuchi for L. L. Bean, Inc., Corporate Strategy; Howard Stevenson for Head Ski Company, Inc.; Nancy Taubenslag for Rockwell International (A); Martha Weinberg for Continental Airlines (A); and H. Edward Wrapp (assisted by L. A. Guthart) for the Texas Instruments, Incorporated cases.

We continue to be indebted to Kenneth R. Andrews for the text material found in this book. His capacity to articulate course concepts and principles for a practitioner is demonstrated not only in this book but in his pioneering volume, *The Concept of Corporate Strategy.*[1]

We owe special thanks to M. Paul R. Jolles, chairman of Nestle Alimentana and chairman of the board of trustees of IMEDE; to M. Jacques Paternot, general manager, Nestle Alimentana, formerly a member of the Harvard Business School Visiting Committee; and finally to Dean Derek F. Abell, director of IMEDE, for their willingness to let us use IMEDE cases in this sixth edition. IMEDE continues as the leader in education for international and European general management.

Edmund P. Learned, a "great" in the development of the Business Policy field of study, continues to enjoy his well-deserved retirement. We rededicate this book to him. All who have been touched by his teaching and research efforts realize his major contributions to private

---

[1] Kenneth R. Andrews, *The Concept of Corporate Strategy,* rev. ed. (Homewood, Ill.: Dow Jones-Irwin, 1980).

and public administration. He was our teacher, counselor, and friend.

Dean John H. McArthur and Professor E. Raymond Corey, director of the Division of Research, provided us with intellectual support and practical administrative assistance. We are in their debt.

Dyanne Holdman took on the management task of producing this edition of *Business Policy: Text and Cases* and carried out this assignment with extraordinary efficiency and good humor.

We also thank Eve Bamford who has been most helpful in making editorial contributions.

We hope this book, in which the efforts of so many good people is compressed, will contribute to constructive concern for corporate purposes and accomplishments and to the continuing and effective study and practice of Business Policy, in private and semiprivate and public organizations.

C.R.C.
K.R.A.
J.L.B.
R.G.H.
M.E.P.

Contents

BOOK ONE
Determining Corporate Strategy   **113**

The Concept of Corporate Strategy   **115**
What Strategy Is. Summary Statements of Strategy. Reasons for Not
Articulating Strategy. Deducing Strategy from Behavior. Formulation
of Strategy. The Implementation of Strategy. Kinds of Strategies: *Low-
Growth Strategies. Forced-Growth Strategies.* Kinds of Companies.
Criteria for Evaluation. Problems in Evaluation. Application to Cases.

Cases

**The Company and Its Environment: Relating Opportunities to
Resources**   **227**
The Nature of the Company's Environment. Tracking the Changing
Environment. The Competitive Environment. Industry Structure.
Threat of Entry. Powerful Suppliers and Buyers. Substitute Products.
Rivalry. Industry Structure and the Formulation of Strategy.
Competitors: *Future Goals. Assumptions. Current Business Strategy.
Capabilities. Picking the Battleground.* Identification of Opportunities
and Risks. Opportunity as a Determinant of Strategy. Identifying
Corporate Competence and Resources. Application to Cases.

Cases

**The Company and Its Strategists: Relating Corporate
Strategy to Personal Values**   **393**
Strategy as Projection of Preference. The Inevitability of Values.
Reconciling Divergent Values. Modification of Values. Awareness of
Values.

Cases
Marks and Spencer, Ltd., 403
*Schlumberger, Ltd.: Jean Riboud Excerpts from "A Certain Poetry"
by Ken Auletta,* 430

The Company and Its Responsibilities to Society: Relating Corporate Strategy to Ethical Values 459

The Moral Component of Corporate Strategy. Categories of Concern: *Review of Management Concerns for Responsibility. Impact of Control Systems on Ethical Performance. The Individual and the Corporation. The Range of Concerns.* Choice of Strategic Alternatives for Social Action. Determination of Strategy.

Cases
Allied Chemical Corporation (A), 470
Consolidated Petroleum Corporation (Revised and Condensed), 486
Noble Objectives—False Means? 506
The Viking Air Compressor, Inc., 520
Peter Green's First Day, 526

BOOK TWO
Implementing Corporate Strategy 529

The Implementation of Strategy: Achieving Commitment to Purpose 531

Distorted Approaches to Implementation. Flexibility in Pursuit of Purpose. Implementation in the Innovative Corporation. Structure, Coordination, and Information Systems. Commitment.

Cases
The Adams Corporation (A), 541
The Rose Company, 546
Texas Instruments, Incorporated (A) (Condensed), 550
Texas Instruments, Incorporated (B), 557
Air, Inc., 567
Introductory Note to DAAG Europe, 572
DAAG Europe (A), 580
Mitek Corporation, 595
Cleveland Twist Drill (A), 620
Marshall-Bartlett, Incorporated (A), 644

The Implementation of Strategy: From Commitment to Results 663

Establishment of Standards and Measurement of Performance: *Need for Multiple Criteria. Effective Evaluation of Performance.* Incentives and Motivation: *Role of Incentive Pay. Nonmonetary Incentives. Constraints and Control: Formal Control. Integrating Formal and Social Control. Enforcing Ethical Standards.* Recruitment and Development of Management: *Continuing Education. Management Development and Corporate Purpose.*

In Retrospect: Strategic Management and Corporate Governance
Strategy as a Process. Managing the Process. The Strategic Function of the Board of Directors.

INTRODUCTION

Introduction

Business Policy as a Field of Study

This book is an instrument for the study of Business Policy. As a field in business administration, Policy is *the study of the functions and responsibilities of senior management,* the *crucial problems* that affect success in the total enterprise, and *the decisions* that determine the direction of the organization and shape its future. The problems of policy in business, like those of policy in public affairs, have to do with the choice of purposes, the development and recognition of organizational identity and character, the continuous definition of what needs to be done, the mobilization of resources for the attainment of goals in the face of competition or adverse circumstance, and the definition of standards for the enforcement of responsible and ethical behavior.

The Policy Point of View

In Business Policy, the problems considered and the point of view assumed in analyzing and dealing with them are those of the chief executive, chairman, or president, whose primary responsibility is the enterprise as a whole. But while the study of Business Policy (under whatever name it may be called) is considered the capstone of professional business education, its usefulness goes far beyond the direct preparation of future general managers and chief executives for the responsibilities of office. In an age of increasing complexity and advancing specialization, and in companies where no person knows how to do what every other person does, it becomes important that the functional specialists—controller, computer scientist, financial analyst, market researcher, purchasing agent—acquire a unique nontechnical capacity. This essential qualification is the ability to recognize corporate purpose; to recommend its clarification, development, or change; and to shape their own contributions, not by the canons of specializations but by their perception of what a cost-effective purposeful organization requires of them. The special needs of individuals and the technical requirements of specialized groups and disciplines inevitably exhibit expensive points of view that ultimately come into conflict with one another and with the central purposes of the organization they serve. The specialists who are able to exercise control over this tendency in organizations and keep their loyalty to the conventions of their own specialty subordinate to the needs of their company become free to make creative contributions to its progress and growth. To be thus effective in their organization, they must have a sense of its mission, of its character, and of its importance. If they do not know the purposes they serve, they can hardly serve them well. Most users of this book will neither be nor become corporate chief executive officers. But virtually all can benefit from the detachment implicit in the impartial, functionally unbiased, results-oriented attitude we will call the chief executive's point of view.

Relevance of Policy to All Organization Members

The purposes of organized effort in business as elsewhere are usually somewhat unclear, apparently contradictory, and constantly changing. Except in abstract language they cannot be communicated once and for all to the variety of persons whose effort and commitment are demanded. It is not enough, therefore, for senior executives to issue statements of policy and for junior managers to salute and go about their business. In each subunit of an organization and in each individual, corporate purpose must become meaningful in ways that announcement and repetition cannot accomplish. It must be brought into balance with individual and departmental needs, satisfactions, and noneconomic aspirations. But if corporate purpose is to be reconciled with (rather than subordinated to) individual and departmental purposes, then there must be widespread knowledge of the considerations on which corporate policy is based and understanding of the risks by which it is threatened. In addition, the adaptation of corporate purpose to changing circumstances, to tactical countermoves by competitors, or to newly identified opportunities is assisted if there can be *informed* participation in policy thinking by subordinate managers from different ranks and groups. This advantage, however, can be realized only if these subordinates are capable of looking beyond the narrow limits of their own professionalization. Thus the study of Policy is not as remote from the immediate concern of apprentice managers or students of business as it first appears. In fact whenever people are challenged—in business or out—by the problem of establishing goals for *themselves* that will shape productive and satisfying lives, they will find the study of the process of determining institutional purpose of central relevance. It is helpful to personal as well as to corporate decision. It permits discovery of the individual's own powers and the purposes to which they might well be devoted.

The study of Business Policy provides, therefore, a direct if distant preparation for performance as a general manager and a less direct but more immediate broadening of the perspective of the technician. In addition, it may be viewed as resulting in certain *knowledge, attitudes,* and *skills.* Some of these are unique to Policy studies. Others may have germinated in other activities in learning. But the latter are brought to fruition by examination of the most fundamental issues and problems that confront the professional manager in the course of a business career. It may prove useful to characterize briefly the expected outcomes.

Objectives in Knowledge

The choice of objectives and the *formulation* of policy to guide action in the *attainment* of objectives depend upon many variables unique to a given organization and situation. It is not possible to make useful generalizations about the nature of these variables or to classify their possible combinations in all situations. Knowledge of what, *in general,* Policy is and should be is incomplete and inconclusive. The knowledge to be gained from Policy studies is, therefore, primarily a familiarity with an approach to the policy problems of business and public affairs which makes it possible, in conjunction with attitudes and skills to be discussed later, to combine these variables into a pattern *valid for one organization.* This pattern may then be examined against accepted criteria and tested for its quality. Policy must first be a study of situations.

Knowledge of Concepts

The basic concept that students of Policy will in time come to understand is the concept of *strategy,* since the design and implementation of strategy provide the intellectual substance of this study. What is meant by *strategy* and, more important, how this concept may be usefully employed in the choice and accomplishment of purpose is the subject of the rest of this book. Strategy will be the idea unifying the discussions in which students will engage. These discussions will involve cerebral activities more important than simply acquiring information.

Knowledge of Situations

An abundance of information about business practice is, nonetheless, a by-product of the study of Business Policy and other cases. In their deliberately planned variety, the cases in this book encompass many industries, companies, and business situations. Although the information contained in these cases is provided mainly to permit consideration of policy issues, the importance of this incidental knowledge should not be underestimated. Breadth of exposure to the conventions, points of view, and practices of many industries is inoculation against the assumption that all industries are basically the same or that all men and women in business share the same values and beliefs. Thus consideration of the policy problems of a number of different industries guards against distraction by the particular in seeking out the nature of the universal.

For this reason it is hoped that students—although they may be, or plan to be, engineers in a utility or vice presidents of a railroad—will not resent learning about retailing in England. Knowledge of the environment and problems of other industries and companies is something that students may never consciously use. It will nevertheless widen the perspective they bring to their own problems. It may stimulate the imagination they put to work in introducing innovation into the obsolescent practices of their own industry. It should provide a broader base for their powers of generalization.

The study of strategy as a concept will be relatively systematic. The acquisition of information about the management problems of the many firms and industries whose strategic problems are presented in this book will be less orderly. Both are important. In particular the time spent in mastering the detail of the cases will ultimately seem to be of greater value than at first appears. Graduates of a demanding Policy course feel at home in any management situation and know at once how to begin to understand it.

The Literature of Policy

A considerable body of literature purporting to make general statements about policymaking and strategic management is in existence. It generally reflects either the unsystematically reported evidence of individuals or the logical projection to general management of concepts taken from engineering, economics, psychology, sociology, or mathematics. Neither suffices. What people wise in practice have to say is often instructive, but intuitive skill cannot be changed into conscious skill by exposition alone. The disciplines cited have much to do with business, but their purposes are not ours. Knowledge generated for one set of ends is not readily applicable to another. Besides reported experience and borrowed concepts, the literature of the field also includes independent research in Business Policy, guided by designs derived from the idea of strategy. Such research has been for some time under way and begins to make a claim on our attention. We shall often allude to the expository literature of Business Policy. The most useful literature for our purposes, however, is not that of general statements, but case studies.[1] These present not illustrations of principle but data from which generalizations may to a limited degree be derived and to which the idea of strategy may be usefully applied. The footnotes of the text portions of this book constitute a useful bibliography for further reading. The books referred to comprise a relevant but incidental source of knowledge. Look to these books in order to learn not information or theory but skills in using both.

Objectives in Attitudes

Knowledge of either concepts or cases is less the objective of the study of Policy than certain attitudes and skills. What managers know by way of verifiable fact about management appears to us less important than the attitudes, aspirations, and values they bring to their tasks. Instructors in Policy do not have a dogma which they force upon their students, but most of them, like their students, appear to be influenced in their analysis and conclusions by characteristic assumptions. Thus indoctrination is implicit in the study of ideas and cases included in this book. This indoctrination—tempered by the authors' exhortation to students to think for themselves—is comprised of some important beliefs of which you should be aware.

The Generalist Orientation

The attitudes appropriate to the resolution of policy problems are several. First, the frame of mind which you will be encouraged to adopt and which will influence the outcome of your thinking is that of the *generalist* rather than the specialist. Breadth, it follows, takes precedence over depth. Since attitudes appropriate for the generalist are not always appropriate for the specialist, the two will sometimes come into conflict. Efforts to resolve this conflict in practice should help to prove that breadth which is shallow is no more satisfactory than depth which is narrow.

The Practitioner Orientation

A second outlook encountered in the study of Business Policy is the point of view of the *practitioner* as opposed to that of the researcher

---

[1] In addition to the cases in this book, the reader is referred to such volumes as C. Roland Christensen, Norman A. Berg, and Malcolm S. Salter, *Policy Formulation and Administration,* 8th ed. (Homewood, Ill.: Richard D. Irwin, 1980); Michael E. Porter, *Cases in Competitive Strategy* (New York: Free Press, 1983); J. Ronald Fox, *Managing Business-Government Relations* (Homewood, Ill.: Richard D. Irwin, 1982); and John B. Matthews, Kenneth E. Goodpaster, and Laura L. Nash, *Policies and Persons* (New York: McGraw-Hill, 1985). Many other cases from a variety of sources are listed in the bibliographies of HBS Case Services, Soldiers Field, Boston, MA 02163.

or scientist. A willingness to act in the face of incomplete information and to run the risk of being proved wrong by subsequent events will be developed in the classroom as pressure is brought to bear on students to make decisions on the problems before them and to determine what they, as the managers responsible, would do about them. Despite the explosion of knowledge and the advance of electronic data processing, it is still true that decisions affecting the business firm as a whole must almost always be made in the face of incomplete information. Uncertainty is the lot of all thoughtful leaders who must act, whether they are in government, education, or business. Acceptance of the priority of risk taking and problem resolution over completeness of information is sometimes hard for students of science and engineering to achieve. Though natural and understandable, hesitation in the face of the managerial imperative to make decisions will impede the study of Policy. At the same time, rashness, overconfidence, and the impulse to act without analysis will be discouraged.

The Professional Orientation

The third set of attitudes to be developed is the orientation of the professional manager as distinct from the self-seeking contriver of deals and of the honest person rather than the artist in deception. The energetic opportunist sometimes has motives inconsistent with the approach to policy embodied in this book. This is not to say that quick response to opportunity and entrepreneurial energy are not qualities to be admired. Our assumption will be that the role of the business manager *includes but goes beyond* the entrepreneurial function. We shall examine what we acknowledge to be the obligations of the business community to the rest of society. We shall be concerned with the *quality* as well as the *clarity* of the alternative purposes we consider and of the values that govern our final choice. Maximum short-run profit is *not* what we mean when we consider the purpose of business enterprise. At the same time it is assumed that profit is indispensable. It is one of the necessary *results* of business activity.

The Innovative Manager

A fourth set of attitudes to be evoked is one that attaches more value to creativity and innovation than to maintenance of the status quo. We have grown accustomed to innovation stemming from new inventions and advancing technology. But suiting policy to changing circumstances includes also the application of a firm's long-established strengths to unexplored segments of the market via innovations in price, service, distribution, or merchandising.

In any course of study that has as its object enabling practitioners to learn more from subsequent experience than they otherwise might, the attitudes appropriate to the professional activity being taught are as important as knowledge. It is therefore expected that students will take time to determine for themselves the particular point of view, the values, and the morality they feel are appropriate to the effective exercise of general management skills. Much more could be said about the frame of mind and qualities of temperament that are most appropriate to business leadership, but we will expect these to exhibit themselves in the discussion of case problems.

Objectives in Skills

Extensive knowledge and positive attitudes, desirable as both are, come to nothing if not applied. The skills that a course in Business Policy seeks to develop and mature are at once analytical and administrative. Since even with a variety of stimulation and the use of case situations drawn from life, the reality of responsibility can only be approximated in a professional school, we may look to make most progress now in analytical power and to use it later in actual experience to develop executive ability.

Analytical Ability

The study of Policy cases, unlike, for example, the effort to comprehend these expository notes, requires the students to develop and broaden the analytical ability brought to the task from other studies. The policy problems of the total enterprise are not labeled as accounting, finance, marketing, production, or human problems. Students are not forewarned of the kind of problem they can expect and of which tool kit they should have with them. They must now consider problems in relation to one another, distinguish the more from the less important, and consider the impact of their approach to one problem upon all the others. They will bring to the cases their knowledge and abilities in special fields, but they will be asked to diagnose first the total situation and to persist in seeking out central problems through all the distraction offered by manifest symptoms.

The study of Policy, besides having its own jurisdiction, has an integrative function. It asks the analyst to view a company as an organic entity comprising a system in itself, but one related also to the larger systems of its environment. In each diagnostic situation, you are asked to pull together the separate concepts learned in functional and basic discipline courses and adapt them to a less structured set of problems. The strategic analyst must be able to see and to devise patterns of information, activities, and relationships. The facts given or the problems observed, if dealt with one at a time, soon overwhelm the mind.

Strategic Analysis

Besides extending to the company as a multifaceted whole the knowledge and analytic skills developed in less comprehensive studies, students of Policy must acquire some additional abilities. These are particularly needed to deal with the concept of strategy. Under the heading of thinking about strategy, you will be asked to examine the economic environment of the company, to determine the essential characteristics of the industry, to note its development and trends, and to estimate future opportunity and risks for firms of varying resources and competence. You will appraise the strengths and weaknesses of the particular firm you are studying when viewed against the background of its competition and its environment. You will be asked to estimate its capacity to *alter* as well as to *adapt* to the forces affecting it. Finally you will be expected to make a decision putting market opportunity and corporate capability together into a suitable entrepreneurial combination.

As you think about this decision you will encounter many feasible alternatives. Your own preferences for kind of product and the level of quality for price to be offered the consumer will influence your choice of product and market. Your values will influence your judgment and the reactions of your associates to your recommendations or decisions.

At this point you will realize the full measure of the new skill required. The strategic decision is the one that helps determine the nature of the business in which a company is to engage and the kind of company it is to be. It is effective for a long time. It has wide ramifications. It is the most important kind of decision to be made for the company. It requires the best judgment and analysis that can be brought to it. Practice in making this decision while still safe from most of the consequences of error is one of the most important advantages offered by an education for business.

Making Analysis Effective

But the analysis is not the whole of the task implied by the concept of strategy. Once the entrepreneurial decision has been determined, the resources of the organization must be mobilized to make it effective. Devising organizational relationships appropriate to the tasks to be performed, determining the specialized talents required, and assisting and providing for the development of individuals and subgroups are essential tasks of strategic management and policy implementation. These tasks, together with prescribing a system of incentives and controls appropriate to the performance required and determining the impetus that can be given to achievement by the general manager's personal style of leadership, demand that you bring to the discussion of Policy everything previously learned about administrative processes.

Administrative skills can be approached, though not captured, in the classroom. Patterns of action will be judged as consistent or inconsistent with the strategy selected according to criteria which must be developed. Students approach the study of Business Policy with skills nurtured in studies like accounting and control, personnel and human relations, financial management, manufacturing, and marketing. The balanced application of these skills to the accomplishment of chosen purpose in a unique organizational situation is the best test of their power. Any failure to see the impact on the total company of a decision based on the tenets of a special discipline will be sharply called to its proponent's attention by the defenders of other points of view. Conflicts of functional bias, which often lead to political stalemate, must yield at last to an integration dictated by corporate purpose.

General Management Skills

General management skills center intellectually upon relating the firm to its environment and administratively upon coordinating departmental specialties and points of view. Some students of business and even some students of Policy believe that these skills cannot be taught. General management is indeed an art to be learned only through years of responsible experience. And even through experience it can be learned only by those with the necessary native qualities: intelligence, a sense of responsibility, and administrative ability.

But if education means anything at all, students with the requisite native qualities can learn more readily and more certainly from experience and can more readily identify the kinds of experience to seek if they have at their disposal a conceptual framework with which to comprehend the analytical and administrative skills they will require and the nature of the situations in which they will find themselves. If, in addition, they have had practice in making and debating the merits of policy decisions, they will be more likely to grow in qualification for senior management responsibility than if they are submerged in operational detail and preoccupied by intricacies of technique.

This book is not a manual for policymakers or a how-to-do-it checklist for corporate planners. In fact it virtually ignores the mechanisms of planning on the grounds that, detached from strategy, they miss their mark. Our book is unaffected by the current backlash against a new kind of strategic planning we have never had in mind. We emphasize the long-term future, the development of superior competence, the recognition and encouragement of noneconomic values and ethical standards, and the need to measure the quality of performance other than by short-term profits and current share price. Our message is a strong challenge to the students of business who will seek wealth in the financial community rather than in building a business providing quality products important to customers or offering services that elevate the comfort, convenience, or quality of everyday life.

The central idea described here will indeed be useful for those more interested in capital markets than in providing goods and services or more interested in extracting personal wealth than increasing corporate wealth. But it is not designed for them. Nor do we think that even for the managers of productive businesses can the conceptual framework described here take the place of informed judgment. All the knowledge, professional attitudes, and analytical and administrative skills in the world cannot fully replace the intuitive genius of some of the natural entrepreneurs you will encounter in this book. Native powers cannot be counterfeited by reading books.

We do not propose the acquisition of knowledge in the usual sense. We plan instead to give men and women with latent imagination the opportunity to exercise it in a disciplined way under critical observation. We expect to prepare people for the assumption of responsibility by exposing them, for example, to the temptation of expediency. We plan to press for clarification of personal purposes and to challenge shoddy or ill-considered values. We expect to affect permanently analytical habits of mind in a way that will permit assimilation of all, rather than part, of experience. The ideas, attitudes, and skills here discussed are adequate for a lifetime of study of one of the most vitally important of all human activities—leadership in organizations. Education is the prelude to true learning.

Universal Need for Policy Skills

The need for general management ability is far too acute to be left to uninstructed development. The ideas, attitudes, and skills that comprise this study are much in demand not only throughout our own economy but also—in this age of rapid economic development abroad—throughout the world. The alleged failure of American management to adapt to new requirements for success in international competition can be traced to various kinds of counter-strategic shortsightedness. Leadership in industries no longer automatically dominated by American technology requires now, in companies large and small, a world perspective on opportunity. A changing society also requires new imagination in achieving productivity in organizations committed to energetic achievement.

In addition to their utility, these ideas are their own reward. For those who wish to lead an active life, or to provide for themselves and their families the material comfort and education that make culture possible, or to make substantial contributions to human welfare, the acquisition of policy skills is essential. Not all who turn to business are called to leadership, to be sure, but all are affected by it. No one suffers from study of its place in business.

The Nature of the Text and Cases

The vehicles here provided for making progress toward these objectives are the text and cases that follow. All the cases are drawn from real life; none is selected to prove a point or draw a moral. Accuracy has been attested to by the sources from which information was taken; disguise has not been allowed to alter essential issues.

The text is designed to assist in the development of an effective approach to the cases. Its content is important only if it helps students make their analyses, choose and defend their conclusions, and decide what ought to be done and how it can be accomplished.

The text is dispersed throughout the book so as to permit a step-by-step consideration of what is involved in corporate strategy and in the subactivities required for its formulation and implementation. The order of cases is only partially determined by the sequence of ideas in the text. Each case should be approached without preconceptions as to what is to come. To make conceptual progress without predetermining the students' analysis of the problem or the nature of their recommendations, the cases focus initially on problems in strategy formulation and later on problems of building the organization and leading it to the accomplishment of the tasks assigned. As the course unfolds, considerations pertinent to previous cases are included in new cases. Students should not feel constrained in their analysis by the position of the case in the book; they are free to decide that an apparent problem of strategy implementation is actually a problem of strategy choice. However, the increasing complexity of the material provided will enable most students to feel a natural and organic evolution of subject matter in keeping with their own evolving understanding, perspective, and skill.

The text suggests only that order is possible in approaching the enormous purview of Policy. The concept of strategy is an idea that experience has shown to be useful to researchers and practitioners alike in developing a comprehension of policy problems and a pragmatic approach to them. It is not a "theory" attended in the traditional sense by elegance and rigor. It is not really a "model," for the relationships designated by the concept are not quantifiable. But in lieu of a better theory or a more precise model, it will serve as an informing idea to which we can return again and again with increasing understanding after dealing with one unique case situation after another. The idea is intended to sharpen the analytical skills developed in the process of case discussion and to serve as the basis for identifying uniformities and generalizations that will be useful later on in practice. Our energies should be spent not so much on perfecting the definition of the concept as on using it in preparing to discuss the cases and in coming to conclusions about their issues. Students will not really learn how to distinguish effective from ineffective recommendations and good from bad judgment by study of these words or any others, but rather by active argument with their classmates under challenge by their instructors. Such discussion should always end in the clarification of standards and criteria. The cases, we know from experience, provide stimulating opportunity for productive differences of opinion.

To see how the complexity of choice among all the possibilities confronting a person or a company can be understood and managed by application of the idea of corporate strategy is an exciting illumination. Such insight banishes irresolution, empowers leadership, and unleashes the suppressed capability of organizations.

The Chief Executive's Job: Roles and Responsibilities

What General Management Is

We pointed out in the introduction to this book that Business Policy is essentially the study of the knowledge, skills, and attitudes constituting general management. *Management* we regard as leadership in the informed, planned, purposeful conduct of complex organized activity. *General* management is, in its simplest form, the management of a total enterprise or of an autonomous subunit. Before we examine some cases presenting the range of decision issues we will consider more thoroughly later on, we should look at the position of the general manager. The senior general manager in any organization is its chief executive officer, who for the purposes of simplicity we will often call the *president.* As we said earlier, the role of the chief executive in examining the situation of a company may be initially an uncomfortable assignment for students of some modesty who think themselves insufficiently prepared for such high responsibility. It is nonetheless the best vantage point from which to view the processes involved in (1) the conception of organization purpose, (2) the commitment of an organization to evolving but deliberately chosen purposes, and (3) the integrated effort appropriate to achieving purpose and sustaining adaptability.

Roles of the Chief Executive Officer

We will therefore begin by considering the *roles* that presidents must play. We will examine the *functions* or characteristic and natural actions

15

that they perform in the roles they assume. We will try to identify *skills* or abilities that put one's perceptions, judgment, and knowledge to effective use in executive performance. As we look at executive *roles, functions,* and *skills,* we may be able to define more clearly aspects of the *point of view* that provide the most suitable perspective for high-level executive judgment.

Many attempts to characterize executive roles and functions come to very little. Henri Fayol, originator of the classical school of management theory, identified the roles of planner, organizer, coordinator, and controller, initiating the construction by others of a later vocabulary of remarkable variety. Present-day students reject these categories as vague or abstract and indicative only of the objectives of some executive activity. Henry Mintzberg, who among other researchers has observed managers at work, identifies three sets of behavior—interpersonal, informational, and decisional. The interpersonal roles he designates as *figurehead* (for ceremonial duties), *leader* (of the work of his organization or unit), and *liaison* agent (for contacts outside his unit). Information roles can be designated as *monitor* (of information), *disseminator* (internally), and *spokesman* (externally). Decisional roles are called *entrepreneur, disturbance handler, resource allocator,* and *negotiator.* [1]

Empirical studies of what managers do are corrective of theory but not necessarily instructive in educating good managers. That most unprepared managers act intuitively rather than systematically in response to unanticipated pressures does not mean that the most effective do so to the same extent. If in fact the harried, improvisatory, overworked performers of 10 roles do not really know *what* they are doing or have any priorities besides degree of urgency, then we are not likely to find out what more effective management is from categorizing their activities. On the other hand it is futile to offer unrealistic exhortations about long-range planning and organizing to real-life victims of forced expediency.

The simplification which will serve our approach to Policy best will leave aside important but easily understood activities. The executive may make speeches, pick the silver pattern for the executive lunchroom, negotiate personally with important customers, and do many things human beings have to do for many reasons. Roles we may study in order to do a better job of general management can be viewed as those of *organization leader, personal leader,* and *chief architect of organization purpose.* As leader of persons grouped in a hierarchy of suborganizations, the president must be taskmaster, mediator, motivator, and organization designer. Since these roles do not have useful job descriptions saying what

---

[1] See Henry Mintzberg, *The Nature of Managerial Work* (New York: Harper & Row, 1973), and for a different pattern of roles, John P. Kotter, *The General Managers* (New York: Free Press, 1982).

to do, one might better estimate the nature of the overlapping responsibility of the head of an organization than to draw theoretical distinctions between categories. The personal influence of leaders becomes evident as they play the roles of communicator or exemplar and attract respect or affection. When we examine finally the president's role as architect of organization purpose, we may see entrepreneurial or improvisatory behavior if the organization is just being born. If the company is long since established, the part played may be more accurately designated as manager of the purpose-determining process or chief strategist.

Complexity of General Management Tasks

The point of this nontechnical classification of role is not its universality, exactness of definition, or inclusiveness. We seek only to establish that general managers face such an array of functions and must exercise so various a set of skills as to require a protean versatility as performing executives. When you see Howard Head invent and perfect the metal ski, set up his company, devise a merchandising and distribution program of a very special kind, you see him in a role different from his arranging for the future of his business, his maintaining year-round production in a cyclical industry in order to meet the needs of his work force, his withdrawal from supervision of the company, and his selection of a successor. We make no claim to definitiveness in distinguishing executive roles as just attempted. It is essential to note, however, that the job of the general manager demands successful action in a *variety* of roles that differ according to the nature of the problem observed or decision pending, the needs of the organization, or the personality and style of the president. The simpleminded adherence to one role—one personality determined, for example—will leave presidents miscast much of the time as the human drama they preside over unfolds.

We are in great need of a simple way to comprehend the total responsibility of chief executives. To multiply the list of tasks they must perform and the personal qualities they would do well to have would put general management capability beyond that of reasonably well-endowed human beings. Corporate chief executives are accountable for everything that goes on in their organizations. They must preside over a total enterprise made up often of the technical specialties in which they cannot possibly have personal expertness. They must know their company's markets and the ways in which they are changing. They must lead private lives as citizens in their communities and as family members, as individuals with their own needs and aspirations. Except for rare earlier experience, perhaps as general managers of a profit center in their own organizations, they have found no opportunity to practice being president before undertaking the office. Only the brief study of Policy, for which this book is intended to be the basis, has been available as the academic preparation for general management. New presidents are obliged to put behind them the specialized apparatus their education and functional experience have provided them. Engineers, for example, who continue to run their companies strictly as engineers will soon encounter financial and marketing problems, among others, that may force their removal.

This book, together with the directed series of case discussions which will bring its substance alive, is intended to provide a way for the observer to comprehend the complexity of the president's job and for the president to put past experience in a new perspective and comprehend the world of which he or she has been put in charge. We will elaborate briefly the functions, skills, and points of view which give force and substance to the major roles we have just designated. This may lay a foundation for later discussion of the performance of chief executives in the cases that follow. In due course we will have an organizing perspective to reduce to practicable order the otherwise impossible agenda of the president.

The CEO as Organization Leader

Chief executives are first and probably least pleasantly persons who are responsible for results attained in the present as designated by plans made previously. Nothing that we will say shortly about their concern for the people in their organizations or later about their responsibility to society can gainsay this immediate truth. Achieving acceptable results against expectations of increased earnings per share and return on the stockholder's investment requires the CEO or president to be continually informed and ready to intervene when results fall below what had been expected. Changing circumstances and competition produce emergencies upsetting well-laid plans. Resourcefulness in responding to crisis is a skill which most successful executives develop early.

But the organizational consequences of the critical taskmaster role require presidents to go beyond insistence upon achievement of planned results. They must see as their second principal function the creative maintenance and development of the organized capability that makes achievement possible. This activity leads to a third principle—the integration of the specialist functions which enable their organizations to perform the technical tasks in marketing, research and development, manufacturing, finance, control, and personnel, which proliferate as technology develops and tend to lead the company in all directions.[2] If this coordination is successful in harmonizing special staff activities, presidents will probably have performed the task of getting organizations to accept and order

---

[2] See P. R. Lawrence and J. W. Lorsch, *Organization and Environment: Managing Differentiation and Integration* (Boston: Harvard University Graduate School of Business Administration, 1967), for a study of the process of specialization and coordination.

priorities in accordance with the companies' objectives. Securing commitment to purpose is a central function of the president as organization leader.

The skills required by these functions reveal presidents not solely as taskmasters but as mediators and motivators as well. They need ability in the education and motivation of people and the evaluation of their performance, two functions which tend to work against one another. The former requires understanding of individual needs, which persist no matter what the economic purpose of the organization may be. The latter requires objective assessment of the technical requirements of the task assigned. The capability required here is also that required in the integration of functions and the mediation of the conflict bound to arise out of technical specialism. The integrating capacity of the chief executive extends to meshing the economic, technical, human, and moral dimensions of corporate activity and to relating the company to its immediate and more distant communities. It will show itself in the formal organization designs which are put into effect as the blueprint of the required structured cooperation.

The perspective demanded of successful organization leaders embraces both the primacy of organization goals and the validity of individual goals. Besides this dual appreciation, they exhibit an impartiality toward the specialized functions and have criteria enabling them to allocate organization resources against documented needs. The point of view of the leader of an organization almost by definition requires an overview of its relations not only to its internal constituencies but to the relevant institutions and forces of its external environment. We will come soon to a conceptual solution of the problems encountered in the role of organizational leader.

The CEO as Personal Leader

The functions, skills, and appropriate point of view of chief executives hold true no matter who they are or who make up their organizations. The functions that accompany presidential performance of their role as communicator of purpose and policy, as exemplar, and as the focal point for the respect or affection of subordinates vary much more according to personal energy, style, character, and integrity. Presidents contribute as persons to the quality of life and performance in their organizations. This is true whether they are dynamic or colorless. By example they educate junior executives to seek to emulate them or simply to learn from their behavior what they really expect. They have the opportunity to infuse organized effort with flair or distinction if they have the skill to dramatize the relationship between their own activities and the goals of corporate effort.

All persons in leadership positions have or attain power which in sophisticated organizations they invoke as humanely and reasonably as possible in order to avoid the stultifying effects of dictatorship, dominance, or even markedly superior capacity. Formally announced policy, backed by the authority of the chief executive, can be made effective to some degree by clarity of direction, intensity of supervision, and the exercise of sanctions in enforcement. But in areas of judgment where policy cannot be specified without becoming absurdly overdetailed, chief executives establish in their own demeanor even more than in policy statements the moral and ethical level of performance expected. At the national level of executive behavior, even presidents reveal in their deportment their real regard for the highest levels of ethical conduct. The results are traceable in the administrations of Presidents Kennedy, Johnson, Nixon, and Carter. Failure of personal leadership in the White House leads to demoralization different only in scale and influence from corporate analogies. The behavior of President Reagan strikingly illustrates the influence of personal style—one which outshines doubts about the wisdom of his foreign policy or his command of economic issues.

Formal correctness of structure and policy is not enough to inspire an organization. Enthusiasm for meeting ethical problems head on and avoiding shoddy solutions comes not so much from a system of rewards and punishments as from the sentiments of loyalty or courage stimulated by the personal deportment of the chief executive. By the persons they are, as much as by what they say and do, presidents and CEOs influence their organizations, affect the development of individuals, and set the level of organized performance. At this moment in the history of American business enterprise, conscious attention to the essential integrity of the chief executive becomes an important requirement if confidence in the corporate institutions of a democratic society is to be restored.

The skills of the effective personal leader are those of persuasion and articulation made possible by saying something worth saying and by understanding the sentiments and points of view being addressed. Leaders cultivate and embody relationships between themselves and their subordinates appropriate to the style of leadership they have chosen or fallen into. Some of the qualities lending distinction to this leadership cannot be deliberately contrived, even by an artful schemer. The maintenance of personal poise in adversity or emergency and the capacity for development as an emotionally mature person are essentially innate and developed capabilities. It is probably true that some personal preeminence in technical or social functions is either helpful or essential in demonstrating leadership related to the president's personal contribution. Credibility and cooperation depend upon demonstrated capacity of a kind more tangible and attractive than, for example, the noiseless coordination of staff activity.

The relevant aspects of the executive point of view brought to mind by activities in the role of personal leader are probably acknowledgment of one's personal needs and integrity as a person and acceptance of the importance to others of their own points of view, behavior, and feelings. Self-awareness will acquaint leaders with their own personal strengths and weaknesses and keep them mindful of the inevitable unevenness of their own preparation for the functions of general management. These qualities may be more important in the selection of a general manager than in the study of general management. But students of the cases that follow will quickly see the personal contributions of M. Bich in BIC Pens and the values of John Connelly in Crown Cork & Seal.

Michael Maccoby, author of *The Gamesman,*[3] once conducted a provocative inquiry into executive character types. Using some terms of dubious usefulness, he designates these as the craftsman, the jungle fighter, the company man, and the gamesman. The craftsman is dedicated to quality but unable to lead changing organizations. The jungle fighter is the antihero who after rising rapidly is destroyed by those he has used. The company man is committed to corporate integrity and success but is said to lack the daring required to lead innovative organizations. The gamesman is the dominant type—able and enthusiastic, a team leader whose main goal is the exhilaration of victory. His main defect is said to be that his work has developed his intellectual but not his emotional gifts. Despite the disclaimer that each person is a combination of types, these attention-getting labels produce caricature in the effort to distinguish overlapping or coexisting traits. Similarly, labels applied to roles suggest distance between them.

Despite the shortcomings of such classification, the work of psychoanalysts like Maccoby and Zaleznik brings support to the thesis developed here that such qualities as generosity, idealism, and courage should accompany the gifts of persons devoted to their company and its objectives. If Maccoby is right in saying that the gamesman (by which he seems to mean quarterback or captain) is the representative type in leading American corporations today, then we have come a long way from the Carnegies, Rockefellers, and Astors of the 19th century. We would still have a long way to go. The route passes directly through the pages that follow.

The prototype of the chief executives we are developing is, in short, the able victory-seeking organizational leader who is making sure in what is done and in the changes pioneered in purpose and practice that the game is worth playing, the victory worth seeking, and life and career worth living. If the stature of corporation presidents as professional persons is not manifest in their concern for their organizations, they will not perform effectively over time either in the role of organization or personal leader. If we concede that the gamesman should be concerned with what the game is for, we are ready to consider the role of the

---

[3] Michael Maccoby, *The Gamesman* (New York: Simon & Schuster, 1976).

president in the choice of corporate objectives. That choice determines what the contest is about.

The CEO as Architect of Organization Purpose

To go beyond the organizational and personal roles of leadership, we enter the sphere of organization purpose, where we may find the atmosphere somewhat rare and the going less easy. We think students of the companies described in these cases will note, as they see president after president cope or fail to cope with problems of various economic, political, social, or technical elements, that the contribution presidents make to their companies goes far beyond the apparently superficial activities that clutter their days.

The attention of presidents to organization needs must extend beyond answering letters of complaint from spouses of aggrieved employees to appraisal (for example) of the impact of their companies' information, incentive, and control systems upon individual behavior. Their personal contribution to their company goes far beyond easily understood attention to key customers and speeches to the Economic Club to the more subtle influence their own probity and character have on subordinates. We must turn now to activities even further out—away from immediate everyday decisions and emergencies. Some part of what a president does is oriented toward maintaining the development of a company over time and preparing for a future more distant than the time horizon appropriate to the roles and functions identified thus far.

The most difficult role—and the one we will concentrate on henceforth—of the chief executive of any organization is the one in which he serves as custodian of corporate objectives. The entrepreneurs who create a company know at the outset what they are up to. Their objectives are intensely personal, if not exclusively economic, and their passions may be patent protection and finance. If they succeed, like Howard Head, in passing successfully through the phase of personal entrepreneurship, where they or their bankers or families are likely to be the only members of the organization concerned with purpose, they find themselves in the role of planner, managing the process by which ideas for the future course of the company are conceived, evaluated, fought over, and accepted or rejected.

The presidential functions involved include establishing or presiding over the goal-setting and resource-allocation processes of the company, making or ratifying choice among strategic alternatives, and clarifying and defending the goals of the company against external attack or internal erosion. The installation of purpose in place of improvisation and the substitution of planned progress in place of drifting are probably the most demanding functions of the chief executive. Successful organization leadership requires great human skill, sensitivity, and administrative ability. Personal leadership is built upon personality and character. The capacity for determining and monitoring the adequacy of the organization's continuing purposes implies as well analytic intelligence of a high order. The president we are talking about is not a two-dimensional poster or television portrait.

The crucial skill of the president concerned with corporate purpose includes the creative generation or recognition of strategic alternatives made valid by developments in the marketplace and the capability and resources of the company. Along with this, in a combination not easily come by, runs the critical capacity to analyze the strengths and weaknesses of documented proposals. The ability to perceive with some objectivity corporate strengths and weaknesses is essential to sensible choice of goals, for the most attractive goal is not attainable without the strength to open the way to it through inertia and intense opposition, with all else that lies between.

Probably the skill most nearly unique to general management, as opposed to the management of functional or technical specialties, is the intellectual capacity to conceptualize corporate purpose and the dramatic skill to invest it with some degree of magnetism. As we will see, the skill can be exercised in industries less romantic than space, electronics, or environmental reclamation. John Connelly did it with tin cans. No sooner is a distinctive set of corporate objectives vividly delineated than the temptation to go beyond it sets in. Under some circumstances it is the president's function to defend properly focused purpose against superficially attractive diversification or corporate growth that glitters like fool's gold. Because defense of proper strategy can be interpreted as mindless conservatism, wholly appropriate defense of a still valid strategy requires courage, supported by detailed documentation.

Continuous monitoring, in any event, of the quality and continued suitability of corporate purpose is over time the most sophisticated and essential of all the functions of general management alluded to here. Because of its difficulty and vulnerability to current emergency, this function may not be present in some of the companies the student will encounter in the pages that follow. Because of its low visibility, this activity may not be noticed at first in cases where it is properly present. The perspective which sustains this function is the kind of creative discontent which prevents complacency even in good times and seeks continuous advancement of corporate and individual capacity and performance. It requires also constant attention to the future, as if the present did not offer problems and opportunities enough.

Enormity of the Task

Even so sketchy a record of what a president is called upon to do is likely to seem an academic idealization, given the disparity between the complexity of role and function and the modest qualifications of those pressed into office. Like the Molière character who discovered that for 40 years he had been speaking prose without knowing it, many managers have been programmed by instinct and experience to the kind of performance that we have attempted to decipher here. For the inexperienced, the catalog may seem impossibly long.

Essentially, however, we have looked at only three major roles and four sets of responsibilities. The roles deal with the requirements for organizational and personal leadership and for conscious attention to the formulation and promulgation of purpose. The four groups of functions encompass (1) securing the attainment of planned results in the present, (2) developing an organization capable of producing both technical achievement and human satisfactions, (3) making a distinctive personal contribution, and (4) planning and executing policy decisions affecting future results.

Even thus simplified, how to apply this identification of executive role and function to the incomparably detailed confusion of a national company situation cannot possibly be made clear in the process of generalization. Students using this text will wish to develop their own overview of the general manager's task, stressing those aspects most compatible with their own insight and sense of what to do. No modifications of the deliberately nontechnical language of this summary should slight the central importance of purpose. The theory presented here begins with the assumption that the life of every organization (corporate or otherwise), every subunit of organization, and every human group and individual should be guided by an evolving set of purposes or goals which permits forward movement in a chosen direction and prevents drifting in undesired directions.

Need for a Concept

The complexity of the president's job and the desirability of raising intuitive competence to the level of verifiable, conscious, and systematic analysis suggest the need, as indicated earlier, for a unitary concept as useful to the generalist as the canons of technical functions are to the specialist. We will propose shortly a simple practitioner's theory which we hope will reduce the four-faceted responsibility of the company president to more reasonable proportions, make it susceptible to objective research and systematic evaluation, and bring to more well-qualified people the skills it requires. The central concept we call "corporate strategy." It will be required to embrace the entire corporation, to take shape in the terms and conditions in which its business is conducted. It will be constructed from the points of view described so far. Central to this Olympian vantage point is impartiality with respect to the value of individual specialties, including the one through which the CEO rose to generalist responsibilities. It will insist upon the values of the special functions in proportion to their contribution to corporate purpose and ruthlessly dispense with those not crucially related to the objectives sought. It necessarily will define the president's role in such a way as to allow delegation of much of the general management responsibility described here without loss of clarity. After students have examined and discussed the roles, functions, and skills evident or missing from the cases that immediately follow these comments, we will present the concept of corporate strategy itself. Our hope will be to make challenging but practicable the connection between the highest priority for goal setting and a durable but flexible definition of a company's goals and major company-determining policies. How to define, decide, put into effect, and defend a conscious strategy appropriate to emerging market opportunity and company capability will then take precedence over and lend order to the fourfold functions of general management here presented.

Despite a shift in emphasis toward the anatomy of a concept and the development of an analytical approach to the achievement of valid corporate strategy, we will not forget the chief executive's special role in contributing quality to purpose through standards exercised in the choice of what to do and the way in which it is to be done and through the projection of *quality* as a person. It will remain true, after we have taken apart analytically the process by which strategy is conceived, that executing it at a high professional level will depend upon the depth and durability of the president's personal values, standards of quality, and clarity of character. We will return in a final comment on the management of the strategic process to the truth that the president's function above all is to be the exemplar of a permanent human aspiration—the determination to devote one's powers to jobs worth doing. Conscious attention to corporate strategy will be wasted if it does not elevate the quality of corporate purpose and achievement.

Head Ski Company, Inc.

The Head Ski Company, Inc., of Timonium, Maryland, was formed in 1950 to sell metal skis which had been developed by Howard Head during three years of research. In the first year six employees turned out 300 pairs of skis. By the 1954–55 skiing season, output reached 8,000 pairs, and by 1965 it passed 133,000. Growth in dollar sales and profits was equally spectacular. When Head went public in 1960, sales were just over $2 million and profits just under $59,000. By 1965 sales were up to $8.6 million and profits to $393,713. In the next two years, volume continued upward, though growth was less dramatic. In the 53 weeks ended April 30, 1966, sales were $9.1 million and profits $264,389. For a like period ending April 29, 1967, sales were $11 million and profits $401,482. (For financial data, see Exhibit 1.)

The Industry

Head was an enthusiastic participant in the growing market generated by leisure-time activities, of which skiing was one of the most dynamic segments. The industry association, Ski Industries America (SIA), estimated that skiing expenditures—including clothing, equipment, footwear, accessories, lift tickets, travel, entertainment, food and lodging—rose from $280 million in 1960 to $750 million in 1966–67. Gross sales were expected to reach $1.14 billion by 1969–70. This growth was attributed

Copyright © 1967 by the President and Fellows of Harvard College
Harvard Business School case 313–120

to both the rising number of skiers and greater per capita expenditures. In 1947 it was estimated that there were fewer than 10,000 active skiers in the United States. SIA estimated that there were 1.6 million in 1960, 3.5 million in 1966–67 and predicted 5 million for 1970. Another industry source estimated that the number of skiers was increasing by 20 percent a year.

As of 1966–67 the $750 million retail expenditures of skiing were estimated to be divided into $200 million going for ski equipment and ski wear, and $440 million going to the 1,200 ski areas and the transportation companies carrying skiers to their destinations. Ninety-eight manufacturers belonged to the SIA. *Skiing International Yearbook* for 1967 listed 85 brands of wooden skis available in 260 models, 49 brands of metal skis in 101 models, and 53 brands of fiberglass skis in 116 models. For each model there could be as many as 15 sizes. Many manufacturers made all three types of skis and some had multiple brands, but even so the industry was divided into many competing units.

The ski business, industry observers noted, was undergoing rapid change. *Ski Business* summed up an analysis of industry trends as follows:

> Imports of low-priced adult wood skis into the United States are skidding sharply.
>
> U.S. metal skis are gaining faster than any other category.
>
> The ski equipment and apparel market is experiencing an unusually broad and pronounced price and quality uptrend.
>
> Ski specialty shop business appears to be gaining faster than that of the much publicized department stores and general sporting goods outlets.
>
> The growth in the national skier population is probably decelerating and may already have reached a plateau.[1]

Supporting these statements of trends, *Ski Business* made some other observations.

> Foreign skis clearly lost in 1966 at the gain of domestic manufacturers. (The total of imported and domestic skis sold in the United States is believed to be running at over 900,000 pairs annually.) By conservative estimate, U.S. metal ski production in 1966 (for shipment to retail shops for the 1966–67 selling season) was up by at least 40,000 pairs from 1965. . . .
>
> But far more important than the domestic American ski gain (which will continue now that American fiberglass ski makers are entering the market) is the remarkable upward price shift. Thus while 10 percent fewer foreign skis entered the United States in 1966, the dollar value of all the skis imported actually rose by more than 10 percent or $700,000. . . . Here was the real measure of growth of the ski market; it was not in numbers, but in dollars.
>
> The principal beneficiary of this remarkable upward shift in consumer preference for higher product quality is, of course, the ski specialty shop.

---

[1] John Fry, *Ski Business,* May–June 1967, p. 25.

The skier bent on purchasing $140 skis and $80 boots will tend to put his confidence in the experienced specialist retailer. The ski specialist shops themselves are almost overwhelmed by what is happening. Here's one retailer's comment: "Just two or three years ago, we were selling a complete binding for $15. Now skiers come into our shop and think nothing of spending $40 for a binding. . . ."

. . . Most of the department store chains and sporting goods shops contacted by *Ski Business* were also able to report increased business in 1966–67, but somehow the exuberant, expansionist talk seems to have evaporated among nonspecialty ski dealers. Montgomery Ward, for instance, says that ski equipment sales have not come up to company expectations. Ward's has specialized in low end merchandise for beginning and intermediate skiers. . . . Significantly, department stores or sporting goods shops which reported the largest sales increases tended to be those which strive hardest to cast their image in the ski specialist mold.[2]

Ski imports for 1966 served both the low-priced and high-priced markets. More than half the Japanese imports of 530,000 pairs of skis were thought to be children's skis which helped to explain the low valuation of the Japanese skis. This value of $6.84 a pair was the FOB price at the door of the Japanese ski factory and does not include shipping, duty, importer's or retailer's margins.[3] *Ski Business* reported imports into the United States as follows:

1966 Ski Imports into the United States (By country of origin)

Country of Origin	Number of Pairs	Change: 1966 versus 1965	Dollar Value	Average Dollar* Value per Pair 1965	Average Dollar* Value per Pair 1966
Canada	7,091	+6,350	$ 149,961	$23	$21.14
Sweden	2,767	+1,131	22,386	9	8.09
Norway	1,125	−698	18,221	6	16.20
Finland	10,184	+5,411	98,275	9	9.65
Belgium	129	+129	6,327	—	49.05
France	5,257	+2,828	265,018	49	50.41
West Germany	44,736	+9,959	1,010,354	18	22.58
Austria	72,536	−20,872	1,511,563	21	20.84
Switzerland	2,835	+1,155	124,068	39	43.76
Italy	7,494	+351	195,723	14	26.12
Yugoslavia	22,540	+5,122	254,962	11	11.31
Japan	529,732	−89,632	3,625,639	5.54	6.84
Australia	2,307	+2,307	114,091	—	49.45
1965 total	785,746	—	6,692,451	—	8.52
1966 total	708,733	−77,013	7,396,588	8.52	10.44

* The average value per pair of skis represents an FOB plant price and does not include charges for shipping and handling, tariff, excise tax, or profit for trading company or wholesaler. Tariff on skis was 16⅔ percent.

Source: *Ski Business,* May–June 1967, p. 31.

---

[2] Ibid.

[3] Ibid.

In the high-price market segment, where skis retailed at $100 or more, the annual market was estimated by industry sources to be approximately 250,000 pairs of skis. Here estimates of the leading contenders according to these industry sources were:

Brand	Type	Estimated Sales (Pairs)	Price Range
Head (United States)	Metal	125,000	$115.00–$175.00
Hart (United States)	Metal	44,000	$ 99.50–$175.00
Kniessl (Austria)	Epoxy	20,000	$150.00–$200.00
Yamaha (Japan)	Epoxy	13,000	$ 79.00–$169.00
Fischer (Austria)	Wood / Metal / Epoxy	13,000	$112.00–$189.00

Source: *Skiing International Yearbook, 1967,* pp. 90–91. Copyright by Ziff-Davis Publishing Co.

Fischer was believed to have $15–$18 million sales worldwide. Kniessl was believed to be about the same size as Head worldwide, but only about one tenth Head's size in the United States. In addition Voit, the recreational products division of AMF, was entering the market with a fiberglass ski. Voit also manufactured water skis, a wide variety of aquatic equipment, and rubber products. AMF's total 1966 sales were $357 million. Recreational equipment accounted for approximately 20 percent, not including bowling equipment which accounted for an additional 22 percent of sales.

The skier's skill level was one determining factor in his choice of skis. (For those unfamiliar with the differences among skis designed for each group, a discussion of ski construction is included as the Appendix.) Of the 3.5 million active skiers, 17,000 were regarded as racers, another 75,000 were considered to be experts, and another 100,000 were classed as sufficiently skillful to be strong recreational skiers.

The Market

Skiing was considered to be a sport which attracted the moderately well-to-do and those on the way up. This conception was borne out by the following market data:

A statistical study released early this year [1965] by the Department of Commerce disclosed that the American skier has a median age of 26.2 and a median annual income of $11,115. Moreover, it showed that about two thirds of all skiers are college graduates.

How do these young, affluent and intelligent men and women spend their skiing dollars? At a typical resort, a person might spend each day

$10 for accommodations, $10 for food, $5 for a lift ticket and $10 for renting everything needed to attack the slopes from pants and parka to skis, boots, poles and bindings. . . .

The initial purchases of a person determined to have his or her own good equipment and to look well while skiing could easily be about $200. For this amount, a skier could buy everything from winter underwear to goggles and perhaps even have a bit left over for a rum toddy in the ski lodge the first night of his trip.

For instance, ski boots cost from $20 to $150 and average $50 a pair. Skis range from $30 to $200 and poles from $5 to $35.

When it comes to apparel, costs vary considerably. Snow jackets or parkas might cost as little as $20 or as much as $1,000 for those made with fur. Many jackets are available, though, at about $30.

Stretch pants have an average price of about $20. Other apparel requirements for skiing include sweaters which retail from $10 to $50, winter underwear which costs about $5, and ski hats and caps which sell for $3 and up.[4]

There was an apparent fashionability to skiing. Fashion consciousness was apparent in the design of ski equipment, ski wear, and the influx of a new type of skier. Under the headline "The Nonskiers: They Flock to Ski Resorts for the Indoor Sports," *The Wall Street Journal* reported as follows:

Want to take up a rugged, outdoor sport?

Cross skiing off your list.

The sport has gone soft. Ski resorts now have all the comforts of home— if your home happens to have a plush bar, a heated swimming pool, a padded chair lift, boutiques and a built-in baby sitter. . . . Skiing, in fact, has become almost an incidental activity at some ski resorts; indeed, some of the most enthusiastic patrons here at Squaw Valley and other resorts don't even know how to ski. They rarely venture outdoors.

So why do they come here? "Men, M-E-N. They're here in bunches, and so am I, baby," answers slinky, sloe-eyed Betty Reames as she selects a couch strategically placed midway between the fireplace and the bar. . . .

Squaw Valley houses half a dozen bars and restaurants and often has three different bands and a folksinger entertaining at the same time. Aspen, in Colorado, throws a mid-winter Mardi Gras. Sun Valley, in Idaho, has a shopping village that includes a two-floor bookstore and boutique selling miniskirts.

Life has also been made softer for those skiers who ski. . . . Also some resorts are making their chair lifts more comfortable by adding foam padding. But even that isn't enough for some softies. "What? Me ride the chair lift? Are you crazy? I'd freeze to death out in the open like that," says blond Wanda Peterson as she waits to ride up the mountain in an

---

[4] *The New York Times*, December 12, 1965. © 1965 by The New York Times Company. Reprinted by permission.

enclosed gondola car. She doesn't stand alone. The line of the gondola is 200 strong; the nearby chair lift, meanwhile, is all but empty. . . .

. . . for beginning skiers most resorts offer gentle, meticulously groomed inclines that make it almost impossible to fall. "We try to make it so that the person who has no muscle tone and little experience can't be fooled, can't make a mistake," says one resort operator. "Then we've got him. He's a new customer as well as a happy man."

Once he gets the hang of it—whether he's any good or not—the happy man starts spending lots of money, and that's what the resorts love.[5]

In line with the concern for style, some manufacturers of skiwear and ski equipment developed new colors and annual model changes to inspire annual obsolescence and fad purchases.

Head Company History

Howard Head, chairman and founder of the company bearing his name, was the man responsible for the development of the first successful metal ski. Combining the experience of an aircraft designer with dedication to a sport which he enjoyed, he spent more than three years developing a ski which would not break, turned easily, and tracked correctly without shimmying and chattering. Others had tried to produce metal skis, but Head succeeded almost five years before his nearest competitors, Hart and Harry Holmberg, introduced the Hart metal skis. *Ski Magazine* described the reason behind Howard Head's success:

He was obsessed, to be sure, and being relatively unencumbered by stock-holders, high overhead and strong yearnings for luxurious living, he was well braced for the long haul. . . .

"I made changes only where I had to make them," he has said of the days when his skis were undergoing trial by fire. "When they broke, I made them stronger only where they broke."[6]

In 1960 Howard Head described the early years of his enterprise and the trials which surrounded it as follows:

Twelve years ago I took six pairs of handmade metal skis to Stowe, Vermont, and asked the pros there to try them out. It had taken about a year to make those six pairs of skis. The design, based on engineering principles of aircraft construction, was radically different from any ever tried before. I thought it was sound but the pros weren't a bit surprised when all six pairs promptly broke to pieces. After all, others before me had tried to make metal skis and all they had proved was what everyone knew anyway— a ski had to be made of wood.

That was in January 1948. Today about 60 percent of all high-grade skis sold in the United States are metal skis. The reasons for this revolution

[5] *The Wall Street Journal,* February 1967.

[6] *Ski Magazine,* January 1964.

in ski manufacturing industry are simple. People like the way metal skis ski, they like their durability, and they like their easy maintenance. . . .

Many small refinements and changes in design have been introduced through the years because of our continued testing and development program and to meet the advances in technique and changes in skiing conditions. But the basic structural design hasn't changed, which speaks well for the original concept.[7]

Mr. Head further indicated that his personal interest in technical problems played a major part in leading him to create his business:

When I started out, I was a mechanical design engineer—the whole origin of the business was the feeling that it should be possible to build a better ski. What started as an engineering puzzle ended as a business.

I distinctly remember wondering at that time whether we would ever grow to the point where we would be making 5,000 pairs of skis a year.

Price-volume considerations exerted small influence over initial marketing policy. Mr. Head priced his first metal skis at $75 in spite of the fact that most skiers were using war surplus skis that cost $20, including bindings. Mr. Head discussed his early ideas on quality, costs, and prices as follows:

The great disadvantage of all metal skis is simply their high price. This became apparent to us when we were pioneering the original metal ski and found it was going to cost a good bit more than a wood ski. We didn't let that stop us because we believed the striking advantages of a metal ski more than compensated for its high price. As it turned out, even with a higher initial price, Head Skis proved to cost less in the long run because they are so durable. . . .

In the early days people had no way of knowing the skis would last so long that they actually ended up costing less than cheaper skis. They simply liked them enough to go ahead and buy them in spite of the price.[8]

Mr. Head found a market which was quite unexpected. In spite of the high price, Head skis appealed more to the average beginner or slightly better skier than to racers. Among skiers, Heads became known as "cheaters." This designation grew out of the skis' ability to make almost anyone look good. "They practically turned themselves." Soon the black plastic top of the Head ski became a ubiquitous status symbol on the slopes.

Product Policy

The keynote of Mr. Head's product policy was quality. His fundamental belief was that the consumer should get all he pays for and pay for all

---

[7] "On Metal Skis" (manuscript by Howard Head, 1960).

[8] Ibid.

he gets. The 17-year history of the company had seen considerable upgrading of the products. Several times in the past the company had called in particular models or production runs of skis which had been found to be defective. One executive commented that this had been done without hesitation, even when the company was in precarious financial condition.

Asked what set Head apart from its competition, Mr. Head replied as follows:

> I believe that it is a tradition of attention to detail which grew out of its entrepreneurial history. In every aspect we attempt to follow through. Service, dealer relations, product quality, style, advertising are all important and must be done in the best way we know how.
>
> We stress continued emphasis on quality of product and quality of operating philosophy. We pay meticulous attention to the individual relationships with dealers and the public.
>
> I have attempted to make creativity, imagination, and standards of perfection apply across the board. This was always our desire, and we only failed to live up to it when the business got too big for the existing staff. The philosophy remained constant, and now we have the people to live up to it.
>
> We get a return on this attention to detail. The feedback from success allows us to maintain the necessary staff to insure continuation of this philosophy.
>
> We allow no sloppiness.

Head skis came in one color—black. There was no special trim to designate the model, only a modification in the color of the name "Head" embossed on the top of the ski and a change in the color of the base: red for some models, yellow or black for others. Although at one time a chrome top was considered, it was rejected because of the glare and because it was difficult to see against the snow. In addition to these factors, one executive described black as being a conservative color which would go with anything. Howard Head explained that he "did not want to complicate the consumer's choice."

> I deeply believe in sticking to function and letting style take care of itself. We have stuck so rigorously to our black color because it is honest and functional that it has become almost a trademark. While we constantly make minor improvements, we never make an important model change unless there is a performance reason for it. In other words, we skipped the principle of forced obsolescence, and we will continue to skip it.

This policy had been consciously chosen and maintained, in spite of competition which had introduced six or eight different colors and yearly color changes to keep up with fashion.

Apart from color and style, skis had to perform well on the slopes. There were three fundamental things which a ski had to do. It had to "track,"[9] "traverse,"[10] and "turn."[11] The need to perform these functions imposed certain constraints on ski design, and the necessity to both track and turn required some compromises in design.

Researcher interviews with ski distributors and retailers noted some of the characteristics which this "balancing" involved. These experts detailed a number of critical features of a ski's design. The ski had to be flexible, designed with a cambered or arched shape to distribute the skier's weight over the entire ski, and manufactured so as to be straight without warp or twist. The tip of the ski played an important role. It had to be pointed and turned up to permit the skier to navigate difficult terrain and soft snow without changing direction. The bottom of the ski was also critical: it had to provide a slippery surface for ease of travel and had to be perfectly flat except for a center groove which helped the skier to achieve tracking stability. The edges of the ski had to be sharp for holding and turning purposes. All of those interviewed stressed that for maximum performance, the skier had to select the proper length ski.

Mr. Head found a proper combination of these elements for the recreational skier in his earliest metal ski. Designated the Standard, this model underwent substantial improvement over its 17-year history. Until 1960, however, the goal of providing the best ski for experts eluded Head and other makers of metal skis. Mr. Head said of this period, "During the early years at Head Ski, we were too busy making the best ski we could for the general public to spend much time developing a competition ski."

For experts, the basic complaint against metal skis was that they were too "soft" and tended to vibrate badly at racing speeds. This problem was substantially solved in 1960, when Head introduced its Vector model, to be followed in 1962 (and later entirely replaced) by the Competition. In these skis, an imbedded layer of neoprene dampened vibrations and considerably improved performance. Whereas in 1960 most competitors in the Squaw Valley Olympics had stuck to their wooden skis, by the end of 1962 Head skis were in wide use, and they had carried 77 racers out of 141 to positions among the top six contenders at races conducted by the International Professional Ski Race Association in Canada and the United States. Also about half the skis used in the U.S. National Junior and Senior Championships that year were Heads.

---

[9] Track: If you point a ski down a slope and allow it to run freely, it should hold a straight course—over bumps and through hollows and on every type of snow surface.

[10] Traverse: A ski should be able to hold a straight line while moving diagonally across a slope over obstacles and various snow conditions.

[11] Turn: When a skier releases the edges of his skis, the skis must be capable of slipping sideways, and when edged, they must bite into the snow evenly. (A skiing turn is nothing more than a slideslip carved into an arc by the controlled bite of the edges.)

By 1966 Head had established itself as an important factor in the ski racing world. Two Americans had set the world speed record—106.527 MPH—on Head skis. In major international competition in 1966, one third of all finishers in the top 10 places at all events were on Head skis, and Head was the outstanding single manufacturer on the circuit with 18 gold medals, 15 silver medals, and 15 bronze medals.

The 1968 Head line included a ski for every type of skier from the unskilled beginner to the top professional racer. The line was described in Head's *Ski Handbook* as follows:

. . . the most important design consideration is you—the type of skier you are and where you ski. That's why your dealer was able to offer you nine different models of Head Skis to choose from. You can be sure the model he helped you select was the optimum—for you.

STANDARD—THE MOST FORGIVING SKI: For beginners of average size and athletic ability up to intermediates learning stem christies. Also for the better, occasional skier who prefers an easy-going, lively, lightweight ski that practically turns for him.

The *Standard* is medium soft in flex overall for easy turning and responsiveness. Engineered side camber and relative overall width contribute to ease and slow-speed stability. Its light weight and torsional rigidity make traversing and other basic maneuvers simple. Thin taper in the tip allows the *Standard* to cut easily through the heaviest snow instead of ploughing.

Standard. $115. Thirteen sizes from 140 to 215 cm. Black top, sidewalls and bottom; white engraving.

MASTER—MORE OF A CHALLENGE: For the skier who has mastered the basic techniques and wants to begin driving the skis and attacking the slope. As lively as the *Standard,* this is also the ski for the heavier, more athletic beginner who wants more "beef" underfoot.

The *Master* is like the *Standard* in basic shape but thicker and heavier. The tip radius is longer for extra shock absorption. Slightly stiffer flex overall acts as a heavy-duty shock absorber over bumps.

Master. $135. Nine sizes from 175 through 215 cm. Black top and sidewalls; blue base and engraving.

THE FABULOUS 360—THE MOST VERSATILE SKI: Finest all-around ski ever made—for the skier beginning stem christies on through the expert class. Remarkable for its ease of turning as well as its steadiness and precision, the *360* is the serious skier's ski for attack or enjoyment on the slope, under any condition of snow or terrain.

With its smooth-arcing flex pattern, the *360* has the supple forebody of the other recreational skis, but is slightly stiffer at the tail. Its side camber is similar to that of the *Giant Slalom.* Narrower overall than the *Standard* or *Master.* Rubber damping in the lightweight top-skin unit makes the *360* a very responsive ski, allowing the expert to control his turns beautifully and set his edges precisely. Tip splay is designed to give easiest entrance through snow and to provide excellent shock absorption, particularly in heavily moguled areas.

The Fabulous 360. $155. Eleven sizes from 170 to 220 cm. Black top and sidewalls; yellow base and engraving.

SLALOM—THE HOT DOG: For the expert skier who likes to stay in the fall-line, slashing through quick short-radius turns on the steepest, iciest, slopes. The *Slalom* has been totally redesigned this year to fit the special needs of the expert recreational skier, who wants the lightest, fastest-reacting, and best ice-holding ski possible.

Slalom is Head's narrowest ski overall. And, thanks to the lightweight top-skin unit and core, it is also one of Head's lightest skis. Lightness and narrowness allow for carved or pivoted turns, reflex-fast changes in direction. Special engineered side camber and relative softness at the thin waist give the ultimate in "feel" and control on ice. Neoprene rubber gives the damping and torque necessary for a top-performance ice ski.

Slalom. $160. Five sizes from 190 to 210 cm. Black top and sidewalls. Racing red base and engraving.

DOWNHILL—BOMB!: Widest and heaviest Head ski, the *Downhill* is for the advanced skier—recreational or competitor—who wants to blast straight down the slope. It offers the ultimate in high-speed performance, tracking ability, and stability over bumps and moguls.

The long tip splay and supple forebody is the secret of the *Downhill's* exceptional speed advantage. It virtually planes over the surface of the slope. With its firm midsection and tail acting like the rudder of a hydroplane, the *Downhill* affords the skier utmost control coupled with great turning ability at slower speeds. Heavy-duty top-skin unit and added rubber damping contribute to the stability and high-speed "quietness" of the *Downhill*. This is the elite international-class racing ski, and experts have found it an excellent powder ski as well.

Downhill. $175. Seven sizes from 195 to 225 cm. Black top and sidewalls. Yellow base and engraving.

GIANT SLALOM—GRACE PLUS SPEED: The *GS* incorporates the best features of the *Downhill* and *Slalom* models. It offers the expert skier—recreational and/or competitor—the optimum in stable all-out speed skiing, combined with precise carving and holding ability in high-speed turns. It is another favorite on the international racing circuit.

The *Giant Slalom's* stability and precision come from a unique combination of sidecut and relatively stiff flex. The *GS* is similar to the *360* in overall dimensions, but has a stiffer flex pattern than the *360*, particularly underfoot. This gives the *GS* the versatility of the *360* but with greater control at high speeds. Tip splay is designed for maximum shock absorption and easy riding.

Giant Slalom. $165. Nine sizes from 175 to 215 cm. Black top and sidewalls. Yellow base and engraving.

YOUNGSTER'S COMPETITION—JUNIOR HOT DOG: Carrying the *Giant Slalom* engraving, this ski is designed for expert youngsters who want, and can handle, a faster, more demanding ski than the small-size *Standard*. Similar in cut and performance characteristics to the *Giant Slalom*, but without the *GS's* neoprene damping, to provide the junior racer with easier turning ability.

Youngster's Competition. $120. Two sizes, 160 and 170 cm. Black top and sidewalls. Yellow bottom and engraving.

SHORTSKI—FUN WITHOUT EFFORT: Not just a sawed-off *Stan-*

dard, but a totally different ski with totally different proportions. Very wide for its length, quite stiff overall, the *Shortski* is the only ski of its kind with an engineered side camber. Ideal for quick learning of the fundamentals of skiing. Also for the older or more casual skier who enjoys being on the slopes and wants the easiest-possible tracking and turning ski ever built.

Shortski. $115. Four sizes from 150 to 190 cm. Black top, sidewalls and bottom. White engraving.

DEEP POWDER—SHEER BUOYANCY ON THE SLOPES: Super-soft flexibility and buggy-whip suppleness allow this specialized ski to float in powder, while maintaining easy turning plus full control and tracking ability on packed slopes.

The *Deep Powder* is very wide and soft overall, with a "hinge-like" effect in the forebody that enables it to glide through the deepest powder.

Deep Powder. $115. Five sizes from 195 to 215 cm. Black top, sidewalls and bottom. White engraving.

Head was constantly experimenting with new designs and introducing minor modifications to improve the performance and durability of its product. When asked about a major change in product construction, such as to the fiber-reinforced plastic-type ski, Mr. Head gave the following reply:

We think that the metal sandwich construction is the best material. We do not see this situation changing in the foreseeable future. Certainly now the other exotic materials are not gaining ground. They lack the versatility of application of the metal sandwich ski. The epoxy or fiber reinforced plastic have low durability and don't have the wide performance range of our skis.

We believe that the advantage of the metal ski is that you can build in any performance characteristic which you desire. Naturally, we have a research department investigating other materials, but until a major improvement is found, we should stick to our basic material. We can always build the best ski for beginners, and we can adapt that ski to get the performance required by experts.

Marketing Policies

Head's emphasis on quality extended beyond the product to the dealer and service network. The company sold through only a limited number of franchised dealers, who had satisfied management that "they know something about skis and skiing." Ten district sales managers were employed, who sold to about 900 dealers throughout the United States. Of these about 85 percent were ski specialty shops, 12 percent were large full-line sporting goods stores, and the remainder were full-line department stores (see Exhibit 2). Head skis were distributed in Europe through an exclusive distributor, Walter Haensli of Klosters, Switzerland.

In 1964 he sold 19 percent of Head's output. This figure appeared to be declining gradually.

Head believed that a Head franchise was valuable to a dealer. Many large stores had wanted to sell Heads but had been turned down. Saks Fifth Avenue had waited eight years before it was given a franchise. Mr. Head commented on dealer selection as follows:

> Getting Saks Fifth Avenue as a dealer is consistent with our operating philosophy of expecting the same quality from our dealers as from ourselves.
>
> Once they become a dealer, however, we get to know the people involved and work closely with them. Increasingly, we are recognizing the business value of providing more assistance and leadership to our dealers in helping them to do a better job for their customers.
>
> Even a large, well-managed department store or sporting goods store may need help in the specialized area of skis. They may need help in display stock selection, or even personnel selection. We are increasingly concerned about the type of personnel who sell skis. There is a high degree of dependence on the salesman. He must be a good skier himself.
>
> We have seen instances of two department stores of essentially identical quality in the same area where one store could sell 8 pairs of skis a year and the other 300 simply because of a different degree of commitment to getting the right man to sell. Skis can only be sold by a floor salesman who can ski and who can sell from personal experience.

The company was committed to the belief that selling skis was an exacting business. The ski size had to be matched to the individual's height and body weight, flexibility had to be chosen correctly depending on use, and bindings had to be mounted properly.

Following up on the initial sale, Head offered extensive customer service. Dealers were expected to have service facilities for minor repairs, and the factory had facilities for sharpening edges, rebuilding the plastic portion of the ski, and matching a single ski if the mate had been broken beyond repair. Even in the busiest part of the season, service time was kept under three weeks.

In March 1967, Mr. Harold Seigle, the newly appointed president and chief operating officer of Head, sent out a "management news bulletin" outlining Head's marketing philosophy:

Marketing Philosophy

1. Our current selective dealer organization is one of Head Ski Company's most valuable assets, next to the product itself.
2. Our continued sales growth will be based on a market-by-market approach aimed at increasing the effectiveness of our present dealers and by the very selective addition of new dealers wherever present dealers prove to be inadequate rather than by mass distribution and merchandising techniques.
3. Our future marketing efforts, particularly personal selling, advertising, merchandising, and sales promotion, will be geared to the specific needs of our dealers to sell all Head Ski products.

4. We want and will have the finest sales forces in the industry . . . who rely upon personal integrity, service, and hard work to do a professional selling job rather than inside deals and short cuts.

5. We feel that, next to quality products, strong personal selling at the manufacturer's level and the retail level is paramount to our continued success and tends to transcend other facets of marketing that contribute to the sale of merchandise.

Advertising was done on a selective basis. An outside source reported as follows:

> The company invests about 2 percent of gross sales in advertising, split between the skiing magazines (50 percent) and *Sports Illustrated, The New Yorker,* and *Yachting*—"the same kind of people like to sail."
>
> The most effective promotion, however, is probably the ski itself. Head is delighted at the growing demand for his skis in the rental market. "We sold 10,000 pairs—almost 10 percent of our business—for rental last year," he points out, "and everyone who rents those skis becomes a prospect."[12]

To aid in placing rental skis, Head gave an additional 12 percent–15 percent discount on skis which a dealer purchased for rental. Ski rental was seen as the best way to introduce a customer to the ease of skiing on Heads.

The Head Ski Company approach was a "soft sell." Unlike many sporting goods companies, Head did not rely on personal endorsements of famous skiers. According to one executive, it was impossible under American Amateur rules even to have posters featuring an amateur skier. Professional endorsements were probably ineffective anyway, since so many other sporting goods companies used them, and most of the public knew that such endorsements could be bought. Head tried to get actual news pictures of famous skiers or racers using Head skis and winning. To make certain that top skiers would use Head skis, the company did lend skis to racers for one year. Even this practice was expensive and had to be tightly controlled. A good skier might need upward of nine pairs of skis a year, which would represent an expenditure of nearly $1,000. Head did feel this type of promotion yielded a secondary benefit of product development information which could not be overlooked.

Head had received many requests for a promotional film made in conjunction with United Airlines showing famous ski slopes. Head was mentioned in the title, at the end, and in a few identifiable spots in the body of the show. This film was used by ski clubs and other organizations to promote interest in the sport.

Other Head promotion came as a result of skiwear and resort advertisements. As *Sales Management* put it:

> So great is the worldwide prestige of Head skis that although Howard Head claims he makes no promotional tie-in deals, the ski buff can hardly

---

[12] *Sales Management,* February 5, 1965.

miss seeing the familiar black skis in ads for anything from parkas to ski resorts. They're status symbols.[13]

Production

Head skis were produced in three steps. The detail department made up the various components which were to go into the assembly, including the core, the nose piece, the tail piece, the top plastic, the top and bottom skins, the running surface, and the edges. The separate pieces were then taken to the cavity department, where they were assembled. Here, too, the various layers were laid into a mold and heated and bonded under controlled time, temperature, and pressure. At this point the skis were roughed out on a band saw. From that time on, all work was done on the skis as a pair. In the finishing department, the skis were ground to final form, buffed, polished, and engraved.

Manufacture involved a great deal of handwork, of which 70 percent was characterized as requiring a high degree of skill. The basic nature of the assembly process meant that operations did not lend themselves to mass production techniques.

In May 1967, Head completed the fifth addition to the plant since its construction in 1959. Prior to the new addition, the plant contained 105,668 square feet, of which 93,040 was devoted to manufacturing and warehouse facilities, and 12,628 to office space. Included were a cafeteria, locker rooms, and shower areas for the workers.

Howard Head commented on the difficulty of the manufacturing process and on the relationship between costs and price:

> [There are] approximately 250 different operations, involving a great number of specially developed machines, tools, and processes. None of the processes is standard. It all had to be developed more or less from scratch.
>
> Some of the special-purpose machines involved are those for routing the groove in the bottom aluminum, for attaching the steel edges, and for profiling the ski after it comes out of the presses. Also there are the bonding procedures which require an unusual degree of control of heat and pressure cycles.
>
> Supplementing all the special-purpose machines, we have learned to make rather unusual use of band saws. A good example of a demanding band-saw operation is the profiling of the plywood and plastic core elements. Since the stiffness of a ski at any point goes up as the square of the spacing between the top and bottom sheets—i.e., the core thickness—a normal band-saw tolerance of about 0.010″ would grossly affect our flexibility pattern and would be out of the question. However, by special adapters and guides, we are actually able to band saw these parts in high production at about 10 seconds apiece to a tolerance of plus or minus 0.002″ over the entire contour.

---

[13] Ibid.

An example of effective but low-cost equipment in our factory is the press used to laminate 3' x 10' sheets of plywood core material to their corresponding sheets of sidewall plastic. This operation requires a total load of some 90,000 pounds. By using a roof beam as the reaction point, the floor for a base, and three screw jacks for pressure, we are able to produce enough material for 600 pairs of skis at one shot with equipment costing a total of about $250.

It's been our policy from the start to put absolute emphasis on quality of product. We never compromise on old material, nor reject a new one on the basis of cost. In principle, if better skis could be made out of sheet platinum, I suspect we would wind up with it. In other words, it is our policy to make the best product we can regardless of cost and then price it accordingly to the trade.

Production at Head was on a three-shift basis throughout the year, with skis being made for inventory during the slow months. There were over 600 employees.

Six attempts had been made to unionize the plant, but all had been rejected, several times by three-to-one majorities. One warehouse employee with 12 years' seniority said, "It's a nice place to work. We don't need a union. If you have a problem, Mr. Head will listen to you."

All employees received automatic step raises based on seniority, as well as merit reviews and raises. In addition there was a profit-sharing trust plan which in the past had generally added 6 percent–7 percent to the employees' salaries. These funds became fully vested after three years.

Another important benefit in which exempt salaried employees participated was the year-end bonus plan. Under this plan, three groups received different bonus rates. For the lowest paid group, the rate was 3 percent if pretax profits on sales were under 2 percent, but 10 percent–11 percent if profits were 8 percent–12 percent. For the middle group, no bonus was paid if profits were 2 percent or below, but the rate was 20 percent–22 percent if profits ranged between 8 percent and 12 percent. For the top group rates were not disclosed, but it was indicated that their bonus plan was even more steeply peaked. For most of the past several years, the payoffs had been at or near the upper range.

Finance

The initial financing of Head Ski Company was $6,000 from Howard Head's personal funds. In 1953 Mr. Head sold 40 percent of the stock in the company for $60,000. This, together with retained earnings and normal bank debt, financed expansion until 1960 when common stock was issued. Additional financing was required to continue the rapid expansion, and in January 1965, a $3,527,500 package was sold, made up of 5½ percent convertible subordinated debentures in face amount of $2,125,000 and 42,500 shares of common stock. Until the stock issue of 1965, Howard Head had owned 42.4 percent of the common stock, and the other directors and officers had owned 46.1 percent. At no time had there been any question about the commanding role of Howard Head when important decisions were made. Full conversion of the new issue would represent 17.1 percent ownership.

Expansion was viewed by many in the company as a defensive tactic. The belief was expressed that "if you do not grow as fast as the market will allow you to, you are taking substantial risk that someone else will come in and take that market away from you." In addition, the new funds provided capital for two diversifications started in 1966: The Head Ski and Sportswear Co. and the Head plastics division.

In spite of the drop in earnings growth, the stock market continued to evaluate Head's prospects at 29 to 60 times previous years' earnings. During the period January 1966 to July 1967, its stock sold in the range from $9\frac{3}{8}$ to $17\frac{3}{4}$. As late as January 1965, however, the stock had sold at $22\frac{3}{4}$.

Organization

As of June 1967, the Head Ski Company was organized along functional lines. Reporting to the president were the vice president for operations, the treasurer, and the directors of marketing, quality control, and personnel. This organization pattern had been introduced by Mr. Harold Seigle when he was named chief operating officer on January 16, 1967 (see Exhibit 3).

Of the 26 men shown on the organization chart, 12 had been with Head one year or less. When asked about the potential difficulties of that situation, Mr. Head responded,

> I would only say that if you are to have a lot of new people, you must have one man in command who is an experienced and gifted professional at utilizing people. My job is to support and use that man.

Mr. Head reviewed the history of the organization which had led to the current structure as follows:

> I think that this is typical of the kind of business that starts solely from an entrepreneurial product basis, with no interest or skills in management or business in the original package. Such a business never stops to plan. The consuming interest is to build something new and to get acceptance. The entrepreneur has to pick up the rudiments of finance and organizational practices as he goes along. Any thought of planning comes later. Initially he is solely concerned with the problems of surviving and building. Also, if the business is at all successful, it is so successful that there is no real motivation to stop and obtain the sophisticated planning and people-management techniques. Such a business is fantastically efficient as long as it can

survive. One man can make all of the important decisions. There is no pyramidal team structure.

In our case this approach worked quite successfully until about 1955 when we sold 10,000 pairs of skis and reached the $500,000 sales level. The next five years from 1955 to 1960 saw a number of disorganized attempts to acquire and use a more conventional pyramidal organizational system. To put it succinctly, what was efficient at the $500,000 level was increasingly inefficient as we reached $1 million, then $2 million in sales. One man just couldn't handle it. I made too many mistakes. It was like trying to run an army with only a general and some sergeants. There were just no officers, to say nothing of an orderly chain of command.

In 1960 came the first successful breakthrough, where I finally developed the ability to take on a general manager who later became an executive vice president. It was hard for me to learn to operate under this framework. The most striking thing missing from this period was a concept of people-management. I spent five years gradually learning not to either over- or under-delegate.

Let me interject that the final motivation necessary to make a complete transition to an orderly company came because the company got into trouble in 1965–66. Even five years after the beginning of a team system, the company got into trouble, and this was the final prod which pushed me to go all the way. It is interesting that it took 12 years. Up until 1960 the company was totally under my direction. From 1960 to 1965 we stuttered between too much of my direction and not enough.

The chief difficulty for me was to learn to lay down a statement of the results required and then stay out of details. The weakness was in finding a formula of specifying objectives, then giving freedom as long as the objectives were met.

The appointment of Hal Seigle as president brought us a thoroughly sophisticated individual who can bring us the beginning of big business methods. On my part, this change has involved two things: first, my finally recognizing that I wanted this kind of organization; second, the selection of a man with proven professional management skills.

Unfortunately, with an entrepreneur, there are only two courses which can be taken if the company is to grow beyond a certain size. He can get the hell out, or he can really change his method of operation. I am pleased that this company has made the transition.

Now more than ever the company is using my special skills and abilities, but I am no longer interfering with an orderly and sophisticated management and planning system. We have given the company new tools to operate with, and I have not pulled the rug out from under them.

I am reserving my energies for two things. First, there is a continuation of my creative input—almost like a consultant to the company. Second, I have taken the more conventional role of chairman and chief executive officer. In this role I devote my efforts to planning and longer range strategy.

I feel that I can serve in both capacities. I can only be successful in the role of creative input if I can be solely a consultant without authority. It has to be made clear in this role that anything said is for consideration only. It has been demonstrated that this role is consultative, since some of my suggestions have been rejected. I like this role because I like the freedom. I can think freer, knowing that my suggestions will be carefully reviewed.

Of course, in areas of real importance like new product lines such as binding or boot, adding new models to the ski line, or acquisitions, etc., I must exert authority, channeled through the president.

Prior to coming to Head, Mr. Seigle had been vice president and general manager of a $50 million consumer electronics division of a $150 million company. His appointment was viewed as "contributing to a more professional company operating philosophy." He hoped to introduce more formalized methods of budget control and to "preside over the transition from a 'one-man' organization to a traditionally conceived functional pattern."

Mr. Seigle introduced a budgeting system broken down into 13 periods each year. Reports were to be prepared every four weeks comparing target with actual for each of the revenue or expense centers, such as marketing, operations, the staff functions, and the three subsidiaries. The hope was eventually to tie the bonus to performance against budget. Previously statements had been prepared every four weeks, but only to compare actual results against previous years' results.

Being new to the company, Mr. Seigle found that much of his time was being spent on operating problems. He believed, however, that as the budget system became completely accepted and operational, he would be able to devote more of his time to looking ahead and worrying about longer term projects. He said: "Ideally, I like to be working 6 to 18 months ahead of the organization. As a project gets within six months of actual operation, I will turn it over to the operating managers." He had hired a manager for corporate planning with whom he worked closely.

Under the previous organization from March 1966 until Mr. Seigle's appointment, Howard Head had presided directly over the various departments and marketing functions. There was no overall marketing director at that time. Even in the period from 1960 to 1966 when there was an executive vice president, Mr. Head indicated that he had concerned himself with the operating details of the business.

A View toward the Future

Head's first diversification was to ski poles. These were relatively simple to manufacture and were sold through existing channels. As with the skis, Head maintained the highest standards of quality and style. The poles were distinguished from competition by their black color and adoption of the tapered shape and extra light weight which at the time were unavailable on other high-priced, quality ski poles. Head's prices were well toward the upper end of the spectrum: $24.50, as compared with as little as $5 for some brands. Success in selling poles encouraged the company to look at other products it might add.

Two further steps taken were toward diversification in late 1966 when Head formed a plastics division and established a subsidiary, Head Ski and Sportswear Co.

The plastic division's activity centered on high molecular weight plastics. In March 1967 a press release was issued concerning this activity:

> Head Ski Co., Inc., has signed a license agreement with Phillips Petroleum Company . . . to use a new method developed by Phillips for extruding ultra-high molecular weight high density polyethylene into finished products. . . .
>
> Developmental equipment has been installed at the Head plant here, and limited quantities of sheet have been extruded and tested in the running surface of Head skis with excellent results. . . . Production of ski base material is scheduled for this Spring. . . .
>
> In addition to its own running surface material, the Head plastics division has been developing special ultra-high molecular weight high density polyethylene compound to serve a variety of industrial applications. . . .
>
> Ultra-high molecular weight high density polyethylene is an extremely tough abrasion-resistant thermoplastic capable of replacing metal and metal alloys in many industrial areas. Compared with regular high density resins, the ultra-high molecular weight material has better stress-cracking resistance, better long-term stress life and less notch sensitivity.

The diversification into skiwear was considered by company executives to be the more important move. Howard Head talked about the logic of this new venture as follows:

> Skiwear is "equipment" first and fashion second. We are satisfied that our line of skiwear is better than anything done before. It represents the same degree of attention to detail which has characterized our hardware line.

The president of the new subsidiary, Alex Schuster, said:

> Many people thought that Head should stay in hardware such as poles, bindings, and wax. As I see it, however, by going into skiwear we are taking advantage of ready-made distribution and reputation. There is no reason why the goodwill developed through the years can't be related to our endeavor.
>
> This new market offers a greater potential and reward than the more hardware-oriented areas. Any entry into a new market has difficulties. These can only be solved by doing things right and by measuring up to the Head standards. Having a Head label commits us to a standard of excellence.
>
> Assuming that we live up to those standards, we shall be able to develop into a supplier in a small market but with formidable potential. We are creating a skill base for further diversification.
>
> Our products are engineered, not designed. We are concerned with the engineered relationship among fabric, function, and fit. The engineering details are not always obvious, but they are related to functional demands.

Emphasis is placed on function over fashion, yet there is definite beauty created out of concern for function. We are definitely in tune with fashion trends.

[See Exhibit 4 for examples of the new products.]

We will provide a complete skiing outfit—pants, parkas, sweaters, accessories, sox, and gloves. We will offer a total coordinated look.

Along with the design innovations, we shall offer innovations in packaging, display and promotion. We have to go beyond simply preparing the proper apparel.

Head Ski and Sportswear did both manufacturing and subcontracting. The products which had the highest engineering content were made in the Head plant. Sweaters, with less engineering, were contract-made to Head specifications by one of Europe's leading sweater manufacturers.

The collection was first shown to dealers in April 1967 and was scheduled for public release for the 1967–68 skiing season. Initial response by dealers and by the fashion press had been extremely encouraging. *Ski Business* reported:

HEAD'S UP.

. . . way up, in fact 194 percent ahead of planned volume on its premier line of skiwear.

Anyone who expected Howard Head's entry into the world of fashion to be presented in basic black was in for a surprise. Ironically the skiwear collection that blasted off with the hottest colors in the market is offered by a man who is totally color blind. . . .

On pants: The $55 pant was the big surprise. It was our top seller—way beyond expectations—and the basic $45 pant came in second in sales. Another surprise was the $70 foam-waisted pant for which we only projected limited sales—it's a winner. . . .

On orders: Way beyond expectations. Ninety percent of the orders are with ski shops and 10 percent with the department stores. Naturally we are committed to selling to Head Ski dealers but it definitely is not obligatory.[14]

The sportswear subsidiary had been set up in a separate plant five miles from Head's Timonium headquarters. It was an autonomous operation with a separate sales force and profit responsibility. The initial premise was that the sportswear should be distributed through current Head dealers, although according to Mr. Seigle, the marketing decisions of the sportswear division would be made independently of decisions in the ski division. Although Head dealers were offered the Head sportswear line, it was not sold on an exclusive basis. Distribution would be directly from factory salesmen to the dealer. Within the company, the necessity for a separated and different type of sales force was acknowledged. As one executive phrased it, "I can't imagine our ski salesmen trying to push soft goods. Our salesmen got into the business first and foremost

---

[14] *Ski Business,* May–June 1967.

because they were excellent skiers." As with skis and poles, the product line was to be maintained at the high end of the spectrum in both quality and price.

When asked about future growth potential, Mr. Seigle replied that he believed Head would continue to grow rapidly in the future. He saw the potential of doubling the ski business in the next five years. Although he characterized the sportswear business as a "good calculated risk," he believed it offered the potential of expanding to $5 to $8 million per year. Beyond that he felt that Head might go in three possible directions. First, he believed that Head should once again explore the opportunities and risks of moving into the other price segments of the ski market, either under another brand or with a nonmetallic ski. Although he believed that by selling in a lower price range Head could sell 50,000 or more pairs of skis, the risks were also high. Second, he felt that Head should explore the opportunity in other related ski products, such as boots or bindings. Third, he felt that eventually Head should expand into other specialty sporting goods, preferably of a contraseasonal nature.

In looking to these new areas, Mr. Seigle had formulated a two-part product philosophy as follows:

Any new product which Head will consider should:
1. Be consistent with the quality and prestige image of Head Skis.
2. Should entail one or more of the following characteristics:
   a. High innovative content.
   b. High engineering content.
   c. High style appeal.
   d. Be patentable.

We will consider getting into new products through any of the normal methods such as internal product development, product acquisition, or corporate acquisition. If we are to move into a new area, we definitely want to have a product edge. For example, if we were to manufacture a boot, we would want to be different. We would only seriously consider it if we had a definite product advantage such as if we were to develop a high-quality plastic boot.

Howard Head, in speaking of the future, voiced the following hopes:

I would like to see Head grow in an orderly fashion sufficient to maintain its present youth and resiliency. That would mean at least 20 percent–25 percent per year. This statement does not preclude the possibility that we might grow faster. We believe the ski business alone will grow 20 percent–25 percent per year. As our staff capabilities grow, we will probably branch into other areas.

As to our objectives for the next five years, I would say that the first corporate objective is to maintain healthy growth in the basic ski business. It is the taproot of all that is good in Head. Second, we must be certain that any new activity is carefully selected for a reasonable probability of developing a good profit and an image platform consistent with the past activity of Head.

Appendix*

Types of Skis

Elements of a Well-Designed Ski

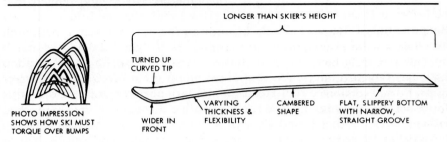

LONGER THAN SKIER'S HEIGHT

TURNED UP
CURVED TIP

PHOTO IMPRESSION
SHOWS HOW SKI MUST
TORQUE OVER BUMPS

WIDER IN
FRONT

VARYING
THICKNESS &
FLEXIBILITY

CAMBERED
SHAPE

FLAT, SLIPPERY BOTTOM
WITH NARROW,
STRAIGHT GROOVE

Wood Skis

If you are on a tight budget, well-designed wood skis at low prices are available from domestic and foreign manufacturers. Wood is a bundle of tubular cellulose cells bound together in an elastic medium called lignin. The internal slippage of wood skis not only lets them torque over the bumps in traverse, but damps any tendency to vibrate or chatter on hard rough surfaces. There are wood skis for any snow, any speed, and they are fun to ski on. Their only problem is a lack of durability. Wood skis are fragile. Besides, as wood skis are used, the internal slippage of the fibers increases, and they lose their life.

Wood Ski Cross-Section

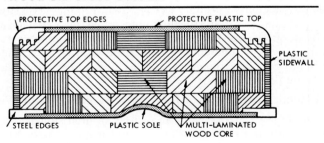

PROTECTIVE TOP EDGES

PROTECTIVE PLASTIC TOP

PLASTIC
SIDEWALL

STEEL EDGES

PLASTIC SOLE

MULTI-LAMINATED
WOOD CORE

In choosing a wood ski, it is probably wise to pay more than the minimum price. Multiple laminations of hickory or ash, a soft flex pattern, interlocking edges, polyethylene base, plastic top and sidewalls, tip and tail protectors are some of the features a beginner or intermediate should

---

* Source: *Skiing International Yearbook, 1967,* pp. 63–68. Copyright by Ziff-Davis Publishing Co.

look for in a better wood ski. When you get past the $40 to $70 range, your own dealer's recommendations will be your best guarantee of value.

FRP Skis

A few years ago there were only a handful of "epoxy" skis on the market, and skiers were eyeing them with mixed interest and distrust. Now the available models have multiplied almost unbelievably. New companies have been formed, and many of the established manufacturers have now brought out versions of their own. The plastic skis are still new enough for most skiers to be confused about their true nature—and with good reason, since there are so many types.

The word *epoxy* is part of the confusion. The true family resemblance of all the skis that are currently being lumped under that designation is the use of glass fibers locked into a plastic medium to create layers of great strength. The plastics engineers use the term *fiber-reinforced plastic* (FRP) to designate this type of structural solution. It is very strong.

The reinforcing layers used in these new designs derive their strength from the combined strength of millions of fine glass fibers or threads locked in the plastic layer. The potential strengths of materials in this family of structural plastics can exceed those of aluminum or steel. Unfortunately, there is no simple way to evaluate them or describe the materials actually in use. The wide variety of glass fibers, resins, and systems of molding and curing the fiber-reinforced layer produces a wide range of results. These can be evaluated only by laboratory tests or, finally, by actual in-service results.

FRP materials are being used for all sorts of sporting goods, industrial, and space-age applications. The strength-to-weight ratio is attractively high, and the possibility of creating new reinforced shapes by means of molding operations has proved to be attractive enough to encourage a great deal of experimentation. Skis seem to adapt to this structural technique.

Metal Skis

In the search for more durable skis, the metal skis took over the quality market about a decade ago and are widely accepted as ideal for both recreational skier and expert. Except for specialized racing uses, the wooden skis have been largely outmoded in the better ski market. Today, the fiber-reinforced plastic designs are the only challengers to the primacy of the metals.

Metal skis obtain their strength from aluminum sheets that are light in weight but very strong. The structure of a metal ski is somewhat like an "I" beam; when the ski is bent, the bottom sheet is stretched and the top sheet is compressed. The core material serves as the web—the vertical portion of the "I"—and must be attached to the top and bottom metal sheets securely enough to resist the shearing stress that occurs when the ski is bent.

Service Potential of Metal Skis

The possibility of rebuilding and refinishing metal skis has been one of the key sales attractions of the metal ski in this country. So long as bonding remains intact, only the effects of wear and tear—rocks, skis banging together, rough treatment in transportation, etc.—limit the life of the skis. The possibility of having the plastic surfaces and edges, or

Metal Ski Cross-Sections

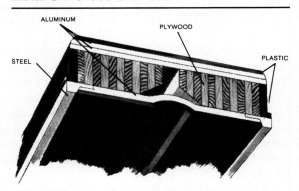

Northland Golden Jet—Cross-laminated fir plywood core with no filler in center, full-length bonded steel edge, aluminum sheets on both the top and the bottom.

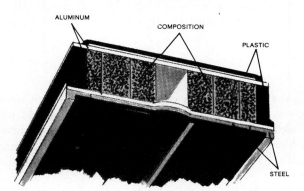

Hart Javelin—Grainless core of pressed particles, continuous full-length steel L edge welded to steel sheet, revealed aluminum top edge, phenolic plastic top.

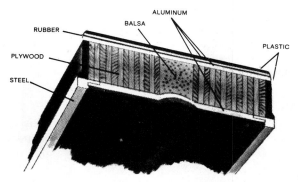

Head Competition—Cross-laminated fir plywood core, rubber damping layer on top of structure, full-length bonded steel L edge, high-density plastic base.

FRP CROSS-SECTIONS

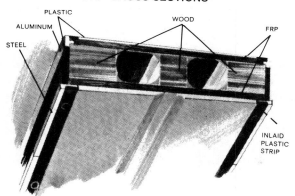

Kneissl White Star—Epoxy sandwich with interrupted wood core for lightness, sectional steel L edge screwed-in, aluminum top edge, two-color inlaid base.

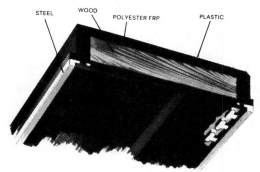

A&T K2—Vestigial core of pine, full wrap-around construction, bonded full-length L edge. ABS plastic top sheet. Bonded edges have tab construction for strength.

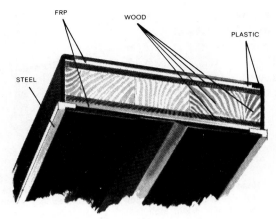

Yamaha Hi-Flex—FRP sandwich, hardwood core with grain running lengthwise, full-length bonded stainless steel L edges on bottom, with top edges of celluloid.

even the structural members themselves, replaced has strong appeal for the skier investing well over $100 in his skis. The rebuilding potential also tends to keep the trade-in and used resale value of the skis higher, making it less expensive for the skier to move to higher performance or more recent models as his skiing ability—or his desire for something new—dictates. The American companies were the first to develop rebuilding techniques, but more recently European factories have been establishing service centers in the United States.

There are three basic elements of FRP construction: the plastic material or resin; the glass fibers themselves; and the method of combining, curing, and shaping the composite reinforcing layer. Variation of any of these three elements affects the characteristics of the end product.

Service Potential of FRP Skis

One of the problems facing the manufacturers of fiber-reinforced plastic skis has been how to service and rebuild them—once the normal wear and tear of skiing has taken its toll. Only the metal skis, it has seemed, could be refinished and rebuilt.

Though it is true that you cannot heat up an FRP ski, melt the glue, resand, recoat, and reconstruct it quite as easily as you can a metal ski, progress has been made in this direction during the past season. Several manufacturers have set up regional service centers.

What these various service centers can accomplish is considerable. They are replacing bases and edges. They are renewing and refinishing top surfaces. In some cases, the structural fiberglass members can be separated from the wood core and replaced, producing in effect a brand-new ski. The sum of all this is real benefit to the average skier, who is unwilling to discard a pair of skis every season or so. The gap between metal and FRP skis, as far as service potential is concerned, is being narrowed. You will find that the costs range over approximately the same spread as the metal skis and that guarantee provisions are similar.

Exhibit 1

HEAD SKI COMPANY, INC.
Consolidated Balance Sheet, 1965–1967

Assets	As of April 24, 1965	As of April 30, 1966	As of April 29, 1967
Current assets:			
Cash	$ 162,646	$ 233,330	$ 263,896
Short-term commercial paper receivable	1,200,000	800,000	1,200,000
Notes and accounts receivable—less reserve	334,503	174,127	242,632
Inventories—valued at lower of cost or market	2,815,042	3,522,235	3,102,069
Prepayments and miscellaneous receivables	207,279	223,864	402,879
Total current assets	4,719,470	4,953,556	5,211,476
Fixed assets, at cost:			
Building—pledged under mortgage	1,014,738	1,012,085	1,010,149
Machinery and equipment	847,974	1,059,274	1,540,707
Other	147,336	213,692	715,089
	2,010,048	2,285,051	3,265,945
Less accumulated depreciation	822,255	892,153	1,123,203
Total fixed assets	1,187,793	1,392,898	2,142,742
Other assets:			
Unamortized bond discount and expenses	277,636	263,564	252,004
Cash surrender value of life insurance	103,117	120,589	133,568
Other	28,583	22,364	70,194
Total other assets	409,336	406,517	455,766
Total assets	$6,316,599	$6,752,971	$7,809,984

Liabilities and Stock-holders' Equity	As of April 24, 1965	As of April 30, 1966	As of April 29, 1967
Current liabilities:			
Accounts payable	$ 521,031	$ 299,040	$ 829,826
Current portion of long-term debt	20,600	21,000	23,100
Accrued expenses	451,062	413,865	549,720
Income taxes payable	39,102	299,452	333,514
Other	94,899	91,271	51,120
Total current liabilities	1,126,694	1,124,628	1,787,280
Long-term debt:			
Mortgage on building—5¾%, payable to 1978	396,646	376,036	331,115
Convertible subordinated debentures	2,125,000	2,125,000	2,125,000
	2,521,646	2,501,036	2,456,115
Less current portion	20,600	21,000	—
Total long-term debt	2,501,046	2,480,036	2,456,115
Commitments and contingent liabilities, stockholders' equity:			
Common stock—par value 50¢ per share (authorized 2 million shares; outstanding 1966, 915,202 shares; 1965, 882,840 shares adjusted for 2-for-1 stock split-up effective September 15, 1965)	220,710	457,601	459,401
Paid-in capital	1,820,323	1,679,700	1,694,700
Retained earnings	647,826	1,011,006	1,412,488
Total stockholders' equity	2,688,859	3,148,307	3,566,589
Total liabilities and stockholders' equity	$6,316,599	$6,752,971	$7,809,984

Consolidated Statement of Earnings

	52 Weeks Ended* April 25, 1964	52 Weeks Ended* April 24, 1965	53 Weeks Ended* April 30, 1966	52 Weeks Ended* April 29, 1967
Net Sales	$6,018,779	$8,600,392	$9,080,223	$11,048,072
Cost of sales	4,033,576	5,799,868	6,357,169	7,213,188
Gross profit	1,985,203	2,800,524	$2,723,054	$ 3,834,884
Expenses:				
Selling, administrative and general	1,169,392	1,697,659	2,029,531	2,756,939
Research and engineering	102,358	303,884	239,851	327,857
Total expenses	1,271,750	2,001,543	2,269,382	3,084,796
Income before income taxes and nonrecurring charges	713,453	798,981	453,672	750,088
Federal and state income taxes	367,542	392,515	221,034	348,606
Income before nonrecurring charges	345,911	406,466	232,638	401,482
Nonrecurring debt expense—after giving effect to income taxes	—	63,678	—	—
Net earnings	345,911	342,788	232,638	401,482
Net earnings as restated	$ 376,788	$ 393,713	$ 264,389	$ 401,482
Earnings per share before nonrecurring charges	0.40	0.51	0.26	0.44
Earnings per share after nonrecurring charges	0.40	0.43	0.26	0.44
Earnings per share as restated	0.48	0.49	0.29	0.44

Earnings per share are based on average shares outstanding of 904,237 in 1966 and 801,196 in 1965 after giving effect to the 2-for-1 stock split-up effective September 15, 1965, and the 3-for-1 stock split on July 7, 1964.

* Earnings restated April 29, 1967, to give effect to an adjustment in the lives of depreciable assets for federal income tax purposes.

	52 Weeks Ended April 27, 1963	52 Weeks Ended April 25, 1964	52 Weeks Ended April 24, 1965	53 Weeks Ended April 30, 1966	52 Weeks Ended April 29, 1967
Net sales	$4,124,445	$6,018,779	$8,600,392	$9,080,223	$11,048,072
Net earnings	191,511	376,788	393,713	264,389	401,482
Expenditures for plant and equipment	272,154	513,130	558,865	304,102	1,027,854
Depreciation	79,719	132,497	211,683	238,161	249,961
Working capital	654,676	1,525,015	3,542,857	3,828,928	3,424,196
Plant and equipment and other assets, net	701,875	1,187,246	1,745,839	1,799,415	2,598,508
Long-term debt	287,245	1,176,647	2,501,046	2,480,036	2,456,115
Shareholders' equity	1,069,306	1,535,614	2,787,650	3,148,307	3,566,589
Earnings per share	0.25	0.48	0.49	0.29	0.44
Average shares outstanding	777,600	777,600	801,196	904,237	916,542

Average shares outstanding reflect the 2-for-1 stock split-up effective September 15, 1965, and 3-for-1 stock split on July 7, 1964.
Statistical data for the years 1963 through 1966, inclusive, have been adjusted to reflect retroactive adjustments.
Source: Company records.

Exhibit 2

Dealer Organization, 1962–1967 (Franchised dealers)

Year	Number at Beginning	Newly Franchised	Terminated or Not Renewed	Number at End
1962	390	105	41	454
1963	454	136	30	560
1964	560	167	57	670
1965	670	96	39	727
1966	727 (est.)	n.a.	n.a.	900
1967	900 (est.)	30	n.a.	—

n.a.—Not available.

Note: In addition the franchised dealers had approximately 300 branches which are not included in the above figures.

Source: Company records.

Exhibit 3

Organization Chart (June 1967)

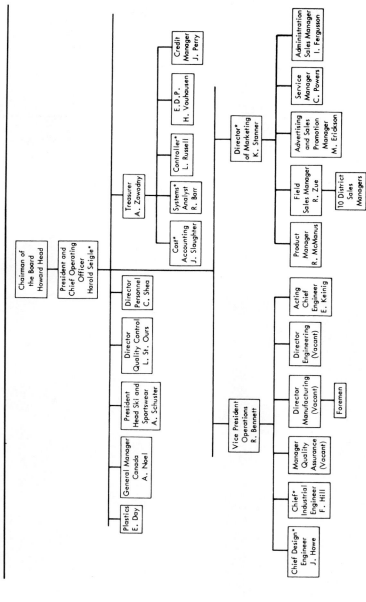

Chairman of the Board — Howard Head

President and Chief Operating Officer — Harold Seigle*

- Plastics — E. Day
- General Manager Canada — A. Noel
- President Head Ski and Sportswear — A. Schuster
- Director Quality Control — L. St. Ours
- Director Personnel — C. Shea
- Treasurer — A. Zawodny
  - Cost* Accounting — J. Slaughter
  - Systems* Analyst — R. Barr
  - Controller* — L. Russell
  - E.D.P. — H. Vouhausen
  - Credit Manager — J. Perry
- Vice President Operations — R. Bennett
  - Chief Design* Engineer — J. Howe
  - Chief* Industrial Engineer — F. Hill
  - Manager Quality Assurance (Vacant)
  - Director Manufacturing (Vacant)
    - Foremen
  - Director Engineering (Vacant)
  - Acting Chief Engineer — E. Keinig
- Director* of Marketing — K. Stanner
  - Product Manager — R. McManus
  - Field Sales Manager — R. Zue
    - 10 District Sales Managers
  - Advertising and Sales Promotion Manager — M. Erickson
  - Service Manager — C. Powers
  - Administration Sales Manager — I. Fergusson

* With Head less than one year.
Source: Company records.

Exhibit 4 Samples of the New Head Skiwear

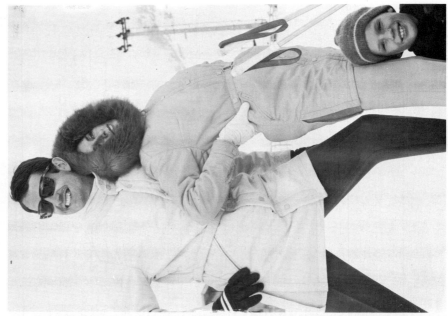

Exhibit 4 (concluded)

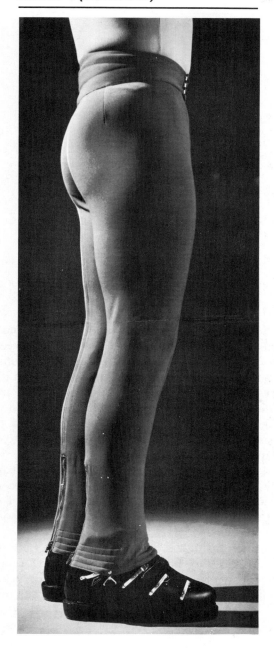

Southern Packaging (A)

Introduction

In early April 1981 David Levine was thinking about what he had learned during his first three months as president and chief executive officer of Southern Packaging (SP), a $40 million producer of customized packaging materials. SP headquarters were in Houston, Texas, and its main production facilities were in Waco, Texas. Levine took office in January 1981 after serving on SP's board of directors since 1975. He replaced W. C. Williams, a founder and major shareholder, who had retired as chief executive officer in January 1981 and had urged Levine to consider taking the job. Williams continued to serve as chairman.

Levine had joined SP after a very successful, 25-year career with a large, diversified forest products company. He decided to join SP because "it was basically an opportunity to be the true CEO of a publicly held company and a real challenge to see what kind of leadership ability I had and how well I could develop other people."

Levine described his first months at SP as "the high point of anxiety in my life." Earnings for the six months ending December 31, 1980, had fallen by almost 40 percent from the previous year, despite a 10 percent rise in sales, and the first half of 1981 promised no improvement. From the day he became president, Levine had moved vigorously to address SP's operating problems, but his efforts had proven frustrating

Copyright © 1984 by the President and Fellows of Harvard College
Harvard Business School case 385–179

and disappointing. He said, "I found a lot of weak managers and a lot of others who were very resistant to me, who just gave me lip service."

Nevertheless, in early April Levine had to decide what action to take on three issues. One was a union organizing effort in SP's largest plant. Another was the possibility of moving SP into the packaging market for high tech consumer electronics products like audio- and videocassettes and floppy disks. The third issue was the question of how he should follow up on a memo he had sent to the heads of SP's operating units specifying how they should prepare strategic profiles of their companies. The memo was one of Levine's first steps in what he expected to be a long-term effort to get SP managers to think "more strategically and less opportunistically." For Levine the difficulty of handling each of these three issues was compounded by his limited familiarity with SP personnel.

The Company

SP (known as Waco Packaging before 1973) was founded in 1933. One of its founders was W. C. Williams, who was chairman of the company and a major shareholder when Levine became president. Williams described the company's history:

> A friend of mine, Robinson Jeffers, bought a printing company that was in receivership in the middle of the depression, and I was its sixth employee. I made two dollars a week. We were a very poor company and lost money for three or four years. What really got us started, around 1937, was selling labels to bakers, and I sold these first in Waco and then in other cities in the south and eventually even in Chicago. For most of the next 20 years, we were a very small, more or less successful Waco company. Our name was Waco Packaging. We continued to sell labels as well as customized boxes for small consumer products. By 1959 we had sales of about $5 million, and we'd had several years of strong growth because we had added flexible packaging—that is, packaging made out of cellophane—to our other products.
>
> It was in the early 1960s that we started having problems. We knew the packaging industry was growing, growing fast, but we just weren't keeping up. So one thing we did was try to become more professional by broadening our board of directors. We added a local investment banker and a friend of mine with a lot of marketing experience. In 1969 when our sales were about $7 million, we went public on the over-the-counter market. After this, Jeffers owned about 20 percent of the company. I owned a little bit more than 10 percent, and several others who had been there from the early years owned 5 percent apiece.
>
> In the early 1970s we made several small acquisitions. These were Puritan Corp., Plastek, Inc., Applied Designs, Inc., New Screen Designs, Inc., and NovelTee, Inc.
>
> In four years or so the acquisitions added about 25 percent to our sales.

We also set up a corporate office, located in the Waco plant, to supervise Waco Packaging—the original packaging business—along with the companies we bought. The headquarters handled personnel policies, long-range planning, and relationships with banks. To distinguish the new corporate office from Waco Packaging, we created a new name, and that was Southern Packaging. In 1975 the corporate office was moved across town to a separate office building, and in 1978 the corporate offices were moved to Houston, which was judged to be a better location for the headquarters of a growing, regional company. Houston was roughly 150 miles from Waco. This is basically the organization we had in place through the rest of the 1970s.

When Levine became CEO in January 1981 SP sales were approaching $40 million (see Exhibit 1). The company was organized into six operating units, which were Waco Packaging and the five acquisitions. SP had two group vice presidents, one for Waco Packaging and the other for the acquisitions known within SP as "the subsidiaries." (See Exhibit 2 for a table of organization.)

Waco Packaging had three separate divisions, all based in Waco. The three divisions shared the same plant and sales force, but each had its own general manager. Its largest division was the Plastic Packaging Division, with 1980 sales of $14.7 million. The division extruded, printed, and laminated a wide range of plastic flexible packaging materials used for products such as snack foods, men's underwear, and coffee. Most of the competitors in the flexible packaging market were small, independent companies. Sales of flexible packaging, in real dollars, were expected to grow 2.3 percent annually between 1980 and 1984.

Despite its slow growth, flexible packaging was a dynamic market in which new products could quickly gain share; both new and old products could lose share just as quickly. Foil, glass, paper, polymers, and composites of these materials competed with packaging that used flexible materials. Polymers were another alternative. Their raw material was cheap, they were available in many forms, and they could be readily adapted by the producer to end-user's specifications for heat, light, shelf life, water- and grease-proof qualities, strength, color, and printing characteristics. SP customers included BIC, Frito-Lay, and Nabisco, along with many smaller companies.

The second largest division was the Paper Division, with 1980 sales of $8 million. Paper used lithographic printing to prepare paperboard and carton packages for small consumer products such as Gillette razors. While average real growth for the entire carton and paperboard industry in the 1970s had been 4.1 percent per year, the estimate for 1980–1984 was 2.4 percent, largely because of competition from alternative materials, especially plastics. SP competitors ranged from large diversified packaging companies to very small operations.

The smallest division in Waco Packaging was the Print Division, with 1980 sales of $5 million. Print made pressure-sensitive labels for textile, health, and pharmaceutical products. Numerous local small- and medium-sized companies supplied such labels.

There were five operating units in SP's subsidiary group. SP had sought to acquire small packaging firms with attractive earnings growth or good earnings potential. (See Exhibit 3 for financial data.) Puritan had facilities in Ohio and North Carolina and 1980 sales of $2.8 million. Puritan produced skin packaging and blister packaging in which products, such as small tools, were immobilized on printed paperboard by a "second skin" of plastic film. SP had acquired Puritan becaue it had a good share of its local market and a successful history of developing new technologies for skin packaging. SP expected Puritan's sales to grow 20 percent per year.

Plastek, Inc., was in the same business as Puritan, selling skin packaging in California. Its 1980 sales were $3 million. Although Plastek had been losing money for two years, SP had hoped to realize scale benefits from their combined market share. However, managers at Puritan had recently purchased equipment suitable for long, low unit cost production runs only to discover that the West Coast market demanded frequent variations in copy, with many short runs and changeovers. Sales went flat for the entire skin market in 1980 as the large companies that had been switching to skin packaging retrenched during the economy's downturn and cut back marketing efforts that would have required new packaging.

Applied Designs, Inc., was based in Louisville, Kentucky, and had 1980 sales of $2.9 million. It was a local company which supplied a varied range of customers with products such as printed vinyl decals and lighted sign panels. New Screen Designs, Inc., based in Memphis, Tennessee, had 1980 sales of $0.8 million. It manufactured pressure-sensitive decals and metal signs used on truck cabs and trailers, heavy equipment, boats, motor homes, and vans. Applied Designs and New Screen Designs had been jointly owned and were acquired together because both seemed like good companies. The smallest subsidiary was NovelTee, Inc., based in Dallas, Texas, with 1980 sales of $0.7 million. NovelTee manufactured informal wear featuring padded, three-dimensional designs applied by an adhesive process. SP acquired NovelTee in 1974.

Each of these six operating units had its own manufacturing facilities, sales force, and administrative organization. None of SP's machinery or manufacturing techniques was proprietary. None of its customers represented more than 10 percent of SP's total sales. SP was generally the second or third supplier to its customers; other suppliers ranged from $200 million packaging subsidiaries of companies like R. J. Reynolds, or larger companies predominantly in the packaging industry, to label suppliers with annual sales of less than $200,000.

The first supplier had the best position: it was usually consulted first on new packaging requirements, and higher volume allowed the first supplier to lower costs. The customers used other suppliers in several ways: to keep the first supplier's prices honest; as backup suppliers so that any failure by the first supplier would not shut the line down; as innovators; and as a buffer to be cut back when business slowed. Typically, the first suppliers would get about half the business, the second, 25 percent, and then several smaller companies (of which SP was usually one) divided the last quarter. SP generally had 10 percent to 15 percent of a large customer's business and half or more of a small customer's. Second and third ranked suppliers received no price premium or other advantages for their precarious "insurance" function; they were simply offered a standard going rate that they could take or leave.

Wallace Stevens, the general manager of Plastic Packaging, gave the following overview of SP's business:

> This is customized work. What we have here is basically a make-and-sell business; every run is different. As our customers change their marketing, even in slight ways, our production has to change. In effect we never run a repeat order. Even though the package may appear to be the same year after year to the consumer, there are always slight changes that we have got to accommodate. This is basically a job shop and our job keeps changing.
>
> We have to be opportunistic and reactive in this business. People here have to enjoy a good crisis. This job is for people who like interruptions and nonroutine, not accounting types. Waco is essentially a link in its customer's chain of manufacturing. This is both a blessing and a curse. We have strong pressure to produce our products at low price. It also has to be functionable, that is, it's got to run on our customer's equipment and a lot of the filling machines run very fast. At the same time it's got to be aesthetically right—we sell color, design, graphics, color consistency, sharpness, everything you can imagine that makes up the picture that the consumer sees. Once we are working with a customer, we are unlikely to be displaced by price competition unless the gap between our prices and others' prices gets too big. Generally, our customers don't want to run the risk of changing firms.
>
> To get new business you've got to be close enough to a customer to understand when new products and new packages are going to be required, and then you've got to get with the engineering people who are designing the packaging and show them what you can do. If you want to try to displace a competitor, which is very hard to do, you've got to have a big change in your recipe for making a package. You've got to save the customer a lot of money, add some new feature that wasn't there before, but there is very little head-to-head competition. Each customer and each supplier watches the other supplier for mistakes and then says, "Give us a try— this is how we'll do a better job." What we try to do is to become consultants to our customers so that we understand their needs and they understand our capabilities.
>
> Most of our competitors are smaller than we are. These are mom-and-pop operations that usually concentrate on a certain region or a certain

kind of package. There are also a few much larger competitors that are generalists like we are and offer a wide range of packaging products, and there are a few large specialists, but not in many markets. Waco is a medium-sized generalist. We have close, long-term relationships with many of our customers, and I guess they see us as "good old boys" who can deliver the goods.

James Dickey, an outside board member and friend of Levine's, commented:

The mom-and-pop operations aren't sophisticated, but owner-operated means the guy is right there, does his own sales; his wife handles the checkbook so he knows he's all right. You can do that up to about $5 to $10 million in sales. They are very tough to compete against. Then you're up against giants like Continental Can and St. Regis. Then there are companies in the $20 to $50 million sales range that are too big for close control and don't sell enough to make it low cost. SP is trying to move to professional management in a low-margin industry.

In the 70s Waco Packaging saw itself as one business unit with three product lines. There was one sales force for all of Waco Packaging, one support staff, one guy to monitor everything, one creative arts department. They told themselves that with this great generalist capability they'd go in to J. C. Penney and they could give them everything they need. But those kinds of accounts buy millions of dollars, for hundreds of products, and with different people making the decisions on suppliers for different products—they couldn't care less about Waco's "full-line capability." When you go in to sell snack food packaging to one of the giants, your competitor is some guy who only sells potato chip bags. Instead, Waco had 26 salesmen each with three or four accounts in snack food.

Wallace Stevens said, "The company has a lot to do with Mr. Williams. He really represented the company, its image, and its style. He was quiet, a real southern gentleman, ethical par excellence. There was no puffery about him at all. He was very fair and generous. He even cosigned home loans for some people who worked here. No one was ever laid off. He also supported the strong selling effort that kept the company going for so long. Salesmen got out and sold all they could sell, they built real relationships with customers, and management was cheering them all the way. This company became very good at taking an order and making it."

Dickey said, "Waco saw themselves as polite, nice guys, an image which followed W. C. and his culture. The company was paternalistic, there'd never been a work cutback, and W. C. wouldn't fire anyone. There's been almost no management turnover, no push for how SP can grow and do better, or how to get ROI up. It just hasn't been a high-level concern."

By the time W. C. Williams decided to retire, his successor faced management problems more complicated and of longer duration than simple uninspiring performance. Dickey reported: "There was a big, deep emotional split between W. C. and the SP staff on the one hand, and Waco's Randall Jarell, the president of SP. Jarell, a 30-year veteran at SP, spent nearly all his time with Waco Packaging. Communication between Jarell and Williams had broken down, and there was no mutual respect. Jarell was an excellent salesman and sales manager, so they kept him on. After SP went public in 1969, W. C. Williams assembled a board of independent and successful executives. The Waco Packaging managers resented the board's active role which was unfamiliar to them, and a barrier developed between W. C. Williams and the Waco managers."

Levine's First Months

David Levine became president of SP in January 1981 after serving as a director since 1975. He began working at SP in mid-January.

Since 1972, Levine had been president of the $225 million Houston-based packaging division of a diversified forest products corporation with corporate headquarters in Connecticut. The division's principal product was paperboard, but it did not compete with SP. Levine was a native of Houston who had received his B.I.E. from the University of Texas in 1951, studied in graduate school there, and joined the forest products company in 1954. He worked in manufacturing, purchasing, administration, and planning before becoming manufacturing manager for its packaging division. He started the company's Asian operations and served as its manager director in Bangkok, responsible for its operations in Southeast Asia, the Philippines, and Indonesia.

When Levine returned to the United States, he was named general manager of the packaging division. In 1972, he became president of the division. At that time, its sales were $48 million, and for the next nine years the division grew at a 30 percent annual rate. The division's major products were labels and paperboard, sold to beverages companies. People who worked with Levine described him as "dynamic . . . aggressive . . . blunt, though thoughtful . . . shrewd . . . kind about people's feelings." He believed that he learned habits of ambition and hard work from his father and mother, who were poor Jewish emigrants from central Europe.

Levine, who had been married 25 years and had three children, was a director of the Houston chapter of the American Red Cross, the National Minority Purchasing Council, the Texas Business and Industry Association, and the Houston Chamber of Commerce. In 1979 Levine was appointed to the Texas Board of Industry and Trade by the governor.

When W. C. Williams decided to retire as CEO, Levine and two other members of the board were asked to serve as a committee to determine whether Randall Jarell could perform satisfactorily as CEO. It was assumed throughout the company that Jarell would succeed Williams. Williams had expressed some reservations on this score, but the board decided that Jarell would get the job unless he demonstrated a lack of capability for the position.

In mid-1979 the three-member committee had interviewed key managers to get their ideas about the company's problems and opportunities. The committee also asked Jarell to prepare a statement describing SP's problems, his view of what the company's objectives should be, and his plans for accomplishing them.

The board was dissatisfied with Jarell's plan. Its members with marketing experience, including Levine, sat down with Jarell to help work out some of the plan's shortcomings. After extended discussions with Jarell during the fall of 1979 and spring of 1980, the members concluded in April 1980 that Jarell should not succeed W. C. Williams. Williams was asked to delay his retirement and to continue as CEO until a successor could be found.

Jarell left SP in June 1980 and ultimately took a job with Frito-Lay, a major SP customer, in February 1981. Board member Dickey reported, "Waco people thought Jarell was 'fired' for purely political reasons, like Watergate or something. People in the company had no concept of 'performance was poor, so Jarell should be out since he had no plan to turn things around.' I asked people I knew what Waco managers thought was the reason Jarell left, and they said, 'Political friction— it was W. C. and the board against the real workers in Waco.' "

The board began looking for other candidates within SP, asking more probing questions than they had the first time around. As the search continued and the board members learned more about the problems SP faced, members began telling Levine, "You know, David, we need a guy like you—in fact, we need you, David!" Levine's initial response was that he was happy and had no desire to leave his job. He even provided the committee with the names of some potential candidates. Eventually, however, he changed his mind.

> Several other board members also asked me to take the job and I started to think about it. Finally I thought, "Why not do it?" Advancing where I was would mean moving to Stamford, and I really wasn't eager to leave Houston. It was also unclear how far someone like myself could advance in a company dominated by the "tree people" from the core business, and there was also political squabbling within the corporation I didn't enjoy. But it was not an easy decision, and I spent about six months thinking it over. There were the attractive challenges, but there were also negatives. I was 50 years old and knew that this job would take a lot of individual, detailed effort. In the recent past, I basically depended on others, and my job was to supervise and help them do their job right. So I had the question of whether I really wanted to get down into the details of operations and, for that matter, the question of whether I really could do it again. After all, I was moving from a $225 million operation to a $40 million operation.

I guess I also wondered about what other people would think. Would they wonder whether I was fired or not?

I think the announcement of my appointment as president was a total shock to the organization, absolutely the most stunning thing they had ever heard. And this shock was followed by a second one when Randall Jarell, who had left the company, went to work for Frito-Lay, a major SP customer. All of this was a bombshell.

Jarell's departure mattered in several ways. For one thing, he had created a lead shield around Waco Packaging and ran it by himself as a kind of fiefdom. In fact, I think that one of the reasons W. C. Williams wanted to build a strong, outside board was to find a way of penetrating this lead shield and resisting Jarell's initiatives. It just wasn't Williams's style to confront this head-on. Within Waco, everything was run on a personal basis by Randall Jarell. I was even told that the group VP for Waco sometimes introduced himself as "the president of Waco Packaging." There were no group meetings to talk about the business or company problems. It was all one-on-one meetings with Jarell, meetings that he could control. And that was part of the motivation for the acquisitions—Jarell really had Waco Packaging under his control. So my first big step was to try to get on the other side of the barriers that Jarell had built up.

I'm an activist, and I really feel I have to get into the details of things. I started out by arranging meetings with the general managers and top people of the divisions and operating units. This was a kind of meeting that had never been held before. In the past, Mr. Williams had dealt with the general managers through the group vice presidents. And members of the SP corporate staff who needed to visit plants had to get permission from the group vice presidents. So I jumped down two whole levels of the organization when I started these meetings. And I'd start out and say, "Tell me about your products." They would talk a bit, and I would take notes. Then I would say, "Stop, explain that a little bit further." They'd explain it further, and I'd ask more questions.

I like to draw things. I like to make charts and put down the basics in diagrams or matrixes. So I would say, "Does it work this way? Does it work that way?"

I also tried to talk about my philosophy of our business. In particular, I stressed that we had to be much more marketing oriented. We couldn't just be generalists with standard technology. I tried to put all of this as positively as I could, but these meetings didn't go very well. We just weren't making any progress. I am very specific, and I asked a lot of pointed questions. I would say, "Explain extrusion, tell me how you laminate this product, and so on and so on." But we just didn't get anywhere.

I did the same thing at the next meeting with people from another operating unit. I found that they were totally antagonistic toward the board, and some of that wore off directly on me. Basically, I asked questions, and I got the idiot treatment. At a set of meetings in the Print Division I found that people were really in over their heads. I asked my questions, and I found out that they knew even less about their competitors and their markets than I did. It seemed to be incomprehensible to them that a CEO would ask about these things. Print in fact was losing money, and I thought they were lucky they weren't doing even worse than they were.

I asked managers why their units had performed poorly. I learned that they had been installing new equipment without having trained people to use it and had huge cost overruns. I asked them about their prices and learned that we weren't price leaders. If anything, we lagged far behind. So I followed up by saying, "Are these good customers?" They would say, "Yes." "Do we have any competition here?" They would say, "No." "How is our service?" "Fine," they would tell me. "Are we in solid?" "Yes, we are." "Are we getting a decent margin?" "No," they would say. Then I would say, "Why didn't we raise our prices?" And I wouldn't get an answer. I suppose the salesmen had such good relationships, doing back-flips for so many years to do things right for the customers, that they never actually thought about raising prices to levels that really were competitive.

There was no sense of urgency. Even though we had had one or two bad quarters, people here explained them away by general economic conditions. Everyone assumed that the company was healthy, was solvent, and had no real problems for the future. Early on I decided I would meet once a month with the four top managers of the company. These were the two group VPs, finance VP, and the human resource VP. I wanted to discuss the basic issues facing SP. This had never happened before, and the people really lacked the capability of having these kinds of discussions. Before, SP had held quarterly information meetings at each division with no questions, no discussion, just reporting. When I started asking questions about variances, problems, or opportunity, I only got specific answers about opportunities.

After about two weeks I found myself asking, "Why did I take this job in the first place?" The more I talked with people, the harder and faster problems kept coming in. At the end of my first month I was very, very frustrated and filled with anxiety. I was also away from home most of the time, in Waco, and I lived in a furnished apartment that had about a 40-watt light bulb, and I ate most of my dinners at Burger King. One thing I realized in these first two weeks was that I needed more information than I had on the managers I was working with. So I spent some time looking at the personnel files.

I was in charge of this operation and had weak managers and resistant managers. Out of the top 14 managers, my guess was that half of them were giving me lip service, another three or four were going to resist me, and the rest might eventually move in the right direction. Some of the resisters were probably using lip service, too. I guess they thought I was intruding and eventually would give in to them or go away. Lip service was the most frustrating, because so far as I could tell, they would say they agreed with me and then would go back to doing what they had been doing before.

James Dickey had a similar perspective on the meetings Levine initiated:

I just assumed that the monthly meetings which David started would go over the division financials. But the division people weren't used to the idea of performance monitoring at all. Capital allocation was pretty informal—mainly on the basis of "I need more equipment because sales are going up." No one wanted to talk about problems. They didn't even talk about some of the important products at Waco that had started losing money. It was considered impolite to ask the guy in charge what was going on if a unit had material costs going through the roof and scrap rate rising— you'd be considered a meddler, hostile, and unfriendly. So they'd talk instead about some new product or some meetings with these great potential customers. Their feeling was, "Hey, we work our rear ends off and do the best we can—if the Fates are against us, that's tough!" Their attitude wasn't, "We produce results, and results can't be changed."

The Union Drive

On Tuesday of the first week in April, Levine learned that a union organizing drive was under way among workers in the Print Division of Waco Packaging. Allen Tate, the group VP for Waco Packaging, and John Ransom, the corporate human resources manager, brought the news to Levine.

Tate and Ransom told Levine they had learned about the union effort one week earlier from Thomas McGrath, production manager in the Print Division. At a regular monthly meeting between McGrath and the 16 hourly workers on one shift, McGrath heard complaints of unfair treatment by supervisors in the department. The workers also told McGrath that some workers were signing union cards.

Later that day, McGrath told the general manager of the Print Division, Gregory Corso, about the meeting. Corso, in turn, contacted Tate and Ransom. Two days later, on Thursday, Corso, Tate, and Ransom met with the same group of workers and heard the same complaints. The workers did not object to their basic pay level, which was comparable to other printing plants in the area. They did complain that their supervisors made recommendations for merit pay increases on the basis of favoritism, while at other companies print workers moved to higher pay levels largely on the basis of seniority. The workers also said that favoritism affected job and shift assignments, and they wanted these decisions to be made on the basis of seniority in the future.

When asked about the union drive, the workers said the Graphics Art International Union had begun a serious organizing effort at SP in November 1980. A union representative had recently told several workers that the union had collected signatures from at least 30 percent of the print workers at the Waco plant. Within a week or two, the union expected to present SP with an approved petition from the NLRB for a union election. Tate and Ransom told Levine they had ended the meeting by thanking the workers for their candor and promising to try to solve the problems.

As Levine discussed the problem with Tate and Ransom, he learned that roughly a quarter of the employees in the Waco Packaging plant were print workers and that a number of them had relatives in the

Paper and Plastic Packaging divisions. He also found out that Corso, the Print Division manager, had hired a Waco lawyer, with experience in labor law, to give advice on tactics. One of the lawyer's first comments was that, in all probability, the union had already signed up at least 50 percent of the print workers. Otherwise, they would not be petitioning the NLRB for an election.

However, as Levine heard more of what the lawyer had said, he found himself wondering how much experience with union organizing drives the lawyer actually had. For one thing, Levine was fairly confident that SP could argue to the NLRB that the print workers alone were not a proper bargaining unit since they made up only a fourth of all the employees in the Waco plant. Levine based these judgments on his own experience: He had managed both union and nonunion operations and had worked personally with union leaders and with Houston labor attorneys.

Levine also knew that there had never been a union at SP, and he strongly believed that workers were much better off at a nonunion company, as long as it was well managed.

Consumer Electronics

The union question arose at a time when Levine's calendar was already very crowded. Moreover, Levine believed that two recurring questions—one involving consumer electronics and the other involving strategic planning—had to be resolved in the near future.

Packaging for consumer electronics had been on Levine's mind ever since a mid-March meeting with Cleanth Brooks, marketing manager in the Paper Division of Waco Packaging. Levine had asked Brooks the same question he had put to many other SP managers: What ideas do you have for new products or markets? Brooks answered the question immediately and enthusiastically. He gave Levine a copy of a report he had made in late 1979 on packaging opportunities for consumer electronics products, such as audio- and videocassettes and floppy disks. Brooks's conclusion was that this market presented an extraordinary opportunity. (Exhibit 4 gives excerpts from Brooks's report.)

As their conversation continued, Levine found that he shared Brooks's enthusiasm. The market was in its earliest phases and promised to grow very rapidly for at least a decade. And aside from several much smaller niche markets, it was the only major new opportunity that Levine had come across during his early inquiries at SP. In fact, Levine had already heard something about the market from a close business acquaintance in Maxcell's U.S. operations. (Maxcell is a major Japanese producer of tapes and computer disks.) In the weeks after his meeting with Brooks, Levine had grown more and more convinced that SP should make a major commitment to this market.

At the same time, however, several considerations tempered Levine's enthusiasm. First of all, the managers of Waco's three divisions had not acted on Brooks's 1979 report. Brooks told Levine that in 1978 Waco Packaging had supplied some consumer electronics packaging to Sony on a trial basis. Sony had rejected the SP products and refused to discuss further supply arrangements. Brooks thought the Waco managers rejected his proposal because they didn't want to risk further humiliation at the hands of the Japanese.

Second, Levine knew that this concern about meeting Japanese standards was quite legitimate. 3M and four Japanese companies—Maxcell, TDK, Fuji, and Sony—were the major packaging buyers in this market. Even though the Japanese manufactured audiotapes, videotapes, and floppy disks at several locations in the United States, they bought their packaging from Japanese companies. From his own experience Levine knew that Japanese packaging companies used the highest quality raw material, bought the latest fabrication and printing equipment, and then modified the equipment to suit their needs. Levine even remembered a conversation in which a Japanese packaging company executive complained that American paper currency was printed sloppily.

Levine knew that if SP were to move into this market, it would have to purchase the same equipment the Japanese had and set up a special production operation just for these products. Levine would probably have to call upon his own business acquaintances to learn more about Japanese equipment suppliers and prospective Japanese customers and gain introductions to them. Setting up the business would also require a number of trips to Japan by SP personnel, including Levine. SP might also need a special sales force for this product, and the managers responsible for the business would have to begin thinking and planning much more aggressively and systematically than they had in the past. The initial investment in the business could easily reach or exceed $2 million.

Despite these reservations Levine wanted to pursue this opportunity. Fundamentally, the product was not much different from other SP products. It simply had to be manufactured to extremely high standards. Moreover, rapid growth in consumer electronics would create many opportunities for packaging suppliers and high margins for the packagers who could compete successfully.

Strategic Planning

In Levine's mind the strategic planning issue was the question of how he should follow up on a memo he had sent to the managers of the six SP operating units in early March. The memo provided an outline showing how each unit would be expected to develop business plans in the future. (Exhibit 5 gives excerpts from the memo.)

In meetings with these managers Levine had told them that he intended to introduce an explicit strategic planning system at SP. Its aim would be "to get everyone in the company to think more strategically and less opportunistically." He also said it would take several years to fully develop the necessary database and get all the bugs out of the system. Nevertheless, he intended to start the process as soon as possible.

Levine's ultimate goal was to divide SP into 10 to 25 product lines and have each of them develop its own detailed business plan. The corporate office would array these in a portfolio and allocate funds among them. Levine had used the portfolio approach before and believed that "planning develops consensus and commitment as to where a company is headed and how it expects to get there. It creates a climate for coordinating the efforts of all businesses in a single corporate strategy."

Levine had considered several ways of following up on his memo. Some involved various series of meetings with the six managers and group VPs to discuss basic approaches and ideas for strategic planning. In time, these discussions could focus on the plans for each operating unit. What concerned Levine about these approaches was that fiscal 1982 would start on July 1, and he had inherited capital spending plans for the year totaling nearly $2 million. Even if SP could fund these plans comfortably, Levine was reluctant to commit such a large amount of money before the company had really started to do systematic planning. Levine thought very highly of the corporate vice presidents for finance and human resources whom he inherited from W. C. Williams, but the corporate office had no strategic planner. Ideally, Levine wanted to find some way of accelerating the planning process while putting brakes on capital spending.

In approaching the planning issues, as well as all the other issues he faced at SP, Levine wanted above all to follow lessons he had learned from his own experience.

> The most rewarding part of the business is seeing your managers embrace the philosophy. It's just like your children, when you see them mature and do the things that are satisfying to them. It's got to be the highest reward one can receive. Early in my career, I had two different jobs, and on each of them I thought I had done pretty good work, but both times I was demoted and no one told me what I did wrong or how I could do better. I don't want to repeat that here. I want to be sure that everybody who wants to be on the team has a fair chance to play.

Exhibit 1

Operation Results

	1980	1979	1978	1977
Net sales	$ 34,961	$ 30,029	$ 26,965	$ 23,463
Cost of sales	27,137	22,844	21,050	17,628
Selling & administrative expense	5,726	4,869	4,355	3,742
Operating income	2,098	2,316	1,560	2,093
Interest expense	(432)	(392)	(229)	(228)
Interest income	140	149	22	44
Other income	80	134	33	95
Income from operations	1,886	2,207	1,386	2,004
Taxes	782	944	614	965
Net income	1,104	1,263	772	1,039
Net/share	.85	.98	.60	.79
Shares out	1,290,368	1,290,368	1,290,368	1,308,024
Cash dividend/share	$ .256	$ .224	$ .189	$ .134
Net fixed assets	6,411	5,121	4,747	4,090
Working capital	6,414	6,669	4,058	4,191
LTD	4,441	4,209	2,243	2,150
Equity	8,786	8,014	7,039	6,512
Number of employees	615	573	539	505
Number of shareholders	848	879	797	710
Capital expenditures	$ 1,712	$ 1,252	$ 1,259	$ 512
Depreciation & amortization	728	659	530	474
Current ratio	2.9:1	3.4:1	2.5:1	2.8:1
LTD/capital	33.6%	34.4%	24.2%	24.8%
Profit margin	3.2%	4.2%	2.9%	4.4%
ROE	13.1%	16.8%	11.4%	16.8%

Exhibit 2

Southern Packaging in 1981 (Years at SP shown in parentheses)

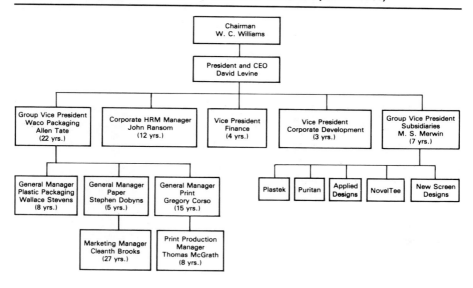

Exhibit 3

Subsidiary Financial Performance

Units	Sales (M)	PBT	ROA (before Tax)	1977–1980 Growth Rate
Puritan Packaging Corporation	$2.8	338	30%	13%
Plastek	3.0	Neg.	Neg.	N/A
Applied Designs	2.9	291	28%	6%
New Screen Designs	0.8	63	28%	7%
NovelTee	0.7	333	130%	11%

Exhibit 4

Audio- and Videotape Market Report (December 20, 1979)

I. Products
    A. Audio
        1. Pressure-sensitive labels.
        2. Audio inserts.
        3. Film overwrap.
        4. Bags and pouches.
        5. Blister cards.
        6. Miscellaneous cartons and labels.
    B. Video
        1. Sleeves.
        2. Inserts.
        3. Pressure-sensitive labels.
        4. Promotional labels and film.

II. Size and Growth
    Cassettes—240 million.
    8-track—28 million.
    Open reel—10 million.
    Growth—13%–20% per year.

III. Videotape Projections—1985
    Blank tapes—75 million.
    Prerecorded—10.5 million.
    1990—150 million.
    1995—300 million.
    2000—500 million.

IV. Why Waco Packaging?
    A. Geography.
    B. Pricing.
    C. Packaging components fit—quantities, size, few changes.
    D. All divisions participate.
    E. Not a totally new market.
    F. Some sales coverage exists.
    G. Little domestic competition.
    H. High value-added market.
    I. Heritage of high standards of quality.
    J. High profit potential.

V. Bottom Line
    A. A market has been identified that has great needs with alternative for potential profitable growth.
    B. Must move immediately and vigorously.
    C. Risk is prevalent.

Exhibit 5

Excerpts from David Levine's Memo on Business Unit Plan and Business Plan Outline

Business unit plan preparation should flow from the general to the specific. Early stages involve reassessing the definition of the business and its strategic direction, examining the business climate outlook, reviewing operations, and identifying broad issues. The middle stages normally involve developing approaches to resolve the issues and making preliminary financial projections. The last stage generally involves detailing action programs, fine tuning the financial projections, and examining and dealing with the risks involved. From this comes the budget or business plans.

Listed below are some thoughts or explanations:

I. *Mission:* The mission statement of a business plan defines the nature and direction of a business in measurable terms. This definition forms the basis for developing the business plan. The mission statement should accomplish the following:

1. Define the classification of the business, such as high growth, low growth, cash generator, cash user, high market share, low market share.
2. Identify the longer range objective of the business.
3. Identify other nonrevenue-related objectives for the business.

II. *General strategy:* General strategy defines the action required to achieve the long-range objectives of the mission. The simplest presentation of a general strategy is through a summary statement of an overall strategy followed by a list of the major long-term strategies comprising it.

The long-term strategies might cover such areas as marketing, product development, new ventures, cost effectiveness, etc.

III. *Situational analysis:* Probably the most important part of the business plan is the situation analysis. This provides a detail base of reference information and analysis supporting the plan. The situation analysis should cover:

1. A market analysis-growth trend, the unit's position in each segment, competition's position, and current strategy in each segment.
2. A technological outlook as it relates to the unit's products, processes, and end users.
3. An operating effectiveness analysis relating to procurement, manufacturing, marketing, distribution, and administration.
4. The social, economic, and political environment outlook, labor concerns, outlook for the business conditions due to the state of the economy, legislative threats and opportunities, pollution control requirements, etc.

IV. *Strategic issues and actions:* The strategic issues evolve from the situation analysis. The strategy actions required to satisfactorily resolve these issues generally fall into three categories:

1. The longer term actions required to support the strategy.
2. The shorter term actions which are key to the needs of the annual plan.
3. The ongoing actions that represent the never-ending effort to improve performance.

Exhibit 5 (concluded)

V. *Capital plan:* The capital expenditure plan should list all capital items needed as specifically as possible.

The capital equipment items should be grouped according to their strategic area and should indicate the approximate ROI and the nature of the investment:

Profit adding
Expansion.
Product improvement.
Cost improvement.

Profit maintenance
Necessary and replacement.
Environmental control.

Other

Continental Airlines (A)

It was shortly after 7:00 A.M. in January 1984 when Frank Lorenzo, chairman of Continental Airlines (CAL) opened a meeting of CAL's top decision makers. The only adornments in the austere Houston conference room were paper cups of lukewarm coffee and the suitcases of the three CAL managers who had arrived on early morning flights from Los Angeles and Honolulu. Indeed, the entire group of six men gathered for the meeting more closely resembled a weary but exhilarated athletic team returning from an out-of-town trip than the prototype top management of a firm with $1 billion in revenues whose tactics and progress were being monitored daily by the national and international media.

Lorenzo launched immediately into the subject of the meeting:

> Even though I was skeptical of the profit potential and strategic value of our South Pacific operations before I was involved with this company, George's proposal to expand our service to the Honolulu–Guam market looks good.
>
> We would need some additional aircraft to do this, and we are stretched a little thin at the moment. But we've done before most of the things we'd have to do to make it successful: I think that we can raise the money, find the right planes and put them in the air. The one new wrinkle is that when we've done this before, we haven't been bankrupt. That fact imposes some constraints and probably allows for some opportunities that we've got to look at carefully.

Copyright © 1984 by the President and Fellows of Harvard College
Harvard Business School case 385–006

I'm particularly concerned that we think about the implications of this proposal for our overall positioning as a business. Will the bankruptcy judge allow us to do it, and how would the proposal affect our ongoing strategy for dealing with the creditors' committees in court? Would it affect what the unions do, both in the courtroom and as they make their case to the public? Is there anything about this kind of move that could be damaging to an increasingly favorable public sentiment about Continental?

History and Background of Continental Airlines

The Continental Airlines of which Frank Lorenzo was chairman was the product of a 1982 merger of Texas International Airlines and "old" Continental, two airlines with different traditions, styles, and positions in the industry. (See Exhibit 1 for a map of the merged routes.)

The "old" Continental was founded in 1934 as Varney Speed Lines. In 1936 Robert Six became the fledgling airline's general manager. Despite a limited route structure and a roster of only 16 employees, Six moved the airline to Denver in 1937 and renamed it Continental, a name that reflected his aspirations for the company. By the mid-1970s, under Six's leadership, Continental had become a medium-sized national carrier with revenues of more than $900 million and a reputation for impeccable service, generous compensation and benefits packages for employees, and high morale.

Throughout the 1970s the "Proud Bird with the Golden Tail" had modest profits. However, with the passage by Congress of the Airline Deregulation Act in 1978 Continental, like many other airlines, found itself floundering in an environment in which all the rules had been rewritten. Before deregulation the federal government through the Civil Aeronautics Board (CAB) had retained jurisdiction over both airline rates and routes and had generally sought to avoid price competition and entry of new competitors. Airlines had competed not on price but on service and frequency of flights. While not immune to the boom-and-bust cycle of the industry Continental had relied on its image as an airline that had focused successfully on providing excellent full-service, frequent cross-country flights. But the company was not prepared to compete on price to attract customers and, with the passage of deregulation, was hard pressed to adapt quickly to market demands. Continental's post-deregulation difficulties were increased because it had a linear route system. Delta and many of the new entrants had in place, or were able to create, "hub-and-spoke" systems in which short-hop flights could feed passengers to a central base for profitable long-haul flights. However, Continental had neither the equipment nor the experience to adapt its system quickly enough to find a niche in this market. Neither did it have the marketing mass, traffic strength, and resources that helped insulate the large carriers such as American and United against low-cost competition.

In addition Continental had internal problems. In 1978 Six announced his wish to retire as CEO and his intention to pick his successor from among the current top management of the company. This announcement set off fierce competition and feuding among several of the leading candidates for the job. In an attempt to stabilize the organization Six changed his mind about his decision to name someone inside the company to be CEO and in 1980 named Alvin Feldman, CEO of Frontier Airlines, to the job. Six's decision precipitated a mass exodus of top management at the time when Continental was beginning to face serious financial stress because of the deregulated environment.

Unlike Continental, Texas International Airlines (TXI) had begun as a regional airline. It functioned in the pre-deregulation era using "hand-me-down" routes and equipment to feed local traffic into the "trunk" system dominated by the major national carriers. In 1972 when it was taken over by Frank Lorenzo and Robert Carney, Houston-based TXI was plagued by many of the problems faced by local service carriers: small markets, short hauls, and an uneconomic mix of aircraft had led to the demise of a number of small regional airlines. While TXI, with its outdated fleet, $7 million negative net worth, $20 million working capital deficit, and nickname of "Tree Top Airlines," might not have appeared to be a particularly attractive takeover candidate, it represented for Carney and Lorenzo a good opportunity to build on their experience.

After graduating from Harvard Business School in 1963 both men had taken jobs in New York—Carney in investment banking and Lorenzo at TWA. In 1970 they raised $1.5 million in a small public offering to form Jet Capital, a firm that initially specialized in providing advice and arranging equipment leases for small, regional airlines. Later they began looking for an airline to buy, an unusual goal in what was then an industry characterized by long-term stability in ownership and management. They first set their sights on troubled, on-strike Mohawk Airlines. When the attempt to take over Mohawk failed they turned in 1971 to TXI and worked out a plan for Jet Capital to acquire 25 percent of TXI's equity and the majority of the voting rights for $1,150,000. However, even after they had arranged the financial transaction to acquire the airline, CAB approval of their purchase was delayed because of opposition by Howard Hughes, who hoped to combine TXI with Hughes Air West to form a southern tier carrier. It was not until September 1972 that Lorenzo as president and Carney as executive vice president gained control of the airline.

The new management immediately began to recruit new personnel and to focus on controlling costs, redeploying aircraft to serve the denser route segments, and petitioning the CAB to be allowed to drop unprofitable service. In 1973 TXI earned $258,000 and in 1974, $317,000. The airline's rebuilding seemed to be successfully under way as they modernized their fleet and began to deliver frequent, reliable service. In 1975 the new management suffered a setback: rather than budge from their position that labor costs had to be lowered and productivity increased in order to improve their competitive position, they took a strike and finished the year with a $4,370,000 loss. In 1976 they rebounded and persuaded the Civil Aeronautics Board to allow TXI to offer off-peak discount "peanuts fares," the first discount fares allowed an interstate carrier in the industry and an early signal of the change in climate that would ultimately accommodate deregulation.

In 1978 TXI earned $13 million, and TXI officials began to look at possibilities for expansion. As Douglas Tansill, a charter director of Jet Capital and at that time an employee of White Weld, described it:

> Frank was always creative about understanding the financial markets and how to use them. In early 1978 we did a unit offering of subordinated debentures and common stock, a new kind of deal for an airline. This increased Frank's awareness that there was money out there, money that could be used, if he chose, to acquire the undervalued assets that he also saw. He wanted to expand in a way that made sense. This included the possibility of looking for an airline to buy, an option that would allow him to expand his business in a quantum leap by purchasing equipment at a discount and increasing the network of routes that fed into his Houston hub.
>
> National Airlines became the target. At this time there hadn't been a takeover, much less a hostile takeover, in the industry in years. But what Frank proposed made sense, and throughout 1978 and 1979 we did a series of creative financings that allowed TXI to build the war chest.

The TXI attempt to take over National turned into a three-way battle with Eastern and Pan American, a battle Pan Am ultimately won. TXI, however, came away from the takeover attempt $47 million richer as a result of its sale of National stock.[1] The cash generated by the run at National gave Lorenzo and Carney an opportunity to expand and restructure. In the period following the takeover attempt they took three significant initiatives.

In 1980 Lorenzo and Carney established Texas Air Corporation (TAC), a publicly traded holding company with majority ownership held by Jet Capital, to serve as a parent not only of TXI but also of the other enterprises they were considering. Also in 1980 they founded New York Air, a nonunion carrier designed to challenge Eastern on its highly profitable Boston–New York–Washington route. In 1981 they took New York Air public, retaining control by Texas Air of a majority of New York Air's stock. Finally, when it became clear that they were

---

[1] In 1981 National Airlines took TXI to court, arguing that TXI was liable under Section 16 (b) of the Securities and Exchange Act of 1934 for "short swing profits." The U.S. District Court determined TXI's liability to be $1,149,195, plus interest and cost, a judgment which was upheld on appeal. Texas Air Corporation assumed the liability in 1982 and paid it in 1984.

not going to win control of National, they began to search for another airline to provide them with longer routes and larger equipment that would complement TXI's short-hop routes and small planes. By 1981 their leading candidate was Continental, and they began to acquire stock.

Though the logic of merging the two airlines into a hub-and-spoke system with focused strength in Houston and Denver may have been compelling, the battle that ensued was one of the bitterest in the history of the airline industry. Continental employees, many of whom had long tenure with the company, proposed and fought for an employee stock purchase plan that, had it been implemented, would have prevented the TXI takeover. The acrimony generated by the battle was further aggravated when Continental's president, Alvin Feldman, desolate because of the recent death of his wife and because of his inability to stop TXI, committed suicide.

On October 31, 1982, Continental and Texas International consolidated operations, becoming the nation's eighth largest airline and a wholly owned subsidiary of TAC, with Frank Lorenzo as chairman and Robert Carney as chairman of the executive committee. (See Exhibit 2.)

The Start-Up of the "New" Continental

The new Continental was a financially troubled company from its inception. The combined companies had a long-term debt of $642 million and equity of $142 million. During the year of the CAL-TXI battle, the management of the old Continental had focused on fighting the takeover rather than responding to the company's mounting losses. The new CAL finished 1982 with net losses of $41.8 million and during the first nine months of 1983 lost $161 million. (Exhibit 3 is a summary of selected financial data for CAL. Exhibit 4 is a summary of selected data for TAC.)

In part Continental's difficulties reflected those of the industry as a whole during this period. Between 1979 and June 30, 1983, the industry had lost $2.2 billion. Several factors had precipitated these losses. Fuel prices had escalated. The downturn in the economy had put a damper on passenger traffic, and rising interest rates had limited airlines' access to the capital markets. The grounding of DC-10 aircraft and the strike and subsequent dismissal of air traffic controllers had limited the flexibility of many airlines to fly the equipment they had to destinations they chose on schedules that made sense. Finally, many established carriers were being pushed hard by the new low-cost, low-priced competitors spawned by deregulation. The new competitors, most of which were nonunion carriers, enjoyed a significant advantage in labor costs: in the first quarter of 1983 the average annual salary paid to an employee of the major national carriers was $42,000, while the average for an employee of a post-deregulated start-up domestic carrier was $22,000.

In addition to having to operate in a difficult industry climate Continental faced a number of problems stemming from its history and place in the industry. One of the reasons the old Continental was a desirable acquisition for TXI was that it allowed TXI access to a second hub, in Denver, with cross-country feeder routes. But CAL's route structure was also an extremely competitive one in which it was forced to go head-to-head both with major carriers such as American and United and with the new, low-cost carriers. In addition 60 percent of Continental's traffic was generated by travel agents using computerized reservations systems controlled by American and United and biased in favor of bookings on the owner airline. Finally, the old Continental was constrained by union contracts mandating some of the highest labor costs in the industry.

The issue of labor costs was particularly pressing, and even before TXI's takeover, George Warde, Alvin Feldman's successor, had begun to call for work-force concessions. But even before the merger was consummated Warde, a former president of American Airlines who had been brought in by Six to shore up the company, found the labor issue intractable:

> Sure, everyone could see the principle, the macro need to cut back on costs. But nobody was willing to say, "For the good of the whole, I'll cut my own salary," especially in light of the fact that the old CAL was dead, filled with the superannuated or people waiting to bail out with their golden parachutes. There was no way we were going to be able to get people to agree readily to take cuts for the good of the company. "What company?" and "Why should I?" were the implicit responses.

The new Continental management continued to focus on decreasing labor costs. In 1982 Continental won nearly $100 million in concessions over two years from its pilots, although neither the unionized machinists nor the flight attendants followed suit. In March 1983, 15 percent of the airline's personnel were laid off. During the summer, the headquarters staff was moved from Los Angeles to Houston, which had become the dominant hub of the company. The move, another effort to reduce costs, caused discontent among many of the "old CAL" employees and became a symbol of what some labeled the "callous" attitude toward employees of the new management.

Despite this effort to cut labor costs, the airline continued to lose money at an increasingly rapid rate. In July 1983 the company lost $8 million; in August, $17 million. On August 12 the machinists, represented by the International Association of Machinists and Aerospace Workers (IAM) went on strike after Continental refused to agree to a union proposal for a 36 percent wage increase with no work-rule concessions. On the first day of the strike, Continental operated at 85 percent of capacity and as the month progressed, returned to full capacity. In the process CAL management eliminated 800 machinist union jobs by hiring outside contractors, primarily in its flight kitchens and cabin cleaning areas.

During August and September Continental officials unsuccessfully sought $100 million in contract concessions from the Airline Pilots Association (ALPA) and the Union of Flight Attendants (UFA). On September 14 CAL management announced its intention to implement a new economic plan to restructure labor cost permanently. The $150 million annual cost-reduction plan included requests for cost savings of $30 million from agent, clerical, reservations, and management groups, $20 million from the mechanics, $40 million from the flight attendants, and $60 million from pilots. In return, CAL management proposed that 4 million shares of CAL stock held by Texas Air be donated to an employee stock ownership plan and that a permanent profit-sharing plan be established. The proposal was turned down by all union representatives, except the TWU (representing several dozen flight dispatchers) which agreed to the plan. In addition the company's nonunion personnel, the largest employee group, voted overwhelmingly for the plan.

On September 21 Continental President Stephen Wolf resigned. On September 22 the Continental board of directors met to consider the position of the company and reached the conclusion that if CAL were to pay salaries, debt service, pension contributions, and some back payments to vendors, the company would run out of working capital by September 30.

(See the Appendix for an example of CAL management's analysis of the situation.)

The Bankruptcy and Its Aftermath

There is no halfway procedure. There is no Chapter 5½.

> Frank Lorenzo, chairman, Continental Airlines,
> *Business Week*, November 7, 1983.

On Saturday, September 24, Continental Airlines filed a petition for reorganization under Chapter 11 of the U.S. Bankruptcy Code. Citing as the precipitating factors in reaching the decision the deteriorating financial position of the airline and inability to reach agreements with union groups on pay and benefit concessions and work-rule changes, Continental ceased all domestic service. At the same time TAC issued a statement saying its management was confident that CAL's filing for reorganization would not cause financial difficulties or problems with creditors for TAC or its other subsidiaries. TAC Senior Vice President Robert Snedeker assured the press and financial community that:

> Texas Air continues to maintain substantial liquidity and significant asset value. The company has always operated and will continue to operate its

subsidiaries independently from one another, and as such, the profitable operations of New York Air, Texas Air's other principal subsidiary, will not be affected.

Throughout the weekend immediately following the bankruptcy filing, CAL's top management cleared the payroll of 8,000 jobs, laying off 65 percent of the work force. At the same time they unilaterally implemented new wage and work rules for all employees: pilots' salaries were cut from an average of $78,000 to $43,000 for captains and $28,000 for flight officers. All employees, including top management, took at least a 15 percent pay cut, and Chairman Lorenzo decreased his own salary from $257,000 to the $43,000 salary of a senior captain. "It all sounds very neat and tidy," recalls Bruce Hicks, the airline's chief spokesman.

But it was like a very bad version of *War and Peace.* On Monday morning there were several dozen employees milling in the lobby of the building waiting to find out if they still had a job and, therefore, would be allowed upstairs to their offices. Because the job cutting was not completed until the wee hours of the morning, a number of people were not notified, and only those whose names were on a master list were being allowed past Security into the corporate offices. And even then there were some people inadvertently left off the working list, and that caused some confusion and obviously very tense moments for those people.

It was a very sad time for everybody. It was sad for those who could not come to work, and it was sad for those who did when their friends could not.

It was a surrealistic world. We had no carefully thought-out plan for how you run an airline in bankruptcy—no one had ever done it before. How many people and which ones do you need in a marketing department that has to shrink 65 percent? It wasn't a question of did we make mistakes: it was a question of trying to control the magnitude of the mistakes as we wrote and executed the plan simultaneously. We were dealing with a world turned upside down.

Two days after the announcement of the Chapter 11 filing, Continental resumed 27 percent of its flights. Before filing for reorganization CAL had flown to 78 cities in the continental United States, as well as providing service between the United States and Mexico, Venezuela, Hawaii, Australia, New Zealand, and the Far East and Micronesia. In addition to continuing international service throughout the filing process, by September 27 Continental had launched limited service to 25 of the 78 cities previously served. Customers stood in long lines to take advantage of Continental's $49 "welcome back fares," good through September 30. "We knew that to keep the airline going we *had* to get people on our planes," recalls Doug Birdsall, vice president of market planning.

That meant we had to price it just right. How did we do it during that hectic time? Not scientifically, I can tell you that: rather, by excellent instinct informed by good experience.

On October 1, four days after Continental resumed flying, the unionized pilots and flight attendants went on strike over the wage cuts and work rules. Both management and union employees recognized that wage reductions and labor cost constituted the most critical issue facing the new Continental. Previously labor costs accounted for 35 percent of Continental's operating expenses; they fell to 20 percent after the bankruptcy filing and promulgation of new work rules. Recognizing that the early days of resumed service would be crucial ones, the pilots' and flight attendants' unions picketed Continental's gates in most major airports. In addition ALPA approved an assessment of its members to cover extraordinary benefits for striking CAL pilots for an unlimited period: a striking captain received $45,000 a year, $2,000 more than a working CAL captain. Continental's management filled its employee ranks by attracting many of the union members who were willing to work on the new wage scale and began to hire flight attendants, many of whom had been laid off by other airlines in the troubled industry.

Following the filing Continental gradually restored service. During October and November, the CAL system expanded to 50 percent of prepetition capacity. By mid-January 1984 the airline was operating at 56 percent, and management was projecting 75 percent by March 1 and 90 percent by midsummer. (See Exhibit 5 for the 1984 CAL route system.) During the rebuilding phase Continental officials staked out the airline's "niche" as a carrier with strong presence in the Houston and Denver hubs, providing low-cost, high-frequency full-service flights.

The airline's special promotional fares continued through mid-October. Continental next offered simplified peak and off-peak coach fares that ranged from 30 percent to 70 percent less than the standard coach fares of other airlines. To be able to hold this position Continental had not only to lower labor costs but to meet a break-even load factor of 65 percent. From November 1983 through January 1984 Continental had the highest monthly load factors of any of the major airlines, with 63.1 percent in November, 66.8 percent in December, and 65.1 percent in January.

In addition to operating and expanding the new Continental, management was heavily involved in legal proceedings. Shortly after filing the reorganization petitions, Continental officials sought the bankruptcy court's approval to reject its union and other employee-related executory contracts. ALPA, UFA, and the IAM, representing the three largest groups of Continental's unionized employees, filed a motion to dismiss the company's bankruptcy petition. During December U.S. Bankruptcy Judge R. F. Wheless conducted hearings that included eight days of testimony by company and union officials. Characterizing Continental's Chapter 11 petition as the "fruit of the poisonous tree," union lawyers argued that the airline, with more than $200 million in total current assets, had been solvent at the time of the petition and that Continental had filed solely and calculatedly to get rid of its collective bargaining agreements. Continental's lawyers argued, on the other hand, that Continental, with a negative net worth of $51.4 million when it filed, was obviously insolvent and that, should the court rule that it had to honor its labor contracts, Continental would be forced to liquidate. Testifying before the judge Lorenzo described the bankruptcy proceedings as "an admission of failure, an admission that we had not been able to turn this company around. . . . Continental filed for Chapter 11 because we had reached the end of the line, the last resort."

The court hearings concluded on January 3. On January 17 Judge Wheless denied the union's motion to dismiss Continental's Chapter 11 petition. Explicitly dismissing the union's argument that Continental's filing was engineered over time by management as the means by which it could reject union contracts, Wheless concluded that "neither the sole nor the primary purpose of filing was to reject these executory contracts." Instead, he suggested, Continental filed for reorganization under Chapter 11:

> . . . for the purpose of attempting to keep the company alive and functioning. . . . The primary purpose in filing these proceedings was to keep the airline operating so as to best utilize its going-concern value. The management of the company owed this obligation to its shareholders and to its creditors.

In the opinion Judge Wheless also agreed to begin hearing the airline's motion to be allowed to dissolve its union contracts.

The Management of Continental Airlines

The bankruptcy and subsequent reemergence of Continental during the fall and winter of 1983 was a subject of widespread interest and controversy. At the center of much of the media and public attention was Continental's chairman, Frank Lorenzo, who seemed to have become a lightning rod for many of the most intense feelings and beliefs evoked by Continental's actions. Continental's pilots picketed at airports and carried posters depicting Lorenzo with a Hitler mustache or behind bars, with a caption that read, "Wanted: For the Murder of Continental Airlines." In describing and analyzing events at Continental the press also often focused on Lorenzo. "Why is Lee Iacocca the most popular business man in America and Frank Lorenzo the most reviled?" asked an editorial writer for the *Denver Post*.

> When Chrysler got into trouble Iacocca saved it the old-fashioned way, by begging for a government handout. . . . Lorenzo, in contrast, knew Continental lacked the political muscle to rescue itself on the backs of American taxpayers. . . . Instead of joining Iacocca at the corporate entrance to the U.S. Treasury Department's soup kitchen, Lorenzo decided to try capitalism. . . .

Free enterprise isn't supposed to be a popularity contest. We'd rather have rough, abrasive Frank Lorenzo playing the game by the rules and saving consumers money in the process than watch smooth, charming Lee Iacocca rewrite them at public expense.

The son of a hairdresser, Frank Lorenzo grew up in New York. He graduated from Columbia University in 1961 and entered Harvard Business School in the same year. "From the time I first knew him, when he was 19 or so, Lorenzo always wanted to run an airline," recalls one of his HBS classmates.

And you have to remember that that was before airlines were interesting, like *real* businesses: they were regulated; they'd been dominated by the old pilots-turned-executives for years. But that's what Lorenzo wanted to do. It was tolerated: you know, there have to be some outliers in every class.

Lorenzo's philosophy about the airline business was shaped by his experience in running Texas International. He recalls two factors as being especially significant in influencing his view of the business:

First, we "grew up" next to Southwest, an airline that, because it was based in a state large enough to generate substantial intrastate business, understood the power of the marketplace early. Those guys were scrappers. Instead of telling customers how they had to behave because they were so big and powerful, they were out aggressively trying to understand their markets. They pioneered the masterful use of the fare structure. And to this day they know how to think about their customers.

The second experience I'll never forget was going to Washington in the middle of the 70s to testify against deregulation. Here I was, the president of a little airline in the middle of Texas with a fleet of old planes. We had a pig in a poke; there was no way that we didn't want the government to continue regulating what we did. But as I talked to the smart staff people who were working on the legislation, I saw several things clearly. First, deregulation was probably going to happen. Second, it would come with the force of a tidal wave and turn the airline business upside down, putting power into the hands of consumers. And third, I thought that it was a wave that could be ridden.

Although Lorenzo had made his career working for airlines and since 1972 had been a chief executive officer, he never was an integral part of, or blended in easily with, the industry leadership. As an industry analyst and long-time observer of the industry explains:

He's never been a member of the club. They don't trust him. His style is so different: he crashes in and takes on the big ones. He took over TXI when you didn't *buy* an airline, pushed for off-peak fares when it was clear that that would add turbulence to the environment—and he took a strike at TXI. . . .

The airline world doesn't (or *didn't* until deregulation) allow for Lorenzo's style. I've been in and watched this business for 30 years. The two cardinal rules have always been: (1) If you can do anything to avoid a strike, do it, but whatever you do, don't try to fly; and (2) when you're in financial difficulties, near bankruptcy, don't fly. The safety of the passengers may be endangered.

Lorenzo just rolls over these canons. Also his attempt to take over National reinforced his image as a renegade. The other guys in the industry regarded him as a pirate, more as a speculator than as someone who wants to operate an airline.

This perception of Lorenzo as not a typical old-boy airline executive was widely shared on Wall Street and was reinforced by his active and innovative involvement in raising money for his companies. Even before taking Jet Capital public in 1970, Lorenzo had been intimately involved in financing new equipment purchases and expansion of his base. Rather than relying on any single investment banking firm, Lorenzo had maintained a close relationship with a long-time associate, Douglas Tansill, a Harvard Business School classmate, who described their relationship as:

. . . unusual, largely because Frank is unique. Through the years, we've done some totally innovative deals with Frank—the first unit offering of subordinated debentures and common stock for an airline, the first Eurodollar convert in the industry, a very creative Eurodollar floating rate note issue. In each case, then and in the future, Frank either readily and quickly embraced an idea presented to him by us, even if it hadn't been done before, or brought the idea to us for execution. He understands finance as well as the best in the business and has a great sense of timing.

But according to another long-time associate, Texas Air's Senior Vice President Robert Snedeker, Lorenzo's facility and talent with finance occasionally proved to be a mixed blessing, especially in dealing with certain elements of the financial community and the media:

The Street at times seems to view negatively those who it perceives to be financially oriented. Perhaps it's a competitive thing. Frank and the senior management have never been viewed as "airline people" by the Street, even though many have spent their whole careers around airlines.

Unfortunately this can lead to some simplistic stereotyping of the company when they analyze its operations. We're never quite sure whether or not the people on the Street have done a full financial analysis, or instead, are just relying on these stereotypes.

These labels often lead them to some conclusions that don't necessarily follow. For example, we sometimes hear, "You must be lousy managers because you're good finance people." Or based on a quick look at the turnover of presidents of our airlines, they seem ultimately to come around to the much-repeated refrain of "even if those guys are right about where the business is going, they'll never get anyone to run their airlines."

The lack of continuity since 1980 among top management of airlines in which he was involved was consistently raised as an indication of what many saw as Lorenzo's weakness as a manager. Certainly the list of former TXI, New York Air, and Continental officials is a distinguished one and includes those who became competitors, such as Don Burr, the founder of People Express, and Steve Wolf, the president of Republic Airlines. One insider explains the turnover as being caused by "the clash of bright, sometimes brilliant, guys with big egos."

Lorenzo's own assessment is:

The turnover in our organizations has to be viewed in the context of the environment at our company at the particular time. Burr was with us for seven years—not exactly a short stint—before leaving to take advantage of the newly passed deregulation laws. While Wolf left after a short 10 months the instability of that relationship is better understood, I believe, when one realizes that the company lost over $100 million during that period—in increasing amounts. While personalities play a role, they don't play nearly the role that some of our critics and ex-managers would have you believe.

In addition we've always tended to hire bright, ambitious guys, guys who you know won't stay forever. We take risks with people. Burr was a money manager from Wall Street. Mike Levine (former president of New York Air) was a law professor. Phil Bakes was a government lawyer, and he'll be great at Continental.

In building our companies and our boards we've always tried to look at what skills we need and at who can give us good direction. Our boards have always consisted of people who can help us understand a piece of the world, not like some other airline boards of civic do-gooders whose only concern is what constituencies they might offend by doing something controversial. For example, Bob Sakowitz (Continental board member and president of Sakowitz, Inc.) is one of the more brilliant marketing people around. It doesn't matter that he runs retail stores and we run an airline. He can give us good advice on marketing.

We've always selected the people in our organization the same way—for their particular skills and to give us a blend.

The CAL Management Team

The top management of Continental Airlines did indeed encompass an eclectic mix of backgrounds. The major holdovers from the old Continental were several senior operating managers. Of this group among the most prominent and active in the major decision making of the new Continental were Richard Adams, senior vice president for operations and a 22-year Continental employee, and George Warde, manager of the Far East region. The younger officers came from more disparate backgrounds. Although the new Continental had no known organizational chart, prominent among this group were Executive Vice President

Phil Bakes, Legal Counsel Barry Simon, Vice President for Market Operations Douglas Birdsall, and Treasurer Mickey Foret. Of this group Birdsall, 40 years old, was the only "career" airline employee, having been recruited to the old Continental from Eastern Airlines shortly before the TXI takeover.

Perhaps prototypical of the new style manager in the TAC companies was Phil Bakes. Bakes, a 39-year-old Harvard-trained lawyer, had worked for the Civil Aeronautics Board and as the chief of staff for Senator Edward Kennedy's Judiciary Subcommittee's hearings on airline deregulation. It was in this context that he first met Lorenzo, who had come to testify against deregulation. As Bakes describes it:

> Working on airline deregulation in the Senate, I'd met just about every airline CEO. Lorenzo was just different: he had a vision. I remember having a conversation with him about deregulation. Unlike many of the other guys, he caught onto it, including its risks and opportunities, right away. It was the most intellectually challenging encounter I had with any of the airline chiefs.
>
> When, years later, he proposed that I join him, I jumped. I'm not in this for security: I've never looked ahead more than two or three years in my own career. I always knew that I eventually wanted to get out of law and into business, especially an entrepreneurial business. Here I saw an opportunity to learn 30 years of business in 30 months, with a group of very smart people who were not afraid to take risks. I won't ever regret having jumped at that.

Also present at many of the meetings involving long-range commitments of CAL resources were Robert Snedeker and Charles Goolsbee, both senior officers of Texas Air. Snedeker, a 41-year-old graduate of Harvard Business School, had been associated with Lorenzo since 1968 and had been a chief strategist in most of TXI's and TAC's capital and financial negotiations. Goolsbee, a lawyer and TAC general counsel and, at 49, one of the senior members of the Lorenzo team, provided legal advice for the parent company. Although TAC had distanced itself from Continental Goolsbee and Snedeker were involved in many key decisions involving equipment purchases and in other resource allocation decisions with long-range implications.

The environment in which the top managers of Continental plied their trade was anything but formal. Housed in a stark new building perched on the edge of one of Houston's major roadways, Continental's headquarters had a lived-in feeling: at six o'clock in the evening the faint aroma of coffee brewing mingled with that of pizza being reheated in a microwave oven. The building bustled with activity at all hours, although much of the activity seemed governed by few formal rules or procedures. This lack of formality and of rigid adherence to calendars or schedules was notable at the highest level of the organization. According to Birdsall:

Our meetings are hard to characterize. We schedule arrival times, no departure times. We finish when everyone gets tired and hungry.

Our meetings go from free-form to rigid-form to no-form, depending on the week. Nobody's much of a stickler for procedures for the sake of procedures. We don't care much about whether the budget information presented in the meetings does or doesn't conform to damn accounting standards or a rigid format, just so long as you convey what you need to convey.

And we certainly don't waste our time writing everything down and then Xeroxing copies to send to everybody. We write down the material on things that involve capital commitments, irreversible decisions. But we have no time for tracking the "no-brainers," the decisions that require no tracks, like the latest personnel procedure or the addition or deletion of 10 computer mnemonics from our system. American would have not one, but two memos on these subjects. But that's just not the way we operate.

The assignment and delegation of responsibility among top management were handled informally and were characterized by one observer as operating "like a good zone defense in football, where players converge on problems in their territory." Bakes's characterization of the organization's modus operandi dovetails with this description:

We're stretched very thin around here. We have about 20 people responsible for running a large airline. People work together without turf battles because we don't have time for them. Each person knows what he's responsible for. We have no notes and no committees. Committees body-check everything useful that might get done. I learned in government that if you organize a task force or a committee you'll get a report in which you *will* find out all the problems. But you'll also become paralyzed. You can't possibly do that with an organization in flux.

Goolsbee describes the TAC enterprises as:

. . . the least institutionalized organizations I've worked for. It's a hard environment to get used to, both because you have to work so hard and because you have to reorient your thinking to the risk-taking aspect. I had to convince myself that security isn't important: what's fun, what's important, is trying something new and challenging.

Frank wants the organization to be able to turn on a dime. As a result, people here sometimes lay back and wait to see what he's going to do, or do something only to have to redo it. This can be costly in extra legal and accounting costs. And one problem with having the organization turn on a dime is that you have to deal with that half of the organization that's still going in the other direction.

Although decisions at Continental were made in a flexible, informal manner, management had a clear view of Continental's corporate objectives. According to Bakes, these included:

1. Achieving profitability.

2. Improving the climate for participatory management by employees.

3. Becoming a low-cost producer.

4. Removing Continental from bankruptcy.

5. Solidifying Continental's position in its defined market niche as a low-cost, full-service airline providing a quality product with a simplified pricing structure.

Both Lorenzo and Bakes emphasized that to solidify Continental's position the airline would have to improve the quality of its product distribution network, particularly its methods of ticketing, and to "put meat on the bones of the company" by growing it to a size that would strengthen its hubs in Denver and Houston and ensure its position as number one or a solid number two in each of its markets served.

As for Lorenzo's own goals, a long-term observer speculated:

I believe that what Frank wants Continental to be is a great big survivor, of a size somewhere between Northwest and American. And Frank wants to control it.

Frank started deregulation with an unplayable hand and he played it as well as he could. He's amassed a large amount of capital and assets in a very short time. Now he really wants a viable airline.

He hasn't made money yet because he hasn't had a chance to. Throughout this enterprise he's emphasized a kind of value added that doesn't produce returns quickly. But ultimately, he has to produce—and he knows it.

Running a Bankrupt Company

Chapter 11 is not pleasant. It's sort of like going through open-heart surgery and brain surgery at the same time.

A Continental Airlines lawyer,
The Wall Street Journal, February 24, 1984.

The thing that's so difficult about the bankruptcy setting is that there are so many people involved, all posturing. Everybody's got turf to defend. It's like having several more boards of directors.

Charles Goolsbee, senior officer, Texas Air.

In addition to facing the financial problems associated with bankruptcy, the most pressing of which was to find sources of cash to continue the company's operations, the CAL management also was confronted with a legal and political contest in which very little was predictable. The environment in which Continental was attempting to carry out its goals had been turbulent even before the company's Chapter 11 filing; its uncertainty increased dramatically after the filing, for the rules and guidelines for management of companies in bankruptcy were in flux.

The 1978 Bankruptcy Code and its predecessor, the 1898 Bankruptcy Act, provide for two kinds of bankruptcy. The first, which can be either involuntary or voluntary, requires liquidation of the property of the debtor; the second, specified in Chapters 11 and 13, provides for debtor rehabilitation. The purpose of such a reorganization is to allow management to restructure the finances and operations of the firm so it can once again become a functioning economic unit and continue to provide jobs, pay off creditors, and give shareholders a return on their investment.

In April 1983 Wilson Foods Corporation, the nation's largest pork butcher, had filed for protection under Chapter 11, announcing that the primary purpose of its filing was to enable the company to reject costly existing collective bargaining agreements. Continental in its filing had picked up on the logic of the Wilson case, arguing that rehabilitation was preferable to liquidation and that the only conceivable way the company could continue to function was to abrogate its employment agreements. At the time of the Continental filing, however, cases based on the Wilson logic were working their way through the court system on appeal; how the court would decide the question of whether companies could use Chapter 11 to terminate employee contracts was unclear.

There was a second source of uncertainty about the broad rules that would govern Continental's bankruptcy proceeding. In the 1978 Bankruptcy Reform Act Congress had established a special set of bankruptcy courts designed to take pressure off the U.S. District Court system. The legislation created positions for special bankruptcy judges, with 14-year terms and jurisdiction only over bankruptcy issues, to replace the bankruptcy "referees" responsible to district court judges in the old system. In 1982 in *Northern Pipeline Construction* v. *Marathon Construction,* the Supreme Court had ruled in favor of a plaintiff who had filed a suit arguing that the bankruptcy judges were not legitimate members of the federal judiciary because they were not appointed for life, as specified in Article III of the U.S. Constitution. Because this ruling called into question the legitimacy of the whole bankruptcy court system, the Supreme Court had given Congress a deadline of April 1, 1984, to rewrite the bankruptcy code to address the issue of jurisdiction. As early as the fall of 1983 it was clear that the impending congressional rewrite would provide an opportunity for special interests to insert provisions and would also serve as a forum for debate about the desirability and legitimacy of using Chapter 11 to abrogate employment contracts.

In addition to the uncertainty about the broad legal parameters that would govern the bankruptcy, Continental's management faced all of the difficulties of running a company governed by the constraints of the bankruptcy court. As a Chapter 11 debtor Continental was required to file a reorganization plan that satisfied both the judge and a committee or set of committees of creditors. The judge could determine the makeup of the committees, and in Continental's case, the committees consisted of separate groups of bank creditors, secured institutional creditors, unsecured creditors, unionized employees, and nonunionized employees.

In addition to being charged with the authority to approve any final proposal for reorganization, the judge and the committees were allowed to become involved with the ongoing business of rehabilitation in a number of ways. They had the right to consult with management, monitor all proceedings in the court, and assess the company's acts, conduct, and financial status. To facilitate this the creditors' committees were permitted to hire staff to be paid for by the debtor. The judge, with the advice of the creditors, was required to monitor monthly financial transactions by the company and to approve any new lending agreements or major commitments of resources. In short Continental had to be prepared to transact much of its business in public, in writing, and under the microscope of the bankruptcy court.

Barry Simon, Continental's counsel, described the situation this way:

> We had some things going for us. The goal of the bankruptcy statutes is to permit rehabilitation of debtors, so we began with a favorable basis in law. Because of this a "success" for the judge would be a revitalized company.
>
> But we had to file a plea in court to do *anything* we wanted to do. And we were faced with the fundamental difference between the Continental management, which wanted to build a successful company and make a profit, and the creditors, who wanted to pull out their money and satisfy their more short-term objectives.

The Issue at Hand: Flying the New Pacific Routes

It was against this backdrop that the meeting was held to consider the proposal to expand Continental's service to the South Pacific.

The old Continental had flown routes in the South Pacific for many years. At the time it was taken over by Texas International, Continental had authority, granted by the Civil Aeronautics Board and foreign governments, to fly a series of routes to Australia, New Zealand, Japan, the Philippines, Taiwan, Hong Kong, Fiji, and a number of Pacific islands in Micronesia. Continental had continued to fly its international routes throughout the bankruptcy, and its operations in both the South Pacific and mid-Pacific had been financially successful.

After the Chapter 11 filing and its attendant cut in labor costs, the routes began to look even more attractive for, unlike CAL's domestic routes, the international routes were highly regulated, and much of CAL's competition came from foreign carriers with high labor costs. In addition in late November 1983 Pan American had announced its intention to cease its Honolulu–Guam nonstop flights on April 1, 1984.

Following Pan Am's announcement, Warde had suggested to Lorenzo and Bakes that an expansion of service be considered, and with their preliminary approval, he and his staff had developed a proposal to expand Continental's routes and establish a Honolulu hub. Having worked with CAL equipment experts, Warde argued that he could add profitable capacity with the addition to the Continental fleet of two DC-10-30s, small, longer-range versions of DC-10-10s that could fly nonstop from Honolulu to Sydney and to Guam without refueling. Specifically, Warde proposed:

— Introduction of nonstop service to Guam from San Francisco and Honolulu.
— Increased nonstop service, with additional nonstop flights to Sydney and introduction of new nonstop flights to Auckland.
— Direct Honolulu–Guam service.

Warde's forecasts for 1984 showed that even without the new aircraft the Pacific route system could generate $10.7 million, a figure that would account for 36 percent of CAL's projected profits. He projected in pro formas that the addition of the 10-30s flying the new South Pacific routes could generate an additional profit of $3.38 million in 1984. (For a summary of management's analysis of important considerations, see Exhibit 6.)

CAL and TAC management had been aware since November that McDonnell-Douglas was willing to sell two used DC 10-30s and also knew that the aircraft might be attractive on the Pacific routes. During preliminary negotiations with McDonnell-Douglas, the price on the aircraft had been established at $15.5 million each. In addition the two aircraft would require an overhaul costing approximately $7 million, bringing the total projected cost to almost $40 million.

It was clear that Continental was in no position to purchase the aircraft. Therefore, Snedeker proposed that it lease the planes through a transaction to be arranged by E. F. Hutton and that the underlying debt be secured by a lien on the aircraft, further supported by a limited "first loss deficiency guarantee" from McDonnell-Douglas and by recourse to Texas Air. (See Exhibit 7 for a summary of the lease proposal.)

Snedeker, in viewing the transaction as one that would require the financial support of TAC, assessed the proposal this way:

The right aircraft are available at the right time. The 10-30s suit Continental's needs, and the opportunity exists to buy them at attractive prices. Also I'm convinced that the aircraft themselves are a good investment. The market seems to have turned around. I'm convinced that the 10-30s have good collateral value.

TAC's involvement is critical. Douglas will only help us finance with the credit of TAC. But it seems like a good venture for TAC because of the aircraft value, and in addition TAC owns 90 percent of Continental, so we have a strong stake in helping them succeed.

Of course there are certain risks. The time frames for arranging the deal and financing are tight: both planes are supposed to be in service by July 1984. TAC could go ahead with the agreement and the bankruptcy court could disallow it. Also in the process of negotiating the agreement, we could set a precedent for there being a tangible linkage between CAL and TAC that creditors might jump on. And of course, we have to anticipate that the decision to acquire the aircraft might create a certain amount of animosity among lower levels of Continental; you can imagine them saying, "Here we are starving, and they're off buying planes."

The piece of this that we haven't really done before is buy equipment in a bankruptcy setting. But the skin gets thick, and overall it doesn't seem too risky.

Vice President for Market Planning Birdsall had mixed reactions to the proposal:

Certainly in terms of a business proposition the numbers seem to make sense. I've been convinced for a long time that the Pacific routes with the right configuration can make money. In fact several years ago we put together a plan to fly Honolulu–Guam in competition with Pan Am but, given all of the difficulties the company was facing, decided not to do it at that time. It just so happened that Pan Am decided to stop serving the route at what was an inopportune moment for Continental.

But I must confess to having the reaction of "I'm busy." I have a bankrupt airline that's growing at a rate of 20 percent a month to run. You can't always follow the Lorenzo rule to "defy all the laws of gravity and do what makes good economic sense."

I'm concerned about controlling risk. For me some of the risk in this comes from flying the routes in that part of the world. I don't know their market, have no intimate understanding of what's going on in Guam and Fiji. In the United States I can put 10 planes in the air in an hour and feel comfortable, but there—I don't know the territory as well. Maybe we should just go for one plane, and between the Mid-Pacific and South Pacific opportunities, one would be relatively certain that one of the two is going to work very well. Of course, that isn't in keeping with what seems to be our motto around here: "If I'm going to die, I'd just as soon not spend 20 years doing it."

Continental's legal counsel, Barry Simon, focused his assessment of the proposal on how it would affect the company's position in court:

There is something a little incongruous about having teams of lawyers fighting in court for every penny and then laying on top of that a proposal to find $40 million to buy new planes.

There seem to me to be several risks associated with this particular proposal. Several of the creditors are pushing us to sell off our assets and become a nice little airline. In light of this, even if we were to get approval from the judge, the unions and some of the creditors are likely to appeal, especially since we're footing the bill for their legal costs. This could cause significant delay, and the delay could make it impossible to get financing and could kill the whole deal.

On the other hand, there are business reasons for the proposal and the judge has so far been receptive to the arguments we have made. (At this point, Continental had won most of its pleas before the court.) I think we could convince him on this matter, too. Also the expansion would create jobs and the unions would be hard pressed to oppose that.

Executive Vice President Phil Bakes was the last to speak:

My first strong reaction is to jump on the opportunity. It's the first time since I've joined the company that we can do something other than keep the blood from flowing. I think a positive decision would provide a very loud answer to the question, "What is your mindset about the future?"

There's compelling logic to it as a business decision, in spite of the risk. I'm very leery of falling victim to the logic of the school of thought that says here are all of the ways that things might go wrong. I'd rather commit to the thing in a wholehearted way, as an opportunity, not as a risk. The more committed we are—to McDonnell-Douglas, the judge, E. F. Hutton, and the rest—the more difficult it will be to stop us. It's for this reason that if we decide to fly the routes, I want to go for both planes, not just one: we don't want the judge to feel that he's being nibbled to death. We should put our cards on the table. We have a growth strategy for the Pacific because of our marketing strength there and our low costs. We already have a significant investment out there. Pan Am's departure and the state of the current used aircraft market present opportunities.

This isn't to say that I don't see some risk in the proposal. If we can't get the aircraft and get them refurbished in the time, we could use up a lot of cash, and although we're improving, we're not exactly flush with money. In addition I think that trying to figure out what our numbers are for places like Hong Kong and Taipei is risky: we don't have years and years of traffic data and history as we do in this country. Also at Continental we haven't really acquired any assets for a long time, and $40 million is a big commitment.

Finally, I see as a major aspect of the risk the possible fallout from the symbolic aspects of this proposal for Continental to expand. In this sense the 10-30s are stalking horses. If we can handle this, it may help us to expand our other parts of the business. But if we can't do it, when the summer comes and we try to put on additional flights and build the airline, we'll have everybody breathing down our necks. If we go with the proposal, one thing is clear to me, and that's that our credibility will be on the line.

Appendix
Frank Lorenzo: Presentation to Continental Airlines' Pilots, September 20, 1983

The company's financial position is most serious. The massive losses that are continuing at the company will very shortly erode our current cash and liquid resources. That liquidity is largely the product of investments made by American General, the public, and Texas Air Corporation. We will not allow this company to deplete its resources. We, therefore, have some immediate choices: implement a new operating plan including dramatic relief from our current cost structure or take steps that protect our cash and other assets while we still have substantial cash resources.

We truly regret that these stark alternatives fall so squarely on the pilot group at Continental. The pilots are the group which approximately one year ago voluntarily revised its contract in hope of reducing expenses and saving the company. Little did we then realize how swiftly the marketplace would be upon us and how harshly it would treat Continental's cost and revenues. The pilots of Continental also continued to fly during our continued efforts to resist IAM strike-backed demands that would result in absurd cost increases. We appreciate both of these efforts in our common interest.

Though we regret the circumstances we now find ourselves in and the role the pilots will play—one way or another—we believe there is no responsible alternative left open to us.

The reasons we have reached this conclusion are basically four.

First, the company is losing money at an alarming rate—$84 million in the first six months and another $7.4 million loss in July. July had originally been projected to bring a $25.5 million profit, and just a few months ago we lowered that to an $8.4 million profit. The economic warfare being waged by the IAM is taking its toll. The company's shareholders' equity or net worth is close to zero, and our cash resources are diminishing rapidly.

Second, our operating costs are too high to ever allow the company to be profitable or to bring a significant return to shareholders. This is true even with the new IAM wages and work rules we implemented. Therefore, unless we can reduce our operating costs very significantly and promptly, it makes no business sense to continue as we have been doing. As a result of the new wages and work rules due to the IAM strike, we will be able to reduce our IAM costs by about $20 million annually. Our goal is an overall annual cost reduction of $150 million; we believe that this requires a $60 million reduction from the pilots, $40 million from the flight attendants, and a $30 million reduction in other costs, including other employee groups.

Third, pilot expenses at Continental are a large portion of total labor expenses. Pilot expenses are about $130 million per year, or over 25 percent of the total annual costs of $520 million, based on the May 1983 cost levels. Pilot wages, benefits, and work rules at Continental create significantly higher costs than we can afford. For example, if the Continental pilots worked under the same contract as the "new" Braniff, our pilot costs would be reduced by $90.0 million per year, or about 70 percent. Completely new-entrant airline pilot cost structures would save even more than that. These are the cost structures we compete against. Other nonpilot cost reduction programs, such as IAM flight attendants, corporate overhead, and so on, although necessary, are not sufficient unless pilot costs are reduced significantly and permanently.

Fourth, if our costs cannot be reduced significantly and immediately, it is not an acceptable business risk to go into the off-peak season without a credible plan to preserve our cash resources. We are not going to go out of business as Braniff did, that is, with no cash. Rather, we are firmly committed to take other steps to protect our remaining liquidity and our assets.

The more basic reason we face these stark choices is because of the new world out there today. Only the efficient airlines with marketplace cost structures will survive. This is certainly true of Continental and carriers like Republic, Western, and Pan Am. And it is also true of carriers even like American and United. The giants realize this fact and are following a strategy unique to themselves in order to survive. They have stockpiled truly awesome financial resources to provide the strength and time to grow. This growth is nourished under new labor contracts that have very low new-hire rates, thus building lower unit cost structures into their entire company. In the meantime, the giants are benefiting from biased travel agent computer reservation systems that distort traffic patterns and competitive market shares. Before that distortion is fully redressed, the giants may or may not be sufficiently prepared for the cost pressures of the marketplace. Delta's recent massive losses show how fickle the marketplace is to even the apparent giants.

No matter how intelligently we manage our business, we cannot have labor costs that are dramatically higher than our competitors' and survive. Although it is perfectly clear that reducing costs *alone* will not solve the company's problems and that much remains to be done on the revenue side, nevertheless it is also true that a precondition to success is a dramatic reduction in our cost structure. Unless we do this, we will run out of the time it takes to improve revenues.

So while we continue to work on revenue improvements and acknowledge that there is much to do, we have concluded that reducing costs dramatically is a necessary first step to survival.

You have often heard me say that I did not author "deregulation." In fact at first I opposed it in the U.S. Congress because I thought it would harm Texas International.

Today I philosophically believe in deregulation. Although it is tough on all of us and on the company we work for—and Continental could perish because of it—I much prefer over the long term to be subject to the rule of the marketplace rather than the bureaucrat.

But we must heed the rule of the marketplace. The latest example of how harsh but inevitable that marketplace is came last week when People Express announced plans to commence Newark–Houston service five times per day at unrestricted fares, a fraction of some of our recent discount fares, to say nothing of our regular fares.

The People Expresses, the Southwests, the America Wests, the Frontier Horizons are drastically altering Continental's marketplace. Unless we change with the marketplace, we will perish.

Other courses of action that are evolutionary, not revolutionary, do not work for Continental.

Exhibit 1

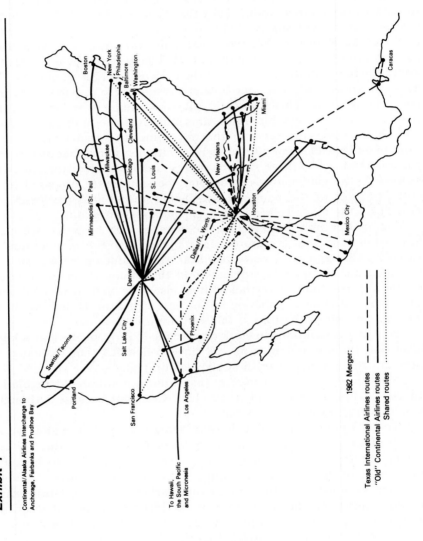

Continental/Alaska Airlines Interchange to Anchorage, Fairbanks and Prudhoe Bay

Seattle/Tacoma

Portland

San Francisco

Los Angeles

To Hawaii, the South Pacific and Micronesia

Salt Lake City

Phoenix

Denver

Minneapolis/St. Paul

Milwaukee

Chicago

St. Louis

Cleveland

Dallas/Ft. Worth

Houston

New Orleans

Mexico City

Miami

Boston

New York

Philadelphia

Baltimore

Washington

Caracas

1982 Merger:

Texas International Airlines routes — — —

"Old" Continental Airlines routes ————

Shared routes ·········

Exhibit 2

Stock Ownership

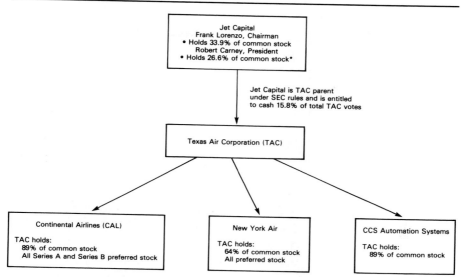

* Remainder of stock is held in small lots.
Sources: 1983 TAC Annual Report; 1981 TAC Proxy.

Exhibit 3

CONTINENTAL AIRLINES (A)
Selected Financial and Statistical Data

	1983	1982	1981	1980	1979
Operating revenues:					
Passenger	$ 995,994	$1,261,642	$1,245,215	$ 879,593	$807,694
Other	116,991	165,373	154,435	112,426	120,288
Total operating revenues	1,112,985	1,427,015	1,399,650	992,019	927,982
Operating expenses:					
Wages, salaries, and related costs	420,600	492,053	532,866	401,481	380,089
Aircraft fuel	321,509	437,560	432,425	295,255	227,614
Depreciation and amortization	75,991	86,950	84,002	59,262	56,353
Other	445,206	445,045	398,823	282,229	271,847
Total operating expenses	1,263,306	1,461,608	1,448,116	1,038,227	935,903
Nonoperating expenses (income):					
Interest expense	69,304	89,152	100,526	42,099	30,182
Capital interest	(181)	(1,348)	(4,521)	(4,974)	(1,673)
Other	(996)	(77,460)	(60,724)	(47,500)	(4,645)
Total nonoperating expenses, net	68,127	10,344	35,291	(10,375)	23,864
Earnings (loss) before income taxes	(218,448)	(44,937)	(83,757)	(35,833)	(31,785)
Income taxes (credits)	—	(3,133)	(3,859)	(15,129)	(18,600)
Net earnings (loss)	$ (218,448)	$ (41,804)	$ (79,898)	$ (20,704)	$ (13,185)

Assets, Liabilities and Stockholders' Equity

Current assets:				
Cash and temporary investments	$ 64,686	$ 37,123	$ 76,082	$ 31,717	$ 34,670
Accounts receivable—net	84,449	152,495	155,306	106,381	118,629
Spare parts and supplies—net	27,728	33,422	42,729	36,938	23,497
Prepayment and other	21,946	26,828	15,661	5,816	5,007
Total current assets	198,809	249,868	289,778	180,852	181,803
Property and equipment:				
Owned property and equipment (net)	546,040	619,758	706,847	482,715	545,590
Capital leases	124,958	134,868	145,365	115,544	—
Total property and equipment	670,998	754,626	852,212	598,259	545,590
Total other assets	38,336	48,575	41,051	5,038	11,314
Total assets	$ 908,143	$1,053,069	$1,183,041	$ 784,149	$738,707
Current liabilities:				
Current portion of long-term debt	$ 17,087	$ 68,780	$ 66,943	$ 38,305	$ 53,484
Current portion of capital leases	3,452	5,116	4,169	1,631	—
Accounts payable	16,812	119,314	111,595	64,549	82,131
Other	63,387	198,857	205,641	141,950	116,061
Total current liabilities	100,738	392,067	388,348	246,435	251,676
Estimated liabilities subject to Chapter 11 reorganization proceedings	737,610	—	—	—	—
Long-term obligations	172,178	583,948	679,629	328,797	243,979
Other (deferred credits)	6,812	27,185	23,391	18,043	30,195
Stockholders' equity:				
Stock and paid-in capital	182,420	121,704	121,704	88,953	88,698
Retained (deficit) earnings	(291,615)	(71,835)	(30,031)	101,921	124,159
Total stockholders' equity	(109,195)	49,869	91,673	190,874	212,857
Total liabilities and stockholders' equity	$ 908,143	$1,053,069	$1,183,041	$ 784,149	$738,707

Note: 1979–1980 Continental Airlines only; 1981—Pro Forma CAL and TXI combined; 1982–1983—CAC.
Source: Continental Airlines Company records.

Exhibit 4

TEXAS AIR CORPORATION
Five-Year Summary of Selected Financial and Statistical Data
(dollars in thousands, except per share data)

	1983	1982	1981	1980	1979
Summary of Operations					
Operating revenues:					
Passenger	$ 1,124,189	$ 1,356,122	$ 649,491	$ 266,837	$ 213,218
Other	122,026	160,198	69,909	24,659	20,943
Total operating revenues	1,246,215	1,516,320	719,400	291,496	234,161
Operating expenses	1,382,087	1,562,289	760,246	284,949	218,825
Operating income (loss)	(135,872)	(45,969)	(40,846)	6,547	15,336
Other income (expense):					
Interest and debt expense—net	(67,785)	(87,107)	(40,964)	(4,238)	(11,067)
Minority interest in subsidiaries	—	20,861	12,077	27	—
Other—net	25,793	60,107	17,755	4,284	44,026
Total other income (expense)	(41,992)	(6,139)	(11,132)	73	32,959
Income (loss) before income taxes	(177,864)	(52,108)	(51,978)	6,620	48,295
Income tax (credit) provision	2,076	(3,133)	(4,793)	2,630	6,900
Extraordinary items	—	—	—	—	—
Net income (loss)	$ (177,864)	$ (48,975)	$ (47,185)	$ 3,990	$ 41,395
Net income (loss) per share:					
Primary	$ (14.58)	$ (7.27)	$ (8.11)	$ 0.55	$ 5.88
Fully diluted	$ (14.58)	$ (7.27)	$ (8.11)	$ 0.55	$ 4.84

Financial Summary

Current assets	$ 304,455	$ 326,391	$ 352,549	$ 195,490	$ 156,927
Current liabilities	134,547	415,956	405,002	82,871	68,452
Property and equipment—net	839,525	839,332	928,358	177,988	158,507
Total assets	1,177,959	1,191,976	1,301,316	385,749	319,201
Long-term debt—net	259,212	515,948	605,001	196,236	154,491
Obligations under capital leases—net	55,656	144,808	156,213	11,347	13,940
Redeemable preferred stock	23,219	24,464	4,400	4,899	5,548
Stockholders' equity	(49,649)	63,477	40,453	84,325	75,670
Common stock price range	11¾–4¾	13⅞–4	15⅛–5⅛	14¾–6⅜	13⅝–7½

Statistical Summary

*Continental Airlines**

Available seat miles (000)	15,396,477	19,270,121	17,474,238	17,865,646	19,175,563
Revenue passenger miles (000)	9,274,257	11,157,365	10,069,734	10,359,077	11,674,282
Load factor	60.2%	57.9%	57.6%	58.0%	60.9%
Revenue passengers	10,236,004	11,335,711	10,285,713	11,404,046	13,192,855
Average fare per passenger	$97.30	$111.30	$121.06	$100.49	$77.38
Average yield per revenue passenger mile	10.74¢	11.31¢	12.37¢	11.06¢	8.74¢
Average length of passenger trip (miles)	906	872	850	828	885
Revenue aircraft miles (000)	110,703	137,678	127,393	135,480	146,097
Average length of aircraft flight (miles)	662	638	620	585	590
Average daily utilization of aircraft (block hours)	7:19	9:02	9:08	9:51	10:46

New York Air†

Available seat miles (000)	1,146,584	1,110,478	735,494
Revenue passenger miles (000)	656,601	606,654	460,832
Load factor	57.3%	54.6%	67.2%
Revenue passengers	2,103,681	1,738,095	1,562,017
Average fare per passenger	$60.94	$54.36	$40.89
Average yield per revenue passenger mile	19.5¢	15.57¢	13.86¢
Average length of passenger trip (miles)	312	349	295
Revenue aircraft miles (000)	10,307	9,878	6,238
Average length of aircraft flight (miles)	300	330	287
Average daily utilization of aircraft (block hours)	8:08	8:45	8:90

* Reflects the combined operations of Continental and Texas International.
† New York Air began service in December 1980.
Source: Texas Air Corporation 1982, 1983 annual reports.

Exhibit 5

Texas Air Corporation
Airline Route System

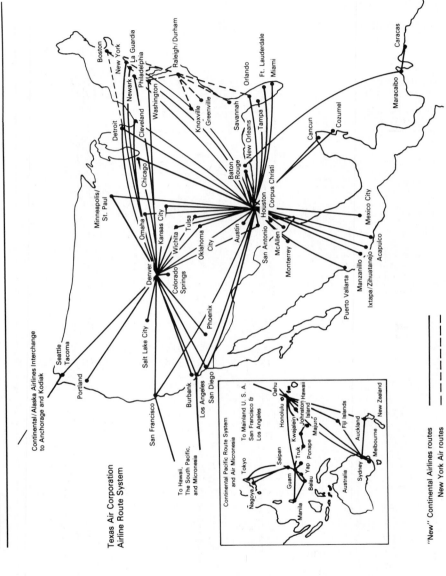

"New" Continental Airlines routes

New York Air routes

Exhibit 6

Continental Airlines: Analysis of South Pacific Route Decision

Mid-Pacific Strategic Factors

Profitable franchise $9.1 million in 1983.[1]
Pan Am withdrawing April 1.
Preempt competitive incursions:
— SPIA.
— Aloha.
— Hawaiian.
Build natural traffic flows between points with strong current
   Continental identity:
— HNL–West Coast.
— Guam–Micronesia, Japan, and Philippines.
Enhances value of Continental's limited entry routes.
Capitalize on Continental's Pacific market identity.
Efficient utilization of resources—no new stations.
Continues the planned development of the Mid-Pacific.

Nagoya	—	Summer 1983
Guam–Tokyo	—	March 1984
Guam–Honolulu	—	April 1984

South Pacific Strategic Factors

Profitable franchise $5.3 million in 1983.[2]
Respond to competitive changes.
— Additional nonstops to Sydney.
— Introduction nonstop service to Auckland.
Build natural traffic flow between United States and South Pacific and Mid-Pacific.
Efficient utilization of existing resources—no new stations.
Fill Honolulu void.
Why now?
   Synergistic with Honolulu–Guam.
   Competitors are strategically redeploying in April.
   Market conditions are correct.
   Implements deferred 1983 expansion.

Potential Risks of Action Considered

Mid-Pacific:
— Deterioration of Guam market.
— Price competition.
— Essential air service requirements.
— Air Micronesia dispute.

---

[1] Eleven months ended November 30, 1983.
[2] Ibid.

BOOK ONE

Determining Corporate Strategy

The Concept of Corporate Strategy

When we were looking at the chief executive's job, we promised that a simple central concept called *corporate strategy* would be developed here. It would be offered, we said, as a means to reduce the general management function to manageable proportions and enable technical specialists to understand the proper relationship between their departmental objectives and the goals of their companies. We come now to the central idea of this course and this book. We will look at what strategy is, what form it takes in different kinds of companies, what tests of validity may be applied to it, and what it is good for. If you think back to your discussion of Head Ski, you may already be able to see or imagine what does or can happen to this idea in living organizations and sense both its inherent difficulties and its power.

What Strategy Is

As the outcome of the decision process we will later analyze in detail, corporate strategy is the pattern of decisions in a company that (1) determines, shapes, and reveals its objectives, purposes, or goals; (2) produces the principal policies and plans for achieving these goals; and (3) defines the business the company intends to be in, the kind of economic and human organization it intends to be, and the nature of the economic and noneconomic contribution it intends to make to its shareholders, employees, customers, and communities. In an organization of any size or diversity, corporate strategy usually applies to the whole enterprise, while business strategy, less comprehensive, defines the choice of product

115

or service and market or individual businesses within the firm. *Business strategy,* that is, determines how a company will compete in a given business and position itself among its competitors. *Corporate strategy* defines the businesses in which a company will compete, preferably in a way that focuses resources to convert distinctive competence into competitive advantage. Both are outcomes of a continuous process of *strategic management* that we will later examine at length.

The strategic decision contributing to this pattern is one that is effective over long periods of time, affects the company in many different ways, and focuses and commits a significant portion of its resources to expected outcomes. The pattern resulting from a series of such decisions will probably define the central character and image of a company, the individuality it has for its members and various publics, and the position it will occupy in its industry and markets. It will permit the specification of particular objectives to be attained through a timed sequence of investment and implementation decisions and will govern directly the deployment or redeployment of resources to make these decisions effective.

Some aspects of such a pattern of decision may be in an established corporation unchanging over long periods of time, like a commitment to quality, or high technology, or certain raw materials, or good labor relations. Other aspects of a strategy must change as or before the world changes, such as product line, manufacturing process, or merchandising and styling practices. The basic determinants of company character, if purposefully institutionalized, are likely to persist through and shape the nature of substantial changes in the allocation of resources and of product policy.

It would be possible to extend the definition of strategy for a given company to separate a central character and the core of its special accomplishment from the manifestations of such characteristics in changing product lines, markets, and policies designed to make activities profitable from year to year. *The New York Times,* for example, after many years of being shaped by the values of its owners and staff, is now so self-conscious and respected an institution that its nature is likely to remain unchanged, even if the services it offers are altered drastically in the direction of other outlets for its news-processing capacity.

It is important not to take the idea of strategy apart—to separate goals from the policies designed to achieve those goals or even to overdo the difference between the formulation of strategy and its implementation. The interdependence of purposes, policies, and organized action is crucial to the particularity of an individual strategy. It is the unity, coherence, and internal consistency of a company's strategic decisions that give the firm its identity and individuality, its power to mobilize its strengths, and its likelihood of success in the marketplace. It is the interrelationship of a set of goals and policies that crystallizes from the formless reality of a company's environment a set of problems an organization can seize upon and solve.

We mean the term *strategy*, therefore, to suggest that *pattern* among goals is more important than any array of separate purposes. The variety of valid and attractive objectives is nearly infinite. Impressionistic selection results in uncoordinated and inefficient pursuit. Superficially attractive financial goals like high return on equity and high profit margins, for example, are in practice or at any one time incompatible with high rates of growth in sales or market share. As we will see, different kinds of objectives limit other kinds. Financial goals may impose constraints on organization development and social goals. An organization objective of maximum decentralization will put limits on short-term attainment of cost control. The objective of continuous employment subordinates at once responsiveness to peaks of demand.

The interrelation among objectives is the key to coherence and consistency. The pattern of goals and policies, rather than their separate substance, is the source of the uniqueness which ideally should distinguish every company from its competitors. Especially when values visibly affect economic choices, the special character of a company becomes apparent to its employees and customers. Breaking up the system of corporate goals and the character-determining major policies for attainment leads to narrow and mechanical conceptions of strategic management and endless logic chopping.

Many popular terms and current buzzwords allude to various aspects of goal setting. Whether you wish to refer to a view of the total corporation as its *vision* or a statement of purpose as its *mission statement*, for example, is up to you. Language has many ways of describing so central an activity as choice of purpose. We should get on to understanding the need for strategic decision and for determining the most satisfactory pattern of goals in concrete instances. Refinement of definition can wait, for you will wish to develop definition in practice in directions useful to you. In the meantime, remember that what you are doing has no meaning for yourself or others unless you can sense and say or imply to others what you are doing it for. The quality of all administrative action and the motives lending it power cannot be understood without knowing their relationship to purpose.

Summary Statements of Strategy

Before we proceed to clarification of the strategy concept by application, we should specify the terms in which strategy is usually expressed. A summary statement of strategy will characterize the product line and services offered or planned by the company, the markets and market segments for which products and services are now or will be designed, and the channels through which these markets will be reached. The means by which the operation is to be financed will be specified, as will the profit objectives and the emphasis to be placed on the safety of capital versus level of return. Major policy in central functions, such as marketing, manufacturing, procurement, research and development, labor relations, and personnel, will be stated where they distinguish the company from others; and usually the intended size, form, and character of the organization would be included.

In a statement of Howard Head's intuitive or consciously designed strategy for Head Ski, some of these categories would be missing (profit objectives, for example) but others stressed (such as quality of product). Each company, if it were to construct a summary strategy from what it understands itself to be aiming at, would have a different statement with different categories of decision emphasized to indicate what it wanted to be or do.

To indicate the nature of such a statement, a student of Heublein, a famous old Policy case, deduced this statement from the account of the company before it was acquired by R. J. Reynolds and when it was about to acquire Hamm's Brewery:[1]

> Heublein aims to market in the United States and via franchise overseas a wide variety of high-margin, high-quality consumer products concentrated in the liquor and food business, especially bottled cocktails, vodka, and other special-use and distinctive beverages and specialty convenience foods, addressed to a relatively prosperous, young-adult market and returning over 15 percent of equity after taxes. With emphasis on the techniques of consumer goods marketing [brand promotion, wide distribution, product representation in more than one price segment, and very substantial offbeat advertising directed closely to its growing audience], Heublein intends to make Smirnoff the number one liquor brand worldwide via internal growth [and franchise] or acquisitions or both. Its manufacturing policy rather than full integration is in liquor to redistill only to bring purchased spirits up to high-quality standards. It aims to finance its internal growth through the use of debt and its considerable cash flow and to use its favorable price earnings ratio for acquisitions. Both its liquor and food distribution are intended to secure distributor support through advertising and concern for the distributor's profit.[2]

Although it might be argued that the statement was not clearly in the chief executive's mind when he contemplated purchasing Hamm's Brewery and therefore did not help him refrain from that unfortunate

---

[1] The Heublein case may be found in earlier editions of this book or obtained from HBS Case Services.

[2] Kenneth R. Andrews, *The Concept of Corporate Strategy*, rev. ed. (Homewood, Ill.: Dow Jones-Irwin, 1980), p. 22.

decision, it was in his experience and in the pattern of the company's past strategic decisions—at least as reported in the case. Note also that this statement must be regarded as only a partial summary, for it omits reference to the kind of human organization Heublein means to be for its members and the responsibility its leaders feel for such strategy-related social problems as alcoholism. But even without mention of organization or social responsibility substrategies, this statement raises a multimillion dollar question about the beer business as a compatible element in the company's marketing mix.

Reasons for Not Articulating Strategy

For a number of reasons companies seldom formulate and publish as complete a statement as we have just illustrated. Conscious planning of the long-term development of companies has been until recently less common than individual executive responses to environmental pressure, competitive threat, or entrepreneurial opportunity. In the latter mode of development, the unity or coherence of corporate effort is unplanned, natural, intuitive, or even nonexistent. Incrementalism in practice sometimes gives the appearance of consciously formulated strategy, but it may be the natural result of compromise among coalitions backing contrary policy proposals or skillful improvisatory adaptation to external forces.[3] Practicing managers who prefer muddling through to the strategic process at the heart of Business Policy would never commit themselves to an articulate strategy.

Other reasons for the scarcity of concrete statements of strategy include the desirability of keeping strategic plans confidential for security reasons and ambiguous to avoid internal conflict or even final decision. Skillful incrementalists may have plans in their heads which they do not reveal to avoid resistance and other trouble in their own organization. A company with a large division in an obsolescent business which it intends to drain of cash until operations are discontinued could not expect high morale and cooperation to follow publication of this intent. Since in any dynamic company, strategy is continually evolving, the official statement of strategy, unless it were couched in very general terms, would be as hard to keep up to date as an organization chart. Finally, a firm that has internalized its strategy does not feel the need to keep saying what it is, valuable as that information might be to new members.

---

[3] For an extended account of incrementalism, see David Braybrooke and Charles E. Lindblom, *A Strategy of Decision* (New York: Free Press, 1963), and James Brian Quinn, *Strategies for Change: Logical Incrementalism* (Homewood, Ill.: Richard D. Irwin, 1980). H. Edward Wrapp's "Good Managers Don't Make Policy Decisions," *Harvard Business Review,* July–August 1984, pp. 8 ff., is a widely read analysis of purposeful incrementalism.

Deducing Strategy from Behavior

The cases in this book enable students of Policy to do what the managements of the companies usually have not done. In the absence of explicit statements, we may deduce from decisions observed what the pattern is and what the company's goals and policies are, on the assumption that some perhaps unspoken consensus lies behind them. Careful examination of the behavior described in the cases will reveal what the strategy must be. At the same time we should not mistake apparent strategy visible in a pattern of past incremental decisions for conscious planning for the future. What will pass as the current strategy of a company may almost always be deduced from its behavior, but a strategy for a future of changed circumstance may not always be distinguishable from performance in the present. For all of Howard Head's skill in integrating a series of product development, distribution, merchandising, service, manufacturing, and research and development decisions around the metal ski, was he as well prepared as he might have been for the advent of the fiberglass ski? The essence of strategic decision is its reach into the future.

Formulation of Strategy

Corporate strategy is an organization process, in many ways inseparable from the structure, behavior, and culture of the company in which it takes place. Nevertheless, we may abstract from the process two important aspects, interrelated in real life but separable for the purposes of analysis. The first of these we may call *formulation;* the second, *implementation.* Deciding what strategy should be may be approached as a rational undertaking, even if in real life emotional attachments (as to metal skis or investigative reporting) may complicate choice among future alternatives (for ski manufacturers or alternative newspapers). The principal subactivities of strategy formulation as a logical activity include identifying opportunities and threats in the company's environment and attaching some estimate or risk to the discernible alternatives. Before a choice can be made, the company's strengths and weaknesses should be appraised together with the resources on hand and available. Its actual or potential capacity to take advantage of perceived market needs or to cope with attendant risks should be estimated as objectively as possible. The strategic alternative which results from matching opportunity and corporate capability at an acceptable level of risk is what we may call an *economic strategy.*

The process described thus far assumes that strategists are analytically objective in estimating the relative capacity of their company and the opportunity they see or anticipate in developing markets. The extent to which they wish to undertake low or high risk presumably depends on their profit objectives. The higher they set the latter, the more willing they must be to assume a correspondingly high risk that the market opportunity they see will not develop or that the corporate competence required to excel competition will not be forthcoming.

So far we have described the intellectual processes of ascertaining what a company *might do* in terms of environmental opportunity, of deciding what it *can do* in terms of ability and power, and of bringing these two considerations together in optimal equilibrium. The determination of strategy also requires consideration of what alternatives are preferred, quite apart from economic considerations, by the chief executive and by his or her immediate associates as well. The acquiescence or, better, the enthusiastic engagement of all whose productivity and creativity are important in achieving superior performance grows out of participation in the process of strategic decision. Personal values, aspirations, and ideals do, and in our judgment quite properly should, influence the final choice of purposes. Thus what the people in a company *want to do* must be brought into the strategic decision.

Finally, strategic choice has an ethical aspect—a fact much more dramatically illustrated in some industries (chemicals and nuclear power, for example) than in others. Just as alternatives may be ordered in terms of the degree of risk that they entail, so may they be examined against the standards of responsiveness to the expectations of society that the strategist elects. Some alternatives may seem to the executive considering them more attractive than others when the public good or service to society is considered. What a company *should do* thus appears as a fourth element of the strategic decision.

The ability to identify the four components of strategy—(1) market opportunity, (2) corporate competence and resources, (3) personal values and aspirations, and (4) acknowledged obligations to segments of society other than stockholders—is nothing compared to the art of reconciling their implications in a final pattern of purpose. Taken by itself, each consideration might lead in a different direction.

If you put the various aspirations of individuals in any organization you know against this statement, you will see what we mean. Even in a single mind contradictory aspirations can survive a long time before the need to calculate trade-offs and integrate divergent inclinations becomes clear. Growth opportunity attracted many companies to the computer business after World War II. The decision to diversify out of typewriters and calculators was encouraged by growth opportunity and excitement. But the financial, technical, and marketing requirements of this business exceeded the capacity of most of the competitors of IBM. The magnet of opportunity and the incentive of desire obscured the calculations of what resources and competence were required to succeed. Most crucially, where corporate capability leads, executives do not always want to go. Of all the components of strategic choice, the combination of resources and competence is most crucial to success.

The Implementation of Strategy

Since effective implementation can make a sound strategic decision ineffective or a debatable choice successful, it is as important to examine the processes of implementation as to weigh the advantages of available strategic alternatives. The implementation of strategy is composed of a series of subactivities which are primarily administrative. If purpose is determined, then the resources of a company can be mobilized to accomplish it. An organizational structure appropriate for the efficient performance of the required tasks must be made effective by information systems and relationships permitting coordination of subdivided activities. The organizational processes of performance measurement, compensation, management development—all of them enmeshed in systems of incentives and controls—must be directed toward the kind of behavior required by organizational purpose. The role of personal leadership is important and sometimes decisive in the accomplishment of strategy. Although we know that organization structure and processes of compensation, incentives, control, and management development influence and constrain the formulation of strategy, we should look first at the logical proposition that structure should follow strategy in order to cope with the organizational reality that strategy also follows structure. When we have examined both tendencies, we will understand and to some extent be prepared to

Figure 1

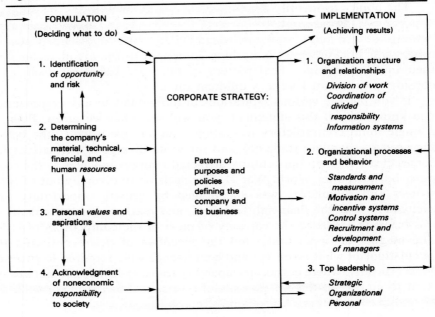

deal with the interdependence of the formulation and implementation of corporate purpose. Figure 1 may be useful in understanding the analysis of strategy as a pattern of interrelated decisions.

Kinds of Strategies

The most important characteristic of a corporate pattern of decision that may properly be called strategic is its uniqueness. A creative reconciliation of alternatives for future development is made unique by the special characteristics of an organization, its central competence, history, financial and technical resources, and the aspirations and sense of responsibility of its leaders. The environment—market opportunity and risk—is more nearly the same for major companies operating in the same geographical regions than are the resources, values, and responsibility components of strategy. For the company unequipped to dominate the full range of opportunity, the quest for a profitable segment of, or niche in, a market is, if successful, also likely to distinguish one company from another. In fact in an industry where all companies seem to have the same strategy, we will find trouble for all but the leaders—as at various times American Motors, Chrysler, and Ford have had different degrees of difficulty following General Motors, which got where it is by *not* following the previous industry leader, Henry Ford.[4]

In seeking its position of uniqueness, there are two fundamental types of competitive advantage that a company can possess: *lower cost* and/or *differentiation.* A lower cost position can potentially come from many sources that reflect the firm's strategy, among them larger scale, favorable raw material supplies, or proximate location. A lower cost position yields the firm higher profitability than rivals at whatever the industry price. Differentiation, or the superiority of the company in meeting special or important customer needs, yields the firm higher profitability than rivals through a premium price. Differentiation may potentially result from many aspects of the company's strategy, including its product quality, servicing ability, or delivery time.

Every truly successful strategy that outperforms competitors exploits one or both of these two sources of competitive advantage, achieved in a manner that is *sustainable* against rivals. We see three possible generic strategies for sustaining competitive advantage:

1. *Overall cost leadership.* While producing a product or service of good quality, the company strives to be the overall cost leader across its entire product line in the industry. This position is achieved through

---

[4] For a basic study in strategy formulation, see Alfred P. Sloan, *My Years at General Motors* (Garden City, N.Y.: Doubleday, 1964).

a range of supporting functional policies compatible with industry economics.

2. *Differentiation.* The company strives to be distinctive in an important aspect of most of its products or services that the customer values. Costs are kept close to those of competitors, but the strategic emphasis is on achieving and maintaining the chosen form of differentiation, quality, or style, for example, through the coordinated activities of each functional department. Again this selective superiority is attempted across the entire product line and in all its markets.

3. *Focus.* Unable to be the low-cost producer industrywide or to achieve comprehensive differentiation, the firm selects a narrower strategic target and concentrates its entire efforts at serving a distinctively defined market segment. In so doing, the firm is able to achieve lower costs, differentiation, or both in serving the chosen market even though it cannot achieve these competitive advantages industrywide or across the broadest possible product line. Possible strategic targets may include portions of the product line, particular customer segments, limited geographic areas, particular distribution channels, or some combination of these. The essential logic of the focused strategy is that the firm competing in this way can serve its target better than the competitor with the divided loyalties of serving a special target along with others in a more broadly based strategy.

Usually, the firm must make a choice among these three fundamentally different approaches to achieving a competitive advantage because the functional requirements and organizational needs of each are different. Generally, for example, the firm achieving differentiation does so at the price of higher costs. In a few industries where the economics allow it, however, a firm can be both cost leader and differentiated at the same time. The enviable position is nirvana, remote from the pain and turmoil of competition.

On the way to this happy state, companies encounter other generic strategies, less universal than low-cost differentiation and focus but more common. The generation of strategic alternatives is sometimes approached with growth the dominant consideration.

Low-Growth Strategies

1. *No change.* The strategy properly identified and checked out against the tests of validity outlined below can be closely monitored, fine tuned for minor defects, managed for maximum cash flows, with low investment in forced growth. Defensive contingencies will be designed for unexpected change, and efficient implementation will be the focus of top-management attention. During recessions and after the onset of conservation and environmental protection, this strategy is more attractive than it was in the heyday of "more is better." The profit to be made from doing better what a company already knows how to do rather than investing heavily in growth is the attraction of this strategy, which can be protected by achievement of low costs. Its disadvantage is the possibility of being overtaken or displaced by new developments and the restriction of opportunity for organization members. Positions in cost advantage and differentiation may be less vulnerable if growth goals are modest.

2. *Retreat.* The possibility of liquidation is not to be sought out but may be for companies in deep trouble a better choice than continuing the struggle. Less drastic alternatives than complete liquidation include discontinuance or divestment of marginal operations or merging with a ceding of management control. This alternative may come to mind as you look at one or two of the cases in this book. It would have come up more often in earlier editions around cases from the farm equipment, typewriter, and sewing machine businesses. Consolidation may protect a market niche.

3. *Focus on limited special opportunity.* A more constructive course of contraction is concentration on a profitable specialty product or a limited but significant market niche, as if Head had elected to concentrate on high-priced, high-quality skis without diversification into ski wear and other equipment. Success in a narrow line almost always tempts a company to broaden its line, but the McIlhenny strategy (Tabasco sauce only) may not be totally obsolete. If the proper focus is chosen, the limits may relax and growth may come in any case. Once the risk of limited life is accepted, the advantages of the no-change strategy can be sought.

Forced-Growth Strategies

1. *Acquisition of competitors.* In the early stages of its development, a company with a successful strategy and proven record of successful execution can acquire small competitors in the same business to expand its market. Eventually antitrust regulation will put an end to this practice, unless the prospective acquisition is very small or on the edge of bankruptcy. Such acquisitions are usually followed by an adaptation of strategy either by the parent or acquired company to keep the total company a single business or one dominated by its original product-market specialization. Lower costs do not follow automatically from growth by acquisition.

2. *Vertical integration.* A conservative growth strategy, keeping a company close to its core competence and experience in its industry, consists of moving backward via acquisition or internal development to sources of supply and forward toward the ultimate customer. When a newspaper buys a pulp and paper mill and forest lands or news agencies for distribution, it is extending its strategy but not changing materially the nature of its business. Increasing the stages of integration provides a greater number of options to be developed or closed out as, for example, the making of fine paper and the distribution of magazines. Vertical integration serves lower costs better than it serves product differentiation.

3. *Geographical expansion.* Enlargement of territory can be accomplished by building new plants and enlarging marketing organizations or by acquisition of competitors. For a sizable company the opportunity to enlarge international operations, by export, establishments of plants and marketing activities overseas, with or without foreign partners, may protect against contraction forced by domestic competition. You could have considered the possibility of Head Ski's seeking growth overseas, where 19 percent of its sales were accomplished by a single agent about whom almost nothing is said in the case.

4. *Diversification.* The avenue to growth which presents the most difficult strategic choices is diversification. Diversification can range from minor additions to basic product line to completely unrelated businesses. It can be sought through internal research and development, the purchase of new product ideas or technology, and the acquisition of companies. It may have nothing to do with either lower costs or differentiation of product or service and detract seriously from both.

Kinds of Companies

The process of strategic decision differs in complexity depending upon the diversity of the company in question. Just as having the range of strategy from liquidation to multinational diversification in mind will stimulate the generation of strategic alternatives, so a simple way of differentiating kinds of companies will help us see why different kinds of companies have different kinds of problems in making their activities coherent and effective and in setting a course for the future.

Bruce Scott has developed a model of stages of corporate development in which each stage is characterized by the way a firm is managed and the scope of strategic choice available to it.[5] *Stage I* is a single-product (or line of products) company with little or no formal structure run by the owner who personally performs most of the managerial functions, uses subjective and unsystematic measures of performance and reward and control systems. The strategy of this firm is what the owner-manager wants it to be.

---

[5] See Bruce R. Scott, "Stages of Corporate Development, Parts I and II" (unpublished paper, Harvard Business School, 1970), and "Can Industry Survive the Welfare State?" *Harvard Business Review,* September–October 1982, pp. 70–84.

Stage II is the single-product firm grown so large that functional specialization has become imperative. A degree of integration has developed between raw materials, production processes, distribution, and sales. The search for product or process improvement is institutionalized in research and development, and performance management and control and compensation systems become systematic with the formulation of policy to guide delegation of operating decisions. The strategic choice is still under top control and centers upon the degree of integration, size of market share, and breadth of product line.

Stage III is a company with multiple-product lines and channels of distribution with an organization based on product-market relationships rather than function. Its businesses are not to a significant degree integrated; they have their own markets. Its research and development are oriented to new products rather than improvements, and its measurement and control systems are increasingly systematic and oriented to results. Strategic alternatives are phrased in terms of entry into and exit from industries and allocation of resources by industry and rate of growth.

If a company grows, it may pass from stage I to stage III, although it can become very large while still in stage II. Its strategic decisions will grow in complexity. The stages of development model has proved productive in relating different kinds of strategies to kinds of companies and has led other researchers into productive classification. Leonard Wrigley and Richard P. Rumelt have carried Scott's work forward to develop suggestive ways of categorizing companies and comparing their strategies.[6]

First, of course, is the *single-business* firm (stages I and II firms) with 95 percent or more of its revenues arising from a single business—an oil company or flour-milling company, for example, or as you will see, Crown Cork & Seal.

Second is the *dominant business* consisting of firms diversified to some extent but still obtaining most of their revenues from a single business. The diversification may arise from end products of integration, with products stemming from strengths of the firm or minor unrelated activities. A large oil company in the petrochemical and fertilizer business would fall in this category.

Third is the *related business* comprising diversified firms in which the diversification has been principally accomplished by relating new activities to old—General Electric and Westinghouse, for example.

---

[6] Leonard Wrigley, "Division Autonomy and Diversification" (Ph.D. dissertation, Harvard Business School, 1970); and Richard P. Rumelt, *Strategy Structure and Economic Performance* (Boston: Division of Research, Harvard Business School, 1974). Malcolm Salter has added a refinement to stage III in "Stages of Corporate Development," *Journal of Business Policy* 1, no. 1 (1970), pp. 40–51.

Fourth is the *unrelated business*. These firms have diversified primarily without regard to relationships between new businesses and current activities. The conglomerate companies fall in this category.

Each of these categories have subdivisions devised by Rumelt which you may wish to examine at a more advanced stage of Policy studies. In the meantime it is interesting to note that Rumelt has found significantly superior performance in the related businesses, suggesting that the strategy of diversifying from the original business to a significant degree has been the most successful strategic pattern among the Fortune 500 under conditions prevailing in recent years.

The range of strategy and the kinds of company which different growth strategies have produced suggest, in short, that the process of defining the business of a company will vary greatly depending on the degree of diversification under way in the company. The product-market choices are crystal clear in Crown Cork & Seal and a single-business oil company; they could not be exhaustively listed for General Electric. That top management decides product-market questions in such a company, except in such instances as entry into nuclear energy, is conceivable only as an oversimplification.

As diversification increases, the definition of the total business turns away from literal description of products and markets (which become the business of the separate product divisions) toward general statements of financial results expected and corporate principle in other areas. A conglomerate firm made up of many different businesses will have many different strategies, related or not depending upon the desire for synergy in the strategic direction of the total enterprise. The overall strategy of a highly diversified firm may be only the total of its divisional strategies. That it should be more than that is a matter for argument. To make it so puts heavy demands on the ability to conceptualize corporate purpose.

The task of identifying the coherence and unity of a conglomerate is, of course, much greater than that of even a multidivision-related business. Students should be prepared, then, to adapt the beginning definition offered here to the complexity of the business they are examining. Since the trend over time is product diversity in growing firms and evolution from stage I to stage III, it is well to have this complication in mind now.

For as Norman Berg makes clear in "Strategic Planning in Conglomerate Companies," strategic choice is not merely the function of the chief executive office.[7] It is of necessity a multilevel activity, with each unit concerned with its own environment and its own objectives. The

---

[7] Norman A. Berg, "Strategic Planning in Conglomerate Companies," *Harvard Business Review,* May–June 1965, pp. 79–92. See also his "What's Different about Conglomerate Management?" *Harvard Business Review,* November–December 1969, and "Corporate Strategy in the Diversified Firm," Chapter 12 in his *General Management: An Analytical Approach* (Homewood, Ill.: Richard D. Irwin, 1984).

process will reflect the noneconomic goals of people at the level at which proposals are made. In a conglomerate of unrelated businesses the corporate staff is small, the divisions are relatively autonomous, and the locus of strategic planning is in the divisions. This makes supervision of the strategic planning process and allocation of resources, depending upon the evaluation of strategies submitted, the strategic role of the corporate senior managers.

The differences in the application of a concept of strategy to a modest single business on the one hand and to a multinational conglomerate on the other—although important—mean that the ability to conceive of a business in strategic terms must be distributed throughout the organization in a complex company. The problems of choosing among strategic alternatives and making the choice effective over time, together with the problems of ensuring that such organization processes as performance measurement do not impede the choice, must be part of the management ability of many people besides the general managers. All those involved in the strategic process, it follows, are vitally concerned with how a strategy can be evaluated so that it may be continued, amended, or abandoned as appropriate. Operating level managers who make a strategic proposal should be able to test its validity against corporate norms if for no other reason than their own survival. Those who must approve and allocate funds to such proposals should have a criterion to evaluate their worth going beyond a general confidence (or lack of it) in the ability of the proponents.

Criteria for Evaluation

How is the actual or proposed strategy to be judged? How are we to know that one strategy is better than another? A number of important questions can regularly be asked. As is already evident, no infallible indicators are available. With practice they will lead to reliable intuitive discriminations.

1. *Is the strategy identifiable and has it been made clear either in words or practice?*

The degree to which attention has been given to the strategic alternatives available to a company is likely to be basic to the soundness of its strategic decision. To cover in empty phrases ("Our policy is planned profitable growth in any market we can serve well") an absence of analysis of opportunity or actual determination of corporate strength is worse than to remain silent, for it conveys the illusion of a commitment when none has been made. The unstated strategy cannot be tested or contested and is likely therefore to be weak. If it is implicit in the intuition of a strong leader, the organization is likely to be weak and the demands the strategy makes upon it are likely to remain unmet. A strategy must be explicit to be effective and specific enough to require some action and exclude others.

2. *Is the strategy in some way unique?*

As we have already said, a fully developed strategy will visibly differentiate any company from its competitors. For producers of commodities, like chlorine or cement, the difference will not be found in the product itself but in the way it is marketed, delivered, produced, or priced. For manufacturers of proprietary products, the problem of differentiation lies in substitute products or in future direct competition when patents expire. The sameness that afflicts companies not strategically managed usually arises from industry structure, from similarities in the technology of production, and from conventions developed to limit competition, regulate market share, and educate newcomers in how things are done. Uniqueness is more the product of imagination than experience.

3. *Does the strategy exploit fully domestic and international environmental opportunity?*

An unqualified yes answer is likely to be rare even in the instance of global giants such as General Motors. But the present and future dimensions of markets can be analyzed without forgetting the limited resources of the planning company in order to outline the requirements of balanced growth and the need for environmental information. The relation between market opportunity and organizational development is a critical one in the design of future plans. Unless growth is incompatible with the resources of an organization or the aspirations of its management, it is likely that a strategy that does not purport to make full use of market opportunity will be weak also in other aspects. Vulnerability to competition is increased by lack of interest in market share.

4. *Is the strategy consistent with corporate competence and resources, both present and projected?*

Although additional resources, both financial and managerial, are available to companies with genuine opportunity, the availability of each must be finally determined and programmed along a practicable time scale. This may be the most difficult question in this series. The key factor which is usually left out is the availability of management for effective implementation or the opportunity cost implicit in the assignment of management to any task.

5. *Are the major provisions of the strategy and the program of major policies of which it is comprised internally consistent?*

A foolish consistency, Emerson said, is the hobgoblin of little minds, and consistency of any kind is certainly not the first qualification of successful corporate CEOs. Nonetheless, one advantage of making as specific a statement of strategy as is practicable is the resultant availability of a careful check on fit, unity, coherence, compatibility, and synergy—the state in which the whole of anything can be viewed as greater than the sum of its parts. For example, a manufacturer of chocolate candy who depends for two thirds of his business upon wholesalers should not follow a policy of ignoring them or of dropping all support of their activities and all attention to their complaints. Similarly, two engineers who found a new firm expressly to do development work should not follow a policy of accepting orders that, though highly profitable, in effect turn their company into a large job shop, with the result that unanticipated financial and production problems take all the time that might have gone into development. An examination of any substantial firm will reveal at least some details in which policies pursued by different departments tend to go in different directions. Where inconsistency threatens concerted effort to achieve budgeted results within a planned time period, then consistency becomes a vital rather than merely an esthetic problem.

6. *Is the chosen level of risk feasible in economic and personal terms?*
Strategies vary in the degree of risk willingly undertaken by their designers. For example, a small food company in pursuit of its marketing strategy once deliberately courted disaster in production slowdowns and in erratic behavior of cocoa futures. But the choice was made knowingly and the return was likely to be correspondingly great. The president was temperamentally able to live under this pressure and presumably had recourse if disaster struck. At the other extreme, another company had such modest growth aspirations that the junior members of its management were unhappy. They would have preferred a more aggressive and ambitious company. Although risk cannot always be known for sure, the level at which it is estimated is, within limits, optional. The riskiness of any future plan should be compatible with the economic resources of the organization and the temperament of the managers concerned.

7. *Is the strategy appropriate to the personal values and aspirations of the key managers?*
Until we consider the relationship of personal values to the choice of strategy, it is not useful to dwell long upon this criterion. But to cite an extreme case, the deliberate falsification of warehouse receipts to conceal the absence of soybean oil from the tanks which are supposed to contain it would not be an element of competitive strategy to which most of us would like to be committed. A strong personal attraction of leisure, to cite a less extreme example, is inconsistent with a strategy requiring all-out effort from the senior members of a company. Or if, for example, a new president abhors conflict and competition, then it can be predicted that the hard-driven firm of an earlier day will have to change its strategy. Conflict between personal preferences, aspirations, and goals of the key members of an organization and the plan for its future is a sign of danger and a harbinger of mediocre performance or failure.

8. *Is the strategy appropriate to the desired level of contribution to society?*

Closely allied to the value is the ethical criterion. As the professional obligations of business are acknowledged by an increasing number of senior managers, it grows more and more appropriate to ask whether the current strategy of a firm is as socially responsible as it might be. Although it can be argued that filling any economic need contributes to the social good, it is clear that manufacturers of cigarettes might well consider diversification on grounds other than their fear of future legislation. That the strategy should not require violations of law or ethical practice to be effective became abundantly clear with the revelation in the mid-70s of widespread bribery and questionable payments, particularly in overseas activities. Honesty and integrity may seem exclusively questions of implementation, but if the strategy is not distinctive, making it effective in competition may tempt managers to unethical practice. Thus a drug manufacturer who emphasizes the production of amphetamines at a level beyond total established medical need is inevitably compelling corruption. The meeting of sales quotas at the distribution level necessitates distribution of the drug as "speed" with or without the cooperation of prescribing physicians. To the extent that the chosen economic opportunity of the firm has social costs, such as air or water pollution, a statement of intention to deal with these is desirable and prudent. Ways to ask and answer this question will be considered in the section on the company and its responsibilities to society.

9. *Does the strategy constitute a clear stimulus to organizational effort and commitment?*

For organizations which aspire not merely to survive but to lead and to generate productive performance in a climate that will encourage the development of competence and the satisfaction of individual needs, the strategy selected should be examined for its inherent attractiveness to the organization. Some undertakings are inherently more likely to gain the commitment of able men of goodwill than others. Given the variety of human preferences, it is risky to illustrate this difference briefly. But currently a company that is vigorously expanding its overseas operations finds that several of its socially conscious young people exhibit more zeal in connection with its work in developing countries than in Europe. Generally speaking, the bolder the choice of goals and the wider range of human needs they reflect, the more successfully they will appeal to the capable membership of a healthy and energetic organization.

10. *Are there early indications of the responsiveness of markets and market segments to the strategy?*

Results, no matter how long postponed by necessary preparations, are, of course, the most telling indicators of soundness, so long as they are read correctly at the proper time. A strategy may pass with flying colors all the tests so far proposed and may be in internal consistency and uniqueness an admirable work of art. But if within a time period made reasonable by the company's resources and the original plan the strategy does not work, then it must be weak in some way that has escaped attention. Bad luck, faulty implementation, and competitive countermoves may be more to blame for unsatisfactory results than flaws in design, but the possibility of the latter should not be unduly discounted. Conceiving a strategy that will win the company a unique place in the business community, that will give it an enduring concept of itself, that will harmonize its diverse activities, and that will provide a fit between environmental opportunity and present or potential company strength is an extremely complicated task.

We cannot expect simple tests of soundness to deliver a complete evaluation. But an analytical examination of any company's strategy against the several criteria here suggested will nonetheless give anyone concerned with making, proving, or contributing to corporate planning more than enough to think about.

Problems in Evaluation

The evaluation of strategy is as much an act of judgment as is the original conception, and it may be as subject to error. The most common source of difficulty is the misevaluation of current results. When results are unsatisfactory, as we have just pointed out, a reexamination of strategy is called for. At the same time, outstandingly good current results are not necessarily evidence that the strategy is sound. Abnormal upward surges in demand may deceive marginal producers that all is well within their current strategy, until expansion of more efficient competitors wipes out their market share. Extrapolation of present performance into the future, overoptimism and complacence, and underestimation of competitive response and of the time required to accommodate to changes in demand are often by-products of success. Unusually high profits may blind unwary managers to impending environmental change. Their concern for the future can under no circumstances be safely suspended. Conversely, a high-risk strategy that has failed was not necessarily a mistake, so long as the risk was anticipated and the consequences of failure carefully calculated. In fact, a planning problem confronting a number of diversified companies today is how to encourage their divisions to undertake projects where failure can be afforded but where success, if it comes, will be attended by high profits not available in run-of-the-mill, low-risk activities.

Although the possibility of misinterpreting results is by far the commonest obstacle to accurate evaluation of strategy, the criteria previously outlined suggest immediately some additional difficulties. It is as easy to misevaluate corporate resources and the financial requirements of a new move as to misread the environment for future opportunities. To be overresponsive to industry trends may be as dangerous as to ignore them. The correspondence of the company's strategy with current environmental developments and an overreadiness to adapt may obscure the opportunity for a larger share of a declining market or for growth in profits without a parallel growth in total sales.

The intrinsic difficulty of determining and choosing among strategic alternatives leads many companies to do what the rest of the industry is doing rather than to make an independent determination of opportunity and resources. Sometimes the companies of an industry run like sheep all in one direction. The similarity among the strategies, at least in some periods of history, of insurance companies, banks, railroads, and airplane manufacturers may lead one to conclude these strategic decisions were based on industry convention more than on independent analysis.

A strategy may manifest an all-too-clear correspondence with the personal values of the founder, owner, or chief executive. Like a correspondence with dominant trends and the strategic decisions of competitors, this one may also be deceptive and unproductive. For example, a personal preference for growth beyond all reasonable expectations may be given undue weight. It should be only one factor among several in any balanced consideration of what is involved in designing strategy. Too little attention to a corporation's actual competence for growth or diversification is the commonest error of all.

It is entirely possible that a strategy may reflect in an exaggerated fashion the values rather than the reasoned decisions of the responsible manager or managers. That imbalance may go undetected. The entire business community may be dominated by certain beliefs of which one should be wary. A critic of strategy must be at heart enough of a nonconformist to raise questions about generally accepted modes of thought and conventional thinking that substitute for original analysis. The timid may not find it prudent to challenge publicly some of the ritual of policy formulation. But even for them it will serve the purposes of criticism to inquire privately into such sacred propositions as the one proclaiming that a company must grow or die or that national planning for energy needs is anathema.

Another canon of management that may engender questionable strategies is the idea that cash funds in excess of reasonable dividend requirements should be reinvested whether in revitalization of a company's traditional activities or in mergers and acquisitions that will diversify products and services. Successful operations, a heretic might observe, sometimes bring riches to a company that lacks the capacity to reemploy them. Yet a decision to return to the owners substantial amounts of capital which the company does not have the competence or desire to put to work is an almost unheard-of development. It is therefore appropriate, particularly in the instance of very successful companies in older and stable industries, to inquire how far strategy reflects a simple desire to put all resources to work rather than a more valid appraisal of investment opportunity in relation to unique corporate strengths. We should not forget to consider an unfashionable alternative—namely, that to keep an already large worldwide corporation within reasonable bounds, a portion of the assets might well be returned to stockholders for investment in other enterprises.

Much more serious misevaluation of strategy stems from a pervasive conflict between the academic interests of financial economics and the practitioner orientation of the concept of corporate strategy. The use of simple ratios, like the relation of debt to equity or simple measures like return on an investment, return on equity, or earnings per share as determinants of decision often lead to shortsighted moves to satisfy a measure rather than to make a strategic investment. (The related misuse of portfolio analysis leads similarly to mechanical appraisal of separate businesses rather than relating the separate businesses to the future of the company as a whole.) Capital budgeting that applies discounted cash flow analysis and hurdle rates to separate projects often bypasses strategic consideration of the project. Improper use of discounted cash flow analysis ignores the difficulties of estimating discount rates, future cash flows, the project's impact on the company's cash flow from other assets, and on the firm's future investment opportunities.

The distortion in evaluating and shaping strategy by overuse of financial formulas and rules of thumb is unwittingly perpetrated by financial analysts, financial economists, and students of financial theory who appear unaware of the need to make financial policy serve rather than dominate corporate strategy. Parochial use of financial expertise, in short, can pervert the strategic process by appearing to justify project-by-project rather than strategy-dominated decisions. It originates in the simplistic assumption (with implicit emphasis on the short term) that the single purpose of corporate enterprise is the enhancement of shareholder wealth.[8]

The identification of opportunity and choice of purpose are such challenging intellectual activities that we should not be surprised to find that persistent problems attend the proper evaluation of strategy. But

---

[8] Students interested in pursuing the relation of financial policy to corporate strategy should read Stewart C. Myers, "Finance Theory and Financial Strategy," in Arnoldo Hax, *Readings on Strategic Management* (Cambridge, Mass.: Ballinger Publishing Co., 1984), pp. 177–88; Richard R. Ellsworth, "Subordinate Financial Policy to Corporate Strategy," *Harvard Business Review,* November–December 1983, pp. 119 ff.; and "Capital Markets and Competitive Decline," *Harvard Business Review,* September–October 1985, pp. 177 ff. For the route to reconciliation, see Gordon Donaldson's important book: *Managing Corporate Wealth: The Operation of a Comprehensive Financial Goals System* (New York: Praeger Publishers, 1984).

just as the criteria for evaluation are useful, even if not precise, so the dangers of misevaluation are less menacing if they are recognized. We have noted some inexactness in the concept of strategy, the problems of making resolute determinations in the face of uncertainty, the necessity for judgment in the evaluation of soundness of strategy, and the misevaluation into which human error may lead us. None of these alters the commonsense conclusion that a business enterprise guided by a clear sense of purpose rationally arrived at and emotionally ratified by commitment is more likely to have a successful outcome, in terms of profit and social good, than a company whose future is left to guesswork and chance. Conscious strategy does not preclude brilliance of improvisation or the welcome consequences of good fortune. Its cost is principally thought and work for which it is hard but not impossible to find time.

Application to Cases

As you attempt to apply the concept of strategy to the analysis of L. L. Bean, Crown Cork & Seal, BIC Pen, and later cases, try to keep in mind three questions:

1. What is the strategy of the company?
2. In the light of *(a)* the characteristics of its industry and developments in its environment, *(b)* its own strengths and weaknesses, and *(c)* the personal values influencing decision, is the strategy sound?
3. What recommendations for changed strategy might advantageously be made to the president?

Whatever other questions you may be asked or may ask yourself, you will wish constantly to order your study and structure your analysis of case information according to the need to *identify, evaluate,* and *recommend.*

By now you have an idea of strategy, which discussion of the cases will greatly clarify. You know how it is derived and some of its uses and limitations. You have been given some criteria for evaluating the strategies you identify and those you propose. And you have been properly warned about errors of judgment which await the unwary.

The cases which immediately follow will permit you to consider what contributions if any the concept of strategy (if mostly missing as a conscious formulation) would have made to these companies. What strategic alternatives can be detected in the changing circumstances affecting their fortunes? Which ones would you choose if you were responsible or asked to advise? By the time these cases have been examined, you will be ready to turn from the nature and uses of strategy to a study in sequence of its principal components—environmental opportunity, corporate capability, personal aspirations, and moral responsibility.

L. L. Bean, Inc., Corporate Strategy

Leon Leonwood Bean, the late founder of L. L. Bean, was fond of saying, "Sell good merchandise at a reasonable profit, treat your customers like human beings, and they'll always come back for more."

"We still adhere to the business philosophy laid down by 'L. L.,' " declared Leon Gorman, his grandson and president of the company. "At L. L. Bean it is our purpose to provide quality apparel, footwear, and equipment to outdoorspeople at the fairest possible prices and with the most efficient and accommodating service."

"L. L." had started his business in 1912 with a borrowed $400 and one product sold around the country by mail. By the time of his death in 1967 the business had grown to $3 million. By 1980 sales had risen to over $120 million. The company recorded a compound growth rate of over 25 percent between 1967 and 1975. Between 1975 and 1980 its average return on equity was over 30 percent.

If company forecasts in April 1981 were reliable, that success would continue through 1985, leading L. L. Bean sales to double every three years. The question that absorbed Mr. Gorman—as well as many outside observers—was how he could achieve this growth without changing the unique character of the company, whose reputation for product quality, personal service, and rugged individualism had become almost legendary in American retailing.

Industry Background

Total U.S. mail-order sales in 1979 amounted to $25.8 billion, or 9.7 percent of all general merchandise sales and 2.5 percent of all retail

Copyright © 1981 by the President and Fellows of Harvard College
Harvard Business School case 581–159

sales.[1] Specialty merchandisers accounted for $17.8 billion and general merchandisers for $8 billion of mail-order sales.

Mail-order sales had grown in excess of 15 percent annually in recent years, or more than twice the rate for the retailing industry as a whole. By 1981 over 10,000 businesses used mail order to market their products, and per capita mail-order expenditures on products and services were estimated at $117. Factors contributing to the success of the mail-order business are summarized in Table 1.

Table 1

Factors Contributing to the Success of Mail-Order Businesses

Socioeconomic Factors	External Factors	Competitive Factors
More women joining the work force	Rising cost of gasoline	Inconvenient store hours
Population growing older	Availability of WATS 800 lines	Unsatisfactory service in stores and inadequate product information
Rising discretionary income	Expanded use of credit cards	Difficulty of parking, especially near downtown stores, and increased cost of transportation
More single households	Low-cost data processing	
Growth of the "me generation"	Availability of mailing lists	"If you can't beat 'em, join 'em" approach of traditional retailers

Source: John A. Quelch and Hirotaka Takeuchi, "Nonstore Marketing: Fast Track or Slow," *Harvard Business Review,* July–August 1981.

Current mail-order growth rates were expected to continue through the mid-1980s.

To capitalize on this growth potential, several large publicly owned companies had entered the field. According to *The New York Times* (December 7, 1980):

A steadily growing number of the estimated 5,000 to 8,000 cataloguers have been acquired by corporate giants such as ITT, Beatrice Foods, and W. R. Grace, which are attracted by such factors as the industry's exceptionally high return on equity. . . . Publicly owned mail-order companies last year achieved a 21 percent return on equity, compared with the 12 percent reported by major retailers.

[1] Maxwell Sroge Company, *1980–81 United States Consumer Mail Order Industry Estimates.*

Company Background

L. L. Bean was still a privately owned company in 1981. Reviewing his organization's history, Mr. Gorman identified three distinct phases: (1) the entrepreneurial phase, from 1912 to 1967; (2) the transitional phase, from 1967 to 1975; and (3) the professional phase, from 1975 through the present.

The Entrepreneurial Phase

Orphaned at the age of 12, the future founder of the L. L. Bean Co. grew up in the hill country of western Maine during the late 1800s. By 1907, after only a few years of formal education, part of which he paid for by selling soap door-to-door, L. L. was working at his brother's haberdashery store in Freeport, earning $12 a week and devoting as much time as possible to hunting and fishing.

The corporation that would one day be the largest mail-order retailer in its industry was born the night L. L. decided he'd had enough of trudging over the deer trails with cold, wet feet. The all-leather loggers' boots of the day gave good support but were heavy and absorbed moisture. All-rubber boots stayed dry but were clumsy and uncomfortable. Experimenting in his brother's basement, L. L. fashioned some lightweight leather uppers on rubber overshoe bottoms and tested the new product with his friends. Reaction was unanimously positive, and L. L.'s first invention was the Maine Hunting Shoe. In 1912 he obtained a mailing list of Maine hunting license holders, set up shop in his brother's basement in Freeport, and prepared a three-page descriptive mail-order brochure. Ninety of the first 100 pairs sold were returned because the rubber bottoms had ripped away from the leather tops. L. L. refunded the purchase price, borrowed $400, corrected the problem, and mailed more brochures.

The eventual success of his hunting shoe convinced L. L. that anything he liked and used himself would also be liked and used by his customers. He added apparel to his catalog in the late 1910s and fishing and camping equipment in the 1920s. By 1924 he was employing 25 people, and sales totaled $135,000. His boots were selected by Admiral MacMillan for his second Arctic expedition. L. L. continued to write his own catalog copy in a highly personal style, informing his customers, for example, that "It is no longer necessary for you to experiment with dozens of flies to determine the few that will catch fish. We have done the experimenting for you."

Discussing his grandfather's operating philosophy, Mr. Gorman recalled:

> Word-of-mouth advertising and customer satisfaction were critical to L. L.'s way of thinking. To hear that one of his products had failed was a shock to his system. He'd charge around the factory trying to find an

explanation. Then he'd write the customer, return his money, enclose a Trout Knife, invite him fishing, or do anything to make the matter right. The customer was a real person to L. L., and he'd put his trust in L. L.'s catalog.

L. L. incorporated his business in 1934. Three years later his annual sales passed the $1 million mark. In 1942 he wrote a book, *Hunting— Fishing and Camping,* which eventually sold 200,000 copies at a dollar each. "That wasn't bad for a boy who never got through the eighth grade," he told his friends. In 1945 he set up a special retail salesroom in the middle of the factory, providing it with a bell for hunters and fishermen traveling through town late at night. Six years later he opened the retail store 24 hours a day, 365 days a year, announcing, "We've thrown away the keys to the place!"

L. L. entered his eighties in the early 1950s. His company was growing older with him, and sales leveled off around the $2 million mark through the late 1950s and early 1960s. When asked about his seeming lack of interest in further growth, L. L. would say, "I'm eating three meals a day and I can't eat four."

The Transitional Phase

When L. L. died in 1967 at the age of 94, America's top-rated television news show devoted eight minutes to the story, and the company received over 50,000 letters of condolence. The average age of his 200 employees was almost 60 years.

Mr. Gorman recalled his early days working under his grandfather:

> I showed up for a job in 1961 after a fine liberal arts education at Bowdoin College and four exciting years as an officer on navy destroyers. In a way it was fortunate I had no prior experience. The only business principles I could learn were those L. L. had practiced for 50 years. His catalog production methods, his style of writing copy, his advertising techniques for getting new customers, and his conservative financing became the basis of my business education.

"Like many great entrepreneurs, however," Mr. Gorman observed, "L. L. had never been able to delegate any responsibilities or plan for any future beyond his own." During the 1960s L. L.'s workdays had become increasingly shorter. Merchandising was falling out of date, lapses in general product quality were starting to appear, and service was becoming erratic. Mr. Gorman tried to incorporate new technology into the products and bring the business back on track. "It was a somewhat frustrating period," he recalled, "because of the limitations imposed by L. L.'s advancing years."

To take advantage of the recreation boom of the mid-1960s, Mr. Gorman convinced L. L. to increase the budget for advertisements that offered customers free catalogs. He also added Christmas and summer catalogs to the company's traditional spring and fall offerings. Sales increased from $3 million in 1967 to $30 million in 1975; the buyer list went from 325,000 to 860,000.

Operations played "catch up" to sales during this period. The catalog mailing list and the order-entry and inventory systems were computerized. The manufacturing operation moved into a modern rented building in 1970, and the retail store went through several expansions. New buildings for the office and distribution center were constructed, and the company's first computer was installed in 1974.

All these changes, however, created fears among some customers that the "old ways" were being abandoned. One old-time customer went directly to the company and demanded, "Not going to put in a computer, are you? I remember 69 when you put the rugs on the stairs. Place hasn't been the same since."[2] Recognizing these concerns, Mr. Gorman stressed the importance of maintaining the store's informal, friendly atmosphere in which customers would not feel pressured to buy. He continued to emphasize the need to respond to every customer request and complaint as helpfully as possible.

"By 1975 our profits were back, our morale was high, and our momentum was up," commented Mr. Gorman. "The average age of our employees was in the forties." Moreover, the market for outdoor apparel and equipment, as well as mail-order retailing, continued to expand. Nevertheless, "We had a pause in our growth rate during the 1974–75 recession [*only* a 19 percent increase over the previous year], and we wanted to get going again," he recalled. "There were a lot of new things we wanted to do, especially in marketing and operations. We were of such a size that there simply wasn't enough time to do them. It was time to go outside for help and become more professionally managed."

The Professional Phase

Leon Gorman made what he called a big decision in 1975 and hired William T. End as marketing director. Mr. End was then a 26-year-old group product manager of the Gillette Company with an MBA from the Harvard Business School. "It took Bill about 24 hours to get indoctrinated in the L. L. Bean way," said Mr. Gorman. In his own words, Mr. End was an "outdoors freak" with a strong conviction that much of the company's marketing potential had not yet been tapped. Another outdoors enthusiast, John Findlay, Jr., joined the company in 1976 at the age of 34 as vice president of operations. He had previously worked for a data processing company.

When Leon Gorman joined L. L. Bean, he had been the only college

---

[2] *The Wall Street Journal,* December 5, 1973.

graduate among management. In 1981 there were 66 college graduates on the management team, including 15 MBAs. All the officers reporting to Mr. Gorman had been hired since 1975 and were in their thirties.

Between 1975 and 1980 sales increased to $120 million, and the buyer list increased to 2.1 million. More than 26 million catalogs were mailed in 1980; some customers received as many as nine full and mini-catalogs a year. Each full catalog contained 128 pages with over 1,800 separate items and over 13,000 stockkeeping units (SKUs). A minicatalog was half that size. In 1980 the company handled about 2.2 million mail orders and 500,000 telephone orders, responded to some 215,000 customer questions, and processed over 14,000 repairs (including a pair of Maine Hunting Shoes about 30 years old) and over 1,800 special orders (including a pair of size 17 triple-E Maine Hunting Shoes). More than 175,000 pairs of Maine Hunting Shoes, still the company's most popular product, were produced that year.

Competition

"When I first came to work here, Abercrombie & Fitch was the big name in sporting goods, and I thought it would be great to be as big as Abercrombie," said Mr. Gorman. "Abercrombie & Fitch has since gone out of business, and we are now the largest mail-order company in the specialty outdoor business."[3]

Among L. L. Bean's immediate competitors, as listed in Exhibit 1, the company's own managers most often drew comparisons with Eddie Bauer, Talbots, Orvis, and Lands' End. Eddie Bauer and Talbots operated 16 stores each in 1980. According to recent press accounts, Bauer planned to more than double its retail outlets in the next five years, opening 30 full-sized stores in major metropolitan areas and several catalog showrooms in smaller communities. Talbots intended to operate 56–65 stores by 1984. Orvis had three retail stores as well as many dealer outlets through its wholesale division. Lands' End, a privately held company, operated only one retail store.

Eddie Bauer, which had been founded in Seattle, Washington, in 1923, competed with L. L. Bean in the outdoor apparel and sporting goods segment. "Bauer is our No. 1 competitor by a long shot," commented Mr. End. "When we ask our customers what other mail-order companies they've bought from, about 27 percent mention Bauer. The next competitor is mentioned by only 8 percent." A 1979 customer awareness survey conducted by the company showed that L. L. Bean had higher awareness than Eddie Bauer in all regions except the Pacific, Bauer's home territory (see Table 2).

---

[3] "Cashing in on 'Down East' Simplicity," *Forbes,* January 23, 1978.

Table 2

Customer Awareness Survey: L. L. Bean and Eddie Bauer

	L. L. Bean		Eddie Bauer	
Region	Awareness*	Index	Awareness*	Index
New England	39.3%	250	5.2%	60
Mid-Atlantic	16.7	106	6.5	76
South Atlantic	15.7	100	4.9	57
East South Central	8.0	51	3.1	35
East North Central	13.6	87	10.1	117
West North Central	14.2	90	13.1	152
Mountain	21.5	137	16.3	190
Pacific	9.8	62	15.4	179
Nation	15.7%	100	8.6%	100

* Percentage of population; aided and unaided awareness combined.
Source: Company records.

In 1980 Eddie Bauer recorded sales of $80 million and estimated net profits of $4 million.

Talbots of Hingham, Massachusetts, competed with L. L. Bean in the women's mail-order apparel business. Its 64-page catalog carried about 360 items for women and 40 items for men. Talbots featured brand names such as Evan-Picone, Gordon of Philadelphia, J. G. Hook, Robert Scott, David Brooks, and Ciao. Its stores recorded estimated sales per square foot of $250 on an average selling space of 5,000 sq. ft.[4]

Vermont-based Orvis, a maker of fishing tackle since 1856, carried higher price points than L. L. Bean and specialized in mail-order sales of fishing and hunting equipment. Its major targets were "serious outdoorspeople"; it published a customer newspaper, operated the "Orvis Record Catch Club," and offered customers three-day courses on fishing and shooting. The company was intent on maintaining its "serious outdoor" image but also sold a substantial amount of country apparel and gifts. The average Orvis order size was about $60.

Lands' End, based in Wisconsin, was an emerging competitor in the mail-order sportswear segment. L. L. Bean conducted four focus group interviews in Washington, D.C., and Dallas among noncustomers of both companies (men and women) in 1980, to determine the perceived differences between the two catalogs. Some of the major findings were as follows:

— The majority of the participants had a strong preference for one catalog or the other. Those who preferred the L. L. Bean catalog usually gave better quality merchandise as their main reason.

---

[4] *Women's Wear Daily,* June 24, 1980.

Those who preferred Lands' End felt that the clothing (particularly the colors) was more fashionable.
— The Lands' End catalog had greatest appeal for participants under 35 and for women. The L. L. Bean catalog was viewed as more suitable for the older men's segment.
— L. L. Bean was described by many as oriented toward fishermen, campers, or serious outdoor sportspeople, and Lands' End as designed for people casually enjoying the outdoors.
— The Lands' End catalog was described by some as more enjoyable to look at; others felt that it was too "flashy" and "hard sell."

Observing his competition, Mr. End commented:

The quality of our products is well known. What people sometimes don't immediately see is how competitive we are on price. We're generally about 10 percent to 15 percent below Bauer, Orvis, and Talbots, particularly if their postage and handling charges are taken into account. The catalog prices of Lands' End items are 5 percent below L. L. Bean—but the customer actually pays more by the time postage and handling are calculated.

L. L. Bean had never charged postage or handling to customers; Mr. End estimated that by 1981 these charges averaged $1.00 to $1.50 per order. "We've always believed that absorbing these costs is an extra service to our customers and makes mail-order purchasing more convenient," explained Mr. Gorman.

Marketing

In 1975 Mr. Gorman and Mr. End had established what they thought was an aggressive goal of doubling the business within five years. After briefly considering three potential areas of expansion—mail-order sales, retail store sales, and manufacturing, they decided, for several reasons, to concentrate on mail-order sales. The mail-order business, in general, was entering a period of rapid growth. Mail order was relatively more profitable—it yielded an average profit after taxes of 7.0 percent, compared with an average 2.5 percent for retailing and 5.4 percent for manufacturing. Mail order was the business L. L. Bean knew best. And because mail-order sales were closely correlated with catalog circulation, management felt more confident in forecasting and controlling this type of growth.

Once the company's direction was set, Mr. End worked on improving the catalog sales. Four major changes took place.

1. Credit cards were accepted. By 1980 credit-card orders accounted for 50 percent of mail-order sales and had an average order value 30 percent higher than cash orders.
2. Telephone lines were added, and the staff of order takers was

increased so that only 2 percent of all incoming calls would get busy signals. Phone orders, which carried an average value 23 percent higher than mail orders, accounted for almost 30 percent of catalog sales in 1980.

3. All catalogs were converted to all-color printing.

4. A professional art director was hired to improve catalog page layouts.

Leon Gorman recalled:

We tried, and succeeded I think, to remain sensitive to the traditional look of the catalog, but those who really knew it could see big changes. Somebody once described L. L.'s catalog display style as throwing a garment against the wall and clicking the shutter before it hit the floor! We improved the layout and used models for the first time, all of them drawn from our own employees.

But more important than any of these specific tactics, according to Mr. Gorman, was the company's ongoing emphasis on improving its product assortments and competitive pricing.

Mr. End conducted studies with a nationally known direct-mail consultant to identify the L. L. Bean customer and determine his or her perception of the company's products and services. Demographically, the L. L. Bean customer was predominantly over 35 years old and highly educated, with very high income (see Exhibit 2). Geographically, customers were skewed strongly to three regions in the East (New England, Mid-Atlantic, and South Atlantic), as shown in Exhibit 3. Penetration was lowest in the western regions. Perceptually, the L. L. Bean customer appeared to be extremely satisfied with the company's high-quality products, reasonable prices, and delivery time (see Exhibit 4).

These findings substantiated Mr. Gorman's conviction that there was no need to change the positioning of the company and that there were no major problems with L. L. Bean's service or product line. Accordingly, he and Mr. End concluded that the best means of increasing sales would be to increase catalog circulation among two target audiences—new prospects and current customers.

To acquire new customers, Mr. End relied primarily on advertising and rented mailing lists. Until 1975 advertising had been by far L. L. Bean's most important means of acquiring new customers. Small ads were run in general-interest publications (such as *The New Yorker, The New York Times,* and *Yankee*) and in outdoors publications (such as *Outdoor Life, Field & Stream,* and *Sports Afield*). The purchases resulting from each ad were then traced over time to determine the cost per buyer for the ad. "This analysis gives us the information to optimize ad dollar spending next year," explained Mr. End. The advertising budget increased from $250,000 in 1975 to $1 million in 1980.

Mr. End simultaneously began testing mailing lists available for rental. He tested 16 lists with customer demographics or product interests similar to those of L. L. Bean. The company expanded rental mailings from 400,000 in 1975 to over 4.7 million in 1980 (see Exhibit 5).

Additional names came from the customer referral program, Freeport store buyers, and general word of mouth. Mr. End also tested L. L. Bean buyers who hadn't purchased for over three years and had been "purged" from the master file. "We found this 'rejuvenated' segment by far the best list we tested," he said.

New L. L. Bean customers exceeded 360,000 in 1976 and 690,000 in 1980. In both years, new customers accounted for about half of existing L. L. Bean customers (see Exhibit 6).

During the customer acquisition program, L. L. Bean's customer mix shifted toward women and buyers under 35. Twenty-five percent of L. L. Bean customers were women in 1976, compared with 49 percent in 1980. Also a majority of new customers added since 1977 were women. The under-35 segment increased from 31 percent in 1977 to 41 percent in 1980. Women tended to purchase L. L. Bean merchandise more for family use, as opposed to personal use, and more for gifts than men did.

This shift in customer mix called for slight modifications in the merchandise mix. Although the total number of pages in the fall catalog remained 128 between 1975 and 1980, about 8 pages were shifted out of sporting goods, 2 pages added to home/camp furnishings, and more than 6 pages added to women's apparel and footwear. "Women's apparel represents, in my opinion, our greatest single growth opportunity, but I don't know how much more we can modify our merchandise mix before we jeopardize our image," noted Mr. End.

To "activate" (in other words, increase the purchases of) current customers, Mr. End analyzed information on each one's purchase history in the computerized master file. The file noted which items were purchased, when the last purchase was made, how often purchases were made, how much a customer ordered each time, whether the order was by mail or phone, and whether the purchase was by cash or credit card. This information was used to identify L. L. Bean's "best" customers. By 1979 the best customers were receiving nine catalogs, compared with four in 1975.

Business quadrupled from 1975 to 1980. "And we had thought that the objective of doubling our business in five years was pretty tough," said Mr. End with a smile. "Of course, we couldn't have done it alone. Our operations coped with that growth extremely well."

Operations

"Many small mail-order companies do not recognize the critical importance of committing resources to the 'back end' of the business as the key to future growth," observed Mr. Gorman. "They continue to be completely product or merchandising oriented and do not take the operational steps required to build superior service." L. L. Bean's customer service was acknowledged to be among the best in the industry. Letters from customers confirmed this assessment. One woman from Illinois wrote, "You are such a pleasure to order from. Your delivery is quick, and you give me no problems or hassles for returning merchandise." Another customer declared: "You are dependable, efficient, and incredible. I think, with the approval of Congress, you should run the country." Mr. Findlay explained:

> At L. L. Bean, we can open and sort over 31,000 mail orders a day. We can process and ship over 35,000 parcels a day. Our average shipping time during our peak season last year was within three working days from the date we received the order.
>
> Our computerized inventory management system enables us to achieve an average initial service level of 90 percent. That is to say, 90 percent of the products will be in stock when the customer makes an order. We fill another 6 percent to 7 percent of orders following a brief back-order period to give us a final service level of 96 percent to 97 percent.
>
> Our outgoing accuracy rate is 99.85 percent which translates into 1.5 errors for every 1,000 parcels. We're striving for 99.99 percent.

To make such fast and accurate service possible, L. L. Bean had expanded its data processing capabilities and its distribution center. It added a second mainframe computer in 1979; by 1981 the data processing department had a staff of 30 and a budget of about $1 million. "The computer edits the keypunched orders, and we make corrections through CRTs [cathode ray tubes]," said Mr. Findlay. "We update our back-order file, refund file, and good order file on a daily basis. Our next project is to bring the master file in-house to reduce data transmission delays, which inhibit the currency and availability of data for market analysis." Mr. Findlay added:

> In the distribution center, which was expanded to 310,000 sq. ft. in 1979, the computer instructs the pickers on how to set up the slots on their picking carts, how many items to put in each slot, and which zone sequence to follow. The computer also selects the size of the box and determines which shipping service will be less expensive—United Parcel Service or the U.S. Postal Service. In both cases, the computer precomputes postage, eliminating the need for a weighing and stamping operation.

Customer service at L. L. Bean went beyond packing and sending. One customer, for example, called and wanted to know if she could obtain another button for her red "Double L" shirt. "Sure," said a staff member of the customer service department, "we keep all the buttons on all our products in stock." Another customer planning a skiing trip called to ask what the weather was like in Sapporo, Japan, during March.

A third customer wrote, "Here is a shirt I bought in 1951. Never worn. Please send refund." A refund was sent. Others contacted the department to check on delivery, to inquire about repair work, or to return a defective product.

"We feel that customer service begins as soon as we receive the products from our vendors or from our own manufacturing facility," said Mr. Findlay. New shipments, for example, were inspected according to a double-sampling plan and, if necessary, subjected to 100 percent inspection. New items were also fit-tested to avoid size discrepancies by "models" of known sizes drawn from company personnel.

Inspection records were kept on all past shipments by vendor and SKU and displayed on a 15 ft. by 10 ft. board. A colored dot before each SKU number indicated whether the item needed tight, normal, or reduced inspection. Records of returns in units and dollars—by vendor, SKU, and reason—were given to the inspectors every month. The company's overall customer return rate, relative to unit sales, was about 9 percent in 1980.

Actual laboratory tests were conducted on selected items as well. In spring 1981, Merv Wyman, L. L. Bean's lab technician, was testing, among other products, down samples just received from China. Mr. Wyman noted that nearly $2 million in down products had been rejected in 1978 because they did not meet company standards. He also had several samples of Duofold underwear stacked in the lab for shrinkage testing. "We are the largest buyer of Duofold underwear in the United States, but we want to make sure of its quality," said Mr. Wyman. "It's preventive medicine."

The company also had an active field testing program. "We encourage our employees to test out new equipment," said Mr. Gorman. "For example, last week seven of us were backpacking up in the Mahoosuc Mountain Range. In addition, guides, game wardens, and professional outdoorspeople from all parts of the country are testing our products."

Personnel

In 1980 L. L. Bean had a full-time staff of 900 and a part-time staff of 500. Of the full-time staff, 800 were hourly employees and 100 were salaried. "They make our systems and our image work," said Mr. Gorman. "Our momentum has generated high morale, and we get hundreds of letters from our customers praising our employees' efforts." All employees were nonunion. Outside agents had made two attempts to organize the company. The last, by the Teamsters in 1978, had attracted only three Bean employees, two of whom were husband and wife.

To attract and retain top-quality people, L. L. Bean paid substantially above-average wages and cash performance bonuses (a single rate paid to all employees) and offered attractive benefits (including pension, profit sharing, savings plan, insurance, tuition reimbursements, and medical and dental coverage). "In my view," observed Mr. Gorman, "paying 20 percent above average in wages will get you a 30 percent to 40 percent above-average employee." The company also stressed job security and individual development through job posting and supervisory assessment programs. Additional benefits included a 33.3 percent discount on all L. L. Bean products; an employee store where defective products or returned items were sold at two thirds off or more; and an equipment pool through which employees could borrow equipment at no cost.

To foster communication with its employees, the company published the *Bean Bulletin* every week and the *Bean Scene* every year. To encourage feedback, L. L. Bean had started the "Employee Speak Up Program" in 1979. "The program generated 135 memos in 1980, half of which dealt with problems and the other half with suggestions," said Austin Farrar, personnel director. "We're now investigating the feasibility of a Quality Circles program among our hourly workers."[5]

The working atmosphere throughout the company appeared relaxed and congenial. "I love to come to work every morning," said a woman on a sewing machine. "I'm proud to be part of a company so committed to our community and to conservation," declared a salesperson at the retail store.[6] Many employees, especially in the store, seemed to personify L. L.'s love for the outdoors. Several certified sports instructors worked in the store, and other in-house experts gave free clinics on sports, camping, and outdoor safety.

Although the number of L. L. Bean employees had grown from 200 in 1967 to 1,400 by 1980, a family atmosphere still prevailed. The Recreation Committee, for example, organized well-attended events for employees, retirees, and their families. At work, there were few barriers among ranks.

Future Growth Opportunities

By April 1981, after a prolonged appraisal of L. L. Bean's possible avenues for growth, Mr. Gorman and his officers had reached the following policy decisions:

— To remain in the same product lines with approximately the same mix.

— To keep the same distribution methods.

---

[5] Quality circles were a bottom-up group approach to solving job-related problems; made popular in Japan.

[6] L. L. Bean contributed 1.5 percent of its pretax profits—approximately double the national average for all industries—to charity and community activities in 1980. It gave over $100,000 to alternative energy and conservation projects that year and worked with environmental organizations on bird and wildlife protection studies.

— To maintain current levels of product quality and customer service.

— To keep up present overall corporate productivity.

Recognizing the conservatism of these guidelines, Mr. Gorman declared:

> We have the obligation to grow as long as we can continue to increase benefits to our customers, employees, stockholders, vendors, and community. But we also have the obligation to maintain the character of our business. Leon L. Bean was innovative in his business and progressive in his community activities. We will continue his tradition and only grow to the extent it does not jeopardize our unique character.

At the end of 1980 the company had recruited as vice president of finance Norman Poole, the former controller of Spiegel, a well-known mail-order general merchandise retailer. Mr. Poole analyzed L. L. Bean's past sales and growth trends and projected sales and income through 1985 (see Exhibit 7). These projections, Mr. Poole observed, represented neither goals nor quotas but the reasonable extension of existing trends. Mr. Gorman noted further that these figures assumed 9 percent to 10 percent annual inflation and a compounded growth rate, deflated, of 11 percent to 12 percent. He believed this growth could be achieved through mail order. Several tactics were open to the company:

1. To expand geographically into regions of lesser L. L. Bean penetration.

2. To develop specialized catalogs for narrower segments of L. L. Bean's existing customers (for example, a catalog for women) or for narrower product lines (for example, an apparel catalog or a sporting equipment catalog).

3. To continue expanding the customer activation program by installing a toll-free 800 number and the customer acquisition program by increasing the advertising budget and/or renting untested lists.

The company could also continue to grow by acquiring other mail-order companies offering noncompeting product lines. Mr. End was very enthusiastic about such acquisitions, and Mr. Gorman believed that by continuing to operate acquired companies under their original names, L. L. Bean might be able to grow without irrevocably changing its own image. Mr. End and others on the management team felt L. L. Bean could become a $300 million organization without seriously changing its traditional ways of doing business.

Retail Sales Options

One growth option was to expand retail store sales. Store sales had grown from about $6.5 million in 1975 to nearly $20.0 million in 1980, but as a percent of total sales, they had declined from 22 percent in 1975 to 16 percent in 1980. The store had expanded its selling space from 15,000 sq. ft. in 1975 to 24,000 sq. ft. in 1980; current expansion would bring the floor space up to 28,000 sq. ft., according to Frederick "Mac" McCabe, director of retail and special sales.[7]

In 1981 the store was still open 24 hours a day 365 days a year and was staffed by people with extensive product knowledge (150 at peak season). On a busy summer day in 1980, the store tallied a record 5,000+ transactions. "About 90 percent of the summer traffic is from out-of-state customers," said Mr. McCabe. "Some will come to Maine simply to tour the store. In fact, we recently had an Alaskan customer who was visiting in Milwaukee. Since he was so close to Freeport, he felt he had to pay us a visit."

Mr. McCabe was constantly receiving requests to open stores outside Freeport. "Department stores want us to open L. L. Bean departments, Quincy Market [a redeveloped downtown mall in Boston] wants us to open a specialty store, and a regional mall operator wants us to open a mall store," he said. L. L. Bean also had the option of opening another free-standing store or a free-standing factory outlet.[8]

The Freeport store recorded a gross profit of 43.6 percent, a labor expense of 10.2 percent, and a contribution of 30.1 percent in 1981.[9] See Exhibit 8 for a detailed report on store revenues and expenses. "Our directly allocatable expenses would be higher if the marketing expenses for the mail-order business were included," explained Mr. McCabe. He felt that the store's profitability would suffer if it expanded to locations outside Freeport.

Mr. End, on the other hand, felt the company had potential in retail distribution. "Currently our Freeport store sales are nearly $850 per square foot, not bad for a town of 5,000 over 20 miles from any major populated area."

Mr. Gorman, however, was not enthusiastic about the idea. He insisted:

> I know of no company that has successfully distributed both ways. As Bauer and Talbots have concentrated on retail, their catalog marketing has suffered. The two approaches require very different kinds of management. Mail-order marketers are very analytic, quantitatively oriented. Retailers have to be creative, promotional, pizzazzy, merchandise oriented. It's tough to assemble one management team that can handle both functions.

---

[7] Mr. McCabe, a 1971 Harvard MBA, had worked for Filene's department store before joining L. L. Bean in 1975.

[8] L. L. Bean operated a 2,200-square-foot factory outlet on the first floor of the store building. In 1980 it had a selling space productivity of over $1,000 per square foot.

[9] *Contribution* in this case is gross profit less all directly allocatable expenses.

Realizing that their single retail outlet might not represent potential profitability for a chain, management had recently been examining the profitability of comparable businesses. One of these was Oshman's Sporting Goods, Inc., a well-regarded, mall-oriented sporting goods and apparel chain. Oshman's, based in Houston, operated over 90 stores in eight southern and western states. Most of these were so-called fun stores targeted to middle- and upper-income consumers. In addition, Oshman's had bought the Abercrombie & Fitch name after that firm went bankrupt and had recently opened several Abercrombie & Fitch stores catering to very high-income customers. In late 1979 Abercrombie & Fitch mailed its first catalog to over 300,000 customers in all parts of the country. A 10-year summary of Oshman's financial statements is presented in the Appendix.

Manufacturing Expansion Options

The second nonmail-order option was to expand L. L. Bean's manufacturing business. Its manufacturing capacity had more than tripled when the new 72,000 sq. ft. factory was completed in 1979. The factory employed 230 employees (mostly hourly workers, with 35 handsewers paid on a piecework basis), who worked a single shift from 7:00 A.M. to 3:30 P.M. In 1980 it produced 175,872 pairs of Maine Hunting Shoes, 164,339 pairs of other handsewn footwear, and 528,574 specialty items, such as tote bags, garment bags, and sheepskin covers. These products accounted for 17 percent of L. L. Bean sales.

The remainder of L. L. Bean's products were bought from outside suppliers: 42 percent were made under contract to L. L. Bean, 23 percent were made under private label, and 18 percent were bought from vendors of branded items (for instance, Pendleton shirts, Nikon binoculars, Coleman stoves, and Bass shoes).

In all, L. L. Bean bought from over 400 vendors. The buying organization consisted of three product managers (or buyers), three assistant product managers, six control buyers, and four administrative assistants. The product managers—responsible for men's and women's apparel, footwear and luggage, and sporting goods and home furnishings—spent most of their time developing and selecting the products. Control buyers, on the other hand, spent most of their time forecasting sales, managing inventories, and supervising purchase orders. "This organizational split makes sense because the creative types give full attention to product selection, and the analytical types give full attention to inventory management," commented Mr. End.

In developing new products, product managers sometimes solicited bids from both the factory and outside vendors. The factory determined its transfer price to L. L. Bean by marking up the sum of all direct and indirect costs (labor, materials, factory overhead, and allocated corporate overhead) by a constant factor. This factor, set by the corporate office in consultation with Mert Greenleaf, director of manufacturing, had recently dropped from 11.10 percent to 5.26 percent.

"I personally think that we'll be missing an opportunity for growth if we don't invest in manufacturing," said Mr. Greenleaf. "I'm obviously biased, but even with the new markup structure, the factory yielded an after-tax return on equity of 17 percent.[10] I think we could invest $1 million to $1.5 million to expand the manufacturing building by another 50,000 sq. ft. and start making our own backpacks, tents, sleeping bags, or even simple apparel items. We could also think of selling more of the products we currently make to outside companies. Just recently, for example, we started manufacturing shoes for another retailer. We currently sell only 0.5 percent of our output to outside companies."

Specialty Growth Opportunities

The third nonmail-order option was to pursue growth opportunities aggressively in two specialty areas—premium sales and international sales. Premium sales to domestic companies reached about $500,000 in 1980. A bank in Virginia, for example, bought tote bags as customer incentives to open accounts. A potato processing company in Idaho bought more than 800 gift certificates, each worth $50, as giveaways to institutional chefs. "These are primarily one-shot deals, but a lot of companies give out premiums, and each order size is huge by mail-order standards," said Mr. McCabe.

The only foreign country in which L. L. Bean had any presence to date was Japan. Mr. McCabe had visited Japan in early 1980 and agreed to work with Sony, which would import selected L. L. Bean products and sell them in L. L. Bean "corners" of stores in several downtown Sony-owned shopping malls. There was an implicit understanding that Sony would eventually move into the mail-order business through its subsidiary, CBS-Sony, one of the most successful mail-order record retailers in Japan.

Mr. McCabe was pleased with the progress in Japan so far. Sony had placed an order of about $1 million in the past year, promoted the L. L. Bean name aggressively through print media (see Exhibit 9 for an ad), and expanded the store network to six (out of the 26 Sony Plazas in Japan). At the same time, both Mr. McCabe and Mr. Gorman were concerned that L. L. Bean products sold in Japan cost at least double the price of those in the United States. Moreover, the Japanese stores had floor spaces of only 500–700 sq. ft. and were not free standing.

---

[10] The markup factor excluded margin on retail. Equity was that portion of the stockholders' total equity employed in the manufacturing operation.

Sony and L. L. Bean were currently discussing an exclusive relationship and expanded program.

The company was also beginning to receive serious inquiries from other countries, such as Australia, Canada, West Germany, Great Britain, and the Scandinavian nations. This increasing interest prompted management to give serious thought to the following questions: (1) whether to pursue a consistent strategy throughout the world or to negotiate a different arrangement in each country; (2) whether to sell primarily through retail stores or by mail order; and (3) what criteria to use in selecting distributors. Exhibit 10 gives mail-order sales data for selected foreign countries.

Concerns

Despite his confidence in the continued growth of mail-order sales, Mr. Gorman was mindful of some marketing concerns Mr. End had voiced recently.

1. Catalog saturation: L. L. Bean catalogs already reached an estimated 33 percent of all mail-order clothing and footwear buyers and 50 percent of such buyers with incomes over $25,000.

2. New buyer growth: The number of new buyers had grown each year, but the annual growth rates were 11 percent in 1978, 14 percent in 1979, and 8 percent in 1980, in contrast to 32 percent in 1977.

3. Rental lists: Outside rental list sources were not growing as rapidly as L. L. Bean. Increased duplication of available names was becoming a more significant problem.

4. Response rate: The response rate from rental lists declined from 2.98 percent in 1978 to 2.48 percent in 1980 and a projected 2.25 percent by the end of 1981. "As you penetrate the lists," Mr. End commented, "you get less and less desirable names. We've already skimmed the cream."

5. Marketing costs: Increased costs of advertising and rental lists were expected to raise marketing costs from 12 percent of sales to 15 percent in a few years. To maintain current profitability levels, L. L. Bean had to consider an increase in gross margin, a decrease in operating costs, or both.

6. Seasonality: Sales per catalog mailed were considerably higher in the fall ($4.12 in 1980) than in the spring ($3.25 in 1980). Fall mailings also generated more contribution to profit per dollar of catalog cost. But the fear of overloading the company's facilities at Christmas forced Mr. End to balance his marketing efforts over the course of the year, even though the company's marketing investment was not optimized by doing so.

In a broader context, Mr. Gorman was concerned with the future ownership of L. L. Bean. It would be another 10 to 15 years before the next generation of the Bean family could participate in managing the company. He was concerned by the risk some family members were taking in tying up their entire assets in L. L. Bean stock. He also had to be concerned about estate taxes. At the moment, the death of any major family stockholder would cause a significant tax loss to the estate.

Many suitors were interested in buying out the company, attracted by its impressive financial statements (see Exhibits 11 and 12). If he were to sell out, should it be to a Fortune 500 company or to a smaller company possibly involved in the outdoors market? When should the move be made?

Seeking to summarize the key strategic issues his company faced, Mr. Gorman developed the following list:

— Given constraints, can we achieve sales projections through list acquisition and activation alone?
— Can we achieve sales growth while maintaining and enhancing product quality and service?
— Can we develop the human resources to meet our growth needs without losing the commitment and motivation of our staff? And is the talent we need available in Maine?
— Can we achieve the requisite productivity levels to meet our profit projections?
— Can we continue as a family-owned company with growth, given potential estate and management succession problems?
— Can we maintain the L. L. Bean image to our customers and to our employees and not change the essential nature of our business?

Mr. Gorman was well aware that a decision to slow growth would exact heavy penalties. "What would happen to the spirit of our young managers?" he asked. "We'd probably lose some commitment and some good people as well." Mr. End confirmed this intuition: "Some people here would leave tomorrow if they thought we were going to plateau at current sales levels."

Again and again, as he pondered his company's course, Mr. Gorman's thoughts returned to his grandfather, the mainspring of the company even after death. Gazing out across his desk at the Maine countryside, he mused:

The most important legacy of L. L.'s genius was the power of his personality. It transcended the buying and selling of products. His personal charisma, based on "down home" honesty, a true love for the outdoors, and a genuine enthusiasm for people, inspired all who worked for him and attracted a fanatic loyalty among his customers. He established an image that was as broad in its appeal and as enduring in its acceptance as any in marketing history. How best can we grow without losing that legacy and turning into another billion-dollar number-crunching machine? How can we keep that magic alive?

Appendix

OSHMAN'S SPORTING GOODS
10-Year Summary 1971–1980
For the Years Ended January 31

	Ten-Year Compound Growth Rate	1980‡	1979	1978	1977	1976	1975	1974
Consolidated sales	21%	$135,006,000	$118,192,000	$85,465,000	$69,782,000	$60,890,000	$49,565,000	$40,991,000
Retail	25	128,398,000	111,814,000	79,508,000	62,972,000	54,259,000	43,420,000	33,737,000
Team	5	6,608,000	6,378,000	5,957,000	6,810,000	6,631,000	6,145,000	5,381,000
Wholesale	—	—	—	—	—	—	—	1,873,000
Consolidated cost of goods sold	20	80,795,000	69,693,000	51,196,000	41,977,000	37,154,000	30,570,000	25,711,000
Consolidated earnings before income taxes	23	11,719,000	10,595,000	7,934,000	6,464,000	5,747,000	3,727,000	3,684,000
Retail	25	11,566,000	10,392,000	7,736,000	6,212,000	5,524,000	3,437,000	3,316,000
Team	(2)	153,000	203,000	198,000	252,000	223,000	290,000	284,000
Wholesale	—	—	—	—	—	—	—	84,000
Income taxes	24	5,379,000	4,800,000	3,720,000	3,031,000	2,766,000	1,678,000	1,684,000
Net earnings	22	6,340,000	5,795,000	4,214,000	3,433,000	2,981,000	2,049,000	2,000,000
Net earnings per share	20	1.41	1.29	.88	.71	.62	.43	.42
Advertising	27	4,514,000	3,506,000	2,705,000	2,146,000	1,757,000	1,444,000	1,107,000
Taxes other than income taxes	27	2,341,000	2,201,000	1,554,000	1,205,000	989,000	820,000	629,000
Rent	26	4,782,000	4,207,000	2,688,000	2,174,000	1,903,000	1,671,000	1,168,000
Depreciation	26	1,547,000	1,176,000	830,000	692,000	555,000	402,000	277,000
Interest	38	760,000	779,000	503,000	203,000	201,000	229,000	74,000
Repairs and maintenance	37	1,232,000	948,000	635,000	530,000	428,000	262,000	152,000
Common stock price range								
High bid		15	18¼	6⅝	9½	9⅝	8⅞	17⅜
Low bid		10½	6⅜	4⅞	6	4⅝	2½	6⅜
Dividends		$.20/share	$.13/share 50% stock	$.09/share	$.06/share	—	—	—
Current assets		$ 44,772,000	$ 45,202,000	$38,022,000	$24,734,000	$22,240,000	$20,060,000	$16,123,000
Current liabilities		$ 16,560,000	$ 19,567,000	$12,727,000	$ 6,837,000	$ 7,748,000	$ 5,526,000	$ 3,972,000
Working capital		$ 28,212,000	$ 25,635,000	$25,295,000	$17,897,000	$14,492,000	$14,534,000	$12,151,000
Current ratio		2.7:1	2.3:1	3.0:1	3.6:1	2.9:1	3.6:1	4.1:1
Inventory		$ 31,630,000	$ 29,404,000	$23,532,000	$17,001,000	$15,598,000	$14,960,000	$10,514,000
Short-term debt		$ 1,096,000	$ 695,000	$ 679,000	$ 12,000	$ 3,000	$ 750,000	—
Long-term debt		$ 7,622,000	$ 8,718,000	$ 8,738,000	$ 1,755,000	$ 521,000	$ 2,250,000	—
Total debt		$ 8,718,000	$ 9,413,000	$ 9,417,000	$ 1,767,000	$ 524,000	$ 3,000,000	—
Stockholders' equity		$ 35,228,000	$ 29,697,000	$26,069,000	$23,269,000	$20,109,000	$17,091,000	$15,049,000
Equity per common share	17%	7.87	6.65	5.51	4.91	4.25	3.62	3.18
Common shares outstanding		4,476,434	4,466,030	4,735,237	4,735,088	4,733,340	4,720,941	4,727,186
Number of employees		2,288	2,270	1,998	1,420	1,335	1,191	988
Number of stores		90	87	81	52	47	44	34
Total square footage of all stores		1,023,732	976,560	919,320	590,788	532,054	486,366	375,810
Retail sales per square foot*		$ 127.56	$ 121.89†	$ 117.21	$ 111.84	$ 106.61	$ 102.17	$ 95.11
Return on stockholders' equity		21.3%	22.2%	18.1%	17.1%	17.4%	13.6%	15.5%

* For stores in operation 12 months or more.
† Includes, for the first time, sales of 23 stores acquired from United Sporting Goods, Inc.
‡ As of February 2, 1980, or for the year ended February 2, 1980.
Source: Annual report.

Appendix (*concluded*)

1973	1972	1971
$32,760,000	$25,365,000	$21,810,000
25,435,000	18,727,000	15,681,000
5,077,000	4,655,000	4,266,000
2,248,000	1,983,000	1,863,000
20,947,000	16,422,000	14,026,000
3,075,000	2,355,000	1,954,000
2,827,000	2,041,000	1,672,000
207,000	265,000	204,000
41,000	49,000	67,000
1,398,000	1,048,000	863,000
1,677,000	1,307,000	1,091,000
.35	.28	.24
771,000	564,000	468,000
439,000	312,000	239,000
931,000	714,000	610,000
211,000	157,000	126,000
37,000	35,000	36,000
84,000	67,000	44,000
19½	9⅞	4⅞
10	2⅞	1⅛
50% stock	50% stock	—
$13,505,000	$13,038,000	$11,799,000
$ 3,315,000	$ 3,404,000	$ 3,164,000
$10,190,000	$ 9,634,000	$ 8,635,000
4.1:1	3.8:1	3.7:1
$ 8,873,000	$ 7,364,000	$ 5,924,000
—	$ 128,000	$ 250,000
—	$ 206,000	$ 148,000
—	$ 334,000	$ 398,000
$12,940,000	$10,453,000	$ 9,147,000
2.75	2.23	1.95
4,700,937	4,679,303	4,679,303
800	540	497
30	19	15
339,569	234,911	195,976
$ 87.36	$ 84.78	$ 84.12
16.0%	14.3%	16.7%

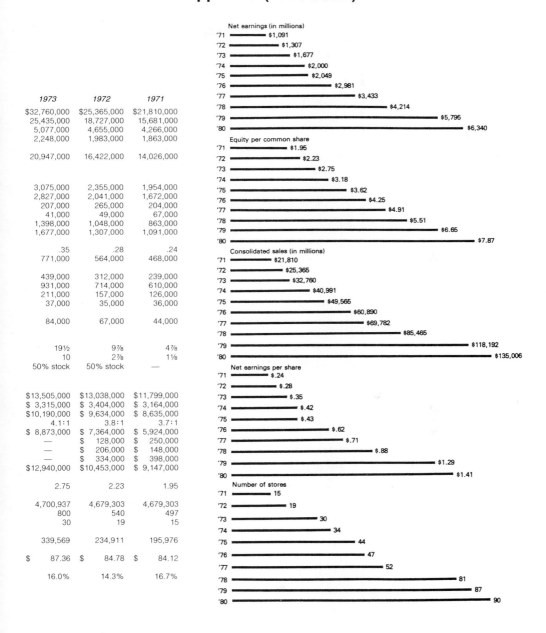

Net earnings (in millions)
'71 $1,091
'72 $1,307
'73 $1,677
'74 $2,000
'75 $2,049
'76 $2,981
'77 $3,433
'78 $4,214
'79 $5,795
'80 $6,340

Equity per common share
'71 $1.95
'72 $2.23
'73 $2.75
'74 $3.18
'75 $3.62
'76 $4.25
'77 $4.91
'78 $5.51
'79 $6.65
'80 $7.87

Consolidated sales (in millions)
'71 $21,810
'72 $25,365
'73 $32,760
'74 $40,991
'75 $49,565
'76 $60,890
'77 $69,782
'78 $85,465
'79 $118,192
'80 $135,006

Net earnings per share
'71 $.24
'72 $.28
'73 $.35
'74 $.42
'75 $.43
'76 $.62
'77 $.71
'78 $.88
'79 $1.29
'80 $1.41

Number of stores
'71 15
'72 19
'73 30
'74 34
'75 44
'76 47
'77 52
'78 81
'79 87
'80 90

Exhibit 1

Review of Selected Competitors, 1980

Company	Sales ($ Millions)	Stores	Estimated Mail Order		Mail Order			Division of
			($ Millions)	Percent of Total	(000)	Free	Fee*	
Eddie Bauer	$ 80	16	$ 40	50%	400	Yes	$2.50	General Mills
Orvis	17	1	14	74	161	No	3.15	
Eastern Mountain Sports	24	29	4	17	75	No	2.20	Franklin Mint
Recreational Equipment, Inc.	49	7	14	29	150	Yes	2.05	
Cabela's	16	1	14	88	234	No	3.25	
Talbots	43	16	23	53	240	Yes	3.00	General Mills
Carroll Reed	25	9	16	64	130	No	2.65	CML Group
Norm Thompson	12	2	10	83	100	Yes	3.50	Parker Pen
Lands' End	17	1	16	94	157	Yes	2.50	
L. L. Bean	120	1	101	84	1,200	No	None	

* Assumes $35.00 average order size.
Sales source: *Dun & Bradstreet*, 1980, 1981.

Exhibit 2

Customer Demographic Profile, 1980

		United States	Survey		Index
Sex:	Male	48%	51%		106
	Female	52	49		94
Age:	Under 35	40	41		103
	35 to 54	31	36		116
	55 and over	29	23		79
Education:	Not graduate of college	84	34		40
	College graduate	16	26	64	400
	Graduate work or degree		38		
Income:	Under $15,000	46	10		22
	$15,000–24,999	32	21		65
	$25,000–39,999	22	33	69	314
	$40,000 and over		36		
Marital Status:	Married	67	71		106
	Single	19	23		121
	Divorced/widowed	14	6		43

Source: Company records.

Exhibit 3

Regional Penetration of Current Customers

	1976			1980		
	U.S. Population	Current L. L. Bean Buyers	Index (Buyers/U.S.)	U.S. Population	Current L. L. Bean Buyers	Index (Buyers/U.S.)
New England	5.7%	19.5%	342	5.4%	16.3%	302
Mid-Atlantic	17.3	26.0	150	16.3	24.6	151
South Atlantic	15.9	16.3	103	16.3	18.2	112
Southeastern Central	6.4	3.6	56	6.5	3.9	60
Northeastern Central	19.0	14.4	76	18.4	14.3	78
Northwestern Central	7.8	4.6	59	7.6	4.6	61
Southwestern Central	9.9	3.9	39	10.5	4.5	43
Mountain	4.6	3.7	80	5.0	4.0	80
Pacific	13.4	8.0	60	14.0	9.6	69
Total	100.0%	100.0%	100	100.0%	100.0%	100

Source: Company records.

Exhibit 4

Customer Perception of L. L. Bean, 1980

	Strongly Agree and Somewhat Agree
Opinions about L. L. Bean:	
Bean has high-quality merchandise.	99%
Bean offers good value.	100
Bean will stand behind its products.	97
Bean provides personal, friendly service.	100
Like most about L. L. Bean:	
Ordering, delivery	29
Variety of merchandise	27
Prices	23
Like least about L. L. Bean:	
No answer	30
Nothing	20
Ordering, delivery	22
Variety of merchandise	17
Prices	9

Opinion of L. L. Bean Compared with Competitors	Much Better	About Same	Much Worse
Good value	44%	54%	2%
High quality	33	64	2
Low prices	38	59	3
Speed of delivery	28	66	6

Source: Company records.

Exhibit 5

Catalog Circulation (In thousands)

	1975	1980	Increase
L. L. Bean buyer	3,800	10,819	7,019
L. L. Bean best customer mailings	N.A.	3,523	3,523
Advertising	800	2,965	2,165
Rental mailing lists	400	4,744	4,344
L. L. Bean prospects			
—Master file inquiries			
—Customer referrals			
—Store buyers	900	4,573	3,673
Total	5,900	26,624	20,724

Source: Company records.

Exhibit 6

Sources of New Customers, 1976–1980

	1976	1977	Percent Change	1978	Percent Change	1979	Percent Change	1980	Percent Change
Advertising	80,094	96,811	+21%	99,767	+ 3%	119,242	+ 20%	159,185	+34%
Rental mailing lists	86,965	111,741	+28	131,638	+ 18	138,317	+ 5	142,038	+ 3
Store buyers	6,075	5,456	−10	8,306	+ 52	10,710	+ 29	12,221	+14
Customer referrals	1,287	762	−41	7,819	+926	24,135	+209	47,553	+97
Gift recipients	5,571	8,341	+50	9,659	+ 16	12,315	+ 28	19,636	+59
Unknown*	183,180	256,768	+40	277,639	+ 8	302,754	+ 9	278,351	− 8
Total new customers	363,172	479,879	+32	534,828	+ 11	607,473	+ 14	658,984	+ 8
Rejuvenated old buyers	N.A.	10,160	—	23,831	+134	29,495	+ 24	36,049	+22
Total existing customers	700,128	902,409	+29	1,045,990	+ 16	1,220,724	+ 17	1,440,440	+18
Grand total buyer list	1,063,300	1,392,448		1,604,649		1,857,692		2,135,473	
New as a percent of existing	51.9%	53.2%		51.1%		49.8%		45.8%	

* Customers of "unknown" origin could be, for instance, old customers appearing on the mailing list under new names or addresses. Customers using plain stationery to place orders or using catalog forms without the preprinted labels were also "unknowns." Mr. End estimated that about half the unknowns were new customers.
  Source: Company records.

Exhibit 7

Strategic Planning Profit and Loss Projections, 1981–1985

	1980 (000)	1981 (000)	% Δ	1982 (000)	% Δ	1983 (000)	% Δ	1984 (000)	% Δ	1985 (000)	% Δ
Net sales	$121,545	$151,820	24.9	$188,485	24.2	$232,275	23.2	$283,940	22.2	$344,320	21.3
Cost of sales	68,545	86,385	26.0	105,550	22.2	130,075	23.2	159,005	22.2	192,820	21.3
Gross margin	53,000	65,435	23.5	82,935	26.7	102,200	23.2	124,935	22.2	151,500	21.3
Operating expense	38,305	46,415	21.2	59,335	27.8	73,130	23.2	89,420	22.2	108,455	21.3
Operating income	14,695	19,020	29.4	23,600	24.1	29,070	23.2	35,515	22.2	43,045	21.2
Other income	460	625	35.9	790	26.4	990	25.3	1,230	24.2	1,515	23.2
Taxable income	15,155	19,645	29.6	24,390	24.2	30,060	23.2	36,745	22.2	44,560	21.3
Income taxes	7,545	9,625	27.6	11,950	24.2	14,730	23.3	18,005	22.2	21,835	21.3
Net income	7,610	10,020	31.7	12,440	24.2	15,330	23.2	18,740	22.2	22,725	21.3
Net income/net sales	6.3*		6.6		6.6		6.6		6.6		6.6
ROE	32.7*		33.6		32.7		31.8		30.9		30.0
Gross margin	43.6		43.1		44.0		44.0		44.0		44.0
Operating expense/net sales	31.5*		30.6		31.5		31.5		31.5		31.5

* Adjusted for accelerated items: Income/sales, 6.6; ROE, 34.3; operating expense/net sales, 30.9.
Source: Company records.

Exhibit 8

L. L. BEAN, INC.
Retail Store Revenue and Expense Statement
February, Year to Date
(dollars in thousands)

Account Name	1981	1980	Variance	Percent
Sales:				
Cash	$12,060.4	$ 9,675.1	$2,385.3	24.7%
MasterCharge	3,059.1	2,602.0	457.1	17.6
Visa	3,204.3	2,574.0	630.3	24.5
American Express	1,933.7	1,361.5	572.2	42.0
Gross Sales	20,257.5	16,212.6	4,044.9	24.9
Returns:				
Cash	560.6	452.8	107.8	23.8
MasterCharge	34.7	33.1	1.6	4.8
Visa	37.7	34.9	2.8	8.0
American Express	14.9	13.3	1.6	12.0
Less: Returns	647.9	534.1	113.8	21.3
Net Sales	19,609.6	15,678.5	3,931.1	25.1
Cost of Goods Sold	11,059.8	9,030.8	2,029.0	22.5
Gross Profit	8,549.8	6,647.7	1,902.1	28.6
Operating Expenses:				
Salaries and Wages:				
Store Order Picking Wages	18.3	16.8	1.5	8.9
Store Salaries	150.1	144.4	5.7	3.9
Store—General	1.9	0.5	1.4	280.0
Inventory	0.1	—	0.1	—
Salesclerks	643.1	499.0	144.1	28.9
Cashiers	181.6	127.8	53.8	42.1
Stock Clerks	132.4	133.7	(1.3)	(1.0)
Support	110.7	50.8	59.9	117.9
Customer Service	64.9	42.2	22.7	53.8
Accounting Wages	20.5	17.3	3.2	18.5
Custodian Wages	27.0	9.3	17.7	190.3
Security Wages	27.9	16.2	11.7	72.2
Data Processing Labor	1.6	1.4	0.2	14.3
Inventory Transport Labor	5.3	5.1	0.2	3.9
D.C. Receipts	4.2	—	4.2	—
Total Salaries and Wages	1,389.6	1,064.5	325.1	30.5
Fringe Benefits:				
Vacation Pay	51.2	55.7	(4.5)	(8.1)
Holiday Pay	46.1	35.0	11.1	31.7
Sick Pay	13.3	13.7	(0.4)	(2.9)
Pension Plan	50.7	38.1	12.6	33.1
Savings Plan	5.5	5.1	0.4	7.8
Health Insurance	25.7	27.0	(1.3)	(4.8)
Group Insurance	4.6	3.9	0.7	17.9
Payroll Taxes	144.4	108.0	36.4	33.7
Workers' Compensation	35.1	19.5	15.6	80.0
Dental Insurance Benefits	1.2	—	1.2	—
Short-Term Disability Pay	1.1	—	1.1	—
Bonus	170.6	113.0	57.6	51.0
Profit Sharing	66.9	34.6	32.3	93.4
Total Fringe Benefits	616.4	453.6	162.8	35.9

Exhibit 8 (concluded)

Account Name	1981	1980	Variance	Percent
Occupancy:				
Depreciation:				
Furniture and Fixtures	$ 20.5	$ 18.4	$ 2.1	11.4%
Machinery and Equipment	39.9	10.9	29.0	266.1
Land Improvements	11.4	4.7	6.7	142.6
Building and Building				
Improvements	57.2	65.3	(8.1)	(12.4)
Cushing Street Warehouse	0.9	1.1	(0.2)	(18.2)
Utilities:				
Fuel	9.2	5.9	3.3	55.9
Electricity	34.1	23.7	10.4	43.9
Water	2.9	2.5	0.4	16.0
Sewerage	4.2	4.4	(0.2)	(4.5)
Property Insurance	36.0	27.7	8.3	30.0
Property Taxes	15.4	14.0	1.4	10.0
Total Occupancy	231.7	178.6	53.1	29.7
Credit Card Service Charges	175.9	149.6	26.3	17.6
Supplies:				
Store Supplies	25.8	21.8	4.0	18.3
Store Allocated Supplies	4.9	1.5	3.4	226.7
Store Packing Allocated				
Supplies	43.9	54.5	(10.6)	(19.4)
Store Packing Supplies	—	0.3	(0.3)	(100.0)
Total Supplies	74.6	78.1	(3.5)	(4.5)
Advertising:				
Advertising	109.2	78.7	30.5	38.8
Promotions	24.3	17.0	7.3	42.9
Total Advertising	133.5	95.7	37.8	39.5
Other Miscellaneous:				
Store Services	4.3	0.8	3.5	437.5
Store Equipment Rental	4.6	3.1	1.5	48.4
Store Equipment Maintenance	9.1	8.4	0.7	8.3
Store Travel	3.5	3.0	0.5	16.7
Store Consultants	25.2	102.1	(76.9)	(75.3)
Store Building Repair	1.0	0.4	0.6	150.0
Store Display Materials	5.3	4.7	0.6	12.8
Store Parking Lot Rent	0.5	2.7	(2.2)	(81.5)
Store Maintenance Services	5.4	—	5.4	—
Total Miscellaneous	58.9	125.2	(66.3)	(53.0)
Total Expenses	2,680.6	2,145.3	535.3	25.0
Operating Income	5,869.2	4,502.4	1,366.8	30.4
Other Revenue and (Expenses):				
Fish and Game License Income	2.6	2.9	(0.3)	(10.3)
Ski Equipment Rental Income	5.0	1.2	3.8	316.7
Snowshoe Rental Income	—	0.1	(0.1)	(100.0)
Cash Short and Over	(1.2)	(1.0)	(0.2)	(20.0)
Total Other	6.4	3.2	3.2	100.0
Total Revenue	$ 5,875.6	$ 4,505.6	$1,370.0	30.4%

Exhibit 9 Sony/L. L. Bean Advertisement

Exhibit 10

Mail-Order Sales in Selected Foreign Countries (Dollars in millions)

	Sales Year	Mail Order	Mail Order as Percent of Retail Sales	Mail Order per Capita Sales	1979 Percent Growth in Dollars
Australia	1978	$ 732	—	$ 52	—
Austria	1978	255	1.9%	34	—
Belgium	1979	307	0.7	31	7%
Brazil	1979	118	—	1	—
Canada	1979	1,900	—	81	11
Denmark	1977	100	1.0	20	—
Finland	1978	129	1.0	27	—
France	1979	3,479	2.2	66	22
West Germany	1979	9,297	4.7	151	10
Great Britain	1979	5,461	5.3	98	35
Italy	1979	469	0.5	8	29
Japan	1977	3,000	0.9	18	—
Netherlands	1979	598	1.4	43	18
Norway	1976	30	—	7	—
Spain	1978	100	2.0	3	—
Sweden	1978	332	—	40	—
Switzerland	1979	449	1.7	79	15
United States	1979	25,775	2.5	117	12

Sources: Association Europeene de vente par correspondance and U.S. Department of State—Bureau of Intelligence and Research.

Exhibit 11

L. L. BEAN, INC.
Statements of Income and Retained Earnings
(For the Years Ended February 22, 1981, and February 24, 1980)

	Amount		Percent	
	1981	*1980*	*1981*	*1980*
Sales:				
Mail-order	$109,525,481	$83,576,796		
Salesroom	20,257,457	16,212,594		
	129,782,938	99,789,390		
Less returns and allowances	8,237,631	6,365,712		
Net sales	121,545,307	93,423,678	100.0%	100.0%
Cost of sales	69,870,940	55,680,148	57.5	59.6
Gross profit	51,674,367	37,743,530	42.5	40.4
Operating expenses:				
Operations	12,628,711	9,993,410	10.4	10.7
Marketing	14,501,024	11,151,398	11.9	11.9
General and administrative	10,272,611	7,298,562	8.4	7.8
Total operating expenses	37,402,346	28,443,370	30.7	30.4
Operating income	14,272,021	9,300,160	11.8	10.0
Other income (expenses):				
Interest income	599,621	300,287	0.5	0.3
Interest expense	(1,335,687)	(834,755)	(1.1)	(0.9)
Miscellaneous, net	274,480	161,476	0.2	0.2
Total other income (expenses)	(461,586)	(372,992)	(0.4)	(0.4)
Income before income taxes	13,810,435	8,927,168	11.4%	9.6%
Federal and state income taxes	6,842,000	4,230,600		
Net income	6,968,435	4,696,568		
Retained earnings, beginning of year	20,607,701	16,617,228		
Cash dividends, $145.00 and $97.50 per share	1,050,090	706,095		
Retained earnings, end of year	$ 26,526,046	$20,607,701		

Exhibit 12

L. L. BEAN, INC.
Balance Sheets,
February 22, 1981, and February 24, 1980

	1981	1980
Assets		
Current assets:		
Cash and cash equivalents	$ 1,963,932	$ 577,902
Certificates of deposit and U.S. Treasury bills	14,181,235	3,700,000
Accounts receivable, net of allowance for doubtful accounts of $11,200 and $44,600	1,086,926	776,933
Inventories	19,761,305	20,330,430
Prepaid federal income taxes, net	27,885	51,733
Prepaid expenses and other assets	905,921	1,541,028
Total current assets	37,927,204	$26,978,026
Property, plant, and equipment, at cost:		
Land	444,119	204,453
Buildings and improvements	1,237,545	942,652
Leasehold improvements	1,762,785	1,721,738
Machinery, furniture, and equipment	4,606,126	4,186,193
Capital leases	6,754,137	7,150,172
Total property, plant, and equipment	14,804,712	14,205,208
Less accumulated depreciation and amortization	3,582,088	2,460,575
	11,222,624	11,744,633
Prepaid federal income taxes, net	528,500	263,748
Prepaid pension	372,005	324,963
Total assets	$50,050,333	$39,311,370
Liabilities and Stockholders' Equity		
Current liabilities:		
Current obligations under capital leases	$ 52,764	$ 46,162
Note payable	146,452	—
Accounts payable	5,989,672	6,167,797
Unfilled customer orders	1,563,763	1,300,498
Dividends payable	398,310	217,260
Total current liabilities	8,150,961	7,731,717
Accrued liabilities:		
Federal and state income taxes	3,550,285	563,736
Payroll and payroll taxes	3,031,776	1,998,796
Pension and profit sharing	1,250,831	812,251
Total accrued liabilities	7,832,892	3,374,783
Total liabilities	15,983,853	11,106,500
Long-term capital lease obligations	7,318,434	7,375,169
Stockholders' equity:		
Common stock, par value $100 per share: Authorized: 8,000 shares Issued: 7,800 shares	780,000	780,000
Retained earnings	26,526,046	20,607,701
	27,306,046	21,387,701
Less cost of 558 shares of reacquired common stock	(558,000)	(558,000)
Total stockholders' equity	26,748,046	20,829,701
Total liabilities and stockholders' equity	$50,050,333	$39,311,370

Crown Cork & Seal Company, Inc.

Strategic Position, 1977

By 1977 Crown Cork & Seal Company was the fourth-largest producer of metal cans and crowns in the United States.[1] Under the leadership of John Connelly, Crown had raised itself up from near-bankruptcy in 1957 and emerged as a major force in the metal container market both domestically and internationally. The year 1977 marked the 20th consecutive year of sales and profit growth (see Exhibit 1).

Crown Cork & Seal had concentrated its efforts on basic tinplated steel cans to hold beer, soft drinks, and aerosol products. During the past 20 years this strategy had helped Crown overcome some tough challenges from large competitors and unfavorable industry trends. However, by 1977 the emergence of the ozone controversy and the trend toward legislative regulation of nonreturnable containers had struck at the heart of Crown's domestic business. Was it time for a change in Crown's formula for success or just time for a reaffirmation of Connelly's basic strategic choices?

To explore these questions, this case looks at the metal container industry, Crown's strategy and position within that industry, and the nature of the problems facing the company during mid-1977.

---

[1] Crowns are flanged bottle caps, originally made with an insert of natural cork; hence the name Crown Cork and Seal.

Copyright © 1977 by the President and Fellows of Harvard College
Harvard Business School case 378–024

The Metal Container Industry

Although the metal container industry included 100 firms and a vast number of product lines, it is possible to focus on a few basic factors which composed Crown's competitive environment. This section will describe the product segments in which Crown competes, examine the industry's competitive structure, and look at three current industrywide trends: (1) increasing self-manufacture, (2) new material introductions, and (3) the effect of the "packaging revolution" on the competitive atmosphere.

The Products

Metal containers made up almost a third of all packaging products used in the United States in 1976. Metal containers included products ranging from traditional steel and aluminum cans to foil containers and metal drums and pails of all shapes and sizes. The largest segment, however, was metal cans which in 1976 reached $7.1 billion in total value, over three fourths of all metal container shipments.

Metal cans were formed from two basic raw materials, aluminum and tinplated steel. The traditional process had been to roll a sheet of metal, solder it, cut it to the right size, and attach two ends forming a three-piece seamed can. In the late 1960s, however, a new process was introduced by the aluminum industry. This was a two-piece can, formed by pushing a flat blank of metal into a deep cup, eliminating a separate bottom and producing a seamless container. The product adopted the name "drawn-and-ironed" can from the molding procedure.

The aluminum companies who developed the process, Alcoa and Reynolds, had done so with the intention of turning the process over to can manufacturers and subsequently increasing their own raw material sales. However, when the manufacturers were reluctant to incur the large costs involved in line changeovers, the two aluminum companies began building their own two-piece lines and competing directly in the end market.

The new can had advantages in weight, labor, and materials costs and was recommended by the Food and Drug Administration, which was worried about lead migration from soldered three-piece cans. Tinplated can producers soon acknowledged the new process as the wave of the future. They quickly began to explore the possibilities for drawing and ironing steel sheets. By 1972 the technique was perfected and investment dollars had begun to pour into line changeovers and new equipment purchases. Exhibit 2 illustrates the rapid switch to the two-piece can in the beverage industry. In the beer segment alone, almost half of the total cans used in 1974 were made by the new drawn-and-ironed process.

Table 1

Metal Can Shipments, 1967–1976 (Thousand base boxes)

	1967	*1972*	*1973*	*1974*	*1975*	*1976*
Total metal cans	133,980	168,868	180,482	188,383	177,063	179,449
By product:						
Food cans	67,283	64,773	68,770	73,104	68,127	64,984
Beverage cans:	42,117	75,916	84,617	89,435	85,877	90,084
Soft drinks	14,580	31,660	35,631	36,499	33,284	39,488
Beer	27,537	44,256	48,986	52,936	52,593	50,596
Pet foods	5,797	6,694	7,121	7,083	6,057	6,121
General						
packaging						
cans:	18,783	21,485	19,974	18,761	17,002	18,391
Motor oil	n.a.	3,095	2,756	2,533	n.a.	n.a.
Paints	n.a.	6,086	5,562	5,202	n.a.	n.a.
Aerosols	n.a.	5,877	6,103	5,765	4,808	5,097
All other	n.a.	6,427	5,553	5,261	n.a.	n.a.

Note: A base box is an area of 31,360 square inches.
n.a. = Not available.
Sources: Standard & Poor's Industry Survey, *Containers, Basic Analysis,* March 24, 1977, p. C123; and *Metal Can Shipments Report 1974,* p. 6.

Growth

Between 1967 and 1976 the number of metal cans shipped grew at an average of 4.3 percent annually. As shown in Table 1, the greatest gains were in the beverage segment, while motor oil, paints, and other general packaging can shipments actually declined. The 6 percent decline in total shipments in 1975 turned around as the economy picked up in all areas except basic food cans. For the future, soft-drink and beer cans were expected to continue to be the growth leaders.

Industry Structure

In 1977 the U.S. metal can industry was dominated by four major manufacturers. Two giants, American Can and the Continental Can Division of the Continental Group, together made up 35 percent of all domestic production. National Can and Crown Cork & Seal were also major forces with market shares of 8.7 percent and 8.3 percent, respectively (see Exhibit 3).

Capital Barriers to Entry. A typical three-piece beer can line cost $750,000 to $1 million. In addition, expensive seaming, end-making, and finishing equipment was required. Since each finishing line could handle the output of three to four can-forming lines, the minimum efficient plant cost was at least $3.5 million in basic equipment. Most plants had 12 to 15 lines for the increased flexibility of handling more than one type of can at once. However, any more than 15 lines became unwieldy because of the need for duplication of setup crews, maintenance, and supervision.

The new two-piece lines were even more expensive. The line itself cost approximately $8.5 million, and the investment in peripheral equipment raised the per line cost to $10–$15 million. Unlike three-piece lines, there was no minimum efficient size, and plants ranged from one line to five lines.

Conversion to these two-piece lines virtually eliminated the market for new three-piece lines. No new three-piece lines had been installed in some time, and the major manufacturers were selling complete fully operational three-piece lines "as is" for $175,000 to $200,000. Many firms were shipping their old lines overseas to their foreign operations.

Pricing. The can industry was heavily price competitive. The need for high-capacity utilization and the desire to avoid costly line changeovers made long runs of standard items the most desirable business. As a result, most companies offered volume discounts to encourage large orders. From 1968 to 1975 industrywide margins shrank 44 percent, reflecting sluggish sales and increased price competition. This trend was particularly hard for the small producer who was less able to spread its fixed costs. Raising prices above industry-set norms, however, was dangerous. Continental tried it in the fall of 1963 with the announcement of a 2 percent price hike. Other manufacturers refused to follow their lead, and by mid-1964 Continental was back to industry price levels with considerably reduced market share.

Distribution. Because of the product's bulk and weight, transportation was a major factor in the canmakers' cost structure. One estimate put transportation at 7.6 percent of the price of a metal can, with raw materials playing the largest part at 64 percent and labor following at 14.4 percent. Choice of lighter raw materials and widely dispersed plant locations could then have a large impact on total costs. Most estimates put the radius of economical distribution for a plant at between 150 and 300 miles.

Suppliers and Customers

Steel companies formed an oligopoly which set the price of the canmakers' raw materials. Although can companies as a whole were major steel buyers (the fourth-largest consumers of steel products), individual companies had only minimal leverage. More important was the competitive position of steel with respect to aluminum or glass containers. Threats of substitute raw materials kept down steel prices and encouraged technological cooperation between the steel and can producers.

On the customer side, over 80 percent of the metal can output was purchased by the major food and beer companies. Since the can was about 45 percent of the total costs of beverage companies, most had at least two sources of supply. This both decreased their risk and increased their leverage with the can manufacturers. For the canmakers, then, poor service and uncompetitive prices were punished by cuts in order size. As plants were often located to supply a customer, the loss of a large order in one area could greatly cut into manufacturing efficiency and company profits. As one can executive caught in the margin squeeze commented, "Sometimes I think the only way out of this is to sell out to U.S. Steel or to buy General Foods."[2]

Industry Trends

Three major trends had plagued the metal container manufacturers since the early 1960s: (1) the continuing threat of self-manufacture; (2) the increasing acceptance of substitute materials such as aluminum, foil fiber, or plastic for standard tinplate packaging needs; and (3) the "packaging revolution" where expansion of the whole industry concept forced the question, "Could one stay only in the tin can business and survive?"

Self-Manufacture

In the last six years there had been a growing trend toward self-manufacture by large can customers, particularly in the low-technology standard items. As shown in Table 2, the proportion of captive production increased from 18.2 percent to 25.8 percent between 1970 and 1976.

These increases seemed to come from companies gradually adding their own lines at specific canning locations rather than full-scale changeovers. However, the temptation for large can users such as food and beer producers to backward integrate into can production was high. Campbell Soup Company, for instance, had long been one of the largest producers of cans in the United States. The introduction of the two-piece can was expected to dampen this trend. Since the end users did not possess the technical skills to develop their own two-piece lines, they often had to purchase these cans from outside sources.

Substitute Materials

Aluminum. The greatest threat to the traditional tinplated can was the growing popularity of the new lighter weight aluminum can. The major

---

[2] *Crown Cork & Seal Company and the Metal Container Industry,* Harvard Business School case 6–373–077.

Table 2

Metal Can Production

	1970	1971	1972	1973	1974	1975	1976
By market:							
For sale	81.8%	80.9%	80.8%	78.2%	76.7%	73.7%	74.2%
For own use	18.2	19.1	19.2	21.8	23.3	26.3	25.8

producers of this can were the large aluminum companies led by Reynolds Metals and Aluminum Company of America (Alcoa). Some traditional tinplate can producers such as Continental and American also produced a small proportion of aluminum cans.

From 1970 to 1976 aluminum went from 11.6 percent to 27.5 percent of the total metal can market. It was expected to reach a 29 percent share in 1977 (see Table 3). In absolute numbers, steel use remained fairly level while aluminum use had tripled since 1970 (see Exhibit 4).

Most of the inroads were made in the beer and soft-drink markets where aluminum held 65 percent and 31 percent shares respectively in 1976. Additional gains were expected as aluminum was in general "more friendly to beer," reducing the problems of flavoring, a major concern of both the brewing and soft-drink industries.

Aluminum had several other important advantages over tinplated steel. First, its lighter weight could help reduce transportation costs. In addition, aluminum was easier to lithograph, producing a better reproduction at a lower cost. Finally, aluminum had the edge in recycling facilities and collection systems and was expected to continue to lead as recycled aluminum was far more valuable than recycled steel.

Aluminum's major disadvantage was in the cost area. The continuation of the trend toward greater utilization of aluminum over steel depended on expected price differentials between the two metals. In 1976 the stock to manufacture 1,000 12-ounce beverage cans cost $17.13 in steel and $20.81 in aluminum. However, steel companies were attempting to widen this gap. One account reported that "in early 1977, steel producers raised the price of tinplate by only 4.8 percent, in contrast to an increase for aluminum can stock of about 9.7 percent." They did this "in an effort to enhance the competitiveness of steel vis-à-vis aluminum

Table 3

Metal Can Production by Material

	1970	1971	1972	1973	1974	1975	1976
Steel	88.4%	86.9%	82.6%	81.4%	79.0%	74.7%	72.5%
Aluminum	11.6	13.1	17.4	18.6	21.0	25.3	27.5

and to persuade companies intending to add canning lines to go with steel."[3] Some industry observers also expected the gap to widen as the auto companies increased their usage of aluminum, thus driving up aluminum prices. The two-piece tinplate cans were also considerably stronger than their aluminum counterparts.

Other Materials. Two other raw materials threatened tinplated steel as the primary product in making containers: the new paper and metal composite called fiber-foil and the growing varieties of plastics.

Fiber-foil cans were jointly developed by the R. C. Can Company and Anaconda Aluminum in 1962 for the motor oil market. They caught on immediately, and by 1977 this composite material was the primary factor in the frozen juice concentrate market as well.

Plastics represented the fastest growing sector of the packaging industry and the principal force in packaging change. The plastic bottle offered an enticing variety of advantages including weight savings, break resistance, design versatility, and lower shelf space requirements. Although most of the competitive impact was on glass bottle makers, can companies could suffer as well if plastic successfully entered the carbonated softdrink market.

The "Packaging Revolution"

Not only was the traditional package being reshaped and its materials reformulated, but the modern container also served a new purpose. From the late 1950s the package itself became increasingly important in the marketing of the product it contained. The container was an advertising vehicle whose own features were expected to contribute to the total product sales. This had serious implications for the metal can industry. Although the tin can was functional, it was not romantic. Aluminum was easier to lithograph, and plastic was more versatile. Pressure for continuing innovation meant the need for greater R&D expenditures to explore new materials, different shapes, more convenient tops, and other imaginative ideas with potential consumer appeal.

Perhaps the greatest long-term significance of the packaging revolution was that metal containers were increasingly becoming just one segment of the overall packaging industry. The implication of this trend was that the metal can companies would have to contend with the research and marketing strength of such giant integrated companies as Du Pont, Dow Chemical, Weyerhaeuser Timber, Reynolds, and Alcoa. In response to the forward integration of these major material suppliers into packaging, some metal can manufacturers began to invest in their own basic

---

[3] Standard & Poor's Industry Survey, *Containers, Basic Analysis,* March 24, 1977, p. C123.

research. In 1963 American announced the start of construction on a research center at Princeton, New Jersey, which would "give major attention to basic research in such areas as solid-state physics and electrochemical phenomena, as a potential source of new products."[4]

The Competition

By the late 1960s all three of Crown Cork & Seal's major competitors had diversified into areas outside the metal container industry. However, in 1977 they still remained major factors in metal can production (see Exhibit 3).

Continental Group

Because of the extent of its diversification, Continental changed its name in 1976 making Continental Can only one division of the large conglomerate. Although only 37.3 percent of the total company sales were in cans, it still held the dominant market share (18.4 percent) of the U.S. metal can market. The remainder of Continental's domestic sales were in forest products (20 percent) and other plastic and paper packaging materials (9 percent).

In 1969 Continental began refocusing its investment spending into foreign and diversified operations. In 1972 the company took a $120 million aftertax extraordinary loss to cover the closing, realignment, and modernization of its canmaking facilities over a three-year period. Of the $120 million loss, close to 70 percent resulted from fixed asset disposals, pension fund obligations, and severance pay. By 1976 almost one third of the company's revenues came from their overseas operations which covered 133 foreign countries. Domestic investment went primarily to the paper products and the plastic bottle lines. Very little was allocated for the changeover to new two-piece steel cans.

American Can

American also reduced its dependence on domestic can manufacture and, even more than Continental, emphasized unrelated product diversification. American competed in the entire packaging area, from metal and composite containers to paper, plastic, and laminated packaging products. In 1972 American "decided to shut down, consolidate, or sell operations that had either become obsolete or marginal . . . [this] resulted in an aftertax extraordinary loss of $106 million."[5]

---

[4] *Crown Cork & Seal Company and the Metal Container Industry,* p. 14.

[5] Annual report, 1972, p. 3.

By 1976 20 percent of the company's sales came from consumer products such as household tissues, Dixie paper cups, and Butterick dress patterns. American also had a large chemical subsidiary (15 percent of sales), and another 15 percent came from international sales. Return on sales for the domestic container segment of American's business remained stable at about 5 percent for the previous five years, but relatively poor performance in their diversified areas gave American the lowest average return on equity (7.9 percent) of all the can manufacturers (see Exhibit 3).

National Can

National's attempt to join in the trend to diversification achieved somewhat mixed results. Up until 1967 National was almost solely a can producer. Since then, acquisitions moved the company into glass containers, food canning, pet foods, bottle closures, and plastic containers. However, instead of generating future growth opportunities, the expansion into grocery products proved a drag on company earnings. Pet foods and vegetable canning fared poorly in the 1974–75 recession years, and the grocery division as a whole suffered a loss in 1976. As a result, National began a stronger overseas program to boost their earnings and investment image.

Crown Cork & Seal

While its three major competitors turned to diversification, Crown Cork & Seal had remained primarily in metal cans and closures. In 1976 the company derived almost 65 percent of its sales from tinplated cans; crowns accounted for 29 percent of total sales and 35 percent of profits. The remaining sales were in bottling and canning machinery. In fact, Crown was one of the largest manufacturers of filling equipment in the world. Foreign sales, which were primarily crowns, accounted for an increasingly larger percentage of total sales (see Exhibit 5).

In 1976 Crown's return on sales was almost twice that of its three larger competitors. Over the past 10 years Crown's sales growth was second only to National Can, and Crown was first in profit growth. The following sections describe Crown's history and strategy.

Crown Cork & Seal Company

In April 1957 Crown Cork & Seal lay on the verge of bankruptcy. The 1956 loss was $241,000 after preferred dividends, and 1957 looked even darker. Bankers Trust Company had called from New York to announce the withdrawal of their $2.5 million line of credit. It seemed that all that was left was to write the company's obituary. Yet by the end of

1957 Crown had "climbed out of the coffin and was sprinting." Between 1956 and 1961 sales increased from $115 to $176 million and profits soared. Since 1961 the company has shown a 15.4 percent increase in sales and 14 percent in profits on the average every year.

Company History

In August 1891 a foreman in a Baltimore machine shop hit upon an idea for a better bottle cap—a round piece of tin-coated steel with a flanged edge and an insert of natural cork. This "crown cork" top became the main product of a highly successful small venture, the Crown Cork & Seal Company. Yet as the patents ran out, competition became severe. The faltering Crown Cork was bought out in 1927 by a competitor, Charles McManus, who then shook the company back to life, bursting upon the starchy firm as one old-timer recalls, "like a heathen in the temple." *Fortune,* in 1962, described the turnaround:

> Under the hunch-playing, paternalistic McManus touch, Crown prospered in the 30s, selling better than half the U.S. and world supply of bottle caps. Even in bleak 1935 the company earned better than 13 percent on sales of $14 million.
>
> Then overconfidence led to McManus's first big mistake. He extended Crown's realm into canmaking. Reasoning soundly that the beer can would catch on, he bought a small Philadelphia can company. But reasoning poorly, he plunged into building one of the world's largest can plants on Philadelphia's Erie Avenue. It grew to a million square feet and ran as many as 52 lines simultaneously. A nightmare of inefficiency, the plant suffered deepened losses because of the McManus mania for volume. He lured customers by assuming their debts to suppliers and sometimes even cutting prices below costs. The Philadelphia blunder was to haunt Crown for many years.[6]

With all his projects and passion for leadership, McManus had no time or concern for building an organization that could run without him.

> Neither of his two sons, Charles Jr. and Walter, was suited to command a one-man company, although both had been installed in vice presidents' offices. Crown's board was composed of company officers, some of whom were relatives of the boss. The combination of benevolent despotism and nepotism had prevented the rise of promising men in the middle ranks. When McManus died in 1946, the chairmanship and presidency passed to his private secretary, a lawyer named John J. Nagle.
>
> In a fashion peculiar to Baltimore's family-dominated commerce, the inbred company acquired the settled air of a bank, only too willing to forget it lived by banging out bottle caps. In the muted, elegant offices on

---

[6] All quotes on the following pages are taken from *Fortune's* article, "The Unoriginal Ideas that Rebuilt Crown Cork," October 1962, pp. 118–64.

Eastern Avenue, relatives and hangers-on assumed that the remote machines would perpetually grind out handsome profits and dividends. In the postwar rush of business, the assumption seemed valid. The family left well enough alone, except to improve upon the late paternalist's largess. As a starter, Nagle's salary was raised from $35,000 to $100,000.

Officers arrived and departed in a fleet of chauffeured limousines. Some found novel ways to fill their days. A brother-in-law of the late McManus fell into the habit of making a day-long tour of the junior executives' offices, appearing at each doorway, whistling softly, and wordlessly moving on. After hours, the corporate good life continued. More than 400 dining and country club memberships were spread through the upper echelons. A would-be visitor to the St. Louis plant recalls being met at the airport, whisked to a country club for drinks, lunch, cocktails, and dinner, and then being returned to the airport with apologies and promises of a look at the plant "next time."

Into the early 1950s Crown ran on a combination of McManus momentum and the last vestiges of pride of "increasingly demoralized middle managers," both powerless to decide and unable to force decisions from above.

Dividends were maintained at the expense of investment in new plant; what investment there was, was mostly uninspired. From a lordly 50 percent in 1940, Crown's share of U.S. bottle cap sales slipped to under 33 percent. In 1952 the chaotic can division had such substantial losses that the company was finally moved to act. The board omitted a quarterly dividend. That brought the widow McManus, alarmed, to the president's office. President Nagle counseled her to be patient and leave matters to him.

Matters soon grew worse. A disastrous attempt at expansion into plastics followed a ludicrous diversification into metal bird cages. Then in 1954 a reorganization, billed to solve all problems, was begun, modeled on Continental's decentralized line staff structure. The additional personnel and expense were staggering, and Crown's margins continued to dip. One observer noted, "The new suit of clothes, cut for a giant, hung on Crown like an outsized shroud." The end seemed near.

John Connelly Arrives

John Connelly was the son of a Philadelphia blacksmith who after working his way up as a container salesman formed his own company to produce paper boxes. His interest in Crown began when he was rebuffed by the post-McManus regime who "refused to take a chance" on a small supplier like Connelly. *Fortune* described Connelly's takeover:

By 1955, when Crown's distress had become evident to Connelly, he asked a Wall Street friend, Robert Drummond, what he thought could be done with the company. "I wrote him a three-page letter," Drummond recalls, "and John telephoned to say he'd thrown it into the wastebasket, which I doubted. He said, 'If you can't put it into one sentence you don't understand the situation.' " Drummond tried again and boiled it down to this formula: "If you can get sales to $150 million and earn 4 percent net after taxes and all charges, meanwhile reducing the common to 1 million shares, you'll earn $6 a share and the stock will be worth $90."

That was good enough for Connelly. He began buying stock and in November 1956 was asked to be an outside director, a desperate move for the ailing company.

The stranger found the parlour stuffy. "Those first few meetings," says Connelly, "were like something out of *Executive Suite*. I'd ask a question. There would be dead silence. I'd make a motion to discuss something. Nobody would second it, and the motion would die." It dawned on Connelly that the insiders knew even less about Crown than he did.

He toured the plants—something no major executive had done in years. At one plant a foreman was his guide. His rich bass graced the company glee club, and he insisted on singing as they walked. Connelly finally told him to shut up and sit down. The warning system silenced, Connelly went on alone and found workers playing cards and sleeping. Some were building a bar for an executive.

At another plant he sat in on a meeting of a dozen managers and executives, ostensibly called to discuss the problem posed by customers' complaints about poor quality and delivery. The fault, it seemed, lay with the customers themselves—how unreasonable they were to dispute Crown's traditional tolerance of a "fair" number of defective crowns in every shipment; how carping they were to complain about delays arising from production foul-ups, union troubles, flat tires, and other acts of God. Connelly kept silent until a pause signaled the consensus, then he confessed himself utterly amazed. He hadn't quite known what to make of Crown, he said, but now he knew it was something truly unique in his business life—a company where the customer was always wrong. "This attitude," he told the startled executives, "is the worst thing I've ever seen. No one here seems to realize this company is in business to make money."

The Crisis

By April 1957 the crisis had arrived. With Bankers Trust calling in their loans and bankruptcy imminent, John Connelly took over the presidency. His rescue plan was simple; as he called it "just common sense."

His first move was to pare down the organization, or put more simply, to fire. Paternalism ended in a blizzard of pink slips. The headquarters staff was cut from 160 to 80. Included in the departures were 11 vice presidents. The company returned to a simple functional organization, and in 20 months Crown had eliminated 1,647 jobs or 24 percent of the payroll. As part of the company's reorganization, Mr. Connelly discarded divisional accounting practices at the same time he eliminated the divisional line and staff concept. Except for one accountant maintained at each plant location, all accounting and cost control was performed at the corporate level, the corporate accounting staff occupying half the space used by the headquarters group. In addition, the central research and development facility was disbanded.

The second step was to make each plant manager totally responsible for plant profitability, including any allocated costs (all company overhead, estimated at 5 percent of sales, was allocated to the plant level). Previously, plant managers were only responsible for controllable expenses at the plant level. Under the new system, the plant manager was even responsible for the profits on each product manufactured in the plant. Although the plant manager's compensation was not tied directly to profit performance, one senior executive pointed out, "he is certainly rewarded on the basis of that figure."

The next step was to slow production to a halt and liquidate $7 million in inventory. By mid-July the banks had been paid off. Planning for the future, Connelly developed control systems. He introduced sales forecasting dovetailed with new production and inventory controls. This took control back from the plant foreman who could no longer continue production to avoid layoffs and dump the products into a bottomless pit of inventory.

However, Connelly was not satisfied simply with short-term reorganizations of the existing company. By 1960 Crown Cork & Seal had adopted a strategy that it would follow for at least the next 15 years.

Crown's Strategy

Products and Markets

Being a smaller producer in an industry dominated by giants, Connelly sought to develop a product line built around Crown's traditional strengths in metal forming and fabrication.[7] He chose to return to the area he knew best: tinplated steel cans and crowns and to concentrate on specialized uses and international markets.

A dramatic illustration of Connelly's commitment to this strategy occurred in the early 1960s. In 1960 Crown held over 50 percent of the market for motor oil cans. In 1962 R. C. Can and Anaconda Aluminum jointly developed fiber-foil cans for motor oil, which were approximately 20 percent lighter and 15 percent cheaper than the metal cans then in use. Crown's management decided not to continue to compete in this market and soon lost its entire market share.

In the early 1960s Connelly singled out two specific applications in the domestic market: beverage cans and the growing aerosol market.

---

[7] In 1956 Crown's sales were $115 million compared to $772 million for American and $1 billion for Continental.

These applications were called "hard to hold" because the cans required special characteristics to either contain the product under pressure or to avoid affecting taste and to be used in high-speed filling lines. In the mid-1960s growth in demand for soft-drink and beer cans was more than triple that for traditional food cans.

Crown had an early advantage in aerosols. In 1938 McManus had tooled up for a strong-walled seamless beer can which was rejected by brewers as too expensive. In 1946 it was dusted off and equipped with a valve to make the industry's first aerosol container. However, little emphasis was put on the line until Connelly spotted high-growth potential in the mid-1960s.

In addition to the specialized product line, Connelly's strategy was based on two geographic thrusts: expand to national distribution in the United States and invest heavily abroad. The domestic expansion was linked to Crown's manufacturing reorganization where plants were spread out across the country to reduce transportation costs and to be nearer the customers. Crown was unusual in that they had no plants built to service a single customer, which was characteristic of other firms in the industry. Instead, Crown concentrated on product and produced to serve a number of customers near their plants. Also, Crown developed their lines totally for the production of tinplate cans, making nothing in aluminum. In international markets Crown invested heavily in underdeveloped nations, first with crowns and then with cans as packaged foods became more widely accepted.

Manufacturing

When Connelly took over in 1957, Crown had perhaps the most outmoded and inefficient production facilities in the industry. In the post-McManus regime, dividends had taken precedence over new investment, and old machinery combined with the cumbersome Philadelphia plant gave Crown very high production and transportation costs. Soon after he gained control, Connelly took drastic action, closing down the Philadelphia facility and investing heavily in new and geographically dispersed plants. From 1958 to 1963 the company spent almost $82 million on relocation and new facilities. By 1976 Crown had 26 plant locations domestically versus 9 in 1955. The plants were small (usually under 10 lines versus 50 in the old complex) and were located close to the customer rather than the raw material source.

Crown emphasized flexibility and quick response to customer needs. One officer claimed that the key to the can industry was "the fact that nobody stores cans," and when customers need them, "they want them in a hurry and on time . . . fast answers get customers."[8] To deal with

---

[8] *Crown Cork & Seal Company and the Metal Container Industry,* p. 28.

rush orders and special requests, Crown made a heavy investment in additional lines which they maintained in setup condition.

Marketing/Service

Crown's sales force, although smaller than American's or Continental's, kept close ties with their customers, and they emphasized technical assistance and specific problem solving at the customer's plant. This was backed by quick manufacturing responses and Connelly's policy that, from the top down, the customer was always right. As *Fortune* described it:

> At Crown, all customers' gripes go to John Connelly, who is still the company's best salesman. A visitor recalls being in his office when a complaint came through from the manager of a Florida citrus-packing plant. Connelly assured him the problem would be taken care of immediately, then casually remarked that he planned to be in Florida the next day. Would the plant manager join him for dinner? He would indeed. As Crown's president put the telephone down, his visitor said that he hadn't realized Connelly was planning to go to Florida. "Neither did I," confessed Connelly, "until I began talking."[9]

Research and Development

Crown's R&D focused on enhancing the existing product line. As Connelly described it:

> We are not truly pioneers. Our philosophy is not to spend a great deal of money for basic research. However, we do have tremendous skills in die forming and metal fabrication, and we can move to adapt to the customer's needs faster than anyone else in the industry.[10]

Research teams worked closely with the sales force, often on specific customer requests. For example, a study of the most efficient plant layout for a food packer or the redesign of a dust cap for the aerosol packager were not unusual projects.

Crown tried to stay away from basic research and "all the frills of an R&D section of high-class ivory-towered scientists." Explained Mr. Luviano, the company's new president:[11]

> There is a tremendous asset inherent in being second, especially in the face of the ever-changing state of flux you find in this industry. You try to let others take the risks and make the mistakes as the big discoveries

---

[9] *Fortune,* October 1962, p. 164.

[10] *Crown Cork & Seal Company and the Metal Container Industry,* p. 30.

[11] Mr. Luviano became president in 1976, while Connelly remained chairman and chief operating officer.

often flop initially due to something unforeseen in the original analysis. But somebody else, learning from the innovator's heartaches, prospers by the refinement.[12]

This was precisely what happened with the two-piece drawn-and-ironed can. The original concept was developed in the aluminum industry by Reynolds and Alcoa in the late 1960s. Realizing its potential, Crown, in connection with a major steel producer, refined the concept for use with tinplate. Because of its small plant manufacturing structure and Connelly's willingness to move fast, Crown was able to beat its competitors into two-piece can production. Almost $120 million in new equipment was invested from 1972 through 1975, and by 1976 Crown had 22 two-piece lines in production, far more than any competitor.[13]

In addition, in its specialized areas, Crown was credited with some important innovations. The company initiated the use of plastic as a substitute for cork as a crown liner, and in 1962 it introduced the first beverage filling machine that could handle both bottles and cans.

Financial

During the crisis Connelly used the first receipts from the inventory liquidation to get out from under the short-term bank obligations. Since 1956 he had steadily reduced the debt-equity ratio from 42 percent to 18.2 percent in 1976.

No dividends were paid after 1956, and in 1970 the last of the preferred stock was bought in, eliminating preferred dividends as a cash drain. Since 1970 the emphasis had been on repurchasing the common stock (see Exhibit 1). Each year Connelly set ambitious earnings goals, and most years he achieved them, reaching $2.84 per share in 1976. The 1976 market was a critical time for Connelly's financial ambitions. He said in the 1976 annual report:

> A long time ago we made a prediction that someday our sales would exceed $1 billion and profits of $60 per share. Since then the stock has been split 20 for 1 so this means $3 per share. These two goals are still our ambition and will remain until both have been accomplished. I am sure that one, and I hope both, will be attained this year [1977].

International

Another aspect of Crown's efforts was its continuing emphasis on international growth, particularly in underdeveloped nations (see Exhibit 6).

---

[12] *Crown Cork & Seal Company and the Metal Container Industry,* p. 29.

[13] In 1976 there were 47 two-piece tinplate and 130 two-piece aluminum lines in the United States.

With sales of $343 million and 60 foreign plant locations, Crown was, by 1977, the largest producer of metal cans and crowns overseas.

In the early 1960s when Crown began its program of expanding internationally, the strategy was unique. At that time Connelly commented:

> Right now we are premature, but this has been necessary in order for Crown to become established in these areas. . . . If we can get 20 percent to 40 percent of all new geographic areas we enter, we have a great growth potential in contrast to American and Continental. . . . In 20 years I hope whoever is running this company will look back and comment on the vision of an early decision to introduce canmaking in underdeveloped countries.[14]

In fact, 10 years later, Crown's overseas position was widely acknowledged to be its "ace in the hole."[15]

In 1976 the international divisions of Crown contributed 36 percent of total company sales and 44 percent of the profits. Growth potential overseas was greater with many countries only recently turning to convenience and packaged foods. There were few entrenched firms, and canning technology was not as well known or understood. Suppliers and customers overseas tended to be smaller than those in the United States.

Margins were particularly good for Crown, and in many cases the company received 10-year tax shelters as initial investment incentives. In addition, manufacturing costs were low as Crown used outmoded but fully depreciated equipment from its U.S. plants. For instance, when the company changed over to the drawn-and-ironed process, much of the three-piece equipment found its way into the foreign operations.

John Connelly—the Person

Many claimed that John Connelly, the person, was the driving force behind Crown's dramatic turnaround and that it was his ambition and determination that kept the company on the road to success. Connelly has been described as a strong-willed individual whose energetic leadership has convinced and inspired his organization to meet his goals.

Yet Connelly was no easy man to please. He demanded from his employees the same dedication and energy that he himself threw into his work. As one observer wrote in 1962:

> At 57 Connelly is a trim, dark-haired doer. The 7-day, 80-hour weeks of the frenetic early days are only slightly reduced now. The Saturday morning meeting is standard operating procedure. Crown's executives travel and confer only at night and on weekends. William D. Wallace, vice president for operations, travels 100,000 miles a year, often in the company plane.

---

[14] *Crown Cork & Seal and the Metal Container Industry,* p. 33.

[15] *Forbes,* September 1, 1967, p. 19.

But Connelly sets the pace. An associate recalls driving to his home in the predawn blackness to pick him up for a flight to a distant plant. The Connelly house was dark, but he spotted a figure sitting on the curb under a street light, engrossed in a looseleaf book. Connelly's greeting, as he jumped into the car: "I want to talk to you about last month's variances."[16]

At 72 Connelly still firmly held the reins of his company.[17] "He'll never retire. He'll die with his boots on," noted one company official.[18] Although he raised John Luviano, 54 (a 25-year veteran at Crown) to the presidency, Connelly's continued presence was a concern of many who watched Crown Cork: "If Connelly wasn't around, we would question who would make those absolutely perfect strategic decisions."[19]

Outlook for the Future

In 1977 observers of Crown Cork & Seal had a favorite question: "How long can this spectacular performance last?" Up to then, Crown's sales and profit growth had continued despite recession, devaluation, and stiff competition from the giants of the industry. However, by 1977 two additional issues had surfaced which directly affected the company's key markets. The ozone scare and the potential legislation on nonreturnable containers threatened the company's beverage and aerosol business. As a result, many wondered if government action might not pull the plug on Crown Cork.

The Ozone Controversy

In 1973 two University of California chemists advanced the initial theory that fluorocarbons, a gas used in refrigerators, air conditioners, and as a propellant in aerosols, were damaging the earth's ozone shield. Ozone formed an atmospheric layer that prevented much of the sun's ultraviolet radiation from reaching the earth's surface. The theory was that the fluorocarbons floated up into the stratosphere where they broke up, releasing chlorine atoms. These atoms then reacted with the ozone molecules causing their destruction. The problem was compounded because after the reaction the chlorine atom was free to attack other ozone molecules causing accelerated breakup of the ozone layer. Proponents of the theory asserted that "fluorocarbons have already depleted ozone by 1 percent and will eventually deplete it by 7 percent to 13 percent perhaps within 50 to 80 years if the use of fluorocarbons continues at recent levels."[20]

---

[16] *Fortune,* October 1962, p. 163.

[17] Connelly reportedly owned or controlled about 18 percent of Crown's outstanding common stock.

[18] *Financial World,* November 26, 1975, p. 12.

[19] Ibid.

[20] *The Wall Street Journal,* December 3, 1975, p. 27.

The Dangers

The theory argued that there was real danger in allowing the destruction of the ozone shield. Ozone filtered out most of the sun's harmful ultra-violet radiation before it could reach the earth's surface. As this shield was depleted and more radiation passed through, the number of cases of skin cancer were expected to rise alarmingly. Dr. Sherwood Rowland, one of the original proponents of the theory, predicted:

> If aerosol use were to grow at 10 percent annually (half the growth rate of the 1960s), stratospheric ozone content would fall by 10 percent by 1994. Scientists figure this would mean a 20 percent increase in ultraviolet radiation reaching the earth and cause by itself at least 60,000 new cases of skin cancer annually in the United States, roughly a 20 percent increase.[21]

Other possible dangers were crop damage, genetic mutation, and climatic change.

Although many studies were in progress, by the end of 1976 the ozone theory had not yet been conclusively proven. There were still some major questions about the types and amounts of reactions that would take place in the stratosphere. Nonetheless, most subsequent tests supported the basic thesis that fluorocarbons were in some way damaging the ozone layer.

Effects

After the ozone theory was publicized, the reaction against aerosols was severe. Aerosols provided about 60 percent of the fluorocarbons released into the air annually. In 1974 aerosol production was off almost 7 percent in reaction to the recession and the fluorocarbon problem. Only 2.6 billion aerosol containers were used, down from 2.9 billion in 1973. Action began immediately on both legislative and scientific fronts to test the ozone theory and restrict the use of fluorocarbons.

Soon a bitter battle broke out between industry spokespeople and those advocating an immediate ban. One industry spokesman, who requested anonymity, said:

> All the scientific theories against fluorocarbons are just that—theories, not facts. What we need is more research before there are any more bans or badmouthing. We don't want another false scare.[22]

A member of the Nature Resource Defense Council looked harshly upon the aerosol industry's tactics: "It's like Watergate," he said. "They want to see a smoking gun. We'll have to wait 25 years for that, and by then the irreparable damage will have been done."[23]

---

[21] Ibid.

[22] *The New York Times,* June 22, 1975, p. F3.

[23] Ibid.

Despite industry protests and with the support of some additional studies, state legislators began to introduce antifluorocarbon bills. Georgia led the way in June 1975 by passing a bill banning fluorocarbon aerosols effective March 1, 1977. Effective industry lobbying kept other actions to a minimum until May 1977 when federal agencies proposed a nationwide ban. Calling fluorocarbons an "unacceptable risk to individual health and to the earth's atmosphere," the commissioner of Food and Drugs outlined a three-step phase out of fluorocarbon manufacture and use.[24] The first step in the ban was to be a halt to all manufacture of chlorofluorocarbon propellants for nonessential uses. This ban would take effect October 15, 1978. In the second step, on December 15, 1978, all companies would have to stop using existing supplies of the chemicals in making nonessential aerosol products. The third step would be to halt all interstate shipment of nonessential products containing the propellant gases. This part of the ban would go into effect April 15, 1979.[25]

The Future for Aerosols

Opinions differed widely as to the extent of the problems the ozone issue would cause the industry. By 1977 the latest estimates were that the fluorocarbon ban would cost container manufacturers over $132 million in lost sales from 1977 to 1980. This was much less than most of the original estimates due to the success of efforts in the last two years in finding fluorocarbon substitutes. Most of these solutions centered around finding substitute propellants or changing the aerosol valve.

New Propellants. A propellant was the pressurized gas used to hold the suspended molecules of aerosol products as they were sprayed out. Up to the early 1970s the most common propellant material was fluorocarbon which was used in about half of the aerosol cans sold. By 1977 the possibility of substituting hydrocarbons was being explored for many applications. However, although they were less expensive, hydrocarbons were more flammable and thus more dangerous to mix with many personal care products that included alcohol. Other proposed alternatives included carbon dioxide and special pressurized cans that did not release propellants at all.

Changing the Valve. In May 1977 one of the most promising ways of eliminating fluorocarbons was the new Aquasol valve. Developed by Robert Abplanalp, the inventor of the original aerosol valve, the Aquasol used a dual duct system (versus the traditional one duct) that kept the product separate from the propellant. Abplanalp claimed that fillers could get twice as much product into a can with a new valve as it did not

---

[24] *The New York Times,* May 12, 1977, p. 1.

[25] Ibid.

have to be mixed with the propellant. This also meant hydrocarbons could be used more safely for many applications.

Industry Recovery

By 1977 recovery had already begun in the aerosol market with shipments for 1976 up 6 percent. It seemed likely that this trend would continue because of the strong appeal aerosols had for the consumer. In a 1974 study over 59 percent of the population had heard of the ozone problem, yet about 25 percent said they would be "very disturbed to do without" aerosol products. Industry optimism was moderated, however, by the growing popularity of pump sprays and other nonaerosol products and by the tendency of the consumer not to differentiate between fluorocarbons and aerosols using other propellants.

Regulating Nonreturnable Containers

The second major threat to Crown's future was the potential legislative restrictions on the use of nonreturnable containers. In 1977 several states had already regulated the use of disposable containers. Laws requiring mandatory deposits for most beverage containers were approved in November 1976 by voter referendums in Maine and Michigan. Three other states, Oregon, Vermont, and South Dakota, already had such laws while they were turned down by narrow margins in Massachusetts and Colorado. The existing laws required a five-cent deposit on all bottles and cans, refundable when the empties were brought back for recycling or reuse. Nationally, the federal Environmental Protection Agency banned throwaways from federal property—parks, federal buildings, and military posts—starting in October 1977.

The main problem was litter. Although it was estimated that only 1 percent of the American population were litterers, the extent of the damage was staggering. Unfortunately, disposable cans contributed significantly to the problem. While containers made up only 8 percent of the solid waste in the United States, they made up 54 percent to 70 percent of highway litter by volume. A second issue was the potential savings of raw materials and energy that could be obtained from reusing containers.

Economic Impact

Part of the controversy centered around the potential economic impact of legislative bans on nonreturnables. Industry sources agreed that the laws would bring an increase in beer and soft-drink prices and eliminate thousands of jobs. The environmentalists countered that consumers paid

30 percent to 40 percent more for beverages in throwaway containers. "Any increased cost due to retooling would be offset by savings in the use of returnable bottles or recycled cans," claimed Mr. Washington of the Michigan United Conservation Clubs. He added that "any jobs lost in the canning or bottling industries would be offset by additional jobs in transportation and handling."[26]

Prospects for the Future

Despite a powerful industry lobby, the fight against nonreturnables was gaining momentum. In July 1977 legislation was being considered by the congressional Committee on Energy and Natural Resources to require deposits on throwaways nationwide. Although the Senate had once rejected a ban on pull tops, some states, including Massachusetts, had passed such bills effective in 1978. Returnable bottles which could be used by more than one manufacturer were being encouraged under the new laws, but it seemed unlikely that cans would be totally banned. Instead, various schemes for deposits and recycling were being emphasized. Metal cans would be collected, crushed, melted, and reused to make new cans. Under the new system it was uncertain who would pay the extra transportation costs and whether lower raw material prices to the canmaker would result. Unfortunately for tinplate users like Crown, the new system favored aluminum cans due to the higher value of the reclaimed metal and the recycling network that already existed for aluminum products.

Crown's Future Growth

Domestically Crown's usual optimistic forecasts continued into 1977. The 1976 annual report all but ignored the aerosol and bottle bill issues. The strategy stayed the same: no major basic R&D efforts but quick attention to customer needs and leadership in new applications, such as the drawn-and-ironed process, which involved the traditional metal can. Thus, despite current problems in its markets, many observers saw no reason why the company's good record wouldn't continue:

> Even with Connelly's eventual retirement, his No. 2 man seems certain to keep Crown on its upward profits growth trend. While others—like National Can—have ventured into uncharted and at times unprofitable waters, Crown has prospered by doing what it knows best. Under that strategy, prosperity is likely to continue reigning for Crown.[27]

---

[26] *The New York Times,* October 30, 1976, p. F1.

[27] *Financial World,* November 26, 1975, p. 12.

Exhibit 1

CROWN CORK & SEAL COMPANY, INC.
Financial Statements, 1956–1976
(dollars in thousands)

	1976	1975	1974	1973	1972	1971	1966	1961	1956
Net sales	$909,937	$825,007	$766,158	$571,762	$488,880	$448,446	$279,830	$176,992	$115,098
Cost of products sold (excluding depreciation)	$757,866	$683,691	$628,865	$459,183	$387,768	$350,867	$217,236	$139,071	$ 95,803
Selling and administrative expense	$ 31,910	$ 30,102	$ 28,649	$ 23,409	$ 20,883	$ 21,090	$ 18,355	$ 15,311	$ 13,506
Percent of net sales	3.5%	3.6%	3.7%	4.1%	4.3%	4.7%	6.6%	8.7%	11.7%
Interest expense	$ 3,885	$ 7,374	$ 6,973	$ 4,407	$ 4,222	$ 5,121	$ 4,551	$ 1,252	$ 1,150
Depreciation expense	$ 26,486	$ 25,402	$ 25,525	$ 20,930	$ 18,654	$ 16,981	$ 9,381	$ 4,627	$ 2,577
Taxes on income	$ 43,500	$ 34,925	$ 33,298	$ 26,725	$ 24,900	$ 24,560	$ 12,680	$ 7,625	$ 105
Net income	$ 46,183	$ 41,611	$ 39,663	$ 34,288	$ 31,193	$ 28,474	$ 16,749	$ 6,653	$ 277
Percent of net sales	5.1%	5.0%	5.2%	6.0%	6.4%	6.3%	6.0%	3.8%	0.2%
Earnings per share of common stock	$ 2.84	$ 2.43	$ 2.20	$ 1.81	$ 1.58	$ 1.41	$ 0.80	$ 0.28	$ (0.01)
Plant and equipment:									
Expenditures	$ 21,568	$ 47,047	$ 52,517	$ 40,392	$ 28,261	$ 33,099	$ 32,729	$ 11,819	$ 1,931
Accumulated investment	$398,377	$401,657	$371,297	$335,047	$316,266	$313,214	$223,153	$107,258	$ 65,196
Accumulated depreciation	$149,306	$143,406	$129,924	$116,191	$105,377	$101,314	$ 68,359	$ 45,004	$ 31,167
Current asset/liability ratio	1.8	1.6	1.4	1.6	1.7	1.6	1.5	2.7	3.2
Long-term debt	$ 25,886	$ 29,679	$ 34,413	$ 37,922	$ 31,234	$ 41,680	$ 57,890	$ 17,654	$ 21,400
Short-term debt	$ 2,984	$ 30,419	$ 45,043	$ 28,504	$ 17,221	$ 31,381	$ 44,784	$ 5,190	$ 6,500
Shareholders' investment	$316,684	$292,681	$262,650	$243,916	$230,366	$211,847	$110,841	$ 77,540	$ 50,299
Preferred shares	0	0	0	0	0	0	79,370	139,540	275,000
Common shares—average	16,235,040	17,137,030	18,000,792	18,894,105	19,726,799	20,211,810	20,606,835	21,594,720	24,155,800

Source: Crown Cork & Seal Company, Inc., 1976 annual report, pp. 4, 5.

Exhibit 2

Beverage Can Shipments (Million cans)

	1972	1973	Percent Change 1972–73	1974	Percent Change 1973–74
Soft-drink cans:					
Total	15,596	17,552	+12.5%	17,980	+ 2.4%
Three-piece	14,217	15,779	+11.0	15,589	− 1.2
Percent of total	91.2%	89.9%	—	86.7%	—
Two-piece	1,379	1,773	+28.6	2,391	+34.9
Percent of total	8.8%	10.1%	—	13.3%	—
Beer cans:					
Total	21,801	24,131	+10.7	26,077	+ 8.1
Three-piece	14,746	14,363	− 2.6	13,237	− 7.8
Percent of total	67.6%	59.5%	—	50.8%	—
Two-piece	7,055	9,768	+38.5	12,840	+31.4
Percent of total	32.4%	40.5%	—	49.2%	—

Source: Can Manufacturers Institute, *Metal Cans Shipments Report 1974,* p. 6.

Exhibit 3

Comparison of 1976 Performance of Major Metal Can Manufacturers
(Dollars in millions)

	Continental Group	American Can	National Can	Crown Cork & Seal
Total company performance:				
Sales	$3,458.0	$3,143.0	$917.0	$910.0
Net income	$ 118.3	$ 100.9	$ 20.7	$ 46.2
Sales growth, 1967–76	147.0%	107.0%	317.0%	202.0%
Profit growth, 1967–76	51.0%	33.0%	160.0%	145.0%
Return on equity, 5-year average	10.3%	7.1%	11.9%	15.8%
Debt-equity ratio	34.0%	35.0%	46.0%	23.0%
Metal can segments (domestic):				
Sales	$1,307.8	$1,177.6	$616.0	$575.00
Pretax income	$ 73.0	$ 64.9	$ 36.4	$ 49.00
As percent of sales	5.6%	5.4%	5.0%	8.5%
Market share	18.4%	16.6%	8.7%	8.3%
Number of can plants	70	48	41	26
International:*				
Sales	$1,147.2	$ 475.1	n.a.	$343.0
Net income (before taxes)	$ 63.4	$ 41.5	Small loss	$ 39.4

n.a. = Not available.
* International sales of *all* products.
Sources: *Wall Street Transcript,* November 3, 1975, pp. 41, 864, and company 10-K reports.

Exhibit 4

Metal Can Shipments (Million base banks used in manufacturing)

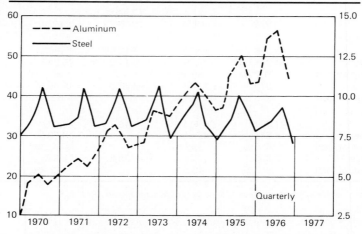

Source: Standard & Poor's Industry Survey, *Containers, Basic Analysis,* March 24, 1977, p. C123.

Exhibit 5

Estimated Breakdown of Crown Cork & Seal's Sales and Pretax Income
(Dollars in millions)

	1974	1975	1976*	1974	1975	1976*
Sales:						
Domestic:						
Cans:						
Beer	$180	$209	$232	23.5%	24.7%	24.6%
Soft drinks	120	128	140	15.7	15.2	14.8
Food	55	65	70	7.2	7.7	7.4
Other (mainly aerosols)	100	91	101	13.0	10.7	10.7
Total cans	455	493	543	59.4	58.3	57.5
Crowns	25	29	32	3.3	3.4	3.4
Machinery	20	24	27	2.6	2.8	2.8
Total domestic	500	546	602	65.3	64.5	63.7
International:						
Cans	46	57	73	6.0	6.7	7.7
Crowns	200	220	242	26.1	30.0	25.6
Machinery	20	24	28	2.6	2.8	3.0
Total international	266	301	343	34.7	35.5	36.3
Grand total sales	$766	$847	$945*	100.0%	100.0%	100.0%
Pretax income:						
Domestic:						
Cans	$ 41.0	$ 43.0	$ 46.0	53.9%	52.2%	50.9%
Crowns	2.0	2.0	3.0	2.6	2.4	3.3
Machinery	1.5	2.0	2.0	2.0	2.4	2.2
Total domestic	44.5	47.0	51.0	58.5	57.0	56.4
International:						
Cans	4.0	6.0	8.0	5.3	7.3	8.9
Crowns	25.6	26.4	28.4	33.6	32.1	31.4
Machinery	2.0	3.0	3.0	2.6	3.6	3.3
Total international	31.6	35.4	39.4	41.5	43.0	43.6
Grand total pretax income	$ 76.1	$ 82.4	$ 90.4	100.0%	100.0%	100.0%
Pretax margins:						
Domestic:						
Cans				9.0%	8.7%	8.5%
Crowns				8.0	6.9	9.4
Machinery				7.5	8.3	7.4
Total domestic				8.9	8.6	8.5
International:						
Cans				8.6	12.5	11.0
Crowns				13.0	12.3	11.6
Machinery				10.0	12.5	10.7
Total international				11.9	11.8	11.5
Grand total pretax margins				9.9%	9.7%	9.6%

* 1976 figures are estimated and thus do not match actual numbers on other exhibits.
Source: *Wall Street Transcript,* November 3, 1975, pp. 41, 865.

Exhibit 6   **Locations of Crown Cork & Seal's Facilities**

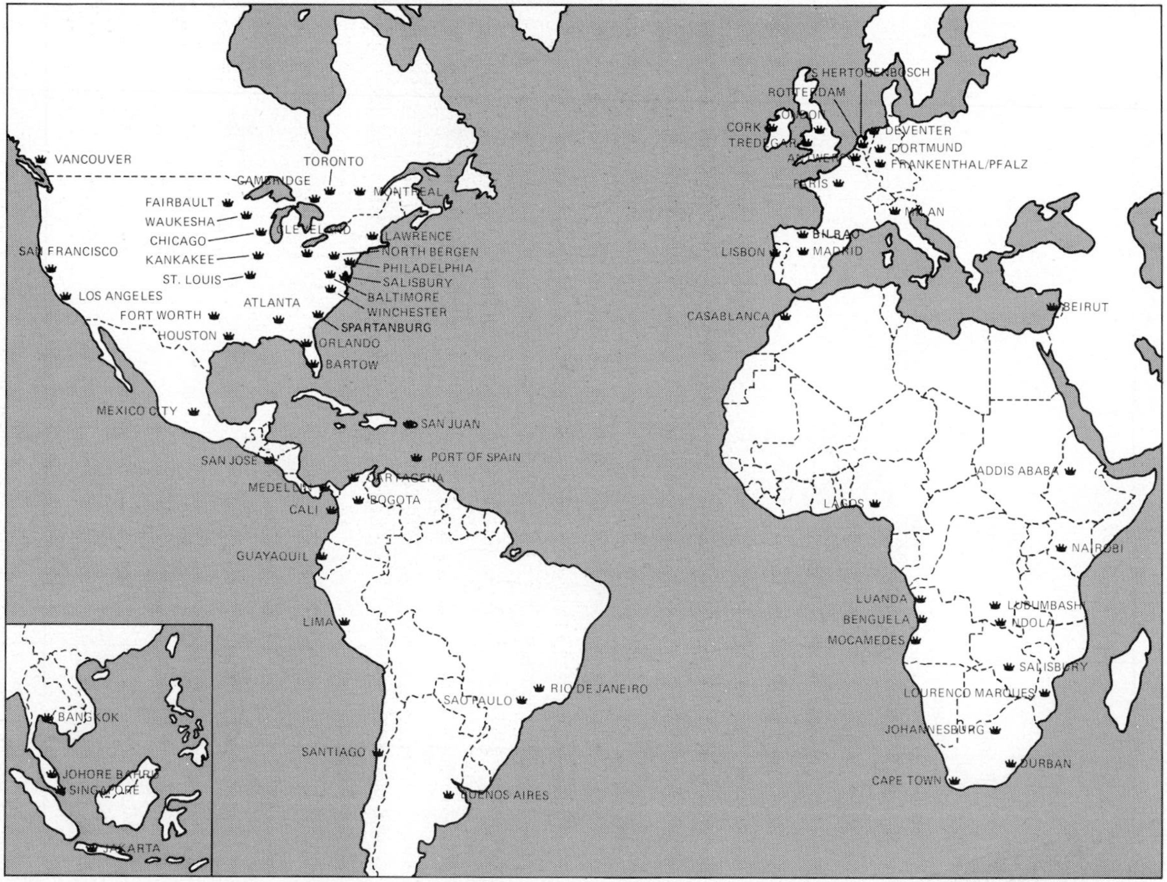

Source: Crown Cork & Seal Company, Inc., 1972 annual report.

BIC Pen Corporation (A)

Described by an economic observer as "one of the classic success stories in American business," the BIC Pen Corporation was widely acknowledged as a leader in the mechanical writing instrument industry in 1973. "The success was dramatic," the observer had said, "because it was achieved from the residue of a deficit-ridden predecessor company, over a short period . . . , in the extremely competitive, low-price sector of the industry. 'BIC' had become a generic name for inexpensive ball-point pens."

Mr. Robert Adler, president of BIC, was extremely proud of the firm's success, which he attributed to "numerous and good management decisions based 40 percent on science and 60 percent on intuition." BIC had reported its first profit in 1964 based on net sales of $6.2 million. Over the following nine years, net sales increased at a compounded rate of 28.2 percent, and the weighted average aftertax profit as a percentage of net sales was 13.2 percent. (See Exhibits 1–3 for a summary of financial data from 1964–73.)

Until 1972, BIC concentrated exclusively on the design, manufacture, and distribution of a complete line of inexpensive ball-point pen products. The most successful pen was the 19-cent Crystal, which accounted for over 40 percent of BIC's unit sales in ball-point pens and about 15 percent of industry unit sales in ball-point pens in 1972. That same year, BIC expanded its writing instrument product line to include a fine line porous point pen. In 1973, it added a disposable cigarette lighter.

Copyright © 1974 by the President and Fellows of Harvard College
Harvard Business School case 374–305

Company History

The name "Waterman" meant a writing instrument since Mr. Louis Waterman invented the first practical fountain pen in 1875. For many years, the Waterman Pen Company led the world in the manufacture of fountain pens. But in the late 1950s, when the shift to ball-point pens swept the United States, the Waterman Company continued to concentrate on its fountain pen line, and its performance slipped substantially.

In 1958 M. Marcel Bich, a French businessman well established as a leading European pen maker, bought the facilities, trademark, and patent rights of the ailing Waterman Company, which then became the Waterman-BIC Pen Company. Believing strongly that the ball-point pen was the writing instrument of the future, M. Bich established the objective of becoming the leading firm in the low-price disposable ball-point pen industry. To obtain that position, management proposed the use of forceful consumer advertising and mass distribution policies.

At the time of M. Bich's purchase of Waterman, ball-point pens constituted only 8 percent of Waterman's unit sales. By 1964, however, all fountain pen and ink products had been eliminated, and most sales came from the 19-cent stick-type ball-point pen. The conversion process was costly, as reflected in the five years of deficits (1959–63). BIC reached its turning point in 1964, marked by the national success of its Crystal pen.

From 1964 through 1973 the company expanded its ball-point pen line to include 12 models of retractable and nonretractable pens offered in varying point sizes, ink colors, and barrel colors at retail prices between 19 cents and $1. A 29-cent fine line porous point pen was added in 1972 and a $1.49 disposable butane cigarette lighter in 1973. In addition to product line expansion, BIC established a 100 percent-owned operation in Canada (1967), joint ventures in Japan (1972) and Mexico (1973), and a distributor arrangement with a firm in Panama (1973).

On May 1, 1971, the company changed its name to the BIC Pen Corporation. The Waterman trademark was subsequently sold to a Zurich firm, and BIC went public with an offering of 655,000 shares of common stock listed at $25 per share on the American Stock Exchange. In 1973, BIC's parent company, Société Bic, S.A., held 62 percent of the BIC stock.

Men of Influence

M. Marcel Bich

M. Marcel Bich has been described as having done for ball-point pens what Henry Ford did for cars: produce a cheap but serviceable model.

In 1945 Bich and his friend Edouard Buffard pooled their wealth—all of $1,000—and started making ball-point refills in an old factory near Paris. Soon it occurred to Bich that a disposable pen that needed no refills would be more to the point. What his country needed, as Bich saw it, was a good 10-cent pen. Today the cheapest throwaway BIC sells for close to that in France—about 7 cents. In the United States the same pen retails for 19 cents, and it is the biggest seller on the market. . . .

Marcel Bich is a stubborn, opinionated entrepreneur who inherited his title from his forebears in the predominantly French-speaking Val D'Aoste region of northern Italy. He abhors technocrats, computers, and borrowing money. At 58, he attributes his business successes to his refusal to listen to almost anyone's advice but his own. Bich says that his philosophy has been to "concentrate on one product, used by everyone every day." Now, however, he is moving toward diversification. A disposable BIC cigarette lighter that gives 3,000 lights is being test marketed in Sweden; if it proves out, Bich plans to sell it for less than 90 cents. . . .

In the United States, Bich is best known for his fiasco in the 1970 America's Cup Race: His sloop *France,* which he captained, got lost in the fog off Newport. He speaks in aquatic terms even when describing his company: "We just try to stick close to reality, like a surfer to his board. We don't lean forward or backward too far or too fast. We ride the wave at the right moment."[1]

Société Bic, S.A., was known as a "one-man empire" which in 1972 accounted for a third of the ball-point pen sales worldwide and included full operations in 19 countries. M. Bich's personal holdings were estimated to be worth about $200 million. "The only way he could control his empire," BIC's treasurer Mr. Alexander Alexiades had said, "was to have certain rules and guidelines. All Société Bic companies were quite autonomous once they had become consistent with his philosophies."

BIC Pen Corporation had been characterized as the "jewel in M. Bich's crown." In the firm's early years, M. Bich had provided much of the machinery, production techniques, and supplies from the French parent company. By 1973 the only substantial business exchange which still remained between the two firms was in research and development. One of the few visible signs of the American company's European heritage was the Renaissance artwork which M. Bich had hung in BIC's reception and board rooms.

Mr. Robert Adler

In 1955, the day after Connecticut's Naugatuck River raged out of control and flooded the countryside, Mr. Adler reported to work at the old Waterman Pen Company as a newly hired junior accountant fresh out of Pennsylvania's Wharton School of Finance. Instead of being shown

---

[1] "Going Bananas over BIC," *Time,* December 18, 1972, p. 93.

to his desk and calculating machine, he was handed a shovel and ordered to help clean out the mud which had collected in the plant during the flood. Nine years later, at the age of 31, he became president of the Waterman-BIC Pen Corporation, which under his leadership became the largest ball-point pen manufacturer and distributor in North America. Mr. Adler was described by a business associate as:

> A president who liked to be totally familiar with and completely immersed in every area of his company's operations, one who felt that he should never quash his instincts with an overdependency on numbers and facts alone . . . a shirt-sleeved president who made it his personal concern to know intimately every facet of the BIC marketing and manufacturing process, including highly technical matters involving complex moulding equipment, advanced production techniques, merchandising, advertising, and sales . . . a do-it-yourself investigator-president who regularly made the rounds of the plant, keeping himself available at all times.

Mr. Adler had stated that he personally selected his colleagues on the basis that they demonstrated aggressiveness and an unswerving belief and conviction that they were serving a company that produced the world's finest writing instruments—products of exceptional quality and value. "A businessman is born, not made," he said, "and education can only enhance and refine what already exists." He attributed much of BIC's success to the fact that in the firm's early years he had consciously hired persons who were unfamiliar with the industry and who therefore did not question BIC's ability to succeed by selling an inexpensive ball-point pen via extensive advertising. He emphasized the importance of his own role in determining BIC's performance by stating:

> A lot of decisions are easy because there is only one way to go. Sometimes you're lucky and sometimes, no matter what, you'll get the same outcome. A president gets paid to make decisions. That's his big job. What's important is once a decision is made is to make sure that it comes out right. The decision is not so important; it's the outcome. A president must say to himself: "I will now make my decision successful."

Writing Instrument Product Line

The BIC Pen Corporation manufactured and sold inexpensive writing instruments in a variety of shapes: stick or pocket pen; ink colors, 1–10; point sizes, medium or fine; and retail prices, 19 cents–$1. All retractable pens were produced in a pocket pen shape; all nonretractables in a stick shape.

The most successful product, the Crystal, accounted for over 40 percent of all ball-point pen units sold in North America. Its sister product, the 25-cent Fine Point Pen, which differed from the Crystal only in point size, accounted for over 15 percent of all ball-point pen units sold.

Table 1

1973 Writing Instrument Product Line

Product Name	Ink Colors	Point Sizes	Retail Price
Ball-point pens:			
Nonretractable/nonrefillable:			
Crystal	4	m	$0.19
Fine Point	4	f	0.25
Reproduction	4	m	0.25
Eraser	4	m,f	0.25
Deluxe Eraser	4	m,f	0.29
Deluxe	4	m	0.39
Accountant	4	f	0.49
Retractable/refillable:			
Clic	4	m,f	0.49
2-Color Pen	2	m,f	0.69
4-Color Pen	4	m,f	0.98
Citation	1	m	1.00
Retractable/nonrefillable:			
Pocket Pen	3	m	0.29
Fine line porous point pen:			
BIC Banana	10	m,f	0.29

Source: Corporate records.

In 1973, writing instruments accounted for approximately 90 percent of BIC's consolidated net sales. Nonretractable pens accounted for 80 percent of the writing instrument unit sales, retractable pens for 6 percent, fine line porous point pens for 12 percent, and refills for 2 percent.

Table 1 presents the 1973 BIC writing instrument product line.

Nonretractable Ball-Point Pens

The Crystal, a nonretractable/nonrefillable ball-point pen, was introduced on the market in 1959 at a retail price of 29 cents. As the first product of the newly formed Waterman-BIC Corporation, the BIC Crystal was intended to become a "brand name replacement for all no-name,[2] disposable pens in a market where no dominant competitor existed." Its retail price was dropped to 19 cents in 1961. In commenting on the success of the Crystal, Mr. Jack Paige, vice president of marketing, remarked:

> We built this company on the 19-cent pen. In 1961 it was selling for 19 cents, and in 1973 it is still 19 cents. One third of all retail sales are from the 19-cent stick. It's a highly profitable business. We've found ways to become more efficient and still maintain our profitability.

---

[2] No-name products were those which were not advertised and were marketed at retail prices far below the comparable, inexpensive, nationally advertised products.

Between 1961 and 1968, BIC expanded its nonretractable ball-point pen line to include six other models of varying point sizes, ink colors, and usages. Nonretractables were priced from 19 cents to 49 cents.

Retractable Ball-Point Pens

In 1968 BIC introduced its first retractable/refillable ball-point pen, the 49-cent Clic.[3] Management felt that the Clic would (1) improve the overall corporate profit margin, (2) enable the company to sell merchandise in multipacks (quantity selling in one package), such as for school specials, and (3) increase distribution—as some retail outlets, particularly those not dependent on BIC for their profits—had been reluctant to sell the 19-cent and 25-cent pens.

Following the Clic, four other retractable ball-point pens were added to the BIC product line. Three imported French pens: the 98-cent 4-Color Pen (1971), the 69-cent 2-Color Pen (1972), and $1 Citation Pen (1973) were introduced to "upgrade ball-point pen sales." The 29-cent Pocket Pen, the only nonrefillable pen in the retractable line, was added to "expand primary demand for ball-point pens."[4]

Fine Line Porous Point Pens

In April of 1972 BIC introduced its first nonball-point pen product, the 29-cent BIC Banana, which was a fine line porous point pen produced in a stick shape. Mr. Paige commented on the Banana decision:

> The development of the concept of entering the porous point pen market was not a sudden decision. Our philosophy was simply that as soon as we had a porous point pen that would reflect BIC quality and could be mass marketed at a popular price that anybody could afford, we would then move into that business.
>
> For openers, we were faced with a couple of major problems. First we were a late entry and the market was dominated by a 49-cent strong brand name of good quality that had a 50 percent market share. Maybe for some companies that stark statistic would have been enough not to enter. However, at BIC there is an aggressive attitude about marketing. That attitude manifested itself a year and a half ago when we began plotting our sales course for the introduction of this new product. (BIC spent $3 million on advertising the BIC Banana in 1972.) We took the attitude that we weren't going to be squeezed into that remaining 50 percent share that the leading brand left for the rest of the field. Our plan was to expand the consumer market

---

[3] In retractable pens, industry sales volume in dollars was concentrated in the high-priced products and in units in the no-name brands.

[4] Despite a major introductory campaign ($1.5 million spent on advertising), sales in the Pocket Pen were "disappointing," according to one company spokesman. He attributed the poor results to styling problems and a lack of room for new products in a market with a declining sales growth rate.

for this type of writing instrument—to make it grow. In a larger market, we felt we would have the opportunity to build a franchise that would give us a substantial share.

In reviewing the same product decision, Mr. Alexiades said:

In 1966 we saw the product opportunity for the soft tip pen, but Marcel Bich owned 90 percent of the company, and we had a difficult time convincing him that this was the right approach. He thought that the soft tip pen was a passing thing and that it was impractical because it wouldn't write through carbon. But we're in a carbon society and there's no logical explanation for the consumer. However, M. Bich's philosophy changed. Years ago, he only wanted to sell ball-point pens. He's now interested in inexpensive, disposable, mass-produced items. He has the marketing know-how, the distribution, the name.

We saw that the porous point pen was not a fad so we got in, perhaps a little late, but at least we entered an expanding portion of the market. The growth rate of ball-point pen sales had leveled off. If we didn't enter the porous pen market, it would have been difficult to grow since we're so dominant in the industry. We knew that the only way to grow was through product line diversification or acquisition.

Our objective is to become the largest producer of fine line porous point pens. We are in ball-point pens. It might be difficult because Gillette's Flair has been there for five years. Papermate brand is not a no-name brand with no resources like those which we initially attacked in the ball-point pen market.

A competitor commented on the market entry of the BIC Banana:

Many people associated BIC with the ball-point pen. BIC had a difficult time because people thought that the Banana was a ball point. It's a stick shape and looks like a ball point. They don't have that problem with the lighter (1973) because it is a different looking product altogether. BIC hasn't done well with the Banana against the Flair. After all, who could enter the stick pen market now and do well against BIC? But at least BIC broke the price point (49 cents) with its 29-cent point which softened the retail and commercial markets. Maybe they'll get smart and get out.

The Markets

Mr. Adler's philosophy had always been "to sell BIC products wherever there was a doorknob." Consistent with that view, marketing efforts had been focused on all writing instrument markets, with special emphasis placed on the "four key sales volume opportunities": the retail, commercial, ad/specialty, and premium markets, which represented about 90 percent of the dollar sales volume in the writing instrument industry in 1973. The other three markets, government, military, and export, accounted for the remaining 10 percent. In 1973 the Writing Instrument Manufacturers Association estimated total industry sales at $353.3 million.

Retail Market

The retail market, or over-the-counter market, was the largest mechanical writing instrument market, accounting for over 50 percent, or $176.6 million, of the total industry dollar sales in 1973. Of significance in the retail market was the growing trend away from indirect selling through retail distributors to independent stores toward direct selling from the manufacturers to mass merchandise outlets.

Since the national success of the 19-cent Crystal pen in 1964, BIC had completely dominated the ball-point pen segment of the retail market. By the end of 1973, BIC held a 66 percent share of that segment, followed by Gillette with 15 percent and Lindy with 5 percent. In fine line porous point pens, Gillette was the front-runner with a 35 percent share followed by BIC with 22 percent, Magic Marker with 8 percent, and Pentel with 5 percent.

Management attributed BIC's successful penetration of the retail market to its aggressive marketing and distribution policies as well as to the low price and high quality of its products.

Commercial Market

The commercial market, or office supply market, was the second largest mechanical writing instrument market, accounting for about 20 percent, or $70.6 million, of total industry sales in 1973. Selling in the commercial market was primarily handled through commercial distributors, who channeled products from the manufacturers to office supply dealers, who in turn sold to commercial customers. Large office supply dealers bought directly from manufacturers and used distributors to fill in inventory gaps.

At the end of 1973 management estimated that the leading market shareholders in ball-point pens in the commercial market were BIC with 50 percent, followed by Berol with 18 percent and Gillette with 5 percent. In fine line porous point pens, it was estimated that Gillette held a 40 percent share, Berol 25 percent, Pentel 10 percent, and BIC 4.5 percent.

In commenting on BIC's 4.5 percent market share in fine line porous point pens, Mr. Adler said:

> We have had difficulty in the commercial market because that market is conditioned to something like the Flair, Pentel, or Berol porous pens which sell for 49 cents and allow good margins to the distributors. The model which BIC manufactures does not compete head on with is the Flair. Ours is a stick model; theirs is a pocket model. Because of the design of the product, it's difficult to get a certain percentage of the market. The Flair product costs twice as much to manufacture (has a clip, etc.). The 29-cent Write-Brothers also has a clip. For us, we're a long way from being Number 1. To get into the porous pen business, we had to use the stick

model. Our problem is that the distributors do not want to push the Banana because they have a 49-cent market. Naturally, they make less on a 29-cent model. It will take time.

Advertising/Specialty and Premium Markets

The ad/specialty and premium markets together accounted for approximately 20 percent, or $70.6 million, of the total industry dollar sales volume in 1973.

Ad/specialty sales referred to special orders made through specialized distributors for products imprinted with a slogan or organization name. Competition in the ad/specialty market was based heavily on price, which accounted for the strength of the no-name brands in that market. BIC held close to a 5 percent share in the ad/specialty market in 1973.

A premium was defined as a free promotional item which was attached to another product in order to promote the sale of that product. Premium sales were made through distributors or direct from the manufacturer to customer. As in the ad/specialty market, competition was based upon price. Unlike that market, it was also based upon brand recognition and included a broader base of product types, not just writing instruments. Although it was a small market, management considered BIC's participation in the premium market as important in "reinforcing the firm's dominant position in the pen business." BIC held close to a 100 percent market share among writing instrument firms in the premium market in 1973.

The Competition

In 1973 approximately 200 firms were engaged in the manufacture and sale of mechanical writing instruments in the United States. Most firms competed selectively in the industry on the basis of (1) product type: fountain pen, mechanical pencil, ball-point pen, or soft tip pen; (2) price range: high (>$1), medium (50 cents–$1.00), and low (<50 cents); and (3) market: retail, commercial, ad/specialty, premium, military, government, and export. Strong advertising programs and mass-distribution networks were considered critical for national success.

In management's view, BIC had four major writing instrument competitors: Berol, Gillette, Lindy, and Pentel.[5] The five firms competed at the following price points with similar products. (See Table 2.)

---

[5] The Magic Marker Corporation was considered a strong competitor in fine line porous point pens with four models selling from 19 cents to 49 cents and comprising an estimated 8 percent share of the retail market. However, Magic Marker was best known for its broad tip markers (10 models, from 39 cents to $1.29). Its ball point pen products were sold strictly as no-name brands.

Table 2

1973 Selected Product Lines

Product Type	BIC	Berol	Gillette Paper Mate	Write-Bros.	Lindy	Pentel
Ball-point pens:						
Retractable:						
Refillable	$0.49	$0.29	$0.98	$ —	$1.00	$2.98
	0.69	0.39	1.50			5.00
	0.98	0.49	1.98			7.00
	1.00	0.59	3.95			8.50
		1.49	5.00			
			5.95			
Nonrefillable	0.29			0.39		0.79
Nonretractable	0.19	0.19		0.19	0.19–	
	0.25	0.25			0.59	
		0.29			(0.20)	
		0.39				
Fine line porous						
point pens	0.29	0.29	0.49	0.29	0.59	0.29
		0.49	0.98			0.35
			1.95			0.49

Source: Corporate records.

The Berol, Lindy, and Pentel corporations were well known for product innovation. In 1973, the Berol Corporation, best known for its drafting products, particularly for its Eagle brand pencils, was the second firm to introduce the rolling writer combination pen, a pen which performed like a regular fountain pen, yet could write through carbons. Lindy Pen Corporation had earned its reputation as an early entrant into new markets, yet lacked the advertising strength to back the sale of its new products. Lindy introduced a 39-cent stick pen prior to the introduction of the BIC Crystal in 1959, a fine line porous point pen in 1969, and a disposable lighter in 1970. Pentel Corporation had earned the reputation of "revolutionizing the U.S. mechanical writing instrument industry" with the introduction of the soft tip in 1964 and the rolling writer combination pen in 1969. Like Lindy, it lacked the resources to support heavy advertising and mass distribution programs.

Gillette

The Gillette Company was considered BIC's major competitor in all writing instrument products. The comparative performance in writing instruments for the two firms from 1968–73 is shown in Table 3.

Table 3

Comparative Performance in Writing Instruments
(Consolidated statements)

	1968	*1969*	*1970*	*1971*	*1972*	*1973*
BIC:						
Net sales ($ millions)	$29.6	$36.6	$37.7	$39.5	$47.6	$52.4
Net income ($ millions)	$ 3.2	$ 4.3	$ 4.0	$ 5.5	$ 6.3	$ 7.3 (est.)
Net income/sales	10.8%	11.7%	10.6%	13.9%	13.2%	14.0% (est.)
Net sales/total assets*	—	—	1.6%	1.4%	1.3%	1.3%
Total assets/total equity†	—	—	1.3%	1.2%	1.1%	1.2%
Gillette (Paper Mate Division):						
Net sales ($ millions)	$33.2	$36.5	$47.0	$51.1	$60.9	$74.5
Net income ($ millions)	$ 2.5	$ 3.3	$ 3.3	$ 2.5	$ 3.0	$ 4.3
Net income/sales	4.5%	9.0%	7.0%	4.9%	4.9%	5.8%
Net sales/total assets*	1.4%	1.4%	1.3%	1.3%	1.3%	1.3%
Total assets/total equity†	1.8%	1.8%	1.8%	1.9%	2.0%	2.1%

* Estimated total assets allocated to writing instruments.
† Total corporate assets and equity.
Source: Corporate 10-K reports.

In 1973 Gillette competed in the high-price market with its Paper Mate products and in the low-price market with its Write-Brothers products. The Paper Mate ball-point pens had been the mainstay of its writing instrument business since the early 1950s. In the late 1960s management at Gillette "recognized the potential of Pentel's new soft tip pens." Backed by a large research and development capability, a well-known corporate name, and advertising and distribution strength, Gillette set out to capture that market with a fine line porous point pen called Flair, which retailed in three models from 40 cents to $1.95. In 1972 Gillette created the Write-Brothers products: a 39-cent retractable ball-point pen, a 29-cent fine line porous point pen, and a 19-cent nonretractable ball-point pen, in order "to take advantage of growth opportunities in the low-price end of the mechanical writing instrument market." The Write-Brothers name was selected to prevent confusion on the part of consumers who had associated the Paper Mate name with high-priced ball-point pen products and middle- to high-priced Flair products.

Retail market share patterns for BIC and Gillette are shown in Table 4. (The BIC Banana was introduced in May of 1972 and the Write-Brothers products in July of 1972.)

Table 4

Bi-Monthly Retail Market Share Patterns (Units)

	JF '72	MA	MJ	JA	SO	ND	JF '73	MA	MJ	JA	SO	ND
Ball-point pens:												
Total BIC	66%	67%	65%	65%	66%	65%	67%	66%	65%	66%	68%	66%
$0.19 Crystal	36	35	34	33	31	31	32	32	31	31	31	31
0.25 Fine Point	12	14	13	13	11	13	13	12	13	13	11	12
0.29 Pocket Pen	—	1	2	2	3	3	3	3	3	2	2	2
0.49 Accountant	8	7	7	8	9	7	8	7	7	8	10	9
0.49 Clic	8	8	7	7	9	8	8	8	8	8	9	7
Other	2	2	2	2	3	3	3	4	3	4	5	5
Total Gillette	8	8	9	13	13	13	13	15	15	14	14	15
$0.19 W-B	—	—	—	3	3	3	4	6	5	5	5	5
0.39 W-B	—	—	1	2	2	2	2	2	2	2	2	2
0.98 Retractable	4	4	4	4	4	4	4	4	4	4	4	4
Other	4	4	4	4	4	4	3	3	4	3	3	4
Lindy	7	7	8	7	6	7	6	6	6	5	5	5
Other	19	18	18	15	15	15	14	13	14	15	13	14
Total	100%	100%	100%	100%	100%	100%	100%	100%	100%	100%	100%	100%
Fine line porous point pens:												
BIC	—	—	5	11	15	16	16	19	19	20	23	22
Total Gillette	49	46	45	43	43	40	39	37	36	37	35	35
$0.49 Flair	45	43	41	36	34	33	32	30	30	30	28	29
0.49 Hotliner	2	2	1	1	1	1	1	1	1	1	1	1
0.29 W-B	—	—	2	5	7	5	5	5	5	5	5	4
Other	2	1	1	1	1	1	1	1	—	1	1	1
Lindy	5	5	4	4	4	4	3	3	2	2	2	2
Magic Marker	—	—	—	—	—	—	6	6	7	8	9	8
Pentel	9	9	9	7	7	7	7	6	6	5	4	5
Other	37	40	37	35	31	33	29	29	30	28	27	28
Total	100%	100%	100%	100%	100%	100%	100%	100%	100%	100%	100%	100%

Source: Corporate records.

Over the five-year period 1969–73, BIC and Gillette made the following advertising expenditures on writing instruments (see Table 5):

Table 5

Writing Instrument Advertising Budget Estimates
(Dollars in millions)

	1969	1970	1971	1972	1973
Gillette	$1.9	$4.0	$6.0	$8.5	$9.0
BIC	3.6	4.0	4.3	7.0	6.8

Source: Case researcher's estimates derived from corporate records, interviews with company officials, and journal articles.

In commenting on advertising programs and the BIC/Gillette competition in general, Mr. David Furman, advertising director at BIC, said:

Our strategy has been to emphasize profit and therefore look for the mass market. Gillette has said: "Let's make the most money and not worry about the size of the market." Gillette had a nice profitable business with Flair. It kept Paper Mate alive. But they can't stay alive with one-dollar-plus pens. We expanded the market so now their unit sales are up. The philosophy of Gillette has been to spend heavily to develop the product, then let the products decay and spend on new product development. Their unit sales continue to go up, but their loss of market share is considerable.

Company Policies and Structure

Mr. Adler had sometimes described his company as a car with four equally important wheels: sales, manufacturing, finance, and advertising, all of which had to be synchronized in order for the car to accelerate and sustain itself at high speed. That car, he claimed, had equal responsibility to its stockholders, employees, and customers. It followed, therefore, that management's attention should be focused on achieving a good return on investment, which Mr. Adler felt was derived by improving: (1) productivity (unit production per hour), (2) efficiency in production (cost savings methods), and (3) quality control standards and checks.

Finance

In the spring of 1971 BIC Pen effected a recapitalization which resulted in an aggregate number of 3.03 million outstanding common shares, 87 percent of which were owned by Société Bic, S.A., 3 percent by M. Bich, 9 percent by Mr. Adler, and 1 percent by other officers and directors (stock bonuses).[6] On September 15 of that year, 655,000 of those common

---

[6] Four million common shares were authorized.

shares were offered to the public at $25 per share, resulting in a new capital structure of 67 percent of the shares owned by Société Bic, S.A., 3 percent by M. Bich, 7 percent by Mr. Adler, 1 percent by other officers, and 22 percent by the public. Proceeds from the public offering after underwriting discounts and commissions amounted to $15.4 million. On July 27, 1972, M. Bich exercised his warrants for the purchase of 210,000 shares of common stock at $25 per share, totaling $5.25 million, which BIC received in cash. That same day the company declared a 2-for-1 share split in the form of a 100 percent share dividend of 3.24 million shares, $1 par value, which resulted in the transference of $3.24 million from retained earnings to common stock. At the end of 1972, 6.48 million shares were outstanding of the 10 million shares authorized in June of 1972; none of the 1 million authorized shares of preferred stock had been issued.

Since 1967, the company paid the following cash dividends as shown in Table 6:

Table 6

BIC Pen Corporation Dividend Payment History

	1967	1968	1969	1970	1971	1972	1973
Consolidated net income (dollars in millions)	$2.862	$3.231	$4.233	$4.033	$5.546	$6.264	$7.430
Dividends (dollars in millions)	2.591	—	1.175	1.166	1.319	1.603	1.750
Adjusted net dividend/ share*	0.43	—	0.19	0.19	0.22	0.26	0.27
Stock price range*	—	—	—	—	12¼–18	16¼–37	11⅝–32½

* After giving retroactive effect to a 2-for-1 share split in 1972.
Source: BIC Pen Corporation annual report, 1973.

Regarding dividend policy, Mr. Alexiades said:

When we were a private firm, there was no dividend policy. Dividends were only given when declared by M. Bich. In 1969 when we knew that we would be going public, we tried to establish a policy to find the proper relationship between earnings and dividends. Twenty percent to 25 percent of earnings seemed like a good target policy. Now we're having trouble increasing our dividends, due to government guidelines, although we would like to increase the payout in accordance with our rise in earnings.

The purchase of the original BIC plant from the Norden Company in 1963 was financed with a 5¾ percent mortgage loan from Connecticut General, payable in monthly installments of $7,749 (principal and interest) until January 1, 1981.[7] The three plant expansions—$1 million for

---

[7] The loan had not been paid off by 1973 because of its low interest rate.

110,000 square feet in 1965, $1.8 million for 100,000 square feet in 1969, and $5–$6 million for 275,000 square feet in 1973—were financed through short-term loans and cash on hand. Regarding the 1973 expansion, Mr. Alexiades said: "We decided to use our own cash so that if something develops in 1974 or 1975, such as an acquisition or new product opportunity, we can always fall back on our credit rating."[8]

In keeping with BIC's informal organizational structure, management used no formalized budgets. "We use goals, not budgets. We just keep surprising ourselves with our performance," said Mr. Alexiades, "although perhaps as we mature, we will need a more structured arrangement."

BIC was known in the New Haven area for its attractive compensation plan. It was Mr. Adler's belief that good people would be attracted by good pay. Plant workers received the highest hourly rates in the area ($4.53 base rate for the average grade level of work). All employees were invited to participate in a stock purchase plan whereby up to 10 percent of their salaries could be used to purchase stock at a 10 percent discount from the market price, with BIC assuming the brokerage commission cost. Executives participated in a bonus plan which Mr. Adler described as follows:

> We have a unique bonus system which I'm sure the Harvard Business School would think is crazy. Each year I take a percentage of profits before tax and give 40 percent to sales, 40 percent to manufacturing, and 20 percent to the treasurer to be divided up among executives in each area. Each department head keeps some for himself and gives the rest away. We never want bonuses to be thought of as salaries because they would lose their effect. So we change the bonus day each year so that it always comes as a pleasant surprise, something to look forward to.

Manufacturing

Manufacturing had emphasized the development over the years of a totally integrated, highly automated production process capable of mass-producing high-quality units at a very low cost. Except for the metal clips, rings, and plungers, all components—even the ink—were produced in the Milford plant. Société Bic had supplied the basic production technology, machinery, and research and development.[9] Some raw materials, particularly the brass, were still imported from France.

The U.S. energy crisis posed a major threat to BIC in 1973. Polysty-

---

[8] BIC borrowed on a seasonal basis to meet working capital needs, using bank lines of credit ($15.5 million available; maximum borrowed was $10.6 million in 1970).

[9] BIC Pen Corporation spent $30,368, $15,254, and $128,553 on R&D in 1971, 1972, and 1973, respectively.

rene, the key raw material used in making pens, was a petroleum derivative. Mr. Adler commented on the shortage of plastic:

> We've reached a point in our economy where it's become more difficult to produce than sell. I mean I have this big new plant out there [pointing to the new $5–$6 million addition], and I may not be able to produce any products. I have to worry about the overhead. I'm reluctant to substitute materials.
>
> I predict that in 1974 polystyrene will cost more than double what it costs in 1973, which is 15 cents per pound. It represents about 10 percent of the manufacturing cost of the ball-point stick pen.

The production process consisted of three stages: (1) manufacture of parts, (2) assembly of parts, and (3) packaging. Porous pens (4 parts) were the simplest instrument to manufacture followed by ball-point pens (7 parts) and lighters (21 parts). Some parts, such as nonretractable pen barrels, were interchangeable, which built flexibility into the production process. Production rates were steady throughout the year, while inventory buildups were seasonal. In mid-1973 BIC was producing on average about 2.5 million ball-point pen units per day and 0.5 million porous pens per day, which was close to plant capacity.

Management felt that production costs were substantially controlled by the strict enforcement of a quality control system. One fourth of the plant's employees participated in quality control checks at each stage of the production process, which was precision oriented, involving tolerances as close as $0.0002\pm$. Mr. Charles Matjouranis, director of manufacturing, had stated that it was his job to search for cost-savings programs which would protect profit margins on products. He said:

> We are in the automation business. Because of our large volume, one tenth of one cent in savings turns out to be enormous. Labor and raw materials costs keep increasing, but we buy supplies in volume and manufacture products in volume. One advantage of the high volume business is that you can get the best equipment and amortize it entirely over a short period of time (four to five months). I'm always looking for new equipment. If I see a cost-savings machine, I can buy it. I'm not constrained by money.

In 1973 there were 700 persons working at BIC in Milford, of which 625 were production personnel represented by the United Rubber Workers Union under a three-year contract. Management considered its relations with employees as excellent and maintained that BIC offered the best hourly rates, fringe benefits, and work environment in the area. Weekly meetings between supervisors and factory workers were held to air grievances. Workers were treated on a first-name basis and were encouraged to develop pride in their jobs by understanding production technicalities and participating in the quality control program and production shift competition. Most assembly-line workers were women. At least 40 percent of the factory workers had been with BIC for over 10 years, and 60–65 percent for over 5 years. Despite increased automation, very few layoffs had occurred because workers were able to be retained for other positions to compensate for the increase in production unit volume. Over 50 percent of the workers had performed more than one job.

Marketing and Sales

In admiring his BIC ring studded with six diamonds, each representing an achieved sales goal, Mr. Ron Shaw, national sales manager, remarked:

> It's almost a dream story here. When I started with the company in 1961 as an assistant zone manager, we were selling 8 million units a year. We now sell 2.5 million units a day. Everyone said that: One, we couldn't sell 5,000 feet of writing in one unit and succeed; two, we couldn't have the biggest sales force in the writing instrument industry and make money; and three, we couldn't advertise a 19-cent pen on TV and make money. Well, we did and we're Number One!

Distribution. The BIC products were sold in the retail and commercial markets by 120 company salesmen who called on approximately 10,000 accounts. Those accounts represented large retailers, such as chains, as well as wholesale distributors. Through those 10,000 accounts, BIC achieved distribution for its products in approximately 200,000 retail outlets of which 12,000 were commercial supply stores. In addition, the salesmen called on 20,000 independent retail accounts which were considered important in the marketplace. In the case of those accounts, the BIC salesmen merely filled orders for the distributors. A specialized BIC sales force sold ad/specialty orders to ad/specialty distributors and most premium orders directly to corporate customers.

The backbone of BIC's customer business had originally been the mom-and-pop stores. They had initially resisted selling BIC pens but were later forced to trade up from the no-name products once BIC had become a popular selling brand. As product distribution patterns moved away from indirect selling toward more direct selling to large chains and discount houses, the mass merchandisers became eager to carry BIC products, which had earned a reputation for fast turnover, heavy advertising support, and brand recognition. In 1973 BIC did 60 percent of its sales volume through distributors and 40 percent through direct sales channels.

Pricing Policy. BIC had never raised the original retail prices of any of its products. Management, therefore, placed a great deal of importance on retail price selection and product cost management. Advertising expenses generally ran 15 percent of the manufacturer's selling price; the combined costs of packaging and distribution approximated 20–30 percent of the manufacturer's selling price. The distributor's profit margin was 15 percent off the listed retail price; the indirect retail buyer's was

40 percent; and the direct retail buyer's was 55 percent. Regarding pricing policy, Mr. Adler said:

> If I increase my price, I help my competition. The marketplace, not ourselves, dictates the price. We must see what people are willing to pay. You must sell as cheaply as possible to get the volume.

Customary Marketing Tools. In a speech made before the Dallas Athletic Club in September of 1972, Mr. Paige remarked: "We're in the *idea* business. Selling is an idea. Many people have products but we have ideas."

BIC used four basic marketing tools to sell its ideas: (1) advertising, (2) point-of-purchase displays, (3) packaging forms, and (4) trade and consumer promotions. Management felt that the only way to enter a new market was to be innovative either by: (1) introducing a new product, (2) creating a new market segment, or (3) using unique merchandising techniques designed specifically for that market. The BIC salesmen were known to be aggressive.[10] Products were always introduced on a regional roll-out basis with the entry into each new region attempted only after market saturation had been achieved successfully in the prior region.

Advertising was considered the most important element of the BIC marketing program. Company research had shown that 7 out of 10 writing instruments sold were impulse purchase items. With that knowledge, management felt that widespread distribution of a generic name product line was essential for success. It was further felt that retailers and commercial stationers preferred to carry nationally advertised brands.

BIC used TV advertising, "the cheapest medium when counting heads," almost exclusively. In 1973 BIC added advertising in *T.V. Guide* and the Sunday supplements "in order to reach more women, the biggest purchasers of writing instruments."

In keeping with the belief that merchandising techniques should be designed differently for each product and market, BIC varied its TV commercials substantially, depending upon the intended product usage, time of entry into the market, and demographic interest. Each advertising message was designed to be simple and to communicate *one* idea at a time. Exhibit 4 presents examples of four different themes: (1) BIC has a lighter (BIC Butane); (2) BIC's products are durable (Crystal); (3) BIC has coloring instruments for children (Ink Crayons[11]); and (4) BIC offers a "new and fun way to write" (BIC Banana).

Another marketing tool was the *point-of-purchase display.* Mr. Paige remarked:

> Merchandise well displayed is half sold, particularly on a low consumer interest item. Displays must be designed to fit every retail requirement be-

---

[10] On average, assistant zone managers earned $12,000, and zone managers earned $22,000 a year. Compensation consisted of a base salary plus commission.

[11] Ink Crayons consisted of a multipack of BIC Banana pens in an array of ink colors.

cause, for example, what's good for Woolworth's may not be good for the corner drug store.

Packaging was considered another form of advertising. "We want to make the 19-cent pen look like a one-dollar pen," Mr. Paige had said. BIC was one of the first firms to use the concept of multipacks. Packaging forms were changed as much as six times a year. Regarding packaging and *promotions,* Mr. Alexiades commented:

> We've created a demand for constant innovation, excitement in the marketplace. Many people say that's the reason for BIC's success. We change the manner in which we sell (blister packs,[12] multipacks, gift packages), which makes our merchandise turn and keeps our name in front of the wholesaler and retailer all of the time. The consumer remembers us because we offer a true value. The retailer and dealer remember us because they receive special incentive offers, free merchandise, and promotional monies, plus their merchandise turns.

Organizational Structure

Throughout its 15-year history, the BIC organizational structure had remained small and simple. (See Exhibit 5 for the 1973 organizational chart.) In 1973 the average tenure (since 1958) of the six key executive officers was 13 years. At least 40 percent of the factory workers had been at BIC for over 10 years. Several of the managers commented on the BIC environment:

> We try to run this company as a family organization. We don't try to run it as a General Motors. We've been very successful with this concept. It's a closely knit management group—very informal. Decisions are made immediately. A young guy comes here. He sees that we [management] exist. We understand him. He gets his decisions immediately. We try to get him to join the family. Inside of two to three years, if he's not in the family, he won't work out.
>
> Mr. Robert Adler,
President

> Part of the success of management is our ability to communicate with one another. We're trying to remain the same. It's one of the regrets that growth has to bring in departments and department heads, but we're trying to maintain a minimum.
>
> Mr. Alexander Alexiades,
Treasurer

> We have few managers, but the best. One real good one is better than two average.
>
> Mr. Charles Matjouranis,
Manufacturing Director

---

[12] Blister packs were product packages which were designed to be displayed on peg boards.

> This company does not believe in assistants. Philosophically, we try to stay away from any bureaucracy. There are no politics involved here, no knifing, no backbiting. Part is a function of size. Everybody knows his place and area of responsibility. We don't want to break from that.
>
> Mr. David Furman,
Advertising Director

> We promote from within. We recognize the abilities of our own people.
>
> Mr. Ron Shaw,
National Sales Manager

The BIC Butane Disposable Cigarette Lighter

The Lighter Decision

In March of 1973 BIC Pen Corporation introduced its first nonwriting instrument product, the BIC Butane disposable lighter, at a retail price of $1.49. Management viewed the BIC Butane as a logical extension of its current product line as it was inexpensive, disposable, of high quality, and able to be mass-produced and distributed through most writing instrument trade channels, especially retail. It differed from writing instruments in that it required 21 rather than the basic 7 assembly parts, required more precise manufacturing, and was subject to strict governmental standards. Mr. Furman made the following statement regarding BIC's decision to enter the disposable lighter business:

> For years we were in the high-level, profitability trap. We had had it as far as that market would go. The Banana was the first break out from the trap and now the lighter. We utilize our strengths, but we're no longer a writing instrument company. We're in the expansion stage where writing instruments are a base from which we are expanding. We're using the skills we've gained and are applying them to any kind of mass-produced product.

Introductory Campaign

The decision to sell a disposable lighter dated back to 1971 when M. Marcel Bich purchased Flaminaire, a French lighter company, with the objective of marketing a substitute for matches in Europe. Matches had never been free in Europe, and for that reason disposable lighter sales had been very successful there far before they caught on in the United States. The BIC Butane was imported from Flaminaire but was scheduled to be produced at the Milford plant on a highly automated production line by March of 1974.

The BIC Butane was introduced first in the Southwest, where management claimed it had captured a 32 percent retail market share by year's end. Management expected its national retail market share of 16 percent to rise to 25 percent when the product reached full national distribution in February of 1974. The regional rollout was backed with a $1 million

Table 7

U.S. Cigarette Lighter Retail Sales (Dollars and units in millions)

	1969	1970	1971	1972	1973 (Est.)
Total lighters ($)	$94.9	$98.1	$106.9	$115.0	$153.0
Disposables ($)	n.a.	$ 8.5	$ 18.0	$ 36.0	$ 50.0
Units (no.)	—	—	13	21	40

Note: n.a.—not available.
Source: Case researcher's estimates based on trade and company interviews and unpublished figures from the *Drug Topics* magazine research group (1972).

advertising campaign. A $3 million campaign was planned for 1974. Lighter sales approximated 10 percent of BIC's consolidated net sales in 1973. An industry source estimated their pretax margin at 15–21 percent.

The Cigarette Lighter Industry

Lighters were categorized in three basic product classes: disposables, regular refillables, and electronics. Disposable lighters contained butane gas; electronic lighters contained butane gas or a battery; regular refillable lighters contained either butane gas (90 percent) or liquid fuel (10 percent). There were three basic price categories: <$2 (all disposables), $2–$12 (most regular refillables), and >$12 (all electronics and fancy regular refillables). It was estimated that 75 percent–80 percent of all cigarette lighters sold in 1972 were priced below $6.95 at retail. (See Table 7.)

Cigarette lighter sales in the middle price range had begun to fall off in the early 1970s. As a replacement for matches, disposable lighters had expanded the primary demand for lighters and represented the major growth opportunity in the U.S. lighter industry.

Major Competitors

By 1973 many firms, particularly manufacturers of writing instruments, had entered the disposable lighter business. Most firms served as distributors of foreign-made products, many of which were reputed by trade sources to be of questionable quality. As with writing instruments, BIC's management believed that industry success was heavily dependent on the strength of a firm's advertising program and distribution network, although most firms did well initially due to the excessive demand for disposable lighters relative to the available supply.

There were three clear contenders for industry dominance in the disposable lighter business: Gillette, Garrity Industries, and BIC, with Scripto a distant fourth. Gillette's Cricket lighter was the leading market shareholder, accounting for one third of all disposable lighter sales in 1973. (See Table 8.)

Table 8

1973 Major Competitors in Disposable Lighters

	BIC	Gillette	Garrity	Scripto*
Market entry (year)	1973	1972	1967	1972
Product	BIC Butane	Cricket	Dispoz-a-lite	Catch 98
Price	$1.49	$1.49	$1.49	$0.98
Product produced in	France ($\rightarrow$1973); U.S. (after)	France ($\rightarrow$1973); Puerto Rico (after)	France	Japan
Ad $ strategy (1973)	Consumer	Consumer ($\frac{3}{4}$) Trade ($\frac{1}{4}$)	Trade	None
Distribution emphasis	Mass/chains	Mass/chains	Smoke shops, hotel stands, drug stores	Independent retailers

* In 1974, Scripto planned to raise the price of the Catch 98 to $1.19, add another Japanese disposable lighter at the $1.39 price point, and produce a $1.69 disposable lighter in its Atlanta plant.
Source: Casewriter's interviews with corporate marketing managers.

In speculating on the future of the BIC Butane lighter, Mr. Paige stated:

> We think that the disposable butane will cannibalize every low-priced lighter. BIC, Dispoz-a-lite, and Cricket will do 90 percent of the business in 1973. Cricket advertises extensively. BIC will compete with Cricket at the $1.49 price point. BIC and Cricket will dominate the industry in the future. The cheaper disposables of lesser quality will only sustain themselves.

Exhibit 1

Financial Highlights 1964–73

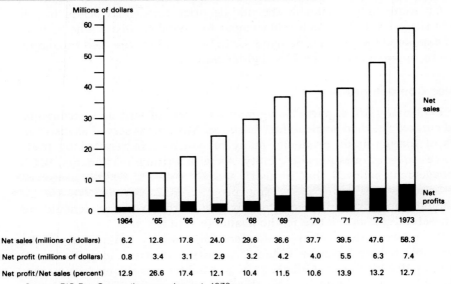

	1964	'65	'66	'67	'68	'69	'70	'71	'72	1973
Net sales (millions of dollars)	6.2	12.8	17.8	24.0	29.6	36.6	37.7	39.5	47.6	58.3
Net profit (millions of dollars)	0.8	3.4	3.1	2.9	3.2	4.2	4.0	5.5	6.3	7.4
Net profit/Net sales (percent)	12.9	26.6	17.4	12.1	10.4	11.5	10.6	13.9	13.2	12.7

Source: BIC Pen Corporation annual report, 1973.

Exhibit 2

BIC PEN CORPORATION
Consolidated Financial Statements
For the years ended December 31, 1973 and 1972
(in thousands)

	1973	1972
Consolidated Statement of Income		
Net sales	$58,326	$47,571
Cost of goods sold	26,564	19,892
Gross profit	31,762	27,679
Selling, advertising, and general and administrative expenses	17,191	15,248
Profit from operations	14,571	12,431
Other income	589	269
Total	15,160	12,700
Other deductions	327	196
Income before income taxes	14,787	12,504
Provision for income taxes	7,357	6,240
Net income	$ 7,430	$ 6,264
Earnings per share	$ 1.15	$ 1.00

Consolidated Statement of Retained Earnings		
Balance—beginning of year	$11,683	$10,262
Net income	7,430	6,264
Total	19,113	16,526
Dividends:		
Cash:		
Common shares	1,750	1,603
Preferred shares	—	—
Total cash dividends	1,750	1,603
Common shares	—	3,240
Total dividends	1,750	4,843
Balance—end of year	$17,363	$11,683

Source: BIC Pen Corporation annual report, 1973.

Exhibit 3

BIC PEN CORPORATION
Consolidated Balance Sheet
December 31, 1973 and 1972
(in thousands)

	1973	*1972*
Assets		
Current assets:		
Cash	$ 683	$ 919
Certificates of deposit and short-term investments—at cost, which approximates market	8,955	10,000
Receivables—trade and other (net of allowance for doubtful accounts, 1973—$143,000, 1972—$102,000)	9,445	8,042
Inventories	9,787	6,299
Deposits and prepaid expenses	644	633
Total current assets	29,514	25,893
Property, plant, and equipment—at cost (net of accumulated depreciation, 1973—$9,687,000, 1972—$7,091,000)	15,156	9,687
Investments and other assets	1,790	1,329
Total assets	$46,460	$36,909
Liabilities and Shareholders' Equity		
Current liabilities:		
Notes payable—banks	$ 21	—
Construction loan payable (due March 21, 1974)	560	—
Accounts payable—trade	3,872	$ 1,245
Mortgage payable	62	58
Accrued liabilities:		
Federal and state income taxes	1,231	815
Pension plan	306	265
Other	488	402
Total current liabilities	6,540	2,785
Deferred liabilities	361	275
Mortgage payable	459	520
Minority interest*	91	—
Shareholders' equity:		
Common shares	6,480	6,480
Capital surplus	15,166	15,166
Retained earnings	17,363	11,683
Total shareholders' equity	39,009	33,329
Total liabilities and shareholders' equity	$46,460	$36,909

* Mexican subsidiary is 80 percent owned by BIC Pen Corporation, 20 percent by Mexican interests.

Source: BIC Pen Corporation annual report, 1973.

Exhibit 4

Television Advertising Themes

BIC BUTANE   BIC CRYSTAL   BIC BANANA   BIC INK CRAYONS

"For $1.49 and thousands of lights, it's a Pretty Good Lighter. BIC Butane."

"Dear BIC . . . You're probably not going to believe this but. . . ."

"You can't write with blueberries, but you can write with a BIC Banana, the new porous tip pen."

"BIC Banana Ink Crayons. In ten bright colors. The only fruit you can draw with."

Source: BIC Pen Corporation annual report, 1972.

Exhibit 5

1973 Internal Organizational Chart

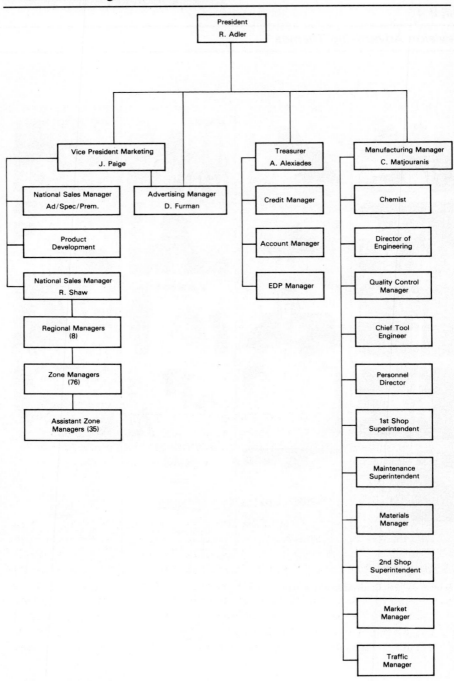

Source: Corporate records.

BIC Pen Corporation (B)

News Release: January 11, 1974

BIC Pen Corporation, which has specialized successfully in mass marketing consumer products, soon will introduce a new product which it will distribute in the $1.3 billion retail pantyhose market, Robert P. Adler, president, disclosed today.

"The sale of pantyhose is for BIC a further expansion into other mass-produced disposable consumer products," Mr. Adler said. "Because of BIC's strong reputation for value and our ability to merchandise successfully to the consumer through more than 200,000 retail outlets, we believe our new pantyhose product will be well received in this marketplace."

The Women's Hosiery Industry

Hosiery had always been the most rapidly consumable apparel item in a woman's wardrobe. For years the women's hosiery industry had been stable in unit sales and repetitive in product offerings. Many low-profile brands were sold in a wide range of sizes and typical colors. The business "kicked up its heels" in the late 60s with the advent of the convenience product pantyhose and miniskirts. Hosiery became a fashion item, costing as much as $10 a pair, depending upon style, texture, color, and brand name. Prosperity did not last, however, and by 1973 the $2 billion women's hosiery business was characterized as "having to run faster to stay

Copyright © 1974 by the President and Fellows of Harvard College
Harvard Business School case 374–306

in the same place." The market had become plagued by an uncertainty in consumer demand, sagging profits, price battles, distribution changes, and the rising fashion trend of women's pants. Hosiery makers claimed that women had begun to go without hose or to wear ripped stockings under pants.

The Pantyhose Market

As an attempt to interject some life into the stable pantyhose market, the three big hosiery makers, Hanes Corporation, Kayser-Roth Corporation, and Burlington Industries, launched an unprecedented $33 million promotional campaign in 1973. They cast aside their established merchandising techniques and began pushing new, low-priced pantyhose in supermarkets. The firms adopted catchy brand names and used dramatic advertising campaigns centering around "trendy" packaging. Their assumption was that women would buy more pantyhose if the products were cheaper, more accessible, and more attractively displayed than before. No longer were branded products available exclusively in department or specialty stores at $3 a pair; rather, they could be purchased at every corner market for 99 cents to $1.39. As a result, pantyhose sales in food outlets rose from 5 percent in 1968 to 28 percent of the industry pantyhose sales in 1973, with analysts predicting a 50 percent share by 1975. Despite the surge in supermarket buying, sales of pantyhose declined by 7 percent in 1973.

The private-label business represented 50 percent of the hosiery sales in food stores in 1973, with some labels selling as low as 39 cents a pair. The supermarket invasion by known brands—"L'eggs" by Hanes, "Activ" by Burlington, and "No-Nonsense" by Kayser-Roth—resulted in a general upgrading in the quality of the private-label brands and an expansion of the branded lines to cover additional market segments, such as pantyhose in large sizes for heavier women and pantyhose for less than $1 for price-conscious women.

In describing pantyhose purchase behavior, one industry source said:

> Generally, all women are interested in quality, price, fit, and availability, but purchasers do tend to fall into three basic categories: (1) women who think that all hosiery is the same and therefore look for the lowest price; (2) women who feel that an extremely low price implies inferior quality; and (3) women who switch off between high and low prices, depending upon their needs.

L'eggs was the largest selling brand name in 1973 with a 9 percent dollar volume share of the total hosiery market. The idea for L'eggs was born out of the recognition that no high-quality name brand dominated the highly fractionated pantyhose market; nor was one available at a reasonable price (<$2) at convenience locations (supermarkets). The L'eggs integrated marketing program centered around the theme, "Our L'eggs fit your legs," and the distinctive egg-shaped package. The L'eggs direct-selling approach leaned heavily on a platoon of 1,000 young delivery women clad in hot pants and traveling their appointed routes in distinctive white vans. Their task was to restock flashy "L'eggs Boutiques" in supermarkets and drug chains. L'eggs retail sales rose from $9 million in 1970 to $110 million in 1973. Hanes spent $20 million on their promotion in 1972 and $13 million in 1973.

Activ and No-Nonsense pantyhose were priced at 99 cents a pair in contrast with L'eggs at $1.39.[1] Both brands were backed by $10 million promotional campaigns in 1973. The "Activ Girls" competed with the "L'eggs Ladies." Similarly clad and driving red vans, they also sold products on consignment. Besides supermarkets, Activ pantyhose appeared in outlets serviced by tobacco distributors, thus supporting Burlington's motto: "Activs are everywhere." Kayser-Roth shunned the distribution system favored by the other two hosiery makers and delivered its No-Nonsense brand-name pantyhose to food brokers at supermarket warehouses. The No-Nonsense approach—without vans, hot pants, and comely delivery women—allowed the retailers a 45 percent profit margin, compared with the 35 percent return guaranteed by Hanes and Burlington.

The Pantyhose Decision

Mr. David Furman, advertising director, commented on BIC's entry into the pantyhose business:

> The hosiery industry used to be dominated by manufacturing, not marketing, companies. L'eggs was the first attempt to change that. The success of L'eggs and other industry leaders has depended on an extremely expensive direct-selling distribution system which is good for large volume outlets but is not feasible for smaller stores or local advertising. BIC intends to use its usual jobbers and make it profitable for them to act as middlemen and garner the independent stores.
>
> Nearly all companies deal primarily with pantyhose as a fashion item. The market is moving away from the fashion emphasis, which cannot be successful in food stores. BIC will address the fit problem by using the slogan: "It fits there, it fits everywhere"; hence the name—Fannyhose. Ours is a utility story as it was with ball-point pens.

In introducing Fannyhose to the trade, management used the theme of "taking a simple idea and making it pay off." The quality product was priced at $1.39, came in two sizes and three colors, and was packaged in a compact little can with a see-through top. The advertising program centered around the "better fit" concept, as was illustrated in animated television commercials and Sunday supplements. Product promotions included cents-off coupons and free samples.

In contrast with its major competitors, BIC planned to act as a

---

[1] Hanes introduced First-to-Last pantyhose at 99 cents a pair to counter the price competition from Activ and No-Nonsense pantyhose.

distributor of pantyhose, rather than as a manufacturer/distributor, and to establish a specialized sales force to sell the product direct or through distributors to its wide variety of writing instrument retail accounts. BIC's supplier was DIM, S.A., one of France's largest hosiery makers ($100 million in sales), which M. Bich bought control of in 1973. Mr. Furman called the BIC plan "a brilliant stroke around L'eggs. Theirs is a fixed system—low profits, no risk, fixed price. We add promotional profits by passing on to the trade the money we've saved by avoiding the need for our own service crews."

BIC's Investors React

An article appearing in the February 4, 1974, edition of *The Wall Street Journal* described the reaction of the investment community to BIC's entry into the pantyhose business. One analyst cited several obstacles which BIC faced in its new venture, namely: (1) the limited pricing flexibility which BIC would have because of import duty costs[2] and (2) the fact that BIC had not been particularly strong in supermarkets. Another analyst took a more positive view, citing the recent market price decline in the BIC stock to "investors' questions over the competitive nature of the pantyhose business without understanding the philosophy of BIC: to produce inexpensive disposable consumer products once there is an established market for them and to use its widespread marketing system to become a powerful force in the industry." A third analyst predicted a bright future for BIC in the pantyhose business because of its "access to materials through Société Bic, its reputation for high-quality products, its well-developed distribution system and its commitment to marketing, rather than manufacturing, pantyhose."

Exhibit 1

U.S. Women's Hosiery Industry Trends

	1964	1965	1966	1967	1968	1969	1970	1971	1972	1973
Numbers of:										
Companies	645	609	576	579	574	530	502	471	457	390
Plants	828	782	750	746	741	734	699	665	604	521
Annual per capita consumption:										
Pantyhose	—	—	—	—	2.3	9.0	13.3	11.0	12.7	11.7
Stockings	14.8	15.7	17.3	19.5	18.1	12.7	6.3	4.2	3.1	2.5
Knee-highs, Anklets	0.1	0.1	0.1	0.1	0.1	0.1	0.1	0.3	0.6	1.2
Total consumption	14.9	15.8	17.4	19.6	20.5	21.8	19.7	15.5	16.4	15.5

Source: National Association of Hosiery Manufacturers.

---

[2] Duty fees averaged 33 percent per unit. One analyst speculated that the pretax margin on Fannyhose was 15 percent.

The Company and Its Environment: Relating Opportunities to Resources

Determination of a suitable strategy for a company begins in identifying the opportunities and risks in its environment. This chapter is concerned with the identification of a range of strategic alternatives, the narrowing of this range by recognizing the constraints imposed by corporate capability, and the determination of one or more economic strategies at acceptable levels of risk. We shall examine the complexity and variety of the environmental forces which must be considered and the problems in accurately assessing company strengths and weaknesses. Economic strategy will be seen as *the match between qualification and opportunity that positions a firm in its environment.* We shall attempt in passing to categorize the kinds of economic strategies that can result from the combination of internal capability and external market needs and to relate these categories to the normal course of corporate development.

The Nature of the Company's Environment

The environment of an organization in business, like that of any other organic entity, is the pattern of all the external conditions and influences that affect its life and development. The environmental influences relevant to strategic decision operate in a company's industry, the total business community, its city, its country, and the world. They are technological, economic, social, and political in kind. The corporate strategist is usually at least intuitively aware of these features of the current environment. But in all these categories change is taking place at varying rates—fastest in technology, less rapidly in politics. Change in the environment of business necessitates continuous monitoring of a company's definition of its business lest it falter, blur, or become obsolete. Since by definition the formulation of strategy is performed with the future in mind, executives who take part in the strategic planning process must be aware of those aspects of their company's environment especially susceptible to the kind of change that will affect their company's future.

Technology. From the point of view of the corporate strategist, technological developments are not only the fastest unfolding but the most far-reaching in extending or contracting opportunity for an established company. They include the discoveries of science, the impact of related product development, the less dramatic machinery and process improvements, and the progress of automation and data processing. We see in technical advance an accelerating rate of change—with new developments arriving before the implications of yesterday's changes can be assimilated. Industries hitherto protected from obsolescence by stable technologies or by the need for huge initial capital investment become more vulnerable more quickly than before to new processes or to cross-industry competition. Science gives the impetus to change not only in technology but also in all the other aspects of business activity.

Major areas of technical advance foreseen by students of the management of technology include increased mastery of energy, its conservation and more efficient use; the reorganization of transportation; technical solutions to problems of product life, safety, and serviceability; the further mechanization of logistical functions and the processing of information; alteration in the characteristics of physical and biological materials; and radical developments in controlling air, water, and noise pollution. The primary impact upon established strategies will be increased competition and more rapid obsolescence. The risks dramatized by these technical trends are offset by new business opportunities opened up for companies that are aggressive innovators or adept at technical hitchhiking. The need intensifies for any company either to engage in technical development or to maintain a technical intelligence capability enabling it to follow quickly new developments pioneered by others.

Economics. Because business is more accustomed to monitoring economic trends than those in other spheres, it is less likely to be taken by surprise by such massive developments as the internationalization of competition, the return of China and Russia to trade with the West, the slower than projected development of the Third World countries and the resulting backlash of poverty and starvation, the increased importance of the large multinational corporations and the consequences of the host country hostility, the recurrence of recession, and the danger of inflation. The consequences of world economic trends need to be monitored in the detail relevant to an industry or company.

Society. Social developments of which strategists keep aware include such influential forces as the quest for equality for minority groups; the demand of women for opportunity and recognition; the changing patterns of work and leisure; the effects of urbanization upon the individual, family, and neighborhood; the rise of crime; the decline of conventional morality; the changing composition of world population; and the role of the professions in society.

Politics. The political forces important to the business firm are similarly extensive and complex—the changing relations between communist and noncommunist countries (East and West) and between the prosperous and poor countries (North and South); the relation between private enterprise and government, between workers and management; the impact of national planning on corporate planning; and the redefinition of conservative and liberal ideology.

Although it is not possible to know or spell out here the significance of such technical, economic, social, and political trends and possibilities for the strategist of a given business or company, some simple things are clear. Changing values will lead to different expectations of the role business should perform. Business will be expected to execute its mission not only with economy in the use of energy but with sensitivity to the ecological environment. Organizations in all walks of life will be called upon to be more explicit about their goals and to meet the needs and aspirations (for example, for education) of their membership.

In any case, change threatens all established strategies. We know that a thriving company—itself a living system—is bound up in a variety of interrelationships with larger systems comprising its technological, economic, social, and political environment. If environmental developments are destroying and creating business opportunities, advance notice of specific instances relevant to a single company is essential to intelligent planning. Risk and opportunity in the last 15 years of the 20th century require of executives a keen interest in what is going on outside their companies. More than that, a practical means of tracking developments promising good or ill, and profit or loss, needs to be devised.

Tracking the Changing Environment

Unfortunately the development of knowledge in a flourishing business civilization has produced no easy methodology for continuous surveillance of the trends in the environment of central importance to a firm of ordinary capabilities. Predictive theories of special disciplines such as economics, sociology, psychology, and anthropology do not produce comprehensive appraisal readily applicable to long-range corporate strategic decision. At the same time many techniques do exist to deal with parts of the problem—economic and technological forecasting, detailed demographic projections, geological estimates of raw material reserves, national and international statistics in which trends may be discerned. More information about the environment is available than is commonly used.

The underuse of technical information appears in Frank Aguilar's research in how managers in the chemical industry obtained strategic information about environmental change.[1] Aguilar found that even in this technically sensitive industry, few firms attempted any systematic means for gathering and evaluating such information. Publications provided only about 20 percent of the information from all sources, with current market and competitive information from personal sources dominating the total input of information. Internally generated information comprised only 9 percent of the total, and more information received was unsolicited than solicited. (Interestingly enough, very few people in subordinate positions felt they were getting useful strategic information from their superiors.)

Aguilar's findings were corroborated by Robert Collings's study of investment firms.[2] The obvious moral of these studies is that the process of obtaining strategic information is far from being systematic, complete, or even really informative about anything except current developments, at least in these industries. These researchers show that it is possible to organize better the gathering and integrating of environmental data through such means as bringing miscellaneous scanning activities together and communicating available information internally.

Certain large companies organize this function. General Electric once maintained a Business Environment Section at its corporate headquarters. It prepared reports on predicted changes for use by GE divisions. Consulting firms, future-oriented research organizations, and associations of planners provide guidance for looking ahead. Databases (electronically accessible) have proliferated beyond the ability to make use of them. The sense of futility experienced by executives in the face of overabundant information is reduced when they begin the task by defining their strategy and the most likely strategic alternatives they will be debating in the foreseeable future. Decision on direction spotlights the relevant environment. You cannot know everything, but if you are thinking of going into the furniture business in Nebraska, you will not be concerned about the rate of family formation in Japan. Clarification of present strategy and the few new alternatives it suggests narrows sharply the range of necessary information and destroys the excuse that there is too much to know.

---

[1] Frank J. Aguilar, *Scanning the Business Environment* (New York: Macmillan, 1967).

[2] Robert Collings, "Scanning the Environment for Strategic Information" (doctoral thesis, Harvard Business School, 1969).

The Competitive Environment

The aspect of the environment that most tangibly affects a company is the competitive environment of the industry or industries in which it does business. In each of its businesses, the company faces an industry structure that shapes the rules of competition it must respond to or try to influence and motivates the attempt to develop an innovatively unique strategy. It also faces a group of competitors who may attack its market position and whose behavior can thwart actions it may take to improve position. The essential task of the strategist is to find a *defensible* position for the company in its competitive environment, or one that addresses or evades the demands of industry structure and is resistant to encroachment by competitors.

Industry Structure

If we look broadly at competition in any industry, whether it produces a product or service or is domestic or international, the state of competition depends on five elemental forces which are diagrammed in Figure 2.[3] The collective influence of rivalry among firms, the threat of new entrants, the bargaining power of customers and suppliers, and the specter of substitute products or services determine the ultimate profit potential of an industry. These pressures range from *intense* in industries like tires, metal cans, and steel, where no company earns spectacular returns on investment, to *mild* in industries like oil field services and equipment, soft drinks, and toiletries, where room remains for quite high returns.

Whatever their collective strength, the strategist's goal is to find a place in the industry where the company can best defend itself against these forces or can influence them in its favor. The strongest competitive force has the greatest impact on the profitability of an industry; it is usually of the greatest importance in strategy formulation. For example, even a company with a superior position in an industry unthreatened by potential entrants will earn low returns if it faces a superior or a lower cost substitute product—as the leading manufacturers of vacuum tubes and coffee percolators have learned to their sorrow. In such a situation, coping with the substitute product becomes the number one strategic priority.

Every industry has an underlying structure, or a set of fundamental economic and technical characteristics, that gives rise to these competitive currents and pressures. Identifying these forces for the industry a company operates in will uncover the critical requirements for success in

---

[3] This approach to competition is elaborated in Michael E. Porter's *Competitive Strategy: Techniques for Analyzing Industries and Competitors* and *Competitive Advantage,* published by The Free Press and Macmillan, New York, in 1980 and 1985, respectively.

Figure 2

Five Elemental Forces of Competition

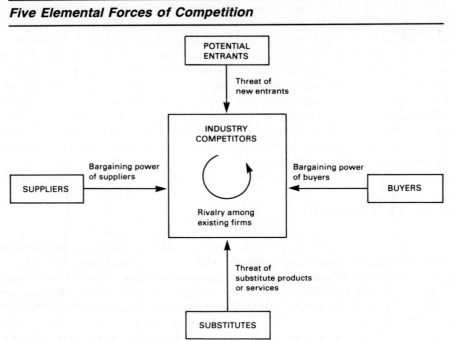

the industry and the areas where creative strategic readjustments will have the greatest impact on the company's profitability.

Threat of Entry

Newcomers to an industry bring new capacity, the desire to gain market share, and often substantial resources. The seriousness of the threat of entry depends on existing barriers to entry and on the likelihood of strong reaction from established competitors. If barriers to entry are high and if a newcomer can foresee sharp retaliation from the entrenched competitors, the threat of potential new entry is reduced.

There are at least seven barriers to entry:

1. *Economies of scale.* These economies, if present in any aspect of operation, deter entry by forcing the entrant either to come in on a large scale or to accept a cost disadvantage. Scale economies in production, research, marketing, and service are probably key barriers to entry in the mainframe computer industry, as Olivetti, Xerox, and General Electric once discovered.

2. *Product differentiation.* Product differentiation creates a barrier by forcing entrants to spend heavily to match the incumbent competitor's product features or to overcome brand loyalty. Product differentiation is perhaps the most important entry barrier in soft drinks, over-the-counter drugs, cosmetics, investment banking, and public accounting.

3. *Switching costs.* A barrier to entry is created by the presence of switching costs or one-time costs incurred by the buyer in switching from one supplier's product to another's. The switching price tag may include the time and money costs of employee retraining, new ancillary equipment, testing or qualifying a new source, and technical help from the seller in engineering, product redesign, or even the psychic costs incurred in severing a long-established relationship. If these switching costs are high, then new entrants must offer a major improvement in cost or performance to persuade the buyer to switch from an incumbent.

4. *Capital requirements.* The need to invest large financial resources in order to compete creates a barrier to entry, particularly if the capital is required for unrecoverable expenditures in up-front advertising or R&D. Capital may be necessary not only for fixed facilities but also for customer credit, inventories, and absorbing start-up losses.

5. *Cost disadvantages independent of scale.* Existing companies may have cost advantages not available to potential rivals, no matter what their attainable economies of scale. These advantages can stem from the effects of the learning curve (and of its first cousin, the experience curve), proprietary technology, access to the best raw materials sources, long-lived assets purchased at preinflation prices, government subsidies, favorable locations, or patents.

6. *Access to distribution channels.* The new competitor must, of course, secure distribution of his product or service. A new food product, for example, must displace others from the supermarket shelf via price breaks, promotions, intense selling efforts, or some other means. Sometimes this barrier is so high that, to surmount it, a new contestant must create its own distribution channels, as Timex did in the watch industry in the 1950s.

7. *Government policy.* The government can control or even foreclose entry to industries with licensing requirements and limits on access to raw materials. Regulated industries like liquor retailing and freight forwarding are obvious examples; more subtle government restrictions operate in fields like ski-area development and coal mining. The government also can play a major indirect role by affecting entry barriers through air and water pollution standards and safety regulations.

The potential rival's estimate of the reaction of existing competitors also will influence its decision whether to enter. The potential entrant may expect strong retaliation if incumbents have previously lashed out at new entrants or if:

— The incumbents possess substantial resources to fight back, including excess cash and unused borrowing power, productive capacity, or clout with distribution channels and customers.
— The incumbents seem likely to cut prices because of a desire to maintain market shares or because of industrywide excess capacity.
— Industry growth is slow, affecting its ability to absorb the new arrival and probably causing the financial performance of all the parties involved to decline.

Entry barriers of all kinds can and do change as industries evolve. The expiration of basic patents on instant photography and xerography, for instance, greatly reduced the barrier of proprietary technology protecting Polaroid and Xerox. Conversely, in the auto industry, economies of scale have increased with post-World War II automation and, recently, the need for enormous product development costs—virtually stopping successful new entry.

Of perhaps even more importance to the strategist is the fact that strategic decisions can have a major impact on the conditions determining the threat of entry. For example, the actions of many U.S. wine producers in the 1960s to step up product introductions, raise advertising levels, and expand distribution nationally surely strengthened the entry roadblocks by creating economies of scale and making access to distribution channels more difficult. Similarly, decisions by members of the recreational vehicle industry to integrate vertically in order to lower costs have greatly increased economies of scale and raised capital cost barriers. A company, then, can enhance the defensibility of its position through strategic actions affecting entry barriers.

Powerful Suppliers and Buyers

Suppliers can exert bargaining power on participants in an industry by raising prices or reducing the quality of purchased goods and services. Powerful suppliers can thereby squeeze profitability out of an industry unable to recover cost increases in its own prices. By raising their prices, for example, soft-drink concentrate producers have contributed to the erosion of profitability of bottling companies because the bottlers, facing intense competition from powdered mixes, fruit drinks, and other beverages, have limited freedom to raise *their* prices accordingly. Buyers likewise can force down prices, demand higher quality or more service, and play competitors off against each other—all at the expense of industry profits.

The power of each important supplier or buyer group depends on a number of characteristics of its market situation and on the relative importance of its sales or purchases to the industry compared with its overall business.

A *supplier* group is powerful if:

— It is dominated by a few companies and is more concentrated than the industry it sells to.
— Its product is differentiated, or if it has built-in switching costs.
— It does not compete with substitutes.
— It poses a credible threat of integrating forward into the industry's business.
— The industry is not an important customer of the supplier group.

A *buyer* group is powerful if:

— It is concentrated or purchases in large volumes.
— The products it purchases from the industry are undifferentiated, and there are few switching costs.
— The products it purchases from the industry represent a significant fraction of its cost. Where the product sold by the industry in question is a small fraction of buyers' costs, buyers are usually much less price sensitive.
— It earns low profits, which create great incentive to lower its purchasing costs. Highly profitable buyers, on the other hand, are generally less price sensitive (that is, of course, if the item does not represent a large fraction of their costs).
— The industry's product is unimportant to the quality or performance of the buyers' products or services. Where the quality of the buyers' products is very much affected by the industry's product, buyers are generally less price sensitive and willing to pay higher prices for desirable performance. Industries in which this fortunate situation exists include oil field equipment, where a malfunction can lead to large losses, and enclosures for electronic medical and test instruments, where the quality of the enclosure can influence the user's impression about the quality of the equipment inside.
— The buyers pose a credible threat of integrating backward to make the industry's product. The Big Three auto producers and major buyers of metal cans have often used the threat of self-manufacture as a bargaining lever.

In view of their potential bargaining power, a company's choice of suppliers to buy from or buyer groups to sell to should be viewed as a crucial strategic decision. A company can improve its strategic posture by finding suppliers or buyers who possess the least power to influence it adversely.

As the factors creating supplier and buyer power change with time or as a result of a company's strategic decisions, naturally the power of these groups rises or falls. In the ready-to-wear clothing industry, as the buyers (department stores and clothing stores) have become more concentrated and control has passed to large chains, the industry has come under increasing pressure and suffered falling margins. The industry has been unable to differentiate its product or engender switching costs that lock in its buyers securely enough to neutralize these trends. As with entry barriers, a prime objective of the strategist is to neutralize the power of buyers or suppliers through artful strategic positioning.

Substitute Products

By placing a ceiling on prices, the availability of substitute products or services limits the potential of an industry. Unless it can upgrade the quality of the product or differentiate it somehow (via marketing, for example), the industry will suffer in earnings and possibly in growth.

The threat of substitutes depends on two conditions. Manifestly, the more attractive the price-performance trade-off offered by substitute products, the more firmly the lid is placed on the industry's profit potential. Sugar producers, confronted with the large-scale commercialization of high fructose corn syrup, a sugar substitute, are learning this lesson currently. The threat of substitution is also modified by switching costs from the industry's product to the substitute. The switching costs of possible substitutions are analyzed in an analogous fashion to those facing buyers when switching brands.

Substitutes not only limit profits in normal times but they also reduce the bonanza an industry can mine in boom times. In 1978 the producers of fiberglass insulation enjoyed unprecedented demand as a result of high energy costs and severe winter weather. But the industry's ability to raise prices was tempered by the plethora of insulation substitutes, including cellulose, rock wool, and styrofoam. These substitutes are bound to become an even stronger force once the current round of plant additions by fiberglass insulation producers has boosted capacity enough to meet or exceed demand.

Substitute products that deserve the most attention strategically are those that *(a)* are subject to trends improving their price-performance trade-off with the industry's product or *(b)* are produced by industries earning high profits. Substitutes often come rapidly into play if some development increases competition in their industries and causes price reduction or performance improvement. A company facing substitution must either improve its product's price-performance characteristics, raise switching costs, or be prepared to cash in its position as the substitute takes a larger and larger fraction of industry demand.

Rivalry

Rivalry among existing competitors takes the familiar form of jockeying for position—using tactics like price competition, product introduction, and advertising battles. Intense rivalry is related to the presence of a number of factors:

— Competitors are numerous or are evenly balanced in size and capabilities.

— Industry growth is slow, precipitating fights for market share triggered by expansion-minded members.

— The product or service lacks differentiation or switching costs, which lock in buyers and insulate one competitor from raids on its customers by another.

— Fixed costs are high or the product is perishable, creating strong temptation to cut prices.

— Intermittent overcapacity is present due to cyclicality of large required capacity additions.

— Competitors are diverse in strategies, origins, and "personalities." They have different goals and ideas about how to compete and continually run head-on into each other in the process.

— Competitors perceive high stakes to succeeding in the particular industry.

— Exit barriers are high. Exit barriers stem from very specialized assets, fixed costs of exits, linkages with sister business units, or management's loyalty to a particular business. Where exit barriers are high, companies remain in a business even though they may be earning low or even negative returns on investment. Excess capacity is not retired, and the profitability of the healthy competitors suffers as the sick ones hang on.

The factors affecting rivalry change as industries evolve. As an industry matures, its growth rate falls, resulting in increasing rivalry and often a shakeout. In the booming recreational vehicle industry of the early 1970s, nearly every producer did well; but slow growth since then has eliminated high returns, except for the strongest members, and wiped out weaker companies. The same profit story has been played out in industry after industry—snowmobiles, aerosol packaging, and sports equipment are just a few examples.

While a company must live with many of the determinants of rivalry—because they are built into industry economics, it may have some latitude for improving matters through strategic shifts. For example, it may try to raise buyers' switching costs or increase product differentiation. A concentration of selling efforts on the fastest growing segments of the industry or on market areas with the lowest fixed costs can reduce the impact of industry rivalry. If it is feasible, a company can try to avoid confrontation with competitors having high exit barriers and can thus sidestep involvement in bitter price cutting.

Industry Structure and the Formulation of Strategy

Once the strategist has assessed the forces affecting competition in his industry and their underlying causes, he can identify his company's strengths and weaknesses. The crucial strengths and weaknesses from a strategic standpoint are the company's position vis-à-vis the underlying causes of each competitive force. Where does it stand against substitutes? Against the sources of entry barriers?

Then the strategist can devise a plan of action that may include (1) positioning the company so that its capabilities provide the best defense against the competitive forces; (2) influencing the balance of the forces through strategic moves, thereby improving the company's position; and (3) anticipating shifts in the factors underlying the forces and responding to them, with the hope of exploiting change by choosing a strategy appropriate for the new competitive balance before opponents recognize it.

The first approach takes the structure of the industry as given and matches the company's strengths and weaknesses to it. Strategy in this sense can be viewed as building defenses against the competitive forces or as finding positions in the industry where the forces are weakest. Influencing the balance is a more aggressive approach designed to do more than merely cope with the forces themselves; it is meant to alter their causes and change the competitive rules of the game. For example, innovations in marketing can raise brand identification or otherwise differentiate the product. Capital investments in large-scale facilities or vertical integration affect entry barriers. The balance of forces is partly a result of external factors and partly in the company's control.

Industry evolution is important strategically because evolution, of course, brings with it changes in the sources of competition that have been identified. In the familiar product life-cycle pattern, for example, growth rates change, product differentiation is said to decline as the business becomes more mature, and the companies tend to integrate vertically.

Technology, a particularly important driver of industry evolution, can affect every one of the five competitive forces, often in dramatic ways. Scientific discoveries can lead to entirely new products that launch whole new industries, as is happening with genetic engineering in the 1980s. Technology can accelerate the development of substitute products, alter process technology in ways that greatly change economies of scale or capital requirements, or enhance the ability of a company to differentiate its product.

Industry trends, in whatever area, are not crucially important in themselves; what is critical is whether they affect the origins of competitive pressures. Consider vertical integration. In the maturing minicomputer industry, extensive vertical integration, both in manufacturing and in software development, is taking place. This very significant trend is greatly enhancing economies of scale and increasing the amount of capital necessary to compete in the industry. This in turn is raising barriers to entry and has driven some competitors out of the industry now that growth has leveled off.

Obviously the trends carrying the highest priority from a strategic standpoint are those that affect the most important sources of competition in the industry and those that elevate new forces to the forefront. In contract aerosol packaging, for example, the trend toward less product differentiation is now dominant. It has increased buyer's power, lowered the barriers to entry, and intensified competition.

Strategic analysis must begin in an examination of present and future industry trends in order to ascertain their impact on fundamental industry structure. This is the starting point for identifying strategic changes that may have to be made. More positively, however, the strategist who can foresee structural change may well be able to turn it to advantage by repositioning the company before the need is obvious to everybody.

Competitors

Strategy then involves positioning a business to maximize the value of the capabilities that distinguish it from its competitors. It follows that a central aspect of strategy formulation is perceptive analysis of competitors' strategy and predictable future behavior. The objective of an analysis of competitive strategy is to develop a profile of the nature and success of the changes in strategy each competitor might make, predict each competitor's probable response to the range of feasible strategic moves other firms could initiate, and forecast each competitor's probable reaction to the array of industry changes and broader environmental shifts that might occur. Sophisticated "competitor analysis" is needed to answer such questions as "Whom should we pick a fight with in the industry and in what sequence of moves?" "What is the meaning of that competitor's strategic move and how seriously should we take it?" and "What areas should we avoid because the competitor's response will be emotional or desperate?"

It is useful to identify four components of an analysis of a competitor's strategy (see Figure 3): *corporate strategy* with emphasis on long-term goals and the interrelation of corporate and divisional goals, *current business strategy* with emphasis on the economic strategy and operating policies of each of the competitor's businesses, *assumptions,* and *capabilities.* Understanding these four components will allow an informed profile of a competitor's likely behavior, as articulated in the key questions

Figure 3

The Components of a Competitor Analysis

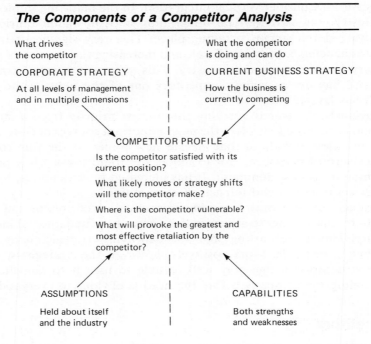

posed in Figure 3. Most companies develop at least an intuitive sense for their competitors' current business strategies and their strengths and weaknesses (shown on the right side of Figure 3). Much less attention is usually directed at the left side, or understanding what is really driving the behavior of a competitor—its future goals and the assumptions it holds about its own situation and the nature of its industry. These underlying elements, which must be deduced from behavior, are much harder to identify than is actual competitor behavior, yet they often determine how a competitor will behave in the future.

Each component of an analysis of a competitor's strategic position will be described briefly below. The same ideas can also be turned around to provide a framework within which a company may analyze its own position in its industry environment. Going through such an exercise can help a company understand what conclusions its competitors are likely to draw about it.

Future Goals

By a competitor's corporate strategy we mean in this context the targets of performance that motivate its striving. Although one most often thinks of financial goals, a comprehensive diagnosis of a competitor's corporate strategy will include, as we have noted before, many more qualitative factors, such as its objectives in terms of market leadership, technological position, social responsibility, and the noneconomic satisfactions it offers its members. Diagnosis of strategy should be carried to all management levels. Corporatewide goals, business unit goals, and goals that can be deduced for individual functional areas and key managers can often be identified or deduced from observable behavior. Finally, any diagnosis of a competitor's goals and their place in its total corporate strategy must include an analysis of the personal objectives that key managers at the competitor company seem to subscribe to.

The identification of a competitor's goals (and the measures they use in recording progress against these goals), the first component of competitor analysis, is important for a variety of reasons. A knowledge of objectives will allow a prediction of the degree of satisfaction each competitor feels with its present position and financial results and, as a result, how likely that competitor is to change strategy and the vigor with which it will react to outside events (for instance, the business cycle) or to moves by other firms. For example, a firm placing a high value on stable sales growth may react very differently to a business downturn or a market share increase by another company than a firm most interested in maintaining its rate of return on investment.

Knowing the priority of a competitor's goals will also aid in predicting its reaction to strategic changes. Some strategic changes will threaten a competitor more than others, given its goals and any pressures it may face from a corporate parent. This degree of threat will affect the probability of retaliation. Finally, identification of the goal components of a competitor's strategy helps the interpretation of the initiatives the competitor takes. A strategic move by a competitor which addresses one of its central goals or seeks to restore performance against a key target is not a casual matter. Similarly, an appreciation of its objectives will help determine whether a corporate parent will seriously support an initiative taken by one of its business units or whether it will back that business unit's retaliation against moves of competitors.

Assumptions

The second crucial component in competitor analysis is identifying each competitor's apparent assumptions about *itself* and about *the industry and the other companies in it.*

Each firm acts out a set of assumptions about its own situation that may not be rooted in fact or in consciously decided strategic intentions. For example, it may see itself as a socially conscious firm, as the industry leader, as the low-cost producer, or as having the best sales force. These assumptions about its own situation will guide the way the firm behaves and the way it reacts to events. If it sees itself as the low-cost producer, for example, it may try to discipline a price cutter with price cuts of its own.

A competitor's assumptions about its own situation may or may not be accurate. Where they are not, the discrepancy provides an intriguing strategic lever. If a competitor believes it has the greatest customer loyalty in the market but it actually does not, a provocative price cut may be a good way for another company to gain position. The competitor might well refuse to match the price cut believing that it will have little impact on its share, only to find that it loses significant market position before it recognizes the error of its assumption.

Just as each competitor holds assumptions about itself, every firm also operates on assumptions about its industry and competitors. These also may or may not be correct. For example, a manufacturer of baby foods is reported to have steadfastly believed that births would increase ever since the 1950s, even though the birth rate had been declining steadily until 1979. There are many examples of firms that have greatly over- or underestimated their competitors' staying power, resources, or skills.

Examining assumptions of all types can identify biases or blind spots that may creep into the way managers perceive their environment. Blind spots are areas where a competitor will either not see the significance of events (such as a strategic move) at all, will perceive them incorrectly, or will perceive them only very slowly. Revealing these blind spots will help the firm identify moves with a lower probability of immediate retaliation and identify moves where retaliation, once it comes, will not be effective.

Current Business Strategy

The third component of competitor analysis is the development of statements of the current economic or business strategy of each competitor, in just the same way as the firm identifies its own strategy as discussed earlier. Each competitor's strategy can then be probed for its implications in terms of the likely future behavior that will reinforce or support that strategy. This analysis will serve to expose likely future moves or areas where the competitor will retaliate vigorously because an essential part of its strategy is threatened.

Capabilities

A realistic appraisal of each competitor's capabilities is the final diagnostic step in competitor analysis. A competitor's goals, assumptions, and current strategy will influence the likelihood, timing, nature, and intensity of its reactions. Its capabilities will determine its ability to initiate or react to strategic moves and to deal with environmental or industry events that occur. We will examine the identification of company competence and resources shortly.

Picking the Battleground

Assuming that competitors will retaliate to the moves a firm initiates to improve its position, its strategic agenda is to select the best battleground for fighting it out with its competitors. The best battleground is the market segment or dimensions of strategy in which competitors are ill prepared, least enthusiastic, or most uncomfortable about competing as a result of the objectives in their corporate strategy, their assumptions, business strategies and capabilities. The best battleground may be competition on costs, for example, centered at the high or low end of the product line.

The ideal is to find a strategy that competitors are frozen from reacting to because of their present circumstances. The legacy of their past and current strategy may make some moves very costly for competitors to follow, while posing much less difficulty and expense for the initiating firm. For example, when Folger's Coffee invaded Maxwell House strongholds in the East with price cutting, the cost of matching these cuts was enormous for Maxwell House because of its large market share.

Realistically, competitors will not often be completely frozen or even torn by mixed motives. In this case, the analysis above should help to identify those strategic moves that will put the initiating firm in the best position to fight the competitive battle when it comes. This means taking advantage of an understanding of competitor goals and assumptions to avoid effective retaliation whenever possible and picking the battlefield where the firm's distinctive abilities represent the most formidable artillery.[4]

Identification of Opportunities and Risks

For the firm that has not determined what its strategy dictates it needs to know or has not embarked upon the systematic surveillance of environmental change, a few simple questions kept constantly in mind will highlight changing opportunity and risk. In examining your own company or one you are interested in, these questions should lead to an estimate of opportunity and danger in the present and predicted company setting.

1. *What is the underlying structure of the industry in which the firm participates?*

---

[4] See Porter, *Competitive Strategy,* chap. 3, for a fuller statement of competitor analysis.

As just pointed out, the company must develop an ongoing diagnosis of five competitive forces in its industry and the underlying economic, physical, and technical characteristics that produce those competitive forces. For example, knowledge that the rigid container industry requires high fixed investment in plant, faces slow growth, enjoys little product differentiation among competitors, and faces buyers with little cost in switching suppliers suggests that competitive rivalry will be intense. Such an analysis suggests that efforts to minimize cost through low overhead and new machinery will be fruitful, as will service and technical assistance that differentiates one company's appeal and performance from others. Knowledge that the cement industry requires high investment in plant, proximity to a certain combination of raw materials, a relatively small labor force, and enormous fuel and transportation costs suggests where to look for new plant sites and what will constitute competitive advantage and disadvantage. The nature of its product may suggest for a given company the wisdom of developing efficient pipeline and truck transportation and cheap energy sources to lower its costs rather than engaging in extensive research to achieve product differentiation or aggressive price competition to increase its market share.

2. What industry trends are apparent that might change this underlying structure?

Industry trends with the greatest impact are those that promise to affect the five competitive forces. Changes in substitute products occurring as a result of research and development, for example, affect the substitution threat facing the industry. For example, the glass container industry's development years ago of strong, light, disposable bottles and, more recently, combinations of glass and plastic recouped part of the market lost by glass to the metal container. The need for the glass industry to engage in this development effort was made apparent by the observable success of the metal beer can. Similarly, the easy-opening metal container suggested the need for an easily removable bottle cap in order to cope with the substitution threat. Increased sophistication of buyers of contract aerosol packaging, coupled with increasing ease of their vertical integration into the business themselves, made buyers increasingly powerful and price sensitive and had a strong depressing effect on industry profits.

3. How might foreseeable changes in the social, political, and macroeconomic context affect the industry or the firm?

Broad changes in society, government policy, or macroeconomic conditions can have a dramatic impact on the industry or on the company's position in its industry. Deregulation has thrown the domestic U.S. airline and trucking industries into bitter price wars and a scramble for consolidation. Both the glass bottle and the metal container face increasingly effective attack by environmentalists, who constitute a noneconomic and nontechnical force to be reckoned with. Container industries should have begun long since, for example, to develop logistical solutions to the legislatively mandated returnable bottle and can.

4. *What are the goals, assumptions, strategies, and capabilities of the important existing and potential competitors in the industry and their likely future behavior?*

Strategy must be developed in the context of informed profiles of competitors, both existing and potential. Competitors' moves can pose a threat to the company's existing strategic position, and the company's planned strategic changes can be nullified by competitive reaction.

A realistic assessment of competitors must guide the goals a company sets for itself. A small rubber company, in an industry led by Uniroyal, Goodyear, Goodrich, and Firestone, will not, under the economic condition of overcapacity, elect to provide the automobile business with original tires for new cars. The capabilities of competitors, quite apart from the resources of the firm, may suggest that a relatively small firm should seek out a niche of relatively small attraction to the majors and concentrate its powers on that limited segment of the market.

5. *What are the critical requirements for future success for the company?*

Industry structure, the capabilities of competitors and their expected behavior, and broader social, political, and macroeconomic trends all define the critical tasks the company must perform to ensure its strategic health and survival. In the ladies' belt and handbag business, style and design are critical, but so (less obviously) are relationships with department store buyers. In the computer business, a sales force able to diagnose customer requirements for information systems, to design a suitable system, and to equip a customer to use it is more important than the circuitry of hardware given the positions of the various competitors.

Although the question of what tasks are most critical for the company may be chiefly useful as a means of identifying risks or possible causes of failure, it may also suggest opportunity. Imagination in perceiving new requirements for success under changing conditions, when production-oriented competitors have not done so, can give a company leadership position. For example, opportunity for a local radio station and the strategy it needed to follow changed sharply with the rise of television, and those who first diagnosed the new requirements paid much less for stations than was later necessary.

6. *Given the analysis of the industry, competitors, and broader context, what range of strategic alternatives is available to companies in this industry?*

The force of this question is obvious in the drug industry. The speed and direction of pharmaceutical research, the structure of the industry, the behavior of competitors, the characteristics of worldwide demand, the different and changing ideas about how adequate medical care should be made available to the world's population, the concern about price, and the nature of government regulation suggest constraints within which a range of opportunity is still vividly clear. Similarly, in a more stable industry, there is always a choice. To determine its limits, an examination of environmental characteristics and developments is essential.

Opportunity as a Determinant of Strategy

Awareness of the environment and analysis of the behavior of competitors is not a special project to be undertaken only when warning of change becomes deafening; it is a continuing requirement for informed choice of purpose. Planned exploitation of changing opportunity ordinarily follows a predictable course which provides increasing awareness of areas to which a company's capabilities may be profitably extended. A useful way to perceive the normal course of development is to use Bruce Scott's stages referred to briefly in a previous discussion.

The manufacturer of a single product (stage I) sold within a clearly defined geographical area to meet a known demand finds it relatively easy to identify opportunity and risk. As an enterprise develops a degree of complexity requiring functional division of management decision, it encounters as an integrated stage II company a number of strategic alternatives in its market environments which the stage I proprietor is too hard pressed to notice and almost too overcommitted to consider. Finally, stage III companies, deployed along the full range of diversification, find even a greater number of possibilities for serving a market profitably than the resources they possess or have in sight will support. The more one finds out what might be done, the harder it is to make the final choice.

The diversified stage III company has another problem different from that of trying to make the best choice among many. If it has divisionalized its operations and strategies, as sooner or later in the course of diversification it must, then divisional opportunities come into competition with each other.

The corporate management will wish to invest profits not distributed to stockholders in those opportunities that will produce the greatest return to the corporation. If need be, corporate management will be willing to let an individual division decline if its future looks less attractive than that of others. The division on the other hand will wish to protect its own market position, ward off adverse developments, prolong its own existence, and provide for its growth. The division manager, who is not rewarded for failures, may program projects of safe but usually not dramatic prospects. The claims regarding projected return on investment, which are submitted in all honesty as the divisional estimate of future opportunity, can be assumed to be biased by the division's regard for its own interest and the manager's awareness of measurement.

The corporate management cannot be expected to be able to make independent judgments about all the proposals for growth which are submitted by all the divisions. On the other hand, all divisions cannot be given their heads, if the corporation's needs for present profit are to be met and if funds for reinvestment are limited. In any case, the greatest knowledge about the opportunities for a given technology and set of markets should be found at the divisional level.[5]

The strategic dilemma of a conglomerate world enterprise is the most complex in the full range of policy decisions. When the variety of what must be known cannot be reduced by a sharply focused strategy to the capacity of a single mind and when the range of a company's activities spans many industries and technologies, the problems of formulating a coherent strategy begin to get out of hand. Here strategy must become a managed process rather than the decision of the chief executive officer and his immediate associates. Bower and Prahalad[6] have shown in important research how the context of decision can be controlled by the top-management group and how power can be distributed through a hierarchy to influence the kind of strategic decision that will survive in the system. The process of strategic decision can, like complex operations, be organized in such a way as to provide appropriate complementary roles for decentralization and control.

To conceive of a new development in response to market information, analysis of competitive strategy, and prediction of the future is a creative act. To commit resources to it only on the basis of projected return and the estimate of probability constituting risk of failure is foolhardy. More than economic analysis of potential return is required for decision, for economic opportunity abounds far beyond the ability to capture it. That much money might be made in a new field or growth industry does not mean that a company with abilities developed in a different field is going to make it. We turn now to the critical factors that for an individual company make one opportunity better than another.

Identifying Corporate Competence and Resources

The first step in validating a tentative choice among several opportunities is to determine whether the organization has the capacity to prosecute

---

[5] See Norman Berg, "Strategic Planning in Conglomerate Companies," *Harvard Business Review,* May–June 1965.

[6] Joseph L. Bower, *Managing the Resource Allocation Process* (Boston: Division of Research, Harvard Business School, 1970); and C. K. Prahalad, "The Strategic Process in a Multinational Corporation" (doctoral thesis, Harvard Business School, 1975), partially summarized in "Strategic Choices in Diversified MNCs," *Harvard Business Review,* July–August 1976, pp. 67–78.

it successfully. The capability of an organization is its demonstrated and potential ability to accomplish, against the opposition of circumstance or competition, whatever it sets out to do. Every organization has actual and potential strengths and weaknesses. Since it is prudent in formulating strategy to extend or maximize the one and contain or minimize the other, it is important to try to determine what they are and to distinguish one from the other.

It is just as possible, though if anything more difficult, for a company to know its own strengths and limitations if it is to maintain a workable surveillance of its changing environment. Subjectivity, lack of confidence, and unwillingness to face reality may make it hard for organizations as well as for individuals to know themselves. But just as it is essential, though difficult, that a maturing person achieve reasonable self-awareness, so an organization can identify approximately its central strength and critical vulnerability.

Howard H. Stevenson has made the first formal study of management practice in defining corporate strengths and weaknesses as part of the strategic planning process.[7] He looked at five aspects of the process: (1) the attributes of the company which its managers examined, (2) the organizational scope of the strengths and weaknesses identified, (3) the measurement employed in the process of definition, (4) the criteria for telling a strength from a weakness, and (5) the sources of relevant information. As might be expected, the process Stevenson was looking at was imperfectly and variously practiced in the half dozen companies he studied. He found that the problems of definition of corporate strengths and weaknesses, very different from those of other planning processes, center mostly upon a general lack of agreement on suitable definition, criteria, and information. For an art that had hardly made a beginning, Stevenson offered a prescriptive model for integrating the considerations affecting definition of strength or weakness. Indicative of the primitive stage of some of our concepts for general management, Stevenson's most important conclusion is that the attempt to define strengths and weaknesses is more useful than the usual final product of the process.

Stevenson's exploratory study in no way diminishes the importance of appraising organization capability. It protects us against oversimplification. The absence of criteria and measures, the disinclination for appraising competence except in relation to specific problems, the uncertainty about what is meant by "strength" and "weakness," and the reluctance to imply criticism of individuals or organizational subunits—all these hampered his study but illuminated the problem. Much of what is intuitive

---

[7] Howard H. Stevenson, "Defining Corporate Strengths and Weaknesses: An Exploratory Study" (doctoral thesis deposited in Baker Library, Harvard Business School, 1969). For a published summary article of the same title, see *Sloan Management Review,* Spring 1976.

in this process is yet to be identified. Both for a competitor and for one's own company, one can inquire into strengths and weaknesses in functional components like marketing, manufacturing, research and development, finance, or control; the impact that growth may have on functional capability and on the quality of management; the capacity to respond quickly to competitive moods and to adapt to the changing environment. Raising questions like these quickens the power of self-awareness, even if definitive judgments are hard to come by.

To make an effective contribution to strategic planning, the key attributes to be appraised should be identified and consistent criteria established for judging them. If attention is directed to strategies, policy commitments, and past practices in the context of discrepancy between organization goals and attainment, an outcome useful to an individual manager's strategic planning is possible. The assessment of strengths and weaknesses associated with the attainment of specific objectives becomes in Stevenson's words a "key link in a feedback loop" which allows managers to learn from the success or failures of the policies they institute.

Although this study does not find or establish a systematic way of developing or using such knowledge, members of organizations develop judgments about what the company can do particularly well—its core of competence. If consensus can be reached about this capability, no matter how subjectively arrived at, its application to identified opportunity can be estimated. Surely as much success can be achieved in developing analysis of one's own company as in preparing the competitor analysis described earlier.

Sources of Capabilities. The powers of a company constituting a resource for growth and diversification accrue primarily from experience in making and marketing a product line. They inhere as well in (1) the developing strengths and weaknesses of the individuals comprising the organization, (2) the degree to which individual capability is effectively applied to the common task, and (3) the quality of coordination of individual and group effort.

The experience gained through successful execution of a strategy centered upon one goal may unexpectedly develop capabilities which could be applied to different ends. Whether they should be so applied is another question. For example, a manufacturer of salt can strengthen his competitive position by offering his customers salt-dispensing equipment. If in the course of making engineering improvements in this equipment, a new solenoid principle is perfected that has application to many industrial switching problems, should this patentable and marketable innovation be exploited? The answer would turn not only on whether economic analysis of the opportunity shows this to be a durable and profitable possibility but also on whether the organization can muster the financial, manufacturing, and marketing strength to exploit the discovery. The former question is likely to have a more positive answer than the latter. In this connection, it seems important to remember that individual and unsupported flashes of strength are not as dependable as the gradually accumulated product- and market-related fruits of experience.

Even where competence to exploit an opportunity is nurtured by experience in related fields, the level of that competence may be too low for any great reliance to be placed upon it. Thus a chain of children's clothing stores might well acquire the administrative, merchandising, buying, and selling skills that would permit it to add departments in women's wear. Similarly, a sales force effective in distributing typewriters may gain proficiency in selling office machinery and supplies. But even here it would be well to ask what distinctive ability these companies could bring to the retailing of soft goods or office equipment to attract customers away from a plethora of competitors.

Identifying Strengths. The distinctive competence of an organization is more than what it can do; it is what it can do particularly well. To identify the less obvious or by-product strengths of an organization that may well be transferable to some more profitable new opportunity, one might well begin by examining the organization's current product line and by defining the functions it serves in its markets. Almost any important consumer product has functions which are related to others into which a qualified company might move. The typewriter, for example, is more than the simple machine for mechanizing handwriting that it once appeared to be when looked at only from the point of view of its designer and manufacturer. Closely analyzed from the point of view of the potential user, the typewriter is found to contribute to a broad range of information processing functions. Any one of these might have suggested an area to be exploited by a typewriter manufacturer. Tacitly defining a typewriter as a replacement for a fountain pen as a writing instrument rather than as an input-output device for word processing is the explanation provided by hindsight for the failure of the old-line typewriter companies to develop the electric typewriter and the computer-related input-output devices it made possible before IBM did. The definition of product which would lead to identification of transferable skills must be expressed in terms of the market needs it may fill rather than the engineering specifications to which it conforms.

Besides looking at the uses or functions to which present products contribute, the would-be diversifier might profitably identify the skills that underlie whatever success has been achieved. The qualifications of an organization efficient at performing its long-accustomed tasks come to be taken for granted and considered humdrum, like the steady provision of first-class service. The insight required to identify the essential strength justifying new ventures does not come naturally. Its cultivation can probably be helped by recognition of the need for analysis. In any case, we should look beyond the company's capacity to invent new products. Product leadership is not possible for a majority of companies, so it is fortunate that patentable new products are not the only major highway to new opportunities. Other avenues include new marketing services, new methods of distribution, new values in quality-price combinations, and creative merchandising. The effort to find or to create a competence that is truly distinctive may hold the real key to a company's success or even to its future development. For example, the ability of a cement manufacturer to run a truck fleet more effectively than its competitors may constitute one of its principal competitive strengths in selling an undifferentiated product.

Matching Opportunity and Competence. The way to narrow the range of alternatives, made extensive by imaginative identification of new possibilities, is to match opportunity to competence, once each has been accurately identified and its future significance estimated. It is this combination which establishes a company's economic mission and its position in its environment. The combination is designed to minimize organizational weakness and to maximize strength. In every case, risk attends it. And when opportunity seems to outrun present distinctive competence, the willingness to gamble that the latter can be built up to the required level is almost indispensable to a strategy that challenges the organization and the people in it. Figure 4 diagrams the matching of opportunity and resources that results in an economic strategy.

Before we leave the creative act of putting together a company's unique internal capability and evolving opportunity in the external world, we should note that—aside from distinctive competence—the principal resources found in any company are money and people—technical and managerial people. At this stage of economic development, money seems less a problem than technical competence, and the latter much less critical than managerial ability. In reading the cases that follow, by all means look carefully at the financial records of each company and take note of its success and its problems. Look also at the apparent managerial capacity and, without underestimating it, do not assume that it can rise to any occasion. The diversification of American industry is marked by hundreds of instances in which a company strong in one endeavor lacked the ability to manage an enterprise requiring different skills. The right to make handsome profits over a long period must be earned. Opportunism without competence is a path to fairyland.

Besides equating an appraisal of market opportunity and organizational capability, the decision to make and market a particular product or service should be accompanied by an identification of the nature of the business and the kind of company its management desires. Such a guiding concept is a product of many considerations, including the man-

Figure 4

Schematic Development of Economic Strategy

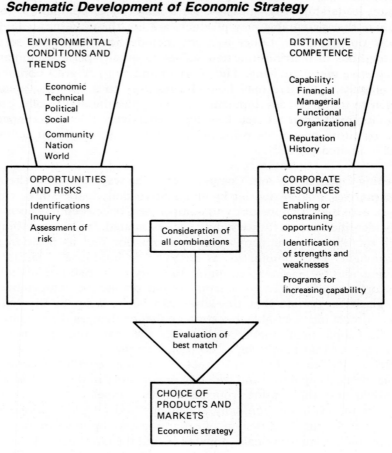

agers' personal values. As such, this concept will change more slowly than other aspects of the organization, and it will give coherence to all the variety of company activities. For example, a president who is determined to make his or her firm into a worldwide producer and fabricator of a basic metal, through policies differentiating it from the industry leader, will not be distracted by excess capacity in developed markets, low metal prices, and cutthroat competition in certain markets. Such a firm would not be sidetracked into acquiring, for example, the Pepsi-Cola franchise in Africa, even if this business promised to yield a good profit. (That such a firm should have an experimental division exploring offshoot technology is, however, entirely appropriate.)

Uniqueness of Strategy. In each company, the way in which distinctive competence, organizational resources, and organizational values are combined is or should be unique. Differences among companies are as numerous as differences among individuals. The combinations of opportunity to which distinctive competences, resources, and values may be applied are equally extensive. Generalizing about how to make an effective match is less rewarding than working at it. The effort is a highly stimulating and challenging exercise. The outcome will be unique for each case and each situation, but each achievement of a viable economic strategy will leave the student of strategy better prepared to take part in real-life strategic decisions.

Application to Cases

Students could profitably bring to the cases they study not only the questions suggested earlier but the following as well:

— What really is our product? What functions does it serve? To what additional functions might it be extended or adapted?
— What is happening to the market for our products? Is it expanding or contracting? Why?
— What are our company's major strengths and weaknesses? From what sources do these arise?
— Do we have a distinctive or core competence? If so, to what new activities can it be applied?
— What are our principal competitors' major strengths and weaknesses? Are they imitating us or we them? What comparative advantage over our competitors can we exploit?
— What is our strategy? Is the combination of product and market an optimum economic strategy? Is the central nature of our business clear enough to provide us with a criterion for product diversification?
— What, if any, better combinations of market opportunities and distinctive competence can our company effect, within a range of reasonable risk?

These questions will prove helpful throughout the course in the task of designing an economic strategy. However, they are never wholly sufficient, for the strategic decision is never wholly economic in character.

Rockwell International (A)

Municipal and Utility Division

Rockwell International's Municipal and Utility division had been the leader in the $160 million water meter industry since 1970, the culmination of a period of improving market position following the introduction of Rockwell's innovative sealed register (SR) product line in 1957. In 1982, however, Rockwell faced new challenges. Competitors had taken a renewed interest in the industry, and Rockwell's return on assets had been falling. It was in this context that Dick Bohlen, M&U president, and John Harriger, vice president of the M&U division, were considering options for improving the division's strategic position.

The Water Meter Industry

A water meter measured and recorded the amount of water flowing from a central utility water source to homes, businesses, or agricultural users. A meter consisted of a maincase, a measuring chamber through which the water flowed, and a register that recorded usage. Maincases were made of bronze or plastic. Desirable characteristics of maincases were durability, resistance to high internal pressure, leakproofness, and insensitivity to temperature extremes. Bronze case meters had greater durability than plastic case meters and were the predominant form of meter sold in 1981. The plastic case meters on the market in 1981 had a number of problems. They were prone to environmental stress, cracking

Copyright © 1982 by the President and Fellows of Harvard College
Harvard Business School case 383–019

after 10 or less years in the field, and the plastic screw threads that interfaced with the water pipes sometimes sheared off, destroying the seal between meter and pipes. Also some plastic resins used in maincase manufacturing in 1981 were weakened by hydrocarbons contained in house paints and in the "pipe dope" compound used by some installers to prevent leakage.[1] On the other hand, plastic maincases were more resistant to corrosion than bronze meters, and municipal water companies in some large cities such as Detroit refused to buy bronze meters because residents were stealing them to sell for scrap.

Four different types of measuring chambers were in common use in water meters in 1981—piston, disc, multijet, and turbine. Piston and disc meters were used for residential applications and counted the number of times the chamber was filled and then emptied. The predominant chamber sizes for residential application were ⅝″ and ¾″. Piston meters retained accuracy for longer periods of time than disc meters. Rockwell was the only major competitor that produced the piston design. Multijet and turbine meters were used in high flow and industrial applications. Fully 52 percent of the U.S. market was accounted for by ⅝″ and ¾″ residential meters, 12 percent was parts, and the balance was split among agricultural, industrial, and special-sized residential meters.

Water meters declined in accuracy over time, as shown in Exhibit 1. Inaccuracy resulted either from chamber erosion that allowed water to pass through unmeasured or from reduced tolerances due to excessive wear. Both causes of inaccuracy always led to underestimation of water usage. Typically for each percentage loss in accuracy, annual revenues per meter declined about $1.00.

An optional feature of water meters was remote meter reading capability. A so-called remote eliminated problems and costs associated with gaining access to a customer's premises to read the meter. An average meter reader could visit about 100 homes a day at an average daily cost of $75. Without remotes the meter reader gained access to only about half the homes visited, while the remotes allowed 100 percent coverage. Remotes were not needed in warmer areas of the United States where meters could be installed outdoors with little danger of damage from frost or extremely cold weather. It was estimated that by 1990 a majority of meters sold nationwide would have remote meter reading capabilities.

The simplest type of remote, called a generator remote, allowed the meter reader to read water usage from a meter installed in an accessible outdoor location. More complex remotes provided for automatic transfer of the reading onto a portable cassette tape (encoded remotes) or even direct to the water utility over telephone lines (centralized remotes).

---

[1] It was rumored that the major meter manufacturers were developing more durable hydrocarbon-resistant plastics for use in manufacturing maincases.

This provided for more accurate reading and reduced billing cost. However, capital costs were significantly higher—perhaps $50 more for each meter and $2,000 for a portable cassette recording device in the case of encoded remotes and to $80–$120 per meter plus $10–$30,000 of central computing costs for a centralized system.

Water utilities were expected to attempt to reduce computer costs by sharing their remote systems with local gas or electric utilities. Centralized systems were expected to save more money in labor and billing costs than encoded systems.

Forty-six percent of all utilities had purchased generator remotes for their systems by 1981, though few, if any, utilities used remotes for all their residential meters. Compared to meter manufacturers' estimates, utilities had been slow to accept the new encoded or centralized remote systems. In fact few centralized remote systems were fully operational in 1981, though many types of centralized systems were being developed and tested.

Customers

In 1980 U.S. water meter sales totaled over $160 million. Over 90 percent of the meters were sold to public and private utilities ranging in size from water departments of large cities to mobile home parks. Municipal governments owned approximately 95 percent of all water utilities, the remainder being owned and operated by groups of private investors. The 10 largest utilities purchased between 40,000 and 70,000 residential meters each per year, while small utilities purchased as few as 10 or 20 meters per year. (See Exhibit 2.)

Before accurate meters, water rates had typically been flat rates based on arbitrary user classifications. The installation of water meters permitted billing based on actual usage. In addition utility experience had shown that water consumption declined about 30 percent when water meters were installed. Of the 60,000 utilities in the United States 95 percent were metered by 1981. More than 4 million residences and businesses were still unmetered, however, and some unmetered utilities were considering meter installation to counteract recent water shortages. In addition, even in metered cities, apartment buildings that were connected to one large meter were candidates for conversion to individual metering of each living unit. It was estimated that there were up to 20 million unmetered individual apartments in the United States.

Water rates and taxes were the two major revenue sources available to most municipalities, since of all municipally owned utilities only water systems were consistently profitable. The average water utility charged 8 to 10 cents per 100 gallons of water used, and annual consumption averaged 100,000 gallons per home. On average, utilities had increased their water rates by about 5 percent a year. Water rates were as or more difficult to raise as other utility prices or taxes because of widespread belief that water cost nothing. For investor-owned water utilities, rates were regulated. There were some utilities that wanted to charge higher rates for usage during peak hours, but the standard meters and remotes available in 1981 could not distinguish between peak and off-peak consumption. Only centralized remotes could potentially be adapted to record the time that water usage occurred, and adaptation of centralized remotes for this purpose was expected to be quite costly for the utilities.

Water departments were almost always independent entities that were under the jurisdiction of city government offices. Water departments handled all functions including installation, purchasing, meter reading, and billing. Installers and meter readers were municipal employees. Larger utilities were organized like companies, while smaller utilities had few personnel and often contracted billing to a local bank.

Annual capital expenditures for water treatment facilities, pipes, meters, and other water utility equipment averaged 20–40 percent of annual water revenues, with meter purchasing costs representing between 5 percent and 10 percent of total capital expenditures. The utilities relied on internally generated revenues, municipal bonds, and taxes for funding. It was estimated that the 756 urban areas with populations over 50,000 would have to spend up to $100 billion in the 1980s and 1990s just to maintain their water systems. For municipal water utilities a large portion of water revenues was used to finance other nonwater services. Federal loans and subsidies to municipalities were expected to decrease through the mid-1980s.

Meters were purchased by utilities for installation in new homes and businesses and for replacement of the utility's installed base. Installation costs averaged $30 per meter. Sales of meters for new homes and businesses, which were directly related to the level of construction activity in the economy, accounted for 40 percent of 1981 residential meter sales. Since 1977 single family housing starts had fallen more than 50 percent and were expected to decline further in 1982. After this it was expected that economic recovery, pent-up housing demand, and increased emphasis on meter replacement programs would raise total demand for residential meters at about 7 percent a year through 1987. In the 1980s meter replacement was expected to represent 50–75 percent of the total residential meter demand, while percentage of remotes sold was expected to rise from 25 percent in 1981 to somewhat greater than 50 percent in 1987.

Replacement sales of water meters were a function of the longevity of previously installed meters, the extent to which the meters retained their accuracy, and the presence or absence of water meter repair facilities at a utility. Approximately 50–60 percent of all utilities with over 50,000 installed meters had their own repair shops, with fewer small utilities doing their own repairs. Repair costs for utility-owned repair shops averaged $20–$35 per visit to remove the meter and $10–$25 to repair it. Manufacturers ran repair programs for utilities that did not have their own repair shops. From a technical standpoint old meters could be replaced with models from different manufacturers, though the prevalence of model switching varied among utilities.

In the 1970s the average utility had increased its time between repair calls from once every 10 years to once every 15 years despite local ordinance and industry association guidelines for repair every 10 years. Meter manufacturers, particularly Rockwell, had been encouraging utilities to replace many meters at one time in "changeout programs" to increase the accuracy of installed base while obtaining quantity discounts on meter purchases.

Purchase decisions by utilities were to specifications written by utility executives or local government officials. Starting in the late 1960s city councils, chief city engineers, and purchasing agents had increasingly become involved in setting specifications for water meters. Accuracy and ease of repair were cited as the most important criteria for purchase (see Exhibit 3).

Specifications differed from utility to utility. Some wrote specifications tight enough to preclude all but one manufacturer while others were loose enough to allow all manufacturers a chance to bid for the business. Specifications could change from year to year due to product and service changes or new decision makers being introduced into the purchase process. However, specifications changed very slowly in water systems, and it could take up to five years or more before dramatically new features were included in specifications.

In the smallest utilities the fire chief or water superintendent was the principal decision maker for meters. In medium-sized and larger utilities, the decision makers were the local water superintendent and/or the utility engineering manager, who relied on technical advice and ongoing service provided by salesmen to set specifications. Water superintendents were generally not political appointees or elected officials and often stayed at their jobs for 20 years or longer. In large cities city engineers or purchasing agents sometimes had a role in meter purchasing.

Larger utilities tended to rely more heavily than smaller utilities on sealed bids when purchasing meters, but direct sales contact was still very important since different manufacturers offered different product features, specifications, and guarantees. Direct marketing was an important tool used to differentiate competing products. Smaller utilities relied more heavily on negotiated bids, single source relationships, and the distributor channel. Exhibit 4 shows the relationship between utility size and average meter cost.

Regulation

Local public utility commissions (PUCs) and other local government bodies regulated water utilities in a variety of ways. Most municipalities imposed price controls on public utilities, and PUCs limited returns for investor-owned utilities. PUCs also ruled on whether utilities could charge customers the full meter cost upon installation or charge meter rental fees as part of the monthly water bill. Local laws also differed on the required frequency of actually reading the meter versus billing on an estimated basis and the frequency of meter accuracy checks which varied from 7 to 15 years. According to *Public Utility Reports,* less than 50 cases disputing water rates had been brought since 1935 compared to many hundreds for electrical and telephone utilities. In general more municipalities were limiting the use of estimated bills, and it was also expected that certain local governments would enact legislation requiring 100 percent metering where water supply was critical.

Utilities were also affected by local ordinances, especially in smaller towns. For example, laws had been passed requiring that only certain manufacturers' meters could be installed. Many small utilities also had to obtain authorization on large meter purchases from their city councils.

The industry association, the American Water Works Association (AWWA), had a water meter standards committee consisting of 25 utility officials and 15 employees from the meter manufacturers. The committee met several times a year and was expected to promulgate new standards in 1982. The AWWA standards had had uneven impact on utilities, however. For example, although the AWWA's standards established in 1977 forbade plastic maincases for PD meters, several manufacturers had been moderately successful selling plastic meters since 1972. In addition meters that did not meet all of AWWA's other stringent performance standards were being sold to price-sensitive customers.

Distribution and Marketing

Water meters were sold direct through manufacturers' sales forces and through more than 200 distributors and agents (see Exhibit 2). Manufacturers' sales representatives worked with utility officials to develop purchase specifications as well as handling technical questions and service requests for existing clients. A sales rep made an average of four visits a day. In general large customers were visited at least once a month, while smaller accounts were seen three to four times a year. Sales reps had some discretion on pricing, but important negotiated bids and all sealed bids were cleared through headquarters.

In addition to regular sales calls, many utility officials were exposed to manufacturers' representatives at the annual AWWA convention and regional conventions. The water meter manufacturers set up information booths staffed with sales personnel to discuss meter features and hospitality rooms where customers were wooed over drinks and bowls of shrimp. At the 1980 annual convention each major meter manufacturer had spent in excess of $100,000 on booths, information dissemination, refreshments, travel, and accommodations.

Water equipment distributors were the other major sales channel. In the late 1970s distributors had increasingly run into financial troubles, and several had gone bankrupt. Water meters comprised less than 20 percent of distributors' revenues, which consisted primarily of high-volume, low-profit pipes, valves, and hydrants.

Distributors did not carry competing water meters in most cases. While they did not handle exclusive territories, distributors had little territorial overlap. Distributors set their own prices based on manufacturers' suggested list price and participated in sealed bids for smaller orders though obtaining some bidding guidance from the manufacturers. While distributor margins in the 1960s and early 1970s averaged 20–25 percent for water meters, some had recently cut their margins to approximately 10 percent in order to match the discounts being offered by direct sales forces.

Meter manufacturers maintained inventories of meters and would ship small lots out of a large order as a utility needed them. Utilities were billed only as meters were actually shipped and not when an order was placed.

Manufacturers advertised meters in trade journals. The leading competitors seldom spent as much as $100,000 per annum on such advertising. The manufacturers also printed annual sales catalogs and brochures and sponsored promotional roadshows, maintenance seminars for repairmen, and informational programs on changeouts. Total sales and administrative costs, including logistics, averaged more than 10 percent of total revenue.

Meters for industrial, commercial, and agricultural uses were sold both to utilities and end users. The same decision makers within utilities usually helped choose both residential and nonresidential meters. Purchasers of industrial commercial water meters were most interested in careful measurement and reducing their water use costs. They purchased more accurate and sophisticated instruments which were often customized for special needs. As industrial users recognized needs for increased accuracy and conservation, demand for turbine and compound meters was predicted to grow 8 percent per annum through 1987. In the agricultural meter market price and availability were key where meters were required by law. Where metering was undertaken for conservation and accountability instead of legal requirements, accuracy was more important to purchasers. Agricultural demand was expected to grow 3 percent a year through 1987.

International Markets

About 25 percent of worldwide water meter sales were in the United States and Canada. Outside of North America water meters had a much lower per capita penetration. Overall world penetration was less than 50 percent of all homes, with world market growth of about 1 percent a year. The highest penetration of water meters outside the United States was in the more industrialized cities in Canada, South America, and Europe.

Three basic sets of water meter standards prevailed outside the United States: American Water Works Association (AWWA) standards, British Standards System (BSS) standards, and the International Standards Organization (ISO) standards originating in the European Economic Community. AWWA standards were considered the most stringent, and often standards were customized by country.

Selection of standards was a function of a number of factors. The country where consulting engineers were trained affected the standards specified as did the source of financing for projects. Historical colonial ties and close relationships among countries also mattered; South America tended to be closer to AWWA specifications, for example, while Arab nations and the West Indies tended toward BSS specifications. Developing countries often bought inexpensive, lower quality meters while the developed world bought higher quality meters though not necessarily meeting strict AWWA standards. Few disc or piston meters were sold outside North America.

Import regulations covering water meters varied by country. Import tariffs ranged from 0–30 percent with 22.5 percent assessed in Israel and other Middle Eastern countries. Local content rules were imposed in most South American, Middle Eastern, and African countries. Because of rigid technical specifications in Japan, no significant quantities of water meters had yet been imported there.

Manufacturing

The manufacture of water meters involved three high-speed precision operations—fabrication of bronze and plastic parts; finishing and subassembly of chambers, registers, and maincases; and final assembly and testing. Plastic parts were injection molded on high-speed automatic injection-molding lines. Except for the oldest machines, employees were only needed for machine setup, monitoring, maintenance, and parts inspection. Manufacturers continually upgraded their processes to reduce cost and improve product quality.

Bronze maincases were fabricated in a continuous process foundry operation using highly skilled labor. In a noisy, hot foundry room melting furnaces were operated 24 hours a day. Molten bronze was poured into sand molds and between 100 and 200 maincases could be produced per hour. After the metal in each mold cooled the sand molds were destroyed and maincases were punched out and cleaned. Materials cost for regular-sized bronze maincases accounted for about one third of direct manufacturing cost (before manufacturing overhead) while maincase materials for downsized meters averaged 10–15 percent less.

Plastic maincases were injection molded on large, semiautomatic numerically controlled machines that could produce two finished parts in less than two minutes. Bronze maincases cost about 10 cents per unit more in labor costs than plastic cases to manufacture due to machining requirements. Materials costs were approximately one third of direct manufacturing costs for plastic maincases.

Numerically controlled injection-molding machines for plastic maincase manufacturing cost approximately $200,000 and required up to $100,000 in molds and tooling. In contrast, costs for establishing a bronze foundry were far greater and required a sustained long-term commitment by the manufacturer. Molds for high-production bronze maincase manufacture cost considerably less than plastic molds but lasted only one third as long.

Finishing operations for maincases and chambers were performed by numerically controlled (NC) machines that removed material from the inside of the maincase and then finished to the proper size, followed by boring, drilling, and threading operations. The investment in NC equipment was substantial and required high volume to justify the investment.

Subassembly and final assembly took place on assembly lines operated by semiskilled and unskilled labor. When the meters were finally assembled they were tested extensively for accuracy, seal, and so forth. Customer orders were sent out on trucks, with most orders filling less than a full truckload. Most manufacturers used independent truckers for transporting meters and parts. Transportation costs were less than 5 percent of total manufacturing costs.

Meter manufacturers produced variations of their standard meter in batches. Common variations included different sized meterpipe connections, different materials for chambers or bottom plates, and different measurement units for registers. Utilities requested variations for cost savings, extra durability, or standardization with other meters in their installed base.

Minimum efficient scale for a residential meter model was approximately 200,000 units a year. As volume decreased plants became less efficient in manpower use, increasing per-meter costs. Depending on sales volume and meter models, manufacturing overhead averaged 20–40 percent of manufacturers' sales price to distributors. In addition manufacturers engaged in regular R&D programs that cost 3–5 percent of total sales. Other miscellaneous fixed costs averaged 5 percent of total sales.

Many operations could be performed at lower cost if manufactured on numerically controlled machines or on automated assembly lines. Current scale did not justify this investment for many of the residential meter manufacturers. Manufacturers had investigated the use of robotics, however, and the major companies were expected to invest heavily to improve their cost position.

A fully integrated bronze meter manufacturing facility with capacity for 1 million meters per year cost on the order of $10–$12 million, while a facility using purchased bronze casting cost on the order of $5–$7 million. An integrated plastic meter manufacturing facility cost $4–$6 million.

Suppliers

Twenty different materials were used in manufacturing water meters, including bronze ingot, plastic resin, stainless steel machined parts and stampings, iron and bronze castings, electrical components, hard and soft rubber, magnets, and metal fasteners. Sales to the meter industry represented a small percentage of suppliers' volume. Meter manufacturers used multiple suppliers for all materials except hard rubber, which comprised less than 5 percent of total materials purchases. In the 1970s the only four domestic hard rubber manufacturers went bankrupt. In 1978 the meter manufacturers had helped subsidize the formation of a new domestic hard rubber company, and after one year product quality was sufficient to satisfy water meter manufacturers' needs.

Water meter manufacturers often obtained discounts on large purchases of bronze and plastic. Large purchasers of bronze ingot, such as the leading water meter manufacturers, received a 5–15 percent discount depending on market conditions in the bronze industry. Large-scale plastic meter manufacturers received 10–15 percent discounts on plastic resin. Bronze prices were highly volatile depending on copper prices and the demand of other users of copper and bronze. Plastic costs were directly related to oil prices and had escalated rapidly since 1973.

Industry History

At the end of World War II, there were eight major competitors in the U.S. water meter industry, most of which had existed since the turn of the century. Several companies had attempted to enter the industry in the late 1940s but exited within a few years of their entry. In the 1950s and 1960s Neptune Water Meter Company was market share leader, followed by Rockwell Manufacturing, Badger Meter, Gamon-Calmet Industries, Carlon Meter Company, and Hersey Products. The 1950s and 1960s were a period of rapid industry growth, stimulated by the development of suburbs around major U.S. cities. Manufacturers sold their products at similar prices and differentiated their products based on meter design and service.

No major product innovation had occurred in residential meters between the early 1900s and 1957. In 1957, however, Rockwell introduced its sealed register (SR) meter. The SR meter incorporated a unique magnetic drive and sealed register concept that retained its accuracy over a longer period of time. In addition the SR had less bronze content and eliminated or modularized two thirds of the parts in the then conventional meters, simplifying manufacture and repair and resulting in considerable manufacturing cost savings.

Acceptance of the SR was slow. Many utilities adopted a wait-and-see attitude since SR field testing by some utilities revealed operating problems. Other manufacturers argued against the meter. In 1963 Rockwell announced a 10-year warranty on its SRs as well as a maintenance plan under which customers could replace worn-out parts at a very low cost. SR sales began to pick up as the operating problems were corrected and service and warranty programs were introduced. In the 1960s the other competitors incorporated similar magnetic drive mechanisms into their designs and began offering extended warranties and maintenance programs similar to Rockwell's. However, by 1970 Rockwell had become the market share leader.

In 1958 Badger had introduced the first remote register meter (generator concept). Other competitors had waited five or more years to introduce their own register remotes. In 1965 Neptune introduced the first system for automated reading and billing (encoded system). As with most metering innovations and new models, the remotes encountered operating problems in their first few years in the field.

In 1972 Badger and Kent Meter, a European-based company, introduced the first plastic maincase meters, selling at prices 30–40 percent below those of comparable bronze meters. Badger had developed the plastic meter to reduce the company's vulnerability to fluctuations in bronze prices, exacerbated because Badger did not have its own foundry. Kent Meter developed its plastic meter for use primarily in the more price-sensitive international marketplace. In the next five years two additional smaller manufacturers had also begun producing plastic meters. As of late 1981, however, Rockwell and Neptune had not introduced plastic meter models.

In the mid-1970s Rockwell had introduced a downsized meter which contained less bronze and was slightly less durable than the SR. In 1980 this model was discontinued, never having sold as many as 100,000 units in a year. Neptune introduced its own downsized meter in 1981. Both downsized meters used smaller maincases and chambers than standard models.

The first major foreign entrant into the United States had been Kent

Meter Sales, the world market share leader in 1981. In 1966 Kent had purchased Engineered Controls Company, a very small U.S. piston meter manufacturer, in order to establish a U.S.-owned and -operated subsidiary. In the late 1970s Arad Meters of Israel also began U.S. production of multijet meters, and Precision Meter, founded by Pont à Mousson, was the only other foreign competitor operating in the United States. Though neither company met AWWA standards, both had gained some sales because of low prices and because their multijet meters met the needs of certain sandy water applications.

Competitors

In 1981 four companies sold 86 percent of all U.S. water meters. Relative market share had fluctuated in the 1970s:

Estimated Market Share of U.S. Water Meter Manufacturers

	1972	1976	1977	1978	1979	1980	1981
Rockwell*	29%	29%	33%	31%	32%	33%	36%
Badger	23	24	24	22	20	19	18
Neptune	20	20	18	20	21	23	24
Hersey	16	15	15	13	11	9	8
Other	12	12	10	14	16	16	14

* Rockwell's share reduction in 1978 was due to a capacity constraint which has since been alleviated through additional investment in the business.

During the 1970s meter prices had remained relatively flat, while costs rose approximately 5 percent a year. Sealed bid prices had sometimes fallen far below meter prices charged to distributors. One casualty was Gamon-Calmet, which went bankrupt in 1978 due to poor quality and high manufacturing costs. In 1979 both Rockwell and Badger tried, without success, to lead bid prices up. Between 1977 and 1981 sealed bid prices for the ⅝" meter had dropped 33 percent in constant dollar terms.

Profiles of the leading competitors in water meters are given below with a summary of their financial positions shown in Exhibits 5 and 6. Briefer profiles of several other firms, including the leading international competitors, are given as well.

Badger Meters

Badger was founded in 1905 to manufacture water meters. During the 1970s Badger had expanded its business into chemical processing, wastewater treatment, and telecommunications. About 80 percent of its total revenues still came from water meters, accessories, and valves in 1981, however. More than 40 percent of the publicly traded Badger stock was either owned by Badger President James Wright or in trust for the Wright family.

While Badger sold a full line of water meters residential meter sales were concentrated in plastic meters. Since the 1972 introduction of its plastic meter Badger's annual residential meter unit sales had more than doubled with more than 4 million plastic meters sold since introduction. However, much of the sales growth of plastic meters had cannibalized the sales of Badger's bronze meters.

According to its 1980 annual report Badger listed its most important strengths as price, quality, and delivery. Total sales had been strongest to small- and medium-sized utilities. In the late 1970s guarantees on plastic meters were improved, and Badger had become more aggressive on bidding for bronze meter business. Beginning in 1977 it had assembled the second strongest distributor and agent network and improved field service levels. At the same time Badger reduced the number of direct sales representatives in its four regional offices. It established a new order entry and distribution system to process customer orders within minutes. A new warehouse and final assembly facility was built in Rio Rico, Arizona, in 1980.

Badger's main manufacturing facility in Milwaukee, Wisconsin, was constructed in the 1950s and expanded in the 1970s to allow increased plastic meter production. Badger did not own its own foundry, purchasing machined bronze maincases, but had an excellent plastic injection-molding facility at the Milwaukee plant. It was believed that Badger had not invested as heavily as Rockwell and Neptune in plant automation. Final assembly of maincases, registers, and chambers was done both at the Milwaukee plant and at three regional distribution centers. Meters assembled in the field were not as thoroughly tested for leaks or coordination between register and chamber. Badger's unionized labor rates were estimated to be equal to or 5–10 percent higher than Rockwell's labor rates at Uniontown, Pennsylvania.

During the early 1970s Badger had expanded internationally through the acquisition of meter companies in Europe and South America. Though several of the European subsidiaries had been divested, Badger maintained a distribution network and participated in European bidding to a small extent since U.S.-designed meters were not competitive in the European market, and plastic meters had not been accepted. Badger also had a very small market share in Canada. Foreign sales represented 11 percent of total Badger revenues with the majority of sales coming from its Mexican subsidiary.

In October 1981 Badger appointed a new president, James Forbes, a CPA with a law degree who joined Badger in 1979 after serving as president of the Will Ross Health Group. Dividends were discontinued in 1981 due to poor results and covenants on outstanding long-term debt.

Neptune Meters

Neptune was founded in 1892 to produce and sell meters. It sold a full line of residential, industrial, and commercial bronze meters, industrial flow meters, electronic weighing systems, process control equipment, and clean water and wastewater treatment systems.

In 1979 Neptune had been acquired by Wheelabrator-Frye (WF), a diversified manufacturer of energy and environmental systems, fertilizer plants, chemicals, and transportation equipment with $1.3 billion in sales and $55.3 million in net income in 1980. In 1980 WF purchased Pullman Equipment, a $133.4 million transportation equipment company with substantial problems caused by damage suits, high debt, and unprofitable operations. By late 1981 it was strongly rumored that WF would divest Pullman within the next year.

Neptune comprised five subdivisions within WF's engineered components division. All activity and strategic planning was supervised by Neptune President Bill Miller, age 35, a long-time WF employee who was appointed to his current position after the acquisition in 1979. Miller ran his operation with a relatively small staff and had lower administrative fixed costs than Rockwell. In 1981 he had expressed confidence in regaining market share leadership in residential water meters and was rumored to believe that Rockwell was harvesting its water meter business.

Neptune had relocated to a nonunionized plant in Tallahassee, Alabama, in the mid-1970s. After the move it had started bidding aggressively for large utility accounts. Some of Neptune's winning bids were estimated to have barely covered variable cost. In 1981 the company introduced its first downsized residential meter, the T-10, which was initially not sold on a sealed bidding basis but only in negotiated or sole source situations. Neptune's public statements stressed product quality, new remote reading technology, and conformance to AWWA standards. It had a strong direct sales force with five regional offices and approximately 30 sales and marketing personnel. Neptune's distributor relations were weak compared to Rockwell and Badger. Neptune's meters were also sold to other divisions of WF.

Neptune had the second highest capacity in the industry with its own semiautomatic bronze foundry and plastic injection-molding facilities. Parts were designed for maximum interchangeability between meter models. Production labor rates were estimated to be as much as 15 percent lower than Rockwell's Uniontown, Pennsylvania, rates.

Neptune had invested heavily in R&D in order to introduce new meters and centralized remote metering. It had optimistic expectations for widespread acceptance of centralized remote systems. Neptune's vice president of engineering had been very vocal in the industry in promoting the use of telephone and two-way cable for centralized metering through retrofit of the Neptune remotes to the current Neptune meter line. Neptune had conducted most of the centralized remote experiments that were publicized in the 1980s, though much of the remote equipment was designed and manufactured by outside electronics and computer firms. Some public statements by Neptune alluded to practical and affordable centralized remote systems to be readily available by 1987. Neptune held over 60 percent of the Canadian market but had been losing share to Rockwell during the past five years. Though Neptune had foreign subsidiaries in five other countries, Neptune achieved only small sales outside North America.

Hersey Meters

Hersey was a small, privately held company started in the early 1900s. Water meters and water safety devices accounted for nearly all of its revenues. In 1981 Hersey was deemphasizing its residential piston meter line due to an antiquated design and manufacturing costs about 40 percent higher than its major competitors. Instead it was attempting to build sales of its turbine meters, which were comparable to Rockwell's in both quality and price. Hersey's direct sales force and distribution were small compared to that of the competition. International sales were also minor compared to its major competitors.

Hersey had a unionized plant in Dedham, Massachusetts, and a nonunionized plant in Spartanburg, South Carolina. In 1979 the Dedham plant had a seven-week strike. Industry observers did not anticipate Hersey introducing any new residential meters in the 1980s.

Kent Meter Sales

Kent Meter Sales was a U.S. subsidiary of Brown Boveri, a Swiss corporation that produced power generators, flow controls, turbo chargers, telecommunications equipment, locomotives, food processing equipment, magnets, home appliances, and nuclear reactors. Of Brown Boveri sales 8.7 percent were in electrical products, measurement, and control devices (in which water meters were classified), and 4.5 percent of total worldwide sales were made in North America. The U.S. meter subsidiary received no financial assistance from Brown Boveri.

While Kent's U.S. sales were only $3 million in 1980, its affiliates in 126 countries had totaled $115 million in water meter sales in 1980 and held high market shares in almost all markets. In the United States Kent distributed a full line of bronze and plastic piston and multijet meters similar to designs of U.S. competitors while selling European meters for industrial and commercial applications. Product quality was judged lower than that of U.S. competitors' products and sold to price-sensitive customers. Kent had U.S. plants and offices in Florida and Puerto Rico. U.S. penetration had been limited by unsuccessful efforts to establish a direct sales force in addition to product quality problems.

Kent had achieved its strong international position through a wide distribution system, numerous joint ventures and licensing agreements, and localized final assembly. Chambers and register parts were produced at central plants in Puerto Rico, U.K., Australia, South America, and Africa, while maincases and other register parts were manufactured on a country-by-country basis. Transport costs from Kent's centralized plants to the local final assembly sites were estimated at about 5 percent of total manufacturing cost.

Rockwell International

Rockwell International was a large diversified manufacturing company with fiscal 1980 sales of $7 billion and aftertax profits of $280 million. It was organized in 1928 to sell products to government and commercial markets. Through aggressive R&D and acquisitions, the company had developed a broad range of products including automotive components, aerospace systems (including the space shuttle, the B-1 Bomber, and Navstar satellite), defense electronics, telecommunications and switching equipment, avionics systems, automatic mailroom equipment, and flow control systems. In fiscal 1980 37 percent of total revenues came from U.S. government contracts and subcontracts.

In 1973 Rockwell Manufacturing Company was merged into North American Rockwell, and the new corporation was renamed Rockwell International. With the merger came a new emphasis on planning and control systems. The M&U division, containing meter operations, became part of Rockwell's General Industries operations which included: components for the oil, gas, and nuclear industries; nuclear-related government work; high-speed printing presses and related graphics equipment; water and gas meters; clamps and couplings; textile machinery; and power tools.

Until 1974 Rockwell was led by members of the Rockwell family. By the mid-1970s, however, Rockwell experienced serious cash flow and debt-to-equity problems due to an aggressive acquisition program and was nearly acquired by Gulf Oil. Nonfamily management had taken over, and the corporation had placed strong emphasis on careful money management. In 1978 Rockwell discontinued its Admiral line of TV sets and other appliances. By 1980 its financial position had improved substantially to where it was receiving A ratings or above from the bond and financial service communities.

Rockwell Manufacturing Company entered the water meter market when it acquired Pittsburgh Equitable Meter Company in 1945. Pittsburgh Equitable was formed through the merger of Pittsburgh Meter Company, founded in 1886 by George Westinghouse, Equitable Meter Company, founded in the 1890s, and National Meter Company, founded in 1870. Many of Pittsburgh Equitable's products were based on George Westinghouse's original patents.

By 1955 Rockwell's then Meter and Valve division included parking meters, gas and water meters, gasoline and oil meters, taxi meters, and valves. That year the company invested more than $2 million in moving its water meter manufacturing from Brooklyn, New York, to Uniontown, Pennsylvania. In 1956 the M&U group was established as a separate division to sell gas and water meters. In 1970 the division added clamps and couplings to its product line. In 1978 an additional plant was built in Texarkana, Arkansas, to manufacture industrial, commercial, and agricultural meters and clamps and couplings. M&U headquarters were located in Pittsburgh, Pennsylvania, near both Rockwell's corporate headquarters and the Uniontown plant.

The water meter group shared accounting, human resources planning, business planning, and research staff with other M&U product groups but used different warehouses and purchasing, manufacturing, engineering, selling, and field repair personnel. John Harriger was vice president in charge of both the water meter and clamps and couplings groups. In addition to the same manufacturing and purchasing facilities in Texarkana, the nonresidential water meter subgroup and clamps and couplings group used the same international sales staff as the rest of the division.

The invention and introduction of the SR meter was stimulated and fully endorsed by the then CEO, Al Rockwell. This commitment had been continued by current corporate management which considered the M&U business as an important business in the Rockwell portfolio. The division had received substantial capital dollars in the past which was expected to continue in the future.

M&U Strategy

Rockwell manufactured and sold a full line of premium quality bronze case meters to about 60,000 utility customers. The SR piston meter line had been the premium meter in the industry with over 11 million sold since its introduction. In 1981 the SR meter carried guarantees of 15-year accuracy and 25-year life on the register and maincase. Rockwell's meter differed from its major competitors' in its use of a more accurate piston chamber (unlike Badger's and Neptune's disc chambers), its tamper-proof design, extensive bronze content, and longer life. Rockwell residential meters contained slightly more bronze than those of the competition, which improved product durability. SRs were promoted on the basis of their durability and life accuracy compared to plastic-cased and other bronze meters.

Rockwell emphasized durability and accuracy in selling meters, more so than other manufacturers who tended to place more emphasis on initial purchase price. Marketing programs utilized by Rockwell included meter leasing and a financial analysis package showing the trade-off among price, length of service, and repair costs. Rockwell had also emphasized encoded remotes and devoted some attention to the development of centralized remote systems. In general Rockwell expected slower utility acceptance of centralized remotes than did Neptune.

Rockwell also produced high-quality turbine, compound, and agricultural meters as well as a full line of instrumentation. Rockwell had been the first to introduce the turbine concept in 1970, and it had gained wide acceptance. Rockwell was one of the highest priced producers of industrial and agricultural meters.

Rockwell had both the largest direct sales force and distributor network in the industry with five sales offices and over 150 active distributors. A majority of water meter sales were made by direct sales force. The sales force had been cut back in 1975 but had regrown to its former size by 1981. Rockwell was believed to have spent more on the AWWA convention and promotional activities than its competitors. Rockwell's penetration in other world markets was small despite some attempts to sell piston meters abroad.

Rockwell utilized a computerized order entry system located in Uniontown. Customers, sales representatives, and distributors called in orders on a toll-free telephone line. As orders came in they were processed in Uniontown or at any of Rockwell's four other regional water meter warehouses. All orders could be processed within 24 hours. Small orders for common models were picked from stock, dispatched, and delivered within one week for a rush order. Larger orders for residential meters were produced and shipped, via Rockwell's own truck fleet, within one month of order entry. Custom orders for specialized industrial meters took up to 60 days from order placement to delivery.

Rockwell also ran repair programs that frequently charged utilities lower rates than the utilities' cost of repair in their own repair facilities. Other manufacturers' repair programs charged higher rates than Rockwell's.

Rockwell had the largest domestic manufacturing capacity in the industry. In 1977 the Uniontown plant had operated at full capacity but was unable to fully meet demand, and Rockwell had charged premium prices for its SR meters. In 1978 the shift of nonresidential meter production to Texarkana and installation of more automated equipment had increased Uniontown's SR meter capacity by 40 percent. Because of the greater use of automation, Rockwell was believed to have 10 percent to 20 percent higher productivity than Badger and Neptune. The Uniontown plant was pursuing a program to increase capacity and productivity with further automation.

The Uniontown plant had its own modern bronze foundry and highly automated plastic injection-molding facility. All maincases were produced internally as were over 90 percent of the small plastic parts. Uniontown also had additional injection-molding capacity that had earlier been used to make plastic parts for Rockwell's Power Tool division.

Rockwell was the largest employer in Uniontown, a manufacturing town located near coal mining and steel producing areas. Workers at the Uniontown plant were all members of the United Steel Workers Union. Though there had been an eight-week strike in 1979, current labor relations were judged to be friendly, and a new contract had been signed without a strike in early 1982. Labor costs were expected to increase 6–8 percent a year in the 1980s.

The M&U division used the Rockwell corporate laboratories, General Industries labs, and its own divisional facilities as sources of R&D. The Rockwell corporate laboratory in Thousand Oaks, California, performed basic R&D on materials, corrosion, and physics, and its services were contracted for on a per-hour basis by M&U. The General Industries lab provided material applications engineering and lab assistance. M&U's research group did applied research on specific questions of mechanical design and electronics. Because of the level of R&D support, Rockwell considered itself to be the technological leader in the water meter industry.

M&U's president, R. W. Bohlen, reported to William Hamilton, president of the General Industries Organization. Division employees prided themselves on spreading M&U-trained managers around the company. Kent Rockwell, grandson of the founder, had been general manager of M&U from 1975 to 1977.

Exhibit 1

Meter Accuracy over Time

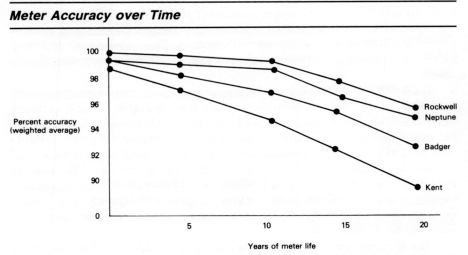

Note: Weighted average based upon a modified domestic water use profile developed by Philadelphia Suburban Water Company in 1970. Actual performance can vary greatly by individual meter.
Source: Interviews with utilities and manufacturers.

Exhibit 2

A. 1981 Sales by Customer Size ($\frac{5}{8}$″ and $\frac{3}{4}$″ meters)

Utility Size (Installed Base)	Number of Utilities	Total Meter Sales (Thousands of Units)
25,000 and greater	1,250	996
10,000–24,999	1,540	395
5,000–9,999	1,876	348
2,000–4,999	4,000	259
Less than 2,000	≅51,000	480
Total	≅60,000	2,478

Source: Rockwell International; Environmental Protection Agency listings.

B. Water Meter Purchasing Channel by Size of Utility

Utility Size (Installed Base)	Direct	Distributor	Both
Less than 500	37%	61%	2%
500–599	36	57	7
1,000–2,249	50	43	7
2,250–5,000	51	40	9
More than 5,000	70	24	6

Source: Harvard Business School Strategic Marketing Study, 1979.

Exhibit 3

Purchase Criteria for Residential Meters

	Percent of Sample Mentioning Factor as:	
	An Important Criterion	Most Important Criterion
Price	49.6%	15.5%
Accuracy	42.6	17.5
Parts availability	41.6	10.3
Ease of repair	36.9	16.0
Quality	31.9	11.0
Guarantee	21.0	4.8
Delivery	19.1	5.7
Reputation	12.3	3.0
Don't know/ other	39.8	16.3

Source: Harvard Business School Strategic Marketing Study, 1979.

Exhibit 4

1982 Selling Prices for Residential Meters

	Mean	Minimum	Maximum
By company:			
Rockwell	$27.00	$18.00	$50.00
Badger	24.00	20.00	50.00
Neptune	25.00	18.00	50.00
Hersey	35.00	24.00	50.00
Kent	25.00	22.00	50.00
Other (velocity type)	24.00	20.00	40.00
By number of units purchased per utility*			
Less than 38–100	$42.00	$35.00	$48.00
100–300	40.00	32.00	48.00
300–500	32.00	30.00	45.00
500–1,000	27.00	24.00	35.00
1,000–2,000	25.00	20.00	30.00
Greater than 2,000	24.00	18.00	28.00
By channel:			
Direct	$27.00		
Distributor/agent	31.00		

* Ranges chosen as quintiles for number of meters purchased.
Source: Harvard Business School Strategic Marketing Study, 1979; Rockwell International.

Exhibit 5

Overall Corporate Financial Performance of Leading Competitors (Dollars in millions)

	1980	1979	1978	1977	1976	1975	1974	1973	1972
Rockwell International:									
Sales	$6,907	$6,176	$5,309	$5,390	$5,043	$4,654	$4,178	$3,179	$2,678
Profit before tax	526	486	415	327	267	213	229	221	171
Total assets	4,431	4,128	3,536	3,392	2,890	2,891	3,043	2,003	1,729
Equity	1,740	1,539	1,355	1,252	1,182	1,131	1,097	953	924
Water meter sales	53	48	45	42	36	31	38	30	27
Pretax ROS (%)	7.6%	7.9%	7.8%	6.0%	5.3%	4.6%	5.5%	7.0%	6.4%
Pretax ROA (%)	11.9%	11.8%	11.7%	9.7%	9.2%	7.4%	7.5%	11.0%	9.9%
Pretax ROE (%)	30.2%	31.6%	30.7%	26.1%	22.6%	18.8%	20.9%	23.2%	18.5%
Badger Meters, Inc.:									
Sales	$58	$59	$58	$54	$47	$43	$41	$37	$34
Profit before tax	2	5	6	6	4	2	3	4	4
Total assets	45	41	37	37	33	31	33	31	28
Equity	22	22	20	18	16	15	14	14	13
Water meter sales	35	37	36	34	29	26	32	24	22
Pretax ROS (%)	2.7%	9.0%	9.8%	10.7%	8.2%	4.2%	7.6%	11.0%	10.4%
Pretax ROA (%)	3.5%	13.0%	15.3%	15.8%	11.6%	5.7%	9.3%	13.2%	12.9%
Pretax ROE (%)	7.3%	24.1%	27.7%	32.6%	24.2%	12.2%	21.5%	29.5%	28.6%
Neptune (Wheelabrator-Frye)*:									
Sales	$1,300	$ 947	$ 781	$ 137	$ 116	$ 118	$ 100	$ 77	$ 68
Profit before tax	87	73	71	14	11	10	8	5	3
Total assets	1,931	650	406	110	91	82	74	65	60
Equity	706	270	219	47	42	38	35	33	32
Water meter sales	38	33	29	24	19	18	19	NA	20
Pretax ROS (%)	6.7%	7.7%	9.1%	9.9%	9.7%	8.3%	7.7%	5.8%	4.8%
Pretax ROA (%)	4.5%	11.2%	17.4%	12.4%	12.4%	12.0%	10.4%	7.0%	5.4%
Pretax ROE (%)	12.3%	27.0%	32.3%	28.9%	26.5%	25.7%	21.9%	13.6%	10.1%
Hersey Meters:									
Sales	NA	$ 33	$ 25	$ 25	$ 24	$ 24	NA	NA	NA
Profit before tax	NA	(2)	(1)	(1)	(FF)	1	NA	NA	NA
Total assets	NA	18	18	18	18	19	NA	NA	NA
Equity	NA	12	12	13	14	14	NA	NA	NA
Water meter sales	15	17	19	19	20	14	NA	NA	16
Pretax ROS (%)	NA	(6.5)%	(3.5)%	(2.7)%	(0.9)%	2.2%	NA	NA	NA
Pretax ROA (%)	NA	(8.4)%	(6.2)%	(5.4)%	(2.9)%	1.4%	NA	NA	NA
Pretax ROE (%)	NA	(13.0)%	(7.0)%	(5.1)%	(1.5)%	3.7%	NA	NA	NA

* Neptune was acquired by Wheelabrator-Frye in 1978.
Source: Annual reports; Rockwell International estimates.

Exhibit 6

Competitive Sales by Business Segment (In millions)

	1980	1979	1978	1977	1976	1975	1974	1973	1972
Rockwell International:									
Automotive	$1,735	$1,838	$1,485	$1,284	$1,214	$1,103	$1,030	$ 883	$ 667
Aerospace	2,042	1,625	1,453	1,991	1,544	1,386	1,209	1,019	759
Electronics	1,696	1,530	1,263	1,107	1,031	951	898	448	504
General Industries:									
Energy (including meters)	584	477	420	382	333	308	254	170	170
Textile, graphic and industrial*	850	706	688	626	397	408	473	551	467
Consumer*	—	—	—	524	498	314	108	81	
Total	$6,907	$6,176	$5,309	$5,390	$5,043	$4,654	$4,178	$3,179	$2,678
Neptune:									
Measurement group	$ 397	$ 307	$ 259	$ 66	$ 55	$ 51	$ 50	$ 44	$ 44
Environmental group	305	314	245	71	61	67	50	33	24
Wheelabrator-Frye segments:									
Engineered components (including meters)	198	93	85						
Engineered systems	133	—	—						
Engineered services									
Transportation equipment									
Chemicals and specialty products	266	233	192						
Total	$1,300	$ 947	$ 781	$ 137	$ 116	$ 118	$ 100	$ 77	$ 68
Badger:									
Flow equipment and controls	$ 49	$ 51	$ 50	$ 46	$ 40	$ 37	$ 36	$ 32	$ 30
Electronic equipment	9	8	8	8	7	6	5	4	3
Other	—	—	—	—	<<	<<	<<	1	1
Total	$ 58	$ 59	$ 58	$ 54	$ 47	$ 43	$ 41	$ 37	$ 34

* In 1979 Rockwell discontinued the Admiral consumer line. 1977 and 1978 restated to include other consumer goods under textile, graphic, and industrial for comparison purposes.

Source: Annual reports and other published financial data.

The Soft Drink Industry in 1985

With retail revenues estimated to exceed $26 billion in 1984, the U.S. soft drink industry had become an integral part of the American way of life. Soft drinks were distributed through a host of outlets and sold in a multitude of products and packages. American per capita consumption had grown to 43.2 gallons per year by 1984.

Populated by companies which sometimes dated back to the 1800s, leading soft drink producers had enjoyed extraordinary success. However, the industry was undergoing change in 1985 that was affecting new and old participants alike.

Industry Structure

Soft drinks consisted of a flavor base, a sweetener, and carbonated water. Some products also contained caffeine and artificial coloring. Cola-flavored drinks accounted for approximately 63 percent of the market in 1983 and lemon/lime, 12 percent. Diet and caffeine-free products were taking a growing share of the market. Exhibit 1 shows the history of

Copyright © 1985 by the President and Fellows of Harvard College
Harvard Business School case 385–320

major soft drink product introductions. Throughout its history, the industry had experienced rapid growth and rising per capita consumption:

Year	Bottler Sales Wholesale and Vending (in Thousands)	Total Cases (288 oz.) (in Thousands)	Per Capita Annual Consumption (in Gallons)
1849	$ 760	1,013	0.1
1889	14,354	17,398	0.6
1929	214,322	181,619	3.3
1969	4,369,664	1,942,073	21.5
1975	9,397,797	2,610,499	31.0
1976	10,375,167	2,952,474	33.7
1977	11,526,810	3,247,722	35.9
1978	13,344,588	3,490,000	37.1
1979	14,872,628	3,664,300	38.1
1980	17,676,648	3,816,575	38.8
1981	20,015,269	3,959,697	39.5
1982	21,156,140	4,065,815	40.1

Source: National Soft Drink Association.

Exhibit 2 shows U.S. consumption trends for all liquids, 1960 to 1984. The consumption of soft drinks varied by age group.

Soft Drink Consumption as a Percent of All Liquid Consumption by Age Group

0–5	6–12	13–19	20–29	30–39	40–49	50+
15%	23%	29%	24%	25%	16%	12%

Source: Beverage Marketing Corporation: Beverage Data Bank National Family Opinion, Inc. Reported in *Beverage Industry,* Annual Manual, 1983. Study conducted in 1981. Research method not described.

The prospects for future growth in U.S. soft drink consumption were being actively debated in 1985. Some believed that disposable personal income was a key determinant for per capita soft drink consumption (see Exhibit 3). Others stressed the aging of the "baby boom" generation (approximately 25–39 years old in 1985). Some had argued for years that U.S. soft drink consumption was approaching its limits. Other observers believed that industry innovation in product development, packaging, advertising, and distribution would fuel continued industry growth.

Three major groups of participants were involved in the production and distribution of soft drinks: (1) concentrate and syrup producers, (2) bottlers, and (3) retail outlets. Exhibit 4 diagrams the industry with estimates where available of the size of different parts of the system in 1984.

Concentrate Producers

Concentrate producers manufactured the basic flavors and sold them to independent franchised or company-owned bottlers. Although there were over 50 concentrate producers in the United States in 1983, the industry was dominated by a few firms, particularly Coca-Cola and Pepsi-Cola.

Corporate Market Shares, 1983 (Units)

Coca-Cola	35.3%
Pepsi-Cola	25.3
Dr Pepper	10.4
Seven-Up	7.3
Royal Crown	3.8
Shasta (Division of Consolidated Foods)	2.0
Sunkist (Division of General Cinema)	1.8
Crush (Division of P&G)	1.2
Others	12.9
	100%

Source: *Beverage Industry* and John C. Maxwell.

Beside these major producers, there were several dozen regional and private label producers. These producers, such as C&C, Polar, and White Rock, tended to sell an extensive line of soft drink flavors—such as cola, grape, orange, cream soda, and ginger ale—that combined to yield a small share of its regional market. They usually sold to major food chains only and distributed their products through the stores' warehouse systems.

Concentrate producers sold the flavor concentrate only in the case of regular soft drinks. For diet drinks, the concentrate was sold together with artificial sweetener. The cost of the diet sweetener was charged to the bottler. Coca-Cola, the exception, had traditionally sold syrup (already containing the regular sweetener) to its bottlers. Coca-Cola charged its bottlers for the concentrate plus the list sweetener price. In 1980 Coca-Cola began to sell concentrate to certain of its largest bottlers representing 15 percent of Coke's sales in 1984. Manufacturing concentrate was a simple process requiring little capital investment, and the cost of concentrate represented approximately 10 percent of a concentrate producer's selling price to bottlers.

A concentrate producer's most significant costs were for advertising, promotion, market research, and bottler relations. Marketing programs were jointly implemented and financed by concentrate producers and bottlers. The concentrate producers usually took the lead in developing the programs—particularly in product planning, market research, and advertising. Bottlers assumed a larger role in developing trade and consumer promotions and usually financed two thirds of promotion costs. Advertising costs were usually split 50/50.

Concentrate producers employed extensive sales and marketing support staffs to work with and help improve the executional performance of their franchised bottlers. Concentrate producers set standards for their bottlers and suggested operating procedures. Concentrate producers also negotiated directly with major suppliers to bottlers—particularly sweetener and packaging suppliers—to encourage reliable supply, faster delivery, or lower prices to bottlers.

Bottlers

Bottlers added carbonated water and sweetener to the concentrate and bottled or canned the resulting soft drink. Bottling was a capital-intensive process involving high-speed bottling lines. Each package type required separate bottling equipment as lines were interchangeable only for packages of similar size and construction. Bottling lines cost from $100,000 to several million dollars depending on volume and package type. Bottlers sometimes arranged with bottlers in contiguous territories to invest in high-volume equipment for new packages and to supply the other bottlers with soft drinks in the new container. Bottler salespersons drove bottling trucks and delivered soft drinks directly to individual retail outlets. Bottlers and salespersons also stocked and maintained food store shelves. All the major concentrate producers utilized direct store delivery by independent bottlers.

Shasta and Faygo, which were small national brands, used warehouse distribution in 1985, just as the regional producers did, and their products sold for 25–30 percent below store door brands. Several major corporations, such as General Foods, had examined the possibilities for circumventing the store door system.

The store door delivery system was controversial with the trade, who earned higher gross margin on the few warehouse delivered soft drinks than on the store door delivered products. The table below gives price and cost comparisons, as estimated by one major bottler, of store door and warehouse delivery for both the retailer and the bottler.

Comparison of Warehouse and Store Door Delivery, 1984 (2-litre size)

	Warehouse Delivery		Store Door Delivery	
Retailer:				
Net retail price	$ .99	100%	$1.29	100%
Net wholesale price	.72	73	1.06	82
Store gross margin	.27	27	.23	18
In-store handling	.18	18	.09	7
Direct product profit* margin	.09	9	.14	11
Annual turns	13×/yr.		48×/yr.	
Direct product profit* for the allocated space	$1.17		$6.72	
Bottler:				
Net wholesale price	.72	100	1.06	100
Variable cost (concentrate, sweetener, packaging, variable manufacturing)	.57	79	.57	54
Selling and distribution	.05	7	.28	26
Net advertising cost (after coop allowances)	.00	0	.03	3
Bottler operating profit (before overhead, depreciation, interest, and taxes)	.10	14	.18	17

*Direct product profit was a method of analysis using computerized cost and inventory turn models developed by McKinsey & Co. to determine the profit margin that a store would earn on product lines it carries.

Concentrate itself accounted for 12 percent of bottler's variable costs, with packaging making up much of the balance. Throughout the 1960s, 1970s, and 1980s, a host of new packages had been introduced. Glass bottles had been supplemented by tin cans and more recently by aluminum cans. The most recent new package was the plastic container. Plastic containers were lightweight and unbreakable and allowed large sizes to be introduced.

Soft Drink Sales by Package Types (Volume of ounces sold)

	Reusable Bottles (Glass)	Nonreusable Bottles		Cans (Aluminum and Steel)
		(Glass)	(Plastic)	
1960	94%	2%		4%
1970	46	25		29
1980	32	33		35
1982	29	16	20%	35
1984	26	14	23	37

Note: Glass and plastic were separated in this analysis only after 1982.
Sources: *Beverage Industry,* Annual Manuals and 1984 issue.

Exhibit 5 provides data on the costs of selected packages in 1984.

Suppliers. Aside from the concentrate producers, packaging and sweetener firms were the bottlers' major suppliers. Three glass container manufacturers dominated sales to the soft drink industry: Libbey-Owens, Anchor-Hocking, and Owens-Illinois. In 1971 Owens-Illinois introduced the "Plasti-shield" bottle, which was protected by a thin sturdy foam cover over parts of the bottle, in order to improve the competitiveness of glass bottles with cans.

Five can companies accounted for 98 percent of the cans sold to the soft drink industry: American Can, Continental Can, Crown Cork & Seal, National Can, and Reynolds Aluminum. Almost all the major sales were to the individual bottling companies, although each of the concentrate producers negotiated with the canning suppliers about the design, availability, and price of the cans. Coca-Cola also operated its own canning company, supplying some of its bottlers with canned soft drinks.

Plastic containers were supplied primarily by the same three firms that supplied glass containers. In early 1985 Owens-Illinois was the sole supplier of the new 3-litre plastic bottle that was introduced in 1984. Owens-Illinois's sales and return on equity were respectively $3.4 billion and 5.1 percent in 1983 and $3.5 billion and 9.9 percent in 1984. (Source: Annual reports.)

The major concentrate producers negotiated directly with packaging suppliers to ensure that new packaging innovations were quickly available in sufficient quantity for their bottlers. Some analysts believed that both Dr Pepper and 7UP sales had been hurt because of their inability to secure sufficient supplies of 32-ounce and 64-ounce bottles in the mid-1970s.

Bottlers also purchased nutritive (or caloric) sweeteners such as sugar for their regular soft drinks. The soft drink industry consumed 85 million hundredweight units, or 8.5 billion pounds, of nutritive sweetener in 1984, accounting for 31 percent of total U.S. consumption. Concentrate producers often negotiated directly with sweetener processors concerning the price that bottlers would be charged. Typical bottler discounts obtained by large concentrate producers were $2.50 to $3.00 off list per hundredweight.

The Franchise Bottler System. Coca-Cola and Pepsi-Cola had both begun granting franchises for the right to bottle their soft drinks early in their history. Franchisees were granted, in perpetuity, the exclusive right to bottle and distribute a concentrate company's line of branded soft drinks in a defined territory as long as conditions of the franchise agreement were met. Franchisees were not allowed to market a directly competitive brand; for example, a Coca-Cola bottler could not sell Royal Crown (RC) Cola. However, franchisees could sell noncompetitive brands and could decline to market a concentrate producer's secondary lines. For example, a Coca-Cola bottler could decide to turn down the Coca-Cola lemon/lime drink Sprite in order to be able to bottle 7UP.

Because the franchise agreements carried exclusive territorial rights, the Federal Trade Commission (FTC) had initiated action in 1971 against eight major concentrate producers, charging that the exclusive territories were illegally preventing intrabrand competition. After nine years of litigation, PepsiCo led a successful effort to persuade Congress in 1980 to enact the Soft Drink Interbrand Competition Act, preserving the right to grant exclusive territories. The proponents argued that *interbrand* competition was sufficiently strong to warrant continuation of the existing exclusive agreements.

Bottling Firms.   The bottler segment of the industry could be divided into four types. First were the privately owned franchise bottlers. Many of these were small and marketed only Coca-Cola or Pepsi-Cola products. However, some of these franchisees, especially those located in medium-sized metropolitan areas, had achieved substantial growth by buying up franchise operations in contiguous areas and by taking on secondary brands such as Dr Pepper or 7UP.

A second group of bottlers consisted of large, publicly owned, multibrand franchise firms based in major metropolitan districts. Coca-Cola Bottling Company of New York, for example, bottled and distributed Coca-Cola products, Dr Pepper, and minor soft drink brands in a five-state area and had twenty-four manufacturing plants. Two large publicly owned multibrand bottlers (Coca-Cola Bottling of New York and Coca-Cola Bottling of Los Angeles) from 1979 to 1983 earned on average aftertax 10 percent return on equity and 4 percent return on assets.

The third category of bottlers were the conglomerates—such as Beatrice Foods, IC Industries, General Cinema, and Procter & Gamble—which owned bottling franchises of Coca-Cola and Pepsi-Cola as one of a number of subsidiaries. Beatrice, for example, owned Coca-Cola franchises in nine states, and its bottling operations accounted for $880 million in sales in 1983.

The fourth category included the bottling operations owned by the concentrate producers themselves. Coca-Cola sold approximately 11 percent of its U.S. volume through its own bottlers; Pepsi-Cola sold approximately 23 percent of its volume through its Bottling Group. Dr Pepper, Seven-Up, and Royal Crown also directly owned some of their bottlers.

The number of bottling franchises granted by the five largest concentrate producers had fallen approximately 15 percent between 1974 and 1984, and the average size of the franchise territory had increased. A more marked decline in the number of plants had occurred during the same period.

	1974	1976	1978	1980	1982	1984
Plants	2,613	2,321	2,079	1,859	1,643	1,522

Source: National Soft Drink Association.

Retail Outlets

Industry analysts divided the retail channels for soft drinks into four types: (1) food stores, (2) fountain, (3) vending, and (4) other. The chart below shows the percent of industry volume that moved through each of these types of outlets in 1982 and the share of each channel's volume obtained by Coca-Cola, Pepsi-Cola, and other soft drink companies.

Retail Outlets for Soft Drinks, 1982

	Food Stores	Fountain	Vending	Other
Percent of industry volume	42%	20%	12%	26%
Share of channel:				
Coca-Cola (all brands)	29	59	41	27
Pepsi-Cola (all brands)	30	22	26	24
Other brands	41	19	33	49

The percent of volume moving through food stores had increased from 39 percent in 1972, the percent through fountain had increased from 18 percent, and the percent through "other" had fallen from 31 percent.

In food stores, rival bottler sales forces fought fiercely for shelf space. Soft drinks were a major product category for food stores, traditionally bringing approximately 20 percent gross margin and accounting for 4.5 percent of food store revenues in 1983. The largest supermarket chain in the United States accounted for approximately 6 percent of total U.S. food retail sales. No regional chain controlled more than 25 percent of the market in a major trading area.

Fountain sales consisted of the sales of syrup to retail outlets, who mixed the syrup with carbonated water on-site for immediate consumption by the end customer. Soft drink sales were extremely profitable for fountain outlets. Many small food stands and mom-and-pop stores were fountain outlets. However, large fast-food chains accounted for one third of fountain sales and were one of the fastest growing channels for soft drinks. Coca-Cola had historically dominated fountain sales and controlled the important McDonald's account. Coca-Cola sold syrup directly to the outlets of large chains, bypassing the local bottler. Local Pepsi bottlers handled fountain accounts, selling a mixture of concentrate and sweetener. Pepsi-Cola had won the Burger King account in 1982.

In the vending channel, bottlers purchased and installed machines, although concentrate producers often offered rebates to encourage bottlers to invest in machines and to allocate all or most of the slots (usually four to six per machine) to their products. On average, bottlers obtained significantly higher margins through vending machines than from stores. One source estimated that Coca-Cola bottlers owned 50 percent more vending machines in the United States than Pepsi bottlers did and that Coca-Cola bottlers often earned over half of their total profits through vending.

There were also a host of other smaller channels for soft drinks. Restaurants, caterers, and institutional buyers such as airlines often served soft drinks in bottles and cans rather than from a fountain. Convenience stores sold an increasing volume, especially through single serve cold cases. Some mass merchandisers also allocated shelf space to soft drinks. Sales to these diverse outlets were handled by local bottlers.

The International Soft Drink Industry

The soft drink industry outside the United States also consisted of concentrate producers, independent local bottlers, and retail outlets. Product lines tended to be less broad and channels less developed, but this varied substantially by country. Both Coca-Cola and Pepsi-Cola had company-owned or franchised bottling operations in over 140 countries in 1984. During the 1960s and 1970s international growth in the consumption of soft drinks exceeded that in the United States. In the first five years of the 1980s, U.S. growth had exceeded that in the international markets because of economic problems in many countries. The international profits of all the concentrate producers have been reduced in the 1980s by these trends.

Coca-Cola, which had gained a substantial head start in the establishment of local bottling companies, held a strong lead overseas. The company estimated in its 1984 annual report that including local soft drinks unique to particular countries, Coca-Cola held the leading market share with 38 percent of the worldwide market. Coca-Cola's lead was particularly strong in Europe where it led Pepsi-Cola, its nearest competitor, by four to one. Coca-Cola received 62 percent of its soft drink revenues from outside the United States in 1984.

Pepsi-Cola began to expand its international operations particularly after World War II. Pepsi's strongest position was in Latin America, the Middle East, and the South Pacific, where it held the market share lead in a number of countries. Approximately 20 percent of Pepsi-Cola's soft drink revenues came from outside the United States.

Seven-Up had also begun after World War II to expand its international operations. It had in 1980 persuaded Cadbury-Schweppes, a major U.K. food company and Pepsi-Cola's bottler in the United Kingdom, to bottle and market 7UP. Seven-Up executives regularly pointed to the promise of the U.K. market, where lemon-flavored drinks were popular. Other U.S. concentrate producers, such as Dr Pepper, had attempted to gain market presence in some specific countries.

Industry History

Soft drinks had existed since the early 1800s when many U.S. druggists concocted blends of fruit syrups and carbonated soda water that they sold at their soda fountains. The formulas for Coca-Cola, Pepsi-Cola, and Dr Pepper were all developed in this way.

Coca-Cola was formulated in 1886 by Dr. John Pemberton, a pharmacist in Atlanta, Georgia. The drink was sold as a refreshing elixir at the fountain counter of Jacobs's Pharmacy, of which Dr. Pemberton was part owner. Eventually Mr. Asa Candler became sole owner of the pharmacy and of the rights to the soft drink. Candler began selling the syrup for the drink to other pharmacies, established a sales force, and began advertising the drink on signs placed in train stations and town squares. The advertising budget reached $100,000 in 1901. Candler granted the first bottling franchise for the drink in 1899 for $1.00, believing that the main future rested with fountain sales.

Coca-Cola's franchise bottler network grew quickly, and a standard 6½-ounce "skirt" bottle was designed in 1916 to be used by all its franchisees. This bottle eventually became one of the best-known images in the world. In 1920 Justice Oliver Wendell Holmes of the United States Supreme Court ruled that the nickname "Coke" could only mean Coca-Cola, because "it means a single thing coming from a single source, and well known to the community. Coca-Cola probably means to most persons the plaintiff's familiar product to be had everywhere."

In 1919 Ernest Woodruff purchased the Coca-Cola Company from Asa Candler's heirs for $25 million. In 1923 his son, Robert W. Woodruff, who was to become the most dominant figure in Coca-Cola's history, was made CEO. Woodruff set out to try to make Coca-Cola available everywhere, anytime a consumer might want to be "in arm's reach of desire." In 1929 Coca-Cola began to offer an open-top cooler for bottled Coca-Cola to storekeepers and gasoline station operators at extremely low prices. In 1937 the company introduced the first coin vending machine. Woodruff also initiated "life-style" advertising for Coca-Cola which emphasized the product's role in a consumer's life rather than its product attributes. The company continued to own its original bottling operations around Atlanta and began to buy back a few of its franchises that it believed were underperforming.

Woodruff also began to develop Coca-Cola's international business, principally through its export company. However, Woodruff's most memorable action may have been his decision, made at the request of General Dwight Eisenhower at the beginning of World War II, to "see that every man in uniform gets a bottle of Coca-Cola for five cents wherever he is and whatever it costs." Coca-Cola bottling plants followed the march of American troops around the world. Woodruff remained on the board of directors and an influential figure on major decisions until his final retirement in 1982.

Pepsi-Cola was invented in 1893 in New Bern, North Carolina, by a pharmacist, Caleb Bradham. Pepsi-Cola followed a pattern similar to Coca-Cola of expansion through franchise bottlers. However, its growth in the early 1900s was not nearly as significant, and the company was on the brink of bankruptcy several times. Pepsi-Cola designed a standard 12-ounce bottle which its bottlers sold at a retail price of 10 cents compared to Coca-Cola's 5 cents for its 6½-ounce unit. In 1933 Pepsi-Cola lowered the price to five cents, and in 1939 it launched its radio advertising jingle, "Twice as much for a nickel, too. Pepsi-Cola is the one for you." In 1940 that jingle was rated by the radio industry as the second best-known song in America, behind only the Star Spangled Banner.

Dr Pepper was formulated by an unknown fountain clerk in 1885 and first dispensed at a drug store in Waco, Texas. Dr Pepper was not a cola but rather a combination of other fruit syrups. During the next eight years Dr Pepper developed much more slowly than Coca-Cola or Pepsi-Cola, but it became firmly entrenched in Texas and other parts of the southwestern United States. The product was bottled by Dr Pepper-owned bottlers or independent Dr Pepper franchisees.

The Seven-Up Company was founded in 1920 in St. Louis, Missouri, as a partnership of three men—C. L. Grigg, E. G. Ridgway, and F. Y. Gladney. Descendants of these three families were still part of the executive group in 1976, and the company continued to reflect the values of the founding families. From its beginning, Seven-Up sold primarily through franchise bottlers who were usually bottlers for the major cola brands as well. By 1976, Seven-Up owned only 13 of the 482 Seven-Up bottler operations.

After World War II Coca-Cola outsold its closest rival Pepsi-Cola by 10 to 1. In 1950 Alfred Steele became CEO at Pepsi-Cola and developed several new package sizes. He also encouraged Pepsi bottlers to invest in vending machines. Pepsi sales increased 131 percent between 1950 and 1955. Competition became even more intense in the 1960s, as Pepsi launched its "Pepsi Generation" advertising theme, positioning its product as the brand choice of the young and young at heart. Pepsi bottler salespeople were praised at meetings as "veterans in the war against Coca-Cola," who "invaded" Coke markets with new "sales weapons."[1] Pepsi-Cola also bought back several of its bottling franchises in order to strengthen their operations.

Coca-Cola continued to grow both domestically and internationally

---

[1] Pat Watters, *Coca-Cola: An Illustrated History* (Garden City, N.Y.: Doubleday, 1978).

after World War II. In 1954 Coca-Cola made the first change in its bottle since 1916, increasing the size to 12 ounces as a direct response to the competitive threat from Pepsi-Cola. In 1960 Coca-Cola purchased the Minute Maid orange juice company, its first diversification effort, moving it into the consumer food processing business. In the 1960s new packages and new products, such as the lemon/lime drink Sprite and the diet drinks Tab and Fresca, were introduced. (See Exhibit 1.)

During this period the Coca-Cola brand remained the focus of the company, and the brand name was used only on regular Coke. Industry observers referred to the efforts of "Mother Coke" to continue to expand distribution and availability of its product in the United States and internationally. Coca-Cola executives were proud that they never voiced the name Pepsi-Cola in meetings with Coca-Cola bottlers but rather discussed only the growth of their own brand.

In 1963 Donald Kendall became CEO of Pepsi-Cola. Kendall had gained fame in 1959 when he convinced Vice President Richard Nixon to bring Soviet Premier Nikita Khrushchev by the Pepsi booth at the American Exhibition in Moscow. Famous photos were taken of Khrushchev and Nixon drinking Pepsi. Under Kendall, Pepsi-Cola Company was renamed PepsiCo, Inc., and diversified into four new lines of business: snack foods (Frito-Lay); food service and restaurants, including Pizza Hut and Taco Bell; Wilson Sporting Goods; and North American Van Lines. The company also began to expand its product line, introducing both Diet Pepsi and Mountain Dew in 1964. (See Exhibit 1.) Andrall Pearson, president and chief operating officer of PepsiCo between 1971 and 1984, described Kendall as a "builder, constantly thinking of ways to make things bigger. He can't live in a negative atmosphere. He's broad and has a real feel for the marketplace. He's willing to bet on new products."[2]

In the early 1970s the company recruited professional marketing managers such as Victor Bonomo (who became president of Pepsi-Cola U.S.A., and eventually executive vice president of PepsiCo). Pearson moved to increase the prices and margins of Pepsi's store door delivered products—soft drinks and snack foods—and to establish stringent and challenging standards by which the salespeople of such products were to gain, keep, and maintain in good form the retail shelf space for Pepsi products. Salespeople were to secure an extensive primary shelf space site and to strive to maintain a "permanent" secondary site, like an end-of-aisle display. By the 1980s the snack food and soft drink areas were widely regarded as the best maintained parts of most retail stores, whereas they were often in disarray in the 1960s.

Pepsi-Cola increased the price it charged its bottlers for its concentrate which had been selling at a price 20 percent below Coca-Cola's

---

[2] *Nation's Business,* May 1981.

price in the early 1970s. Pepsi secured the price increases without fierce opposition because it used the extra margin to increase advertising and promotion for Pepsi brands.

Dr Pepper also made major strides in the 1960s and 1970s. In 1962 the Pepsi-Cola Company sued Dr Pepper for alleged trademark infringement over Dr Pepper's use of the word *pep*. Pepsi-Cola won the suit; however, Dr Pepper countersued, and the court ruled that Dr Pepper was not a cola drink but a unique and separate flavor. Coca-Cola and Pepsi-Cola franchised bottlers could now also bottle Dr Pepper without violating their cola franchise.

Led by W. W. ("Foots") Clements who became CEO in 1967, Dr Pepper aggressively moved to build distribution by signing up Coca-Cola and Pepsi-Cola bottlers. The success of this effort was perhaps best exemplified in 1969 when Clements convinced the Coca-Cola Bottling Company of New York, the world's largest distributor of Coca-Cola, to bottle and sell Dr Pepper to the 20 million Americans in its market area. By the mid-1970s Dr Pepper had secured nationwide distribution with the following bottler network:

Dr Pepper Bottler Configuration, 1976

Brands Bottled	Number of Franchises
Dr Pepper only	45
Coca-Cola and Dr Pepper	192
Pepsi-Cola and Dr Pepper	164
Dr Pepper and other brands	96
	497

Dr Pepper sales grew from $17 million in 1962 to $152 million in 1976 on the strength of widening distribution and innovative, heavy advertising. Dr Pepper also placed great stress on providing excellent service and support to its bottlers. Coca-Cola introduced a drink tasting similar to Dr Pepper, called Mr. PiBB, testing it first in Waco, Texas, in 1972.

7UP by the mid-1960s was the third largest selling soft drink in the United States, behind only Coke and Pepsi. Consumer surveys showed that 7UP consumption was skewed toward an older segment who saw the drink as a mixer with liquor more than as a soft drink. In 1968 Seven-Up began to gain increased market share when it launched its "Uncola" advertising campaign. This campaign, which benefited from memorable execution, clearly positioned 7UP as a soft drink alternative to Coke and Pepsi.

Royal Crown Cola, which was the fifth leading concentrate producer, was introduced in 1935. It also employed independent franchise bottlers who also often marketed 7UP, Dr Pepper, and other smaller brands. Royal Crown was strongest in the midwestern United States, where its bottlers were most numerous. Many analysts considered RC the most innovative concentrate producer. It had introduced the first diet soft drink, Diet Rite, in 1962. The company continued to produce primarily its regular and diet cola.

A number of firms had entered the soft drink business after the five majors. Consolidated Foods, based in Chicago, Illinois, bought a small concentrate company in 1960 and created the Shasta Beverage Division. Consolidated Foods operated in a number of diverse, food-related areas: sugar refining, meat packing, convenience food stores, and institutional feeding operations. Some of its well-known brand names included Sara Lee frozen foods and Popsicles.

Shasta sold soft drinks directly to retail stores who operated their own warehouse facilities. Shasta produced 20 standard flavors, both diet and conventional formulations, primarily in cans but also in 1-litre and 2-litre bottles. A 300-person sales force worked with large chain store personnel, assisting them in product display, pricing, and promotion. The company often gave discounts off list price to chains. More than 80 percent of Shasta's business was to food stores; the company did not attempt to sell to the fountain or to the single service cold case market. Shasta did not impose geographic restrictions on its wholesale purchasers who could resell Shasta products to whatever area they liked.

The Cola Wars

During the 1960s and early 1970s the rivalry between Coca-Cola and Pepsi-Cola intensified, eventually earning the description, "The Cola Wars." Bottlers' sales forces began to visit retail stores to stock and maintain shelves and displays as often as five times a week. The importance of soft drinks as a product category to the food stores increased during this period, and total shelf space allocated increased commensurately.

Pepsi decided to concentrate on the food store channel and on the larger bottles that were becoming more popular for in-home consumption. Pepsi continually introduced new "big ideas," such as new packages or promotional campaigns, and worked with its bottlers to focus intensified advertising and selling efforts to promote that idea.

Coca-Cola began using periodic discounting to combat Pepsi in the food stores. In 1975 for the first time, the Pepsi brand of regular cola exceeded the Coca-Cola brand of regular cola in sales volume, according to Nielsen Audits. In 1976 Paul Austin, CEO of Coca-Cola, stated in an article that U.S. soft drink consumption had matured and that Coca-Cola's largest growth would come from the international market.

The Pepsi Challenge

In Dallas, Texas, Pepsi-Cola was the third largest selling soft drink in 1974, behind both Coke and Dr Pepper. The sales manager for that

district had seen the Pepsi market research that indicated that the majority of consumers in blind taste tests preferred Pepsi over Coke by approximately 58 percent to 42 percent. The Pepsi manager initiated in-store
"Challenge Booths" to persuade consumers to take the blind taste test
themselves. Pepsi-Cola began immediately to move up in share and eventually became the Number 2 brand.

Victor Bonomo, president of Pepsi-Cola U.S.A., decided to employ
the Pepsi Challenge in other markets in which Pepsi was weak. The
total marketing program was tailored to fit cohesively—gearing advertising, store displays and banners, the message that the bottlers' salespeople
were educated to convey to the trade, and the in-store Challenge Booths
all to highlight the Challenge. Coca-Cola responded to the extension
of the Pepsi Challenge by initiating major price discounts in selected
markets where Pepsi was weak, the Pepsi bottler was an independent
franchisee, and the Coca-Cola bottler was company owned.

Pepsi then launched the Pepsi Challenge nationwide in 1977. By
1980 the regular Pepsi brand had gained an additional 1.3 percent share
of market lead over the Coca-Cola brand in food stores, building on
the initial lead that it had first gained in 1975. Coca-Cola used price
only selectively as a competitive weapon during the remainder of the
1970s. The cost of price promotions continued to be split approximately
two thirds bottler and one third concentrate producer. Advertising expenditures increased significantly during the late 1970s as Pepsi-Cola moved
to explain the Pepsi Challenge and Coca-Cola moved to discredit it.

Philip Morris, a major international marketer of cigarettes, acquired
the Seven-Up Company in 1978. Within the first year, Philip Morris
had installed new management at Seven-Up who increased advertising
by over 50 percent that year.

The 1980s

Pepsi-Cola worked to exploit the success of the Pepsi Challenge to motivate and improve the performance of its bottlers. John Sculley, who
succeeded Bonomo as president of Pepsi-Cola U.S.A., urged Pepsi bottlers
to expand sales through vending and fountain outlets. Sculley was quoted
in 1980 as saying, "I want our bottlers to defend their competitive position
in food stores but also to go for the competitor's jugular by attacking
its high-margin vending business." Sculley also increased the price of
the concentrate for Diet Pepsi and used the margins to increase Pepsi
advertising in the growing diet segment.

Industry observers were surprised in 1980 when Roberto Goizueta,
a Cuban immigrant, was tapped to become CEO of Coca-Cola. As one
of his first acts, Goizueta issued a 1,200-word strategy statement that
called for dramatic changes at Coca-Cola. Coca-Cola was to look for a
growth in the U.S. soft drink market. Price discounting would be used

when necessary to retain Coke's dominant position in that market. While Coca-Cola would remain committed to independent bottlers, the company would replace bottlers in key markets where they were not deemed "sufficiently aggressive," sometimes taking an equity position in the new ownership. Coca-Cola would also seek to amend its franchise agreement, permitting the price of Coca-Cola concentrate, which had been frozen by the agreements for 60 years despite inflation, to be increased. Coca-Cola would use the increased gross margins for advertising and promotions. In exchange, Coca-Cola agreed to sell concentrate rather than syrup to some of its largest bottlers. The company would use the Coca-Cola brand name as competitive "equity" and would no longer treat it as sacrosanct. Finally, Columbia Pictures was acquired, thus adding a third major business to the Coca-Cola portfolio. (In 1984 soft drinks comprised 68 percent of Coca-Cola's revenues; entertainment, 12 percent; and food processing, 20 percent. Soft drinks provided 85 percent of operating profit.)

Price discounting began to reach a new level of intensity in 1980 as Coca-Cola and its bottlers raised their discounts. By the end of 1980 approximately 50 percent of Coke and Pepsi in the food store channel were sold at discount. In 1981 Nielsen Audits indicated that Coca-Cola cost an average of 15 cents less per 192-ounce case than Pepsi-Cola.

In 1980 Royal Crown introduced RC 100, a diet caffeine-free cola. At that time surveys indicated that approximately 15–20 percent of American consumers expressed a serious concern about caffeine consumption. The diet segment of the soft drink market had been growing steadily, comprising 13 percent of the market in 1980. Seven-Up in 1981 decided to exploit the fact that 7UP had never contained caffeine. Its advertising was changed to the theme, "Never had it, never will." It also played ads showing other soft drink brands, stating that they contained caffeine and implying that caffeine was bad for the consumer. Pepsi-Cola management wrote angry letters to its franchise bottlers who marketed both Pepsi-Cola and 7UP, demanding that they not run the ads disparaging Pepsi-Cola. Some bottlers complied; some did not. Seven-Up attempted to carry this theme further by introducing Like in March 1982. Like was a caffeine-free regular cola. In response to a suit initiated by Coca-Cola, Like was determined to be in fact a cola, and therefore bottlers of Coca-Cola, Pepsi-Cola, and RC Cola could not market it.

Pepsi-Cola introduced Pepsi Free and Sugar Free Pepsi Free in July 1982. The company announced that it intended these products to become the leaders in the caffeine-free segment. The company significantly increased advertising for these products in 1983. (In 1982 PepsiCo incurred an unusual charge of $79.4 million due to problems in its Philippine and Mexican operations. In 1983 international soft drink losses—resulting largely from devaluations of the Mexican and Venezuelan currencies—had offset strong results from Pepsi-Cola U.S. operations.)

In August 1982 Coca-Cola introduced "diet Coke" in the New York City area and certain other lead markets. Surveys showed that most consumers found the diet Coke formula far superior to Tab. Many observers believed that Coca-Cola had developed the diet Coke formula years earlier, but management was said to have hurried its introduction in response to the introduction of Pepsi Free and Sugar Free Pepsi Free.

Some Coca-Cola bottlers voiced strong resistance to the use of the Coke brand name. However, the introduction of diet Coke in New York City, which was accompanied by a lavish advertising campaign, proved successful beyond even the company's expectations. Diet Coke had gained national distribution by early 1983 and had become the largest selling diet soft drink by the end of 1983. Coca-Cola also introduced diet Coke in 20 countries in 1984.

Dr Pepper also took a series of steps in 1982. W. W. Clements announced that his goal was to increase Dr Pepper's market share to 7 percent. The company acquired two of its franchised bottlers, in Florida and Alabama, and also acquired the Canada Dry Company, a concentrate producer of ginger ale and various mixers.

Victor Posner, a financier, acquired the Royal Crown Company in 1982. Speculation persisted into 1985 whether, or when, Posner would sell Royal Crown. The company, headquartered in Chicago, retained its greatest strength in the Midwest.

Procter & Gamble, a major consumer products company with revenues of $14 billion in 1984, acquired Crush orange drink and Hires Root Beer in 1982 and two Coca-Cola bottling franchises in Kentucky in 1983. Procter & Gamble had shown signs of beginning to work more cooperatively with the trade than had been its tradition or reputation. P&G had begun to employ direct product profit analysis to make changes in its packaging and operations to improve trade profits. The company was seen as making a comeback from heavy competition in its basic detergent and household paper product businesses and had introduced several new products including Citrus Hill orange juice. The soft drink operations were small, but the CEO, John Smale, stated that the operations were satisfactory and that P&G had "learned a good deal about the beverage industry."[3]

Price discounting grew more intense in 1982. The trend was led by Coca-Cola, particularly in the early months of the year before the introduction of diet Coke. Dr Pepper, in its annual report for 1982, attributed lower earnings directly to the effect of competitive discounting. Coca-Cola also moved in 1982 to engineer changes in the ownership of nine of its franchise bottlers, including the largest, Coca-Cola Bottling of New York. In several cases the company took an equity position but resold the majority of the bottling company to a contiguous franchise.

---

[3] *Fortune,* February 4, 1985.

As an industry rule of thumb, bottling franchises usually sold in 1984 for $8 to $10 for each 288-ounce case of annual volume. Some industry observers believed that Coca-Cola intended to consolidate its bottling system significantly. One even projected that Coca-Cola wanted to reduce its franchises from approximately 400 local to 20 regional operations. Pepsi-Cola management continually reaffirmed their support for their franchises.

Coca-Cola also changed the advertising theme in 1982. Goizueta stated: "With our new slogan—Coke is it—we're saying we're Number 1 and not ashamed of it. Our former slogan—Have a Coke and a smile—was wonderful, but we were in a fight, and our slogan was a ballad. The momentum has now shifted from Purchase (headquarters of PepsiCo) to Atlanta."[4]

Discounting had been established as a permanent characteristic of the industry by 1984. In most areas of the United States, both Coca-Cola and Pepsi-Cola were on discount all the time in all major food stores. Exhibit 6 shows the average net prices that consumers actually paid for soft drinks in four types of packages.

Pepsi-Cola changed its advertising theme for regular brand Pepsi in 1984—positioning the brand as the "Choice of a New Generation." Pepsi-Cola secured endorsements from the stars Michael Jackson and Lionel Richie and, in 1985, from former Democratic vice presidential candidate Geraldine Ferraro. The endorsements by Jackson and Richie gained extensive free publicity and were used to generate excitement and motivation at the large conventions of Pepsi-Cola bottlers.

In mid-1984 Brian Dyson, president of Coca-Cola U.S.A., declared that diet Coke had become the third largest selling soft drink in the United States, surpassing both the regular 7UP brand and the regular Dr Pepper. Dyson then predicted that diet Coke would become the second largest selling soft drink in the United States. Some industry observers believed that the bravado of this statement was intended to motivate the Coca-Cola bottlers and to reduce the effects of the Michael Jackson and Lionel Richie endorsements for Pepsi-Cola.

Pepsi-Cola had begun in 1984 testing of a new lemon/lime drink named Slice, which contained 10 percent fruit juice distinguishing it from both 7UP and Sprite which contained no fruit juice. Industry publications indicated that the drink appeared successful in test markets in Wisconsin. Spurred by the innovation of one of its bottlers, Pepsi-Cola was also the first to introduce the 3-litre plastic bottle in 1984, gaining a four-month window before Coca-Cola could secure supplies from Owens-Illinois for its own bottlers. Pepsi-Cola and Coca-Cola products packaged in 3-litre bottles sold at retail for significantly less per ounce in late 1984 and early 1985 than the same products packaged in 2-litre bottles.

---

[4] *Industry Week,* November 1982.

In November 1984 Coca-Cola began in-home testing of a new 12-ounce "plastic can," which the 1984 annual report indicated would be introduced nationally in 1985. Coca-Cola had apparently negotiated a special supply agreement with Petainer, S.A., the developer of the container.

In early 1984 W. W. Clements engineered a leveraged buyout of Dr Pepper by Forstmann Little & Co., a closely held private investment firm that reportedly had approximately $500 million in capital invested by pension funds and other institutional investors. The total purchase price for Dr Pepper was $622.5 million. Dr Pepper managers provided 10 percent of the capital, and the majority was borrowed against Dr Pepper assets.

Later in 1984 Clements told industry journalists that Dr Pepper sales in 1983 had increased 8.5 percent over 1982 to $560 million, and earnings had increased 73 percent in 1983 to $21.6 million. He believed that Dr Pepper had found new marketing clout in its first year as a private company and that private ownership "increased the strength of our resources and our ability to concentrate on the basics of the business." He also stated that the company would consider selling its Canada Dry unit and some of its bottling operations in order to return the company to "a single focus." Clements asserted that Dr Pepper had no intention of "retreating" to become "merely a regional producer" just in Texas and the Southwest and that it intended to continue working with Coca-Cola and Pepsi-Cola bottlers.[5]

Aspartame, a sweetener derived from natural ingredients which could be used in diet soft drinks, was rapidly becoming the industry standard in 1984. In 1969 the Food and Drug Administration had banned the use of cyclamates. Soft drink companies began using saccharin as the sweetener in their diet drinks. Surveys indicated that consumers thought soft drinks with aspartame tasted far superior to those with saccharin, and saccharin was also suspected by some researchers to be a carcinogen. Aspartame, with 200 times the sweetness of sugar, was marketed by G. D. Searle & Co., which had a patent on it until 1992. However, it was far more expensive than saccharin and at the $90/pound price listed by Searle was three times as expensive as the cost of the equivalent amount of sugar. A cost analysis showed that the variable cost of concentrate plus aspartame would at $90 per pound cost more than the price that major concentrate producers were charging their bottlers in late 1984 for concentrate plus saccharin. The four largest concentrate producers, led by Pepsi-Cola, decided to use 100 percent aspartame in 1984. Industry sources believed that they had all secured significant but varying discounts off the list price.

Pepsi-Cola was able to secure delivery of aspartame from G. D. Searle before Coca-Cola did, and Pepsi undertook a concerted effort to

---

[5] *Advertising Age,* October 10, 1984.

use its six-week lead to promote Diet Pepsi against diet Coke. Coca-Cola responded by launching a national advertising campaign stating that diet Coke had 100 percent aspartame, even though it was available only in certain packages and areas. Pepsi-Cola responded by emphasizing at the point of purchase that the labels of its Diet Pepsi actually contained the announcement of "100% Nutrasweet" (the brand name of Searle's aspartame), while the Coca-Cola labels could not make this claim. Industry sources indicated that the growth of Diet Pepsi had exceeded that of diet Coke during these two months.

Exhibit 1

Chronology of Major New Soft Drink Brand Introductions

Year	Brand	Company	Description
1885	Dr Pepper	Dr Pepper	Regular Pepper
1886	Coca-Cola	Coca-Cola	Regular cola
1898	Pepsi-Cola	Pepsi-Cola	Regular cola
1920	7UP	Seven-Up	Regular lemon-lime
1934	Royal Crown Cola	Royal Crown	Regular cola
1961	Sprite	Coca-Cola	Regular lemon-lime
1962	Diet Rite Cola	Royal Crown	Diet cola
1962	Diet Dr Pepper	Dr Pepper	Diet Pepper
1963	Tab	Coca-Cola	Diet cola
1964	Diet Pepsi	Pepsi-Cola	Diet cola
1964	Mountain Dew	Pepsi-Cola	Regular "hillbilly" flavor
1970	Diet 7UP	Seven-Up	Diet lemon-lime
1971	Sugar-Free Dr Pepper	Dr Pepper	Diet Pepper
1972	Mr. PiBB	Coca-Cola	Regular Pepper
1974	Welch's Grape Soda	Welch's*	Regular grape soda
1974	Diet Sprite	Coca-Cola	Diet lemon-lime
1977	Pepsi Light	Pepsi-Cola	Diet cola with lemon
1978	Sunkist	General Cinema	Regular orange soda
1979	Mello Yello	Coca-Cola	Regular "hillbilly" flavor
1980	RC 100	Royal Crown	Diet caffeine-free cola
1980	Diet Sunkist	General Cinema	Diet orange soda
3/82	Decaffeinated RC	Royal Crown	Regular caffeine-free cola
3/82	RC 100 Regular	Royal Crown	Regular caffeine-free cola
3/82	Like	Seven-Up	Regular caffeine-free cola
7/82	Pepsi Free	Pepsi-Cola	Regular caffeine-free cola
7/82	Sugar Free Pepsi Free	Pepsi-Cola	Diet caffeine-free cola
7/82	Diet Coke	Coca-Cola	Diet cola
10/82	Sugar-Free Like	Seven-Up	Diet caffeine-free cola
1/83	Pepper Free	Dr Pepper	Regular caffeine-free Pepper
1/83	Sugar Free Pepper Free	Dr Pepper	Diet caffeine-free Pepper
5/83	Caffeine-Free Coke	Coca-Cola	Regular caffeine-free cola
5/83	Caffeine-Free Diet Coke	Coca-Cola	Diet caffeine-free cola
5/83	Caffeine-Free Tab	Coca-Cola	Diet caffeine-free cola

* Brand acquired by Dr Pepper in 1982.
    Source: Cola data from Jesse Meyers's *Beverage Digest*, April 27, 1983. Other data from various magazine articles and company annual reports.

Exhibit 2

U.S. Liquid Consumption Trends 1960–1984 (Per capita annual consumption in gallons)

	1960	1965	1970	1975	1976	1977	1978	1979	1980	1981	1982	1983	1984
Soft drinks	17.5	20.3	27.0	31.0	33.7	35.9	37.1	38.1	38.8	39.5	40.1	42.0	43.2
Coffee	40.2	37.8	35.7	33.0	29.4	28.0	27.0	29.2	26.8	26.7	26.1	25.9	27.3
Beer	15.4	15.9	18.5	21.6	21.8	22.5	23.1	23.8	24.3	24.6	24.4	24.6	24.0
Milk	28.0	26.0	23.1	22.1	22.1	21.5	21.3	21.0	20.7	20.4	20.0	19.8	21.1
Juices	4.0	3.8	5.2	6.9	6.9	6.9	6.6	6.7	6.9	6.7	6.6	6.8	8.1
Tea	6.0	4.9	5.5	6.2	6.4	6.9	6.7	6.6	6.6	6.5	6.3	6.4	7.3
Powdered drinks	NA	NA	NA	4.8	5.5	5.9	6.1	6.0	6.0	6.0	6.0	6.5	6.3
Wine	NA	1.0	1.3	1.7	1.7	1.8	2.1	2.2	2.3	2.3	2.3	2.4	2.5
Bottled H_2O	NA	NA	NA	1.2	1.2	1.3	1.4	1.5	1.6	1.9	2.2	2.7	3.0
Distilled spirits	1.3	1.5	1.8	2.0	2.0	2.0	2.0	2.0	2.0	2.0	1.9	1.8	1.8
Subtotal	112.4	111.2	118.1	130.5	130.7	132.7	133.4	137.1	136.0	136.6	135.9	138.9	144.6
Imputed H_2O consumption	70.1	71.3	64.4	52.0	51.8	49.8	49.1	45.4	46.5	45.9	46.6	43.6	37.9
Total*	182.5	182.5	182.5	182.5	182.5	182.5	182.5	182.5	182.5	182.5	182.5	182.5	182.5

* This analysis assumes that each person consumes on average liquids totaling one half gallon per day.
Source: *Beverage Industry* and John C. Maxwell.

Exhibit 3

Disposable Income and Soft Drink Industry Growth

	1965	1970	1975	1978	1979	1980	1981	1982	1983
Disposable income (billions)	$475.8	$695.3	$1,091.1	$1,474.0	$1,650.2	$1,828.9	$2,041.7	$2,180.5	$2,340.1
		1965–1970	*1970–1975*	*1975–1978*					
Annual growth rate		7.9%	9.5%	10.4%	12.0%	10.8%	11.6%	6.8%	7.3%
Real disposable income (1967 dollars)	$503.5	$597.9	$ 680.0	$ 754.4	$ 759.1	$ 741.0	$ 749.5	$ 754.2	$ 784.2
		1965–1970	*1970–1975*	*1975–1978*					
Annual growth rate		3.5%	2.6%	3.5%	0.6%	−2.4%	1.1%	0.6%	4.0%
Annual soft drink volume		7.9%	4.9%	10.2%	5.0%	4.1%	3.8%	2.7%	4.5%

Sources: *Statistical Abstract of the United States, 1985; Beverage Industry,* 1985 Annual Manual.

Exhibit 4

Soft Drink Industry Structure, 1984

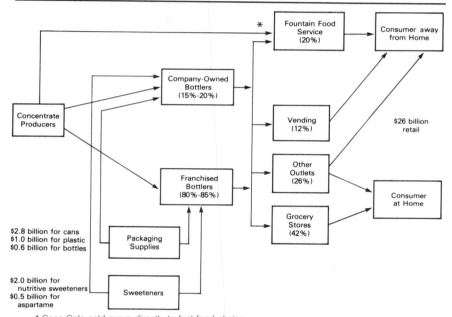

* Coca-Cola sold syrup directly to fast food chains.

Exhibit 5

Estimated Packaging Costs in 1984

Package Type	Price†	Price per Unit	Price per Ounce
Aluminum can	$90.00 per 1,000	$0.090	$0.0075
1-litre glass*	$2.55 per 12	$0.213	$0.0064
16-ounce glass	$2.29 per 24	$0.095	$0.0059
1-litre plastic	$2.41 per 12	$0.201	$0.0060
2-litre plastic	$1.95 per 8	$0.244	$0.0036
3-litre plastic	$2.45 per 6	$0.408	$0.0040

* Glass refers to the plasti-shield glass bottles.
† Price includes all labeling and secondary packaging such as cartons and boxes.
Source: Major soft drink bottler.

Exhibit 6

Average Retail Prices of Soft Drinks in Food Stores

	1977	1978	1979	1980	1981	1982	1983	1984
16-ounce returnable bottles, 8-pack	$1.54	$1.66	$1.82	$1.97	$2.12	$2.08	$2.09	$2.13
Percent change		7.8%	9.6%	8.2%	7.6%	-1.9%	.5%	1.9%
16-ounce nonreturnable bottles, 6-pack	$1.50	$1.65	$1.81	$2.14	$2.42	$2.51	$2.61	$2.68
Percent change		10.0%	9.7%	8.2%	13.1%	3.7%	4.0%	2.7%
2-litre nonreturnable plastic bottles	$ .93	$1.00	$1.10	$1.23	$1.31	$1.30	$1.28	$1.26
Percent change		7.5%	10.0%	11.8%	6.5%	-.7%	-1.5%	-1.5%
Aluminum cans, 6-pack	$1.37	$1.51	$1.66	$1.85	$2.00	$2.01	$2.00	$2.04
Percent change		10.2%	9.9%	11.5%	8.1%	.5%	-.5%	2.0%
Consumer Price Index 1967 = 100	181.5	195.3	217.7	247.0	272.3	288.6	300.4	310.0
Percent change		7.6%	11.5%	13.5%	10.2%	6.0%	4.1%	3.2%

Sources: Neilsen Store Audits; Bureau of Labor Statistics.

Exhibit 7 — Advertising Spending by Brand (In millions)

Brand	1983	1982	1981	1980	1979	1978	1977	1976	1975	1974	1973
Coca-Cola Company											
Coca-Cola	$ 41.7	$ 44.9	$ 38.3	$ 35.6	$ 41.7	$ 35.0	$ 25.0	$ 22.1	$ 20.3	$ 22.1	$ 24.0
Diet Coke	20.9	38.0									
Sprite	21.2	16.2	11.5	10.7	9.6	7.9	4.5	2.7	2.6	2.5	1.7
Tab	25.2	22.0	15.2	12.6	12.6	8.6	4.2	5.2	6.5	5.3	5.3
Fresca	—	0.6	3.7	7.3	6.3	6.1	1.3	2.0	2.4	2.6	2.6
Others	10.7	3.3	4.8	4.9	3.5	2.1	1.3	2.8	2.6	2.9	3.9
Total	119.7	125.0	73.5	71.1	73.7	59.7	36.3	34.8	34.4	35.4	37.5
Pepsi-Cola U.S.A.											
Pepsi-Cola	22.8	39.1	31.2	39.7	35.0	25.7	24.5	17.5	15.0	14.9	13.4
Diet Pepsi	20.6	15.0	13.8	11.6	8.7	6.4	6.4	4.1	3.7	4.1	4.1
Pepsi Free (reg. & sf)	23.0	4.2	—								
Mountain Dew	8.4	8.4	13.0	10.2	8.4	6.8	4.5	3.3	2.8	0.6	0.4
Pepsi Light	6.2	5.4	5.1	5.2	6.3	3.7	6.5	2.9	0.9	—	—
Teem			0.1	0.1	0.6	0.5	0.2	0.1	0.1	—	—
Others	3.2	3.2	2.5	0.5	1.5	0.4	0.1	1.6	2.9	5.5	5.5
Total	84.2	75.3	65.6	67.3	60.5	43.5	42.2	29.5	25.4	25.1	23.4
Dr Pepper Company*											
Dr Pepper	6.0	10.0	9.7	11.0	9.0	10.2	7.0	5.2	4.9	5.4	5.3
Pepper Free	2.6										
Diet Dr Pepper	3.5	4.5	3.1	2.9	2.8	1.9	1.8	1.6	1.6	1.8	1.2
Canada Dry	0.8	8.9	7.9	10.1	4.6	5.5	4.5	5.1	5.2	4.9	5.4
Barrelhead	0.1	0.1	0.8	1.3	0.7	1.0	1.2	1.4	1.3	0.6	0.2
Welch's	0.1	0.3	1.6	2.6	2.3	1.8	1.5				
Others				0.2	0.4	0.3					
Total	13.1	23.8	25.3	25.9	19.8	20.7	16.0	13.3	13.0	12.7	12.1
Seven-Up Co.											
7UP	21.2	19.6	23.4	25.5	24.6	15.6	13.2	11.1	10.2	10.4	10.4
Diet 7UP	11.9	7.8	7.1	7.9	5.7	3.7	1.5	3.0	3.3	2.0	2.1
Like	9.0	3.7	—								
Others	2.6	1.1			1.2	1.1					
Total	44.7	32.2	30.5	33.4	31.5	20.4	14.7	14.1	13.5	12.4	12.5
Royal Crown Cola Co.											
Royal Crown	4.0	6.2	3.0	6.5	7.3	7.3	7.6	11.7	10.5	5.7	4.9
Diet Rite Cola	5.4	4.2	5.1	3.4	3.0	3.1	2.3	4.2	3.5	2.1	2.4
Others	5.6	6.0	0.1	0.1	0.6	0.5	0.4	0.4	0.4	0.3	0.2
Total	15.0	16.4	8.2	10.0	10.9	10.9	10.3	16.3	14.4	8.2	7.5
Shasta total	6.1	6.1	4.1	4.4	4.6	4.1	4.1	3.0	2.8	2.3	—
All others	24.0	38.4	29.5	26.3	25.0	21.2	11.4	11.0	10.5	10.1	9.6
Industry total	$306.8	$317.2	$236.7	$238.4	$226.0	$180.5	$135.0	$122.0	$114.0	$106.2	$102.6

* Dr Pepper acquired Barrelhead and Welch's in 1976 and Canada Dry in 1982.
Sources: *Beverage Industry; Advertising Age;* company annual reports.

Exhibit 8

U.S. Soft Drink Market Shares (Percent) by Volume (All channels, major brands)

Brand	1983	1982	1981	1980	1979	1978	1977	1976	1975	1974	1973
Coca-Cola Co.											
Coca-Cola	22.4%	23.9%	24.2%	24.3%	23.9%	24.3%	24.5%	24.3%	24.2%	24.4%	24.8%
Diet Coke	3.2	0.3	—	—	—	—	—	—	—	—	—
Tab	2.7	3.8	3.6	3.2	3.0	2.7	2.6	2.6	2.5	2.2	2.1
Sprite*	2.8	3.2	2.9	2.9	2.9	2.9	2.8	2.7	2.5	2.2	2.0
Fresca	0.2	0.3	0.4	0.4	0.4	0.5	0.5	0.6	0.6	0.6	0.8
Mello Yello	0.6	0.8	0.9	0.8	0.7	—	—	—	—	—	—
Others	3.4	2.2	2.5	2.8	3.1	3.2	3.5	3.2	3.0	3.1	2.9
Total	35.3	34.5	34.5	34.4	34.0	33.6	33.9	33.4	32.7	32.1	32.2
Pepsi-Cola U.S.A.											
Pepsi-Cola	16.9	18.1	18.3	17.9	17.9	17.6	17.2	17.0	17.4	17.5	17.5
Diet Pepsi	2.4	2.9	2.9	2.6	2.5	2.3	2.1	1.9	1.6	1.5	1.4
Pepsi Free	2.5	0.3	—	—	—	—	—	—	—	—	—
Mountain Dew	2.7	2.8	3.0	2.9	2.8	2.4	1.9	1.5	1.1	1.1	0.9
Teem	0.2	0.2	0.2	0.3	0.3	0.3	0.2	0.2	0.3	0.3	0.3
Others	0.2	0.2	0.2	0.3	0.3	0.3	0.4	0.3	0.3	0.3	0.4
Total	25.3	25.0	25.1	24.4	24.2	23.3	22.3	21.4	20.8	20.7	20.5
Dr Pepper Company											
Dr Pepper	4.9	5.1	5.4	5.5	5.5	5.4	5.3	5.0	4.9	4.8	4.8
Diet Dr Pepper	1.1	1.3	1.3	1.2	1.1	1.1	1.0	0.8	0.6	0.4	0.3
Canada Dry	2.8	2.2	2.1	1.9	1.8	1.8	1.9	2.0	2.1	2.0	1.9
Others	1.6	2.0	2.2	2.7	3.0	3.2	3.1	3.1	3.3	3.5	3.6
Total	10.4	10.6	11.0	11.3	11.4	11.5	11.3	10.9	10.9	10.7	10.6
Seven-Up Co.											
7UP	5.4	5.2	5.0	5.4	5.6	5.9	6.0	6.3	6.6	7.0	7.2
Diet 7UP	1.3	1.3	1.2	1.1	1.1	1.1	1.2	1.2	1.0	0.6	0.3
Like	0.4	0.3	—	—	—	—	—	—	—	—	—
Others	0.2	0.1	0.1	0.2	0.2	0.2	0.2	0.2	0.2	0.2	0.3
Total	7.3	6.9	6.3	6.7	6.9	7.2	7.4	7.7	7.8	7.8	7.8

Royal Crown Cola Co.										
RC Cola	2.1	2.3	2.5	2.8	2.8	3.0	3.2	3.3	3.4	3.4	3.7
RC 100*	0.6	0.8	0.2	0.1	—	—	—	—	—	—	—
Diet Rite	0.4	0.6	0.6	0.6	0.7	0.7	0.8	0.8	0.8	0.8	1.0
Others	0.6	0.6	0.7	0.8	0.9	1.0	1.0	1.2	1.2	1.2	1.2
Total	3.8	4.3	4.1	4.3	4.4	4.7	5.0	5.3	5.4	5.4	5.9
General Cinema										
Sunkist	1.8	1.9	1.6	1.3	0.6	0.2	—	—	—	—	—
Crush International	1.1	1.2	1.1	1.1	1.1	1.1	1.0	0.9	0.9	0.8	0.8
Shasta	2.0	2.1	1.8	1.8	1.8	1.9	2.0	1.9	2.5	2.6	2.5

* Includes both regular and diet versions.
Source: John C. Maxwell and *Beverage Industry*.

Exhibit 9

Financial Data for the Major Soft Drink Competitors, 1971 to 1983 (Dollars in millions)

	1971	1972	1973	1974	1975	1976	1977	1978*	1979†	1980	1981	1982§	1983
Coca-Cola Co.													
Corporate sales	$1,729.0	$1,876.0	$2,145.0	$2,522.0	$2,773.0	$2,928.0	$3,328.0	$4,013.0	$4,588.0	$5,475.0	$5,699.0	$6,021.0	$6,829.0
Corporate net income	$ 168.0	$ 190.0	$ 215.0	$ 196.0	$ 249.0	$ 294.0	$ 331.0	$ 375.0	$ 420.0	$ 422.0	$ 482.0	$ 512.0	$ 559.0
Income/sales	9.7%	10.1%	10.0%	7.8%	9.0%	10.0%	9.9%	9.3%	9.2%	7.7%	8.5%	8.5%	8.2%
ROE	21.4%	21.5%	21.0%	19.1%	20.9%	20.5%	21.0%	21.6%	21.9%	20.3%	21.2%	18.4%	19.1%
Long-term debt/total capital	4.5%	4.8%	5.0%	5.5%	3.1%	3.5%	3.5%	3.8%	6.8%	9.9%	9.3%	17.3%	17.5%
Soft drink sales	NA	NA	NA	NA	NA	NA	$2,702.0	$3,306.0	$3,765.0	$4,522.0	$4,683.0	$4,516.0	$5,101.0
Soft drink operating income	NA	NA	NA	NA	NA	NA	$ 562.0	$ 634.0	$ 676.0	$ 732.0	$ 804.0	$ 873.0	$ 894.0
Operating income/soft drink sales	NA	NA	NA	NA	NA	NA	20.8%	19.2%	18.2%	16.2%	17.2%	19.3%	17.6%
PepsiCo, Inc.													
Corporate sales	$1,369.0	$1,560.0	$1,913.0	$2,409.0	$2,709.0	$3,109.0	$3,649.0	$4,300.0	$5,089.0	$5,975.0	$7,027.0	$7,449.0	$7,896.0
Corporate net income	$ 69.0	$ 80.0	$ 87.0	$ 100.0	$ 124.0	$ 162.0	$ 197.0	$ 223.0	$ 251.0	$ 261.0	$ 298.0	$ 224.0	$ 284.0
Income/sales	5.0%	5.1%	4.5%	4.2%	4.6%	5.2%	5.4%	5.2%	4.9%	4.4%	4.2%	3.0%	3.6%
ROE	16.5%	16.3%	15.8%	16.8%	18.3%	20.4%	21.0%	20.6%	20.8%	19.8%	20.3%	14.0%	16.5%
Long-term debt/total capital	34.4%	33.5%	37.8%	36.3%	34.9%	30.6%	29.2%	26.3%	29.2%	31.4%	27.2%	28.4%	23.7%
Beverage sales	$ 592.0	$ 661.0	$ 829.0	$ 982.0	$1,065.0	$1,161.0	$1,407.0	$1,698.0	$2,014.0	$2,768.0	$2,772.0	$2,908.0	$2,940.0
Beverage operating income	$ 76.0	$ 85.0	$ 101.0	$ 114.0	$ 111.0	$ 144.0	$ 180.0	$ 227.0	$ 254.0	$ 244.0	$ 252.0	$ 218.0	$ 126.0
Operating income/sales	12.8%	12.9%	12.2%	11.6%	10.4%	12.4%	12.8%	13.4%	12.6%	8.8%	9.1%	7.5%	4.3%
Philip Morris/													
The Seven-Up Co.													
Philip Morris sales	$1,853.0	$2,131.0	$2,603.0	$3,011.0	$3,642.0	$4,294.0	$5,202.0	$6,633.0	$8,149.0	$9,650.0	$10,722.0	$11,586.0	$12,976.0
Net income	$ 102.0	$ 125.0	$ 149.0	$ 176.0	$ 212.0	$ 266.0	$ 335.0	$ 409.0	$ 507.0	$ 549.0	$ 660.0	$ 782.0	$ 904.0
Income/sales	5.5%	5.9%	5.7%	5.8%	5.8%	6.2%	6.4%	6.2%	6.2%	5.7%	6.2%	6.7%	7.0%
ROE	17.6%	18.0%	18.3%	18.1%	17.3%	18.6%	19.8%	19.3%	20.5%	19.4%	20.4%	21.3%	22.4%
Long-term debt/total capital	40.4%	41.3%	42.6%	44.5%	42.9%	41.7%	40.9%	42.1%	41.0%	40.9%	42.2%	40.1%	36.8%
7UP sales	$ 124.0	$ 133.0	$ 147.0	$ 191.0	$ 214.0	$ 233.0	$ 251.0	$ 186.0	$ 296.0	$ 353.0	$ 432.0	$ 531.0	$ 650.0
Net income	$ 11.3	$ 12.0	$ 14.1	$ 16.6	$ 10.3	$ 24.8	$ 25.8	$ 2.6	$ 7.0	$ (7.1)	$ (1.7)	$ (1.2)	$ (10.8)
Operating income	—	—	—	—	—	—	—	—	—	—	—	—	—
Net income/sales	9.1%	9.1%	9.6%	8.7%	9.5%	10.6%	10.3%	14.0%	2.4%	(2.0%)	(0.4%)	(0.2%)	(1.7%)
Operating income/sales	—	—	—	—	—	—	—	—	—	—	—	—	—

ROE	27.8%	23.7%	23.6%	23.9%	23.6%	24.0%	23.1%	—	—	—	—	—	—
Long-term debt/total capital	3.4%	4.1%	4.5%	3.4%	2.3%	3.1%	4.2%	—	—	—	—	—	—
Dr Pepper Company‡													
Sales	$64.0	$77.0	$99.0	$128.0	$138.0	$152.0	$227.0	$271.0	$292.0	$333.0	$364.0	$516.0	NA
Net income	$6.8	$8.1	$9.7	$9.9	$11.9	$15.5	$20.3	$23.6	$23.6	$26.5	$29.4	$12.5	NA
Income/sales	10.7%	10.5%	9.8%	7.7%	8.6%	10.2%	8.9%	8.7%	8.1%	8.0%	8.1%	2.4%	NA
ROE	26.9%	26.0%	25.4%	22.7%	24.0%	27.0%	26.5%	26.9%	24.5%	25.5%	25.2%	9.2%	NA
Long-term debt/total capital	0%	0%	0%	0%	0%	0%	0%	0%	0%	0%	0%	0%	NA
Royal Crown Cola Co.													
Sales	$125.8	$191.4	$195.4	$223.2	$257.5	$295.1	$349.6	$390.7	$421.4	$438.1	$450.4	NA	NA
Net income	$8.4	$11.7	$12.2	$8.2	$13.3	$15.2	$18.6	$1.4	$16.4	$10.1	$15.5	NA	NA
Income/sales	6.7%	6.1%	6.2%	3.7%	5.2%	5.2%	5.2%	0.4%	3.9%	2.3%	3.4%	NA	NA
ROE	23.8%	22.1%	19.8%	12.0%	17.4%	15.4%	18.8%	1.5%	16.4%	9.9%	14.2%	NA	NA
Long-term debt/total capital	NA	NA	NA	NA	NA	NA	28.3%	38.3%	38.3%	38.2%	34.3%	NA	NA
Soft drink sales	NA	NA	NA	NA	NA	NA	$202.7	$213.0	$204.0	$221.0	$230.0	NA	NA
Soft drink operating income	NA	NA	NA	NA	NA	NA	$21.0	$11.1	$14.8	$13.9	$22.7	NA	NA
Operating income/sales	NA	NA	NA	NA	NA	NA	10.4%	5.2%	7.3%	6.3%	9.9%	NA	NA
Consolidated Foods													
Corporate sales	$1,545.0	$1,783.0	$2,042.0	$2,282.0	$2,443.0	$2,755.0	$2,892.0	$3,536.0	$4,720.0	$5,343.0	$5,614.0	$6,039.0	$6,572.0
Net income	$59.0	$69.0	$76.0	$72.0	$13.0	$89.0	$88.0	$101.0	$111.0	$128.0	$140.0	$159.0	$171.0
Income/sales	3.8%	3.9%	3.7%	3.2%	0.5%	3.2%	3.0%	2.9%	2.4%	2.4%	2.5%	2.6%	2.6%
ROE	13.3%	13.5%	13.8%	11.9%	2.2%	14.3%	13.2%	14.3%	14.8%	15.6%	16.1%	17.3%	18.4%
Long-term debt/total capital	21.7%	22.9%	22.2%	25.0%	33.9%	21.8%	19.8%	26.5%	31.8%	25.4%	26.1%	22.5%	20.3%
Beverage division sales (including Shasta)	$188.0	$213.0	$239.0	$239.0	$213.0	$239.0	$238.0	$251.0	$1,111.0	$1,402.0	$1,348.0	$1,346.0	$1,440.0
Operating income	$2.4	$3.4	$0.6	$3.4	$12.8	$15.2	$17.2	$18.6	$84.0	$97.0	$88.0	$58.0	$69.0
Operating income/sales	1.3%	1.6%	0.3%	1.4%	6.0%	6.4%	7.2%	7.4%	7.6%	6.9%	6.5%	4.3%	4.8%

* In 1978 Consolidated Foods acquired 65 percent of Douwe Egberts, B.V., a company which roasts and markets branded coffee in France and the Benelux countries. Beginning in 1979 C.F. reported the results of Douwe Egberts and Shasta as one beverage division.

† Philip Morris purchased the Seven-Up Co. in 1979 and consolidated earnings back to 1978.

‡ Acquired Welch's and Barrelhead in 1976 and Canada Dry in 1982; went private through a leveraged buyout in 1983.

§ In 1982 Victor Posner purchased Royal Crown Cola.

The Seven-Up Co., Division of Philip Morris Incorporated

Philip Morris Incorporated was a leading international marketer of cigarettes and had increased its share of the U.S. cigarette market from 15 percent in 1970 to 35 percent in 1984. Philip Morris acquired the Miller Brewing Company in 1970 and engineered its growth from the seventh largest to the second largest U.S. brewer by 1977. In 1979 Philip Morris acquired the Seven-Up Co., the number three concentrate producer in the United States. After four years of losses, Seven-Up had registered an operating profit in 1984. Industry analysts were debating the role that Seven-Up would play in Philip Morris's future. (See Exhibit 1.)

History of the Seven-Up Co.

The Seven-Up Co. was founded in 1920 in St. Louis, Missouri, as the partnership of three men—C. L. Grigg, E. G. Ridgway, and F. Y. Gladney. Originally the company produced an orange drink, but in 1929 it introduced its "BIB Label Lithiated Lemon-Lime Soda." Renamed 7UP in 1937, the drink had to compete with over 600 lemon-lime drinks in the U.S. market. The company designed an attractive green bottle for 7UP, which was clear, unlike the caramel colored colas.

Seven-Up began to work to persuade bottlers of other soft drinks to market 7UP. Seven-Up managers took pride in the close, cooperative relations that they worked to establish with their bottlers. They always

Copyright © 1985 by the President and Fellows of Harvard College
Harvard Business School case 385–321

referred to their bottlers as "Developers" in order to demonstrate the importance that they placed on their bottlers' sales effort.

World War II sugar rationing helped to increase 7UP's U.S. sales because 7UP, using less sugar, was able to produce relatively more units than Coca-Cola and Pepsi-Cola were allowed during this period. After the war, Seven-Up emphasized its product's medicinal benefits, both for children (with such slogans as "Tune Tiny Tummies") and for adults (with such slogans as "Cure for Seven Hangovers"). The product was also widely used as a mixer for alcoholic beverages. 7UP plus Seagram's Seven Crown whiskey became a particularly popular drink.

By the 1950s Seven-Up had achieved national distribution through its franchise network. Seven-Up established and owned a small number of bottling operations. The vast majority of 7UP developers were bottlers for Coca-Cola, Pepsi-Cola, and RC Cola. Like Royal Crown, 7UP was particularly strong in the U.S. Midwest. Seven-Up sold its concentrate for approximately 15 percent more than Coca-Cola did because 7UP used less sugar, thus saving its bottlers some of the cost of sweetener. At retail, 7UP sold at prices comparable to Coca-Cola.

In the 1960s the company found through research that its consumption was significantly skewed toward older buyers and that the product was frequently viewed as an aid for indigestion or as a mixer but not as a soft drink. In 1968 Seven-Up launched its "Uncola" advertising campaign, designed to position 7UP as a soft-drink alternative to colas. The target market for the effort was the 16- to 24-year-old age group. The campaign used Geoffrey Holder, a Jamaican actor with a distinctive sound and style, to convey the message. The television advertisements received high advertising recall ratings. 7UP became the dominant soft drink in the lemon-lime category, which comprised approximately 12 percent of the total soft drink market during the 1960s and the 1970s. The second best selling lemon-lime soft drink was Sprite, introduced by Coca-Cola in 1961. Seven-Up also introduced a diet version of its product in 1970.

Seven-Up, like other concentrate producers, adopted many new packages during the 1960s and 1970s. In 1971 Seven-Up was the first company to use the plasti-shield glass bottle, introducing it in 12-ounce and 16-ounce sizes. In 1974 and 1975 Seven-Up could not obtain sufficient supplies of 32-ounce and 64-ounce plasti-shield glass bottles, which were the fastest growing package sizes.

Seven-Up did not enter the fountain market until 1960. However, by 1970, fountain sales represented 7 percent of Seven-Up unit sales, and by 1974 they were 12 percent. Seven-Up succeeded in convincing most of the major fast-food chains to direct their outlets to allocate one or two of their fountain dispensers (usually four or five per outlet) to Seven-Up products. In 1975 Seven-Up persuaded McDonald's to distribute sugar-free 7UP to all its outlets, the first time a major chain had taken on a diet drink. 7UP bottlers handled distribution of the product to individual fountain outlets. By 1976 Seven-Up had achieved the following distribution in the top 10 fast-food chains:

Seven-Up Distribution in Leading Fast-Food Chains, 1976

Chain	Share of Fast-Food Market	Type of 7UP Sold
1. McDonald's	20.0%	Sugar-free
2. Kentucky Fried Chicken	11.7	Regular
3. International Dairy Queen	6.0	Regular
4. Burger King	4.8	Both
5. Burger Chef	2.8	Sugar-free
6. A&W International	2.7	Both
7. Hardy's	2.6	Sugar-free
8. Denny's	2.6	Regular
9. Jack-in-the-Box	2.5	Not sold
10. Pizza Hut	2.5	Regular

7UP also began to expand internationally during the 1960s and 1970s. It was sold in 89 countries by 1977, holding a minor share in each market, smaller than its share in the United States. As in the United States, 7UP was usually bottled internationally by bottlers of Coca-Cola or Pepsi-Cola.

In the late 1970s, the three founding families of the Seven-Up Co. still controlled 55 percent of the company. The other 45 percent had been sold in 1967 through a public stock offering. The company sold 9 of its 13 company-owned bottlers between 1975 and 1979. In 1979 Philip Morris bought the Seven-Up Co. for $520 million.

Philip Morris Incorporated

Philip Morris was founded before the turn of the century and held a minor share of the U.S. tobacco market before World War II. The industry was dominated by the American Tobacco Company, which held over 40 percent of the market. After decades of mediocre performance Philip Morris decided in 1953 to reposition its Marlboro brand, which had been introduced in 1924 and previously targeted toward women. The new positioning and advertising theme employed the image of the American cowboy, and the brand immediately began to gain market share.

Cigarettes were highly subject to taxation. *Tobacco Industry,* a trade journal, estimated the following distribution of the end consumer dollar for cigarettes in 1981 and 1983:[1]

---

[1] *Tobacco Industry,* February 22, 1985.

Cents Out of Each Consumer Dollar Spent for Cigarettes

Sector	1981	1983
Federal, state and local taxes (excise, sales, and corporate income)	39%	44%
Wholesale and retail markups (excluding state and local taxes)	18	16
Product costs (leaf, labor, distribution, advertising, nontobacco materials, interest and general business overhead, net earnings, costs necessary to make and market the product)	43	40
Total	100%	100%

Tobacco leaf accounted for approximately 40 percent of the full production cost of cigarettes. Philip Morris engaged in extensive research and development regarding the growing, selection, curing, and blending of tobacco leaf. Tobacco leaf needed to be cured and dried for one year after it was purchased by the cigarette manufacturers before it could be used. At the end of 1984 Philip Morris had $2.2 billion in tobacco leaf inventory. The cigarette manufacturing process was capital-intensive and highly automated.

Manufacturers sold their cigarettes to independent wholesalers who in turn distributed the cigarettes along with hundreds of different products to many kinds of retail outlets and directly to major retail store chains. The companies employed sales forces who worked with wholesalers and retail chains to help gain fuller distribution for products and in particular to gain distribution for new brands.

In 1964 the U.S. Surgeon General announced findings that cigarette smoking was potentially hazardous to one's health, and by 1967 the Food and Drug Administration (FDA) ruled that cigarette packages sold in the United States would have to carry a health warning. In 1971 by act of Congress, cigarette advertising was banned from television. Throughout this growing controversy many large cigarette manufacturers began to diversify (see Exhibit 2).

After the ban on television and radio advertising Philip Morris and R. J. Reynolds were the only cigarette manufacturers to introduce entirely new cigarettes. Later in 1980 Brown & Williamson introduced Barclay, a brand that already was established in the United Kingdom. In the early 1970s Philip Morris and R. J. Reynolds began to fund extensive research concerning the question of smoking as a possible cause of cancer and lung and heart diseases. Both companies continued to assert that no scientific evidence existed to prove that smoking did cause health problems. R. J. Reynolds also increased its advertising expenditures to introduce new brands and support its best-selling established brands.

Philip Morris had grown in the 1960s under the leadership of Joseph Cullman, CEO from 1961 to 1978, and held 15 percent of the U.S. cigarette market in 1970. Philip Morris had also expanded its international cigarette business, fueled by the growth of the Marlboro brand, which grew by 1971 to become the largest selling brand in the world. Like Coca-Cola, Marlboro came to be one of the world's best-known brand names.

During the late 1960s and the 1970s Philip Morris set out to expand the number of brands and types of cigarettes that it sold in the United States. Its stated plan was to identify different segments of the cigarette market and to design and target new products to these segments. It introduced, among others, the following brands: Virginia Slims in 1967, a brand targeted toward women; Benson & Hedges in 1969, a 100-millimeter cigarette; and Merit in 1975, a low tar and nicotine cigarette. (See Exhibit 3.)

Philip Morris also developed new types of blends and packages for its best-selling brands. In particular Philip Morris expanded the breadth of offerings marketed under its Marlboro brand to include Marlboro Lights, a lower tar blend introduced in 1971, and three different kinds of packages. Each different tobacco blend and package was designed to fit a segment of the market that Philip Morris marketing research had identified as a discrete group. By 1984 the Marlboro brand in all its forms had become by far the leading U.S. cigarette brand, and Philip Morris had three of the top 10 selling brands (see Exhibit 4).

Philip Morris advertised heavily to build its Marlboro brand and to establish new brands (see Exhibit 5). Because television and radio advertising was banned Philip Morris made extensive use of magazine and billboard advertising and also began to sponsor sporting events and concerts, even though these media were viewed as cost inefficient relative to television in introducing new cigarette brands. The cost of introducing advertising for a new cigarette brand had grown to the point that Brown & Williamson spent $150 million to launch the Barclay brand in the United States in the 1980s.

Throughout the 1970s and 1980s Philip Morris invested heavily to expand and modernize its cigarette manufacturing plants (see Exhibit 1). In 1984 Philip Morris, with cigarette revenue of $9.8 billion, carried on its books $2.5 billion in plant and equipment dedicated to cigarette manufacturing. (See Exhibit 6.)

The Miller Brewing Company

In 1969 Philip Morris bought the Miller Brewing Company, the seventh largest U.S. beer manufacturer. This was the company's first investment outside the cigarette business except for a small industrial packaging company that had been purchased during the 1960s. The U.S. beer industry was populated by over 150 regional brewers. Most were family-owned operations that had been started before the turn of the century by emigrants from Europe.

Males accounted for 60 percent of all beer purchases and 80 percent of all beer consumption. Beer was sold in bottles and cans as well as in kegs. Beer consumption was moving toward the take-home market and bottles and cans. Kegs, or draft beer, accounted for 14 percent of consumption in 1975 and 10 percent in 1983.

Brewers bottled and canned their own beer. Beer tended to be packaged in more expensive bottles and cans than were soft drinks, and packaging comprised the largest portion of a brewer's costs. The following estimates were made of a "typical"—or regional—brewer's cost structure in 1975:[2]

Typical Brewer's Cost Structure

Production costs:		90%
Agricultural inputs	17%	
Packaging	49	
Direct labor	13	
Depreciation and other	11	
Selling and administration:		10
Delivery	5	
Advertising	1.5	
Other	3.5	
Total		100%

Beer was distributed via independent regional beer distributors. The largest national brewers had exclusive distributorships, while small national brands used distributors that handled several brands at once. Regional brands usually distributed their own beer. Distributors sold to liquor stores, bars, restaurants, and other retail outlets.

Anheuser-Busch, with approximately 20 percent of the market, was the industry leader in every region of the United States. Majority ownership still belonged to descendants of the original Busch family. Anheuser-Busch sold three major brands: Budweiser, its flagship brand in the premium category, Michelob in the super-premium category, and Busch in the popular category. During the 1960s Anheuser-Busch invested in several new plants, increasing its total capacity by 50 percent during the decade. It incorporated the most modern, cost-efficient production techniques in its plants and also began to integrate backward into the production of aluminum cans in order to reduce costs. (See Exhibits 7, 8, 9, and 10.)

Miller Brewing Company's lead brand, Miller High Life, had carried

---

[2] *The Wall Street Journal,* October 13, 1975.

the slogan, "The Champagne of Bottle Beer," since the early 1900s. The brand had held a constant share of approximately 4 percent throughout the 1960s. W. R. Grace, which had owned the brewery, had neither increased capacity nor advertised extensively. Chief Executive Officer W. R. Grace, Jr., stated that he did not want to play Anheuser-Busch's "capacity game." He initiated the sale to Philip Morris when he read that Joseph Cullman was considering buying the largest brewery in Canada.

In explaining the acquisition Philip Morris stated the following in its 1970 annual report:

> The product is a low-cost, mass-produced, disposable consumer good. It passes through many of the same outlets—supermarkets, convenience stores, even bars—and is enjoyed by many of the same customers (male, aged 18–44) and has good margins. The technology, processing wet agricultural products as opposed to semidry as in the case of tobacco, is not foreign to us.

After the acquisition Philip Morris initially kept the existing Miller management. Philip Morris marketing executives, who were sent by Cullman to help Miller with its plans, suggested introducing a new 7-ounce pony bottle that would be sold in an eight-bottle "Pony Pack." Miller executives resisted, arguing that the bottle was too expensive on a per-ounce basis.

In 1971 Philip Morris installed a new president of Miller, John Murphy, who had been the executive vice president in charge of the Philip Morris International cigarette business. Murphy introduced the Pony Pack in 1973. Murphy also changed the slogan of Miller High Life to "Champagne of Beer." In 1974 Miller introduced a new advertising campaign around the theme, "Now, It's Miller Time." Murphy stated that Miller would reposition Miller's premier brand from the champagne bucket to the lunch bucket. The intent was to target working males and to use life-style advertisements emphasizing Miller High Life's role in the consumer's life after a successful day of work.

In 1975 Miller introduced Miller Lite, a beer with fewer carbohydrates. Lower carbohydrate beer had been introduced by some regional brewers in 1971 and promoted as containing fewer calories. Miller first introduced its Lite beer with little advertising. Through research and auditing, Miller executives discovered that the beer had become most popular not where it was viewed as a diet beer but rather in some working neighborhood bars where it was viewed as less filling. In 1976 Miller launched an extensive advertising campaign for Lite using well-known male sports stars endorsing the beer in witty commercials as good tasting and less filling. The execution proved highly memorable.

Miller invested heavily in new brewing capacity to meet the rapid growth of both Miller High Life and Miller Lite (see Exhibit 7). Miller designed larger plants than the industry to achieve economies of scale through new production techniques, involving a minimum-efficient scale of 4 million barrels annually. With high transportation costs for bottled beer, that capacity necessitated approximately a 10 percent share of a region's market. Miller could brew both Miller High Life and Miller Lite in its new plants. Despite these investments, Miller could not keep up with demand throughout the late 1970s. Miller also invested in aluminum can manufacturing and had become 50 percent backward integrated into aluminum canning by 1979.

Miller also purchased the rights to brew domestically a brand named Lowenbrau which had previously been imported from West Germany. The domestically brewed Lowenbrau was introduced nationally by Miller in late 1977, establishing Lowenbrau in the small but rapidly growing super-premium beer segment. By 1977 Miller had become the second largest brewer in the United States.

Murphy also moved to strengthen Miller's distribution. Miller had already achieved national distribution through a network of independent distributors dedicated to Miller. Murphy, however, increased the size of the Miller sales force that worked with the distributors to ensure that Miller products obtained extensive distribution in retail outlets in every region of the country. By 1979 Miller was the second largest brewer, behind Anheuser-Busch, in five of seven regions of the country and the third largest behind Anheuser-Busch and Coors in the Rocky Mountains and Pacific Coast regions.

In reviewing its performance in the cigarette and beer business Philip Morris made the following comments in its 1979 annual report:

> Ten years ago in this company's most profitable unit, Philip Morris U.S.A. held a 15 percent share. 1970 was the year all television and radio advertising of cigarettes was terminated. Philip Morris U.S.A. now holds approximately 29 percent of this market, with the total market itself in units almost 20 percent larger now than it was then.
>
> For Philip Morris International the 10-year story has been much the same. Revenues have increased at a compounded rate of 26 percent. Operating income has increased at 21 percent compounded, and market share has more than doubled.
>
> During 1970 Philip Morris acquired full control of the Miller Brewing Company. The next few years were a period of trial and preparation during which Miller revenues remained flat while operating income dropped steadily. But by then the early learning years had begun to produce results, and the second half of the decade has been a period of spectacular success for Miller. In 1979 barrel shipments were more than seven times larger than 1970, and operating income was almost 16 times as great. Market share has quintupled to about 21 percent of the U.S. market, which itself grew more than 40 percent in units in the decade. In 1970 Miller ranked seventh among domestic brewers; today, it is a strong second.

During the early 1970s Anheuser-Busch continued its strategy of steady capacity expansion and cost reduction through modern plants and backward integration into can manufacturing. By 1975 Anheuser-Busch had achieved full backward integration into aluminum cans. It focused on the expansion of its Budweiser and Michelob brands, rather than on introducing any new brands, and increased advertising from $10 million in 1970 to $26 million in 1976.

In 1976 the Busch family recruited new marketing managers from General Mills and Procter & Gamble. The managers introduced a new advertising campaign in 1977 for the Budweiser brand with the theme, "This Bud's for You." The advertisements were designed to portray Budweiser as a reward for good, hard work and were targeted at the same consumer segment as Miller targeted in its "Miller Time" campaign. Anheuser-Busch increased advertising expenditures for this campaign. In 1982 Anheuser-Busch introduced Bud Light with an extensive advertising campaign saying that this was the first light beer worthy of the Budweiser name. This brand gained 2.1 percent and 2.3 percent of the U.S. market in 1983 and 1984, respectively (see Exhibit 11).

The Seven-Up Co.

In 1979 Philip Morris completed the acquisition of the Seven-Up Co. for $520 million. In discussing the acquisition management stated the following in its 1978 annual report:

> Many of the characteristics of the soft drink industry are similar to those of our other businesses. Essentially, soft drinks—like cigarettes and beer—are reasonably priced, relatively low-cost consumer items that give pleasure to users, who repeat their purchases often when the quality of the product satisfies their expectations.
>
> Our major priority in soft drinks will be the 7UP brand in the United States. The first move to improve the position of the brand was the appointment by Seven-Up management of a new advertising agency and the creation of a new advertising campaign and marketing program for the 7UP brand. The campaign, introduced early in 1979, is designed to capitalize on the national trend to more active outdoor lifestyles. The theme, "America's Turning 7UP," is intended to develop a large and growing base of consumers whose primary soft drink is 7UP.

Following its first year of ownership Philip Morris described its moves at Seven-Up as follows:

> — For the Seven-Up Co. 1979 was a significant year, principally characterized by a major restructuring program designed to position the Seven-Up organization for the future.
> — Advertising was the principal component of Seven-Up's enlarged marketing program. The campaign—"America's Turning 7UP"—

was intended not only to improve the awareness and product positioning of 7UP but also to assist our bottlers in improving distribution and retail availability of our products. The campaign, now featuring endorsements by such prominent athletes as Earvin "Magic" Johnson, Larry Bird, John McEnroe, and Earl Campbell, has created substantial consumer awareness. It has also helped to strengthen our relationship with our bottlers.

— In addition Seven-Up has restructured and increased its staff—particularly its field sales force—and has substantially improved its product research activities.[3]

— In March William E. Winter, previously president, became chairman, and Edward W. Frantel, previously vice president-sales of Miller, was appointed president and chief executive officer of Seven-Up. During the remainder of the year a number of other organizational changes were made to establish the marketing, distribution, quality control, finance, and planning organizations needed for further growth consistent with Philip Morris long-term objectives. To the extent that new senior positions could not be filled by existing Seven-Up personnel, they were largely filled by people from other divisions of Philip Morris.

— Also during the past year a sweeping graphics design program was begun, and the resulting new graphics will be introduced in the spring of 1980.

— For the Seven-Up Co. 1979 was a difficult year of transition. We restructured the Seven-Up organization adding new personnel to strengthen both our marketing and research capabilities and our relationships with bottlers in the United States, Canada, and Puerto Rico. In addition Seven-Up International was integrated into Philip Morris International in order to take full advantage of the latter's long experience in the worldwide marketplace.

— As in the early stages of our Miller acquisition we do not expect Seven-Up to be a significant contributor to our profits for a few years. But we do not believe that this will adversely affect the trend lines of the corporation's overall performance.

In 1980 Seven-Up expanded the advertising for its "America's Turning 7UP" campaign. The company also initiated a $12 million investment in a new research and development facility that would focus on both product and packaging innovation.

In 1981 Seven-Up bought two of its franchise bottlers which had performed below sales projections. These investments began a series of other bottler acquisitions, resulting in a total of six by 1984. The Seven-

---

[3] The field sales staff were the people who worked with Seven-Up bottlers in developing and helping to improve the execution of advertising and promotion campaigns.

Up bottler system had the following configurations in 1975, 1979, and 1984:

Seven-Up Bottler System

Bottlers	1975	1979	1984
7UP company-owned franchisees	13	4	10
7UP independent franchisees*	102	102	103
Coca-Cola and 7UP	97	99	84
Pepsi-Cola and 7UP	153	149	143
Royal Crown and 7UP	104	92	81
Total	482	446	421

* Some also bottle Dr Pepper or smaller brands.

These acquisitions represented the vast majority of Philip Morris's investments in Seven-Up during these three years (see Exhibit 1).

In 1981 Ed Frantel, president of Seven-Up, announced a new advertising campaign that would emphasize the caffeine-free issue. The theme, "Never Had It, Never Will," was designed to emphasize that the major colas all contained caffeine and that 7UP did not. This campaign proved more effective than the "America's Turning 7UP" and helped to increase the share of the soft drink market accounted for by the lemon-lime flavor.

Each Flavor's Share (Percent) of Total U.S. Market by Year

	1977	1978	1979	1980	1981	1982	1983
Cola	62.4%	62.3%	62.3%	62.4%	62.6%	62.1%	63.6%
Lemon-lime	12.4	12.3	12.1	11.8	11.6	12.0	12.5
Pepper	7.2	7.5	7.5	7.5	7.4	7.0	6.8
Orange	7.4	7.4	7.3	7.4	7.4	7.6	7.4
Root beer	5.3	5.4	5.5	5.5	5.5	5.4	5.0
Others	5.3	5.1	5.3	5.4	5.5	5.9	4.7

Source: John C. Maxwell and *Beverage Industry.*

The 7UP brand's share also increased from 5.0 percent in 1981 to 5.4 percent in 1983.

In 1982 Seven-Up introduced Like, a caffeine-free cola. Seven-Up attempted to gain distribution through its franchised bottlers who also bottled other colas, contending that Like was not a regular cola. Upon a civil suit by Coca-Cola, a U.S. court determined that Like was a cola. Seven-Up spent $12.7 million in advertising for Like in 1982 and 1983. The product gained a 0.4 percent share of the market.

In 1983 Coca-Cola persuaded McDonald's to replace Diet 7UP on its list of required fountain soft drinks with Diet Sprite. The regular brand 7UP was placed on a list of authorized optional soft drinks.

In 1984 Seven-Up moved to adopt aspartame for its Diet 7UP soft drink. Ed Frantel stated that his decision was based on the need to remain competitive with Pepsi-Cola and Coca-Cola, which were also adopting 100 percent aspartame.

In March 1985 Ed Frantel reflected on the company's progress as follows:

> We had to take a few years to learn more about the business. When we came to 7UP, bottlers who believed 7UP had no share of voice in the media said to us, "You advertise, we'll promote." We're now doing both. Our marketing spending is at an all-time high. Bottlers have been very responsive to our marketing plans. They have noted the plans' flexibility for individual markets, and have increased their dollar participation as well. . . .
>
> The only constant is change. Anything is possible, because nobody is infallible. I just don't believe that Coca-Cola and Pepsi-Cola are incapable of mistakes. Executives make dumb decisions. There is always the challenge.
>
> We dare to be different. When you're not the leader, you have to be. To be different you have to do it with substance. Caffeine was an example of that; and Like was also a different approach to the cola business. When I went out personally and talked to some of the key retailers about Like cola, there was great interest in having another brand, someone else in that particular category that had some staying power to maintain the competitive position. I don't think that would change.[4]

Recent Developments

In 1984 Hamish Maxwell, who had headed the international cigarette unit, became chairman and chief executive of Philip Morris. He obtained the job over John Murphy, whose fortunes had apparently diminished with the problems of Miller High Life during the 1980s (see Exhibit 11). Some beer industry analysts believed that the "Miller Time" campaign had become ineffective and was relied upon for too long. In 1984, Philip Morris wrote down the asset value of a new $450 million Miller brewery that had never been used. Miller was operating at 83 percent capacity in 1984.

Maxwell stated in early 1985:

> I can say unequivocally that 7UP and Miller have never been for sale. And I promise you, we will keep Miller and 7UP for the foreseeable future.
>
> To protect our earnings growth we must use our resources to succeed in other businesses. It would be very shortsighted to get out of a business every time there is a downturn.[5]

---

[4] *Beverage World,* March 1985.

[5] *Fortune,* March 18, 1985.

Exhibit 1

Financial Statistics on Philip Morris Incorporated

	1973	1974	1975	1976	1977	1978	1979	1980	1981	1982	1983	1984
Corporate												
Total revenues	$2,603.0	$3,011.0	$3,642.0	$4,294.0	$5,202.0	$6,633.0	$8,149.0	$9,650.0	$10,722.0	$11,586.0	$12,976.0	$13,814.0
Net income	$ 149.0	$ 176.0	$ 212.0	$ 266.0	$ 335.0	$ 409.0	$ 507.0	$ 549.0	$ 660	$ 782.0	$ 904.0	$ 889.0
Net income/sales	5.7%	5.8%	5.8%	6.2%	6.4%	6.2%	6.2%	5.7%	6.2%	6.7%	7.0%	6.4%
Return on equity	18.3%	18.1%	17.3%	18.6%	19.8%	19.3%	20.5%	19.4%	20.4%	21.3%	22.4%	21.7%
Long-term debt/ total capital	41.3%	42.6%	44.5%	42.9%	1.7%	40.9%	42.1%	41.0%	40.9%	40.1%	36.8%	34.8%
Total operating income	$ 329.0	$ 404.0	$ 493.0	$ 635.0	$ 783.0	$ 968.0	$1,191.0	$1,273.0	$ 1,446.0	$ 1,716.0	$ 1,958.0	$ 2,346.0
Total capital expenditures	$ 174.7	$ 215.8	$ 244.5	$ 220.2	$ 279.8	$ 566.2	$ 629.4	$ 750.8	$ 1,018.5	$ 918.2	$ 566.2	$ 298.1
For tobacco	$ 105.2	$ 127.4	$ 149.9	$ 101.3	$ 143.2	$ 327.8	$ 321.7	$ 415.3	$ 633.5	$ 498.9	$ 319.9	$ 163.1
For beer	$ 59.6	$ 79.6	$ 88.9	$ 111.9	$ 126.3	$ 221.2	$ 259.3	$ 261.1	$ 328.9	$ 286.3	$ 174.6	$ 93.6
For 7UP	—	—	—	—	—	—	$ 29.1	$ 41.2	$ 35.2	$ 86.5	$ 49.9	30.9
For industrial packaging	$ 9.9	$ 8.8	$ 5.7	$ 7.0	$ 10.3	$ 17.2	$ 19.3	$ 33.2	$ 20.9	$ 46.5	$ 21.8	$ 10.5

Source: Philip Morris annual reports.

Exhibit 2

Diversification of U.S. Tobacco Companies in 1980

	Percentage of Total Sales*	Percentage of Total from Operations*
R. J. Reynolds Industries, Inc.:		
Domestic tobacco	34%	60%
International tobacco	20	13
Transportation (sea-land)	13	5
Energy operations (Aminoil)	9	14
Foods and beverages (Del Monte, etc.)	22	7
Packaging (RJR Archer)	2	1
Philip Morris Incorporated:		
Domestic and international tobacco	65	86
Beer (Miller)	26	11
Soft Drinks (7UP)	4	(-)
Paper and chemical products	3	1
Land development	2	2
B.A.T. Industries Ltd.:		
Tobacco (Brown & Williamson)	57	72
Retail* (International Supermarkets, Koh, Gimbels Bros., Saks Fifth Avenue)†	23	9
Paper (Wiggins Tape)	9	11
Other (cosmetics, domestic products, investment, insurance)	5	4
American Brands Inc.:		
Domestic tobacco	17	37
International tobacco (Gallaher)	47	22
Hardware (Master Lock)	3	5
Distilled beverages (James B. Beam)	3	4
Engineering	3	2
Food products (Duffy-Mott, Sunshine Biscuits‡)	8	4
Office services and supplies (Swingline)	2	3
Optical goods and services	1	1
Toiletries (Andrew Jergens)	1	1
Golf products (Achushnet)	1	1
Retail	7	1
Wholesale	5	3
Life insurance (Franklin Life)	—	15
Other	2	2
Loews Corp.:		
Domestic tobacco (Lorillard)	23	36
Timing devices (Bulova)	4	1
Insurance (CNA Financial)	63	27
Hotels	5	18
Theaters	1	3
Consumer finance	3	11
Other (real estate)	1	4
Liggett Group:§		
Tobacco	32	38
Spirits and wines (J&B Scotch, Grand Marnier, etc.)	17	26
Pet foods (Alpo)	22	9
Soft drinks (bottling and distribution)	18	27
Other (sporting goods, food ingredients)	11	10

* Figures are approximate, derived from 1980 annual reports, Standard & Poor's, and Moody's *Industrial Manual.*
  † Also acquired Marshall Field, March 1982.
  ‡ Sold to Cadbury Schweppes Ltd. for $60 million, March 1982.
  § Acquired by Grand Metropolitan Ltd. in 1980.
  Source: HBS Case Services, "U.S. Tobacco Companies: Smoking and Health," case 382–155.

Exhibit 3

Share of U.S. Cigarette Market (In units sold of the six major manufacturers)*

Company	1963†	1970‡	1980‡	1983‡
Philip Morris	9.4%	16.5%	30.9%	35.2%
R. J. Reynolds	34.3	31.7	32.6	34.1
Brown & Williamson	10.9	16.7	13.7	10.2
American Brands	24.8	19.6	10.8	8.8
Lorillard	10.9	8.7	9.7	10.2
Liggett Group	9.7	6.8	2.3	1.5
Total	100.0%	100.0%	100.0%	100.0%

* The six large U.S. cigarette manufacturers accounted for 98 percent of the U.S. market.
† *Printer's Ink,* February 14, 1968, p. 27.
‡ Lehman Brothers Kuhn Loeb Research.

Exhibit 4

Top Ten Brands in the U.S. Cigarette Market
(Unit share of market)

	Percent	
	1983	1984
Philip Morris:		
Marlboro	20.1%	21.1%
Benson & Hedges	5.0	4.8
Merit	4.4	4.1
Total	29.5	30.0
R. J. Reynolds:		
Winston	11.9	12.0
Salem	8.1	8.1
Camel	4.6	4.5
Vantage	3.7	3.5
Total	28.3	28.1
Brown & Williamson:		
Kool	7.2	7.0
American Brands:		
Pall Mall	4.1	3.8
Lorillard:		
Kent*	3.9	3.3
Grand total	73.0%	72.2%

* Recalculated to include Golden Lights brand family.
Source: John C. Maxwell and Laidlow Ansbacher, published in *Tobacco International,* December 28, 1984.

Exhibit 5

Major Media Advertising Expenditures of the Six Large Cigarette Manufacturers* (In millions)

	1974	1975	1976	1977	1978	1979	1980	1981	1982	1983	Nine Months January–September 1984
American Brand	$ 18.1	$ 18.6	$ 24.3	$ 31.2	$ 29.6	$ 31.6	$ 36.3	$ 37.8	$ 33.4	$ 39.4	$ 24.5
Brown & Williamson	45.2	34.2	39.6	49.1	48.8	41.7	67.2	115.9	135.1	78.3	37.8
Liggett Group	11.9	10.6	11.1	12.0	15.1	5.2	0.6	3.2	6.3	6.9	7.3
Lorillard	19.6	30.1	29.3	33.9	35.9	64.3	61.3	51.8	45.2	74.1	53.1
Philip Morris	58.7	65.9	69.7	89.2	85.1	119.0	126.0	156.1	205.6	215.2	143.5
R. J. Reynolds	68.6	82.2	95.0	111.7	135.8	182.2	167.2	141.9	159.7	243.3	218.2
Total six major media	$222.3	$237.6	$269.2	$327.1	$350.3	$444.0	$458.6	$506.7	$585.3	$657.2	$474.4

* The six media—which LNA researched—were estimated to account for 75–80 percent of all cigarette advertising. Other advertising expenditures included promotion through the sponsorship of sporting events and musical concerts.

Source: BAR/LNA (Leading National Advertisers) Multi-Media Service, years 1974–1984.

Exhibit 6

Statistics on Philip Morris Cigarette Operations (Revenues in millions; cigarette units in billions)

	1972	1973	1974	1975	1976	1977	1978	1979	1980	1981	1982	1983	1984
United States:													
U.S. cigarette industry unit sales	543	565	490	595	601	605	608	615	624	629	625	595	600
Philip Morris U.S.A.:													
Operating revenues	$1,165	$1,304	$1,501	$1,722	$1,963	$2,160	$2,737	$2,767	$3,272	$3,762	$4,330	$5,520	$6,133
Operating income	$ 194	$ 227	$ 295	$ 337	$ 401	$ 474	$ 568	$ 701	$ 786	$ 906	$1,012	$1,338	$1,745
Operating income/ revenues	17%	17%	20%	20%	20%	22%	21%	25%	24%	24%	23%	24%	28%
Unit sales	81	103	124	142	152	163	170	180	197	201	206	202	212
Unit share of market	17%	18%	21%	24%	23%	27%	28%	29%	30%	32%	33%	34%	35%
International:													
Non-U.S. world cigarette industry unit sales	3,470	3,447	3,335	3,290	3,522	3,472	3,527	3,683	3,854	3,735	4,050	4,016	3,954
Philip Morris International													
Operating revenues	$ 624	$ 823	$ 860	$1,040	$1,084	$1,349	$1,811	$2,561	$3,205	$3,400	$3,564	$3,647	$3,741
Operating income	$ 84	$ 92	$ 96	$ 113	$ 130	$ 154	$ 189	$ 261	$ 318	$ 397	$ 446	$ 366	$ 421
Operating income/ revenues	13%	11%	11%	11%	12%	11%	10%	10%	10%	12%	13%	10%	11%
Unit sales	125	131	140	148	169	184	201	221	239	249	243	245	253
Unit share of market	3.6%	3.8%	4.2%	4.5%	4.8%	5.3%	5.7%	6.0%	6.2%	6.7%	6.0%	6.1%	6.4%

Source: Philip Morris annual reports.

Exhibit 7

Statistics on Miller Brewing Company Operations (Revenues in millions)

	1972	1973	1974	1975	1976	1977	1978	1979	1980	1981	1982	1983	1984
U.S. beer industry barrel shipments (in millions including imports)	131	137	147	151	154	161	167	194	177	180	181	183	181
Miller Brewing Company:													
Operating revenues	$276	$211	$404	$653	$983	$1,328	$1,835	$2,236	$2,542	$2,837	$2,929	$2,922	$2,928
Operating income	$ 0	$ (2)	$ 6	$ 29	$ 76	$ 106	$ 150	$ 181	$ 145	$ 116	$ 159	$ 227	$ 116
Operating income/ revenues	0.0%	(0.9%)	1.5%	4.4%	7.7%	8.0%	8.2%	8.1%	4.6%	8.0%	5.4%	4.0%	5.0%
Millions of barrel shipments	5.8	6.9	9.3	13.0	18.8	24.5	31.6	36.5	37.3	41.2	40.0	38.2	38.2
Unit share of market	4.5%	5.0%	6.3%	8.6%	12.2%	15.2%	18.9%	21.0%	21.1%	22.2%	22.0%	20.9%	21.1%
Share rank	7th	6th	5th	4th	3rd	2nd	2nd	2nd	2nd	2nd	2nd	2nd	2nd

Sources: Philip Morris annual reports; *Beverage Industry* and John C. Maxwell.

Exhibit 8

Volume Share of U.S. Beer Market (Including imports)

Company	1970	1971	1972	1973	1974	1975	1976	1977	1978	1979*	1980†	1981	1982	1983*
Anheuser-Busch	20.5%	19.2%	20.9%	21.6%	23.4%	23.7%	22.9%	23.3%	25.6%	26.8%	28.2%	30.0%	33.0%	33.5%
Miller	4.1	4.1	4.2	5.0	6.2	8.6	12.2	15.2	18.9	21.0	21.1	22.2	22.0	20.9
Stroh	4.1	4.2	4.3	4.4	4.3	4.4	4.5	4.3	4.1	5.4	4.8	4.2	5.3	13.4
Heileman	8.0	8.1	8.0	8.2	8.5	8.4	8.4	8.2	7.8	6.6	7.5	7.7	8.1	9.7
Coors	7.5	7.6	7.8	7.9	8.5	8.6	10.5	10.2	9.5	7.5	7.8	7.3	6.6	7.5
Pabst	8.5	8.7	8.8	9.5	9.8	10.6	11.3	10.0	11.1	8.8	11.9	10.5	9.8	7.3
Genesee	2.0	1.9	1.9	1.9	2.0	1.9	1.9	1.8	1.8	2.0	2.0	2.0	1.9	1.7
Schmidt	4.5	4.1	3.9	3.7	3.5	3.2	3.1	3.0	2.4	2.2	2.0	1.6	1.8	1.7
Pittsburgh	NA	NA	NA	NA	NA	NA	NA		NA	0.4	0.6	0.5	0.5	0.5
Schlitz	14.3	14.9	15.2	15.4	15.6	15.7	16.1	14.0	11.5	9.9	9.1	8.0	7.5	—
Others	26.5	27.2	25.0	22.4	18.2	14.9	9.1	10.0	7.3	9.4	5.0	5.3	3.5	3.8
Total	100.0%	100.0%	100.0%	100.0%	100.0%	100.0%	100.0%	100.0%	100.0%	100.0%	100.0%	100.0%	100.0%	100.0%

NA = Not available.

* Stroh acquired the Schaefer Brewing Company in 1979 and the Schlitz Brewing Company in 1983.

† Pabst bought two regional brewers in 1980.

Sources: *Beverage Industry* and John C. Maxwell; annual reports of companies; *Modern Brewery Age*; U.S. Brewers Association.

Exhibit 9

U.S. Beer Industry Advertising Expenditures (Dollars in millions)

Company	1970	1973	1976	1977	1978	1979*	1980†	1981	1982	1983*
Anheuser-Busch	$10.1	$15.0	$ 25.7	$ 45.2	$ 63.1	$ 82.3	$111.4	$132.0	$155.4	$180.8
Miller	3.5	14.1	29.0	42.4	64.3	79.1	90.5	106.2	119.1	138.9
Stroh	2.2	3.3	5.0	7.2	9.0	20.9	25.1	29.4	32.0	54.4
Heileman	2.3	3.1	3.5	4.7	6.7	7.8	10.1	11.9	15.9	19.1
Coors	1.1	1.3	1.6	4.0	8.1	12.3	15.4	17.9	22.1	30.3
Pabst	8.1	8.9	9.1	10.9	18.1	20.2	23.1	25.1	26.0	26.2
Genesee	NA	NA	NA	2.8	3.0	4.5	4.7	5.1	5.4	7.5
Schmidt	NA	NA	NA	3.9	3.1	4.4	3.1	2.6	1.6	4.6
Others	25.3	29.4	65.1	75.4	79.7	50.1	41.5	37.9	28.5	32.9
Total	$52.6	$75.1	$139.0	$196.5	$255.1	$281.6	$324.9	$368.1	$406.5	$494.7

NA = Not available.

* Stroh acquired the Schaefer Brewing Company in 1979 and the Schlitz Brewing Company in 1983.

† Pabst bought two regional brewers in 1980.

Sources: Leading National Advertisers, Inc.; LBKL Research. The six major media researched by LNA accounted for approximately 60–75 percent of total advertising expenditures for beer. Other expenditures included the sponsorship of sporting events and musical concerts.

Exhibit 10

1983 Profitability of Leading Brewers (Brewery Business Only)
(Dollars in millions)

Brewer	Net Sales	Operating Income	Percent of Sales
Anheuser-Busch	$4,907.7	$649.9	13.24%
Miller	2,922.1	227.3	7.78
Pabst	799.9	13.7	1.70
Coors	1,110.4	154.3	13.90
Stroh	1,318.0	54.7	4.15
Heileman	870.8	82.9	9.50

Source: Company annual reports.

Exhibit 11

Top Ten Beer Brands (By unit share of market)

	1980		1981		1982		1983		1984	
	Share (Percent)	Rank	Share (Percent)	Rank	Share (Percent)	Rank	Share (Percent)	Rank	Share (Percent)	Rank
Budweiser	19.1%	1	20.6%	1	21.6%	1	22.8%	1	24.0%	1
Miller High Life	13.6	2	12.2	2	11.2	2	9.7	2	7.8	3
Miller Lite	7.5	3	9.0	3	9.5	3	9.5	3	10.0	2
Coors	6.5	4	6.1	4	4.9	4	5.2	4	5.0	4
Pabst Blue Ribbon	6.4	5	5.4	5	4.8	5	4.3	5	3.4	7
Michelob	4.9	6	4.6	6	4.6	6	3.9	6	3.8	6
Schlitz	4.3	7	3.1	7	2.3	10	—	—	—	—
Old Milwaukee	2.3	8	2.7	10	3.2	7	3.7	7	3.8	5
Busch	2.6	9	—	—	—	—	—	—	—	—
Michelob Light	1.5	10	—	—	—	—	—	—	—	—
Old Style	—	—	3.0	8	3.1	8	3.0	9	2.9	9
Stroh	—	—	3.0	9	2.9	9	3.1	8	3.2	8
Bud Light	—	—	—	—	—	—	2.1	10	2.3	10

Sources: *Beverage Industry* annual manuals; *Beverage World*, March 1985.

Exhibit 12

Financial Statistics on the Seven-Up Co. (Revenues in millions)

	1972	1973	1974	1975	1976	1977	1978*	1979	1980	1981	1982	1983	1984
Seven-Up sales	$133.0	$147.0	$191.0	$214.0	$233.0	$251.0	$186.0	$296.0	$353.0	$432.0	$531.0	$650.0	$734.0
Net income	$ 12.0	$ 14.1	$ 16.6	$ 10.3	$ 24.8	$ 25.8	$ 2.6	$ 7.0	$ (7.1)	$ (1.7)	$ (1.2)	$ (10.8)	$ 5.3
Operating income	—	—	—	—	—	—	—	—	—	—	—	—	—
Net income/ sales	9.1%	9.6%	8.7%	9.5%	10.6%	10.3%	—	—	—	—	—	—	—
Operating income/sales	—	—	—	—	—	—	14.0%	2.4%	(2.0%)	(0.4%)	(0.2%)	(1.7%)	0.7%
Return on equity	23.7%	23.6%	23.9%	23.6%	24.0%	23.1%	—	—	—	—	—	—	—
Long-term debt/ total capital	4.1%	4.5%	3.4%	2.3%	3.1%	4.2%	—	—	—	—	—	—	—

* Philip Morris bought the Seven-Up Co. in 1979 and consolidated earnings back to 1978.
Sources: Philip Morris annual reports; Seven-Up Co. annual reports.

Note on the Major Home Appliance Industry in 1984 (Condensed)

Major home appliances had sales in excess of $12 billion in 1984 in the United States and represented one of the largest consumer goods industries. At one time many of the major automotive and consumer electronics manufacturers had participated in the business, but all of them (except General Electric) had withdrawn. By early 1983 with the Japanese gaining a foothold in the United States in the microwave oven market and most of the domestic manufacturers operating at 50 percent to 60 percent of their overall capacity, the future of the industry seemed uncertain.

Products

The products of the appliance industry could be classified in terms of customer use and technology. Based on customer use, appliances were sold for the kitchen (refrigerators, freezers, ranges, dishwashers, and disposers); for the home laundry (washers and dryers); and for room air conditioning. Technologically, appliances fell into three categories: water bearing (dishwashers, disposers, clothes washers, and some dryers); refrigerating (refrigerators, freezers, and room air conditioners); and cooking (ranges).

Refrigerators. Refrigerators had historically been the largest selling appliance (see Exhibits 1 and 2). Since the product's average life expectancy

Copyright © 1984 by the President and Fellows of Harvard College
Harvard Business School case 385–211

Table 1

Percent of Refrigerator Shipments by Size

Size (Cubic Feet)	1982	1981	1980	1979	1978
6.5–11	4.0%	3.7%	5%	6%	8%
12–13	7.8	7.8	9	9	10
14–15	25.7	24.7	23	22	21
16–17	24.7	24.0	23	22	21
18–19	18.8	19.2	19	18	19
20–21	10.8	11.4	11	12	12
22 and over	8.2	9.2	10	10	10

Source: *Merchandising* magazine, November issues, 1978–82.

was 15 years, manufacturers expected that replacement sales alone would come to about 5.5 million units a year during the 1980s. But with sales of only about 4.3 million, 1982 turned out to be the worst year since 1963. Refrigerators were the only appliance product whose saturation exceeded 100 percent. Some households had two or more units, and many nonhousehold entities like offices and dorm rooms also had a refrigerator.

Manufacturers seemed to disagree as to likely future trends in refrigerators. In the regular-size segment, which represented about 90 percent of the market, a key issue was whether customers would shift future purchases toward smaller sizes. Until 1981 customers making replacement purchases had tended to upgrade to slightly larger models (see Table 1). But in 1982 there was a definite shift downwards in the three largest size categories.

The argument for downsizing was based on three trends. First, the average size of the household was declining as the number of divorces, childless couples, and single-person households increased. In addition, the prices of refrigerators had risen considerably, and consumers with a limited budget might prefer to give up size rather than features or quality. Finally, rising energy costs had created an incentive to use appliances with lower operating costs. On the other hand, despite trends in household size, kitchens were not getting any smaller. People were doing more entertaining at home, and kitchens were increasingly becoming the focal point in the home. As Charles Dowd, vice president, sales and marketing, for Admiral (Magic Chef), remarked, "I have yet to meet a consumer who said her refrigerator was too large."[1]

Compact units of less than 6.5 cubic feet had been gaining share of the overall refrigerator market since 1978. Though sales of the two-cubic-foot models were declining, the three- to five-cubic-foot models

---

[1] "Mart Money Maker," *Mart,* January 1982.

had been growing consistently. These small undercounter refrigerators were characteristically used in four situations: (1) by students, retirees, and single people living in dorms, retirement homes, and even studio apartments; (2) in professional and business offices; (3) as a second home unit outside the kitchen; and (4) in boats, recreational vehicles, motel rooms, and so forth.

Imports had gained a strong position in the compact segment, representing 40–48 percent of the market of the previous five years. Imports also played a small but growing role in the standard-size segment, though most of these units were refrigerator-freezer combinations, which have traditionally been more popular abroad than in the United States.

Three companies—Whirlpool, GE, and White—together represented 80 percent of the market and had traditionally controlled it. The top five—including Admiral and Amana—made up 95 percent of the market. (See Exhibit 3.)

Freezers. Freezer sales had been in the doldrums since the recession of 1975 (see Exhibit 1). Until then freezer sales had maintained momentum even when the overall industry was depressed. In difficult times people tended to economize by buying food in larger quantities during special sales and in larger packages with lower unit costs; thus they needed more freezer space. In the late 1970s, one of the worst inflationary-recessionary periods, freezer sales languished. After continued gains since 1961, saturation leveled off at around 45 percent. Freezers had the longest life expectancy of any appliance, and the product features had not changed in decades. Sales of compact freezers had also remained constant over the last 10 years.

Whirlpool was the clear leader in freezers, followed by White, with Admiral (Magic Chef) a distant number 3 (see Exhibit 3). These three companies controlled 80 percent of the market. In 1981 Magic Chef had acquired Revco but had not been able to hold on to all of Revco's market share.

Air Conditioners. Air conditioner sales were more volatile than those of any other appliance since demand was seasonal and dependent on the weather. The 1970s had illustrated this pattern. In 1974 retailers got caught with excess inventory which was reflected in their orders for 1975 and 1976.

The energy crisis had hurt air conditioner sales after the all-time high of 5.9 million units sold in 1970. As an industry analyst noted:

> Air conditioners were the first to feel the brunt of the energy issue . . . utilities not only virtually discontinued their promotional support but even in many areas seemed to discourage air conditioner purchases by harping on the theme of using them as little as possible. . . . Whirlpool officials

also make the point that room air conditioners use something less than 1 percent of residential energy yet are "drawing about 90 percent of the fire."[2]

Despite the volatility of the business, competitors' market share positions had remained remarkably stable. The three full-line appliance manufacturers—GE, Whirlpool, and White—together had just over 50 percent of the market; the three specialists—Fedders, Friedrich, and Addison—together had slightly under 40 percent (see Exhibit 3).

Cooking Appliances. The introduction of microwave ovens represented the most radical technological change in the appliance industry. Traditionally the choice had been between gas and electric ranges, each with its own merits and limitations with regard to cost, cleanliness, efficiency, safety, and so on. Until the late 1960s gas ranges had had a slight edge over electric ranges in the number of units sold. Recently, however, the trend had moved toward electric ranges and ovens.

During the early 1970s microwave ovens were introduced by electronics companies outside the traditional appliance industry. At first the microwave was seen primarily as a novelty or luxury item rather than a basic cooking medium, and its use was limited to the quick reheating and defrosting of foods. From the mid-1970s on, however, microwave oven sales took off. Despite stagnation of the overall appliance industry, overall, microwave oven sales continued to grow steadily until 1982 when microwaves became the single largest selling appliance product. The growth would not have been possible without significant technological improvements including improved electronic controls and the overcoming of a major safety scare; although all manufacturers complied with stringent government safety tests, some concerns about microwave radiation still lingered.

Microwave ovens represented one of the only two real growth markets for appliance manufacturers, as shown in Table 2.

In 1977, the two leaders were Litton, with a 25 percent market share, and Amana, with 20 percent. (See Exhibit 4.) Litton, a conglomerate, offered no home appliance other than cooking products in its entire product line. Amana, owned by Raytheon, had a larger stake in the home appliance business. Of the dedicated major appliance manufacturers, GE and Tappan each had only 10 percent of the microwave market.

In 1979 GE introduced the "Spacemaker," which could be installed on the wall over a range. This product, the only microwave oven that did not require counter space, enabled GE to move into first place, while Litton and Amana, despite heavy advertising, dropped back to second place. The other significant competition came from Japanese manufacturers (Sharp, Sanyo, Panasonic, and others).

---

[2] "Air Treatment," *Merchandising,* November 1982.

Table 2

Percent of U.S. Households Owning a Microwave Oven

1972	1973	1974	1975	1976	1977	1978	1979	1980	1981
0.4%	1.1%	2.1%	3.5%	5.9%	8.7%	11.7%	15.2%	19.4%	24.4%

Source: Home Furnishing: Standard & Poor's Industry Surveys.

Laundry. The market for laundry products, though less saturated than for some other appliance products, seemed to be growing more slowly than most. Industry observers felt that washer saturation of a little over 70 percent and dryer saturation of about 65 percent would not be surpassed in the foreseeable future (see Exhibit 2). Those who currently did not own laundry appliances (mainly apartment dwellers) had access to coin-operated machines. Even if they wanted to buy washers and dryers for their exclusive use, few apartments had the necessary space and plumbing facilities.

Since laundry equipment constituted more than 25 percent of total major appliance unit sales, manufacturers were continually striving to introduce innovations that would boost sales. Some new products reduced water and energy consumption; others improved dependability and performance. Manufacturers had also developed more compact, stackable appliances. The expanding use of microelectronics, though not a major feature, allowed elaborate cycle control options on the higher priced models.

Market share had remained remarkably stable in laundry products in the past six years (see Exhibit 5). Almost 90 percent of the market was controlled by the big four—Whirlpool with 40 percent and GE with 20 percent, followed by White and Maytag with 15 percent each.

Dishwashers. With a saturation level of under 45 percent and the best-selling models retailing between $400 and $500 (with the top of the line being between $700 and $800), dishwashers appeared to offer true growth potential in contrast to other appliances. Dishwashers were one of the most complicated of all appliances to manufacture, because they involved a combination of electrical, mechanical, and hydraulic (plus electronic in some models) technology.

The dishwasher market had been dominated by Design and Manufacturing (D&M). A privately held firm specializing in dishwashers, D&M had consistently maintained a market share of 45 percent for the past decade. GE had been a steady number 2 with 25 percent market share, while Hobart-KitchenAid followed with 15 percent. (See Exhibit 6.)

Because of the product's high price and low saturation level, GE had targeted the dishwasher for future investments. In 1982 it was in the process of improving its technology by switching from a porcelain tub to a plastic tub, based on earlier successes on high-end models. It also seemed possible that Whirlpool, who previously had not been a major participant, could make a strong bid for some of the Sears business, which was presently sourced entirely from D&M.

Disposers. In contrast to all other appliances, disposers were sold primarily through plumbing contractors. Until 1980 GE was the leader in this market, followed by In-Sink-Erator, a wholly owned subsidiary of Emerson Electric. Disposers were Emerson's only home appliance product. When GE decided to exit disposers, In-Sink-Erator became the leader, with a 65 percent market share, followed by Anaheim Manufacturing with a 25 percent share. Anaheim was acquired by Tappan in 1965.

Compactors. The trash compactor market was dominated by Whirlpool and GE, with a combined market share of 75 percent. Although saturation is less than 5 percent, potential growth seemed limited, and manufacturers did not attach much importance to this product.

Product Design and Innovation

Innovations in product design took three forms: (1) customer-oriented features; (2) reducing manufacturing costs through process improvements, and (3) new products that expanded the market.

Feature innovations had been plentiful. Because many appliance markets were highly saturated, features were a useful way of speeding up replacement demand and differentiating products from those of competitors. Examples include the self-cleaning oven, pilotless gas ranges, side-by-side refrigerators, "Servadoor" refrigerators, and so on. In recent years there had been an emphasis in almost all appliances on electronic timers and controls and on energy efficiencies. Most often features were introduced at the top of the line and made available on lower-priced models within a few years. Generally the manufacturers' brands had the newest and most elaborate features, followed by the national retailers, who usually copied the previous year's successful top-of-the-line features.

In the area of process innovations a trend toward the use of plastic rather than metal, foam rather than fiberglass insulation, coiled rather than flat steel, prepainted rather than in-house painted cases, and so forth, had helped reduce manufacturing costs. Occasionally these changes had made the product intrinsically better as well (for example, lighter, slimmer, or more spacious).

The only true new product innovation that had been successful since the microwave oven was developed outside the appliance industry. The combination washer-dryer was an innovation that had not proved popular in the United States, though it had sold well in Europe. In 1982 the market verdict was not yet in for the compact and mini models of refrigerators, freezers, washers, dryers, and so on. Innovations of a sort, these products had been introduced chiefly by the foreign manufacturers.

Markets

There were two major end-use markets for appliances in the United States: retail and contract. A wide variety of retail outlets sold to the consumer. A significant share of appliances moved from manufacturer to consumer through the private-brand market, which consisted of mass merchandisers and other manufacturers that needed certain products to make up a full line. In the contract market, construction firms, builders, contractors, mobile home manufacturers, or kitchen remodelers made the purchase decision.

The Contract Market.[3] Contract sales were directly related to new housing starts. Since World War II this segment had grown to a peak in 1973 when it represented 33 percent of total appliance shipments. With the collapse of new housing construction during 1973–75, contract sales dwindled and in 1976 accounted for about 25 percent of shipments where they had remained through 1982.

Manufacturers sold appliances to the contract segment both directly to the large builders and indirectly through local builder suppliers. Direct sales to construction firms and mobile home manufacturers were made by corporate salesmen for most of the full-line companies and to a limited extent by independent distributors for the smaller manufacturers. Direct sales accounted for 80 percent of contract sales, and it was thought that the trend toward apartment living could increase their importance.

Appliances were crucial in selling homes even though they represented no more than 10 percent of total home costs. In the industry it was generally believed that consumers did not have the knowledge to evaluate objectively the quality of the dwelling units; on the other hand they had opinions as to the quality of various brands of appliances and associated this judgment with the quality of the dwelling unit. Because of the perceived importance of appliance brand image, builders seldom bought private brands.

Builders, however, were very cost conscious. They typically bought the middle and lower end of the product line. By buying all the appliances from one manufacturer they could save on transportation costs and also establish the leverage to command a lower price. When a dwelling unit was ready for the appliance, it was crucial that the appliance be there.

---

[3] Parts of this section are taken from Michael S. Hunt, "Note on the Major Home Appliance Industry," 1972. (Prepared under the supervision of Professor Joseph L. Bower.)

By maintaining a relationship with one manufacturer, the builder could apply pressure for timely delivery.

All the major companies active in the contract market sold full product lines. Some manufacturers also provided kitchen designing services to large builders, and all were able to advise builders how to match the quality of the appliance to the dwelling unit. Highly trained salesmen attempted to convince the builders of the merits of a particular brand.

Not all appliances were of equal importance to the housing market. Builders typically concentrated on three products: standard range/oven, dishwashers, and disposers. Of buyers surveyed, 53.1 percent felt a refrigerator should also be a standard feature, and another 34 percent were willing to pay for it as an option. Microwave ovens also seemed to be of some importance, as more than half of buyers felt they should be either standard or optional. A survey by the National Association of Home Builders also suggested that the builders and manufacturers might not be fully tapping the home buyer's willingness to pay extra for optional products such as refrigerators, washers, and dryers.

The Retail Market. A study of the major home appliance and TV set market concluded that the purchase decision was precipitated by four major events (household move, family change, product failure, and wealth increase) and three catalysts (initial homemaking, seasonal gift giving, and promotional offer).[4] The precipitating event was ordinarily preceded by an extended period of low-level involvement in information gathering (from parents, relatives, friends, media, and so forth). For a short time after the stimulus event, purchasers sought information more intensively (visiting stores, looking in catalogs, calling up family and friends, and so forth), trying to learn about available brands, price, performance (features), credit, and so on. Sales skills at the retail level were found to have a considerable influence on the purchase decision.

The study also shed light on several other aspects of appliance purchasing behavior. First, although people who had moved recently accounted for only 21 percent of the population, they purchased 60 percent of all the ranges, 53 percent of the refrigerators, 49 percent of the dryers, 47 percent of the dishwashers, and 43 percent of the washing machines. They were only slightly more likely than others to purchase air conditioners (25 percent) and freezers (22 percent). Second, while most appliance decisions were made jointly by the husband and wife, it was the wife who played the major role in the early stages: initiation, search, and determination of style and size. The husband became more involved in choosing a brand and determining how much to spend. Third, family, friends, and neighbors exercised considerable influence on the decision

---

[4] Peter Dickson and William Wilkie, "The Consumption of Household Durables: A Behavioral Review."

makers, since their advice was considered trustworthy, and they had a knowledge of the prospective buyers' needs and life-styles. Neighbors also exerted a subtle pressure to "keep up with the Joneses." Fourth, most appliance purchasers visited only one store, which indicated a significant level of store and brand loyalty. The growth in the market share of private brands also reflected this tendency.[5] Fifth, appliances had a good performance record in use. In 1976 appliances accounted for just 4 percent of consumer grievances as measured by the Office of Consumer Affairs, compared with 19 percent for automobiles. Finally, appliances like old soldiers, seldom died; they just faded away. A survey of refrigerator disposition found that 25 percent were sold, 19 percent given away, 20 percent traded, 8 percent converted, 4 percent rented or loaned, and only 23 percent thrown away.

Appliances were sold under the brand names of both retailers and manufacturers (either the original manufacturer or one that had sourced it from the original maker). National retail chains like Sears and Penney's carried the Kenmore, Coldspot, and Penncrest lines as their only brands. Especially in the case of Sears, these national retail brands were designed by the retailer, manufactured according to its specifications, and heavily advertised. Sears accounted for more than half of the sales for Whirlpool, Roper, Sanyo, and D&M and had recently started sourcing particular appliance types from more than one manufacturer. Some retailers, primarily large department stores, which sourced private-label products to be used as a bottom-of-the-line brand and sold primarily on price, discontinued this practice in the 1980s.

Appliances were sold through four major kinds of retail outlets: appliance dealers, national chain stores/mass merchandisers, discount stores, and department stores. Since the mid-1970s the national chain stores had gained share in almost all product lines (see Exhibit 7), primarily because of deeper penetration by Sears, which accounted for 50 percent of the sales in this category. Appliance stores also gained share, to a lesser extent, because of the emergence of large regional chain stores specializing in appliances (for example, Lechmere, Polk Brothers, Trader Horn). Small independent appliance dealers held their own by providing personalized, special service which the large retailers could not offer. The biggest losers were the traditional department stores, many of which had gradually phased out their major home appliance departments. After significant gains in the 1960s and early 1970s, the discount stores (K mart, Korvette, Caldor) had started to slip in the standard-size appliances but had maintained or improved their position in compact appliances, microwave ovens, and room air conditioners.

---

[5] From 1966 to 1970 a survey found that private brands grew from 36 percent to 43 percent of the total for freezers, 38 percent to 42 percent for washing machines, 35 percent to 40 percent for dryers, 14 percent to 24 percent for refrigerators, 12 percent to 13 percent for ranges, and 10 percent to 14 percent for dishwashers.

Consumers showed considerable brand loyalty in their appliance purchases. Asked whether they would buy the same brand again when purchasing a new appliance, 70.1 percent of a survey sample said they would, 13.6 percent would not, while 16.3 percent did not know.[6] These figures represent an average for 10 different appliance products, with dishwashers at the very top with 81.3 percent. Interestingly enough, dishwashers were one of the products most likely to have been sourced externally by the manufacturer or retailer. A mid-1970s survey found that the most important factor in the purchase of cooking appliances was "reputation of brand."[7] Other significant factors included "special features," "overall appearance/styling," "good value for money/price," and so on. Less often cited factors were "manufacturer/store reputation for service" and "past experience with brand."

Companies exploited the importance of brand names in several ways. Maytag, GE, and other top-of-the-line firms used a "pull" strategy to get the customer committed to the brand before entering the store, thus making switching difficult. The "push" strategy, in contrast, encouraged switching in the store, by offering some unique product attribute and most often a lower price to clinch the sale. Manufacturers at the middle or lower end of the line, like White and Magic Chef, gave the retailer higher margins and advertising allowances to encourage them to push their products. Finally, the "sell-up" strategy used heavy advertising of low-priced models to pull customers into the store, where the salesmen were trained and financially motivated to push them into the higher-priced models. This combination strategy was characteristically practiced by the national retailers like Sears.

Distribution and Service

Manufacturers, retailers, and independents all had a stake in appliance distribution. GE was the only manufacturer that owned its entire distribution network. Some large manufacturers owned their distribution networks only in the high-volume areas, and used independent distributors elsewhere. Whirlpool, for example, owned 50 percent of its distribution, mainly in the Sunbelt states and otherwise worked through independents. Most of the other manufacturers and retailers relied heavily on independent distributors. Sears, though, was the exception in having a 100 percent retailer-owned distribution.

Even the very largest manufacturer could not match the costs of an independent distributor that represented several noncompeting manufacturers, since the distributor could spread its warehousing, transporta-

---

[6] *Look,* National Appliance Survey, 1963.

[7] "Cooking Appliance Survey," *Newsweek,* 1975.

tion, sales, and collections costs across its entire product mix. On the other hand, whoever owned the distribution had substantial influence over the retailers in areas such as inventory, pricing, selection of dealers, and advertising. Certain smaller manufacturers, like Maytag and Hobart-KitchenAid, bypassed the independent distributor as they concentrated on the high-price, high-quality image with top-of-the-line products. They sold and shipped directly to carefully selected, exclusively franchised dealers with whom they had a very close working relationship.

Two recent developments were complicating the wholesale and distribution side of the appliance industry. The first was a trend toward more drop shipments direct from the factory to the dealer, bypassing the distributor's warehouse. One large Whirlpool distributor estimated that in 1982 60 percent of the units sold in his region did not pass through his warehouse. These direct dealer shipments cut costs about $18 per unit. The second trend was the emergence of buying groups. Sometimes dealers grouped their purchases and pressed the distributor for volume discounts. Similarly, large chains could shop for prices across several distributors' territories to get the best possible deal. Finally, some individual entrepreneurs had begun to act as subwholesalers, spotting imperfections in the marketplace and making deals wherever the opportunity arose.

GE was the only manufacturer and Sears and Penney's were the only retailers with their own appliance service networks. Other firms relied on franchised or free-lance independent service agents. These service agents had no connection with independent distributors.

The Appliance Value Chain

The appliance business could be broken down into six major activities: product design; purchase or manufacture of components; manufacturing, final assembly and testing; distribution and warehousing; sales and advertising; and after-sales service. For a typical appliance product, costs broke down as follows:

Sales	100%
Manufacturing cost:	65–75
(a) Fully integrated:	
— Raw materials	30–40
— Labor	6–10
— Plant and equipment	12–20
— General administration	12–20
(b) Not integrated:	
— Components	35–45
— Labor and overhead	30–40
Transportation and warehousing	5–7
Advertising	1–2
Sales and other marketing	4–8
Service	2–5
Product R&D	2–5
Overhead	3–10

The optimum size of a finished goods plant was thought to be an annual capacity of 500,000 units for refrigerators, ranges, dishwashers, and washer/dryers and 100,000 units for air conditioners. Though at one time production costs were estimated to be 10 percent to 40 percent higher in plants one half to one fifth the optimal size, the advent of robotics had led to current thinking that the optimum plant size could be much smaller than what it used to be. Plants were dedicated facilities, since each product category required its own specialized equipment on the assembly line. Even within a plant, different model configurations (for example, top mounted versus side by side) required their own dedicated lines, and some large manufacturers found it more efficient to manufacture them in separate plants. Vertically integrated manufacturers produced their own compressors, plastic molding, wiring harnesses, electronic controls, and so on. Even the most integrated manufacturer bought many components outside, however, since there were many efficient and competitive suppliers.

Full-line manufacturers that had concentrated their production and/ or distribution facilities in one location were able to achieve economies (approximately 8–10 percent of transportation costs) by shipping full carloads loaded with different kinds of appliances. On the other hand those whose production facilities were geographically dispersed had the advantage of shipping shorter distances to reach their markets. Producers of more than one line tended to use shared sales forces and brand names.

Economies were achieved in installation and after-sales service by companies that had sufficient volume to justify providing their own service rather than relying on independent service agents. Having its own service facility could also enhance the appliance maker's brand image. Although economies of scale were theoretically possible in product design, they had the least impact on overall cost position.

Most appliance companies offered a full range of products even if they did not produce all items themselves. A firm would fill the gaps in its line by putting its own brand name on products it purchased from another manufacturer. This practice was not confined to partial-line producers: everybody in the industry bought some product from someone else (see Exhibit 8).

Industry History

Prior to World War II most appliance manufacturers produced a limited line of appliances developed from the original products of their companies.[8] General Electric started a refrigerator business, Maytag made washers, and Hotpoint produced electric ranges. The lines broadened,

---

[8] This section has been compiled from: Hunt, "Note on the Major Home Appliance Industry."

but not until after World War II did manufacturers begin to offer full lines of products. Expansion continued in the following decade.

After 1955, however, the industry experienced overcapacity, leading to concentration through mergers and acquisitions among the manufacturers and a proliferation of brands, both national and private. By the mid-1970s there was some feeling that home appliances were destined to become commodities, allowing the Japanese to become a dominant industry force. Others thought that certain peculiar industry forces, such as the giant vertically integrated retailers (for example, Sears Roebuck), would lead to the development of a unique structure. Finally, some believed that entirely new products and revolutionary changes in existing products would drastically alter the industry.

The industry almost doubled in size as several products grew very rapidly during the 1960s. (See Exhibit 1.) Room air conditioner and dishwasher unit sales almost quadrupled, and clothes dryers more than tripled. Even products in highly saturated markets—like refrigerators and ranges, which were already present in 99 percent of wired homes—experienced an increase of roughly 50 percent in unit sales over the decade. At the same time the individual products themselves were changing. New features were added, and the capacity of home appliances increased (witness the trend toward larger refrigerators and air conditioners). Product reliability also improved, and real prices declined about 10 percent. Interestingly, these advances came during the period of mounting public criticism of the automobile industry's failure to produce a better and less expensive product.

The major home appliance industry in 1970 shipped 28.2 million units with a retail value slightly over $6 billion. This represented an 82 percent increase in units and a 62 percent increase in dollar sales since 1961. It was believed that the coming decade promised even greater growth. In the next three years the industry achieved real growth of almost 30 percent. In 1973 some 39 million units were shipped, and the average price level was less than in 1961. Consumers seemed to sense the great value, as even appliances with a high saturation rate continued to score steady gains, buoyed by a robust economy.

As 1973 ended economists began to project a slowdown in the economy, and consumer confidence surveys suggested a restraint in future spending. The Arab oil embargo had created considerable uncertainty about energy supply, and it was feared that fuel shortages might lead to material shortages as well. On the bright side, however, the market for dishwashers, air conditioners, and freezers was far from saturated, and new appliance products like microwave ovens and trash compactors seemed well positioned to take off.

By the close of 1974 the economy was in a recession, and consumers were not buying. The only bright spot seemed to be freezer sales, which were helped by the high price of food, along with the impact of the oil embargo on shopping trips. As real disposable incomes continued to decline, buyers deferred hard goods purchases as long as possible and simply did not replace their older appliances.

In 1975 as new housing starts fell to their lowest level in more than a decade, appliance shipments were lower than in any of the past seven years. Sales were down almost 30 percent from 1973 levels. Recognizing its vulnerability to downturns in housing construction, which accounted for an estimated 20 percent to 30 percent of appliance sales, the industry began paying greater attention to the replacement market in 1976 and 1977. However, the housing market rebounded in 1977 and 1978. Concurrently, consumers' disposable income was rising, and credit was becoming more readily available, together with increased consumer confidence due to a robust economy. As a result of these trends, 1978 and 1979 were two of the three best years the industry had seen (1973 remained the all-time high).

Inflation put an end to the long period of stable retail price levels after 1975, however. Manufacturers found their profit margins squeezed by rising operating costs. Compounding the problem of rising costs, growth slowed in 1980. Housing starts were lower than in any year since 1975 and in 1981 declined further to the lowest level in more than 20 years. The industry also seemed to be a victim of its own sturdy quality. The average life expectancy of an appliance was 10–15 years, and many functioned adequately for quite a bit longer. During tough economic times consumers tended to invest in repair jobs to prolong their appliances' lives a few more years. It was estimated that about 40 percent of these repairs were of the do-it-yourself variety.

On a more positive note, 1983 began and as the economy recovered, all signs seemed to be pointing to a significant upturn in housing and a surge in appliance sales. The domestic appliance manufacturers were ready for the long-awaited turnaround. And according to some, so too were the Japanese.

Competitors

All the major automobile manufacturers except Chrysler had appliance divisions at one time: Frigidaire of General Motors, Philco of Ford, Kelvinator of American Motors, Franklin of Studebaker. The other two major automotive-related companies in the appliance business were Bendix and International Harvester. All of these firms had divested their appliance business units, most of which had been acquired by White Consolidated.

The giants in the electric/electronics industry—GE, RCA, Westinghouse, McGraw Edison, Emerson Electric—had also been involved in the appliance business. Only GE remained as a major force, while Emerson Electric, through its subsidiary, In-Sink-Erator, manufactured only disposers. Diversified companies in the appliance business included Rockwell, United Technologies, Borg-Warner, Litton, Raytheon, and Dart & Kraft. Still participating in 1982 were Litton, Raytheon (Caloric, Amana, Speed Queen, and Modern Maid) and Dart & Kraft (Hobart-KitchenAid).

According to a long-time industry observer, there had been approximately 300 specialist appliance manufacturers in the United States at the end of World War II. Almost all were quite small, regional, and focused on a single product area. Only about 15 remained active in 1982, most notably Whirlpool, Magic Chef, Maytag, Tappan (acquired by Electrolux of Sweden in 1979), D&M (Design and Manufacturing), and Roper (41 percent owned by Sears).

Current appliance industry participants fell into three broad categories: *(a)* those that manufactured a full range of appliance product groups (General Electric, Whirlpool, White Consolidated, and Magic Chef); *(b)* those that manufactured a partial line, one or two groups of appliances (Raytheon, Maytag, Tappan, Hobart-KitchenAid, and Thermador-Waste King); and *(c)* specialists that concentrated on only one product (In-Sink-Erator for disposers; D&M for dishwashers; Litton, Sharp, Sanyo, and Panasonic for microwave ovens; Fedders, Friedrich, Addison, and Emerson for room air conditioners).

GE and Whirlpool, with sales of over $2 billion each, had traditionally led the industry. As an analyst put it, "To gain market share, you need a pricing edge, and no one can have a lower price structure than GE and Whirlpool."[9] GE had a powerful name and brand image and was the most vertically integrated of all the appliance companies. It manufactured some of its components and was the only appliance manufacturer that owned its entire distribution and service facilities. Whirlpool owed its leadership position to its unique 50-year relationship with Sears, which accounted for just over half of Whirlpool's sales at the factory level. At retail, Sears was the leader in most product categories. Since Whirlpool was the prime manufacturer for most Sears products, it had the economies of scale needed to compete head-to-head with GE.

The third-ranked position belonged to White Consolidated, with approximately $1.5 billion in sales. White had built its position exclusively through acquisitions. While antitrust considerations prevented GE and Whirlpool from acquiring other appliance businesses, White was able to take over the troubled appliance divisions of all the automobile manufacturers and of Westinghouse in rapid succession as they were put up for sale. However, White had not yet integrated the acquired companies into a single organization. The company's brand names included Frigidaire, White-Westinghouse, Gibson, Kelvinator, and Philco. Tradition-

---

[9] James Majid of Shearson Loeb Rhodes Inc., quoted in *Industry Week*, January 21, 1980.

ally dealers have been reluctant to carry many lines, which may become a problem for White.

Less than half the size of White were Raytheon, Magic Chef, and Maytag (number 4, number 5, and number 6 in the industry). Raytheon had entered the business only in 1965 and had grown mainly by acquisition, its distinctive advantage being high technology. Magic Chef and Maytag, two long-established names in the industry, had historically stayed away from any acquisitions and concentrated on their special markets: ranges and laundry products, respectively. With recent acquisitions, however, both firms had become almost full-line manufacturers. Maytag had acquired Jenn-Air and Hardwick, both range manufacturers. Magic Chef acquired Admiral and Revco-Rheem. Both Maytag and Magic Chef shared with White and Raytheon the problems of having diverse locations and brand names. As a top executive of Whirlpool put it: "It'll take those people five years to digest those purchases, to find the right kind of distribution . . . but when they do—with the volumes they can get—it'll give them a better cost structure and make it tougher for specialist companies."[10] Tappan by itself ranked number 7, but its acquisition by Electrolux made it a strong potential competitor. A leading appliance manufacturer in Europe, Electrolux had been rapidly expanding through acquisition and had strong product lines precisely where Tappan had a gap—in the refrigerator business.

The remainder of the industry consisted of a few specialists focused on microwave ovens and dishwashers, the least saturated markets, which offered the greatest potential for further growth. Litton and three Japanese firms—Sharp, Sanyo, and Panasonic—had a considerable stake in the microwave market. The dishwasher specialist was the last of the true independents—privately held D&M (1982 sales, $170 million), which over the last decade had been the unchallenged leader in this segment.

One observer summed up the competitive rivalry and industry consolidation aptly:

> You can't see the change on the showroom floor, but the appliance industry has been through a turbulent period of mergers and purchases. Many of those familiar brands now belong to a new owner. The industry's leaders, GE and Whirlpool, are being pursued by a crowd of competitors. Every firm is trying to emphasize its lineup's strengths and shore up its weak points. Not everyone will succeed.[11]

International Competition

Unlike the other major consumer durable products—especially automobiles and consumer electronics—major home appliances had resisted be-

---

[10] *Industry Week,* January 21, 1980.

[11] Michael A. Verespej, "Appliances' New Lineups for the '80s," *Industry Week,* January 21, 1980.

coming vulnerable to imports and had not globalized in spite of many formidable manufacturers in the United States, Europe, and Japan.

Europe

The European market though in a state of flux was very much dominated by the Europeans. The six major markets were Italy, West Germany, the United Kingdom, France, Sweden, and Holland.[12]

Italy produced more appliances than any other European nation, 42 percent of total unit output. Efficient mass production techniques and design quality had allowed Italian manufacturers to take over the middle and low end of the European market. Zanussi was by far the largest manufacturer in Europe. The other major Italian appliance producers were Indesit, Merloni, Candy, and Philips (a subsidiary of the Dutch Philips).

Germany was a large, rich market with high-quality products. Its industry was the second largest in Europe, accounting for 21 percent of all units produced. The two full-line producers, Siemens-Bosch and AEG Telefunken, dominated their home market and used this base to export aggressively in high-quality product segments.

Though the United Kingdom was the third largest European appliance producer, a large part of its domestic market went to imports. More than three quarters (78 percent) of domestic refrigerator and freezer sales in 1979 were imports, primarily from Italy. The two largest full-line producers, Hoover and General Electric, were not among the top 10 in Europe (see Exhibit 9A). Both were in the process of closing some plants as the U.K. producers were squeezed between low-cost imports at the bottom end of the market and high-quality German products at the top.

France was a large and fairly rich market, with significant imports from Italy and Germany. Recently nationalized, Thomson-Brandt was the sole French appliance manufacturer, covering the entire product spectrum. It used product differentiation to protect its position from low-priced imports and had a 40 percent market share in refrigerators and washing machines. (Philips claimed to be a close second in France.) Increasingly, Thomson-Brandt was looking toward export markets.

There were two other countries of significance, each dominated by a major domestic producer. One was Sweden, a large, developed market with very demanding consumers, where Electrolux had nationalized the industry. The second was Holland, a small though rich market, with Philips being the sole Dutch manufacturer. Philips also had extensive multinational operations. While the U.S. industry had seen a steady trend

---

[12] The description of each of the countries is based on Catherine Barre's "Merloni Group," HBS case 383–152, 1982.

toward consolidation and nationalization, the European market was quite fragmented. According to an industry observer:[13]

> [This is] not just the end of one upheaval but the opening of another that could last for the rest of the decade. . . . The European market is now similar in size and maturity to that of the United States. But there are at least 400 companies involved in the manufacture of white goods. The industry is still painfully out of gear with its marketplace.

In Germany AEG had bought up about 50 companies in an attempt to become the market leader. In 1982, however, it was close to financial collapse and was being dismembered, with Zanussi, Philips, Electrolux, and Siemens-Bosch negotiating to purchase various parts. The third largest German company, Bauknecht, was in the bankruptcy courts, and Philips had acquired a minority share in the firm with the option of buying future control. In response to the increasing success of low-cost Italian imports in the Scandinavian market, Electrolux had nationalized the industry by buying up many smaller manufacturers and consolidating their operations. It hoped to challenge Zanussi's leadership in Europe and through its acquisition of Tappan had gained a foothold in the United States (the only European appliance manufacturer to do so). In 1984 Electrolux was attempting to buy Zanussi. Since certain creditors objected it was not certain whether it would succeed. Thomson-Brandt, the recently nationalized French producer, also had ambitious plans for exports outside Europe. The company's director of exports commented:

> Our domestic market is Europe, and it is saturated; demand is on the decline. . . . Therefore, it is only logical that any company that can afford to invest in other markets should do so. . . . I believe the U.S., Canada, and Japan all offer an opportunity for our products. But at this stage, we are only evaluating the feasibility.[14]

The success of European appliances in the U.S. market seemed likely to depend on whether a trend toward downsizing developed. European manufacturers had considerable experience in producing versatile, well-designed compact appliances with the latest in electronic features. As in the United States, the fastest-growing appliances in Europe were microwave ovens and dishwashers. (See Exhibit 9B for saturation levels in European countries.) For example, in Germany, fewer than 1 percent of households reportedly had microwave ovens.

Japan

There were at least six major Japanese companies that manufactured appliances: Hitachi, Mitsubishi, Panasonic, Sanyo, Sharp, and Toshiba.

---

[13] Christian Tyler, *The Financial Times.*

[14] Jules Arbose, *International Management,* December 1979. *Appliance Management,* April 1983.

Considering the success of Japanese consumer durable goods in the U.S. market, appliance executives were cautiously looking over their shoulders in 1982.[15]

The Japanese had about 30 percent of the microwave oven market and 40 percent of the compact refrigerator market and had just introduced a miniwasher. While the compact refrigerator market had remained steady at less than 1 million units for the past five years, the market for microwave ovens had been growing consistently, becoming the second largest selling appliance product in the United States in 1981.

The Japanese strategy for the U.S. appliance market seemed to be two-pronged: exports and setting up manufacturing plants in the United States. As reported by an industry analyst:

> Matsushita, Sharp, and Sanyo will soon be making about 50,000 ovens a month in the United States—20 percent of total annual sales. Toshiba America Inc. may join them later this year. And Sanyo's San Diego plant is making 1,000 compact refrigerators a day, approximately 40 percent of the U.S. market. The Japanese appear to be picking their targets carefully, avoiding head-to-head competition with major U.S. manufacturers in mature product lines. . . . However, Sanyo does have plans to add a full-size refrigerator.[16]

U.S. Response

Daniel Krum, CEO of Maytag, assessed the impact of changing demographics in the 80s and summed up the challenge facing the appliance industry:

> Our historic average customer is changing. Families consisting of both parents plus children are now a minority in the United States. They have been outnumbered by the combined total of one-parent families, childless married couples, persons living alone, and groups of unrelated people living together. . . . This means that the appliances we designed for families in the 1960s and 1970s may not do for the 1980s and 1990s. Living in smaller housing with fewer children suggests a need for appliances that are different. Perhaps stackable, and storable, and smaller, but still offering all the features and amenities that go with today's sophisticated appliances.
>
> Up until now many of the products we make have not been seriously challenged from abroad. Foreign makers have not been inclined to produce and export the full-size major appliances that the American market requires, without a viable domestic market of their own. But as we in the United States edge closer to what is being manufactured abroad, to perhaps produce a "world appliance"—one that can be sold throughout the United States, Europe, and Japan—the possibility of greater competition may grow. The

---

[15] The Japanese made 93 percent of all motorcycles sold in the United States, 21 percent of automobiles (40 percent in California; 50 percent in subcompacts), 34 percent of color TVs. *Merchandising,* May 1982.

[16] "An Appliance Boom that May Not Last," *Business Week,* March 10, 1980.

potential would grow for vast new markets for U.S. manufacturers, but it also may well invite increased foreign competition within the United States.[17]

Prospects for the Future

Future growth prospects for appliances are shown in Exhibit 10. Halfway through 1983 it appeared that the appliance industry may just turn out to be the unlikely leader of a renaissance in U.S. manufacturing. According to a major business publication:

America's appliance industry is headed for sparkling good times. After a long brutal shakeout in which even such heavyweights as General Motors finally called it quits, a handful of survivors are poised to reap the benefits of a boom fueled by a burst of housing starts and a long-awaited resurgence of replacement demand. Sales have already turned up, and the appliance makers, long renowned for high levels of productivity, are beginning a ferocious battle for market share.

The major appliance industry is stronger than ever. The struggle that winnowed out inefficient producers left a group of bigger and better-capitalized companies. There may be a lesson here for the increasing number of politicians and business leaders who espouse the notion that government should assume a larger role in protecting and reviving American industries. Left to its own devices, at least one mature industry has managed to revitalize itself.[18]

---

[17] "AHAM: Execs Wrestle with Tough Problems," *Mart,* June 1982.

[18] Lisa Miller Mesdag, *Fortune,* July 25, 1983.

Exhibit 1

Summary of Total Shipments (Domestic and Exports) in Millions of Units and Their Retail Value in Millions of Dollars

	1961	1966	1971	1972	1973	1974	1975	1976	1977	1978	1979	1980	1981	1982
Refrigerators	3.48	4.98	5.69	6.32	7.01	6.27	4.90	5.37	6.39	6.81	6.54	6.05	5.87	5.10
	$1,027	$1,328	$1,542	$1,706	$1,936	$1,819	$1,474	$1,748	$2,585	$3,461	$3,413	$3,359	$3,510	$3,161
Freezers	1.05	1.10	1.44	1.58	2.70	3.52	2.74	1.79	1.89	1.83	2.19	2.08	1.93	1.54
	$ 293	$ 256	$ 311	$ 342	$ 580	$ 804	$ 653	$ 469	$ 549	$ 566	$ 786	$ 840	$ 836	$ 706
Air conditioners	1.50	3.35	5.44	4.51	5.35	4.56	2.67	2.96	4.15	4.93	4.39	3.79	4.14	3.12
	$ 389	$ 699	$1,147	$ 911	$1,069	$ 931	$ 641	$ 741	$1,166	$1,563	$1,527	$1,393	$1,654	$1,312
Gas ranges	1.81	2.18	2.55	2.66	2.48	1.95	1.62	1.83	1.75	1.80	1.79	1.53	1.50	1.38
	$ 272	$ 421	$ 517	$ 565	$ 544	$ 447	$ 383	$ 484	$ 537	$ 619	$ 643	$ 583	$ 619	$ 585
Electric ranges	1.55	2.01	2.71	3.12	3.64	3.23	1.36	2.73	3.35	3.60	3.29	2.81	2.63	2.12
	$ 411	$ 447	$ 601	$ 707	$1,016	$ 844	$ 657	$ 817	$1,078	$1,293	$1,309	$1,170	$1,134	$ 932
Microwave ovens	—	—	.10	.33	.44	.64	.84	1.49	2.25	2.55	2.92	3.69	4.53	4.27
	—	—	$ 45	$ 130	$ 167	$ 217	$ 337	$ 626	$ 995	$1,171	$1,338	$1,639	$2,140	$1,999
Dishwashers	.62	1.53	2.48	3.20	3.70	3.32	2.70	3.14	3.36	3.56	3.50	2.72	2.57	2.23
	$ 155	$ 330	$ 542	$ 676	$ 800	$ 759	$ 697	$ 855	$ 994	$1,082	$1,138	$ 960	$ 952	$ 858
Disposers	.80	1.41	2.29	2.77	2.97	2.55	2.08	2.52	2.94	3.31	3.32	2.89	3.07	2.69
	$ 64	$ 85	$ 138	$ 172	$ 193	$ 194	$ 187	$ 252	$ 324	$ 285	$ 295	$ 277	$ 321	$ 293
Compactors	—	—	.10	.21	.32	.32	.23	.25	.28	.30	.29	.23	.21	.18
	—	—	$ 26	$ 48	$ 70	$ 66	$ 52	$ 57	$ 66	$ 72	$ 74	$ 62	$ 60	$ 52
Washers	3.44	4.45	4.61	5.11	5.98	5.34	4.48	4.75	5.12	5.28	5.18	4.71	4.67	4.18
	$ 882	$1,018	$1,077	$1,212	$1,434	$1,349	$1,399	$1,621	$1,830	$1,831	$1,832	$1,765	$1,812	$1,757
Dryers	1.24	2.36	3.38	3.93	4.55	3.89	3.06	3.37	3.62	3.68	3.60	3.19	3.16	2.82
	$ 245	$ 422	$ 583	$ 689	$ 821	$ 741	$ 762	$ 887	$1,000	$ 938	$ 980	$ 935	$2,003	$ 964
Total	15.49	23.37	30.79	33.85	39.04	35.59	27.68	30.20	35.10	37.65	37.01	33.69	34.28	29.04
	$3,738	$5,006	$6,529	$7,158	$8,630	$8,171	$7,242	$8,552	$11,124	$12,881	$13,335	$12,983	$14,044	$12,139
Average price	$ 241	$ 214	$ 212	$ 212	$ 221	$ 230	$ 262	$ 283	$ 317	$ 342	$ 360	$ 385	$ 410	$ 418

Source: *Merchandising* magazine.

Exhibit 2

Product Line Data—1982

	Total Units (Millions)	Retail Value (Millions of Dollars)	Import Units (Millions)	Import Value (Millions of Dollars)	Saturation (Percent)	Average Life Expectancy (Years)	Expected Replacement Demand 1984
Refrigerators:							
Standard	4.37	$2,937	.16	$ 19	99.9%	13	5.46
Compact	.49	100	.41	29			
Freezers:							
Standard	1.29	621	.10	16	42.8	15	1.19
Compact	.23	70					
Room air conditioners	2.75	1,173	—	—	27.0	11	3.20
Gas ranges	1.38	585	—	—	42.7	16	3.67
Electric ranges	2.04	902	—	—	58.2		
Microwave ovens	4.20	1,979	1.15	204	25.6	12	.44
Smooth-top ranges	.10	64	—	—	2.0	—	
Washers:							
Standard	3.79	1,641	—	—	73.6	12	4.49
Compact	.25	74	—	—			
Dryers:							
Standard	2.61	898	—	—	65.3	13	2.70
Compact	.17	56	—	—			
Dishwashers	2.18	846	—	—	44.5	11	3.0
Disposers	2.69	293	—	—	49.7	10	2.78
Compactors	.18	52	—	—	3.1	10	.10

Sources: For "Units Shipped," "Retail Value" and "Saturation": *Merchandising* magazine. For "Saturation (percent) (1979 and 1982)," "Life Expectancy," and "Units to be Replaced": *Appliance* magazine.

Exhibit 3

Analysis of Company Market Share, Refrigeration (Percent)

Company	Refrigeration	1982	1981	1980	1979	1978	1977	1969	1964	1954
Whirlpool	Refrigerator	30%	31%	31%	27%	27%	25%	27%	24%	8%
	Freezer	36	36	30	30	30	30	*	31	13
	Air conditioner	17	17	17	17	17	15	*	25	10
GE/Hotpoint	Refrigerator	25	28	26	30	30	30	21	21	26
	Freezer	*	*	*	*	*	*	*	6	7
	Air conditioner	20	20	20	20	20	20	*	12	8
White	Refrigerator	21	21	21	25	25	30	27	18	19
	Freezer	34	34	25	25	25	25	*	5	5
	Air conditioner	15	15	15	15	15	15	*	4	10
Magic Chef (Admiral)	Refrigerator	14	11	11	12	12	10	7	6	*
	Freezer	13	13	9	9	9	15	*	*	*
Revco	Freezer	—	—	15	15	15	15	*	*	*
Raytheon (Amana)	Refrigerator	5	5	5	*	*	*	*	*	*
	Freezer	7	7	*	*	*	*	*	*	*
Fedders	Air conditioner	14	15	15	15	15	15	*	11	4
Friedrich	Air conditioner	12	12	12	12	12	10	*	*	*
Addison	Air conditioner	10	10	10	10	10	10	*	*	*
Others	Refrigerator	5	4	6	6	6	5	20	37	47
	Freezer	10	10	21	21	21	15	*	51	75
	Air conditioner	12	11	11	11	11	15	*	48	68

* Could mean either does not manufacture, insignificant market share, or figures not available and hence included in "others."
Sources: (a) For years 1977 to 1982—Appliance magazine.
(b) For years 1954, 1964, and 1969—Michael S. Hunt, "Note on the Major Home Appliance Industry," 1972.

Exhibit 4

Analysis of Company Market Share, Ranges and Ovens (Percent)

Company	Ranges/Ovens	1982	1981	1980	1979	1978	1977	1969	1964	1954
Whirlpool	Electric	9%	9%	9%	9%	*	*	19%	20%	9%
	Microwave	5	4	*	*	*	*	*	*	*
GE/Hotpoint	Electric	33	35	35	35	35%	35%	15	13	12
	Microwave	16	19	21	13	13	10	*	*	*
White (includes	Gas	6	*	*	*	*		*	*	*
Frigidaire)	Electric	18	18	18	18	18	20	11	9	7
Magic Chef	Gas	20	20	20	20	20	25⟩	13	6	5
(Admiral)	Electric	5	5	5	5	13	10⟩			
	Microwave	4	4	*	*	*	*			
Maytag	Gas	11	10	10	10	10	10			
(Jenn-Air and	Electric	7	5	5	5	*	*			
Hardwick)	Microwave	1	1	*	*	*	*			
Raytheon	Gas	18	15	12	12	12	10			
(Amana and	Electric	8	*	*	*	*	*			
Caloric)	Microwave	10	14	13	20	20	20			
Electrolux	Gas	20	20	20	20	20	20⟩	12	6	7
(Tappan)	Electric	6	6	6	6	10	10⟩			
	Microwave	12	8	8	13	13	10			
Roper	Gas	15	15	15	15	15	15⟩			
(41 percent owned	Electric	7	8	8	8	10	10⟩	2	*	*
by Sears)	Microwave	1	*	*	*	*	*			
Litton	Microwave	11	14	14	23	20	25			
Sharp	Microwave	10	11	8	13	13	15			
Sanyo	Microwave	15	9	*	*	*	*			
Matsushita	Microwave	5	4	*	*	*	*			
Others	Gas	10	20	23	23	23	20⟩			
	Electric	7	14	14	14	14	15⟩	25	46	60
	Microwave	10	10	36	18	21	20			

* Could mean either does not manufacture, insignificant market share, or figures not available and hence included in "others."

Sources: (a) For years 1977 to 1982—*Appliance* magazine.
(b) For years 1954, 1964, and 1969—Michael S. Hunt, "Note on the Major Home Appliance Industry," 1972.

Exhibit 5

Analysis of Company Market Share, Washers and Dryers (Percent)

Company	Washers and Dryers	1982	1981	1980	1979	1978	1977	1969	1964	1954
Whirlpool	Washers	41%	40%	40%	40%	40%	45%	46%	27%	18%
	Dryers (E)	40	40	40	40	40	40>	45	43	26
	Dryers (G)	40	40	40	40	40	40>			
GE/Hotpoint	Washers	20	20	20	20	20	20	16	11	8
	Dryers (E)	20	20	20	20	20	20>	14	8	6
	Dryers (G)	15	15	15	15	15	15>			
White	Washers	14	14	14	14	14	*	12	8	8
	Dryers (E)	15	15	15	15	15	10>	9	8	9
	Dryers (G)	15	15	14	14	14	10>			
Magic Chef (Norge)	Washers	5	5	5	5	5	*			
	Dryers (E)	5	5	5	5	5	*			
	Dryers (G)	5	5	5	5	5	*			
Maytag	Washers	15	15	15	15	15	15	10	11	8
	Dryers (E)	15	15	15	15	15	15>	9	9	2
	Dryers (G)	15	15	15	15	15	15>			
Others	Washers	5	6	6	6	6	20	16	43	58
	Dryers (E)	5	5	5	5	5	15>	23	32	57
	Dryers (G)	10	10	11	11	11	20>			

* Could mean either does not manufacture, insignificant market share, or figures not available and hence included in "others."

Sources: (a) For years 1977 to 1982—*Appliance* magazine.
(b) For years 1954, 1964, and 1969—Michael S. Hunt, "Note on the Major Home Appliance Industry," 1972.

Exhibit 6

Analysis of Company Market Share, Clean-Up Products (Percent)

Company	Clean-Up Products	1982	1981	1980	1979	1978	1977	1969	1964	1954
Whirlpool	Dishwashers	7%	6%	*	*	*	*	5%	10%	*
	Compactors	45	45	45%	45%	45%	45%	*	*	*
GE/Hotpoint	Dishwashers	22	20	25	25	25	25	29	30	38%
	Disposers	—	—	35	35	35	40	*	*	*
	Compactors	30	30	30	30	30	30	*	*	*
White	Dishwashers	4	4	*	*	*	*	15	7	12
Maytag	Dishwashers	6	6	6	6	*	*	*	*	*
	Disposers	2	2	*	*	*	*	*	*	*
Hobart-	Dishwashers	15	15	15	15	15	15	20	10	11
(KitchenAid)	Disposers	4	3	10	10	10	10	*	*	*
	Compactors	10	10	*	*	*	*	*	*	*
Thermador	Dishwashers	2	2	*	*	*	*	*	*	*
(Waste King)	Disposers	7	6	*	*	*	*	*	*	*
	Compactors	1	1	*	*	*	*	*	*	*
Design and Manufacturing	Dishwashers	42	45	45	45	45	45	25	18	*
In-Sink-Erator (Emerson Electric)	Disposers	60	60	25	25	25	18	*	*	*
Tappan (Anaheim)	Disposers	20	25	20	20	10	15	*	*	*
	Compactors	7	7	*	*	*	*	*	*	*
Others	Dishwashers	2	2	9	9	15	15	6	25	31
	Disposers	7	4	10	10	20	17	*	*	*
	Compactors	7	7	20	20	20	20	*	*	*

* Could mean either does not manufacture, insignificant market share, or figures not available and hence included in "others."

Sources: (a) For years 1977 to 1982—*Appliance* magazine.
(b) For years 1954, 1964, and 1969—Michael S. Hunt, "Note on the Major Home Appliance Industry," 1972.

Exhibit 7

Percent of Appliance Sales by Type of Outlet, 1982

	Standard Refrigerator	Standard Freezer	Air Conditioner	Compact Refrigerator	Compact Freezer	Gas Ranges	Electric Ranges	Microwave	Standard Washer/ Dryer	Compact Washer/ Dryer	Dishwasher	Disposer	Compactor
Appliance stores	33%	15%	28%	25%	18%	42%	40%	36%	34%	49%	26%	9%	26%
Catalog/chain stores (Sears, Penney's, etc.)	29	47	22	38	41	31	22	27	39	14	25	17	28
Department stores	8	14	13	9	12	3	5	8	8	11	3	2	11
Discount stores	5	13	25	18	16	5	3	11	8	12	7	—	2
Furniture stores	5	4	2	2	5	6	4	4	4	10	2	—	—
Catalog showroom	—	—	3	7	4	1	1	4	3	5	—	—	1
Builder/contractors	12	1	4	1	—	7	10	2	4	1	28	28	21
Kitchen remodeler	2	—	1	1	—	5	9	4	—	—	6	11	9
Plumbing contractor	—	—	—	—	—	—	—	—	—	—	1	23	1
Home improvement centers	—	—	—	—	—	—	—	—	—	—	—	—	—
Other	7	6	2	5	4	1	5	4	—	—	2	10	3
	—	—	—	—	—	—	—	—	—	—	—	—	—

Source: Merchandising.

Exhibit 8

The Private Brand Picture: Manufacturers Who Produce for the Various Private Branders

1. Refrigerators:
   Admiral (Magic Chef)
   — Crossley Group
   — Magic Chef
   — Montgomery Ward
   — O'Keefe & Merritt
   — Tappan
   — Western Auto
   General Electric
   — Firestone Tire & Rubber Co.
   — J. C. Penney [out of business]*
   Whirlpool
   — Sears [also from White]
   White Consolidated
   — Gamble Skogmo
   — Marquette

2. Freezers:
   Admiral (Magic Chef)
   — Crossley Group
   — Montgomery Ward
   — O'Keefe & Merritt
   — Tappan
   — Western Auto
   General Electric
   — Firestone Tire & Rubber
   — J. C. Penney [out of business]*
   Whirlpool
   — Sears
   White Consolidated
   — Gamble Skogmo
   — Marquette

3. Dishwashers:
   Design and Manufacturing
   — Admiral [from GE]*
   — Caloric
   — Chambers [from KitchenAid]*
   — Gaffers & Sattler
   — Magic Chef [from GE]*
   — O'Keefe & Merritt
   — Roper
   — Sears
   — Tappan
   General Electric
   — J. C. Penney [out of business]*

4. Disposers:
   Anaheim Manufacturing (Tappan)
   — Admiral
   — Caloric
   — Earl's Plumbing
   — Gaffers & Sattler
   — GE/Hotpoint
   — Magic Chef
   — Modern Maid
   — O'Keefe & Merritt
   — Tappan
   In-Sink-Erator
   — Elkay [from Kelvinator]*
   — Frigidaire
   — Granger (Dayton)
   — Kelvinator
   — Roper
   — Sears
   — Tru-Value
   — Wards [from Waste-King]*
   — White-Westinghouse

5. Compactors:
   General Electric
   — J. C. Penney
   Tappan
   — Caloric
   — Modern Maid
   Whirlpool
   — Modern Maid
   — Sears

6. Ranges (electric):
   Litton
   — J. C. Penney (microwave combinations)
   Magic Chef
   — Crossley Group
   — Gamble Skogmo
   — Sears
   — Montgomery Ward
   White Consolidated
   — J. C. Penney

7. Ranges (gas):
   Magic Chef
   — Crossley Group
   — Gamble Skogmo
   — Sears
   Roper
   — Jenn-Air
   Tappan
   — Montgomery Ward
   White Consolidated
   — J. C. Penney [out of business]*

8. Microwave ovens:
   Litton
   — North American
   — Phillips (Norelco)
   Magic Chef
   — Crossley Group
   — Gamble Skogmo
   Sanyo
   — Sears
   Sharp
   — Montgomery Ward

9. Washers:
   General Electric
   — J. C. Penney [out of business]*
   Norge (Magic Chef)
   — Admiral
   — Crossley Group
   — Magic Chef
   — Marquette
   — Montgomery Ward
   — Western Auto
   Whirlpool
   — Sears

10. Dryers:
    General Electric
    — J. C. Penney [out of business]*
    Norge (Magic Chef)
    — Admiral
    — Crossley Group
    — Magic Chef
    — Marquette
    — Montgomery Ward
    — Western Auto
    Whirlpool
    — Sears [also stackable from White]

* Telephone conversation with publisher of *Appliance* magazine on February 21, 1984, for [recent changes].
Source: *Appliance,* September 1982.

Exhibit 9A

Top 10 Appliance Manufacturers in Europe

	Manufacturer	Country	Appliance Sales (000 Units)	
			1977	*1981*
1.	Zanussi	Italy	3,872	4,000
2.	Philips	Holland	2,583	2,800
3.	Siemens-Bosch	Germany	2,200	2,300
4.	AEG Telefunken	Germany	2,050	2,200
5.	Electrolux	Sweden	1,540	2,000
6.	Thomson-Brandt	France	1,950	1,600
7.	Indesit	Italy	2,120	1,300
8.	Merloni	Italy	773	1,200
9.	Bauknecht	Germany	1,430	1,200
10.	Candy	Italy	805	900

Exhibit 9B

Saturation Levels for Selected Appliances in Europe (1978–1979)

	Washers	Dishwashers	Refrigerators	Freezers	Electric Ranges
Germany	88%	20%	95%	47%	70%
Italy	88	16	89	28	3
U.K.	77	3	91	44	41
France	72	13	83	23	10
Sweden	65	21	94	66	89
Holland	87	11	98	44	8

Exhibit 10

Six-Year Forecast by Appliance Manufacturers

	1982 Projected	1983	1984	1985	1986	1987	1988
Refrigerators							
— Standard	4,418	4,640	4,965	5,288	5,432	5,586	5,806
— Compact	540	560	570	580	590	600	610
Freezers							
— Standard	1,423	1,487	1,591	1,627	1,691	1,753	1,805
— Compact	270	280	295	305	310	315	320
Air conditioners	2,850	2,978	3,267	3,270	3,435	3,500	3,633
Ranges/ovens							
— Gas	1,387	1,445	1,529	1,580	1,620	1,672	1,752
— Electric	2,061	2,213	2,343	2,458	2,551	2,634	2,710
— Microwave	3,864	4,485	4,892	5,188	5,150	5,300	5,446
Dishwashers	2,066	2,226	2,464	2,699	2,798	2,875	2,989
Disposers	2,600	2,856	3,055	3,236	3,113	3,197	3,260
Compactors	151	165	193	205	216	230	250
Washers							
— Standard	4,083	4,183	4,348	4,494	4,477	4,547	4,693
— Compact	269	282	295	307	312	320	330
Dryers							
— Standard (Electric)	2,167	2,245	2,349	2,441	2,428	2,483	2,578
— Standard (Gas)	574	498	626	649	646	653	679
— Compact	176	194	204	210	215	220	225

Source: *Appliance* magazine, January 1983.

Competitive Positioning in the Dishwasher Industry (A)

The Dishwasher Market

Dishwasher sales rose dramatically—up to 40 percent—during the first quarter of this year [1983] compared with the same period in 1982, merchants told *Merchandising*. . . . Most said they have done little to spark the upturn in sales . . . when homes and apartments are built, they said dishwashers are bought. Also making purchases, merchants added, are consumers who can't afford to move. Instead they are remodeling their kitchens and putting in new dishwashers.[1]

As the economy recovered in 1983 increases in dishwasher sales led the appliance industry to a long-awaited turnaround. With a saturation level of under 45 percent and the best-selling models retailing between $400 to $500 (with the top of the line being between $700 and $800), dishwashers appeared to be a true growth opportunity for an otherwise mature industry that seemed to be on the decline.

The manufacture of dishwashers is one of the most complicated of all appliances because it involves the combining of electrical, mechanical, and hydraulic (plus electronic in some models) technology. Ironically, the clear market share leader for dishwasher manufacturing was neither GE nor Whirlpool, who between them were either number 1 or number

---

[1] Liz Leshin, "Dishwasher Sales Soar 40% Thanks to Construction Surge," *Merchandising,* May 1983.

2 in almost all appliance categories (see Exhibit 1). Nor was it any of the top seven appliance manufacturers, who between them controlled anywhere from 80 percent to 90 percent of the appliance industry, but instead a small privately held company called D&M (Design and Manufacturing).

D&M got its start in the 1950s because GE, who was the leader then, and Hobart and Frigidaire, who were far behind tied for the number 2 position, were all pursuing similar strategies of higher price and brand image in the dishwasher market. None of them was willing to serve the needs of retailers like Sears, whom they saw as their direct competition.

This series of cases is designed so that discussion can focus on the major decision facing Sears in 1983 concerning its source for dishwashers. The (B) case describes the basic operation of its historical supplier, D&M. The (C) case introduces Sears in 1983. The (D) case describes GE, Sears' major competitor in home appliances. And the (E) case describes the alternatives under consideration at Sears in 1983.

Exhibit 1

	GE	Whirlpool
Refrigerators	# 2	# 1
Freezers	—	# 1
Air conditioners	# 1	# 2
Gas ranges	—	—
Electric ranges	# 1	# 3
Microwave ovens	# 1	# 6 or # 7
Washers	# 2	# 1
Dryers (E)	# 2	# 1
Dryers (G)	# 2	# 1
	(3-way tie)	
Dishwashers	# 2	# 4
		(2-way tie)
Disposers	—	—
	(# 1 until 1980)	
Compactors	# 2	# 1

Competitive Positioning in the Dishwasher Industry (B)

Design and Manufacturing Co. (D&M)[1]

In 1959 Samuel Regenstrief left Philco to purchase the appliance division of Avco. Like so many of the other major manufacturers after World War II, Avco had gotten into the appliance business. And like many of these same manufacturers, Avco's appliance division started incurring substantial losses for want of effective distribution, and so Avco decided to sell out.

A D&M executive described the purchase of the Avco Division as follows:

> The Avco Division had a good production facility and a good dishwasher. What it lacked was a viable approach to the market. In simple terms it lacked management. The Avco Division was precisely what Sam was looking for. Its book value was low because the plant was almost fully written off. It was also incurring heavy losses. Hence Sam could afford to buy it and Avco could afford to sell it. Sam had the management capability to turn it around and turn it around he did.

Regenstrief described why he decided to go into the dishwasher business:

---

[1] This case is excerpted from HBS case "Design and Manufacturing" (D&M) (4–372–343).

Copyright © 1984 by the President and Fellows of Harvard College
Harvard Business School case 385–046

It was clear to me that the dishwasher market was going to take off. The dishwasher accomplished a chore most families disliked and gave the housewife more free time. It also was beneficial from a health standpoint since very hot water could be used.

I also felt that the national retailers offered a very attractive market. Originally manufacturers were creating the need for a specific brand of appliance. The "Frigidaire refrigerator" and "GE range" were examples of this. But as consumers came into closer contact with a wider range of appliances and appliances became more uniform in quality, the need that was being created was the need for the appliance. Value became key. National retailers gave the most value per dollar. In my opinion their success will continue because they are catering to the needs of today's consumers—the need for value.

There was another more philosophical reason for my interest in dishwashers. Home appliances like dishwashers improve the quality of life. I feel that the social problems that face this country arise from the great divergence in the quality of life. In the late 1950s dishwashers were too expensive to be purchased by any but the rich. This in my opinion contributed to the divergence in the quality of life.

Yet the only measure of performance available to a businessman is profits. The dishwasher business offered a unique opportunity. By going into it with the intention of mass producing appliances and selling to national retailers and other manufacturers, I would make a profit only by continually lowering my production costs. Dishwasher prices would fall and dishwashers would quickly become available to any consumer that wanted one. Hence by concentrating on profits I could make a positive contribution to society.

In commenting on D&M's strategy, Mr. Regenstrief stated:

Our basic approach hasn't really changed over the last 12 years. We are in business to make as high profits as possible by fashioning and manufacturing a quality dishwasher and selling it to national retailers and other manufacturers. To succeed we have to have a product of competitive quality and a low-cost position in the industry.

The reason that the low-cost position is crucial is that we can succeed only if we can sell a product for less than our customer can make it or buy it elsewhere. Our maximum margin is determined entirely by our production efficiency relative to our customers, our present competitors, and our future competitors.

Given the importance of cost to this approach, I have been concerned with getting volume up and costs down since day one. We needed volume to have the operating efficiencies necessary for low cost. But we also need the most efficient product facility possible. As a result we often scrap a piece of machinery a year or two after we buy it if we can replace it with a better machine.

The whole reason for starting D&M was that I felt that we could get the volume to make the strategy work. GE was skimming the cream off the market and no one was around to do what I wanted to do. The market had obvious growth potential. By getting in first and getting the volume we could have a natural advantage.

Things have changed in the last 12 years. GE, for example, is now willing to slug it out on a cost basis where volume is involved. But we have the volume and the efficiency now to play this game profitably. No one can match our production costs today.

To achieve this strategy D&M had a very lean, informal, and flexible organization structure, where communication and responsibility cut across functional and hierarchical lines. This resulted in a strong commitment throughout the company to getting costs down and volume up by whatever means were necessary. As Regenstrief commented:

I could draw you an organization chart, but it would be meaningless. . . . If I see that production costs are out of line for a given day, I don't call up Bud Kaufman, my production vice president. I call the foreman responsible and find out why. If his explanation doesn't suit me, or it happens again, then I talk to Bud. . . . This goes all the way down to the worker. If he is going to run out of parts it is his responsibility to get them—not just tell his foreman.

To ensure that he got the best out of his people, Mr. Regenstrief used bonuses and profit sharing (97 percent of the stock was owned by company employees, with the vast majority owned by Sam Regenstrief). As he put it:

Our executives are rewarded heavily on the basis of corporate performance. Bonuses in a good year may be greater than salary. We carry this philosophy down to the worker level. A worker may earn 25 percent of his salary in bonus during a good year. Since our basic wage is competitive with other manufacturers, this means that we are among the highest paying firms in the industry. We do this not out of a sense of altruism but rather to guarantee that we get maximum effort out of everyone.

My general approach is to keep the corporate overhead as low as possible. I want the best possible managers, but as few as possible. The same is true with our data collection. I want to know exactly what is going on in as few numbers as possible.

All of D&M's functional policies reflected the personal philosophy of Sam Regenstrief:

Our approach to production is based on two concepts—simplicity and standardization. We want to produce the least complicated product and get as much standardization as possible in the parts. This allows us longer production runs and lower costs.

We are continually installing new, more efficient equipment. The age of the equipment we replace is not important. We scrap equipment and take a capital loss whenever we find a better way to make the product. When we wanted to speed up the production flow by combining several of our operations which were in outlying buildings, we could not afford to build a new plant. So we figured out an ingenious way of building the new plant over the existing ones (which were later torn down), without slowing up production.

I handle sales. The crucial three factors in each contract are price, volume, and design specification. In setting the price I start with a margin I am trying to achieve for our total sales. But with regards to each of 13 companies I set the price based on what they could produce it for and/or what it will take to keep them in business. Hence I have to consider the companies' volume and their marketing and distribution costs. I want to supply as many companies as possible but only if each of them can give me the volume I need. With regards to design I give more leeway to the companies with higher volume. I occasionally will give a new company more leeway than their volume deserves to get them established in the market. But if the volume doesn't come I won't carry them.

It was generally agreed at D&M that the chief thrust of their product development was defensive. However, having a good defense resulted in occasional innovations. They only introduced a new feature or product (for example, the counter top dishwasher) where they felt that there could be considerable demand and being first would be a strong advantage.

"Our basic philosophy in this area is to maintain D&M's position in the industry by helping our customers maintain theirs," stated Dr. Harold DeGroff, vice president of new product development and professor of business policy at Purdue University. He continued:

We basically work in three areas—new features, environmental acceptance (for example, noise and safety), and new processes. The first area is handled by our engineering staff at Connersville while the second two areas are handled at a facility we built in Lafayette, Indiana, near Purdue University, because they draw heavily on Purdue for part-time consultants.

To understand our approach you have to understand the needs of our customers. The large national retailer we sell to needs a product of competitive quality that he can sell at a low price. He is particularly concerned with having unique features, and he also needs to have those successful features that his competitors have. With the rest of our customers dishwashers serve the purpose of broadening their product line. They need the dishwasher especially for the builder market, and this market is highly competitive.

In areas like noise and safety we are continually faced with the threat of new standards or tightening of old standards. We have to be ready to respond. In the area of new processes we are faced with the threat of a whole new way to clean dishes. We are periodically working on ultrasonics and other approaches to protect ourselves from being out of business should one of these new technologies come to market.

Since D&M was responsible for repairs incurred during warranty, they had a rigid quality control inspection system, and they also engaged in training their customers' service personnel. This enabled them to minimize the service expense for any given breakdown.

D&M had no substantial long-term debt. The rapid expansion in output and hence plant and equipment throughout the 1960s was financed almost entirely out of current profits. As one D&M executive described it, "After the first couple of years, the capital needed for expansion didn't really make much of a dent in current profits."

In commenting on the first 12 years of D&M, Mr. Regenstrief stated:

When I acquired the Avco Division it had a core of good engineering and production talent as well as the physical plant. With this as a base, we got rid of everything but the dishwasher, sink, and cabinet business. The latter two we kept until the mid-60s before dropping them because of their contribution to overhead. This contribution helped in the early days.

Starting with less than 100 employees and 60,000 units we have grown to a position of being the largest producer of dishwashers in the world with over 25 percent of the U.S. market. Our sales go to a leading national retailer and to 12 manufacturers. We now have in excess of 1,600 employees.

Prices have fallen over the last 12 years. We have, however, at the same time reduced costs considerably, but our margin has also decreased. Total profits have definitely increased.

Between 1961 to 1971 D&M's unit volume grew by 800 percent, while its revenues grew by 730 percent. As 1971 ended, Samuel Regenstrief, who by then was in his early 60s, commented on the future of D&M:

The future looks good. Only 25 percent of the U.S. homes have dishwashers. This means that there is considerable growth potential for the product. If anything, the market share of national retailers will expand because they offer the greatest value. Hence I see no reason to expect our growth to slow.

Of course I am concerned about competition. A lot of companies would like to take our business away from us. To do that they would need our volume. The only way they could get it is if they introduced a significantly better product and could match our costs. Since we are continually improving our product I doubt if anyone could do this. But it is certainly something we are always looking at. It is one reason we stay lean and flexible. We must be able to move quickly to match any major changes in the product.

My biggest problem is to develop the management capability of D&M so that we can continue to fashion a better product at a lower cost. Our success over the last 12 years has been based on accomplishing these two tasks, and I see no reason for any change in the future.

Competitive Positioning in the Dishwasher Industry (C)

Sears Roebuck & Co.

Though Sears does not manufacture a single appliance product, it is the largest seller of major home appliances, with a reported market share of approximately 35 percent. For Sears the problem has always been how to compete with the branded manufacturers, on both cost and features, when some leading manufacturers have been unwilling to sell to Sears on terms that can allow it to compete.

This case begins with Sears's early history and its strategic uncertainty in the early 1970s. Then it examines some of the forces that lie behind Sears's success in the major home appliance business, the most important of which is its sourcing strategy.

Early History[1]

In 1895 Richard Sears in partnership with Alvah Roebuck began the profitable exploitation of the rural American market. "In his semiannual catalog Sears offered the American farmer a wide variety of goods and, because he purchased in large quantities and often directly from the

---

[1] This section is excerpted from the HBS case "Sears Roebuck & Company," (373–010).

Copyright © 1984 by the President and Fellows of Harvard College
Harvard Business School case 385–047

manufacturer, offered them at a lower price than did the local merchants and storekeepers."[2]

In 1925 Sears initiated under General Wood a strategy of entry into direct retail selling based on store location, concentration on hard goods, mass purchasing, and limited backward integration into the production of these goods. To guarantee supply and eliminate the middlemen Sears also purchased common shares (often a controlling interest) of its suppliers of "big ticket items."

Sears's growth placed increasing pressure on its highly centralized, functional organization. In the 1920s and 1930s a new form of organization developed. The merchandising functions (for example, purchasing, designing, and advertising) were controlled at the corporate level, while the retail operations were each organized into profit-center territories with each store manager having considerable autonomy as to his actions.

A second major change after World War II was the move away from factory ownership. With the increasing complexity of the product and production process and Sears's rapidly increasing retail volume, backward integration became less attractive. Furthermore, it was to Sears's advantage to have its suppliers sell their own national brand because it forced the manufacturer to keep up on new product development and achieve economies from higher volume. Since Sears needed products with competitive features, it required its suppliers to have strong product development capability.

Sears also began to adopt distinctive brand names (for example, Coldspot and Kenmore) under which to sell its appliances nationally—thereby creating the concept of a retail national brand. One observer commented that, "the mutual dependency between these suppliers and Sears allows Sears to buy at a low price while allowing the suppliers a fair profit, especially when the cost savings on their other sales are considered. And then," he said, "the organization takes over."

Appliance Organization

Two segments of the Sears organization were of crucial importance to its appliance business—the buying department at the corporate level and the department managers' offices at the store level. The merchandising department was responsible for the development, procurement, and promotion of all merchandise sold in Sears stores or catalogs. Reporting to each merchandising vice president were national merchandising managers, each with responsibility for a given group of products such as home laundry, freezers, air conditioners, and dehumidifiers, refrigerators, and kitchens (including ranges, disposers, and dishwashers).

The two key positions under the national merchandising manager

---

[2] Chandler, *Strategy and Structure,* p. 226.

were the buyer and retail sales manager. The buyer was responsible for everything having to do with his product. He determined the source of the product, the purchase price, product design, product research and development, retail pricing, service, and most important of all, sales and profit. The retail merchandising office was responsible for advertising, promotion, placement within the store, and so on. Though the merchandising manager and his staff had no power to compel the retail stores to use their services or products, the stores typically followed the appliance policies set by the buyers.

At the retail end of the chain each retail store was also a profit center. Reporting to the store manager were department heads responsible for various product groups within the store. These department heads, with the store manager's approval and within the corporate policy guidelines, had the power to set product policy for that store, but they usually followed the buyers' guidelines. A bonus based on profits was a large part of total compensation for the store managers, which many believed was crucial to Sears's success in the appliance field.

Appliance Strategy

Sears's appliance strategy was characterized as a focused approach to retailing through merchandising. In order to get the sales and profit growth expected from appliances, Sears concentrated on heavy advertising to generate traffic, maintaining consistent quality and providing good service, and taking advantage of the natural traffic a Sears store generates. The product line design was based on the top-of-the-line product having the most advanced features, while the lowest price product, though of the same quality, had the least features. In between would be carefully spaced pricing points, each associated with a separate feature. Sears believed this gave their customers the opportunity to get the best buy at whatever level they could afford. It also contributed to Sears's financial success.

A second part of Sears's strategy also was based on volume. The higher the volume, the lower the cost to the manufacturers in selling to Sears, and the lower would be Sears's distribution costs. The latter cost reduction was based on the savings achieved from shipping full carloads both to regional warehouses and the larger Sears stores. This saving could be as much as 8 percent to 10 percent of the freight cost.

In describing Sears's pricing policy the national merchandising manager for Home Laundry stated:

> After we have established the top-of-the-line and the bottom-of-the-line (our opening price point) we ask, "How many models do we need to fill the gap?" On the one hand each price point must give the consumer real benefits as compared to the price point below it. On the other hand the jump between price points must not be so great that the consumer will

not be willing to move up. And we do not want to have too many price points, since every increase in stockkeeping units increases inventories. On automatic washing machines we have six basic retail price points.[3]

There were two key aspects to the pricing policy: the bottom-of-the-line price was set to be as low or lower than any of Sears's competitors, and there were a limited number of carefully spaced pricing points—each point associated with a separate feature.

Prior to the late 1960s service represented Sears's clearest competitive advantage. Only Sears offered a service contract backed up by its own servicemen, while other manufacturers were forced to rely on franchised service operations. Just as important, the ability to locate service facilities in or near its stores allowed Sears store managers to supervise the service operation. Sears suppliers, however, were responsible for breakdowns during the warranty period, which motivated them to design as reliable a product as possible as well as one that was easily serviceable. This competitive advantage for Sears began to erode by 1970, as GE started developing factory service outlets in most metropolitan areas with a population over 100,000.

Competitive Environment in the 1960s and 1970s

While in the past Montgomery Ward had been thought of as Sears's closest retail competition, by 1970 J. C. Penney had become the second largest retailer in the United States. Penney had been growing more rapidly than Sears in both sales and profits during the 60s and early 70s.

Penney was tied in with GE, Sears's largest competitor in the appliance market. GE had contracted to sell appliances to Penney for resale under the Penncrest name. This alliance between the largest national full-line appliance manufacturer and the second largest retailer was expected to be a source of trouble for Sears's appliance business in the future. At the least such an arrangement would help both GE and Penney make inroads on Sears's current volume advantage.

This threat was especially great if Sears suppliers were unable to attack the builder market successfully. If the suppliers' volume would drop, with this decline would come loss of scale economies. On the other hand if Sears suppliers did penetrate this market segment successfully, Sears's business would not be as important to them. Hence Sears was in danger of losing its buying power.

Despite these changes in the environment, Sears management did not appear to be directing a large part of its attention to the appliance business. Indications were that the primary changes in Sears's strategy went in the opposite direction—placing heavier relative emphasis on soft

---

[3] Ibid., p. 302.

goods. A *Business Week* article suggested that Sears's new strategy was to maintain growth despite bigness, by broadening their market and diversifying.[4] To accomplish this, as the company approached saturation of its traditional middle-class market, Sears planned to aim for the low- and high-income segments of the market which it had previously eschewed. Soft goods, especially clothing, were expected to lead the way.

Strategic Reversal—1970–1980[5]

By 1975 Sears was reporting sudden reverses in its sales and earning trends, while its competitors were having rising earnings. The business press attributed this to Sears's awesome size, the apparent drift in its strategic thrust and the resulting image confusion it created among its customers. Some speculated that the 1960s' move into higher priced merchandise and toward soft goods had hurt the company. The higher prices were eroding Sears's solid base of "needs" shoppers but failing to attract upper-income buyers. Sears for too long had been identified not with leather jackets and cocktail dresses but with pliers, refrigerators, and linens. Between 1967 and 1974 Sears's overall market share relative to its competitors had decreased from 35 percent to 30 percent, while Penney's went from 14 percent to 16 percent, Kresge's 7 percent to 13 percent, and Woolworth's 8 percent to 10 percent.

Along with the setback in market share and earnings there were changes in management and strong internal dissension about Sears's new strategic directions. This led to McKinsey & Co. being called in as consultants, as Sears felt that among other things "we needed an independent referee." McKinsey spent three months trying to convince Arthur Wood (CEO of Sears) and Charlie Meyer (VP Planning) to first focus on strategy. At the end of that time McKinsey realized that they could not have been more wrong. "If we had worked on strategy first, it would have taken until 1983 to get any action," the McKinsey partner in charge admitted. He added: "The *impact of structure* and process at Sears was greater than any other situation I have seen in shaping the strategy and in inhibiting the consideration of new strategic directions."

McKinsey made two major recommendations. The first was that the 51 buying departments be organized into nine merchandising groups, each headed by a vice president. In addition the territory managers were to significantly reduce their role in merchandising decision making, which put the group and zone managers, who were closer to the marketplace, in more direct communication with headquarters buyers.

In 1977 a new strategy was launched to regain market share, to

---

[4] "How Giant Sears Grows and Grows," *Business Week,* December 16, 1972.

[5] This section is excerpted from HBS cases "Sears Roebuck & Co. (B) and (C)" (580–131 and 132) written by Professor E. Raymond Corey.

reestablish the Sears value image, and to build store traffic. The strategy was to use price promotions frequently and in depth. In retrospect, the emphasis on promotions and the severity of the price cuts exceeded prudent norms and led to a profit collapse. "But," according to one Sears executive, "1977 proved that the system worked. The field delivered what was asked of it." The 1978 goals, however, gave high priority to regaining margin percentage points as opposed to increasing market share.

On February 1, 1978, Edward Telling was named by Arthur Wood as his successor, becoming the 10th chairman in Sears history. Telling, who had worked his way up from the selling floor, described Sears's retail strategy for the 1980s:

> Sears strategy? First, you have to recognize that this is an exceedingly difficult retail climate. The expansion in square footage of retail store space in the last decade is unbelievable. It's very important for us to know exactly where we fit.
>
> To the customer Sears is a state of mind: we serve the middle 60 percent on the economic scale. We offer quality at a reasonable price; we build goods to last. We offer fashion but not high style.
>
> We compete against K mart, Penney's, Ward's, a lot of specialty shops (but not fashion shops), and in many towns, the local department store.

Thus Sears returned to its identity of 15 years earlier: a store for middle-class, home-owning America, offering quality at low prices.

Appliance Strategy for the 1980s

By 1983, of the nine Sears merchandising groups, the Home Appliance group was the second largest, contributing 19 percent of the total sales. The Home Appliance group consisted of four major product categories: (1) ranges and cooking equipment; (2) laundry, refrigeration, and air conditioning; (3) home entertainment (brown goods); and (4) vacuum cleaners and sewing machines. Dishwashers, disposers, and compactors were not part of the Home Appliance group but, instead, were part of the Kitchen Improvement section, which was part of the Building Materials group.

At the retail level the appliance products took up 5 percent of the store space while generating 20 percent of its volume and contributing even greater to its profitability. The major home appliance strategy was based on "having a captive product, a captive sales organization, and a captive service network."

Product Planning

Sourcing Relationships. The foundation of Sears's appliance strategy was its strong relationship with its suppliers. And of all its suppliers, none has been more important than Whirlpool. Sears in 1982 accounted for just over 50 percent of Whirlpool's sales. Whirlpool supplied 100 percent of Sears's laundry products, 70 percent of the air conditioners, and 65 percent of the refrigerator and freezer products—the other 35 percent of refrigerators and freezers and 30 percent of the air conditioners being supplied by White. Since Whirlpool in the 1950s did not manufacture either ranges or dishwashers, Roper supplied most of Sears's electric and gas ranges, and sales to Sears accounted for 78 percent of its total. D&M (Design and Manufacturing) supplied all their dishwasher requirements.

A senior executive recalled the Whirlpool-Sears partnership as it has evolved over time:

> It is an interesting paradox that when Sears started in the retail business, the big companies were not interested in supplying to us, so we had no choice but to deal with the little guys. We started buying from a lot of small companies, and one such company was the 1900 Corporation, which made a tub with a hand device for washing clothes. That was Sears's first entry into selling laundry appliances.
>
> During this time Bendix was the first to come out with an automatic washer. But it had a lot of problems. At that time there were no detergents, and the housewives used soap instead. The soap in those days contained quite a bit of grease, and grease was not compatible with the mechanical parts of the washing machines.
>
> The 1900 Corporation invented an automatic machine that would solve the problem that the Bendix machine was having, but they needed $1 million to gear up for production. This they did not have nor could they raise. General Wood, the head of Sears at that time, decided to give them $1 million in return for an equity position, and thus began a long-lasting relationship. Soon was born the first of many millions of "Kenmore" machines. In its early days the Kenmore washing machine was called a "jeep," because when it went into its spin cycle, it moved around like a jeep. The Bendix machine was a front load, while the Kenmore was a vertical access top load, and though Kenmore had fewer mechanical difficulties, it did have the problem of moving around during the spin cycle, which became obvious if the clothes were not evenly distributed. This problem was solved not in the factory but in the customer's home by the Sears salesmen. The salesmen would go into each customer's home, see where the machine was to be placed, and bolt the machine firmly to the floor. In homes where the machine could not be bolted to the floor, they would bolt it to a concrete base and then place it in position.
>
> Just as it was buying laundry machines from the 1900 Corporation, Sears bought refrigerators from the Seeger Corporation. Since Seeger wanted to become more of a full-line company, Sears arranged for the merger of the two companies, which was called Whirlpool. However, neither of the companies had any distribution or sales network to market their products to the general public. At that time RCA, which was heavily into brown goods, had no white goods (unlike GE, which had both white and brown goods), but they had the distribution expertise, so these two companies

were put together. Thus in the early 1950s Sears was instrumental in the creation of RCA/Whirlpool, which enabled Whirlpool to get launched under its own brand into the marketplace using RCA's distribution and sales network. In the 1970s RCA decided to concentrate on the brown goods and cashed in its RCA/Whirlpool equity, leaving Whirlpool to manage on its own. However, to this day Whirlpool and RCA share many of the same distributors.

Though Sears no longer has any equity in Whirlpool either, its relationship has grown stronger over the years and exemplifies Sears's philosophy of wanting its suppliers to grow with it. This bond is further cemented by the management relationships between the companies. When Whirlpool needed someone to head up its marketing for outside sales, they took John Hurley from Sears for the job. Hurley then brought some other Sears people. The ex-CEO of Whirlpool, Bud Gray, was a store manager for Sears in New York at one time. His successor, John Platt, was responsible for the Sears account at Whirlpool.

Roper, too, in which Sears had a 41 percent equity, was a Sears creation.

We were buying electric ranges from Newark Manufacturing, and we were buying farm equipment from David Bradley and some other products from a third company, so we put the three companies together to form the Roper Corporation.

When relationships with domestic suppliers have not worked out, Sears has turned to Japanese manufacturers. Unable to devise a satisfactory supply arrangement with a major U.S. television manufacturer, Sears invested in Warwick for its TV sets. But Warwick was unable to produce to Sears's satisfaction. So Sears arranged for Whirlpool to acquire Warwick. However, Whirlpool's strength was in metal bending, and they could not make Warwick successful, either. So Sears assisted Whirlpool in finding Sanyo to buy Warwick and took equity in the Sanyo Manufacturing Co. of USA, which has a plant in Arkansas.

Sears did not seem to feel that its equity positions in its suppliers created any conflict of priorities:

Our buyers have the independence to make their decisions based on their criteria. We have only taken equity positions when that was the only way to make sure that the supplier provided us with what we needed. White goods are highly capital-intensive, and so we would much rather invest $10 million to open a new store than take an equity position in a supplier.

In keeping with its sourcing philosophy Sears generally preferred to work with one rather than multiple suppliers:

If we are going to penetrate an industry we must get the economies of scale. So we want to simplify. Why should we be buying from different manufacturers? Because at the servicing level this would complicate the process!

When a Sears supplier does not offer a specific type of appliance, Sears may source it elsewhere, especially if it feels the product represents a limited market. While Whirlpool made the icemaker refrigerator, it did not sell well in the East because it required special piping and water connections that were not feasible or permitted in many apartment buildings. Hence Sears went to White for its purchases of these models. But when Sears perceives a major trend in the market not currently met by its supplier, it will try to induce its primary supplier to begin manufacturing the product. Thus when Sears wanted to carry side-by-side refrigerators, it persuaded Whirlpool to make them. Sometimes the decision to go to another manufacturer comes down to costs:

> If we want a 28-inch refrigerator, and Whirlpool says it would cost $350,000 to tool up for it, and if Gibson [part of White Consolidated] already has an acceptable product, then we buy it from Gibson.

Product Design. Features are what distinguishes Sears's products from their competitors' at the consumer level. They facilitate full-line selling, allowing the Sears sales force to demonstrate different features available at different price points. At the design stage Sears tries to structure its product line so that the value of the features to the customer at the higher priced models will outweigh the increases in sales price.

Even in product design, Sears maintains its partnership relationship with its suppliers who can also be its competitors:

> We take a major share of Whirlpool's products, so we get top choice of their latest designs. Sunburg and Farrar are the designers who do design work for both Whirlpool and Sears. The critical evaluation of their design work is that an objective group of persons can look at the two designs and say they are quite different though designed by the same firm. We also have our in-house designers who make sure that when the Sears identity comes on, there is no similarity in our product as compared to anyone else's.

However, Sears's approach to product planning is quite conservative:

> In product planning we use a lot of field input on what's selling, what the customers want, and what the competitors are selling. But overall we don't stray too far from our successful products. We would much rather stay with the tried and true products than be on the cutting edge.

Cost Leverages. A key element of Sears's sourcing strategy is its price negotiations with its suppliers. Sears buys most of its appliance products on a negotiated cost plus basis. It constantly works with its suppliers to make them the most cost-efficient producers. Hence Sears knows generally what its suppliers' costs are for material, labor, and burden (overhead) for each product. To obtain economies of scale Sears encourages its suppliers to sell a distinctly different line of merchandise to others, and so Sears competes with its suppliers downstream on the value chain where its real strengths lie. The point at which Sears stops being its supplier's partner, and instead becomes its competitor, is when the product acquires the Sears identity on the production line.

Sears's goal is to share as much of the production and assembly process with the suppliers' products as possible, as all costs are shared in cost plus contracts until the point at which the Sears product is differentiated from the manufacturers' product. From this point on Sears starts to absorb all the costs for its product line.

Most Sears products have a 15 percent to 20 percent cost advantage over the manufacturer's product, because it costs the manufacturer at least that much more than Sears to distribute, market, sell, and service their product. While Sears can spread its distribution, warehousing, advertising, and selling costs across its entire retail product offerings, the manufacturer has far more limited economies of scale and, perhaps more important, has less expertise in retailing.

> We use this cost advantage to either put some of it back into product design or we use it to be more price competitive. For example, we recently made some design improvements in our washing machines by putting in an access panel on top of the machine. Now for most repairs the serviceman only has to open the panel instead of having to turn the machine around. This saves eight minutes of a service call, and we have about a thousand service men working an average of eight calls a day. We are continuously trying to take the costs out of this business. We want to be the residual legatee of the appliance business.

Marketing and Sales

Sears looks upon the major home appliance marketplace as "a bell-shaped curve" according to one of the national merchandising managers:

> Ten percent of each end is not our market, it's the remaining 80 percent that we consider our major marketplace. We are number 3 in brown goods but number 1 in white goods. (The number 1 and number 2 in brown goods—RCA and Zenith—were not willing to sell to Sears, "the way we like to buy".)

At the retail level 85 percent of the appliance sales are made directly at the stores, and 15 percent are through catalog sales. However, these catalog sales are made through small outlets where the models are displayed, so the customer can look at both the catalog and the merchandise before ordering.

There are two forces that are critical to their market share leadership

> our drawing power and selling power. Drawing power is the percent of people who shop our brand. Selling power is the percent of people who buy our brand, as a percent of those who were drawn to our brand. The

key to achieving significant drawing power is advertising and price, while the key to selling power is the ability of the sales force to sell.

This is a very advertising-sensitive market, and we have found in market after market that the biggest advertiser is often the market share leader. There is a direct correlation between advertising spending and market share vis-à-vis each of the competitors.

But Sears's main advantage is that we have a highly trained sales force of product specialists who know their products and have a strong incentive to sell. Moreover we have a wide range of well-organized and orderly price point increases.

For contract sales Sears has a separate marketing effort concentrating on the builder market. The importance of this market to Sears is the volume, which contributes to higher economies of scale (for example, it was estimated that in 1981 contract sales volume lowered the overall cost of manufacturing and as a result the cost of all refrigerators was reduced $3.75 per unit). Though it is not a leader in the contract market Sears had two things going for them. One, the Sears name and service capabilities and, two, the ability to provide the builder with a total package that nobody else could: appliances, sinks, tubs, carpets, other home improvements, and furnishings.

Service Network

The capability of providing service and repair for the appliances sold is a key factor in developing consumer loyalty. Sears is the only retailer and one of the only three appliance sellers to own its service network (the other two being GE and Whirlpool). This control over one's own service network contributed a great deal to Sears's leadership position and also has discouraged other retailers from getting into appliances.

> The great advantage of having your own service network is that every time a serviceman enters your home, he is a silent salesman. In the eyes of the housewife he is a very credible source and thus can greatly influence future buying decisions while repairing or servicing the appliance. This makes him quite an important cog in the wheel of building the replacement market for Sears.

Prospects for the Future

With J. C. Penney's recent decision to leave the major home appliance marketplace, Sears occupies a unique position as the only retailer with such tremendous influence in the industry. Surveying Sears's position as the residual legatee, a senior executive explained:

> What is meant by being the residual legatee? Sears is committed to the appliance business like no other national retailer. Penney's could no longer

afford to remain in appliances. In a major strategic move, they decided to concentrate on soft goods and get out of products that are Sears's strengths—automotive, home improvement, and major home appliances. Ward's are deflating their thrust in home appliances.

Sears, on the other hand, features home appliances very strongly. If you will go into any of our "stores of the future," you will find the finest presentation of home appliance products anywhere. For us there is no national competition; there is only local competition like Lechmere in Boston or Polk Brothers in Chicago or local dealers, many of whom have a high turnover.

GE has always thought of Sears as their major competition, but their real competitor is going to be Whirlpool. Besides, GE is at the mercy of its local dealers, and the local dealers sell a mix of products. Nobody controls its sales like Sears does.

Montgomery Ward has recently started buying from Maytag. But they are not using Maytag as a private brand. Instead they are using the Maytag brand to draw people into their stores so that they can then sell them Ward's own lower priced private brand products, as frequently their Maytag prices are not locally competitive.

This is a mature business, and the industry in 1983 was functioning between 65 percent and 70 percent capacity. If there is any market share change it will be the big guys who will take away from the smaller ones. After Sears, GE, and Whirlpool, there really is no full-line name of any significance.

White does not make a single product under its own name, and that is their major problem. Presently McKinsey & Co. are doing a major strategy study for them. Magic Chef meanwhile faces financial problems.

Maytag, though quite profitable so far, is now attempting to become full line. They have gone into dishwashers and ranges, but they are going to have problems finding distributors, because their present distributors and dealers are already handling KitchenAid or Amana or some other line.

Raytheon still is not full line and could be a candidate to purchase KitchenAid but will still have problems at the service end because they provide service through independent contractors.

So there still is more settling in the industry to happen. It probably will be like the automobile industry with the "Big Three" remaining, with the other small companies like American Motors and others just struggling to get along.

Competitive Positioning in the Dishwasher Industry (D)

General Electric (GE)

General Electric, which neglected its major-appliance business from 1978 to 1981 while it debated about whether to be in appliances at all, is gunning to reassert itself. . . . Now that it has decided to stay in the appliance business, GE strikes terror in the hearts of smaller players. Its dishwashers and microwave ovens are nudging their way to big market shares in the two fastest-growing segments of the industry. (*Fortune,* July 25, 1983.)

Early Background[1]

GE entered the appliance field in 1918 with the acquisition of Hotpoint. Hotpoint, which produced and marketed irons and ranges, operated as a separate division and constituted GE's sole effort to that time in the appliance field. Hotpoint's business grew rapidly through the 1920s. In the 1930s with the advent of the electric refrigerator, GE introduced its own appliance brand. Gradually during the 1930s and after the war, the GE and Hotpoint lines expanded independently and began to compete with one another. Independent development continued through the 1950s under GE's decentralized organization structure although the two appliance divisions were formally merged in 1952.

---

[1] This section is from HBS cases, "Note on the Major Home Appliance Industry" (372–349) and "Associated Electrical Manufacturers" (372–344).

Copyright © 1984 by the President and Fellows of Harvard College
Harvard Business School case 385–048

In the 1950s GE adopted a policy of building capacity ahead of demand. Construction of the vast Louisville manufacturing facility was the result. The goal seemed to be to achieve high market share and attendant scale manufacturing economies. Low unit production costs thus attained later gave GE a distinct competitive advantage in the increasingly price-sensitive appliance industry. This advantage was not shared as fully by the Hotpoint line which maintained separate and more modest production facilities into the 1960s.

In the 1960s development of the appliance business took a back seat at GE to three new capital-intensive businesses: computers, breeder reactors, and heavy jet aircraft engines. However, 1965 did see the merger of Hotpoint and GE production facilities.

As GE entered the 1970s the appliance business again moved to the forefront as a potential money-maker in the wake of disappointments and even some outright failures in three glamour businesses in the 1960s. Organizationally, GE integrated Hotpoint and GE appliance lines into one centrally coordinated appliance group. This merely gave official recognition to the informal working arrangements followed since the merger of production facilities in 1965.

In the 1970s GE strove for maximum coverage in the marketplace with three product brands—GE, Hotpoint, and Penncrest (made for J. C. Penney). With these three brands, they believed they could cover the major market segments. In the retail market GE was able to get its products into more stores with three brands than they could with one. The GE brand had a larger number of models, which were higher featured–higher priced than the Hotpoint brand models. The Penncrest brand was the private-label brand for Penney's. As one Hotpoint executive explained: "We needed volume, and Sears's success suggested that this area would give us volume. We could go after the Penney's account without substantial risk to our brand image."

GE believed its biggest competitor was not any of the other appliance manufacturers, but Sears. According to a senior GE executive:

> Sears has the advantage of directly controlling retail price and advertising as well as their salesmen. This allows Sears to advertise low-feature/low-price products and then sell the customer up to more expensive items. Along with the traffic a Sears store generates Sears will get a chance to sell to most classes of purchasers. We want to maximize coverage so that we get a shot at them also. By being in most of the important retail appliance stores and by selling through Penney's we feel we will get a chance to sell our products.

The other major thrust of GE's appliance strategy was in the contract (new construction) segment of the appliance market. Here the GE brand and reputation for innovation were a tremendous asset in competing for the business of home builders. Manufacturing and distribution muscle also helped in fighting for share in this highly price-sensitive market. With Sears absent, both the GE and Hotpoint brands had achieved important market positions. As one of the executives described GE's strength in 1971:

> We have now and have had since the very beginning good relations with the big builders. This not only has educated us to their needs but also guarantees us a good chance to sell to the largest part of the market. We have a strong brand image which is very important for the builders. We have a very fine logistic system and can provide reliable service. Finally, we are the volume producer—an important advantage in a highly competitive industry.
>
> In this market Sears is not an important threat as of now, and because of its poor brand image we do not anticipate it becoming one in the near future. In this market segment we feel confident that we can grow and grow profitably.

To this the group executive added:

> If the growth over the next decade in the appliance industry is going to come up from the contract market segment, then our success as a group is highly dependent on our success in this market.

Summarizing what most executives felt to be GE's prime weakness—lack of control over retail salesmen, advertising, and price—one GE executive commented:

> The main area where we are at a disadvantage is in direct control over retail strategy. We just can't do what Sears can do. Even if we wanted to forward integrate we wouldn't have the talent to make the move successfully. We just don't have retail skills.

In the early 1970s the strategic planning system at GE had been completely revised, and the strategic planners for the appliance group had, after careful consideration, prepared two growth strategies for the next decade. The first was the conservative position, where the goal was to grow by 75 percent in terms of unit volume over the next decade. This was the rate at which they expected the industry to grow, and hence in this scenario GE would maintain its market share. The second strategy was more ambitious, as its goal was to grow faster than the industry and increase market share in several product categories.

Either alternative entailed a significant increase in manufacturing capacity, with a capital investment of several hundred million dollars. So the only real choice was whether to continue this expansion on a normal or an accelerated basis, as the commitment to expansion had already been made. This was to be a repeat of the successful strategy followed by GE after World War II, when they had decided to build capacity ahead of demand. Their goal was to achieve high market share by becoming the most efficient producer. This meant achieving economies of scale in manufacturing. Hence GE decided to build another huge appliance manufacturing complex similar to the one in Louisville—this time in Columbia, Maryland. It was to be called "Appliance Park East"; however, it never became fully operational.

Manufacturing Base

The Louisville appliance park when built was considered by GE to be the largest, most efficient appliance facility in the world. In contrast, their major manufacturing competitors—Whirlpool and White—had acquired their plants which were geographically scattered. Moreover, GE was the most vertically integrated. It had integrated backwards into various components—compressors, plastic moulding, wiring harnesses, electronic controls, and so forth, and had integrated forward into distribution, sales, and service. However, the twin strategies of economies of scale and vertical integration seemed to require a high capacity utilization to result in least cost production. But instead, according to an industry executive well versed in plant functions, the Louisville complex was suffering from diseconomies of scale. He believed that the difference between an 85 percent capacity operation and a 50 percent capacity operation would amount to a 20 percent increase in labor and overhead costs on a per unit basis. The next thing he felt one has to recognize is that there are almost no economies of scale in purchasing that would not be available to most of the appliance manufacturers.

He added that even at the theoretically optimum utilization, there were trade-offs between large plants and smaller plants that were often not recognized. In coming down to half the plant size from the minimum efficient scale one would not incur that big a penalty—a 5–10 percent theoretical cost efficiency—but this would be more than compensated for in having a more manageable plant, less chances of unionization, more flexible work practices, higher productivity of all workers, and even better quality control. A GE executive admitted: "We would not build another Louisville-size plant."

As for multiplant locations he said:

> There are relatively negligible economies of scale, once you are past full carload shipments. Ideally there would be separate plants located centrally around the country, specializing in one product type.

As for the threat from Japanese manufacturers, one of the GE executives who had just returned from a trip to Japan commented:

> There is no secret to having a world class manufacturing plant. It's just that the United States made a big mistake of letting their plants get 30 years old. Japanese plants are now state-of-the-art. They have power and free system on their lines, all foot pedals instead of hand controls, automatic

screwdrivers, and so forth, and moreover they devote 25 percent of their assembly line for testing.

He felt that the reason the Japanese had made an entry into small refrigerators is because "the domestic manufacturers have left a window open in the small-size, high-feature niche of the market." He felt that they had a much easier entry in microwave ovens than they would have in larger appliances because "in major appliances one winds up paying shipping costs for transporting cubic feet of air." He believed that their main thrust would be in the area of electronic components. "The Japanese content of U.S. appliances will grow as components can be shipped efficiently. Also, Korean manufacturers [of components] will become important."

Under this backdrop GE in the early 1980s moved toward a strategy of more outside sourcing and away from vertical integration, especially for the electronic components in microwave ovens. GE had divested itself of the disposers business and would be sourcing them from outside in order to maintain its full-line posture. They had also divested themselves of the central air conditioning business in order to focus on their other major home appliances. Their investment priorities were to be in dishwashers and microwave ovens, with dishwashers being the area of major focus. The thrust in dishwashers was twofold: "First, to achieve the highest level of automation in the factory and, second, to make a major switch to a plastic tub." According to a GE executive:

> In the dishwasher market the key requirements are: reliability, cost, noise, wash performance, and energy use. Since dishwashers are a water-bearing product plastics are definitely superior from a corrosion, cost, and noise viewpoint. The major hurdle for every manufacturer has been to make the plastic more durable. This is where we made the R&D investment. Our biggest competitor, D&M, is making a major investment in the powder porcelain process and is staying with porcelain tubs. Whirlpool, on the other hand, is going partially plastic with their doors.

Structure and Strategy

To implement their strategy of growth and in keeping with GE's philosophy of decentralization, the appliance group was reorganized in 1970. The most important change then was the elimination of separate sales divisions for GE and Hotpoint and, instead, the setting up of separate sales divisions for retail and contract to emphasize the importance of the latter. Also a staff function for strategic planning was added. The four major product divisions—Air Conditioning, Refrigerators, Home Laundry, and Kitchen Appliances—continued as profit centers.

Ten years later in what industry observers considered a major revamping, GE decided to centralize and cut back its organization structure. The individual profit centers which by 1981 had grown to six (Kitchen

Appliances was split into Ranges and Dishwashers, and Compressors was added) ceased to exist. Instead all manufacturing, marketing, sales, and technology were centralized by function. Paul Van Orden, the executive vice president in charge of the Consumer Products Sector and to whom the Home Appliance Group reported, put it this way:[2]

> What we have encountered has been three tough years. . . . In response we have restructured several of our businesses internally. . . . As the consumer business went through its growth phase, there was a tendency to keep adding structure. We did it, and we weren't the only ones. . . .
>
> We were structured by product category. We've now recognized that major appliances are essentially one business . . . and we've reorganized along functional lines. . . . Our major appliance group has gone through some organizational turmoil . . . but Roger Schipke has a strong group of people.

This organization turmoil Van Orden referred to was most likely the matrix organization structure that preceded the centralization structure. One veteran GE executive, commenting on the matrix organization, felt "it was a disastrous experiment. It was the worst possible form of organization. It had great problems." This was also the period when GE was totally enamored by strategic planning and developed the Strategic Business Unit (SBU) concept. As reported in the *New York Times* Reginald Jones, then GE's chairman, explained:[3]

> We couldn't plan for refrigerators independently of ranges. So we superimposed over the organizational structure a strategic planning structure of SBUs—single departments or several as long as they were unique from a planning point of view. . . . That's what strategic planning is all about: How you allocate resources for optimum growth.

The *New York Times* went on to note:

> The GE way is to assign different priorities to different SBUs forming a matrix of enterprises, some of which are always weaning, and some of which are always nurturing. The budget reflects these priorities. The result, theoretically at least, is continued growth with steady profits.
>
> GE categorizes all its SBUs into one of four classifications which the SBUs, in turn, use to categorize each of their individual product lines. First come "invest/grow" businesses. . . . Then there are "selectivity/ grow" and "selectivity/earnings" businesses. . . . Finally, there are "harvest/divest" businesses. . . .
>
> To all this Mr. Jones has now added yet another layer of strategic planning. He has grouped the SBUs with five broad "sectors" that amount to super SBUs.

---

[2] "GE: Tough Times, Tough Decisions," *Home Furnishings Daily,* February 14, 1983.

[3] Anthony J. Parisi, "Management: GE's Search for Synergy," *New York Times,* April 16, 1978.

The Major Appliance SBU was a part of the Consumer Products Sector. (The other SBUs in the sector were Lighting Products, Houseware and Audio Products, Room Air Conditioners, Television Receivers, and Broadcasting and Cablevision.) Heading up the Major Appliance SBU was Roger Schipke who formerly was the general manager of the laundry and dishwasher product division.

With the major home appliance plants operating at 50 percent capacity, the future outlook of the industry a little uncertain, and Jack Welch's well-publicized management philosophy—of not wanting to remain in a business where GE is not, nor has prospects of becoming, number 1 or number 2—looming in the background, the centralized organization structure reflected the appliance division's new priorities. As Paul Van Orden, executive vice president Consumer Products sector, put it:[4]

> If you are going to be a significant factor you are going to have to cut costs and take away business from the others. . . . In the hard goods business you have to be careful that you don't get too wrapped up in the product engineering and manufacturing processes and neglect the consumer. . . . We also want to pay more attention to the retail structure and product positioning.

Comeback in the Marketplace

The major challenge facing GE in 1982, as stated by a product management executive, is "how to achieve better capacity utilization." The way they hoped to achieve this was through a two-pronged approach: "First, increase volume. Second, rationalize the factories."

In the late 1970s and early 1980s the housing market took a real downturn, and GE's strength became its vulnerability. Historically the appliance market had been retail 70 percent and contract 30 percent, with GE's mix being retail 60 percent and contract 40 percent. By 1981 the contract market was down to 20 percent of the total and GE was hurting badly. An industry publication reported:[5]

> General Electric's major-appliance sales were the "biggest difficulty" in the firm's consumer products sector last year, according to GE chairman John Welch. "We were hit perhaps harder than anyone else in the industry as a result of our strong contract position and the downturn in housing completion," Welch said recently. "It was a tough year for GE in the appliance business, and we lost a point or two of market share as a result of the relative weakness in the contract vs. retail segments."

On the retail side, too, there were troubles, as Penney's, which was GE's largest customer, decided in 1982 to get out of selling major appli-

---

[4] "GE: Tough Times, Tough Decisions," *Home Furnishings Daily,* February 14, 1983.

[5] "Newswatch," *Mart,* February 1982.

ances as a result of a strategic shift in their merchandising policy. In November 1982 looking back on what went wrong over the past decade, one of the general managers for product management at GE appliance division said:

> During the peak years of the mid-1970s some significant errors were made in projecting the growth of the industry. First, the projections on housing starts were way too high. Second, too much importance was put on the "keeping up with the Joneses" factor; instead, the replacement cycles have stretched out significantly further than projected with a 40 percent rate of do-it-yourself repairs. While the corrosion factor in dishwashers and laundry washers reduced their life, there is very little that breaks down in refrigerators and ranges, so there is no definite "have to replace in" number of years. Third, the projections were made on a straight line trend of the past basis rather than on a saturation basis.

One of the general managers for the plants commented:

> Having a correct perception of the market is of great significance. The market has contracted, and the critical issue is how grossly people misforecasted the market. There is a dramatic difference between where people perceived the market would be and where it finally ended up. We were late in facing up to the realities of the situation.

According to *Business Week*[6] it was more than just poor forecasting:

> Far more pervasive, however, has been the effect of bottom-line pressure on the quality of many of its consumer products. GE spending decisions for several years have clearly underlined the cash-cow status of that sector. In 1976, for example, consumer products contributed 22 percent of GE's net income while receiving only 12 percent of the company's $740.4 million capital budget for new plant and equipment.
>
> CEO Welch conceded that the drop in quality was reflected in a loss in consumer approval.
>
> Welch has wrestled with this problem since 1977, when he first took over management of consumer products. His most ambitious program to date is under way right now at a dishwasher manufacturing plant in Louisville. There, GE is investing $38.6 million to create a new showcase factory for use as a model for other GE appliance operations. The object is to build the premier quality dishwasher in the United States at a reasonable price—not only by giving workers the latest tools and technology but also by allowing workers to stop the line at key points to prevent defects from being built in. GE's program emphasized dishwashers.
>
> The new plan envisions making GE's Building 3, already the largest dishwasher plant in the world, the most modern facility as well by 1983. About 60 percent of the current equipment will be replaced with more sophisticated machines and automated assembly systems.

---

[6] "Corporate Strategies: General Electric—The Financial Wizards Switch Back to Technology," *Business Week,* March 16, 1981.

But management hinted that as much as $1 billion might be invested in the next decade. Already the appliance group accounted for half of the industrial robots in the company.

As major manufacturers such as Westinghouse, GM, and Rockwell International sold their appliance businesses, GE gained share. But GE's dishwasher line dropped to 18 percent in 1980 from its 26 percent share in 1974, and its washing machines dropped to 16 percent of the market from their 18 percent share. "A consumer punch in the eye," Welch notes, "does not go away for maybe a decade." Moreover, he adds, if quality is not improved, "we will not be a major factor in the appliance business in the mid-1980s."

By early 1983 GE appeared to be on the brink of a comeback as it heralded its modernized dishwasher plant as the most technologically advanced dishwasher manufacturing system in the world. In rebuilding this plant it may have signaled a new trend for U.S. manufacturing. As an industry publication reported[7]:

It all began about four years ago—the work culminated in Project C, the remodernization of General Electric's dishwasher plant in Louisville, Kentucky. "We had two objectives," says Raymond L. Rissler, manager, Project C programs operation. "Our first was to build a better product—one that could be produced with consistent high quality, hour after hour, day after day. And second, to build the product better—to provide a method of manufacture that would enable it to be built at a high rate of productivity with a substantial gain over traditional approaches. The concepts we applied to meet these objectives began with a focused factory—focused on the manufacture of Perma-Tuf built-in dishwashers.". . .

"The first thing we did was change our organization," said Schipke, "we made our structure leaner, more agile. Not the usual pruning, but a complete turnaround. Then we turned to technology. Instead of applying technology for technology's sake we went after low cost and high quality with products that were right for today's consumer. Then we rebuilt the manufacturing system while production continued. Last year we produced over 600,000 dishwashers while the plant was being remodernized.". . .

In 1977–78 management began to become more aware of automation, particularly in Japan. "A number of us visited leading companies in Japan and began to give more thought to the need for concurrent product and process design so we could come out winning on all objectives," said Rissler. "We began some information exchange with some Japanese firms, taking a priority view of it. . . . We borrowed films from Japanese firms; one showed a line that makes washer motors. Only two people work on the line—one a step-up man and the other a quality auditor.". . .

"When I returned from Japan in 1981," says Moeller, "I was convinced that we had to make major changes in the way we assemble products if we were going to be a world-class competitor. This modernized plant was

---

[7] James Stevens, "Forging the Focused Factory," *Appliance,* June 1983.

to be a role model. We set our sights very high and were willing to take risks! We had very high expectations for the people, the product, and the process . . . and, believe me, we achieved them."

To make sure that it would not lose in the marketplace the gains it was making at the plant, GE demonstrated that it was just as willing to learn from its competitors as it was willing to learn from the Japanese. A major business publication reported:[8]

> General Electric, which has not been particularly responsive to dealers, is now following Whirlpool's lead and beefing up its dealer support systems. Says one security analyst, "GE made a study of everything Whirlpool was doing right and copied it."
>
> This year GE will give up its single-brand status, having won contracts to make dishwashers for Magic Chef and Tappan under their brand names. GE has stopped Maytag's growth in dishwashers and is even threatening KitchenAid: the last rating of dishwashers by *Consumer Reports* back in 1980 gave the GE model higher marks, and GE has been feasting on that rave review ever since.

However important these gains were for GE, the bigger opportunity was to get some of Sears's business, which in the past might have been unthinkable. Sears was currently in the process of evaluating all the dishwasher manufacturers and had even approached GE. Roger Schipke believed GE not only had the most advanced product but a new philosophy to go with it:

> The GE challenge is to enter the private-label arena more strongly than in the past. This objective combined with a philosophic change that recognized Sears as a *customer,* and not a competitor, led to the opening of discussion with them on several products.

---

[8] Lisa Miller Mesdag, "The Appliance Boom Begins," *Fortune,* July 25, 1983.

Competitive Positioning in the Dishwasher Industry (E)

Sears's Dishwasher Dilemma

By mid-1983 though Sears was in a commanding position in its home appliance business, there was one area where they felt they might be vulnerable. It was the dishwasher product line. As part of a major companywide reorganization, Sears's top management had decided to move dishwashers and compactors from the Building Materials group to the Home Appliance group. Though the formal organization change was to be effective January 1, 1984, to all intents and purposes the shift in responsibility had already occurred.

Sears bought 100 percent of its dishwasher products from Design and Manufacturing (D&M), which was still privately owned, and had done so ever since Sam Regenstrief founded D&M. However, for the past 10 years there had been a steadily increasing concern at Sears on what would happen to D&M after Sam Regenstrief. Thus Sears found itself in a dilemma. One important component of Sears's sourcing strategy was to ensure that its suppliers have stable top management over a long term, and one-man shows were always a big concern. On the other hand the success of Sears's merchandising strategy was based on buying from the lowest cost producer, who would meet acceptable quality standards and specifications.

Copyright © 1984 by the President and Fellows of Harvard College
Harvard Business School case 385–049

> Over the years we had many discussions at Sears to consider whether we should have other sources, but it always comes down to the fact that because of D&M's cost position, it does not make economic sense to go anywhere else. Sam was one of the outstanding small entrepreneurs in this country. He was extremely innovative and cost conscious, and he had one thought in mind—to make a very good dishwasher at low cost.

In the past five years the leadership situation at D&M had become Sears's primary concern, especially after Sam Regenstrief began to suffer health problems around 1978. This meant he had to turn the reins over to someone else, though he retained ownership control of the company. He chose as his successor his nephew-in-law, Marvin Silberman, who had worked at D&M. When Silberman left the company he was replaced by Lee Burke, 67, who was one of Sam's long-time trusted lieutenants. The day-to-day operations were managed by Lee Burke.

Eighty to 85 percent of D&M stock is owned by the Regenstrief Foundation, whose board consists of Sam, his wife, and some of Sam's friends. (The Regenstriefs have no children.) The foundation is engaged primarily in medical research in conjunction with Indiana University.

Another concern that Sears had from time to time about D&M was in the area of product quality. As D&M's volume with Sears and its overall market share grew over the years, they seemed to have a constant problem of monitoring their quality. In the mid-1970s Sears had to have an extensive product recall of its dishwashers because of a wiring defect. According to a Sears executive:

> D&M through Lee Burke seems to have rededicated itself to quality in the last few years, and as a result their quality has vastly improved. But this has also increased their costs.

Because of Sears's lead position in the dishwasher consumer market, a third area of concern for Sears was GE's significant investment in the dishwasher product and manufacturing process. GE was the only manufacturer to come out with a plastic tub and had invested $38 million in modernizing their dishwasher plant with robotics and other state-of-the-art technology. Historically, dishwashers were loaded from the top into a porcelain tub inside. D&M was the first to come out with a front-loading dishwasher which the other manufacturers soon followed. Just prior to the oil crunch of 1974–75, GE started experimenting with the plastic tub which tested out successfully, and so they began phasing out of porcelain and getting into plastics for their tubs and door liners on all their models. D&M remained with porcelain though it improved its technology to go to a powder-coated porcelain product (see Exhibit 1). Whirlpool, too, remained with porcelain for its tub but went with plastics for its door liner.

In the plastics versus porcelain debate both materials had their pros and cons though it seemed porcelain was quite meaningful to the consumer. According to an industry expert:

> From the customer's viewpoint our research shows that white porcelain has always represented high quality and comes out ahead of plastic, especially for the tub; for the door liner, the plastic is fine and well accepted. Not only does the porcelain tub have a higher aesthetic value in appearance it can also last longer. However, it has one major problem: unlike plastic, it is prone to developing nicks (due to contact with dropped metal utensils) which then start to rust. So, with plastics, even though it stains over the years you can put a 10-year guarantee, which you cannot put on porcelain. GE has a unique advantage, and today it would be rather prohibitive for any other manufacturer to convert totally to plastics.

By the beginning of 1981 Sears decided that no longer could they jeopardize their future in the dishwasher product line with a business-as-usual approach:

> For the first time we decided that we better go out and look over the entire dishwasher industry with a fresh perspective, and so we decided to visit the various manufacturers: KitchenAid, Maytag, White Consolidated, Whirlpool, and GE. After some initial discussions the first three companies were out of the running. And so it came down to Whirlpool and GE, both being acceptable manufacturers. Now it was up to Sears decision makers to decide whether we should be taking on a secondary supplier to D&M, or even making one of them our primary supplier. Because of unusual circumstances this decision has taken a long time.

One member of the decision-making group who would be responsible for this decision described his dilemma:

> You have to really understand our history of relationships with these three companies (D&M, Whirlpool, and GE) to appreciate how tough this decision is.
>
> GE had always looked at Sears as an intense competitor. To them, selling to Sears was just not compatible. The policy at GE was that the GE product would only carry the GE name, and so even what they made for Penney's was made by Hotpoint.
>
> GE today has a different attitude in doing business with Sears than they had even a few years ago. Now they are looking at us as a customer and for the past six months have been bidding for our business with an eagerness that we never expected. Our buyers have made several trips to the GE plant, and they are really impressed with their modernized plant which is by far the most advanced of any. More important, they found the people at GE much more open to satisfying our needs, and their costing is in line, too. Additionally, at our testing laboratory, where our engineers test models that they randomly buy from retail outlets, they approved the GE model, so now they even have a very satisfactory, quality product, which was not true for their older products. What has happened almost overnight is the beginning of a new relationship between GE and Sears.

The folks in Louisville [GE's appliance division headquarters] are going to be disappointed if they don't get at least some of Sears's business.

Now Whirlpool, as you know, has been doing business with us—the Sears way—for decades, so the working bond between the two organizations is very strong, which is an important factor. For many years Whirlpool has been interested in Sears's dishwasher business and presented various models, though none of them was good enough for us. It was not until Sears started to look at GE and others that Whirlpool realized that Sears would be amenable, so they became conscious of a better featured, lower cost private brand for Sears. They have put emphasis on quality, and as for their costing, it is comparable to GE. You really don't know the true costs, anyway, for the first couple of years of doing business together, until things settle down. So a lot depends on the product. Whirlpool has been working on a product with the self-cleaning filtering system which they claim is superior.[1]

There is no question it would be very hard for Sears to pull back from D&M after all these years. As you know, Sears is very loyal to its suppliers, and we have all the confidence in D&M. But who is there after Lee Burke? More important, is D&M going to be able to match Whirlpool and GE in R&D investments? Though D&M hesitated at first, when they fully grasped that we were seriously looking around, they put in an extra effort on quality and material cost-effectiveness. But they are still behind on development of product innovation, features, and so forth. I am told our people have been telling D&M for many years to invest in improving product quality and features, and we have even gone so far as to offer to pay more for a higher caliber product. But Sam had his philosophy, which was: "I pay my people top money to make a quality product. I don't need to build up my overhead." There is no question that D&M is still the lowest cost producer and that their quality is not only acceptable but has improved recently.

Our marketing people tell us that in the 1980s, dishwasher sales will grow faster than any other appliance, and they want something with a little more pizzazz and quality, especially at the top of the line.[2]

In the effort to evaluate all possibilities, the Sears's buyers even looked beyond the United States. One of them commented:

---

[1] Both Whirlpool and GE have a filtering system that reuses the water, while D&M has a direct flush-out system. In the past, dishwashers used up to eight water changes; however, with the emphasis on energy conservation, many manufacturers have got it down to four water changes. The main advantage of a reusable water system is not in the saving of water but in the saving of energy that goes to heat the water.

[2] The Sears dishwasher line consisted of 15 models as follows:

— Six 24″ under-the-counter models.
— Three 18″ under-the-counter models.
— Three 24″ portable models.
— Three 18″ portable models.

The very top of the line would be the most feature-laden, 24″ under-the counter model, followed by the 18″ under-the-counter model.

We feel that some day someone is going to come up with a totally new system to clean dishes. We went to Switzerland to look at the "Ultrasonic" system, which cleans dishes with high-speed sound waves. But at this point it is too expensive and not feasible for us.

Since both GE and Whirlpool had made it a high priority to win some of Sears's dishwasher business, top management from both the companies were involved in pitching for the account. Recognizing the high sensitivity of their decision, the Sears buyers reiterated what they have always expected from their suppliers:

We have to be very conscious of our customers' desire for top quality but at an affordable price. The price-value trade-off is still the number 1 motivation. In the final analysis, who gets how much of our business depends a great deal on who earns it in this arena.

Exhibit 1

Dishwasher

	1970	1976	1982
KitchenAid		Redesigned tub & door	
Maytag	Introduced first dishwasher	Redesigned cost reduced	
D&M	18″ dishwashers	Electronics Powdered porcelain	
Whirlpool	Silverware on door	Plastic door	Electronics
WCI	Purchased Westinghouse design		Electronics
General Electric	P/T 'A'	P/T 'B'	Electronic GSD2500

The Company and Its Strategists: Relating Corporate Strategy to Personal Values

Up to this point we have argued that an awareness of purpose and a sense of direction strengthen a company's ability to survive in changing circumstances. We have seen, to be sure, the difficulties of understanding clearly both a company's circumstances and its strengths and weaknesses. The action implied by these difficulties is an objective and alert surveillance of the environment for threats and opportunities and a detached appraisal of organizational characteristics in order to identify distinctive competence. We have considered the suitable combination of a company's strengths and its opportunities to be a logical exercise characterized by perhaps not precise but reasoned, well-informed choices of alternatives assuring the highest possible profit. We have been examining the changing relationship of company and environment almost as if a purely economic strategy, uncontaminated by the personality or goals of the decision maker, were possible.

Strategy as Projection of Preference

We must acknowledge at this point that there is no way to divorce the decision determining the most sensible economic strategy for a company from the personal values of those who make the choice. Executives in charge of company destinies do not look exclusively at what a company might do and can do. In apparent disregard of the second of these considerations, they sometimes seem heavily influenced by what they personally *want* to do.

We are ourselves not aware of how much desire affects our own choice of alternatives, but we can see it in others. In the 1950s George

393

Romney, then president of American Motors, began a dramatic promotion of economic sensible transportation which might have early developed the market for small cars later sensationally exploited by the Japanese. After the solvency of his company was assured he preferred to repay every dollar of debt to investing in research and development of variations in the small car that might have retained leadership in even then a growing segment of the market. Almost certainly we see reflected here the higher value Romney placed on economy than on consumer preferences, on liquidity over debt, and other values derived more from his character and religious upbringing than from an objective monitoring of the best course for American Motors to follow. Romney's successors, with less distinctive personal values, reverted to the General Motors big-car strategy.[1]

Frank Farwell came from IBM to the presidency of Underwood in 1955, it has been reported, saying that he would be damned if he would spend his life peddling adding machines and typewriters. This aversion may explain why Underwood plunged into the computer business without the technical, financial, or marketing resources necessary to succeed in it. Similarly, when Adriano Olivetti purchased control of Underwood after three days of hurried negotiations, he may well have been moved by his childhood memory of visiting Hartford and by the respect for the world's once leading manufacturer of typewriters that led his father to erect in Ivrea a replica of the red-brick, five-story Hartford plant.[2] That he wanted to purchase Underwood so badly may explain why he and his associates did not find out how dangerously it had decayed and how near bankruptcy it had been brought.

The three presidents of J. I. Case in the years 1953 and 1963 seem to have been displaying their own temperaments as they wracked the company with alternating expansionism and contraction far beyond the needs of response to a cyclical industry environment.[3] In all these cases the actions taken can be rationalized so as not to seem quite so personal as we have suggested they are.

The Inevitability of Values

We will be able to understand the strategic decision better if we admit rather than resist the dimension of preference. If we think back over

---

[1] See "American Motors," in Edmund P. Learned, C. Roland Christensen, Kenneth R. Andrews, and William D. Guth, *Business Policy: Text and Cases* (Homewood, Ill.: Richard D. Irwin, 1965), p. 103. This classic case is also available from Harvard Business School Case Services.

[2] See "Underwood-Olivetti (AR)," in Learned et al., *Business Policy: Text and Cases,* p. 212, and HBS Case Services, case 312–017.

[3] "J. I. Case Company," in Learned et al., *Business Policy,* pp. 82–102, and HBS Case Services, case 309–270.

the discussions of earlier cases in this book, the strategies we recommended for the companies probably reflected what *we* would have wanted to do had we been in charge of those companies. We told ourselves or assumed that our personal inclinations harmonized with the optimum combination of economic opportunity and company capability. The professional manager in a large company, drilled in analytical technique and the use of staff trained to subordinate value-laden assumptions to tables of numbers, may often prefer the optimal economic strategy because of its very suitability. Certain entrepreneurs, whose energy and personal drives far outweigh their formal training and self-awareness, set their course in directions not necessarily supported by logical appraisal. Such disparity appears most frequently in small privately held concerns or in companies built by successful and self-confident owner-managers. The phenomenon we are discussing, however, may appear in any company, especially if it is large, in its divisions.

Our problem now can be very simply stated. In examining the alternatives available to a company, we must henceforth take into consideration the preferences of the chief executive. Furthermore, we must also be concerned with the values of other key managers who must either contribute to or assent to the strategy if it is to be effective. Finally, at a higher level of sophistication, the strategy should appeal to all employees. Their detailed exposure to opportunity for superior implementation can contribute, under receptive leadership, to improved productivity and continuous adaptation to customer needs. Bureaucratic constraints and autocratic multilayered supervision often choke off the constructive by-products of the kind of enthusiastic cooperation that convergence of individual and corporate goals produces.

We therefore have three levels of reconciliation to consider—first, the divergence between the chief executive's preference and the strategic choice which seems most economically defensible; second, the conflict among several sets of managerial personal values which must be reconciled not only with an economic strategy but with each other; and third, the difference in motivation of management and the work force that must be transcended by participation in and acceptance of at least the organization components of the strategy.

Thus when Mr. Edgar Villchur, inventor of the acoustic suspension loudspeaker, founded Acoustic Research, Inc.,[4] in 1954, he institutionalized a desire to bring high-fidelity sound to the mass market at the lowest possible cost. He licensed his competitors freely and finally gave up his original patent rights altogether. He kept not only his prices but his dealer margins low, maintained for a considerable time a primitive production facility and an organization of friends rather than managers,

---

[4] "Acoustic Research, Inc.," in Learned et al., *Business Policy,* pp. 466–519, and HBS Case Services case 312–020.

and went to great lengths to make the company a good place to work, sharing with employees the company's success. The company was dominated by Mr. Villchur's desire to have a small organization characterized by academic, scientific, and intellectual rather than "commercial" values. Product development was driven by some of these values away from the acoustical technology which Mr. Villchur's personal competence would have suggested into development of record players, amplifiers, and tuners which were to offer less in superiority over competitive products than did his speakers. Again these were priced far below what might have been possible.

Mr. Abraham Hoffman, for years vice president and treasurer, had the task of trying to overcome his superior's reluctance to advertise, to admit the validity of the marketing function, and of maintaining the business as a profitable enterprise. That the company had succeeded in at long last developing and producing a music system of great value in relation to its cost and in winning the respect of the high-fidelity listener market does not alter the fact that the first determination of strategy came more from Mr. Villchur's antibusiness values than from an analytical balancing of opportunity and distinctive competence. The latter would have led, with perhaps much greater growth and profitability, into acoustical systems, public-address equipment, long-distance communications, hearing aids, noise suppression, and the like—all areas in which technical improvement in the quality of available sound is much needed.

We must remember, however, that it is out of Mr. Villchur's determination and goals that his company came into being in the first place. The extraordinary accomplishments of an antimarketing company in the marketplace are directly traceable to the determination to innovate in quality and price. The reconciliation between Mr. Villchur's values and Mr. Hoffman's more business-oriented determination to manage the company's growth more objectively occurred only when the company was sold to Teledyne, Mr. Villchur retired to his laboratory, and Mr. Hoffman became president. The quality achievements of this firm have been rewarded, but the economic potential of its strategy was for years unrealized.

We should in all realism admit that the personal desires, aspirations, and needs of the senior managers of a company actually *do* play an influential role in the determination of strategy. Against those who are offended by this idea either for its departure from the stereotype of single-minded economic man or for its implicit violation of responsibilities to the shareholder, we would argue that we must accept not only the inevitability but the desirability of this intervention. If we begin by saying that all strategic decisions must fall within the very broad limits of the manager's fiduciary responsibility to the owners of the business and perhaps to others in the management group, then we may proceed legitimately to the idea that what a manager wants to do is not out of order.

The conflict which often arises between what general managers want to do and what the dictates of economic strategy suggest they ought to do is best not denied or condemned. It should be accepted as a matter of course. In the study of organization behavior, we have long since concluded that the personal needs of the hourly worker must be taken seriously and at least partially satisfied as a means of securing the productive effort for which wages are paid. It should, then, come as no surprise to us that the president of the corporation also arrives at his work with his own needs and values, to say nothing of his relatively greater power to see that they are taken into account.

Reconciling Divergent Values

If we accept the inevitability of personal values in the strategic decision governing the character and course of a corporation, then we must turn to the skills required to reconcile the optimal economic strategy with the personal preferences of the executives of the company. There is no reason why a better balance could not have been struck in Acoustic Research without sacrifice to the genius of the founder or the quality of life in his company. It is first necessary to penetrate conventional rationalization and reticence to determine what these preferences are. For without this revelation, strategic proposals stemming from different unstated values come into conflict. This conflict cannot be reconciled by talking in terms of environmental data and corporate resources. The hidden agenda of corporate policy debates makes them endless and explains why so many companies do not have explicit, forthright, and usefully focused strategies.

To many caught up in the unresolved strategic questions in their own organizations, it seems futile even to attempt to reconcile a strategic alternative dictated by personal preference with other alternatives oriented toward capitalizing on opportunity to the greatest possible extent. In actuality, however, this additional complication poses fewer difficulties than at first appear. The analysis of opportunity and the appraisal of resources themselves often lead in different directions. To compose three, rather than two, divergent sets of considerations into a single pattern may increase the complexity of the task, but the integrating process is still the same. We can look for the dominant consideration and treat the others as constraints; we can probe the elements in conflict for the possibilities of reinterpretation or adjustment. We are not building a wall of irregular stone so much as balancing a mobile of elements, the motion of which is adjustable to the motion of the entire mobile.

As we have seen, external developments can be affected by company action and company resources, and internal competence can be developed. If worst comes to worst, it is better for a person to separate from a management whose values he or she does not share than to pretend agreement or to wonder why others think as they do. Howard Head, whose passionate dedication to the metal ski not only produced a most successful business but delayed unnecessarily its entry into plastic skis, realistically retired from his now diversified business and sold his holdings. It is not necessary, however, for all members of management to think alike or to have the same personal values, so long as strategic decision is not delayed or rendered ineffective by these known and accepted differences. Large gains are possible simply by raising the strategic issues for discussion by top management, by admitting the legitimacy of different preferences, and by explaining how superficial or fundamental the differences are.

Collision between a management-determined change in strategy and the organization that is charged with carrying it out is not a feasible subject for one-on-one discussion with everyone. We must deal now not with the personal preferences of individuals but with the culture that develops in organizations to establish certain values as dominant with unimportant variations left untouched. *Culture* has become a buzzword among consulting firms, especially as the importance of implementation has been recognized by those previously concerned with portfolio analysis, competitive strategy, and other logical or analytical approaches to strategy formulation.

Every organization develops an informal pattern of relationships in which authority is recognized and traditional ways of doing things evolve. Some organizations like Lincoln Electric, which prizes individual achievement and rewards it handsomely, are spare, no-nonsense, highly productive organizations more than holding their own against competition. Others, like Du Pont, become institutions in which research and development, safety, and corporate uniformity tend to homogenize scores of divisions in dozens of industries. This process makes them more culturally Du Pont than ready to succeed in the stringent rough and tumble of their own competitive environments. In many such instances an admirable history has produced a dominant culture that displaces the succession of strategic decisions that changes in the marketplace require. Rather than attempt a classification of cultures, we ask you to look at Head Ski and Crown Cork & Seal reflecting now on those elements of their culture which would be difficult to change, should your recommendations require such change. When you come to the NIKE cases, you should be well prepared for a searching inquiry into the interconnection of strategy and institutionalized values.

Modification of Values

The question whether individual values can actually be changed or corporate culture modified during the reconciliation process is somewhat less clear. A value is a view of life and a judgment of what is desirable that is very much a part of a person's personality and a group's morale. From parents, teachers, and peers, we are told by psychologists, we acquire basic values, which change somewhat with acquired knowledge, analytical ability, and self-awareness but remain a stable feature of personality. Nonetheless the preference attached to goals in concrete circumstances is not beyond influence. The physicist who leaves the university to work in a profit-making company because of a combined fondness for his work and material comfort, may ask to continue to do pure rather than applied research, but he presumably does not want his company to go bankrupt. The conflict in values is to some degree negotiable, once the reluctance to expose hidden agendas is overcome. Retaining the value orientation of the scientist, the ambivalent physicist might assent to a strategic alternative stressing product development rather than original investigation, at least for a specified time until the attainment of adequate profit made longer range research feasible.

The recent restructuring of American industry has forced drastic changes in the culture of organizations. Foreign competition has revealed that American wage rates are often uncompetitive in relation to productivity. The architects of hostile takeovers, looking to sell assets of target companies, identify and dispense with what they consider to be unproductive assets, divisions, jobs, and people. The staff sections of corporate headquarters, grown large in the attempt to give expert attention to everything that might well rather than must be done, have been slashed. Downsizing and consequent layoffs, painful as they are to contemplate, attract attention to the problem being addressed. Survivors, however demoralized, are energized by the struggle to survive and become aware of the need to develop new ways to get done what must be done. It is unfortunate in such instances that less drastic measures were not undertaken earlier. Strategic innovation is a practical alternative to violent restructuring.

Even so large a company as General Motors, in trouble not yet deep, is self-consciously restructuring itself for leadership in an industry changing in ways that make its previous organization structure, procurement, labor relations, and production methods obsolete. Du Pont is attempting to define its mission, adapt its culture-shaping policies to the conditions of the industries in which it participates, and differentiate its management style to suit the needs of subsidiaries. The merger of a large international oil company with its oil-field and market cultural characteristics has undoubtedly dramatized the decorum and stability of Du Pont. General Electric has recently radically reduced its corporate staff and assigned responsibility to its divisions to succeed on their own against their competitors rather than to view themselves as under the protection of the corporate monogram. A new kind of giant corporation is in the making.

That under adversity the culture of an organization and the values of its leaders can change has been recently established beyond doubt. Units divested dramatically from their corporate parents have often become more profitable and pleasant to work in as the burden of corporate allocations and compliance with corporate policy has been lifted. The opportunity wasted by our basic industries is that presented by this book. The conditions confronting the automobile, steel, chemical, textile, and footwear industries have been visible for years. The failure to adapt to change that had become clearly inevitable reflects the triumph of habit and short-term measurement of results over strategic assessment of company position in a changing world. The faltering of American industry, affected to be sure by forces other than managerial ineptness, is a dramatic background to the need to devise a strategy proof against a conservative culture suppressing innovation and adaptation.

Awareness of Values

Our interest in the role of personal values in strategic formulations should not be confined to assessing the influence of other people's values. Despite the well-known problems of introspection, we can probably do more to understand the relation of our own values to our choice of purpose than we can to change the values of others. Awareness that our own preference for an alternative opposed by another stems from values as much as from rational estimates of economic opportunity may have important consequences. First, it may make us more tolerant and less indignant when we perceive this relationship between recommendations and values in the formulations of others. Second, it will force us to consider how important it really is to us to maintain a particular value in making a particular decision. Third, it may give us insight with which to identify our biases and thus pave the way for a more objective assessment of all the strategic alternatives that are available. These consequences of self-examination will not end conflict, but they will at least prevent its unnecessary prolongation.

The object of this self-examination is not necessarily to endow us with the ability to persuade others to accept the strategic recommendations we consider best; it is to acquire insight into the problems of determining purpose and skill in the process of resolving them. Individuals inquiring into their own values for the purpose of understanding their own positions in policy debates can continue to assess their own personal opportunities, strengths and weaknesses, and basic values by means of the procedures outlined here. For a personal strategy, analytically considered and consciously developed, may be as useful to an individual as a corporate strategy is to a business institution. The effort, conducted by each individual, to formulate personal purpose might well accompany his or her contributions to organizational purpose. If the encounter leads to a clarification of the purposes one seeks, the values one holds, and the alternatives available, the attempt to make personal use of the concept of strategy will prove extremely worthwhile.

Introducing personal preference forces us to deal with the possibility that the strategic decision we prefer (identified after the most nearly objective analysis of opportunity and resources we are capable of) is not acceptable to other executives with different values. Their acceptance of the strategy is necessary to its successful implementation. In diagnosing this conflict, we try to identify the values implicit in our own choice. As we look at the gap between the strategy which follows from our own values and that which would be appropriate to the values of our associates, we look to see whether the difference is fundamental or superficial. Then we look to see how the strategy we believe best matches opportunity and resources can be adapted to accommodate the values of those who will implement it. Reconciliation of the three principal determinants of strategy which we have so far considered is often made possible by adjustment of any or all of the determinants.

The role of self-examination in coming to terms with a conflict in values over an important strategic determination is not to turn all strategic decisions into outcomes of consensus. Some organizations—you can see them in this book—are run by persons who are leaders in the sense that they have power and are not afraid to use it. It is true that business leaders, in Zaleznik's words, "commit themselves to a career in which they have to work on themselves as a condition for effective working with other people."[5] At the same time a leader must recognize that "the essence of leadership is choice, a singularly individualistic act in which a [person] assumes responsibility for a commitment to direct an organization along a particular path. . . . As much as a leader wishes to trust others, he has to judge the soundness and validity of his subordinates' positions. Otherwise, the leader may become a prisoner of the emotional commitments of his subordinates, frequently at the expense of making correct judgments about policies and strategies."[6]

When a management group is locked in disagreement the presence of power and the need for its exercise conditions the dialogue. There are circumstances when leadership must transcend disagreement that cannot be resolved by discussion. Subordinates, making the best of the inevitable, must accept a follower role. When leadership becomes irresponsible and dominates subordinate participation without reason, it is usually ineffective or is deposed. Participants in strategic disagreements must know not only their own needs and power but those of the chief

---

[5] Abraham Zaleznik and Manfred F. R. Kets de Vries, *Power and the Corporate Mind* (Boston: Houghton Mifflin, 1975), p. 207.

[6] Ibid., p. 209.

executive. Strategic planning, in the sense that power attached to values plays a role in it, is a political process.[7]

You should not warp your recommended strategy to the detriment of the company's future in order to adjust it to the personal values you hold or observe. On the other hand you should not expect to be able to impose without risk and without expectation of eventual vindication and agreement an unwelcome pattern of purposes and policies on the people in charge of a corporation or responsible for achieving results. Strategy is a human construction; it must in the long run be responsive to human needs. It must ultimately inspire commitment. It must stir an organization to successful striving against competition. People have to have their hearts in it.

---

[7] See Abraham Zaleznik, "Managers and Leaders: Are They Different?" *Harvard Business Review,* May–June 1977, pp. 67–78.

Marks and Spencer, Ltd.

The principles on which the business was founded do not change. The original ideas have been expanded to conform to the changing requirements of a more knowledgeable and discerning public—a public that has broadened to include wider strata of the community.

In the course of the years, we have built up three great assets:

1. The goodwill and confidence of the public.
2. The loyalty and devotion of management and staff throughout the system.
3. The confidence and cooperation of our suppliers.

The principles upon which the business is built are:

1. To offer our customers a selective range of high-quality, well-designed and attractive merchandise at reasonable prices.
2. To encourage our suppliers to use the most modern and efficient techniques of production and quality control dictated by the latest discoveries in science and technology.
3. With the cooperation of our suppliers, to enforce the highest standard of quality control.
4. To plan the expansion of our stores for the better display of a widening range of goods and for the convenience of our customers.

Copyright © 1975 by the President and Fellows of Harvard College
Harvard Business School case 375–358

5. To foster good human relations with customers, suppliers, and staff.

These five tenets constituted the fundamental operating principles of Marks and Spencer (M&S), according to Lord Marks of Broughton, chairman of the firm from 1916 to 1964. Through application of these principles, M&S had achieved outstanding success. By 1974 M&S was the largest retail organization in the United Kingdom. Each week more than 13 million customers made purchases at the firm's 251 stores, which offered some 700 food and 3,000 nonfood (primarily textile) items. Textiles supplied 71 percent of M&S sales in 1974; food, 27 percent; and exports, 2 percent. The company accounted for 12 percent of British consumer expenditures for clothing and footwear and held over one third of the market in women's lingerie and men's underwear.

Despite the disappointing British economic situation, M&S prospered in 1974. While national income declined 2 percent and inflation rose 15–18 percent, M&S posted record sales, with pretax profit climbing 10 percent (see Exhibit 1). While sales per square foot for Britain's top retailers averaged $180 per year, M&S's reached $260. The company's Marble Arch outlet in London achieved sales per square foot of $1,000, earning it a listing in *The Guinness Book of World Records* as the most profitable store in the world.

A board of 22 executives managed M&S from the firm's offices in Baker Street, London, where buying, merchandising, distribution, quality control, and finance were centralized. M&S sold all of its merchandise under the exclusive St. Michael brand name. The company owned no production facilities, relying instead on a broad network of suppliers from whom it ordered some $25 million worth of goods each week.

M&S's major competitors included a supermarket chain with food sales nearly twice M&S's; two retailing firms that imitated M&S but sold cheaper, lower-quality goods; and an American-style department store that emphasized more fashion-oriented goods at lower prices and quality.

The Early Years

The business principles enunciated by Lord Marks originated in the experiences of his father, Michael Marks, the founder of M&S. In 1884 the elder Marks, a Polish Jew, began visiting the town markets of northern England, setting up stalls that featured the sign, "Don't Ask the Price— It's a Penny." The slogan proved so popular that Marks adopted the penny price in all his stalls. The simplicity of the single fixed price allowed Marks to give up keeping accounts and inspired him to search continually for goods as varied and excellent as could be sold for a penny. High turnover counterbalanced the low profit margins.

Marks's business flourished, and in 1894 he took Thomas Spencer into partnership. By 1903, when Spencer retired, the company boasted 40 branches. In that year Marks and Spencer, Ltd., was formed, with control entirely in Marks and Spencer family hands, and the headquarters was moved to Manchester. Spencer died in 1905, Marks in 1908. After Marks's death, control of M&S temporarily passed out of family hands.

1914–1939

When the founder's son Simon Marks (later Lord Marks) regained control of the firm in 1914, it was a national chain with 140 branches. Although only 10 percent were in market halls, M&S maintained its traditional policies of open display, easy accessibility to goods, and self-selection. Management also strove to make M&S a place where employees were happy and proud to work. Each store had a manageress (term used by M&S management) in charge of training. A heated room was provided for the staff as a place to eat and relax.

With the accession of Simon Marks, a strong family influence returned to M&S. Simon exercised overall direction while his brother-in-law, Israel Sieff (later Lord Sieff) took charge of buying and merchandising. After their deaths their descendants continued to dominate M&S into the 1970s. (In 1975 M&S had no outside directors.) Two outside influences also had profound impact on M&S in the decade after 1914: first, Chaim Weizmann, the brilliant chemist and famous Zionist leader, encouraged Marks and Sieff in commitments that became cornerstones of the modern M&S. Weizmann interested them in the applications and benefits of new technologies and inspired them to regard their business as a social service to both customers and employees. Second, a 1924 visit to the United States allowed Simon Marks to study American chain stores. He returned to England determined to transform M&S into a chain of "super stores" featuring continuous merchandise flow and a central organization acutely sensitive to consumer needs.

M&S went public in 1926 and within 10 years had a branch in every major town. Enhanced staff amenities accompanied this rapid growth. The welfare department, founded in 1933, supervised a variety of employee facilities and expanded medical and dental services that included chiropody (especially significant to people who spend hours on their feet). A pension plan was initiated in 1936.

Changes also occurred in M&S's relations with its suppliers. In 1928 M&S registered the St. Michael brand name (honoring M&S's founder) and became the first department store in the United Kingdom to set the goal of selling only "own-brand" merchandise. To assure the highest product quality, M&S insisted on close cooperation with suppliers and stressed the use of technological advances in materials and production processes. In 1928 M&S's large orders enabled the company to overcome

Table 1

Company Growth, 1946–1974

	Sales* (£000)	Profits (£000)	Number of Stores	Total Store Space (000 square feet)
1946	£ 19,693	£ 2,027	224	1,407
1955	108,375	9,168	234	2,461
1968	282,308	33,871	241	3,939
1974	571,650	76,825	251	5,489

* Including exports. Food sales ranged from 14 percent of total sales (1957) to 27 percent (1974).

traditional wholesale opposition and place orders directly with producers. Food purchases, upon which management imposed extremely strict standards, followed a similar pattern.

1945–1955

In the decade following the war, M&S's sales rose 450 percent, and pretax profits, 351 percent. The St. Michael brand gradually emerged on all products and became increasingly identified in consumers' minds with quality and value. Concentrating on a limited product range, M&S developed a dominant position in many textile lines.

Sales growth led to store modernization and expansion. After postwar controls were abolished in the 1950s, growth accelerated rapidly (see Table 1).

Operation Simplification, 1956

On February 16, 1956, Lord Marks, chairman of M&S, was presented with a budget that exceeded the previous year's by millions of pounds. He reacted strongly to the increases and launched a companywide campaign to eliminate the burgeoning load of paperwork, which appeared to be chiefly responsible for rising overhead. As Lord Marks remarked to Israel Sieff, "It's not a law of business growth that administrative costs continue to increase." The campaign, known as Operation Simplification, aimed at liberating staff, management, and supporting services from paperwork so that they could focus on one task: increasing sales in pounds sterling.

The general principles of Operation Simplification were:

1. Sensible approximation: The price of perfection is prohibitive; approximation often suffices and costs less.
2. Exception reporting: Events generally occur as arranged, and only exceptions need be reported.

3. Never legislate for exceptions: Detailed manuals are unnecessary (M&S went from 13 manuals to 2), and local decision making enhances willingness to assume responsibility.

4. Decategorization: Those below management and supervisory levels are more useful in a "general staff" category than as specialists.

5. People can be and need to be trusted: Eliminating checks and controls saves time and money, while improving staff self-confidence and sense of responsibility. Management control is more effectively exercised by selective spot checks.

Lord Marks set a goal of allowing store staff, management, and support services to focus on one task—increasing sales in pounds sterling. The new system made senior executives responsible for profitability. They determined one markup target for food and another for textiles. With margins thus standardized, the selectors focused on finding goods of acceptable quality that would turn over rapidly. Stores then worked to use space and to serve customers in ways that would achieve maximum sales.

To ensure the effectiveness of the system, Lord Marks enlisted the personal support of head office managers, who then assumed responsibility for improving efficiency in their areas. The campaign, which culminated in a symbolic bonfire of old records, eliminated 26 million pieces of paper—120 tons—per year and reduced the staff from 32,000 to 22,000. The abolition of countless forms and routines freed senior managers to get personally involved in their departments.

On the drive for simplicity, Lord Sieff wrote: "Both the executives and the merchandisers of the department should *probe* into the goods in the stores *with seeing eyes and a critical mind.* The department supervisor and the salesgirl are his best sources of information. To depend on statistics is to asphyxiate the dynamic spirit of the business."

Lord Sieff described the process as "the method whereby the interested and inquiring mind of the executive and his colleagues penetrates beneath the surface of things and discovers the facts."

The emphasis on probing became an integral part of the M&S management philosophy. Brian Howard, director of foods, illustrated the merits of probing,

We get concerned when statistics get on paper, because they hide things. For example, suppose I had a report on sales at a store that showed for a day

	Beginning Stock	Sales	Ending Stock, End of Day
Item A	100	100	0
Item B	50	20	30

I might conclude on the basis of a day's sales that sales of A to B were 5:1 and act accordingly. But if I looked after lunch, I might find that the sales for the morning showed

	Beginning Stock	Sales	Ending Stock, End of Morning
Item A	100	100	0
Item B	50	10	40

I have to ask the store manager to learn that the proper order is more like 10:1. That's why we distrust statistics and value probing.

Simplicity remained a touchstone for M&S management in the 1970s. In 1974 M&S inaugurated a "Good Housekeeping" campaign to limit paperwork, with probing still occupying an important place. It was conducted not only at the head office but also, and especially, in the stores. All senior executives frequented stores, many stopping on their way home from work. In 1974 only 10 of M&S's 251 stores failed to receive a visit from a senior board member.

Each director was expected to wear M&S clothes and every weekend received a hamper of M&S food. Both policies allowed executives to monitor product quality personally. On Saturdays each board member and senior executive toured two or three stores. Managers frequently encountered other executives in stores while probing. For example, a researcher accompanied Howard on a Saturday tour of the Uxbridge store. Over coffee Howard assembled a textile sales manager, junior executives in food and textiles, a food technologist, and the store manager. All were headed for other stores. As a head office employee remarked about the directors, "They work 60 hours during the week, they visit stores on Saturday, and they talk about it on Sunday. They live, eat, and breathe M&S."

During the Saturday visits executives spent a great deal of time talking with employees. The following describes incidents during a 1974 store tour conducted for the casewriter by the chairman, Sir Marcus Sieff, and Brian Howard:

Staines was a small store but did £40,000 per week. We arrived around 9:15 and were greeted by one of the supervisors. The store traffic seemed brisk but the staff manageress thought it a little below normal.

A very young food department supervisor was asked to take us around. She was flustered but did her best to answer questions. It was easy to see what was meant by the necessity at M&S of being able to give straight, clear answers. Brian Howard expected her to know her numbers and her situation. There were problems of short produce deliveries, and he wanted them described. He also offered comments on store layout.

Later the staff manageress took us around upstairs. The warehouse space floor was spotless. The atmosphere was one of easygoing efficiency and competence.

Leaving Staines, Howard drove on to the Reading store to meet Sir Marcus Sieff. Sir Marcus led his party around the store. All that he was wearing that day, except his shoes—slacks, shirt, sweater, and jacket, were available on the racks in the store. His questions dealt entirely with merchandise and people. What was moving? The store manager offered from memory current sales numbers representing percentage comparison with previous weeks and years. Department managers added comments.

Of a shirt, Sir Marcus Sieff commented, "Here's one of our mistakes. Have you reduced this?"

"Yes, but it still isn't moving. We'll have to take it down another pound."

"Why isn't there a price notice?" Sir Marcus asked a young sales supervisor.

"We just got these this morning, chairman, and the sign is being made. We buy this from Burlington. We've ordered 2 million yards of this fabric so far. It's moving very well."

Looking at a child's snowsuit jacket at £6.25 (approximately $15.00), Sir Marcus said, "Is that our price? We've *got* to get a less expensive range. Our customers can't afford that."

Everyone had a pad, from the chairman down, and all took their own notes.

"Did your boss come in to work today?" he asked a warehouse foreman whose wife worked as a sales clerk. "Yes, chairman."

"How is Mary?"

"She's well, thank you."

On a tour of the lunchroom and offices, Sir Marcus asked for the hairdresser by name ("She's the queen of Reading") and gave numerous directives.

"I want 'switch the lights out please' signs near the doors whenever the switches aren't near the door. They have to learn we have a balance of payments problem. When do our window lights go off?"

"6:30."

"When do we close?"

"6:00."

"I want them off at 6:00."

Driving to his home for lunch, Sir Marcus commented on what he had learned. "Some lines we like don't move—like this jacket. We have to find out why. We have a problem on having enough stock for the period after New Year's without carrying too much inventory. And that store has some good people. They're doing a good job."

Other Developments

Personnel

The fifth point of the general principles of Operation Simplification reemphasized M&S's traditional commitment to the well-being of its employees. M&S implemented this commitment by establishing company-financed social and recreational clubs at Baker Street and in each store and by upgrading medical and pension benefits. When Lord Sieff succeeded to the chairmanship in 1964, he reiterated the company's concern: "M&S started with people. We—Lord Marks and I—both felt that making people happy was the great thing in life. So when we got into the stores, we automatically thought in these lines. For instance, we found that the girls were going without lunch when they were broke or busy. So we put in lunchrooms and saw to it that they got time to eat their meals."

A 1969 speech by Managing Director (later Chairman) Sir Marcus Sieff reflected similar sentiments:

> The guiding light of business enterprise is attention to human relations within the business. Firms, like our own, that study human relations—in some places they are called labor relations or industrial relations—are often asked to supply people to lecture on the subject. It is very difficult. How can you tell people to do things that you know they are not doing because they are the way they are? You cannot get the goodwill of the people who work for you by changing words such as *canteen* into *dining room, navvy* to *worker, office boy* to *junior clerk,* and so on, or even just by paying higher wages. In the last analysis, good labor relations come from workers approving of the kind of people they believe their employers to be.
>
> Good human relations can only develop if top management believes in its importance and then sees that such a philosophy is dynamically implemented. They must come in a sensible way, which we have found brings in response, with few exceptions, from all grades of staff. This response expresses itself in loyalty to the firm's cooperation with management, greater labor stability, and a willing acceptance of new and more modern methods. The majority of workers under such conditions take pride in doing a good job. All this results in greater productivity and higher profits. This enables management to provide all those facilities that make for contented and hard-working staff and to pay better wages based on genuinely increased productivity.

Management designed the M&S personnel organization to implement their philosophy of concern (see Exhibit 2). In each outlet, a store personnel executive oversaw the training, movement, and welfare of the store's staff. The job of the head office personnel executive was similar but somewhat less structured due to the close relationships between headquarter's top executives and staff. Of particular importance was the post of pension and welfare executive, who not only ran M&S's pension plan but also looked after retired M&S employees. Retired employees remained attached to a particular store from which the company provided various services, including a free medical plan and periodic lunches. The pension plan itself—long noncontributory—provided well above average benefits.

Concerning these policies Sir Marcus commented, "The word *welfare* has an old-fashioned sound reminiscent of the Victorian era, but I do not know a better one to replace it. People do have troubles, and it is a fundamental part of a good staff policy to be able unobtrusively and, above all, speedily to give help and advice when needed."

M&S also offered current employees a rich and varied program of free activities including riverboat trips, table tennis, and bowling and concert tickets. Of these amenities Sir Marcus said, "They should be of such a nature that executives are pleased to take advantage of them. . . . If the facilities are not good enough for top management, then they are not good enough for staff whatever the grade." By 1972 annual welfare costs at M&S exceeded £4.5 million.

Ultimate responsibility for the company's personnel and welfare policies rested with a welfare committee of nine senior managers. The committee, which met weekly, handled those cases that exceeded local store authority or that required a "common handwriting." The committee's decisions were never questioned.

M&S's emphasis on family atmosphere and employee welfare resulted in a distinctive work environment. An employee described M&S's "house rules":

1. The first thing to remember is that it is a *family* business. Because we're a family business, we care for people. It's a paternal business. How does that affect the professional? You have to receive your inoculation. If you get a violent reaction, you'd better go. And then you grow with the business. It comes back to a recruitment policy. We have to get them young and train them ourselves.

2. You can't be a loner. You have to be part of the team.

3. You have to spread your decisions around. Some in-house decisions are "I don't like it." You learn to accept a decision and wait your time to come back with it.

4. You have to learn how to handle people in an ordinary, decent way.

5. Nobody succeeds who can't talk clearly and simply to the management.

Marketing

M&S's marketing philosophy, like its personnel policy, developed from traditional antecedents. The late Lord Israel Sieff summarized it thus:

The future of the business depends on quick imaginative study of what the people need—not of what the public can be persuaded to buy. Only in supplying real needs will a business flourish in the long term. Only by giving the people what on reflection they continue to want will a business earn the respect of the customer, which is essential to anything more durable than a cheapjack's overnight success. So long as Marks and Spencer continues to study what the people need, and efficiently produces it by means of a staff humanely organized, we can meet any economic trend and challenge.

M&S believed in offering the customer a selective and streamlined range of products aimed at rapid turnover. In Lord Sieff's words, "In each section there are a few lines which do a large percentage of the business, and generally speaking, it is these items whose development merits our first consideration. It is no use wasting time on articles that can have no future." The 3,000-item range of textile products included women's clothing and lingerie, men's clothing and underwear, children's clothing, footwear, domestic furnishings, floor coverings, accessories, and toiletries. Among the 700 food offerings were bakery goods, confectionaries, produce, poultry and meat, dairy products, beverages, and frozen foods. The articles selected typically offered the consumer very high quality at moderate—rather than low—prices. This combination of quality and price encouraged customers to associate M&S with "value for money."

Though M&S had always attempted to maintain a policy of one markup percentage for all merchandise, the range of markups had been expanding. Markups for food ranged from 18 percent to 24 percent with a target of 23 percent; textiles, from 26 percent to 33 percent with a target of 30 percent. In 1974 the annual report announced that margins had been "deliberately and substantially" cut, with "attendant loss of profit" to counteract rising prices and costs.

M&S never held sales, and it reduced merchandise for clearance purposes only. It did little advertising (0.3 percent of sales versus 2–3 percent in the United States), which was limited to information (i.e., new product line). Executives believed that the products sold themselves and so relied largely on word of mouth.

Sales within the store were for cash only, as executives believed that credit only increased costs. The company provided no fitting rooms but did maintain a liberal refund policy. M&S accepted virtually all returns on face value, thus eliminating customers' anxieties.

President J. Edward Sieff summarized M&S's basic marketing principles: "We do what's best for our suppliers, staff, and customers, and we get better at it all the time."

Production and Product Line Organization

In 1960 Lord Marks stated, "It is easy enough to test goods when they are made. What is more important is to be sure they will be well made from the start. What we want to have is process control and testing at the point of production."

Although M&S did not manufacture the goods it sold, it was often responsible for 75–90 percent of a supplier's output. The company worked closely with the approximately 175 food and 400 nonfood independents providing St. Michael merchandise to M&S specifications. Indeed, according to Brian Howard, "Management at M&S is concerned with a flow that begins with the manufacture of synthetic fibers or the import of raw goods and ends with what we hope is a steady movement of merchandise across store counters."

Supplier relationships often stretched back 30 years or more, allowing many suppliers to share in M&S's growth. In 1975 the company employed over 250 scientists, engineers, and support staff, working in teams with merchandising departments and suppliers to develop product specifications and monitor product quality. Suppliers manufactured goods according to an M&S-planned schedule and held them until the company requested delivery to specific stores, at which time M&S accepted title.

Responsibility for handling the flow from suppliers to M&S rested with the merchandise teams (see Exhibit 3). Within the textiles division two subdivisions existed, each headed by a managing director. One director supervised men's and boys' wear, home furnishings, footwear, accessories, and new products; the other, women's and girls' wear. Reporting to the managing director of each subdivision were one or more senior executives, each of whom had charge of one or more product lines handled by the division. Each line was further subdivided into segments overseen by junior executives (e.g., menswear subdivisions included knitwear and outerwear). Junior executives, in turn, supervised selectors responsible for developing merchandise ranges and merchandisers responsible for sales estimates, production, packaging, and distribution.

The food division, though more centralized, adhered to the same basic philosophies and procedures as did textiles. Each product group within the food division had a selector and merchandiser. Merchandise teams tested new items with recipes and tasting panels. Product shelf life frequently required a shorter time span for food division operations than for textiles.

At the store level food operations differed slightly from textiles. Store staff, responsible for determining the merchandise they carried, prepared weekly lists of stock on hand that indicated what they wanted delivered on each day of the following week. The merchandisers who controlled distribution edited these orders. After the individual store orders were submitted a computer, programmed weekly with the production capacity and location of each supplier, generated a production plan for each supplier and geographical area. The merchandise was subsequently ordered. All food orders were transported to the stores via depots operated by independent contractors. Perishable goods were delivered daily. Each product bore a clear sell-out date, and it was the responsibility of the merchandise and store staffs to monitor the freshness of the food continually. In addition to testing all new products and resampling trial lines, M&S staff randomly selected items from stores and brought them to the laboratory for inspection.

Merchandising began with semiannual estimates for the coming season, including budgets for sale, stock, and production. Merchandisers, selectors, and merchandise executives held joint responsibility for estimates. The board of directors calculated the total estimate for the company and for each major decision. All estimates were made exclusively in pounds sterling.

Senior executives monitored sales performance personally and by means of reports. Of particular interest was the Stock Checking List Summary, which was used in both foods and textiles and circulated weekly to the directors (see Exhibit 4). Most merchandise executives believed that the basics needed monitoring while fashion items would "take care of themselves." Senior management was reluctant to accept external conditions as justification for results below plan. Generally if department sales were unsatisfactory, internal procedures were evaluated first. Senior management constantly monitored departments when performance was smooth and eased up in the face of difficult problems. The reasoning was that good performance deteriorated easily if not continually pressured.

Store Divisional Organization

In 1974 M&S had 251 stores divided into 11 divisions, each under a corporate director with responsibility for store operations, building and equipment, transportation, packaging, and real estate. Twelve divisional superintendents, covering regional groups of stores, acted as Baker Street's field representatives and helped store managers as needed. The store managers were the senior line managers in each store and were held responsible by the board for implementing its policies.

In practice the store manager concentrated on sales. Relieved of responsibility for profit margins and usually ignorant of individual margins, managers strove to increase volume, control store expenses, monitor turnover, eliminate "counter cloggers," and ensure adequate stock in fast-moving items. The staff manageress was responsible for staff selection, training, assignment, development, and welfare. Most store managers were men, but some women had recently been promoted to that position.

The dual authority structure was designed to instill a family spirit in each store. The manager and manageress of a new store always had comparable experience in other stores and were expected to achieve a family spirit within six months.

The typical store in 1973 had a manager, an assistant manager, a staff manageress, 2 or 3 department managers, a warehouse manager, a cashier, 10 department supervisors, and 150 general staff. All managerial staff received training in company stores. By age 30, however, most staff and line managers embarked on different career paths, with staff people centralized at headquarters (see Exhibit 5).

The sales assistant occupied one of the most important positions in the company. Assigned to specific departments and attired in identical uniforms, sales assistants monitored product quality, kept stock plentiful and neat, operated the cash registers, and assisted customers. They had authority to replenish stock and to reject goods that seemed of poor quality or inappropriate for the department. However, rejection of stock seldom occurred.

A Look at a Store

A tour of a large downtown London store began in the unusually clean and tidy stock and receiving area. Merchandise was received on conveyor belts, spot-counted, and immediately put into stock. A large, spotless area, used for food stock and storage, included freezers and cold storage rooms. Unique baskets enabled stacking so that food products would not be damaged.

Staff amenities included a medical room and a nurse, with periodic visits from a physician, dentist, and chiropodist; a one-room infirmary; a hairdressing salon (charge, 75 cents), where women were served lunch under the dryers; a cloakroom with security lockers; shower and bath-room facilities; a staff refrigerator; a recreation room; and a staff dining room. The dining room provided lunches, coffee, and afternoon tea, and the charge for all three was 25 cents per day. The food compared favorably with that served in executive dining rooms (see Exhibits 6 and 7).

The main sales floor was arranged to reflect shopping behavior rather than production process (for example, knitwear was separated into men's, women's, and children's). Except for area identification signs, there were no graphics or displays. Merchandise was displayed on tables and gar-ments racks (see Exhibit 8).

The food department had a separate checkout but no barriers to the department store. All food was packaged in see-through containers. Many shelves were completely empty because M&S ordered only a one-day supply plus minimal stock for the next (see Exhibit 9). When shelf life expired unsold goods were available to staff at half price or less.

Movement of both textiles and foods was continuously monitored by the store manager. He remarked, "By 12:00 noon I know the fastest-moving item in the store. It's my job to move that merchandise and make sure we get enough of it. The major problem I face is that if I can't get what I know to be the best, what will I settle for as next best?"

Finance

According to John Samuel, financial officer, M&S's financial policy aimed to provide sufficient resources for capital development, retained earnings, and dividends. The board determined the specific amounts to be committed. A pretax profit goal of 10–10½ percent and an expense level of about 12 percent together implied need for about a 25 percent gross profit margin. Only senior board members dealt with profitability, but even they regarded profit as a required residual and focused on sales volume and expenses in pounds sterling. They tried to balance food and clothing sales as related to margins and overall volume. Store-level goals were set in relation to sales and expenses, while merchandising and buying dealt with production and distribution cost and quality.

Despite growth major percentage relationships changed little over time. For example, expenses remained at 11–12 percent of sales from 1970 to 1974. Samuel indicated that M&S's size minimized the effects of change and eliminated the threat of violent shifts.

The company made every effort to finance its continual growth internally. Although dividend payout was high, Samuel reported a "massive scaling down of proportions paid out to the shareholders in order to finance continued growth."

During the period of domestic expansion, M&S also built up exports to 159 retailers in 41 countries who operated St. Michael shops in departments stocked exclusively with M&S merchandise. In 1974 exports rose 31 percent to $31,920,050. The company was also beginning to move directly into foreign markets. In 1972 a 50 percent joint venture was formed with People's Department Stores of Canada under the name St. Michael Shops of Canada. Major developments were also under way for France (two stores) and Belgium (one store). Although these operations required local borrowing, retained earnings remained the major source of investment funds for both Canadian and European expansion.

In recent years the company's freedom in financial matters had been increasingly circumscribed by government actions which included (1) raising the corporate tax rate from 40 percent to 52 percent in 1974; (2) mandating, under the provisions of the Counter-Inflation Act of 1973, that the gross equivalent of ordinary dividends declared in 1973 could not exceed those of the previous year by more than 5 percent; and (3) forcing all retailers to reduce gross margins by 10 percent in the spring of 1974.

Management Style

A typical week at Baker Street began with an 8:30 A.M. meeting in the chairman's office. Generally eight or nine of the senior members met daily with the chairman, M&S's chief operational director. The members most frequently in attendance included the president, J. Edward Sieff;

the vice chairmen and joint managing directors, M. Sacher and Michael Sieff; joint managing directors, Henry Lewis and Derek Rayner; and directors, R. Greenbury, W. B. Howard, and G. D. Sacher.

Upon entering the chairman's office, each member received sales and stock figures for the previous week. The chairman generally started the meeting by relating a particular incident he had observed during the previous several days. He frequently spoke for several minutes on one or two particular problems and how they related to the business. General comments were then interchanged by all present. The chairman then went around the room and asked each director if he had anything he wished to discuss, starting with the vice chairman, Michael Sacher. The following excerpts are from a meeting held on January 15, 1975.

Sir Marcus (chairman): We are not taking our markdowns fast enough or sharp enough.

Henry Lewis (joint managing director): That's related to some problems we discussed yesterday. The production cutoff date is not in adequate control. We must be able to learn from production sheets so we don't make mistakes. Production changes and cutoffs should be noted for reference next year.

Sir Marcus: If you go away from the principle, it costs you more than you gain 9 times out of 10.

Brian Howard (director): We are moving further into computers in food. From July 1975 to November 1975 stores will be converted from a daily indent (order) system to a weekly system. The computer then translates the weekly ordering into daily projections. It reduces paperwork, and by 1976 the stores probably won't be ordering at all. It's going to take a lot of training to get people to think in total terms. The one system will, however, simplify the stores' life.

J. Edward Sieff (president): I want to make a plea for self-restraint in cloth buying on price points. There's no point in buying more expensive fabrics. We are only interested in the desirability of the article. Once we see the retail price in print, it qualifies the cost price, which doesn't necessarily represent value. We should ask ourselves, "Is it better, of more value, and better quality?"

Sir Marcus: I think the president is absolutely right. It's a matter of self-restraint. Anything else, Teddy?

J. Edward Sieff: I ran across a fabric yesterday, 5–8. I think it's inferior. I hear our people saying it's lousy. It may be an achievement for technology but not for women. And ICI [major fabric supplier] is pushing it.

Sir Marcus: Are we telling them?

Michael Sacher (vice chairman and joint managing director): We have a meeting Thursday.

Sir Marcus: We must be frank with our suppliers.

J. Edward Sieff: We must be frank with ourselves.

Derek Rayner (joint managing director): I've been trying to work our priority stores for 1975. Over two thirds of the sales will come from 95 stores. We need good stock composition of basic merchandise. Can we carry both basic merchandise in all stores and specialized lines in selected stores?

Sacher: I'm concerned about two operations in the stores—training of the cashiers and methods of filling up the displays. For £45 million of goods, we handle £180 million at Marble Arch. We accept too much of this and take too many things for granted. We handle everything four times before it gets to the customer.

R. Greenbury (director): I have set up a team to look at the handling of bread and crisps [potato chips].

J. Edward Sieff: Anything to learn from Safeway or Migros [grocery chains]?

Sir Marcus: Let's ask them. Or Sainsbury. They'll tell us. No need to invent everything ourselves.

Greenbury: I've asked them.

Sir Marcus: O.K., but let's *do* something. I don't want to see the perfect solution.

On Mondays only, after the 8:30 meeting, those meeting with the chairman proceeded to a conference room for the 10:00 A.M. meeting of all directors and senior executives. A total of approximately 25 to 30 people gathered around a long table. The meeting was conducted similar to the 8:30 A.M. meeting. The following are excerpts of the January 30 meeting:

Sir Marcus: Henry Lewis and I visited nine of the Nottingham Manufacturing factories [the largest M&S supplier]. They are an outstanding operation, but they have failed to innovate in the design area. However, they had no criticism of our criterion in this respect. Also they were making a line of ladies' nylons, three in a package, for 75 pence that was not making enough money for them. They asked us if we really wanted them to make lines at a substantial loss. We said certainly not, and we canceled the line.

My second point is that we brought back goods that were of appalling quality—not poor in make but in conception. Are we sufficiently self-critical? Are our standards high enough? Do we probe enough in our eating and wearing? You must see that it applies to you—we've got to be critical.

Another point concerns customers' criticism and complaints. Ninety-four percent of them are replied to by me within a maximum of 48 hours. This procedure should apply around this table.

It is a job for the senior members, not the subordinate members. "A soft answer turneth away wrath."

J. Edward Sieff: I've heard complaints about hosiery that doesn't stay up. We must look at the technicians' role. We are not calling on our technicians sufficiently. Secondly, I'd like to talk about our taste, which should be one of classic simplicity. We give too much credibility to gimmicks that we see in foreign fairs. I know the young people want the showy goods, but we must draw the balance. What are the parameters of taste?

Sir Marcus: Decent taste, reasonably up-to-date taste.

Michael Sieff (vice chairman and joint managing director): The opening of Paris—we have very poor stock conditions. The outstanding orders aren't being filled. I want to know what's happening. Next, markdowns. The trial reports and evaluations are important. We must be cautious to avoid markdowns. Thirdly, price increases. Some of our margins have been increased to 32 percent or 33 percent, which makes up for the budget line of 24 percent. To talk to the stores about margin is difficult. Should we bring in margin? It may not be wise.

Sacher: Their job is to sell whatever they've got at whatever price, including the reduced items. I don't think they should be told.

Sir Marcus: I received a letter from the Wolverhampton store about our plan for extension there. As you know, we canceled plans to extend the operation. The letter was written by departmental supervisors asking for an extension of their store. It's a very well-written letter. Let me read it to you [*reads the letter*]. I think we should look into the situation again. [Sir Marcus noted in March 1975 that the supervisors' letter led to an investment of over £1 million.]

At the conclusion of the general meeting, many directors and senior executives met with their respective groups. Senior directors often joined such gatherings. At a food meeting attended by a researcher, one of the vice chairmen came in and threw a package of rhubarb crumble on the table. He scathingly commented on the poor taste and consistency of the dish. "This is the most disgusting thing I have ever had the pleasure of serving to guests. The rhubarb was unripe and overcooked—it was inedible. Also the product is overpackaged. We should take a closer look at our packaging policies."

Elsewhere at Baker Street, a constant parade of people went in and out of offices. Standard procedure was to knock and immediately enter without awaiting a response. The object was to project an open-door policy; often the visitor would get an answer to a question and leave. Outside each door was an "engaged" sign that could be lit from the occupant's desk to avoid being disturbed. Executives were constantly available to anyone who wanted to work with them. In each office and in the halls was a light with four colors (much like a traffic light). Each board member and senior executive was assigned a combination of colors. These lights flashed whenever someone wanted to reach an executive who was not in his office. Those without a light combination carried pocket beepers.

Most executive offices featured two phones. One could be used for any purpose. The other was answered by an operator; the executive told the operator whom to look for, hung up, and was called back when the party was located. Thus all executives, unless off the premises, were available to anyone who wanted to see or talk with them.

Concerns about the Future

The executives of M&S were figures of considerable public importance, well known in the business community. Asked about the future the chairman spoke of his concern for the economic future of M&S and the nation.

> We believe that if we guard the standards of our goods, improve our systems, and look after both our staff and our customers, we shall continue to grow and to make profits.
>
> We need profits, after paying taxes:
>
> 1. To improve the pay and working conditions of our staff and to take care of them during retirement. The high morale and productivity of our staff owe much to these factors; most of them take pride in working for a successful business that is quality oriented.
> 2. To have funds for investment in the development of the business, which is clearly desired by our many customers.
> 3. To pay a proper dividend to our 240,000 shareholders, who include many small savers, individual pensioners, and pension funds.
>
> Marks and Spencer has, over the years, under a private enterprise system, made a significant contribution to the economic life of the country and has helped to raise the standard of living. We doubt whether we could have achieved this under any other system.

Sir Marcus was particularly upset with inept government interventions in business. When asked what these actions would mean to his basic strategy of expansion in Britain, he commented:

> First we have to be concerned with our liquidity. We will not spend our reserves. The result is, whereas we were going to spend £40 million a year to upgrade our stores, we're now going to spend £20 million. We have to preserve our position. The consequences will not be important in the short term. But as a pattern they will hurt Britain severely in three to four years' time.

A particularly clear expression of Sir Marcus's views was made in a corporate statement issued on October 8, 1974, two days before the 1974 parliamentary elections. The statement made headlines in all of Britain's major papers.

> Retailing performs a major role in the chain of production and distribution. We cooperate with whatever government is in office, but some ministers and their advisers do not seem to appreciate the significant contribution which a healthy and competitive retail industry can make in stemming the rise in the cost of living. We are not helped in this task by misguided interference.
>
> Corporation tax takes more than half our profits. The Government criticizes the private sector for its failure to invest, but it omits to explain that much investment is financed out of our profits. If our profits are subject to politically motivated restrictions and massively reduced, confidence is eroded, and investment on which the maintenance of employment and the future prosperity of the country depends slows down.
>
> The remaining profit [after tax and dividends] is retained in the business to finance its future growth. Present Government policy has substantially reduced the money available for such development in the immediate future.

Michael Sacher, vice chairman, commented on some of the firm's internal issues and problems:

> What has always astounded me is how few people have learned the simple principles on which we operate. I think we have carved a market out here which is quality goods at lower prices. As long as we stick to that we'll be okay, as long as the younger people learn the principles of the business. You have to have a clear policy where you upgrade areas in which you are weak and stay out of the caviar business. The board can help here but there are so many things distracting us from being shopkeepers—bombs, the government, and so on. But we implement by generalizing from the particular. That is how you teach young people.
>
> I always try to pick out one thing and then work on it. Take frozen canneloni; it's a new line that I think will move very well. People like canneloni and it's hard to make. Someone else suggested spaghetti. The housewife can make perfectly good spaghetti with ease, why should we? It just requires a bit of common sense. It's no good developing a slip department if everyone's wearing pants.

> **Researcher:** Isn't it inevitable that you sell the spaghetti as well?
>
> **Michael Sacher:** No, I don't think so. We don't believe in a high degree of specialization, and it has always been our practice to move selectors around the business. So much of selection is taste, feel, and common sense.
>
> I was going to say something else, also immodest, and it's true of other senior colleagues. You have to become expert in a wide variety of activities: selecting goods, feel for merchandise,

know what's coming, principles of building, and rudimentary technological questions.

I hear a lecture in Israel about tomatoes, so I know something about them. I've been shown cell sections of frozen material, so I can ask why our beans and sprouts have such lassitude. I've acquired enough garbage to ask technological questions that they can't throw out.

In the end, the decision has to be taken by management, not the experts. And you have to be humble. I just try to take a jolly good look at everything that's been here a long time in the same place. Repotting is healthy managerially if not horticulturally.

I do see problems: you can't help but lean on the strengths that you have. Take Teddy. He has an astronomic knowledge of textiles, and he applies himself. His taste is not perfect, but he knows what an M&S range should be. He's done a wonderful job in his new role.

The family is a binding force. Members of the family can talk to each other in a candid way that I find extremely difficult to discover with professional managers. It happens with some, but it takes time.

Researcher: How much does great wealth have to do with it?

Michael Sacher: Well, there is something to that. We know what good taste is. We see fashion as it emerges and whether it lasts. I once suggested that we send our selectors to the Caribbean for the winter holiday to see what is being worn.

Another problem is that most of our executives have joined us straight from the university. It compels you to have a series of graded courses outside the university. Not so much for what they learn, but they can test themselves against peers. My generation had the war in which to measure themselves.

Senior members of the board agreed that the major question facing M&S concerned the proper rate of expansion in Britain and the moves into the Common Market and Canada. Sir Marcus articulated his reasons for the moves. "First, as an opportunity for more profit. Given the deteriorating situation in Britain we think Canada can become very important for us. Second, as a chance to expand British exports. And finally, should things be really bad, it's a lifeline for us abroad."

Exhibit 1

Financial Data, 1973–1974 (£000)

	Years Ended March 31	
	1974	1973
Profit and Loss Account		
Gross store sales	£591,570	£511,934
Export sales	13,583	10,370
Net sales	605,153	522,304
Operating profit	76,825	70,036
Taxation	39,900	24,900
Profit after taxation	36,925	45,136
Extraordinary item:		
Surplus on disposal of fixed assets	2,383	176
	39,308	45,312
Dividends	19,008	21,388
Undistributed surplus	£ 20,300	£ 23,924
Earnings per share	11.4p	13.9p
Balance Sheet		
Assets		
Current assets:		
Inventory	£ 31,472	£ 29,638
Cash and short-term deposits	18,460	44,612
Debtors and prepayments	10,502	8,150
Tax reserve certificates	—	4,000
Total current assets	60,434	86,400
Fixed assets:		
Properties	221,895	182,710
Fixtures and equipment	19,825	15,668
Total fixed assets	241,720	198,378
Total assets	£304,364*	£284,830†
Liabilities		
Current liabilities:		
Creditors and accrued charges	£ 28,055	£ 29,971
Corporation tax	28,237	23,359
Dividends (interim payable and final proposed)	12,255	21,283
Total current liabilities	68,547	74,613
Long-term liability:		
Deferred taxation	18,400	13,100
Debenture stock	45,000	45,000
Total long-term liability	63,400	58,100
Net worth:		
Shareholders' interest	172,417	152,117
Total liabilities	£304,364	£284,830

* Investment in subsidiary companies was £1,040,000; investment in associated company was £1,170,000.

† Investment in associated company was £52,000.

Exhibit 1 (concluded)

Ten-Year Financial Statement (£000)

	1965*	1966	1967	1968	1969	1970	1971*	1972	1973	1974
						Years Ended March 31				
Turnover†	£208,636	£226,135	£242,954	£268,607	£299,672	£338,843	£390,915	£438,600	£522,304	£605,153
Operating profit	27,506	29,618	30,659	33,871	38,123	43,705	50,115	53,766	70,036	76,825
Profit after taxation	12,706	18,268	18,959	20,121	21,773	26,005	31,215	34,416	45,136	36,925
Corporation tax rate	nc	40%	40%	42.5%	45%	42.5%	40%	40%	40%	52%
Earnings per share	nc	5.6p	5.8p	6.2p	6.7p	8.0p	9.6p	10.6p	13.9p	11.4p‡
Dividend payments										
to shareholders	£ 9,258	£ 9,928	£ 9,950	£ 10,266	£ 10,609	£ 11,928	£ 13,904	£ 15,528	£ 17,826	£ 19,008
Retained profit	3,246	4,322	2,461	2,536	3,667	5,747	8,220§	9,132	23,924	17,917§
Depreciation	1,844	1,993	2,177	2,488	2,987	3,534	4,177	4,620	5,055	5,464
Ordinary share capital										
and reserves	105,468	109,790	112,251	114,788	118,455	123,152	127,711	136,843	150,767	171,067
Total sales area										
(000 square feet)	3,337	3,471	3,635	3,929	4,214	4,408	4,708	4,944	5,059	5,489

Note: nc = Not comparable.
* 53 weeks.
† Turnover for the year ending March 31, 1974, is shown after deduction of VAT. For the purpose of comparison, turnover figures for previous years have been shown after deduction of purchase tax.
‡ Earnings per share are not comparable by reason of the change in basis of taxation.
§ Excluding surplus on disposal of assets: 1971 = £2,393,000; 1974 = £2,383,000.
Source: Company records.

Exhibit 2

Organization Chart, 1975

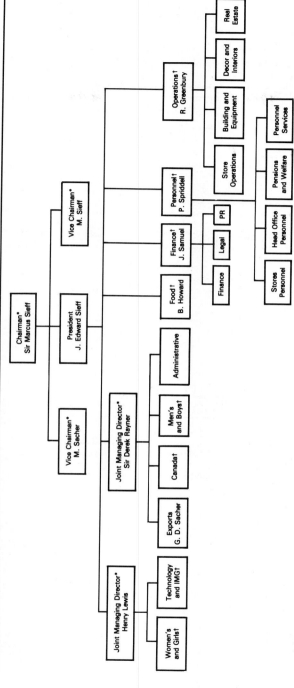

Chairman*
Sir Marcus Sieff

President
J. Edward Sieff

Vice Chairman*
M. Sacher

Vice Chairman*
M. Sieff

Joint Managing Director
Henry Lewis

Joint Managing Director*
Sir Derek Rayner

Women's and Girls†

Technology and IMG†

Exports
G. D. Sacher

Canada†

Men's and Boys†

Administrative

Food†
B. Howard

Finance†
J. Samuel

Personnel†
P. Spriddell

Operations†
R. Greenbury

Finance

Legal

PR

Stores Personnel

Head Office Personnel

Store Operations

Pensions and Welfare

Building and Equipment

Personnel Services

Decor and Interiors

Real Estate

* Joint managing director.
† There were 22 directors altogether.
Source: Casewriter's notes.

Exhibit 3

Textiles Division Organization Chart with Detailed Organization for Menswear

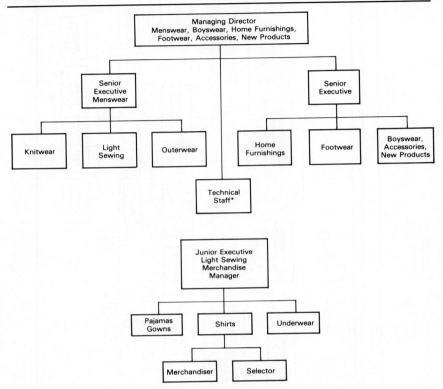

* For all individual merchandise groups.
Source: Casewriter's notes.

Exhibit 4   Stock Checking List, Summary

This Year FIVE Week(s) Ending DECEMBER 30, 1974
Last Year FIVE Week(s) Ending DECEMBER 31, 1973

C.L. Item	Article	Selling Price £	5 WEEKS Sales £	5 WEEKS Stock £	5 WEEKS On Order £	This Period Stock at Mfrs (Including Warehouses) £	This Period Production Planned Next 8 Weeks	No. of Stores	2 WEEKS Sales £	2 WEEKS Stock £	2 WEEKS On Order £	Last Period Stock at Mfrs (Including Warehouses) £	Last Year Sales £	Last Year Stock £	Last Year 5 WEEKS Selling Price £	Remarks
	KNEE NYLON SOCKS															
62A/B	**NYLON**															
62A/B	White	22p/35p	226319	249968	38938	260000	370000		53764	210470	131998	320000	189116	191386	18p/29p	
62C	Colours	22p/25p	22123	26529	1016	10000	75000		8485	31076	5840	5000	36595	42063	18p/29p	
62D 64	Grey/Beige	22p/35p	15234	24685	1203	5000	70000		3635	41002	5367	10000	15606	55012	22p/32p	
	WOOL/NYLON															
56	T.O.T.	44p/49p	41817	39758	586	20000	50000		14149	39167	19864	15000	38672	63445	35p/40p	
63	St. Top	33p/44p	48685	55146	1386	45000	50000		14829	41252	30460	45000	41315	43567	28p/37p	
	ORLON/NYLON															
61	Plain	30p/40p	30905	10180	420	25000	40000	200	8768	56510	16114	30000	60651	104163	27p/35p	
59	Pattern	40p/49p	77388	30577	2185	5000			32407	92217	21707	15000	31681	37063	37p/45p	
	TOTAL KNEE-HIGH SOCKS		462471	432843	45734	370000	655000	C.L. 31/12/74 Reduced 13/12/74	136037	511694	231350	440000	413636	536699		
81/82 83/84	Heavyweight Tights	ALL	149960	162994	14395	10000			52735	178273	69730	70000	198133	98655	55p/70p	
77	Girls' One Size Tights	23p	24607	7783				140	6803	17504	6137	10000				
65/66 72	Boys' Socks	24p/45p	20112						5622	32840	2549	20000	45595	74419	27p/45p	
65/47/48 52/55/58 68/98	Experimental & Unseasonable	ALL	42542	138793	53703	375000	29000		2561	67240	7633	335000	18277	86555	ALL	
	TOTAL FULL SELLING PRICE		698692	742413	113832	755000	945000		203758	807551	317399	875000	675601	796328		
	Reduced	ALL	28542	75303					334	2343			8931	8152	ALL	
	GRAND TOTAL	ALL	727234	817716	113832	755000	945000		204092	809894	317399	875000	684532	804480		
	Stock Target 28th December 1974		750000			750000										
	Estimated Intake for Period £780,000															

Source: Company document.

Exhibit 5

Organization for Store Operation

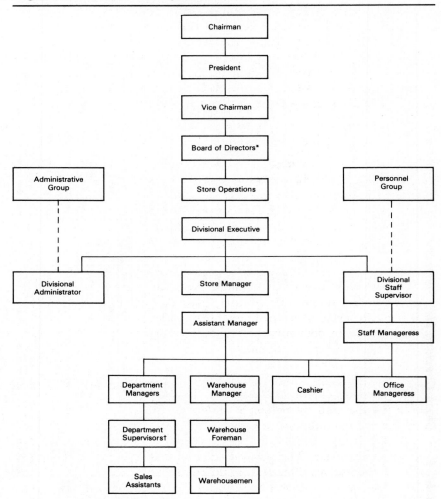

* Including managing directors.
† Present only in larger stores, but in some instances numbering 10.

Exhibit 7   Store Dining Facilities

Exhibit 9   Food Area

Exhibit 6   Store Hairdressing Salon

Exhibit 8   Textile Area

Schlumberger, Ltd.: Jean Riboud
Excerpts from "A Certain Poetry"
by Ken Auletta

Jean Riboud

From the windows of Jean Riboud's New York office on the 44th floor at 277 Park Avenue, one can see the buildings that house the headquarters of such corporate giants as Warner Communications, Gulf & Western, Citicorp, International Telephone & Telegraph, Colgate-Palmolive, United Brands, Bankers Trust, CBS, RCA, and International Paper. All of them are better known than Schlumberger, Ltd., the company that Riboud is chairman and chief executive officer of, but none of them can match Schlumberger's profits. In stock-market value—the number of outstanding shares multiplied by the price per share—only three companies were worth more than Schlumberger at the end of 1981. They were AT&T ($48 billion), IBM ($34 billion), and Exxon ($27 billion). Schlumberger was then worth $16 billion.

Riboud has offices in New York and Paris, and both are rather ordinary except for the art on the walls—works by Picasso, Klee, Max Ernst, Magritte, Jasper Johns, Victor Brauner, Janez Bernik. His New York office is a snug corner—16 feet by 20 feet—with beige walls. An adjoining conference room, 17 feet by 18 feet, has one couch and a round wooden table with six chairs. Riboud's office has a single telephone with just two lines and no private bathroom; there are white blinds on the windows and a simple beige sisal carpet on the floor. His desk is a long, rectangular teak table with chrome legs; on it are a few memorandums but no "in" or "out" box and no books. His personal New York staff consists of one secretary, Lucille Northrup, to whom he rarely dictates; memorandums and paperwork are frowned upon at Schlumberger, and when Riboud wants to send out a memorandum, he first writes in longhand. His Paris office is equally uncluttered.

Riboud is 63 years old. He is 5 feet 10 inches tall and slight of build with wavy gray hair combed straight back. His nose is long and thin, his lips are narrow. His suits come in conservative shades, and his shirts are usually quiet solid colors. He speaks softly, sometimes almost inaudibly, in accented English, rarely gesticulates, and is an intense listener, usually inspecting his long fingers while others speak. Everything about Riboud conveys an impression of delicacy except his eyes, which are deep brown and cryptic. He arrives at work around 10 A.M., and he takes at least six weeks' vacation annually. Yet he is no figurehead; rather, he believes in delegating authority—a principle that no doubt accounts for the calm of Schlumberger's offices in New York and Paris. Schlumberger employs 75,000 people, and of that number only 197 work at the two headquarters.

* * * * *

This case was excerpted from "A Certain Poetry—Parts I and II," copyright 1983, Ken Auletta, by permission of *The New Yorker* and Ken Auletta.

Copyright © 1983 by the President and Fellows of Harvard College
Harvard Business School case 384–087

As the chief executive of a multinational corporation—Schlumberger does business in 92 countries, Riboud has a somewhat surprising talent for avoiding publicity. He is a stranger to most other corporate executives, deliberately keeping his distance from them. He sits on no other company's board of directors.

Riboud has been the chief executive of Schlumberger for the past 18 years. Because the corporation does no mass advertising, of either the consumer or the institutional sort, because it retains no lobbyist in Washington and no public-relations agency in New York or Paris, and because it has never been involved in a public controversy, Schlumberger (pronounced "shlum-bare-zhay") remains one of the world's lesser known major corporations. It is a high-technology company that generates the bulk of its income from the oil-field-service business—making tools that enable oil companies to find and drill for oil with great precision. The information gained and the techniques learned in oil-field services have helped the company to expand into such fields as electric, gas, and water meters; flight-test systems; transformers and semiconductors; automatic test equipment for integrated-circuit chips; electronic telephone circuits; computer-aided design and manufacturing processes; and robotics. Schlumberger is recognized on Wall Street as one of the world's best-managed multinational companies, and financial analysts can point to a number of facts to document its success. Its net income has grown by about 30 percent in each of the past 10 years up to 1981. Its earnings per share rose by more than 30 percent annually between 1971 and 1981, even though the price of oil remained stable or declined in several of those years. Its profit in 1982 totaled $1.35 billion on revenues of $6.284 billion, for a profit as a percentage of revenue of 21 percent—higher than that of any of the thousand other leading industrial companies in the world. Its return on equity in 1981 was 34 percent, while the median for the Fortune 500 companies was 13.8 percent. Schlumberger has relatively little long-term debt: it amounted to just $462 million at the end of 1982, or 3 percent of the company's total capitalization. And while the profits of most oil and oil-field-service companies fell sharply in 1982, Schlumberger's net income rose by 6 percent.

Science is the foundation of Schlumberger. Science is the link between the various corporate subsidiaries, for the task of most of them is collecting, measuring, and transmitting data. Science, and particularly geophysics, was at the core of the careers of Conrad and Marcel Schlumberger, the company's founders. Ever since the first oil well was drilled, in 1859, oil companies had longed for a technology that would help them find oil. Initially prospectors had to painstakingly extract core samples and drill cuttings from rock formations, haul them slowly to the surface, ship them to a laboratory, and await a chemical analysis. This tedious, expensive process enabled the oil companies to determine whether there was oil in a given area and even to determine its quality but not its precise quantity or the exact shape of the well, and it did not enable them to pinpoint where to drill. Conrad, having discovered a new geophysical principle, assigned the job of fashioning a tool and testing it to Henri Doll, who was a brilliant young engineer and also the husband of Conrad's daughter Anne. Doll's task was to chart the electric current as it encountered various kinds of rock, water, and oil. By comparing the actual current coursing through the earth with records showing the electrical resistivity of each substance, the brothers and Doll hoped to produce what amounted to the world's first X-ray of an oil well.

Today the tools are more refined, but the basic process—wireline logging, as it came to be known—is a measurement taken on just about every oil or gas well drilled in the world. And today without benefit of a patent on its basic logging process, Schlumberger—as the original partnership was renamed in 1934—has a near-monopoly on this business, logging some 70 percent of the world's wells. In the United States alone, in 1981 the company hired 1 percent of all the engineers graduating from American colleges.

Over the years, Schlumberger's oil-field business has expanded beyond logging measurements to include a broad range of other services: drilling, testing, and completing wells; pumping; cementing. The company's Forex Neptune subsidiary, formed in the 1950s, is now the world's largest oil-drilling company. The Johnston-Macco and Flopetrol subsidiaries provide an assortment of testing and completion services after drilling has started. A subsidiary called The Analysts provides continuous detailed logs of oil wells from the moment drilling begins, in contrast to most logs, which are prepared only before drilling begins or after it ceases. The Dowell Schlumberger company, which is jointly owned by Schlumberger and Dow Chemical, offers pumping and cementing services. Together with the Wireline division, these companies make up the Oilfield Services—one of two major parts of the Schlumberger empire. The other major part is known as Measurement, Control & Components. Its subsidiaries include the world's largest manufacturer of electric, gas, and water meters; a leading manufacturer of transformers; a producer of valves and safety controls for nuclear power systems; and a manufacturer of flight-control and signal-processing systems for aerospace and military use. The Fairchild Camera & Instrument Corporation, a California-based semiconductor company that Schlumberger acquired in 1979, manufactures, among other products, integrated circuits such as microprocessors and memories; advanced bipolar microprocessors for the F-16 fighter plane; and electronic telephone circuits. Applicon, another subsidiary, is among the pioneers in computer-aided design and other efforts to automate factories.

Schlumberger has a total of 43 major subsidiaries, most of which rely on science and technology. The jewel in Schlumberger's crown is the Wireline, which in 1981 generated 45 percent of the company's $6 billion in revenues and about 70 percent of its $1.2 billion in profits. Many of Schlumberger's subsidiaries rank at or near the top of their various industries. The investment banker Felix Rohatyn, who serves on the boards of eight major corporations, including Schlumberger, and is a close friend of Riboud, says, "By the standard of profit margins, return on investment, compound growth rate, remaining ahead of the state of the art technically and having an efficient management structure over the last 20 years—until the recent drastic change in the energy environment—Schlumberger might well have been the single best business in the world." Rohatyn's enthusiasm is shared by independent analysts at the major Wall Street brokerage firms, and their judgment has been reflected in research reports issued by, among others, Morgan Stanley, Merrill Lynch, Paine Webber, Wertheim, L. F. Rothschild, Unterberg, Towbin. An analysis issued by Barton M. Biggs, managing director of Morgan Stanley, in January of 1982 reads, "Here is this immense, superbly—almost artistically—managed company booming along with a 35 percent compound annual growth rate in earnings and 37 percent in dividends between 1975 and 1980. . . . Our analysis of earnings variability from growth trend shows Schlumberger as having the most consistent, high-growth track of any company in the 1,400-stock universe of our dividend discount model."

Even though Schlumberger is a competitive company devoted to ever-higher profits, over the years its executives have shown a predilection for the politics of the left. Paul Schlumberger urged his sons to share the profits of their company with employees. He financed his sons only on the condition that "the interest of scientific research take precedence over financial ones." Conrad was a pacifist and a socialist until Stalin's Russia disillusioned him. Rene Seydoux, the husband of Marcel's daughter Genevieve, who ran Schlumberger's European wireline operations and to whom Riboud reported after Marcel's death in 1953, was an ardent and active supporter of the French Socialist Party. Jean de Menil, who supervised all South American operations in the period after the Second World War, supported various liberal causes in the United States. Along with his wife, Dominique, a daughter of Conrad Schlumberger, de Menil became a major financial contributor to Martin Luther King, Jr., and the American civil-rights movement. And in 1981 Jean Riboud, as an intimate of President Mitterrand, supported the Socialist government's proposed nationalization of 46 enterprises.

* * * * *

Riboud is a man of contrast. He is a hugely successful capitalist, with an annual salary of $700,000 and Schlumberger stock worth about $33 million, yet he calls himself a socialist. He loves business, yet most of his friends are from the worlds of art and politics. He was born into a French banking family in Lyons, the historical birthplace of the

French ruling class, yet he says that one of his principal goals in life is to battle this class. He has deep roots in France, yet he considers himself an unofficial citizen of India and of the United States. He places a premium on loyalty and sentiment, yet he is a tough businessman who has unhesitatingly fired loyal executives and has had a hand in easing out four members of the Schlumberger family. He is charming yet distant. He is a strong and independent man, yet he has a history of "more or less falling in love"—in the words of his friend the writer Françoise Giroud—with leading French politicians of the left.

Even to many of his friends, Riboud is an enigma. They do not understand his success as a capitalist—in part because he does not speak of Schlumberger to them. "Jean Riboud impersonates a businessman who is trying to hide a certain poetry," Saul Steinberg says. "He is in some sort of Sydney Greenstreet business, as far as we see it—oil, Arabia. I say, 'What's this pussycat doing as director of this company? I can see the pussycat. But where is the crocodile?' Now, no pussycat becomes officer in charge of such a company, and I tell myself that in order to be good on the highest level of anything, you need mysterious sources."

Few cities dominate nations the way Lyons once dominated France. A city of over half a million people in the center of France, Lyons was synonymous with the French business establishment. The Ribouds were Roman Catholic—the right religion—and comfortable. The family lived in an apartment in Lyons until 1929 when they moved to a spacious house in the suburb of Ecully. Summers were spent 55 miles north of Lyons at La Carelle, an estate of 1,300 acres of farmland and wooded hills which has been in the family since 1850. Like many members of the French establishment, Camille Riboud, Jean's father, attended L'Ecole des Sciences Politiques in Paris, where his circle of friends included Georges Boris, who became a close associate of Pierre Mendes-France; Andre Istel, a future banker; Maurice Schlumberger, who became a banking partner of Istel's; and Jean Schlumberger, who became a writer of some distinction. Maurice and Jean Schlumberger were brothers of Conrad and Marcel. Jean Riboud says, "My father was an enlightened conservative. He was really part of the establishment and wanted to be part of the establishment, and yet he wanted to be entirely independent-minded—independent of the establishment." His days were devoted to commerce. At night he read to his children: Homer, Euripides, Baudelaire, Verlaine, Rimbaud.

Camille's wife, Helene, grew up in Lyons and spent her summers in the nearby town of Givors, where her father's family owned a bottling factory. Helene Riboud was taught to be a devout, unquestioning Catholic, to obey her husband, to control her emotions, and to organize a good home. She "was not a silly woman," Antoine Riboud says, but she was "ordinary"—without "the sparkle of my father." Jean Riboud offers a different memory of Helene. "She was a lively, attractive, gay woman, without the culture of my father," he says. "But she was not an ordinary person." The qualities that Jean remembers most vividly are "an extraordinary dignity and an extraordinary sense of duty." Krishna Riboud remembers her mother-in-law, who died in 1957, as a woman of "great determination and great character," but she also says that Jean has a romanticized view of his father. "He feels that all his cultural background comes from his father," she says. "All the authority he has comes from the mother. I see more of the mother in him than the father."

In 1939, at the age of 53, Camille Riboud died of a heart attack, and Jean, who was then 19, became the de facto head of the family. "Jean is exactly the portrait, the figure of my father," Antoine Riboud says. "He has the same intellectual way of thinking as my father. To all the children, he was the second father."

In 1939 after graduating from L'Ecole des Sciences Politiques, he volunteered for the army but was rejected because, at 19, he was too young. The next year, though, he joined the army as a tank officer, and when Germany invaded France he was sent into battle in the Loire Valley. He was captured in June of 1940, but he escaped. In the spring of 1941 he went to the Sorbonne to study law and economics and prepare for the Civil Service. He studied and lived for two years in occupied Paris, and during this time he kept in touch with the budding Resistance movement in Lyons, attending organizational meetings and slipping back and forth between occupied France and Vichy France.

In the summer of 1943 he and a fellow student, Yves Le Portz, were urged by others in the Resistance to join the Free French Army in North Africa. To get there they decided to take a route that had been used by, among others, Georges Schlumberger, a son of Maurice: to Perpignan, in the south, by bicycle, and from there the 25 miles or so to Spain by kayak. On a moonless August night Riboud and Le Portz hid their bicycles at the top of a cliff, put their kayak into the water, and paddled furiously, hoping to parallel the coastline just out of sight. But a storm came up, sending water crashing into their tiny craft and shoving them out into rough seas. Frantically they struggled back toward the shore, where the water was calmer, and then they made their way south to a point where the Pyrenees plunged straight down into the Mediterranean. They spotted a cave and, leaving their kayak outside, crawled in to sleep. They were awakened a short while later by officers from a German patrol boat who, after one look at the detailed maps of the coast of Spain the two were carrying, arrested them. The Germans took them to be interrogated by a colonel, who first saluted their bravery and then turned them over to the Gestapo in Perpignan. After two weeks of questioning, they were taken to the city of Compiegne, north of Paris, and in September they were among 1,200 prisoners shipped by train to Buchenwald.

When Riboud and Le Portz arrived at Buchenwald, experienced prisoners gave them some advice: The Gestapo will ask if you are able to do mechanical work. Say yes. "We had no idea of mechanics at all," recalls Le Portz, who is today chairman of the European Investment Bank. But they followed the advice and were sent to an aircraft construction plant near Buchenwald. Prisoners who said they were ignorant of mechanics were sent on to Dachau, the extermination camp. Buchenwald was brutal—particularly the long hours working outdoors in winter without a coat. In addition to the cold, the hard labor, and the Gestapo, prisoners of war had to contend with common criminals whom the Germans had rounded up and sent to the camps. "To divide us, they mixed ordinary criminals with members of the Resistance," Le Portz says. "There were as many conflicts among inmates as between inmates and guards. Unity among the prisoners was essential."

Riboud recalls that in many of the camps "some of the Christians and the Communists became forces of order." They helped their fellow prisoners not to lose faith and to accept discipline and solidarity. Riboud himself soon emerged as a leader at Buchenwald. "We didn't speak German," Le Portz says. "Yet a few months after entering the camp Jean was the official German interpreter for the prisoners—and he'd read German newspapers to them. Moreover, he was a man of extraordinary humor. He tried to make life as easy as possible for other prisoners. Jean managed to establish contact with the outside world and get information to the camp. He was not a passive man."

Of his years at Buchenwald, Riboud says, "I've seen the worst and the best of human beings, to an extent that I never thought could be as bad and as good, as ominous and as perfect." The experience contributed to a lifelong conviction that, in Riboud's words, "in the presence of death there are the ones who fight and the ones who give up, the ones who survive and the ones who do not." Antoine Riboud says that Buchenwald made his brother "more liberal" and also made him "very strong, very capable of resisting anything."

* * * * *

With the war behind him, Jean assumed that a job in his father's bank awaited him. A career in banking had been Camille Riboud's wish for him, and though Jean had no ambitions along those lines he decided to fall in with his father's plan. He recalls, "I went to see the man who was the head of the bank"—his father's partner—"and he said to me, 'There is no room in the bank.'" The partner also told Riboud that he had "no gift for banking." Unsure of what he wanted to do, he went to Paris to have an interview for a job in industry, and while he was there he also went to see Andre Istel, who had been a banking partner of Maurice Schlumberger. Istel, a French Jew, had fled to the United States during the war, and now he planned to open a New York banking office, to be called Andre Istel & Company. Among Istel's clients was the oil-field-service company Schlumberger.

Two months later, in September of 1946, Riboud opened Istel's New York office, working at a salary of $200 a month. "It was another planet," he says. "Europeans had absolutely nothing. I took all my belongings to America, and I remember that they were one pair of shoes and two shirts. That's all I had—that was everything." For a year, Riboud rented a furnished room on the East Side, and then, his salary having risen, he moved into a $125-a-month apartment on Sixty-third Street between Madison and Fifth Avenues. A number of art galleries were nearby, as was the Museum of Modern Art, which he particularly enjoyed. Again as at Buchenwald, Riboud quickly learned the language being spoken around him.

As a young man, Riboud had become accustomed to meeting his father's literary friends, and he had read the classics; he had always cared about art and about politics; and now he shared the passions and interests of his new friends in the New York literary and artistic community.

* * * * *

Riboud did well at the bank. He came to know some conservative businessmen and formed friendships with several—notably Garrard Winston, an attorney whose bloodline stretched back to the early days of the American republic. But investment banking did not inspire Riboud the way politics did. His was a generation that had been dominated from its early years by political questions: by Fascism, the Spanish Civil War, Hitler, the Second World War, the Holocaust, the United Nations, and colonialism, and now by Senator Joseph McCarthy. "We had to choose," Riboud says. He wanted the left to remain united, to remain focused on traditional enemies, to help prevent the Cold War. When Riboud thought of Communists, he thought not of a Stalin Gulag but of Buchenwald, populated in part by Communists "who had convictions and integrity," and who had saved his life.

* * * * *

The Schlumberger family had been keeping an eye on Jean Riboud. Glowing reports arrived from Andre Istel and Maurice Schlumberger. The Schlumbergers had come to know Riboud directly, because a third of the investment bank's financial-advisory business was with their company or with the family itself. Riboud was invited to family dinners and impressed other guests with his knowledge of politics, art, and literature. One day Marcel Schlumberger arrived at the house of his niece Anne in Ridgefield, Connecticut. She recalls that he seemed depressed. Schlumberger had always been a family company, and Mr. Marcel, as he was called, usually hired its engineers himself. But the company was growing rapidly—it now had offices not only in Paris but also in New

York, Ridgefield, and Houston, and Marcel worried that it was becoming too successful, too bureaucratized, and would lose its sense of intimacy and fall into the hands of men without character. Anne listened to Marcel's lament, and after a while the talk turned to Jean Riboud. "You see him now and then," he said. "What do you think of this lad?"

In "The Schlumberger Adventure," a family memoir published in the United States in January of 1983, Anne (who, divorced from Henri Doll, had become Anne Gruner Schlumberger) writes that she replied, "I think he has a heart—a feeling for humanity, I guess I want to say. That's rare enough in someone committed to high finance. If you're thinking of taking him on, I'll be surprised if he disappoints you."

"Oh, I find him *sympathique,*" Marcel said. "We'll see." He paused, then added, "I wouldn't know how to use him. Finance is not our business, and I don't believe in it."

Marcel arranged to have lunch with Riboud in Paris in July of 1950. Jean and Krishna had had a son, Christophe, that year and had talked often of starting a new life in France. Riboud felt unfulfilled as an investment banker. He was restless in America and was concerned that he was losing touch with France. Moreover, he had never been to India; he wanted to go there and then settle in Paris and maybe open a bookstore. Earlier that year he had notified Andre Istel that he planned to leave the banking business and go to India for six months. Now when Marcel learned of these plans, he offered Riboud an undefined position with Schlumberger. "I haven't the foggiest idea what you'll do," he said at lunch. He offered to pay Riboud $500 a month—$2,500 a month less than he was then making. He proposed to send him to Houston as an assistant to his son, Pierre, but Riboud, because of his Indian-born wife, preferred not to live in the South. Still he was intrigued by Schlumberger and by the sense of adventure that the oil business promised. He agreed to go to work for the company but on two conditions: he must first visit India, and he must work at Schlumberger's Paris office. Marcel accepted his terms.

Upon returning to France in May of 1951 Riboud went to work at Schlumberger. He worked on finances, on merging what had become four independent Schlumberger companies into one, but mostly he listened. "For the first year, I really did nothing except listen to Marcel," he says. "Marcel used him as a gadfly," says Paul Lepercq, who is also from Lyons and was recruited by Riboud as his replacement at the New York bank; today Lepercq is the second longest serving member of the Schlumberger board of directors. Riboud watched Marcel—the "adapter," as Paul Schlumberger called him—spend hours asking penetrating questions or sit through meetings without saying a word, his eyes unreadable under thick eyebrows, his expression blank. Marcel focused on personnel decisions which, he told Riboud, were the most important decisions an executive had to make. Even though Marcel was approaching 70, he would cross the ocean to attend meetings of engineers and managers. William Gillingham, a British-born engineer who had been hired by Marcel in 1934 and had become the head of Schlumberger's oil-field-service operations, recalls saying, "Mr. Marcel, you must enjoy coming over here and hearing these technical papers," and that Marcel glared at him and said, "Mr. Gillingham, I don't come here to hear these papers. I can read them in my office. I come here to see what kind of people are running *my* company."

* * * * *

Despite his flaws, Marcel communicated to Riboud his almost religious devotion to Schlumberger. As with other corporate pioneers—Thomas J. Watson of IBM, A. P. Giannini of the Bank of America, Henry Ford—this devotion became a legend. Riboud speaks of an incident that took place in 1940, when the Germans had invaded Belgium and were poised to overwhelm France. Erle P. Halliburton, the head of the Halliburton Oil Well Cementing Company, which was Schlumberger's chief oil-field-service rival, paid a visit to Marcel. "Everybody knew that France was going to be defeated, that Paris would be totally cut off from Houston, and that Houston wouldn't survive by itself, without Paris," Riboud says. Halliburton offered to buy Schlumberger for $10 million. Marcel made no reply but slowly rose from his chair and beckoned Halliburton to follow him. They walked silently to the elevator, where Marcel thanked his visitor and said goodbye. Another executive might have hesitated, Riboud says. Why didn't Marcel? "Because there are some questions you never discuss," he says. "If somebody were to come and ask you to sell your wife, you wouldn't hesitate, would you?" Riboud draws a lesson from this tale: Marcel Schlumberger was never swayed by passing storms, because he remained anchored to a set of beliefs. "The first was: think for yourself," Riboud says. "Whatever is happening at the moment, try to think for yourself." In the summer of 1953, at the age of 69, Marcel died of heart failure.

* * * * *

Although Marcel's corporate heirs shared his sense of the company's special mission, his death robbed Schlumberger of its central authority. Feuds surfaced among the branches of the Schlumberger family. No one emerged as chief operating officer to replace Marcel. Instead, the company was divided into four fiefdoms, each ruled by a family member. The technical side of the business was the domain of Henri Doll. But Doll was a scientist, not a corporate manager; although he ranked first in seniority when Marcel died, he chose not to assume the leadership of the company.

* * * * *

Pierre Schlumberger, the only son of Marcel—and the only son of either founder—ruled the most profitable division: Schlumberger's North

American wireline operations. Schlumberger came out of the war a weakened company, with its executives scattered. In 1946 Pierre set up an organization in Houston that would keep pace with the growing American oil market. Like his father, Pierre was a man of simple convictions. With his father gone, he came to believe that if Schlumberger was to grow it had to become a public company rather than remaining a family one and that it had to make its financial operations more professional—to codify a set of rules rather than follow the whims of one man. Pierre had ambitious plans, but the other family members resisted them.

A third sector—Schlumberger's wireline operations in South America and the Middle East—was run from Houston by Jean de Menil, the husband of Conrad's daughter Dominique. For eight years after his marriage, de Menil, a Paris banker, resisted Marcel's importunings to join the company, but in 1939 he did and became responsible for Schlumberger's financial structure. During the war de Menil successfully schemed with Marcel to free the company from potential Nazi control by shifting its base of operations from France to Trinidad. And after the war de Menil played a large part in making Schlumberger a truly international corporation by requiring that all business be conducted in English and that the dollar be the common currency, as is now customary in the oil business. Like Conrad Schlumberger, de Menil was an idealist and lent his financial support to political and artistic movements that challenged the status quo. And also like Conrad, he believed that Schlumberger's ability to help others find oil was a natural extension of his political beliefs. "You were bringing to human frontiers technology that helped people," says his son George de Menil, who is a professor of economics. "During the war, it contributed something crucial to the war effort. After the war, it contributed something crucial to the growth of the world economy."

Schlumberger's European operations—the fourth fiefdom—were run by Marcel's son-in-law Rene Seydoux. Like de Menil, he had intense political convictions, and he became a supporter of the French Socialist Party. During the war he was captured by the Germans and sent to a prisoner-of-war camp. After the war he returned to Schlumberger and was made head of its Paris office. Among those who worked for him following Marcel's death was Jean Riboud, who admired his gentle nature. Through Seydoux, Riboud came to know many Socialist Party leaders. Of the four family members, a person who knew them well says, "The others were stronger personalities in a sense, but Rene Seydoux was always the cement, trying to hold things together."

The cement did not adhere. For three years after Marcel Schlumberger's death, the company remained divided into four parts. Relations among the family members were amicable, professional, often affectionate. The four parts were united in their devotion to Schlumberger and its mission, but there was no central planning and coordination. Riboud and other executives disliked this arrangement and campaigned to restructure the corporation. Finally, in 1956, a new parent company, Schlumberger, Ltd., was created to unify operations. Pierre Schlumberger became president; Henri Doll was elected chairman of the board. The company was incorporated on the island of Curaçao, in the Netherlands Antilles, which was then becoming one of the world's major tax havens.

In 1959, however, Pierre's wife died, and over the next 18 months Pierre stayed at home most days. When he did come to the office, he was irritable and autocratic. "Pierre was very fragile and lost his balance," observes his cousin.

The branches of the Schlumberger family disagreed about many things but not about the value of Riboud. Everyone saw in him familiar qualities. In early May of 1965 the family asked Riboud to replace Pierre Schlumberger. Riboud says that he immediately resigned, declaring, "I will not replace Pierre, because I owe too much friendship to him. The only decent thing for me to do is to resign." The family prevailed on Pierre to resign first and then asked Riboud to become president and chief executive officer of Schlumberger. He did so on May 13, 1965.

For 18 years Riboud has ruled Schlumberger, in the words of one company executive, "like an absolute constitutional monarch." Felix Rohatyn says, "He is the absolute, unquestioned boss in the company. His authority is as absolute as that of any chief executive I've seen." When Riboud speaks of Schlumberger, he often does so in the first person singular. Explaining, for example, Schlumberger's 1979 acquisition of the Fairchild Camera & Instrument Corporation, he says, "It seemed to *me* . . ." Although he is not a Schlumberger, his authority within the family is comparable to that of Conrad or Marcel. "He has the unanimity of the family behind him," according to Dominique de Menil, who is now 75 and is a close friend of Riboud. Since the Schlumberger family owns about a fourth of the company's stock, the support of the family is significant. Still, because Schlumberger has generated consistently higher profits under his reign, because he has succeeded in completing the transformation of a family enterprise into a public company, because he is acclaimed on Wall Street, and because he has at times ruthlessly asserted his authority, Riboud has assured his independence.

The only overt challenge to Riboud's reign has come from Jerome Seydoux. From the time Jerome was a little boy, Marcel Schlumberger had urged his grandson to become an engineer. By the end of the 60s he had caught the attention of Riboud. In 1969 Jerome's father, Rene, retired from the board of directors, and Riboud invited Jerome to join it. He hailed the younger Seydoux as one of the brightest men of his generation, valued his advice, and took him into his counsel, as Marcel Schlumberger had done with Riboud.

In 1969 while Seydoux was vacationing in the South of France, Riboud phoned and asked to meet him on a matter of urgency. Seydoux still remembers the date of the meeting—the first day of May. Riboud offered Seydoux a job with Schlumberger. Some months later Schlumberger acquired the Compagnie des Compteurs, a French manufacturer of electric meters and other instruments, and Riboud offered Seydoux the job of president. The company had been losing money, but Riboud believed that it could become profitable. Riboud remembers telling Seydoux that if he succeeded with the new acquisition, he would have "a big future." Seydoux remembers Riboud's saying that he would become president of Schlumberger. In any case, Seydoux did succeed, transforming the company into a profitable operation that is now known as Measurement & Control–Europe. Five years later, in September of 1975, Riboud appointed Seydoux president of Schlumberger, retaining the positions of chief executive officer and chairman of the board. Seydoux remained president for just 18 weeks. His memory of his tenure remains vivid. Now president of Cargeurs S.A., a Paris transportation company, Seydoux recently told a visitor to his office, "I always worked very well with Riboud. We talked easily and communicated well. Yet a few days after I became president he wasn't happy. It lasted four and one half months, but I really think it lasted only a week. Very soon after I became president, we stopped communicating."

In the opinion of people who knew him then, Seydoux began acting as if he were the chief executive—as if the family dynasty had been restored. When he moved into his new office, one of his first acts was to hang on the wall over his desk a picture of his grandfather, Marcel Schlumberger. Riboud thought that Seydoux was acting like someone who believed that his station was inherited and not earned. Riboud's unease was intensified by complaints from executives who had been instructed to report to Seydoux. Jerome was too officious, too brusque, they protested. William Gillingham says that Jerome lacked "the human touch." Some executives were doubtless unhappy that they no longer reported directly to Riboud, and Riboud himself was unhappy because he had discovered that at the age of 55 he did not want to step aside.

Riboud, having decided to dismiss Seydoux, carefully met with or telephoned every other member of the board—there were 16 members—and said that there was not room for two corporate heads at Schlumberger and that he planned to dismiss Seydoux. With the board's approval, he visited and won the concurrence of five of the six branches of the Schlumberger family. And then one winter morning he summoned Seydoux to his New York apartment at the Carlton House on Madison Avenue. In his soft, polite way, Riboud said that he was unhappy with the current arrangement and asked Seydoux to leave.

Riboud, as he demonstrated with Seydoux, is not timid about firing people. "Jean has less difficulty facing up to tough personnel decisions than any other executive I know. Most executives dread it," Felix Rohatyn says. Carl Buchholz, an American who started as an engineer, was once vice president of personnel and is now president of The Analysts, says, "One of my predecessors sat outside Riboud's office all day, and Riboud wouldn't talk to him. If someone was blowing hot air in my office, I'd say, 'Get the hell out of here!' If you're blowing hot air around Riboud, he'll smile and put his arm around you and walk you to the door and make you feel good—and you'll never get in there again."

A man who sulks after losing at golf or at gin rummy—something that Riboud does—is capable of holding grudges. "When something goes wrong, it's finished," says Jeanine Bourhis, Riboud's secretary in Paris for the past 13 years. "Jerome Seydoux was family. He liked Jerome very much, too. And all of a sudden—*phiff!*"

* * * * *

"Riboud handles personnel matters as if no personalities were involved," says Benno Schmidt, who is a managing partner of J. H. Whitney & Company and was a member of Schlumberger's board from 1973 to 1982. "If he considers you the wrong man, he'll remove you in five seconds. He's invariably generous as far as the personal welfare of the person is concerned, but he feels no obligation to keep people in jobs they're not doing. It's matter-of-fact." Several months after making those remarks, Schmidt himself felt the cold side of Riboud. Riboud visited Schmidt in his office on Fifth Avenue and told him that after prolonged deliberation he had decided that Schmidt and three other board members should retire. (Board members who were not also employees of the company received $24,000 annually for their services and $9,000 more if they served on the executive committee, the audit committee, or the finance committee.) Riboud did not ask whether Schmidt, a sometime golfing partner and a member of the Schlumberger executive committee, wanted to step aside. He simply told Schmidt politely that he must go.

* * * * *

Whatever personal pain Riboud feels is soothed by the conviction that loyalty to the company outweighs personal loyalties. He believes that he is simply doing his duty. "If you want to be St. Francis of Assisi, you should not head a public company," he says.

At the beginning of 1982 70 percent of the world's active oil-drilling rigs outside the Soviet bloc were in the United States and Canada. Because of the current oil glut, the number of active drilling rigs in North America fell from 4,700 in January of 1982 to 1,990 in March of 1983, but that was still more than the 1,200 active rigs operating in the rest of the non-Communist world. The United States produces more barrels of oil daily (about 8.6 million) than Saudi Arabia (about 4.6 million). And Schlumberger's Wireline division generates 45 percent of the corporation's revenues and an estimated 70 percent of its net profits. It is therefore not surprising that this division occupies much of Riboud's time.

On a recent Friday afternoon Riboud, accompanied by Andre Misk, a former field engineer who is a vice president and the director of communications, went to Teterboro Airport in New Jersey and boarded one of six jet airplanes belonging to the company for a flight to Houston.

On Monday morning at nine Riboud went to the office of Ian Strecker, who has been in charge of Schlumberger's wireline, engineering, and manufacturing operations in North America since the beginning of 1982. Strecker is a burly, gregarious man of 43 whose normal work outfit consists of cowboy boots, an open-necked sports shirt, and slacks. He joined Schlumberger 21 years ago in England, where he was born, and has since held 20 jobs in 18 different locations. Part of Riboud's purpose in meeting with Strecker was to get a feel for him and other employees in order to gauge, in Marcel Schlumberger's words, "what kind of people are running *my* company." One of Riboud's preoccupations is that Schlumberger will lose its drive as a company and grow complacent—a concern he had discussed on the plane to Houston. "Any business, any society has a built-in force to be conservative," he said. "The whole nature of human society is to be conservative. If you want to innovate, to change an enterprise or a society, it takes people willing to do what's not expected. The basic vision I have, and what I'm trying to do at Schlumberger, is no different from what I think should be done in French or American society." In other words, sow doubt. Rotate people. Don't measure just the profits in a given division—measure the man in charge, too, and his enthusiasm for change. Strecker's predecessor, Roy Shourd, learned at first hand just what Riboud means. Shourd headed the North American Wireline division from 1977 through 1981, and in those years its profits rose an average of 30 percent annually. But Riboud worried that Shourd was growing complacent with success, that he was surrounding himself with an inbred group of executives and becoming too clubby with the Houston oil establishment, so late in 1981 he suddenly shifted Shourd to New York and a staff job. (Typically, one year later, in another surprising move, Riboud elevated Shourd to the position of executive vice president for drilling and production services. Riboud was satisfied that Shourd's year in exile had reignited his competitive spirit.)

This visit to Houston allowed Riboud to take the measure of Strecker, whom he did not know well. Strecker's office is in a three-story, red brick building overlooking Houston's Gulf Freeway. Strecker and Riboud sat down at an oval cherrywood conference table, and then Riboud, who had arrived with no reports or notes, silently inspected his fingernails, formed his long fingers into a steeple on which he rested his chin, and began the meeting. He asked how Strecker's wife, Elaine, had adjusted to Houston, how their two sons, who had remained in school in England, were getting on, how the Streckers had enjoyed a recent visit to England. Before long, the meeting got around to specific employees. Riboud made detailed comments on them, giving not only his impression of their abilities but also his impression of how well their abilities were matched to their jobs. He emphasized that final judgments on all employees were Strecker's to make. After Riboud had finished with the personnel matters, he asked Strecker if he had been spending much time in the field—among 1,800 field engineers whom Schlumberger employed in North America.

"I feel that my biggest challenge here in the next couple of years is engineering," Strecker replied, referring to engineering research. "So I'm spending most of my time there now." He said that the next day he would join all the engineering department heads for a three-day retreat in California at which they would evaluate priorities and challenges. Riboud suggested that the engineers might want to consider pushing the manufacturing section of Schlumberger Well Services, in Houston, which produces 60 percent of the equipment used by the Schlumberger field engineers. Even though this is more than the company's other manufacturing plant, in Clamart, France, produces, Riboud is not satisfied. He wants Schlumberger to become totally self-sufficient—to farm out less work to such companies as Grumman and International Harvester, which makes the frames for Schlumberger's trucks.

There was a long silence. Riboud sat inspecting the fingers of one hand, and finally Strecker asked if Riboud had any further questions.

"I've got a major concern about what happens to your business in the next few years," Riboud said. He then noted that Strecker's monthly report for January, which he had received in New York, revealed that North American logging operations were 11 percent below plan and that operations in completed wells—so-called cased-hole explorations—were 5 percent below plan. "The January report blames the weather," he said. "But then I read and see that the biggest decline was in log interpretation, and you can't blame the weather for that." Riboud said he was confident that the world would remain dependent on oil for at least 50 years longer, but he added that two unknowns threatened oil exploration—and thus Schlumberger revenues—in the immediate future. One was the faltering American economy. The other was a decline in the price of oil.

Even in a recession, Strecker said, independent oil drillers can earn enough to continue searching for oil as long as the price is at least $30 a barrel. He observed that after President Carter began to decontrol the price of oil in 1979, the number of oil rigs in North America climbed from 2,500 to 4,750 between 1979 and 1981. "Decontrol caused that rapid growth," Strecker said. But now, with the real price of oil declining, with the economy in recession, and with abundant, if perhaps temporary, oil surpluses, the number of rigs was back down to just under 2,500. Strecker said the natural gas picture was totally different, with supplies plentiful but the price "probably too high."

"It's funny—the gas manufacturers are lobbying in Washington today against decontrol of all gas prices," Riboud said.

If gas should be fully decontrolled, Strecker said, gas producers would not be able to sell all their supplies in this sluggish economy, and the price should drop. (It has not yet done so.) With lower prices, gas producers would concentrate on shallow-well drilling, which was less expensive. Deep-well drilling would become prohibitively expensive, just as it was for independent oil prospectors whenever the price dipped below about $30 a barrel.

Riboud and Strecker, their session over, walked to the office of Robert Peebler, the North American Wireline's vice president of finance, to review the division's business projections for February. Surveying the expected rig counts of Schlumberger and of its competitors, Riboud seized on the figure of 90 rigs credited to competitors off the Gulf Coast. "I'm always surprised by how many offshore rigs our competitors have," he said. Peebler replied that competitors had only 10 percent of the offshore market, but this did not seem to appease Riboud; he asked Peebler to forward an analysis of the situation to his New York office. Riboud's message was clear: Only total victory counts. Schlumberger could lose its edge; competitors with more to prove could be hungrier and more aggressive. Already Wall Street analysts who examined oil-field-service companies had reported that Dresser Industries' Atlas Oilfield Services Group, a worldwide competitor, was leading in the development of the Carbon/Oxygen log and the Spectralog—two advanced logging tools. Gearhart Industries, which was bidding for a larger share of the American market, claimed to have hired 300 graduate engineers in 1981—an increase of 100 percent over 1980. (Because of the drop-off in drilling and the recession, the number fell to 140 in 1982.) Schlumberger remains far ahead of its competitors, but to stay there, Riboud feels, it must continue to challenge its employees.

After Riboud's meeting with Peebler came a slide presentation by engineers and scientists, who talked about such things as a "neutron porosity tool," a "Gamma Spectroscopy Tool," the "radial geometric factor," and the "finite element code." The advanced technology that such arcane terminology represents is perhaps the major reason that Schlumberger stays ahead of its competitors—who concede that Schlumberger's tools are generally more advanced than theirs. And since Schlumberger spends $125 million annually on wireline research—a sum greater than the profits of any wireline competitor—its lead will be difficult to overcome. Much of the research is designed to perfect drilling and logging tools that help identify hard-to-reach oil in already drilled wells and help extract it. This residual oil is expensive to recover, and oil companies claim that as long as the price per barrel stays below $30, pursuing it is not profitable. But if the price rises above $30 and if supplies become scarce (they are now abundant), new opportunities await the oil companies and Schlumberger. An analysis made by Philip K. Meyer, a vice president with the Wall Street firm F. Eberstadt & Company, in April of 1981 explains why: "We have found in the United States roughly 450 billion barrels of original-oil-in-place of which only some 100 billion barrels have been produced to date. This means we know the location of 350 billion barrels of remaining (residual)-oil-in-place. . . . If only a third of this residual-oil-in-place were to economically respond to tertiary recovery, over 100 billion barrels would be added to U.S. reserves."

Riboud listened intently to the engineers and scientists, and when the presentation was over, he said, politely, "I have read all this. You are just preaching motherhood. Where are the problems?"

Not long after the engineering presentation, Riboud had lunch in the executive dining room with three dozen section heads, most of them in their late 20s or early 30s. A number of them said that at Schlumberger they didn't feel isolated in their offices or laboratories, as they had at other places they had worked, and that they weren't dependent on memorandums or rumors to gauge the reactions of their superiors.

"I was at Bell Labs for four years, and I don't think I ever met the vice president of research," said Dennis O'Neill, who was head of the informatics section and had been with Schlumberger for five years. "Here within six months I was making presentations to the executive vice president of the Wireline." James Hall, who had been employed by Schlumberger for 10 years, said he had had the same experience. "It's a lot more personal at Schlumberger," he said. With a Ph.D. in nuclear physics from Iowa State University and two years of advanced doctoral work at the Swiss Federal Institute of Technology in Zurich, Hall was the head of the engineering-physics section. While he was completing his studies, he worked for Mobil Oil. "You felt more isolated there, because contact with management was much less," he said of that experience. "You had contact just with your bosses. You didn't feel the direct contact with your managers you have here. It tends to build more of a team spirit when not only your boss comes to talk to you about a project but several levels of command above as well. To me, in engineering that's what the Schlumberger spirit is. The individual design engineer feels that the responsibility of the company is placed on him."

In Riboud's field visits, time is often set aside for questions from employees like Hall. During the lunch in Houston, the first question was from a young engineer-researcher, who asked for Riboud's "view of the non-wireline" part of the Schlumberger's empire.

"You are an engineer," Riboud said. "Be a little more precise in your question." Riboud did not wait for the young man to rephrase the question. He apparently sensed that, like many Wireline employees, the young man was concerned about Schlumberger's purchase, for $425 million, of the Fairchild Camera & Instrument Corporation—a giant semiconductor company, which lost $30 million the second year after the purchase. Now Riboud went on, "The question is really: When we have this little jewel of a wireline business, why do we bother à la Fairchild and so forth? It's really a philosophical problem. Why does the company have to grow, and in which direction? I'm not saying I'm right, but I feel two things—two dangers. One danger is of becoming a conglomerate and trying to do everything. The other danger is of just staying a Wireline company. I don't think we could have maintained the profit margin we had and the motivation of our people if we'd done that. The real problem in any organization is to have new challenges, new motivations.''

Lunch was followed by a session with department heads from the manufacturing division, which employed 950 people and produced $400 million worth of field equipment annually. The heads of the materials-management and purchasing sections presented Riboud with flow charts and graphs showing a steady rise in their productivity and spoke in the self-assured language of American business schools. Riboud's eyes narrowed. He listened politely but impatiently; finally, he leaned forward with his elbows on the conference table and explained why the company could not measure productivity by price or sales alone. "Since we are selling equipment to ourselves, it is hard to measure," he said. There was no competition over price or product or speed of production, he said, and the charts were therefore relatively worthless.

Later that afternoon Riboud met with the 27 executives and department heads who supervise the North American Wireline division. Many of them also inquired about the acquisition of Fairchild and about Schlumberger's stock. And they asked why Schlumberger had organized a division in the Far East much like the one in Houston. Japan and the rest of the Far East, Riboud repeated, are the frontier of the 80s, as Houston was in the late 40s and 50s. There are vast reserves of oil in China. The Japanese have moved ahead of the West in consumer electronics and office automation; they are threatening to move ahead in the development of computers, semiconductors, and genetic engineering. Singapore, Hong Kong, South Korea, Taiwan, and Japan manufacture goods more cheaply and more efficiently than the West does. If Schlumberger does not feel the threat of competition in North America or the Middle East, then it will feel it from the Far East. Schlumberger has been so successful for so long, he said, that it risks losing its "intellectual humility." He added, "We have the King Kong attitude."

Riboud toured the center and then went to the company cafeteria, where he had coffee with several dozen employees. Gene Pohoriles, the general manager of this unit, was a veteran Schlumberger engineer and, like many old-timers, wore in his lapel a gold Schlumberger pin with stars that symbolize the number of years he had served the company. Pohoriles introduced Riboud to the employees and then asked the first question: Why did Schlumberger dilute the value of its stock by buying Fairchild?

"Let me be blunt about it," Riboud answered. "What people in the

Wireline are asking is: Why did Riboud screw up the Schlumberger stock by purchasing Fairchild?"

"Close," Pohoriles said.

Fairchild was a necessary acquisition, Riboud told him. "I felt strongly that 20 years down the road we had to have a semiconductor capacity." Schlumberger's basic business, he went on, is information, not oil, and what the Wireline does is provide information to oil companies to help them make accurate decisions. The next generation of wireline and meter equipment, he said, will be more dependent on tiny microprocessors and semiconductors.

* * * * *

Riboud's reaction to Pohoriles—admiring his courage while excusing what Riboud thought was an ignorant question—hinted at Riboud's style of management at Schlumberger. On several occasions he has said that the company's goals should be "to strive for perfection." To this end he searches for fighters, for independent-minded people who don't, in his words, "float like a cork." In 1974 when he appointed Carl Buchholz his vice president of personnel, it was largely because Buchholz was not afraid to speak out. Riboud recalled first seeing Buchholz at a Schlumberger management conference near Geneva. "All the people were reciting the Mass, and suddenly Buchholz said, 'You're full of it!' I said, 'This is a fellow who speaks his mind.'" The subject under discussion at the conference, Buchholz later recalled, was the development of managers. The executives in attendance rose, one after another, to congratulate themselves on their success, and finally Buchholz stood up and said that in fact the executives were not successfully developing managers at all. A debate ensued, and Riboud sided with Buchholz. Afterward Riboud made a point of getting to know him, and not long after the conference Buchholz, who had been assistant vice president of operations for Schlumberger Well Services, in Houston, was promoted to vice president of personnel and transferred from Houston to New York, where he quickly developed a reputation as an in-house critic.

* * * * *

Of all the people who have surrounded Riboud at Schlumberger over the years, probably none has been closer than Claude Baks, who was hired by Marcel Schlumberger as an engineer in 1946 and left the company only in the fall of 1982. An enigmatic man with a blunt manner, Baks had no official duties, but he could enter any meeting uninvited, and he reported only to Riboud. He was born in 1917 in Latvia. His parents were Jewish, and with the outbreak of the Second World War he joined the Free French Army, fighting in North Africa and Europe. On assignment for the company in Venezuela some years after he was hired, Baks met Krishna and Jean Riboud, who were traveling there.

When he returned to Paris on holiday, he looked up the Ribouds and became close to them and their son, Christophe. Riboud, who was then general manager of Schlumberger's European operations, had a hand in getting Baks transferred from Venezuela to Paris, where he was given a staff job. Admiring Baks's independence, Riboud asked him to become his adviser. At this time Riboud, with Henri Langlois, was raising money to finance a 12-hour film, directed by Roberto Rossellini, about the history of the world. (They raised $500,000, including $100,000 from Schlumberger.) Baks shared Riboud's interest in film and worked closely with both Langlois and Rossellini on Riboud's behalf. Baks had no family of his own, and the Ribouds in effect became his family.

Riboud and Baks were an unlikely pair. Riboud is a man of delicate appearance and subdued manner. Baks has bushy black eyebrows, a stubbly black beard, and a bulbous nose; he is missing a few front teeth. He has a deep, raspy voice, which some find intimidating, and he is usually wearing a dirty raincoat and a baggy sports jacket and baggy pants. His office, a cubicle on the fourth floor of Schlumberger's Paris headquarters, was just two doors from Riboud's. He kept the blinds closed and would not open the windows, and visitors seldom stayed long. The walls were bare, the desk top was clear, and besides the desk, the only furniture was two chairs and three metal file cabinets. Yet fellow employees went to Baks's office to try out ideas, to get clues to Riboud's thinking, to learn something of the company's history, to ingratiate themselves with Baks.

In trying to explain the role that Baks played, Riboud has said, "His main contribution at Schlumberger has been to prevent Schlumberger from becoming an establishment." He went on, "He has never had a title in 35 years. He has never had a secretary. He has never written a letter. He has no responsibilities. Schlumberger is not a bank where everyone has to have a niche. Over the years he's had more purpose than 90 percent of the people I know. He forces people to think." What Baks helped do was keep alive, under chairman Riboud, a sort of permanent "cultural revolution" at Schlumberger.

* * * * *

"Generally, after a while people repeat themselves," observes Michel Vaillaud, who until December of 1982 was one of two Schlumberger executive vice presidents for operations, his sphere being all oil-field services. "You know what they will ask you. With him, you never feel safe. Never." Vaillaud, who is 51 years old, is a lean, regal-looking man. When he met Riboud in 1973 he was a career civil servant. He had graduated first in his class from L'Ecole Polytechnique, which Conrad Schlumberger attended and which is acknowledged to be the best scientific school in France. He then received an advanced degree from mining and petroleum schools and, entering the Civil Service, rose rapidly in the French Ministry of Industry. When Riboud and Vaillaud met, Vaillaud was the ministry's director for oil and gas. Some weeks later, Vaillaud recalls, Riboud offered him a position at Schlumberger. Although Vaillaud's training and experience were in petroleum, Riboud asked him to move to New York and become vice president of Schlumberger's electronics division. Vaillaud spoke little English, and he felt unsure of himself in electronics, but he accepted the offer.

Two months after Vaillaud took the job, Riboud called and asked to spend the day with him in New York. Vaillaud remembers feeling that he gave inadequate answers to persistent questions from Riboud. "I came back and told my wife, 'We should pack—I'm going to be fired.' Then I heard nothing the next day, or the next." At the time, Vaillaud did not understand that his uncertain technical answers to Riboud's questions were secondary. Riboud was taking his measure as a man, not as a technocrat. Computers could give out data; Riboud was searching for character. Two years later Vaillaud returned to France as president of the Compagnie des Compteurs. Then in 1981, when Riboud decided to divide Schlumberger into two basic parts—the Oilfield Services and Measurement, Control & Components—Vaillaud and most Schlumberger executives expected him to make Vaillaud the head of the electronics division and Roland Genin, who had been an executive vice president and manager of Drilling and Production Services, the head of the oil-field division. These appointments would have had a certain logic to them, for Vaillaud had mastered electronics and Genin had spent his career in the oil-field division, beginning in 1950 when he joined Schlumberger as a field engineer. Riboud did just the opposite: Vaillaud became the head of the oil-field division; Genin, the head of the electronics division. Riboud picked the less experienced man for each job, because, he says, each would bring a "totally different view," a "fresh imagination" to his new task. Riboud had taken a similar unexpected step a year earlier when he chose Thomas Roberts, a West Point graduate who had become the vice president of finance, to be the new president of Fairchild. Roberts had asked him why, and Riboud had answered, "I like to shake the tree."

If an eagerness to shake the tree is one of Riboud's most prominent management traits, another one—allied to it—is, obviously, his preoccupation with personnel matters. As his meetings in Houston showed, he is familiar with people at many levels of the organization. Instead of closeting himself with a few top executives, he meets with large groups of employees. The vice president of personnel at Schlumberger—the job is now held by Arthur W. Alexander—reports to the president, not to an executive vice president as is often the case at other companies. "Riboud spends more time on people and people problems, in contrast to business and business problems, than any other chief executive I've ever seen," says Benno Schmidt. "I think the thing he's most concerned with in running this vast business is coming as near as possible to having exactly the right man in the right place all the time. Most people who run a company are much more interested in business, new products, research—all that."

When it comes to evaluating individuals, Riboud can be quite blunt. Once a year he meets with each of his top executives to offer an evaluation of their performance. Carl Buchholz remembers one of his evaluations: "He said, 'Let's talk about the Buchholz problem.' He talked about my relations with other people and how I ought to improve them. He talked about what he wanted done that wasn't being done. He was quite specific."

Like his predecessors, Riboud wants people at Schlumberger to have a feeling of independence. Day-to-day decisions are left to those in the field. Riboud's job, as he sees it, is primarily to think 5, 10, 20 years ahead and to set the basic direction of the company. On September 30, 1977, at a celebration of the 50th anniversary of the Schlumberger's first log, he remarked, "I should say that the most important thing I learned from Marcel Schlumberger was to have an independent mind— to think for oneself, to analyze by oneself, not to follow fashions, not to think like everyone else, not to seek honor or decorations, not to become part of the establishment." On another occasion, he said, "When you fly through turbulence, you fasten your seat belt. The only seat belt I know in business turbulence is to determine for oneself a few convictions, a few guidelines, and stick by them."

Riboud the businessman puzzles many of his nonbusiness friends. For years Henri Cartier-Bresson has wondered why Riboud worked in a corporation instead of plunging full time into art or politics. Cartier-Bresson—a shy man with pale blue eyes, gold-framed eyeglasses, and close-cropped white hair—recalls asking Riboud, "What are you doing there? You're not a scientist. You have no passion for making money," and that he replied, "I'm a corkscrew."

"It means he knows how a bottle must be opened—delicately and firmly," Cartier-Bresson says.

*   *   *   *   *

Riboud sees his work at Schlumberger as an extension of his political views. "Running a company is like politics," he says. "You are always balancing interests and personalities and trying to keep people motivated." On being asked how he would like to be characterized as an executive, he replied, "I would like it to be said that I'm bringing about in my professional life what I'm trying to bring about with myself— it's one and the same thing." Like Marcel and Conrad Schlumberger, the two brothers who founded the company in 1926, Riboud thinks of the company as an extension of personal values—humility, loyalty, preserving faith in an idea, serving people, being trusting, being open-minded to different cultures, being ambitious and competitive and yet mindful of tradition. The key in a corporation or in government, Riboud says, is "motivating people" and forging a consensus. "We are no longer in a society where the head of a corporation can just give orders," he says. People need to believe in something larger than themselves. To be successful, he thinks, a corporation must learn from the Japanese that "we have the responsibility that religion used to have." A good company must not be just a slave to profits; it must strive to perform a service and to beat its competitors. But more, he feels, it must measure itself against a higher standard, seeking perfection.

There is another way in which Schlumberger is an extension of Riboud's political philosophy—in its international character. Riboud says that with the possible exception of the oil company Royal Dutch/Shell, Schlumberger is "the only truly multinational company that I know of." Schlumberger has long since ceased to have a single national identity. "If I have one purpose today," Riboud says, "it is to expand the concept of merging together into one enterprise Europeans, Americans, and citizens of the Third World; to bring in Asians, Africans, and Latin Americans so they feel at home with their own culture, their own religion, and yet feel that Schlumberger is their family."

$$* \quad * \quad * \quad * \quad *$$

"I think politics is a contradiction in Riboud," says Bernard Alpaerts, who began his career with Schlumberger 30 years ago as an engineer and retired this year as executive vice president of the company's Measurement & Control operations worldwide. "Politics is far removed from the management of this company. Schlumberger is almost a company without a nation. Riboud knows very well that most of his managers don't have the same political opinions he has. And, honestly, he doesn't mind. Sometimes you don't recognize in his business decisions the political opinions he has." The investment banker Felix Rohatyn, says, "Riboud is complicated. There is this mixture in the man of being the hardheaded manager of a huge company that is as intensely capitalistic as any organization I know, and at the same time being clearly involved with the Socialist government of France."

This is one of several contradictions in Riboud. He is, for example, a loyal family man—devoted to his wife, to his son and daughter-in-law and their three children, yet he has had sometimes stormy relationships with his brothers and sisters. He takes pride in being open-minded and a foe of bigotry, yet Christophe Riboud says that his father is "one of the most determined and prejudiced men I know."

$$* \quad * \quad * \quad * \quad *$$

Why is it that a company like Schlumberger succeeds? In order to answer this, one should probably first inquire into the degree of success of the company's various components. Schlumberger, according to Wall Street analysts, had a near-monopoly on the wireline business—about 70 percent of the world market. (Its nearest wireline competitor, Dresser Industries' Atlas Oilfield Services Group, has just over 10 percent.) And Schlumberger retains its near-monopoly even though it charges higher prices than its competitors. "We believe we are entitled to a certain return on investment, which we intend to maintain, and we price accordingly," says D. Euan Baird, who is 45, Scottish-born, and, like most of the company's top executives, started as a Schlumberger field engineer. A policy first established by Marcel Schlumberger remains in force today: Schlumberger charges its wireline customers twice the amount of its costs. Because Schlumberger does not sell, or even lease, its equipment, and because its equipment is the most technologically advanced, so that the company provides the best technical service, it remains the most highly regarded company in the oil-field-service industry. Of course, oil companies can afford to pay its prices. Since the cost of logging a well—the wireline process—is only 2 percent to 5 percent of the oil company's cost, wrote John C. Wellemeyer, managing director of the investment-banking firm of Morgan Stanley, in 1973, "Schlumberger should be able to increase prices as much as required to maintain its margins." Until the current oil shock, that is what it has done.

To isolate the specific reasons for Schlumberger's success, one needs to start where Conrad and Marcel Schlumberger did—with technology. Competition in the oil-field-service business hinges on technology. Marvin Gearhart, president of Gearhart Industries, an aggressive domestic competitor of Schlumberger, says, in reference to the industry and Schlumberger, "It's a high-technology business, and they've been the leader in high technology."

Helped by the Fairchild subsidiary and by a heavy investment in what is called artificial intelligence, Schlumberger may be nicely positioned for the future. In recent years, advanced technology has brought about an explosion of the well-log data that are generated at every well site. Concurrent advances in data processing have helped cope with this explosion, but an isolated field engineer cannot quickly interpret so much data, and none of Schlumberger's 44 data processing centers—which may be hundreds, or perhaps even thousands, of miles away from an oil well—can entirely replicate the skills of a trained field engineer. Consequently, a bottleneck has formed in the oil-field-service industry, with clients desperate for all possible information before they make their expensive decisions and logging companies unable to provide a complete on-the-spot analysis of their complex logs. Enter the new world of artificial intelligence. Fairchild is at the center of a strategy to forge ahead in artificial intelligence.

Schlumberger's reliance on research and technology suggests a second reason for the company's success: Schlumberger executives are trained to think in 10-year and 20-year cycles. "The time horizon there is longer than that of any other company I know in being willing to wait for a return on their investment," says Felix Rohatyn. Riboud points out that after the Compagnie des Compteurs was acquired in 1970 it took Schlumberger seven years to transform it into a success. "We could afford to take the seven years, because we had our basic business," he says. "If it had been 10 or 12 years, though, people would have lost faith in what we were doing." The Compagnie des Compteurs is actually one of relatively few companies that Schlumberger has acquired: 15 or so over the past 20 years—a tiny number for a company of such size and cash reserves. This is in marked contrast to the current trend among American corporations. Between 1978 and 1982 American corporations spent an estimated $258 billion to acquire other companies, many of them in unrelated fields.

Schlumberger, on the other hand, has not assumed that because it was successful in one field it could succeed in unrelated fields. This refusal to shed its basic identity is a third reason for its success. Schlumberger, Riboud says, will not engage in an unfriendly takeover of another company, believing that the hostility generated poisons the corporate atmosphere required for success.

Schlumberger's determination to stick with what it knows best contributes to a fourth reason for its success: it is relatively unburdened by debt. Unlike, say, the Du Pont company, which had long-term corporate debts of $5.7 billion in 1982, Schlumberger's long-term debt as of December 1982 was a mere $462 million; moreover, it had a readily available cash pool of $2.3 billion in short-term investments. Such a balance sheet, says Elizabeth Taylor Peek, of Wertheim & Company, is "incredible for a company of that size." Interest income alone brought Schlumberger $254 million in 1982.

Schlumberger is exceptional in a fifth way: It is in good standing in the Third World. There are several reasons for Schlumberger's standing in the Third World. "You can't nationalize a spirit or brains," Riboud has said. "They could nationalize a few trucks, but what would they have? The concept from the beginning was to do everything ourselves—to manufacture the equipment and deliver the services. We never sold equipment. So how do you nationalize a service?" Schlumberger has escaped troubles of the sort that befell many oil companies in the Middle East and the United Fruit Company in Latin America, partly because it has striven to remain inconspicuous. It does not own natural resources (oil) in any nation but services those who do. It does not engage in consumer advertising, and it does not lobby governments, so it is less of a target than the well-known big corporations.

The key executives of most multinational companies tend to be of a single nationality. For example, IBM has 23 members on its board of directors, all but one of whom are Americans. Exxon has three non-

Americans on its 19-member board. General Electric has only Americans on its 18-member board. This has not been the case at Schlumberger. Its board was evenly divided in 1982 between French and American nationals.

What Riboud has called "the will to win" hints at a final reason for Schlumberger's success—what employees refer to as "the Schlumberger spirit." Riboud likens the Schlumberger spirit to a religion. "It is our greatest asset, our unique strength," he says. The reason the Japanese have done so well, he told the New York Society of Security Analysts in March of 1980, is so simple and so obvious that it has been overlooked. It has less to do with their technological prowess, their productivity growth, the assistance they receive from their national government than with spirit. "They had the same faith that the great religions had in past centuries," he said. Riboud then tried to define what makes up the Schlumberger spirit:

> (1) We are an exceptional crucible of many nations, of many cultures, of many visions. (2) We are a totally decentralized organization. . . . (3) We are a service company, at the service of our customers, having a faster response than anybody else. (4) We believe in the profit process as a challenge, as a game, as a sport. (5) We believe in a certain arrogance; the certainty that we are going to win because we are the best—arrogance only tolerable because it is coupled with a great sense of intellectual humility, the fear of being wrong, the fear of not working hard enough.

Where does this spirit come from? Surely, in part at least, from the personalities at the top: from the Schlumberger brothers and from Jean Riboud. "Conrad and Marcel created this spirit of friendship and honesty, and Riboud kept it," says Anne Gruner Schlumberger, a daughter of Conrad Schlumberger. "Riboud is loved because he is very friendly. It is the love of people and the interest in their life. When people left for America and Russia, Conrad escorted the engineers to the railroad station to give them advice. He knew their families, their children." The brothers communicated shared democratic values within the Schlumberger hierarchy, as Riboud does today.

The company's spirit also comes in part from the special nature of Schlumberger's business. From the start, Schlumberger has been the only wireline company to refuse to turn over raw data to clients, insisting that it alone must process these data, for it is producing a service, not a commodity. Anne Gruner Schlumberger has written that "the high quality of human relations" at the company "took its start from a 'noble' activity, in the sense that nothing produced there was mere merchandise." She goes on, "The object conceived and made there was not such as fall into an anonymous market and in their turn became anonymous. This sonde, the galvanometer, were not for sale. The tie between the man who makes and the thing made was not cut." The Schlumberger brothers stipulated at the outset that the company would not own oil wells or permit employees to buy shares in oil companies. Schlumberger was to be trusted to keep oil-company secrets, it had to be "pure." Dominique de Menil, another daughter of Conrad, who was trained as an engineer and worked closely with her father, has recalled, "You had to be totally honest and independent of any interest." Engineers at Schlumberger sensed that they were embarking not just on a career but a calling. They were not just merchants but missionaries.

* * * * *

Summing up, Riboud said, "If we lose the drive and fear searching for new technologies or fear taking incredible gambles on new managers" or fear to heed the voices of "other countries and cultures, then we will become an establishment." If that happens, Schlumberger may remain powerful and profitable for the moment, but ultimately it will decline. "It's easy to be the best," Riboud has said many times. "That's not enough. The goal is to strive for perfection."

* * * * *

In sum, Riboud remains a mystery even to his friends. "He is a man who cannot be classified in any way," says Charles Gombault, the former editor of *France-Soir,* who came to know Riboud through Pierre Mendes-France. "Is he an intellectual? I don't think so. Is he a merchant? I don't think so. Is he an industrialist? It doesn't show. He is one of the few men with a strong influence over the president of France, but he will never talk about it. He never shows off. If you see La Carelle, you will understand. It's a beautiful old house with lots of antiques everywhere, extremely comfortable. But if you want to have the feeling of fortune you do not have it looking at the house. You have it looking at the ground as far as you can see. He is a man of the earth."

The Company and Its Responsibilities to Society: Relating Corporate Strategy to Ethical Values

We come at last to the fourth component of strategy formulation—the moral and social implications of what once was considered a purely economic choice. In our consideration of strategic alternatives, we have come from what strategists *might* and *can* do to what they *want* to do. We now move to what they *ought* to do—from the viewpoint of various leaders and segments of society and their standards of right and wrong.

Ethical behavior, like the exercise of preference, may be considered a product of values. To some the suggestion that an orderly and analytical process of strategy determination should include the discussion of highly controversial ethical issues, about which honest differences of opinion are common and self-deceiving rationalization endless, is repugnant.

Even when public scandal erupts over apparent overcharges to the government by General Dynamics, forged time cards in a division of General Electric, exaggerated and organized overdrafting in E. F. Hutton, the business community stands silent. Good reasons, including the vulnerability of all organizations to wrongdoing by subordinates under pressure, make such silence prudent. Unfortunately it suggests to the press and general public complicity in illegal, unethical, and irresponsible behavior.

The Moral Component of Corporate Strategy

The emerging view in the liberal-professional leadership of our most prominent corporations is that determining future strategy must take into account—as part of its social environment—steadily rising moral

459

and ethical standards. Reconciling the conflict in responsibility which occurs when maximum profit and social contribution appear on the same agenda adds to the complexity of strategy formulation and its already clear demands for creativity. Coming to terms with the morality of choice may be the most strenuous undertaking in strategic decision.

Attention is compelled to the noneconomic consequences of corporate power and activity by a combination of forces constituting the environment of business. Most dramatic is the decline in public confidence in public and private institutions accompanying the prosecution of the Vietnam War, Watergate, and the forced resignation of a vice president and president of the United States. Distrust of business flared with the revelation by the Watergate Special Prosecutor of illegal political contributions. The Securities and Exchange Commission's probe of other illegal and questionable payments has publicized the illegal or questionable behavior of scores of well-known companies. The deposition of the top leadership of such companies as the Gulf Oil Corporation and the Lockheed Aircraft Company was a blow to the supposition that our respected companies were abiding by the law and professional standards of ethical conduct. The quick confessions of other companies to avoid prosecution were given wide publicity.

Discussions of the responsibility of business have usually until now taken individual personal integrity for granted or have assumed that the courts were adequate discipline to ensure compliance with the law. The obvious necessity for explicit company policy now makes it necessary for decision to be made about at least how compliance with the law can be ensured. The first step is a stated policy that illegality will not be condoned and enforcement provisions will begin with corporate action rather than waiting for the law and the courts.

Since political contributions and bribery are neither illegal nor even unusual in other parts of the world, explicit policy must be made with respect to other marginal, technically legal, but in American eyes, improper kinds of payments. The Foreign Corrupt Practices Act deals with the difference between American and foreign law and custom. It includes a requirement that companies report its confidence in the adequacy of its control systems. Once embarked on this sea of uncertainty, companies are forced to include policy decisions about other corporate and personal ethical behavior.

In most reputable companies it has long been assumed that economic objectives would be pursued within the law and the bounds of ethical custom. The present-day necessity to articulate and enforce an unspoken assumption leads to detailed consideration of the ethical quality of an organization's culture and to decisions governed by noneconomic criteria. Specifying and securing ethical behavior is not easy in a large company in which responsibility is delegated through many levels of authority and degrees of autonomy. The first step is to break the custom of silence to make possible the assertion of ethical concern.[1]

The morality of personal behavior, however, is not our only concern. The dominant position of the corporation in our society, the influence it has on all citizens, its inevitable relations with local, state, and national governments make it increasingly important to consider, company by company, what its social responsibility will be. Milton Friedman, to be sure, still argues that the only social responsibility of business is to pursue profit as vigorously as possible (within the law and an undefined "ethical custom").[2] For a number of reasons, it is no longer possible to conclude that consideration of strategic alternatives should be exclusively economic and free of concern for the impact of economic activity upon society.

First, corporate executives of the caliber, integrity, intelligence, and humanity capable of coping with the problems of personal morality just cited are not happy to be tarred with the brush of bribery and corruption. They are not likely to turn their backs on other problems involving corporate behavior of the late 70s and early 80s. The recurring energy crises, the growing sensitivity to environmental damage by industrial and community operations, the protection of the consumer from intended or unwitting exploitation or deception, the extension of social justice, as exemplified by the demands of minority populations and women for opportunity and recognition, the general concern for the limits of growth and the so-called quality of life—all these cannot be ignored. The need is widely acknowledged to respond as a matter of conscience as well as a matter of law.

Second, it is increasingly clear that government regulation is not a good substitute for knowledgeable self-restraint. As expectations for the protection and well-being of the environment, of customers, and of employees grow more insistent, it is clear that if corporate power is to be regulated more by public law than by private conscience, much of our national energy will have to be spent keeping watch over corporate behavior, ferreting out problems, designing and revising detailed laws to deal with them, and enforcing these laws even as they become obsolete.

Executives assuming top-management responsibility today may be more sensitive on the average than their predecessors to the upgrading of our goals as a society and more responsive to the opportunity to relate corporate and public purposes. But if not, they can be sure that

---

[1] For useful notes on ethical analysis in the practice of general management and an excellent bibliography of writings in the field, see John B. Matthews, Kenneth E. Goodpaster, and Laura L. Nash, *Policies and Persons: A Casebook in Business Ethics,* (New York: McGraw-Hill, 1985).

[2] The classic statement of this position, which is hardly susceptible to modernization, is still Friedman's *Capitalism and Freedom* (Chicago: University of Chicago Press, 1962).

new regulation will force this concern upon their strategic processes. Extending the reach of strategic decision to encompass public concerns is either a voluntary response permitting latitude in choice or acquiescence to law which may involve none. New forms of regulation or effective enforcement come late to the problem without regard for feasibility or cost. The strategist can consider much earlier whether the problem is susceptible to effective and economically satisfactory solution.

Categories of Concern

If you elect to admit responsiveness to society's concern about corporate power and activities to your definition of strategy, you come face to face with two major questions. What is the range of corporate involvement available to a company? What considerations should guide its choice of opportunity?

The World. The problems affecting the quality of life in the society to which the company belongs may usefully be thought of as extending through a set of densely populated spheres from the firm itself to the world community. The multinational firm, to take world society first, would find (within its economic contribution to industrialization in the developing countries) the need to measure what it takes out before it could judge its participation responsible. The willingness to undertake joint ventures rather than insist on full ownership, to share management and profits in terms not immediately related to the actual contributions of other partners, to cooperate otherwise with governments looking for alternatives to capitalism, to train nationals for skilled jobs and management positions, to reconcile different codes of ethical practices in matters of taxes and bribery—all illustrate the opportunity for combining entrepreneurship with responsibility and the terms in which strategy might be expressed. Even small firms now face the opportunity and necessity to export. In smaller ways they also must negotiate with host countries and pursue their self-interests in an environment of give-and-take.

The Nation. Within the United States, for a firm of national scope, problems susceptible to constructive attention from business occur in virtually every walk of life. To narrow a wide choice, a company would most naturally begin with the environmental consequences of its manufacturing processes or the impact of its products upon the public. Presumably a company would first put its own house in order or embark upon a long program to make it so. Then it might take interest in other problems, either through tax-deductible philanthropic contributions or through business ventures seeking economic opportunity in social need—for example, trash disposal or health care. Education, the arts, race relations, equal opportunity for women, or even such large issues as the impact upon society of technological change compete for attention. The proper role of government in providing support for American industry now under attack by foreign competitors is of immediate concern to business leaders. In beleaguered industries like textiles, they must weigh the short-term advantages of protectionism versus the long-term superiority of free trade. Through organizations like the Business Roundtable, the American Business Conference, and the National Manufacturers Association, they find themselves making recommendations to the executive branch and the Congress which must address public as well as corporate interest. Our agenda of national problems is extensive. It is not hard to find opportunities. The question, as in product-market possibilities, is which ones to choose to work on.

The Local Community.   Closer to home are the problems of the communities in which the company operates. These constitute the urban manifestations of the national problems already referred to—inadequate housing, unemployment in the poverty culture, substandard medical care, and the like. The city, special focus of national decay and vulnerable to fiscal and other mismanagement, is an attractive object of social strategy because of its nearness and compactness. The near community allows the development of mutually beneficial corporate projects such as vocational training. Business cannot remain healthy in a sick community.

Industry.   Moving from world to country to city takes us through the full range of social and political issues which engage the attention of corporate strategists who wish to factor social responsibility into their planning. Two other less obvious but even more relevant avenues of action would be considered—the industry or industries in which the company operates and the quality of life within the company itself. Every industry, like every profession, has problems which arise from a legacy of indifference, stresses of competition, the real or imagined impossibility of interfirm cooperation under the antitrust laws. Every industry has chronic problems of its own, such as safety, product quality, pricing, and pollution in which only cooperative action can effectively pick up where regulation leaves off or makes further regulation unnecessary.

The Company.   Within the firm itself, a company has open opportunity for satisfying its aspirations to responsibility. The quality of any company's present strategy, for example, is probably always subject to improvement, as new technology and higher aspirations work together. But besides such important tangible matters as the quality of goods and services being offered to the public and the maintenance and improvement of craftsmanship, there are three other areas which in the future will become much more important than they seem now. The first of these is the review process set up to estimate the quality of top-management decision.

The second is the impact upon individuals of the control systems and other organization processes installed to secure results. The third is a recognition of the role of the individual in the corporation.

Review of Management Concerns for Responsibility

The everyday pressures bearing on decisions about what to do and how to get it done make almost impossible the kind of detached self-criticism which is essential to the perpetuation of responsible freedom. The opportunity to provide for systematic review sessions becomes more explicit and self-conscious. At any rate, as a category of concern, how a management can maintain sufficient detachment to estimate without self-deception the quality of its management performance is as important as any other. The proper role of the board of directors in performing this function—long ago lost sight of—is undergoing revitalization.

The caliber and strategic usefulness of a board of directors will nonetheless remain the option of the chief executive who usually determines its function. How much he uses his board for the purposes of improving the quality of corporate strategy and planning turns, as usual, on the sincerity of his interest and his skill. Recent research has illuminated the irresponsibility of inaction in the face of problems requiring the perspective available only to properly constituted boards. This organization resource is available to general managers who recognize dormancy as waste and seek counsel in cases of conflicting responsibility. A number of large corporations, including General Motors, have established Public Responsibility Committees of the board to focus attention on social issues.

The effective provision by a board of responsible surveillance of the moral quality of a management's strategic decisions means that current stirrings of concern about conflicts of interest will soon result in the withdrawal from boards of bankers representing institutions performing services to the company, of lawyers (in some instances) representing a firm retained by the company, and other suppliers or customers, as well as more scrupulous attention to present regulations about interlocking interests. As much attention will soon be given to avoiding the possibility of imputing conflict of interest to a director as to avoiding the actual occurrence. Stronger restrictions on conflict of interest will also affect employees of the firm, including the involvement of individuals with social-action organizations attacking the firm.

Impact of Control Systems on Ethical Performance

The ethical and economic quality of an organization's performance is vitally affected by its control system, which inevitably leads people, if it is effective at all, to do what will make them look good in the terms of the system rather than what their opportunities and problems, which the system may not take cognizance of, actually require. We will examine the unintended consequences of control and measurement systems when we come to the implementation of corporate strategy; in the meantime we should note that unanticipated pressures to act irresponsibly may be applied by top management who would deplore this consequence if they knew of it. The process of promotion by which persons are moved from place to place so fast that they do not develop concern for the problems of the community in which they live or effective relationships within which to accomplish anything unintentionally weakens the participation of executives in community affairs. The tendency to measure executives in divisionalized companies on this year's profits reduces sharply their motivation to invest in social action with returns over longer times. Lifelong habits of neutrality and noninvolvement eventually deprive the community, in a subtle weakening of its human resources, of executive experience and judgment. Executive cadres are in turn deprived of real-life experience with political and social systems which they ultimately much need.

The Individual and the Corporation

The actual quality of life in a business organization turns most crucially on how much freedom is accorded to the individual. Certainly most firms consider responsibility to their members a category of concern as important as external constituencies. It is as much a matter of enlightened self-interest as of responsibility to provide conditions encouraging the convergence of the individual's aspirations with those of the corporation, to provide conditions for effective productivity, and to reward employees for extraordinary performance.

With the entry of the corporation into controversial areas comes greater interest on the part of organization members to take part in public debate. It becomes possible for individuals to make comments on social problems that could be embarrassing to the corporation. It is at best difficult to balance the freedom of individuals and the consequences of their participation in public affairs against the interests of the corporation. The difficulty is increased if the attitudes of management, which are instinctively overprotective of the corporation, are harsh and restrictive. Short-run embarrassments and limited criticism from offended groups—even perhaps a threatened boycott—may be a small price to pay for the continued productivity within the corporation of people whose interests are deep and broad enough to cause them to take stands on public issues. The degree to which an organization is efficient, productive, creative, and capable of development is dependent in large part on the maintenance of a climate in which the individual does not feel suppressed and in which a kind of freedom (analogous to that which the corporation enjoys in a free enterprise society) is permitted as a matter of course.

Overregulation of the individual by corporate policy is no more appropriate internally than overregulation of the corporation by government. On the other hand, personal responsibility is as appropriate to individual liberty as corporate responsibility is to corporate freedom.

The Range of Concerns

What corporate strategists have to be concerned with, then, ranges from the most global of the problems of world society to the uses of freedom by a single person in the firm. The problems of their country, community, and industry lying between these extremes make opportunity for social contribution exactly coextensive with the range of economic opportunity before them. The problem of choice may be met in the area of responsibility in much the same way as in product-market combinations and in developing a program for growth and diversification.

The business firm, as an organic entity intricately affected by and affecting its environment, is as appropriately adaptive, our concept of corporate strategy suggests, to demands for responsible behavior as for economic service. Special satisfactions and prestige, if not economic rewards, are available for companies that are not merely adaptive but take the lead in shaping the moral and ethical environment within which their primary economic function is performed. Such firms are more persuasive than others, moreover, in convincing the public of the inherent impossibility of satisfying completely all the conflicting claims made upon business.

Choice of Strategic Alternatives for Social Action

The choice of avenues in which to participate will, of course, be influenced by the personal values of the managers making the decision. In the absence of powerful predispositions, the inner coherence of the corporate strategy would be extended by choosing issues most closely related to the economic strategy of the company, to the expansion of its markets, to the health of its immediate environment, and to its own industry and internal problems. The extent of appropriate involvement depends importantly on the resources available. Because the competence of the average corporation outside its economic functions is severely limited, it follows that a company should not venture into good works that are not strategically related to its present and prospective economic functions.

As in the case of personal values and individual idiosyncrasy, a company may be found making decisions erratically related to nonstrategic motives. However noble these may be, they are not made strategic and thus defensible and valid by good intentions alone. Rather than make large contributions to X University because its president is a graduate, it might better develop a pattern of educational support that blends the company's involvement in the whole educational system, its acknowledged debt for the contributions of technical or managerial education to the company, and its other contributions to its communities. What makes participation in public affairs strategic rather than improvisatory is (as we have seen in conceiving economic strategy) a definition of objectives taking all other objectives into account and a plan that reflects the company's definition of itself not only as a purveyor of goods and services but as a responsible institution in its society.

The strategically directed company then will have a strategy for support of community institutions as explicit as its economic strategy and as its decisions about the kind of organization it intends to be and the kind of people it intends to attract to its membership. It is easy and proper, when margins allow it, to make full use of tax deductibility, through contributions, from which it expects no direct return. The choice of worthy causes, however, should relate to the company's concept of itself and thus directly to its economic mission. It should enter into new social service fields with the same questions about its resources and competence that new product-market combinations inspire. In good works as in new markets, opportunity without the competence to develop it is illusory. Deliberate concentration on limited objectives is preferable to scattered short-lived enthusiasm across a community's total need.

Policy for ethical and moral personal behavior, once the level of integrity has been decided, is not complicated by a wide range of choice. The nature of the company's operations defines the areas of vulnerability—purchasing, rebates, price fixing, fee splitting, customs facilitation, bribery, dubious agents' fees, conflict of interest, theft, or falsification of records. Where problems appear or danger is sensed specific rules can be issued. As in the case of government regulation of the firm, these should not be overdetailed or mechanical, for there is no hope of anticipating the ingenuity of the willful evader. Uncompromising penalties for violations of policy intent or the rarely specified rule will do more to clarify strategy in this area than thousands of words beforehand. The complexity of elevating individual behavior is thus a matter of implementation of strategy more properly discussed in the context of organization processes such as motivation and control.

Determination of Strategy

We have now before us the major determinants of strategy. The cases studied so far have required consideration of what the strategy of the firm is and what, in your judgment, it ought to be. Concerned so far with the problem of formulating a proper strategy rather than implementing it, you have become familiar with the principal aspects of formulation—namely, (1) appraisal of present and foreseeable opportunity and risk in the company's environment, (2) assessment of the firm's unique combination of present and potential corporate resources or competences, (3) determination of the noneconomic personal and organizational preferences to be satisfied, and (4) identification and acceptance of the social responsibilities of the firm. The strategic decision is one that can be reached only after all these factors have been considered and the action implications of each assessed.

In your efforts to analyze the cases, you have experienced much more of the problem of the strategist than can be described on paper. When you have relinquished your original idea as to what a company's strategy should be in favor of a more imaginative one, you have seen that the formulation process has an essential creative aspect. In your effort to differentiate your thinking about an individual firm from the conventional thinking of its industry, you have looked for new opportunities and for new applications of corporate competence. You have learned how to define a product in terms of its present and potential functions rather than of its physical properties. You have probably learned a good deal about how to assess the special competence of a firm from its past accomplishments and how to identify management's values and aspirations. You may have gained some ability to rank preferences in order of their strength—your own among others.

The problem implicit in striking a balance between the company's apparent opportunity and its evident competence and between your own personal values and concepts of responsibility and those of the company's actual management is not an easy one. The concepts we have been discussing should help you make a decision, but they will not determine your decision for you. Whenever choice is compounded of rational analysis which can have more than one outcome, of aspiration and desire which can run the whole range of human ambition, and a sense of responsibility which changes the appeal of alternatives, it cannot be reduced to quantitative approaches or to the exactness which management science can apply to narrower questions. Managers contemplating strategic decisions must be willing to make them without the guidance of decision rules, with confidence in their own judgment, which will have been seasoned by repeated analyses of similar questions. They must be aware that more than one decision is possible and that they are not seeking the single right answer. They can take encouragement from the fact that the manner in which an organization implements the chosen program can help to validate the original decision.

Some of the most difficult choices confronting a company are those which must be made among several alternatives that appear equally attractive and also equally desirable. Once the analysis of opportunity has produced an inconveniently large number of possibilities, any firm has difficulty in deciding what it wants to do and how the new activities will be related to the old.

In situations where opportunity is approximately equal and economic promise is offered by a wide range of activities, the problem of making a choice can be reduced by reference to the essential character of the company and to the kind of company the executives wish to run. The study of alternatives from this point of view will sooner or later reveal the greater attractiveness of some choices over others. Economic analysis and calculations of return on investment, though of course essential, may not crucially determine the outcome. Rather, the logjam of decision can only be broken by a frank exploration of executive aspirations regarding future development, including perhaps the president's own wishes with respect to the kind of institution he or she prefers to head, carried on as part of a free and untrammeled investigation of what human needs the organization would find satisfaction in serving. That return on investment alone will point the way ignores the values implicit in the calculations and the contribution which an enthusiastic commitment to new projects can make. The rational examination of alternatives and the determination of purpose are among the most important and most neglected of all human activities. The final decision, which should be made as deliberately as possible after a detailed consideration of the issues we have attempted to separate, is an act of will and desire as much as of intellect.

Allied Chemical Corporation (A)

In June 1976 Richard Wagner, president of the Specialty Chemicals Division at Allied Chemical, faced two difficult decisions. He had to recommend whether Allied should support passage of the Toxic Substances Control Act then pending before Congress. He also had to decide whether to implement a proposed new program, called Total Product Responsibility, in his division.

Wagner found these decisions especially difficult because of the variety of factors he had to consider, including Allied's business prospects, recent developments in the chemical industry, and the increasing public and government concern about the health, safety, and environmental effects of chemical production. Another important factor was the set of problems related to Kepone, a pesticide produced until 1974 by Allied and afterwards by an outside contractor.

Allied Chemical

Allied Chemical was a major producer of chemicals, fibers and fabricated products, and energy. With headquarters in Morristown, New Jersey, the company operated over 150 plants, research labs, quarries, and other facilities in the United States and overseas. In 1975 Allied earned $116 million on sales of $2.3 billion. (See Exhibit 1 and Tables 1 and 2 for Allied's organization and recent financial performance.)

During the late 1960s and early 1970s Allied had changed dramati-

Copyright © 1979 by the President and Fellows of Harvard College
Harvard Business School case 379–137

Table 1

Financial Performance, 1972–1975 (Dollars in millions except per share data and ratios)

	1975	1974	1973	1972
Sales	$2,333	$2,216	$1,665	$1,501
Aftertax income	$ 116	$ 144	$ 90	$ 64
EPS	4.17	5.19	3.27	2.30
Debt/equity	0.59	0.45	0.49	0.54
Gross margin/sales	22%	23.3%	24.6%	24.3%
R&D/sales	1.51%	1.39%	1.73%	1.89%
Pollution control facilities cost	$ 34.4	$ 29.0	$ 28.0	$ 25.0

Table 2

Line of Business Performance, 1974–1975 (Dollars in millions)

	1975		1974	
Line of Business	Sales	Income from Operations	Sales	Income from Operations
Energy (petroleum, nuclear, coal, and coke)	$ 581	$ 28	$ 511	$ 32
Fibers and fabricated products	504	46	484	81
Chemicals (inorganic, plastics, organic, and agricultural)	1,248	144	1,221	135
Totals	$2,333	$218	$2,216	$248

cally. One company official said Allied was run as "a loose feudal barony" in the 1960s. *Forbes* called the company "a slow-moving, low-growth, low-profit producer of basic inorganic chemicals, fertilizers, and dyestuffs."[1] Changes began in 1967 when John T. Connor resigned as Secretary of Commerce and became chairman of Allied. Over the course of several years Connor brought in 250 new executives, pruned failing businesses, established systematic planning and tight cost control, and increased corporate supervision of the divisions. At the same time he stressed decentralized decision making and said that innovation and flexibility were crucial to Allied's future.

Connor's most important step was an $800 million commitment to find and develop oil and gas supplies throughout the world. According to Connor this strategy would be financed with new capital and with funds "from existing businesses that were losing, had poor prospects, or had severe environmental risks."[2] The largest investments were in Indonesian gas fields and North Sea oil fields. In Indonesia Allied had

---

[1] "Risk Rewarded," *Forbes,* March 15, 1977, p. 101.

[2] Ibid.

a 35 percent interest in a joint venture with Pertamina, the Indonesian government petroleum agency. The British government had announced its intention to obtain a voluntary 51 percent participation in the North Sea oil fields, but the form that participation might take had not been determined then.

This energy investment was very risky. Finding and developing new reserves was highly competitive, technically difficult, and very costly. Changes in government regulations or tax laws, either domestic or foreign, could cut profits. And problems with weather, technology, or politics in host countries could delay the start of production. These risks seemed justified as shortages of energy and chemical feedstocks occurred during the 1970s and as the potential payoff from the investment grew. Connor stated that energy could provide as much as half of Allied's profits by the early 1980s.

In mid-1976, however, the return on the energy investment was still small. In fact it appeared that Allied's energy businesses, taken altogether, would just about break even in 1976. Allied's U.S. natural gas pipelines lost money because of federal price controls on interstate gas shipments. Its coal and coke business had chronic operating problems, and following a plea of no contest, the company had been fined approximately $100,000 for allegedly failing to meet the Environmental Protection Agency (EPA) air pollution requirements. Finally, obtaining government approval to operate Allied's nuclear fuel reprocessing plant could prove difficult. Company officials then hoped that 1977 would bring the first profits from North Sea oil, and they expected profits from Indonesian gas sales in 1978.

While Allied had invested heavily in energy, chemicals provided the foundation of company earnings. In 1976, for example, chemicals most likely produced 75 percent of company profits, even though they were only 50 percent of total company sales. Allied produced approximately 1,500 chemicals and sold them to all major industries. These sales were primarily to other chemical manufacturers for use in making their products. Other sales were to dealers, who sometimes resold them under their own names, and ultimately to consumers. The two best years in the history of Allied's chemical business were 1974 and 1975. Sales were expected to weaken later in 1976, however, as a result of the recession that began in 1975.

Allied's fiber and fabricated products had been a steady contributor to company profits. On average, this business accounted for one fifth of total sales and profits during the early 1970s. Allied made fibers for clothing, carpeting, and auto tires. The company was also the world's largest manufacturer of auto seat belts and shoulder harnesses.

Overall Allied's record in the early 1970s did not compare favorably with chemical industry standards. Between 1971 and 1975 Allied's return on equity, sales growth, and return on total assets were the second lowest among the 13 major diversified U.S. chemical companies. EPS growth was exactly the average of the 13 companies. On the positive side Allied improved its relative performance in 1974 and 1975, and its energy investment offered the prospect of major improvements in the future.

The Chemical Industry

In 1976 chemicals was one of the largest U.S. industries, with annual sales of more than $100 billion. In the 20 years after World War II chemicals became a high-profit, glamour industry that often grew twice as fast as the GNP. From the mid-1960s to the mid-1970s, however, industry growth had slowed and financial performance dimmed. Among the reasons were higher raw material costs, increased government regulation, the slowdown in U.S. economic growth, and what many considered the maturity of major segments of the industry. Nevertheless, the industry continued to contribute $3–5 billion per year to the U.S. balance of payments.

Roughly 80,000 chemical compounds are sold in the United States and 500 to 1,000 new ones are added each year. More than 12,000 companies manufacture these chemicals, and most of these companies have sales of less than $5 million per year. The major customer for chemical products is the chemical industry itself. A typical chemical company will buy the product of one chemical company, process it, and sell its product to yet another chemical company. In most cases, a long chain of intermediate processors connects a chemical raw material with its ultimate consumer.

The industry is highly competitive. Many chemicals are commodities and compete on price. Competition comes from both natural products (such as cotton fabric) and close chemical substitutes. Chemical firms also face competition from suppliers—especially oil companies—that integrate forward and from customers integrating backward. For a highly capital-intensive industry chemicals have a low degree of concentration. The 10 largest chemical companies account for roughly 35 percent of industry shipments. Low concentration encourages competition by limiting oligopolistic pricing. The industry is also highly cyclical, lagging the business cycle by a few months, and vigorous price cutting usually occurs during recessions.

In the past successful chemical companies tended to follow a basic pattern of growth. They made large investments in research and development, resulting in new products or better processes. These innovations lowered prices and took markets from other chemicals and from natural products. In turn new markets permitted larger-scale operations, further economies, and further R&D. The R&D investments were the key to successful performance. The importance of innovation to the industry is indicated by the fact that half of all chemical products sold in 1970 were not produced commercially in the 1940s. Ammonia fertilizers, sulfa drugs, Dacron, and nylon are some of the results of chemical industry R&D.

Industry prospects were especially uncertain in 1976. The industry earned record profits in 1974 and 1975—an abrupt change from its sagging performance from 1967 to 1973. In response to these profits and to shortages in 1974 a $25 billion capital spending boom took place. This new capacity raised the specter of industrywide overcapacity and renewed price cutting. In fact the new capacity came on line just as the economic slowdown affected chemical sales in 1976.

At the same time costs were rising. Environmental laws and high construction costs raised the price of new plant and equipment. Companies were testing more of their products and raw materials for harmful effects, and testing costs were escalating. It was not unusual then for tests on just one substance to take several years and cost $500,000. Most important, the days of cheap and plentiful oil and natural gas had ended. Chemical companies are disproportionate users of fossil fuels because they need energy to run plants and to use as feedstock for their products. Higher energy costs meant that chemical products in general lost some of their price competitiveness against nonchemical products.

Industry executives were also concerned about an "innovation shrinkage." R&D spending in 1976 would be roughly $1.4 billion, up from $800 million 10 years before. But a higher percentage of this spending was going to modify products already on the market or into government-required health and safety research. Reduced R&D seemed to threaten future industry growth.

Kepone

Wagner had to make his decisions at a time when Allied was in the middle of the Kepone affair. Problems related to Kepone had preoccupied Allied executives for nearly a year and seemed to be growing rather than subsiding. Kepone was a DDT-like pesticide used in ant and roach bait in the United States and as a banana pest killer abroad. It looked like fine, white dust and was toxic. Between 1966 and 1973 Allied made Kepone at its Hopewell, Virginia, plant or had Kepone made for it by outside contractors. Profits were under $600,000 a year, and Allied had no health or safety problems with its Kepone production.

In early 1973 Allied needed more capacity at Hopewell for other products, so it sought bids from companies willing to produce Kepone for Allied. This was not unusual: twice before outside contractors had made Kepone for resale by Allied. The lowest bid by far was submitted by Life Science Products (LSP), a new company owned by two former Allied employees. Both of them had been involved in the development and manufacture of Kepone. LSP leased a former gas station near the Hopewell plant, converted it, and began making Kepone in March 1974.

For 16 months LSP produced Kepone under conditions that might have shocked Charles Dickens, according to most accounts. Brian Kelly, a reporter for the *Washington Post,* described the plant as "an incredible mess. Dust flying through the air . . . saturating the workers' clothing, getting into their hair, even into sandwiches they munched in production areas. . . . The Kepone dust sometimes blew . . . in clouds. A gas station operator across the street said it obscured his view of the Life Science plant. . . . Two firemen in a station behind Life Science say there were times when they wondered if they could see well enough to wheel their engines out in response to a fire alarm."[3]

Two months after LSP started operations, Hopewell's sewage treatment plant broke down because Kepone allegedly killed the bacteria that digested sewage. LSP employees soon developed the "Kepone shakes"; some saw doctors provided by "informal agreement"[4] with LSP, but they were diagnosed as hypertensive. This continued until July 1975, when one worker saw a Taiwanese doctor who sent blood and urine samples to the Center for Disease Control (CDC) in Atlanta. The Kepone levels in the samples were so high that the CDC toxicologists wondered whether they had been contaminated in transit. The CDC notified the Virginia state epidemiologist.

Five days later the epidemiologist examined several workers at LSP. He later said, "The first man I saw was a 23-year-old who was so sick, he was unable to stand due to unsteadiness, was suffering severe chest pains . . . had severe tremor, abnormal eye movements, was disoriented. . . ."[5] The next day LSP was closed by the Virginia state health authorities.

In early 1976 a federal grand jury in Richmond, Virginia, was called to consider the Kepone events. In May it indicted Allied, LSP, the two owners of LSP, four supervisors at Allied, and the City of Hopewell on a total of 1,104 counts. Most of the counts were misdemeanor charges. Hopewell was indicted for failing to report the massive Kepone discharges and for aiding and abetting LSP. Allied was also indicted for aiding and abetting LSP, for violating federal water pollution laws by dumping Kepone and non-Kepone wastes into the James River before 1974 and for conspiring to conceal the dumping. These cases would then be prosecuted by William B. Cummings, U.S. attorney for Virginia. Allied faced penalties of more than $17 million if convicted.

By the end of June there had been several more legal developments. Allied had publicly denied any wrongdoing. The City of Hopewell had pleaded no contest to the charges against it. Allied's attorneys favored

---

[3] Christopher D. Stone, "A Slap on the Wrist for the Kepone Mob," *Business and Society Review,* Summer 1977, p. 4.

[4] Ibid., p. 5.

[5] Ibid., p. 6.

a no contest plea on the pre-1974 dumping charges, but they were confident the company would be found innocent of the other charges. The case would not come to trial until the early fall. Allied also expected suits from the LSP workers, local fishermen, and seafood companies, as well as a large class action suit. These suits would claim damages of astronomical proportions—more than $8 billion.

The Kepone toll had been mounting week by week. The LSP workers were now out of the hospital, but more than 60 of them still reported symptoms of Kepone poisoning. (Mice fed high levels of Kepone had developed tumors that were characterized as cancerous.) The James River was closed to fishing because Kepone tends to accumulate in many species caught for seafood. The James had tens of thousands of pounds of Kepone in its bed, and sales of seafood from the Chesapeake Bay (into which the James flows) were hurt badly. A "60 Minutes" TV report on Kepone damaged Allied's image and reinforced a growing public view that chemicals equaled cancer. Finally, publicity about the Kepone incident increased the likelihood that the Toxic Substances Act would become law.

The impact of Kepone on Allied was traumatic. The company's reputation for environmental safety and responsibility seemed shattered. Settling the court cases could have a significant effect on earnings, and uncertainty about this cost would result in a qualified auditors' statement. Morale was low and hiring had become difficult. Problems also developed in Allied's dealings with federal regulatory agencies, such as the EPA and Occupational Safety and Health Administration (OSHA). These relations depended on good faith bargaining, and Allied met with increasing skepticism and even suspicion. Costly delays resulted in getting permits for new construction. Officials feared the cost of new oxime production facilities at Hopewell would rise more than $10 million because of these delays. (Oximes were organic chemicals used to produce biologically degradable pesticides.)

Allied management felt a strong sense of moral responsibility to the LSP workers, their families, and the Hopewell community. The company already funded research aimed at finding a way to eliminate Kepone from the bodies of the LSP workers. Allied also planned to establish a multimillion-dollar foundation to help with the Kepone cleanup and make grants for other environmental improvements.

Wagner found it hard to understand how the Kepone affair happened in the first place. Allied had made Kepone without any health or safety problems, and the LSP owners should have been able to do the same. Hopewell officials knew about the discharges when the sewage facility began having trouble, yet they took no action. The Virginia Air Quality Resources Board had an air-monitoring filter within a quarter of a mile of LSP, but it was not checking Kepone emissions. Virginia's Water Quality Control Board knew there was a serious problem in October 1974. The board did not use its authority to shut down the LSP plant but tried to use persuasion to get changes.

Federal agencies were also involved. In autumn 1974 the Occupational Safety and Health Administration received a letter from a former LSP employee, who claimed he was fired for refusing to work under unsafe conditions. OSHA responded by writing to the LSP owners. They, in turn, wrote back that there was no problem, and OSHA accepted their assurances. The Environmental Protection Agency had sent an inspector to LSP in March 1975. The inspector was uncertain whether the EPA had jurisdiction over pesticides. His letter of inquiry to the EPA regional office in Philadelphia was unanswered in July when LSP was closed.

Toxic Substances Control Act

In less than a week Wagner would report to Allied's executive committee on the Toxic Substances Control Act (TSCA). He had to recommend company support for the act, or opposition, or continued neutrality. A neutral stand meant Allied would keep a low profile and issue public statements saying the company supported some features of the act and opposed others.

TSCA was a new approach to government regulation of harmful chemicals. Past legislation aimed at remedial action, while TSCA aimed at prevention. Senator James B. Pearson (R., Kansas) made this distinction:

> Existing legislation simply does not provide the means by which adverse effects on human health and the environment can be ascertained and appropriate action taken before chemical substances are first manufactured and introduced into the marketplace. At present the only remedy available under such Federal statutes as the Clean Air Act, the Federal Water Pollution Control Act, the Occupational Safety and Health Act, and the Consumer Product Safety Act, is to impose restrictions on toxic substances after they have first been manufactured.[6]

TSCA was intended to *prevent* unreasonable risks to health and the environment. It gave the Environmental Protection Agency two new powers. The EPA could compel companies to provide information on the production, composition, uses, and health effects of the chemicals they made or processed. Using these data the EPA could then regulate the manufacture, processing, commercial distribution, use, and disposal of the chemicals.

TSCA had three key provisions. Section 4 (testing) authorized the EPA to require testing of a chemical for any of several reasons. The reasons included clarification of health effects, toxicity, and carcinogenicity. Before requiring tests the EPA had to show that (1) the chemical

---

[6] Library of Congress, *Legislative History of the Toxic Substances Control Act* (Washington, D.C.: U.S. Government Printing Office, 1976), p. 215.

could pose an unreasonable risk to health or the environment or that human or environmental exposure to the chemical would be substantial; (2) there was insufficient data for determining the health and environmental effects of the chemical; and (3) the only way to develop these data would be by testing the chemical. The manufacturer would pay for the testing.

The most controversial provision of TSCA was section 5—premarket notification. This required a manufacturer to report its intent to produce any new chemical to the EPA 90 days before doing so. A manufacturer had to make similar notice of plans to produce a chemical for a "significant new use." These reports had to disclose the chemical's name, chemical identity and molecular structure, its proposed categories of use, the amount to be made, its manufacturing by-products, and its disposal. The manufacturer was also required to submit available data on health and environmental effects.

If the EPA found that there was not enough information to judge the health or environmental effects, it could prohibit or limit the manufacture, distribution, or use of the chemical until adequate information was provided. This was the third key provision of TSCA. It gave the EPA broad new powers to regulate the operations of more than 115,000 establishments that made or processed chemicals. TSCA also directed the EPA to weigh the costs and benefits of the testing and regulations that it required under these new powers.

Wagner had to sort out a number of complicated issues to make his decision. He had to ask whether, as a citizen, he thought TSCA was in the public interest. As an Allied executive, he had to consider how support for TSCA would affect Allied's image and how the act itself would affect Allied's chemical business. This last question was especially difficult since TSCA could help business in some ways and hurt it in others. For example, TSCA might cut the chances of another Kepone incident. The costs of testing and reporting might give large chemical companies, like Allied, a competitive edge over smaller firms. But these costs would also hurt Allied's bottom line and make chemical products, particularly new ones, less competitive with natural products. Wagner had his assistant, a recent graduate of a leading eastern business school, summarize the major arguments for and against TSCA. The assistant's report is presented in the following two sections.

For TSCA:

1. TSCA closes gaps in current laws. The act will require testing *before* exposure, so workers and communities will not be used as guinea pigs.
2. TSCA's cost will be low. The EPA and the General Services Administration estimate total costs to industry of $100–200 million a year. Industry sales exceed $100 billion a year.

3. TSCA will reduce national health care costs by preventing some of the health effects of harmful chemicals. Care for cancer patients alone now costs more than $18 billion per year.

4. Under current laws the incidence of cancer has been rising, and many chemical disasters and near-disasters have occurred.

5. The act offers protection for the interests of chemical companies. When companies disagree with EPA regulations, they can file a timely law suit and seek a court injunction.

6. TSCA may reduce the risks of doing business in chemicals. The act may, in effect, put a "government seal of approval" on hazardous chemicals. It could also cut the risk of a company being sued because a customer used its products in a dangerous way.

7. Public support for the act will help restore Allied's image as a responsible community-minded company.

8. The act is likely to pass this year, so Allied might as well get on the bandwagon. The Senate has already passed the act, and the current version lacks several features that caused House opposition in past years. Public pressure for passage is building, especially in the wake of the Kepone headlines. The membership of the Manufacturing Chemists Association, the major industry trade group, is split over the act.

Against TSCA:

1. The industry is already sufficiently regulated. Twenty-seven major federal laws now cover almost every aspect of company operations. Large chemical companies like Allied already deal with more than 70 government agencies.

2. Companies already do extensive testing of chemicals before marketing them. The tests sometimes cost several hundred thousand dollars and take several years. They are performed by highly trained scientists working in the most modern labs. Furthermore, companies have a strong incentive to do sufficient testing: they want to avoid the many heavy costs imposed by incidents like Kepone.

3. TSCA will be extremely costly. Dow puts the cost at $2 billion annually; the Manufacturing Chemists Association estimates $800 million to $1.3 billion. There will be less innovation because of excessive testing burdens on new chemicals. U.S. chemical exports will become more costly and less competitive, U.S. jobs will move overseas, and the testing and reporting requirements will hurt or even close many small companies. This will also affect large companies like Allied. We rely on small companies as suppliers, and Allied itself is basically a composite of 60 or 70 small specialty chemical companies.

4. The act is dangerously vague. The EPA gets very broad powers with few restrictions.

5. Reporting to the EPA under TSCA will require us to disclose trade secrets and other confidential data.

6. Supporting the act to aid our image or get on a bandwagon won't fool many people. It will be taken as a public relations move and could raise even more suspicions about Allied's motives.

7. It's not even clear there's a bandwagon. The Senate passed the act in 1972 and 1973, and the House killed it both times. Even though the EPA is lobbying hard for TSCA, the Commerce Department and the Office of Management and Budget oppose it. There is as yet no indication whether President Ford will sign or veto the act.

8. Many of the reports of chemical "disasters" have been exaggerated by the media and by environmental groups. We should not give in to pressures based on this sort of misinformation.

Total Product Responsibility

Wagner also had to decide whether to implement a new program called Total Product Responsibility (TPR). This program had been developed in 1975 by the engineering and operations services unit in the Specialty Chemicals Division. This 17-person staff unit developed policies and procedures related to health, safety, maintenance, and quality control (see Exhibit 2). TPR would use "tools of policy, procedure, control, and review" to help Allied "properly discharge its legal and moral responsibility to protect its employees, customers, the public, and the environment from harm."

TPR was first proposed in 1975 by R. L. Merrill, vice president of engineering and operations services. Merrill had come to Allied after several years with Dow Chemical and was impressed by Dow's Product Stewardship Program. According to *Business Week* product stewardship meant Dow would assume "total responsibility for how its products affect people" and Dow's products would carry "a virtual guarantee of harmlessness."[7] Dow had 600 people involved in setting up product stewardship in 1972. They prepared environmental and safety profiles for all 1,100 of Dow's products. Then film cassettes were made for presentations to Dow employees, customers, and distributors. In its first year, product stewardship cost $1 million.

Merrill's original proposal was not for a program as extensive as Dow's. Merrill had suggested a survey of information currently available to Allied on the health and environmental effects of its products. This

---

[7] "Dow's Big Push for Product Safety," *Business Week,* April 21, 1973, p. 82.

survey would then be followed by whatever tests were needed to supplement existing information. But during 1975 and early 1976, an expanded TPR slowly took shape around this original suggestion. If it was important to get complete health and safety information about Allied's products, it also seemed important to get similar information on raw materials, processes, and customer uses of Allied products. And, in turn, it seemed important to make sure all this information was reflected in Allied's everyday operating procedures.

The first step in implementing TPR would be for Wagner to issue a 25-page memorandum on TPR to all management personnel in his division. The memo would set out standards of operating and business practice that covered virtually every aspect of division operations. Line management would then have to make sure that operating procedures conformed to these standards. The following excerpts are from the TPR memorandum.

Specifications: Specifications should exist for every raw material . . . and every finished product. . . . No specifications may be changed without the approval of the director of operations/general manager after review with operations services.

Testing: All of the division's products will be reviewed on a priority basis, as determined by our toxicology specialists, to determine the known or suspected undesirable toxic effects which those products may have on our employees, customers, the public, and the environment.

Plant SOPs: Standard operating procedures will be developed by plants for each product area. Procedures will be designed by engineering, technical, and operations groups to provide capability of producing uniform product quality and to ensure process continuity. Use of approved procedures will be mandatory, and revisions to accepted methods will require approval of preestablished authority levels.

Equipment Testing: Testing procedures and frequencies are to be developed to ensure reliability of equipment at the 95 percent confidence level to minimize the possibility of unforeseen problems arising.

Change Procedure: Changes in R&D, product development, manufacturing, distribution, and marketing that may adversely affect the process, employees, product, customer, the public, or the environment should not be made without the approval of the director of operations, director of marketing, or research laboratory director, as appropriate, and after review with operations services.

Technical Bulletins: Technical literature and bulletins should include all safety and environmental statements necessary to protect employees, customers, the public, and the environment. Operations services is to receive, edit, and approve all literature and bulletins to assure that all such proper statements are included.

Advertising: Advertising copy should reflect true and accurate statements about our products. Advertising copy should be reviewed by operations services to prevent misleading statements concerning claims in the areas of environmental products' safety, health, and quality assurance.

Product End Use: Marketing departments should make every effort to determine the end use application of each product sold. Consideration should be given to the desirability of using the product in that application and the customer's understanding of the effect of such use on the operation. . . . A product should not be sold to a customer where it is known that the end use application is not proper.

Capability of Existing Customers: Marketing departments have the responsibility to establish the capability of our customers concerning their competency to handle our products in a manner that protects the customers' process, employees, the public, and the environment. Hazardous products should not be sold to customers whose capability is deemed inadequate. If it is determined that an application or end use of the product is improper .. . the sales of this product to that customer should be discontinued immediately.

New Customers: Hazardous products should not be sold to new customers until the capability of that customer is deemed adequate.

Outside Contractors: When outside contractors are to be used to process, reprocess, repackage, or manufacture materials for us, the review should include a determination of the toxicity and hazards of the materials to be handled and an in-depth study of the contractor's capability to perform the work such as not to endanger the contractor's employees, the public, or the environment. . . . When a contractor is retained it is the responsibility of the appropriate business area to arrange for periodic inspections and reviews of that contractor's operations by the operations services department.

Wagner had distributed the draft memo within the Specialty Chemicals Division and discussed the program with a variety of line and staff personnel. Reaction was mixed. Leonard Warren, director of marketing services, said:

I don't know where I come down on this. I know that chemical companies are getting burned in the newspapers and in court, and the result is more and more government people telling us how to do business. We've got to stop this, but we've also got to make money. As I read TPR it says we're going to say "no" to some people who want to buy from us. We'll also be harassing our current customers and prospects by asking them how they use our products, who they sell to, and what their customers do with their products. Some of them are going to tell us to keep our noses out of their businesses. A lot of our products are virtually commodities, and they're already hard enough to sell without the burdens of TPR paperwork, TPR costs, and the mixed signals we'll be giving to our reps.

Now I'm not completely opposed to TPR in some form. After Kepone, it will make Allied's reputation a little better. There are probably some customers that we shouldn't sell to, because they're too risky, and this program will help us get rid of them. In some cases, it might even help sales because it would be a reason for our reps to have even further contacts with customers, and more information about uses of our products could be a useful kind of market research for us.

Another hesitant view came from Joe DeStefano, a production manager at the Hopewell complex:

My first reaction is that we already do a lot of the things in the TPR memo. The difference is that our current procedures are not formalized and we don't have to get as much clearance before making changes. I can't help wondering whether TPR isn't going to make business a lot more bureaucratic. It seems to me that the government already does enough of that. Under TPR, we would have to go through operations services to do almost anything. We could end up with more paperwork, buck-passing, and bureaucracy. Sometimes I'm not sure what's more important: getting a good product out the door at a profit or complying with a thousand rules and restrictions.

Janet Baker, an associate corporate counsel who handled environmental cases, supported TPR:

Allied has to do something like TPR. Kepone costs are skyrocketing, and we can't afford to let another Kepone happen. TPR sends a clear message throughout the division that health and safety are top priority. We've sent the message before, but it needs vigorous emphasis. If we don't take steps to run our business as safely as possible, the government will do it for us.

But there are problems. Customers and suppliers could well resent our sanctimonious attitude when we poke our noses into their businesses. Refusals to deal have to be handled unilaterally and without publicity or else we may be liable for conspiracy allegations, antitrust, trade disparagement, or libel suits.

Despite these objections and misgivings, Merrill remained enthusiastic about TPR; he argued:

Of course TPR won't be free of problems, but it does much more good than harm. It will help our image and cut our risk of environmental and safety problems. Besides, the government is likely to require most of what's in TPR in just a few years. By starting now, Allied can learn to do business under these inevitable new conditions.

It's also absolutely essential that the attitude of Allied managers and workers toward the government start to change. The government is going to be a major factor in the chemical industry for the indefinite future. We can either take an adversary approach and comply with regulations in a minimal, grudging way, or we can recognize that the government is here to stay, learn to cooperate with federal agencies, and as a result, get better results in regulatory proceedings and lower our risks of future Kepones.

In making his decision Wagner also had to consider the views of Allied's chairman and the executive committee. There was strong support among these executives for "some concrete steps" that would prevent another Kepone and change company attitudes toward government health and environmental rules. At the same time Wagner could not ignore his division's earnings and performance. In the summer of 1976 sales were weakening as a result of the recession that began in 1975. Wagner wondered if this was the right time to divert managerial time and attention from the chemical business. He was also concerned about the possible impact of TPR on the flexibility, decentralized decision making, and innovation he had been trying to encourage in his division. He also wondered whether TPR would have kept the Kepone problem from happening in the first place.

Further Developments

Since 1976 was an election year Wagner had been paying some attention to the positions candidates took on regulation in general and the chemical industry in particular. Senator Vance Hartke (D., Indiana), who then faced a serious reelection challenge, campaigned hard for greater regulations of chemicals. One of his speeches included the following remarks:

> The hazards associated with chemicals like PCB's vinyl chloride, BCME, and asbestos have all dramatically illustrated how important it is to get early warning with respect to new chemical substances. . . .
>
> During this (last) five-year period, there have been in excess of 1 million deaths in this country from cancer. Over a million infants have been born with physical or mental damage. . . . While many of the grave health risks to human beings have declined in recent years, cancer statistics have done just the opposite. In fact, the incidence of cancer was estimated in 1975 to be some 2½ percent above the previous year. . . .
>
> It is no accident that the hot spots for cancer in this country are in close proximity to those locations where the chemical industry is most highly concentrated.
>
> . . . It is tragic that those who rely upon the industry for jobs have essentially become guinea pigs for discovering the adverse effects of chemical substances. It is also tragic that much of the information which has shown the cancer-producing potential of many chemicals has come from death records of employees. For example, of 1 million current and former American asbestos workers who still survive, fully 300,000 have been projected to die of cancer. This death rate is 50 percent higher than that of the U.S. population at large.[8]

At the same time Wagner was also aware of growing opposition to government regulation. The leading presidential contenders then—Ford, Carter, and Reagan—all sounded the theme of "too much government interference." Academic studies had documented the large indirect costs of regulation and even reformers like Ralph Nader were very critical of agencies such as the FTC, which Nader said was basically a captive of the industries it regulated. Industry also joined this movement against regulation. Dow Chemical, for example, announced completion of its own "catalogue of regulatory horrors" and claimed it had spent $50 million in 1975 to meet regulations it considered excessive.[9]

---

[8] Library of Congress, *Legislative History of the Toxic Substances Act,* p. 216.

[9] "Dow Chemical's Catalogue of Regulatory Horrors," *Business Week,* April 4, 1977, p. 50.

Exhibit 1

Company Organizational Chart

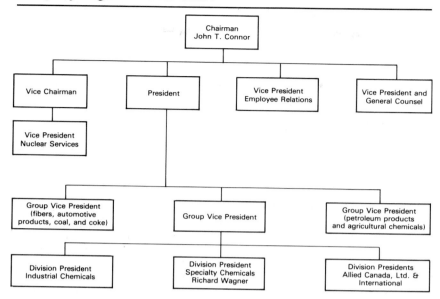

Exhibit 2

Specialty Chemicals Division Organization Chart

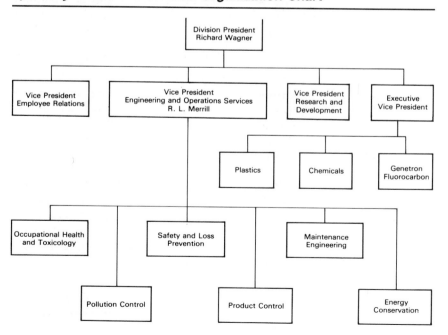

Consolidated Petroleum Corporation (Revised and Condensed)

The board of directors of Consolidated Petroleum Corporation met at the call of its chairman in a special session at the company's New York City headquarters at 10 A.M. on Monday, May 3, 1976. As they entered the board room that morning several directors sensed and commented on the tension in the air. Prior to the appearance of the chairman outside directors talked quietly together at one end of the room while inside officer-directors clustered at the other end. Background for the meeting was a number of disturbing developments during the preceding year. One of the developments—the revelation that Consolidated, like some other large business organizations, had made illegal political contributions and possibly had bribed foreign government officials—had led a few months earlier to the creation of a Special Review Committee of outside directors. On April 23 the committee transmitted to the full board a report embodying findings, conclusions, and recommendations, together with a statement of a minority view of one member of the committee.

When the chairman entered the room the directors took their customary seats around the long oval table. The chairman opened the meeting by saying, "Gentlemen, I've called you together because this company is facing a crisis—probably the most serious and urgent situation that has arisen in the entire history of the business. I don't think I'll get any argument about that description of our position. I hope you're all

This case, a condensation of Consolidated Petroleum Corporation (Revised), copyright 1979 by Columbia University, was developed for use in the Corporate Governance Workshop, Harvard Business School. Used with permission.

486

prepared to continue this meeting through the rest of the day and, if necessary, into the evening until we decide what we are going to do and how we are going to do it."

Consolidated Petroleum Corporation, an integrated oil company (ranking 13th in 1975 sales among U.S. oil companies), was engaged in the production, procurement, transportation, refining, and marketing of petroleum and natural gas and products derived therefrom. The company also participated, through wholly owned subsidiaries as well as through joint ventures and minority investments, in the chemical, plastics, and minerals industries.

For the fiscal year ended December 31, 1975, Consolidated Petroleum reported total revenues of $4.8 billion, the second highest in the company's history, although down 12 percent from 1974. Net income of $210 million was the third highest ever recorded but 34 percent less than in 1974. Earnings per share were $1.08 against $1.64 in 1974.

The following information was excerpted from Consolidated's 1975 annual report and SEC Form 10-K:

1. The company's principal resources were its capability as a finder, producer, refiner, and marketer of petroleum; its reserves of petroleum and various minerals; its diversification into other industries with strong growth and profit potential; and its healthy financial position.

2. The company's balance sheet showed cash and marketable securities aggregating more than $500 million. A major part of this resource would be committed to reversing the decline in Consolidated's U.S. petroleum production. Developmental work would also be pushed for the company's discoveries in the North Sea petroleum field and in certain nonpetroleum properties. In addition a substantial investment would be made in chemical operations.

3. The fall in revenues and even greater decline in net income during 1975 were attributed to several developments. First, while earnings from U.S. petroleum operations were more than 9 percent higher than in 1974, foreign petroleum profits fell 65 percent. The U.S. gain was caused principally by improved margins on petroleum products. The falloff in foreign earnings was attributed partly to nationalization of company properties in several Middle East and Latin American countries, loss of certain markets to nationalized producer-country sales organizations, and in some countries, high government-mandated costs that reduced normal selling margins. In addition refining and marketing operations in Europe suffered from that region's then generally stagnant economy. Second, chemical earnings fell because of sluggish demand in both the United States and abroad. Finally, losses from minerals operations were reduced in 1975, but these activities continued to be unprofitable, as they had been for a number of years.

4. Effective July 1, 1973, the company had entered into a partnership under which the company and David Chemicals Corporation owned and operated on a 50–50 basis the plastics business previously conducted by Con-

solidated. Provision was made for the company's 50 percent share of anticipated future losses in certain commitments of the partnership; the company's share was projected to be $72 million. The provision for losses reflected continuing and additional anticipated difficulties in achieving a consistent level of control over quality of output in the production of the principal product of the business, a specialty plastic compound of high market potential but extremely erratic behavior under large-scale continuous-flow processing.

Consolidated Petroleum's board had undergone one shocking and several seriously disturbing experiences during 1974 and 1975. The shocking experience was the revelation, initially in news reports and later in testimony before the SEC and various congressional committees, that corporate funds had been contributed to political parties and candidates in the United States and several foreign countries, and alleged bribes paid to certain foreign government officials had been recorded as commission payments to agents and other legitimate business expenses. This matter became the subject of an investigation by the Securities and Exchange Commission when it was revealed that some of the contributions and alleged bribes had been hidden in various operating accounts, while others had been handled through funds that were never incorporated in the company's official accounting records.

Less shocking, but clearly disturbing to some outside directors, were several other developments that surfaced in 1973, 1974, and 1975.

1. A Federal Trade Commission complaint was issued in July 1973 against several petroleum companies of which Consolidated was one, charging violation of Section 5 of the Federal Trade Commission Act and alleging a combination or agreement to monopolize the business of refining crude oil. This proceeding remained in a relatively early stage of development in 1976.

2. In June 1975 a class-action suit was filed by the State of California in the United States District Court for the Northern District of California alleging violations of federal antitrust laws by a group of petroleum companies including Consolidated. Early in January 1976 this suit was consolidated for purposes of discovery in the United States District Court for the District of Connecticut with class-action suits previously filed by the attorneys general of Connecticut and Kansas against a number of petroleum companies including Consolidated, alleging multiple violations of state and federal antitrust laws.

3. In 1975 a number of U.S. senators and representatives began vigorously to promote legislation that would dismember vertically integrated petroleum companies.

4. A class-action suit was filed in 1974 on behalf of all members of the United Steel Workers in the Federal District Court for the

Northern District of Indiana against several large petroleum companies including Consolidated, charging the defendants with violations of the federal antitrust laws and seeking damages in the amount of $750 million before trebling and injunctive relief.

5. Several suits against Consolidated were filed in 1975 in various states charging violations of federal, state, and local antipollution legislation and regulations.

6. During 1975 a number of derivative actions were filed by shareholders on behalf of the company, later consolidated into a single complaint which alleged that certain directors and officers of the company had violated various sections of the Securities Exchange Act of 1934 and had permitted waste of corporate assets. In general the complaint charged that since 1960 the defendants were responsible for the unauthorized disbursement of almost $4 million of corporate funds for unlawful political contributions and other similar unlawful purposes in the United States and abroad and that the disbursements were concealed by means of false entries in the books of the company and its subsidiaries, with the result that reports filed with the Securities and Exchange Commission and proxy statements disseminated to shareowners during this period were false and misleading. The complaint alleged that the company's independent accountants knew or should have known that such irregularities existed and that they aided in the concealment of such matters by failing to conduct a proper audit or to disclose matters known to them.

7. A number of actions were brought against the company and its officers during 1975 alleging discriminatory or other inequitable employment and promotion policies and practices prejudicial to the rights of members of minority groups and women.

Shaken by these developments, several outside directors proposed that the board establish a Special Review Committee to investigate thoroughly (1) the use of corporate funds for political purposes, (2) other matters which the committee might judge essential in relation to the legality and morality of the behavior of the company officers and managers, and (3) the role of the board in the management of the company. It was proposed that the committee be composed of five outside directors—Mr. Perrine as chairman, Mr. Appleton, Dr. Count, Mr. Walden, and Dean Yost—and be authorized to draw upon internal and external staff assistance to the extent required to complete its assignment.

The chairman, supported by the president, objected to this proposal on the following grounds: (1) To the extent that corporate funds had been disbursed for purposes or in a manner contrary to law in the United States or in foreign countries, the actions were not in accord with established company policy, were concealed from and were unknown to senior officers, and were the subject of investigations already in progress under top management direction. (2) Allegations about the illegality of certain of the company's trade practices were without merit, and all charges would be successfully rebutted. (3) Established company policies and practices governing environmental pollution and employment conditions were in full compliance with relevant laws and administrative rulings. (4) The Consolidated board, and in particular its outside members, could not properly and effectively play a larger role in the management of the business, nor would the outside directors be able or willing to invest the substantial additional time required to become more closely involved in ongoing affairs. (5) The appointment of the proposed committee would inevitably be reported in the business press and would be widely interpreted as an expression by outside directors of lack of confidence in operating management, with consequent unfortunate repercussions on the price of the common stock and on the morale of all management personnel.

In the ensuing lively discussion, the chairman expressed the view that the appropriate and only viable responsibility of the board was to select the chief executive officer, to maintain a general familiarity with his performance as evidenced by overall financial results and similar measures, to support his policies and strategies if they produced satisfactory results, and to discharge him and install a successor CEO if his performance was judged unsatisfactory. Several outside directors disagreed with this view as unduly restrictive and unresponsive to newly emerging public pressures for a more active role for corporate boards.

When the chairman discovered the strength of the contrary position, he stated that despite the fact that the outside directors were a minority of the board's membership he was unwilling to take the issue to a vote that would divide a board that had always found it possible to act unanimously. He therefore agreed to the appointment of the proposed Special Review Committee. He suggested, however, that the committee's mission be restricted to items (1) and (2) of the initial proposal. Several outside directors objected to such a restriction and said that it would be useful to extend the committee's task to include a broad assessment of the board's functions and responsibilities. One of the group observed that he could no longer accept as satisfactory Consolidated's financial performance, which he described as below average for the industry for several years. Another outside director was critical of the company's diversification program and added that the board had never had an opportunity to evaluate that strategy in depth, with detailed staff analysis of alternative investment opportunities, risks, and projected payouts. After further discussion, which one director characterized as "sharp but not belligerent," the chairman agreed to give the Special Review Committee the proposed broad mission.

In January 1976 before the Review Committee had completed its investigation, without either admitting or denying the allegations in the complaint, the company consented to the entry of a Final Judgment of Permanent Injunction, Consent, and Undertaking in the matter of the *Securities and Exchange Commission* v. *Consolidated Petroleum Company* before the United States District Court for the District of Columbia. The judgment enjoined the use of corporate funds for unlawful political contributions or other unlawful purposes and also enjoined the company from violating Sections 13(a) and 14(a) of the Securities Exchange Act of 1934 and the applicable rules thereunder by filing materially false and misleading annual or other periodic reports or proxy statements which failed properly to reflect such expenditures.

The board of directors of Consolidated Petroleum Company was composed of the following members in 1976 (see Exhibit 3 for further detail):

— *Edwin Huntington,* 63, Chairman and Chief Executive Officer. He was elected president and chief operating officer in 1965 and chairman and chief executive officer in 1968. Mr. Huntington had two years to serve before mandatory retirement. He was largely responsible for bringing to the board all of the outside directors serving in 1976 except Mr. Perrine and Dean Yost.

— *Paul Gallery,* 58, President and Chief Operating Officer. Mr. Gallery was Mr. Huntington's choice for president when that position was vacated by Mr. Huntington's election as chairman of the board. He was expected to succeed Mr. Huntington as chairman in 1978.

— *Lewis Appleton,* 63, Chairman of the Board, Union Commercial National Bank of New York. An old friend of Mr. Huntington's and the head of the company's lead bank, Mr. Appleton joined the Consolidated board in 1969.

— *David Count,* 62, President, Atlantic Institute of Technology. He became dean of the faculties at A.I.T. in 1955 and was elected president in 1963. A director of several major corporations he accepted an invitation from Mr. Huntington to join the Consolidated board in 1971.

— *Arthur Gallon,* 56, Senior Vice President. He was responsible for the company's petroleum and gas activities. He was elected a director of the company in 1969.

— *Monroe Howard,* 61, Senior Vice President. He was the chief financial officer of the company. He became a director in 1972.

— *Walter Johnson,* 58, Senior Vice President. He was in charge of administrative services and planning. Mr. Johnson accepted an invitation in 1965 from Mr. Huntington's predecessor as chairman to assume responsibility for implementing a reorganization plan he had proposed as a consultant to the company. He joined the board in 1972.

— *Crosby Kennedy,* Senior Partner, Kennedy, Swift, Rose & Christianson (one of the larger New York corporate law firms and principal outside counsel for Consolidated Petroleum). A longtime friend of Mr. Huntington's he was invited to join the Consolidated board in 1971.

— *Philip Lewis,* 57, Chairman, President, and Chief Executive Officer, Inter-Continental Aerospace Corporation. A graduate of West Point and a career military officer he attained the rank of brigadier general in the air force. He became Inter-Continental chief officer in 1970. General Lewis met Mr. Huntington as a fellow member of a yacht club on Long Island's North Shore. After the acquaintance developed into friendship General Lewis accepted Mr. Huntington's invitation to fill a vacancy created by the retirement of an outside member of the Consolidated board.

— *William Perrine,* 68, retired from his position as chairman of the board, Whipple Industries (a very large, diversified company with divisions in a number of industries). Mr. Perrine was a self-made man who had gone to work at the age of 16 in a small manufacturing company. His hard work, aggressiveness and ability to learn from every experience supported his rise through foreman and factory management ranks until, at the age of 27, he was asked to become general manager of the company when the owning family could no longer provide for its effective administration. He proceeded to buy out the family interest and then carried through a public stock offering and the first of a series of acquisitions and mergers that built the giant organization from which he retired in 1973. Mr. Perrine joined the Consolidated board in 1962 and participated in the selection of Mr. Huntington to serve as president and then chairman.

— *John Rosterman,* 60, Senior Vice President. He was in charge of chemical and mineral activities. He joined Consolidated in 1962 and in 1968 was made a senior vice president in charge of both chemicals and minerals. He joined the board in 1974.

— *Thomas Thompson,* 62, Senior Vice President. He was responsible for foreign operations. Mr. Thompson entered the Foreign Service and served several duty tours in the Middle East. In 1954 he left the State Department and joined Consolidated as a vice president responsible for relations with Mid-East and North African governments. In 1965 his assignment was broadened to include all foreign operations. He became a director in 1974.

— *Carl Walden,* 55, a director of several large corporations, was formerly managing partner of a major international management consulting company. He retired from his firm at the age of 50 in order to work as a "professional director," serving on the boards of a number of large companies where his earlier experience with the problems of companies across a broad spectrum of industries and his accumulated knowledge and wisdom might be valuable. He accepted an invitation to join the Consolidated board in 1971.

— *Joseph Yost,* 64, Dean, Graduate School of Business, Colharstan University. Dean Yost's career included an early period teaching management after acquiring an MBA and Ph.D. at Columbia, a middle period when he served as senior staff officer and assistant to the president of a large manufacturing company, and a third period in which he returned to academia as dean of a major business school. He was brought on the Consolidated Petroleum board by Mr. Huntington's predecessor as chairman and was involved in the selection of Mr. Huntington as president and later as chairman.

— *Carroll Ziegler,* 50, Senior Vice President. He was responsible for technology and research. He became a director in 1971.

Consolidated Petroleum's board of directors met six times annually on the first Thursday of every second month. Meetings typically began at 10:00 A.M. and continued through a working lunch. Committees of the board usually scheduled their meetings for the afternoon preceding a regular meeting of the full board, although on occasion they met at other times. The board had five standing committees. The Executive Committee was empowered to act for the board in emergencies between regular meetings and, from time to time, specifically authorized to act for the board with respect to a defined decision situation. The other four carried out functions typically assigned to such a board committee.

The Executive Committee was composed of the chairman, the president, and one outside director, an assignment rotated annually among outside directors. The Executive Compensation and Audit committees were composed exclusively of outside directors.

Directors received monthly financial and operating reports in considerable detail for the corporation as a whole and also for the operating divisions. These reports were accompanied by analytical material prepared by the corporate finance staff, noting and explaining trends and deviations from standards. Consolidated had a formal long-range planning system generally covering a five-year planning horizon with annual review and updating. The updated plan was submitted annually to the board for its review and approval and on these occasions was the subject of verbal explanation. Special reports were made to the board from time to time when a significant decision such as a proposed acquisition was under consideration by management.

The regular bimonthly meetings of the board were conducted in accordance with the discipline of a planned and familiar agenda. At a typical meeting the chairman, after disposing of the minutes of the preceding meeting and other formalities for the record, would open with a general review of operations during the preceding two months and comments on near-term prospects for the business. He would then invite the president to supplement his remarks on the basis of his closer familiarity with specific operating details. At each meeting two or three senior line managers—some board members and others, not—would address the board on performance and prospects in their areas of responsibility. These presentations were carefully prepared, typically with elaborate supporting array of visual aids, and board members, particularly outside members, had an opportunity to make observations and raise questions. Outside directors usually posed few questions. Such questions as were raised were ordinarily directed at eliciting explanations of developments and prospects in somewhat greater depth than had been offered in the original presentations.

Comments of several outside directors described the character of board meetings and the environment in which the board fulfilled its obligations prior to 1975. One outside director observed: "This is an orderly and gentlemanly group. The inside members clearly know their place in relation to the chairman, and the outside members generally hold to the view that their principal responsibility is to select competent people to run the company and then support them as long as they bring in acceptable results. That has certainly been the case in this organization as long as I have been a director."

Another outside director described the board as "passive but prudently observant. We have all the information necessary to maintain our appropriate watching brief. We could have more information if we asked for it. We never have the feeling that we might be refused anything we wanted."

A third director observed, "With competent management, there is really very little for outside directors to do except in crises. Competent management seldom permits a crisis to occur. Even when the Arabs decided to change the whole petroleum ballgame in 1973, there was little that any outside director of this company could contribute. Management was on top of the situation, kept the board informed about what was happening and what they were doing about it, and none of us knew enough about the business to develop any original ideas or even to suggest significant alternatives to management."

A fourth director said, "I've been on boards where there was acrimonious discussion, political maneuvering, and even aggravating nitpicking. In general, these situations occurred because management was not delivering a satisfactory performance or because management was divided within its own house or because an external force—such as a radical technological change that disrupted a major market or a threatened unfriendly takeover bid—impacted on the business. Or even because one or two outside directors didn't understand their proper role. But we haven't seen any of that here at Consolidated Petroleum."

The report of the Special Review Committee, made available to the full board on April 23, 1976, concluded that during the period 1960–75 a total of approximately $4 million of corporate funds had been used for political contributions and related purposes. The report stated that at least $2 million of this amount was expended by the company in foreign countries, mostly in circumstances which the committee concluded were lawful or as to the legality of which the committee expressed no judgment. The remaining expenditures for political purposes in the United States and in a few foreign countries were characterized by the committee as illegal.

The committee's report also commented on its investigation of knowledge of such contributions both abroad and in the United States on the part of certain of the company's executives. The report noted that all senior executives denied any knowledge of illegal contributions in the United States, and most of them denied any knowledge of contributions, whether legal or illegal, in other countries. Nevertheless, the report concluded that senior officers, even if ignorant of the payments, could not completely disavow responsibility for them and indeed should have taken steps to assure that such contributions were not made and, if made, were brought to their attention.

With respect to the allegations of bribes given to certain foreign government officials and others, the report concluded that deficiencies in financial reporting and control systems, absence of policy guidance from the corporate level to country-level operating managers, and the committee's inability to make clear distinctions between legitimate and valuable agents and illegitimate interveners who received payments to which no specific business services could be related combined to render any judgment cloudy. Bribery had probably occurred, the report stated, but its magnitude and pervasiveness could not be determined. It was beyond dispute, however, that Consolidated's management and information systems lacked both qualitative and quantitative standards and controls that would outlaw the use of bribes to advance the interests of the business—particularly in national cultures which traditionally had a relaxed attitude toward bribery—and identify the prohibited practice if it occurred.

The committee recommended the establishment and implementation of policies and procedures that would preclude unlawful political contributions in the future and proposed changes in internal accounting and reporting procedures that would strengthen information and control systems in this area, including termination of all "off-the-books" funds for any purposes. The committee further recommended that the board consider additional steps to assure a more rigorous control over the behavior of managers at all levels in their relationships with governmental organizations, political parties, and their personnel. It proposed the creation of a committee of the board on business principles and policies with specific responsibility for formulating a code of ethical behavior applicable to managers at all levels of the company in both U.S. and foreign operations.

The report stated that the committee had not undertaken to appraise the weight of the evidence for the charge that almost $4 million of corporate funds had been expended for unlawful purposes and without proper authorization and that certain disbursements had been concealed by false accounting entries or otherwise. That was a matter for judicial determination. The committee's great concern was for the future. It observed that the committee found no indication that the practice of making such disbursements without authorization or proper recording was recently initiated; it might have been going on for some time. The committee did not address the question of whether outside auditors might reasonably have been expected to uncover such practices. This was an issue for consideration by the board's Audit Committee. To the committee's knowledge, the company's U.S. political contributions had not been "washed" through a foreign subsidiary.

The report noted that decisions about political contributions had apparently been made in Consolidated's organization one or two levels below the vice presidential level in both the United States and foreign countries. How far up the line such actions were known, or might reasonably be expected to have been known, was not investigated. It clearly appeared, however, that there was no evidence of explicit prohibition of such actions.

The committee found that the general feeling among Consolidated's managers was that Consolidated's behavior in the questioned areas was no different from that of other companies in the petroleum and other industries and that the people engaged in the criticized practices were acting in ways they sincerely believed to be in the best interests of the company.

The report also observed that Consolidated's principal outside legal counsel were not engaged in defending directors and officers against the shareholders' complaint. Another law firm was specifically employed by Consolidated for this assignment. Directors' liabilities, if any, arising from this and other suits would be covered, at least in part, by insurance paid for by Consolidated.

The report then turned from the issues of political contributions and bribery to what it described as "fundamental considerations related to the general governance of the company and particularly the role of the board of directors." It presented the following principal conclusions:

1. Consolidated's board has not satisfactorily implemented its responsibility for maintaining effective oversight of the conduct of the

business. The outside directors have not been furnished, nor have they requested, essential information about critical aspects of company policies and practices.

2. Important strategic decisions involving basic changes in the company's business and investment and potential future investment of resources have not been adequately reviewed by the board at the formative stage, with opportunity to consider options and trade-offs. The normal procedure has been to ask the board to approve programs that have been fully developed at lower management levels and have been endorsed by senior management.

3. Outside directors were a minority of the board, and new directors have generally been selected by the chief executive officer with no more than formal approval by the existing directors.

4. Inadequate attention has been given by the board—because of its relatively passive role in the governance of the company—to the company's responsiveness to new societal expectations and demands for corporate policies and practices in such areas as personnel administration and environmental hygiene.

5. The audit responsibility has been fulfilled at no more than a bare minimum level of compliance.

Each of these conclusions was supported by considerable detail of facts and observations compiled by the committee in carrying out its assignment. Discussion of conclusion (2) included extensive criticism of the company's chemicals, plastics, and minerals operations, covering both program commitments and management performance. A major thrust of the criticism was the failure to bring outside directors into a knowledgeable position about these diversifications early in the planning stage and to project long-term programs and alternatives.

The report then presented for board consideration a number of specific recommendations which amounted, in the committee's judgment, to a major change in the membership, structure, and work of Consolidated's board—a change described as "essential for the effective implementation of the board's responsibilities as defined by the relevant laws and the demands laid upon business by our evolving society." The principal recommendations follow:

1. At the earliest possible date two additional outside directors should be added to the board.

2. Within three years the composition of the board should be further changed by the removal from board membership of all inside directors except the chairman, the president, and two other officers designated by the chairman. The removed inside directors should be replaced by new outside directors.

3. The new outside directors referenced in (1) and (2) above should be selected by a special committee of outside directors. The chair-

man could, if he desired, propose individuals for the committee's consideration and could also indicate to the committee his objection to any prospective board member under consideration by the committee.

4. The specific responsibilities and duties of outside directors should be described in writing and that description, after review and approval by the board, should be incorporated in the board's minutes. The description should include a statement declaring the right of any outside director to request information in any desired detail on any aspect of the company's plans and operations and, at the director's choice, to address the request to the chairman, president, or directly to any company officer.

5. A new committee composed of outside directors (the Agenda Committee) should be responsible, in consultation with the chairman, for preparing the agenda for all board meetings.

6. The composition of the Executive Committee should be changed to consist of the chairman and two outside directors, with all outside directors serving, in turn, annual assignments as members of this committee.

7. The board should be involved in Consolidated's formal long-range planning system, not, as heretofore, simply as audience giving brief, formal assent to a completed plan but at an earlier stage, with presentation to the board of principal planning options and trade-offs and an opportunity for directors to question line officers about planning assumptions and conclusions and to propose alternatives.

8. The responsibility of the Audit Committee should be broadened to include oversight of the thoroughness and integrity of all management information and control systems and the implementation of corporate policies. Further, the enlarged assignment should be formally described in writing and incorporated in the board's minutes.

9. A new board committee of outside directors (the Committee on Public Affairs) should be created, with responsibility for reviewing policies and practices in such socially and politically sensitive areas as political contributions, environmental hygiene and safety (both within Consolidated facilities and in the communities surrounding facilities), personnel administration, product safety, governmental relationships (at all levels in the United States—federal to local—and in other countries), and relations with various "publics"—for example, customers and suppliers.

This comprehensive program for redesigning the membership, organization, and work of the Consolidated board reflected primarily the ideas of Mr. Appleton, Dr. Count, and Dean Yost. At the committee's final meeting before concluding its work and submitting its report, these three directors argued that:

The complex and demanding requirements of corporate governance today and tomorrow—with multiple responsibilities to shareowners, employees, and local and national publics—requires a board that is capable of being objective toward and independent of operating management. The membership, structure, and duties of such a board must be clearly defined. Without intervening in the detail of operations, the board must function in a way that facilitates and compels its involvement in the formulation of fundamental corporate goals, policies, and strategies.

Mr. Perrine then stated:

I am going to join with Messrs. Appleton, Count, and Yost in recommending the full list of our committee's proposals because I think the company needs strong shoring up, and this will be the means to get it. I'm particularly in favor of getting a majority of outsiders on the board as soon as possible, vigorously policing our ethics program and moving ahead with a much broader and deeper approach through the Audit Committee. This is only the beginning of things, however, as far as I am concerned.

What we should be primarily concerned with as directors of Consolidated is that the company has not been delivering the kind of bottom-line performance it should be delivering, that it has to do better, and that top operating management must accept that responsibility and deliver on it. If it doesn't, then the board should discharge the management and replace it with more competent people. In short, I think we should appraise management in terms of the results it achieves. And I think the correct measuring stick is the performance recorded by, say, the top three or four performing companies in the industry. A professional baseball manager or a professional football coach holds his job when he produces a winning team and loses it when he doesn't. That's an appropriate rule in business, too.

I think we have to be very careful when we start getting the board involved in long-range planning. We can't afford to relieve management of any responsibility here. It's their job to present the plans, and we'll review them. It's our job then to hold their feet to the fire—above all, the feet of the chief executive officer and the chief operating officer—and demand outstanding accomplishments. Then we will be in the proper position to do what the shareowners fundamentally expect from the board— to hire the best managers we can find for the company, pay them appropriately when they perform effectively, and replace them when they don't. When we discuss our report with the full board I'm going to say these things to everybody, including Ed Huntington. But I don't consider this to be in any sense a minority report, as I understand Carl Walden proposes to write.

Mr. Walden then read aloud to his committee associates his proposed minority report, as follows:

I am in substantive agreement with many—even most—of the recommendations of the majority of this committee. However, because I am so concerned about the timing of the various moves and the way the moves are made, I want to record my opinions in a minority report. I'd like to stimulate full board consideration and discussion of my two key points.

The first issue is timing. If we who are the independent directors of Consolidated do all of the things that our committee has recommended, we are going to be overwhelmed. I just don't see how we can organize and serve on so many new committees, lay down intelligently their detailed functions and responsibilities, dig deeper into the planning and managerial programs of the company, and simultaneously bring several new outsiders on to the board. Some things we should start on immediately—the vigorous enforcement of an ethics policy, a reconstituted and freshly mandated Audit Committee, and the formation of a Nominating Committee, for example. Other things should evolve, I believe, as we work out longer term relationships between the board and management.

This brings me to my second point, which is a matter of overall philosophy. The worst thing that could happen to Consolidated Petroleum right now would be to have a showdown between the senior management group and the board, with the result that one side has to get out. We have not reached this point in either the financial or the operating condition of the company—nor have we in the state of our communications with Mr. Huntington and his top associates. Yet if we too dictatorially insist upon an excessively rapid implementation of all our recommendations, we are in grave danger of establishing an adversary relationship between board and management which would have only harmful results.

On the contrary side I think we have an unusual opportunity here to do something that will be of lasting benefit to the company. I believe we should begin to discuss among ourselves—outside directors, inside directors, and even some other members of the senior management—what the role of the board really should be in Consolidated Petroleum. And I mean in the exact circumstances in which this company finds itself. We need to ask ourselves a number of questions such as, "What information should the board be getting, and when and how should it be presented to us? What kind of benchmarks should be established for management so that we can appropriately measure their performance? And over what period of time?" We have a very delicate balance here—and we're not the only U.S. company in this situation—between guiding and doing, between evaluating and supporting, between the short run and the long run, between management interests and prerogatives and shareowner interests and prerogatives. And I don't want us to rush into a lot of fast decisions without careful and deliberate thought.

Accordingly, I propose that for at least the next year we begin the dialogue that will lead us in orderly fashion to greater trust and understanding between outside directors and operating management. I suggest that we move the board to a monthly meeting schedule, with formal meeting times from 9:30 to at least 12:30. I suggest that we actively seek out new outside directors who can bring us special expertise in areas where the company has acknowledged problems. Above all, let us present a united front to the press and to our shareowners, not criticizing management and ourselves but openly stating that we are moving professionally and harmoniously toward the development of a company that has set for itself higher goals in all areas and has established logical and rational programs and timetables to achieve those goals.

When Carl Walden had completed reading his proposed minority report, Chairman Perrine said, "Fine. I think Carl's viewpoint should go to the full board along with the majority report. As far as I'm concerned, however—speaking as one member of this committee and of the board—the whole situation, and I mean especially the operating situation, demands prompt action, not further time-consuming discussion. I think we have a responsibility to the shareowners and to ourselves to act, to act promptly, and to get results."

Exhibit 1

CONSOLIDATED PETROLEUM CORPORATION
Consolidated Statement of Income and Retained Earnings
(in millions except per share data)

	Year Ended December 31	
	1975	1974
Revenues:		
Sales and other operating revenues	$4,751	$5,386
Interest income	55	54
Other revenues	8	24
	4,814	5,465
Deductions:		
Purchased crude oil, products, and merchandise	2,192	2,641
Operating expenses	393	445
Exploration and dry hole expenses	95	77
Selling, general, and administrative expenses	366	343
Taxes on income and general taxes	1,268	1,417
Federal Energy Administration entitlements	67	4
Depreciation, depletion, amortization, and retirements	189	183
Interest on long-term financing	34	36
	4,604	5,146
Net income	210	319
Retained earnings at beginning of year:		
As previously reported	1,557	1,330
Restatement	(72)	(72)
As restated	1,485	1,258
Cash dividends	(99)	(92)
Retained earnings at end of year	$1,596	$1,485
Per share data:		
Net income	$ 1.08	$ 1.64
Cash dividends	$ .51	$ .47

Exhibit 2

Representative Sample of U.S. Petroleum Companies—1971–1975 (Dollars in millions)

	Sales					Percent Earned Total Capital				
	1975	1974	1973	1972	1971	1975	1974	1973	1972	1971
Large:										
Exxon	$44,864	$42,062	$25,724	$20,309	$18,701	12.8%	17.3%	15.5%	10.9%	11.2%
Texaco	24,507	23,255	11,407	8,693	7,529	8.3	15.1	13.8	10.9	11.7
Mobil	20,620	18,929	11,390	9,166	8,243	10.0	13.4	13.0	9.7	9.6
Mid-range:										
Shell	8,144	7,634	4,884	4,076	3,892	10.8	14.3	8.8	7.3	7.3
Continental	7,500	7,041	4,215	3,415	3,051	12.1	12.2	10.6	8.3	7.3
Phillips	5,134	4,981	2,990	2,513	2,363	11.1	15.5	9.3	6.6	6.0
Union	5,086	4,419	2,552	2,098	1,981	9.7	12.0	8.7	6.5	6.3
Consolidated	4,814	5,465	2,805	2,081	1,980	9.7	14.3	10.1	6.1	7.1
Small:										
Getty	2,984	2,742	1,601	1,405	1,343	12.4	14.3	7.9	5.0	8.1
Marathon	2,878	2,882	1,579	1,278	1,183	10.8	14.8	12.2	8.2	9.3
Standard-Ohio	2,507	2,207	1,507	1,447	1,394	5.5	7.1	5.9	5.1	4.9

Exhibit 3

Board of Directors Membership 1976

Edwin Huntington, Chairman and Chief Executive Officer, Consolidated Petroleum Company. Employed by the company as a petroleum engineer after graduating from the University of Texas, Mr. Huntington rose through technical and management ranks, served in a variety of assignments in the United States and overseas in all parts of the petroleum and gas area, but not in other divisions, was elected president and chief operating officer in 1965 and chairman and chief executive officer in 1968. He was 63 years old in 1976, with two years to serve before mandatory retirement. Mr. Huntington was largely responsible for bringing to the board all of the outside directors serving in 1976 except Mr. Perrine and Dean Yost.

Paul Gallery, President and Chief Operating Officer, Consolidated Petroleum Company. Employed by the company as a geologist after graduating from Colorado School of Mines, Mr. Gallery was assigned, after about five years in petroleum exploration, to the refinery function where he worked under Mr. Huntington's direction. Thereafter his career followed Mr. Huntington's in the senior man's various assignments. He was Mr. Huntington's choice for president when that position was vacated by Mr. Huntington's election as chairman of the board. He was 58 in 1976 and was expected to succeed Mr. Huntington as chairman in 1978.

Lewis Appleton, Chairman of the Board, Union Commercial National Bank of New York (one of the six largest banks in the city). An old friend of Mr. Huntington's and the head of the company's lead bank, Mr. Appleton joined the Consolidated board in 1969. All of his career was spent in commercial banking after graduating from Princeton with a major in economics and the Harvard Business School where he concentrated in banking. First employed by Chase Manhattan in New York, he transferred to Union Commercial in mid-career with a principal responsibility for the development of the bank's national account business with major corporations. He was 63 in 1976.

David Count, President, Atlantic Institute of Technology (one of the country's leading scientific and engineering schools). Following his doctoral work in organic chemistry at Cornell, he pursued an academic career of increasing distinction in research at Cornell, Columbia, and A.I.T. He became dean of the faculties at A.I.T. in 1955 and was selected as president by the Institute's trustees in 1963. A director of several major corporations, he accepted an invitation from Mr. Huntington to join the Consolidated board in 1971. He was 62 in 1976.

Arthur Gallon, Senior Vice President, Consolidated Petroleum Company, responsible for the company's petroleum and gas activities. Mr. Gallon was employed by Consolidated as a refinery process engineer in 1945 after graduating from Baylor and completing two years of military service. He advanced through management ranks in a variety of U.S. and international assignments. He took command of the petroleum and gas activities on Mr. Gallery's promotion to president in 1968 and was elected a director of the company the following year. He was 56 in 1976.

Monroe Howard, Senior Vice President, Consolidated Petroleum Company. The chief financial officer of the company, Mr. Howard was responsible for the treasury and controller functions. Trained in accounting at the Wharton School, Mr. Howard worked for several years for one of the largest public accounting firms, which included Consolidated Petroleum as one of its clients. Having become acquainted with a number

Exhibit 3 (continued)

of Consolidated's controller and financial staff people as a result of his work on the Consolidated account, Mr. Howard was recruited by the company's controller as a principal deputy in 1952 and later served as controller and then treasurer before accepting appointment as senior vice president in charge of both departments in 1968. He became a director in 1972. He was 61 in 1976.

Walter Johnson, Senior Vice President, Consolidated Petroleum Company, in charge of administrative services and planning. A graduate of Williams College and the Columbia Graduate School of Business, Mr. Johnson worked for a number of years for a large international management consulting firm, first as staff associate and then as partner. In the late 1950s he headed a consulting team that studied the administrative and planning process in Consolidated Petroleum. With the acceptance by the client of the team's recommendations for reorganizing and redirecting the company's headquarters staff services and planning activities, Mr. Johnson accepted an invitation in 1965 from Mr. Huntington's predecessor as chairman to assume responsibility for implementing the reorganization plan. He was named a senior vice president in 1970 and joined the board in 1972. He was 58 in 1976.

Crosby Kennedy, Senior Partner, Kennedy, Swift, Rose & Christianson (one of the larger New York corporate law firms and principal outside counsel for Consolidated Petroleum). A graduate of Harvard College and Harvard Law School, Mr. Kennedy joined the firm of which his father was a founder and was continually associated with it thereafter except for service in the navy during World War II. He became senior partner following his father's death in 1970. A long-time friend of Mr. Huntington's, he was invited to join the Consolidated board in 1971.

Philip Lewis, Chairman, President, and Chief Executive Officer, Inter-Continental Aerospace Corporation. A graduate of West Point and a career military officer, he had attained the rank of brigadier general in the air force before electing early retirement to accept a position as vice president of Inter-Continental. He became that company's chief officer in 1970. Inter-Continental was a high-technology company, an important subcontractor on a number of military prime contracts in the aerospace field. General Lewis met Mr. Huntington as a fellow member of a yacht club on Long Island's North Shore where they were small-boat racing enthusiasts and competitors. After the acquaintance developed into friendship, General Lewis accepted Mr. Huntington's invitation to fill a vacancy created by the retirement of an outside member of the Consolidated board. He was 57 in 1976.

William Perrine, retired from his position as chairman of the board, Whipple Industries (a very large, diversified company with divisions in a number of industries). Mr. Perrine was a self-made man who had gone to work at the age of 16 as an apprentice machinist in a small manufacturing company. His hard work, aggressiveness, ambition, and ability to learn from every job experience supported his rise through foreman and factory management ranks until, at the age of 27, he was asked to become general manager of the company when the owning family could no longer provide for its effective administration. He proceeded to buy out the family interest within three years and then carried through a public stock offering and the first of a series of acquisitions and mergers that built the giant organization from which he retired in 1973. Mr. Perrine joined the Consolidated board in 1962 and participated in the selection of Mr. Huntington to serve as president and then chairman. He was 68 in 1976.

Exhibit 3 (concluded)

John Rosterman, Senior Vice President, Consolidated Petroleum Company, in charge of chemical and mineral activities. A graduate of the University of Michigan Engineering School, Mr. Rosterman worked up through management levels from his start as a process engineer in a medium-sized chemicals company. When the company was acquired by Consolidated Petroleum in 1962 as a building block in its plan for developing a petroleum-based chemical business, Mr. Rosterman was second in command of the company. Within a few years he was promoted to the top position in Consolidated's chemicals division. In 1968 he was made a senior vice president in charge of both chemicals and minerals. He joined the board in 1974. He was 60 in 1976.

Thomas Thompson, Senior Vice President, Consolidated Petroleum Company, responsible for foreign operations. A graduate of Yale, Mr. Thompson entered the Foreign Service of the State Department and served several duty tours in the Middle East where he became acquainted with officers of a number of U.S. petroleum companies. At the age of 40 in 1954 he left the State Department and joined Consolidated as a vice president responsible for relations with Mid-East and North African governments. In 1965 his assignment was broadened to include all foreign operations. He became a director in 1974. He was 62 in 1976.

Carl Walden, a director of several large corporations, formerly managing partner of a major international management consulting company. As a young graduate of the Harvard Business School, Mr. Walden helped to found what became over the next 25 years one of the leading consulting organizations—a firm he was largely responsible for developing in its early years and for administering in the following period when its size was substantial and its reputation secure. He retired from the firm at the age of 50 in order to work as a "professional director," serving on the boards of a number of large companies where his earlier experience with the problems of companies across a broad spectrum of industries and his accumulated knowledge and wisdom might be valuable. He accepted an invitation to join the Consolidated board in 1971. He was 55 in 1976.

Joseph Yost, Dean, Graduate School of Business, Colharstan University (one of the country's leading institutions of higher learning). Dean Yost's career included an early period teaching management after acquiring an MBA and Ph.D. at Columbia, a middle period when he served as senior staff officer and assistant to the president of a large manufacturing company, and a third period in which he returned to academia as dean of a major business school. He was brought on the Consolidated Petroleum board by Mr. Huntington's predecessor as chairman and was involved in the selection of Mr. Huntington as president and later as chairman. He was 64 in 1976.

Carroll Ziegler, Senior Vice President, Consolidated Petroleum Company, responsible for technology and research at the corporate level and in the divisions. Dr. Ziegler earned his doctorate in molecular biology at MIT and thereafter worked as research administrator in several major corporate research laboratories. He joined Consolidated in the capacity of director of research and technology in 1967, was elected senior vice president in 1969, and became a director in 1971. He was 50 in 1976.

Noble Objectives—False Means?

The company Agro-Pharma S.A., situated in Schaffhouse, Switzerland, manufactured fertilizers and other specialized chemical products, as well as veterinary goods. Its consolidated sales amounted to Swiss Fr 500 million at the end of 1981, of which 35 percent were sold on the national market. The rest of the products were either exported from Schaffhouse or manufactured and sold through various affiliated companies abroad, especially in the United States, Latin America, Japan, and Africa.

In 1981 the Agro-Pharma group of companies employed 2,640 people. During the last five years the growth of sales and profits had varied from between 10 percent and 20 percent per year. On the other hand 1982 looked as though it would be much less positive due to the world recession. Competition was becoming fierce, particularly from Japan, which was extremely active in the developing countries.

The financial situation, which was very healthy in 1981 (see Exhibits 1 and 2), showed a tendency to deteriorate in 1982, principally with regard to profitability. Not only were the profit margins narrower but the repatriation into Switzerland of dividends and other incomes from subsidiaries abroad was subject to the hazards of exchange rates, devaluations, and monetary controls.

The firm was organised on the basis of regional divisions and their heads were located in Schaffhouse.

This case was prepared by Professor P. Goetschin as a basis for class discussion rather than to illustrate either effective or ineffective handling of an administrative situation. Copyright © 1983 by IMEDE (International Management Development Institute), Lausanne, Switzerland. Reproduced by permission.

The African Zone Division was in charge of all the exports to North Africa and Black Africa. The transactions with the Republic of South Africa were also the responsibility of this division but went through the intermediary of a separate company registered in Geneva.

The sales effected in Africa amounted to Fr 80 million 1981, that is, nearly 16 percent of the total sales of the group. Out of this 80 million turnover, 25 million came from South Africa, where a subsidiary situated in Bloemfontein, 100 percent owned, was in charge of imports and also carried out various production and finishing operations.

About 80 people were employed by this subsidiary, the production of which contributed 10 million of the 25 million sales. Of the 80 people employed, 10 were white senior managers, amongst which 8 were English speaking and Afrikaner South Africans and 2 were Swiss who had settled in South Africa with their families within the past seven to eight years. As to the rest, 60 percent of the workers and employees were Coloureds, Indians, and Blacks. The majority of the supervisors were Whites, two were Blacks. The qualifications of the personnel were fairly high, and one Black with a University degree and trained in Schaffhouse, worked in a small control laboratory for veterinary products. The subsidiary contributed to the financial support of two professional schools opened and organised by Swiss firms for young Blacks.

The wages and social benefits were well above the legal norms, and the subsidiary had never, up till now, been affected by racial conflicts arising out of "apartheid," even though the management was, on the whole, conforming to the segregationist laws of the country. As much as possible, the management followed the guidelines set out in the charter of the company and in foreign and South African codes of conduct relating to labour relations.

In 10 years, the subsidiary had achieved a rapid development. It had realised a net profit on sales which was proportionally superior to that of the group as a whole (6 percent compared to 5.5 percent). It paid a modest dividend to the head office and reinvested completely the rest of the cash flow in the company. In spite of the economic sanctions taken with regard to South Africa by several governments and the socio-political risks resulting from apartheid, the general management in Schaffhouse, as that of the subsidiary, had estimated that the South African market was promising. Notwithstanding the uncertain situation, foreign capital had not really stopped flowing into South Africa, even if the rate of economic growth there had slowed down. According to a study by the United Nations, loans of almost $3 billion had been made to South Africa between 1979 and 1982, involving 180 banks, mostly Western. By prudence, however, Agro-Pharma had decided that its South African subsidiary would develop by self-financing and would not rely on new funds from head office. There was an important problem concerning the recruitment of supervisory and management personnel. It was almost impossible to promote Coloured people. Proposals to Swiss employees were usually met with a refusal on the part of those who, having a family, feared the outbreak of violence and would feel unhappy with apartheid.

The man responsible for the African Zone Division was Mr. Max Mayer, who was a member of the Board of Management of the group, which was chaired by a senior officer and composed of all the division heads.

Mr. Mayer had often had the opportunity to discuss the South African case with his colleagues. The board was of the opinion that the company, which conformed strictly to the laws of the host countries and which had adopted a certain number of ethical rules relating, among other things, to the management of people, bribery, and product quality, had no reason to proceed differently in South Africa than in the other countries of the world where it was active (see Exhibit 3).

Nevertheless, Mr. Mayer was somewhat disturbed by the fact that the social situation seemed to be deteriorating in South Africa and that pressure groups, which condemned apartheid, notably in the name of human rights, were more active than ever and were directing their attacks against the headquarters of multinationals operating in South Africa. Mr. Mayer was asking himself whether he ought to take steps regarding the South African subsidiary. What should they be and according to which criteria? Was it that the ethics of his company were too lax? On the other hand, should he do nothing and let events take their course or, on the contrary, take measures to counter the arguments and the methods of hostile groups?

In order to clarify his own ideas Mr. Mayer had gathered in his office on 26 February 1983, in a strictly private capacity, two of his acquaintances. One, Peter Schwab, was a Catholic priest and former missionary in Africa; the other, Klaudius Arndt, was an economic journalist attached to a large daily in Basle. The following conversation took place between the three men:

Mayer: I am struck by the fact that numerous pressure groups, especially religious ones, are showing signs of a growing activism towards multinationals, particularly in relation to apartheid in South Africa. Dissatisfied no doubt with the verbal condemnations of the international organisations, these groups have passed, if I may say so, to direct action. This began, certainly, at the end of the 60s, especially in the United States, but their interventions seem to me to be getting more frequent and more vigorous. Recently in Switzerland a socialist weekly, from the French-speaking part of the country, suggested that public authorities and private clients should withdraw their money from the three main banks of the country, accompanying their decision by a written protest denouncing these establishments' links with South Africa. A similar incident seems to have recently involved Barclays Bank in London, which holds a majority shareholding in one of the biggest South African banks. An Anglican diocese is reported to have been the initiator of this move. A few weeks ago, the American General Electric company had to renounce an investment project in a coal mine in the Kwazulu Homeland as the result of an intervention, if I'm not mistaken, of the Methodist Church of Connecticut, the state where GE has its headquarters, and of some of the black personnel employed by the company. As far as I know, however, Chief Buthelezi, who is responsible for the Homeland, would have approved the investment in question. All this seems to me to be extremely paradoxical and complicated!

Finally, last Sunday, at the end of the church service, I was approached by the Protestant minister, who is a friend of mine, and asked to sign a petition condemning racial segregation in South Africa. I did not sign it because I do not like this kind of thing, and I do not want to involve my company even indirectly.

I have no sympathy for apartheid, but I am responsible for people and economic interests in that country. It is difficult for me to accept the idea that religious communities fall back on such methods as the boycott of products, the withdrawal of bank deposits, spectacular interventions during general meetings of shareholders, or other pressure means in order to stop trade with South Africa and advocate the dismantling of foreign investments in that country. I asked myself what my policy should be if my company were the object of such attacks! Can I do anything to prevent them? I would also like to clarify my own thoughts, in order to be able to give clear replies, both to my personnel and to anybody else who would question me about these matters.

Schwab: Dear friend, I detect in your proposals a certain bitterness with regard to the Churches and I presume that I am here, what a dreadful expression, to play the role of devil's advocate. The Church, and I include under this heading all Christians, is also of this world. Has it not been, from the outset, on the side of the poor and the oppressed! It is the Church of Corinth, described by St. Paul, which was mainly made up of destitutes! Inspired by Holy Scriptures, the great Encyclicals, from Rerum Novarum to Populorum Progressio, including Mater et Magistra, have they not affirmed the evangelical requirement to promote greater justice and to contribute to the liberation of man in the political, economic, and social domains, so that he can devote himself more to the divine objectives which are his.

The Churches have, in general, approved the Universal Declaration of Human Rights, adopted by the United Nations in 1948, even if they are aware that this declaration does not encompass man in his totality, the reason for which the Vatican did not adhere formally to the declaration. For the first time, however, the ethical objectives of an international lay organisation have been in symbiosis with the Christian message. The religious communities have not remained indifferent to this convergence, which could only help to comfort them in the affirmation of their Faith and of their acts.

The Church announces the Truth, and its means towards salvation are above all love, prayer, and forgiveness. However, the Gospel does not condemn man to passivity; it is not neutral, as Cardinal Marty said in 1968. The Church being on the side of the poor, it is its duty to participate in their liberation from all forms of oppression, especially from racism, which is one of the most serious threats to the dignity of man.

On earth, one does not only advance through speech, however powerful the Word can be. St. Paul said: 'do not become the slave of men,' which means that obedience has its limits and that beyond, disobedience and rebellion can be justified.

In the past, the Churches have often been accused of remaining silent and doing nothing. Now many of them voice opinions and act. Faced with false ideologies, contradictions, vested interests, misunderstandings, and oppressions, it is normal that the religious world should not be content only with edifying declarations. My Protestant colleagues from the World Alliance of Reformed Churches, not without some internal controversies, have proposed more than one justification for what you call direct action, including the methods that you have pointed out. In Latin America, the Roman Church has found itself very close to the liberation movements. The World Council of Churches is even supposed to have extended financial support to revolutionary movements. In Gaudium et Spes, it is written that 'if a person is in extreme necessity, he has the right to take from the riches of others what he himself needs,' from which one can understand that the Christian is not simply condemned to resignation.

I am not personally a partisan of violence, and I cannot approve acts of terrorism from whatever source. Nevertheless, if the road towards more justice and dignity calls, for example, for the public expression of criticisms or for boycotts, which I would call soft violence, I believe that the means are not at all disproportionate to the ends.

Arndt: You know me, I am rather more cynic than religious, and, perusing several studies prepared by national or international Christian organisations, I have asked myself whether the Churches were not in the process of appropriating the philosophy of human rights, in order to refurbish their own image, to enhance their credibility, and to check the decline in the number of the faithful. God and Faith even seem to be somewhat pushed aside or to be only a pretext in this plethora of petitions, of condemnations, not to speak about this use of capitalistic mechanisms such as the sale of shares of sinful companies. It should not be forgotten that the Christian Churches are less and less European or North American. Theology is influenced by demography. Henceforth one condemns more easily the acts of white Westerners than those of people from other ethnic groups.

I would not go as far as saying that the ways to exercise pressure, which we are talking about, are always without effect. If the Arab boycott of Israel had practically no consequences, on the other hand, the increase in the price of oil has been more effective, but it has principally fallen on innocent targets like certain developing countries. The only result of the embargo on the export of arms to South Africa has been to encourage the creation, through the state company Armscor Ltd., of an armament industry in this country, which has even become an exporter, in some cases, to developing countries.

However, let us come back to the sale of shares: those who get rid of them on the Stock Exchange are naturally forced to find buyers; they, therefore, pass on to them the evil from which they themselves wish to be freed. Even if the shares were given away, it would still be a poisonous gift. The only convincing solution would, therefore, be to burn them publicly as witches and heretics were burnt in previous times! One offers a rather easy sop to one's conscience by selling "dirty" shares with a view to buying "clean" investments.

What about the withdrawal of bank deposits? Here again the real efficacity is small; the money remains in the banking system, and a part of it will almost inevitably find its way back to the guilty bank.

Much more serious is the pressure to disinvest. Imagine that this is forced on Mayer. He will have to dismiss 80 people, including the Blacks, and he will repatriate the 2 Swiss. On the other hand, he will not be able to take home his company's money, which will certainly be blocked by the South African government. In his closing speech, his only conclusion will be: 'I am packing up and sacking you on the imperative demand of a religious congregation in my country which disapproves of the racist policy of your state but which offers you all its love.' Enlightening isn't it?

I believe that those who resort to such measures think more of their effect on public opinion than of their real efficacity. They forget sometimes that there are also perverse consequences of such steps. Thus, as I have already said, the dismantling of economic investments will create unemployment amongst the Blacks and the Whites, who are modest players in this drama, and as a result, this act will conflict with the famous right to development, which is so often spoken about in the United Nations assemblies. Is this really what we want? For some, however, who have absorbed, willy nilly, bits of Marxist ideology, this state of affairs could, in accordance with their belief in the concept of class struggle, hasten finally the bloody revolution that they hope for. Is this outcome the one which is eagerly expected? The confusion of minds and of acts transforms into travelling companions the faithful and the atheist, unintentionally united on the road paved with good and bad intentions.

I can, no more than you, reconcile myself to apartheid, but, and this is going to horrify you, I cannot help feeling a certain sympathy and fear for those dreadful South Africans. Four million Whites facing 20 million Blacks, Coloureds and Indians! The white race, which comprises now barely 20 percent of the world population and which will be no more than 10 percent in 2100 gets infuriated with this remnant of European stock, as if it wanted to expunge its alleged feelings of culpability linked with colonialism? What would be the problems and the speeches of the prelates of Birmingham and the ministers of Connecticut if they were living in the middle of a community where those with a skin of a different colour to theirs were largely in the majority? Moreover, why attack South Africa specially? There are also Indians ill-treated by black populations! Recently, Nigeria has expelled some 2 million Togolese, Ghanaians, and other foreigners from neighbouring countries, under very inhuman conditions. Have you heard any rough and tough protests from UNO, from the Churches, or from other great proponents of human rights on this issue? Practically nothing!

But let us come back to economics. Not only I do not believe in sanctions but I think also that it would be unwise to link human rights too much with the pursuance of economic transactions unless these rights are incorporated explicitly in legal norms respected by all. In June 1982 a report dealing with Switzerland's policy regarding human rights was published and the Federal Council recalled that "our country has not taken as criteria for the export of goods abroad, whether or not a country respects human rights," except in the case of the export of arms and development aid. After all the freedom of trade and industry is a fundamental civil right, guaranteed by the Constitution.

This principle of universality is wise, otherwise our country would end all economic ties with the USSR, Argentina, the Islamic

Republic of Iran, Bulgaria, Turkey, the two Irelands, where two competing religions unceasingly violate these rights, or finally with anyone whomsoever, even with the Vatican which does not recognise the right of women to be ordained priests. The same goes for Pakistan, which cuts off the hands of robbers! Equally for France, which supplies missiles to the Argentinians, a nuclear plant to South Africa, and pipeline equipment to the USSR! Apparently such arguments have not hindered the International Monetary Fund from recently granting a loan of more than $1 billion to South Africa.

My dear friend Mayer, you should, with prudence, continue your work in South Africa. It seems to me that the concept of President Reagan, of "constructive involvement," is a formula which can help both Botha and the South African Republic to progress towards a more harmonious solution in the future. This country does not only have to solve a racial problem; it must still overcome the consequences of the Boer war, for Dutch farmers were, and still are, opposed to British businessmen. The situation is very complex, and I think that the state of isolation to which South Africa is being condemned will, in the end, have more negative results than positive ones for everyone. It can only lead to a radicalisation of the problems on all sides, therefore to violence, which is not what the most reasonable people among the Black elite want. Only the Marxist revolution can derive benefit from a possible epidermic reaction of Pretoria. It should also be remembered that the exodus of Whites from Mozambique did not provoke any movement of sympathy on the part of those who extol human rights *ad nauseam.*

In this context one cannot help smiling when one reads, in the reports of the Commission on Human Rights of the United Nations, that the Russian delegate pleads in favour of the right of self-determination and freedom of movement for individuals in South Africa, that the delegate from Zimbabwe disparages police violence just before his country uses it, that the representative of the Palestinian Liberation Movement also decries terrorism and violence. One would be delighted to hear the delegate from Argentina rail against torture and the representative of Nigeria defend the individual right of free establishment!

Within the limits of the laws, you have shown proof of what today one would qualify as social responsibility. As a businessman, you seem to me to have acted correctly. You are making profits, which is, obviously, your goal, and you pay taxes to the government, which is an unavoidable way of reinforcing it; but you create, at the same time, employment and training possibilities. As a result of your activities, Blacks feel less humiliated, more respected, and you contribute modestly to their economic promotion. Your presence in South Africa and the open approach of your managers there leads one to believe that you could also contribute, however humbly it may be, to the search for acceptable democratic and human solutions. In fact, it is one or two of the oft attacked multinational companies and liberal South African businessmen who are some of the most important factors for change in this part of the world. That being said, an explosion could take place, and you must prepare contingency and protection measures for your personnel and your assets.

Schwab: Arndt has made a vicious thrust with his allusion to the nonordination of women in the Catholic Church. I will not take up the gauntlet here; but what can you say about the position of the Dutch Reformed Church[1] of South Africa which succeeded at one point in proving that the Old Testament justifies apartheid! I wish to come back to the argument of Arndt: internal pressures will finally be strong enough to influence the South African authorities! Perhaps, but I believe that, without an overall awakening of conscience, provoked from the outside, nothing would happen, and there would be new Sowetos. Look at the infant food case: without pressure from the outside, the World Health Organisation would not have prepared a code! Without the ecologists, there would have been no environmental protection! Without the Church, human relationships would be deprived of any ethical contents! All this, therefore, requires declarations, manifestations, and pressure forces.

For instance, the modern version of human rights, after the independence of the United States and the French revolution, was in large part directed against the Church itself, which was thus obliged, first of all unwillingly, to revise its theology and its vision of the world. Rerum Novarum is, after all, a reply to Das Kapital; without the Communist Manifesto, the social doctrine of the Church might still not be written. This illustrates Toynbee's theory of 'historical challenges' which explains, perhaps, the path of progress of the human mind in which religions, moreover, have also played an essential role.

My dear Arndt, I do not want to run counter to your proposals. It remains for our dear friend Mayer to decide. I would, however, like to remark that many businessmen whom I have met often seemed to me to show arrogance, contempt, and indifference for the problems that we have raised. They only react when there is a crisis. How many times have I heard that stupid expression: 'You look after the spiritual side and we'll take care of the tempo-

---

[1] Nederduitse Gereformeerde Kerk.

ral,' as if the two sides of the coin were not closely linked! Can one not read on the U.S. $1 bill: 'In God we trust'? If Mayer is sincerely preoccupied with his social responsibilities, it is necessary that he should be able to refer to some principles and values which are generally accepted. If racism is contemptible, he must fight to abolish it, even more so as he is a Christian. He must strive for more democracy in South Africa, for a more balanced participation of today's bullied majority, for recognition of the black trade unions, to ensure promotion on an equal footing for his coloured managers. This could lead him to disobey the South African authorities in the name of individual rights and of economic and social rights.

I could to some extent accept that he continues his activities in South Africa as long as his company there has a strategy which goes beyond the mere production and sale of pharmaceutical products. The legitimacy of his firm is not defined only by its profitability; it must cater to the common good in the widest sense of the term. He has, anyway, only to read again the statutes of his firm and to behave accordingly.

This said, as a member of one of the oldest multinational organisations, I must also refer to our own turbulent history. Down through the ages, Rome has learnt the value of time. This is why we are more inclined to prudence and sometimes to compromise than our Protestant colleagues who, like American managers, want immediate results. Conciliation is better than violence, even when the latter limits itself to boycotts or other similar measures.

In fact, it should be up to the Churches to suggest various possible solutions for South Africa, with full regard for the rights of both Blacks and Whites, for God speaks to all. It is not easy, but why not encourage Botha and his people to look for such solutions rather than only to condemn what they do? In this the attitude of Christians of all races in South Africa is decisive. Nevertheless, it is also necessary to find adequate institutions and rules of the game which could be conducive to an overall agreement, calling probably for international guarantees in favour of all the ethnic groups. After all, the Rhodesia/Zimbabwe experience, which finally took place with a certain calm, allows one to hope that solutions can be found, even though bloody battles between black ethnic groups could not be avoided.

Mayer: This exchange of views disturbs me as much as it comforts me. I would sincerely like to offer to my South African collaborators conditions which would give them every assurance of dignity and equality. I fear, however, that I have very little influence on the evolution of affairs there. I am sensitive to the arguments of Schwab. All the same, I have the feeling that one cannot be absolute with regard to human rights. Their concretisation is an evolving process, and contradictions cannot be avoided. The free Western world and the Marxist East conceive them from opposite angles, depending upon their own view of history. But even at home there are contradictions: Is the right to life compatible with abortion or not? I am also struck by the fact that one abundantly refers to these rights but passes over in silence the corresponding obligations.

If the principles are not of the clearest, it must be also admitted that the daily reality places us before a thousand ambiguities. What meaning can be attributed to the right to work when there is a push for the withdrawal of investments? What does the right to live signify when one creates revolutionary conditions? More concretely still, I believe that boycotts, sales of shares, and so forth, are dysfunctional. This does not prevent me from recognising that the Churches have the right to speak out. I am ready to listen to theological arguments, but I also want my interlocutors to be aware of the dilemmas with which businessmen are confronted in situations such as those we are now describing. All multinationals are not ferocious brigands, greedy for exploitation. We, heads of companies, are no doubt too encased in our problems, and sometimes we show arrogance towards those who criticise us because we imagine that they are working quietly in shelter behind their university desks or hidden in their vicarages. While we are struggling on the markets, we see hundreds, thousands of diplomats take, in comfortable palaces, admirable resolutions which they are often the first to disregard.

Finally, as a result of this discussion I am coming to believe that the policy we have adopted up till now has been just and responsible. We have tried to apply, in South Africa as well as elsewhere, the principles of our company's charter. However, the fact remains that to behave oneself well in a country does not free you from accusations or attacks. That certain groups want to exert pressure on a state, which does not respect, for example, human rights, and that they do it by means of threats against companies does not seem to me to be justifiable.

At present, one is constantly referring to human rights, sometimes with intentions other than to enforce their respect. One sees also how much they are flouted, principally by the states. But is it not also curious to see that fervent defenders of these rights often reach the point where, carrying their missionary spirit to the extreme, they themselves leave justice behind? The theologians of liberation, who uphold revolutions, do they not threaten the right to life, to property, to security, and to employment?

It is a good thing to take inspiration from great principles, but one has to follow the road step by step pragmatically. The efforts towards the moralisation of economic, political, and social life are highly commendable, but human nature remains ambiguous and circumstances complex. I see this myself in my company, for example, in the case of our attempts to promote women. It is going better now, but it is not automatic.

With regard to my personnel in South Africa, I must decide clearly. Am I going to tell them that we will continue our activities and nothing more; that we are going to expand the business or, on the contrary, cut back? Must I formulate a "political statement" for the firm with regard to the social situation in South Africa, and if so, what should it be, with what risks? Should our headquarters take a public stand and in what direction? Should one practise the policy of "wait and see"? Finally, there are some very practical problems: How can we protect our South African personnel and the assets that we have there? We could repatriate more funds, but how do we explain that to our collaborators? An easy solution would be to sell our subsidiary to a South African company. I believe personally that economic development, if it takes place, will help us to solve these problems better than economic depression and violence.

I am now better aware of the scale of the problems, but I also have somewhat the impression of being in a maze.

Thank you for your remarks and advice.

Exhibit 1

AGRO-PHARMA S.A.
Profit and Loss Account
31st December 1981
(in thousand Swiss francs)

Net sales	SFr 503.000	100%
Gross profit on sales	186.115	37.0
Income from licences	16.610	3.0
Income from participations	10.037	2.0
Other income	12.899	3.0
Total income *(a)*	225.661	
Salaries	62.123	12.0
Social charges	12.433	3.0
Overheads and other fixed costs	69.249	14.0
Cost of subcontracting	17.120	4.0
Taxes and financial costs	13.653	3.0
Depreciation	23.255	5.0
Total costs *(b)*	197.833	
Net profit *(a − b)*	27.828	5.5
Carried over 1980	633	
Disposable profit	SFr 28.461	
Cash flow:		
Net profit	27.828	
Depreciation	23.255	
	SFr 51.083	10

Exhibit 2

AGRO-PHARMA S.A.
Balance Sheet
31st December 1981
(in thousand Swiss francs)

Assets		Liabilities	
Fixed assets:		Equity:	
Land, buildings	SFr 18,400	Share capital (shares with nominal value of SFr 1,000 each)	SFr 42,000
Equipment, machines	4,320	Legal reserve	28,000
Trademarks (pro forma 1.—)	—	Special reserve	26,000
Total fixed assets	22,720	Loss and profit account, disposable	28,461
Participations*	51,528	Total equity	124,461
Current assets:		Provisions:	
Inventories	28,135	Provision for foreign risks	22,000
Receivables	34,362	Provision for doubtful debtors	4,500
Cash, banks, etc.	93,742	Provision for economic risks	4,000
Total current assets	156,239	Provision for R&D expenditures	16,000
		Various other provisions	1,000
		Total provisions	47,500
		Foreign funds:	
		Pension fund	300
		Foundation for personnel	1,250
		Banks	8,225
		Payables	43,639
		Other debts	5,112
		Total foreign funds	58,526
Total assets	SFr 230,487	Total liabilities	SFr 230,487

* The participation of 100 percent in the South African subsidiary was reported at its initial nominal value of SFr 3 million. In 1981 the total of the balance sheet of this company was equivalent to SFr 11 million at the end-of-the-year rate of exchange for the Rand.

Exhibit 3

Excerpts (Summarized) from the Company Charter

1. The management of business is not an end in itself. It must be viewed as a service to man and society, but only economic success allows the accomplishment of such a mission.

5. Although we wish to maintain the Swiss identity of our firm, we want to develop our activity on all continents in order to ensure our economic success and to contribute to the development of the country in which we are present.

12. We encourage, as much as possible, the promotion of our collaborators by constantly increasing their responsibilities and offering them opportunities for further education and training.

19. In all countries where we are present, we consider ourselves as a member of the community, fully conscious of our responsibilities. We maintain a loyal collaboration with the national and local public authorities.

22. We inform our collaborators, our shareholders, and public opinion about our activities in a suitable manner.

25. The Group's affiliated companies are autonomous entities, which operate within the framework of principles and global objectives incorporated in our business policy.

The Viking Air Compressor, Inc.

As he left the president's office, George Ames wondered what he ought to do.[1] His impulse was to resign, but he knew that could be a costly blot on his employment record. Moreover, there was the possibility that he was seeing things in a distorted way, that he might later regret leaving Viking before he really knew all the facts bearing on his position and its future. He decided to wait for another week before making up his mind, and in the meantime he made an appointment with Professor Farnsworth of the Amos Tuck School of Business Administration at Dartmouth College to get his advice. Mr. Ames had received his MBA degree from the Tuck School the previous June.[2]

The Viking Air Compressor company was founded in Bradley, Connecticut, in 1908 by Nels Larsen, an inventor and engineer who left the Westinghouse Electric Company to start his own organization. Mr. Larsen had both a successful design for a new type of air compressor and a talent for management. He led Viking to steadily increasing successes in the air compressor industry.

In 1971 Viking held a steady 25 percent of the air compressor business in the United States, with total annual sales of $180 million. Mr. John T. Larsen, grandson of the founder, was chairman of the board and chief executive officer. Three other descendants of the founder were officers of the company, and the rest of the management team had been

---

[1] Most of the names in this case have been disguised.

[2] Mr. Ames received his A.B. from the University of Michigan in June 1966. He spent three years as an army officer, concluding as a captain in Vietnam, before entering Tuck in September 1969. He was married in June 1971.

520

developed from Viking employees who rose through the ranks. The ownership of Viking was substantially in the Larsen family hands.

In March 1971 Mr. Oscar Stewart, vice president for personnel administration of Viking, visited the Amos Tuck School to talk with MBA candidates interested in a new position to be created in the Viking structure the following June. Mr. Stewart explained to Dean Robert Y. Kimball, Tuck's director of placement, that Viking had never hired MBAs directly from business schools but wanted to experiment in 1971 with this method of bringing fresh ideas and new techniques into the firm.

The corporate officers had decided, according to Mr. Stewart, to begin to test the effectiveness of the recruitment of MBAs by hiring a business school graduate to become director of public affairs, with the assignment of coordinating the relationships between Viking and outside agencies seeking financial contributions from the company.

As Mr. Stewart described the job to the students he interviewed at Tuck in March 1971, it would contain such tasks as *(a)* proposing to the board of directors the best criteria to use in deciding how to make corporate gifts to charitable organizations of all kinds, *(b)* supplying the chief officers of the company with information about the participation of Viking employees in public service activities, *(c)* recommending future strategy for Viking in the employment of women and members of minority groups, and *(d)* serving as secretary to the newly formed committee on corporate responsibility which consisted of five members of the board of directors.

George Ames accepted the post of director of public affairs at Viking. He had been chosen by Vice President Stewart as the most promising of the five attractive Tuck applicants for the new position. After a short vacation, Mr. Ames reported for work on July 1, 1971, and immediately plunged into the difficult task of gathering information about his new assignment. It soon became clear that his primary task would be to work with the board committee on corporate responsibility, mainly to propose new policy guidelines to the board at its September 10 meeting. Mr. Stewart said there were two other areas of high priority: (1) the corporation's attitude toward public service of employees and (2) developing criteria for corporate philanthropic giving.

As Vice President Stewart explained to George in early July, the committee on corporate responsibility was created at the January meeting of the Viking board after unanimous endorsement of the suggestion made by Dr. Thomas A. Barr, pastor of the local Congregational Church and one of the four outside members of the 12-man board. Dr. Barr's major support for his recommendation was the observation that the General Motors Corporation had taken a similar step, under some pressure, and that corporate responsibility was an idea whose time had come on the American scene. In response to the question, what will such a committee do, Reverend Barr replied that there need be no hurry in defining the detailed responsibilities of the committee but that furthermore there could not possibly be any harm or drawbacks from setting it up as soon as possible. He added that the public relations value of such a gesture should not be underestimated. In establishing the committee on corporate responsibility, the board voted to require the first progress report from the committee in September 1971.

The committee on corporate responsibility met following the February meeting of the board of directors and decided to delay any definite action until an executive secretary could be hired. Vice President Stewart was asked to keep this post in mind as he interviewed MBA graduates of several of the leading business schools, and so he did.

George Ames met with the chairman of the committee on corporate responsibility at a luncheon on July 21, 1971, arranged by Vice President Stewart. The committee chairman was Mr. Paul Merrow, one of the most respected lawyers in northern Connecticut and the son of one of the first board members of Viking when the company was incorporated in the 1920s. Mr. Merrow expressed his pleasure that George Ames was working on the corporate responsibility question and asked him to prepare a report that might be reviewed by the committee just prior to the September board meeting. What he wanted, he explained to Mr. Ames, was an analysis of the three or four possible approaches to corporate responsibility which the directors ought to consider. He asked for a listing of the pros and cons of these various approaches. He said that Mr. Ames should consider this very much like an assignment in a course at the Tuck School. He would be performing a task which none of the board members had the time or academic background to do, and thus he would substantially improve the decision making of the board of directors.

Mr. Merrow concluded the luncheon by saying that he would like Mr. Ames to proceed on his own during the summer but that he would be glad to confer with him in early September. Mr. Merrow explained that he was leaving the next day for a legal conference in Europe and would be on an extended vacation until September 6. He said that he had "the proxies" of the other committee members and that they would prefer not to get involved in working on the committee tasks until after the September board meeting.

George Ames worked assiduously during August, reading all the articles and books he could find in the area of corporate responsibility, including the background of developments in the General Motors situation. He decided not to talk about this particular assignment with other officers of the company, primarily because of Mr. Merrow's injunction that the committee itself would prefer not to engage in substantive talk about the issues until the September board meeting. George feared he would do more harm than good by talking before he knew his subject well.

In early September John Larsen asked George to see him and the following conversation took place:

John Larsen: I've asked you to see me this morning and tell me what progress you have been making in developing background materials for the work of the committee on corporate responsibility. Mr. Merrow told me he had asked you to do some digging and that you would have a brief report to make at the September 10 meeting of the board. I know Mr. Merrow hoped he would be back from Europe in time to talk with you before the board meeting, but it now appears he will be lucky to make the meeting at all. He expects to arrive in town about noon on the 10th.

George Ames: Mr. Larsen, I appreciate the opportunity I have been given to help Viking by developing recommendations about possible strategies for the company to follow in the area of corporate responsibility. Mr. Merrow told me I ought to develop alternative proposals for recommendations to the board and I have as recently as yesterday finally been able to narrow the field so that I can make four recommendations with confidence.

I realize the board may prefer to consider them one at a time, at different meetings, but I would like to tell you about all four so that you will know what my report will contain.

I have decided that the most important issue in the area of corporate responsibility is equal-opportunity hiring. I have been able to develop statistics from the personnel records which show that Viking is rather far behind most major national corporations in the percentage of blacks and women now employed, and although I am sure conscientious efforts have been made by all officers to remedy this, I cannot stress too strongly how much of a time bomb the present situation is. There will be wide ramifications if we do not improve our record.

The second item of priority which I see is the development of corporate sanctions for public service activities of employees. I believe the company should grant paid leaves of absence for employees who wish to accept public-service posts. At present we have done that only for two vice presidents who have been in charge of the Northern Connecticut United Fund. In each case the man was lent to the charitable organization for two full weeks. What I have in mind is a much wider program which would grant employees leaves of absence to work in poverty programs in urban ghettos or in VISTA projects in Connecticut or neighboring states.

It seems to me a third priority is to develop a committee of consumers who will monitor the safety features and other quality items having to do with our products. If we do not do this we will have Ralph Nader breathing down our necks as has already happened in the automotive industry and some others.

Finally, I strongly recommend that we close our sales contact in Capetown, South Africa, and establish policies which will avoid our being embarrassed as a corporation by discriminatory or dictatorial policies of foreign governments which become critically important political and social issues here in this country.

I feel sure these are great issues of our times, and I hope the board will be willing to debate them at the September 10 meeting. I know I could learn a great deal in my position if such a debate could take place.

Mr. Larsen: Young man, I want to congratulate you on how articulately you have told me about some of the things you have learned in the MBA program at the Tuck School. I envy fellows of your generation who go through MBA programs because you get an opportunity to think about policy problems at a much earlier age than my generation ever did. Indeed my only complaint is that the business schools go too far to educate young men to think they know how to run a company long before they have enough real experience to be even a first-line supervisor.

Now I think you have your assignment all backwards as secretary to the committee on corporate responsibility, and I will tell you why I think that. The committee hasn't even met yet, and your remarks make it sound as if you have written the final report. Worse than that it sounds like the final report of the committee on corporate responsibility of the General Motors Company, not Viking. Everybody knows we've done as good a job as we can to hire blacks and women. There just aren't many such people in the work force in our part of Connecticut who could fit our talent standards, and we are going to follow our historical policy of nondiscrimination as we hire the best people to do Viking jobs. We owe it to our stockholders to make a profit, and if we don't do that we don't have the right to do anything else.

Your remarks on public-service activities for our employees are equally off target. The first obligation of our employees is to give a fair day's work for a fair day's pay. All public-service activities are extracurricular activities, and that's the way they must be. In order for us to sponsor public service on company time we would have to discriminate between good and bad activities and that would get us into partisan politics and preoccupy all of our executive time. How would the company have done if I had been a part-time chief executive officer in the last five years? That is a preposterous idea! At the same time, by working harder on my regular job I have been able to work some evenings and some weekends in fund-raising activities for the Boy Scouts, YMCA, and heaven knows how many other charitable organizations. I would expect every employee to do the same and not to expect the corporation to subsidize activities in their roles as private citizens. As far as public service is concerned, live and let live should be our corporate motto. If we encourage public-service activities and include them as part of our compensation and promotion system, we will be bogged down in a fantastic collection of information about private lives which will lead to chaos. Even the most superficial examination of this question should have led you to see the problems with the route your theory took you.

As far as the safety of our products and other demands consumers might make, that's all done through the marketplace, as you will come to understand. If our products were not safe or durable, they wouldn't sell. You could have found this out had you talked with our production and marketing people as you certainly should have done by now. It's our responsibility to decide after careful market research what the air compressor needs of America are and will be in the future. We don't need a special panel of bleeding hearts to lead us along paths where we are already expert.

As for our selling operations in South Africa, I'm afraid you just don't know what you are talking about. As long as there is no plank of American foreign policy or federal law which tells corporations where they can and where they can't sell their products, American businesses must depend on the free market system. President Nixon is talking about opening the trade doors to mainland China. Do you think for one moment the practices of the Chinese government are any less nefarious in some respects than the practices of the South African government? Of course not. And yet you would probably urge me in your liberal way to establish a selling office in Peking just to go along with the new liberal ideas of our president, and I call that kind of pragmatism ridiculous.

Come to think of it, how could you miss this opportunity to lecture the board on our responsibilities for pollution control and our obligations to get out of the military-industrial complex by cancelling all of our air compressor contracts with the federal government!

Young man, you have shown yourself to be a wooly-minded theoretician and I want to tell you that bluntly now so that you will not think me hypocritical at any later point. I will tell the committee on corporate responsibility that you have not had time to prepare your first briefing of the board of directors and then I want to have a meeting with you and the chairman of the corporate responsibility committee on Monday morning September 20.

That's all I have time for now, I'll see you later.

Peter Green's First Day

Peter Green came home to his wife and new baby a dejected man. What a contrast to the morning, when he had left the apartment full of enthusiasm to tackle his first customer in his new job at Scott Carpet. And what a customer! Peabody Rug was the largest carpet retailer in the area and accounted for 15 percent of the entire volume of Peter's territory. When Peabody introduced a Scott product, other retailers were quick to follow with orders. So when Bob Franklin, the owner of Peabody Rug, had called District Manager John Murphy expressing interest in "Carpet Supreme," Scott's newest commercial duty home carpet, Peter knew that a $15,000–$20,000 order was a real probability and no small show for his first sale. And it was important to do well at the start, for John Murphy has made no bones about his scorn for the new breed of salespeople at Scott Carpet.

Murphy was of the old school. In the business since his graduation from a local high school, he had fought his way through the stiffest retail competition in the nation to be district manager of the area at age 58. Murphy knew his textiles, and he knew his competitors' textiles. He knew his customers, and he knew how well his competitors knew his customers. Formerly, when Scott Carpet had needed to fill a sales position, it had generally raided the competition for experienced personnel, put them on a straight commission, and thereby managed to increase sales and maintain its good reputation for service at the same time.

Copyright © 1980 by the President and Fellows of Harvard College
Harvard Business School case 380–186

When Murphy had been promoted eight years ago to the position of district manager, he had passed on his sales territory to Harvey Katchorian, a 60-year-old mill rep and son of an immigrant who had also spent his life in the carpet trade. Harvey had had no trouble keeping up his sales and had retired from the company the previous spring after 45 years of successful service in the industry. Peter, in turn, was to take over Harvey's accounts, and Peter knew that John Murphy was not sure that his original legacy to Harvey was being passed on to the best salesperson.

Peter was one of the new force of salespeople from Scott's Sales Management Program. In 1976 top management had created a training program to compensate for the industry's dearth of younger salespeople with long-term management potential. Peter, a college graduate, had entered Scott's five-month training program immediately after college and was the first graduate of the program to be assigned to John Murphy's district. Murphy had made it known to top management from the start that he did not think the training program could compensate for on-the-job experience, and he was clearly withholding optimism about Peter's prospects as a salesperson despite Peter's fine performance during the training program.

Peter had been surprised, therefore, when Murphy volunteered to accompany him on his first week of sales "to ease your transition into the territory." As they entered the office at Peabody Rug, Murphy had even seemed friendly and said reassuringly, "I think you'll get along with Bob. He's a great guy—knows the business and has been a good friend of mine for years."

Everything went smoothly. Bob liked the new line and appeared ready to place a large order with Peter the following week, but he indicated that he would require some "help on the freight costs" before committing himself definitely. Peter was puzzled and unfamiliar with the procedure, but Murphy quickly stepped in and assured Bob that Peter would be able to work something out.

After the meeting, on their way back to the Scott Carpet's district office, Peter asked Murphy about freight costs. Murphy sarcastically explained the procedure: because of its large volume, Peabody regularly "asked for a little help to cover shipping costs," and got it from all or most suppliers. Bob Franklin was simply issued a credit for defective merchandise. By claiming he had received second-quality goods, Bob was entitled to a 10–25 percent discount. The discount on defective merchandise had been calculated by the company to equal roughly the cost of shipping the 500-pound rolls back to the mill, and so it just about covered Bob's own freight costs. The practice had been going on so long that Bob demanded freight assistance as a matter of course before placing a large order. Obviously, the merchandise was not defective, but by making an official claim, the sales representative could set in gear the defective merchandise compensation system. Murphy reiterated, as if to a two-year-old, the importance of a Peabody account to any sales rep and shrugged off the freight assistance as part of doing business with such an influential firm.

Peter stared at Murphy. "Basically, what you're asking me to do, Mr. Murphy, is to lie to the front office."

Murphy angrily replied, "Look, do you want to make it here or not? If you do, you ought to know you need Peabody's business. I don't know what kind of fancy thinking they taught you at college, but where I come from you don't call your boss a liar."

From the time he was a child, Peter Green had been taught not to lie or steal. He believed these principles were absolute and that one should support one's beliefs at whatever personal cost. But during college the only even remote test of his principles was his strict adherence to the honor system in taking exams.

As he reviewed the conversation with Murphy, it seemed to Peter that there was no way to avoid losing the Peabody account, which would look bad on his own record as well as Murphy's—not to mention the loss in commissions for them both. He felt badly about getting into a tiff with Murphy on his first day out in the territory and knew Murphy would feel betrayed if one of his salespeople purposely lost a major account.

The only out he could see, aside from quitting, was to play down the whole episode. Murphy had not actually *ordered* Peter to submit a claim for damaged goods (was he covering himself legally?), so Peter could technically ignore the conversation and simply not authorize a discount. He knew very well, however, that such a course was only superficially passive and that in Murphy's opinion he would have lost the account on purpose. As Peter sipped halfheartedly at a martini, he thought bitterly to himself, "Boy, they sure didn't prepare me for this in management training. And I don't even know if this kind of thing goes on in the rest of Murphy's district, let alone in Scott's 11 other districts."

BOOK TWO

Implementing Corporate Strategy

The Implementation of Strategy: Achieving Commitment to Purpose

We now turn our attention to ideas and skills essential to the accomplishment of purpose. An idea is not complete or even completely understood until it is put into action. A unique corporate strategy is only rhetoric until it is embodied in organization activities which are actually guided by it but in turn continually reshape it. Goal-directed implementation, the essence of strategic management, is seen today as far more complex than the execution of directions implied in the classic model of the hierarchical corporation.

The determination of strategy, as we have said before, can be usefully thought of as a combination of four primarily analytical subactivities: examination of the company's environment for opportunity and risk, careful assessment of corporate strengths and weaknesses, identification and weighing of personal values built into the character of the company and its leaders, and establishment of the level of ethical and social responsibility to which it will hold itself.

The implementation of strategy may also be thought of as having essential subactivities. On the action side of corporate strategy these are primarily administrative rather than analytical in nature. Administrative action involves relationships among people, achievement and acceptance of authority, and much else, like energy or morality, that is not the product of mind alone. Implementation consists most broadly of achieving and sustaining commitment to purpose. Secondly, it is directed toward organized achievement of results through three universal structural processes: the specialization of task responsibilities, the coordination of divided responsibility, and the provision of a system of information enabling specialists and general managers alike to know what they need to know to act strategically. Each of these processes tends to develop counterstrategically by elevating its own special purposes above the needs of the total company.

Thirdly, the essential balance between individual and organization needs is sought through four familiar processes: measurement of performance, provision of incentives and rewards, establishment of constraints and controls, and recruitment and development of persons for operating and managing positions. These processes also tend to seek out their own separate purposes; they must be reined in and harnessed to corporate goals.

Finally, the role of leadership throughout the company in the accomplishment, modification, and extension of purpose in the innovative and adaptive corporation will become clear in the discussion of cases as all the more crucial as participation in strategy formulation becomes more extensive. We will come to see corporate strategy as, in part, the evolving product of commitment, vindicating and adapting to reality its initial formulation. We will see it also as the key to simplicity, economy, and superiority in the management of what would otherwise be confusing and needlessly complex affairs.

Distorted Approaches to Implementation

In part, because of the neglect of implementation as integral to strategy, the concept itself has been battered by distortion over the last 20 years. False hope, oversimplification, and naïveté, as well as zest for power, have often led, for example, to the assumption that the chief executive officer conceives strategy single-mindedly, talks the board of directors into pro forma approval, announces it as fixed policy, and expects it to be promptly executed under conventional command and control procedures by subordinates. This unilateral dominance is often at least partly true in the entrepreneurial start-up stage, but when the company grows to something other than a one-person show, it becomes a political and social entity. When an established corporation is long dominated by strategic dictatorship, resistance both outspoken and covert eventually limits achievement.

That strategy formulation, under the name of strategic planning, is primarily a staff activity, assisted by consulting firms, is a related distortion made possible by ignoring the problems of implementation. The assumption that strategy is essentially a value-free appraisal and choice of economic opportunity and evaluation of results without reference to company capability, personal values, and entrenched cultural loyalties often led to strategic recommendations by staff departments and consulting firms that companies were neither able nor willing to carry out. Many planning techniques, useful in limited application, developed as quick-fix solutions to the need for better performance in competition.

Goals often tended to be expressed in terms of high growth rates in sales and profits, mindlessly compounded over future years. Economic objectives were chosen more for their theoretical growth potential than from company capability to attain them. Acquisitions were pursued for the sake of growth in the 70s, just as hostile takeovers are undertaken in the 80s in pursuit of financial strategies largely unrelated to the distinctive competence to make them work. Financial strategies, in fact, following a modern finance theory divorced from the concept of corporate strategy, focus on the acquisition and divestment of assets, the extension of leverage to its limits without reference to impact on human resources, future development, and the capacity to service enormous debt should economic adversity put pressure on the company.

The catalog of strategic mismanagement made possible by ignoring the human, social, and ethical elements in the pattern of corporate purpose would make dreary reading if it were ever to be completely compiled. Even without it, poor performance in the marketplace has in due course exposed overrated techniques and fashionable shortcuts. The backlash against strategic planning occurring in the 1980s is largely justified and wholly understandable, but it has produced its own distortions. It has led to sweeping criticisms of American management and business education. Extreme incrementalism, understood as reactive improvisation, muddling through, or following one's nose, has been disinterred from the conceptual graveyard to justify avoidance of all forms of conscious planning.[1]

That organization cannot have purposes as distinct from the special interests of individuals forming coalitions of rival aspirations is a venerable antistrategic position revived by disillusion with formal planning techniques so misapplied as to elevate quantitative analysis over qualitative appraisal of the needs of an organization viewed as a whole. Other process distortions lead to finessing strategic decision by inspiring the entire organization in folkloric simplicities like "moving close to the customer," "managing by walking around," and "fostering continuous innovation." These are attractive vacuities. What direction leadership should take, and what their substance should consist of, is missing from these prescriptions. An implicit or explicit strategy is required to encourage something to happen in the close relationship to customers, to identify what managers should have in mind when they walk around, and to suggest constructive direction and completion of innovations.

Flexibility in Pursuit of Purpose

Intelligent implementation of the more comprehensive and substantive strategy proposed here presumes a balance between focus and flexibility,

---

[1] This position is not to be confused with the purposeful incrementalism recommended in James Brian Quinn's *Strategies for Change: Logical Incrementalism* (Homewood, Ill.: Richard D. Irwin, 1980).

between a sense of direction and responsiveness to changing opportunities. It is of course true that announcing very specific and restrictive objectives can close out participation. Overspecific topics can lead to centralized decision making, politicized opposition, and rigidity.[2] Such goals should neither be adopted nor announced. Corporate strategy need not be a straitjacket. Room for variation, extension, and innovation must of course be provided. General goals, like the intention to be the leading producer in the technical product line serving a broad class of customer needs, imply product development, related innovations, and even unexpected additions that creativity may produce. In the multibusiness corporation, like General Electric, broad goals, like being first or second in every industry in which it participates, leaves the full development of a more specific business strategy to achieve or maintain that position in the hands of GE's division management. Determination of even more detailed goals falls to the managers of strategic business units. The definition of special character, a common set of values, and expectations for performance does not keep IBM, Hewlett-Packard, Xerox, and, these days, even General Motors from being innovative.

Strategic planning is indeed a legitimate staff activity, but strategic decision is a line function. Much information gathering, competitive intelligence, and exploration of required investment, costs, and potential return can come from good staff work. The decision process is properly presided over by the executives responsible, whose judgment includes, but is not confined to, quantitative analysis. Correction to analytical distortion comes from constant reference to corporate capability and to the relevance of proposed strategic alternatives to company character and culture, either as they are or as, under leadership, they might become.

Our practitioner's theory, which you are asked to test, amend, or extend in the examination of the companies' situations described in this book, postulates conceptually that strategy formulation and implementation should be allowed to interact with each other. The formulation of strategy is not finished when implementation begins. Feedback from operations gives notice of changing environmental factors to which strategy should be adjusted. Unless it is to decline in competitiveness and performance, a business organization will change in response to the contribution of its new members, the changes in the markets and customer needs it services, and in response to success or failure in shaping its environment.

Implementation in the Innovative Corporation

The reciprocal relationship of strategy formulation and implementation makes middle management and employee involvement essential in both. The achievement of planned results means that goals must be known;

---

[2] See, for example, James Brian Quinn, "Strategic Goals: Process and Politics," *Sloan Management Review,* Fall 1977, pp. 21–37.

the achievement of superior goals means they must be so wholly accepted that extraordinary effort or ingenuity, unforeseeable by distant planners, is induced. Sales or service persons often encounter in the field early clues to the need for change. In a company in which they doubt the interest of top management in responding, they may shrug their shoulders and shift their attention to other products. In a company oriented to innovation, they may report the opportunity through channels deliberately opened up to them by people prepared to listen. The development of greater individual capability and the distinctive competence of a company that is the source of competitive advantage comes from experience, the successful solving of problems, and superior service to customers.

Such a moving capability will not occur unless companies acknowledge in their behavior, if not in so many words, that their purpose is as much to maintain and develop a cooperative and creative organization and to foster effective execution as it is to lay plans and measure performance against plan. Committed team players can be involved in strategic determination by inviting their comment on the feasibility of strategic alternatives when secrecy and security are not at stake. Resistance to change, which in such discussion often produces negative response to new ideas, can be turned to constructive use by considering such objections before it is too late and attempting to achieve amendment, acceptance, and understanding beforehand rather than encounter unexpected opposition later on.

It becomes apparent that company organization structure and administrative policies and practices should permit and sustain involvement and the resultant commitment to company purposes. Being given a clearly defined job with lateral and upper limits becomes less and less attractive to present generations of educated employees and middle managers.[3] The values they bring to a company include independence, aversion to arbitrary or unreasoned authority, and ambition to do something important enough to deserve recognition. They expect to be treated as persons capable of responsibility and judgment. They will wish to have room to experiment and explore as they carry out their assignments and reach beyond them. If a company is to profit from their spontaneous contributions, it must involve them in the strategic planning process. One of the ways to do this is to go beyond exposing new possibilities for comment by asking such middle managers for a strategy for their division, department, section, or office and to deal sympathetically with the virtues and shortcomings of the outcome.

The cases you will examine offer many opportunities for such involvement. You will have occasion to observe the everyday ways in which constructive engagement in strategic management is frustrated by what

---

[3] D. Quinn Mills, in *The New Competitor* (New York: John Wiley & Sons, 1985), describes the expectations of what he calls the new generation of managers and the conflict between these and the traditional organization.

you may well conclude are archaic notions of authority, responsibility, hierarchy, status, and centralized decision making. Consider as you read "Texas Instruments" and "The Rose Company" how much or how little the strategy of the plant and company informs the thinking of the profit center and plant managers, respectively—or their seniors, for that matter. Do you think the structure and processes evident there reflect an appropriate strategy and the appropriate involvement by the key people who must carry it out?

The structure of the innovative organization in which we expect people to make creative contributions must clearly be dominated by relevant aspects of the corporate strategy. The way in which the structure is administered will reflect the kind of organization deemed appropriate for the nature of the contribution expected. It is becoming clear that the corporation of the 21st century will be a different kind of organization from the giant, formally controlled, and relatively centralized company of the present day. But before we examine that possibility, and before you use it in appraising and making recommendations for better performance in the cases that follow, we should pause to consider what by way of structure and process needs to be done in a conventional 1985 organization.

A reasonable profile of implementation activities goes as follows:

1. Once strategy is tentatively or finally set, the key tasks to be performed and kinds of decisions required must be identified.

2. Once the size of operations exceeds the capacity of one person, responsibility for accomplishing key tasks and making decisions must be assigned to individuals or groups. The division of labor must permit efficient performance of subtasks and must be accompanied by some hierarchical allocation of authority to assure achievement.

3. Formal provisions for the coordination of activities thus separated must be made in various ways, for example, through a hierarchy of supervision, project and committee organizations, task forces, and other ad hoc units. The prescribed activities of these formally constituted bodies are not intended to preclude spontaneous voluntary coordination.

4. Information systems adequate for coordinating divided functions (that is, for letting those performing part of the task know what they must know of the rest, and for letting those in supervisory positions know what is happening so that next steps may be taken) must be designed and installed.

5. The tasks to be performed should be arranged in a sequence comprising a program of action or a schedule of targets to be achieved at specified times. While long-range plans may be couched in relatively general terms, operating plans will often take the form of relatively detailed budgets. These can meet the need for the establishment of standards against which short-term performance can be judged.

6. Actual performance, as quantitatively reported in information systems and qualitatively estimated through observation by supervisors and judgment of customers, should be compared to budgeted performance and to standards in order to test achievement, budgeting processes, the adequacy of the standards, and the competence of individuals.

7. Individuals and groups of individuals must be recruited and assigned to essential tasks in accordance with the specialized or supervisory skills which they possess or can develop. At the same time, the assignment of tasks may well be adjusted to the nature of available skills.

8. Individual performance, evaluated both quantitatively and qualitatively, should be subjected to influences (constituting a pattern of incentives) which will help to make it effective in accomplishing organizational goals.

9. Since individual motives are complex and multiple, incentives for achievement should range from those that are universally appealing—such as adequate compensation and an organizational climate favorable to the simultaneous satisfaction of individual and organizational purposes—to specialized forms of recognition, financial or nonfinancial, designed to fit individual needs and unusual accomplishments.

10. In addition to financial and nonfinancial incentives and rewards to motivate individuals to voluntary achievement, a system of constraints, controls, and penalties must be devised to contain nonfunctional activity and to enforce standards. Controls, like incentives, are both formal and informal. Effective control requires both quantitative and nonquantitative information which must always be used together.

11. Provision for the continuing development of requisite technical and managerial skills is a high-priority requirement. The development of individuals must take place chiefly within the milieu of their assigned responsibilities. This on-the-job development should be supplemented by intermittent formal instruction and study.

12. Energetic personal leadership is necessary for continued growth and improved achievement in any organization. Leadership may be expressed in many styles, but it must be expressed in some perceptible style. This style must be natural and also consistent with the requirements imposed upon the organization by its strategy and membership.

Structure, Coordination, and Information Systems

The most fundamental processes that shape any organization structure consist of dividing the work and responsibility, coordinating the divided effort, and providing, in an organization of any size, the essential information to enable people to do their part of the total job in ways that fit the whole. You will have studied elsewhere organization design and the management of information systems; we will not take up those subjects here. The implementation of corporate strategy requires that the division of responsibility facilitate the efficient performance of the key tasks identified by the strategy. The formal pattern by which tasks are identified and authority delegated should have visible relationship to corporate purpose, should fix responsibility in such a way as not to preclude teamwork, and should provide for the solution of problems as close to the point of action as possible.

In an organization governed by purpose, responsibility will usually exceed authority; the resulting ambiguity provides opportunity for initiative and clarification in terms of shared objectives rather than separate fiefdoms.

The specialization of function made necessary by the growth of organization opens the door to counterstrategic departmental loyalties. Accountants behave like accountants and engineers like engineers more than is necessary; this specialized zeal has its advantages in the performance of a specialty but can be frustrating to general managers when departmental biases and narrowness produce conflict or impede consensus in the consideration of critical issues. Functional specialists tend to interpret corporate purpose to suit themselves.

It follows, therefore, that in all organizations provision must be made to resolve differences in perspective, clarify strategy against misconceptions and special interpretations, and above all, to provide for discussion of alternatives that satisfy both departmental and organization needs. Committees, task forces, operations reviews, and planning meetings are the ordinary vehicles of common understanding. When such suborganizations are ill run, they are decried as time wasting and unproductive and make strong-willed individuals impatient. In the hands of a skilled chairman, task forces and special purpose committees can be a principal source of creativity. The more informal the distribution of authority and the more ambiguous the boundaries between functions, the more important coordinating committees can become. The innovative company of the future provides much opportunity for people to talk to each other about what new undertakings should be launched, how they should be managed, and how old undertakings can be made more successful. Such meetings become more informative than the routine information provided to the organization by its reporting system.

The design of the formal structure of an organization will reflect corporate purpose, but it is the working of the informal organization that is not only central to productive cooperation but will suggest what the formal structure should be. Landscape architects laying out sidewalks in a park or campus will wait to let people walk on the grass and then either pave the resulting paths or plant out superfluous or unacceptable routes. The entrepreneurial corporation, well represented here by NIKE, begins in a small group of people whose understanding of what they are doing is constantly developed by close communication. What they are trying to accomplish is commanding; they have the resources to do only what most needs to be done. As such an organization grows, informality continues to dominate hierarchical distinctions, but eventually unclear separation of responsibility confuses people. The challenge becomes to clarify separate responsibilities without absolving the marketing people, for example, from knowing the strategically critical problems of production or product development.

The organization growing out of successful entrepreneurial chaos into a more structured company must somehow avoid the stultification of bureaucracy that comes from mismanaged size and complexity.[4] Incentive and reward systems have to be developed to introduce fairness into what was once intuitive recognition of the work of individual contributors justified by daily observation no longer possible. But rigidity need not come on stage with systems. If the latter fall into the hands of bureaucrats who are technically educated in the intricacies of the system and dedicated to its extension for its own sake, then the relation of incentives, for example, to the kind of behavior that is most relevant to successful accomplishment of purpose is lost.

What an organization is trying to accomplish can become recognized if the formalities of hierarchical organization are kept to a minimum. Assignments should never be so clear or restrictive that persons cannot contribute, within the limits of their capability, what most needs to be done. Every functional assignment should include its relevance to corporate purpose; general management perspective can be assigned to persons by evaluating their performance in teamwork terms. The conduct of inquiries into new possibilities by interdepartmental task forces, in addition to their regular duties, should be a way of life for middle managers and professional people, just as quality circles are a symbol of innovative potential on the factory floor. Independent business units, skunk works, pilot operations, high-risk experiments in which failure without penalty is possible, competitive product championing, improvisatory off-budget product development—all characterize the innovative company.

It is the assumption of the authors that you look forward to a management career in an innovative company. In any case, the large American corporation in industries undergoing massive restructuring is in the process of remaking itself. The pressure for becoming slimmer, faster, more responsive, and more profitable may come more from the need for cost reduction under intense foreign competition than from voluntary aspirations to excellence. But becoming and maintaining a position as a world-class company in selected market segments is an opportunity to any entrepreneur capable of devising an innovative strategy and developing an organization to extend the strategy rather than fall into the frustrations of formality, political conflict, and other aberrations of conventional organizations.

---

[4] See James Brian Quinn, "Managing Innovation: Controlled Chaos," *Harvard Business Review,* May–June 1985, pp. 73ff.

Commitment

The essence of successful implementation is commitment. Commitment comes from wanting to do something and from the satisfactions of having its importance recognized. As tasks become more difficult, wanting to contribute is not enough; greater capability is required. But most observers of established companies see a greater potential for cost reduction, product innovation, and quality enhancement than is ever fully recognized.[5] The effort to reexamine corporate capability can result in new ideas for at least minor additions to the product line or range of services, to quality, and to cost effectiveness that cumulatively support or extend market share and help bond customers to their suppliers as partners.

Strategic management is thus now being redirected toward making use of and extending organization's strengths and the innovative resilience of committed persons continually challenged to excel competitors and to improve on past performance. It becomes part of every manager's job. How well an organization can implement purpose becomes critical. Success depends on how much the persons assigned to achieve have been involved in the process of setting the goals and how deeply they have become committed to overcoming unexpected obstacles to success. They should not be deflected from common purpose by a company's organization structure or by its measurement, compensation, incentive, and control systems.

But such systems are required. Informality cannot be absolute. Cooperation in a clearly understood common endeavor rarely occurs by chance. We will look in the next note more closely at the processes through which commitment is expected to produce results. In the meantime the cases that follow now will give you the chance to test out, challenge, or reshape for your own use the ideas expressed here. You are in the process of deciding how you will make use of the concept of strategy and its power in shaping administrative systems toward relevance and simplicity in particular companies and unique situations. Nothing will help you more than examination of the kind of real-life combinations of theory and reality that appear in the next set of cases.

If you are not, yourself, to attack your management responsibilities with a set of unrealistic textbook assumptions about how your associates should respond to your leadership, you will think carefully about the need in any organization for clarity of mission, commitment to purpose, and careful preparation for changes in direction. Your awareness that strategy formulation and implementation must be interdependent, simultaneous processes is fundamental to mastery of the art of management and indispensable to understanding the nature of organization.

---

[5] For a research-based account of innovative practices in the management of work, see Richard E. Walton, "From Control to Commitment in the Workplace," *Harvard Business Review,* March–April 1985, pp. 77ff.

The Adams Corporation (A)

In January of 1972 the board of directors of The Adams Corporation simultaneously announced the highest sales in the company's history, the lowest aftertax profits (as a percentage of sales) of the World War II era, and the retirement (for personal reasons) of its long-tenure president and chief executive officer.

Founded in St. Louis in 1848, the Adams Brothers Company had long been identified as a family firm both in name and operating philosophy. Writing in a business history journal, a former family senior manager comments: "My grandfather wanted to lead a business organization with ethical standards. He wanted to produce a quality product and a quality working climate for both employees and managers. He thought the Holy Bible and the concept of family stewardship provided him with all the guidelines needed to lead his company. A belief in the fundamental goodness of mankind, in the power of fair play, and in the importance of personal and corporate integrity were his trademarks. Those traditions exist today in the 1960s."

In the early 1950s two significant corporate events occurred. First, the name of the firm was changed to The Adams Corporation. Second, somewhat over 50 percent of the corporation shares were sold by various family groups to the wider public. In 1970 all branches of the family owned or "influenced" less than one fifth of the outstanding shares of Adams.

Copyright © 1972 by the President and Fellows of Harvard College
Harvard Business School case 372–263

The Adams Corporation was widely known and respected as a manufacturer and distributor of quality, branded, and consumer products for the American, Canadian, and European (export) markets. Adams products were processed in four regional plants located near raw material sources,[1] were stored and distributed in a series of recently constructed or renovated distribution centers located in key cities throughout North America, and were sold by a company sales force to thousands of retail outlets—primarily supermarkets.

In explaining the original long-term financial success of the company, a former officer commented: "Adams led the industry in the development of unique production processes that produced a quality product at a very low cost. The company has always been production-oriented and volume-oriented, and it paid off for a long time. During those decades the Adams brand was all that was needed to sell our product; we didn't do anything but a little advertising. Competition was limited, and our production efficiency and raw material sources enabled us to outpace the industry in sales and profit. Our strategy was to make a quality product, distribute it, and sell it cheap.

"But that has all changed in the past 20 years," he continued. "Our three major competitors have outdistanced us in net profits and market aggressiveness. One of them—a first-class marketing group—has doubled sales and profits within the past five years. Our gross sales have increased to almost $250 million, but our net profits have dropped continuously during that same period. While a consumer action group just designated us as 'best value,' we have fallen behind in marketing techniques; for example, our packaging is just out of date."

Structurally, Adams was organized into eight major divisions. (See Exhibit 1.) Seven of these were regional sales divisions with responsibility for distribution and sales of the company's consumer products to retail stores in their area. Each regional sales division was further divided into organizational units at the state and county and/or trading area level. Each sales division was governed by a corporate price list in the selling of company products but had some leeway to meet the local competitive price developments. Each sales division was also assigned (by the home office) a quota of salesmen it could hire and was given the salary ranges within which these men could be employed. All salesmen were on straight salary and expense reimbursement salary plan, which resulted in compensation under industry averages.

A small central accounting office accumulated sales and expense information for each of the several sales divisions on a quarterly basis and prepared the overall company financial statements. Each sales division received, without commentary, a quarterly statement showing the number

---

[1] No single plant processed the full line of Adams products, but each plant processed the main items in the line.

of cases processed and sold for the overall division, sales revenue per case of the overall division, and local expenses per case for the overall division.

Somewhat similar information was obtained from the manufacturing division. Manufacturing division accounting was complicated by variations in the cost of obtaining and processing the basic materials used in Adams products. These variations—particularly in procurement—were largely beyond the control of that division. The accounting office did have, however, one rough external check on manufacturing division effectiveness. A crude market price for case lot goods, sold by smaller firms to some large national chains, did exist.

Once a quarter, the seven senior sales vice presidents met with general management in St. Louis. Typically, management discussion focused on divisional sales results and expense control. The company's objective of being "number one," the largest selling line in its field, directed group attention to sales versus budget. All knew that last year's sales targets had to be exceeded—"no matter what." The manufacturing division vice president sat in on these meetings to explain the product availability situation. Because of his St. Louis office location, he frequently talked with Mr. Jerome Adams about overall manufacturing operations and specifically about large procurement decisions.

The Adams Company, Mr. Millman knew, had a trade reputation for being very conservative with its compensation program. All officers were on a straight salary program. An officer might expect a modest salary increase every two or three years; these increases tended to be in the thousand dollar range regardless of divisional performance or company profit position. Salaries among the seven sales divisional vice presidents ranged from $32,000 to $42,000, with the higher amounts going to more senior officers. Mr. Jerome Adams's salary of $48,000 was the highest in the company. There was no corporate bonus plan. A very limited stock option program was in operation, but the depressed price of Adams stock meant that few officers exercised their options.

Of considerable pride to Mr. Jerome Adams had been the corporate climate at Adams. "We take care of our family" was his oft-repeated phrase at company banquets honoring long-service employees. "We are a team, and it is a team spirit that has built Adams into its leading position in this industry." No member of first-line, middle, or senior management could be discharged (except in cases of moral crime or dishonesty) without a personal review of his case by Mr. Adams. In matter of fact, executive turnover at Adams was very low. Executives at all levels viewed their jobs as a lifetime career. There was no compulsory retirement plan, and some managers were still active in their mid-70s.

The operational extension of this organization philosophy was quite evident to employees and managers. A private family trust, for over 75 years, provided emergency assistance to all members of the Adams organization. Adams led its industry in the granting of educational scholarships, in medical insurance for employees and managers, and in the encouragement of its "members" to give corporate and personal time and effort to community problems and organizations.

Mr. Adams noted two positive aspects of this organizational philosophy. "We have a high percentage of long-term employees—Joe Girly, a guard at East St. Louis, completes 55 years with us this year, and every one of his brothers and sisters has worked here. And it is not uncommon for a vice president to retire with a blue pin—that means 40 years of service. We have led this industry in manufacturing process innovation, quality control, and value for low price for decades. I am proud of our accomplishments, and this pride is shown by everyone—from janitors to directors." Industry sources noted that there was no question that Adams was "number one" in terms of manufacturing and logistic efficiency.

In December of 1971 the annual Adams management conference gathered over 80 of Adams's senior management in St. Louis. Most expected the usual formal routines—the announcement of 1971 results and 1972 budgets, the award of the "Gold Flag" to the top processing plant and sales division for exceeding targets, and the award of service pins to executives. All expected the usual social good times. It was an opportunity to meet and drink with "old buddies."

After a series of task force meetings, the managers gathered in a banquet room—good naturedly referred to as the "Rib Room" since a local singer, "Eve," was to provide entertainment. At the front of the room, in the usual fashion, was a dais with a long, elaborately decorated head table. Sitting at the center of that table was Mr. Jerome Adams. Following tradition, Mr. Adams's vice presidents, in order of seniority with the company, sat on his right. On his left sat major family shareholders, corporate staff, and—a newcomer—soon to be introduced.

After awarding service pins and the Gold Flags of achievement, Mr. Adams announced formally what had been a corporate "secret" for several months. First, a new investing group had assumed a "control" position on the board of Adams. Second, Mr. Price Millman would take over as president and chief executive officer of Adams.

Introducing Mr. Millman, Adams pointed out the outstanding record of the firm's new president. "Price got his MBA in 1958, spent four years in control and marketing, and then was named as the youngest divisional president in the history of the Tenny Corporation. In the past years he has made his division the most profitable in Tenny and the industry leader in its field. We are fortunate to have him with us. Please give him your complete support."

In a later informal meeting with the divisional vice presidents, Mr. Millman spoke about his respect for past Adams accomplishments and the pressing need to infuse Adams with "fighting spirit" and "competitiveness." "My personal and organizational philosophy are the same—the name of the game is to fight and win. I almost drowned, but I won my first swimming race at 11 years of age! That philosophy of always winning is what enabled me to build the Ajax division into Tenny's most profitable operation. We are going to do this at Adams."

In conclusion he commented, "The new owner group wants results. They have advised me to take some time to think through a new format for Adams's operations—to get a corporate design that will improve our effectiveness. Once we get that new format, gentlemen, I have but one goal—each month must be better than the past."

Exhibit 1

Organization Chart

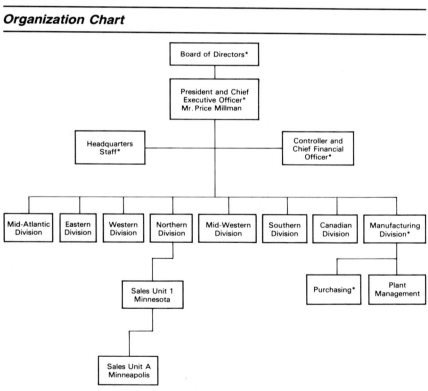

* Located in St. Louis.

The Rose Company

Mr. James Pierce had recently received word of his appointment as plant manager of Plant X, one of the older established units of the Rose Company. As such, Mr. Pierce was to be responsible for the management and administration at Plant X of all functions and personnel except sales.

Both top management and Mr. Pierce realized that there were several unique features about his new assignment. Mr. Pierce decided to assess his new situation and relationships before undertaking his assignment. He was personally acquainted with the home office executives but had met few of the plant personnel. This case contains some of his reflections regarding the new assignment.

The Rose Company conducted marketing activities throughout the United States and in certain foreign countries. These activities were directed from the home office by a vice president in charge of sales.

Manufacturing operations and certain other departments were under the supervision and control of a senior vice president. These are shown in Exhibit 1. For many years the company had operated a highly centralized functional type of manufacturing organization. There was no general manager at any plant; each of the departments in a plant reported on a line basis to its functional counterpart at the home office. For instance, the industrial relations manager of a particular plant reported to the

Copyright © 1953, 1981 by the President and Fellows of Harvard College
Harvard Business School case 453–002

vice president in charge of industrial relations at the home office, the plant controller to the vice president and controller, and so on.

Mr. Pierce stated that in the opinion of the top management the record of Plant X had not been satisfactory for several years. The board had recently approved the erection of a new plant in a different part of the city and the use of new methods of production. Lower costs of processing and a reduced labor force requirement at the new plant were expected. Reduction of costs and improved quality of products were needed to maintain competitive leadership and gain some slight product advantage. The proposed combination of methods of manufacturing and mixing materials had not been tried elsewhere in the company. Some features would be entirely new to employees.

According to Mr. Pierce the top management of the Rose Company was beginning to question the advisability of the central control of manufacturing operations. The officers decided to test the value of a decentralized operation in connection with Plant X. They apparently believed that a general management representative in Plant X was needed if the new equipment in manufacturing methods and the required rebuilding of the organization were to succeed.

Prior to the new assignment Mr. Pierce had been an accounting executive in the controller's department of the company. From independent sources the case writer learned that Mr. Pierce had demonstrated analytical ability and general administrative capacity. He was generally liked by people. From top management's point of view he had an essential toughness described as an ability to see anything important through. By some he was regarded as the company's efficiency expert. Others thought he was a perfectionist and aggressive in reaching the goals that had been set. Mr. Pierce was aware of these opinions about his personal behavior.

Mr. Pierce summarized his problem in part as follows:

I am going into a situation involving a large number of changes. I will have a new plant—new methods and processes—but most of all I will be dealing with a set of changed relationships. Heretofore all the heads of departments in the plant reported to their functional counterparts in the home office. Now they will report to me. I am a complete stranger, and in addition this is my first assignment in a major "line" job. The men will know this.

When I was called into the senior vice president's office to be informed of my new assignment, he asked me to talk with each of the functional members of his staff. The vice presidents in charge of production planning, manufacturing, and industrial relations said they were going to issue all headquarters instructions to me as plant manager and they were going to cut off their connections with their counterparts in my plant. The other home office executives admitted their functional counterparts would report to me in line capacity. They should obey my orders, and I would be responsible for their pay and promotion. But these executives proposed to follow the common practice of many companies of maintaining a dotted line or functional relationship with these men. I realize that these two different patterns of home office-plant relationships will create real administrative problems for me.

Exhibit 2 shows the organization relationships as defined in these conferences.

Exhibit 1

Old Organization

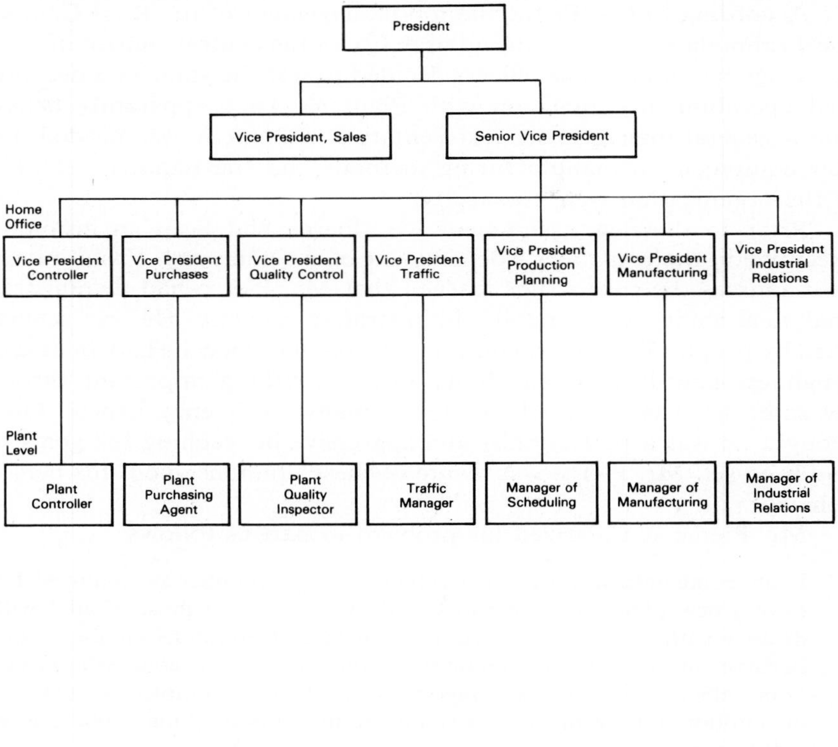

Exhibit 2

New Organization

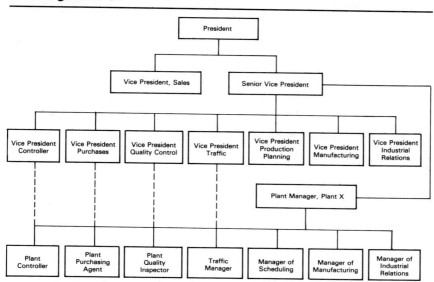

Texas Instruments, Incorporated (A) (Condensed)

On April 17, 1959, Texas Instruments Incorporated (TI) of Dallas, Texas, merged with the Metals & Controls Corporation (M & C) of Attleboro, Massachusetts. One of the fastest growing large corporations in the country, TI had achieved a compound annual growth from 1946 through 1958 of 38 percent in sales and 42 percent in net income. The president had publicly predicted that volume would more than double in 1959 to a sales level near $200 million. Almost half this growth, he added, might come through mergers, with M & C contributing $42 million to $45 million. To date TI's principal business had been in electronic and electromechanical equipment and systems, semiconductors and other components, and exploration services for oil, gas, and minerals.

So highly was TI regarded by the market that in May 1960 its common was selling at about 70 times the 1959 earnings of $3.59 a share.

M & C Activities

Itself the product of a 1932 merger and a postwar diversification, M & C had three major groups of products: clad metals, control instruments, and nuclear fuel components and instrumented cores. The company had grown steadily and in 1959 had plants in two U.S. locations and five foreign countries. Reflecting predecessor corporation names, the clad

Copyright © 1960 by the President and Fellows of Harvard College
Harvard Business School case 312–030

metal lines were known as General Plate (GP) products, and the control instrument lines were known as Spencer products. Included in the former were industrial, precious, and thermostat metals; fancy wire; and wire and tubing. Included in the latter were motor protectors, circuit breakers, thermostats, and precision switches. Among these Spencer lines there were some that utilized GP products as raw materials; that is, GP thermostat bimetals and GP clad electrical contacts.

Apart from a portion of GP's precious metal products which went to the jewelry trade (where appearance and fast delivery from stock were key considerations), most GP and Spencer products had to be designed to specific customer requirements and produced to customer order. Thus engineering know-how and close coordination between the sales and production departments on delivery dates were important. Owing to the technical nature of the products and also to their fast-changing applications, a company sales force with a high degree of engineering competence was essential. To serve its several thousand customers, many of whom purchased both Spencer and GP products, the company maintained a force of 50 men in the field, divided into Spencer and GP units.

With Spencer products facing important competition from four other firms in the $10 million to $40 million annual sales bracket, tight control of costs was important for securing the large orders generally placed by the kinds of customers to whom these products were sold. Buyers included manufacturers of fractional horsepower motors, household appliances, air conditioning, and aircraft and missiles. In contrast, GP industrial metals met no direct competition, although clad metals for industrial uses met with competition from alloys.

M & C's Premerger Organization

At the time TI took over M & C a task force of four junior executives had just completed, at the acting president's request, a critical study of M & C's organizational structure. So far its nuclear activities had been conducted by an entirely separate subsidiary, and the GP and Spencer activities had been organized as shown in Exhibit 1.

Under the acting president at the top level came a tier of predominantly functional executives (the vice presidents for marketing, engineering, and finance, the treasurer, and the controller). At the third and fourth levels of command the structure increasingly showed a breakdown by product lines. For example, at the fourth level in manufacturing there were four separate groups corresponding to the major Spencer lines, and six separate groups corresponding to the major GP lines. Approximately the same breakdown appeared among the fourth-level product specialists in marketing. Although there was no profit responsibility at this level, the controller had been sending marketing's product specialists a monthly P & L by product line, in the hope of encouraging informal meetings among the people in marketing, engineering, and production who were working on the same lines.

Even at the second level the predominantly functional division of responsibilities was neither complete nor unalloyed. Thus the vice president for marketing was also the vice president of Spencer Products, and in this capacity he had reporting to him the Spencer engineers. As a result the company's vice president of engineering was, in effect, the vice president only of GP engineering, although he also served in an other-than-functional role by acting as the vice president of M & C International. (In 1958 exports and other foreign sales totaled about $2 million.)

After confidential interviews with 140 people, members of the M & C task force reportedly concluded that this organizational structure was causing or contributing to a number of company problems. Accordingly the task force recommended sweeping changes, first to the acting president by whom they had been appointed, then to his successor, Mr. Edward O. Vetter, a 39-year-old TI vice president brought in following the merger.

Mr. Vetter's Review and Appraisal

As soon as he arrived at M & C Mr. Vetter spent most of four days in closed meetings with task force members. At the same time he scheduled public meetings with all executives; these sessions he devoted to general discussions of his aims for the organization and to reassurances that drastic changes would not be made.

From these discussions Vetter learned that a great many people at M & C felt that the three major functional departments were not cooperating well enough in the exploitation of new product opportunities based on existing markets and skills. Although in a few isolated instances marketing, engineering, and production personnel concerned with a particular product had formed small informal groups to work on common problems, the three departments had not been seen as working together with maximum effectiveness, particularly in new product development. To blame, besides top management's inattention and the absence of a comprehensive plan, was a lack of clear-cut responsibility and authority.

Other problems, too, provided additional evidence of the failure of functional groups to work together harmoniously and effectively. Thus there was continued squabbling between process engineers and production supervisors, with neither group being willing to accept the other's suggestions for improvements in manufacturing methods. With both groups reporting to different vice presidents, conflicts too often came up for resolution at top levels. Here many times decisions were postponed and issues left unresolved.

Vetter was also told by many members of the organization that the personal influence of marketing's product specialists played too large a role in company decisions. Formally assigned to coordinate certain aspects of factory-customer relations (see notes to Exhibit 1), these specialists were said to determine the amount of R&D time given to particular lines, with the result that some lines had grown quite strong while promising opportunities elsewhere were neglected. Similarly personal relationships between product specialists and production personnel largely determined scheduling priorities.

After becoming familiar with these problems Mr. Vetter decided that M & C provided a golden opportunity for applying TI's philosophy of organization by what TI called "product-customer centered groups." Basically this plan involved putting a single manager in charge of sales, manufacturing, and engineering on a particular product line and making this manager responsible for profits. This type of structure, Mr. Vetter noted, was what had been proposed by M & C's own task force on organization. According to TI's president, it offered advantages not only in managing existing lines but also in finding new opportunities for discerning and serving new customer needs.

As he was collecting information on M & C's organizational arrangements, Mr. Vetter had dictated the following set of notes for his own use:

It appears as if natural product groups already exist here. General Plate, Spencer, and Nuclear have always been separate, and International sales are set apart under Richard Myers. Within these major groupings there is also a somewhat parallel division of the manufacturing and marketing facilities along product lines. There are 10 production departments that are each organized to produce a particular product line, while there is an almost parallel organization of marketing product specialists under James Bradford.

Bringing together product managers and production supervisors for similar product lines would seem to be the logical implementation of TI's management philosophy. Of course one problem would be the rearrangement of some of the production facilities in order to locate all the equipment under a product manager's control in one area. While we do have 10 product-manufacturing departments, some of these share facilities and perform work for one another. In addition, the parts department performs fabrication operations for several production departments. In spite of this there are no major pieces of equipment that would have to be physically relocated. We estimated that some duplicate equipment will have to be purchased if we go ahead with product-centered decentralization; in order to accomplish this about $1.5 million will have to be spent almost three years before it would otherwise have been committed.

I believe that the "inside" product specialist—the man at the factory who lives with both the manufacturing and the marketing problems for his line—is a key man. Our products are mainly engineered to customer order and, as such, require a great deal of coordination on delivery dates, specifications, and special applications. In addition to performing this liaison, the product managers could be the men who sense ideas for new product applications from their marketing contacts and then transmit these to the product engineering personnel at the factory.

These men would not be salesmen. A field sales force would still be needed to make regular calls on all of our clients and to cultivate the associations with our customers' engineering staffs. One significant question here is how to organize the sales force. These men are highly skilled and quite expensive to employ—each salesman should enter commitments of at least $1 million yearly in order to justify his expenses. Since our customers are spread all over the country, it would appear economical to assign field salesmen by geographical areas, each to sell all, or at least a number of, our products. Unfortunately, this system might take a good measure of the responsibility for the sales supervision. Our problem here is to leave sales responsibility at the product group level without having an undue duplication of field sales personnel.

The filtering down of responsibility and authority would mean that we would need more "management skill" in order for the product managers to be able to manage the little companies of which each would be in charge. The product manager must be capable of making sales, manufacturing, financial, and engineering decisions. He is no longer judged against a budget but becomes responsible for profits. We would need talented men to fill these positions—a shift in the organizational structure would undoubtedly force us to hire some new people. Nevertheless, there are tremendous benefits to be gained in terms of giving more people the chance to display their talents and in just plain better functioning of the M & C division.

The organization of engineering personnel brings up a whole hornets' nest of questions. First of all, there are two distinct engineering functions: product engineers, those concerned with current product designs and new applications for existing products, and advanced engineers, those who work on long-term product development. There is little doubt that the new applications sales effort would benefit from placing the product engineering personnel in close organizational contact with the marketers. This would mean splitting engineering up among all the product groups and would probably make for a less efficient overall operation. Decentralization of the advanced engineering groups is easily as ticklish a problem. Again it would probably receive more marketing-oriented stimulus if it were placed under the supervision of the product manager. I wonder, however, if he might not be motivated to cut long-term development more drastically than top management normally would in times of business recession. Furthermore I wonder if the economies of centralized advanced engineering and research in terms of combined effort and personnel selection are not so great as to make decentralization of this function an extremely poor choice. The basic question we have to answer here is to what degree should we sacrifice operating economy in order to give our engineering personnel a greater marketing orientation.

* * * * *

Scheduling has long been a bone of contention here wherever facilities are shared. Conflicts for priorities between product specialists are always occurring. If we decentralize, however, the amount of facilities that are shared will decrease substantially, and this problem should be alleviated. Again we have the basic choice of retaining the centralized scheduling groups or splitting the function up among the various product groups.

In addition to the above issues, Mr. Vetter was considering the proper timing for an organizational change. He was debating whether a change should be made by gradual steps or whether the transfer in corporate ownership provided a convenient opportunity for making radical changes with a minimum of employee resentment. In general, the M & C personnel expressed some regrets because the family that had founded the company was no longer associated with it. They recognized, however, that the continual top management conflict of recent years necessitated a change and were pleased by the fact that a recognized leader in the industry had taken over the company.

Exhibit 1

Premerger Metals & Controls Organization

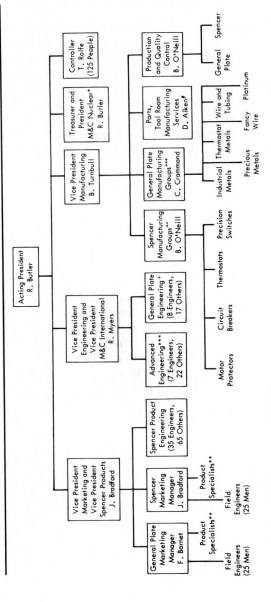

* Detail on M & C Nuclear not disclosed.
** Responsible for factory-customer coordination on specifications, prices, delivery, and new applications on different product lines (broken down about as shown in the manufacturing department).
*** Responsible for long-range product development for GP lines.
† Worked on new applications and process designs for GP lines.
†† Principal operations in Spencer production departments were parts-making and assembly.
††† Principal operations in GP industrial, precious, and thermostat metal departments were bonding and rolling; in GP wire and fancy wire departments, drawing; and in GP platinum department, melting and refining. Some GP facilities were shared, and roughly 5 percent of direct labor hours for each GP department were devoted to work for other departments.
# Reporting to Aiken were units making two GP and three Spencer parts.
Source: Interviews and company records.

Texas Instruments, Incorporated (B)

In May 1960 Tom Pringle, the manager of the Industrial Metals product department at Texas Instruments' Metals & Controls division, was considering several courses of action in the face of his department's failure to meet forecasted sales and profits during the first four months of 1960. The rebuilding of inventories by M & C's customers, which had been expected as an aftermath of the settlement of the 1959 steel strike, had not materialized, and shipments from Pringle's product department were running about 12 percent below forecast. Furthermore, incoming sales commitments during these four months were 15 percent below expectations. The product department's direct profit, according to preliminary statements, was 19 percent below plan.

In light of these adverse developments Pringle was studying the advisability of three specific moves which would improve this profit performance: (1) eliminating his $30,000 advertising budget for the latter half of 1960, (2) postponing the addition of two engineers to his engineering group until 1961, and (3) reducing further purchases of raw materials in order to improve his department's return on assets ratio. Until now Pringle had been reluctant to make any concessions in his department's scale of operations since there was a very strong accent on rapid growth throughout the Texas Instruments organization. This attitude toward expansion also appeared to prevail in the new top management group in the Metals & Controls division. The enthusiasm of the Texas Instru-

Copyright © 1960 by the President and Fellows of Harvard College
Harvard Business School case 306–066

ments management had caught on at Metals & Controls with the formation of the product-centered decentralized organization.

The 1959 Reorganization

In June 1959, just three months after Metals & Controls Corporation had become a division of Texas Instruments, Incorporated, Mr. Edward O. Vetter, the division vice president, instituted a product-centered organization. This decentralization was carried out in accordance with Texas Instruments' policy of placing ultimate responsibility for profitable operation at the product level. The framework that emerged was similar to that which existed elsewhere in the company.

Mr. Vetter organized four major product groups at Metals & Controls: General Plate, Spencer Controls, Nuclear Products, and International Operations. To augment these groups, six centralized staff units were organized at the division level: Research and Development, Legal, Industrial Engineering, Control, Marketing, and Personnel (see Exhibit 1). The four managers of the product groups and the six managers of these staff departments, along with Mr. Vetter, comprised the management committee for the Metals & Controls division. This committee was a sounding board for helping each responsible manager make the proper decision as required by his job responsibility. In the case of profit performance, the ultimate responsibility for the division was Vetter's.

Within each product group several product departments were established. The General Plate products group, for example, included the Industrial Metals, Electrical Contacts, Industrial Wire, and Precious Metals departments (see Exhibit 2). The manager of each of these departments was responsible for its "profit performance." He was supported by staff units such as Industrial Engineering and Administration which reported directly to the group manager (Burt Turnbull for General Plate products). The expense of these staff units was charged to the individual product departments proportionally to the volume of activity in the various departments as measured by direct labor hours or by sales dollars less raw materials cost. The product departments were also charged with those expenses over which the manager and his supervisory group were able to exercise direct control, such as labor and materials.

The field sales force of 50 men was centralized under the manager for marketing, Al Scofield (see Exhibit 1). These men were divided about evenly into two major selling groups: one for General Plate products, and the other for Spencer products. The 25 salesmen assigned to General Plate and the 25 salesmen assigned to Spencer were shared by the four General Plate and four Spencer product departments. Each individual product department also maintained "inside" marketing personnel who performed such functions as pricing, developing marketing strategy, order follow-up, and providing the field sales engineers with information on new applications, designs, and product specifications for its particular line.

The Industrial Metals Department

Tom Pringle was manager of the Industrial Metals department of the General Plate products group. Sales of this department in 1959 were approximately $4 million.[1] Pringle was responsible for the profitability of two product lines: (1) industrial metals and (2) thermostat metals. His department's sales were split about evenly between these lines, although industrial metals had the greater growth potential because of the almost infinite number of possible clad metals for which an ever-increasing number of applications was being found. He was in charge of the marketing, engineering, and manufacturing activities for both these lines and had six key subordinates:

Industrial Metals Department (Years of service with the Metals & Controls Organization)

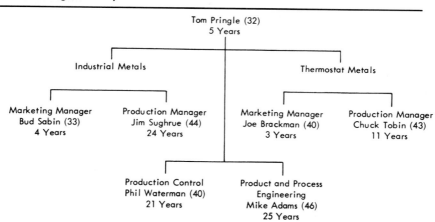

The function of the marketing managers in the Industrial Metals department (Bud Sabin and Joe Brackman) was to supervise the "inside selling units." These units were responsible for developing marketing strategy, pricing, contacting customers on special requests, and factory problems; for promotional activities; and for coordinating product development and sales. In May 1960 in addition to its regular work, the Industrial Metals inside selling unit was developing a manual of special applications for its products which it hoped would improve the ability

---

[1] All figures have been disguised.

of the field sales force to envision new uses. The production managers had line responsibility for the efficient use of manufacturing facilities, for meeting delivery promises to customers, and for expenses incurred in producing the department's products. The product and process engineering group had responsibility for designing new products and devising new production processes. The production control manager formulated guidelines to aid the foremen in scheduling work through the plant, supervised the expediters and clerks who served as a clearinghouse for information on delivery dates, and was responsible for ordering raw material and maintaining a balanced inventory.

In accordance with Texas Instruments' policy of placing ultimate responsibility for profitable operation at the product level, Tom Pringle's performance was measured, to a large extent, by the actual profits earned by the Industrial Metals department. The old M & C system of evaluating performance according to fixed and variable department budgets had been supplemented by the establishment of these "profit centers." Although the system passed actual profit responsibility to the product department manager level, the Texas Instruments' top management had always retained some control over the profit centers by requiring each manager to formulate a one-year plan which was subject to review by higher management. As a result profit planning was instituted whereby each manager set forth a detailed plan for the year's operations under the direction of the management committee. His actual performance was continually being evaluated against the plan.

Formulation of the Profit Plan. In October 1959 Tom Pringle began to prepare his department's profit plan for 1960. This was part of a companywide effort in which all department managers participated. The first step in the process was to prepare a detailed estimate of expected sales for the year. These estimates were gathered from two sources: the inside selling units and the field sales force. Management felt that one would serve as a good check on the other and, furthermore, believed that widespread participation in preparing the plan was one way to ensure its effectiveness. Bud Sabin and Joe Brackman, then, began to prepare estimates of 1960 sales by product lines with the help of the individual product specialists within the inside marketing group. Sabin and Brackman were also aided by the Texas Instruments central marketing group which prepared a report that estimated normal growth for their product lines. Pringle suggested that they prepare their estimates by subdividing the market into three parts: sales resulting from normal industry growth at current levels of market penetration; increased sales resulting from further penetration of the market with existing products; and increased sales from new products detailed by specific customers. At the same time Herb Skinner, the manager of the General Plate field sales force, asked the field engineers to predict the volume of orders that each Industrial Metals customer would place in 1960, without referring to the reports being readied by the product marketing groups. In this way the marketing managers made forecasts by product line and the field force made forecasts by customer.

The field selling force came up with estimated thermostat metal sales of $2,350,000 for 1960, and the inside group estimated sales of $2,420,000. Pringle felt that these two estimates were in reasonably good agreement. On the other hand Bud Sabin, the Industrial Metals marketing manager, estimated sales of $3,050,000, while the other group predicted only $2,500,000. Sabin predicted that 20 percent of the increase would come from normal growth, 50 percent from increased market penetration with existing products, and 30 percent from new products. Sales for Sabin's group had been $1.4 million in 1958 and $2.1 million in 1959. Pringle felt that the disparity between the two estimates was significant, and he discussed the matter with both men. All three men finally decided that the sales force had submitted a conservative estimate and agreed that Sabin's figure was the most realistic goal.

Once the sales estimate of $5,470,000 was agreed upon by Pringle and his marketing managers, the process of estimating manufacturing costs began. The manufacturing superintendents, Chuck Tobin and Jim Sughrue, were furnished the thermostat and industrial metals sales estimates and were instructed to forecast direct labor costs, supervisory salaries, and overhead expenses. These forecasts were to be made for each manufacturing area, or cost center, under their supervision. Sughrue was responsible for five cost centers and Tobin for four, each of which was directly supervised by a foreman. These expenses were to be forecast monthly and were to be used as a yardstick by which the actual expense performance of the manufacturing personnel could later be measured.

Jim Sughrue had previously calculated the hourly labor cost and the output per hour for each of his cost centers for 1959. To estimate 1960 salaries and wages, he then increased 1959 expenses proportionately to the expected sales increase. He followed the same procedure in determining 1960 overhead expenses, such as expendable tools, travel, telephone, process supplies, and general supplies. Chuck Tobin's task was somewhat simpler since the sales projection for his cost centers required a level of output that exactly matched the current production level. For salaries and wages he merely used as his 1960 estimate the actual cost experience that had been reported on the most recent monthly income statement he received. For overhead he applied a historical percent-of-sales ratio and then reduced his estimate by 3 percent to account for increased efficiency. In discussing the overhead estimate with his foremen, Tobin informed them that he had allowed for an 8 percent efficiency increase.

Since this was the first time any attempt at such detailed planning had been made at M & C, and since the M & C accounting system had recently been changed to match Texas Instruments', very little historical information was available. For this reason Pringle did not completely delegate the responsibility for the various marketing and manufacturing estimates to his subordinates. Instead he worked in conjunction with them to develop the forecasts. He hoped that his participation in this process would ensure a more accurate forecast for the year. Furthermore he hoped to develop the ability of his supervision to plan ahead.

Pringle estimated direct materials cost and consumption factors himself. Since it was impossible to predict what all the various strip metal prices would be, he calculated the ratio of materials expense to sales for 1959 and applied it to the 1960 sales projections for each of the product lines in his department.

The marketing, administration, and engineering groups that serviced Pringle's Industrial Metals group forecast their expenses by detailing their personnel requirements and then applying historical ratios of expenses to personnel to estimate their other expenses. From these dollar figures Pringle was able to estimate what proportions of these amounts would be charged to his department.

With the various forecasts in hand Pringle estimated a direct profit of $1,392,000 on a sales volume of $5,470,000. Once this plan had been drawn up, it was reviewed by the division management committee in relationship to the specific profit and sales goals which it had established for the division. In reviewing the plans for each product department in terms of the specific group goals, it became obvious that the combined plans of the General Plate product departments were not sufficient to meet the overall goal and that based on market penetration, new product developments, and other factors, the planned sales volume for Industrial Metals should be revised upward to $6,050,000 and direct profit to $1,587,000 (see Exhibit 3). This was discussed among Vetter, Turnbull, Scofield, and Pringle, and they agreed that it was a difficult but achievable plan.

Actual Performance, 1960. On May 10 Tom Pringle received a detailed statement comparing the actual performance of his department for January through April with his budget (see Exhibit 4). Sales were 12 percent below plan, and direct profit was 19 percent below plan.

In addition to these figures manufacturing expenses by cost centers were accumulated for Pringle. He passed these along to the production superintendents after he had made adjustments in the budgeted expense figures to allow for the sales decline. Pringle had devised a variable budget system whereby he applied factors to the forecast expenses to indicate what an acceptable expense performance was at sales levels other than the planned volume. Chuck Tobin and Jim Sughrue then analyzed the actual expenses and, one week later, held meetings with their foremen to discuss the causes of both favorable and unfavorable variances. The most common explanation of favorable manufacturing variances was either extremely efficient utilization of labor or close control over overhead. Unfavorable variances most frequently resulted from machine delays which necessitated overtime labor payments.

Specific Problems. Pringle was currently faced with three specific problems. In light of his department's poor performance these past months, he was considering the effects of eliminating his $30,000 advertising budget for the remainder of 1960, postponing the addition of two new engineers to his staff for six months, and reducing raw materials purchases in order to decrease inventory and thus improve his department's return on assets performance.

He had discussed the possibility of eliminating the advertising budget with Bud Sabin and Joe Brackman but had not yet reached a conclusion. Advertising expenditures had been budgeted at $30,000 for the final six months of 1960. The Industrial Metals department ads were generally placed in trade journals read by design engineers in the electrical, automobile, and appliance industries. Pringle did not know for certain how important an aid these advertisements were to his sales force. He did know that all of his major competitors allocated about the same proportion of sales revenue for advertising expenditures and that Industrial Metals ads were occasionally mentioned by customers.

In late 1959 Pringle had made plans to increase his engineering staff from 8 men to 10 men in mid-1960. He felt that the two men could begin functioning productively by early 1961 and could help to revise certain processes which were yielding excessive scrap, to develop new products, and to assist the field engineers in discovering new applications for existing products. Pringle estimated that postponing the hiring of these men for six months would save $20,000 in engineering salaries and supporting expenses.

Pringle also knew that one of the important indicators of his performance was the department's ratio of direct profit to assets used. This figure had been budgeted at 40 percent for 1961, but actual results to date were 31 percent. Pringle was considering reductions in raw materials purchases in order to decrease inventories and thus improve performance. He had discussed this possibility with Phil Waterman, the production control manager for Industrial Metals. Pringle knew that significant improvements in the overall ratio could be made in this way since raw materials inventories accounted for almost 20 percent of total assets and were at a level of 10 months' usage at present consumption ratios. He recognized, however, that this course of action required accepting a greater risk of running out. This risk was important to assess since most customers required rapid delivery and Pringle's suppliers usually required four months' lead time to manufacture the nonstandard size metals in relatively small lots required for the Industrial Metals' cladding operation.

The Purpose of the Profit Plan. The degree to which the plan was used as a method for evaluating performance and fixing compensation was not completely clear to Pringle. Everyone seemed to recognize that this first effort was imperfect and had errors built in because of inadequate historical data. He had never been explicitly informed of the extent to which top management desired product department decision making to be motivated by short-run effects on planned performance. Pringle stated that during the months immediately following the initiation of the plan he had concluded that short-term performance was much less significant than long-run growth and that he had preferred to concentrate on the longer run development of new products and markets.

Pringle knew that the Metals & Controls operating committee met every Monday to review the performance of each product department from preliminary reports. Customarily Burt Turnbull, the manager of the General Plate group, discussed both Pringle's incoming sales commitments and actual manufacturing expenses with him before each meeting. Pringle also knew that each manager was given a formal appraisal review every six months by his superior. It was common knowledge that the department's performance in relation to its plan was evaluated at both these sessions. Furthermore, Pringle was aware of the fact that Turnbull's performance as product group manager would be affected by his own performance with Industrial Metals. Over a period of months Pringle had learned that the management committee utilized the comparison of actual and planned performance to pinpoint trouble spots. On occasion Vetter had called him in to explain any significant deviations from plan, but normally he was represented at these meetings by Burt Turnbull. It was Pringle's impression that Vetter had been satisfied with the explanation he had given.

In their day-to-day decisions Pringle's subordinates seemed to be influenced only in a very general way by the profit plan. They reviewed their monthly performance against plan with interest but generally tended to bias their decisions in favor of long-run development at the expense of short-run deviations from the plan. More recently, however, Pringle realized that top management was not satisfied with his explanations of failure to meet plans. The message, though not stated explicitly, seemed to be that he was expected to take whatever remedial and alternate courses of action were needed in order to meet the one-year goals. He was certain that real pressure was building up for each department manager to meet his one-year plan.

In commenting on the use of planning at M & C, Mr. Vetter, the division vice president, stated four major purposes of the program:

> To set a par for the course. Vetter believed that performance was always improved if the manager proposed a realistic objective for his performance and was informed in advance of what was expected of him.
>
> To grow management ability. Vetter believed that the job of manager

was to coordinate all the areas for which he was given responsibility. He saw the planning process as a tool for improving these managerial skills.

To anticipate problems and look ahead. Vetter felt that the planning process gave the department managers a convenient tool for planning personnel requirements and sales strategy. It also set guideposts so that shifts in business conditions could be detected quickly and plans could be altered.

To weld Texas Instruments into one unit. The basic goals for each division were formulated by Vetter in recognition of overall company goals as disseminated by Haggerty, the company president. These were passed down to the product department level by the product group manager at each Texas Instruments division. Profit planning was thus being carried out by the same process by every department manager in the corporation.

Vetter recognized, however, that many reasons could exist for performance being either better or worse than planned. He stated that in his experience extremely rigid profit plans often motivated managers to budget low in order to provide themselves with a safety cushion. In his view, this made the entire profit planning process worthless.

Exhibit 1

Organization Chart, Metals & Controls Division

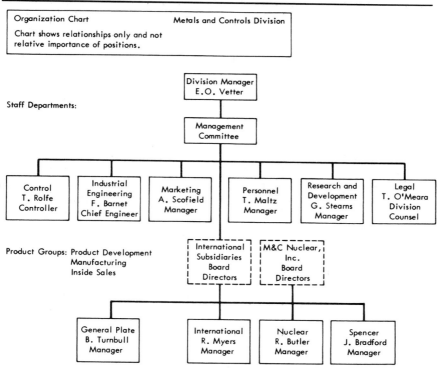

Exhibit 2

Organization Chart, General Plate Products Group

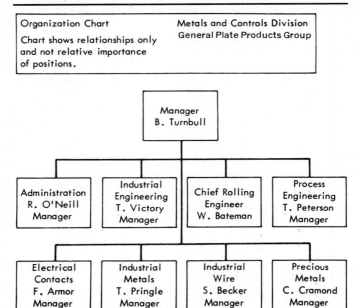

Organization Chart	Metals and Controls Division
Chart shows relationships only and not relative importance of positions.	General Plate Products Group

Exhibit 3

Industrial Metals Department: Initial and Revised Profit Statements for 1960*

	Initial	Revised
Sales	$5,470,000	$6,050,000
Direct labor	435,000	480,000
Direct material	1,920,000	2,115,000
Overhead	875,000	968,000
Marketing	305,000	346,000
Administration	161,000	161,000
Engineering	382,000	393,000
Direct profit	1,392,000	1,587,000

* All figures have been disguised.

Exhibit 4

Comparison of Actual and Budgeted Performance, January–April 1960*

	Budgeted	Actual
Sales	$2,020,000	$1,780,000
Direct labor	160,000	142,400
Direct material	704,000	593,000
Overhead	322,000	287,000
Marketing	100,000	116,400
Administration	54,000	55,800
Engineering	126,000	136,600
Direct profit	554,000	448,000

* All figures have been disguised.

Air, Inc.

In 1971 the board of directors of Air, Inc., Chicago, the oldest and one of the largest manufacturers of air filtration equipment in the world, nominated David Palma, 55, vice president as head of international operations. The International Division supervised about 50 companies throughout the world, which together generated a sales volume roughly equal to that of the U.S. operation.

David Palma, an Italian national who had worked for Air, Inc., for 20 years, took on his new job at a moment when international operations were clearly in a bad way. During the preceding year they had netted only $50,000 profits on $300 million of sales; and although Air, Inc., was still the world leader in market share (with about 20 percent of the world market), its position was weakening.

David Palma noted the reasons for the situation to be the following:

1. Competition was cutthroat: as the industry was labor-intensive, and as its products were old, without patent protection, and often custom-made, there seemed to be little advantage of size against hundreds of small local competitors.

2. Air, Inc., had made no thorough analysis of its competition nor of the different markets it served.

3. There was no product policy; most products were developed in the United States and did not meet local needs nor local building

---

The case was prepared by Professor Alexander Bergmann as a basis for class discussion rather than to illustrate either effective or ineffective handling of an administrative situation. Copyright © 1975 by IMEDE (International Management Development Institute), Lausanne, Switzerland. Reproduced by permission.

code specifications; for lack of competitive products, Air, Inc. found itself excluded from a series of growing markets; there was no product diversification.

4. Management at all levels was inadequate; it was complacent (in many cases, managers of local subsidiaries were not able to give even a gross figure on the financial performance of their unit). They had not been asked for this information even when a company lost money for several years. There was almost no turnover in management and no outside recruiting; there was no management development and training.

5. Controls were inadequate; there were no performance goals and standards, no job descriptions, no performance appraisal (nor rewards for outstanding work or punishment for poor performance).

6. Coordination between and control of the different local subsidiaries was almost nonexistent, as was any organization at division headquarters where no one was specifically assigned to head Marketing, Production, Finance; adequate staff support was lacking in a situation where one had to turn to corporate staffs for the solution of almost every major functional problem.

David Palma, who immediately moved international headquarters to Milan, decided at once to turn the situation by taking dramatic action. He believed two major steps to be essential to realize a recovery and expansion: the introduction of a new product policy and a reorganization of structure and procedures.

As to products, one would revolutionize the industry, he believed, by trying to apply a new concept: Air, Inc., would build standardized models in a module system. This would allow for substantial economy through mass production of different standardized parts in different factories; it would allow for centralized R&D; and it would lead to better service performance. David Palma, himself an engineer, decided to focus all his attention on this strategic change in Air, Inc.'s traditional operations as well as on possibilities of diversification through mergers and acquisitions.

He decided, therefore, to leave the organizational and administrative problems to somebody else. He hired Joe Pfeffer as a director of human resources and gave him "carte blanche" to implement these goals.

Joe Pfeffer, 38, was an American with a good record as a personnel administrator. He was the first manager to be hired from outside the company and only the third personnel administrator in the company's history. He described himself as a compulsive achiever who had struggled to advance in business ever since he was a young man. He had earned his MBA in evening courses and had written two books on management, between 10 P.M. and 3 A.M., as he said. When he moved to Milan, he left his wife and child in New York so that he could concentrate all his energy on his new job. Work was his primary hobby. He considered business an exciting adventure and tough challenge.

He described how he approached the challenge at Air, Inc., International in the following way:

My job was to turn this organization around from a paternalistic institution to a dynamic, successful, healthy, profitable, growing business.

This meant, above all, to bring professionalism into the firm. Air, Inc., was at best 20, at worst 50 years behind in modern management techniques, with managers lacking discipline, drive, professional skills, the ability to work in teams.

Far-reaching changes were necessary. But you have to go slowly and not make mistakes. You have to establish a base from which to operate. You try to learn as much as possible. And as a human resources manager you must be as comfortable with a financial statement as a financial vice president; otherwise, nobody will listen to you.

The first thing I did was to ask management at the operating companies controlled by Air, Inc., International to prepare action plans to improve their productivity and to reduce costs and expenses immediately. These plans were then discussed in Milan or, in the case of larger subsidiaries, at their local headquarters. If in these meetings someone came up with a watered-down budget, he was in trouble; we kicked the hell out of him. Note, however, that in a confrontation with a line man (especially one who is making money) the staff man always loses. So you have to know when to back off and wait until he makes a stupid mistake (they always do) and then sack him.

We set the objectives at headquarters—time was short; inertia had to be removed; we knew that South Africa was performing poorly and should have improved 200 percent; so we set a target of 100 percent. You have to be reasonable and practical. You can't let these people set their own goals; they'll set them too low.

I like to deal with people one by one. We had only two staff meetings in 3½ years. But we do have individually tailored management seminars which I conducted personally. These were really MBO sessions—very simple, basic, and completely authoritarian. We gave as an assignment to the participants to state their greatest problems at the present; we then selected from the problems mentioned a few which seemed most important and discussed possible solutions. We have come up with ideas which have saved the company millions, and I made sure that they were implemented. That is, I visited the companies frequently, giving them usually two months' advance notice so they could shape up before my arrival.

We wanted the different companies to compete with each other. So we called, for instance, the Latin Americans together. The Mexicans were selling $11 million with 1,100 people; the Argentinians, $35 million with 600— very embarrassing. . . . When I went to Australia for the first time, at 4:30 P.M. everybody was gone—no competitive spirit. Now with my new man there, everybody works until 7:00 P.M.

As I met all these executives, I started to establish a worldwide manpower inventory. I interviewed systematically the 350 people in top positions. Interviews took typically about two hours. You give a guy the benefit of the doubt, but actually you know after 30 minutes what the man is like. In one case, I increased a man's salary by 20 percent on the spot (without even checking with his superior), and sometimes I started to look for a replacement the same day. Altogether we had to replace almost all of top management. Keeping them in their positions would really have been too costly. Either we kept them in an advisory function compatible with their technical expertise, or we just had to let them go. We hired only people from outside who had a good job; smart people . . . people who already earned $40,000 but were looking for better promotion prospects. The man on the top is decisive. I focus all the effort on him. If you have good top managers, you don't have to worry much more; they will not tolerate mediocrity down the line; you can leave them alone until they lack in performance. I have had no problems with them—I hired these guys. And none of them ever quit of his own desire.

I'll train the new men; then they'll report directly to me during the first year; and after that I maintain a heavy dotted-line relationship to them. Some may say that this is not my business—I answer that everything involving people is my business.

As to performance, I don't care what a man does (short of stealing from the company) as long as he gets results. That's why I like to hire locals as financial managers (while in many multinationals the finance men come from HQ). For they know the local conditions and how to circumvent the law, legally or illegally.

It's hard to measure the long-term impact of managers on an organization. I don't worry about the uncontrollable; there is enough of what is controllable to worry about—we measure performance; that's what counts. What happens in five years is an illusion, anyway.

After about two years Joe Pfeffer started to *(a)* initiate a more formalized manpower planning system, *(b)* establish standard personnel policies (although he avoided having all policies down in writing—"often it is too dangerous to commit yourself"), and *(c)* reorganized Air, Inc., International's headquarters operations.

More specifically he developed position descriptions and performance standards for many key management positions; he introduced a uniform worldwide performance appraisal and review program (he established an incentive plan and formal annual salary reviews based on worldwide salary survey data); he encouraged on-the-job training of new managers away from their home country (while not supporting the attendance of training programs outside the company—"we can't afford to let our people go for two weeks training"); and he has made it an obligation for every manager to identify and develop high-potential young executives.

He also has worked on the (re)organization of the Milan headquarters. Operations were divided into four regional divisions: Europe, Far East, Latin America, and Other. Each of these new divisions had to be provided with sizable marketing, finance, and engineering staffs which were recruited either from the "cream" of what was available in the operating units or from outside the company. Joe Pfeffer did not create a large personal staff noting he did not have the budget to hire first-rate people and preferred to work alone rather than with second-rate people. The development of a strong group in Milan had the purpose of helping the International Division to gain more independence from Chicago (which he said lacked understanding of the international business) and at the same time of gaining control over the local operating units (which were believed to be drifting).

With all this, Air, Inc., International attained, in 1973, sales of $530 million and profits of $35 million, thus overtaking the North American operations, for the first time, both in sales volume and profitability. Employment was down 13 percent (since 1970) to 33,000.

Introductory Note to DAAG Europe

This note provides a brief description of the elevator business in Western Europe as viewed by executives of the Deutsche Aufzugs A.G. European regional headquarters (DAAG Europe) located in Frankfurt, Germany. It pertains primarily to passenger elevators and relates to events only up to 1969.

The Passenger Elevator

With the arrival of the high-rise building, the passenger elevator passed from being a convenience to being a necessity. While usually an unobtrusive element of such large buildings, the elevators often occupied over 5 percent of the available volume in a building and accounted for about 3 percent to 7 percent of the total building cost.

The elevator system was made up of three major subsystems: (1) the electromechanical system, which guided and propelled the elevator; (2) the electrical/electronic system, which controlled the elevator movement in terms of acceleration, deceleration, and direction; and (3) the elevator cab itself with its moving doors. There were two basic lifting systems (the hydraulic type for low and slow applications, and the electric, cable-driven type for any applications) with many technical variations, a dozen or so basic circuits for the command controls, and countless configurations for the cab.

Copyright © 1973 by the President and Fellows of Harvard College
Harvard Business School case 374–036

While the technology associated with each of these systems had remained fundamentally the same over the past 30 years, the product nonetheless called for relatively demanding technical content and expertise. First, since elevators transported people vertically and were exposed to the possibility of falling, they had to be absolutely safe and reliable. As one observer noted, "If your elevator ever should fall, it could ruin your whole day." Second, an elevator was a means of public transportation. As such, it was essential that it be "idiot proof" (that is, the mechanism should not be damaged or cause injury because of an error by the operator) and also be vandal resistant. Third, for reasons of safety as well as of comfort, the elevator shaft and guide rails had to be straight within reasonably small tolerances and had to remain so. The difficulties in this regard were that the dimensions of buildings were far from exact, and large buildings often sagged or were otherwise distorted over time. One of the most skillful jobs in the elevator business was trueing up the system when it had been installed. Fourth, accelerating and decelerating an elevator for comfortable riding posed difficult propulsion and braking problems for the larger and faster units. For example, in a high-rise office building an elevator might travel at speeds as high as 30 feet per second (the equivalent of about three stories). The system had to be capable of decelerating the cab weighing anywhere from one ton empty to almost three tons fully loaded from that speed to a dead stop within one quarter inch of a given point in space and do all this in such a way as to maintain passenger comfort.

Passenger elevators were generally classified as class A or class B units. Class A elevators were defined within the industry as the large and high-speed (over 300 feet per minute) units with relatively sophisticated electronic controls. These were typically employed in large office buildings, large hotels, and other high-rise buildings where pedestrian traffic was heavy. Class B elevators were defined as the small, slow-speed (around 200 feet per minute) units with manually operated swing doors found in small office buildings and apartments. In most cases, class B units did not have complex "memory" systems.

The Western European Customers

The markets for class A and class B elevators were distinct and had to be approached differently. In most cases, the customer for class B elevators was the general contractor. The contractor in smaller building projects in Europe was often responsible for the design, the costs, and the overall management of the building, including the elevator.

Government agencies were another major customer for class B elevators, especially for apartment buildings. In dealing with this market, a DAAG elevator salesman would call on the local housing authority, the project coordinator, and the general contractor. The general contractor was again considered to be the most important link in this highly price-oriented market.

In contrast to the class B market, there were usually several people involved in the purchase decision for class A elevators. These people typically included several high-ranking managers of the company owning or planning to use the building, the architect, and the general contractor. In the opinion of DAAG management, the architect was the person most influential in selecting an elevator.

Dr. Robert Pelz, managing director of DAAG Europe, described DAAG's approach to this market:

> Our salesmen learn about possible contracts in several different ways. For example, our marketing department monitors the future building activity in a given region and alerts the appropriate salesmen to upcoming projects. However, there are not many potential contracts which the salesmen learn about for the first time in this manner. Most of our contracts are brought to the salesmen's attention by the architects themselves. DAAG, after all, is well known throughout Europe.
>
> It is our policy to have the DAAG salesman contact the architects in his region on a regular basis, whether or not they know of a definite contract possibility at the time of calling. After all, there are not all that many people who deal with larger building projects. The nature of the salesman's work brings him into contact with architects on a regular basis anyway as most of our salesmen already have contracts in progress. We estimate 80 percent of our sales in Europe are made to about 2,500 individual customers, who are constantly involved in the design of major buildings.

Another important source of information for DAAG salesmen was when architects called on the company to provide elevator engineering consultancy service for their building projects. To encourage this practice, it was company policy for salesmen to urge the architect to call for competitive bids. "In this way," noted the DAAG executive, "he can see for himself that DAAG can best supply his needs."

DAAG generally commanded a 10 percent premium in price over local competitors, as did the other major elevator manufacturers (Otis, Schindler, and Westinghouse). In selling elevators DAAG salesmen stressed quality and service and played down price considerations. Although price was discussed in broad terms early in the contract negotiations, the actual price was not set until all specifications had been described. This delay of three to six months was enough time, according to DAAG management, to show why the extra cost was justified. Dr. Pelz described the advantages DAAG offered:

> You see, an elevator can cause an architect more trouble than most anything else in his building. If the president of a company who is housed in a particular building has trouble with an elevator—for example, if a door doesn't work properly—he will probably complain directly to the owner. The owner will, in turn, blame the architect. The architect not only wants

to avoid such nuisances but he also has to guard his reputation for quality work.

DAAG elevators can also save the architect and the building owner money in the long run. The installation of elevators is one of the last steps in the construction of a building. Any delays in installing elevators will therefore cause a similar delay in making the building serviceable, and this could be extremely costly. For example, we have a 15 million German mark contract to install 20 elevators in the Lorelei Tower in Frankfurt. This is a 46-story-high office building costing over 300 million marks. Now if the elevators were to cause a month's delay in opening the building, the additional cost just in terms of one month's extra interest charges on the full investment would run about 3 million marks. Even more impressive would be the rental income lost for that month which would come to about 5 million marks. These figures give you some idea how valuable our rapid and dependable installation can be for the architect and building owner.

Finally, DAAG offers one of the finest maintenance services in the trade. Even though the price of our service contracts runs about 10 percent above our competitors' in many European countries, we service virtually all the installed DAAG class A elevators and about 80 percent of the class B units. In many respects, we consider ourselves as primarily a service company. And while we sell our service contracts quite separately from elevators, the architect has it in mind when he selects an elevator.

Overall, I would say that an architect will usually make his decision on a DAAG elevator on the basis of past experience with the product and his relationship with a particular DAAG salesman.

With the exception of the largest high-rise buildings, the typical period of time for DAAG to be involved with a given class A elevator installation in Europe was about three years. A year would normally elapse between the initial proposal and the signing of the contract. The materials would be shipped from the factories roughly a year later, and finally installation would be completed after another year.

Because elevator sales often involved large sums of money and tended to be made at irregular intervals, DAAG salesmen were paid straight salaries. A well-qualified salesman for class A equipment earned about $14,000 per year. Salesmen for class B equipment and for maintenance service received about $7,000 to $8,000 per year.[1] Salesmen were also reimbursed for all out-of-pocket expenses. By way of comparison, the average DAAG factory worker earned about $3,000 per year.

Manufacturing Operations

An elevator system was made up of many individual parts, such as mechanical relays, motors, ropes (suspension cables), sheet metal, steel railing, and electronic circuitry. Most smaller firms purchased these parts

---

[1] In Germany DAAG employed five class A salesmen, about 40 class B salesmen, and 25 service salesmen. Total annual sales cost in 1969 amounted to almost 2 million German marks for sales of 130 million German marks.

for assembly and even subcontracted certain subassembly work. In contrast, the largest elevator firms had traditionally manufactured almost all of the required parts. According to one DAAG executive, this extensive backward integration was almost a matter of pride for these companies.

The variety of parts to be produced and handled was many times greater than that needed for current operations because of maintenance service requirements. DAAG, for example, serviced units which had been produced as much as 40 years earlier. In addition to its own units, DAAG typically provided parts for elevators which had been produced by the many companies it had acquired over the years. The resulting high number of different components required DAAG and the other major elevator manufacturers to carry large parts inventories.

Field operations were another salient characteristic of the elevator manufacturing business. The extent of field operations was indicated by the composition of DAAG employment in Europe. Out of a total force of 13,000 employees, 6,000 were manual workers in the field compared to about 3,700 factory workers. About half the field workers were responsible for elevator erection and the other half for maintenance service. Because of their deep involvement with building construction, elevator manufacturers shared the building industry's special problems with respect to weather conditions, scattered sites, and sensitivity to economic conditions.

The Elevator Market and Industry Structure in Europe

The elevator business in Europe tended to be subdivided into national markets because of different building codes and in some cases because of tariff barriers. The codes generally defined the nature of the safety features which had to be employed. For example, car doors were not required for certain class B elevators in France. Such an elevator, called a flush hoistway, was prohibited in Germany.

The suppliers of these markets differed between class A and class B elevators. The class B sector was largely served by many small firms which competed in a local or national area. The class A sector in Europe was dominated by the multinational firms: Otis, Schindler, DAAG, and to some extent, Westinghouse. A number of strong local competitors also existed in many European countries. The size of each national market for all elevators in 1969 and DAAG's principal competitors for class A elevators are given in Exhibit 1. European expenditures for construction and for elevators are forecasted by country in Exhibit 2.

The Otis Elevator Company was the world's largest manufacturer of elevators. In addition to passenger and freight elevators, the company also produced escalators worldwide and a line of material handling equipment, automobile hydraulic lifts, and golf carts in the United States.

Founded as a U.S. company in 1853, the company began a rapid extension of operations overseas at the turn of the century. By 1969 affiliated companies in 46 countries and sales representatives in 69 other countries generated almost half of the company's total sales of $536 million.

Schindler A.G. was a family-owned and -operated Swiss elevator firm with sales of approximately $170 million in 1969. It produced a line of high-quality products and was represented in all the European markets. Schindler held a 90 percent share of the Swiss elevator market (both class A and class B) and also held important positions in Germany and France. Most of Schindler's manufacturing facilities were in Switzerland, although it did have plants in several other European countries.

DAAG Europe was a subsidiary of the Pace Garner Corporation (referred to simply as Pace), a large, diversified U.S. firm with a major division which manufactured elevators, escalators, and conveyor equipment for the U.S., Canadian, and Latin American markets. Pace was represented in almost all major European countries by independent subsidiaries which, for management purposes, reported to DAAG Europe. With few exceptions, all these European subsidiaries, with combined sales in 1969 of about $160 million, produced class A and class B elevator equipment under the DAAG name.

Westinghouse Elevator (a subsidiary of the Westinghouse Company) had estimated worldwide elevator sales of about $150 million in 1969. Seventy percent of these sales were made in the United States. DAAG management did not consider Westinghouse as strong a competitor in Europe as Otis or Schindler.

While competition among the big four in Europe was keen, each knew the strengths and the limits of the others. Looming as unknown adversaries were the large Japanese companies, such as Mitsubishi, which had developed excellent class A elevator equipment and were beginning to compete for contracts abroad. As of 1969 the Japanese had not yet bid for elevator contracts in Europe, but European elevator manufacturers considered the Japanese first attempt as imminent.

The potential severity of the Japanese threat was yet to be gauged. Some European elevator people believed that the structural requirements of the business (namely the close relationships between salesmen and architects and the need to provide extensive maintenance service) would block or at least greatly curtail Japanese entry. Others disagreed, arguing that the Japanese had learned to provide quality service from their experience in selling automobiles and various industrial equipment in the United States and Europe. According to the latter, the Japanese could develop a strong position in the European elevator market in four or five years.

Exhibit 1

Estimated European Elevator Sales in 1969 and DAAG's Major Competitors for Class A Equipment

Country	Sales (Class A and Class B)			DAAG's Major Competitors
	Units (000)	Value ($ millions)	Average Value ($000)	
Austria	2.0	$ 23	$11.5	Wertheim, Sovitch, Otis
Belgium	1.4	21	14.9	Westinghouse, Schindler, Otis
Denmark	0.3	6	18.4	n.a.
France	11.4	102	9.0	Otis, Westinghouse, Schindler, Soretex
Germany (West)	11.0	165	15.0	R. Stahl, Schindler, Otis, Haushahn, Manessman
Italy	11.1	57	5.2	FIAM, Schindler, SABIEM, Otis
Netherlands	1.7	20	11.8	Schindler, Otis
Norway	0.4	5	13.2	Kone
Portugal	2.1	10	4.6	Comportel, Esacec, Otis
Spain	10.1	52	5.1	Schindler, Zardoya
Sweden	1.2	14	12.1	Kone
Switzerland	3.4	38	11.2	Schindler, Schlieren
U.K.	5.2	87	16.8	General Electric (U.K.)
Total	61.3	$600	$ 9.8	

n.a. = Not available.
Sources: Official statistics and company data.

Exhibit 2

Average Annual European Building Construction and Elevator Sales Forecast for 1970–1974

| | Construction ($ billions) | | | Elevator Sales ($ millions) | | | Ratios (Percent) | | |
	(A) Total	(B) Residential	(C) Nonresidential	(D) Total	(E) Residential	(F) Nonresidential	D/A	E/B	F/C
Austria	$ 2.1	$ 0.9	$ 1.2	$ 28	$ 11	$ 17	1.33%	1.24%	1.40%
Belgium	4.1	1.3	2.8	27	11	16	0.11	0.83	0.58
Denmark	2.2	1.0	1.2	8	3	5	0.36	0.32	0.40
France	25.6	9.6	16.0	141	56	85	0.55	0.59	0.53
Germany (West)	29.4	10.4	19.0	194	78	116	0.66	0.74	0.61
Italy	14.8	6.5	8.3	69	28	41	0.46	0.42	0.50
Netherlands	5.8	2.5	3.3	24	10	14	0.41	0.38	0.44
Norway	1.9	0.7	1.2	7	3	4	0.37	0.40	0.35
Portugal	1.5	0.7	0.8	13	5	8	0.87	0.74	0.98
Spain	4.5	2.3	2.2	67	27	40	1.49	1.17	1.91
Sweden	4.6	1.5	3.1	18	7	11	0.39	0.48	0.35
Switzerland	1.5	0.6	0.9	48	19	29	3.20	3.20	3.20
U.K.	12.6	4.3	8.3	113	45	68	0.89	1.05	0.82
Total	$111.6	$42.6	$69.0	$758	$303	$455	0.68%	0.71%	0.66%
				(100%)	(40%)	(60%)			

Source: Official statistics except Switzerland and Portugal, for which company estimates were used.

DAAG Europe (A)

Dr. Robert Pelz, managing director of Deutsche Aufzugs A.G. European regional headquarters (DAAG Europe), faced a dilemma as he reviewed the preliminary financial statements for 1969. These showed a continuing deterioration of the company's current accounts. Accounts receivable and inventories had increased during 1969 by 42 percent and 48 percent, respectively, with a sales increase of only slightly more than 10 percent for the same period. Moreover, the company had failed to show profits on contracted sales of new elevators for the fourth consecutive year. Some action would have to be taken to improve DAAG's financial performance in Europe.

Yet Dr. Pelz fully realized that these financial results were a direct consequence of the company's long-term strategy to develop low-cost operations through a European-wide rationalized manufacturing operation. This strategy had brought related changes to every aspect of doing business.[1] Dr. Pelz did not wish to jeopardize the major transformation still under way by any action he might take to remedy the immediate financial problems.

Origins of the DAAG Europe Strategy

The changes in progress in 1969 with respect to organization, marketing, and manufacturing could be traced back to a series of moves initiated

---

[1] See "Introductory Note to DAAG Europe" for a description of the European elevator business.

Copyright © 1973 by the President and Fellows of Harvard College
Harvard Business School case 374–037

580

in the early 1960s by Dr. Pelz, the then managing director of the German operating company, DAAG. One of the early moves occurred in 1964 when he proposed to the U.S. corporate management (Pace Garner Corporation, located in Chicago, Illinois) that the company acquire the rival German firm, Rechtbau A.G. The most compelling reason for this acquisition was that it would boost DAAG's share of the German market from 20 percent to a commanding 35 percent.

Rechtbau itself had been formed in 1960 through a merger of three German elevator companies. Dr. Wagner, managing director of Rechtbau, had engineered this merger in an effort to create a company which could compete with Otis, Westinghouse, DAAG, and Schindler. When Rechtbau was still unable to support the costly engineering and development work necessary to extend its operations from supplying elevators for small apartment and office buildings to the more profitable market for high-rise buildings, Dr. Wagner next attempted to form a multinational coalition with some of the larger independent elevator firms in other major European countries. Failing to interest these firms in joining forces with Rechtbau, Dr. Wagner decided to sell the company to one of the four dominant firms. Thus, if DAAG did not merge with Rechtbau, one of its key competitors would presumably pick up the German firm's 15 percent market share.

Dr. Pelz, who had been a member of the German Diplomatic Corps prior to joining DAAG, won his case. Mr. M. B. Bentley, president of Pace Garner, approved the acquisition on Pelz's terms. Dr. Wagner was appointed president of the new firm and Dr. Pelz, vice president. The two men were given three years to make the merger work without interference from Chicago. Aside from the requirement to reconcile its accounting system with that of Pace, the new German company was on its own. As a DAAG executive later remarked, "Pelz had put his neck on the line. He had to make the merger work."

In taking over Rechtbau A.G., DAAG acquired the largest manufacturer of class B elevators in Germany. While each of DAAG's major European affiliates manufactured and sold class B elevators, these efforts (almost always representing a continuation of business carried out by firms acquired in earlier years) were generally played down and assumed only secondary importance among DAAG's activities. This policy could be attributed to the generally low profitability associated with the class B elevator as well as the fragmented nature of the market. DAAG was organized to deal with the limited number of large and relatively sophisticated architectural and construction firms in Europe. The class B market, requiring contact with each of many small, local building contractors, had traditionally been served by small elevator manufacturers in their locality. The distinctly different requirements for selling and servicing class B elevators had long dissuaded DAAG from entering this market. Moreover, many DAAG executives were of the opinion that DAAG's image as a manufacturer of high-quality and highly sophisticated elevators might be tarnished were DAAG to enter the class B market in a major way.

Dr. Pelz believed that DAAG was wrong in neglecting this market segment, especially in Europe, where it accounted for about 50 percent of the industry's total elevator sales.[2] He argued that DAAG could not afford to ignore one half of its potential market in Europe. He thus set out to launch an attack on this sector of the market from the enlarged base of Rechtbau's class B business and with some ideas on how a large, multinational firm might compete for these sales.

The Move to Standard Models

Elevators had always been custom designed for each building project. The elevator had to fit the space allotted—or left over—for this purpose. Elevator companies competed on the basis of their ability to meet these architectural specifications.

Around 1961 Dr. Pelz became attracted by the possibility of manufacturing and selling standardized elevator models. He knew as did others in the industry that elevators, although designed and manufactured to customers' individual specifications, were basically similar in design, engineering, and construction. This similarity was especially true for class B elevators. Dr. Pelz reasoned that if a line of elevator models similar to a line of automobile models could be developed, major savings would result from reduction in design costs and from economies associated with multiple production. Important savings would also accrue from the opportunity to standardize the technical and administrative processing of contracts. For example, the extensive engineering documentation required for an elevator system and its working parts had to be prepared for each custom unit. The original documentation would serve for repeat sales of a standard model.

The idea of standard models was not entirely novel to the elevator industry. One of DAAG's German competitors had attempted in 1952 to introduce standard models. This effort met with little success and was abandoned. Nonetheless, Dr. Pelz was convinced of the need to move in this direction and consequently initiated in 1962 the design of the first standard elevator model for the German apartment building market. This model, the MOD-S, was introduced in early 1963.

The new model met with some resistance from customers. It met with much more resistance from the DAAG organization and its sales force. Despite this lack of enthusiasm, the company managed to sell

---

[2] Pace headquarters management estimated class B elevators to represent less than 30 percent of total elevator sales in the United States. This estimate was only approximate because of the limited availability of market data.

about 230 units the first year, and Dr. Pelz planned to build a factory at Mainz to produce the MOD-S. The acquisition of Rechtbau provided DAAG with a new factory at Köln which was well suited for producing the standard elevator model and also with a large clientele for class B elevators. Access to an operating factory represented a gain of two years for DAAG, and the Mainz project was consequently abandoned.

While the acquisition of Rechtbau admittedly gave impetus to DAAG's concept of standard models, Dr. Pelz firmly believed that the move to standard models was the only way DAAG could make the Rechtbau acquisition successful. He agreed with the general sentiment that a company like DAAG could not compete effectively against the small firm for class B elevator business under the present way of doing business. It would be necessary to change the nature of the class B elevator business so as to suit DAAG's strengths. In Dr. Pelz's opinion, the standard elevator model was the way to effect such a change.

His experience with the MOD-S convinced Pelz that standard class B elevator models would be successful only when manufacturing and installation costs could be reduced sufficiently to permit prices to be some 10–15 percent lower than current levels while still enabling the company to make a profit. Some of these cost savings would come from a reduction in parts inventories, special jigs and tools, and from a simplification of fabrication procedures. However, important additional savings could only be gained with an appreciably increased production volume compared to the volume handled by the individual DAAG companies in 1964.

The needed volume could be generated reasonably quickly, Pelz reasoned, if the other DAAG European subsidiaries were to join Germany in developing standard models for their own markets as well. Eventually, if the standard elevator model concept proved out, maximum advantage would be gained as models were extended to the class A part of the business and as both class A and class B models could be standardized for all of Europe.

The Beginnings of a European Concept

Dr. Pelz had already begun to lay the groundwork for his idea of a European regional organization during his discussions in Chicago concerning the Rechtbau acquisition. Heretofore each of Pace's foreign subsidiaries had reported directly to Pace Elevator divisional headquarters in Chicago. The large headquarters staff customarily became deeply involved with operations in each of the subsidiaries. Functional staff members at Chicago tended to work directly and closely with their functional counterparts in the field.

Dr. Pelz had found these relationships cumbersome and frustrating as he tried to manage his company in Germany. This centralized organizational arrangement would be even more dysfunctional were the European subsidiaries to try to coordinate their actions. Thus, Dr. Pelz argued for a European regional management on two grounds. First, the move to standard elevator models in Europe would require a great deal of coordinated effort best supervised on the spot. Related to this point was the rapid integration taking place in the European Common Market which undoubtedly would call for other forms of coordinated action on the European continent. Second, an increasingly important part of DAAG's business in Europe would come from class B elevators, and the Chicago staff was not particularly competent to advise the Europeans concerning this type of business.[3]

Although the newly formed German DAAG had yet to prove itself, Dr. Pelz had once again been sufficiently persuasive to gain his point. In late 1965 the general managers of Pace's European elevator companies were to report to Dr. Pelz as managing director of DAAG European regional headquarters. The subsidiaries remained legally independent entities owned by Pace.[4]

Shaping the New Relationship

Dr. Pelz saw his first task as managing director of DAAG Europe to be that of convincing each subsidiary to offer a line of standard elevator models for the class B market segment. By 1966 the German DAAG had developed a product line of eight models for the German apartment building market. He acknowledged, however, that it might not be feasible to market German elevators in other European countries where tastes, building codes, and market conditions were different. Moreover, while the subsidiaries had for years done little more than adapt the company's U.S. elevator designs to meet local needs, Dr. Pelz anticipated that country managers might tend to resist were he to try to relieve them of this engineering and design function. Consequently, in order to lessen resistance as well as to give the national companies an opportunity to gain experience with standard models, he decided as the first step to permit each subsidiary to develop its own national line of standard class B elevator models.

Dr. Pelz's persuasive powers were put to the test as he tried to sell the standard model concept to the national companies reporting to him.

---

[3] Class A business accounted for almost 90 percent in value of all new elevator installations by Pace Elevator division in the United States.

[4] With few exceptions, all these European subsidiaries, with combined sales in 1969 of about $160 million, produced class A and class B elevator equipment under the DAAG name.

The general managers voiced doubt as to the applicability of German experience with elevator models to their national markets. Moreover, even in Germany the results were only preliminary and certainly not clear-cut.

The resistance voiced by each country manager no doubt reflected an opposition by his selling organization. The salesmen were proud of the DAAG reputation for being able to produce the highest quality equipment for whichever design the architect specified. The idea of selling standard, "off-the-shelf" elevators, even if only for the class B business, was somewhat repugnant to them. Furthermore, most salesmen doubted that standard models would catch on—at least rapidly enough to maintain sales performance.

These attitudes were too deeply ingrained, these men too important to his purpose, and their arguments too valid for Pelz to turn them aside. He knew that he had not only to sell the customer on the idea of standard models but, more important, he had to sell each of the DAAG sales forces.

Lowering Price

In 1965 Dr. Pelz moved to induce the DAAG salesmen in Germany to sell the MOD-S line of standard models by lowering prices by about 9 percent from an already artificially low base. (The price in 1963 had been set to reflect prospective cost savings.) He made this reduction in order to create the widest possible price spread between the standard and traditional elevator models. As a result of this move, annual MOD-S sales in Germany almost trebled in 1965 to a volume of 1,321 units.

Shortly after the price cut for MOD-S elevators, DAAG began to lower its prices on class A elevators as well. While Pelz wanted his salesmen to switch from selling traditional class B elevators to standard models, he did not want to divert their energies from selling class A elevators. The MOD-S price cut had that effect to some extent, and he believed it necessary to make a comparable price reduction for the class A equipment if a proper balance of sales effort were to be maintained between the two. Quite apart from this reasoning, as a DAAG executive later explained, the company's prices for class A elevators were lowered throughout Europe almost unconsciously at this time because of the general enthusiasm in DAAG for expansion and growth. By bringing its prices down, DAAG once again increased unit sales.

Competitors in both markets soon countered with price cuts of their own. Dr. Pelz knew the lower DAAG prices could only be justified and maintained when manufacturing costs had been fully driven down by means of large economies of scale.

The European Models

These economies of scale could in Dr. Pelz's view be achieved by moving to the next major phase of his plan—standard European models. By 1968 the development of class B models had been successfully completed on a national basis. Germany, France, Italy, and the U.K. each had a line of between 10 and 15 models. The smaller DAAG companies—such as Austria, Belgium, and Holland—adopted variations of the models designed in larger neighboring companies. As a result, 80 standard models accounted for 90 percent of the DAAG total class B elevator sales on the European continent.[5]

The transition to standard models had been helped, as a DAAG executive pointed out, by increasing the company's class B elevator business through acquisitions. From 1965 through 1969 Pace had expanded the European elevator operations by establishing five additional subsidiaries in Sweden, Denmark, Switzerland, Portugal, and Austria. During this same period of time the DAAG European region had also acquired through its existing subsidiary companies some 30 small, local elevator firms which manufactured or serviced class B elevators. Exhibit 1 shows the expansion of the DAAG European region from 1965 through 1969.

In 1968 DAAG management began working on the development of European models to replace the class B national models and the class A customized units. One of its major tasks for this purpose was to build up an engineering group in Europe which would be capable of developing the new designs. Because of the need to satisfy the half dozen different (and sometimes even conflicting) construction codes to be found on the European continent, the technical demands for designing a compatible model would exceed anything the DAAG engineers in Europe had formerly been called upon to do.

Early on, management decided to give the class A development program higher priority for several reasons. Class B national models were already beginning to produce some economies of scale. The incremental savings to be gained from further standardization of these elevators would therefore be much less than would be the case for the class A elevators. Moreover, the managers and salesmen for each subsidiary would probably object to any change from their national models so soon after bringing them to the market. Finally, the tangle of local building regulations for apartment buildings was proving to be much more difficult to deal with than was true for major high-rise building projects.

The DAAG line of European class A elevator models, the Europa,

---

[5] While the differences in national building codes at the time limited the standardization of design in several important respects, management estimated that a line of 20 to 25 standard European-oriented models would have been sufficient to deal with most of the conflicting requirements.

was scheduled to be introduced in 1970. This product line was to comprise 15 models. The different models would carry between 8 and 24 passengers and have several configurations with respect to such features as speed of travel, door widths, and maximum number of floor stops.

The introduction of a DAAG line of European class B models, to be known as the Continental, was projected for 1973. The development of this line was to take place in three stages. In the first stage, the 90 or so national models, including those in the U.K., would be replaced with 30 European models. The second stage would witness a reduction of European models to 20. The ultimate objective was to have 10 European models. This final objective was based on the fact that 5 to 7 models accounted for about 80 percent of class B sales in each major market. The actual timing for the second and third stages would depend in large measure on the rate at which building codes in the EEC could be harmonized.

Production Rationalization and DAAG Europe

The major payoff in a move to standard elevator models would come from the economies of scale associated with a rationalized production arrangement. As a DAAG executive noted:

> We do not know exactly what the increased savings through greater mass production will be, but common sense tells us it will be a lot. The largest selling German model has sales of about 1,500 units per year. We estimate the largest European model will have sales of between 3,000 and 4,000 per year.

Dr. Pelz's objective was to have each factory specialize in the production of standardized components which could then be sold to DAAG assembly plants within each market. Prior to 1965 each plant manufactured or purchased locally all the necessary components it needed to manufacture all the elevators sold in its market area. By 1969 DAAG had begun to implement the first phase of its plan to rationalize production, whereby the company's EEC factories (two in Germany, one in France, and one in Italy) were to specialize in producing and exchanging a number of basic components. These components were priced at full cost plus a 25 percent charge for intercompany transfers.

The second phase, to be completed around 1974, would also bring the factories in the U.K., Spain, and Austria into the arrangement. At that time, each factory would produce certain major elevator subunits (such as the motor, relays, and the control mechanism) to supply other plants. To ensure safety of supply, critical components were to be made in two plants.

A Deteriorating Financial Position

As Dr. Pelz reviewed the situation in 1969, he was impressed with the progress that DAAG had shown in four short years in its attempt to move to standard models and to rationalize production facilities. Moreover, the company's strategy had led to a better than threefold increase in unit sales and to a more than doubling of DAAG's share of the European elevator market since its inception in 1963. Exhibit 2 graphically shows the decline of the average unit price during the period 1965 to 1969 and the corresponding increase in unit sales.[6]

Profits, however, had suffered as a consequence of the failure to achieve cost savings sufficiently high to cover the decline in prices during this period of time. An even more pressing financial problem in Dr. Pelz's opinion was the rapidly deteriorating working capital position for DAAG Europe. Exhibits 4 and 5 contain the financial results for DAAG Europe during the period 1965 to 1969.

New equity and additional debt were generally ruled out by Dr. Pelz as viable financial moves at this time. DAAG Europe had just assumed additional long-term debt of $3 million in 1969. Moreover, this financing had been arranged contrary to the advice of corporate headquarters in Chicago, which had a long-standing policy of keeping the firm's capital structure as debt free as possible. Pace's policy to hold 100 percent ownership of its overseas subsidiaries wherever possible precluded selling equity on the market.

One possible response to the financial problem was for DAAG simply to raise the prices of elevators. DAAG management felt certain that the competition was experiencing financial pressures similar to those of DAAG since they had also dropped their prices. The principal question in Dr. Pelz's mind was how quickly and how far the competition would follow DAAG in raising prices. A unilateral price increase by DAAG could give the competitors an opportunity to make inroads in important markets at a time when DAAG was attempting to effect economies of scale through volume production.

A tightening of credit terms had been considered by DAAG management as another possible avenue for relieving the current financial burden on the company. Payments normally stretched out over a two- to three-year period with a major portion due after the completion of the job. Dr. Pelz had a proposal before him recommending that DAAG adhere to the industry's pro forma payment schedules, which for Germany involved collecting a down payment of 30 percent at the time the contract was signed, an additional 30 percent when the elevator was delivered,

---

[6] Since the price decline shown in Exhibit 2 resulted from a combination of actual price cuts and an increasing proportion of less costly class B business, price changes for a single unit (the MOD-S) are shown in Exhibit 3. The price changes for the MOD-S were said to be representative of most DAAG elevator units during this period.

30 percent at the completion of the job, and the final 10 percent when the building received official approval (see Exhibit 6). Actual payment schedules had long been more liberal than the announced formula. Moreover, as Dr. Pelz knew, his competitors had employed increasingly generous payment schedules to counter DAAG's aggressive pricing. For example, Westinghouse had reportedly required only 10 percent down payment and no further payment until completion of the project on certain occasions. In other instances Westinghouse had not even required the customer to make a down payment.

Another possible step for DAAG was to reinstate a price escalation clause in new elevator sales contracts to protect against inflation. Customer pressure during the competitive battle of the middle 1960s had led DAAG and the other elevator manufacturers to accept fixed price contracts. Increasing inflation rates during the late 1960s led to losses for major projects which had been negotiated anywhere between two and five years earlier. In Dr. Pelz's opinion, for DAAG to tighten credit terms or to press for escalation clauses would have it run risks similar to those it would run in raising prices.

Exhibit 1

Composition of the DAAG European Region, 1965–1969

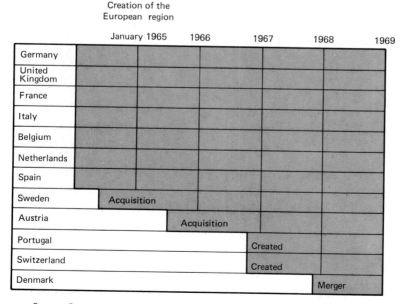

Source: Company document.

Exhibit 2

DAAG Western European Region Elevator Unit Sales and Average Price per Unit

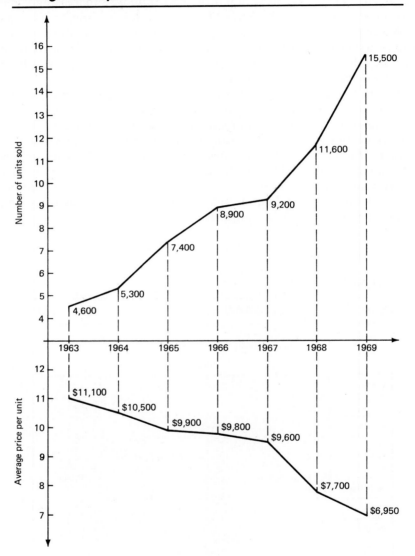

Exhibit 3

Index of Average Price and Manufacturing Cost of the MOD-S German Model

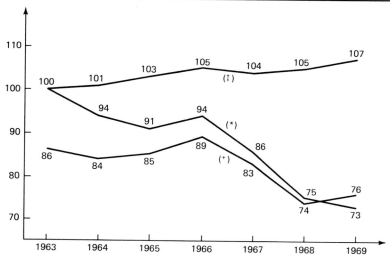

(*) Average selling price of a MOD-S; index 100 = 6,500 DM.
(†) Standard manufacturing cost of a MOD-S.
(‡) Index of price for industrial goods in Germany after 1967 including VAT.
Source: Company document.

Exhibit 4

DAAG Europe Balance Sheets
For the Years Ending 1966–1969
(in millions)

	1966	1967	1968	1969
Assets				
Current assets:				
Cash and marketable securities	$ 1.1	$ 1.9	$ 1.4	$ 0.8
Net notes and accounts receivable	36.0	36.9	39.4	56.5
Associated companies receivables	6.1	7.1	11.3	15.0
Total receivables	42.1	44.0	50.7	71.5
Inventories	31.5	25.0	27.2	40.1
Cost of contracts in progress	64.2	65.8	74.1	88.1
Total inventories	95.7	90.8	101.3	128.2
Prepayments	0.7	0.6	0.5	0.8
Less billings on contracts in progress	(71.5)	(73.0)	(75.5)	(86.2)
Total current assets	68.2	64.4	78.4	115.2
Property, plant, equipment	38.8	40.7	41.3	50.7
Less: Depreciation	(14.7)	(17.0)	(18.4)	(21.1)
Net plant, equipment	24.1	23.7	22.8	29.6
Deferred charges	3.0	2.7	2.8	3.6
Total assets	$ 95.3	$ 90.9	$104.2	$148.5
Liabilities and Capital				
Current liabilities:				
Short-term loans	$ 23.2	$ 17.0	$ 23.0	$ 41.2
Notes and accounts payable	12.5	10.3	12.3	21.9
Associated company payables	4.7	5.6	7.6	7.7
Accrued liabilities	4.5	6.5	9.3	14.6
Income tax	2.5	2.5	2.1	2.5
Total current liabilities	46.7	42.2	54.4	88.1
Long-term notes and				
accounts payable	9.5	8.8	6.9	12.9
Total liabilities	57.1	51.1	61.5	100.9
Reserves for pensions and				
severance indemnities	—	4.2	4.2	4.6
All other reserves	7.3	3.5	9.4	11.0
Capital stock	17.0	17.0	17.2	19.3
Surplus	13.8	14.9	11.7	12.4
Net worth	38.1	39.8	42.6	47.5
Net worth exclusive of				
reserves for pensions	38.1	35.5	38.4	42.9
Total liabilities and capital	$ 95.3	$ 90.9	$104.2	$148.5

Note: Figures may not add due to rounding.
Source: Company records. The figures represent a consolidation of individual company accounts.

Exhibit 5

DAAG Europe Profits and Bookings for the Years 1965–1969, and a Financial Analysis of the Statements (In millions)

	1965	1966	1967	1968	1969
Net profit before tax*	\$ 3.6	\$ 3.3	\$ 3.7	\$ 3.9	\$ 4.0
New sales bookings	73.0	87.0	88.0	89.0	108.0
Service bookings	33.0	38.0	43.0	46.0	51.0
Total bookings	\$106.0	\$125.0	\$131.0	\$135.0	\$159.0

Analysis of the Financial Statements

	1966	1967	1968	1969
$\dfrac{\text{Current assets}}{\text{Current liabilities}}$	1.46	1.53	1.44	1.31
$\dfrac{\text{Cash plus receivables}}{\text{Current liabilities}}$	0.93	1.09	0.96	0.82
Collection period in days	121	121	135	162
Inventory/sales (excluding cost of contracts in progress)	0.25	0.19	0.20	0.25
Debt/net worth	0.25	0.22	0.16	0.27

* Net profit reflected the results of elevator contracts completed and service contracts performed during the year as well as manufacturing variances for the year.

Source: Company records. The figures represent a consolidation of individual company accounts.

Exhibit 6

Pro Forma Payment Schedules on Class A Contracts in Germany, France, and Switzerland, 1969

	Percent
Germany:	
Signing of contract	30%
Delivery to job site*	30
Completion†	30
Final acceptance‡	10
Switzerland:	
Signing of contract	30
Three months prior to delivery	30
During the course of erection	10
Completion	30
France:	
Signing of contract	30
Delivery to job site	30
Completion	40

* DAAG management estimated the time between booking a contract and delivery of the elevator to the job site ran an average of one year. The actual order usually did not arrive until six months after the closing of the contract. This one-year figure did not include the three to six months that normally elapsed between the time a bid was submitted and a contract was closed.

† Erection time (from delivery to completion) for class A elevator projects ranged between two months and two years with an average of one year. The Lorelei Tower, the tallest building in Germany, required about 2½ years for erecting elevators.

‡ Final acceptance was when both the owner and the building authorities approved the building. Final acceptance normally followed the completion of building construction by one to four months.

Source: Company document.

Mitek Corporation

Robert Tweed, president of the Mitek Corporation, knew that the company was at a critical point in its history. There was no question that the company was a success, more so than any of the three founders had allowed themselves to imagine a mere five years ago. But now was not the time to fall back on past laurels or reminisce about past challenges met and surpassed. Now was the time to decide the future direction of the company so as to continue the record of success. To begin this task, Tweed had written a major statement of policy to his managers, "Goals for the Future of Mitek Corporation." Now stacked in front of him was the pile of written responses he had received in return. To his surprise these responses had been frank, critical, and hardly supportive of his plans for the future. They betrayed a lack of cohesiveness and team spirit amongst his senior executives. Apparently, the camaraderie, excitement, and energy that had characterized the early building years of the company had disappeared. Without that energy and cohesiveness, Tweed knew any plans for the future growth of the company would be undermined. Indeed, one of the responses had ended with: "I doubt if any goals can be achieved until the management discord and organizational deficiencies are resolved. The management team is talking to everyone but each other. The atmosphere exists today in which you are in serious jeopardy of losing every senior manager you have."

Copyright © 1979 by the President and Fellows of Harvard College
Harvard Business School case 379–110

The Company and Industry

The Mitek Corporation was a comparatively young, rapidly growing company in a high-growth, high-technology industry. In its five-year history, the company's revenues had grown steadily to $40 million. A healthy economy had made raising external capital relatively easy. Such a steady stream of external funding was needed to support the high R&D and manufacturing costs characteristic of a highly competitive industry with short product life cycles. Such life cycles were partly the logical outcome of readily obtained and widespread technical know-how needed to design and produce the products. Patent protection for new products was thus fairly ineffectual. Indeed, so long as outside capital was available, an engineer with an idea for a small improvement over an existing product could set up an independent shop and begin producing a "me-too" product with relative ease.

Learning curve pricing was a characteristic of the industry and led to competition on the basis of manufacturing cost structures. Success in the market was less a result of the product itself than of quick and timely product introduction, financial and quality control, and well-managed manufacturing operations. Further, companies in the industry suffered from a severe shortage of experienced general managers to coordinate and lead all of these activities. Lacking these abilities, many of the entrepreneurial companies were short-lived, often being acquired by larger, better-managed companies.

The First Five Years

The Mitek Corporation's beginnings were similar in kind to others in the industry. The three founders all worked for the Ohmex Corporation, a large, multiproduct, multinational company and leader in several segments of the industry, with annual revenues in the $500 million range and manufacturing plants in several locations around the globe. The three men—Robert Tweed, assistant treasurer, and George Morrison and Harvey Knight, engineers from the technical R&D staff—were all in their late 30s or early 40s and had met each other socially outside of work. Their conversation revealed a similar dream to run a company of their own. The group was more determined than most, and so these off-hour musings eventually evolved first into a serious search for a small, failing company to acquire and turn around and finally to the idea of starting a company from scratch. It was felt that the technical know-how of the two engineers, coupled with the marketing and finance background of Tweed, would form a good management team.

Initially, three different ideas for possible product areas were suggested. Off-hour discussions about which of these ideas was most feasible were heated and progressed slowly. It was discovered that evening meetings were not sufficient to perform the analysis needed to make a timely decision on the definition of the business. Thus, all three quit Ohmex in order to devote full time to the project.

During the first month Mitek was incorporated with each founder investing $6,000 in return for the same number of shares of stock. Bob Tweed was elected president since it was through his contacts in the financial world that future funding would be found. The major task of that first month was clearly deciding what the product line would be. After long discussions at the homes of one or the other of the group (money was not to be wasted on office space), the original favorite of the three ideas was rejected as technically possible but unmarketable. Instead, it was decided to try to make a go with the second product area, a failing line of the old Ohmex company. All three founders had experience with this product line while at Ohmex. Both Morrison and Knight had proposed improvement projects for this line, although these were rejected due to the low expected return on investment. Tweed had conducted several studies on how best to organize and run operations in the business. Conclusions from these studies had not been implemented, however, due to the cost of changing a large organization.

The engineers were convinced they could develop a much better product than currently available anywhere in the market. The Mitek product was based on a completely new technology and, for extra measure, used cheaper components. Although the new technology was the creation of Morrison and Knight, Mitek was now competing with the former employer of the principals. To avoid any suggestion of violating trade secret laws, the founders discussed their project with Ohmex, but the company was unconcerned inasmuch as it believed that no one could make money in the area anyway.

During the second and third months, the initial investment was used to rent an old warehouse, buy some used equipment, and begin to develop some prototype products. The burden of this task fell primarily on the shoulders of Morrison and his small team of technical people.

At the end of this period sample products had been produced that could provide the basis for a prospectus of sufficient sophistication to present to investment bankers and other potential investors. Tweed then went to New York and Texas to raise capital. The market potential of Mitek's innovative product was immediately obvious to investors, who placed $2 million with the company.

For the next year and a half Morrison and his research team pushed to bring the prototype products to a commercializable stage. Knight and Tweed meanwhile put their efforts to the construction and setting up of a manufacturing facility. After much search a relatively inexpensive site for a plant was found in a small, rather unattractive town 30 miles away. The location had the benefit of a ready labor supply. The advantage of experience and knowledge of manufacturing operations now became significant. An expert in high-precision manufacturing processes, Knight designed all of the manufacturing and quality test equipment as well as the production process itself. The plant was then designed and built around this process. Even with all of this effort, it was found that it was relatively easy to produce prototypes of superior quality in the lab but extremely difficult to manufacture a large quantity on a continuously processed run of sufficiently consistent quality. Consequently, more time and money was being spent debugging and perfecting the processes than developing the product itself, an unforeseen situation. Delays reached a critical point in the middle of year 2 as the initial money ran out before a single successful manufacturing run had been completed.

Tweed, forced to return to the money markets, focused his efforts on venture capital firms. Fortunately he was able to secure another $2.5 million from one such firm in New York that represented a large wealthy family. Afterward, Tweed said of this period:

> We had to bring forward the effort of getting that financing to an extent we hadn't contemplated. We had to get as much money as we could to build our facilities, to provide our working capital, to establish the business. It was the fallacy of our planning, that we originally planned that we could be in production for sale of a commercial product 9 months after we started. As it turned out it took 18 months—twice as long. The cost of the facilities and the equipment was twice as much, too.
>
> We had capitalized the company with a contingency to take care of unforeseens; as it happened we used all of the contingency and still needed more. I was facing a situation where the technical people were saying, "We have this excellent product and we know we are going to be able to sell it, a lot of it. And the thing that's not permitting us to do that is the lack of capital. We've done our job right, now you do yours." Luckily for me and the company, I was able to find more capital.

With the infusion of new capital, the next few months saw the completion of the first successful manufacturing run and the hiring of a marketing vice president, Ted Rowman. The product was an instant success. Orders flowed in from an aggressive, efficiently organized field sales force faster than they could be filled. The emphasis on marketing with the early building of a direct sales force was seen later as a key to the company's rapid growth.

By the end of the second year Mitek's new product had brought in over $800,000 in revenue. Significantly, in year 3 Mitek's bottom line was positive for the first time, with revenues of $8.2 million and net profits after tax of $1.1 million.

For the next couple of years the Mitek Corporation concentrated on the research and development, manufacturing, and marketing of this single line of products. Much effort was expended in developing improved manufacturing processes, extensive quality control, and the further expansion of the field sales force. Indeed, as the company quickly gained market share, a reputation was developed as the price quality leader. Growth continued with revenues of $8.2, $17.8, and $40 million in years 3, 4, and 5 (see Exhibit 1).

For Tweed, the pleasures of starting his own company certainly included monetary ones. Indeed, during year 5, the directors voted a stock split of 30 to 1. But it had always been Tweed's intention for Mitek to be a publicly owned company. Consequently, at the end of year 5, the company went public with the sale of 1 million shares of stock at $25 per share, which were soon listed on the New York Stock Exchange. The success of the stock particularly pleased the New York investors who found their reputations for picking future high flyers greatly enhanced.

The President

One unique factor in the company's early growth and recognition was its president. On first acquaintance, Robert Tweed did not look the hard-hitting businessman and self-made millionaire that he was, but rather he had the abstracted air more common to a professor. Since his youth in the Midwest, however, a desire to excel and win at whatever he did motivated Tweed. He was driven to be "a success," which he understood as having money and a position of leadership. From a large, financially strapped family, he worked his way through the state university and law school by running several boarding houses for students. His college advisor remembered him as one of the most dogged workers he had ever counseled. At the end of law school, Tweed decided that the practice of law would not provide the kind of active role that he sought. He then went on to a well-known eastern business school where he received his MBA with an emphasis in finance.

Like many of his colleagues, he left business school to join a prestigious firm on Wall Street. Early in his career he was transferred to Texas where he helped set up a new sales office. This proved to be a very exciting experience for Tweed. The uncertainty and early difficulties of a new operation, while intimidating to some, were an inspiration to Tweed. The New York home office had other ideas, however, and in recognition of the fast growth of the branch office, promoted Tweed to vice president and transferred him back to New York. This presented a problem for Tweed. If he went back to New York, he would become a prosperous investment banker. He knew that he would remain with the firm because the position would be an interesting one and the cost of leaving the firm would soon be too great. However, if he left the company now and started his own business, he foresaw two great disadvantages: no expertise in any particular business and inexperience in managing any type of manufacturing firm (no "line-type" experience).

In the end, his desire to be his own boss and to be responsible for a large organization prevailed, and he left investment banking. He decided to work for Ohmex first and gain some experience in a manufacturing company operating in a high-growth industry. He reasoned that working for such a company would make up for his deficiency in experience and would be a good training ground for starting his own company.

Tweed was a soft-spoken man but very articulate. He prided himself on his knowledge of up-to-date management practices and particularly enjoyed giving speeches both to outside groups and to his own managers on his ideas for management innovations and methods to stimulate cohesion, hard work, and quality for employees. Perhaps unfairly, such speech-making led some managers to comment that the president did not listen to input from them and that corporate policy meetings of the president's advisory committee tended to be rather one-sided forums.[1] Tweed was generally viewed as very hard working, a believer in the Protestant work ethic. He believed that one's work and family should be strictly separated. Indeed, his wife and six children were rarely seen at the company, if at all. Consistent with these priorities, when asked about the risks encountered in starting a new venture like the Mitek Corporation, Tweed spoke primarily in terms of risks to his family and personal career:

> The sum of $18,000 doesn't sound like a lot of money. I didn't have a lot of money. And that was the risk, but that wasn't the major risk.
>
> I think the major risk was the career risk. I think all of us were doing very well in industry, and I think had we continued in industry in the normal mode, I think most of us could have expected to graduate to one of the higher levels of industrial management.
>
> The risk is that when you try a new venture and you fail, you not only forego the opportunity that you might have had but you penalize yourself because if you reenter an industry, you come down at a lower rung on the ladder, and that was a risk.
>
> There's also a risk in terms of the families. My recollection is there were 20 children under the age of 14 or 15 among the founders, and when you are not working for salary there's a little bit of concern about doing that, and you know the kind of problems, everybody knows the kinds of problems that that can engender. So there was a risk of that.

For a president of a new company, Tweed was perhaps unique in the industry in being a financial man, rather than an engineer or scientist. He saw his early responsibilities as those of finding financial backing for the company and marketing the product, leaving the product definition, development, and manufacturing to the co-founders. Indeed, in the early years of the company he was away much of the time raising capital from friends on Wall Street and elsewhere.

He saw the role of the president as providing leadership and financial motivation for growth. He thought that most people underestimated

---

[1] See Exhibit 2 for makeup of committee.

their own abilities. The president's job was to call upon this extra effort from his employees and reward them for such performance. Thus, for example, he set revenue goals for the corporation which were realistically beyond the reach of the company. By hiring "good" people (defined as intelligent, energetic, and enthusiastic individuals), he believed that he could then leave the "how" of reaching these goals to the managers. Where his managers were concerned, Tweed was interested in results, not methods.

Early Diversification and Expansion

Despite the early success of the company, Tweed was fully aware of the short product life cycles in the industry. By the end of year 4, the business was starting to mature, the initial success of the product having attracted new competitors. Hence, after the original product was released to marketing, Tweed hired a dynamic young scientist, recommended by a friend, to head up a new R&D department. Because of the shortage of such high-caliber personnel, Tweed had to offer to provide a liberal stock option plan to attract him. Fifteen percent of the revenue dollars was allocated for this department to be spent on product improvements. As a consequence, the second generation of the original product line was well on its way toward introduction by the beginning of year 5.

Tweed did not ignore the obvious path for growth for a young company: to increase market size and penetration. Through the first four years, marketing opened sales offices in 25 major cities across the country. Then, in year 5, Tweed was surprised by a visit from one of the early investors, a young man whom Tweed had known at Ohmex. John Hawley was now selling for Ohmex in Europe but, seeing the quick acceptance of Mitek's products, was eager to work for Tweed. Tweed was impressed with Hawley's energy and spirited attitude and decided that the company could benefit from Hawley's knowledge of the European market. With the advisory committee's assent, Tweed hired Hawley, with a very attractive incentive and bonus pay structure, to set up a European sales network. And indeed, in year 5, expansion continued with the opening of the first of several European offices. However, as orders from Europe began to be filled, the costs of transatlantic shipping proved to be quite high. To solve this problem, Tweed initiated planning for a European manufacturing plant. Tweed did not perceive Europe as a major growth area or a solution to the innovation problem, however. European sales branches were useful sources of income but could not solve the longer term growth problem, since the same competitive forces were at work abroad. The European expansion was not without costs either, as both the domestic manufacturing and sales departments were aggravated by the organizational separation of these new operations from their American counterparts.

Tweed started to be concerned about the vulnerability inherent in his single-business firm. He recognized that continued high growth had to be supported by new product innovation. Therefore, toward the end of year 4, Mitek's top executives on the president's advisory committee met and decided to diversify through entry into a related product area, which promised much growth in the future.

A few weeks later, Tweed was taking one of his frequent trips to New York to meet with his investment bankers. On the way home, he happened to sit next to a young engineer from a competing company who not only was a known expert in Mitek's desired new product area but was looking for a way to leave his employer and head up his own operation. Tweed was impressed with the man's ability. Within the month, with the help of a substantial stock option plan, he was able to hire him. The new business was set up in a different location, with its manager reporting directly to Tweed.

While Tweed was actually quite excited about the new R&D developments, the European expansion, and the new business, he was concerned with the way the moves had been made. Rather than the result of a controlled planning process, which had weighed the pros and cons of alternatives, the decisions had been made in a loose, ad hoc manner. Tweed was aware that the expansion and diversification moves had caused much bickering among the key executives, particularly by those who felt the decisions were made because of chance hiring of new key people. Tweed tended to ignore this bickering, expecting that any growth would cause some strain between executives.

Plans for Year 6—The President's "Goals for the Future"

Tweed's key concerns—how to sustain growth in the core business, where to expand after the European extension, and how and when to diversify—were very much on his mind as the company approached the regular annual budgetary process in the last quarter of year 5.

The budget process was a rather uncomplicated affair. In the first few years of the company's history, the primary goal had been one of survival. The management perspective was perforce extremely short term, and many planning activities were handled in an informal manner between senior executives. Within the perspective and scope of these informal discussions, top executives would create a budget during the third or fourth quarter of each year for both old and new projects. After the treasurer's office had consolidated them, the budgets would be submitted to Tweed, who reviewed and presented them to the board of directors. Given the expansion into Europe and the first diversification efforts during year 5, which had been constant topics of conversation in the company, Tweed expected that his executives would address the issue of growth and present plans for expansion in their budgets. Therefore, he was very disappointed as he began reviewing final budgets coming in from the various departments. While the numbers were all in place, the plans, when put together, did not make a cohesive whole. The plans did not address the diversification issue but were myopic, one-year extensions of year 5 activities. There was a distinct lack of analysis. The plans lacked an understanding of financial, market, and operating risks, a discussion of markets and market opportunities, and any strategies as to how to maintain growth.

Tweed realized that the output of the budget cycle was partially his own fault in not specifying his expectations. Given the increasing size of the company and its management staff, it was becoming necessary to instill a longer term perspective and more formal planning process and analysis into the company. Tweed was suspicious, on the other hand, that the lack of cohesion between the plans was due to the internal rivalries and bickering that had built up during the year. Tweed realized that the budgets had to be redone under his leadership. He had to set short- and long-term goals to guide managers in this process. He prepared a set of guidelines and policies entitled "Goals for the Future of the Mitek Corporation," a document which consisted of 25 pages plus exhibits (excerpts and summaries are in Exhibit 4). The "Goals" was sent to approximately 50 people, including the board of directors, all of the first- and second-line senior managers—vice presidents, division heads, the treasurer, and the secretary to the corporation—the key third-line managers, and a few fourth-line managers from the manufacturing division. The guidelines were also sent to McDougal Consulting Company. Recognizing that growth was putting strains on the management structure, Tweed had brought McDougal in to study and recommend changes in the organization design.[2]

The "Goals" document began by stating that its function was to provide a basis for dialogue concerning next year's budget and longer term plans. Written responses directed to the goals themselves were invited. Tweed then presented a corporate purpose and a long-term growth objective. In the growth projections, Tweed even included the sales of a second new business venture to spur the development of new ideas by the managers. Finally, corporate policies on organization, employment, management philosophy, plans and controls, U.S. operations, R&D, marketing, European operations, and acquisitions were discussed.

---

[2] See Exhibits 2 and 3 for organization chart of addresses and makeup of board of directors.

Reaction to "Goals for the Future"

The presentation evoked written responses from more than half of the company's managers. These were primarily negative in tone. What surprised Tweed most, however, was not the reaction to the growth goals or other policies, which were by and large objective in nature. In fact he found them predictable. But the vehemence of the reaction to the management policy section in which Tweed had emphasized the need to decrease bickering and discord and increase teamwork and openness was a disturbing surprise. Excerpts from two of the typical responses are included in Exhibits 5 and 6: both of the authors were on the president's advisory committee, one being the vice president, marketing, Ted Rowman, and the other the vice president, administration (operations and R&D), Harvey Knight, one of the original founders.

Exhibit 1

MITEK CORPORATION
Statement of Income
(in thousands)

	Year 1	Year 2	Year 3	Year 4	Year 5
Net sales	—	$ 801	$8,212	$17,798	$39,453
Cost of sales	—	836	5,138	10,534	21,825
Gross profits (loss)	—	(35)	3,074	7,264	17,628
Operating expenses:					
Preproduction costs	$ 616	805	—	—	—
Research	—	168	678	1,015	2,350
Marketing and advertising	—	219	862	2,321	5,381
General and administrative	—	64	297	380	929
Total expenses	616	1,256	1,837	3,716	8,660
Operating income (loss)	(616)	(1,291)	1,237	3,548	8,968
Other expenses:					
Interest expense	12	81	174	178	596
Net income (loss) before taxes	(628)	(1,372)	1,063	3,370	8,372
Provision for taxes	—	—	556	1,562	3,970
Net income before loss carryforward	(628)	(1,372)	507	1,808	4,402
Reduction in taxes from loss carryforward	—	—	600	400	—
Net income (loss)	$(628)	$(1,372)	$1,107	$ 2,208	$ 4,402

Exhibit 2

Organization Year 5

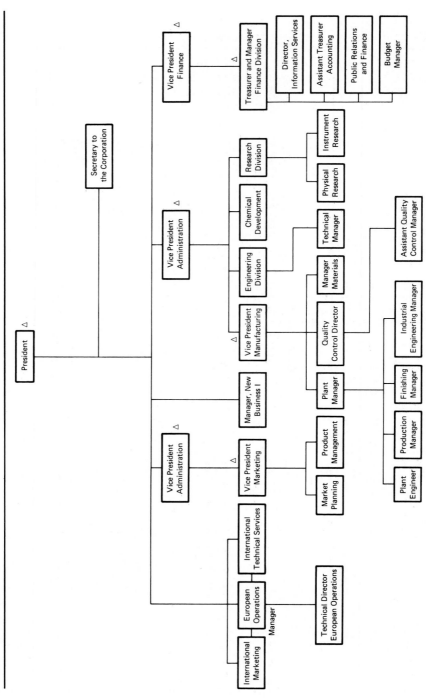

$\triangle$ = President's Advisory Committee.

Exhibit 3

Description of Members of Mitek Board of Directors

Member 1: Robert Tweed, president, Mitek

Member 2: Harvey Knight, vice president administration, for research and development and manufacturing, Mitek.

Member 3: Vice president administration, for marketing, Mitek.

Member 4: Vice president, marketing, of a manufacturing firm in a related industry.

Member 5: Vice president of a major Wall Street investment banking house (had investments in Mitek).

Member 6: Vice president of a large research lab.

Member 7: Partner of a venture capital firm (which had placed the second $2.5 million in Mitek).

Member 8: Professor of engineering from a prestigious engineering school.

Member 9: Chairman of the board of a manufacturing company.

Exhibit 4

Goals for the Future

Introduction

In writing this statement of corporate goals, I am aware of a kind of pontification in establishing them. I sense the lack of "position papers" and the debating of alternatives, except with respect to the statements of organization policy and European operations which have been much discussed.

In connection with the objectives stated herein, as with other objectives in the past which have been benefited by the study and propositions of others, I solicit the ideas of every member of management. Cross-fertilization of each other's thinking can only produce superior results, and this process applied to this statement of objectives will evolve more definitive, solidly grounded, and well-reasoned goals for the company.

For the present, however, this statement of objectives represents the only basis for our planning and preparation of operating budgets for year 6. Undoubtedly in the review of submitted plans and budgets, the evolutionary process toward improvement of our objectives will begin.

Robert Tweed,
President

Corporate Purpose

The purpose of Mitek is to operate an international business pursuant to policies and practices which represent the balanced best interests of customers, employees, and shareholders.

Because of the dynamic character and rapidly expanding opportunities of

Exhibit 4 (continued)

the company's field of interest, the ambitions and vitality of its people, and the capital gain profit motivation of its shareholders, the special emphasis of Mitek's operations is growth.

Long-Term Growth Objectives

Mitek Corporation's corporate objective for growth is to realize the potential which now exists within the existing operating units to achieve sales of $150 million four years from now (the target year).

This objective reflects a significant reduction in the past rate of growth of the company's core business in the United States and projected radical growth of International Operations (principally Europe), our current new business venture, and other new businesses yet to be defined. The sales objectives of each unit, which are set forth below, have been proposed by the several managers who have the responsibility for achieving them and, hence, should be regarded as realistic targets.

Core business sales in the United States are targeted at $80 million in the target year, which reflects a compounded annual growth rate of 25 percent. This, of course, compares to a growth rate of three or four times the projected figure during the past four years.

International sales are projected to increase to $20 million in the target year. After completion of the European manufacturing plant project, which will develop our capacity to transfer know-how overseas, it is likely that we shall undertake a Far East project.

Four-Year Sales Objectives (In millions)

	Core Business			New Business			
	United States	International	Core Sales Subtotal	I	II	New Business Subtotal	Total Mitek Sales
Year 5	$33	$ 6	$ 39	—	—	—	$ 39
Year 6	45	12	57	$ 8	—	$ 8	65
Year 7	58	15	73	18	$ 8	26	99
Year 8	70	18	88	27	15	42	130
Year 9 (target year)	80	20	100	38	22	60	160

The current new business (I) objective is below its potential as a result of our increasing familiarity with the technology and market potential for the product. Sales can anticipate a sharply rising curve because the product will have the important advantages of our quality reputation and immediate international marketing efforts.

Other new business objectives are conjectural because other new products are only in the development stage, and no consensus exists as to which direction expansion should take.

Exhibit 4 *(continued)*

Net profits from these operations should be most satisfactory if their respective technical, manufacturing, and marketing programs are successful. U.S. core business operations and European operations will face declining profit margins as the core business industry engenders the competitive conditions of a mature industry. Reduced profit margins may be countered periodically by new product improvements which do not represent technological breakthroughs, but these will not change the long-term results. Technical managers must calculate, in terms of market potentials and expected payoffs, the division of its resources between product improvement programs, programs which seek fundamental breakthroughs in core business technology, and other R&D programs which may be related to our existing technology but involve extension of our business into other fields.

During the coming year an objective of top management of the company will be to prepare a definitive long-term corporate strategy and integrated operating and capital plans which will bring about consensus on the direction the company shall take to achieve maximum growth.

Organization Policy

The businesses of European operations, core business operations, and new business opportunities will be organized, under the "federal principle" of organization, into decentralized operating units.

Each unit will be a profit center, responsible to its own top management which enjoys full responsibility for success or failure.

In many, if not most, ways each unit will function in a manner similar to an independent business. It will function subject to a framework of policies, guides, and controls fixed by the president. These will differ for each operating unit. Two expected benefits are better decisions because decisions will be made as close to the operating level as possible, and better performance because managers will perform best when objectives are set, resources provided, and operations are left unfettered.

Management

One of the company's principal objectives will be to improve our decision-making processes and to develop the kind of teamwork and achievement-oriented behavior that attract, motivate, and retain talented management people.

Unfortunately, Mitek's growth has been accompanied by increasing occurrences of management discord which are not in the company's best interests and for which we can no longer afford to make allowances. The indictment against our organization is long, but it should be repeated to emphasize the extent of the problem. Too often, problems that might have been approached from a more detached, factual base have been viewed as personal contests with all the attendant secretiveness, petty jealousies, exaggerations, and lack of common courtesy that are part of this unfortunate approach. Moreover, decisions, once made, have often not been followed and in some instances have been

Exhibit 4 (continued)

deliberately ignored or undermined. Finally, accomplishments and difficulties have been exaggerated to make realistic performance appraisal impossible.

Elimination of these practices will not be easy because misconduct always has its roots in unclear causes. However, we must make every effort to identify these causes and improve our ability to work together. To the extent the causes lie within our management system, we shall improve the situation by:

1. Developing a better understanding of what is expected of each manager.
2. Improving communication channels to facilitate more open discussion of common problems.
3. Evaluating performance, in qualitative as well as quantitative terms, against responsibilities.
4. Rewarding teamwork with promotion and favorable compensation and imposing penalties, financial and otherwise, upon those who persist in misconduct.

Top management must set the example in this responsibility for proper business conduct. I am personally dedicated to this course in terms of my own practices. I shall also enjoin it upon other members of management through the rewards system. No amount of tangible accomplishment will excuse anyone's future misconduct, because without mutual respect and cooperative undertaking, an effective management team cannot be welded together to achieve our programs.

Plans and Controls

A principal objective of management will be to perform satisfactory planning and to develop a control system to verify the conformance of actions taken to the plans.

The corporate performance objectives which I have set forth herein will be fractionated by the vice presidents of administration, division managers, and department managers into subgoals, both qualitative and quantitative. Such subgoals, to be prepared in narrative and statistical form, will be the bases for division and department operating plans and their requests for year 6 budgets. This work shall be completed three weeks from this policy statement. When functional subgoals, plans, and budgets have been accepted by top management, individual performance targets will be stipulated for each key manager to serve as a basis for performance appraisals and compensation adjustments.

A principal objective of top management, assisted by the finance division and by the management information systems group yet to be organized, will be to develop reports, standard costs, project costing, expense analyses, and other control measures. To this end it is essential that a top caliber staff for the MIS function be recruited immediately.

In implementing improved controls the purpose will be to present key information to management, highlight exceptions from planned operations, and direct attention to operating difficulties.

Exhibit 4 *(concluded)*

U.S. Operations

The plans from the manufacturing department do not place enough emphasis on cutting costs. Slowing the rate of capacity expansion, achieving economies of scale, better efficiencies, and cost cutting is required. The new target to decrease overhead expense will be 15 percent, as opposed to the 10 percent increase proposed by manufacturing.

Last year we set as our objective an increase in R&D activity of approximately 25 percent over that of the prior year. Our failure to achieve this objective is undoubtedly attributable to the effects of hiring the new director of R&D, which resulted in suspension of new programs and projects and reassignment of certain functions, the necessity to replace resigned personnel, and the difficulty of recruiting additional technical staff of high caliber.

Further, a new market research department will be established, and each researcher will be required to justify programs on the basis of market potential.

U.S. Marketing Operations

Competition has increased. We can no longer skim the cream. A strong marketing effort is required. However, granting the necessity for a significant increase in unit marketing expenses, the submitted budgets from marketing for this year's expenses are untenable. From a three-year level of $1.50–$1.80 per unit sold, the budgets propose an increase to $2.28 per unit. Marketing management must review its programs upon which this projected increase has been based to determine where expenditures are beyond the point of diminishing returns. Lacking factual basis for alternatives, I shall fix the reasonable objective for year 6 to increase marketing expenses to no more than $2 per unit.

Policy Related to Acquisitions

The company will not enter the acquisition game but will grow from within.

Only in the unlikely event of an acquisition opportunity which is possessed of good growth potential, demonstrated profit-making capability, and competent management, and which operates in an area similar or closely related to our current line of business, shall we consider diversification by acquiring another company. In short, our acquisition policy shall be one of disinterest and high opportunism.

Exhibit 5

Comments on Tweed's "Goals for the Future"
(By Ted Rowman, vice president, marketing)

Corporate Purpose

There can be no controversy over the statement of purpose. All of the loyal employees are indeed conscious of the emphasis placed on growth desires. The possibility of being outstripped by superior development by our competitors does indeed highlight the need for efficient operation of all divisions of the company.

Long-Term Growth Objectives

None can quarrel with the burning desire of management to achieve sales of $150 million by the target year, and while there are many methods of achieving this figure, there will be little room for error. Our industry is no longer forgiving. When one considers the changes our industry has seen, the compounded annual growth rate of 25 percent per year in the face of the industry growth of approximately 15 percent per year, we should be able to continue increasing our market share which we all agree is mandatory (but it must be done profitably).

With regard to the international forecast of $20 million by the target year, it is imperative that no more time be wasted in getting our European facility on stream. My personal feeling is that we have delayed far too long and that the effects of our procrastination will be felt sooner than any of us would imagine.

Four-Year Sales Objectives

It is my opinion that the new business venture must be carefully monitored by the corporation, and I feel the current method of monitoring is unsatisfactory. I am concerned that a small company cannot afford the expensive R&D necessary to develop innovative products as envisioned by new business I. We are best equipped to imitate the advances of other companies.

Organization Policy

With regard to the organization of the "federal principle," I feel there is room for debate. In my opinion, the marketing division should be under one manager, and a corporate marketing staff should be established to market our products worldwide. Hawley's operation in Europe should not be his autonomous barony.

Our principal competitor is currently operating under separate marketing organizations and is in the process of reorganizing its marketing division into a centralized marketing force with individual product managers. I feel this is the proper way to operate. The marketing strategies of our competitors overseas are becoming increasingly similar to the domestic marketing strategies.

With regard to the general organization of the company, it is very apparent that McDougal & Company will offer specific recommendations concerning our organization, and while they report directly to the president, it is my feeling

Exhibit 5 (continued)

that the pros and cons of any suggested reorganization be discussed and carefully weighed by all officers of the company.

I will prepare proposed organization charts for consideration and will submit them at a later date.

I feel that our employment policies, in general, are good. However, I have the feeling that we are not aware of the problems at the lower echelon . . . the fact that we are cognizant of top-management problems is evident. I feel that we overrate the morale of our second- and third-line management. The gung ho spirit still seems to be here and I sincerely hope this is true, but with the tremendous growth Mitek has enjoyed, I cannot help but wonder if we truly have a handle on our employee policies. I feel there is the possibility that many of our employees will leave to start their own ventures.

Management

I feel that the management discord is undoubtedly the biggest problem facing us today. We will never reach the $150 million market without establishing a greater degree of harmony.

International, marketing, manufacturing, and new business I each operate as an independent company. This is an impossible situation. The comments made regarding personal contests, secretiveness, petty jealousies, and exaggerations are indeed factual. The comment regarding the lack of common courtesy is one of the most noticeable conditions prevalent at Mitek today and has been commented upon quite frequently.

Another serious situation exists when corporate decisions have been made and not followed or deliberately ignored. One can agree that independent thinkers are a necessity, but once the decision has been made, the book should be closed and every effort should be made to support the final decision. I personally find that old wounds are continually being reopened, but only to the benefit of our competitors. There is simply not enough energy available to fight our competitors and our associates too!

Your report listed a series of steps to be taken to improve the situation. None can quarrel with these proposals, but one can only pray that these suggestions are implemented.

You have stated that you are personally dedicated to this course of action in terms of your own practices. It is often said that an organization is the reflection of its leader. If this statement is true, then you are the one that has to change and lead the way.

Plans and Controls

The three-week deadline placed on each division for subgoals both qualitative and quantitative does not permit sufficient time to adequately do the job. You ask for analysis but allocate no time or money to do it.

We have repeatedly stated that controls must be placed on our expenditures. In years 3 and 4 we were faced with the identical problems facing us today— overhead percentage outstripping profit margins. You vowed then that this would

Exhibit 5 (continued)

never happen again, and here we are at the end of year 5 with the very same problems. Why? We do not know, because we do not have the kind of management information to give us timely warning when things are going wrong, nor a way to systematically correct problems when they are discovered. Unfortunately, the sweet smell of success spoils us and permits us to don rose colored glasses.

U.S. Operations

It would appear now that we have indeed reached the point whereby we will have to reduce profit margins to increase our share of the market. We have steadily felt that we wanted to skim the cream, but the cream is much thinner now. We cannot have our cake and eat it too. If we are to reach the $150 million figure as a corporation, we must adjust to economy of scale in all divisions, not just marketing.

U.S. Marketing Operations

While I understand the need to justify the increased marketing costs to $2.28 per unit, the arbitrary setting of the budget to $2 per unit is typical of the autocratic methods you employ in this company. I do not accept this limitation and am preparing a justification for the budget submitted earlier.

Policy Relating to Acquisition

I feel the basic underlying statement concerning acquisitions is due to the lack of confidence in Mitek's ability to adequately manage and staff the acquired companies. I do not feel the door should be closed on this matter, and if indeed we can clear up our existing management problems, Mitek has sufficient talent to carry out a modest acquisition program and more rapidly achieve a position of a multiproduct company.

General Policies

I agree basically with the general statement of policy. In fact, even greater emphasis could be placed on some of the statements made. It is a known fact that many people at Mitek have responsibility without authority . . . an impossible situation. The statement that no one person shall be given direction by more than one other person cannot be overemphasized. We have conditions whereby employees are giving orders to other employees that are not under their area of jurisdiction, unless our organizational charts are completely erroneous.

Summary

In summary, I should like to quote several excerpts from our facilities brochure written in year 2.

Exhibit 5 (concluded)

"Mitek enjoys the inherent selling advantages of a small company—no rigid procedures, no sacred cows, no ponderous decision making, no cross-purposes."

"It is ambitious to be responsive to the needs of its customers as only a small enterprise with singleness of purpose is able."

"The distinguishing mark of Mitek people—research scientists, engineers, sales force, and accountants—is that we are user-oriented. We mean to prove it to you."

"Although intensely proud of our capabilities, we work by the rule that man's reach should exceed his grasp. In this sense, we shall never realize our ambitions."

I believe Mitek has drifted severely from this spirit.

Exhibit 6

To: Robert Tweed

From: H. Knight, vice president administration for manufacturing and R&D

Re: RT's "Goals for the Future"

Summary

These objectives, while in many ways the best and most comprehensive that you have produced, contain statements and implications, apparently directed toward several individuals, which I feel would be better discussed privately than to be included in a document distributed as widely as this one. Unsubstantiated charges such as "accomplishments and difficulties have been exaggerated" or "decisions . . . have been ignored or undermined" should be discussed forthrightly with the individuals being accused rather than be included in "Goals for the Future." It is quite true that management morale is very poor. It is also quite true that the morale of a ship is the reflection of the policies and practices of her officers and, to a very large extent, the captain. You have had it within your power to restore a high level of management morale and determination by removing several demotivating influences and situations, and by dealing forthrightly with your people. Mitek, in my opinion, must have a leader who will work with and motivate his management, engender management commitment to carefully developed operating plans, and effectively delegate meaningful authority and responsibility to his management. Loyalty and commitment cannot be ordered, can only tenuously and ineffectively be bought, and must be created, nurtured, and won through just and forthright participative and empathetic intercourse with people.

It had been my understanding, or perhaps only my hope, that decisions relative to corporate organization and operating management would be deferred until the McDougal Company report was completed. I was therefore disappointed to find that certain decisions, which I cannot honestly support and which I feel strongly are not in the company's best interests, have apparently

Exhibit 6 (continued)

already been made. In particular I cannot agree with decisions regarding the European operation. Hawley has been given too much autonomy. With the addition of a plant, which apparently will be under his control, not under my manufacturing division, he will be even more difficult to control than he is now. This man is too young and unproven a manager to have such uncontrolled responsibilities. I feel that Mitek should be exploiting its new business opportunities at home to a much greater degree than it appears to be going to. However, the advisory committee has been excluded from forthright discussion on the domestic expansion and diversification as well.

I would like to see more specific goals as to acceptable return on investment, payout period, or other criteria by which discretionary projects in all areas of the company may be evaluated and ranked in order of priority, rather than the ad hoc opportunistic decisions that have been made by you recently.

Introduction

It was my understanding, shared by others, that you wished these proposed goals to stimulate some provocative thinking and that they would be discussed with and modified by members of management before being finalized. I am completely in agreement with you that you cannot have commitment to, nor wholehearted support of, goals unless management participates in their formulation and is permitted an opportunity to freely discuss them. I personally feel the lack of factual and sincere objective discussions regarding certain of the goals and that if they are finalized as they now stand, they will seriously suffer from not having been arrived at by listing all of the pros and cons before arriving at the conclusion. You complain about the department plans being without analysis, but then you give us none either.

Long-Term Growth Objectives

It is my personal feeling that $150 million sales goal in the target year is a relatively conservative figure. We have grown more than 40 percent per year in the past. However, as you have often pointed out, the real goal should not be sales but should be profitability. I believe it is important that, rather than talk about sales volume objectives for each unit, profit and return on investment objectives be discussed and established. The question of whether to enter new areas should be approached not from the concept of the size of market available but from the concept of realizable profit and return on investment.

There can be really no question but that core product profitability per unit will tend to decline in the forthcoming years and that substantial technical and managerial effort will be required to increase plant yields and efficiency, reduce working capital requirements, and improve return on capital invested. It is particularly important for these reasons that the new business venture succeeds. The separation of the old, core product R&D from the newer research efforts (in new business I for example) with more incentives given to the new groups only hurts the cohesiveness of the company, however. The critical importance of preparing early in year 6 a forthright, long-term corporate strategy

Exhibit 6 (continued)

and integrated operating and capital plans, corporate organization plans, corporate facilities plans, an objective evaluation of people and their capabilities and how they may be motivated cannot be overstressed.

Organization Policy

While I cannot argue with the logic of profit centers, the concept is not being applied equitably. The core business division is conspicuous by its absence from consideration as a separate profit center with the same type of management incentive that has been provided for the new business venture and European operations. The stock options and incentive pay, offered to the new managers, are extremely generous and not available to the older, original group, which after all made Mitek what it is today.

If, as you say, managers perform best when objectives are set, resources provided, and operations are left unfettered in the new business areas, it would appear to me to be equally true in the core business area. I believe that whereas Mitek is striving to produce creative environments in its new businesses, it is in fact successfully striving to produce exactly the opposite in its parent corporation. It is obviously stifling the ambitions, aspirations, and vitality of its core business people and encouraging and forcing them to consider possibilities other than long-term Mitek employment.

Management

I believe that in this area a much more specific discussion involving people and situations is in order. I do not believe that the causes of the management discord are unclear. I think they are quite clear. You have had it within your power to correct or remove these causes any time you so desired. The communications amongst the top-management people, and particularly between the president and his staff, are extremely poor and have been lacking in honesty, candor, and objectivity. In a list of ills stated, no one, including RT, is above reproach, and indeed in my opinion RT himself has been the biggest offender in viewing problems as personal contests and in failing to adhere to decisions once made. I am particularly concerned about performance evaluations in qualitative terms. Too high an emphasis on the qualitative leads only to nonfactual judgments and strongly emphasizes the personal contest viewpoints. In view of your request that the goals be viewed provocatively, I believe that the primary source of difficulty within the management group in the company lies within the president's office, in part because of his qualitative, nonfactual judgments of certain people—in some cases highly favorable, in some cases highly unfavorable—and in part because of his opportunistic nature and aversion to true planning. I do not believe that any successful management team can be developed until these matters are openly aired and the problems of secrecy, lack of forthrightness, lack of time, and apparent lack of interest in developing a truly participative performance-based management are resolved.

If unquestioning obedience is desired instead of tangible accomplishment, then initiative, creativity, and growth in Mitek will not persist. The statement

Exhibit 6 (continued)

"accomplishments and difficulties have been exaggerated" should not be made without reference to specific situations and the accused permitted a rebuttal. Actually, I suppose that there may even be those who feel that financing the company may not have been nearly as difficult as it has been made to appear.

Plans and Controls

This section is contradictory within itself from the very start. Its initial paragraph states, "To perform satisfactory planning . . ." and in the next paragraph it states, "subgoals to be prepared in narrative and statistical form . . . shall be completed in three weeks." This is a totally unrealistic date, and it will result, as have such unrealistic dates in the past, in completely unsatisfactory planning and the preparation of unrealistic operating plans which cannot be adhered to, with the resulting management and operating confusion as to what is actually to be done.

Mitek has never been able to complete a satisfactory operating plan. It has never been able to grope through the last step of planning, of completing the loop and comparing what the technical capabilities are relative to the marketing requirements on the basis of economic evaluations and justifications, and to select an overall composite course of action for marketing-technical-manufacturing on the basis of need and profitability. Its top management has never been united in an understanding of the probability of achieving goals or the implication of its achieving or not achieving goals. A recent unsolicited sampling of junior managerial opinion relative to plans and controls and goals indicated that between 75 and 85 percent of the members of a particular meeting did not believe that any meaningful plans and goals would ever be prepared and that, even if they were, 90 percent felt there would be no follow-up on suggested changes in the plans or alterations indicated by the results of planning.

The company has tended to be highly opportunistic and unrealistic in its planning, has never appreciated the problems which it faced and the difficulties associated with their solution. Typically, all recent entry into new areas has been made in an ad hoc manner, following merely informal discussion and approval.

If today we were to spend substantial sums on a management information system, we must be prepared to implement and correct findings pointed out by the system.

U.S. Operations

I cannot abide by the constant cost reductions demanded from manufacturing. While efficiency is always laudable, increasing the overhead reduction to 15 percent is not comprehensible, and most of the cost is passed on to us from finance. Indeed the finance department's projects (like the MIS system) are always approved without question, while many new technical and manufacturing projects are being passed over.

Exhibit 6 (concluded)

European Operations

To attempt to establish Tweed's desired European empire in complete autonomy is in my opinion a most serious and erroneous technical judgment and one which has a high probability of failure. The probability of maintaining product uniformity and product interchangeability between autonomous plants operating in different hemispheres is quite low.

Policy Relating to Acquisitions

It is quite apparent from the whole tenor of the goals that the core business manufacturing personnel are to be confined to the original operation and are to be denied any growth potential. This is particularly evident in the policy relating to acquisitions.

With regard to the comment that "until Mitek has mastered its own basic problems of organization, planning, communications, and control," it must be remembered that the morale and effectiveness of an organization are a direct reflection of the effectiveness and human relations capability of the man leading that organization. The statement, "Our acquisition policy shall be one of disinterest and high opportunism" is precisely the type of planning which has characterized top-management organization with regard to all aspects of the business. One of the commodities which Mitek could export to one or two growing businesses would be experienced management which could take a company and put it into a sound growth situation. Unfortunately, it is not recognized that this management capability exists here, and indeed there appears to be substantial effort directed toward driving it out of the company.

General Policies

The goals are certainly desirable. Unfortunately RT is probably the most flagrant violator of all of these statements, and until he corrects this and accepts the fact that the company reflects his image and that he must provide leadership and must devote sufficient time to the operations of the business or seriously delegate authority to his subordinates, these general policies are ineffective. He frequently appears not to assume that the other person also wants to do a good job. RT has within his control the power to correct the management ills at Mitek if he truly desires to do so.

Cleveland Twist Drill (A)

When Jim Bartlett assumed the presidency of Cleveland Twist Drill (CTD)—a subsidiary of Acme-Cleveland Corporation—in August 1981, the mandate from Acme-Cleveland CEO Chuck Ames was seemingly uncomplicated. Ames had said: "Run a tight ship and manage for cash."

As the economy soured, however, sales and profitability declined considerably. Rather than fine tuning a sound business, Jim Bartlett soon found himself overhauling CTD's entire organization and strategy. He realized that his immediate priorities had to be to make CTD competitive in labor costs and to rationalize a product line that had proliferated to over 16,000 products.

But his approach to these goals had somewhat disoriented the old-line management, who found it difficult to accept the dramatic change in the character and direction of this 107-year-old company. Consequently, Bartlett brought in a new team and replaced virtually all of the inherited department heads, many of whom had devoted their entire careers to the company.

Though Bartlett felt he had been able to formulate the main elements of a turnaround, he knew some major unresolved problems still stood in the way of his achieving his objectives. To address the issue of labor costs, Bartlett had to decide whether to request from the Acme-Cleveland board $17 million to build new manufacturing facilities in lower cost locations or whether to attempt to win concessions from the existing

Copyright © 1983 by the President and Fellows of Harvard College
Harvard Business School case 384–083

work force in Cleveland. Even if Bartlett got the relocation funds, he was unsure how he should handle the prospect of major work-force reductions in Cleveland. In addition Bartlett faced a host of other problems in consolidating CTD's operations and changing its strategy: How could the unwieldy product line be rationalized? How could he maintain morale and a sense of purpose during a period of retrenchment? How could he turn a manufacturing-driven company into a marketing-driven one?

Industry Background

In 1981 Cleveland Twist Drill was the second largest U.S. manufacturer of cutting tools. The high-speed drills, reamers, taps, dies, gauges, end mills, saws, cutters and other products of this approximately $1 billion industry were used primarily in metalworking, where they were expendable "razor blades" in machining and metal removal (see Exhibit 1).

The cutting tool industry was mature with little prospect of long-term real growth. In fact, unit demand had declined approximately 1–2 percent per year during the 1970s. Three major trends were evident:

- Conglomerate acquisition of privately owned firms.
- A change in product demand.
- Increasing foreign competition.

Change in Ownership

Until the late 1960s all of the firms in the expendable cutting tool industry were privately owned. Between 1965 and 1970, however, most were acquired by conglomerates such as Litton, TRW, and Bendix. During this period Cleveland Twist Drill merged with National Acme, a machine tool manufacturer, to form Acme-Cleveland and reduce the probability of being acquired by a much larger company. Since more than half of Acme-Cleveland's top management came from Cleveland Twist Drill, the latter was able to remain relatively unchanged. But CTD's competitors changed rapidly from family-owned and family-managed concerns to publicly owned and professionally managed firms.

In the early 1970s United Greenfield, a TRW subsidiary and CTD's largest competitor, built a major new facility in Augusta, Georgia. CTD did not build its first southern plant until almost nine years later, and even then the new plant's output was a very insignificant percentage of the company's total production.

Change in Product Demand

New materials, technologies, and methods were steadily reducing demand for the industry's "bread-and-butter" product, high-speed steel drills.

Titanium nitride coatings and carbide solid and tipped tools, while higher priced than steel, had a significantly longer wear life. Lasers were being used increasingly as a cutting medium, and a shift from fastening to bonding of metal parts eliminated the need for drills.

Also affecting demand was a trend from specialty to commodity products in much of the market. Traditionally, cutting tool manufacturers had established close working relationships with the manufacturing and engineering departments of their customers. This enabled them to demonstrate the technical superiority of their products and qualified them to bid on high-quality jobs that commanded a price premium. The entry of new competitors and the centralization of purchasing in many large companies increased the importance of price in the buying decision. This, together with a shrinkage of perceived quality differentiation between top-line manufacturers like CTD and the new entrants, had divided the marketplace into a large commodity-like segment and a small high-quality segment. In the commodity segment, service was less valued, and many manufacturers sold directly to the end users through their sales force.[1]

Increased Competition

In the mid-1970s CTD's major end-user customers, such as Boeing, began informing CTD of the availability of good-quality tools at a lower price from Canada, Japan, and Yugoslavia. CTD management felt that this competition was in the lower price quality end of the market and hence not a significant threat. Competition continued to increase, however, as Japanese and Western European manufacturers increased their shares of the American market. In addition, automated equipment for producing cutting tools eliminated many key skills normally required in manufacturing a quality product, thus opening the door for competition from Third World and Eastern Bloc countries. Also, small, "short-line" specialists based in the United States were gaining ground against major competitors like CTD.

History of Cleveland Twist Drill

Cleveland Twist Drill was founded in 1876 by Jacob Dolson Cox in partnership with C. C. Newton. Although neither of Cox's two sons followed in his father's footsteps, the business continued to grow under family ownership. CTD's growth paralleled the growth of industrial distributors, and it was through its distributor network that CTD became the dominant force in the industry. Bert Finlay, the vice president for sales and marketing who had joined the company in 1956, recalled:

---

[1] In 1981 approximately 60 percent of cutting tools were sold through industrial distributors and 40 percent by company sales forces.

From 1930 to 1950 CTD concentrated on building market share and distribution channels. When I came aboard in 1956, CTD had control of the marketplace and maintained that position right up to the Vietnam War. The distributors having the CTD line had virtual entree to any other line [of complementary industrial products].

In 1968 Arthur Armstrong, Cox's son-in-law and CTD's chief executive, engineered a merger with the slightly larger National Acme. As stated in their first combined annual report:

The result is a major resource for production systems, know-how, tools, and automated machines which increase efficiency and reduce costs. Virtually every product manufactured by industry, from surgical needles to automobiles to spacecraft, requires products such as we design, produce and market throughout the free world.

The new company grew rapidly, from combined sales of $109 million in 1968 to $405 million by 1980. Profits increased more slowly, from $9 million to $16 million. (See Exhibit 2 for financial highlights.) In the eyes of some of the old-timers this merger was a turning point for CTD. According to one:

This was the beginning of the decline. There really was no synergy in the two businesses getting together. National Acme was the sick company which never got well. The top management of the merged company tried to bail out National Acme's business by using CTD's resources. As a result they did not pay enough attention, or allocate enough resources, to keep CTD in the forefront. As business boomed we could not make our delivery commitments. Though the product quality was good, manufacturing was not responsive to the needs of the customer; the product and applications engineering and sales would want to respond to the customers' needs and manufacturing would not, and therein lay the conflict.

Enter Jim Bartlett

After graduating from the Harvard Business School in 1961, Jim Bartlett joined McKinsey & Co. in New York City. Two years later he was selected to move to Cleveland, where McKinsey was opening a new office. The partner in charge was Chuck Ames.

After five years with McKinsey Jim went into the venture capital business, first with Laird & Co. and then with a group of partners. Their business was essentially one of acquiring privately held companies ranging from $2 million to $30 million in revenues. Jim's group increased the companies' profitability, installed professional management, and then sold them at a gain. In his 15-year involvement in venture capital Jim and his partners actively invested in and managed roughly 20 privately held manufacturing businesses. Not only did they achieve a solid return on their investment, but Jim found this work quite challenging and satisfying. A minority investor and participant in some of Jim's ventures was Chuck Ames, his old boss and mentor from McKinsey.

In 1972 Ames left McKinsey to become president and chief operating officer of Reliance Electric Company. In 1976 he was made chief executive officer. During his tenure Reliance's sales rose from $339 million in 1972 to $1.34 billion in 1979, net earnings rose from $13.6 million to $67.9 million, and ROE went from 11 percent to 22 percent. In 1979 Reliance was acquired by Exxon for $1.2 billion. Chuck Ames resigned a year after the acquisition was completed.

For over 10 years Arthur Armstrong, the chief executive officer of Acme-Cleveland, had been a member of the board of directors at Reliance. By 1980 Armstrong and his key associate and successor, Paul Cooper, decided to reach out to Chuck Ames to lead Acme-Cleveland through the coming difficult period. Ames, having served on the board of Acme-Cleveland, was familiar with the situation facing the firm.

Shortly after he became president in January 1981 Ames called Jim Bartlett and offered him the presidency of his Cleveland Twist Drill division. "I need management," Chuck said to Jim, but Jim Bartlett was not interested. His venture capital firm had just bought another company, which he was in the process of guiding through the transition to professional management. Despite Jim's initial lack of interest Chuck continued to pursue him. Finally in March 1981 Jim agreed to join Acme-Cleveland as president of Cleveland Twist Drill. But he could not start until August, because he had to wind up his affairs and help find some professional management for the company he was running.

Between March and August Bartlett had several discussions with Chuck Ames about CTD's history, present status, and mission. According to Jim, Ames's perception was that CTD was a very solid business that merely needed a good general manager who could set an explicit long-term strategy. Ames and the rest of Acme's board considered CTD as "solid as the Bank of England . . . number one in the industry . . . a flagship company . . . with unassailable strength."

Jim Bartlett's First Nine Months

Strategic Planning at CTD

When Bartlett arrived CTD was in the midst of preparing its 1982 budget and sales forecasts. He decided to involve himself in the process right away and asked to see management's strategic plans. Bartlett described what he found:

> For at least three years prior to my arrival, the strategic planning process had consisted primarily of the top management of the division getting to-

gether at a hotel and committing to some broad goals which did not change much from year to year, except for increased sales and profit projections. Their strategy could best be captured by the opening statement of the five-year, long-range plan developed in 1978: "In 1983 CTD will be the same as it is today but different. The essential difference will be REAL GROWTH in sales and profits, as compared with 1978." The opening sentence of the 1980 five-year, long-range plan was exactly the same: "In 1985 CTD will be the same as it is today but different. The essential difference will be REAL GROWTH in sales and profits, as compared with 1980 results."

This real growth in sales was projected as follows:

	1978	1979	1980	1981	1982	1983
1978 plan ($ million)	$ 92	$103	$114	$126	$146	$160
1980 plan ($ million)	—	—	126	133	156	183

Profit growth was projected at 6 percent of sales in the 1978 plan and in the 1980 plan was raised to 6.5 percent. As for the actual strategies to achieve these projections, Bartlett said:

This was merely an exercise where the outside consultant who had been brought in would ask the managers everything they would like to do during the next five years. As a result the major strategies for the last three years were generalizations that did not amount to much. Their key strategy statements were:

1. To achieve increased productivity in manufacturing and throughout all division operations.
2. To achieve conversion from purchased to manufactured for major items now resold.
3. To provide management depth and skilled employees required to achieve the division's long-range growth goals.
4. To be more responsive to the physical, emotional, and social needs of employees and to the needs of our communities.
5. To expand international market participation.

Upon learning this I immediately came to the conclusion that planning would have to change because we needed to develop much more relevant strategies. Besides, Chuck Ames had already suspended these kinds of long-range planning efforts and asked the divisions to focus on their short-term results. In a memo to the division heads Chuck had written:

I would suggest that the operating division heads begin to think through the strategy they will employ to raise the return on sales of their division to 7 percent, on a continuing basis. And that all of us think in terms of the strategy required to achieve, on a continuing basis, returns of 7 percent on sales, 22 percent on equity, and 14 percent growth rate in earnings per share.

Bartlett indicated how the 1982 plans were completed:

> When I arrived CTD was about to complete fiscal 1981. At that time we expected the sales volume for the year to come in at about $120 million, and the people there had viewed the results for the year as being pretty good. Like most others at that time the people in the division had assumed that the economy would rebound in 1982, and so the forecast of $140 million for 1982 seemed pretty reasonable to me.

Within six months into the fiscal year Bartlett realized that not only would he not achieve his forecast, but he would be hard-pressed to even do as well as the last year. He felt the plan relied too heavily on assumptions about economic recovery, which did not happen. Bartlett believed, however, that this downturn was a double-edged sword. He explained:

> The bad edge of the sword was that the decline in sales had caused considerable profit pressures on the business. The good or opportunity edge of the sword was that these results produced a climate that made it easier to institute strategic changes which otherwise would have been much more difficult to get people to accept.

Manufacturing

Since CTD was basically a manufacturing company, the next task Bartlett set for himself was to learn about its manufacturing capabilities and vulnerabilities. CTD's facilities comprised 10 acres of manufacturing floor space, including 19 buildings. The main plant, a five-story 500,000-square-foot building on top of which sat CTD's headquarters, was located on East 49th Street, just one block from Lake Erie, in a heavily industrialized section of Cleveland. The Cleveland plant complex accounted for 75 percent of domestic production. Another 15 percent was produced in Mansfield, Massachusetts, and plants in Cranston, Rhode Island, and Cynthiana, Kentucky, produced the remaining 10 percent.[2] There were also three foreign plants, but they were of only minor importance.

CTD had traditionally organized its manufacturing operations by process. Grinding was done in one area, testing in another, milling in another, and finishing in yet another. Many of the processes were not even in the same building. One department did nothing but move goods in process from one floor to another, from one building to another, and even between plants in Cleveland, Cynthiana, and Cranston. One result of the practice and the plant layout was that CTD had more indirect than direct labor cost.

When Jim Bartlett arrived he got involved in the manufacturing

---

[2] In total, CTD had 524,000 square feet of manufacturing space in Cleveland; 65,000 square feet in Mansfield; 49,000 square feet in Cranston; and 145,000 square feet in Cynthiana. The number of hourly employees at these locations was approximately 530, 100, 50, and 90, respectively.

budget right away and targeted a $5 million reduction in manufacturing wages. He asked the manager of industrial relations, Gordon Streit, for ideas on how to achieve this. Streit, who was 57 years old and had spent his entire career at CTD, seemed to be confused by this approach and was at a loss for suggestions. According to Bartlett Streit made some suggestions like "maybe we should cut salaries by 10 percent across the board." Bartlett, finding such responses totally inadequate, fired Streit during his first week at CTD. Needless to say Streit was shocked and asked Bartlett, "How can you do this to me? No one has ever told me I was not doing my job well."

Streit was the first among Bartlett's inherited, nine-member top management team to be dismissed. Bartlett commented: "Firing Gordon was an unpleasant and difficult thing to do, and I sensed that most of the employees felt I was shooting from the hip. But I couldn't tolerate a key executive who could not give me any good ideas on the major problems we faced. Of course, we made a generous severance arrangement with Gordon."[3]

Streit was replaced by Jack Sims from the corporate industrial relations staff at Acme-Cleveland. Bartlett asked Sims to investigate how CTD's wages compared with those of competitors. By contacting the Metal Cutting Tool Institute, the industry trade association, Sims was able to develop a comparison between CTD's wages (excluding benefits) and the industry averages, as shown in Table 1. When benefits were included the gap between CTD and its competitors widened to $4.50 per hour in the Cleveland area.

Table 1

Comparative Wage Analysis: Industry versus CTD

Industry Average		CTD Average Wages	
United States (excluding CTD)	$7.51		
New York, New England,		Mansfield, Mass.	9.89
Mid-Atlantic	7.15	Cranston, R.I.	7.32
Chicago and West	7.55	Cynthiana, Ky.	7.65
Cleveland and Detroit (excluding CTD)	8.30	Cleveland	10.67

In addition CTD's productivity and quality were compared with competitors' levels. These studies showed that productivity varied little throughout the industry and that CTD's quality ran somewhat higher. From these studies Bartlett concluded that CTD was at a competitive

---

[3] Streit was given one year's salary as severance pay, was allowed to begin to collect retirement benefits as if he were 65, and was offered the services of an outplacement company at CTD's expense.

disadvantage and that significant changes in manufacturing strategy would be required:

> When I started at CTD I thought the company was in reasonably good shape and that I would be addressing the longer term issue of substitute products. Instead, within the first month or two I realized that the company faced a very serious and dangerous cost situation that had to be corrected. And with our industry actually decreasing in size and with very tough competition, I concluded that our survival was at stake.

The head of manufacturing was Sam Colt. Colt was 42 years old and described as articulate, soft-spoken, well liked by the rank and file, and a hard worker. He had started as a trainee at CTD, had worked his way up, and was considered the number one candidate to succeed to the top position—so Bartlett had been informed upon joining the company. All the manufacturing plants reported to Colt. As a hands-on manager he knew the production output for every plant on a shift-by-shift and product-by-product basis.

According to Bartlett when he and Colt started discussing manufacturing strategy, Colt wanted to talk only about operating data. Bartlett had to steer the conversation around to CTD's comparative cost position to impress on Colt that CTD was not cost competitive in its present facilities and would always have trouble catching up with competitors that had more efficient facilities.

In October 1981 Bartlett asked Colt to begin work on a change in CTD's manufacturing strategy. In a four-page memo a month later Bartlett spelled out specifically what he was looking for. The memo began:

> The presentation for preliminary five-year plans by each product group is now scheduled for February 25, 1982. These plans will have a major influence on the direction CTD will take in the location and very nature of its manufacturing base. However, as we discussed earlier, there are a number of questions that must be addressed, the answers to which will have a major impact on how we should reposition our manufacturing base. Your responsibility in preparing for the late February meeting is to develop the clearest possible answers to these questions.

There followed a series of questions (see Exhibit 3) listed under four headings: (1) East 49th Street Dispersion; (2) Plant Network Design; (3) Organization and Staffing; and (4) Capital Investment. This memo was never answered to Bartlett's satisfaction, and in February 1982 Sam Colt was fired. Bartlett commented:

> This was a very difficult decision because Sam was so well liked and because he really was just a product of the corporate culture he had grown up in. When I called my first staff meeting, for example, Sam and his people got up to leave when the marketing people arrived. Cross-functional discussion just wasn't part of the culture. Despite all my sympathy and efforts

I realized that it would be impossible to achieve what we had to without someone else in Sam's position.

Sam Colt was replaced by Pete Manzoni, formerly vice president of manufacturing for Bailey Controls, a division of Babcock & Wilcox. Manzoni explained how he came to join CTD:

I have always played the stock market, and my investment philosophy is to buy shares in companies where there is some major change or chance for change going on. In about half of the situations I am able to win big, and in the other half I hope to break even by getting out in time. Thus when Chuck Ames joined Acme-Cleveland, knowing of his track record at Reliance, I bought a large block of shares in Acme-Cleveland. A year later when Acme's stock had gone down and having read in the local papers about management changes at Acme and CTD, I wrote a letter to Ames stating that all he had done was fire a lot of people and changed around positions, but the business meanwhile had continued to go downhill. As a result of this letter Ames contacted me, and soon I was talking to Jim Bartlett about joining CTD, which I did on March 1, 1982.

After about a month on the job Manzoni, with Bartlett, had started to formulate a manufacturing strategy for CTD.

Labor Relations

Only the Cleveland and Mansfield plants were unionized, though with different unions and separate labor agreements. Management's relationship with the workers in Cleveland was not only conflict-free but benevolent and harmonious. While the Mansfield workers were represented by the United Steel Workers union, the Cleveland plant had its own house union.[4] The company's relationship with this union was quite good and rather informal. Until 1969 there was not even a written labor contract. Instead, verbal agreements and clarifying memos were used. All through the 1960s and 1970s, as CTD prospered it shared its gains generously with its workers. The company was one of the first to provide dental insurance and unlimited medication coverage. The cost of living allowance (COLA) provision in its contract was without a cap to enable the workers to recover fully increases in the consumer price index (CPI); moreover the company had agreed in 1972 to an 8 percent minimum annual COLA, which in 1980 turned out to be slightly higher than the increase in the CPI. CTD also had a long tradition of providing piece-rate incentives for increased productivity ranging from 25 percent to 40 percent of base salary.

There had never been a layoff in the company's history. During the 1974–75 recession the salaried employees took a 10 percent cut,

---

[4] A house union is an independent union organized solely within a specific company and has no affiliation with international unions.

but the hourly workers kept working full time and built up inventory that was used later when business picked up. Morale was high, and management and the workers were close; not only the plant manager but also the president spent considerable time on the shop floor and knew people by their first names.

Management's benevolence toward its workers included not only financial rewards but also psychological and social benefits. In the 1970s CTD had a bowling league with about 40 teams, two golf leagues, and a softball league. There were also an annual sports awards banquet, a big Christmas dinner, and a Christmas party for the children. The personnel department kept track of all the employees' children's ages and sexes to ensure that they received the appropriate presents. A club for retirees offered medical checkups, social events, and other benefits.

Other employee assistance programs listed in the company's 1978 and 1980 long-range plans were alcohol and drug abuse counseling, physical fitness courses, CPR and first aid classes, preretirement counseling, financial planning and tax return preparation at company expense, legal referrals, and marital, family, and personal counseling. Social activities included photography and radio classes, picnics, open houses, and family activities. To serve the community there were plans for trial job interviews for high school students, summer jobs at CTD for local teachers, economics courses for employees and students, and encouragement for employees to serve on local community agencies and educational boards.

But all was not a bed of roses. Roy Martin, 38, newly promoted Cleveland plant manager and a 20-year veteran, provided a perspective on CTD's culture and the changes Jim Bartlett had made:

> Even before Jim came things had started to change. In the recession of 1975 they cut out the Christmas party for the kids. Also for the banquet, instead of the shrimp cocktail and steaks we had a spaghetti dinner in the basement. There were also some management layoffs and a 10 percent salary cut. Basically these were the easy things. The tough things had not been done and the tough questions were: Do we really need all these levels of management and do we even need all these managers?
>
> I was one of the last of the manufacturing guys left, and I suddenly went from a Young Turk to the last of the good old boys. This put me in a peculiar position. I was Sam Colt's lieutenant, and when Sam was fired by Bartlett this was a real blow culturally to the organization because Sam was well liked. Conceptually I did not have a problem with what Jim wanted to get done, and so in a way I had one foot in either camp; one camp wanted to continue as before and not make too many changes, while the other camp wanted to do things differently and change the business practices. So the new team basically wanted to make all the changes, and the old people were in a way divided.
>
> What hurts us the most is the COLA provision, which was negotiated in 1972, that went out of control. The incentive program was out of control,

too. Previously it was about 25 percent of the base; now 10 years later it is 42 percent of the base, and the problem is that everyone expects to get it, so it is no longer a real incentive. When people don't get the incentives that they have come to expect, we get grievances that our standards are too tight.

Having collected comparative wage data, management was in a quandary on how to proceed, because contract negotiations were not due until November 1983. Some of the senior management wanted to seek immediate wage and work rule concessions from the union bargaining committee,[5] but there was legitimate concern that the rank and file would resist even if the union leadership went along, because they had never been told there were any real problems. The workers' perception of the company and their part in it was that they produced the best quality goods, and as a result CTD was the leader in the industry. Other members of senior management felt CTD should communicate the grim realities directly to the workers.

Against this backdrop Pete Manzoni, with Bartlett's concurrence, began informal discussions with the union bargaining committee in the middle of March. The committee was headed by Greg Thompson, who had recently been reelected president of the house union. Thompson was a decent, understanding sort of person who was sympathetic to CTD's problems. So far not much had been accomplished by these talks. According to Manzoni:

> Thompson's reaction to our proposals has been one of absolute shock, followed by disbelief and anger. His reaction has been something like this:
>
>> You guys are new here, and you don't know what's going on. We have been here for 25 years, and we have never been treated like this by past management. They never told us there was any big wage or benefit differential problem. I don't know where you got your numbers from, but they can't be right. Besides, our productivity and quality are much higher than our competition, so the numbers are not even comparable.

Bartlett soon realized that they had placed Thompson in a terrible bind:

> Thompson is a very intelligent, sensitive man, who is well respected by his union members. He is a real statesman. He has calmed many management-labor problems and relationships in the past. Now we're telling him to convince his rank and file that a major concession has to be made before the contract expires.

---

[5] The most important work rule change would be a reduction in the over 500 job classifications, which seriously reduced plant flexibility.

Marketing and Sales

CTD's traditional market objectives were to serve as broad a market as possible and to maintain the highest product quality. To achieve these goals, it supplied a very large distributor network with a product line that included about 16,000 standard products and many specials. CTD also had on its own payroll 70 highly trained service representatives who worked directly with end users to solve problems with the existing products and to design new ones for special applications.

Largely because of the sales reps' work, CTD had established a reputation for superior quality. In recent years, however, other manufacturers had improved the quality of their products considerably, and CTD had not sufficiently kept abreast of technological advances to maintain its position. It became increasingly difficult for CTD to obtain a price premium for its products, and top management began questioning the wisdom of an annual outlay of approximately $5 million to maintain a specialized service force.

Drills accounted for 40 percent of CTD's product. Four other important product groups each accounted for between 10 percent and 13 percent of the total:

1. Reamers.
2. Taps, dies, and gauges.
3. End mills and aircraft specials.
4. Assembled threading tools (ATT).

Three other categories—Nobur, saws and cutters, and miscellaneous tools—accounted for the remaining 10 percent. (See Exhibit 4 for market segment analysis and seven-year market share trends.)

Before Jim Bartlett arrived, P&L responsibility at Acme-Cleveland rested primarily with the president of each division or subsidiary. Both Chuck Ames and Bartlett believed, however, that product managers should also have profit responsibility. (See Exhibit 5: Bartlett's memo, The Role of the Product Manager.) Accordingly, Bartlett, shortly after his arrival, appointed three product managers who would have P&L responsibility for major segments of the business: one for drills and reamers; one for end mills, taps, dies, gauges, and Nobur; and one for ATT, saws, and cutters. Before, the product-manager position had reported to the vice president for sales and was basically a staff position (see Exhibit 6); now they would report directly to the president (see Exhibit 7).

Although the product managers had P&L responsibility, they had no product-line P&Ls to manage with. As Jack Massey, the vice president of finance, put it:

There are big problems in getting product-line profitability data. When I got here I started looking at the financial systems, and there was no way to do a good analytical job. The people in the financial department were just bookkeepers. There were no proper information systems. All we had was a P&L and balance sheet, one for the United States, one for Canada, one for Mexico, one for Germany, and one total consolidated. There were no other operating reports to identify profitability, inventory turnover, variance analysis, or efficiency. All they were used to doing was looking at inventory cycles. Also there was no way to identify opportunities or problems. We thought we would have product-line performance in place within six months. Now it seems it's going to take us two years. The problem is that people don't report against the routings; they just produce pieces and get paid, and there are no cost standards. Also with business going down we can't afford to allocate the resources to develop the information we need.

Besides the problem of establishing profitability figures, the product managers also found themselves spending more time responding to short-term pressures. One said:

As demand began to fall, more and more of our time is being spent in reforecasting sales figures and renegotiating production targets with manufacturing. Also pricing issues have become quite important in the face of declining demand. There was, for example, pressure to lower prices so as to keep up demand. However, analysis showed that each 10 percent cut in prices would require 20 percent more sales to make up the lower level of profit. In light of declining overall demand such a sales increase would have been most unlikely.

The product managers did not have an easy time dealing with the sales organization, either. The vice president for sales, Bert Finlay, had been with CTD for over 20 years and was described as "a very bright, energetic guy, though he was not on board with the new concept." Over time the product managers hired product specialists to help them with their jobs. When they tried to fill these positions from the field sales and service organization, they encountered considerable opposition from Finlay, who resisted the development of the product-manager organization at the expense of field sales.

The product managers also faced a difficult task in developing strategies for growth markets. In addition to finding a very broad product line that was almost unmanageable, they found their competitors firmly entrenched in the commodity segment of the drill market (see Table 2). At the high-quality end of the market, in spite of a strong engineering

Table 2

1982 Estimated Sales of the High-Speed Steel Drill Commodity Segment (Figures in millions)

CTD	Company A	Company B	Company C	Company D	Company E	Others
$4	$40	$20	$15	$15	$10	$25.5

and R&D department, CTD found itself far behind in seeking growth opportunities outside high-speed steel tools. As one of the product managers summed it up:

> The market perception of CTD is one of a high-cost producer resting on past successes, with little growth or technological drive. Though our premier product line—Cleforge—is still well respected in the industry, it is too high priced for the price-conscious buyers.
>
> Our lower priced line—Cleline—with which we can be price competitive, is not broad enough. We consistently have trouble putting together complete packages in this line. We really have no choice here. The commodity segment is now more than half the market and growing. We must have a complete, price-competitive line.

Bartlett's Options

In the past nine months Jim Bartlett had dramatically changed the organizational structure of CTD and put new people in most of the key management positions. The administrative staff had also been cut back, and there had been significant volume-related layoffs in manufacturing. Even before Bartlett took over, Chuck Ames had begun restructuring and cutting back the entire Acme-Cleveland organization, and CTD had received a taste of the new management style when 75 management positions had been pared away.

Jack Sims, the vice president of personnel, described how there had been opportunities to do away with entire departments:

> Since June 1981 341 salaried people have been let go, for an annual savings of $10.6 million. For example, there was the wage standards department with 15 people who spent all their time administering the incentive system and writing job descriptions. This department was cut to one person. There was a customer service department with 70 people; these people did nothing but order processing and order entry. That responsibility has now been put into the hands of the sales offices, and the customer service department has been cut to 10 to 12 people. They also had 17 people in the personnel department administering all sorts of programs. That has now been cut to 5 people. And the company also employed its own cafeteria workers, paying them a wage rate of $10 per hour and $5 per hour in benefits; in addition, the cafeteria operation was being subsidized by $300,000 a year. All of these workers were let go, and a food service company was hired to run the cafeteria.

Sims continued:

> I am thoroughly convinced that we are doing the right thing here. We should have addressed these issues many years ago. Of our salaried people about one half of them were in shock when we started to make the changes, but the other half felt that it was about time. I think that the greatest risk of what we are doing is that we may be doing too much too soon. There is just a lot of change all at once.

While Bartlett was pondering the pros and cons of the various options he knew he had to act fast because of CTD's poor performance. For the first six months of fiscal 1982 sales were already 10 percent below the previous year and 15 percent below budget. While earnings were slightly above the previous year, they were considerably below budget. More disturbing was that the trend in both sales and earnings had been deteriorating.

Jim Bartlett realized that many of CTD's problems were rooted in the sharp decline in demand caused by the recession, but he also felt that the recession only highlighted CTD's underlying weaknesses. As Bartlett looked back he realized he had got into more than he had bargained for. The industry had matured. CTD's sales were on the decline, and he had a major problem with the union on wages and benefits.

By early April 1982 Bartlett felt he knew what had to be done. First, he had to improve CTD's competitive cost position dramatically in its core markets while maintaining service and delivery. Achieving a competitive cost position was essential for CTD to compete effectively in the large and growing commodity segment and maintain its position in the high-quality segment. As he wondered how he could pull this off, three possibilities kept churning in his mind.

1. He could step up the pace and pressure of negotiations with the union bargaining committee and hope for an early breakthrough.

2. He could bypass the bargaining committee and appeal directly to the union employees.

3. He could immediately seek board approval for the necessary funds to proceed with plans to transfer work to other locations without involving the union leadership or its members.

None of these alternatives was particularly attractive. Whether Greg Thompson could persuade his union members to accept something as traumatic as wage concessions was an open question. For Thompson to endorse or recommend pay and benefit givebacks might seem tantamount to selling out to the new management.

Going directly to the rank and file might have been feasible a couple of years earlier, when there was still a very strong family feeling. But recently, because of the firings and forced retirements of many of the managers who had spent their entire careers with the company and because many of the company's beneficences, like Christmas dinner and other social activities, had already been cut out, the production employees were already wary.

Requesting board approval for funds to transfer work at this stage also concerned Bartlett. He had a mandate to "manage for cash," and to request $15–$20 million, when Acme-Cleveland was considering several acquisitions, might be viewed as contradicting that mandate. Since Acme-Cleveland was having a bad year, all capital requests were given very close scrutiny. And since most of the board had strong ties to Cleveland, a major move out of Cleveland might not be looked on favorably. Finally, although CTD had begun limited production at its Cynthiana, Kentucky, plant in early 1979, Bartlett wondered how responsible it would be to his employees and the community in Cleveland to launch a full-scale "southern strategy" before at least exploring all possible alternatives to gain wage and benefit concessions.

Complicating these alternatives were the facts that the current contract wasn't due to expire for 18 months and that it would take one to two years to bring any new facilities to competitive levels of productivity. Bartlett feared a three-year delay in achieving a competitive cost position if he waited to negotiate a new contract and then was unable to gain the necessary concessions.

Bartlett's second major objective was to maintain CTD's position in the marketplace because its sales and customer order backlog were dropping precipitously. What the company needed here were sound product-line strategies. But this component still perplexed him because CTD had no financial analysis or history on the profitability of its product lines.

The third major element of Bartlett's program was to move CTD into established growth markets. To accomplish this CTD needed to develop a capability in new technologies, such as titanium nitride coatings, powdered metallurgy, and ceramics, rather than continue its investments in high-speed steel.

Thus, as shown in Exhibit 8, Bartlett felt he had conceived the main aspects of his strategy. What he needed to establish now was how the key elements of each aspect would be realized.

Exhibit 1

Products Manufactured by the Cleveland Twist Drill Co.

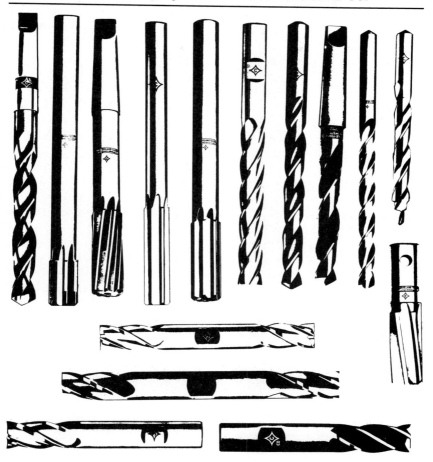

Exhibit 2

CLEVELAND TWIST DRILL
A. Financial Performance 1973–81: Acme-Cleveland

	1981	1980	1979	1978	1977	1976	1975	1974	1973
Summary of operations:									
Net sales	$400,743,537	$405,235,999	$344,460,395	$289,509,329	$218,191,699	$194,088,642	$231,489,665	$169,442,363	$127,850,966
Cost of products sold	318,721,315	301,847,698	246,286,255	210,201,261	160,159,308	143,008,384	170,670,207	126,022,710	90,417,166
Interest expense less interest income	6,942,653	6,651,559	3,592,141	4,328,008	4,756,829	4,756,829	6,569,948	3,102,128	672,111
Earnings before taxes	18,145,346	27,931,887	35,832,636	24,971,294	8,753,201	5,389,716	12,771,499	10,493,880	12,563,828
Income taxes	7,214,000	10,949,000	16,357,000	11,813,000	3,915,000	2,478,000	5,816,000	4,785,000	5,876,000
Net earnings	10,931,346	16,982,887	19,475,636	13,158,294	4,838,201	2,911,716	6,955,490	5,708,880	6,687,828
Net earnings to net sales	2.7%	4.2%	5.7%	4.5%	2.2%	1.5%	3.0%	3.4%	5.2%
Earnings per common share	2.41	3.96	4.34	2.96	1.08	.65	1.56	1.43	1.74
Dividends per common share	1.40	1.35	1.15	.80	5.25	.50	6.25	1.00	.82
Other financial information:									
Current assets	168,751,234	182,884,833	156,791,868	132,945,224	123,794,140	100,570,415	129,570,415	133,731,029	72,362,351
Current liabilities	70,964,020	71,953,727	59,461,457	39,394,887	41,166,527	26,264,216	46,884,880	47,980,021	27,206,073
Working capital	97,787,214	110,931,106	97,330,411	93,550,337	82,627,613	74,306,199	82,316,089	85,751,008	45,156,278
Property, plant and equipment—net	75,596,288	75,120,585	56,196,074	47,716,898	44,352,655	44,259,575	47,054,224	43,890,446	31,169,157
Capital expenditures	16,299,044	26,097,516	14,732,829	9,005,924	4,608,876	8,528,286	8,235,977	5,968,552	5,023,718
Depreciation	8,042,833	6,370,516	5,340,020	5,032,188	4,817,117	4,925,867	4,757,590	3,706,216	3,234,652
Long-term obligations	53,082,173	70,534,284	49,737,582	47,017,089	42,195,043	38,849,752	45,153,231	51,075,644	9,679,581
Total assets	252,437,417	263,712,017	219,574,767	184,463,445	171,071,286	150,001,052	178,141,229	179,894,704	105,258,535
Redeemable preferred shares	162,874	162,874	–0–	62,215	62,215	62,125	62,215	62,215	–0–
Shareholders' equity	121,668,098	116,330,248	107,079,591	93,964,096	84,255,799	81,800,056	81,160,550	77,028,520	66,855,616
Shareholder's equity per common share	27.15	26.37	23.81	21.10	18.92	18.37	18.22	17.28	17.42

B. Financial Performance 1973–81: Expendable Products Segment*
Fiscal Years Ended September 30 (in thousands of dollars)

	1981	1980	1979	1978	1977	1976	1975	1974	1973
Total sales	$148,360	$148,045	$144,521	$115,207	$97,277	$89,854	$91,416	$94,620	$80,653
Operating profit	14,188	10,795	21,665	17,092	11,895	10,516	7,155	10,901	11,325
Identifiable assets	86,444	95,071	72,741	69,135					
Depreciation	3,845	3,347	2,940	2,799					
Capital expenditures	7,321	13,338	8,113	3,947					

* This includes products other than those manufactured by Cleveland Twist Drill.

Exhibit 3

Excerpts from Jim Bartlett's Memo (November 13, 1981) to Sam Colt on Manufacturing Strategy

East 49th Street Dispersion

— What are the common manufacturing operations at East 49th Street to *all* the products manufactured there? How many hourly persons function in relevant departments and what are the costs associated today?

— What skills are required by hourly operators in these departments? What is the age and seniority profile of these persons performing these operations today? Which of these skills will disappear via attrition over the next five years that are not being replaced through training?

— Through matrix analysis, where does each major product group produced at East 49th Street depart from a list of operations common to all? Which of these product groups, by virtue of their separate (or separable) manufacturing process, lend themselves to relatively easy exit?

— Of those products that are readily separable from a process viewpoint, which represent the highest content of critical manual skills? Which represent a high "automation cost" if duplicated elsewhere?

Plant Network Design

— How many plants should we have? What is the optimum size of a plant?

— How many different product lines should be produced in each plant? To what extent can we continue to do early stage operations on a tool class in one plant to support the production of other plants?

Organization and Staffing

— What should the organization be for each of our plants presently on line, including East 49th Street?

— What management resources are available to us in developing the necessary details to execute a major series of manufacturing moves (plant start-ups, line relocations, and so forth)? What must be done to shore up these resources in time to have knowledgeable people making decisions and carrying out the required actions?

— What services, support, or direction will manufacturing require from outside its own organization?

Capital Investment

— What are the major elements of our existing in-place capital structure for manufacturing? Which of these elements (heat treating, centerless grinding, NC equipment, broaching, and so forth) will require major overhaul or substantial capacity upgrading during the next five years?

Exhibit 3 (concluded)

— Again using matrix analysis, where do we have duplication of facilities or equipment today? What additional duplication (or capacity) is already programmed through our present Cranston and Cynthiana moves?

— Are there major segments of capital equipment capability missing in our present plants that impair our competitive ability? What investments might we make to add to our productivity today?

Exhibit 4

A. Market Segment Analysis

Segment	CTD Mix	CTD Market Share	Competitive Market Share	
Drills and reamers	52%	14%	Company A	15%
			Company B	13
Taps and dies	13	9	Company B	15
			Company C	
End mills and aircraft specials	11	10	Company D	20
			Company B	20
			Company E	10
			Company F	10
ATT (assembled threading tools)	10	33	Company B	35
			Company G	20
Saws and cutters	4		(Over 100 domestic manufacturers)	
Other/miscellaneous	10			
	100%			

B. Seven-Year Market Share

	1981	1980	1979	1978	1977	1976
Drills	21.4%	21.2%	22.3%	22.9%	21.3%	21.6%
Reamers	21.5	21.5	22.2	23.0	21.8	22.8
End mills	10.9	11.6	10.3	10.7	10.5	10.8
Taps and dies	10.7	11.7	10.7	10.0	10.0	9.9

Note: Some figures have been disguised. Key relationships have been preserved.

Exhibit 5

Bartlett's Memo on Product Management Concept

Date: March 31, 1982

To: Field Selling Organization   Office:

From: J. T. Bartlett   Office:

Subject: Role of the product manager in our business

Even though we have done considerable communicating about the role of the product manager in our business, I think we have a way to go in making this concept work to produce solid benefits. I am therefore writing to underscore some fundamental points about the product management function and how it should work in CTD's business.

The first and most important point you should understand is our product managers' function as general managers. They have profit and loss responsibility for major segments of our business. Whenever there is a problem in the field, whenever a customer is not being served, whenever we are missing a promised delivery date, whenever a competitor is introducing a product or launching a new initiative in pricing or promotion, the product managers should know. When you are not receiving the kind of support you need from the managers of manufacturing, engineering, or customer service, you should immediately contact your area manager who in turn will call the appropriate product manager. If your area manager is not available and the situation is urgent, you should reach Bert Finlay or one of the product managers directly. Let me stress that this does not mean that the product managers are a "dumping ground" for minor complaints and petty gripes. On the contrary we expect you to handle that level of customer dissatisfaction.

However, if we are about to miss a major opportunity because of our inability to respond in a timely manner, the product manager should know. Only by communication at this level will it be possible for the product managers to be effective.

Secondly, it is impossible for our product managers to function unless they are aware of our competitors' moves and your thoughts on how we should serve our customers or markets better. I never cease to be impressed when I'm with you to hear your ideas and market intelligence. These ideas, particularly those coming from your knowledge of competitors, are invaluable input for our tactical planning as well as our long-term strategic thinking. We need to hear as much as we can from the field about these activities. Without a keen sense of competition we are surely going to hit endless foul balls in our marketing direction. Hence everything you know relating to our competition must be communicated to the product managers. A written format for this information will be forthcoming.

Exhibit 6

Organization Chart as of January 1981

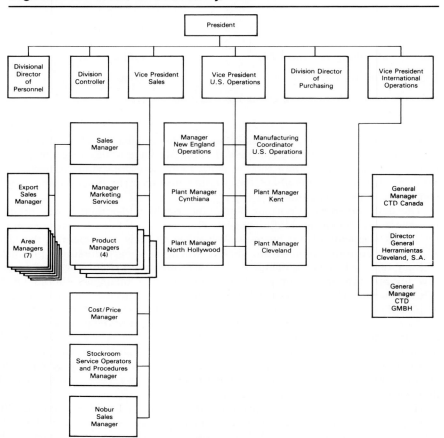

Exhibit 7

Organization Chart as of April 1982

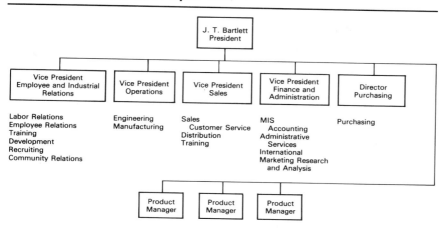

Exhibit 8

CTD Five-Year Strategic Plan Summary

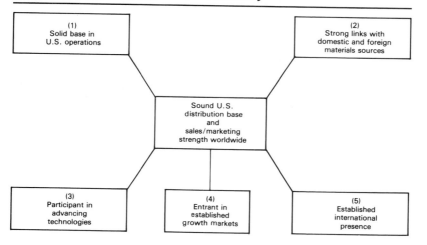

Marshall-Bartlett, Incorporated (A)[1]

After an 18-month search for an operating company, Paul Marshall and his partner John Anderson had acquired Harco Associates, a small firm that designed printed circuit boards[2] and had sales of $1.5 million in 1982. The acquisition had become final on July 26, 1983.

On August 4, little more than a week after the closing, a potentially serious rift had developed between Ken Stinson, Harco's general manager, and Tom Haven, Harco's president/founder, concerning their respective duties in the newly acquired firm. Marshall and Anderson faced a wide array of operational problems at Harco, and these were tough enough to solve without a quarrel between Harco managers. Another cause for concern was the confusion and anxiety that reportedly spread among Harco employees following a memo they had received from Ken Stinson a few days earlier, on August 1 (see Exhibit 1). Marshall had been unable

---

[1] All names have been disguised except for Paul Marshall, John Anderson, and Marshall-Bartlett, Incorporated.

[2] A printed circuit board was a flat piece of plastic clad in a very thin layer of copper. Electric-circuit patterns were made on the board, normally by photoengraving, using the copper as a conductor to route electrical signals. Printed circuit boards were first introduced just after World War II and by 1983 had become a standard item in a vast array of applications. Simple, single-sided boards were found, for example, in radios, TV sets, automobiles, and many home appliances. Multilayered boards were used in computers, process-control equipment, navigation systems, and many other complex devices.

Copyright © 1984 by the President and Fellows of Harvard College
Harvard Business School case 385–158

644

to contact Tom Haven, who had left with his wife, Susan, on a week's Caribbean vacation soon after the closing of the Harco sale.

Marshall and Anderson had high expectations for this acquisition and hoped it would be the first of several. They were aware that the period immediately after the acquisition could set the tone for their future relationship with Harco, and they wondered what they should do.

Marshall-Bartlett, Incorporated

Paul Marshall was president of Marshall-Bartlett, Incorporated (MBI), a consulting firm with 11 employees, located in Lexington, Massachusetts. Founded in 1981, MBI counseled senior managers in both private and public sector organizations and had revenues in 1982 of almost $1 million. The firm's practice covered a wide range of management areas, including strategic planning, marketing, operations, and general economic and financial analysis. MBI's principals also provided expert testimony in complex legal cases involving international trade and the management of very large projects. For example, Paul Marshall spent much of the summer of 1983 testifying in litigation concerning the Alaska Pipeline.

Marshall was an electrical engineer with an MBA and a DBA from the Harvard Business School (HBS). He had joined the HBS faculty in 1968 and had co-authored textbooks on production/operations management and managerial economics. He had been a popular teacher, and his courses had been frequently oversubscribed. In 1976 he left Harvard and founded a management consulting firm, which he left after five years to form MBI. A gregarious man with infectious enthusiasm, Marshall was an expert in the technology and economics of the steel and oil industries and in the management of large-scale projects.

John Anderson was MBI's treasurer, responsible primarily for its financial policies and operations. Anderson was a quiet, good-natured man who shared with Marshall a quick intellect, sense of humor, and an appetite for hard work. Anderson had a BA in marketing and an MBA from Michigan State University. He had 15 years of experience as a manager in both large and small companies and had served in a variety of functions, including operations, engineering, and sales. He had founded two successful retail businesses of his own, one in 1971 and another in 1975. In both cases he had designed the accounting systems, set up and implemented the marketing programs, and hired the initial personnel.

From the start of their partnership, Marshall and Anderson had intended to expand beyond the traditional bounds of management consulting and to acquire a series of operating companies. "I recognized that management consulting was a good field for me," Marshall said, "but I also wanted to build some equity through private ownership of operating firms. In this way I could have income that did not depend on my selling my time." The two men had sought small- or medium-sized local firms that lacked general management expertise and access to capital. Because of their training and experience, Marshall and Anderson were confident they could supply these qualities. The two men, who were both 42 years old, had extensive contacts in the Boston area among both academics and practitioners in business. They were at ease with bankers and accountants and understood the process of raising capital.

Acquisition Strategy

Eighteen months earlier Marshall and Anderson had defined the kind of company they wished to acquire. Their acquisition plan contained the following characteristics:

1. A proven historical earnings performance.
2. A strong balance sheet, with limited long-term debt, and a substantial portion of total assets in equipment, plant, and machinery.
3. A clear competitive advantage.
4. Competent functional management, especially in sales and operations.
5. A stable product and process technology.
6. Growth potential that would not require major increases in working capital.
7. Limited cyclicality and seasonality in product demand.

Essentially Marshall and Anderson were looking for small, healthy companies that had outgrown the general management skills of their owners and that were being sold for those owners' convenience. The two partners had decided to limit their search to the greater Boston area and to firms with sales between $2 and $10 million annually. They wanted to concentrate in metalworking and assembly, plastic fabrication, electronic assembly, or some related manufacturing operation. They had also decided that their acquisitions would be friendly. The original management would be offered an ownership share, and Marshall and Anderson wanted to retain effective personnel.

MBI planned to make their acquisitions by borrowing heavily against the assets of the acquired companies. The major use of the acquisitions' cash flows after purchase would be to repay debt and reduce the investors' exposure. Therefore, the partners needed to have cash flows that were stable and reliable. (For MBI's financial status in 1982–83, see Exhibits 2 and 3.)

Marshall and Anderson were aware that the market was by no means crowded with the kind of firm they sought. Still they had been surprised and frustrated by the difficulty of their 18-month search and had begun to grow impatient by the time they spotted Harco Associates, which was for sale for $445,000 through Boston Business Brokers.

Harco Associates

Harco Associates was located in Burlington, Massachusetts (15 miles northwest of Boston). The firm was the creation of Tom Haven, who with his wife, Susan, had built it from an operation in the basement of their home. Haven was 45 years old and had an associate's degree in electrical engineering from Wentworth Institute. He had worked for several years at Hanscom Air Force Base, near Boston. Dissatisfied with his modest government salary, Haven had turned to designing printed circuit boards (PCBs) part-time. He soon discovered he had a remarkable talent for this work and enjoyed a growing reputation among the high-tech firms that dotted Boston's Route 128.

In 1974 Tom Haven opened Harco Associates in partnership with a close friend. The partner became unhappy with his own inability to attract business, and Haven bought him out a year later. Susan Haven assisted the firm as bookkeeper and administrative director. While she had no formal training in these areas, her intelligence, resourcefulness, and organizational skills helped keep the little company on track as orders mounted.

By 1977–78 Haven had become convinced that the next level of growth would require a shift from manual circuit board design to computer-aided design (CAD). He sensed he was losing orders to his main competitor, Farley Corporation, which had moved toward automating the design process, reducing its costs dramatically. This presented Haven with a dilemma, for he had no idea how to go about buying a design computer. Also for a small firm such machines were a very large investment, costing up to $250,000. Haven needed more money but didn't know how to raise it, and found that he did not enjoy dealing with bankers, lawyers, and others whose participation was required if Harco was to expand. In fact Haven did not seem to want to deal with money at all. He felt uncomfortable if he had to ask his customers to pay their overdue bills, and some of his accounts receivable were lagging badly. He said later, "If I loaned a person $10 and he didn't return it, I would rather let him keep it than ask him to pay me back. I just don't like talking about this kind of thing." In the summer of 1979 Haven nearly quit the business out of frustration.

At this point Haven met Ken Stinson, who was then employed as a management consultant in the accounting firm that assisted Haven with Harco's business accounts. Stinson persuaded Haven not to quit and helped him with the computer purchase decision by suggesting sources of financing and by negotiating with Haven's bankers for a loan of about $90,000 for initial computer equipment. Before the bank would loan Haven this money it required him to submit a business plan. Haven had never heard of business plans and had no idea how to develop one. The accounting firm assigned the task of writing a Harco business plan to Ken Stinson, who later assisted Haven part-time for about two years before becoming Harco's general manager in February 1982.

The computer system Haven selected was the Gerber system, similar to the one Farley was using. By 1980 the new machine plus a growing number of employees required Harco to move from its offices above a liquor store in Wilmington, Massachusetts, to larger quarters in Burlington. These new offices gave Harco about 8,000 square feet of space.

By the end of the year Harco had 42 employees and three Gerber systems. Haven had also retained a manual design capability, positioning his firm as a "full service" electronic and electromechanical design bureau. His list of customers was growing. By 1982 Harco was averaging between 45 and 55 orders per month from nearly 100 different firms. Of its 1982 sales of about $1.5 million roughly one quarter came from two big customers (Digital Equipment Corporation and Wang Laboratories), with the rest scattered among 95 other companies. The accounts ranged in size from $35 to over $250,000. (A profile of Harco's accounts in 1982, factored by size, is shown in Exhibit 4.)

Tom Haven realized he needed some kind of distinctive advantage over Farley and his other competitors. He developed a close relationship with the Telesis Corporation, a young and rapidly growing company founded in 1980. Telesis produced PCB design computers that were far more powerful and flexible than the Gerber systems Harco, Farley, and other design firms had been using. Harco had purchased its first Gerber machine in February 1980 for $35,000, a second in the fall of 1980 for $35,000, and a third in March 1982 for $40,000. It acquired its first Telesis computer in February 1982 for $68,000 and a second in March 1982 for $72,000. Tom Haven found the Telesis machines to be a major advantage, so he rented a third, and Telesis loaned him a fourth one without charge later. These two were eventually purchased in May and August 1983. In return for Haven's help in testing its new computers Telesis recommended his services to its other customers and gave Harco discounts on the two Telesis computers purchased in 1983. Telesis was located only 20 minutes away by car from Harco, and relations between the two firms were mutually supportive.

With this improvement in capability, Harco continued to grow. Haven recalled:

> The business just snowballed on me. I never really thought it would get as big as it did. As time went by I realized more and more that I really didn't enjoy dealing with lawyers, bankers, and accountants, who seemed to have an increasing impact on how this company was being run. Also I can now see that competition is heating up, and there are emerging areas related to PCB design that are going to become more important. I am

not sure I will be able to get into these areas or even identify them in time. I want very much for the firm to succeed, yet I know I do not have the general management skills required for the future.

At the same time I want a buyer I can get along with, since I want to stay on here and continue doing what I'm good at, which is dealing with customers, interpreting their needs, and supervising the design process to get quality products out the door.

The Printed Circuit Board Design Industry

During the 1960s and 1970s the dramatic growth of high-tech industry around Boston had spawned a number of subordinate industries. Among them was printed circuit board design. Designers translated engineering concepts into photographs of each layer of the PCB for use in fabricating the boards. In a sense the board designers acted as architects, and their "product" was a set of drawings and plans for the manufacture and assembly of these increasingly complex devices. The boards themselves were then used in an enormous variety of electronic applications. The use of printed circuit boards in place of the hand-wired electrical connections that they replaced made it possible for manufacturers to achieve far greater performance in smaller space and at dramatically lower cost.

Small, independent firms like Harco Associates provided excess capacity for large companies like IBM, DEC, and Wang. These large firms had their own design staffs, but they often preferred to contract out some work during peak demand rather than hire designers who might prove redundant if orders diminished. There were two other sources of orders for the independent designers: manufacturing firms too small to have their own design staffs and other design firms, which were sometimes competitors and sometimes customers of each other.

The PCB design industry had developed nationally alongside the high-tech manufacturing firms that required design services. The design firms were thus concentrated around Boston, in California's "Silicon Valley," and in parts of Texas, Colorado, and North Carolina. Customers often preferred to have face-to-face contact with the independent designers since the design process frequently required detailed consultations. It was an industry in which a designer's personal reputation was very important.

In the Boston/New York area Harco had half a dozen competitors. The smallest had annual sales of a few hundred thousand dollars, while the largest had sales of several million. There was no single dominant firm. All competed along three dimensions: timeliness of delivery, quality, and price. The first two were most important since delays in design work could mean missing significant shifts in market demand. Price was the third dimension; the cost of PCB design was normally a small part of the total cost of the end product. These three dimensions were often in conflict, and designers had to balance them in each situation to suit their customer's needs. At Harco this balancing was performed by Tom Haven, usually in consultation with his designers and sales personnel, in direct meetings with a technical representative from the customer's staff.

Demand for the independent firms' services was growing steadily and strongly in the early 1980s. Tom Haven pointed out that Harco's business grew both when the computer and other high-tech business was very good (since Harco received overflow work from its customers) *and* when business was very sluggish (since companies using PCBs, especially the smaller ones, then quickly pared the size of their own design staffs). Also many customers were reluctant to invest in highly specialized design equipment, the cost of which would have to be spread over a fairly small number of designs.

The Printed Circuit Board Design Process

The design of printed circuit boards was a vital step in the production of any electronic or electromechanical device. The way the boards were laid out had a major impact on the size, shape, speed, reliability, cost, and other aspects of the end product.

The PCB began with an engineer's concept of a new electronic device and its electrical characteristics. The engineer produced a schematic drawing, using symbols to indicate connections among the integrated circuits and other components. This schematic, together with a description of the mechanical constraints (such as size) to be observed, was delivered to a free-lance PCB designer or a design firm like Harco to be translated into a set of instructions for the PCB manufacturer.

The first step in the design process was called "placement." It required great skill, creativity, and experience to lay out the many components so that they could be connected as simply and logically as possible and still stay within the design parameters described by the customer. Often this step required detailed consultations with the customer to ensure that all expectations were being met and to minimize the need to make changes later. (In spite of this effort, changes were common.)

The second step involved "routing" the electrical conductors among the various elements on the PCB so that electrical current would flow among them properly. The routes were portrayed as lines connecting the electronic components. The result was something like an architect's drawing of a highly complicated plumbing system. Routing had been done by drawing lines of different colors to represent conductors of different widths. This drawing was then covered with a piece of mylar, and opaque tape in appropriate widths was laid over the penciled lines.

Finally, the whole process had to be inspected for accuracy. The taping procedure was tedious, errors were common, and designers tried to discover them before the photos were sent off to a PCB house for manufacture.

This entire process had originally been manual, but by the early 1980s computer-aided design was rapidly pushing manual design into the background. Computer-aided design had been introduced by Gerber Scientific's "digitizing" system. The chief technological contribution of this change was to improve the laborious taping procedure. With Gerber digitizing equipment, an operator could specify the locations of all the elements and their connections by assigning them X-Y coordinates, working from the manually generated pencil design and transferring it into a computer-controlled photo-plotter that produced photographic instructions needed by the manufacturer. The Gerber system still required checking, however, since errors in placing the elements or routing the connections could be digitized without being discovered.

A new and even more powerful computer design capability improved on digitizing. It was called interactive design, because the designer or operator could intervene at any time during the design process to inspect the work for accuracy and make changes if necessary. Further, the new interactive computers were capable of actually routing the lines—a task previously performed by the designers. These high-performance design computers followed one of two concepts. The first concept was based on a large central processing unit with terminals. These systems were priced at $250,000 and up. The second concept called for a small computer system within a single unit. These systems were priced between $50,000 and $70,000. Companies producing high-performance design computers included Computervision, Applicon, Gerber, and Telesis.

MBI's Evaluation of Harco

On first hearing of Harco's availability in the spring of 1983, neither Paul Marshall nor John Anderson were enthusiastic. Harco did not have many of the characteristics they sought. Nonetheless, Harco was about the right size, and they both instinctively liked and trusted Tom Haven.

John Anderson was primarily responsible for evaluating MBI's acquisition alternatives. In his judgment Harco Associates had a number of important advantages. The first of these was the firm's personnel, chiefly Tom Haven himself. Haven had an excellent reputation in an industry where this mattered a great deal. In addition to being a masterful designer, Haven was outstanding at customer relations, able to determine what the customer needed and how best to achieve the desired results.

The unusually familial atmosphere at Harco also impressed the MBI partners. Susan Haven was a major asset. She was bright, hardworking, and her administrative skills contributed substantially to Harco's growth. In addition to his wife Haven employed his son, Dave, who was Harco's most accomplished Gerber system operator, and Dave's wife, Joan, who worked at the firm as a secretary. Most of the Harco designers and computer operators were young men in their 20s, and many of them had known Tom Haven from their Little League baseball days when he had been their coach. Still others had been high-school classmates of the Haven children. This atmosphere, Anderson reasoned, must have had something to do with Harco's low employee turnover, unlike the high turnover throughout the PCB design industry where designers were in heavy demand.

"The employees obviously like and respect Haven," Anderson told Marshall. "He is fair and completely open with them, and he doesn't play favorites." In a conversation that echoed these opinions an experienced Telesis operator at Harco added that Haven was also demanding, sometimes, she thought, excessively so. "He has a short temper and can really explode," she said. "But the storms blow over fast, and he never holds a grudge." This young woman said she had been offered more money by other firms but had never considered leaving Harco. "Tom hired me after one year of college and taught me this business from the ground up. Sure, I could get more money elsewhere, but I'm already making more than I ever thought possible, and I like it here."

Another Harco officer was Ken Stinson, Harco's 36-year-old general manager. Stinson was a certified public accountant with an MBA from Tulane University. He had been hired as Harco's general manager in early 1982 at the insistence of Haven's bankers, who had been concerned over Harco's lack of financial expertise. He was a "numbers man," skilled at the kinds of tasks Haven most disliked. Stinson had prepared a business plan for Harco covering fiscal years 1983–85, and the plan had been the single best source of information during the MBI evaluation of Harco. Marshall and Anderson considered the plan to be thorough, accurate, and well written. In a curious incident that baffled Anderson, Stinson had displaced Haven from his office upon joining the firm, although Haven retained the title of president. There was no doubt, though, that Anderson was impressed with Stinson's abilities. In his report to Paul Marshall, Anderson described Stinson as "very sophisticated in financial planning and accounting."

Harco's marketing effort was led by Ed Giroux, who was the lead salesman in addition to supervising two other salesmen. Giroux was a close friend of Tom Haven's. "I look to Ed for help in major decisions here," Haven said. "He takes a great deal of pressure off me and is a first-rate salesman." Stinson did not share Haven's impression of Giroux's value, telling Anderson that Giroux was not very effective. Most of the business came in on the strength of the firm's excellent reputation, Stinson said, and not because the sales force made any kind of integrated effort to obtain it.

A second major advantage Harco possessed was its technological position in the industry. By cultivating a close relationship with the nearby Telesis Corporation, Harco had moved ahead of its rivals. The interactive process was far more powerful than digitizing, and since Telesis equipment of this type was less expensive than its alternatives, Anderson believed it was bound to become more popular. A design produced on Telesis equipment could be altered by another firm using similar computers, but not on machines produced by other manufacturers. Therefore, increasing market share for Telesis might well result in more work for design firms like Harco, equipped and experienced with these computers. Haven had seen this development coming and had been training his Gerber system operators to become familiar with the more difficult interactive process. It required two to six months to train a Gerber operator to master the Telesis machine, depending on the capability of the operator.

Finally, there was Harco's demonstrated record. Sales had been growing rapidly since 1978 and had increased more than 50 percent between 1981 and 1982. (For Harco's financial performance between 1978 and 1982, see Exhibits 5 and 6.) Marshall and Anderson realized that fast growth was not among their original criteria for acquisitions, since growth implied the need to invest increasing amounts of money in the operation rather than the stable cash flows called for in their plan. Still they believed they could achieve better returns by improving Harco's performance with its present CAD computers than by purchasing more of these expensive machines. The chief source of this improvement, they believed, would be more efficient scheduling.

With these advantages Anderson originally wondered why Harco was being sold. He learned there were two reasons. First, Tom Haven simply disliked dealing with the business aspects of the operation. Haven was a designer and a supervisor of designers, and *that* was what he enjoyed, not being "hassled" by accountants and bankers. Second, Haven realized that Harco's need for funds could no longer be met solely through internal sources, the only method with which he felt comfortable.

According to Boston Business Brokers, the asking price for Harco was $445,000. In addition Haven wanted a five-year contract at approximately his current salary of $50,000. Haven also wanted the buyer to replace his personal guarantee for Harco bank loans amounting to $454,000. Finally, Haven insisted on retaining a number of key employees, including Susan Haven, Dave Haven, and Ed Giroux.

MBI Buys Harco

In July 1983, after considering Harco and negotiating with Tom Haven for four months, Marshall-Bartlett, Incorporated completed the purchase. As Paul Marshall and John Anderson had promised, the acquisition was friendly. The two consultants were aware of Tom Haven's strong attachment to the company he and his wife had built. The MBI partners were also aware that Harco's future profitability rested in large part on retaining Haven himself, since much of Harco's business was drawn in on the strength of his talent and reputation.

MBI did not pay the full $445,000 asking price. Rather the partners paid $150,000 in cash and gave Haven a five-year employment contract at the salary he had specified, plus a company car. Tom Haven was also offered incentive compensation equal to 25 percent of Harco's annual net profits before deduction of income taxes, management fees, and interest expenses above the existing level of interest. This incentive compensation paid quarterly was not to exceed an aggregate of $350,000 over the five-year period. MBI also replaced Tom Haven as guarantor of Harco's bank notes. Finally, Marshall and Anderson agreed to retain certain Harco employees for periods ranging from six months to two years.

In return, MBI became the sole owner of Harco Associates. Tom Haven promised not to compete in any way with Harco for five years. He remained president of Harco and was also a director. The other directors were Paul Marshall and John Anderson.

In addition to the purchase offer from Marshall-Bartlett, Incorporated, Haven had received an offer from another buyer that substantially met his terms. He chose to sell to MBI, however, even though MBI did not offer him the full up-front price. He did this for a number of reasons. First, he was impressed with Marshall's and Anderson's credentials and experience and was convinced that MBI had what it would take to carry Harco into the next level of growth and beyond. Second, he admired Marshall and Anderson personally and felt comfortable with them. Third, MBI's terms enabled Haven to make more money in the long run, if Harco turned out to be as successful under MBI as Haven believed it would be. Finally, the MBI partners were willing to let him remain independent; they would intervene, he thought, as little as necessary.

Haven changed his mind on this last point after the acquisition when he began to comprehend what would need to be done if the hoped-for growth were to be realized. After Haven understood the problems described below, he wanted Marshall and Anderson to spend more rather than less time at Harco. But the MBI partners, who were running their consulting business at the same time, simply could not spend the time that Haven desired. Indeed, the problems of managing this acquisition turned out to be much more difficult than Marshall or Anderson had foreseen. Since MBI was so small their resources were spread very thin during the period following the acquisition. Both Marshall and Anderson were each working well over 80 hours per week for much of that period and were exhausted.

Identifying Problem Areas

As Marshall and Anderson studied Harco in greater detail, they began to identify the specific problems that had to be solved if Harco was going to be a profitable acquisition. It was by solving these problems that Marshall and Anderson intended to add value to Haven's operation. Despite their considerable training and experience, both were surprised at how difficult it was to apply their resources to the situation at Harco. "I had taught production and operations management at the Harvard Business School," Marshall said later, "and I could easily see that this was a classic job shop. But it is clear that we'll have to go well beyond this label in order to be able to solve real problems. It is surprising how little the label really helps!"

The partners decided to focus on the areas they had earlier suspected would benefit most from their contribution: financial administration, operations, and marketing. By achieving better performance in these areas, they believed Harco could reach $2–$2.5 million in sales by 1984 without major capital expenditures.

The MBI partners had expected to find financial administration in fairly good order, since Ken Stinson—an MBA and CPA—had been at Harco for almost three years. What they found in the weeks following the Harco purchase in fact surprised them. Stinson had set up a computerized accounting system but had never bothered to show Susan Haven how to use it. Further, Stinson had asked a number of lower level employees to enter data into his system but did not seem to have explained the process to them well enough. The result was a set of computerized files full of information of dubious value. Meanwhile, Susan Haven, inexperienced with and distrustful of computers generally, had simply ignored Stinson's efforts and continued with her homemade manual accounting procedures. Her system had been effective as long as Harco stayed small, but to Marshall and Anderson it was clear it would collapse beneath the sales that MBI intended to produce.

As Marshall and Anderson became increasingly familiar with Harco they found that the lack of reliable data on Harco operations was even worse than they had feared. Although Harco now had four Telesis and three Gerber systems, scheduling and cost estimating were basically intuitive. No one knew Harco's capacity. "Tom Haven thinks he knows what the various jobs cost and how long they take," Anderson said, "because he has been doing this a long time. But he has no numbers." Earlier Haven and his assistants had established standard costs for the many kinds of jobs that came in and had these standards filed in an Apple computer at Harco. But as Haven explained to the MBI partners, standards were very difficult to define in a business like this in which each job was different and changes were likely to occur as the work progressed. Harco's standard costs appeared to have come from Tom Haven's judgment of how long it would take *him* to complete a job. Haven was obviously faster and more skillful than most, if not all, of his employees, so Marshall and Anderson were concerned that Harco's "standards" might seriously understate the actual expenditure of time and effort. This was a particularly important area for it was here that Marshall and Anderson expected to achieve the greatest improvements in productivity.

"Haven had never thought of his business as a pool of labor that must recover not only its own costs but also overhead costs," Paul Marshall said. "The key to reaching our profit goals at Harco is to get more work through the present facility. Yet the data needed to analyze this are not available. I don't believe that Harco has ever had a way to set priorities for jobs based on profitability."

In marketing Marshall and Anderson learned that Ed Giroux and his fellow salesmen had been on straight salary plus a small commission. Specifically, Giroux received a base salary of $26,000 plus a commission of 1 percent of the firm's net sales. The other salesmen had base salaries of $22,000 and commissions of 1.5 percent of their own sales. Marshall and Anderson wondered if this made sense since it did not seem to provide much in the way of incentives to the sales force. Another marketing question that intrigued them was the percentage of job bids that led to successful contracts.

In late July 1983 Marshall and Anderson had to deal with a problem that did not fit neatly into any of the three categories they had identified. This problem involved the conflict between Tom Haven and Ken Stinson. Relations between the two men had never been cordial, and the takeover by MBI brought their long-simmering quarrel to the surface. Just after the acquisition had occurred, and before Haven's trip to the Caribbean, there was an exchange of sharply worded memos between Haven and Stinson. John Anderson observed wryly that since they occupied adjoining offices, their memos could not possibly have been written to communicate but had to be "for the record."

Marshall and Anderson had just learned about the conflict between Haven and Stinson when they received a copy of Stinson's August 1 memo that had been sent to the Harco employees. The memo had arrived at a time when most of Harco's employees were about to be reviewed for salary and wage increases and for profit-sharing distribution. Although innocuous on the face of it, the memo caused many Harco employees to wonder what was going on. Some even began to be concerned about their continued employment with the firm. John Anderson, who was handling the day-to-day details of the acquisition, was shocked. "We were at a delicate point right then," he said. "The last thing we needed was to have Harco employees getting worried about their jobs."

Goals for the Future

In addition to their involvement with day-to-day problems, Marshall and Anderson needed to make decisions about future directions for Harco. Tom Haven was aware of activities closely related to Harco's basic business, and he wanted to expand into some of these before Harco's competitors beat him to it. One of these activities was computer-aided engineering (CAE). This referred to the automation of the process that preceded PCB design and that resulted in the engineering schematic that served as a PCB designer's basic instructions. The equipment needed for such an expansion was not as expensive as the interactive CAD computers: CAE systems cost between $30,000 and $40,000 each. A move into CAE would also require Harco to hire engineers to operate the new equipment. Skilled design engineers were paid $40,000 or more per year.

Using CAE an engineer could create a schematic on a computer, which would also run a diagnostic test to be sure the concept would function as intended. In fact, Haven pointed out, the computer-generated schematics could be "dumped" directly into the CAD machines Harco had been using, improving both speed and accuracy in the production of PCB designs. If Harco owned some of these newly available CAE computers, the company could also rent time on them for use by its customers' engineers.

Computer-aided engineering would make the whole process faster in another way. Ordinarily a PCB went from schematic to design to prototype to production. At the prototype stage somewhere between half a dozen and 50 boards might be manufactured. It was not uncommon to go through three or four iterations with a design before all the errors and electrical quirks were ironed out. With CAE these intermediate prototypes would be eliminated.

Haven was also interested in the possibility of expanding Harco into the manufacture of PCB prototypes. At the prototype stage customers were not at all sensitive to price but were very concerned with speed. "You can name your price with prototypes," Haven said. "A customer was in here recently, and he wanted a board in two days. I told him we could do it—for $2,400. That's about six times what it would cost if done on a normal schedule. We could do that job because I know some prototype manufacturers I can count on for really fast work. But I don't see why Harco couldn't both design the board *and* build the prototype."

In spite of his enthusiasm for Harco's future growth, Tom Haven said he had no interest in being the firm's general manager. "Titles don't mean anything to me," he said. "I sold Harco because it was getting too big for me. I just want to get design work done."

Paul Marshall and John Anderson had a set of goals that differed somewhat from Haven's. From the MBI partners' point of view the greatest needs were to increase sales, to improve productivity, and, finally, to consider Harco's future general management needs.

Marshall and Anderson wanted to achieve a 25 percent increase in sales during the 1984–85 period. "We need to generate more sales to have enough profits to pay down our debt," Marshall explained. "We need to get our ratio of debt to total capital down from around 80 percent, where it is now, to about 50 percent."

Reaching this first goal depended heavily on achieving the second, which was to realize dramatic improvements in capital productivity. "We'll need a major effort to train people," Anderson commented. "We may have to do some hiring or possibly go to more than one shift. We need to get more output from our machines."

The MBI partners' plans did not include significant expansion, at least in the short term. "We do not plan to expand into other areas for the next 12 to 18 months," Marshall said. "After that we might consider expanding Harco into PCB fabrication or perhaps into a new geographic area or into some related service type of operation. Further down the road, perhaps in the spring of 1985, we might also acquire some other company."

Exhibit 1

MEMORANDUM

To: All employees

From: Management

Date: 1 August 1983

Subject: Salary and wage reviews and profit-sharing distribution

Salary and wage reviews and profit-sharing distribution have been postponed for consideration. The most likely time for a decision appears to be between the fiscal year-end (31 October) and the calendar year-end.

If you have any questions or comments, please see Ken.

Exhibit 2

MARSHALL-BARTLETT, INCORPORATED
Income Statement
For 1 July 1982–30 April 1983

Sales	$899,623	
Interest income	12,563	
Other revenue	922	
Total sales		$913,108
Project expenses		90,111
Gross profit		822,997
Operating expenses:		
Salaries and wages	326,901	
Profit sharing	158,370	
VHI	54,247	
Taxes—payroll	21,829	
Insurance	19,701	
Medical reimbursement	10,773	
Professional services	29,356	
Rent	44,633	
Depreciation	17,100	
General and administrative	40,826	
Total operating expenses		723,736
Net profit*		$ 99,261

* Interim unaudited financials for nine months.

Exhibit 3

MARSHALL-BARTLETT, INCORPORATED
Balance Sheet*
30 April 1983

Assets

Current assets:		
Cash	$ 3,617	
Money market fund	76,291	
Accounts receivable	191,685	
Loans to officers	46,430	
Other	2,380	
Total current assets		$320,403
Fixed assets:		
Leasehold improvements	19,245	
Equipment and improvements	92,562	
Motor vehicles	12,717	
Organization expenses	4,000	
Miscellaneous reserves	(30,082)	
Total fixed assets		98,442
Total assets		$418,845

Liabilities and Equity

Current liabilities:		
Profit-sharing payable	54,370	
Accrued salaries payable	46,798	
Accounts payable	5,307	
Taxes payable	4,620	
Total current liabilities		111,095
Total liabilities		111,095
Equity:		
Common stock	167,670	
Retained earnings—prior	40,819	
Retained earnings—current	99,261	
Total equity		307,750
Total liabilities and equity		$418,845

* Investment in Harco Associates not shown.

Exhibit 4

Harco Associates 1982 New Sales by Size of Customer Account

	$0–1,000	$1,001–5,000	$5,001–25,000	$25,001–100,000	+$100,000	Total
Number of different customers	16	29	38	11	3	97
Revenue	$9,933	$85,155	$426,109	$490,716	$514,019	$1,525,932
Percent of total revenue	0.7%	5.6%	27.9%	32.1%	33.7%	100%

Note: The number of different customers should not be confused with the number of jobs. Many customers contracted for more than one job.

Exhibit 5

HARCO ASSOCIATES
Income Statements for 1978–1982

	1978	1979	1980	1981	1982
Net sales	$263,661	$534,562	$741,344	$987,671	$1,525,932
Cost of sales:					
Subcontractors	136,169	253,773	383,177	403,561	565,185
Salaries and wages	76,752	206,614	239,575	279,687	413,905
Payroll taxes	5,271	15,145	12,765	24,145	32,884
Purchases and leases	4,422	8,823	22,427	27,485	62,766
Amortization and depreciation	1,284	1,360	4,305	14,330	49,472
Inventory adjustment	(4,094)	(7,211)			
Total cost of sales	219,804	478,504	662,249	749,208	1,124,212
Gross margin	43,857	56,058	79,095	238,463	401,720
Operating expenses:					
Rent	3,750	6,000	7,833	13,809	15,420
Insurance	3,042	4,388	12,264	16,308	31,094
Interest	2,984	4,463	5,485	35,277	70,253
Office administration	12,371	17,582	20,841	70,009	100,339
Bad debt expense	17,535	1,445	474		16,496
Salaries—selling				36,776	64,901
Salaries—other				17,502	80,059
Total operating expenses	39,682	33,878	46,897	189,681	378,562
Income before taxes	4,175	22,180	32,198	48,782	23,158
State and federal taxes	890	2,367	7,624	1,884	2,512
Net income	$ 3,285	$ 19,813	$ 24,574	$ 46,898	$ 20,646

Exhibit 6

HARCO ASSOCIATES
Balance Sheets for 1978–1982

Assets	1978	1979	1980	1981	1982
Current assets:					
Cash	$13,173	$ 15,489	$ 23,476	$ 29,051	$ 36,877
Accounts receivable	40,613	130,207	128,111	228,300	274,063
Inventory	8,593	15,805	18,416	63,838	42,213
Other		1,767	2,784	7,378	27,048
Total current assets	62,379	163,268	172,787	328,567	380,201
Fixed assets:					
Computers				99,050	185,910
Equipment and vehicles	5,142	9,384	21,983	40,638	78,413
Leasehold improvements				26,144	36,904
Leased property					196,670
Less: accumulated depreciation	(2,391)	(3,751)	(8,056)	(29,190)	(85,461)
Total fixed assets	2,751	5,633	13,927	136,642	412,436
Total assets	$65,130	$168,901	$186,714	$465,209	$792,637

Liabilities	1978	1979	1980	1981	1982
Current liabilities:					
Notes payable	$ 25,000	$ 31,000	$ 31,000	$100,000	$158,479
Accounts payable, trade	24,544	84,074	79,985	140,927	108,416
Accrued expenses	3,352	11,895	2,400	37	27,354
Accrued taxes payable	690	1,663	5,093	2,516	2,512
Current portion LT debt		2,794	5,114	20,417	34,555
Other current liabilities					31,931
Total current liabilities	53,586	131,426	123,592	263,897	363,247
Long-term debt		6,118	7,191	98,483	305,096
Total liabilities	53,586	137,544	130,783	362,380	668,343
Stockholders' equity	11,544	31,357	55,931	102,829	124,294
Total liabilities and stockholders' equity	$65,130	$168,901	$186,714	$465,209	$792,637

The Implementation of Strategy: From Commitment to Results

Our study of strategy has brought us to the prescription that the way work and responsibility are divided, the choice of means for directing specialized attention to interdepartmental issues, and the design of information systems should not be allowed to divert attention from strategic goals. Structure should follow strategy, but structure once sufficiently well established to influence behavior and decision will then tend to arrange that strategy also follows structure. The latter tendency can go too far. Making flexibility and informality values of high rank, turning frequently to temporary ad hoc teams and task forces, involving specialists and interdepartmental inquiries—all help prevent organization structure from dominating and routinizing behavior. The effort to avoid the rigidity that limits the innovative capacity of static organizations means, for example, that job descriptions should never be regarded as anything more than a snapshot of the current status of a job designed to grow in responsibility as its performer grows in capability. The presumption in a developing organization is that as jobs expand with personal growth, routine activities can be delegated to junior persons with activities requiring judgment and decision performed by fewer people at senior level. The route to lean organizations is through expansion of responsibility, with higher levels of compensation rewarding the efforts of fewer people.

But deliberately checking the counterstrategic influence of bureaucratization will not in itself ensure that people assigned to different tasks in different locations will spontaneously choose the best course toward

663

even those goals to which in principle they are all committed. They will not automatically seek out the new skills they need as what they must accomplish becomes more complex. The innovative corporation is bent, to be sure, on preserving creativity, initiative, and the individual autonomy that makes original contribution possible. But even such an organization, one more typical of the 1990s than the 1970s, will need a set of administrative systems that will attempt equitable evaluation of performance, effective stimulus and reward for achievement, reasonable discipline and enforcement of policy, and the development of management, technical specialists, and producers at all levels.

The first purpose of such systems is to focus individual energy on organizational goals in such a way that individual goals are not needlessly thwarted. Another function of such systems is to acquaint new members of the organization, before they are qualified to be autonomous contributors to innovation, with the ways things are done currently, the kind of organization they have joined, and the standards by which they will be judged. A less attractive but necessary purpose is to constrain behavior that is irrelevant or destructive. Commitment to purpose will prosper if it is rewarded but founder if it is taken for granted or ignored.

When you come to appreciate the need of the NIKE organization, an extraordinarily successful marketer of athletic and leisure footwear and apparel, to develop structure and systems, you will encounter one of its officers making an interesting statement of the need of all contemporary organizations to communicate their requirements to young new-generation potential managers:

> Unless new employees, for example, are capable of assimilating NIKE expectations of centered hard work and caring, creative thought, NIKE will stagger under the weight of a jet-setting, self-centered arrogant—and average—middle management, who aggrandize themselves on a past they were not a part of, instead of striving for future successes in which they can share.

As you have probably observed, the processes we will look at have been studied and developed by specialists of several kinds. We will not attempt to summarize the state of the separate arts involved in influencing organizational behavior. We are concerned first with the limited but important ways in which the specialized bodies of knowledge can be put to use in the implementation of a given strategy rather than in the homogenization of organized activity. We will be suspicious of formality, rigidity, and uniformity but remain mindful that policy in the management of human resources is necessary for fairness and equitable opportunity for growth and advancement, for the protection of individuals against eccentric or biased management behavior, and for the defense of corporate strategy against willful opportunists pursuing their own purpose.

Establishment of Standards and Measurement of Performance

In any organization the overall corporate strategy must be translated into more or less detailed plans that permit comparison of actual to predicted performance. Whether standards are being set at exactly the proper level is never demonstrable. Commitment to attainment comes from negotiation to strike the balance between unreasonable expectations and unchallenged potential. The establishment of a plan will usually include improvement in performance over previous levels, but problems in the marketplace may make plans unattainable. Evidence that plans may not be achieved by the time predicted should be the occasion for inquiry into the problem rather than immediate conclusion that performance is defective. Your discussion of Tom Pringle's predicament in "Texas Instruments (B)" must have made clear the insecurity that short-fall produces in a manager aware of measurement and the kinds of counterstrategic action that such anxiety can produce.

The most urgent duty of any manager is to see that properly planned results are indeed accomplished. The pressure of this duty may lead to exaggerated respect for specific measures and the short-run results they quantify and thus to ultimate misevaluation of performance. Ready recourse to alibis and refusal to admit the validity of changed circumstances as excuses are equally inappropriate. So too is too quick a tendency to pass judgment rather than to take stock of the problem and to find new ways to deal with it. The problems of measurement cluster about the fallacy of the single criterion. When any single measure like return on investment, for example, is used to determine the compensation, promotion, or reassignment of a manager, the resultant behavior will often lead to unplanned and undesired outcomes. No single measure can encompass the total contribution of an individual either to immediate and longer term results or to the efforts of others. The sensitivity of individuals to evaluation leads them to produce the performance that will measure up in terms of the criterion rather than in terms of more important purposes. Since managers respond to the measures management actually takes to reward performance, mere verbal exhortations to behave in the manner required by long-range strategy carry no weight and cannot be relied upon to preclude undesirable actions encouraged by a poorly designed measurement and reward system.

Faith in the efficacy of a standard measure like return on investment can reach extreme proportions, especially among managers to whom the idea of strategy is apparently unfamiliar. Instances in which performance is measured in terms of just one figure or ratio are so numerous as to suggest that the pursuit of quantification and measurement as such has overshadowed the real goal of management evaluation. If we return to our original hypothesis that profit and return on investment are terms that can be usefully employed to denote the results to be sought by business, but are too general to characterize its distinctive mission or purpose, then we must say that *short-term profitability is not by itself an adequate measure of managerial performance.* Return on investment, when used alone, is another dangerous criterion since it can lead business-people to postpone needed product research or the modernization of facilities in the interest of keeping down the investment on the basis of which their performance is measured. Certainly we must conclude that evaluation of performance must not be focused exclusively upon the criterion of short-run profitability or any other single standard which may cause managers to act contrary to the long-range interests of the company as a whole.

Need for Multiple Criteria

As you discuss the cases that follow, you will be concerned with developing more adequate criteria. Our concern for strategy naturally leads us to suggest that the management evaluation system which plays so great a part in influencing management performance must employ a number of criteria, some of which are subjective and thus difficult to quantify. It is easy to argue that subjective judgments are unfair. But use of a harmful or irrelevant criterion just because it lends itself to quantification is a poor exchange for alleged objectivity.

If multiple criteria are to be used, it is not enough for top management simply to announce that short-term profitability and return on investment are only two measures among many—including responsibility to society—by which executives are going to be judged. To give subordinates freedom to exercise judgment and simultaneously to demand profitability produces an enormous pressure which cannot be effectively controlled by endless talk about tying rewards to factors other than profit.

The tragic predicament of people who, though upright in other ways, engage in bribery, "questionable payments," price fixing, and subtler forms of corruption, and of their superiors who are often unaware of these practices, should dramatize one serious flaw of the profit center form of organization. Characteristically management expects this format to solve the problems of evaluation by decentralizing freedom of decision to subordinates so long as profit objectives are met. Decentralization seems sometimes to serve as a cloak for nonsupervision, except for the control implicit in the superficial measure of profitability. It would appear to preclude accurate evaluation, and the use of multiple criteria may indeed make a full measure of decentralization inappropriate.

Effective Evaluation of Performance

To delegate authority to profit centers and to base evaluation upon proper performance must not mean that the profit center's strategic decisions are left unsupervised. *Even under decentralization, top management must remain familiar with divisional substrategy, with the fortunes—good and bad—that attend implementation, and with the problems involved in attempting to achieve budgeted performance.* The true function of measurement is to increase perceptions of the problems limiting achievement. If individuals see where they stand in meeting schedules, they may be led to inquire why they are not somewhere else. If this kind of question is not asked, the answer is not proffered. An effective system of evaluation must include information which will allow top management to understand the problems faced by subordinates in achieving the results for which they are held responsible. And certainly if evaluation is to be comprehensive enough to avoid the distortions cited thus far, immediate results will not be the only object of evaluation. The effectiveness with which problems are handled along the way will be evaluated, even though this judgment, like most of the important decisions of management, must remain subjective.

The process of formulating and implementing strategy, which is supervised directly by the chief executive in a single-unit company, can be shared widely in a multiunit company. It can be the theme of the information exchanged between organization levels. Preoccupation with final results need not be so exclusive as to prevent top management from working with divisional management in establishing objectives and policies or in formulating plans to meet objectives. Such joint endeavor helps to ensure that divisional performance will not be evaluated without full knowledge of the problems encountered in implementation.

When the diversified company becomes so large that this process is impracticable, then new means must be devised. *Implicit in accurate evaluation is familiarity with performance on a basis other than through accounting figures.*

A shared interest in the problems to be overcome in successfully implementing departmental and individual strategies makes possible a kind of communication, an accuracy of evaluation, and a constructive influence on behavior that cannot be approached by application of a single criterion. For one manager as for a whole company, the quality of objective and of subsequent attempts to overcome obstacles posed by circumstance and by competition is the most important aspect of a manager's performance to be evaluated.

Incentives and Motivation

Of the varieties of incentives available to influence behavior toward the attainment of results, monetary compensation is the most conspicuous and important. Whatever the necessity for and the difficulties of performance evaluation, the effort to encourage and reward takes precedence over the effort to deter and restrain.

Unfortunately for the analyst of executive performance, it is harder to describe for executives than for operators at the machine what they do and how they spend their time. The terminology of job descriptions is full of phrases like "has responsibility for," "maintains relationships with," and "supervises the operation of." The activities of planning, problem solving, and directing or administering are virtually invisible. And the activities of recruiting, training, and developing subordinates are hardly more concretely identifiable.

In any case it is fallacious to assume that quality of performance is the only basis for the compensation of executives. Many other factors must be taken into account. The job itself has certain characteristics that help to determine the pay schedules. These include complexity of the work, the general education required, and the knowledge or technical training needed. Compensation also reflects the responsibility of job incumbents for people and property, the nature and number of decisions they must make, and the effect of their activities and decisions upon profits.

In addition to reflecting the quality of performance and the nature of the job, an executive's compensation must also have some logical relationship to rewards paid to others in the same organization.

Furthermore, in a compensation system, factors pertaining to the individual are almost as important as those pertaining to performance, the job, or the structure of the organization. People's age and length of service, the state of their health, some notion of their future potential, some idea of their material needs, and some insight into their views about all of these should influence either the amount of total pay or the distribution of total pay among base salary, bonuses, stock options, and other incentive measures.

Besides the many factors already listed, still another set of influences—this time coming from the environment—ordinarily affects the level of executive compensation. Included here are regional differences in the cost of living, the increments allowed for overseas assignment, the market price of given qualifications and experience, the level of local taxation, the desire for tax avoidance or delay, and the effect of high business salaries on other professions.

Just as multiple criteria are appropriate for the evaluation of performance, so many considerations must be taken into account in the compensation of executives. The company which says it pays only for results does not know what it is doing.

Role of Incentive Pay

In addition to the problem of deciding what factors to reward, there is the equally complex issue of deciding what forms compensation should take. We would emphasize that financial rewards are especially important in business, and no matter how great the enthusiasm of people for their work, attention to the level of executive salary is an important ingredient in the achievement of strategy. Even after the desired standard of living is attained, money is still an effective incentive. Businesspeople used to the struggle for profit find satisfaction in their own growing net worth.

There is no question about the desirability of paying high salaries for work of great value. But in addition, profit-sharing, executive bonuses, stock options, performance shares, stock purchase plans, deferred compensation contracts, pensions, insurance, savings plans, and other fringe benefits have multiplied enormously. Regarded as incentives to reward *individual* performance, many of these devices encounter two immediate objections. First, how compatible are the assumptions back of such rewards with the aspirations of the businessperson to be viewed as a professional? The student who begins to think of business as a profession will wonder what kind of executive will perform better with a profit-sharing bonus than with an equivalent salary. We may ask whether doctors should be paid according to the longevity of their patients and whether surgeons would try harder if given a bonus when their patients survived an operation. Second, how feasible is it to distinguish any one individual's contribution to the total accomplishment of the company? And even if contribution could be distinguished and correctly measured, what about the implications of the fact that the funds available for added incentive payments are a function of total rather than of individual performance? In view of these considerations, it can at least be argued that incentives for individual performance reflect dubious assumptions.

If, then, incentives are ruled out as an inappropriate or impractical means of rewarding individual effort, should they be cast out altogether? We believe not. There is certainly merit in giving stock options or performance shares to the group of executives most responsible for strategy decisions, if the purpose is to assure reward for attention to the middle and longer run future. There is some rationale for giving the same group current or even deferred bonuses, the amount of which is tied to annual profit, if the purpose is to motivate better cost control. Certainly, too, incentive payments to the key executive group must be condoned where needed to attract and hold the scarce managerial talent without which any strategy will suffer.

In any case, as you examine the effort made by companies to provide adequate rewards, to stimulate effective executive performance, and to inspire commitment to organizational purposes, you will wish to look closely at the relation between the incentive offered and the kind of performance needed. This observation holds as true, of course, for nonmonetary as it does for financial rewards.

Nonmonetary Incentives

The area of nonmonetary incentive systems is even more difficult to traverse quickly than that of financial objectives. Executives, as human as other employees, are as much affected as anyone else by pride in accomplishment, the climate for free expression, pleasure in able and honest associates, and satisfaction in work worth doing.

The climate most commonly extolled by managers is one in which they have freedom to experiment and apply their own ideas without unnecessary constraints. Given clear objectives and a broad consensus, then latitude can be safely granted to executives to choose their own course—so long as they do not conceal the problems they encounter. In other words, executives can be presumed to respond to the conditions likely to encourage the goal-oriented behavior expected of them.

We may not always know the influence exerted by evaluation, compensation, and promotion, but if we keep purpose clear and incentive systems simple, we may keep unintended distractions to a minimum. Above all we should be able to see the relevance to desired outcomes of the rewards offered. The harder it is to relate achievement to motives, the more cautious we should be in proposing an incentives program.

Constraints and Control

Like the system of incentives, the system of restraints and controls should be designed with the requirements of strategy in mind, rather than the niceties of complex techniques and procedures. It is the function of penalties and controls to enforce rather than to encourage—to inhibit strategically undesirable behavior rather than to create new patterns. Motivation is a complex of both positive and negative influences. Working in conjunction, these induce desired performance and inhibit undesirable behavior.

The need for controls—even at the executive level—is rooted in the central facts of organization itself. The inevitable consequence of divided activity is the emergence of substrategies, which are at least slightly deflected from the true course by the needs of individuals and the concepts and procedures of specialized groups, each with its own quasi-professional precepts and ideals. We must have controls, therefore, even in healthy and competent organizations manned by people of goodwill who are aware of organization purpose.

Formal Control

Like other aspects of organizational structure and processes, controls may be both formal and informal, that is, both prescribed and emergent. Both types are needed, and both are important. It is, however, in the nature of things that management is more likely to give explicit attention to the formal controls that it has itself prescribed than to the informal controls emergent within particular groups or subgroups.

Formal and informal controls differ in nature as well as in their genesis. The former have to do with quantifiable data, the latter with subjective values and behavior. Formal control derives from accounting; it reflects the conventions and assumptions of that discipline and implies the prior importance of what can be quantified over what cannot. Its influence arises from the responsiveness of individuals—if subject to supervision and appraisal—to information that reveals variances between what is recorded as being expected of them and what is recorded as being achieved. If the information depicts variances from strategically desirable behavior, then it tends to direct attention toward strategic goals and to support goal-oriented policy. But if, as is more often the case, the information simply focuses on those short-run results which the state of the art can measure, then it directs effort toward performance which, if not undesirable, is at least biased toward short-run objectives.

To emphasize the probable shortcomings of formal or quantifiable controls is not to assert that they have no value. Numbers do influence behavior—especially when pressures are applied to subordinates by superiors contemplating the same numbers. Numbers are essential in complex organizations since personal acquaintance with what is being accomplished and personal surveillance over it by an owner-manager is no longer possible. As we have seen, the performance of individuals and subunits cannot be left to chance, even when acceptance and understanding of policy have been indicated and adequate competence and judgment are assured. Whether for surveillance from above or for self-control and self-guidance, numbers have a meaningful role to play, and well-selected numbers have a very meaningful role. We in no way mean to diminish the importance of figures but only to emphasize that numerical measurement must be supplemented by informal or social controls.

Integrating Formal and Social Control

Just as the idea of formal control is derived from accounting, the idea of informal control is derived from the inquiries of the behavioral sciences into the nature of organizational behavior. In all functioning groups, norms develop to which individuals are responsive if not obedient. These norms constitute the accepted way of doing things; they define the limits of proper behavior and the type of action that will meet with approval from the group. In view of the way they operate, the control we have in mind is better described as *social* rather than *informal.* It is embedded in the activities, interactions, and sentiments characterizing group behavior. Sentiments take the form of likes and dislikes among people and evaluative judgments exercised upon each other. Negative sentiments, of great importance to their objects, may be activated by individual departure from a norm; such sentiments can either constitute a punishment in themselves or can lead to some other form of punishment.

The shortcomings of formal control based on quantitative measurements of performance can be largely obviated by designing and implementing a system in which formal and social controls are integrated. For example, meetings of groups of managers to discuss control reports can facilitate inquiry into the significance of problems lying behind variances, can widen the range of solutions considered, and can bring pressure to bear from peers as well as from superiors. All these features can in turn contribute to finding a new course of action which addresses the problem rather than the figures.

Enforcing Ethical Standards

One of the most vexing problems in attempting to establish a functional system of formal and social controls lies in the area of ethical standards. In difficult competitive situations, the pressure for results can lead individuals into illegal and unethical practices. Instead of countering this tendency, group norms may encourage yielding to these pressures. For example, knowing that others were doing the same thing undoubtedly influenced highly competitive branch managers, rewarded for profit, in a national brokerage firm to overdraft systematically their bank accounts to secure, in effect, interest-free loans of funds to invest. Recurring violations of price-fixing regulations, in industries beset by overcapacity and aggressive competition, are sometimes responses to pressures to meet sales and profit expectations of a distant home office.

When top management refuses to condone pursuit of company goals by unethical methods, it must resort to penalties like dismissal that are severe enough to dramatize its opposition. If a division sales manager, who is caught having arranged call-girl attentions for an important customer, against both the standards of expected behavior and the policy of the company, is not penalized at all, or only mildly because of the volume of his sales and the profit he generates, ethical standards will not long be of great importance. If he is fired, then his successor is likely to think twice about the means he employs to achieve the organizational purposes that are assigned to him. When, as has happened, a regional vice president of a large insurance firm is fired for misappropriating $250,000 of expense money but is retained as a consultant because he controls several millions of revenue, mixed signals are given which may confuse the communication but call attention to the dilemmas of enforcement.

But there are limits to the effectiveness of punishment, in companies as well as in families and in society. If violations are not detected, the fear of punishment tends to weaken. A system of inspection is therefore implicit in formal control. But besides its expense and complexity, such policing of behavior has the drawback of adversely affecting the attitudes of people toward their organizations. Their commitment to creative accomplishment is likely to be shaken, especially if they are the kinds of persons who are not likely to cut corners in the performance of their duties. To undermine the motivation of the ethically inclined is a high price to pay for detection of the weak. It is the special task of the internal audit function and the audit committee of the corporate board of directors not only to make investigation more effective but to minimize its negative police-state connotations and distortions.

The student of general management is thus confronted by a dilemma: if an organization is sufficiently decentralized to permit individuals to develop new solutions to problems and new avenues to corporate achievement, then the opportunity for wrongdoing cannot be eliminated. This being so, a system of controls must be supplemented by a selective system of executive recruitment and training. No system of control, no program of rewards and penalties, no procedures of measuring and evaluating performance can take the place of the individual who has a clear idea of right and wrong, a consistent personal policy, and the strength to stand the gaff when results suffer because he or she stands firm. His or her development is greatly assisted by the systems that permit the application of qualitative criteria and avoid the oversimplification of numerical measures. It is always the way systems are administered that determines their ultimate usefulness and impact.

Recruitment and Development of Management

Organizational behavior consistent with the accomplishment of purpose is the product of interacting *systems* of measures, motives, standards, incentives, rewards, penalties, and controls. Put another way, behavior is the outcome of *processes* of measurement, evaluation, motivation, and control. These systems and processes affect and shape the development of all individuals, most crucially those in management positions. Management development is therefore an ongoing process in all organizations, whether planned or not. As you examine cases which permit a wide-angled view of organizational activities, it is appropriate to inquire into the need to plan this development, rather than to let it occur as it will.

The supply of men and women who, of their own volition, can or will arrange for their own development is smaller than required. Advances in technology, the internationalization of markets, the progress of research on information processing, and above all, the unexplored territory into which the innovative corporation will repeatedly venture make it absurd to suppose that persons can learn all they will need to know from what they are currently doing. In particular, the activities of the general manager differ so much in kind from those of other management that special preparation for the top job should be considered. In addition to assignment to a planned succession of jobs in different areas, this may include attendance at university programs of executive education, custom-tailored opportunity to study business-government relationships, or membership on the board of another company or a public service organization.

Strategy can be our guide to (1) the skills which will be required to perform the critical tasks; (2) the number of persons with specific skill, age, and experience characteristics who will be required in the light of planned growth and predicted attrition; and (3) the number of new individuals of requisite potential who must be recruited to ensure the availability, at the appropriate time, of skills that require years to develop.

No matter what the outcome of these calculations, it can safely be said that every organization must actively recruit new talent if it aims to maintain its position and to grow. These recruits should have adequate ability not only for filling the junior positions to which they are initially called but also for learning the management skills needed to advance to higher positions. Like planning of all kinds, recruiting must be done well ahead of the actual need. The choice of new members of an organization may be the most crucial function of management development and the most telling test of judgment.

The labor force requirements imposed by commitment to a strategy of growth mean quite simply that men and women overqualified for conventional beginning assignments must be sought out and carefully cultivated thereafter. Individuals who respond well to the opportunities devised for them should be assigned to established organization positions and given responsibility as fast as capacity to absorb it is indicated. To promote rapidly is not the point so much as to maintain the initial momentum and to provide work to highly qualified individuals that is both essential and challenging. The innovative company will find challenge for rapidly developing competence; it cannot remain innovative without doing so.

Continuing Education

The rise of professional business education and the development of advanced management programs make formal training available to men and women not only at the beginning of their careers but also at appropriate intervals thereafter. Short courses for executives are almost always stimulating and often of permanent value. But management development as such is predominantly an organizational process which must be supported, not thwarted, by the incentive and control systems to which we have already alluded. Distribution of rewards and penalties will effectively determine how much attention executives will give to the training of their subordinates. No amount of lip service will take the place of action in establishing effective management development as an important management activity. To evaluate managers in part on their effort and effectiveness in bringing along their juniors requires subjective measures and a time span longer than one fiscal year. These limitations do not seriously impede judgment, especially when both strategy and the urgency of its implications for manpower development are clearly known.

In designing on-the-job training, a focus on strategy makes possible a substantial economy of effort in that management development and management evaluation can be carried on together. The evaluation of performance can be simultaneously administered as an instrument of development. For example, any manager could use a conference with his superiors not only to discuss variances from budgeted departmental performance but also to discover how far his or her suggested solutions are appropriate or inappropriate and why. In all such cases discussion of objectives proposed, problems encountered, and results obtained provide opportunities for inquiry, for instruction and counsel, and for learning what needs to be done and at what level of effectiveness.

Besides providing an ideal opportunity for learning, concentration on objectives permits delegation to juniors of choice of means and other decision-making responsibilities otherwise hard to come by. Throughout the top levels of the corporation, if senior management is spending adequate time on the surveillance of the environment and on the study of strategic alternatives, then the responsibility for day-to-day operations must necessarily be delegated. Since juniors cannot learn how to bear responsibility without having it, this necessity is of itself conducive to learning. If, within limits, responsibility for the choice of means to obtain objectives is also delegated, opportunity is presented for innovation, experimentation, and creative approaches to problem solving. Where ends rather than means are the object of attention and agreement exists on what ends are and should be, means may be allowed to vary at the discretion of the developing junior manager. The clearer the company's goals, the smaller the emphasis that must be placed on uniformity and the greater the opportunity for initiative. Freedom to make mistakes and achieve success is more productive in developing executive skills than practice in following detailed how-to-do-it instructions designed by superiors or staff specialists. Commitment to purpose rather than to procedures appears to energize initiative.

Management Development and Corporate Purpose

A stress on purpose rather than on procedures suggests that organizational climate, though intangible, is more important to individual growth than the mechanisms of personnel administration. The development of each individual in the direction best suited both to his or her own powers and to organizational needs is most likely to take place in the company where everybody is encouraged to work at the height of his or her ability and is rewarded for doing so. Such a company must have a clear idea of what it is and what it intends to become. With this idea sufficiently institutionalized so that organization members grow committed to it, the effort required for achievement will be forthcoming without elaborate incentives and coercive controls. Purpose, especially if considered worth accomplishing, is the most powerful incentive to accomplishment. If goals are not set high enough, they must be reset—as high as developing creativity and accelerating momentum suggest.

In short, from the point of view of general management, management development is not a combination of staff activities and formal training designed to provide neophytes with a common body of knowledge or to produce a generalized good manager. Rather, development is inextricably linked to organizational purpose, which shapes to its own requirements the kind, rate, and amount of development which takes place. It is a process by which men and women are professionally equipped to be—as far as possible in advance of the need—what the evolving strategy of the firm requires them to be, at the required level of excellence.

Chief executives will have a special interest of their own in the process of management development. For standards of performance, measures for accurate evaluation, incentives, and controls will have a lower priority in their eyes than a committed organization, manned by people who know what they are supposed to do and committed to the overall ends to which their particular activities contribute.

*   *   *   *   *

In examining the cases that follow and in reflecting on the companies already examined, try to identify the strategy of the company and the structure of relationships established to implement it. What pattern of possible incentives encouraging appropriate behavior can be identified? Do they converge on desired outcomes? What restraints and controls discouraging inappropriate behavior are in force? What changes in measurement, incentive, and control systems would you recommend to facilitate achievement of goals? If your analysis of the company's situation suggests that strategy and structure should be changed, such recommendations should, of course, precede your suggested plans for effective implementation.

Basic Industries

In May 1966 Pete Adams, plant manager of Basic Industries' Chicago plant, was worried about the new facilities proposal for toranium. His division, metal products, was asking for $1 million to build facilities which would be at full capacity in less than a year and a half (if forecasted sales were realized). Yet the divisional vice president for production seemed more interested in where the new facility was to go than in how big it should be. Adams wondered how, as plant manager, his salary and performance review would look in 1968 with the new facility short of capacity.

Basic Industries, Metal Products Division

Basic Industries engaged in a number of activities ranging from shipbuilding to the manufacture of electronic components. The corporation was organized into five autonomous divisions (see Exhibit 1). In 1965 these divisions had sales totaling $500 million. Of the five, the metal products division was the most profitable. In 1965 this division realized an aftertax income of $16 million on sales of $110 million and an investment of $63.7 million.

This position of profit leadership within the company had not always been held by metal products. In fact, in the early 1950s Basic's top management had considered dropping the division. At that time the

Copyright © 1968 by the President and Fellows of Harvard College
Harvard Business School case 313–121

division's market share was declining owing to a lack of manufacturing facilities, high costs, and depressed prices.

A change in divisional management resulted in a marked improvement. Between 1960 and 1965, for example, the division's sales grew at 8 percent a year and profits at 20 percent a year. The division's ROI during this period rose from 12 percent in 1960 to 25 percent in 1965.

Ronald Brewer, president of metal products division since 1955, explained how this growth had been achieved:

> Planning goes on in many places in the Metal Products Division, but we do go through a formal planning process to establish goals. We establish very specific goals for products and departments in every phase of the business. This formal and detailed planning is worked out on a yearly basis. We start at the end of the second quarter to begin to plan for the following year.
>
> We plan on the basis of our expectations as to the market. If it's not there, we live a little harder. We cut back to assure ourselves of a good cash flow. Our record has been good, but it might not always be. Some of our products are 30 years old. We've just invested $5 million, which is a lot of money for our division, in expanding capacity for a 25-year-old product. But we're making money out of it and it's growing.
>
> Along with detailed planning for the year to come, we ask for plans for years three and four. Our goal is to make sure that we can satisfy demand. Any time we approach 85 percent of capacity at one of our plants, our engineers get busy.
>
> They will give the plant manager the information as to what he needs in the way of new equipment. The plant manager will then fit the engineer's recommendation into his expansion plans. The plant manager's plan then goes to our control manager. The marketing people then add their forecasts, and by that time we have built up the new facilities proposal. On the other hand the marketing people may have spearheaded the project. Sometimes they alert the plant manager to a rapid growth in his product and he goes to the engineers. In this division, everyone is marketing minded.

*   *   *   *   *

> We measure plants, and they measure their departments against plan. For example, we have a rule of thumb that a plant must meet its cost reduction goals. So if one idea doesn't work out, a plant must find another one to get costs to the planned level. We make damned sure that we make our goals as a division. Our objective is to have the best product in the market at the lowest cost. It's a simple concept, but the simpler the concept, the better it's understood.
>
> Well, on the basis of his performance against plan, a man is looked at by his superior at least once a year, maybe more. We take a pretty hardnosed position with a guy. We tell him what we think his potential is, where he is going to go, what he is going to be able to do. We have run guys up *and* down the ladder. In this division it's performance and fact that count. We have no formal incentive plan, but we do recognize performance with salary increases and with promotions.

You know, we have divisions in this company which are volume happy. We here are profit conscious. We had to be to survive. What I'd like to see is interest allocated on a pro rata basis according to total investment. I grant you that this would hurt some of the other divisions more than us, but I think that treating interest as a corporate expense, as we do, changes your marketing philosophy and your pricing philosophy.

For example, most new facilities proposals are wrong with respect to their estimates of market size—volume attainable at a given price—and timing. You can second-guess a forecast though, in several ways, and hedge to protect yourself. There is a feeling at Basic Industries that there is a stigma attached to coming back for more money. That means that if you propose a project at the bare minimum requirement and then come back for more, some people feel that you've done something wrong. Generally this leads to an overestimate of the amount of capital required. It turns out that if you have the money you do spend it, so that this stigma leads to overspending on capital projects. We at metal products are trying to correct this. First, we screen projects closely. We go over them with a fine-tooth comb. Second, internally we set a goal to spend less than we ask for where there is a contingency.

Also when a project comes in at an estimated 50 percent return, we cut the estimate down. Everyone does. The figure might go out at 30 percent. But this practice works the other way, too. For example, in 1958 Bill Mason [metal products' vice president of production] and I worked like hell to get a project through. Although it looked like 8 percent on paper, we knew that we could get the costs way down once it got going, so we put it through at 12 percent. We're making double that on it today. We haven't had a capital request rejected by the finance committee [see Exhibit 1] in eight years.

Of course, every once in a while we shoot some craps, but not too often. We are committed to a specific growth rate in net income and ROI. Therefore, we are selective in what we do and how we spend our money. It's seldom that we spend $500,000 to develop something until we know it's got real market potential. You just don't send 100 samples out and then forecast a flood of orders. New products grow slowly. It takes six or seven years. And given that it takes this long, it doesn't take a lot of capital to develop and test our new ideas. Before you really invest, you've done your homework. Over the years we've done a good job in our new products, getting away from the aircraft industry. In 1945 70 percent of our business was based on aircraft. Today it's 40 percent. The way we do things protects us. We have to have a very strong sense of the technical idea and the scope of the market before we invest heavily.

The metal products division's main business was producing a variety of basic and rare nonferrous metals and alloys such as nickel, nickel-beryllium, and titanium in a myriad of sizes and shapes for electrical, mechanical, and structural uses in industry. One of the division's major strengths was its leadership in high-performance material technology. Through patents and a great deal of proprietary experience, metal products had a substantial technological lead on its competitors.

Toranium

In the late 1950s metal products decided to follow its technological knowledge and proprietary production skills into the high-performance materials market. One of metal products' most promising new materials was toranium, for which Jim Roberts was product manager (see Exhibit 1).

Roberts was 33 years old and had a Ph.D. in chemical engineering. Prior to becoming a product manager, he had worked in one of metal products' research laboratories. Roberts explained some of toranium's history:

> Developing toranium was a trial-and-error process. The lab knew that the properties of the class of high-performance materials to which toranium belonged were unusually flexible and, therefore, felt such materials had to be useful. So it was an act of faith that led R&D to experiment with different combinations of these materials. They had no particular application in mind.
>
> In 1957 we developed the first usable toranium. Our next problem was finding applications for it. It cost $50 a pound. However, since a chemist in the lab thought we could make it for less, we began to look for applications.
>
> In 1962 I entered the picture.
>
> I discovered it was an aerospace business. When the characteristics of our material were announced to the aerospace people, they committed themselves to it. Our competitors were asleep. They weren't going to the customer. I went out and called on the customers and developed sales.
>
> In 1963 we decided to shift the pilot plant from the lab and give it to the production people at Akron. We decided that we simply were not getting a good production-oriented consideration of the process problems. The people at Akron cut the costs by two thirds and the price stayed the same.
>
> In 1963 I also chose to shut off R&D on toranium because it couldn't help in the marketplace. We had to learn more in the marketplace before we could use and direct R&D.
>
> I ought to mention that under the management system used by Mr. Samuels [vice president of R&D], the product manager, along with R&D and production, shares in the responsibility for monitoring and directing an R&D program. This arrangement is part of an attempt to keep everyone market oriented.
>
> From 1962 to 1965 sales of toranium increased from $250,000 a year to $1 million a year just by seeking them, and in 1965 we put R&D back in.
>
> This material can't miss. It has a great combination of properties: excellent machinability, thermal shock resistance, and heat insulation. Moreover it is an excellent electrical conductor.
>
> We can sell all that we can produce. Customers are coming to us with their needs. They have found that toranium's properties and our technical capabilities are superior to anything or anyone in the market.
>
> Moreover pricing has not been a factor in the development of markets to date. In fact, sales have been generated by the introduction of improved grades of toranium at premium prices. Presently, General Electric represents our only competition, but we expect that Union Carbide will be in the

marketplace with competitive materials during the next few years. However, I don't expect anyone to be significantly competitive before 1968. Anyway, competition might actually help a little bit in expanding the market and stimulating the customers as well as in educating our own R&D.

Now if one assumes that no other corporation will offer significant competition to toranium until 1968, the only real uncertainty in our forecasts for toranium is related to metal products' technical and marketing abilities. R&D must develop the applications it is currently working on, and production will have to make them efficiently.

This production area can be a real headache. For example, R&D developed a toranium part for one of our fighter bombers. However, two out of three castings cracked. On the other hand we've got the best skills in the industry with respect to high-pressure casting. If we can't do it, no one can.

The final uncertainty is new demand. I've got to bring in new applications, but that shouldn't be a problem. You know, I've placed toranium samples with over 17 major customers. Can you imagine what will happen if even two or three of them pay off? As far as I'm concerned, if the forecasts for toranium are inaccurate, they're underestimates of future sales.

New Facilities Proposal

Sam Courtney, district works manager (to whom the plant managers of the Chicago, Akron, and Indianapolis plants reported), explained the origin of the new toranium facilities proposal:

The product manager makes a forecast once a year, and when it comes time to make major decisions, he makes long-range forecasts. In January 1965 we were at 35 percent of the toranium pilot-plant capacity. At that time we said, "We have to know beyond 1966; we need a long-range forecast. Volume is beginning to move up."

The production control manager usually collects the forecasts. Each year it is his responsibility to see where we are approaching 85 percent or 90 percent of capacity. When that is the case in some product line, he warns the production vice president. However, in this instance toranium was a transition product, and Akron (where the pilot plant was located) picked up the problem and told the manager of product forecasting that we were in trouble.

The long-range forecast that Courtney requested arrived at his office about March 1, 1965, and clearly indicated a need for new capacity. Moreover, Roberts's 1966 regular forecast, which was sent to production in October 1965, was 28 percent higher than the March long-range projection. It called for additional capacity by October 1966.

Courtney's first response was to request a new long-range forecast. He also authorized the Akron plant to order certain equipment on which there would be a long lead time. The district works manager explained, "It is obvious we are going to need additional capacity in a hurry, and the unique properties of toranium require special, made-to-order, equipment. We can't afford to lose sales. Producing toranium is like coining money."

At the same time, Courtney began discussions on the problem with Bill Mason, vice president of production for metal products. They decided that the Akron plant was probably the wrong location in which to expand the toranium business. Courtney commented, "There are 20 products being produced in Akron, and that plant cannot possibly give toranium the kind of attention it deserves. The business is a new one, and it needs to be cared for like a young child. They won't do that in a plant with many important large-volume products. We have decided over a period of years that Akron is too complex, and this seems like a good time to do something about it."

The two locations proposed as new sites for the toranium facilities were Pittsburgh and Chicago. Each was a one-product plant which "could use product diversification." While Pittsburgh seemed to be favored initially, Mason and Courtney were concerned that the toranium would be contaminated if it came in contact with the rather dirty products produced at Pittsburgh. Therefore, Courtney asked engineering to make studies of both locations.

The results of these initial studies were inconclusive. The Pittsburgh plant felt that the problem of contamination was not severe, and the economic differential between the locations was not substantial.

After the initial studies were completed, Roberts's new long-range forecast arrived. The following table compares this forecast with Roberts's previous long-range forecasts:

Actual and Projected Sales (Dollars in millions)

Date of Forecast	1965	1966	1967	1968	1969	1970	1971
March 1964	$1.08	$1.30	—	—	$2.20	—	—
March 1965	1.17	1.40	$1.60	—	—	$2.80	—
March 1966	—	1.80	2.50	$3.40	—	—	$5.60
Actual	1.00	—	—	—	—	—	—

In response to this accelerating market situation, Courtney and Mason asked Adams (plant manager at Chicago) to make a "full-fledged study of the three locations" (Akron, Pittsburgh, and Chicago). At the same time Mason told Brewer (president of metal products), "We're now about 90 percent certain that Chicago will be the choice. Associated with the newness of the material is a rapidly changing technology. . . . The metal products R&D center at Evanston is only ten minutes away. . . . Another important factor is Adams. Titanium honeycomb at Chicago was in real trouble. We couldn't even cover our direct costs. Adams turned it around by giving it careful attention. That's the kind of job toranium needs."

Peter Adams was 35 years old. He had worked for Basic since he graduated from college with a B.S. in engineering. After spending a year in the corporate college training program, Adams was assigned to the metal products division. There he worked as an assistant to the midwestern district manager for production. Before becoming Chicago plant manager in 1963, Adams had been the assistant manager at the same plant for two years.

In working through the financial data on the toranium project, Adams chose to compare the three sites with respect to internal rates of return. He made this comparison for the case where capacity was expanded to meet forecasted sales for 1967 ($2.5 million), the case where capacity was expanded to meet forecasted sales for 1971 ($5.6 million) and the case where capacity was expanded from $2.5 to $5.6 million. The results of Adams's analysis are summarized in the following table:

	Chicago	*Pittsburgh*	*Akron*
	(Dollars in Thousands)		
1. Incremental capital investment for capacity through 1967	$ 980	$1,092	$ 765
Internal rate of return	34%	37%	45%
2. Incremental capital investment for capacity through 1971	$1,342	$1,412	$1,272
Internal rate of return	52%	54%	55%
3. Incremental capital investment to raise capacity from $2.5 to $5.6 million	$ 710	$ 735	$ 740
Internal rate of return	45%	47%	46%

While the economics favored Akron, Adams was aware that Mason favored Chicago. This feeling resulted from conversations with Courtney about the toranium project. Courtney pointed out the importance of quality, service to customers, liaison with R&D, and production flexibility to a new product like toranium. Furthermore, Courtney expressed the view that Chicago looked good in these respects, despite its cost disadvantage. Courtney also suggested that a proposal which asked for enough capacity to meet 1967 forecasted demand would have the best prospects for divisional acceptance.

By the end of April 1966 Adams's work had progressed far enough to permit preparation of a draft of a new facilities proposal recommending a Chicago facility. Except for the marketing story which he obtained from Roberts, he had written the entire text. On May 3 Adams brought the completed draft to New York for a discussion with Mason and Courtney. The meeting, which was quite informal, began with Adams reading his draft proposal aloud to the group. Mason and Courtney commented on the draft as he went along. Some of the more substantial comments are included in the following excerpts from the meeting.

Meeting on the Draft Proposal

Adams: We expect that production inefficiencies and quality problems will be encountered upon start-up of the new facility in Chicago. In order to prevent these problems from interfering with the growth of toranium, the new facilities for producing toranium powder, pressing ingots, and casting finished products will be installed in Chicago and operated until normal production efficiency is attained. At that time existing Akron equipment will be transferred to the Chicago location. Assuming early approval of the project, Chicago will be in production in the first quarter of 1967, and joint Akron and Chicago operations will continue through September 1967. The Akron equipment will be transferred in October and November 1967, and Chicago will be in full operation in December 1967.

Mason: Wait a minute! You're not in production until the first quarter of 1967, and the forecasts say we are going to be short in 1966!

Adams: There is a problem in machinery order lag.

Mason: Have you ordered a press?

Adams: Yes, and we'll be moving by October.

Mason: Well, then, say you'll be in business in the last quarter of 1966. Look, Pete, this document has to be approved by Brewer and then the finance committee. If Chicago's our choice, we've got to *sell* Chicago. Let's put our best foot forward! The problem is to make it clear that on economics alone we would go to Akron . . . but you have to bring out the flaw in the economics: that managing 20 product lines, especially when you've got fancy products, just isn't possible.

Courtney: And you have a better building.

Mason: All of this should be in a table in the text. It ought to cover incremental cost, incremental investment, incremental expense, incremental ROI, and the building space. And Sam's right. Akron is a poor building; it's a warehouse. Pittsburgh is better for something like high-pressure materials. But out in Chicago you've got a multistory building with more than enough space that is perfect for this sort of project.

Courtney: Pete, are we getting this compact enough for you?

Mason: Hey, why don't we put some sexy looking graphs in the thing? I don't know, but maybe we could plot incremental investment versus incremental return for each location. See what you can do, Pete.

Courtney: Yes, that's a good idea.

* * * * *

Mason: Now, Pete, one other thing. You'll have to include discounted cash flow on the other two locations. Some of those guys [division and corporate top management] are going to look at just the numbers. You'll show them they're not too different.

* * * * *

Mason: The biggest discussion will be, "Why the hell move to Chicago?"

Courtney: You know, Pete, you should discuss the labor content in the product.

Mason: Good. We have to weave in the idea that it's a product with a low labor content and explain that this means the high Chicago labor cost will not hurt us.

Adams: One last item: Shouldn't we be asking for more capacity? Two and one half million dollars only carries up through 1967.

Mason: Pete, we certainly wouldn't do this for one of our established products. Where our main business is involved, we build capacity in five- and ten-year chunks. But we have to treat toranium a little differently. The problem here is to take a position in the market. Competition isn't going to clobber us if we don't have the capacity to satisfy everyone. If the market develops, we can move quickly.

After the meeting, Courtney explained that he and Mason had been disappointed with Adams's draft and were trying to help him improve it without really "clobbering" him. "Adams's draft was weak. His numbers were incomplete and his argument sloppy. I've asked him to meet with Bob Lincoln [assistant controller for metal products] to discuss the proposal."

The result of Adams's five meetings with Lincoln was three more drafts of the toranium proposal. The numerical exhibits were revised for greater clarity. The text was revised to lessen the number of technical terms.

Adams, however, was still very much concerned with the appropriate size of the new facility. "Mason is only interested in justifying the location of the new facility!" Adams exclaimed. "We plan to sell $5.6 million worth of toranium in 1971. Yet we're asking for only $2.5 million worth of capacity. It's crazy! But, you know, I think Mason doesn't really care what capacity we propose. He just wants 'sexy looking graphs.' That's O.K. for him, because I'm the one who's going to get it in the neck in 1968. So far as I can see, Brewer has built his reputation by bringing this division from chronic undercapacity to a full-capacity, high ROI position."

The next step in the toranium facilities proposal was a formal presentation to the top management of metal products on June 2, 1966. There were two capital projects on the agenda. Brewer began the meeting by announcing that its purpose was to "discuss the proposals and decide if they were any good." He turned the meeting over to Mason, who, in turn, asked Adams to "take over and direct the meeting."

Adams proceeded by reading the draft proposal, after first asking for comments. He got halfway down the first page before Brewer interrupted.

> **Brewer:** Let me stop you right here. You have told them [the proposal was aimed at Basic Industries' finance committee] the name, and you have told them how much money you want, but you haven't told them what the name means, and you haven't told them what the products are.

At this point a discussion began as to what the name of the project was going to be. The meeting then continued with Adams reading and people occasionally making comments on his English and on the text.

> **Brewer:** Look, let's get this straight. What we are doing in this proposal is trying to tell them what it is we are spending their money on. That's what they want to know. Tell me about the electronic applications in that table you have there. I have to be able to explain them to the finance committee. I understand "steel" and "aerospace," but I don't understand "electronic applications," and I don't understand "electronic industry." I need some more specific words.
>
> **Samuels:** [vice president of R&D]: Let me ask you a question which someone in the finance committee might ask. It's a nasty one. You forecast here that the industry sales in 1971 are going to be about $7 million, or maybe a little less. You think we are going to have 75 percent or 85 percent of this business. You also think we are going to get competition from GE and others. Do you think companies of that stature are going to be satisfied with sharing $1.5 million of the business? Don't you think that we may lose some of our market share?

This question was answered by Roberts and pursued by a few others. Essentially Roberts argued that the proprietary technology of the metal products division was going to be strong enough to defend its market share.

> **Brewer:** Let me tell you about an item which is much discussed in the finance committee. They are concerned, and basically this

involves other divisions, with underestimating the cost of investment projects. I think, in fact, that there was a request for additional funds on a project recently which was as large as our entire annual capital budget.[1] Second of all, as a result of the capital expenditure cutback, there was a tendency, and again it has been in other divisions, to cut back on or delay facilities. Now it's not really just the capital expenditure cutback that is the reason for their behavior. If they had been doing their planning, they should have been thinking about these expenditures five or six years ago, not two years ago. But they didn't do the estimates, or their estimates weren't correct, and now they are sold out on a lot of items and are buying products from other people and reselling them and not making any money. It's affecting the corporate earnings, so the environment in the finance committee today is very much (1) "Tell us how much you want, and tell us *all* that you want," and (2) "Give us a damned good return." Now I don't want us to get *sloppy,* but, Bill, if you need something, ask for it. And then make Pete meet his numbers.

Adams: Well, on this one, as I think you know, the machinery is already on order and we are sure that our market estimates are correct.

Brewer: Yes, I know that. I just mean that if you want something, then plan it right and tell them what you are going to need so you don't come back asking for more money six months later.

* * * * *

Brewer: I am going to need some words on competition. I am also going to need some words on why we are ready so soon on this project. We are asking for money now, and we say we are going to be in operation in the fourth quarter.

Samuels: Foresight [*followed by general laughter*].

Mason: Well, it's really quite understandable. This began last October when we thought we were going to expand at Akron. At that time it was obvious that we needed capacity so we ordered some machines. Then as the thing developed, it was clear that there would be some other things we needed, and because of the timing lag we had to order them.

Brewer: OK . . . now another thing. Numerical control is hot as a firecracker in the finance committee. I am not saying that we should have it on this project, but you should be aware that the corporation is thinking a lot about it.

* * * * *

---

[1] Metal products division's capital budget in 1965 was $7.9 million.

Brewer: [*Much later on in the discussion.*] There are really three reasons for moving. Why not state them?

1. You want to free up some space at Akron which you need.
3. There are 20 products at Akron, and toranium can't get the attention it needs.
3. You can get operating efficiencies if you move.

If you set it out, you can cut out all of this crap. You know, it would do you people some good if you read a facilities proposal[2] on something you didn't know beforehand. You really have to think about the guy who doesn't know what you're talking about. I read a proposal yesterday that was absolutely ridiculous. It had pounds per hour and tons per year and tons per month and tons per day and—except for the simplest numbers, which were in a table—all the rest were spread out through the story.

Adams indicated that he was disappointed with the meeting. Brewer seemed to him to be preoccupied with "words," and the topic of additional capacity never really came up. The only encouraging sign was Brewer's statement, "Tell us all that you want." But it seemed that all Mason "wanted" was $2.5 million worth of capacity.

Adams saw three possibilities open to him. First, he could ask for additional capacity. This alternative meant that Adams would have to speak with Courtney and Mason. The Chicago plant manager viewed the prospect of such a conversation with mixed feelings. In the past his relations with Courtney and Mason had been excellent. He had been able to deal with these men on an informal and relaxed level. However, the experience of drafting the toranium proposal left Adams a little uneasy. Courtney and Mason had been quite critical of his draft and had made him meet with Bob Lincoln in order to revise it. What would their reaction be if he were to request a reconsideration of the proposal at this late date? Moreover what new data or arguments could he offer in support of a request for additional capacity?

On the other hand Adams saw a formal request for additional capacity as a way of getting his feelings on the record. Even if his superiors refused his request, he would be in a better position with respect to the 1968 performance review. However, Adams wondered how his performance review would go if he formally requested and received additional capacity and the market did not develop as forecasted.

As his second alternative, Adams believed he could ask that the new facilities proposal specify that metal products would be needing more money for toranium facilities in the future.

This alternative did not pose the same problems as the first with

---

[2] The finance committee reviewed approximately 190 capital requests in 1965.

respect to Courtney and Mason. Adams felt that saying more funds might be needed would be acceptable to Courtney and Mason, whereas asking for more might not be. However, the alternative introduced a new problem. Brewer had been quite explicit in insisting that the division ask for all that was needed so that it would not have to come back and ask for more in six months. To admit a possible need for additional funds, therefore, might jeopardize the entire project.

In spite of this problem, Adams felt that this alternative was the best one available. It was a compromise between his point of view and Mason's. If top management felt that the future of toranium was too uncertain, then why not ask for contingent funds? This would get Adams off the hook and still not actually increase metal products' real investment.

As his third alternative, Adams decided he could drop the issue and hope to be transferred or promoted before 1968.

Exhibit 1

Organization Chart for Basic Industries

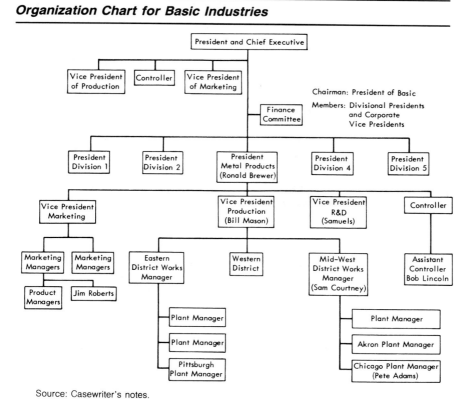

Source: Casewriter's notes.

Industrial Products, Inc.

On April 5, 1967, the finance committee of Industrial Products, Inc., approved its Equipment Division's capital request for $5.8 million to build a new plant for FIREGUARD, a line of fire protection equipment. However, in October 1967 Mr. Robert Kendall, manager of the Chemical Process Department (see Exhibit 1), the department in which FIRE-GUARD was produced, was considering the possibility of killing the expansion project. Divisional pressure for improved departmental earnings and FIREGUARD's continued record of substantial operating losses argued for not using the appropriated capital funds. On the other hand Kendall was well aware that many people in his department were committed to growing the FIREGUARD business and would be quite upset if the project were killed. The context in which Kendall had to make his decision was the following.

Equipment Division, Industrial Products, Inc.

Industrial Products, Inc., was founded in 1949 as a producer of refrigeration equipment. Since that time, the company had diversified its activities into areas such as material handling systems, machine tools, heavy industrial equipment, and laboratory instruments. In 1966 the company's sales were in excess of $350 million.

The Equipment Division was the largest of Industrial's divisions mea-

Copyright © 1969 by the President and Fellows of Harvard College
Harvard Business School case 369–019

sured in terms of sales revenue. In 1966 the Equipment Division's sales were $135.4 million, and its net income before taxes was $31.2 million on an investment of $96.5 million. FIREGUARD, the division's new fire protection line, contributed sales of $2.2 million but produced a net loss before taxes of $1.1 million in 1966. However, with forecasted potential sales in excess of $30 million per year and forecasted net income before taxes in excess of $6.0 million per year, FIREGUARD was considered one of the most promising new products in the Equipment Division.

FIREGUARD

In its continuing work on refrigerants, the Equipment Division's Refrigeration Department had developed a number of new plastic materials that exhibited superior fire extinguishing properties. At the same time the division already produced some of the kind of equipment needed to extinguish fires. Because both the equipment and materials required were readily available in existing businesses, experimental and then commercial sales soon followed. The brand name under which the division developed this business was FIREGUARD.

The division management was highly optimistic concerning FIREGUARD's commercial prospects. Whereas all automatic fire extinguishing equipment required extensive piping to create a system, FIREGUARD was able to operate with a number of physically independent modules. Thus the size of a FIREGUARD system depended principally on the number of module units in the area to be protected.

The source of FIREGUARD's advantage lay in the chemical process used to extinguish fires. The Equipment Division's scientists had discovered a relatively inexpensive chemical substance they called NO-OX that expanded with explosive speed when exposed to air, reacting with the oxygen to free a heavy inert gas. The fire extinction properties of the gas were immediately recognized as superb.

The attack on the fire protection and extinguishing market called for early sales of single module equipment to the "traditional" market for portable extinguishers (local governments, schools, fire departments, industrial plants, commercial offices). Sales of automatic fire protection systems to the same users would follow. Finally, the strategy called for expanding primary demand by eventually introducing automatic residential systems. Exhibit 2 shows sales of the portable units from 1961 to 1966. The automatic systems market was entered for the first time during 1966.

The FIREGUARD business was the responsibility of Mr. Robert Kendall, manager of the Equipment Division's Chemical Process Department (see the organization chart, Exhibit 1). The department manufactured and sold equipment for chemical manufacturing processes. In 1960 the division's general manager, Mr. Lon Fischer, had become concerned with the quality of performance in the manufacturing and construction of chemical process equipment while it was part of the general refrigeration area and had reorganized the activity in a new department—chemical processes—so that "the chemical phase of the business could get separate attention." Because FIREGUARD was a "chemical" business, it was moved into the Chemical Process Department at the time of its formation.[1]

The Equipment Division's assessment of the market was described by George Kramer, product manager for FIREGUARD.

> When we went into FIREGUARD we thought we knew a great deal about the fire protection business. However, we discovered that we knew very little and our customers knew less. They couldn't have cared less about the product. They were protected because they had to be according to the law or the insurance company. So we have had to study the job for the customer. The result has been that we have had a big learning and education program.

Commenting on Mr. Kramer's description, Mr. Kendall observed:

> We got into the FIREGUARD business because we knew how to build some equipment, and we had superior extinguishing materials. In fact we know how to build the containers very well. We make them at our Akron, Ohio, factory. But we're still learning how to put together the support equipment.
>
> The difficulty in engineering has been to learn the requirements of different applications. We are marketing a system, not equipment, and not extinguishing material. Thus most of our learning has to be in the field in a sequence of trial-and-error steps.
>
> Out of the first 300 units, we had to take back 100 over time. Now it's 200 out of 3,000. The engineers are still worried: they can explain what happens after the fact, but the problem of responding in a controlled way to undesired fires or explosions is still there.
>
> The other aspect of FIREGUARD planning has been market definition. It has been going on for five or six years as we have tried to move from fire departments to industrial plants to office building systems to homeowners. Each area is a different problem in the field. Different costs can be cut, different customers have to be educated, and in some instances different parts of our division have to be educated.
>
> For example, we have had an endless series of arguments with our automatic systems design group trying to define what fire protection was. When we finally got it settled, we found that we needed a larger container unit.
>
> However, the decision to build a larger container posed an important facility problem for us. We knew we were going to have to expand because FIREGUARD was already using 250,000 out of 750,000 production man-

---

[1] The NO-OX business remained in the Refrigeration Department. The Chemical Process Department "purchased" the chemical from the Refrigeration Department at a negotiated "market" price.

hours available at Akron. By 1970 the forecasts indicated that FIRE-GUARD would require 650,000 man-hours. And our other lines were growing.

Add to this the problem of the large containers, and it's clear we needed a new facility. We really weren't up to handle them in the existing facility. Therefore, I asked Steve Matthews, facilities planner for FIREGUARD, to study the Akron plant and make recommendations.

Steve Matthews's career at Industrial Products had begun at Akron. He left the company only to rejoin it later to work on a task force which introduced a new data processing system to the Cleveland facility. His performance on that job led to his assignment in February 1966 to head a team put together to study the organization and operation of the Equipment Division's activities at their Cleveland and Akron locations. This assignment was later expanded to cover a study in depth of the FIREGUARD facilities at Akron. Matthews commented on his approach to the study.

My problem was to get a feel for each of Akron's businesses out of marketing. I wanted a definition of the way we did business in each of these markets. It was not easy. For example, in FIREGUARD, George Kramer's forecast was the greatest problem. It was absurdly conservative. I needed to know everything about the business, the way it was going to grow, the role of the parts business, the nature of customer service, and exactly how the business was going to be run so we could design a facility that would meet these needs.

We started the study on the assumption that the business would expand at Akron (location) because it appeared economic to do so. It seemed that the question of relocation costs, the problem of building a new building, and the location of the market indicated that we stay at Akron.

So we were evaluating existing facilities in the light of the markets of 1970 and beyond. If our product managers didn't give us the forecast, we interpolated as best we could. We wanted to build a facility which would enable us to do business the right way in 1970.

Matthews had found the major elements of his problems to be (1) Akron was poorly run, the data available were poor and the manpower available to gather data not always adequate; (2) problems at Akron resulted from the way in which the relationship between engineering and production were organized, an issue outside the scope of the study; (3) many of the study group's findings reflected unfavorably on Akron management and therefore raised political problems; and (4) the group came to feel that the need was for a "mass production" type activity although Akron was typically "job shop" oriented. As a result, the facility being planned looked as if it would be a radical departure from existing facilities both in terms of physical design and the mode of operation.

In fact, by November 1966, when Matthews was to meet with Kendall for a final review of the FIREGUARD project, he had been ready to recommend a new plant in the Carolinas.[2] It was Matthews's judgment that it would be easier to implement the critical nonfacility[3] part of the FIREGUARD expansion project in the new location. He had explained to Kendall that "failure to undertake and effectively implement nonfacility programs would negate the effects of the proposed physical facility plan."

The last part of the meeting with Kendall held November 15 had concerned the size of the capital investment and its timing. An excerpt from that conversation is reproduced below:

> **Matthews:** . . . And I may be wrapping it up too soon, but we strongly recommend going to South Carolina. The existing manufacturing facilities are theoretically adequate to meet the FIREGUARD market demands through 1969. But, practically, we believe that conditions demand the acceleration of this project. Expanded production to meet 1967 and 1968 forecasts plus inventory build-up in anticipation of moving the production lines will be very difficult to achieve under the existing conditions. The new factory will be needed as soon as it can be constructed. We prefer to schedule the physical construction program to fit into the program for an orderly transfer of personnel, equipment, and procedures. Systems and procedures are to be completely worked out before this move is made. Our schedule calls for completion of the plant in the late fall of 1968, assuming that authorization to proceed is obtained in the first quarter of 1967.
>
> **Kendall:** There is no way we can invest incrementally?
>
> **Matthews:** I don't really think so.
>
> **Kendall:** What are we going to do when they won't give us $5.8 million?
>
> **Matthews:** You either bet on a business or you don't. You either believe the forecasts or you don't.
>
> **Kendall:** What if you believe half a forecast?
>
> **Matthews:** You couldn't build half a plant. You save some, but not a lot. What's a half? What forecast are you going to hang your hat on?
>
> **Kendall:** Half: I'll commit myself for half but want to be able to

---

[2] While Matthews formally reported to the Akron plant manager, he kept in close contact with Kendall throughout the FIREGUARD study. The Akron plant manager attended many of these meetings and was aware of Matthews's assessment of the Akron facility and its management. However, since the demand for Akron's other products was growing and their production caused less problems than FIREGUARD's, the Akron plant manager was not upset at the prospect of losing FIREGUARD.

[3] Accounting and information systems, inventory and production control systems, and material handling systems.

make the whole thing. Can't you build one plant for 1971 and then another just like it for 1975? Or what about some added subcontracting? Why can't we do more subcontracting since our manufacturing process isn't that unique?

Matthews: As for two plants, you put machines in for the product, and you don't need more than one, even for peak volume. As for subcontracting, our make-or-buy analysis shows that if we realize forecasted sales, we can improve our return by manufacturing some parts that we now subcontract.

Kendall: Well, yes, but if we really don't have a proprietary position in terms of knowledge and so on, why can't we subcontract our expansion in this area?

Matthews: The trouble with subcontracting is that you never make your delivery promises. It's just impossible to get yourself organized so that you can produce the kind of customer service you need.

Bob, I know your problem. You're thinking about our original estimate of $1.9 million back in June. The original facility was just a factory. This is also a warehouse and a service center. And given the nonfacility expenditures for systems, the investment per unit of capacity is the same as the original proposal.

Kendall had accepted Matthews's argument and arranged to have the FIREGUARD project presented to a meeting of the Equipment Division's executive committee on December 16.[4] Matthews began that meeting by describing the basic strategic assumptions of the FIRE-GUARD business. He described it as "a business selling hardware at a profit, based on warehousing, service, and parts." He noted that at the rate the business was growing, by 1969 they would be handling 5 million parts. That meant, he argued, that FIREGUARD was a large-volume production-oriented operation rather than the traditional job shop kind of business typical of Akron.

Excerpts from the meeting included the exchange below:

Briggs (Gen. Mgr.): The rumor mill had it that the new facility at Akron was going to cost only $2 million. Why is it that your proposal is so expensive?

Kendall: The original facility the people were talking about was simply a plant for the large containers. This is a much larger operation with many more products.

Matthews: Also the original facility was just a factory. Not only are there more products but this is a warehouse and service center.

---

[4] The divisional executive committee consisted of the division's general manager, assistant general manager, department managers, and top functional managers.

A substantial discussion of labor costs and related problems led to the question of systems.

Hughes (Mgr. Eng.): What about systems, do you have any allowance for the cost of all these systems you are installing?

Matthews: You have $175,000 project costs and $185,000 engineering, and that ought to cover it.

Hughes: That's not enough; how many programmers do you have?

Matthews: Five, I think.

Hughes: I think that is low. We had 10 programmers at East St. Louis [an earlier project] if I am not mistaken.

Golden (Asst. Gen. Mgr.): How many accountants do you have?

Matthews looked the figure up in his back-up notebook. He explained that the nature of the FIREGUARD operation was such that it would produce for a full warehouse rather than on the basis of meeting customer demand. Therefore, the demand on accounting was different from traditional equipment businesses.

Golden: I think traditionally we have had our overrun (spent more than budget) on systems and accounting.

Matthews: I think I understand your point, Bill, and we will do our best to take care of it.

After this discussion. Matthews presented the project summary shown below.

	1967	1968	1969	1970	1975
			(Millions of Dollars)		
Sales	$ 3.6	$ 9.0	$17.7	$24.5	$41.5
Net income before taxes	(1.1)*	(.4)*	.8*	3.9	7.5
ROI	—	—	7.4	26.0	32.0
Fixed investment	1.0†	1.2†	4.3†	6.9†	8.0‡
Working capital	2.5	4.7	6.5	8.1	15.5
Total investment	3.5	5.9	10.8	15.0	23.5

* Includes $1.1 million for noncapital items associated with the move: that is, costs of transfers, layoffs, training, equipment moving, and project management.

† Will provide space to satisfy forecasted sales through 1975 and equipment to satisfy forecasted sales through 1970.

‡ $1.1 million additional equipment will be needed to satisfy 1975 forecasted sales.

On April 5, 1967, Briggs presented the FIREGUARD project to the corporate finance committee. While questions of subcontracting, poor current performance, and future ROI were raised, the general feeling of the group was that the project was a good one and the business very promising. Therefore, after a short discussion, the project was approved.

Second Thoughts

However, Kendall was still uneasy about the FIREGUARD project. Matthews argued that the future market for FIREGUARD products was large and lucrative. Yet the earnings record of FIREGUARD since its inception in 1961 had been poor. Moreover, as sales for the product grew, so did the losses. (Exhibit 3.)

Kendall's concern was intensified when the review of his department's 1968 business plan was conducted in October 1967.[5] Divisional executives had expressed concern with the department's recent earnings record (see Exhibit 4). Moreover, Kendall was well aware that the corporation had specifically asked about the FIREGUARD business the previous fall. Since corporate requests for detailed information on an individual business were quite unusual, Kendall knew that FIREGUARD was in the limelight and that most likely there was pressure on the division officers to see that the business' performance improved.

In an effort to secure some guidance in this matter, Kendall asked Mike Richards, corporate director of planning, to discuss FIREGUARD with him. While Richards reflected corporate thinking he did not represent it. Therefore, the meeting between Kendall and Richards was in the nature of "informal advice" rather than "formal corporate review."

The October 27 meeting began with Kendall expressing his concerns to Richards.

Kendall: Mike, Briggs is putting pressure on me to raise the department's profits. But if FIREGUARD goes ahead with the approved expansion, earnings are not going to get much better. On the other hand, Matthews has some convincing arguments for FIREGUARD's market potential. To tell the truth, I'm perplexed.

Richards: Well, . . . from my point of view, FIREGUARD doesn't fit with the rest of our products. We make machine tools, material handling systems, and refrigeration equipment. We enjoy a close relationship with our customers so that we can understand and help solve their technical problems.

On the other hand, FIREGUARD is a mass-produced, standard-design product. Moreover, compared to our existing product

---

[5] The Equipment Division's business plan attempted to answer the questions "What will happen to our products next year and the year after that?" and "What do we plan to do about it?" Departmental plans were reviewed each fall by the division. (Performance against current plan was reviewed quarterly.) This plan review was a formal meeting in which departmental managers made presentations of their business plan to divisional officers. Officers were free to make comments and often did.

Plans were typically concerned with market size, market share, product volume, product price, and profit. Return on investment was sometimes used as a tool to measure the quality of a "business," but the business plans did not include specific investment planning. At most, a crude forecast of "capital requirement" was included.

line, FIREGUARD is mass marketed. That means problems of distribution and service that we haven't faced before.

Kendall: OK, but FIREGUARD's got a fantastic future potential. Its sales in 1975 could easily exceed the total department's sales today.

Richards: Look, I'm not arguing that you drop FIREGUARD completely. I'm merely saying that you don't really know how to market or produce the product very well. If I were you, I would be inclined to concentrate on improving FIREGUARD's profits and then grow the business after you've learned how to run it profitably.

Kendall: That's easier said than done. We've already asked for and received approval for a new plant. The division will not be too pleased if I now say that FIREGUARD should not be expanded for a while. Moreover, I'm sure Matthews will hit the roof.

Richards: Mike, you asked for my opinion and I've given it to you. I think it's better to retrench now rather than sacrifice current earnings to a project that has yet to make a profit.

Following his conversation with Richards, Kendall decided to speak with Matthews about the FIREGUARD project. Kendall began the meeting by explaining his concern over FIREGUARD's past and current performance and expressing pessimism about its future performance. To support this view, Kendall used many of Richards's arguments. Matthews responded quickly.

Matthews: First, it seems to me that the issue is closed since the corporation approved our request for capital funds. Moreover, I think their decision was a wise one. It takes money to build the marketing and systems capabilities we need to take advantage of the FIREGUARD opportunity. If we don't spend money today, we'll surely fail in the years to come.

Anyway, we've carefully timed our expenditures for capital and noncapital items so that we can cut back if the assumed market doesn't develop. For example, by December we will have ordered about $1.1 million in equipment and spent about $160,000 on noncapital items. Yet since the penalty for cancelling the equipment order is only $290,000, our total exposure as of the beginning of 1968 will be $450,000. (Cancellation of equipment was not allowed after January 1, 1968.) Moreover, while the entire capital budget of $5.8 million will be irrevocably committed by the end of 1968, we will have spent only $650,000 of our $1.1 million noncapital budget by that time. In fact, we wouldn't spend our entire noncapital budget until September 1969.

Also, even if FIREGUARD doesn't make it, you've always got a new plant even though most of the machinery is specially designed for the FIREGUARD product line. [The plant represented 70% of the capital budget.]

But this isn't going to happen. FIREGUARD has an enormous business potential. Moreover, the division will make as much on the NO-OX as it does on the equipment. But we both know that FIREGUARD is a new kind of product for the Equipment Division. It depends on the sales and servicing of hardware. This coupled with distribution are major factors to cope with. It's just going to take time and money to develop the capabilities we need.

Kendall: But we haven't done very well in the six years we've been trying to date.

Matthews: That's because we've been producing at Akron. Our new plant in South Carolina will solve many of our problems. Bob, it take time to develop a new business. The payoff doesn't come right away.

Kendall: Steve, that all sounds very good, but have you looked at Kramer's monthly reports for the first seven months of this year? [See Exhibit 5.] After six years it still sounds as if we just began.

Matthews: Even a great business can do poorly if it's mismanaged. We haven't been coordinating design with production. We haven't had a production line suitable for high-volume manufacturing. We haven't had adequate part standardization. We haven't put nearly enough money into developing the needed management and production control systems. Bob, I could go on like this for 10 minutes, but you know these problems as well as I do. How do you expect to make money given this situation? And you certainly can't blame Kramer for a manufacturing problem.

Kendall: You've got a point, but then where the hell does Kramer get his forecasts? Doesn't he take the production constraint into consideration?

Matthews: OK, you've got a point. However, I don't think that should influence your view of the future of FIREGUARD. A lot of people here have spent a lot of time on this project.[6] We have finally got it out from under Akron and have the resources to make it. I don't see how you can even consider changing it at this late date.

---

[6] While Matthews and about a dozen other men had spent over a year and half on the project, the possibility of moving the operation to South Carolina had been kept highly confidential because of its potential impact on the Akron work force. Thus, in addition to the people planning the facility, only the top division and corporate officers were aware of the decision to move the FIREGUARD production operation.

However, while the construction of the new plant had not begun by the time of the Matthews-Kendall meeting, some equipment had been ordered and options had been taken on a piece of land. The cost of cancelling the equipment order and the land option would be $105,000. Moreover, $114,500 had already been spent for noncapital items.

Exhibit 1

Equipment Division Partial Organization Chart as of March 1966

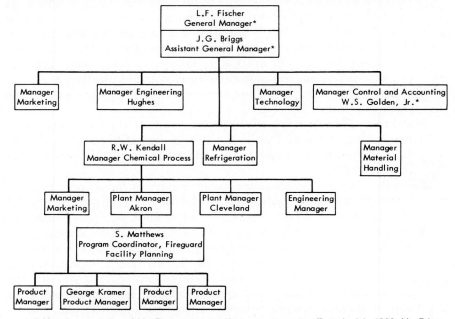

*After the promotion of Mr. Fischer to a position as a corporate officer, in July 1966, Mr. Briggs was made division general manager and Mr. Golden, assistant general manager.

Exhibit 2

Sales of Portable FIREGUARD Units, 1961–1966 (In number of units)

1961	400
1962	820
1963	1,450
1964	1,985
1965	3,775
1966	4,362

Exhibit 3

Forecasted Sales for FIREGUARD (Millions of dollars)

Date of forecast	1964	1965	1966	1967	1968
September 1964	$1.1	$2.5	$4.3		$13.3
July 1965		2.2	4.2	$8.1	
July 1966			3.4	4.8	9.2
April 1967				3.6	

Actual Sales and Earnings for FIREGUARD (Millions of dollars)

Year	1961	1962	1963	1964	1965	1966
Sales	$ .20	$ .41	$ .73	$ 1.0	$ 1.9	$ 2.2
Net income before taxes:						
Actual	(.05)	(.15)	(.38)	(.45)	(.8)	(1.1)
Plan					(.3)	.1

Exhibit 4

Chemical Process Department Sales and Income (Millions of dollars)

	1960	1961	1962	1963	1964	1965	1966
Sales	$ 12.4	$13.4	$15.1	$16.2	$17.8	$20.4	$23.2
Net income before taxes	(.50)	.04	.75	1.72	2.3	3.0	3.1

Exhibit 5

Product Manager's Written Comments on the Monthly Progress Reports for FIREGUARD

January 1967: Equipment sales are 49 percent of plan because of large factory backlog ($790,000 on 1/31/66 from $439,000 on 12/31/65).

February 1967: Total equipment shipments are only 46 percent of plan. While Akron backlog has risen $500,000 this year, part of this is the customary seasonal build-up. It appears we may well be 20 percent below plan.

March 1967: Total shipments continue to lag with year-to-date sales at 50 percent of plan, up only 4 percent from February. We continue to have new equipment production difficulties as represented by a backlog of orders at Akron of $850,000. Backlog as a result of shipments withheld due to production difficulties is $450,000 leaving sales to date substantially below plan as reflected by the latest yearly forecast.

April 1967: Sales continue to lag due to a continuing sales failure to penetrate the commercial market. Automatic systems sales have been delayed due to a lack of production of the new sensing device. Year-to-date total sales have improved 7 percent from March due to heavy overseas shipments. This foreign business is accomplished at significantly lower margins accounting for the continuing higher manufacturing cost versus sales.

May 1967: Sales continue to lag as reported in April with only slight improvement (0.4 percent). Equipment backlog is $725,000, about $300,000 above normal for sales to date. All costs to date are in line with the latest forecast except for development where there will be an overrun of $120,000 for 160 percent of plan due to automatic systems problems.

June 1967: The above listed low sales have been reflected in our 1968 business plan. Our entry into the industrial market has been set back at least one year for lack of satisfactory sensing equipment and is reflected in our 1968 business plan by a 94 percent reduction in plan sales in this area.

July 1967: The high manufacturing costs were due to accounting errors at Akron. One group of costs was cleared prior to sales clearing. Another group was cleared to cost of product when it should have been transferred to an inventory account. When these are corrected in August, the net effect will be to increase our August gross margin by about $75,000.

PC&D, Inc.

When we promoted you to the presidency five years ago, we expected that there would be changes, but we never expected you to diminish the importance of the old line businesses to the extent that you have. I think you have erred in doing so. . . .

The new entrepreneurial subs are certainly dynamic and have brought positive press to the company. But by investing all new resources in them, you are jeopardizing the health of the company as a whole. . . .

My division's reputation has been built over the past 50 years on the superior quality of its products and sales force. But as the leadership of our products begins to erode, my salesmen are beginning to leave. Without resources, I cannot stop this trend, and as much as it saddens me to say so, I am losing my own motivation to stay with the company.

These were some excerpts from a letter that the senior vice president and head of the machinery division, George McElroy, 58, sent to John Martell, president of PC&D, Inc., in February 1976. McElroy was highly respected in both the company and the industry, a member of the board of directors, and a senior officer of the company for 20 years. Therefore, Martell knew that it was important to respond and resolve the issues with McElroy successfully. At the same time, Martell had no intention of giving up his own prerogatives to direct the company.

Copyright © 1979 by the President and Fellows of Harvard College
Harvard Business School case 380–072

History of PC&D, Inc.

Payson & Clark Company

Payson & Clark, the forerunner of PC&D, Inc., was founded during the merger movement around the turn of the century. Four regional machinery companies merged to form a national industrial machinery manufacturing corporation named after the two largest enterprises in the merger, Payson and Clark. With the growth of industry across the country at the time, the demand for heavy machinery took off. The new company benefited from economies of scale, both in production and distribution, and grew and prospered.

By 1965 Payson & Clark Company was an old, stable company, still producing machinery. With revenues of $300 million and net aftertax profits of $6 million, it was still the largest firm in the industry. (See Exhibits 1 and 2 for additional financial information.) The company offered the most complete line of heavy industrial equipment in the industry, the different available configurations of standard and custom models filling a large, encyclopedic sales manual. The consistently high quality and unusual breadth of the product line had made attracting high-caliber salesmen relatively easy. These people were highly knowledgeable in the applications of the product line and saw themselves as consultants to their industrial customers.

While Payson & Clark was the leader in quality and breadth of its product line, it was not the leader in innovations. It left expensive R&D to others, copying products after they were widely accepted. It could afford to follow others primarily because the industry itself was slow moving. In 1965 the business was essentially the same as when the company was founded. Its growth depended on the general growth of industry in the United States, efficiencies in purchasing raw materials, and the scale and automation of production. Indeed, the company's major innovation came in the early 50s with the introduction of plastics in some of the models.

The company was structured in 1965 as it had been in the 20s, with a standard functional organization and highly centralized chain of command. Its top executives were old-time managers, the average age being 55. Many had spent their entire careers with the firm and could remember the days when old Mr. Payson had kept tight reins on the company in the 30s and 40s. Harold C. Payson IV, aged 53 in 1965, was president of the company from the late 40s and president and chairman since 1955. Although the company was publicly held, the Payson family still owned a considerable amount of the stock.

In the early 1960s Harold Payson began to consider succession. He wanted to leave the company in good condition not only for his own personal pride but for the betterment of his heirs. From discussions with his investment bankers and friends in the business world, Mr. Payson had recognized that an association with a high-technology, high-growth industry would strengthen Payson & Clark's image. One way in which Mr. Payson sought to implement this suggestion was to use some of the excess capital thrown off by the machinery business to enter into joint ventures with young, new companies developing high-technology, innovative products. Several such investments were made in the early 1960s, including one with the Datronics Company in 1962.

Datronics Company

In 1965 the Datronics Company was 10 years old with revenues of $50 million. (See Exhibits 3 and 4 for additional financial information.) The company had started as an engineering firm subsisting on government research grants and contracts. As a by-product of the government projects, the company also developed several types of sophisticated electronic equipment with wide applications to industry. The company concentrated its efforts on R&D, however, and subcontracted the production and bought marketing services for its commercial products. The lack of control over marketing and production and the lost profits passed to the marketers and subcontractors displeased the company's young president, John Martell. In his opinion, the growth of the company was limited until the right product emerged to justify going to a full manufacturing and marketing company.

Following Payson & Clark's investment in 1962, Datronics's engineers developed an exciting new product toward the end of 1964 which promised to sell extremely well due to its increased capacity and lower cost. John Martell saw the promise of the new product as the waited-for opportunity to expand the company. It was clear, however, that a major influx of capital was needed to bring the product to the market, build a sales force, and begin volume production. Therefore, Martell began a search for external capital that included a presentation to the joint venture partner, Payson & Clark, which already owned 20 percent of Datronics's stock.

Meanwhile, Harold Payson had been following the activities at Datronics closely and was quite aware of the growth potential of the company before John Martell's visit. Further, he recognized that Datronics, once its manufacturing operations started, would have a continual need for new capital. If Payson & Clark invested once, it would not be long until another request for resources came from Datronics. With these factors in mind, Payson decided that the most beneficial arrangement for both parties would be for his company to acquire Datronics. Martell agreed to this offer, and negotiations for a friendly takeover were consummated. Payson & Clark acquired Datronics for $42 million in November

1965. John Martell himself received $8.4 million in cash, notes, and securities.

The acquisition provided an opportunity for the Payson & Clark Company to update its image. Patterning itself after other successful growth companies of the time, it changed its name to PC&D, Inc., to denote the beginning of a new era in the company.

PC&D, Inc., 1965–1970

After the acquisition, Harold Payson restructured the company with the help of consultants, setting up a divisional organization. The old Payson & Clark Company now became the machinery division, headed by George McElroy, formerly vice president, manufacturing. The Datronics Company became the electronics division, headed by John Martell.

The Electronics Division

At the time of the acquisition, the Datronics Company consisted of several scientific labs, some test equipment, 10 professional engineers, administrative staff, and John Martell.

Martell, an electrical engineer by training, was a man in his mid-30s. He was energetic and a risk taker by nature, and even as a child in Iowa could not imagine working for someone else all his life. After college at MIT he worked for eight years at a large, scientific equipment company in the Boston area. Initially, he was hired for the research group, but he was more attracted to the management positions in the company. He transferred first to the corporate planning office and then became plant manager for one of the divisions. With his technical competence and management experience, it was not surprising that he was approached by several of the more innovative of the company's research engineers to invest in and head up a new, independent R&D company. Martell bought in for 25 percent of the founding stock, and thus began the Datronics Company.

During his term as president of Datronics, Martell was highly regarded by the small group of employees. While he had a respectable command of the technology, he left the research to the engineers, devoting his time to developing sources of challenging and lucrative contracts.

After the acquisition by the Payson & Clark Company, Martell retained full control of the operations of his old organization that was now the electronics division. He hired an experienced industrial marketer from a large technical firm to set up the marketing operations and a friend of his from his old employer to head up the production operations. As expected, the demand for the division's new product was very high. Five years later, by 1970, the division was a successful growing enterprise, having expanded into other electronics fields. It had 700 employees; marketing offices established or opening throughout the United States, Europe, and Japan; plants at three different sites; and revenues of over $160 million. The business press reported these activities very favorably, giving much credit to the leadership of Martell.

The Machinery Division

Meanwhile, the machinery division continued to be the stalwart of the industry it always had been, retaining its structure and activities of the earlier time. George McElroy, division manager and senior vice president, was considered the mainstay of the division. He had joined the company in the early 1950s and was primarily responsible for the plastics innovations of that time. Advisor and confidant of Payson, McElroy was thought by his subordinates to be the next in line for the presidency.

As for Harold Payson himself, he limited his involvement in the company's internal affairs to reviewing budgets and year-end results and spent most of his time with community activities and lobbying in Washington. He felt justified in this hands-off policy because of the quality of both his division vice presidents, McElroy and Martell. PC&D's performance further supported Payson's approach. Revenues climbed to $530 million and profits after tax to $14 million by 1970. The solid 26 multiple of its stock price reflected the confidence in PC&D's prospects (see Exhibits 5 and 6).

The compensation schemes reflected the extent to which Harold Payson allowed the division managers to be autonomous. McElroy's compensation was 90 percent salary, with a 10 percent bonus based on ROI. Martell received two thirds of his pay as a bonus based on growth in revenues. Compensation policies within each division were entirely at the discretion of either Martell or McElroy. In general, Martell made much greater use of incentive compensation than McElroy.

1970 Change at PC&D

Toward the end of 1970 Harold Payson decided that it was time to limit his involvement to that of chairman of the board and to name a new president of PC&D. He, himself, supported the appointment of George McElroy as the next president. McElroy was the next senior officer in the company and, after years of working with Harold Payson, held many of the same views as to the traditional values of PC&D. However, Payson agreed with the school of thought that chief executives should not choose their own successors. He, therefore, established a search committee, consisting of three outside members of the board of directors. (See Exhibit 7 for a list of board members.) A thorough job was done. The committee interviewed several candidates within PC&D, including John Martell and George McElroy. Outside candidates were also considered. The committee utilized executive search firms and consultants to identify candidates and carefully compared external and internal prospects. The result was the nomination of John Martell. While his relative youth was a surprise to some, the search committee's report explained the thinking behind the choice that "during the past five years PC&D has experienced an exciting and profitable period of growth and diversification. But it is essential that the company not become complacent. One of our major criteria in choosing a new president was to find a person with the energy and vision to continue PC&D's growth and expansion." The board unanimously approved the selection of John Martell as president and CEO.

Martell began his new position with the board's mandate in mind. He planned to continue the diversification of PC&D into high-growth industries. He expected to follow both an acquisition mode and a start-up mode, using the excess funds from the machinery division and PC&D's rising stock to finance the growth. For start-ups, Martell planned to use joint ventures supporting newer companies, much as the old Payson & Clark Company had supported his venture in its early days.

Martell brought to his position a very definite management style. He was a strong believer in the benefits accruing from an opportunistic, entrepreneurial spirit, and he wanted to inject PC&D with this kind of energy. However, he was concerned that the kind of people with this kind of spirit would not be attracted to work with PC&D because of the stigma, real or imagined, of being attached to a large company. As Martell commented:

> It was my experience that there are two worlds of people, some of whom are very secure and comfortable and satisfied in their career pursuits in large institutionalized companies and others of whom are, I think, wild ducks and who are interested in perhaps greater challenges that small companies present in terms of the necessity to succeed or die.
>
> In many work environments, the constraints placed upon the individual by the nature of the institution are such as to sometimes make people uncomfortable.
>
> The decision-making process is long and involved, sometimes not known, in the sense that the people who act upon decisions are not in close proximity to those who benefit or suffer from the effects of those decisions.
>
> The formalization of the decision-making process is frequently an irritant, and for people who are unusually energetic and demanding, in the sense of desiring, themselves, to take action and to have their actions complemented by the actions of other people upon whom they are dependent, I would characterize these people as perhaps being wild ducks rather than tame ducks. In that sense, I wanted more "wild ducks" in our company.

Martell himself credited the success of the electronics division to Payson's willingness to turn the reins completely over to him. The secret, Martell thought, was in spotting the right person with both ability and integrity.

Corporate headquarters' role should be to provide resources in terms of both money and expertise as needed, to set timetables, to provide measurement points and incentive, and then to keep hands off.

While the board's directives were clear to Martell, the specifics for implementation were not. Not only were the larger questions of which way to diversify or how to encourage innovation unanswered, but how to plan and who to involve were also unclear. Martell was not given the luxury of time to resolve these issues. Within the first week in his new position, three professionals from the electronics division called on Martell. Bert Rogers and Elaine Patterson were key engineers from the research department, and Thomas Grennan was head of marketing, western region. They had been working on some ideas for a new product (not competing with any PC&D current lines) and were ready to leave the company to start their own business to develop and market it. Indeed, they had already had a prospectus prepared for their new venture. They were hoping either Martell personally or PC&D, Inc., might be able to provide some venture capital. The president particularly liked these three and admired their willingness to take such personal risks with a product as yet unresearched as to market or design. Indeed, with his energy and "can do," aggressive style, Tom Grennan reminded Martell of himself just a few years ago when he left to start the Datronics Company.

Martell liked the product and saw the idea as a possible route for continuing the diversification and growth of PC&D. But there was a problem. It was clear from the presentation of the three that much of their motivation came from the desire to start their own company and, through their equity interest, to reap the high rewards of their efforts if successful. Martell did not fault this motivation, for it had been his as well. He could not expect PC&D's managers to take large personal risks if there was no potential for a large payoff. Further, a fair offer to the group, if in salary, required more than PC&D could afford or could justify to the older divisions. Martell told Rogers, Patterson, and Grennan that he was very interested and asked if he could review the prospectus overnight and get back to them the next day. That night he devised a plan of which he was particularly proud. The major feature of the plan Martell called the entrepreneurial subsidiary. Martell presented this proposal to Grennan, Rogers, and Patterson the next day. They readily accepted, and a pattern for most of PC&D's diversification over the next five years was begun.

The Entrepreneurial Subsidiary

Martell's plan was as follows: When a proposal for a new product area was made to the PC&D corporate office, a new (entrepreneurial) subsidiary would be incorporated. The initiators of the idea would leave their old division or company and become officers and employees of the new subsidiary. In the current example, the new subsidiary was the Pro Instrument Corporation with Grennan as president and Rogers and Patterson as vice presidents.

The new subsidiary would issue stock in its name, $1 par value, 80 percent of which would be bought by PC&D, Inc., and 20 percent by the entrepreneurs involved—engineers and other key officers. This initial capitalization, plus sizable direct loans from PC&D, Inc., provided the funds for the research and development of the new product up to its commercialization. In the case of Pro Instruments, Patterson and Rogers hired 10 other researchers, while Grennan hired a market researcher and a finance/accounting person. These 15 people invested $50,000 together, and PC&D invested another $200,000.

Two kinds of agreements were signed between the two parties. The first was a research contract between the parent company and the subsidiary; setting time schedules for the research, defining requirements for a commercializable product, outlining budgets, and otherwise stipulating obligations on both sides. In general, the sub was responsible for the R&D and production and testing of a set number of prototypes of a new product, while the parent company would market and produce the product on an international scale. Pro Instruments's agreement stipulated two phases, one lasting 18 months to produce a prototype, and another lasting 6 months to test the product in the field and produce a marketing plan. Detailed budget and personnel needs were outlined, providing for a $900,000 working capital loan from PC&D during the first phase and $425,000 during the second.

While PC&D, Inc., had proprietary rights on the product and all revenues received from marketing it, the agreement often included an incentive kicker for the key engineers in the form of additional stock to be issued if the finished product produced certain specified amounts of revenue by given dates. Indeed, this was the case for Pro Instruments: 5,000 shares in year 1, to be issued if net profits were over $250,000; 20,000 shares in year 2 if profits were over $1 million; and 10,000 in year 3 if profits were over $3 million.

The second agreement specified the financial obligations and terms for merger. Once the terms of the research contract were met, PC&D, with board approval, had the option for a stated period of time (usually four years) to merge the subsidiary through a one-for-one exchange of PC&D stock for the stock of the subsidiary. The sub was then dissolved. To protect the interests of entrepreneurs, PC&D was required to vote on merger of the sub within 60 days if the sub met certain criteria. For Pro Instruments, the criteria were (1) the product earned cumulative profits of $500,000 and (2) if the earnings of PC&D and the sub were consolidated, dilution of PC&D's earnings per share would not have occurred over three consecutive quarters. If PC&D did not choose to merge during the 60 days, then the sub had a right to buy out PC&D's interest.

Since PC&D's stock was selling for $103 in 1970 and subsidiary stock was bought for $1 per share, the exchange of stock represented a tremendous potential return. Depending on the value of PC&D's stock at the time of merger, the net worth of the entrepreneurs who originally invested in the sub multiplied overnight. Indeed, as subs were merged in ensuing years, typical gains ranged from 100 to 200 times the original investments in the entrepreneurial sub. For example, PC&D exercised its option to merge Pro Instruments when its product was brought to market in 1972. Thomas Grennan, who had bought 6,000 shares of Pro Instruments stock, found his 6,000 shares of PC&D valued at $936,000 (PC&D common selling for $156 on the New York Stock Exchange at the time). By the end of 1974, Pro Instruments's new product had earned $50 million in revenue and $4.8 million in profits, thus qualifying the original entrepreneurs for stock bonuses. Grennan received another 4,200 shares valued at $684,600. Thus, in four years, he had earned about $1.6 million on a $6,000 investment.

By setting up entrepreneurial subs like Pro Instruments, Mr. Martell had several expectations. In the process of setting up a subsidiary with the dynamics of a small, independent group, Martell hoped to create the loyalty, cohesion, and informal structure conducive to successful research and development efforts. The sub would have a separate location and its own officers who decided structure and operating policies. Further, it provided the opportunity to buy into and reap the benefits of ownership in the equity of a company. In Mr. Martell's words:

> I think the concept of the entrepreneurial subsidiaries was the outgrowth of the insight that in many industrial corporations the system of rewards is perhaps inverted from what many people think it should be; that the hierarchy of the institution commends itself to those people who are capable of managing other people's efforts and those people at lower echelons who are unusually creative and who, as a result of their creativity and innovation and daring in the technical sense or perhaps in a marketing sense, are unusually responsible for the accomplishments of the business and are very frequently forgotten about in the larger rewards of the enterprise.
>
> I, on the other hand, recognized that such persons are frequently, perhaps by training, inclination, or otherwise, not capable of marshaling the financial resources or organizing the manufacturing and marketing efforts required to exploit their creativity. Without the kind of assistance that PC&D was capable of lending to them—an assured marketing capability was often a key concern—they are wary of undertaking new ventures.

Further, it was Mr. Martell's opinion that the organizational and incentive structure of the entrepreneurial sub would attract the best engineers from older, more secure firms to PC&D—the so-called wild ducks.

More important, Martell hoped to encourage the timely development of new products with minimal initial investment by PC&D. If Pro Instruments, for example, did not meet its timetable with the original money invested, its officers would have to approach PC&D for new money just as if they were an outside company. PC&D would then have multiple opportunities to review and consider the investment. If the entrepreneurial sub failed or could not get more money from the parent, PC&D was under no obligation to keep the company alive or to rehire its employees. If loans were involved, PC&D could act as any other creditor. As Martell observed,

> The benefit to PC&D shareholders was in the rapid expansion of PC&D's products, the size of the company, the ability of the company to compete in the marketplace in a way which PC&D, dependent upon only internal development projects, could never have achieved or could have achieved only at much greater costs and over a longer period of years.

However, Martell felt the stock incentives would properly reward the genius of creative engineers for the service performed without having to pay high salaries over a long potentially unproductive period after the initial product was developed. Employees did not have to be rehired, nor were they obligated to continue employment, even if the sub was merged. Those that were rehired would be paid at the normal salary levels of comparable people at PC&D. The reasoning here was that:

> . . . there were two criteria for establishing an entrepreneurial subsidiary. The first criterion was that the R&D objectives of the subsidiary could not be reached except under the aegis of the subsidiary, because it involved people who were not involved in PC&D's main lines of business.
>
> The other criterion was that considerable career risk must exist for the people who would leave their established positions within the management structure of PC&D to undertake the entrepreneurial venture of the new subsidiary. Also, the people, in some part, had to be new talent who came from outside PC&D. When I refer to career risk, I mean for example that if a director of engineering at PC&D left his or her post to join an entrepreneurial subsidiary, a new director of engineering would be appointed, and given the lack of success of the entrepreneurial subsidiary, there would in effect be no position of director of engineering to which the person could return. Moreover, it is probable that we would not want the individual to return.

The stock incentive also motivated the engineers to produce without having to commit any resources of the parent company for the future, since the corporation was not required to merge the sub or to produce and market the new product. The incentive kicker, moreover, would ensure quality. A product that was rushed through development would be more likely to have problems and not reach revenue goals.

Another advantage of the entrepreneurial sub was its effect on decision making. Without the need to go through the entire corporate hierarchy, decisions would be made closer to the operating level. This would enhance the quality of decisions because managers performed best, according to Martell, when given objectives and resources from top managers but with operating decisions left unfettered.

Finally, Martell expected that the entrepreneurial sub would be the training and proving ground of PC&D's future top managers. By providing the means for these executives to gain great personal wealth, Martell expected to gain their loyalty and continued efforts for both himself and PC&D.

PC&D, Inc., 1970–1975

During the first five years of Martell's presidency, PC&D's growth was quite impressive. With revenues topping the billion dollar mark in 1975, growth had averaged about 15 percent in revenues and 35 percent in profits after tax during the five years. (See Exhibits 8 and 9 for financials.) Such growth had been achieved, to a large extent, from new products developed in entrepreneurial subsidiaries. In 1975 sales of $179.2 million and profit before taxes and interest of $22.1 million came from these new products.[1] All together, 11 entrepreneurial subsidiaries had been organized during the 1970–75 time frame. Of these, four had successfully developed products and had been merged into PC&D—one in 1972, one in 1973, and two in 1974. The other seven were younger, and work was still in process. None had failed so far.

Most subsidiaries grew out of needs of the electronics division or Pro Instruments. Competitors in the electronics equipment industry were beginning to integrate backward, lowering costs by producing their own semiconductors. The need to remain cost competitive caused PC&D to establish entrepreneurial subs to develop specialized components including semiconductors, assuming that these could be used both by PC&D and sold in outside markets. In the process of selling semiconductors to outside customers, ideas for new products using PC&D components were stimulated, and new subs were formed to develop these equipment products. The cost of merging the two types of subs, components or equipment, differed, however. Equipment subs were cheaper insofar as they could share the already existent sales force of the electronics division; many parts could be standard ones already utilized in other products; and the processes were similar to other electronics products. But with semiconductors, new plants, new sales channels, new manufacturing processes, and new skills at all levels had to be built. While to Martell

---

[1] Of PC&D total assets in 1975, approximately 40 percent were devoted to the machinery division, 35 percent to the traditional electronics division, and 25 percent to the entrepreneurial subsidiaries.

the move into semiconductors promised a large cash flow in the future in a booming industry, some in the company were concerned that the current cash drain was not the best use of scarce cash resources.

When Martell first became president, he made few changes in PC&D's organization structure. McElroy continued as vice president, machinery division, and retained control over that division's structure and policies. Martel himself retained his responsibilities as manager of the electronics division. This he did reluctantly and with all intentions of finding a new executive for the job; however, the unexpected nature of his promotion left Martell without a ready candidate.

As the subs began to be merged, beginning with Pro Instruments in 1972, questions of organization began to arise. In typical fashion, Martell wanted to pass involvement in these decisions down to the appropriate managers. There was also no question that Pro Instrument's president, Tom Grennan, had proven himself with the new subsidiary. So in 1972 Martell appointed Grennan to division vice president, electronics, based on Grennan's superlative performance. Further, because the products were complementary, all of the subs that were merged in this period were placed in the electronics division. Moreover, in recognition of the increased number of products, Grennan did reorganize the electronics division. He appointed his Pro Instruments colleague, Bert Rogers, to director of research which was organized by product area. Manufacturing, also organized by product, reflected the development by subsidiary as well. Marketing, on the other hand, was organized by region as it had been previously. Until they were merged, however, subsidiary presidents went directly to Mr. Martell for resolution of problems that arose. (See Exhibit 10 for an organization chart in 1975.)

By 1975 the electronics division's enlarged marketing and production departments employed 4,000 people with production plants in three different locations. Electronics now had sales of $561.4 million as compared to machinery's $440.6 million.

While successful development projects from subsidiaries had been largely responsible for the sales growth at PC&D, this result had not come without costs. First, the subsidiaries required funds—$60 million by the end of 1975. Some of these funds came from retained earnings, but much was new money raised in the form of long-term debt. Further, stock issued to capitalize subs and pay bonuses to entrepreneurs had a diluting effect on PC&D's shares. If all subsidiaries were merged and successful, the number of new shares could be significant. While raising such a sizable amount of new funds was not particularly difficult for a company as large as PC&D, the needs arising from the subsidiaries left little new money for the core businesses of PC&D. The machinery division, for example, had not had their development budget increased at all during the five years ending 1975.

Current Concerns

Despite PC&D's recent successes, Mr. Martell was not without worries. Several problem areas had appeared in both the electronics and machinery divisions.

In electronics, personnel and products originating in subsidiaries now equaled or surpassed those from the original division. It had been part of the strategy of the entrepreneurial subsidiaries to use them as devices to attract talent from other firms. A key researcher hired from outside was encouraged to hire, in turn, the best of his or her former colleagues. Thus the loyalty and friendships between key entrepreneurs and their staffs were often strong and of long standing. As the entrepreneurial subsidiaries were merged, their personnel tended to retain this loyalty to the president or key officers of the old sub rather than transferring it to PC&D. Thus several warring spheres of influence were developing in the division, particularly in the research department and between research and other departments. Martell was concerned that such influences and warring would lead to poor decisions and much wasted energy in the division.

Turnover in electronics was also increasing. This was of particular concern to Martell for it was just those talented engineers that the entrepreneurial subsidiaries were meant to attract that were beginning to leave. For example, Elaine Patterson, formerly of Pro Instruments, left during 1975 to start her own company, taking 20 research engineers with her. The source of the turnover was unclear, but possible factors included distaste for the kind of warring atmosphere mentioned above and the inability to be a part of a large corporate R&D department with its demand for budgets and reports.

For many employees, however, the sudden absence of monetary incentives changed the climate drastically. This lack of incentive, coupled with the discovery that the most challenging projects were taken on by newly formed subsidiaries which favored hiring outside expertise, caused dissatisfaction. For Martell, such turnover was of greatest concern in the long run, for the inability to create a strong central R&D department in electronics created a continuing need for more entrepreneurial subs. These subsidiaries were still too new an idea for Martell to want to risk his entire future R&D program on their successes. Further, most of the new products were in highly competitive areas. Without continuing upgrades, these products would soon become obsolete. A strong central R&D department was needed for follow-up development of products started by subsidiaries.

Finally, Martell was concerned by recent indications of rather serious operating problems in the electronics division. This was particularly disturbing in that Martell had placed complete faith in Grennan's managerial ability. The most recent cost report, for example, indicated that marketing, G&A, and engineering expenses were way out of line in the division. Further, the marketing and production departments reported problems in several products originating in the subs. One product, with expected obsolescence of four years, now showed a six-year breakeven just to cover the engineering and production costs. Another product, completing its first year on the market, had been forecasted by the subsidiary to achieve $20 million in sales in its first two years. However, during the first six months, losses had been incurred because of customer returns. A report on the causes of the returns showed a predominance of product failures. The chances for breakeven on this product looked bleak. While none of these problems had affected operating results yet, Martell was especially concerned that these operating problems would have a negative impact on first quarter 1976 earnings.

Martell had not confronted Grennan with these operating problems as yet. He had wanted to see how the division itself was attacking these issues through its long-range plan. Martell had requested Grennan to prepare a long-range plan (five years) as well as the usual one-year operating plan. The product of this effort had only arrived recently (February 1976), and Martell had not had a chance to study it. (Table of contents is reproduced in Exhibit 11.) Its 100-page bulk loomed on Martell's desk. Quick perusal had indicated maybe four pages of prose scattered through the plan and dozens of charts, graphs, and tables of numbers, every one of which manifested an upward trend.

In an attempt to get employee feedback on all of these problems, Martell had contracted an outside consulting firm to carry out confidential interviews with personnel in the electronics division. The interviews found middle managers quite concerned over the "confusion in the division" which was causing a loss of morale there. The consultant's report cited concrete problems, including lost equipment, missed billings, and confusion in the plant. Typical comments from lower level personnel included:

— Either upper management is not being informed of problems or they don't know how to solve them.
— Morale is very poor, job security is nil.
— There is little emphasis on production efficiencies.
— Scrap is unaccounted for.
— Market forecasts are grossly inaccurate.
— Production schedules have a definite saw-tooth pattern. There is very little good planning.
— There are no systematic controls.

These were not the sort of comments Martell expected from the division responsible for the major portion of PC&D's future growth. His concern, at this time, was not so much the problems themselves but what was being done about them. His preferred policy was obviously to stay out of day-to-day operating problems. He wondered how long it was prudent to allow such problems to continue without some intervention on his part.

Meanwhile, the machinery division had its own problems. The last major construction of new plant had been in the early 1950s. Since that time, McElroy had upgraded production methods, which succeeded in checking rising costs. However, since 1965 resources for such improvements had not been increased; and with inflation in the 1970s less and less could be done on a marginal basis. McElroy was currently of the opinion that capacity was sufficient for the short term but that it was impossible to remain state-of-the-art.[2] Indeed, the machinery division's products were beginning to fall behind the new developments of competitors. Further, the costs of the machinery division's products were beginning to inch up. As the production line aged, quality control reported an increasing percentage of defective goods. In contrast to the situation in the machinery division, the rather extensive investment in new plant for the production of semiconductors did not sit too well with McElroy, who was concerned with the lack of flexibility that could result from backward integrating and thought component needs should be farmed out to the cheapest bidder from the numerous small component firms. Martell was concerned how long he could keep McElroy satisfied without a major investment in the machinery division and how long he could count on the cash flow from the machinery division for other users.

Also turnover, a problem never before experienced in the machinery division, had appeared. Here, however, it was the salespeople who were leaving. Martell worried over this trend, for the sales force was the strength of the division. According to the head of marketing the salespeople considered themselves the best in the industry, and they did not wish to sell products which were not the best. They saw the machinery division's products no longer as the best in quality or state-of-the-art. Further, they did not wish to work for a company where they felt unimportant. Whether true or not, the sales force certainly appeared less aggressive than in previous times.

Thus Martell was not overly surprised to receive McElroy's letter, nor was he certain that some of McElroy's anger concerning the electronics division was not justified. Martell knew he had to do something about McElroy, as well as Grennan and the electronics division. He also had to decide whether entrepreneurial subsidiaries should continue to be part of PC&D's research and development strategy. Finally, all of Martell's decisions concerning the divisions and subsidiaries needed to be consistent with a strategy that would continue PC&D's growth.

---

[2] McElroy suspected that the machinery division would require an investment of $100 to $125 million over two to three years to revitalize the product line and plant and equipment. McElroy felt that in the long term the return on this investment would match the division's historic ROI.

Exhibit 1

PAYSON & CLARK COMPANY
Income Statement, 1956–1965
(in millions)

	1956	1957	1958	1959	1960	1961	1962	1963	1964	1965
Sales	$177.6	$190.7	$205.0	$220.5	$237.2	$247.9	$259.1	$273.3	$288.1	$302.7
Cost of goods sold	136.1	145.8	157.6	171.0	184.4	192.4	202.1	218.7	230.8	243.6
Gross profit	41.5	44.9	47.4	49.5	52.8	55.5	57.0	54.6	57.3	59.1
Expenses:										
Depreciation	5.0	5.0	5.0	4.0	4.0	4.0	4.0	4.0	3.5	3.5
Marketing and G&A	18.2	19.7	20.5	22.2	25.6	27.5	28.4	28.0	30.0	33.3
Engineering and product development	8.1	8.6	9.9	10.1	10.6	11.0	11.4	8.8	9.2	7.1
Total expenses	31.3	33.3	35.4	36.3	40.2	42.5	43.8	40.8	42.7	43.9
Profit before interest and taxes	10.2	11.6	12.0	13.2	12.6	13.0	13.2	13.8	14.6	15.2
Interest	3.0	4.0	4.0	4.0	3.0	3.0	3.0	3.0	3.0	3.0
Profit before tax	7.2	7.6	8.0	9.2	9.6	10.0	10.2	10.8	11.6	12.2
Tax	3.6	3.8	4.0	4.6	4.8	5.0	5.1	5.4	5.8	6.1
Profit after tax	$ 3.6	$ 3.8	$ 4.0	$ 4.6	$ 4.8	$ 5.0	$ 5.1	$ 5.4	$ 5.8	$ 6.1
Earnings per share	$1.29	$1.36	$1.44	$1.65	$1.72	$1.80	$1.83	$1.94	$2.08	$2.19
Average stock price	$18	$22	$19	$30	$29	$29	$27	$31	$35	$33

Exhibit 2

PAYSON & CLARK COMPANY
Balance Sheet, 1956–1965
(in millions)

	1956	1957	1958	1959	1960	1961	1962	1963	1964	1965
Assets										
Current assets:										
Cash and securities	$ 6	$ 7	$ 3	$ 1	$ 2	$ 2	$ 2	$ 1	$ 1	$ 1
Accounts receivable	33	36	38	39	41	43	45	47	51	55
Inventories	56	61	64	66	69	74	78	82	88	91
Total current assets	95	103	105	106	112	119	125	130	140	147
Plant and equipment	65	60	60	61	63	67	65	65	64	65
Investments in joint ventures							5	10	11	14
Total assets	$160	$163	$165	$167	$175	$186	$195	$205	$215	$226
Liabilities and Net Worth										
Current liabilities:										
Accounts payable	$ 31	$ 33	$ 36	$ 38	$ 46	$ 54	$ 62	$ 65	$ 70	$ 75
Accrued liabilities	7	9	10	11	13	17	22	25	31	36
Long-term debt due	6	6	6	6	6	6	6	6	6	6
Total current liabilities	44	48	52	55	65	77	86	96	107	117
Long-term debt	52	47	41	35	29	23	18	12	6	—
Total liabilities	96	95	93	90	94	100	104	118	113	117
Common stock	27	27	27	27	27	27	27	27	27	27
Retained earnings	37	41	45	50	54	59	64	70	75	82
Total liabilities and net worth	$160	$163	$165	$167	$175	$186	$195	$205	$215	$226

Exhibit 3

DATRONICS COMPANY
Income Statement, 1956–1965
(in millions)

	1956	1957	1958	1959	1960	1961	1962	1963	1964	1965
Contracts	$ 1.2	$6.4	$8.2	$7.5	$ 8.0	$ 7.9	$ 6.0	$ 4.3	$ 3.4	$ 2.4
Sales			0.2	2.1	4.4	8.1	14.3	22.5	34.2	48.1
Revenues	1.2	6.4	8.4	9.6	12.4	16.0	20.3	26.8	37.6	50.5
Cost of goods sold	1.0	4.5	6.0	6.9	8.9	11.5	14.7	19.6	27.8	37.9
Gross profits	0.2	1.9	2.4	2.7	3.5	4.5	5.6	7.2	9.8	12.6
Expenses	0.5	0.6	0.7	0.7	0.7	0.7	0.9	0.9	1.0	1.1
R&D		0.7	0.8	1.0	1.2	1.5	2.2	3.0	4.0	5.1
Profit before tax	(0.3)	0.6	0.9	1.0	1.6	2.3	2.5	3.3	4.8	6.4
Tax	(0.15)	0.2	0.4	0.5	0.8	1.1	1.2	1.6	2.4	3.2
Net profit	$(0.15)	$0.4	$0.5	$0.5	$ 0.8	$ 1.2	$ 1.3	$ 1.7	$ 2.4	$ 3.2
Earnings per share	($1.50)	$4	$5	$5	$8	$12	$10.40	$13.60	$19.20	$25.60

Exhibit 4

DATRONICS COMPANY
Balance Sheet, 1956–1965
(in millions)

	1956	1957	1958	1959	1960	1961	1962	1963	1964	1965
Assets										
Current assets:										
Cash	$0.05	$0.10	$0.10	$0.40	$0.20	$ 0.60	$ 0.60	$ 0.65	$ 1.56	$ 0.70
Inventories	0.20	2.60	2.70	3.70	5.20	6.20	6.80	10.15	15.22	20.10
Accounts receivable		0.30	0.50	1.00	2.00	2.20	3.00	4.00	5.12	6.00
Total current assets	0.25	3.00	3.30	5.10	7.30	9.00	10.40	14.85	21.90	26.80
Plant and equipment	0.50	1.00	1.20	1.40	2.00	3.10	5.10	7.50	8.50	9.00
Total assets	$0.75	$4.00	$5.50	$6.50	$9.30	$12.10	$15.50	$22.35	$30.40	$35.80
Liabilities and Net Worth										
Liabilities:										
Accounts payable	$0.10	$2.15	$2.20	$2.60	$3.65	$ 4.75	$ 5.50	$ 8.78	$12.10	$14.25
Accrued liabilities	0.10	1.00	1.05	1.25	1.65	2.25	1.70	2.77	3.80	3.85
	0.20	3.15	3.25	3.85	5.30	7.00	7.20	11.55	15.90	18.10
Notes payable	0.60	0.50	1.40	1.30	1.85	1.75	2.50	2.20	3.50	3.50
Total liabilities	0.80	3.65	4.65	5.15	7.15	8.75	9.70	13.75	19.45	21.60
Additional paid-in capital	—	—	—	—	—	—	1.125	2.225	2.225	2.225
Common stock ($1 par)	0.10	0.10	0.10	0.10	0.10	0.10	0.125	0.125	0.125	0.125
Retained earnings	(0.15)	0.25	0.75	1.25	2.05	3.25	4.55	6.25	8.65	11.85
Total liabilities and net worth	$0.75	$4.00	$5.50	$6.50	$9.30	$12.10	$15.50	$22.35	$30.40	$35.80

Exhibit 5

PC&D, INC.
Income Statement, 1966–1970
(in millions)

	1966	1967	1968	1969	1970
Sales:					
Machinery division	$315.1	$327.5	$340.2	$354.1	$368.2
Electronics division	66.1	84.7	106.7	132.3	161.4
Total sales	381.2	412.2	446.9	486.4	529.6
Cost of goods sold:					
Machinery division	251.7	264.3	271.8	284.7	297.9
Electronics division	49.6	63.0	79.6	96.8	118.5
Total cost of goods sold	301.3	327.3	351.4	381.5	416.4
Gross margin	79.9	84.9	95.5	104.9	113.2
Expenses:					
Marketing G&A expense	46.1	48.3	50.3	51.6	53.1
Product development—					
machinery division	4.9	4.6	4.7	4.1	4.5
R&D—electronics division	4.2	5.3	10.3	17.8	27.3
Total expense	55.2	58.2	65.3	73.5	84.9
Profit before interest					
and taxes	24.7	26.7	30.2	31.4	28.3
Interest	3.0	3.0	0.2	0.2	0.2
Profit before tax	22.7	23.7	30.0	31.2	28.1
Taxes	10.8	11.8	15.0	15.6	14.0
Net profit	$ 10.9	$ 11.9	$ 15.0	$ 15.6	$ 14.1
Earnings per share	$3.63	$3.97	$5.00	$5.20	$4.70
Average stock price	$94	$111	$145	$146	$103

Exhibit 6

PC&D, INC.
Balance Sheet, 1966–1970
(in millions)

	1966	1967	1968	1969	1970
Assets					
Current assets:					
Cash and securities	$ 2	$ 5	$ 9	$ 7	$ 11
Accounts receivable	67	71	77	87	101
Inventories	118	128	145	166	180
Total current assets	187	214	231	260	292
Plant and equipment	83	95	97	108	120
Investments in joint ventures	10	11	12	12	10
Goodwill	6	6	5	5	5
Total assets	$286	$320	$345	$385	$427
Liabilities and Net Worth					
Current liabilities:					
Accounts payable	$ 90	$ 96	$103	$111	$127
Accrued liabilities	31	33	31	32	35
Long-term debt due	1	1	1	2	3
Total current liabilities	122	130	135	145	165
Long-term debt	16	30	35	49	57
Total liabilities	138	160	170	194	222
Common stock and paid-in capital	55	55	55	55	55
Retained earnings	93	105	120	136	150
Total liabilities and net worth	$286	$320	$345	$385	$427

Exhibit 7

Members, Board of Directors, 1970

Harold Payson IV, president—PC&D
George McElroy, senior vice president—machinery division, PC&D
John Martell, vice president—electronics division, PC&D
Carl Northrup, treasurer—PC&D
David S. Curtis, partner—Barth & Gimbel, Wall Street brokerage firm
Elizabeth B. Payne, partner—Payne, Bartley & Springer, Washington law firm
Charles F. Sprague, president—Forrest Products, Inc. (large manufacturing firm)
Gardner L. Stacy III, Dean, Business School, State University
James Hoffman, vice president—Baltimore Analysts Association (international firm)

Exhibit 8

PC&D, INC.
Income Statement, 1971–1975
(in millions)

	1971	*1972*	*1973*	*1974*	*1975*
Sales:					
Machinery division	$382.9	$397.8	$412.5	$426.9	$ 440.6
Electronics division*	193.6	235.6	300.1	397.4	561.4
Total sales	576.5	633.4	712.6	824.3	1,002.0
Cost of goods sold:					
Machinery division	311.3	322.6	338.2	350.9	359.1
Electronics division	145.2	174.3	216.1	282.2	421.1
Total cost of goods sold	456.5	496.9	554.3	633.1	780.2
Gross margin	120.0	136.5	158.3	191.2	221.8
Expenses:					
Marketing G&A expense	54.7	56.3	59.1	63.3	67.7
Product development—machinery division	5.0	5.1	5.2	5.2	5.3
R&D—electronics division	28.4	29.5	30.7	31.9	33.5
Total expenses	88.1	90.9	95.0	100.4	106.5
Profit before interest and taxes	31.9	45.6	63.3	90.8	115.3
Interest	0.2	3.0	3.0	7.0	11.0
Profit before tax	31.7	42.6	60.3	83.8	104.3
Taxes	15.8	21.3	30.1	41.9	52.1
Net profit	$ 15.9	$ 21.3	$ 30.2	$ 41.9	$ 52.2
Earnings per share	$5.30	$6.45†	$8.39	$10.47	$13.05
Average stock price	$106	$156	$158	$163	$238

* Sales figures for electronics include both sales by the original division plus sales of new subsidiaries after they are merged. Thus in 1975 the $561.4 million in sales for electronics includes $179.2 from products developed in subs. Profit before interest and taxes from new products was $22.1 million.

† Number of shares increased in 1972 by 0.3 million from the merger of Pro Instruments. They increased in 1973 by 0.3 million from merger of sub 2, and again by 0.4 million in 1974 from the merger of subs 3 and 4. Thus in 1974 there was a total of 4 million shares outstanding. In late 1973, there was a secondary offering of 1 million shares.

Exhibit 9

PC&D, INC.
Balance Sheet, 1971–1975
(in millions)

	1971	1972	1973	1974	1975
Assets					
Current assets:					
Cash and securities	$ 10	$ 5	$ 2	$ 2	$ 3
Accounts receivable	117	131	155	171	213
Inventories	200	223	270	327	401
Total current assets	327	359	427	500	617
Plant and equipment	122	124	125	178	232
Investments in joint ventures	10	8	10	9	6
Investments in subsidiaries	5	10	21	16	25
Goodwill	4	4	3	3	2
Total assets	$468	$505	$586	$706	$882
Liabilities and Net Worth					
Current liabilities:					
Accounts payable	$151	$160	$179	$193	$243
Accrued liabilities	37	41	46	51	65
Long-term debt due	4	4	4	6	7
Total current liabilities	192	205	229	250	315
Long-term debt	55	58	84	138	193
Total liabilities	247	263	313	388	508
Common stock and paid-in capital	55	55	56	57	57
Retained earnings	166	187	217	261	317
Total liabilities and net worth	$468	$505	$586	$706	$882

Exhibit 10

Organization Chart, 1975

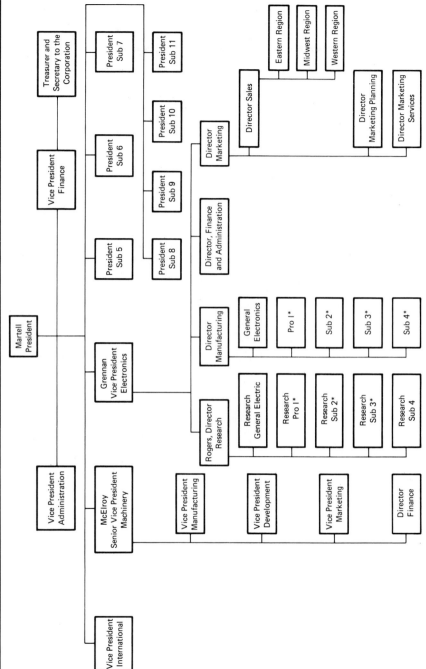

* Reference to subsidiaries indicates origin of personnel and product.

Exhibit 11

Electronics Division 1976 Operating Plan: 1977–1980 Long-Range Outlook

Table of Contents

Exhibit 11 (concluded)

International Harvester (A)

May 17, 1977.

The intercom buzzed. Ed Spencer, president of Honeywell and member of the board of directors at International Harvester Company (IH or Harvester) arrived for an appointment with his friend Archie McCardell, president and chief operating officer of Xerox Corporation.

Spencer entered, smiled, and opened with, "Archie, I've come down today to see if I couldn't get you to take the job at International Harvester that we've been working so hard to get you to consider for the last few months."

Sensing that he was cornered, McCardell laughed, "Wait a minute, Ed, I thought we were going to talk computers. What's this about IH? I've already had at least three approaches from headhunters. One even discovered I was in New York at a meeting, and I ended up at lunch with him. And another managed to get me to dinner with Brooks McCormick [CEO and chairman of IH] in Chicago. I've said no to all of them. I was in that industry when I was at Ford, and it's just a lousy business. I'll admit I don't know anything about International Harvester specifically but just take a look at the balance sheet and income statements—they speak for themselves—the company's in bad shape."

Spencer jumped in, "That's just the point. The challenge is a big one. If you could revitalize a company like Harvester, it would be a very real accomplishment. Besides, the compensation package will put

Copyright © 1980 by the President and Fellows of Harvard College
Harvard Business School case 381–052

you among the very highest paid executives in the country. And while the initial appointment will be as president and COO, part of the deal will be to make you chief executive officer within the first year of your joining IH."

McCardell admittedly was intrigued. But before he could even begin to make a decision on such a major change, he needed to understand exactly what the challenges were at IH and what was going to be expected of him. He needed to have a better idea what people such as Ed Spencer and Brooks McCormick would expect, if the company had enough resources to meet the challenges, and what a reasonable plan of attack could be. After all, what could any one person do with a "venerable dinosaur" like International Harvester?

History of the Company

International Harvester traced its antecedents back to 1831 when Cyrus Hall McCormick invented the reaper in Virginia, the first of many agricultural equipment inventions of those times. McCormick founded a company, moving the headquarters in 1846, when volume manufacturing was set up, to the "frontier" city of Chicago to serve the opening of the midwestern farmlands. McCormick farm equipment was distributed throughout the country and even to Canada and Europe from the 1850s onward. Despite this early presence in international markets and the strength such an image gave to the company, International Harvester retained its "American," indeed midwestern, tone—a tone audible even to this day. As a recent IH publication stated, "International Harvester is a distinctly American enterprise. It has grown with the nation and helped the nation grow."

In 1902 the current company was incorporated through the merger of several agriculture equipment companies, with raw material resources and a steel mill completing the package. Cyrus McCormick's son became the first president. The purpose of the merger was to develop new products, diversify the product line, and develop foreign markets.

The initial Harvester products were all agricultural implements, the majority being used for harvesting (for example, reapers). By the 1900s, however, a full line of equipment was offered. While the first motorized tractor dated back to the first decade of the century, World War I provided the real stimulus for the development of tractors. The first all-purpose tractor that might look familiar today appeared in 1922. IH was the recognized leader in agriculture equipment until the early 1960s.

IH produced a "truck" for farm use in 1907, but again it was the stimulus of World War I that saw the development of nonfarm trucks. Heavy-duty trucks became a separate product line in the early 1920s, and Harvester was the leading producer of a complete line of trucks by 1925. In 1977 the company was still the volume leader in certain segments of the truck industry.

Another outgrowth of agricultural equipment was construction and industrial equipment. Bulldozers, for example, could be configured by adding different attachments or crawlers to a standard farm tractor. The full line of construction equipment was not developed until the early 1950s, however.

After the basic engine technology (both gas and diesel) was established in the 20s and the development of pneumatic tires in the early 30s, the rate of technological change in all IH industries slowed and took on the familiar characteristics of a maturing industry—longer product life cycles and technological evolution rather than revolution. The trends that developed were toward lighter, bigger, and more powerful vehicles, whether in agriculture, trucking, or construction.

Throughout IH's history, sales have shown some volatility around an upward trend. The volatility was due not only to the dependence on the welfare of the farmer, which cannot be characterized as stable, but to the advent of war or depression. Harvester had always received a major boost in sales during wartime, not only from sales of its standard product line but also from the use of its plants for production of munitions. The readjustment to a civilian economy had similarly led to a decrease in sales.

By 1950 IH employed about 90,000 people. It had a reputation for quality, service, and good employee relations. Indeed, one executive who had joined the company around that time described Harvester as a "company with all these traditions. In 1950 people were still talking about the Depression, how everyone was so well treated. No one was ever fired. The company was as solid as the Rock of Gibraltar. Indeed, when I first joined the company and was in a management training program I was told by one of the group, a son of an executive, that I had already achieved the most important thing in my career and that was getting hired."

The tradition was to join the company as a young person and spend one's entire career there. Indeed, on its 50th anniversary, a dinner was given for 26 men who were still working at Harvester after those entire 50 years.

From Postwar Strength to 1970 Hard Times

From its Rock of Gibraltar position of strength after World War II, International Harvester deteriorated and lost its market leadership. Such declines are always complex, but several factors that contributed include its very size, its leadership, and several poor product-market decisions. (For historical sales and income data see Exhibit 1.)

Right after the war, Harvester was still essentially a farm implement company. A strategy of diversification was started with a major investment in the home appliance industry which was enjoying a huge postwar boom. While on the product side, the move made some sense—Harvester had produced cooling equipment for dairy farms for many years—it was not experienced in the selling of refrigerators and similar appliances to consumers. Large capital investment was required, but sales never amounted to more than 5–6 percent of total sales and made little, if any, profit. The assets were sold to the Whirlpool-Seeger Corporation in 1956.

In the construction equipment line, Caterpillar Tractor Company and International Harvester had had an equal share of the market prior to World War II. But during the war, the U.S. government favored Caterpillar for military use throughout the world. Caterpillar thus gained a strong position for international distribution after the war with a developed and reliable product line that emphasized the largest sizes of construction equipment. In an attempt to catch up and regain its parity with Caterpillar, Harvester made large investments in their construction equipment line, particularly in more capital-intense, large machines. Unfortunately, less investment was placed in quality control, and there were problems of reliability.

Other investments were made in new plant, in minor businesses (for example, twine), and new plant or purchases of smaller companies in an effort to backward integrate (for example, foundries or the Solar Turbine Company). While none of these investments was necessarily poor, taken one at a time, the end result was relative inattention to R&D in the core agriculture business. At the same time major competitors, particularly Deere, had made large investments in product improvements of agriculture equipment.

By the mid-50s, the postwar shortages were gone, and the sellers' market became a competitive buyers' market. "Selling is our major challenge," claimed the annual reports of the era. But Harvester products no longer sold themselves, and competitors made major inroads into the company's market share. Perhaps the inevitable changes were masked in the early 50s because sales continued to grow. But the growth was the result of increasing Korean War-related contracts, the value of which reached 18 percent of revenues. Domestic sales meanwhile remained flat. When defense sales dried up in the mid-50s and the company was hit by several severe strikes (one for 10 weeks, another for 4 months), it was obvious that Harvester was falling behind. To top it all, Harvester geared up for a predicted boom in small tractor demand just as the over-100 horsepower tractor market was taking off. One executive described the situation, "We did more for Deere in the period than they did for themselves. As the ratios began to fall, panic set in, and a defensive management style started to appear. It was catch-up psychology from then on."

The problems of the 50s were compounded by the choice of leadership in the 60s. Harry O. Bercher became president in 1962. While he had been with the company for many years, most of his tenure had been in the Wisconsin steel division, the same steel capacity that had been part of the original 1902 merger. It produced steel solely for IH, and because of accounting practices, its profitability could not be determined exactly but was probably not very great. One executive commented, "We just misconstrued Bercher's experience. We thought he understood the Harvester business better than he apparently did." Whether he understood the business or not, large investments were made in capital improvements at the steel plant. Further, he managed by becoming very involved in day-to-day operations. One description portrayed him as "so involved in operations that it stifled us. He would have weekly meetings to go over the extreme details of operations. He even made hiring decisions down four levels into the divisions. There were no administrative systems, no planning, no position descriptions, no long-term view."

By the end of 1970 the company was "in the process of liquidation. Net income had dropped 52 percent from 1967–71 to $45 million, while sales had gone up 20 percent." Debt as a percentage of debt plus equity had increased from 19 percent to 28 percent. Or as another executive claimed, "We were heading down the path of the Penn Central."

The McCormick Era: 1971–1977

During 1971 Brooks McCormick, great-grandnephew of Cyrus H. McCormick, took over the presidency of International Harvester. Having joined the company in 1940, he was 54 when he gained the position of president. One executive surmised that this must have been "a traumatic experience for some executives. Brooks had been ignored for 30 years, and many executives found their career expectations cut short as the balance of power shifted." The situation could have created dissension in the leadership and stifled any attempts at change, particularly if McCormick lacked a power base. But he had the loyalty of the company. The many third- and fourth-generation employees felt a McCormick was properly the rightful heir to the presidency. "Brooks McCormick was Mr. Harvester," explained one older employee. On his side McCormick was "determined to save the company and rejuvenate it." It was a big task: the financial picture was weak, and the company's organization and management systems had remained the same since the 1940s.

Further, Brooks McCormick was a product of the very environment that he was trying to change, an environment described in an early consultants' report to him as "staid, old-fashioned, conservative, inbred, highly centralized, and nonentrepreneurial . . . an atmosphere of strict observance of protocol, status consciousness, and stuffiness." The same report characterized Harvester as having "little sense of direction," making "decisions from a short-term perspective rather than weighed against long-term goals," and having a "general focus on activities rather than results."

McCormick started with the basics. As one executive recalls, "It was a classic MBA situation—elementary textbook stuff: there were no business planning, strategic planning, or management systems to speak of." The core of McCormick's program centered around curing problems of people and planning, triggered by a series of consultants' studies.

Strategic Planning. A consultant was brought in to help establish a corporate strategic planning process, a project that had been attempted several times by McCormick and his executive vice president, James Doyle. By 1975 the first strategic plans were made by the divisions. As one executive commented, "While this was certainly a step in the right direction, the company still lacked the infrastructure for proper planning. These first attempts tended to produce reams of paper with all the blanks filled out but planning was still not a part of management." McCormick also showed his willingness to bring outside talent to Harvester by hiring a corporate planning officer with strong academic and business credentials.

Hay Study. Hay Associates was hired to carry out a climate study and then to set up a system of individual accountability. Using the standard Hay methodology, position descriptions were written, positions were reevaluated, and a salary policy was established which would place Harvester's compensation in the top quarter compared to other companies. An incentive system for management was established that gave credit for individual achievements, a company first. Previously bonuses were based on overall corporate performance.

The changes in the incentive system created conflicts between individuals and the units they worked for. As one executive described it, "The incentive system raised questions for the first time about interdependencies between the divisions as manifested in such areas as transfer prices. Many people wanted to scrap the system, but McCormick realized that organization change was what was really needed."

Reorganization. Brooks McCormick asked Booz Allen to perform an organization study. One description of this study claimed that "the consultants came in and we started having all these meetings—a first at Harvester—I mean it was still all very paternalistic, but we were included—and the consultants started by asking us what business we were in, what our goals were, what our strengths and weaknesses were. We all thought they were out of their tree . . . but we were really developing a common vocabulary for the first time."

In 1976 Booz Allen recommended a complete reorganization of the company. Included was a recommendation that Harvester needed a new president, preferably from outside of the company.

Brooks McCormick announced the reorganization to management in December 1976, following the year-long study of the company by Booz Allen. The plan to be implemented basically followed the consultants' recommendations.

The company was to be organized around five product groups. Four were end-product groups: trucks, agricultural equipment, construction equipment, and turbine engines. The fifth group, components, supplied the other groups. It was created from operations in agriculture, truck, and construction and was responsible for the manufacture of engines and castings and the distribution of parts. Besides creating the components group, the major change in the reorganization was the dissolution of the overseas division. Foreign operations were divided by product area and profit responsibility placed in the worldwide product groups. In one sense, the biggest losers in the reorganization were the old country managing directors, who found their scope of responsibility much reduced.

The five group presidents were chosen by Brooks McCormick. They were all insiders but were not necessarily chosen from the product areas they were to manage. Thus Pat Kaine, formerly president of the agricultural/industrial equipment division, became president of the truck group; Ben Warren, formerly group vice president with corporatewide responsibilities, became president of the agricultural equipment group; Bob Musgjerd, the new president of construction equipment, was formerly president of the overseas division; Keith Mazurek, as the president of the new components group, switched from being president of the truck division; only Morris Seivert continued as president of the solar group.

McCormick then asked each new president to recommend as starters three people for each of the jobs on the Booz Allen charts. They were told that they could staff their organizations with anyone they wanted from either inside or outside the company. In a sort of "players draft," McCormick and the group presidents got together with the corporate human resource executives and negotiated who would go where. The first three levels of the group organizations were determined in this manner. The reorganization was causing much turmoil in the spring of 1977, and shifts in jobs, facilities, and reporting were expected to continue through 1977 and 1978.

The Booz Allen plan essentially recognized Brooks McCormick's desire to decentralize, provide for truly autonomous operations, and assign accountability to the groups. Not only was the role of the corporate staff thereby much reduced but an entire tier of management was removed between the president and group presidents. Each group was allowed to organize as they saw fit, but with the guidelines set down by Booz Allen. Thus the agriculture and truck groups were organized geographically, construction and solar were organized functionally, and components was organized by product line. (For pre- and post-1976 organization charts, see Exhibits 2 and 3.)

How much decentralization was really affected is another question. As one executive commented, "Brooks took over a company that was used to very autocratic systems . . . everything was centralized. So even though there was an attempt to decentralize, it can't be done overnight and is hard to do. The senior managers really didn't have any leeway." Another climate study was taken, and improvement was found, but there was still "a short-term perspective and a management style that was hindering open communication and initiative."

While planning and human resources systems had now been instituted, there was the need to learn to use them judiciously and to ask some critical strategic questions, questions often best asked by a newcomer. As one executive described it, "We were still following the mushroom theory of decision making—keep managers in the dark and requests for resources will pop up all over the place, at random and with no relation to each other. We had to think about the relations."

Other Changes. Beyond the major programs in the planning and human resources areas, McCormick also hired a consultant in mid-1976 to conduct a study of plant-level manpower utilization. The purpose of the study was to pinpoint the sources of excess labor costs which were known to be extensive. The report was received in 1977, indicating some $300 million in excess costs.

Capital and engineering investments were also given higher priority. Because of cash constraints, high interest costs, and lack of borrowing capacity, however, investments were kept to a minimum and emphasized end-product development rather than plant improvement, manufacturing process . . . innovation, or intermediate product research.

Finally, McCormick began to look for ways to divest some unprofitable operations. In 1975 it was decided to sell the Wisconsin steel division, but the sale was not consummated until 1977. IH received $15 million in cash and $50 million in notes, but the effect on net income was a loss of $37.6 million.

In the five years 1971 to 1976 net income had grown from $45.2 million to $174.1 million, return on sales from 1.5 percent to 3.2 percent, and most impressively, return on equity from 3.9 percent to 12.1 percent. As one executive commented, "Brooks saved this company. He did a tremendous job of initiating change and getting the new programs going. His actions showed a lot of fortitude."

International Harvester in 1977

In trying to assess the company in the spring of 1977, Archie McCardell had available to him the following kinds of information from public sources concerning the financial position of the company as a whole, the various industries in which it participated, and its internal resources.

In FY 1976 the company had sales of $5.5 billion and ranked 27th in sales in the Fortune 500, while net income was $174 million which ranked 51st, and return on equity ranked 340th. (For 1976 balance sheet, income statement, key statistics for 10 years, and comparative statistics, see Exhibits 4, 5, 6, and 7.) International Harvester's basic products were in three industries: heavy-duty trucks, agricultural equipment, and construction equipment. The company produced many of the components for these products. On a smaller scale, the company made medium-sized turbine engines mostly for the oil and gas industry. There was also a finance subsidiary to support sales.

Trucks

Trucks were usually segmented by their weight. There were eight different weight classes ranging from pickups and vans (class 1 or class 2) to long-distance tractor trailers (class 8). (See Table 1.) Market growth had been 8–11 percent in the late 60s and early 70s. The growth rate was expected to slow to 3–6 percent in the United States due to several factors: higher prices for fuel and trucks and the slowing of highway construction and population growth.

In the heavy-duty segment of the truck market (classes 6, 7, and 8), trucks were either straight trucks or tractor trucks. A straight truck consisted of a cab, frame, two or three axles, driveshaft, transmission, and engine. A body was added by another manufacturer. Typical straight trucks were dump, garbage, or construction trucks. A tractor truck was meant to pull trailers and had the same components as a straight truck but the frame was shorter. Trailers were bought elsewhere.

Cab design could either be conventional (engine in front) or cab-over engine (COE). Conventional models were generally cheaper to build, less complicated, simpler to maintain, smoother to ride and safer. The COE had better maneuverability, capacity for longer trailers, and higher visibility.

Table 1

U.S. Truck Market Factory Sales by Weight Class—1976 (Trucks and buses; weight in pounds)

Class 1	Class 2	Class 3	Class 4	Class 5	Class 6	Class 7	Class 8
6,000	6,000–10,000	10,000–14,000	14,000–16,000	16,000–19,500	19,501–26,000	26,001–33,000	33,000+
			Unit Sales				
1,248,034	1,389,707	22,444	1,129*	11,416	164,796	24,961	118,048

* 1975 figure.
Source: Motor Vehicle Manufacturers Association.

Within the heavy-duty segment, class 6 trucks were differentiated from class 7 and class 8 by use, mileage, and engine type. Class 6 trucks were used for agriculture, wholesale, and retail trade (intracity delivery). Their annual mileage was lower, and they were more often gasoline powered. In 1976 10 percent of class 6 trucks were diesel powered as compared to more than 95 percent for class 7 and class 8 trucks. But with gasoline prices on the rise, growth of diesel engines in class 6 trucks was predicted. Class 7 and class 8 trucks were found in intercity hauling, mining, construction, and lumbering. They had much greater annual mileage and were diesel powered.

The truck market could also be segmented by buyer. Heavy-duty truck buyers were either private owner-operators or fleet operators. The demarcation between the two was ownership of 10 or more trucks. Light-duty truck buyers were fleet operators (for example, telephone repair trucks) or the consumer market (for pickup, recreational vehicles, or four-wheel drive vehicles).

American manufacturers were not a major factor in the European market in 1976 since their trucks were mostly too large for foreign roads. The European market was highly competitive, with many firms. Consolidation was predicted there, however. There was much opportunity for expansion, particularly in the Third World, but competition was stiff. European firms were threatening to enter the U.S. market with diesel trucks of the class 6 variety. Daimler Benz had started operations in the United States and IVECO (Fiat, Magerius-Deutz) was to team up with Mack. Joint ventures also were allowing U.S. firms to enter the European market, for example, IH with DAF (Holland). (See Exhibits 8 and 9 for European market data.)

Industry Characteristics. Manufacturers of trucks were generally not backward integrated but merely assemblers of parts purchased elsewhere. For example, heavy-duty engines were purchased from Cummins, Detroit Diesel (GM), and Caterpillar. Manufacturers relied heavily on components suppliers not only for the parts but also for R&D of new engineering designs. Only Mack was fully backward integrated, making all its own components, specifically engines, transmissions, and axles, where there were higher profit margins. IH was also unusual in that it made some of its own components for trucks, primarily engines. IH still purchased 70 percent of its truck parts from outside sources, however.

Buyers of trucks were quite sophisticated. Owner-operators specified many of the parts to go into a truck, and fleet operators, who had their own engineering staff, sometimes even indicated how the truck should be designed and built. Hence product differentiation between companies was based more on advertised image and reputation than substance. (See Exhibit 10 for an analysis of the structure of the truck industry.)

Competition. In 1976 International Harvester competed in the heavy-duty market with classes 6, 7, and 8 trucks and in the light-duty market with the four-wheel drive, class 2 vehicle, the Scout.

In the heavy-duty market, a shakeout of competitors occurred in the 50s. At that time there had been some 30 truck manufacturers in the United States, many of them operating only in one region of the country. By 1976 the market contained three giants—International Harvester, Ford, and General Motors; two or three smaller but profitable specialists—Paccar and Mack; and a handful of smaller companies clinging to specialized niches.

In class 7 and class 8 trucks, IH was the industry leader. Twenty-five percent of all class 8 trucks on the road were IH trucks. IH was strongest in the fleet-only segment. Major competitors were GM and Ford, and competition was on price. The rivalry was made stiffer since GM and Ford were lower cost producers and were backed by their parent companies.

Paccar was the leader in the owner-operator segment of the market. Paccar produced Kenworth and Peterbilt trucks which were considered the Rolls Royces of trucking. The company had lower market share than some competitors but the highest profitability in the industry. The lower market share was explained in part by the company's operations being concentrated in the western half of the country. Other analysts explained Paccar's performance as the result of remaining a pure assembler and very specialized. While higher margins were possible through component manufacture (Mack's strategy), a pure assembler retained maximal ability to respond to customer demands on product design. Other companies focusing on the owner-operator market were Mack, Freightliner, and White Motor. Competition in this segment was on service and features (customization) rather than price, and there was a significant degree of brand loyalty.

IH was uniquely positioned as the only major producer specializing in a full line of trucks as a major business. In a market where reputation was important, IH's reputation was as a manufacturer for fleet buyers. The company was known for an ability to produce a wide product range from standard components which lowered the cost and simplified maintenance. IH's strong sales and service dealerships and part distribution network were a major advantage with 800 dealerships versus GM or Ford's 300. However, IH could not match GM or Ford on price in the fleet market. In the owner-operator market, IH did price below competition; but as pointed out above, perceived reputation and product quality and customization were more important to owner-operators.

In class 6 trucks, Harvester, GM, and Ford were the only competitors. Market share estimates varied, but the following were representative (see Table 2):

Table 2

1976 Market Share Estimates (Factory sales)

	Class 6	Classes 7 and 8
International Harvester	15%	26%
General Motors	45	12
Ford	36	19
White	—	12
Paccar	—	9
Mack	—	17

Source: Wainwright Securities.

IH was the major factor for some time in the utility/sport vehicle area, represented by the Scout. But GM and Ford entered that market aggressively in the early 70s and considerably weakened IH's position. In 1976 the Scout had about 14 percent of the market, and volumes were not high enough to support efficient costs. Further, IH's dealerships for the Scout were weaker than that for the two automakers.

In 1976 International Harvester's most popular truck was the Transtar, a COE class 8 truck aimed at the fleet market. IH had introduced a premium COE, the Eagle, for the owner-operator. The S series of medium- and heavy-duty conventional models was to be introduced in 1977. The latter had many standardized components and provided the opportunity for the first serious U.S.-made entry into class 6 diesel-powered trucks. A line of construction trucks under the Paystart name finished out the product line.

IH's strengths were its dealer network and established market leadership. But capital spending had been low in the past, which had limited the ability for integration and modernization of plant and processes. Product proliferation had been somewhat high, increased by some rather random entries in various foreign countries. The S series promised to begin consolidation of the line. Sales in 1976 for the truck group were $2.3 billion, which represented 42 percent of total IH sales (the largest share). IH's operating margin (all groups combined) was 5.9 percent but only 1.4 percent (estimate) for trucks.

Agricultural Equipment

The agricultural equipment industry included combines, tractors, and a wide range of attachments for crop production and harvesting and hay and forage harvesting. Combines and tractors represented the largest share of sales. The worldwide market was relatively mature, with the major markets being North America, Europe, and certain Third World countries. North American manufacturers were strongest in the large

Table 3

Estimated Worldwide Tractor Market, 1977

	Units	Average Horsepower	Total Horsepower	Long-term Annual Growth Potential
United States and Canada	200,000	100	20 billion	0–2%
Europe	350,000	75	26 billion	5%
Third World	280,000	40	11 billion	Mixed
Japan	200,000	40	8 billion	Closed to United States

Source: First Boston Research.

equipment end of the market, such as tractors with over 100 horsepower, which were largely inappropriate for foreign markets because of smaller field sizes.

Tractors represented 52 percent of industry sales and were used as a barometer of market trends. The size and growth potential of the major geographical segments of the tractor market are shown in Table 3.

As Table 3 suggests, different geographical regions were more attractive than others in terms of growth. Other factors also affected the market risks. Over time the market for agricultural equipment in North America was essentially flat, but it was also highly cyclical. In Europe the size of the equipment used on farms had increased rapidly. Four percent of the tractors in Europe were over 70 horsepower in 1972, and 16 percent by 1976. This trend benefited North American manufacturers. Also Europe was not as cyclical as North America. The Third World seemed to offer strong opportunities. A problem there, however, was government's insistence on local production. Economies of scale required a plant to operate at 5,000 units per year at minimum. Few Third World countries offered a market of that size. In addition the usual uncertainties caused by commodity prices, weather, and government regulation of farms made the Third World markets risky at best.

Industry Characteristics. Farm equipment was sold on the characteristics and availability of the products and service. Thus competition centered on the strength of the dealer network. Agricultural equipment manufacturers were more integrated than truck assemblers. For example, IH made its own engines and purchased only 20 percent of its parts from outside sources.

As users of the equipment, buyers were fairly knowledgeable (though this varied by size of farm). Some training was provided by dealers, however.

The industry was cyclical. Sales of farm equipment were highly dependent on farm income. The ability to purchase new farm equipment was dependent in turn on a multitude of interconnected variables, including the weather, commodity prices, and government agricultural policies. Even in good times, purchases were financed, and such financing was usually provided by the manufacturer.

The trend in agriculture was toward larger and larger farms which in turn supported larger and more powerful farm equipment. With the consequent increase in the economies of scale, these trends were adding pressure for an increase in the concentration of the industry. (See Exhibit 11 for a structural analysis of the agricultural equipment industry.)

Competition. For a slow-growth industry, the number of firms in the agricultural equipment industry was large and perhaps greater than the market could support at an efficient scale. The North American companies in order of sales were Deere & Company, International Harvester, Massey-Ferguson, Allis-Chalmers, J. I. Case, White Motor, and Ford. (For pertinent comparative data see Exhibit 12.)

The industry leader was Deere & Company. Prior to 1963, when Deere became number one, International Harvester had been the leader. IH had maintained a strong number two position since the early 60s. One estimate gave Deere about 36 percent and Harvester about 33 percent of the domestic market. The remaining five companies battled for the remaining 30 percent. With its long history of penetration in foreign markets, Harvester was the industry leader in Europe and was strong in several other countries, particularly ex-Commonwealth countries. (Actually, Harvester sold a few units less than Massey-Ferguson in Europe in 1976, but sales of Massey, who had followed a strategy of trying to penetrate foreign markets, had trended steadily downward while Harvester's position had steadily improved.) Deere had begun a major and expensive effort to enter Europe but was not as yet a strong presence in foreign markets. Competitive positions in mid-1977 were estimated as shown in Table 4.

Table 4

Estimated Domestic Farm Equipment Market Share

	Deere	IH	Massey	Case	Chalmers	Other
Tractors (100 HP+)	37%	33%	9%	14%	5%	2%
Combines	37	20	18	—	15	10
Tillage plows	30	23	6	n.a.	n.a.	41
Cotton pickers	50	50	—	—	—	—
Balers	28	18	—	n.a.	n.a.	54

Source: Wainwright Securities and First Boston Research.

Table 5

Comparative Dealer Statistics, 1977

	Pretax Return on Sales		Return on Net Worth	
	All	Hi Performers	All	Hi Performers
Deere	3.9%	6.9%	25.6%	35.6%
International Harvester	2.5	5.5	20.7	38.6
Industry	1.3	5.7	18.6	37.6

Source: First Boston Research.

Both International Harvester and Deere & Company had strong dealer networks unapproached by any others in the industry. Deere's dealerships were considered superior (see Table 5), but IH had been investing in dealer improvement particularly in its XL program, which included certified service through training, parts supports, audiovisual aids, formal planning, and computerized systems. Brand loyalty was particularly strong for IH and Deere but was relatively absent for other equipment makers. One analyst estimated that 90 percent of first-time buyers of IH equipment returned to IH for future purchases of the same brand.

Deere was a formidable opponent. The company emphasized the high end of the product line (big 100+ horsepower tractors, for example) targeted at the 20 percent of the farmers who produced 75–80 percent of farm output. As one analyst put it, "Deere had the biggest share of the biggest machines with the biggest profitability." Deere was the low-cost producer but had chosen not to compete on price but to maintain high margins. They emphasized plant utilization. Indeed, one industry observer claimed that in the attempt to hold back overexpansion, Deere had become capacity constrained to the extent that it was limiting both its sales and market share below obvious potential.

IH produced a full line of such products for the farm market plus lawn and garden tractors for the consumer market. Sales for the agricultural equipment group in 1976 were $2.26 billion or 41 percent of total sales. The group's operating margin was slightly above the company average (estimated at 6–8 percent). According to one financial analyst, agricultural equipment should have been IH's cash generator, but with the intensity of competition and the large investments needed for upgrading facilities and foreign expansion, this had not been possible.

Construction Equipment

Products falling in the construction equipment category covered a broad range of end uses, power ranges, sizes, and size and needs of customers.

Bulldozers, loaders, excavators, cranes, road-building and logging equipment, and forklift trucks were all included in the industry. Manufacturers varied in the breadth of their product line—some specializing in only one type, but none produced the entire range.

The construction equipment market was highly segmented, first by product line and then by weight, size, or capacity. For each of these products and within different geographic areas, a slightly different group of companies competed. The largest segment (about 25 percent) was crawler tractors (bulldozers) and loaders, another 15 percent went to wheel (or rubber-tired) loaders and loaders with a backhoe attachment, and finally excavators (hydraulic or cable) were 10 percent of the market. The other 50 percent was made up of many specialty products, like road scrapers, building construction cranes, off-highway trucks, logging or pipelaying equipment. By custom, industrial machinery such as forklift trucks was usually included in the construction equipment industry though the market followed different dynamics.

The market was also segmented by customer industry: residential building construction, highway construction, energy production (strip mining), and waste treatment. The relative size of these various markets is shown in Table 6.

Understanding the demand for construction equipment required understanding the dynamics of all of these very different markets. The end markets were changing in different ways: the end of the Interstate Highway program in the late 60s slowed the road construction market. Skyrocketing building costs and a problematic economy slowed the building construction industry (particularly the residential sector). Fuel shortages supported the resurgence of strip mining. With these factors added together, demand was predicted in the mid-70s to continue at a 6–8 percent growth rate domestically and at a 10–12 percent rate overseas.

Table 6

Estimated End Markets for Construction Equipment

	Relative Size
Construction:	
Building	20–25%
Nonbuilding (highways)	20–30
Mining all types	20–35
Forestry	5–10
Industrial	2–5
Government (includes waste treatment)	2–5

Source: First Boston Research.

The international market was a tough but lucrative one. Europe was a mature market and, because of the age and congestion of its cities, required different (mostly smaller) equipment than the United States. Most growth potential overseas was in developing and communist countries which required sizable capital to support the distribution and service networks required. Entry was made difficult in most countries, however, by the presence of strong, entrenched local manufacturers.

Industry Characteristics. In the construction equipment industry, the customer was best viewed as not buying a piece of machinery alone but rather a package of a machine and service, or in industry parlance, so many machine hours per day. This was because construction equipment always experienced breakdowns. Such breakdowns were very costly for the customer. Thus when purchasing construction equipment, a customer was not so much price sensitive as concerned with the speed and quality of repairs. Indeed, fully one third of industry sales were for attachments and parts. This aftermarket for parts and service was not only important to the customer but to the manufacturer who earned higher margins on these sales. (Parts support was another aspect of the difficulty of entering foreign markets.)

Customers for construction equipment varied considerably both within and among segments: governments were major procurers of equipment, but at the same time there were hundreds of small builders buying just a few pieces of equipment, particularly for the residential construction market. Key issues for the government buyer were price, parts availability, and dealer reputation; while for private customers, issues were parts availability, a personal dealer relationship, and production experience.

Excluding the aftermarket sales discussed above, profitability was higher on sales of larger equipment, but production for this equipment was also very capital-intensive. There were segments within the industry which were not so capital-intensive as evidenced by the multitude of smaller companies competing in them. Over 16 firms competed in the United States alone in the hydraulic excavator area, for example. Backward integration varied but was an advantage. Caterpillar purchased only 10 percent of their parts outside while Harvester purchased from 50–70 percent outside parts. (See Exhibit 13 for a structural analysis of the construction equipment industry.)

Competition. With the high degree of segmentation in the market, obtaining a clear picture of the competitive environment was difficult. One thing was clear—the worldwide market was dominated by Caterpillar Tractor Company (CAT). Depending on the market segment, CAT's share was anywhere from 35 percent to 65 percent. CAT maintained a price umbrella and followed a full product line strategy. Assuming the presence of the Justice Department would keep CAT in the range of 45–55 percent of the total market, the question was how and who would survive in the remaining half.

In 1977 there were seven other major contenders in the industry and a myriad of smaller, local specialists. The seven majors were J. I. Case (a division of Tenneco), John Deere, International Harvester, Komatsu (Japan), Clark Equipment, Allis-Chalmers, and Massey-Ferguson. In the worldwide market, consolidation in the industry was a recent phenomenon. In Europe, as equipment became larger and economies of scale caused export to become essential, major national firms, specializing in smaller equipment for the home market, merged with the weaker North American firms to fill out product lines. Negotiations were not one-sided by any means as the North American firms were gaining strong distribution systems abroad. The early 70s saw the merger of Allis-Chalmers and Fiat (Italy), Massey-Ferguson and Hannomag (Germany), J. I. Case and Poclaine (France). In a similar vein, IH had a joint venture with Komatsu to gain entry into the large Japanese market, and Komatsu was expected to break into the U.S. market.

Obviously the strategic problem was how to coexist in a market dominated by CAT and still make a profit. Three strategies had succeeded in the industry thus far: (1) offer a full line of all types of products (CAT); (2) offer a full line of one type of product [Clark in loaders, or Terex (GM) in scrapers]; or (3) offer one model of each type of product (Deere). Most companies followed a targeting strategy, finding niches CAT did not occupy. For example, competitors brought out either a larger or smaller version of a given product. How long these strategies would remain successful was questionable as a trend toward the expansion of company product lines was apparent, as shown in Exhibit 14. IH was considered in the strongest position productwise in head-to-head competition with CAT, IH having the second broadest product line.

Other essential ingredients for competitive success were a strong distribution system with excellent parts and after-sale services, strong manufacturing facilities for profitability and price competitiveness, and a strong balance sheet to support the necessary capital investment. CAT had 226 dealers with 950 outlets worldwide, and in the United States filled 99.6 percent of its parts orders within 48 hours. By comparison, IH, which was considered to have a good distribution system, had about 70 dealers with about 200 outlets worldwide. CAT was low-cost producer and was strong financially. While not an innovator, CAT spent a higher percentage of sales on R&D than the rest of the industry. Indeed, the company tended to let others take the market risks of product innovation and entered after a product was established in the marketplace with a slightly better version. With its reputation and superior distribution, CAT could then usurp the number one position. (Exhibits 15 and 16 give some idea of competitive positions in terms of financial indicators and market shares in certain product lines.)

Komatsu, the second largest company worldwide, was a fairly new entrant on the world scene, though it had long dominated Japan. It now threatened to enter the U.S. market.

IH was the number two domestic firm, primarily because it had a strong presence overseas in Asia and the Communist Bloc countries. IH had a decent distribution system and parts support. IH products included crawler tractors, both rubber-tired and crawler loaders, tractors with hydraulic backhoe attachments, excavators, scrapers, off-highway trucks and haulers, logging equipment, and industrial forklift trucks. As mentioned earlier, this was the broadest product line after CAT, although sales volume was only 15 percent of CAT's. IH's weaknesses stemmed from capital starvation in the past. As a consequence, its plant was old and generated high costs. Sales for the construction equipment group were $0.7 billion in 1976 (12 percent of IH total sales), but it had a history of volatile earnings: a $33.6 million profit in 1975, a $4.6 million loss in 1976, and an estimated $10–$12 million profit in 1977. The 1976 loss compared to CAT's average and steadier 14 percent return.

Components

When the components group became a separate entity in 1976, it followed the pattern of CAT and GM in the early 60s and Deere in the late 60s. Sales were almost entirely internal and lumped into the end-product groups for reporting purposes. Products included gas and diesel engines, foundry products (castings), other components (fasteners, bearings, and hydraulics, for example), and repair products. Parts distribution (as the sole cost center) was also part of the group's responsibility.

Turbine Engines

The Solar Company, a California-based specialist in welding of exotic metals and turbine engine technology, was bought in the late 50s to develop turbine engines for other IH products. While this project never came to fruition, the division took off in the 60s, becoming the leading manufacturer of gas turbine engines. It sold its smaller engines primarily to the oil and gas industry on a worldwide basis, for pumping in gas pipelines or off-shore drilling rigs, for example.

A large (10,000 horsepower) turbine was under development in 1976–77 for use in power generation. Solar was its industry's leader. Further market growth potential was probably high—around 10 percent.

Solar's sales in 1976 were $0.25 billion or 3.5 percent of total IH sales. It was a highly profitable, if somewhat volatile, enterprise, having 1976 earnings of $20.7 million which compared to the $20.9 million for trucks.

IH Credit Company

Following industry custom, IH provided customer financing for their major product lines through the financing subsidiary, IH Credit Company. In 1977 IH Credit Company represented 13.3 percent of company assets and 29.1 percent of equity. In comparison, the numbers were 5.4 percent and 11.7 percent, respectively, for Deere. IH Credit had greater profitability than much of the manufacturing operation and provided a profit stabilizer for IH's financial position.

* * * * *

Archie McCardell interrupted Ed Spencer's latest monologue. "Well, Ed, all this information is certainly intriguing, indeed overwhelming. And I must say that I already have some ideas of what I might do. But ideas require capital to make them happen. So the question is, can I get the capital to do anything major or can Harvester only plod along—too big to go under but not profitable enough to become a major factor in any market?"

Spencer replied:

That depends, of course, on how much you think you need. As you said yourself, the financials speak for themselves. The company is capital constrained. One thing to think about though, when looking at the financials, is the age of the company's plant. The average age of tooling, for example, is 23 years which is a lot older than the industry standard of 10 years. The company uses the average cost method for inventory valuation as opposed to the more conservative LIFO method used by the rest of the industry. The credit company should not be ignored either. It finances both retail and wholesale receivables. Realize that CAT doesn't have a credit subsidiary (its dealers are too strong to need one), and Deere only finances retail. You might consider this a $1.5 billion addition to short-term debt. Finally, there is about $900 million in unfunded pension-vested benefits that's a potential liability. For all these reasons and others, Harvester's rating was downgraded to BBB. And as I'm sure you're aware, IH common has been selling below book for years. [For data on capital expenditures, stock price history, profitability, and performance per employee see Exhibits 17, 18, 19, and 20.]

But finances aside, the company may be in somewhat of a turmoil internally, as they are in the throes of a companywide reorganization.

And as you can see, Archie, a lot has already started happening at Harvester, and a lot remains to be done. One person cannot turn around a company alone—but he can, with proper background and emphasis, speed the momentum that already exists.

Archie McCardell smiled slightly and added, "And I take it, you think I'm that person. We'll just have to wait and see."

Exhibit 1

Historical Performance (Dollars in millions)

	Sales	Net Income	Return on Sales	Equity	Return on Equity
1910	$ 102.0	$16.1	15.8%	$ 156.1	10.3%
1920	225.0	16.7	7.4	218.4	7.6
1930	n.a.	25.7	—	316.6	8.1
1940	247.7	23.2	8.4	337.9	6.9
1945	622.0*	24.5	3.9	396.6	6.2
1950	942.6	66.7	7.1	614.5	10.9
1955	1,165.8	55.5	4.8	761.3	7.3
1960	1,683.2	53.8	3.2	1,020.9	5.3
1965	2,336.7	97.7	4.2	1,088.7	9.0
1970	2,711.5	52.7	1.9	1,146.8	4.6

n.a. = Not available.
* $290 million of sales were war related.

Exhibit 2

Organization Chart, October 31, 1974

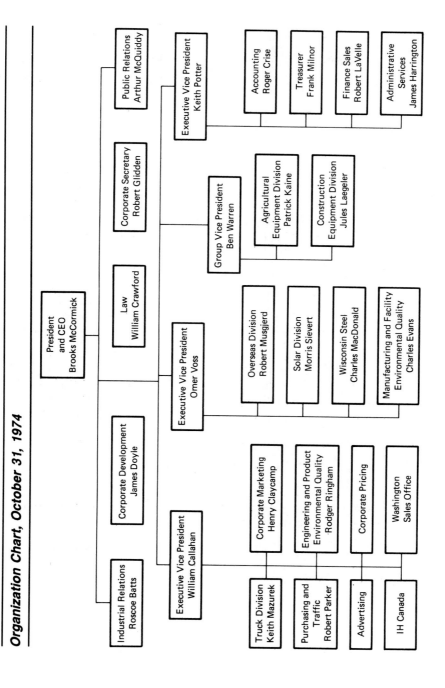

Exhibit 3

Organization Chart, June 1, 1977

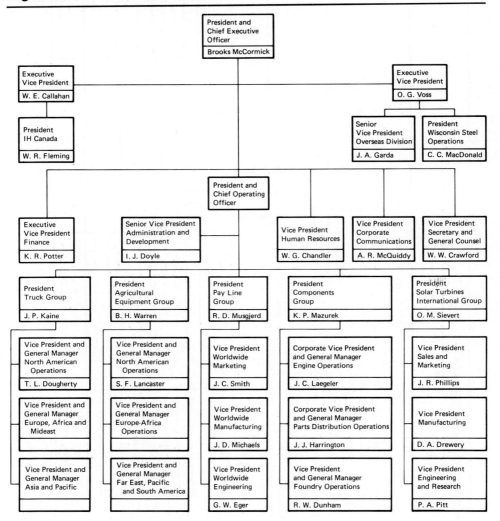

Exhibit 4

INTERNATIONAL HARVESTER
Balance Sheet, 1976
(in millions)

Assets

Current assets:	
Cash	$ 40.0
Marketable securities principally at cost	0.5
Net receivables	603.0
Inventories	1,584.4
Total current assets	2,227.9
Investments	495.8
Property	710.3
Wisconsin steel division	65.8
Other	75.0
Total assets	$3,574.8

Liabilities and Stockholders' Equity

Current liabilities:	
Notes payable	$ 266.5
Accounts payable	282.4
Accrued liabilities	319.6
Current maturities of long-term debt	35.7
Total current liabilities	1,004.2
Long-term debt	922.9
Deferred income taxes	66.9
Total liabilities	1,994.0
Stockholders' equity:	
Preferred stock	50.0
Common stock, $20 par	576.9
Capital in excess of par value	4.0
Income retained	964.7
	1,595.6
Less 464,954 shares of common in treasury at cost	14.8
Total stockholders' equity	1,580.8
Total liabilities and stockholders' equity	$3,574.8

Exhibit 5

INTERNATIONAL HARVESTER
Income Statement, 1976
(in millions)

Sales and other revenues:
Sales $5,488.1
Interest and other income 49.1
Total revenues 5,537.2

Costs and expenses:
Cost of sales 4,536.7
Marketing and administrative 547.3
Interest expenses 121.3
Other 110.5
Total costs and expenses 5,315.8

Income of consolidated group:
Income before taxes 221.4
Taxes 95.6
Net income 125.8

Income of nonconsolidated companies:
Income before taxes 93.6
Taxes 45.3
Net income 48.3
Total net income from continuing operations 174.1
Dividends . . . . $ 5.0
Earned on common stock . . . . $ 169.1
Income per share of common stock . . . . $ 6.02

Exhibit 6 10-Year Statistical Data

	1976	1975	1974	1973	1972	1971	1970	1969	1968	1967
Sales by major product group (continuing operations):										
Trucks	$2,310.4	$1,999.0	$2,282.9	$2,118.1	$1,780.4	$1,522.8	$1,335.6	$1,318.7	$1,145.0	$1,116.9
Agricultural equipment	2,262.0	2,105.7	1,656.7	1,242.1	1,028.0	857.1	775.6	762.0	847.4	898.2
Construction and industrial equipment	668.4	886.8	751.9	627.2	497.3	447.6	426.5	408.8	383.0	386.7
Turbo machinery	247.3	254.5	172.0	104.4	107.2	102.4	97.3	85.1	84.4	72.8
Total	$5,488.1	$5,246.0	$4,863.5	$4,091.8	$3,412.9	$2,929.9	$2,636.0	$2,574.6	$2,459.8	$2,474.6
Sales by area of final sale (continuing operations):										
United States	$3,457.6	$3,167.8	$3,375.0	$2,921.6	$2,551.2	$2,201.5	$1,955.8	$1,903.5	$1,823.4	$1,823.1
Canada	486.8	422.1	407.9	338.8	269.1	199.6	150.9	172.2	158.7	182.4
Europe and Africa	1,057.2	1,097.5	651.0	536.1	358.5	301.3	285.1	263.9	249.8	253.3
Latin America	147.5	183.5	127.4	76.4	79.7	72.7	82.6	74.4	69.5	60.3
Pacific area	359.0	375.1	302.2	218.9	154.4	154.8	161.6	160.6	158.4	155.5
Total	$5,488.1	$5,246.0	$4,863.5	$4,091.8	$3,412.9	$2,929.9	$2,636.0	$2,574.6	$2,459.8	$2,474.6
Net income:										
Amount	$ 174.1	$ 79.4	$ 124.1	$ 114.3	$ 86.6	$ 45.2	$ 52.4	$ 63.8	$ 75.4	$ 93.0
Percent of sales	3.17%	1.51%	2.55%	2.79%	2.54%	1.54%	1.99%	2.48%	3.07%	3.76%
Return on stockholders' equity, beginning of year	12.06%	5.82%	9.66%	9.54%	7.53%	3.94%	4.54%	5.54%	6.67%	8.52%
Other statistical data:										
Working capital	$1,223.8	$1,214.9	$ 947.3	$ 888.7	$ 845.3	$ 791.8	$ 766.4	$ 751.0	$ 768.7	$ 747.1
Long-term debt	922.9	938.2	625.3	497.0	465.1	431.3	402.2	312.7	298.1	264.4
Total net assets	$1,580.8	$1,443.9	$1,364.2	$1,284.6	$1,198.0	$1,149.5	$1,146.8	$1,155.2	$1,151.9	$1,130.0
Capital expenditures	$ 168.4	$ 173.2	$ 180.6	$ 106.5	$ 61.3	$ 62.7	$ 88.5	$ 97.0	$ 102.0	$ 93.5
Per common share:										
Net income	$ 6.02	$ 2.77	$ 4.46	$ 4.13	$ 3.17	$ 1.65	$ 3.92	$ 2.30	$ 2.69	$ 3.31
Dividends paid	$ 1.70	$ 1.70	$ 1.60	$ 1.50	$ 1.40	$ 1.60	$ 1.80	$ 1.80	$ 1.80	$ 1.80
Book value, end of year	$ 53.94	$ 50.14	$ 49.08	$ 46.21	$ 43.87	$ 42.10	$ 42.06	$ 41.70	$ 41.14	$ 40.23
Market price range:										
High	32½	30½	32½	40½	39	33⅞	29	38¾	38	41
Low	21½	18½	16¾	26	23	22⅝	22	25⅛	30⅜	33¾
Ratios:										
Current assets to current liabilities	2.2–1	2.1–1	1.7–1	1.9–1	2.0–1	2.2–1	2.2–1	2.4–1	2.7–1	2.8–1
Long-term debt as a percent of stockholders' equity plus long-term debt	37%	39%	31%	28%	28%	27%	26%	21%	21%	19%

Exhibit 7

1976—Comparative Statistics and Ranking within the Fortune 500

	IH		Deere		Caterpillar		Paccar	
	Amount	Rank	Amount	Rank	Amount	Rank	Amount	Rank
Sales*	$5,488.1	27	$3,133.8	66	$5,042.3	36	$1,001.4	227
Assets*	$3,574.8	43	$2,893.2	48	$3,893.9	35	$ 473.2	305
Sales/assets	1.5%	n.a.	1.1%	n.a.	1.3%	n.a.	2.1%	n.a.
Net income*	$ 174.1	51	$ 241.6	38	$ 383.2	24	$ 50.6	215
EBIT/interest expense	3.2%	n.a.	9.0%	n.a.	9.7%	n.a.	32.3%	n.a.
Equity*	$1,580.8	40	$1,378.8	48	$2,027.3	34	$ 271.9	277
Long-term debt/capital	35.9%	n.a.	26.1%	n.a.	33.7%	n.a.	7.6%	n.a.
Number of employees	97,550	22	55,242	52	77,793	31	10,747	336
Net income/sales	3.2%	360	7.7%	82	7.6%	87	5.1%	218
Net income/equity	11.0%	340	17.5%	79	18.9%	56	18.6%	59
Earnings per share	$ 6.02	—	$ 4.04	—	$ 4.45	—	$ 6.14	—
Ten-year growth rate of EPS	4.54%	318	11.42%	124	9.72%	168	10.91%	137
Total return to investors	55.10%	138	25.79%	295	27.88%	278	97.32%	33
Total return 10-year average	5.46%	294	10.19%	165	12.48%	109	n.a.	—
Sales per dollar of equity	$3.47		$2.27		$2.48		$ 3.68	
Sales per employee	$56,260		$56,728		$64,810		$93,180	
Assets per employee	$36,646		$52,372		$50,055		$44,032	

n.a. = Not available.
* In $ millions.

Exhibit 8

Estimated Share of Market—Trucks over Nine Tons* (As percent total)

	North America	Worldwide
Mercedes group	—	18%
GM	27%	17
Ford	28	15
IH	25	11
Iveco	—	8
Mack	6	3
Paccar	5	—
White	3	—

* Prior to the SAAB-Volvo merger.
Source: Wainwright Securities.

Exhibit 9

Estimated Production—over 15 Tons— 1975 (Units)

	Company	Units
1.	Daimler Benz	65,687
2.	Saab-Scandia & Volvo	40,181
3.	Iveco (Fiat, Magerius-Deutz)	38,760
4.	Mack (U.S.)	24,103
5.	Hino (Japan)	20,444
6.	International Harvester (U.S.)	19,723
7.	Renault (Saviem, Berliet)	18,728
8.	Mitsubishi (Japan)	14,993
9.	General Motors (U.S.)	14,261
10.	Ford (U.S.)	14,045
11.	White (U.S.)	12,356
12.	Nissan (Japan)	12,350
13.	British Leyland	12,061

Source: Wainwright Securities.

Exhibit 10

Structural Analysis of the Heavy-Duty Truck Industry—Domestic

ENTRY/MOBILITY BARRIERS ARE HIGH BUT DEPEND ON SEGMENT:
- Lower economies of scale/easier entry in owner-operator market, but higher costs for required service/dealer network.
- Higher economies of scale/tougher entry in fleet market, but dealer/service network not so important.
- High investment in capital equipment required to upgrade existing plant and build new plant.
- Some R&D necessary to keep up with government regulations and emission controls.

POWER OF BUYERS IS STRONG BUT VARIES BY SEGMENT:
- Owner-operators purchase small quantities, but are highly sophisticated, and together are a sizable market.
- Fleet buyers are large and buy large quantities.
- Fleet buyers tend to integrate backward into service, thus limiting the aftermarket.
- Price sensitivity varies but is higher for large fleet buyers and newer owner-operators.
- No threat of manufacturers integrating forward.

POWER OF SUPPLIERS IS MODERATE:
- Truck manufacturers differ in degree of backward integration.
- If backward integrated, manufacturers meet material shortages.
- If not backward integrated, suppliers are large but multiple sources exist.
- If manufacturer is active in other vehicle (e.g., autos), leverage over suppliers is increased by joint purchasing.

RIVALRY AMONG COMPETITORS IS STRONG BUT DIFFERS BY SEGMENT:
- Few firms in each segment, but more firms in the owner-operator market and fewer in the fleet and medium-heavy-duty markets. Some markets (C1.6) are being entered by foreign manufacturers.
- Growth is slow (1–2 percent per year) and cyclical.
- Physical product differentiation within segments is fairly low, high between segments.
- Some differentiation by brand name, image, and aftermarket services.

SUBSTITUTION THREAT IN NEAR TERM IS WEAK:
- Some intercity competition from rail and perhaps some air.
- All intracity and most intercity distribution dependent on trucks at least for next decade or two.
- Substitution pressure mostly from fuel shortages, but substitution of fossil fuels not in near future.

Exhibit 11

Structural Analysis of the Agricultural Equipment Industry—Domestic

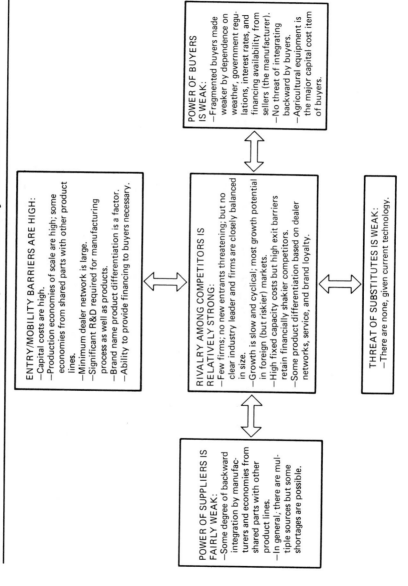

ENTRY/MOBILITY BARRIERS ARE HIGH:
- Capital costs are high.
- Production economies of scale are high; some economies from shared parts with other product lines.
- Minimum dealer network is large.
- Significant R&D required for manufacturing process as well as products.
- Brand name product differentiation is a factor.
- Ability to provide financing to buyers necessary.

POWER OF BUYERS IS WEAK:
- Fragmented buyers made weaker by dependence on weather, government regulations, interest rates, and financing availability from sellers (the manufacturer).
- No threat of integrating backward by buyers.
- Agricultural equipment is the major capital cost item of buyers.

RIVALRY AMONG COMPETITORS IS RELATIVELY STRONG:
- Few firms; no new entrants threatening; but no clear industry leader and firms are closely balanced in size.
- Growth is slow and cyclical; most growth potential in foreign (but riskier) markets.
- High fixed capacity costs but high exit barriers retain financially shakier competitors.
- Some product differentiation based on dealer networks, service, and brand loyalty.

POWER OF SUPPLIERS IS FAIRLY WEAK:
- Some degree of backward integration by manufacturers and economies from shared parts with other product lines.
- In general; there are multiple sources but some shortages are possible.

THREAT OF SUBSTITUTES IS WEAK:
- There are none, given current technology.

Exhibit 12

North American Farm Equipment Producers—1976

	North American Farm Equipment Sales—1976(p)	Total Farm Equipment Sales—1976	Pretax, Pre-Interest on Net Assets *	Ratio Debt to Capital	Capital Expense 1975 and 1976 as Percent 1976 Gross Plant	R&D as Percent Sales
Deere	$1,900	$2,523	26%	30%	32%	3.5%
International Harvester	1,295†	2,106	13	43	25	1.8
Massey-Ferguson	670	2,000	25	47	37	1.8
Allis-Chalmers	525	550	17	26	23	3.0
J. I. Case (division of Tenneco)	385	700	13‡	41	25‡	n.a.
White	332	332	12	60	30	1.0
Ford	270	960	21	24	11	3.2

n.a. = Not available.
* On prior years net assets (total assets less current liabilities).
† United States only.
‡ For J. I. Case only.
(p) Partially estimated.
Source: First Boston Research.

Exhibit 13

Structural Analysis of the Construction Equipment Industry—Domestic

ENTRY/MOBILITY BARRIERS ARE HIGH:
—High production economies of scale.
—Many opportunities for economies of shared parts with other product lines.
—Capital-intensive business requiring large capital expenditures.
—Continuing capital expenditures needed for upgrades of capacity.
—Some R&D required.
—Entry possible with a specialized product or limited region, but very difficult on full product line basis.

POWER OF SUPPLIERS IS FAIRLY WEAK:
—Companies vary as to the degree of backward integration and economies of shared parts with other product lines, but are more so than in the truck industry.
—Like the truck industry, material shortages may be a problem.
—Multiple suppliers usually exist.

RIVALRY AMONG COMPETITORS IS MODERATE:
—Few firms: market dominated by Caterpillar; but strong rivalry for number 2 position among several closely matched firms.
—Growth is relatively slow and cyclical (6–8 percent average); 3 key segments (road, housing, and mining) vary in any given year.
—Product differentiation by brand name is low except for visibility of Cat.
—High fixed costs support pressure for volume and for international expansion where competition is stiff.
—Threat of foreign firms entering market is strong, particularly from Japan.

POWER OF BUYERS IS MODERATE BUT DEPENDS ON SEGMENT:
—Mining and large-scale construction or road building: buyers are large and buy large quantities.
—Buyers are sophisticated.
—Small-scale construction (housing): many small buyers who buy smaller quantities.
—Speed and quality of service more important than price.
—No threat of either backward integration by buyers or forward integration by sellers.

THREAT OF SUBSTITUTES IS WEAK:
—There are none.

Exhibit 14

Product Lines of Major Construction Machinery Manufacturers

1966 - 1976 ●

1966 ○

	IND TRACTOR	FORK-LIFTS	SKIDDER	WHEEL LOADERS	COMPAC-TORS	CRAWLER TRACTOR	CRAWLER LOADERS	EXCAVA-TORS	GRADERS	SCRAPERS	HAUL TRUCKS
CAT		○	○	●	○	●	●	○	●	●	●
KOMATSU		●		●	○	●	●	○	●	●	●
IH	●	○	●	○		●	●	○		●	●
CASE	●	●	○	○		●	●	○			
FIAT-ALLIS		●		●		●	●	○	●	●	
CLARK		●	●	●	○			○	○	○	
DEERE	●	●	○	○	○	●	●	○	○	○	
TEREX				○		●				○	○
MASSEY F	●	●	○	○	○	○	○	○			

Source: Wainwright Securities.

Exhibit 15

Construction Equipment Industry—1976 (Dollars in millions)

	Construction Equipment Sales[p]			Total Sales	Pretax, Pre-Interest Return on Net Assets	Total Debt to Capital	Capital Spending 1975–76 as Percent 1976 Gross Plant	R&D as Percent Sales
	U.S.	Foreign	Total					
Caterpillar Tractor	$1,840	$2,585	$4,425	$ 5,042	28%	34%	34%	3.7%
Komatsu[g]	90[b]	375[c]	945[d]	1,050	28	64	25[e]	n.a.
International Harvester	300	368	668	5,488	13	43	25	1.8
J. I. Case (Tenneco)	290[a]	357	647	6,423	13[h]	51	25[h]	n.a.
Fiat-Allis	175	381	556	556	2	37	22	2.0
Deere	302	105	452	3,134	26	30	32	3.5
Clark Equipment[f]	200	200	400	1,261	18	32	25	1.1
Massey-Ferguson	89[a]	291	380	2,772	25	47	37	1.8
Terex (GM)	175	200	375	47,181	38	11	12	2.7
Ford	90	170	260	28,840	21	24	11	3.2

n.a. = Not available.
[a] North America.
[b] North and South America (but excluding Brazilian and Mexican production).
[c] Outside Japan.
[d] Including Japan.
[e] Estimated.
[f] Excludes Melrose.
[g] At average exchange rate for the year.
[h] For J. L. Case division only.
[p] Partially estimated.
Source: Wainwright Securities.

Exhibit 16

Estimated U.S. Market Share—Selected Products

	Crawler Tractors		Rubber-Tired Loaders		Conventional Scrapers	
	Under 90 HP	Over 90 HP	Under 5 Yards	Over 5 Yards	7–18 Yards (Struck)	Over 18 Yards (Struck)
Caterpillar	0%	60%	35%	45%	45%	65%
International Harvester	20	10	10	20	15	—
Deere	40	—	15	—	—	—
Case	25	5	5	—	—	—
Fiat-Allis	—	10	—	—	—	—
Clark Equipment	—	—	—	—	—	—
Terex	—	5			35	30

Source: Wainwright Securities.

Exhibit 17

Selected IH Stock Data, Fiscal 1967–1976

Year	Earnings per Share	Dividend	Price Range High	Price Range Low	P/E Range High	P/E Range Low	Book Value per Share*	Price as a Percent of Book Value High	Price as a Percent of Book Value Low
1967	$3.31	$1.80	41	34	12.4X	10.2X	$40.23	102%	84%
1968	2.69	1.80	38	30	14.1	11.3	41.14	92	74
1969	2.30	1.80	39	25	16.8	10.9	41.70	93	60
1970	1.92	1.80	29	22	15.1	11.5	42.06	69	52
1971	1.65	1.60	34	23	20.5	13.7	42.10	80	54
1972	3.17	1.40	39	23	12.3	7.3	43.87	88	52
1973	4.04	1.50	41	26	10.0	6.4	45.66	88	57
1974	4.41	1.60	32	17	7.3	3.8	48.47	66	35
1975	3.95	1.70	31	19	7.7	4.7	49.57	62	37
1976	5.98	1.70	33	22	5.4	3.6	53.34	61	40

* Year-end book value.
Source: Goldman Sachs.

Exhibit 18

Selected IH Asset Efficiency and Profitability Ratios, Fiscal 1967–1976

Year	Asset Turnover	As a Percent of Revenues		Capital Expenditures as a Percent of Net Plant	Return on Average Equity	Sustainable Growth Rate
		Working Capital	Inventory			
1967	1.14	29.4%	30.0%	3.9%	8.3%	4.7%
1968	1.10	30.3	31.0	4.0	6.6	3.8
1969	1.10	28.3	31.0	2.9	5.5	2.2
1970	1.07	28.3	34.0	2.5	4.6	2.0
1971	1.14	26.3	30.0	1.6	3.9	1.3
1972	1.24	24.2	32.0	1.5	7.4	2.9
1973	1.37	21.2	31.0	2.6	8.6	2.8
1974	1.46	19.1	30.0	3.7	8.9	2.7
1975	1.45	23.2	31.0	3.3	8.4	2.8
1976	1.52	22.3	29.0	2.9	11.6	8.3

Source: Goldman Sachs.

Exhibit 19

International Harvester's Capital Spending Program (Dollars in millions)

Year	Capital Spending	Gross Plant	Capital Spending as Percent Gross Plant*	Capital Spending as Percent Gross Plant*	
				Deere	Caterpillar
1976	$168.4	$1,452.8	12.3%	12.8%	21.8%
1975	173.2	1,373.4	12.1	27.4	19.7
1974	180.6	1,433.3	13.6	14.4	19.6
1973	106.5	1,329.1	8.4	8.9	20.2
1972	61.3	1,271.3	4.8	5.7	9.8
1971	62.7	1,275.1	5.0	4.6	9.9
1970	88.5	1,257.9	7.4	5.9	9.7
1969	99.2	1,200.4	8.7	7.2	10.2
1968	102.2	1,139.4	9.6	15.3	20.2
1967	93.5	1,063.1	9.0	12.3	31.1
1966	99.2	1,039.9	10.0	11.9	23.8
1965	120.4	989.4	13.2	17.6	18.6
1964	80.6	913.8	8.6	19.7	12.7
1963	76.1	934.0	8.5	10.7	10.3

* At previous year-end.
Source: Wainwright Securities.

Exhibit 20

Value Added and Gross Margin per Employee for International Harvester and Selected Companies, 1968–1976*

Year	International Harvester		Deere & Company		Caterpillar		Paccar	
	Value Added per Employee	Gross Profit Margin	Value Added per Employee	Gross Profit Margin	Value Added per Employee	Gross Profit Margin	Value Added per Employee	Gross Profit Margin
1968	$ 4,836	20.2%	$ 6,377	26.1%	$ 7,595	26.6%	$ 4,987	12.2%
1969	4,688	18.4	6,295	24.9	8,767	28.0	8,743	12.2
1970	4,888	18.4	7,480	28.0	8,801	27.3	6,510	11.2
1971	5,106	16.7	8,708	27.7	8,994	25.9	8,516	13.2
1972	5,866	16.9	9,499	28.5	10,692	27.4	9,333	13.0
1973	6,658	17.1	11,222	28.1	10,556	24.7	10,884	13.5
1974	7,516	16.8	10,817	24.3	11,554	21.8	8,381	9.9
1975	8,888	17.6	13,670	24.9	15,882	25.4	10,462	12.1
1976	10,677	19.0	15,986	28.2	17,222	26.5	14,526	15.6
Average	7,141	18.0	10,714	26.9	11,987	26.0	10,303	12.9

* Gross profit margin excludes depreciation.
Source: Goldman Sachs.

Exhibit 21

Archie R. McCardell

Archie R. McCardell was born on August 29, 1926, in Hazel Park, Michigan, and attended elementary and high schools there. Following service in the U.S. Air Force during World War II, he entered the University of Michigan where he graduated with a bachelor of business administration degree in 1948 and a master of business administration degree the next year.

Mr. McCardell began his business career with the Ford Motor Company in 1949 and served in a variety of financial positions with that organization until 1960 when he was appointed secretary-treasurer, Ford of Australia. Three years later, he became director of finance for Ford of Germany.

In 1966 he joined Xerox Corporation as group vice president for corporate service and chief financial officer. Subsequently, he was elected executive vice president of Xerox and was named president of that organization in 1971.

Mr. McCardell currently serves on the boards of the American Express Company, American Express International Banking Corporation, and General Foods Corporation. He is also a member of the Business Council, the Conference Board, and the Advisory Council of the Stanford University Graduate School of Business. He previously served as chairman of the National Advisory Committee of the Blue Cross Association.

Mr. McCardell and his wife, Margaret, are the parents of three children.

General Electric

Strategic Position—1981

On December 21, 1980, the General Electric Company announced that John F. Welch, Jr., 45, would become chairman and chief executive officer effective April 1, 1981. Welch had spent 20 years in GE's operating organization—first in the plastics business, later in consumer products, and then as vice chairman. He would be replacing the retiring Reginald H. Jones, a man described by some as a "legend." Indeed, *The Wall Street Journal* reported that GE had "decided to replace a legend with a live wire."

The company that Jack Welch would be leading was the 10th largest industrial corporation in the United States and the only firm among *Fortune's* 10 largest that could be characterized as diversified. Its financial performance was solid—AAA bond rating, 19.5 percent return on equity, and $2.2 billion in cash and marketable securities. In addition GE's management systems and in particular its strategic planning system were most highly regarded; the following comments were typical:

> Probably no single company has made such a singular contribution to the arts and wiles, the viewpoints, and the techniques of large-scale corporate management as GE. . . . Today the technique uppermost in the minds of GE top management is planning—a preoccupation in which GE is again an acknowledged master and innovator among corporate giants.

> *Management Today,* August 1978

Copyright © 1981 by the President and Fellows of Harvard College
Harvard Business School case 381–174

Shortly after I took this job, I visited some people at the Defense Department because I had heard that they had just finished an exhaustive survey of industrial planning systems. They told me I was probably inheriting the world's most effective strategic planning system and that Number Two was pretty far behind.

> Daniel J. Fink, senior V.P., Corporate Planning
> and Development, General Electric

When Japanese managers come to visit us, they don't ask to see our research centers or manufacturing facilities. All they want to know about is our management system.

> A General Electric executive

GE's excellent performance and reputation were no guarantee of future success. Jack Welch would be challenged to meet the company's long-term objective of increasing earnings per share 25 percent faster than the growth in GNP in the face of tougher foreign competition and a continued slowdown in the growth of GE's traditional businesses. To meet this challenge, he would have to decide how to stimulate and promote growth and what role GE's famed planning system would play in the years ahead.

Origins of Strategic Planning

As the decade of the 1960s was nearing a close, a number of circumstances came together which led to a major reexamination of the way General Electric was being managed. One of the more salient of these was the company's profitless growth (see Exhibit 1 for financial information). While sales in 1968 of $8.4 billion were 91 percent higher than in 1960, net income had increased only 63 percent, and return on total assets had fallen from 7.4 percent to 6.2 percent. This lackluster profit performance came at the same time that three major ventures—commercial jet engines, mainframe computers, and nuclear power systems—were demanding more and more of the company's financial resources. Pressure on corporate management was mounting: GE's "sacred Triple A bond rating" was in jeopardy.

Improving this financial situation was no easy task. In 1968 GE was widely diversified, competing in 23 of the 26 two-digit SIC industry categories, and was decentralized into 10 groups, 46 divisions, and over 190 departments. Indeed diversification and decentralization had been the major strategic and organizational thrusts of GE's two prior CEOs— Ralph Cordiner, 1950 to 1963, and Fred Borch, 1963 to 1972. Under decentralization, GE's departments became organizational building blocks, each with its own product-market scope and its own marketing, finance, engineering, manufacturing, and employee-relations functions. One GE executive noted:

In the 1950s Cordiner led a massive decentralization of the company. This was absolutely necessary. GE had been highly centralized in the 1930s and 1940s. Cordiner broke the company down into departments that, as he used to say, "were a size that a man could get his arms around." And what the company would say after giving a man his department was, "Here, take this $50 million department and grow it into $125 million." Then the department would be split into two departments, like an amoeba.

In addition to decentralization, Cordiner pushed for expansion of GE's businesses and product lines. With growth and diversity, however, came problems of control:

The case for Cordiner lies in his improvement of GE's numerators and in his creation of a truly remarkable "can-do" organization. He was the champion of volume and diversity and of make rather than buy. He built a company unmatched in American business history in the capacity to pursue those objectives. In the sense of home grown know-how, GE *could* do almost anything; and in the sense of in-house capacity, GE could do a lot of a lot of things, simultaneously.

But the very expansiveness and evangelism that were Cordiner's strengths were flawed by permissiveness and lack of proportion. "We can do it" too often became "we should do it." For example, massive investments with long payback periods were undertaken simultaneously in nuclear power, aerospace, and computers, with a blithe self-confidence in GE's ability to "do-it-ourselves." A sort of "marketing macropia" persisted in which previously constrained market segmentations and product definitions were escalated beyond experience or prudence.[1]

As Fred Borch faced the challenges of leading General Electric in the mid-1960s, internal studies of the company's problems began to proliferate. One such study set out to give management a tool for evaluating business plans by delineating the key factors associated with profitable results.[2] Another study undertaken by GE's Growth Council tried to determine how the company would properly position itself to meet its long-time goal of growing faster than the GNP. Despite these and other staff studies, however, profitless growth continued.

Reg Jones assessed the company's situation at the time:

Our performance reflected poor planning and a poor understanding of the businesses. A major reason for this weakness was the way we were organized. Under the existing structure with functional staff units at the corporate level, business plans only received functional reviews. They were not given a *business* evaluation.

---

[1] James P. Baughman, "Problems and Performance of the Role of Chief Executive in the General Electric Company, 1892–1974" (mimeographed discussion paper, July 15, 1974).

[2] This approach eventually led to the **PIMS** model that has been made available to industry at large by the Strategic Planning Institute.

True, we had a corporate planning department, but they were more concerned with econometric models and environmental forecasting than with hard-headed business plan evaluation. Fortunately, Fred Borch was able to recognize the problem.

In 1969 Borch commissioned McKinsey & Co. to study the effectiveness of GE's corporate staff and of the planning done at the operating level. He commented on McKinsey's study:

They were totally amazed at how the company ran as well as it did with the planning that was being done or not being done at various operating levels. But they saw some tremendous opportunities for moving the company ahead if we devoted the necessary competence and time to facing up to these, as they saw it, very critical problems.

In their report, they made two specific recommendations. One was that we recognize that our departments were not really businesses. We had been saying that they were the basic building blocks of the company for many years, but they weren't. They were fractionated, and they were parts of larger businesses. The thrust of the recommendation was that we reorganize the company from an operations standpoint and create what they call Strategic Business Units—the terminology stolen from a study we made back in 1957. They gave certain criteria for these, and in brief what this amounted to were reasonably self-sufficient businesses that did not meet head-on with other strategic business units in making the major management decisions necessary.[3] They also recommended as part of this that the 33 or 35 or 40 strategic business units report directly to the CEO regardless of the size of the business or the present level in the organization.

Their second recommendation was that we face up to the fact that we were never going to get the longer range work done necessary to progress the company through the 70s unless we made a radical change in our staff components. The thrust of their recommendation was to separate out the ongoing work necessary to keep General Electric going from the work required to posture the company for the future.

Introduction of Strategic Planning

In reporting the results of the McKinsey study to GE's management in May 1970, Fred Borch noted: "We decided that their recommendations on both the operating front and the staff front conceptually were very sound. They hit right at the nut of the problem, but the implementation that they recommended just wouldn't fly as far as General Electric was concerned. We accepted about 100 percent of their conceptual contribution and virtually none of their implementation recommendations."

---

[3] The general characteristics of an SBU were defined as follows: a unique set of competitors, a unique business mission, a competitor in external markets (as opposed to internal supplier), the ability to accomplish integrated strategic planning, and the ability to "call the shots" on the variables crucial to the success of the business.

To develop an approach for implementing the McKinsey recommendations in a way suitable for GE, Borch had set up a task force headed by Group Vice President W. D. Dance. This group spent two intensive months preparing alternatives and recommendations for consideration by the corporate executive office.

As a result of these efforts, a decision was made to restructure GE's corporate staff into two parts. The existing staff units, which provided ongoing services to the CEO[4] and to the operating units, were grouped as the corporate administrative staff reporting to a senior vice president. The administrative staff would deal with functional, operational matters. As a counterpart, a corporate executive staff was created to help the CEO plan the future of the company. It comprised four staff components—finance, strategic planning, technology, legal and governance—each headed by a senior vice president.

Establishing Strategic Business Units

The task force anticipated several problems in implementing McKinsey's recommendation to create strategic business units reporting directly to the CEO. One problem had to do with GE's existing line reporting structure of groups, divisions, and departments. McKinsey's proposal had been to abandon GE's current organizational structure and to reorganize on the basis of SBUs. The task force was concerned that such a change might seriously jeopardize the successful functioning of GE's operational control system. To avoid this risk management decided to superimpose the SBU structure on the existing line reporting structure. For ongoing operations, managers would report according to the group-division-department structure. However, only units designated SBUs would prepare strategic plans.

As shown in Figure 1, a group, division, or department could be designated an SBU. This overlay of a strategic planning structure on the operating structure resulted in a variety of reporting relationships. When a department was named an SBU, for example, the department manager would report directly to the CEO for planning purposes but to a division manager for operating purposes. GE managers expressed the opinion that this approach provided the company with the best of both worlds—tight operational control on a comprehensive basis and planning at the relevant levels. One manager commented:

> In theory, the intervening layers of management were supposed to be transparent for planning purposes and opaque for control purposes. In practice, they were translucent for both. Even though the department or division

---

[4] The CEO here refers to the corporate executive office, which included the chairman and chief executive officer and the vice chairmen. GE usually had two or three vice chairmen.

Figure 1

SBU Overlay on Existing Organization

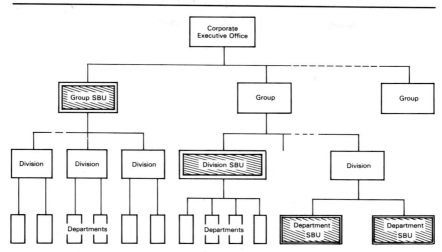

SBU managers were to report directly to the CEO for planning, they would normally review their plans with the group executive. In a sense, we loosened the SBU structure to allow personal influence and power to shape the important strategic decisions.

The designation of SBUs posed a second problem for the task force. According to GE executives, about 80 percent of the SBU designations could be readily agreed upon. The remaining 20 percent required considerable judgment whether the appropriate SBU level was the department, division, or group. In these cases Fred Borch would make the final judgment, often based on his "comfort index" with the business and with the manager running the business. Not until the end of 1972 were all of the SBU designations completed. Of the 43 SBUs, 4 were groups, 21 were divisions, and 18 were departments. Two other problems on the task force's agenda concerned the kind of information to be contained in an SBU plan and the numbers and kinds of people to staff the planning effort.

Defining a Business Plan

Even with the reduction in the number of business plans from 190 departments to 43 SBUs, the CEO faced a formidable task of review. One GE manager noted that "Borch had a sense that he wasn't looking for lots of data on each business unit but really wanted 15 terribly important and significant pages of data and analysis."

To deal with this problem, three of the group vice presidents were asked to work with three different consulting companies (Arthur D. Little, Boston Consulting Group, and McKinsey & Co.) to find a way to compress all of the strategic planning data into as effective a presentation as possible. For example, GE's collaborative effort with McKinsey led to the development of the nine-block summary of business and investment strategy shown in Figure 2.[5] One GE executive commented that "the nine-block summary had tremendous appeal to us not only because it compressed a lot of data but also because it contained enough subjective evaluation to appeal to the thinking of GE management."

The only instructions for the SBU manager on the content of a business plan was a listing of the topics to be covered. Over time new topics were added and some were deleted. But the corporate office never specified how each topic should be treated. The following list contains the topics specified for the 1973 SBU plans:

1. Identification and formulation of environmental assumptions of strategic importance.
2. Identification and in-depth analysis of competitors, including assumptions about their probable strategies.
3. Analysis of the SBU's own resources.
4. Development and evaluation of strategy alternatives.
5. Preparation of the SBU strategic plan, including estimates of capital spending for the next five years.
6. Preparation of the SBU operating plan, which detailed the next year of the SBU strategic plan.

Reg Jones, who became GE's chairman and chief executive officer in December 1972, added a proviso on how the plans were to be presented:

> At our general management conference in January 1973, I stirred up quite a few members of that audience when I said that I expected every SBU manager to be able to stand before a peer group and, without benefit of visual aids, give a clear and concise statement of his strategic plan. And that every manager reporting to him should fully understand that statement and be able to explain it to his troops. I meant it. When that happens, then you can say that planning has become a way of life.

Staffing the Planning Effort

With the new SBU planning approach in place, the question remained of how to staff the effort. Here two important actions were taken. First, each SBU manager was required to hire an SBU strategic planner. Because

---

[5] See Exhibit 2 for a description of GE's 1980 criteria for assessing industry attractiveness and business position.

Figure 2

Investment Priority Screen

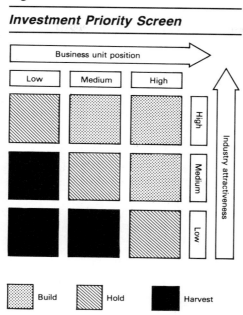

of the limited number of experienced strategic planners in the company at that time, many of the people filling these posts were hired from outside the company, an unusual practice for GE.[6]

Second, both the SBU general managers and strategic planners were required to attend special strategic planning seminars set up at GE's Management Development Center in Crotonville, New York. Each department and division general manager (over 240 in number) was also given a metal suitcase with a slide and tape show to present to subordinates after taking the course.

Acceptance of Planning: 1972–1977

In the 1950s and 1960s a characteristic of GE was the belief that the company could succeed in all of the businesses in which it competed. A frequently voiced reaction to strategic planning and particularly to the nine-block analysis, on the other hand, was that it legitimized exiting from certain businesses. According to *Fortune,* "GE stopped making

---

[6] Over time many of the SBUs developed planning staffs, and the planning positions were filled internally. By 1980 there were approximately 200 senior level planners in GE. About half of these were career planners, while the others rotated through the position as part of their career development.

vacuum cleaners, fans, phonographs, heart pacemakers, an industrial X-ray system, and numerous other products that failed to deliver the returns Jones demanded." During Jones's entire tenure as CEO, a total of 73 product lines were exited.

GE's successful exit from the mainframe computer business in May 1970 also played a pivotal role in legitimizing divestitures; as one manager commented:

> While the sale of GE's computer business actually preceded the adoption of strategic planning, somehow people began to connect the two. From then on it became fashionable to prune businesses. And Jones's subsequent promotion gave even more credibility to those managers who were willing to face up to the fact that certain businesses had to be exited.
>
> The planning system was just another tool which enabled a manager to face up to certain inevitabilities. Prior to this we had really operated with a "floating J curve." In other words, businesses would forecast two or three years of flat or declining profitability, but then all of the numbers would point upwards. What Jones was able to do with the computer business and what strategic planning revealed was that the floating J curve was a fantasy.

Impact on the Business Mix

As shown in Table 1, one impact of strategic planning was a shift in GE's mix of businesses. Reg Jones commented:

> Another source of confidence for us is the continued development of a strategic planning system that provides a strong discipline for differentiating the allocation of resources—that is, investing most heavily in areas of business that we identify as offering the greatest leverage for earnings growth

Table 1

GE's Business Mix (Percent)

	Sales		Earnings	
	1970	1977	1970	1977
Consumer products and services	22.8%	23.5%	29.6%	29.6%
Power systems	21.5	18.0	26.5	6.9
Industrial components and systems	23.1	20.6	28.4	17.6
Technical systems and materials	28.5	23.1	9.1	22.7
Natural resources	0.0	5.4	0.0	18.0
International	15.9	14.3	20.1	6.5
Corporate eliminations	(11.8)	(4.9)	(13.7)	(1.3)

Source: General Electric 10–K reports for 1970 (recast for organizational changes) and 1977.

while minimizing our investments in sectors we see as growing more slowly or remaining static. [1973 annual report]

Comparing the company today with the General Electric of only a few years ago shows that, in selectively allocating our resources to the growth opportunities identified through strategic planning, we have developed decidedly different sources of earnings and a different mix of businesses, whose potentials for profitable growth exceed those of our historic product lines. [1976 annual report]

As Table 1 illustrates, a major contributor to the shift in GE's business mix was the acquisition in 1976 of Utah International, a billion dollar mining company with substantial holdings of metallurgical coal.[7] Many saw in Utah a potential hedge against inflation and numerous opportunities for synergy with GE's other businesses. While not denying these benefits, *Fortune* reported:

Jones wanted to make a lasting imprint on his corporation by providing a new source of earnings growth and creating what he likes to call "the new GE." Utah provided him with a means to make that concept credible. When the opportunity arose, he relied not on his hallowed planning staff but rather seized the chance to personally lead his company into its biggest move in many years. As Jones himself now acknowledges: "Nothing in our strategic planning said that we should acquire Utah International."[8]

Internal developments also contributed to the shift in business mix, as described by one of GE's senior executives: "Much of the recent growth has come from the internal development of businesses brand new to GE. For example, engineered materials didn't even exist as a business in 1960. It was just a bunch of research projects. Now it will have sales of $2 billion, it will make $200 million net, with a ROI of 18 percent, and it will have plants all over the world. The company's experiences with aircraft engines, information services, and several other businesses have been much the same."

Impact on Management Systems

By 1977 the impact of strategic planning was being felt by GE's other management systems. For example, manpower evaluation and selection had been keyed to the strategic plans. A manager in the executive man-

---

[7] General Electric's 1976 annual report related a pooling-of-interest exchange of 41 million shares of GE common stock for all outstanding shares of Utah International, effective December 20, 1976. Utah International's 1976 earnings were $181 million, and sales were $1,001 million. The company's principal operations included the mining of coking coal, steam coal, uranium, iron ore, and copper. By far the most important contribution to 1976 earnings came from Australian coking coal supplied under long-term contracts to Japanese and European steel producers.

[8] "General Electric's Very Personal Merger," *Fortune,* August 1977.

power department noted: "The strategic plans gave us, for the first time, a means by which we could evaluate if a manager really delivered on what he said he would do. All we have to do is check the previous plans. This also helps when there are job changes. We can now determine what current problems are caused by earlier mistakes, so the wrong person doesn't get blamed."

In the area of incentive compensation, performance screens were developed that separated financial and nonfinancial objectives for the business. This was intended to provide greater emphasis on longer term considerations and it did to some extent, but as one manager noted, "It's a great theory, but in a crunch it's the financial results that matter."

In terms of GE's organization structure, only one major change was apparent. This was the dissolution of the corporate executive staff and the return to a number of separate functional staff components. Reg Jones explained: "The corporate executive staff was originally set up with two major objectives: to straighten out the venture messes and to devise a planning system to prevent those troubles in the future. By 1974 the venture problems were solved, and we had a planning staff that was managing the new strategic planning process. By 1975 we dissolved the [corporate executive] staff."

Assessment of Strategic Planning

By 1977 strategic planning had won widespread management support for a variety of reasons. GE executives commented as follows:

> In the views of some managers, there was more planning being done in the mid-1960s than today. There was lots of futurism, scenario writing, contingency planning, and model building. But those efforts were not related to the problems of our ongoing businesses as is the SBU analysis.

> Not specifying the precise format of a strategic plan turned out to be very useful. For one thing, it enabled the SBUs to avoid spending time on issues that weren't important to them. More important, it provided room for some creativity and originality in the writing of the plans.

> Since strategic planning was implemented, our real growth businesses have been funded, even when we were cash short in 1974 and 1975. The key is for the guy who is running a growth business that requires resources to gain the confidence of the people at the top of the organization. Strategic planning can help to get that confidence.

An internal audit of strategic planning, completed in December 1974, reported that "the overwhelming feeling is that strategic planning has become ingrained in General Electric: 80 percent felt there would be no slippage and 16 percent only minor slippage if corporate requirements for SP [strategic planning] were removed."

Not surprisingly, complaints of shortcomings in GE's strategic planning were also voiced. Some of the complaints reported in the audit had to do with the excessive effort devoted to cosmetics and upward merchandising of strategic plans. Another set of complaints had to do with a perceived ineffective review of SBU plans. The audit reported, "One issue is clear: the operations managers feel that corporate-level reviewers do not understand their businesses well enough to be competent reviewers."

The earlier review of strategic plans at the division and group levels was also considered by many managers as ineffective. The reason for this failing was attributed to the fact that managers at these levels typically "were really participants in generating the plans and thus were not objective reviewers." At the CEO level, on the other hand, the review of all 43 SBU strategic plans was requiring an inordinate amount of time and effort.

Pressures for current earnings were also cited as undermining the strategic planning process. One executive, quoted in the audit, commented: "Strategic planning process won't work in General Electric, at least not in the context in which we are trying to make it work. The company needs to project an attractive financial and cash-flow image. The pressure to provide a steady profit growth and a sustained P/E ratio results in short-term demands on operations which disrupt long-term programs."

A Single General Electric and Value Added

The problem corporate management had in evaluating 43 SBU strategic plans was coupled with a growing concern about a lack of integration and cohesiveness among the many business initiatives under way. By the mid-1970s SBU planning, while helping to strengthen GE's competitive positions and to improve profits, was also leading to a balkanization of the company. GE appeared to be moving in the direction of becoming a holding company.

This development ran directly counter to a basic GE management tenet. As early as 1973 Jones addressed management about the need to work "with the grain" rather than against it in reshaping the company. Prominent among the "abiding characteristics of General Electric," according to Jones, was "a strong preference for a single General Electric identity, despite our broad diversification." The world-famous GE monogram symbolized this core identity.

Coupled with the concept of a single GE identity was the notion of "value added." The recurrent attacks on big business, aimed at dismantling U.S. industry giants in the interest of increased competition, posed a serious potential threat to GE. As one senior GE executive explained: "The whole has got to be significantly greater than the sum of its parts. We have nothing to defend (against increasing external pressures to break up or, at a minimum, harass very large companies) unless we have a very effective, productive corporate level." Given top management's strong preference for a cohesive General Electric, SBU strategic planning, good as it was, was not adequate for GE's needs. Something more was needed.

Integrating Strategic Planning: 1977–1980

At the general management conference in January 1977 Reg Jones announced his intention "to revise GE's strategic planning system and to establish a 'sector' organization structure as the pivotal concept for the redesign effort." The proposed changes aimed to improve the strategic planning review process and to develop a cohesive plan for GE as a single, integrated entity.

Improving the Strategic Planning Review Process

In Jones's mind corporate review of SBU plans suffered from overload. He explained:

> Right from the start of SBU planning in 1972 the vice chairmen and I tried to review each plan in great detail. This effort took untold hours and placed a tremendous burden on the corporate executive office. After awhile I began to realize that no matter how hard we would work, we could not achieve the necessary in-depth understanding of the 40-odd SBU plans. Somehow, the review burden had to be carried on more shoulders.

Creating the sector structure was Jones's way of spreading the review load. The sector was defined as a new level of management which represented a macrobusiness or industry area.[9] The sector executive would serve as the GE spokesperson for that industry and would be responsible for providing management direction to the member SBUs and for integrating the SBU strategies into a sector strategic plan. The sector strategic plan would focus heavily on development opportunities transcending SBU lines but still within the scope of the sector. The corporate executive office would thereafter focus its review on the strategic plans of the six sectors.

Below the sector the SBU continued to be the basic business entity. To permit greater competitiveness (and visibility) for important strategic businesses within certain SBUs, however, GE introduced the concept of business segments. For example, the Audio Department became a business segment within the Housewares and Audio SBU because it was a unique business that could operate more effectively within the SBU than on its own.

---

[9] Robert Frederick, the executive who had been assigned the tasks of introducing the sector structure and making it work, explained the new nomenclature: "We picked the word *sector* because no one knew what it meant. In that way there would be no preconceived notions of what the sectors would do."

Figure 3

Sector-SBU Structure

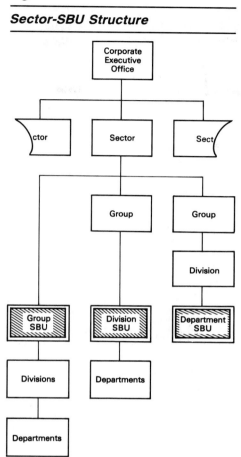

The new organizational line structure is depicted in Figure 3. The dual organization in use since 1971—SBUs for planning; group, divisions, and departments for operations—was supplemented by the sector-SBU structure. The earlier designations of group, division, and department were retained to indicate the relative size of an SBU.

Along with improved review, the new sector structure was also seen as clarifying the responsibilities for business development in GE. According to a senior corporate strategic planning staff executive: "Conceptually, SBUs are expected to develop new business opportunities by extending into contiguous product-market areas. Sectors are expected to develop new SBUs by diversifying within their macroindustry scopes. And corporate is expected to develop new sectors by diversifying into unserved macroindustries."

Improving strategy review and business development were two visible reasons for the new sector structure. (The organization chart in Figure 4 shows the new sector structure and management assignments.) Jones also had a private reason for this organizational change:

> I had a personal road map of the future and knew when I wanted to retire. Time was moving on, and I could see a need to put the key candidates for my job under a spotlight for the board to view. The sector executive positions would provide the visibility.
>
> The men were assigned to sectors with businesses different from their past experience. I did this not only to broaden these individuals but also to leaven the businesses by introducing new bosses who had different perspectives. For example, major appliances had long been run by managers who had grown up in the business. I put Welch, whose previous experience had been with high-technology plastics, in charge to see if he could introduce new approaches.

Strategic Integration and Corporate Challenges

Along with improving strategic review, Jones saw a need to develop a cohesive plan for GE as a single, integrated entity. His concern reflected two problems that appeared to be growing in parallel with SBU planning itself:

> Over the years we were discovering serious discontinuities among the SBU plans. At the operating level we were suffering unnecessary costs from duplication and from uncoordinated actions.
>
> At the strategic level we seemed to be moving in all directions with no sense of focus on what I saw as major opportunities and threats for the 1980s. For example, I saw a need to push forward on the international front, a need to move from our electromechanical technology to electronics, and a need to respond to the problems of productivity. We needed a way to challenge our managers to respond to these pressing issues in an integrated fashion.

To provide corporate direction and impetus on such issues, GE introduced the concept of corporate planning challenges. As shown in Figure 5, the planning challenges set the stage for the annual strategic planning cycle. Each year the CEO would issue a number of specific challenges that had to be addressed in the strategic plans of the SBUs and the sectors. For example, a 1980 corporate challenge called for SBUs and sectors to plan for a productivity improvement appropriate for their industry to counter worldwide competitive threats. The productivity target for GE as a whole was set for 6 percent.

The selection of challenges was seen by Jones as a vital function of the chief executive officer:

> It's the job of the CEO to look ahead. Planning can be helpful, but it is really our job to look at the decade ahead. You look at the environment

Figure 4 Organization Chart, June 1, 1978

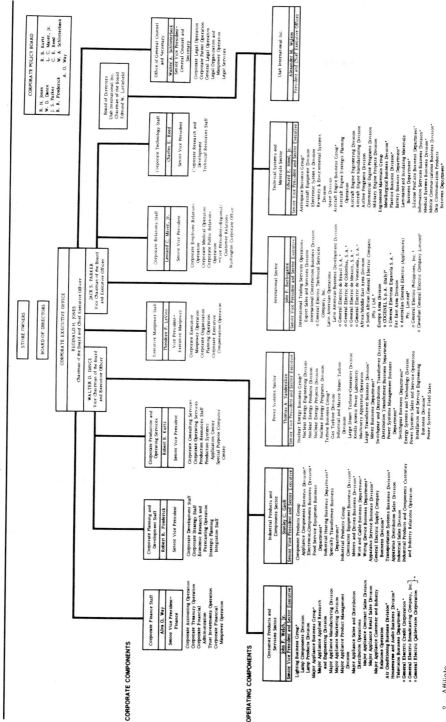

° —Affiliate.

* —Strategic Business Unit.

Figure 5

Annual Planning Cycle

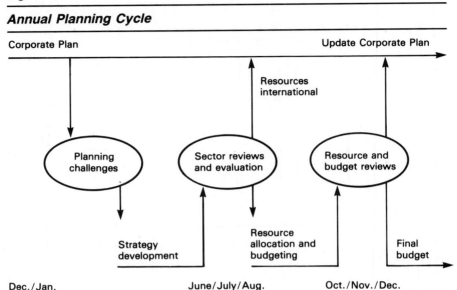

and couple that with your knowledge of the operations. You begin to see gaps that are beyond the plans. You have studies made to examine the possible shortcomings.

For example, as a defrocked bookkeeper, I have always had a concern about technology. In 1976 I commissioned a companywide study of our strengths, weaknesses, and needs in technology. The findings—16 volumes of them—triggered a technological renaissance in GE. We stepped up our R&D budgets, built up our electronic capabilities, and reoriented our recruiting and training activities. Now every SBU has a firm technological strategy integrated with its business strategy.

In addition to the CEO as a source of challenges, the restructured management system included two new approaches for generating planning challenges. One element aimed at fostering GE's international activities, the other at integrating GE's planning for critical resources.

International Sector. To increase the importance and the visibility of international operations in GE, Jones set it up as a sector. It was, however, to play a special role among sectors. In addition to preparing a sector plan for GE's overseas affiliates, the international sector was also given responsibility for fostering and integrating international business for General Electric as a whole.

A subsequent effort to integrate electric iron manufacturing on a worldwide basis illustrates one of the roles that the international sector was intended to play. The SBU responsible for irons had developed a newly designed iron which it planned for production in a single small country. At international sector urging, the SBU reconsidered and ultimately decided on rationalized multicountry production in three countries, including two larger countries with international sector affiliates. This approach improved cost and market share potentials in affiliate countries as well as cost effectiveness on a total GE system basis. This intervention led to an internal joint venture for irons between the international sector and the SBU to share risks and rewards on a worldwide basis.

Resource Planning.   Corporate management's concerns with GE's handling of critical resources were to be dealt with through another company-wide integrating mechanism. For this purpose senior corporate staff executives were given responsibility "for an objective assessment of key resources and the identification of issues impacting the company's strategic strengths." These assessments of financial resources, human resources, technology resources, and production resources would lead to planning challenges to the sectors and SBUs wherever practices needed to be improved.

Planning for human resources illustrated how this approach was to work. The vice president in charge of this planning described two of the issues he had subsequently raised for management consideration:

> One of the major human resources issues GE has had to face had to do with the potential impact of transferring work and jobs to overseas locations. This practice has important implications for the company, for the employees, and for the communities involved which had to be thought through beforehand. Another important issue had to do with GE's image as it relates to recruiting college graduates. In the next few years GE has to hire some 2,800 scientists and engineers, competing with some glamorous firms for the good people.

Implementing the New Structure

In characteristic fashion GE management recognized the need to allow time for the new structure to take root. As the initiating report stated: "The objective of integrated levels of planning is just that—an objective. It may take two or three cycles to accomplish."

True to this schedule Jones made the following assessment three years later: "The sector approach has turned out to be very successful. It even exceeded my expectations. Now I can look at six planning books and understand them well enough to ask the right questions. I could not do that before. The sectors also gave the board and me an excellent means for deciding on my successor. By 1979 the competition had been narrowed down to Burlingame, Hood, and Welch, and these men were moved up to vice chairman positions." (Exhibit 3 contains biographical data on Jones, Welch, Burlingame, and Hood.)

Jones was also pleased with the progress GE had made in responding to a number of corporate challenges. He pointed with particular pride to the "technological renaissance" that had been launched at GE:

> These past few years we have pressed hard the challenge to change the company's basic technology from electromechanical to electronics. Today we have a true companywide effort to apply the new microelectronics and the related information-based technologies to every possible product, service, and process in GE.
>
> The proposed purchase of Calma, a leading producer of interactive graphics equipment, and the acquisition of Intersil, a maker of advanced microelectronic chips, give evidence to this commitment.[10] Perhaps our commitment to broad-based innovation is best expressed by our rising investment in research and development. Since 1977 we have increased GE-funded R&D expenditures 85 percent to $760 million. Total R&D, including external funding, reached $1.6 billion in 1980.

GE in 1980: A Call for Growth

In a presentation to the financial community at the Hotel Pierre in New York City on December 11, 1979, Jones pointed to how GE was "positioned to achieve the objective of sustained earnings growth, faster than the growth of the U.S. economy, in the 1980s." He added: "General Electric is embarked on a course of large-scale innovation, productivity improvement, and business development for the 1980s, and we have built up the financial resources to bring that bold and entrepreneurial strategy to a successful conclusion."

Challenging Static Forecasts

This public promise of rapid growth carried major implications for strategic planning. At the annual general management conference at Belleair held a month later, Daniel Fink, the newly appointed senior vice president for corporate planning and development (development had been added to stress the growth objective), questioned the adequacy of the existing strategic plans to meet Jones's growth challenge. He began by reviewing the recent and projected changes in business mix. The relative earnings figures are summarized in Table 2. (See Exhibits 4 and 5 for more detailed financial statements.) Armed with these figures, Fink then argued:

> Our implied strategy seems to be one of slowing, or even halting, the aggressive and successful diversification of the past decade. The vision of GE in

---

[10] According to GE's 1980 annual report, Intersil was acquired for $235 million. The Calma acquisition was cleared by the Federal Trade Commission in early 1981. The purchase agreement called for an initial payment of $100 million and additional payments of up to $70 million with the exact amount determined by Calma's sales over the next four years.

Table 2

GE's Business Mix (Percent)

	1968	1979	1984	Projected Change
Electrical equipment	80%	47%	44%	−3%
Materials	6	27	27	0
Services	10	16	19	+3
Transportation	4	10	10	0
International	16	40	43	+3

1984 that we get from the long-range forecasts is very much like GE in 1979—same product mix, same international mix, same strategy of leveraging earnings over sales growth.

How can that be? And—more important—do you believe it? Do you believe we'll really have the same product mix in view of even the most obvious technological changes we can see ahead? Do you really think that international mix will hold, despite the faster growth of many world markets? And that we can have the same strategy of leveraging earnings over sales, just as if that last tenth of a point was as easy to achieve as the first?

It's that contradiction of a steady-state GE and a rapidly changing world that gives us, I think, the key strategic issue as we enter the 80s. How do we attain the vision now to reject that static forecast and then take the strategic actions that will move us forward in the 80s, just as we did in the 70s?

Fink next disputed the basis on which the existing strategic plans had projected growth:

Back in '68 we earned 4½ percent on sales, by '74 it was 5 percent, 6 percent in '78, and the LRFs [long-range forecasts] say 7 percent in 1984, but it doesn't follow that just because the company went from 5 percent to 6 percent in the 70s, it will easily move up to 7 percent in the 80s.

There are several reasons for caution. First, most of our SBUs, urged on by last year's business development challenge, carry the expense burden of major investment plans. And finally, we'll be twice as dependent on productivity, rather than price, for inflation recovery. So under these circumstances, we certainly must consider the 7 percent at risk.

Just suppose we hold our ROS at the current 6 percent level. The difference in '84 would be almost $400 million of net income and widening each year. To compensate for that shortfall, we would have to add something like $6–$7 billion of sales. That's another sector.

These are big increments. They aren't going to be achieved by simple extensions of our current businesses. They do demand a period of unprecedented business development in the 80s. Unprecedented business development. Consider what that has to mean to a company that has already made the largest acquisition in U.S. business history; that has produced more patentable inventions than any other company in the world; and that already is the largest diversified corporation on Fortune 500 list.

Realigning GE's Resources

The first step to generating unprecedented business growth in the 1980s was to select the target areas with the greatest potential for GE. In-depth corporate planning staff analysis led to the definition of six broad business areas. These areas, called arenas, were identified as follows:

- Energy.
- Communication, information, and sensing.
- Energy applications-productivity.
- Materials and resources.
- Transportation and propulsion.
- Pervasive services (nonproduct-related services such as financial, distribution, and construction).

A common characteristic of the arenas was that they cut across sector organizational lines. Fink described the dilemma and indicated a need for new approaches:

> How are we going to tackle these new opportunities which cut across organization lines? Sometimes the solution is to reorganize and collect those synergistic businesses under single management. But there are too many opportunities out there. We'd have to reorganize every three days just to keep up with them.
>
> How many times have you heard customers, or even competitors, say, "If you guys could only get your act together!" Well, we're going to have to get our act together if we're to tackle some of these new opportunities. We're going to have to develop coventuring techniques, motivation and measurement techniques that have thus far eluded us. It won't come easy; it's nontraditional. It's not traditional for those of us who learned to manage at the John Wayne school of rugged individualism.

To get GE's "act together," the CEO issued explicit arena-related challenges to launch the 1981 planning cycle. Each challenge listed the specific sectors and corporate staff units to be involved and designated the sector responsible to lead the effort. One of the specific challenges related to the energy applications-productivity arena, for example, was to develop a strategic business plan to exploit the growing opportunities associated with factory automation and robotics. The industrial products and components sector, which was already heavily involved with factory automation, was given lead responsibility for this factory of the future challenge. Support roles were assigned to the information and communications systems group (a unit in the technical systems and materials sector) because of its experience with mobile communications and to the corporate production and operating services staff unit because of its responsibility for improving productivity within GE itself.

Just how this cross-organizational business development would function still had to be worked out. Jones clearly viewed this approach as preliminary and evolving: "I don't want operating managers worrying about arenas for a while. At this point in time arenas are for our use at the corporate level. They help to give us another view of the company." The provisional nature of the arena approach was also indicated in the following comment by a senior executive: "The success or failure of the arena concept will depend to a great extent on how hard corporate management pushes it."

The Next Steps

The General Electric Jack Welch was preparing to lead in 1981 was in the midst of actively probing a panoply of new technology businesses. Lively discussions were being held in offices throughout the company on what GE should do about the factory of the future, the office of the future, the house of the future, the electric car, synthetic fuel, and the like. The list of opportunities seemed endless. Clearly GE would have to make some hard choices. In this connection Welch was reported to have said: "My biggest challenge will be to put enough money on the right gambles and to put no money on the wrong ones. But I don't want to sprinkle money over everything."[11]

What kind of management system would he need to meet this challenge? Jack Welch had used SBU and sector planning to build businesses and later had a hand in shaping GE's approach to strategic management. He laid to rest any idea of dismantling the apparatus in place: "GE was a well-run company before anyone ever heard of John Welch. Most of the corporate revolutions you hear about are when a guy moves from company X to company Y and tips it upside down. Sometimes it works and sometimes it doesn't. That won't happen here."

Despite this commitment, Welch was inheriting a management system undergoing major changes. Crossroad choices would have to be made here as well. The 1981 management audit indicated numerous important management system issues for attention:

- Can the sectors as presently defined accommodate the size and diversity of company operations in 1985? In 1990? Alternatives?
- The 1981 corporate strategy was developed through an arena segmentation which is deliberately different from the GE sector segmentation. Is this useful to the CEO in developing a vision for the company? Will it be a workable approach that leads to truly integrated strategies?
- Is there a better way than our international integration process to determine and pursue company international objectives?

---

[11] *Business Week,* March 16, 1981.

How these management system issues were handled would be influenced by the broad substantive issues GE faced. While opinions differed as to priorities, senior managers agreed on several key challenges. Reg Jones put dealing with inflation at the top of his list. Increasing productivity and increasing international business were also high on his and everyone else's list of major issues. For many senior executives, increasing entrepreneurship and new ventures in GE were also a major challenge in view of the company's ambitious growth goals.

The list of issues—both those having to do with substance and those having to do with management systems—was long, far too long for all to be dealt with in depth. Management would have to be selective in choosing areas for attention. One executive neatly summed up his views of the situation with the comment: "GE is going to be a very exciting company these next few years. You can just feel the electricity in the air."

Exhibit 1

Ten-Year Statistical Summary, 1961–1970 (Dollars in millions, except per share amounts)

	1970	*1969*	*1968*	*1967*	*1966*	*1965*	*1964*	*1963*	*1962*	*1961*
Sales of products and services	$8,726.7	$8,448.0	$8,381.6	$7,741.2	$7,177.3	$6,213.6	$5,319.2	$5,177.0	$4,986.1	$4,666.6
Net earnings	$ 328.5	$ 278.0	$ 357.1	$ 361.4	$ 338.9	$ 355.1	$ 219.6	$ 272.2	$ 256.5	$ 238.4
Earnings per common share	$ 3.63	$ 3.07	$ 3.95	$ 4.01	$ 3.75	$ 3.93	$ 2.44	$ 3.05	$ 2.89	$ 2.70
Earnings as a percentage of sales	3.8%	3.3%	4.3%	4.7%	4.7%	5.7%	4.1%	5.3%	5.1%	5.1%
Earned on share owners' equity	12.6%	11.0%	14.8%	15.9%	15.7%	17.5%	11.5%	14.9%	15.0%	14.8%
Cash dividends declared	$ 235.4	$ 235.2	$ 234.8	$ 234.2	$ 234.6	$ 216.7	$ 197.7	$ 183.1	$ 177.5	$ 176.4
Dividends declared per common share	$ 2.60	$ 2.60	$ 2.60	$ 2.60	$ 2.60	$ 2.40	$ 2.20	$ 2.05	$ 2.00	$ 2.00
Market price range per share	94½–60¼	98¼–74⅛	100⅜–80¼	115⅞–82½	120–80	120¼–91	93⅝–78¾	87½–71¾	78½–54¼	80¾–60½
Current assets	$3,334.8	$3,287.8	$3,311.1	$3,207.6	$3,013.0	$2,842.4	$2,543.8	$2,321.0	$2,024.6	$1,859.7
Current liabilities	$2,650.3	$2,366.7	$2,104.3	$1,977.4	$1,883.2	$1,566.8	$1,338.9	$1,181.9	$1,168.7	$1,086.6
Total assets	$6,309.9	$6,007.5	$5,743.8	$5,347.2	$4,851.7	$4,300.4	$3,856.0	$3,502.5	$3,349.9	$3,143.4
Total share owners' equity	$2,665.1	$2,540.0	$2,493.4	$2,342.2	$2,211.7	$2,107.0	$1,944.2	$1,889.2	$1,764.3	$1,654.6
Plant and equipment additions	$ 581.4	$ 530.6	$ 514.7	$ 561.7	$ 484.9	$ 332.9	$ 237.7	$ 149.2	$ 173.2	$ 179.7
Depreciation	$ 334.7	$ 351.3	$ 300.1	$ 280.4	$ 233.6	$ 188.4	$ 170.3	$ 149.4	$ 146.0	$ 131.6
Total taxes and renegotiation	$ 309.4	$ 313.2	$ 390.5	$ 390.1	$ 409.1	$ 403.8	$ 277.3	$ 331.4	$ 298.7	$ 289.9
Provision for income taxes	$ 220.6	$ 231.5	$ 312.3	$ 320.5	$ 347.4	$ 352.2	$ 233.8	$ 286.7	$ 254.0	$ 248.9
Employees—average worldwide	396,583	410,126	395,691	384,864	375,852	332,991	308,233	297,726	290,682	279,547
Gross national product (current $ billions)	$ 982	$ 936	$ 869	$ 796	$ 753	$ 688	$ 636	$ 595	$ 564	$ 523

Source: General Electric annual reports; *Business Statistics,* U.S. Department of Commerce, p. 245, for GNP.

Exhibit 2

GE's 1980 Criteria for Investment Priority Screen

Criterion	Measure	Criterion	Measure
Industry Attractiveness		**Business Position**	
1. Market size	■ 3-year average served industry market dollars	1. Market position	■ 3-year average market share (total market)
2. Market growth	■ 10-year constant dollar average annual market growth rate		■ 3-year average international market share
3. Industry profitability	3-year average ROS, SBU, and "Big Three" competitors ■ Nominal ■ Inflation adjusted		■ 2-year average relative market share (SBU/"Big Three" competitors)
		2. Competitive position	Superior, equal, or inferior to competition in 1980: ■ Product quality ■ Technological leadership ■ Manufacturing/cost leadership ■ Distribution/marketing leadership
4. Cyclicality	■ Average annual percent variation of sales from trend		
5. Inflation recovery	■ 5-year average ratio of combined selling price and productivity change to change in cost due to inflation	3. Relative profitability	3-year SBUs ROS, less average ROS, "Big Three" competitors ■ Nominal ■ Inflation adjusted
6. Importance of non-U.S. markets	■ 10-year average ratio of inter-national to total market		

Note: Boxes indicate measure used for the first time in 1980.

Exhibit 3

Biographical Data

Reginald Harold Jones: Born Stoke-on-Trent, Staffordshire, England, 1917. B.S. in Economics, University of Pennsylvania, 1939. Joined the General Electric Company in 1939 as a business trainee and traveling auditor, 1939–1950; assistant to controller, Apparatus Department, 1950–1956; general manager, Air Conditioning Division, 1956–1958; general manager, Supply Company Division, 1958–1961; vice president, General Electric, 1961; general manager, Construction Industries Division, 1964–1967; group executive, 1967–1968; vice president finance, 1968–1970; senior vice president, 1970–1972; vice chairman, 1972; president, 1972–1973; chairman of the board and chief executive officer, 1973–1981.

John F. Welch, Jr.: Born Massachusetts, 1935. B.S.Ch.E., University of Massachusetts, 1957; M.S.Ch.E., University of Illinois, 1958; Ph.D., 1960. Joined the General Electric Company in 1960 as a process development specialist for chemical development operations; process development group leader, 1962; manager—manufacturing polymer products and chemical development operations, 1963; general manager, Plastics Department, 1968; general manager, Chemical Division, then Chemical and Metallurgical Division, 1971; vice president and general manager, Chemical and Metallurgical Division, 1972; vice president and group executive, Components and Materials Group, 1973; senior vice president and executive, Consumer Products and Services Sector, 1977; vice chairman and executive officer, 1979; chairman of the board and chief executive officer, 1981.

John Francis Burlingame: Born Massachusetts, 1922. B.S., Tufts University, 1942. Joined GE in 1946; vice president and general manager, Computer Systems Division, 1969–1971; vice president—employee relations, 1971–1973; vice president and group executive, International, 1973–1977; senior vice president, International sector, 1977–1979; vice chairman, 1979–.

Edward Exum Hood, Jr.: Born North Carolina, 1930. M.S., Nuclear Engineering, North Carolina State University, 1953. Joined GE in 1957 as a powerplant design engineer; vice president and general manager, Commercial Engine Division, 1968–1972; vice president and group executive, International, 1972–1973; vice president and group executive, Power Generation, 1973–1977; senior vice president and sector executive, Technical System and Materials, 1977–1979; vice chairman, 1979–.

Exhibit 4

Ten-Year Statistical Summary, 1971–1980 (Dollars in millions, except per share amounts)

	1980	1979	1978	1977	1976	1975	1974	1973	1972	1971 (2-for-1 Stock Split)
Summary of operations:										
Sales of products and services to customers	$24,959	$22,461	$19,654	$17,519	$15,697	$14,105	$13,918	$11,945	$10,474	$9,557
Operating margin	2,243	2,130	1,958	1,698	1,528	1,187	1,171	1,070	877	772
Earnings before income taxes and minority interest	$ 2,493	$ 2,391	$ 2,153	$ 1,889	$ 1,627	$ 1,174	$ 1,181	$ 1,130	$ 963	$ 847
Taxes	958	953	894	773	668	460	458	457	385	333
Net earnings	$ 1,514	$ 1,409	$ 1,230	$ 1,088	$ 931	$ 688	$ 705	$ 661	$ 573	$ 510
Earnings per common share	$ 6.65	$ 6.20	$ 5.39	$ 4.79	$ 4.12	$ 3.07	$ 3.16	$ 2.97	$ 2.57	$ 2.30
Dividends declared per common share	$ 2.95	$ 2.75	$ 2.50	$ 2.10	$ 1.70	$ 1.60	$ 1.60	$ 1.50	$ 1.40	$ 1.38
Earnings as a percentage of sales	6.1%	6.3%	6.3%	6.2%	5.9%	4.9%	5.1%	5.5%	5.5%	5.3%
Earned on average share owners' equity	19.5%	20.2%	19.6%	19.4%	18.9%	15.7%	17.8%	18.4%	17.5%	17.2%
Dividends	$ 670	$ 624	$ 570	$ 477	$ 333	$ 293	$ 291	$ 273	$ 255	$ 250
Market price range per share	63–44	55⅛–45	57⅝–43⅝	57¼–47⅜	59¼–46	52⅞–32⅜	65–30	75⅞–55	73–58¼	66½–46½
Price/earnings ratio range	9–7	9–7	11–8	12–10	14–11	17–10	19–9	24–17	25–20	26–18
Current assets	$ 9,883	$ 9,384	$ 8,755	$ 7,865	$ 6,685	$ 5,750	$ 5,334	$ 4,597	$ 4,057	$ 3,700
Current liabilities	7,592	6,872	6,175	5,417	4,605	4,163	4,032	3,588	2,921	2,894
Share owners' equity	8,200	7,362	6,587	5,943	5,253	4,617	4,172	3,774	3,420	3,106
Total capital invested	10,447	9,332	8,692	8,131	7,305	6,628	6,317	5,679	5,118	4,754
Earned on average total capital invested	17.3%	17.6%	16.3%	15.8%	15.1%	12.5%	13.4%	13.7%	12.7%	12.3%
Total assets	$18,511	$16,644	$15,036	$13,697	$12,050	$10,741	$10,220	$ 9,089	$ 8,051	$7,472
Property, plant, and equipment additions	$ 1,948	$ 1,262	$ 1,055	$ 823	$ 740	$ 588	$ 813	$ 735	$ 501	$ 711
Employees—average worldwide	402,000	405,000	401,000	384,000	380,000	380,000	409,000	392,000	373,000	366,000
Gross national product (current $ billions)	$ 2,626	$ 2,414	$ 2,128	$ 1,900	$ 1,702	$ 1,529	$ 1,413	$ 1,307	$ 1,171	$1,063
Common stock performance	$ 44–63					General Electric common share price				$47–67
	759–1000					Dow Jones Industrial Index				798–950
	111–161					Standard & Poor's Industrial Index				99–116

Source: General Electric annual report, 1980; U.S. Department of Commerce for GNP; Moody's.

Exhibit 5   Financial Statements, 1979 and 1980 (In millions)

Balance Sheets

Assets	1980	1979
Cash	$ 1,601	$ 1,904
Marketable securities	600	672
Current receivables	4,339	3,647
Inventories	3,343	3,161
Current assets	9,883	9,384
Property, plant, and equipment	5,780	4,613
Investments	1,820	1,691
Other assets	1,028	956
Total assets	$18,511	$16,644

Liabilities and Equity

	1980	1979
Short-term borrowings	$ 1,093	$ 871
Accounts payable	1,671	1,477
Progress collections and price adjustments accrued	2,084	1,957
Dividends payable	170	159
Taxes accrued	628	655
Other costs and expenses accrued	1,946	1,753
Current liabilities	7,592	6,872
Long-term borrowings	1,000	947
Other liabilities	1,565	1,311
Total liabilities	$10,157	$ 9,130
Minority interest in equity of consolidated affiliates	154	152
Common stock	579	579
Amounts received for stock in excess of par value	659	656
Retained earnings	7,151	6,307
	$ 8,389	$ 7,542
Deduct common stock held in treasury	(189)	(190)
Total share owners' equity	8,200	7,362
Total liabilities and equity	$18,511	$16,644

Income Statements

	1980	1979
Sales:		
Sales of products and services to customers	$24,959	$22,461
Operating costs:		
Cost of goods sold	17,751	15,991
Selling, general, and administrative expense	4,258	3,716
Depreciation, depletion and amortization	707	624
Operating costs	$22,716	$20,331
Operating margin	2,243	2,130
Other income	564	519
Interest and other financial charges	(314)	(258)
Earnings:		
Earnings before income taxes and minority interest	2,493	2,391
Provision for income taxes	(958)	(953)
Minority interest in earnings of consolidated affiliates	(21)	(29)
Net earnings applicable to common stock	$ 1,514	$ 1,409
Earnings per common share (in dollars)	$ 6.65	$ 6.20
Dividends declared per common share (in dollars)	$ 2.95	$ 2.75
Operating margin as a percentage of sales	9.0%	9.5%
Net earnings as a percentage of sales	6.1%	6.3%

NIKE (A)

Founded in 1964 NIKE emerged from obscurity during the 1970s, riding on (and, some observers suggested, helping to stimulate) the physical fitness boom that was sweeping the United States. The company gained enormous visibility with its high-performance sports shoes. By the end of 1982, for example, every world record in men's track from the 800 meters to the marathon had been set by athletes wearing NIKE shoes. In addition to serving the serious athlete, the company had broadened its product line, and its "Swoosh" logo adorned the feet, legs, and chests of average participants in a wide range of sports as well as millions of consumers who simply found the products comfortable or fashionable.

Some observers called NIKE the success story of the 1970s. Sales rose from $2 million in 1972 to $694 million in 1982, net earnings from $60,000 to $49 million, and several millionaires were created when the company went public in 1980 (see Exhibit 1 for a financial summary from 1976 to 1982). The company emerged as the dominant force in the U.S. market, displacing the worldwide leader, and long-time rival, Adidas (a West German company). In his 1982 letter to the company's shareholders, founder and President Philip Knight described NIKE's first decade as "a race across the athletic scene."

As the company began a second decade, it faced three challenges. First, market growth in the core domestic athletic footwear business appeared to be slowing. Second, the company's rapid growth continued

Copyright © 1984 by the President and Fellows of Harvard College
Harvard Business School case 385–025

to stretch the organization's systems and people. Third, the original entre-preneurial team now had to manage a public company. On a lunchtime run in the January 1983 drizzle near NIKE's Oregon headquarters, Knight reflected:

> As we've looked ahead over the years it's been clear that we would run out of feet in the United States at some point. Perhaps that point is coming sooner than we expected, although we believe there is still a lot of opportunity in shoes here, both for athletes and in some new directions such as the leisure area. But we've also, of course, been looking for some other things to do, for we see ourselves as a growth company. We're excited about the potential in the international market and in the apparel business. The former is proving tougher to penetrate than we thought, and we're still miles from where we want to be in apparel, but we believe we can do it.
>
> I've always felt that if we have the right product at the most economical cost, we'll figure out a way to sell it. Everybody talks about our marketing, and it has been good. But it's been good because we've had a good product with enough margin for the right marketing expense. And it's all worked because of the people we've had. As we get bigger and more spread out, it's harder for our people to understand what they are supposed to be doing, where their job fits in the game plan. This may be a tougher problem than the market.

The following sections of this case describe the competitive arena in which NIKE operated, the company's entrepreneurial history, and the evolution of its business strategy through 1982.

Athletic Footwear and Apparel

Think of NIKE's business as a tree. Its roots lay in the small, specialized performance athletic shoe market that served serious athletes in the 1960s. Its trunk grew dramatically during the jogging boom of the 70s, as millions of Americans started to exercise. And its branches spread widely in the late 70s and early 80s, as many more Americans found the shoes, and then the related athletic apparel, comfortable and "in fashion."

This competitive arena was on the fringes of the traditional footwear, sporting goods, and apparel industries. It evaded conventional business-economic reporting categories. What standard business data were avail-able were elusive and often unreliable. More fundamentally, the future dimensions and shape of this arena were quite ambiguous. As the tree's branches continued to spread, they became intertwined with those of the surrounding forest. As one observer mused, "Will NIKE's major competitor in the future be Adidas or Levi Strauss?"

The Evolving Competitive Arena

During the 1960s the ubiquitous canvas sneaker dominated the U.S. athletic footwear market. Largely unchanged since its introduction in the 1920s, the sneaker was used by professional basketball players and (in a $2.99 version) lived in by American kids. Other types of performance shoes, for sports such as soccer and running, held less than 10 percent of the market and were sold primarily by foreign-based firms.

Moving up the body, the grey sweatsuit was *the* athletic clothing of the 60s, with jeans the popular informal wear of American youth. On a more formal level, sportswear became increasingly fashionable and dressy—such as the colorful jacket and slacks worn to the Saturday afternoon game with loafers, or perhaps "Hush Puppy" shoes.

In the 1970s this scenario changed dramatically. Increasingly concerned about health and physical fitness, millions of Americans began to jog. Millions more took up other sports, both old (softball and bowling, for example) and new (Nautilus workouts and aerobics). Industry sources estimated that half of all Americans—primarily the younger, more affluent half—were active exercisers by 1982. Approximately 35 million were thought to run "with some frequency." Participation at these levels also reflected increased affluence and leisure time as well as significantly greater sports activity by women.

These athletes wore a new generation of sports shoes and clothing that had largely replaced the traditional sneaker and sweatsuit. The new products were designed to aid performance and prevent injury. A lighter running shoe or a sleeker speed skating suit could cut important tenths of a second from the time of a world-class competitive athlete. For the average runner, proper cushioning and support were important factors in reducing injury to feet, shins, and knees. (Figure 1 illustrates a technical running shoe.)

Beyond the growth in athletic participation, two other factors fueled the dramatic change in this market. First, the *comfort* of the shoes and clothing appealed to the millions of American consumers who were developing more casual life-styles. One observer commented:

> Running was never the lifeblood of running shoe sales. Comfort was. And anyone who tried on a running shoe was reluctant to step back onto a less comfortable conventional shoe. No wonder women want to walk to work with high heels under their arms and running shoes on their feet.[1]

Second, the athletic look became socially acceptable, indeed fashionable, for a wide range of activities. Many "followers" began to purchase particular brands in imitation of star athletes or movie stars—or the opinion leaders at a high school.

Comfort and appearance formed the basis for the "ath-leisure" segment of the market. Products sold to these consumers were designed with color, styling, and general comfort as the primary criteria. While they resembled "authentic" products, they were not intended to be worn

---

[1] "Shoemakers: Casual Is In," *Boston Globe,* February 15, 1983, p. 35.

Figure 1

A Technical NIKE Running Shoe

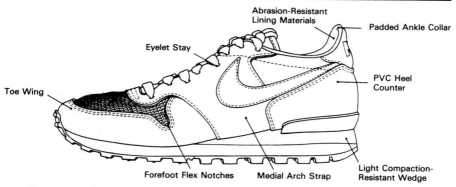

The *upper* provides a protective wrap for the bony structures of the foot, giving support (the medial arch strap, for example), flexibility (forefoot flex notch), breathability (Duro-mesh material), blister protection (padded ankle collar), and snugness (lacing system). The stiff heel counter is responsible for controlling rearfoot motion.

The *midsole* provides full-length protection from the impact forces generated during running.

The *heel wedge* provides additional shock protection as well as heel lift to prevent strain.

The *outsole* contributes to cushioning and shoe stability, provides traction, and protects the foot from the running surface.

Shoe manufacture centers around the *last,* a wooden, metal, or plastic form over which the shoe is shaped. NIKE used different last shapes and lasting methods to create shoes that fulfilled specific performance requirements.

Source: Company records.

while actually participating in many sports. The ath-leisure segment was thought to be many times larger than the authentic, participation-based segment.

While statistics were elusive, observers estimated that the overall branded athletic footwear market in the United States grew from $800 million in 1978 to $1.9 billion in 1982. This represented about half of the total athletic shoe dollar volume (the other half consisted of cheap, unbranded shoes from dozens of sources) and 15 percent of all footwear sales. Similarly, observers estimated that the activewear apparel market grew from $3 billion in 1977 to $6 billion in 1982, which represented less than 10 percent of the total apparel market.

The Branded Athletic Footwear Business

As the market took off in the mid-70s, demand was met by the performance shoe companies, rather than the sneaker makers. Rapid innovation flourished as the companies sought to develop shoes that the top athletes would wear and that influential trade sources, such as *Runner's World,* would rate highly. As one observer explained: "In the emerging market for an unfamiliar product, consumers relied on a brand name, established by the implicit or explicit endorsement of an athlete or by the ratings. And later, as the shoes became fashionable, that brand name again sold the shoes." Athletes and organizers of sporting events discovered that the shoe companies were willing to pay for this visibility, and such "promotion" (as it was called) became a lucrative—or expensive, depending upon your side of the fence—proposition.

Competitors differed most strikingly in their product lines. One issue was the range of product to be offered in a market that consisted of several sport-based submarkets, including running, basketball, racquet (tennis and squash), and field (such as baseball, football, and soccer), as well as children's, and leisure (see Table 1). A second issue was price, with a range from the $20 to $30 ath-leisure shoe to the $60 to $100 sport-specific competitive shoe. Along these dimensions some competitors offered a full line, while others were more specialized. Competitors also made different sourcing decisions, ranging from self-manufacture in domestic plants to purchase from contract factories in the Far East.

At the retail level, branded athletic shoe sales were approximately evenly divided among four channels: *athletic specialty shops,* which typically were small operations run by ex-athletes, selling innovative, high-priced running and court shoes to active athletes; *sporting goods stores,* which sold more of the team-oriented shoes (football, for example) as well as a broad line of sporting goods; *department stores,* which sold the higher-volume, mid- and low-price-point shoes to the family purchaser or to the fashion customer in an "activewear boutique" setting; and *shoe stores,* which served the family at the mid- and low-price points, with more of a focus on children. The branded companies tried to avoid mass merchandisers, which sold cheap, unbranded imports at the low end of the market. Observers believed that the retailer had a significant impact on high-end buying decisions but little impact at the low end.

The Competitors

NIKE dominated the branded athletic shoe market, with an estimated 30 percent share in 1982, followed by Adidas (19 percent), Converse (9 percent), and Puma and Keds (both 7 percent).[2] NIKE's primary competitors fell into three groups: the foreign companies, the specialty companies, and the old sneaker companies. These groups are described below, with one company in each group profiled in some detail. Within these groups companies still differed on a number of dimensions, including the breadth of the product line which they offered and their distribution strategy, as well as on size. See also Table 1.

---

[2] Estimates derived from data in *Sportstyle,* a trade paper published by Fairchild Publications of New York.

Table 1

Branded Athletic Footwear Submarkets (1982)

Submarket	Racquet	Running	Basketball	Field	Other
Percent of total market	35%	30%	15%	15%	5%
Leading competitors (market share)	NIKE 40% Adidas 20 Tretorn 6	NIKE 50% New Balance 15 Adidas 10	Converse 36% Puma 30 NIKE 20	Puma 30% Adidas 20 Hyde 10	HIKING and WALKING: Small but growing as older people discover walking.
Comments	Common for street use; tennis has not been growing but may in coming years.	Growth of 6 to 8% expected, depending on how long people continue to run and how many are diverted to home exercise.	Beginning to decline: fewer teens; Title IX* bulge over.	Team sports, so depends on increase in industrial leagues; soccer will grow but at expense of football.	LEISURE: Moderate growth, unless a model captures imagination of young people.

Note: Data based on sales in athletic specialty and sporting goods channels only.

* Title IX, a federal statute, required that educational institutions provide athletic programs and facilities for women similar to those traditionally provided for men.

Source: Researchers' discussions with industry sources.

The foreign companies had deep roots in the performance athletic footwear business, high-quality brand reputations, and strong manufacturing backgrounds but faced the difficulty of competing in the United States as a foreign market.

Adidas was the worldwide leader in the athletic footwear and apparel business, with 1982 sales estimated at $2 billion of which 40 percent was from apparel. The company was founded in the 1920s by shoemaker Adolph Dassler. Dassler, who made the shoes in which Jesse Owens won four gold medals at the 1936 Olympics, developed many firsts in shoe design over the years. Adidas proudly noted that shoes with its "three stripes" logo were worn by an overwhelming number of Olympic athletes. Dassler died in 1978 leaving the closely held company in family hands.

Adidas developed as a manufacturing company with plants, both owned and under exclusive contract, throughout the world, including the United States. Its product line was the widest in the business, with shoes for virtually every known sport, priced from the lower middle to the high end of the spectrum, and a full range of sports apparel. In the domestic market these products were distributed by four exclusive privately owned companies.

Observers praised Adidas's quality and criticized the company's marketing. As one explained, "In the early days, Adidas was *telling* the dealers, from Germany, what products they should carry. As soon as the market provided an alternative, the dealers snapped it up." By 1982, however, the U.S. distributors had become significantly more influential in domestic product and marketing decisions, and the company was regarded as a powerful long-run competitor.

Puma (estimated 1982 sales of $1 billion) was founded by Dassler's brother Rudolph after a dispute between the two in 1948. The company developed an excellent reputation during the 50s and 60s, especially in soccer, but did not keep up with the expansion of the U.S. market. Although it established a wholly owned distributor in the United States in 1980, observers continued to believe that the brand name was stronger than the company's current operations.

Tiger shoes, best known in the running submarket, were introduced in the United States in 1964 but remained poorly distributed during the late 70s. Even after the Japanese company (properly Asics Tiger) established a U.S. distribution subsidiary in 1981, its U.S. sales remained small ($30 million of a worldwide total of $400 million).

The specialty companies had developed strong brand reputations in specific market segments. These firms typically had more limited resources than the larger companies and faced a dilution of their focus as they expanded their relatively narrow product lines.

The *New Balance Athletic Shoe Company* (NB) entered the arena in 1972 when runner Jim Davis purchased an old orthopedic and specialty athletic shoe company located in a Boston suburb. It received a real boost in 1976 when *Runner's World* gave a NB shoe its number one ranking. By late 1978, however, that shoe had died on the market, and the company experienced a difficult six months until a new model was launched. Company sales grew to $50 million in 1982 (from $1.6 million in 1976), and the product line broadened somewhat, both within the running line and to basketball, tennis, and leisure shoes and running apparel.

NB manufactured its shoes in the United States. An in-house sales force sold primarily to specialty running shops, which used trained personnel to explain the shoes' unique features (such as availability in widths); the company was also beginning to sell through better department and sporting goods stores. NB consistently commanded a price premium in the market and caused a stir with the introduction of a $100 shoe in 1982. "You can't be all things to all people," Davis explained, "and we've concentrated on performance and function."

Brooks ($16 million) also rode the crest of the running shoe wave in the mid-70s, but to disaster. The company declared bankruptcy in 1981 after major quality problems destroyed its credibility with retailers. The company subsequently was purchased by Wolverine World Wide (a $316 million shoe manufacturer specializing in leisure shoes with its famous Hush Puppies brand) and began an aggressive campaign to reenter the market, with some early success. *Etonic* ($37 million), an established, quality golf and tennis shoe manufacturer acquired by Colgate-Palmolive in 1976, developed a performance running shoe line that was well received at the high end of the market. *Hyde Athletic Industries* ($37 million), a long-time supplier of quality team sports shoes, sold under three brand names. Its Saucony running shoe also did well at the high end of the market. Hyde used a mixture of U.S. manufacturing and Far East contracting.

The old sneaker companies, which had been asleep when the running boom took off, later began to exploit their brand names aggressively under new management.

Converse, founded in 1908, was a leading sneaker company. After its 1976 acquisition by Allied Chemical (now the Allied Corporation), Converse suffered, as one observer noted, "from Allied's apparent lack of interest in a consumer business that had been an unwanted part of a larger package purchase." The situation changed dramatically when a group of managers and investors bought it out in 1982 when sales reached $200 million.

The company's strength lay in basketball, although it offered a wide range of other athletic shoes and an apparel line. Unlike most of its competitors, Converse advertised broadly and purchased the designation as "Official Shoe of the 1984 Olympic Games." Observers believed the company was trying to use its well-known brand name and upgrade its image.

Converse manufactured about 70 percent of its shoes in its own plants in the United States, with the remainder sourced in the Far East. The company maintained its own sales force, which was strongest in the sporting goods channel.

Keds ($83 million), the premier sneaker company, had been owned, and finally neglected, by Uniroyal. In 1979 the company was purchased by Stride Rite ($300 million sales in 1982), considered one of the strongest marketers in the shoe industry (with its own brand of children's shoes, as well as Herman's boots and Top-Sider boat shoes). Early attempts to expand the product line and build on the brand name were only partially successful. "I don't know if you can take a name like Keds uptown," one observer commented.

The Activewear Apparel Business

In the late 1960s Adidas became the first athletic footwear company to exploit its brand name by introducing sports clothing for athletes. By 1982 almost every competitor had entered this business. While most had initially viewed it as "a logical opportunity to explore"—reasoning that their shoe customers could be persuaded to wear clothing with the same brand name—several, with a more aggressive orientation, came to view it as a potentially very lucrative business.

Observers agreed that a strong brand awareness was a necessity for a footwear company as it took the plunge into apparel. "Fundamentally," one explained, "the brand name conjures up an authentic, athletic image that appeals to the athlete for his or her on- and off-the-track wear and to the consumer who doesn't actively participate but who values a sense of identification with athletes and the active life-style."

Performance clothing was less sophisticated than performance footwear, although there were technical dimensions of importance to athletes. These included the proper design of seams to avoid chafing while running and the use of particular materials, such as lightweight nylon tricot fabric or "rain-proof but breathable" Gore-Tex fabric. Analysts emphasized, however, that apparel was a different business from shoes. As one remarked, "The apparel world is driven by fashion, not technical performance. It is fast paced; products die quickly; and there is an army of copiers waiting in the wings to knock off whatever design is hot."

Several of the footwear companies, including New Balance and Etonic, chose to supply only authentic, performance clothing. Others, including NIKE and Adidas, sold a full line that included both performance and ath-leisure items. At the authentic end of the activewear spectrum, the footwear companies competed with a number of small specialty outfits that focused on high-performance clothing for athletes. These included Frank Shorter Sports Wear (running), CB Sports (skiing), and Fila (tennis). At the ath-leisure end of the activewear spectrum, they competed with the major sportswear houses, including Levi Strauss, Izod La Coste, and Merona, as well as the hundreds of smaller sportswear firms that were aggressively developing activewear lines.

Trends

In early 1983 many executives and analysts described the athletic footwear market as beginning to mature. The game seemed to be changing, with price competition becoming more important, for example. Maturity also underscored the question, implicit for some time, of where future directions for growth lay.

Although it was difficult to find supporting public numbers, a slowing of market growth was widely assumed. "For the first time," a leading consultant reported, "there is more product out there than demand for it. We noted a slowing in the market 18 months ago, but it's been hard for the companies to believe that the high growth they had seen wouldn't last forever." Similarly, the president of one athletic footwear company reported: "The world has changed dramatically in the last four or five months. We think we're seeing a major shift from a seller's market to a buyer's market."

In light of this change observers expected price competition to become more severe, both among the branded companies and from unbranded sources at the low end of the market. It was also anticipated that retailers would gain power, at the expense of suppliers, and that real innovation would command a greater price premium.

In looking to the future observers emphasized that the nation's concern for physical fitness was an important and enduring trend. "Although the big increases in participation won't be there," one analyst summarized, "Americans are not going to stop exercising—and almost all athletic activity requires shoes." Observers expected growth of 6–8 percent in this participation-based segment of the market through the 80s and a need for continued innovation in both footwear and apparel.

Observers also felt the trend toward a more casual and fashionable American life-style would persist, but the link to athletic footwear and apparel was more tenuous. "Running shoes set a new standard for comfort," one executive noted, "but comfortable shoes do not have to look like running shoes." Recognizing this, many companies began to expand their product lines in more casual and fashionable directions. Inevitably this brought them into increasing competitive contact with companies with more marketing and merchandising experience in fashion-oriented business such as Levi's or Stride Rite.

A final dimension was the worldwide market for athletic footwear and apparel which was considered firmly within Adidas's grip—but observers expected the grip to be challenged by many competitors. It was not clear to what extent the American experience of the 70s would be mirrored in other countries.

The Company

NIKE's colorful story was preserved in the memories of many early employees who remained with the firm in the early 1980s. The company's start-up, through 1972, is briefly summarized in the first section below. Its evolution through the first decade (1972–1982) is presented in the following segments.

The Early Years

Company folklore traces the beginnings of NIKE to a business school paper behind which lay an interest in running and a commitment to sports. Phil Knight, the author, was a shy, 4:13 miler on Bill Bowerman's Oregon track team in the late 1950s. Knight absorbed both Bowerman's passion for competition and his values that kept competition in perspective and observed his continuing creative attempts to craft a better running shoe for his runners. In the now famous paper, for a small business management course in the MBA program at Stanford, Knight wrote about an opportunity he saw. He recalled:

> Adidas shoes were beginning to dominate the U.S. market, and that didn't make any sense, because Germany was not the place to put shoe machinery. I thought it might be possible to take over the market with low-priced but high-quality and smartly merchandised imports from Japan, as had already happened with cameras and other optical equipment.

In 1962 during a visit to Japan on a postgraduation round-the-world trip, Knight started the wheels in motion to test his hypothesis. Selecting the Tiger brand, he presented himself to the shoe's manufacturer, Onitsuka, as a shoe importer. A deal was quickly struck in which Knight's company, Blue Ribbon Sports (BRS)—"the name made me think of winning," Knight recalled—became the exclusive distributor for Tiger shoes in the western United States. The first shipment (50 pairs) finally arrived in early 1964, and Knight and Bowerman officially formed BRS, with each investing $500.

For the next eight years, BRS was primarily athletes selling shoes to athletes. "We'd have a base," remembered Jeff Johnson, the first full-time employee, "which ranged from Knight's basement in Portland to a couple of rooms behind a mortician's place in Wellesley, Massachusetts. But the business was getting out to the tracks, to the locker rooms, showing the coaches and athletes our shoes, putting on clinics."

The BRS folk, in touch with the athletes, found ways to innovate.

A runner's problem with cushioning during the 26-mile marathon, for example, led to Bowerman's development of the first midsole (see Figure 1), which Tiger agreed to incorporate in several of its models.

Knight continued to work as a CPA and later a business professor until 1969, when he turned his full attention to BRS. The company was order rich and cash poor, caught in what Knight described as a reverse leverage situation—operating on a nine-month business cycle with six-month financing. One crisis came in 1971. In Knight's words:

> We asked the bank for so much in terms of a letter of credit. I pushed this, pushed it like I always did, as far as I could. One day the loan officer with whom I'd been working, who liked us, I think, called up: "I've been up to the loan committee," he said, "and the committee not only doesn't approve the letter of credit, they don't want to do business with you any more. You're kicked out of this bank, Phil." There it was. The end staring me in the face. Things became pretty real: the provisions of the law; responsibilities to the people who were trying to make this company go. . . . So we put together a financial package and eventually found another bank.

Another more serious crisis came in 1972. The company's success—sales had reached $2 million—had not gone unnoticed by Onitsuka. Deciding that it wanted to distribute Tiger shoes in the United States, the Japanese company offered to buy 51 percent (at book value) of BRS—and threatened to stop doing business with them if the offer was refused.

These storm clouds hovered in the air for several months while BRS began development of its own shoe. Old-timers recalled a frantic period when the ultimatum finally came. Knight finally struck a deal with Nissho-Iwai, Japan's sixth largest trading company, in which Nissho agreed to find manufacturing sources for the new design and to provide financing and export-import services to BRS. The first shoes—bearing the NIKE brand name (which had come to Johnson in a dream) and the Swoosh logo (created for $35 by a graduate design student)—arrived in the United States in time for the 1972 Olympic trials. The company proudly noted that "four of the first seven finishers" in the marathon event at the trials (actually, numbers 4, 5, 6, and 7) wore the NIKEs. "It was clear to me," Knight recalled, "that to see name athletes wearing NIKE shoes was more convincing than anything we could say about them."

This transformation of BRS from an importer of Tiger shoes to a shoe company in its own right closed the first phase of the company's history. Knight recalled, "We knew that the original concept was right and were enormously excited about marketing our own line even though its acceptance in the market was unknown." But there were dreams. Bob Woodell, who joined BRS in 1967, told the story:

> I remember the night I was at Knight's place on New Year's Eve. He and Penny [Knight] and I were drinking Mai Tais. We had added up the sales and realized we'd just sold a million dollars in the last 12 months.

Big deal. So we had another drink to that. We were sitting there, just marveling at a million dollars and how big that was. I said, "Imagine that some day we are going to be a $10 million company." Knight looked at me and said, "Do you realize how big 10 million is?" And I said, "Yeah, but I think we can make it."

With the company competing in a small market segment—performance athletic shoes—this might have been an unrealistic goal. But America had started to run.

Footwear

NIKE continued to compete primarily in the branded athletic footwear business, although revenues from this segment decreased to 84 percent of the company's total in fiscal 1982 from 97 percent in 1978 (see Exhibit 1). The following sections explore NIKE's strategy in this business, highlighting the functional areas of marketing, R&D, sourcing, and sales and distribution, after an initial look at the product line.

The Product Line. As NIKE followed the market that exploded around it in the 1970s its product line evolved in four directions from the original

Figure 2

Evolution of the NIKE Product Line

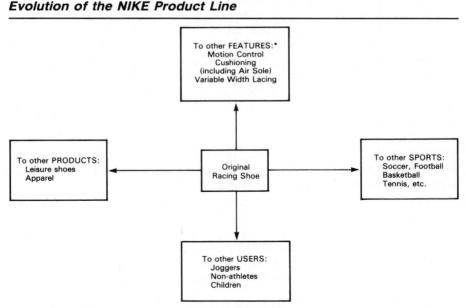

* Jeff Johnson explained: "The idea that different people needed different shoes was revolutionary. A shoe good for one person's physiology may actually hurt another."
Source: Researchers' discussions with company executives.

racing shoe, as shown in Figure 2. This evolution was based on the company's growing knowledge of shoemaking and sports; market factors such as segment size and competitiveness; and the demonstrated transferability of the NIKE brand name.

During the company's first decade, the product line grew from 13 to 156 basic models or, with color and material variations, to 270 separate products (see Table 2). NIKE shoes were offered in a standard range of sizes (each in one width) at suggested retail prices that ranged from $15 to $90. About 100 models had registered sales of over $1 million each in 1982.

Table 2

NIKE Footwear Product Line

Fiscal Year	Basic Models	Total Products, with Variations
1978	63	81
1979	90	136
1980	99	150
1981	139	225
1982	156	270
1983 (est.)	185	340

Source: Company records.

NIKE's products fell naturally into groupings based largely on the type of sport for which the shoes had been designed. In 1982 these groupings, known as product lines, included running, court sports, field sports (cleated), and emerging (or "everything else"). (Exhibit 1 summarizes product line sales from 1978 to 1982, and the appendix gives a more detailed description of the product lines and pictures of representative shoes.)

Running was the largest group, with sales of $236 million in fiscal 1982. NIKE sold a broad line of men's and women's running shoes in three major categories: racing, training, and track and field. The technical shoes, such as the *American Eagle, Mariah,* and *Odyssey,* provided serious runners with features such as lightness, cushioning, motion control, and breathability.[3] The low-end training shoes, such as the *Oceania,* provided ath-leisure users a comfortable fit without any of the "bells and whistles." At the high end of the line, where continued innovation was critical, the company faced stiff competition from the specialty companies. At the low end, competition came from the other full-line companies and

---

[3] Excessive ankle roll during the foot's contact with the ground could be transferred up the leg, causing injury to the knee. Motion control devices sought to limit this movement.

from unbranded imports (as well as from low-end court shoes and more fashionable leisure shoes).

Court shoes ($203 million in 1982) differed from their running brethren in that they had to supply the complex support required by the rapid twists and turns, starts and stops, that characterize basketball, tennis, volleyball, and racquetball. NIKE executives acknowledged that the company's court product line had become dated by 1982 (with older designs and mostly canvas uppers), and a significant initiative was mounted to develop more competitive shoes, including ones that used the Air-Sole technology. The first result of this effort was the *Air Force I* basketball shoe, which was introduced in 1982.

The third group was *cleated* shoes ($14 million in 1982) for field sports such as football, baseball, and soccer. While this submarket was much smaller than running or court (in part because cleated shoes were of limited use for street wear), it was believed important for the exposure provided by professional (and college-level) football and baseball. In addition the company was trying to "learn" soccer, a popular worldwide sport that was growing in importance in the United States.

The *emerging* product line ($120 million) included "everything else." Most prominent was the children's line, which grew very rapidly to $106 million by 1982. These shoes were primarily scaled-down versions of the adult shoes, although some models, such as *Flavors* (watermelon, grape, lemon, mint, and vanilla) catered more to children's colors. A second emerging line was casual shoes which included several leather models.

Over the years these groups were formally defined as product lines within the organization. "Heavyweight" managers were appointed to head each line in early 1982, reflecting concerns that strategic and operational responsibility had become too diffuse. Knight explained:

> Running and the low-end shoes have such volume that it has been easy to neglect the newer and smaller lines that may well be important to us down the road, such as our line of children's shoes. And at the operational level we're all tired of screw-ups like the sales reps pushing a shoe that we're trying to phase out.

The key responsibility of the product line managers, according to several executives, was to protect the integrity of their line. "We've got to have the best shoe at the top of the line," one said, "even though it will, almost by definition, never make money. But without it, the market for the lower priced shoes will go away."

Marketing. NIKE managers viewed the footwear market as a pyramid with a small peak (serious athletes) and a broad base (the millions of

Figure 3

The Market Pyramid

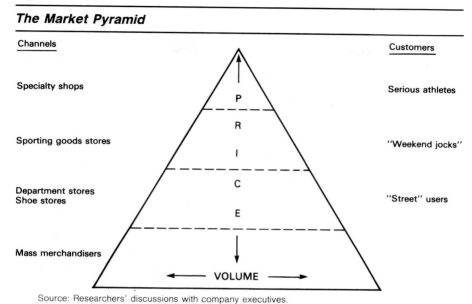

Source: Researchers' discussions with company executives.

Americans who wore athletic footwear in a casual, or "street," way). (See Figure 3.)

During the 1970s the company maintained its strong position at the top of this pyramid. In addition it extended its presence downward to much larger segments—although it continued to avoid the low-end mass merchandiser base. Its success in achieving this expansion, managers believed, was based on the strength of the NIKE brand name. And this, they insisted, was based on the company's reputation at the top.

NIKE's marketing activities, therefore, consistently focused on the top of this pyramid. Most, falling under the rubric of "promotion," involved getting the NIKE shoes on the feet of visible athletes (see Figure 4) and the NIKE name associated with sport—Knight's old word-of-foot policy. *Forbes* described the intended impact:

> Sunday, October 25. This will be one fine day for Philip Knight. [He] positions himself in front of the tube. Morning. Turn on ABC. Alberto Salazar breaks the world marathon record in New York. Early afternoon: Switch to NBC. Dallas Cowboy defensive line rolls back Miami in a 28–27 come-from-behind cliff-hanger. Later: Back to ABC for the World Series. Dodgers stun Yankees 2–1 with a late-inning home run by catcher Steve Yeager.

Not that Knight gets a racing pulse from watching Salazar, the Dallas Cowboy front four, or the Dodgers. His heart leaps for television exposure of NIKE.

Perhaps 100 million viewers have seen parts of these three TV sports events. Millions more will see the pictures in the following days.[4]

NIKE spent 3 percent of its revenues (about $20 million in 1982) on promotion. Major elements of this program were the contracts with professional players and coaches, agreements with amateur athletes and teams, sponsorship of numerous prominent sporting events, and the underwriting of a world-class track club, *Athletics West.*[5] Many outside observers

Figure 4

Source: Company records.

viewed these activities in a crass, commercial light—and, to be sure, the endorsement game had its tales of athlete stealing and shoe doctoring. NIKE executives, however, believed their approach was different, and they consistently added a dimension of caring to the obvious business one. As one executive put it:

> We feel our promotions program is built on a core ethic of decency. Unlike some companies, we'll stick with athletes and not just use them when they're hot. The athletes like our shoes, but they also like our people and service.

---

[4] "NIKE's Fast Track," *Forbes,* November 23, 1981, p. 59.

[5] Based in Eugene, Oregon, this club provided training facilities, coaching equipment, travel expenses, medical support, physiological testing, and assistance in job placement to over 70 top American athletes, including world marathon record holders Alberto Salazar and Joan Benoit and sensational middle-distance runner Mary Decker.

Or in the words of an Olympic athlete, "Phil Knight loves sports and wants to see sport progress. He doesn't look at it like some other executives might."[6]

Less visibly, but still powerfully, NIKE remained active at the grass-roots level, sponsoring local races, presenting clinics for area high school coaches and trainers, and giving shoes to promising local athletes. The NIKE employees themselves, typically athletes or former athletes, added an element of authenticity to these business efforts.

The company's advertising budget (about $6 million in 1982, with 60 percent earmarked for co-op programs with dealers) focused on serious participants through specific sports media such as *The Runner* magazine. Messages ranged from quite technical (see Exhibit 2) to more mood-oriented. Signaling a gradual start to broader advertising, the company sponsored a national TV ad during the New York marathon in October 1982.

As the company began its second decade executives were concerned lest NIKE lose its franchise at the top of the pyramid by seeming too big and interested primarily in the larger volume market segments. Some comments made to the researchers during their field work indicate the reality of the threat:

- "Hey, I don't want to be just another NIKE guy. I want to stand out a little more." [A well-known athlete who had chosen to endorse another shoe.]
- "I don't see how NIKE can be the best anymore. They're so big now." [A moderate runner explaining a decision to purchase another shoe.]

Executives were also sensitive to the success of companies such as New Balance, Hyde Athletic Industries, and Etonic, which had taken visible aim at just the high end of the market. "The bottom line," one NIKE executive concluded, "is that we've simply got to constantly design and build the best shoe."

Research and Development. With Bill Bowerman's heritage of tinkering and early advances such as the full-length midsole, innovation was always an integral and essential part of NIKE's business. Perhaps the most significant success was the waffle-patterned outsole. The idea germinated during Bowerman's breakfast one morning and was implemented with his wife's waffle iron later that day. The sole was widely introduced on NIKE shoes in 1975 and helped put the company on the map with the new wave of jogging enthusiasts.

NIKE's R&D program soon outgrew Bowerman's kitchen, and the company opened a research and development center in Exeter, New

---

[6] Marty Liquori, "Take the $hoes and Run," *Boston Globe,* July 31, 1982, p. 25.

Hampshire, in 1978. One result of the increasingly sophisticated research was the patented Air-Sole. The concept—a gas, under pressure, encapsulated within the midsole material to provide superior cushioning—was purchased from an aerospace engineer; was successfully developed in the lab in great secrecy by a group known as the "airheads"; and was introduced in the *Tailwind* running shoe in 1979 and the *Air Force I* basketball shoe in 1982.

"We're the dreamers here," said Ned Frederick, who directed the R&D Center. "We've got the best lab in the business. The Advanced Concept folks, for example, are really out on the edge of the possible. They have lots of screwball ideas. But those ideas bring the innovation . . . and the big market."

The center had four departments. The *Advanced Concepts Department* studied NIKE's potential use of new and advanced materials resulting from in-house research as well as from the submission of ideas by inventors, designers, and medical professionals. The *Chemistry and Materials Research Department* tested the characteristics and durability of materials used in NIKE footwear. At the *Sport Research Laboratory* scientists analyzed performance athletic shoe characteristics such as flexibility, cushioning, rearfoot and forefoot control, and energy economy (see Figure 5). The lab also analyzed the feedback from athletes who participated in extensive field tests of NIKE prototypes. The *Product Development Department* used the data, information, and testing results received from the other departments to design and develop new NIKE shoes.

Figure 5

Source: Company records.

The product development people in Exeter worked closely with the marketing groups in Oregon to set broad priorities at the senior level and to develop particular products at the middle level. Frederick explained:

R&D for the low-end shoes is driven by the market. The marketing people in Beaverton handle that directly with the plants—the so-called design by telex. We'd have a tendency to overdesign a $30 shoe.

But the products that will lead the line come out of here. I spend a lot of time on the phone with my peers in Beaverton, and what emerges is a common sense of the broad product categories we need to focus on for the next year or so. Then the people here take over, drawing on the research, the input from athletes, and their own knowledge of sports and ingenuity.

When we do it right, the shoe has magic. You pick it up, and it glows with the concern that NIKE has with the athlete, the care we take in designing and making the shoe. There is something in our shoe that is special.

NIKE spent $5.7 million (slightly under 1 percent of its revenues) on R&D in 1982, significantly more than its competitors (with the possible exception of Adidas), all of whom had either in-house or consultant-based R&D programs. The technological revolution in running shoes spawned by these businesswide efforts unquestionably improved the performance and injury prevention characteristics of shoes in many sports. One enthusiastic NIKE manager exclaimed, "And we've only scratched the surface of what can be done." Contrasting these programs, an outside observer noted, "While all the companies are doing some research, NIKE, from my perspective, will tend to produce the more revolutionary advances and the others the more evolutionary ones."

Critics, however, wondered if some advances were related more to marketing than to foot science. One wrote:

> [Runners] need protection of two different sorts. First, they need physical protection. The typical runner with two feet lands on each foot 800 times a mile. . . . The second need for protection relates to that area of the body north of the feet where the wallet resides. . . .
>
> Of all areas of running-shoe design, the most remarkable profusion and ballyhoo involve heel stabilizers, in all their remarkable incarnations. The purpose of a heel stabilizer is both straightforward and laudable. It is intended to limit the heel's movement within the shoe. . . . [But to do this] and to generate consumer enthusiasm, the shoe companies have invented a complete lexicon of heel stabilization to better capture the qualities of their respective devices. . . . Thermoplastic Heel Counter . . . Dynamic Reaction Plate . . . Stabilizing Pillar . . . Dual-Density Tri-Wedge System . . . These features may amount to more than a hill of beans, but they rarely amount to more than a piece of rubber or plastic costing 35 to 50 cents in materials and labor.[7]

From another viewpoint, a supportive but hassled specialty store owner commented, "It's great what NIKE's doing. But I'd like to see those R&D people come down and try to explain the differences among their models to *my* customers."

Sourcing.   Sourcing shoes in the low-cost Far East was a cornerstone of Knight's original concept, and it remained the dominant practice as the company grew through the 1970s, though it required some ingenuity to handle the intricacies of growing trade protectionism and import quotas. The key to making this system work, executives believed, was the

---

[7] "The Birth of Pronation," *Harper's,* May 1983, p. 87.

Figure 6

NIKE Shoe Sources by Country, Fiscal 1982
(40 million pairs)

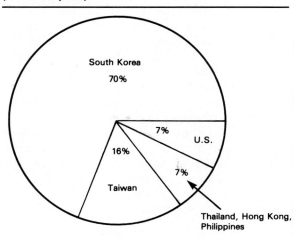

Source: Company records.

company's ability to find and develop contract factories, closely monitor them for quality, and forecast production needs effectively.

Contract factories in South Korea and Taiwan emerged as the major suppliers (see Figure 6), although NIKE had continually sought to diversify sourcing to minimize political risk and to reflect changing economics. Thus just as Korean factories replaced the original Japanese sources in the mid-70s, it was expected that lower wage countries, such as China, would displace some of the Korean volume in the 80s.

Developing new sources was a complex process, combining the usual business problems (including training workers, installing equipment, developing local materials sources, and assuring containerized transportation) with the often difficult challenge of working in a vastly different political and social culture. Vice President David Chang, who had led NIKE's move into the People's Republic of China, commented in early 1983:

We have four factories starting up in China now. It's been slow, hard work. Some of that is due to the inevitable Beijing–Washington–Seoul–Taiwan tensions, but a lot is learning how to do business in such a different environment. For example, we rejected a few thousand outsoles that were off-color and assumed they would be shredded. To the Chinese, however, this was an unthinkable waste, and we later found them used on Chinese shoes going to a different market. It's been critical, as we develop this relationship, to have good people on-site there.

Once a source had been developed NIKE expatriate technicians continued to work closely with it. "This has been the real key," production executive Ron Nelson explained. "Our people are living there and working with the factories as the product is going down the lines. This is a lot different from accepting or rejecting the product at the end of the line—especially at the end of a three-month pipeline to the United States!"

The heart of NIKE's production scheduling system was the Futures sales program. Started in the early 1970s it eventually accounted for about 65 percent of footwear sales. Under the program a retailer ordered five or six months in advance of delivery. In return the retailer received a 5–7 percent discount and guaranteed delivery during a two-week window around the target date. This was valuable to retailers who competed in a rapidly growing business notorious for unreliable suppliers. As one said, "You can count on three things in this world—death, taxes, and Futures." And it was valuable for NIKE: retailer shelf space was committed to NIKE, the company received reliable, early information on trends, and, most important, 65 percent of production was presold goods.[8]

Although NIKE used many nonexclusive factories, company executives believed that work on NIKE footwear was well segregated from that for other customers. These executives acknowledged that NIKE had clout with the factories but consistently described working hard to develop and maintain good business relationships with them. As Executive Vice President Del Hayes noted:

> Most of the factories are heavily committed to NIKE, and we respect that. We want them to make money, too—though not a windfall, of course!—and will do our damnedest, for example, to level production for them. I guess that's part of the company, part of how we want to be perceived. We believe there should be sense of fairness involved.

Some outside observers were less sanguine about NIKE's (and its competitors') Far East production. One athletic footwear buyer commented: "From my viewpoint, the lower end shoes are all the same. I think it's like tennis balls that only find out what kind they are when they get a logo stamped on them at the end of the line."

NIKE established its own manufacturing operations in Exeter, New Hampshire, in 1974 and in Saco, Maine, in 1978. The initial impetus for this move had been an uncertainty about production quality and capacity in other Far East countries following the revaluation of the yen in 1973 (which removed the cost advantage of Japanese sourcing). In fact Korean and Taiwanese factories developed their capability quickly. The New England operation, however, became important for the learning opportunities it offered NIKE executives. Through it they developed

---

[8] The remaining 35 percent, called fill-ins, were projected from current Futures orders and from experience.

Table 3

**Typical Cost Buildup—
Moderate Price NIKE Shoe**

Labor	$ 1.10
Materials	5.20
Overhead and profit	2.70
Factory cost	9.00
Shipping and duty	$ 1.50
NIAC commission*	.36
NIKE cost	10.86
NIKE margin	$ 5.87
Retailer cost	16.73
Retailer margin	12.22
Retail price	28.95

* NIAC—Nissho-Iwai American Corp.
Source: Company records.

an understanding of the manufacturing business and its economics that was invaluable in negotiations with the contract factories (see Table 3). And "tech-rats" got the hands-on understanding critical to effective work as an expatriate technician with the sourcing factories. In addition the New England operation manufactured many shoes at the high end of the product line. It was advantageous, executives reported, to have a source close to the R&D facility (although the expansion of the model shop within the research unit made this factor less important).

With market growth slowing as 1983 began, NIKE executives reached the painful decision to close the manufacturing plant in Exeter, consolidating U.S. production in the larger Saco facility. This decision emerged from a careful look at worldwide production, which also resulted in concluding business with five marginal factories in the Far East. The economics had been clear, although the result spurred one analyst to comment, "This confirms my sense of NIKE as a 'foreign company.' And it certainly doesn't do anything to support their bid in trade hearings to avoid quotas on footwear from the Far East."

The slowdown in growth also changed the pattern in Futures orders, which dropped to about 40 percent of sales in early 1983. The full effect of this change on the company's production scheduling operation was unclear.

Sales and Distribution. The basic pattern for NIKE's sales and distribution was set in the early years. The company used independent sales representatives, paid entirely on commission, to reach an expanding base of accounts. The reps were largely order takers, and NIKE itself performed all order processing, credit, and physical distribution work from three increasingly automated regional warehouses/offices in Oregon, New Hampshire, and Tennessee. The Futures program was the key sales program.

By 1982 the NIKE sales management team supervised 26 independent rep agencies. Most agency heads, typically entrepreneurs who employed 7 to 10 salespersons (often athletes), had been with NIKE for several years. While several reps sold other products, none was allowed to carry lines that competed with NIKE. Many reported that they made "a lot of money," occasionally a sore point with inside managers. NIKE held regional agency head meetings several times a year and a national sales meeting extravaganza for all reps annually.

By early 1983 the account base had expanded to 9,500 accounts (operating 13,000 outlets) in the four relevant retail channels (see Table 4). Executives described the opening of the J. C. Penney account in 1977 as the most significant step in broadening this base. They had been approached by other large national retailers but had not yet signed a distribution agreement with any.

NIKE itself provided several dealer support services which focused on the specialty shops. Key dealers, for example, were given advanced delivery of new performance shoe models (the so-called Torch program). The company also operated seven retail stores in strategic locations across the country. Descendants of the early bases from which people like Johnson and Woodell had worked, these stores functioned more as a source of market research, sales support, and promotion than of significant or profitable sales.

In the growth market of the 1970s the aggressive reps consistently exceeded the sales goals set for them by NIKE management. As market growth started to slow, however, two sources of uncertainty emerged. The first, expressed by numerous outside observers, concerned the dynamics of NIKE's relationship with its accounts. As one specialty shop owner summed it up, "Some of us have been with NIKE for a long time. We like them and feel loyal to them. That personal relationship can't exist

Table 4

Summary of Accounts

Type	Percent of Accounts	Percent of Sales
National accounts*	—	15%
Specialty shops	15%	14
Sporting goods stores	29	26
Department stores	27	19
Shoe stores	29	26
	100%	100%

* Major customers such as J. C. Penney and Footlocker.
Source: Company records.

with the bigger chain and department store accounts. But it's also scary to depend, as we and many other small stores do, on one company for over 50 percent of your business." The second, expressed by several NIKE managers, was how a potentially new and more competitive retail environment would change the selling task and the degree of control the company needed over the selling function.

Leisure Shoes

NIKE had also entered the market for leisure shoes. The leisure shoe was distinguished from an athletic or "ath-leisure" shoe by the fact that the product made no pretense of possible athletic use. The upper was typically a tanned or sueded leather, and the sole, smooth leather or rubber. In 1980 the company introduced the "Air Casual" shoe, which utilized the Air-Sole technology originally developed for running shoes. The shoe was designed by Corporate Technology Center in Exeter, New Hampshire, and manufactured on a contract basis by U.S. factories with leather shoe experience.

By 1982 NIKE managers acknowledged that the shoe had been a failure. It was poorly styled for the leisure market, which was fashion—not performance—oriented. This early lack of success had slowed NIKE's entry into the leisure shoe business which accounted for roughly $14 million of NIKE's sales in 1982.

Apparel

As it became apparent that the bloom would eventually fade from the domestic athletic footwear market, active apparel emerged as one potential area of major growth for the company. Indeed the separate apparel division grew very rapidly in its first years, with sales projected to reach $100 million in fiscal 1983. "It's a huge market," one executive said, "and we're really pumped about it!" But it was also quite a different business.

NIKE T-shirts were introduced at the 1972 Olympic trials, but the company did not seriously enter the business until 1978. Its first steps were faltering. As *Fortune* reported, "The company made an almost fatal first step when it aimed the introductory line at lower middle class consumers instead of its usual, richer buyers. 'The look,' sniffs Bart Stolp, Adidas's U.S. advertising manager, 'was atrocious.' "[9] Bob Woodell was assigned to the division in early 1980, and a new look took shape. With a strong brand name, NIKE's apparel line grew quickly. Sales rose from $2 million in 1979 to an estimated $100 million in 1983, while the number of styles increased from 45 (in 1980) to 270. Observing this growth,

---

[9] "NIKE Starts the Second Mile," *Fortune,* November 1, 1982, p. 160.

Table 5

NIKE Apparel Division

Fiscal Year	Sales ($ millions)	Styles	SKUs*
1979	$ 2	n.a.	n.a.
1980	8	45	480
1981	33	115	1,464
1982	70	215	3,272
1983 (est.)	100	270	4,774

* A stockkeeping unit measures the total number of product variations, not only style but color and size as well.

Source: Company records.

one specialty store owner commented, "NIKE apparel is nothing special in and of itself. But it has the NIKE name on it." (See Table 5.)

The line ranged from authentic performance clothing to comfortable ath-leisure wear for men, women, youths, and children. The company presented a line for both the fall and spring seasons each year, targeted to the young person (aged 14 to 25) who was, or wanted to look, athletic.

The line was sourced from domestic and Far East apparel manufacturers. While less technical than shoe manufacturing, apparel production was complicated by the difficult task of matching and coordinating color on different materials and from different sources (as fashion required); by the notorious unreliability, and too frequent sloppiness, of many American vendors; and by the intricacies of textile quotas on imports from the Far East. In a fast-paced, fashion-oriented business, orders to vendors had to be based largely on gut instinct rather than the solid base of Futures bookings NIKE had established in shoes.[10]

NIKE used the same independent rep agencies to sell the line, although the agencies were usually forced to hire salespeople who handled only apparel. Sales were concentrated in department and specialty stores. The limited advertising appeared in magazines such as *Seventeen* and *Rolling Stone.*

Managers acknowledged that the product line suffered from design, quality, and delivery problems, tracing back to the early directions of the division, but asserted that these were being addressed and solved, with each season's line showing an improvement over the previous one. In addition NIKE executives were excited about potential initiatives at each end of the product line.

The line had few serious high-tech products, such as a Gore-Tex

---

[10] NIKE developed an "Advance Booking" program in apparel that accounted for about 25 percent of orders in 1982.

running suit—a shortcoming galling to many in a company that prided itself on its high-performance footwear. Various programs, such as the development of an "Exeter R&D Center" for apparel, were being discussed in an effort to ensure that the company took more of a lead in high-end products. At the other end of the spectrum NIKE introduced a line of leisure pants in 1982, and executives expected to mount a significant effort to develop this market segment. Summarizing the Apparel Division's strategy, Woodell explained:

> The NIKE name is valid, it's authentic. . . . It's not that people have to buy the authentic apparel. They just need to identify with it, and then we've won.

International

The international market emerged in the early 1980s as the second major area in which NIKE might grow—and the area in which it hoped to challenge Adidas's global leadership in athletic footwear and apparel sales. In fiscal 1982 the international division's sales reached $43 million, almost entirely from footwear (see Table 6). Executives expected this figure to double in fiscal 1983.

NIKE entered the international market in the late 1970s and rapidly lined up local distribution (supported by marketing assistance from regional NIKE offices and sourcing from NIKE contract factories in Asia) in a number of countries in Europe, Latin America, and the Asia/Pacific region. Sales grew quickly, but the company found the reality of building a business in these foreign markets more expensive, complex, and time-consuming than expected. Executives noted several issues:

- *Market strategy.* In the U.S. market, NIKE established its consumer acceptance in running and then expanded its product line into other sport shoes. In most foreign countries, however, running was significantly less popular than in the United States. Would consumer acceptance of the NIKE brand name be more effectively sought by developing credibility in running or by directly tackling the most popular sport in a region (for example, soccer in Europe)?
- *Operations.* Many executives believed that some distributors (typically private companies that marketed, sold, and warehoused the NIKE products) were undercapitalized and/or unwilling to tackle the market as aggressively as NIKE wanted. One option under consideration was the purchase of several distributors. This would provide greater control but would also, of course, require significant capital expenditures and pose the challenge of managing foreign operating units.

Table 6

FY82 Revenues
(In millions)

Europe	$27
Japan	12
Latin America	3
Other	1
	$43

■ *Product strategy.* There was disagreement about the appropriate level of country-specific products in major markets such as Europe or Japan. Typically managers in the countries argued for more market-tailored products, and those in the domestic operation, responsible for the (relatively centralized) development and production operation, argued for less.

■ *General business conditions* differed widely from area to area and often presented significant business challenges to NIKE. In Europe, for example, the Common Market tariff barrier forced the company to source many shoes from European factories, including two it had purchased in 1981–82.

Because of the complexity of the international business, NIKE executives were considering focusing the company's efforts on three major foreign markets (Japan, Europe, and Canada) rather than continuing to push aggressively on so broad a scale.

Administration

Finance. As a small and rapidly growing company with a voracious appetite for ever more credit, NIKE careened through several financial crises until its record of success and a stock offering brought a measure of stability to the picture in the early 1980s. NIKE's unusual financial structure was built primarily on short-term financing, in the form of interest-bearing trade payables from Nissho-Iwai and short-term debt from U.S. banks. This reflected, the company believed, the liquid nature of its assets, which were primarily inventory and accounts receivable rather than "bricks and mortar" (see Exhibits 1 and 3 for financial data).

NIKE's relationship with Nissho-Iwai continued over the decade since Knight first did business with them during BRS's break with Tiger. And in true NIKE fashion it grew along personal as well as business dimensions. "They came over in 1977," Corporate Counsel Rich Werschkul recalled, "and gave Phil a $14 million line of credit as a birthday present." Nissho retained the right to terminate its relationship with

NIKE under certain circumstances, such as Knight's ceasing to be CEO at a time when he did not own a majority of the stock.

Technically NIKE placed orders in the Far East with Nissho's subsidiary, Nissho-Iwai American Corporation (NIAC), which retained title to the goods until they cleared U.S. customs. NIAC's financing took the form of interest-bearing trade payables generally due 115 days after product shipment from the foreign port (ocean transit was typically one month). NIKE also entered a domestic revolving credit agreement with a group of five commercial banks (see Exhibit 3 for a summary of these borrowings). NIKE financial managers viewed both of these relationships from a long-term perspective. They were careful to spread the business between both sources rather than play a "short-term interest rate game." Over time these executives were able to negotiate more favorable terms with both groups. In 1982 the agreements were amended to provide the borrowings on an unsecured basis. As Financial Vice President Jim Manns explained, "We believe, and have been able to convince others, that there is very little risk in our financial structure."

NIKE went public in December 1980 with an offering of common stock at 28 times fiscal 1980 earnings. The company created two classes of stock with the offering: a publicly traded Class B and a closely held Class A, which elected a majority of the directors. At the end of 1982 Knight owned 42 percent of the outstanding stock, including over two thirds of the Class A stock. The initial offering, and a second one in October 1982 at 18 times fiscal 1982 earnings, raised a total of about $80 million for the company—and made millionaires of several key and early employees. "While I trust we have the wisdom to avoid playing the quarterly earnings game," one senior executive commented, "I know that the stock price is important to us." (See Exhibit 3 for data on NIKE's stock market performance.)

Management. NIKE retained a significant degree of its youthful informality as it grew. Dress, language, spirit, relationships—all still carried the flavor of the old NIKE. Increasing organizational size, however, had started to insist, in a voice growing ever more strident, that the old ways be supplemented with more formal management systems. Such systems were being developed, sometimes with hope, as when one takes a vitamin pill, and sometimes with resignation, as with a dose of castor oil. "We shy away from overtones of structure," Executive Vice President Del Hayes noted.

Within NIKE areas of responsibility at first were defined largely along functional lines, although jobs eventually started to coalesce around a product line organization in the 80s with the formation of the apparel and international divisions and the footwear product lines (see Exhibit 4).

Top management watched a daily report on shipments (in effect, sales) and orders as a first and key indicator of whether things were tracking right. The monthly accounting report was also studied as a more in-depth indicator. Lower in the organization, systems were developed as needed. The sales order entry group, for example, was linked to the distribution operation with a "data processing bloodline," as one manager described it. The annual budget process was driven by the sales forecast (developed by Ron Nelson's production scheduling group in conjunction with Knight). Individual department budgets were ultimately approved by Knight, following preparation by the department manager and staff work by Treasurer Gary Kurtz. The company had not instituted formal strategic planning or capital budgeting systems.

Company Goals

Observers agreed that NIKE's first decade was a dazzling success. Sales were approaching $1 billion, far above the $10 million level Knight and Woodell had dreamed of 11 years earlier. Observers believed, however, that the second decade would prove more challenging and pointed to the maturing U.S. athletic footwear market as an indication of tougher times.

Woodell, in describing NIKE's goals to the researchers, told this story:

> Once, years ago, I asked Knight, "What's the goal? Is it to put so many shoes on so many people?" He said, "No. The goal is to maximize profits in the long run." I thought, "My God, that's pretty simple. And it makes sense too."
>
> It's easy to forget that goal and get caught up in getting shoes on 8 zillion athletes in the next Olympics or whatever. But profit is how this game is scored. We're a competitive group and play this game in good part for the competition of it, not just to have more money or so the stock will be worth more. We'd really like to believe that the young whipper-snappers from Oregon, who everybody thinks are country bumpkins, can be best in the world.

Reflecting on this, Knight commented:

> Profit is like the score in a dual track meet. It's the way you decide if you've won or lost. But how you get there—that is through your values, the training, the trying to take every step better than anybody else. We'd like to be the biggest and best in our business in the world. And we're a growth company, not 15 percent but 30 percent or more. Sure, we could slow down our growth, tighten up, and pay some dividends—but that's not who we are, not who we intend to become.

Appendix
Footwear Product Line Description

Men's and women's *running* shoes fell into three major categories—racing, training, and track and field. Racing flats were designed for serious road racing, such as the marathon. NIKE's lightest racing shoe was the *American Eagle* (suggested 1982 retail price, $49.95; see Figure A–1). The *Mariah* ($61.95), another popular model, sacrificed some lightness for the additional cushioning provided by a full-length Air-Sole (a patented midsole with encapsulated air bubbles). Training flats sacrificed lightness to provide more significant cushioning and support. Training models ranged from very technical shoes used for day-in and day-out training by serious racers to basic shoes purchased for comfortable street use. At the upper end of this spectrum NIKE offered a range of shoes designed to meet specific runner needs. The *Equator* ($59.95), for example, provided exceptional motion control (support) for runners with severe pronation problems, while the *Tailwind* ($51.95) provided exceptional cushioning for runners training primarily on roads. For the moderate runner the *Yankee* ($34.95) provided a good combination of cushioning and stability at an economical price. For the consumer purchasing a running shoe for street use the *Oceania* ($24.95; see Figure A–2) provided comfort without the more specialized running features. Track and field shoes were designed for serious competitive use. Models ranged from the *Zoom S* ($59.95), for sprinters, to the *HJ8L* ($58.95), for high jumpers who took off on their left foot.

The flagship of the NIKE *court* line was the *Air Force I* ($89.95; see Figure A–3), a new leather basketball shoe with an Air-Sole that provided significant cushioning. Although it largely missed the 1982–83 season, early reactions from professional players were very favorable. At the inexpensive end of the line, the *Bruin Canvas* ($24.95) was a modest shoe for occasionally "shooting some hoops" and for street wear. Other shoes in the court line included the new *Air Ace* (to be introduced in 1983), a high-performance tennis shoe with an Air-Sole; the *All Court* ($24.95), a popular all-around shoe for street and moderate court use; and the *Aerobic* ($29.95), a new shoe for the increasingly popular aerobics.

The much smaller *cleated* line included shoes for baseball, softball, football, and soccer, including the *Euromatch D* soccer boot ($64.95; see Figure A–4). The *emerging* product line included children's shoes (such as *Flavors*—$23.95—in watermelon, grape, lemon, mint, and vanilla; see Figure A–5), leather casual shoes with the Air-Sole (such as the *Pathfinder*—$72.95; see Figure A–6), and recreational shoes (including the *Approach* hiking boot ($66.95; see Figure A–7).

Figure A

American Eagle
Figure A-1.

Oceania
Figure A-2.

Air Force I
Figure A-3.

Euromatch D
Figure A-4.

Flavors
Figure A-5.

Pathfinder
Figure A-6.

Approach
Figure A-7.

Source: Company records.

Exhibit 1

Recent NIKE Financial Statements
1976–1982 Income Statement and Selected Financial Data (Fiscal year ending May 31—dollars in thousands)

	1982	1981	1980	1979	1978	1977	1976
Net sales	$693,582	$457,742	$269,775	$149,830	$71,001	$28,711	$14,100
Cost of sales	473,885	328,133	196,683	103,466	50,560	20,004	10,036
SG&A	95,354	61,045	39,917	22,372	11,000	4,963	2,526
Interest expense	24,538	17,859	9,144	4,569	1,598	637	348
Income taxes	50,589	24,750	11,526	9,700	3,987	1,585	590
Minority interest	180	—	—	—	—	—	—
Net income	49,036	25,955	12,505	9,723	3,856	1,522	600
Less preferred dividends	—	—	30	30	30	11	—
Net income available	49,036	25,955	12,475	9,693	3,826	1,511	600
Average number of common shares	35,708	34,031	16,140	16,828	17,135	16,843	16,192
Net income per share	$ 1.37	$ .76	$ .77	$ .58	$ .22	$ .09	$ .04
Return on equity	37%	31%	45%	60%	59%	NA	NA
Employees at year end	3,600	2,700	2,300	1,600	720	NA	NA

Note: No dividends have been paid on common shares.
Source: Company annual reports, 10-Ks, and prospectus.

Sales Summary by Product Line (Fiscal year ending May 31—dollars in millions)

	1982		1981		1980		1979		1978	
	Dollars	Percent	Dollars	Percent	Dollars	Percent	Dollars	Percent	Dollars	Percent
Revenues:										
Footwear:										
Running*	$236	34%	$149	33%	$108	40%	$ 80	54%	$39	56%
Court:										
Basketball	144	21	105	23	62	23	28	18	14	20
Racquet sports	59	9	61	13	47	17	26	17	12	17
Cleated (field sports)	14	2	9	2	4	2	2	1	1	1
Emerging:										
Children's	106	15	64	14	21	8	6	4	2	2
Leisure	14	2	8	2	2	1	1	1	1	1
Total footwear	581	84	399	87	245	91	144	96	70	97
Apparel	70	10	33	7	8	3	2	1	1	2
International	43	6	26	6	17	6	4	3	1	1
Total revenues	$694	100%	$458	100%	$270	100%	$150	100%	$71	100%

* About 17 percent of the Running category were high-end shoes specifically designed for serious athletic use.
Source: Company annual reports and 10-Ks.

Exhibit 1 (concluded)

NIKE
Balance Sheet
As of May 31
(in millions)

	1982	1981	1980
Assets			
Cash	$ 5	$ 2	$ 2
Accounts receivable	130	87	64
Inventory	203	120	56
Other	7	4	2
Current assets	345	213	124
Property, plant, and equipment	41	24	14
Less accumulated depreciation	(12)	(8)	(4)
	29	16	10
Other	1	1	1
Total assets	$375	$230	$135
Liabilities and Stockholders' Equity			
Current portion of long-term debt	$ 4	$ 7	$ 4
Notes payable to banks	113	61	37
Accounts payable*	74	42	37
Other	42	28	17
Current liabilities	233	138	95
Long-term debt	9	9	11
Other	1	0	0
Total liabilities	243	147	106
Common stock at stated value	2	2	0
Capital in excess of stated value	27	27	0
Retained earnings	103	54	29
Stockholders' equity	132	83	29
Liabilities and stockholders' equity	$375	$230	$135

* Includes NIAC.
Source: Company annual reports and 10-Ks.

Exhibit 2

Footwear Advertisement

"WE HAVE LIFTOFF."

To be honest, our Columbia isn't *exactly* like their Columbia.

But talk about thrust. Wait until you're atop that refined Air-Sole™. It's not quite the same as 6.65 million pounds of rocket propellant. But it's enough to move you about two percent faster, or two percent farther.*

And the ride. It's awesome.

Even if you don't experience total weightlessness.

Equally important, it's a ride that will last. Because we built this Columbia strictly for training flights. Big, long ones. After more than 800 miles, laboratory tests showed virtually no loss of cushioning. And wear on the new Anatomical outsole — minimal.

We've even come out with a model that has the exact same per-

formance characteristics. The Aurora. For women only.

Now, you don't see NASA doing that.

Naturally, this kind of technology doesn't come cheap.

But look at it this way. You can buy one of theirs. Or about 20,000,000 of ours.

*Compared to shoes of similar weight.

NIKE

Beaverton, Oregon

Source: Company records.

Exhibit 3

Additional Financial Data (Dollars in millions)

	1982	1981	1980	1979	1978
A. Sources and uses:					
Net income	$ 49.0	$26.0	$12.5	$ 9.7	$ 3.8
Depreciation	5.1	3.8	2.2	1.2	.5
Other	.3	.1	—	—	—
Operations, total	54.4	29.9	14.7	10.9	4.4
Increased long-term					
debt	.5	0.0	8.7	1.3	0.8
Stock offering	.6	28.3	0.0	0.0	0.0
Disposal of assets	.3	.1	.1	0.0	0.1
Total sources	$ 55.9	$58.3	$23.5	$12.2	$ 5.3
Decreased long-term					
debt	$ 0.0	$ 2.6	$ 0.0	$ 0.0	0.3
Property, plant, and					
equipment	18.2	9.9	6.8	4.1	2.2
Increased working					
capital	37.5	45.1	16.4	7.9	2.7
Other increased assets	.2	.7	.4	.2	.1
Total uses	$ 55.9	$58.3	$23.5	$12.2	$ 5.3
B. Working capital changes:					
Accounts receivable	$ 43.2	$23.4	$30.9	$15.9	$11.3
Inventory	82.6	64.3	17.5	21.4	10.2
Other	6.7	1.4	1.6	.4	1.6
Total increases in					
current assets	$132.5	$89.1	$50.0	$37.7	$23.1
Accounts payable*	31.6	$ 5.6	$16.7	$ 9.5	$ 5.2
Banks	51.5	24.7	19.3	11.3	5.5
Other	11.9	13.7	(2.4)	9.0	9.7
Total increases in					
current liabilities	$ 95.0	$44.0	$33.6	$29.8	$20.4
Net change	$ 37.5	$45.1	$16.4	$ 7.9	$ 2.7
C. Short-term borrowings					
summary:					
Banks:					
Credit line	$110	$70	$38		
Total borrowings	$203	$61	$37		
Interest rate	16.25%	21.50%	15.25%		
NIAC:					
Credit line	$110	$70	$38		
Total payables	$ 52	$37	$32		
Interest rate	16.25%	19.25%	21.00%		

* Mostly NIAC payables.
Source: Company annual reports.

Exhibit 3 (continued)

NIKE Public Equity Offerings and Market Performance

NIKE went public on December 2, 1980, at $11 per share.* In anticipation of a public offering, the company had created two classes of stock: A-voting and B-nonvoting.

Management maintained control of the voting shares, while the class B shares were sold to the public. The class B shareholders did, however, retain the limited right to elect one of the seven members of the board.

The company offered its B shares to the public for a second time on October 14, 1982, at a price of $24.31 per share.

A summary of the equity offerings and the stock's performance is offered below.

* All data adjusted for 2:1 split January 1983.

NIKE Public Offering Summary (Thousands of shares)

		1st Offering	2nd Offering
Number shares outstanding prior to offering	32,352		
Shares outstanding after offering		35,072	37,272
Class A		30,318	22,532*
Class B		4,754	14,740
Share price at offering		$ 11.00	$24.31
Shares sold (all class B)		4,754	3,000
Primary		2,720	2,200
Secondary		2,034	800†
Funds raised ($ millions)		$ 52.3	$ 72.9
Primary		$ 29.9	$ 53.5
Secondary		$ 22.4	$ 19.4
Company valuation ($ millions)		$385.7	$906.1
Directors' and officers' percent of shares			
Total		57%	50%
Class A		65%	83%‡
P. H. Knight's percent of shares			
Total		46%	42%
Class A		53%	69%‡

* The total number of class A shares is decreasing as these shares are converted to class B shares and sold to the public.

† The sale of secondary shares does not represent a net increase in shares outstanding as existing A shares are converted to B shares and then sold by these shareholders to the public.

‡ Both the directors'/officers' and Knight's percentage share of the class A stock is increasing over this period as other (nondirector and nonofficer) class A shareholders sell their class A shares.

Source: NIKE prospectus and annual report.

Exhibit 3 (concluded)

NIKE Stock Market Performance Summary

Quarter Ending	Price/Share*		P/E†	
	High	Low	High	Low
12/80 offering	$11		13.75	
2/28/81	$11.62	$ 8.75	18.6	14.2
5/31/81	11.50	8.50	14.0	10.4
8/31/81	12.50	9.25	7.8	5.8
11/30/81	13.88	8.88	10.8	6.9
2/28/82	15.36	13.50	12.4	10.9
5/31/82	15.25	12.36	11.2	9.1
8/31/82	20.12	14.75	8.7	6.4
11/30/82	27.12	20.00	20.5	15.1
2/28/83	28.00	15.75	28.0	15.8

* Reflects 2:1 split in January of 1983.
† Based on annualized earnings per share for quarterly period stated.

Exhibit 4

Researchers' Sketch of the NIKE Organization

*The board consisted of Phil Knight, Del Hayes, Bill Bowerman, and the following outsiders: Richard Donahue, partner—Donahue & Donahue, Attorneys, Lowell, Massachusetts; Douglas Houser, partner—Bullivant, Wright, Leedy, Johnson, Pendergrass & Hoffman, Attorneys, Portland, Oregon; Jon Jaqua, partner—Jaqua, Wheatley, Gallagher & Holland, Attorneys, Eugene, Oregon; Charles Robinson, chairman, Energy Transition Corporation, Santa Fe, New Mexico.

† Inside member of the board.

‡ Member of the top management group.

Source: Company records.

NIKE (B)

Yeah, there are a lot of business challenges out there now, and there will certainly be more. Some will be real tough. But I think we can solve those problems. The greatest threats to our continued success may well be internal.

You see, NIKE, more than anything, is a group of people who have learned how to work well together, how to bring the best out of each other. NIKE is a spirit that means being smart about what you do and busting your butt to do it well. It means talking to your friends and sharing ideas and not trying to go off and be a hero by yourself. It means trying things and having the freedom to recognize your mistakes and not be fired for them.

And there's the danger.

As we get used to being Number One, I worry that we'll become arrogant and start to believe we deserve the success; that we'll get lazy and stop reading the market.

But more, as we continue to get larger and more spread out, I worry that we'll start to create our own little fiefdoms and stop talking to each other; that we'll substitute a two-inch thick policy manual for some broad principles and a lot of deep *thinking;* that we'll become just another big company.

Bob Woodell, March 1983

NIKE emerged during the fitness boom of the 1970s as the dominant athletic footwear supplier in the U.S. market and a major contender for worldwide honors. Sales grew from $2 million in 1972 to $694 million in 1982. Of its 1982 sales 84 percent came from the company's domestic footwear business (34 percent from running alone), 10 percent from the

Copyright © 1984 by the President and Fellows of Harvard College
Harvard Business School case 385–027

new activewear apparel line, and 6 percent from the international market. The number of employees increased from 45 to 3,600 during this decade.

By early 1983 it was clear that NIKE's primary market, domestic athletic footwear, was maturing. NIKE executives remained optimistic, however, about the opportunities for continued growth, not only within the U.S. footwear market but especially in the domestic activewear apparel and international athletic footwear/apparel markets, each of which the company was vigorously pursuing. Although these executives identified many external threats to NIKE's continued success (ranging from the skills of particular competitors to political instability in the Far East), they consistently singled out the internal, organizational dimension as the most critical challenge. Most believed that NIKE's success to date was due in large part to the unconventional, freewheeling, entrepreneurial people it had attracted and the collegial style of working together it encouraged. And yet as the company grew larger and its operations became more complex, NIKE senior managers accepted—sometimes grudgingly, sometimes readily—the need for more "formal" management thinking, organization, and practices; and they took steps to move in this direction. Many of these changes were personally difficult. "We all see the need," one executive admitted, "but none of us wants to give up any freedom." These changes also touched a more fundamental, business nerve. "It's fine to develop structures and plans and policies," one senior executive explained, "if they are viewed, and used, as tools. But it is so easy for them to become substitutes for good thinking, alibis for not taking responsibility, reasons to not become involved. And then we'd no longer be NIKE."

This case explores the organizational dimension of NIKE. It introduces several NIKE people and describes their ways of working and working together. The purpose is both to enrich the student's understanding of NIKE as a complete business entity and to provide a backdrop to these managers' concerns, summarized at the end of this case, about the challenges created by increasing organizational size and business complexity.

One final note: The researchers found the NIKE language system studded with expletives. We have attempted in these pages to find that perhaps elusive line between scholarly accuracy and out-of-context impropriety.

NIKE People

Founder Phil Knight and a number of other NIKE managers ran on Coach Bill Bowerman's teams during their college days at the University of Oregon. They learned much more than technical skills from him. "It wasn't anything magic," Knight recalled, "just his ideas of competitive response, of working hard, of having character, or all those corny things that your parents teach you. But he put them on you like a tattoo so that you'd never forget them." (For a tribute to Bowerman in NIKE advertising, see Exhibit 1.)

> You can't make a silk purse out of a sow's ear, as the saying goes. But you can take an athlete with some talent, and with motivation and desire, he can do much more than a super talent who sits on his ass.

In its early years NIKE lacked the money to hire experts, and there was no traditional industry from which to draw people. Knight simply found good people, including many accountants ("with personality") and lawyers ("who could count"), and found the good *in* people. These people jumped in and tackled a wide variety of tasks within the company, often moving quickly from one position to another to bring a person's particular skills to bear on the latest problem or crisis.

Over the years this managerial style became an established company philosophy. Initially perceived as a weakness, the approach clearly yielded benefits. "It is unusual," one observer commented, "to find an organization in which so many people perceive problems and issues broadly, as company issues, rather than narrowly, as functional or territorial ones." Or in Knight's words, "We tend to have specialists in the company, not the job."

Managers were also conscious of the costs. "There's a limit," Knight commented, "to the sins you can cover up with enthusiasm." Gradually the company began to hire more managers with specific experience and skills, although with only modest success. In part managers attributed this to the difficulty of tailoring old experiences to a new situation rather than trying to do the reverse. "People want to do things the way they used to," one senior manager explained. "It's hard to get them to forget that and learn NIKE." The ability to fit within NIKE, to be "a good guy," remained a key requirement.

Senior Management

NIKE's senior group was unique. In the words of one inside observer, "They are entrepreneurs—with a capital *E.*" While many were athletes, or at least read the sports pages first, the strong bonds among them seemed to reflect a camaraderie based on deeper, shared values: a desire to accomplish something of value, a healthy cynicism, self-confidence, a willingness to be a part of a team. They were proud of their achievements, but most could step back and poke a little fun at themselves, too. As Bob Woodell commented, "Jeff Johnson, our first employee, used to say, 'We're definite park bench material,' and I think there's a lot of truth in that."

In early 1983 the 11 members of the senior management group (the "Friday Club") included the heads of the several functional areas within NIKE (see Table 1 and Exhibit 2). Six of these men are introduced in greater depth in the following pages.

Table 1

NIKE Senior Management, 1983

Executive	Age	Joined Company	Background	Current Responsibilities
Phil Knight	44	Founder, 1964	MBA, CPA	President and chairman
Bob Woodell	38	1967	College	Vice president and worldwide marketing
Del Hayes	47	1975 (part-time from 1971)	CPA	Executive vice president, manufacturing and development
Rob Strasser	35	1976 (association from 1972)	Lawyer	Vice president, marketing projects
Ron Nelson	40	1976	CPA	Production
Rich Werschkul	36	1977	Lawyer	Corporate counsel
Jim Manns	44	1979	CPA, Business	Vice president, finance
Gary Kurtz	36	1979	Banker	Treasurer
David P. C. Chang	52	1981	Architect	Vice president, Far East manufacturing
Neil Goldschmidt	41	1981	Public management	Vice president, international
George Porter	51	1982	CPA, Business	Vice president, administration

Phil Knight, 44, was clearly in charge at NIKE. Indeed, many spoke of NIKE as his company. But they spoke of him with immense loyalty and affection. Knight, a Portland native, was shy but very warm; keenly competitive but deeply caring. He believed his greatest strengths lay in longer term thinking rather than day-to-day operations and described himself as a worrier by nature. As he talked of the company, he spoke with enormous pride and with a sense of perspective:

> I had to give a speech recently at a big trade meeting, and a number of people told me beforehand that everyone was eager to hear what NIKE's secret is. Hell, there isn't a secret; there's just the basic paying attention to details and doing all the parts of the business right.

One interested observer remarked, "Phil is very different from most of the CEOs that I've known—but he's been a highly effective general manager and leader for this company." A more detailed profile of Knight, and of the general management task within the company, appears in the NIKE (C) case.

Bob Woodell, 38, was one of the earliest NIKE employees. Raised in Portland, he attended the University of Oregon where he was a champion long jumper under Bill Bowerman until he suffered a broken back in an accident, resulting in permanent leg paralysis. He had determinedly fought back from that accident and was both fiercely independent and supercompetitive.

Over the years Woodell held every major position within NIKE except accounting and legal. Many saw him as an effective administrator. "Woodell has a lot of organizational strengths," one peer noted, "and does more creative, practical thinking than anyone I know." He was also a peppery speaker and a storehouse of anecdotes. He explained to the researchers:

> Somehow we've found a way to work together, to bring the best out of each other. People have said, "Yeah, but you have a great product." Well the product didn't exist until the people invented it. And on and on. As Knight keeps saying, "No one person ever did anything at NIKE. It's the group that does it." He's found a way to let us, within reason, be ourselves and not fit a mold but continue to work together.
>
> Del Hayes has an expression we quote a lot: "We like people who aren't afraid to strap on a tin bill and pick s—— with the chickens." We really like that. One of my frustrations is that I don't get to *do* anything anymore. I just *talk* to people all the time. In the olden days we had shipping problems once, and Hayes and Knight and I started going over to the warehouse at night to help ship shoes. We probably f—— up more orders than we got out, but we felt great—we were *doing* something about a problem. Actually, we did get a few more shoes out, and we had fun ourselves; and I think we sent a signal to some people.
>
> Knight, Hayes, Strasser, me—we're each a very strong-willed individual. We've worked together long enough that we understand each other's strengths. We can communicate reasonably quickly because we know what the other person means when he uses a certain word, and we know how to communicate through humor. We've all done a number of things within this company and understand the problems and frustrations in each area because we were probably in that job once before.
>
> But all four of us look at things from different points of view, too. We're able to challenge each other and fight like hell. But there is never ever a

doubt that you are arguing and fighting with one of the best friends you've got in the world, so the issue is not the friendship, not the human being. The issue is the issue. We just argue like hell and have the ability to come to a common agreement, if that in fact is what's required.

Del Hayes, 47, a Minnesota native and CPA, was Knight's boss at Price Waterhouse in the mid-60s. He kept in touch with Knight, which led to part-time work with Blue Ribbon Sports, NIKE's predecessor company, in 1971 and full-time work with NIKE in 1975. Over the years Hayes worked broadly within the manufacturing area and did a short stint in marketing. A very large man with a full beard, Hayes was described by one peer as "brilliant, with a totally quantitative mind, maybe the best in the world in things having to do with shoe factories and production." Reflecting on NIKE, Hayes said:

We hear a lot about the NIKE way. It may be the philosophy of how we perceive ourselves, the kind of mark we intend to leave in the marketplace, how we believe the consumer and the retailer should be treated, carried forward to the general management of the company. There's a little bit of fairness involved, a little bit of equity.

The one thing Knight did very well, I think, was the original concept of maintaining an off-shore source of supply that would enable us to provide a quality and an economy that the consumer previously hadn't known. That was a cornerstone. From there on NIKE became a collection of people who were, for the most part, driven in the same direction; who had quite a desire to do well in the marketplace; who wanted to be associated with a business that had some heavy overtones of funness to it, recognizing *certainly,* that there was always a profit motive. But the timing was right in the marketplace, and there was an inherent profitability in the business, so we didn't really have to worry about the profit as long as we were doing a reasonable job at the other aspects of the business.

Generally speaking, the top group tries to have some knowledge of and feeling for what is going on in areas that may not be their direct responsibility. We try to do this through a series of meetings and through a continual interplay and exchange of ideas. You get a better grasp of what is happening on the whole and more of an appreciation for a problem in one area that may have a ripple effect in your area. In addition you tend not to develop an overly protective sense of *your* empire, because you're more concerned with what's happening in the team and what can be the best bottom-line result. That has worked fairly well.

Rob Strasser, 38, a Portland native, earned a law degree at Berkeley in 1972 and returned to a Portland law firm. Within two months, he was assigned to the *Blue Ribbon Sports* v. *Tiger* suit,[1] which then dragged on for three and a half years.

Strasser joined NIKE in 1976 as its first corporate counsel. In 1977 he moved into marketing and has worked in this general area ever since, including a stint as managing director of NIKE Europe (1980–82). Peers described him as incredibly creative— and equally "off-the-wall." "Seven of ten Strasser ideas may be crazy," one colleague explained, "but the other three will be just incredible." Others referred to him as "a cheerleader in the organization" and "the vice president in charge of stirring the pot." One remarked, "Every company needs one Strasser . . . and probably can't handle more than that."

Strasser, a large, exuberant, quick-witted man with a sense of command, described NIKE this way:

It's the best American capitalism has to offer, a "no bull——, let's get out and solve the problem" frame of mind. We didn't make something out of thin air, though. Conditions were right—we saw them, were a part of them, grew up in them. When it runs right, it's a real special place. We'll dream the undreamable, then get down to reality again. It's less Wall Street and more street-street.

But there are *threads,* too. Everybody wants to be a part of something that is done right, that is done uniquely, that is done in an atmosphere that is a little bit cynical, that recognizes bull—— quickly. I know it sounds corny, but it's true.

It's a tough place to play, though, because a lot of people know each other *real* good. I don't mean from cocktailing or from golf but from a lot of shared experiences over a long time. You can't pull any stuff off. We're like a big check-and-balance system here but one that lets you go further rather than limiting you.

I think we got a little sterile last year, maybe started to put ourselves in boxes: There's Europe; there's production; and so forth, I think we started

---

[1] BRS, NIKE's predecessor company, sued Onitsuka, the Japanese manufacturer of Tiger shoes, when Onitsuka terminated its distribution agreement with BRS in 1972. The successful outcome (a settlement of $400,000) provided an important source of cash for the growing company.

to miss the interaction, because when each of us is left alone, we're not that f—— good. It's tougher and lonelier and not as fun a deal. But put us together . . . and that's starting to happen again.

David Chang smiled. "Why did I become a shoemaker? Well, as Knight says, 'None of us studied shoemaking in college, either.' " Born in the People's Republic of China, Chang, 52, studied architecture in the United States and had a successful practice in New York for 22 years. As relations between this country and China thawed in the 70s, he reestablished ties there. This led to several consulting projects, including one with NIKE in 1981 to help the company establish production sources there. A year later he joined the company full time. Knight explained, "I don't like consultants, as a general rule, because they tend not to be involved in whether their thing really works or not. But we turned on to Chang during the first trip to China. He wanted to get this project going. There wasn't extra money or anything else in it for him—he just wanted to get the job done, and done well." In fact Chang accomplished a "miracle" in getting NIKE quickly established in China, with salable product first shipped in early 1983. A man of medium height and warm countenance, Chang was observant and articulate. Reflecting on his experience in joining NIKE at a senior level, he said:

Despite all this seemingly jocular, fraternity house sort of thing, there is a great deal of pressure on new people. It's not the pressure of an IBM or ITT but the pressure of lack of direction, of not having the familiar accoutrements of job descriptions, performance goals, and organization charts to tell you what you're supposed to do. After being at NIKE a couple of weeks, for example, I went into Del's office and said, "Could you give me a little direction as to what I'm supposed to do?" Strasser was there, and he broke into peals of laughter. For months he would poke his head into my office and ask, "Have you gotten any direction yet?" as if that was the most absurd thing in the world to ask for.

A new person needs to have a strong sense of self, yet not be defensive. You can't be afraid to say, "I don't know," or to ask for help. There's a feeling here that nobody knows it all; this is a business where we're writing the book from scratch.

A new person shall also be sensitive to the kind of loyalties that the firm has engendered in people. There's a group that has paid their dues, has earned its stripes. They've been through a lot together. I can go to a meeting, for example, and not understand half of the things the old-timers are talking about; there's almost a subculture among them.

But I've also found a *real* core of kindness here. You've got to get through the first layers, but underneath, it's there. As Jeff Johnson said, "There is a lot of love within NIKE," corny as that sounds. And I feel a total trust that no one is going to do me in for his own personal gain.

George Porter, 51, joined NIKE in late 1982 to head up a collection of administrative areas (including distribution, transportation, management information systems, personnel) that, some managers noted, "the top four just aren't interested in." Porter came to NIKE with a significant business background (at Boise Cascade and Evans Corporation) and, earlier, 12 years of experience as a CPA at Price Waterhouse, where he had been Hayes's and, briefly, Knight's boss. "I was," he chuckled, "a known quantity to these guys." Tall, thin, and a thoughtful speaker, Porter said of NIKE:

Part of the success of the company has been a good concept—innovation, aggressive marketing, a good source of supply at reasonable prices—and the ability to follow through on that concept. And the timing was just fantastic. Another part of the success has been that this is a group of extremely intelligent people—and *smart,* too. Another thing has been the sense of being the leader in the market—like being the runner out in front. A lot of confidence flows from that.

But perhaps the real strength is the reliance on people. There's a willingness and faith to let people do things themselves, to make their own decisions, and to feel the satisfaction if the decision is a success or the extreme disappointment if it fails. For example, a subordinate and I just made a presentation to the top four guys about a $20 million distribution project. We'd been into this for about 10 minutes, and Woodell looked at me and asked, "Do you agree with this?" I said, "I wouldn't have brought it to you if I didn't." He responded, "Well, what in hell are we talking about then? Go do it."

There's a lot of that attitude here. I've made some major decisions and could have made more, but I'll let Phil know what I'm doing in case it's contrary to any basic philosophies he has—since it takes a while to learn them. This is in such contrast to my past experience, in which managers always inflated projects to get the right ROI or whatever—it was just a game. But here you have to live with your decisions. As the story goes, for example, when Hayes bought the Saco [Maine] plant to start manufacturing there, Knight told him, "Okay, Hayes, you bought it, now go make it work."

Middle Management

NIKE's middle managers were young, diverse in background, vigorous in their approach to the management task, and increasingly important to the growing company. Knight explained:

> The other guys and I at the top know less and less of what is happening at the middle levels. People there have to understand how this whole thing fits together, what the basics are, what their jobs are, and how they fit into the whole, so that good decisions get made.

Within the middle group—whose size was variously estimated at 40 to 120—a core had been with NIKE for years; the rest had joined the company more recently. Most were college graduates and under 40. Some had worked only for NIKE; others had experience in other companies or professions. Turnover was almost nonexistent.

For most of the middle group NIKE presented a special opportunity to contribute, to accomplish something; many spoke of the company (and of senior management) with great caring and loyalty. Yet this group was also an emerging, younger generation that, like its counterpart in society at large, was increasingly forceful in stating—and working for—its own ideas and beliefs.[2] The following profiles introduce several middle managers and summarize their views of NIKE.

David Kottkamp, 40, from Portland, joined Blue Ribbon Sports in 1969. He left in 1971 to work in a successful Portland political campaign and returned to NIKE in 1978, working in product development in Exeter and product line management and apparel sales in Beaverton. An enthusiastic sportsman, he was both direct and reflective. Talking of NIKE on an afternoon run, he said:

> This may be simplistic, but I think NIKE is a group of pretty good people working together on interesting and important puzzles. Knight has assembled some bright people from all over the spectrum in terms of personality and capability and has harnessed that energy and creativity in a way that seems to have worked, although it sometimes looks pretty ragged. The working together part is really substantial.

Kirk Richardson, 30, joined NIKE in 1979 as a sales supervisor and subsequently had charge of national account sales, product development in Exeter, and the product lines in Beaverton. An Oregon native, he worked as a supervisor in a steel foundry before joining NIKE. Tall, with a warm smile, Richardson was an avid mountaineer. "I feel good about our product," he said. "People are going to benefit from it in ways I can relate to." Of the company he said:

> Its roots are really sports oriented. It was started by a group of runners who were trying to improve on products they used and understood, and

---

[2] See Exhibit 3 for a summary of a meeting of middle managers.

we're unbeatable there. I worry that we may be getting pretty far afield today with some of the ath-leisure stuff.

But the top guys listen. Indeed, there's a feeling around here that maybe we're all learning, from the president on down to the peon level, and that we're all capable of coming up with good ideas. You feel like you're a part of something here. In the foundry I would have had to wait 35 years before getting to a position where I could *do* something.

Mary Anne White, 28, held a textile-related degree from Oregon State University. She had joined NIKE's fledgling apparel operation in early 1978 and worked in that group ever since. "Apparel used to be thought of as Siberia," she chuckled, "but now it's getting to be a lively spot in the company."

Quiet and determined, White, a product design manager, coordinated the development of the NIKE apparel line. At a 7:00 A.M. breakfast meeting, she reflected:

Success at NIKE is measured more by respect from peers than by dollars. There's not a lot of stroking, so you have to be pretty independent. And you have to be aggressive enough to ask questions, because people won't tell you what to do. Perhaps we're more like a family—brothers and sisters who can and do fight but know that we care about each other—than a traditional organization. It's important to see the top guys, to see that they're still that way, that they're still enjoying it, that they still believe in it.

Ned Frederick, 36, had a Ph.D. in functional morphology (the study of the function of the human anatomy). He consulted with NIKE from 1978 to 1980, when he left his academic career to head up NIKE's new sports research lab in Exeter, New Hampshire. In 1982 he became director of research and development (which included the product development effort as well as the lab). Frederick was soft-spoken and reflective and had a zany sense of humor. He commented:

If your ambition is to be *someone,* you're going to have to go somewhere else because you don't succeed at NIKE by climbing the ladder. I don't think there is a ladder. There are just a bunch of jobs out there that need to get done. Your satisfaction is the approval of your peers and that sense of a job well done, not the big promotion with the raise and not the sign on the door and not the bigger office and all that horse———. There's also been an understanding that the leaders, the people you're responsible to, are looking out for your best interests.

In one way or another I think four simple principles explain how people feel about NIKE. When we're feeling good, it's because we feel a part of it, feel we are getting a fair deal, have a way to keep score, and get a chance to show our stuff.

Jim Gorman, 35, joined BRS in 1972 with a background in store location research. He initially worked in one of the company's early retail stores. "It was in a real low-rent district," he recalled. "Maybe we sold some shoes, but mostly we were out on the road telling people about NIKE." He was the first NIKE expatriate in the Far East and later worked on special projects in R&D and in international licensing. "I've had 10 jobs in the last seven years," he noted. In early 1983 he was asked to head a special apparel project. Reflecting on NIKE, Gorman said:

> The shakers and movers still control it, thank goodness. We grew up believing, perhaps out of ignorance, that anything could be done, and we did the impossible. This attitude is slowly eroding, I fear, and we're starting to see an assumption that things can't be done. We're all doers, but I think the time is coming for the top guys, and for us who have been around a while, to pull back and do more teaching.

Jack Joyce, 41, joined NIKE in mid-1982 after leaving a successful legal career that had become frustrating. "Basically," he recalled, "that system didn't make a whole lot of sense to me any longer." He also was lured by the opportunity, in his words, "to work with friends who have proven that success can be achieved without three-piece suits and sustained without stifling corporate structures."

Dynamic and confident, Joyce spent his first six months at NIKE as an assistant to Del Hayes. In early 1983 he was assigned to head up the promotion department (which worked with NIKE athletes) and made significant changes in it. Commenting on NIKE, Joyce wrote:

> NIKE's awesome success, in a large part, is the result of efforts by a synectic group of loose canons with keenly sensitive hearts and minds who busted their butts.
>
> Nostalgia assumes this dynamic can be sustained as the prime mover for continued success. Conventional wisdom holds that the current size, projected growth, and public nature of NIKE necessitate the substitution of a more traditional, institutionalized mode of obtaining efficiency and profit. Both nostalgia and convention are flawed as wellsprings for analysis, and neither of their prescriptions will prevail at NIKE. But the future structure of NIKE needs far more concentrated attention than it is currently receiving.
>
> Unless new employees, for example, are capable of assimilating NIKE expectations of centered hard work and caring, creative thought, NIKE will stagger under the weight of a jet-setting, self-centered, arrogant—and average—middle management who aggrandize themselves on a past they were not a part of, instead of striving for future successes in which they can share.

NIKE Ways of Working

NIKE leadership found its own way to accomplish the fundamental tasks of getting product designed, sourced, and sold at a profit (described in the NIKE (A) case). The company relied less on formal systems (in Strasser's words, "Wall Street techniques") than on informal methods ("street savvy"). Components of the NIKE method—setting direction, dividing up the work, pulling it together, establishing the rules of the game, and providing rewards—are described in the following sections.

Setting Direction

The fundamentals of the NIKE strategy—innovative product, economical sourcing, aggressive marketing, innovative financing—remained relatively constant through the years; its managers believed that these fundamentals were now well understood within the company. Like the harmonies that support a melody, many individual decisions, of course, had been made to develop and embellish these fundamentals as the business had expanded. An example was the decision to develop factories in the People's Republic of China as the "ultimate" low-cost source.

From the beginning Knight took the lead in setting corporate direction. "He's a dreamer, the Christopher Columbus out trying to find the new worlds," one manager explained. "And he's got pretty good instincts, a good nose for these things." Knight's preferred pattern was to spend time alone thinking and then to work with particular people in the organization to address threats and opportunities he had identified. He usually involved several senior managers, often Woodell, Strasser, and Hayes, with whom he had worked for a long time, in direction-setting discussions.

Ned Frederick (director of research and development) explained how corporate directions were communicated:

> Direction in this company, as I see it, comes from being sensitive to, and aware of, what's going on in NIKE. You tune into what other people are doing, and if you're receptive, you start to see the need for something to be done. For example, when I moved from the lab to this position, everything seemed to point toward a big push in court shoes—the promo people were concerned because the athletes were getting bored with the old product, the salespeople were seeing some declines, and so forth. So we put a group together, and a year later we have some great products coming out.
>
> This wasn't the result of a unilateral decision from above. I talked to people in the product lines, advertising, promo, production, and it just seemed obvious. There was a strong consensus that this was the thing to do.
>
> It would have been nice, in a way, if Knight had come along and said, "This is what you ought to do," but he won't do that. He'll ask what I think, and I'll tell him. He'll ask some questions and then tell me to go do whatever I think is right. This kind of thing promotes a "give-it-a-try" attitude, a trust in your judgment and instincts. It tends to encourage people to jump into situations they perhaps wouldn't have attempted in a more structured environment, and it means we can be much more responsive.

But it also means we can be off base, if people don't think or don't understand how it fits together.

Dividing up the Work

The business fundamentals at NIKE (see Figure 1) historically were organized along functional lines. In the 80s this structure began to shift toward a product line organization, as the apparel and international businesses emerged as separate divisions and the domestic footwear marketing operation split into four product lines (see Exhibit 2).

Within this basic format, the formal organizational structure shifted frequently as the company adapted to changing issues, external circumstances (such as the 1984 Summer Olympics in Los Angeles, which prompted the formation of a special ad hoc marketing group), and personnel assignments. For example the promotions function was decentralized to the new product line managers in early 1982 and nine months later

Figure 1

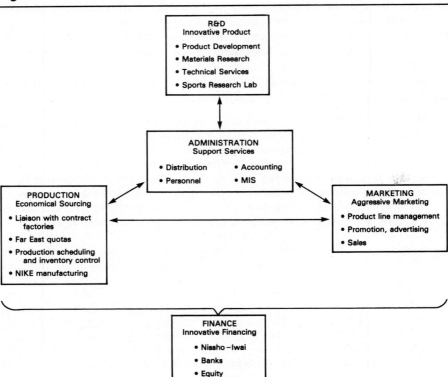

recentralized into a promo department. "We were worried when we set it up that it might consume too much of the line manager's time," one manager explained. "But it had some advantages, and it seemed worth a try. It didn't work, so we changed it."

Knight explained, "In an organization our size, the structure we choose clearly depends on the people we have to make it work." Several managers used the following anecdote to illustrate this point about organization:

> A college football team with a great quarterback won the national championship one year using the T-formation, which capitalized on the quarterback's skills. The following year the team again won the championship, but this time with the single wing offense, which used the skills of the two strong tailbacks it then had.

Pulling Things Together

As the company grew and jobs were divided into smaller, more manageable, and increasingly more specialized chunks, NIKE developed three primary mechanisms to pull its business tasks together into a reasonably coherent whole: meetings, defined coordinating roles, and management reports/systems.

Meetings were the primary communication and problem-solving mechanism within NIKE. They occurred at all management levels in the organization and ranged from informal conversations in the hallway to more formal reviews of the product lines. They tended to be scheduled in response to particular needs rather than according to preset cycles. From the researchers' perspective, the meetings were refreshingly open and productive, combining liberal doses of humor with a drive to get the job done. Managers appeared able to discuss issues along multiple dimensions, and several often took the lead in moving a session forward. "We don't invite the organization chart to a meeting," Bob Woodell said. "We invite people who can contribute to the issue."

The Friday Club (see Table 1) met approximately biweekly (or as needed) for a couple of hours. During these meetings, which Knight chaired, executives reported on their areas of responsibility and/or discussed relevant issues in greater depth. Twice a year this group went off-site for a week. "This is about the most enjoyable part of the business for me," Knight reported. "Many of us have been together for a long time and understand each other pretty well." The discussions were reported to be quite frank and open, and executives spoke of these sessions as critical opportunities to put their heads together, deal with some issues, and generally get back in touch with what everyone was doing and where the company was headed. Representative issues discussed during one meeting, for example, included:

- Production and R&D: Ways to improve the new product transition from design to production; R&D priorities; factory capacities and capabilities.
- Control: The excess inventory situation; the growing space requirements in the Beaverton area.
- Marketing: The appropriate advertising/promotion balance (currently 1 to 3 in dollars); the Los Angeles Olympics; the overall marketing focus; the defective product return policy; broadening the sales pyramid (should retailers such as Sears be added?).
- People: Are the right people in the right slots?

A more impromptu meeting was described by Kirk Richardson, who was in charge of the product lines at the time:

> Several of us had been getting real concerned that we were sapping our brand strength with some bonehead decisions and poor control in the sales area. We'd hammer away at this in staff meetings, and finally Woodell and Strasser said, "S——, let's get together and hash this thing out." So we got the relevant people from across the country together off-site for several days. Bob and Rob gave us a little direction, and we helped fill them in on what the problem seemed to be from our perspective. We then worked on it for a couple of days and identified a series of concrete steps we thought we should take. We got back together with Woodell and Strasser, and they poked at us pretty hard and then said, "Let's do it."

Although various individuals, particularly the senior managers, had served informally in coordinating roles over the years, the company had recently begun to define this job formally. For example, a major responsibility of a product line manager was to coordinate all activities relating to that line—R&D, advertising, promotion, selling, and so forth. "We were tired," one noted, "of screw-ups like the sales reps pushing a shoe that we were phasing out."

Although traditional management reports and systems were relatively little used at NIKE, the managers, many of whom were CPAs, seemed able to keep in touch with "whether things were tracking or not." Although much of their information came from talking with people, two reports were of particular importance to top management. A daily summary of orders and shipments (in effect, Futures and sales) was a key indicator of whether things were going as expected. A substantial monthly accounting report presented a detailed picture of the whole operation from which trouble spots could be identified.

Over time an increasing variety of management systems was developed, typically in response to specific needs. For example, in early 1983 middle managers in the production scheduling, product line management, product development, and sales areas developed a formal planning tool to help coordinate their increasingly interdependent work with the product line.

It was easier to install these systems than to gain full acceptance of, and adherence to, the discipline they imposed. Treasurer Gary Kurtz commented on the introduction of an annual budgeting process in 1978:

> Budgets are a part of the evolution of any company, and we're moving toward more bottom-line accountability by product area. There's been a reluctance to get involved initially, but we find it's a matter of education, of trying to get people to the point at which they understand the process and don't just treat it as a bureaucratic procedure. As I try to explain, running a business without good numbers would be like trying to manage a baseball team without the statistics.

Knight approved the department budgets;[3] formal reviews with the department managers were seldom conducted. Kurtz provided significant staff and coordinating work in this process.

Woodell saw the budget as a "scorecard":

> It's a kind of a financial plan with checkpoints so we can look at our results during the year and ask, "How are we coming, are we ahead or behind, what's happening?" It's not an authorization in advance to go spend money. As each decision comes along, you have to rethink it. We'll either decide to do it or we won't, and that process doesn't have a whole lot to do with budgets.

R&D Director Ned Frederick felt the budget system had brought a greater emphasis in product line accountability:

> There is more of an orientation toward managing profits today. We see this mostly from the product line folks, in a decision not to go with a particular product or to change a product in some way so as to improve the gross profit margin. We've always had a lively dialogue with those folks, but the dialogue didn't use to be about gross profit margins.

Establishing the Rules of the Game

Understandings evolved at NIKE that, in essence, created the ground rules by which the game was played, ranging from guidelines on vacation time to limits on spending authorization. For the most part these norms were not captured on paper; their transmission depended on people's sensitivity to "the way things are done here."

As the organization grew there were inevitable pressures for more explicitness, more consistency—and in some ways, more fairness—than the informal practices provided. A Policy and Procedures Committee was formed in late 1982 to address this issue in the personnel area.

---

[3] The budgets were prepared by the department managers on the basis of the sales forecast developed by Nelson and Knight.

Providing Rewards

For most people NIKE was an exciting place to work, not only at the top but down through the ranks. The company, in effect, asked people to join a team. As Woodell expressed it, "What we like is for people to come in and say, 'I want to contribute. However I can contribute most to this place is how I'd like to do it.'" In return management "took care of" people, in part with pay, but more with opportunities for growth, responsibility, and contribution. As Knight explained, "It's really not so much salary as it is job responsibility or the perception of it."

Wages and salaries were considered roughly comparable to those of other local companies. Each employee (including all managers) was reviewed once a year, a practice that Knight, in a legacy from his days as a junior accountant at Price Waterhouse, strongly favored. Annual raises were awarded at this time, with managers asked to tie the increase given to a person's performance. There was no organized incentive compensation program. Inevitably there was some variation in how well such procedures were administered. "Some managers," Knight noted, "do a real good job. Others aren't perhaps as willing to take the time or to make some of the hard decisions that such matters often require." Yet the researchers found a general sense within NIKE that the company was "fair" and a "great place to work."

Growing Larger

NIKE's growth had been spectacular, and managers expected it to continue, although at a slower rate. This growth—in sales, products, geographical spread,[4] and employees—and a changing market brought the need for change within the organization. Many managers told stories illustrating a "crack" through which something had recently fallen or a warning of a thunderhead seen on the horizon. David Chang, for example, had his doubts about the recent expansion of offices for Knight, Hayes, himself, Porter, Manns, and Kurtz on the top floor of the home office building.

> In the old days, I'm told, people drifted into the top management area after five and talked over the day. As a result people knew enough about what others were doing that they weren't making cold calls in their own area. But people don't drift up to this "elephants' graveyard" today, and I worry that we may be getting out of touch.
>
> Each decision, such as these larger offices or the reserved parking places, is made to correct a problem and is usually too small to argue against. But taken as a whole we're starting to establish a caste.

---

[4] There were nine NIKE locations in the Beaverton area alone.

Excerpts from an informal internal document summarizing a number of managers' concerns are presented in Exhibit 4.

As NIKE managers discussed their company and the internal challenges it faced, the researchers noted three primary areas of concern: the continuing need to "emphasize the basics"; the necessity of continuing to "talk to each other"; and the challenge of "remaining a team."

Emphasizing the Basic

"People aren't dumb," Bob Woodell protested, with a sigh. "It's just that the momentum here can carry good people off base." He explained:

> We've got to keep going back and teaching people the principles: the goal is to maximize profits. We do it with people, by thinking better and working harder, through an innovative product, economical sourcing, aggressive marketing, innovative financing. . . . But it's tough, even for all of us who have been around for a while, to keep on the right track. You get sucked up in the day-to-day stuff.

As Knight put it, "We need to do a better job, in Vince Lombardi's terms, of saying, this is a football, here's how you run, this is a block, here's how to tackle."

Talking to Each Other

"When NIKE was a small company," Corporate Counsel Rich Werschkul noted, "communication used to just happen—in the hallways, over a beer on the way home, at the basketball game. Now we have to go out of our way to make it happen." While managers often spoke of the need for communication in horizontal terms, several noted the importance of the vertical dimension as well. "I'm a little concerned," George Porter said, for example, "that Phil may be getting insulated from the people. He's always been close enough to have a feel for what the thinking is down in the bowels of the company, and I worry that we'll lose that."

Communication, however, was not just a matter of emitting words. Those words had to be understood. Jim Manns, financial vice president, noted:

> People who have joined NIKE in recent years have a very different perspective on the world. We've had plenty of money, and it's been pretty rosy for them. So this winter, when we say we've got to be tough with expenditures, they don't know what that means. The old-timers, however, who lived through the early years when there just wasn't any money, really do *know*.

Rob Strasser offered another illustration:

> We had some newer people working in promo around the time of the 1980 Olympic trials. We were all down there, of course, and I think the new

people, looking up in the stands and seeing Knight really excited as some runners in our shoes won their events, sort of said to themselves, "Boy, we're going to get everybody in our shoes next time." So they went out and spent a zillion dollars and said that Knight had given them direction to do it. They didn't give the guy a chance just to be himself. What's worse, they felt he was too much of a god to go and talk to, to check if they had understood. It's so easy to misread signals.

Ron Nelson, who handled production scheduling, summed it up: "It all boils down to people being not afraid to talk about what's right and what's wrong. Then there's never an end to the ideas."

Remaining a Team

As the company grew larger, managers spoke of the need to remain a team—with all employees involved and working together—as NIKE confronted its challenges. Interviewed by the company paper, Bob Woodell warned:

Recently we've been working against ourselves by becoming too compartmentalized. A proprietary feeling about "my area" seemed to be developing in many places. That's like running on two cylinders. The minute a person says, "I can make this thing work in my little department and it will be a miracle and I'll be a hero," we're in trouble.

Another part of the task was keeping people—at all levels—involved in a company that was now larger and more successful. Rich Werschkul commented:

It's imperative that we, as senior managers, build that next group of 40 or 80 or however many middle managers. We've got to make them feel a real part of this thing. Some of this is communication, so people are informed and included. But some is compensation, and we can't ignore it. As much as we've liked to think that working at NIKE is enough compensation in and of itself—and it is worth a lot—it is not enough. The top people obviously have financial security, and that's no secret. Once the company went public, however, the hope of a founder's equity interest disappeared, so we've got to do something else as a potential reward for this next group whom we're asking, in effect, to devote their lives to NIKE.

This concern was echoed by several middle managers. One noted:

Yeah, there has been some upheaval caused by the instant millionaires, the BMW fleet, the private parking places. For most of us that's not in the cards. But a lot of folks who go back a ways had carried around the hope that this was a possibility and have run up against the reality that they're probably not going to achieve that kind of independence.

It's real important for the health of the company that the middle be strong, healthy, and committed. This place has remained pretty intact so far, and one of the most important questions is how do we keep doing this thing together.

The issue of involvement affected the top and bottom as well. Several middle managers expressed a worry about the impact of financial success on top management. "How much longer," one asked, "will they continue to work so hard and deal with all the hassles?" And one critical internal observer noted, "We want everybody to be on the NIKE team and have the NIKE esprit de corps that many of the old-timers feel. But I worry that a lot of employees don't have a clue about what it really is." As one middle manager put it, "Each layer is a little more insulated from the rays coming down from the top."

Researchers' Observations

"This is a hard place to describe," Rob Strasser commented. "You have to feel it." After many months with the company, the researchers came to feel that this response symbolized both the intuitive level of thinking and decision making that prevailed at NIKE and the company's distinctive intangible qualities. These included a sense of differentness; an identification with an athletic metaphor, if not athletics itself; little formality; and a real sense of openness and honesty.

While NIKE operated around the world, and many managers had spent time abroad or in the eastern United States, there was a distinct sense within the company of being a small, "anti-Establishment" group from Oregon. A number of managers noted their dislike of "the bull—— we see in Establishment companies"; there was also a desire to show how well NIKE could do without the support of the traditional community. ("Where were you established businessmen when we needed you?") NIKE managers expressed a sense of trying to find their *own* way to do things. In the early days one employee said, "We really didn't have any idea what we were doing, but when we looked around at the other companies making athletic shoes, we sure as hell knew that they didn't know what they were doing either. So we did it our own way." Today another observer noted, "We're not trying to cram ourselves into a mold either; we're trying to be a little creative internally."

The company's identification with athletics extended far beyond its primary product and was deeper than the fact that many employees were themselves athletes or former athletes. A contribution to athletics provided a "worthy" goal. "We think of ourselves as people who make shoes for the top athletes in the world."

The team ethic was very strong. Woodell spoke of NIKE with phrases such as "for competition's sake," "find daylight and run," "play the game," and "change the rules"; his old coach Bowerman was "my professor of competitive response." Woodell saw his own role as that of a coach. "People are here to play the game for the competition of it," he believed.

The researchers found little formality in the company, although this dimension was changing. Dress was generally casual, ranging from jogging suits to business suits, and most people seemed to be on a first-name basis with each other. Titles and formal organization charts were downplayed. As Woodell explained, "I'd just as soon not have a title." A middle manager observed: "At its best this place stands for collaboration that goes beyond title, race, creed, or color. And the reality is pretty close to that."

The researchers were struck particularly by NIKE's openness and honesty. The organization's attitude toward "mistakes" encouraged openness. A senior manager said, "People aren't chastised for making mistakes, because we all are going to. Repetitious mistakes of the same type, of course, are another story." Similarly the company discouraged jockeying for internal position. Del Hayes noted: "We try to be a nonpolitical company; we don't like people who are attempting to better their position at the expense of someone else." An industry analyst, accompanying Knight and Kurtz on a three-day trip through Chicago, New York, and Boston, described these managers and the company as a whole as "open and refreshingly honest."

The Challenge

The challenge of size and complexity was demanding new skills and thinking within NIKE organization. One middle manager offered a subtle perspective:

> The top guys are good guys. They want to do the right thing, are pretty smart about things, and have the best interests of the people of NIKE at heart. But they are getting far enough separated from the masses that they've got to look at their actions less in terms of the intent behind them and more in terms of their impact. I think there is a difference.

From his vantage point, Knight concluded:

> A lot of people think we were lucky. That certainly played a part, but we had a heavy hand in it, too. The early people were really good. The question for the next five years is how good are the people at the next level and the next? I happen to think they are pretty good. But there's more to it than that. The real question is can we continue to find ways of working together that draw out their potential?

Exhibit 1

The Spirit that Moves Us

THE SPIRIT THAT MOVES US.

For 24 years at the University of Oregon, he never recruited. And when athletes came to him, he put them to work in sawmills. Cut anyone who couldn't keep up the grades. He knew more people succeed because of mental toughness than physical ability.

He took the U.S. Track and Field team to Munich in '72. And came back complaining the Olympic games aren't conducted for athletes. But for aristocrats and pseudo-aristocrats.

To the A.A.U. and now the Athletics Congress, he remains a thorn in the side. Fighting in the courts for what he calls the emancipation of the athlete.

His literary career has been sporadic at best. But for thousands of Americans he is the writer who convinced them to take to the streets. And pound it out, year after year.

At Nike, we know him as the renegade inventor. Who made an excuse to his wife so he could skip church and fool around with a waffle iron.

He's the guy on our board of directors who comes prepared to raise hell. Share a laugh. And to never let us forget the real point of the whole thing — to help athletes perform.

Bill Bowerman. Stubborn, demanding. Given to sudden outbursts and moments of magical insight.

We wouldn't be the same without him.

NIKE

Beaverton, Oregon

Source: Company records.

Exhibit 2 **Researchers' Sketch of the NIKE Organization**

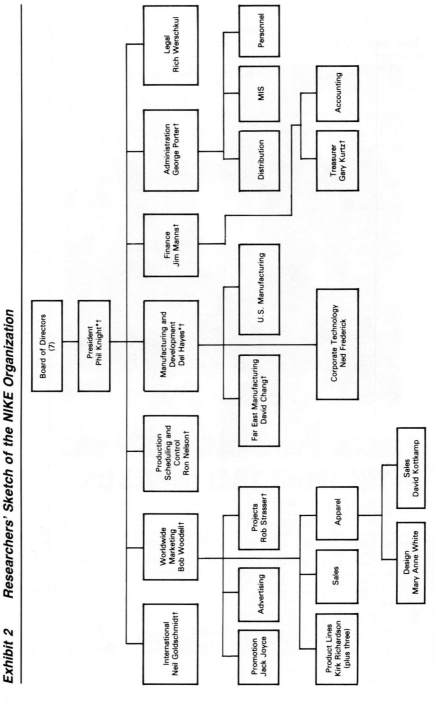

Board of Directors (7)

President
Phil Knight*†

International
Neil Goldschmidt

Worldwide
Marketing
Bob Woodell†

Production
Scheduling and
Control
Ron Nelson†

Manufacturing and
Development
Del Hayes*†

Finance
Jim Manns†

Administration
George Portert

Legal
Rich Werschkul

Promotion
Jack Joyce

Advertising

Projects
Rob Strasser†

Far East Manufacturing
David Chang†

U.S. Manufacturing

Corporate Technology
Ned Frederick

Distribution

MIS

Personnel

Treasurer
Gary Kurtz†

Accounting

Product Lines
Kirk Richardson
(plus three)

Sales

Apparel

Sales

Design
Mary Anne White

Sales
David Kottkamp

* Inside member of the board.
† Member of the top management group.
Source: Researchers' interpretation.

Exhibit 3

Excerpts from a Meeting of Middle Managers

Vice President David Chang took the initiative in early 1983 to get a group of about 20 middle managers in the Beaverton area together for an afternoon of talking. Presented below are excerpts from his memo to the participants before the meeting and from the summary of the meeting prepared afterwards by one of the participants.

Chang's Memo:

I want to hold a "shadow Friday Club" discussion. I look forward to this being a forum for freewheeling, uninhibited discussion—on issues and subjects which concern, preoccupy, amuse, please, displease, and frustrate some of us. Since so often attempts at these skull-sessions end up in bitching, which I hope this does not, I have listed some suggested topics below.

If the "shadow" session works, we shall have others and with other participants. If it does not, no great harm done; we will have enjoyed each other's company and had a few beers and perhaps shared a pizza together.

Suggestions: [excerpts]

- What is NIKE? What should we be that we aren't? How do we get there?
- What made NIKE what it is?
- Are we still a company with a "bias for action," or have size and other factors made us "safe"?
- One significant difference is that we are now a public company. Has this affected us, and in what way?
- How can we capture (recapture) the benefits of a small, dedicated group, now that we are much larger? Is it possible to have the best of both worlds? If not, what are the alternatives?
- What is or should be the technology for maintaining "open communications" when we are 4,000 people in 19 countries (and nine locations in Portland alone)?

Meeting Summary

Though the group did not attempt to draw any conclusions, there was an obvious sense of pride in working for and being a part of NIKE. There is a sincere feeling that we have had a "very good thing" going but that we must work extremely hard to retain and improve it as we continue, as a public company, to expand and grow.

The major concern which surfaced during the discussion revolved around an apparent lack of communication among top management, middle management, and all employees within NIKE. General observations made included the following: [excerpts]

- Some top managers are not available and approachable enough. They may simply be too busy to communicate enough with management, and possibly

Exhibit 3 (concluded)

there should be more delegation or additional top management to share the chores.

- Some people believe growth is necessary, while others think it more important to make the best products.
- The NIKE name cannot sell everything, and we must accept that fact.
- It is a myth to believe that NIKE/NIKE management truly has a vision.
- There is a perception that insiders will not become vice presidents, since several have come in from the outside recently. However, there is a recognition that certain skills are required and that we may have to go outside for them.
- The management group is shrinking rather than expanding. Middle managers should be used more, and there should be more feedback on our performance, strengths, and weaknesses.
- We must retain that strong sense of "doing it together."

Exhibit 4

What We Should Be

A model for American business—an aggressive, growing American public company.

The chance to:

- Be a part of something not done before.
- Grow and be allowed to do things you never thought you'd do.
- To THINK and keep thinking.

What We Were	*What We Are Now*
■ Honest, authentic, fun, dreamers, innovative.	■ Desire to be better but don't know what "better" means.
■ Small, American, unconventional, never satisfied.	■ Secure about the company, insecure about their position—the exact opposite of what you want (feel secure in your place but don't know if the team is going to win).
■ Knew what mattered most; identified problems and opportunities; attacked them without preconceptions or no-can-do's (and sometimes without enough facts).	■ Too much wishing for a Ten Commandments—a set of rules and ideas to make everything easy.
■ Made decisions on what could work for us, not on what did or didn't work for someone else; used insight, instincts, judgment—call it what you want but it wasn't just "logical" business.	■ No enemy like Adidas; Levi's too American, too likable, and too product-remote for most people.
■ Run by people who were comfortable with each other and who weren't comfortable in places they had come from. Like each other—the best f—— guys to do business with in the whole wide world.	■ Too much refuge in rules or buzzwords when judgment is needed.
■ Personal achievement, team victory.	

We're Getting Better, Slowly and in Pockets

Source: Company records.

NIKE (B1): Business Class Travel

After a brief break for a buffet supper, the managers settled back into their comfortable chairs in the hotel suite, and the discussion turned to the finance area, where NIKE continued to grapple with several growth-related accounting/data processing problems. Next the topic shifted to several accounting "policies," including guidelines for business travel. Steve, a middle manager who traveled to the Far East frequently, began, "One of the things that irritates me is our policy on coach fare. . . ."

Background

This meeting, held in mid-1983, was one in a series of irregularly scheduled get-togethers of selected middle managers in the Beaverton area. They met primarily to exchange information about what was going on in the several functional areas. Approximately 30 middle managers attended, joined by four senior managers (Strasser, Nelson, Werschkul, and Chang) as their schedules permitted. In typical NIKE fashion participation was spirited, frank, and intense (with no breaks, for example, from 3:00 to 9:30 P.M. except for 15 minutes for dinner in the room).

NIKE's "Travel and Entertainment Policy" had been formulated in a nine-page 1979 document by managers reporting to the financial vice president. It began with a statement of company philosophy:

Yearly employee travel and entertainment expense involves a substantial outlay of cash. The company is concerned with controlling this activity in order to properly account for expenses and prevent unnecessary expenditures. To aid the company in achieving these goals, employee cooperation in abiding with prescribed guidelines and procedures is crucial. It is the policy of NIKE to reimburse employees for all reasonable and necessary travel and entertainment expenses incurred in the conduct of company business that comply with IRS regulations. A good rule to follow: "Spend the company's money like it was your own."

In discussing travel, the policy stated: "Good business judgment should be practiced in selecting the type of transportation required. Cost and time should be considered before you select your mode of transportation." Section IV.a.2. then spelled out the guidelines for air travel:

Commercial air travel: Employees should arrange trips through their department manager's secretary, if possible. Every effort should be extended to take advantage of special rates offered by airlines. Remember that coach class is not necessarily the least expensive. First-class service may be used only when the above service is not available, and with approval of the employee's supervisor.

Although many managers did not realize a written policy existed, the researchers found they did report a common understanding that employees were to travel coach class. Informal stories were told of managers being called on the carpet for upgrading to business class.

A Summary of the Discussion

Steve: One of the things that irritates me is our policy on coach fare. I travel over to Korea fairly often, and it's a bitch to fly for 10 hours one day and have to do business the next day. I really believe we should fly business class—not first class, but business class—in situations like that.

Doug (senior manager): I'm going over to Hong Kong next week on a flight that experience suggests won't be too full. The coach return fare is $900, business class is $1,795. I feel it would be unconscionable to spend twice as much to make that trip.

Peter: I agree. What would you do if it were your own company, Steve?

Steve: Go business class. Have you ever flown for 10 hours in one of those seats? [He scrunches up to dramatize the effect.]

Devon: You're just too damn tall, Steve!

Steve: F—— you, Devon. Seriously, it's a real bitch to do business after those flights. And most of us fly on our own time, too. Don't most of you guys fly over on a Saturday or Sunday?

Several: Yeah. . . .

Susan: Where do you think we should draw the line, Steve? 1,000 miles? 3,000 miles?

Ed: No, it would have to be hours. Anything over five hours.

Susan: Would it make any difference if the guy were going over to sign a $5 million deal or just on a routine, touch-bases trip?

At this point, the middle manager who was moderating the meeting asked Ray, a representative of the controller's office, to find out what other companies' policies in this area were.

Ted (senior manager): Wait a minute. In the old days, this wasn't an issue. First, we didn't have the money anyway. But more, you talked to people and made the call yourself. If it was the right thing to do, you did it. If it wasn't, you didn't. We were good because we were flexible, could respond quickly, could do the right thing to get the job done. I'm afraid that these policies we're seeing more and more of will undermine that.

Bill: But if we don't have them, Ted, you know some jerk's going to decide that he needs to travel first class, and then other people will see that and think they should be doing it. . . . At some point, it gets to be real money.

Ted: If someone has to go first class, great. If someone doesn't, and he keeps doing it, fire the bastard. He's not a part of the team and doesn't understand.

Ray: But how the hell do we get people to understand? I think that's what the policy is—something down in black and white that communicates a common expectation about the way something is supposed to be done. And it provides a consistency that people can count on. That is only fair.

Ted: Yeah, I know, Ray. And we have to have it. But it's really just a rule, a written statement. That isn't enough. We want people to understand the thinking that lies behind it. Without that, what do you have? What do you get?

NIKE (C): Phil Knight

In a mid-1983 interview, Phil Knight talked about his job . . .

Researchers (HBS): Is NIKE still fun for you? As we listen to the tapes that you and Johnson and Woodell and Hayes made . . .

Knight (PHK): Hell, we were going to go through the whole history [of the company] that night and we managed to get through a year and a half!

HBS: It's a different ball game now.

PHK: It's not all still fun.

The NIKE story—a graduate school paper transformed into a company within shooting distance of a billion dollars—is a fairy-tale example of entrepreneurial success. Phil Knight, 44, wrote that paper in 1962, formed Blue Ribbon Sports (BRS) in 1964, and served as its president and chairman as BRS evolved into NIKE and grew into the 1980s. "For me personally," Knight reflected, "I can't think of any other thing I could possibly have done that would have been as enjoyable and rewarding as this has been."

While proud of NIKE's accomplishment, Knight did not take continued success for granted. "It's a very competitive world in business," he said, "and there are a lot of companies that grew fast and then went away. I don't want NIKE to be one of those." In mid-1983, as described in the NIKE (A) and NIKE (B) cases, managers believed that the com-

Copyright © 1984 by the President and Fellows of Harvard College
Harvard Business School case 385–029

pany faced challenges that ranged from stiffened competition in a maturing marketplace to the organizational growth that threatened the core of NIKE's entrepreneurial spirit. NIKE managers were most concerned about the latter.

This case introduces Phil Knight in greater depth and presents his perspective on the impact of organizational growth on his job and on the company.

A Short Biography

Knight, 44, was the son of a Portland, Oregon, newspaper publisher. He attended the University of Oregon in Eugene, where he ran on Coach Bill Bowerman's track team and was sports editor of the university paper and president of his fraternity. He continued on to the MBA program at Stanford, from which he graduated in 1962. He found this experience a "real confidence builder," discovering that he could relate to people whom he perceived to be "real smart" and enjoying the practical problem-solving atmosphere in several of the courses.

Knight and Bowerman founded NIKE's predecessor company in 1964. Knight worked as a CPA and accounting professor until 1969, when he began to devote himself full time to the fledgling company. "We started in a basement," he recalled with sparkling eyes, "and we can tell hours and hours of stories about those early days." He continued:

> There have been some real triumphs along the way. I can remember in 1976 . . . we'd never had a guy make the Olympic team in NIKE shoes and thought we had a good chance in the Olympics trials down in Eugene. In the first event, we went 1, 2, 3, and I just went berserk! While you can feel good about the financial performance and things like that, moments of elation like that race in Eugene are real treasures.
>
> And I'm proud of the whole China thing. I'm idealistic enough to think that we're building bridges and generating hard currency that they will use to buy more things from us—and all those good things we say about world trade. But when we can do that in a place that is as difficult to do business in as China is—that's a real thrill.
>
> But there have certainly been lows, too. I've been scared, and I've been really sad. And there have been periods of several months when I've said, God, this job is getting to be awful. But you have to wake up from that, and say, well, whose fault is that??

With his wife and two sons, Knight lived in a modest house in a rural area west of Beaverton. He was an avid sportsman and particularly enjoyed running and tennis. Observers described him as having a deeply ingrained "competitive response" but the commitment of a team player. He exuded a pride in the company—he often spoke movingly about it—but seemed personally shy and averse to the limelight. A demanding manager, Knight also had a reputation as a practical joker with a sense of humor and a willingness to laugh at himself. While he was active in several outside activities, including the U.S.–China Trade Commission and The Conference Board, his primary vocation and avocation was NIKE.

A tall man with a runner's body frame, Knight was a cameraman's delight with his tousled blond hair and infectious smile. NIKE management at all levels accorded him high respect for his judgment, his fairness, and his leadership in building NIKE. Just as the Swoosh logo unmistakably marked NIKE products, Knight's presence—his mystique—imbued the organization.

"It's Not Magic"

Knight kept NIKE's formal structure relatively flat, functional, and flexible. He believed that this "simpler setup" had been a help to the growing company, yet he was aware that increasing size was driving managers to divide jobs into smaller components, which inevitably made the organization more complex (for example, the product line reorganization in 1982 broke down one "unmanageable" job into four). Knight was clear, however, that structural actions could not be divorced from a consideration of the people involved.

> **HBS:** We've sensed from your description of the product line reorganization that you see organization structure and people as integrally bound together.
>
> **PHK:** It's like so many things around here; it has been colored a great deal by the athletic world. There was a football coach at Oregon State who was recognized as one of the greatest single wing teachers in history. He knew that system inside out. Then he had a great quarterback show up on campus and he became one of the best T-formation coaches in the country.[1]
>
> I don't think you can say that there is one best structure for a billion dollar company selling sport shoes. It depends on the personnel you've got. They have an enormous impact on how you decide to organize.
>
> **HBS:** What sort of people do you look for?
>
> **PHK:** Well, we've always tried to look for ability more than specialties. In the beginning we didn't have an industry to draw on and never had enough money to hire guys that were expert in an area. We just sort of all banded together, recognizing that maybe we weren't good enough individually to do this but somehow, collectively, we could make this thing go okay. I think that's a lot of the message of NIKE's success.

---

[1] A single wing system in football relies on the strength and abilities of the team's running backs; a T-formation's success depends on the quarterback's skills.

But as we get bigger and bigger, people know less and less about the different areas—and the areas get more sophisticated. It gets harder to help each other as much as we used to.

HBS: We've also noted that NIKE has moved people around far more than many companies seem to. For example, Woodell's moved from marketing to R&D to apparel and now back to marketing.

PHK: Well, that whole process really came about out of necessity. There were holes being left that just had to be filled, and we'd see guys who could fill them working in some other roles. So we took the chance and moved them. But after a while we began to see certain benefits in the very fact of moving. People developed a broader understanding, and that's helpful. We've sort of liked people to become specialists in the company rather than the job. We don't intend to move people in less than a year—and it should be two—but sometimes it just doesn't work out that way.

I think we've kind of taken both of these areas to an extreme, and it's not the ideal way to manage a company. Perhaps a combination of traditional management practice and the way we've done it would be best. On the other hand, I think companies have a tendency to try to find, for lack of a better word, a textbook answer to the problem of organizing while overlooking the enthusiasm and human side of the whole equation.

Knight felt that NIKE morale has been aided by the product. "There's a feeling of 'We did it!'" he explained, "when you see the product on the feet of someone crossing the finish line on TV. That's different not only from widgets but from something that isn't related to sports, something that doesn't make you feel really proud." That tie to the values and ideals of sports was an underlying foundation of NIKE.

HBS: Phil, you and others have frequently spoken of Coach Bowerman as a teacher, as a wellspring from which many NIKE values have flowed.

PHK: He was a marvelous teacher—and always referred to himself that way even when he was national coach of the year and Olympic coach and everything. You don't forget his whole thing about competitive responses and working hard and character—he put them on you like a tattoo.

And it carried over into how I view employees. For example, we have fired three sales managers who had increased their sales by 50 percent to 100 percent in a year. They weren't being measured by sales alone. You can kind of tell whether a guy is any good or not, and they weren't.

HBS: NIKE has attracted some very good people.

PHK: We've tried not to buy people. We don't ask them to sacrifice, but there is a feeling—and maybe it is dissipating a bit down in the ranks—that they will be treated fairly. I don't think people are motivated by money, particularly. They are a little bit, but if you are not hung up on an ostentatious living style, there's not an enormous gap in the way people live. So I think that what people really want to do with their lives is accomplish something. We have a pretty good history of giving people a chance to do that. They've liked the challenge and have trusted us. And a lot of people have been taken care of. Those that are close enough see that, understand it. But again, with growth, as people get farther away, maybe they don't understand that as well.

A deeply ingrained aspect of the Bowerman legacy was a belief that, for an individual, hard work and desire counted for more (and produced more results) than raw talent, and teamwork accomplished more for the organization than individual heroism. This belief had been a leveling influence within the organization. Knight reflected:

The idea that the brains are all at the top of an organization is really kind of silly. And nobody at the top ever *does* anything—it's the folk down the line that make it work. I learned that early. I had a great concept about bringing in shoes from Japan to compete with the German shoes, but I wouldn't have gotten far with it if I hadn't bumped into Jeff Johnson. He *really* made it work. And Jeff in turn had to rely on other people. I have a lot of respect for how we did that, and I guess that's the way this company has always worked. There has been a basic honesty between people, and all anybody has wanted is what works.

That sort of pragmatism, Knight felt, was the key to NIKE's success. "It isn't magic," he assured the researchers.

Working with Knight

The researchers observed an immense loyalty to, and affection for, Phil Knight at NIKE. As Vice President Rob Strasser explained:

We know Knight's in control, that he's the boss. But he knows it's a big world, that he makes mistakes, too. He has accepted guys here that wouldn't fit well anyplace else. We're not geniuses, but we do have intuitive smarts, and he knows when to pull in and when to let go. He identifies your strengths and weaknesses early on and cares about you enough to hope you do better. He's a great leader.

Knight's work pattern seemed, to the researchers, to be driven by three primary factors:

— The basic areas of interest in which he had been most active: trade with the Far East, working with the athletes, and product innovation.

— Situations brought to the fore by his own longer term thinking or by operating pressures in which he then became involved.

— His close relationship with longer term managers with whom he felt most comfortable.

Knight's days were busy but remarkably free of formal, prescheduled appointments. Among his formal duties Knight chaired the board and led the Friday Club meetings, but he disliked ceremonial tasks. A trade paper described him as an elusive shadow. He traveled extensively and spent four to six weeks in the Far East each year. Formal reviews and presentations were rare at NIKE, yet Knight kept in close touch informally with the company as a whole and with particular projects, issues, and people. Some managers with whom Knight was not particularly close found him difficult to approach, yet most respected his "creativity, brilliance, instincts, and drive."

While NIKE managers often found it hard to articulate the experience of working with Knight, three common observations emerged: he tended to provide *general direction,* rather than specific orders; he expected people to *keep in touch* with him on relevant issues; and he was, like Bowerman, often referred to as a *teacher.*

Knight was clearly in charge and would make decisions when he believed it appropriate or necessary. One close observer, however, noted that a major strength was his ability to induce a consensus—at the highest practical level. A senior NIKE manager remarked:

> His style is to give some general direction. He doesn't give you a lot of specifics; rather, you get a general feeling and that's what you go out and try to do. For example, I've been working on a contract with an athlete. Knight told me, "Don't spend much money, but don't let anybody else sign her." What the hell does he mean by that? It may be impossible, but I'll try to do something of that nature.

Another said:

> His style, as best I know it, is to encourage and stimulate discussion among others. He gives some direction in terms of keeping some semblance of order to a meeting but allows people to have a full discussion. He'll listen, and he'll ask some questions.

While Knight routinely saw several formal reports [see NIKE (B)], his "control system" was largely informal, based upon keeping in touch. For this approach to work, of course, both Knight and his subordinates had to be sensitive to which issues were sufficiently important to keep in touch about and able and willing to be reasonably open about them. Clearly, these characteristics took time to develop.

Knight typically talked with his closest associates every couple of days. "With those who really understand this place," he said, "I can count on being told about what's going right *and* what's going wrong in their area." One senior manager explained, "On major things you touch base with him, just keep him generally informed. He doesn't need a lot of details. If he has confidence in you, on many things you just do it." As an example of this interaction, a brief meeting between Woodell and Knight is summarized in Exhibit 1.

Managers often alluded to what they had learned from Knight. For example, one senior manager said:

> One of the things Knight has taught us is that you can always do something better. Sure, there are some good moments, but you can always do it better. He's not a stroker, doesn't let you gloat on a success. "Not bad!" is a supreme accolade. Perhaps that's where we avoid some of the phoniness, some of the saccharine bull—— found in so many places.

Knight's attitude reflected his belief that there was always more to learn—and inevitably mistakes to be made. In the words of another senior manager:

> You don't just have one shot here. I mean, you've got to have some victories, but there will be mistakes, too. We've all got a ton of them, every single one of us, including Knight. He's not above being teased about his mistakes. He takes it and laughs.

Knight had worked a long time and formed very close relationships with several of his managers—Woodell, Strasser, and Hayes in particular, but also a wider group of senior and middle managers. As Woodell described it:

> We go back a ways, and he is comfortable with us. We're real different but have worked together long enough that we understand each other's strengths, can communicate reasonably quickly, have all done a lot of the jobs in the company.
>
> Knight's a difficult person to get to know, and few people are close to him. With most people he avoids conflict and confrontation. But with Strasser, Hayes, and me, he'll absolutely seek it out. At one point, for example, I was overseeing distribution, although it was a small part of what I was doing. One day Phil called me up on the phone and was just whaling on me for something in distribution. Finally I said, "Knight, so and so are integrally involved in this problem; they're the ones who can do something about it. Why the hell are you calling and beating on me?" He said, "Because they're no fun to give s—— to and you are." And he just kept beating on me for another five minutes. Once I understood that, I was fine. At the end I said, "Well, nice talking to you," and he said, "Yeah," and hung up. He didn't want to talk to those other guys then, he wanted to get it off his chest so he called me and yelled at me about it. It took me a lot of years to really understand that.

"Thinking Conceptually"

The researchers spoke with Knight about how his job had changed over the years.

PHK: In some ways, I guess, it hasn't changed. I've always felt that if we have the right product at the most economical cost, we'll figure out a way to sell it. Innovation and sourcing have been really important, and most of my time has been spent in those two areas. Everybody talks about our marketing, and it's been good. That isn't to say that we haven't done some pretty awful things along the way. But we've been able to do this because we've had a good product with enough margin for the right marketing expense.

HBS: Are you as strong in terms of cost and price as you were several years ago?

PHK: Of course, the more innovative the shoe is, the less the price has to be competitive. But no, I don't think we're as strong now as we were a couple of years ago. On the other hand, the potential savings in China are just enormous. China has been a really great concept, but it wouldn't have been worth a damn unless you had some guys who were willing to say, "Send me in, Coach!"

HBS: Was it your concept?

PHK: I guess I am a worrier. And one of the things I worry about is government stability in our source countries. We've been trying, with some success, to get the production spread out. But the most meaningful place, if we're really going to have a good future, is China. It was Chang who made it work. I couldn't even get into the country.

HBS: How do you decide what to worry about?

PHK: I don't know. I suppose, on an ongoing basis, people keep me informed about the areas they are in, either at a Friday Club meeting or as Woodell did. If I am alarmed about something, I'll probably go and get involved.

HBS: Phil, people in the company have consistently described you as a long-range thinker.

PHK: When I'm at what I would consider my best, I am thinking in conceptual terms—where we want to be, how we are going to get there. Then I'll go out and spend some time in the area I've been thinking about and really probe in depth. Actually this is what I think I ought to be doing. It's a constant fight to avoid getting overwhelmed by the daily operating types of things and the ceremonial types of things. Obviously if I don't win at least some of those battles, we're in real trouble.

HBS: Can you give us an example of what you call conceptual thinking?

PHK: I tend to think the conceptual thoughts when I'm alone. Two or three years ago, I guess, after spending some time thinking, I woke up one night and said, "A real vulnerability for us is the proposed quotas on shoe imports from the Far East. But it's also an area of enormous opportunity, because there's not another shoe importer that's thinking more than three months down the road in this area." So I spent some time with Nelly [Ron Nelson] and Dewey [Shelly Dewey] going over the production in Korea and Taiwan, which were the countries in danger. Later we sent a negotiating team over there to set up a quota base that was far superior to anybody else's.

More generally this is basically thinking about where you're going and where you want to be. For example, we looked three or four years down the road and said, "Well, we're going to run out of feet in the United States so we have to do something else." And we've identified some directions, such as apparel and international, that will continue to let us grow, and we're trying to get them going.

HBS: Do you distinguish between this conceptual thinking and planning?

PHK: A plan is more a list of where we are going to be: Point A, Point B, Point C. The problem is that the plan never kind of works out the way you thought it would. When we look ahead over the next three or four years and say, "Here's a plan"—and we've done this a little bit—the guys in the middle read it and think it is cast in stone. And then the plan becomes a substitute for thinking. They stop thinking about why they are doing what they are doing. This leads to all kinds of bad decisions.

We tell a little story to illustrate this. With his team buried on their own five-yard line, a coach sent in explicit instructions to the quarterback to pass on the first play, run on the second, and punt on the third. On the first play, the quarterback completed a 45-yard pass. On the second, he gave the ball to the fullback, who ran for a 40-yard gain, bringing the team to the opponent's 10-yard line. On the third play, he punted.

HBS: But somehow, through this process of thinking—your going out there and just mucking around in things—people in the middle get some direction without the imposition of a plan.

PHK: What we've done has worked very well historically. The hard part now is that we have guys in the middle that aren't a part of the strategic sessions. If we just get the message out to them, that's essentially a plan. And if we don't get the message out, they don't have any idea what we're doing. What we have to do is get them to understand the *thinking* behind the message: to get those guys to *understand* why they are doing what they are doing and how it all fits together.

HBS: How are you working on this?

PHK: Recognition of the problem is part of it. We've kind of attacked it in different ways, but I'm really not satisfied with any of them. For example, one of the things we've done over the last month is to go out and touch the "peeps" and tell them where we see this place going and some of the thought processes behind that. This kind of gets everybody's morale up, but it's a one-time shot.

HBS: The peeps?

PHK: The people. Hayes always calls them the peeps. But this thing is a problem. The flow of communications in the past has been very, very good. Listening on both sides. Up, down, crosswise. But there hasn't been a formal procedure to do this. We're getting big enough now to begin to see the cracks—and bigness is not a number, it's when our ways of communicating, of working together, that nobody can quite define, start to slip.

HBS: Can you give us an example of a crack?

PHK: Sure. _____, who's in charge of one of the product lines, decided that we will not have a shoe in that line at a price of more than $39.95. He didn't ask anybody. He interpreted the message that way. If you look at the line, 80 percent of it sells at less than $30. But the whole concept is that you have to be at the high end and do well there. If we aren't, we're not going to have the good athletes in our shoes, and we're not going to have any reason to exist. Understanding that is fundamental. But he told the R&D people, "We're not going to have a shoe in *my* line that sells for more than $39.95. We lose money on them." My God!

HBS: Should his boss have checked that?

PHK: What should have happened was that he should have talked to some people about it. But on his own, he just came up with that decision for "his line."

HBS: Isn't that the irony? You want people to take responsibility, but . . .

PHK: Sure. But there ought to be some kind of dialogue, up, down, sideways, about this sort of thing. That's why we have meetings; that's why we try to talk a lot. He was doing what he thought he was supposed to be doing, but he didn't do it right.

As I think about it, I realize that a lot of the people who do pretty well for us have been around for a while, have been close enough to see the thought processes that go on here, see how and why decisions are made.

HBS: Which is back to what you said earlier about the middle people understanding.

PHK: Yeah. If the people are good enough—and I think they are— then it gets to be, simply, an educational process. The job is to get the word out to these people somehow. The concept's not complicated, but getting the word out is.

HBS: So they'll do what they're supposed to do.

PHK: It's broader than that. When we get together with guys, they'll tell us the major things happening in their departments. The problem is, there may be things happening whose significance is beyond their perspective. They're not afraid to tell you—it just boils down to their having to know what is significant.

And even they are often so consumed with getting product out the door, or whatever they do on a day-to-day basis, that they forget about it, and it's not a part of their thought process.

HBS: Could you explain that a little more?

PHK: It's the things they think about all the time: what shows up on the daily sheets, what shows up on the financial statement. That's okay, but you have to make sure they understand, for example, that even though apparel does not have an opportunity right now to be the innovator that we would like it to be, it has not gone away as a company goal. We may make a short-term decision that is in conflict with these goals, but you don't want them to lose sight of what the company is trying to be and how we can make sure it will still be here in 1990 and doing well then.

HBS: In what ways has your job changed over the years?

PHK: Since we went public I've been spending a lot of time, which I didn't before, in what I call ceremonies. I don't add a damn thing, but customers or investment bankers or vendors like to say they met a chief executive, and you sort of get obligated into those things. It's a constant fight. If I could manage my schedule the way I would like to, I would have every day clean to go to what was important.

HBS: Do you know what's on the docket next week?

PHK: Unfortunately, I do. On Monday I've got to fly down and meet with a big customer with some of our guys. It's one of those ceremonies. Strasser keeps saying we could accomplish the same thing by getting a plastic doll at Disneyland that looks like me and sticking a tape recorder in it.

On Tuesday what I'd really like to do is turn it over to Nelson's office and get back into apparel. We're facing the same situation with quotas in apparel now that we did with shoes several years ago. You can play offense with that quota.[2] But what I will do is spend some time with an employee who's coming back from the Far East. There are a couple of choices about where he can

---

[2] Within the foreign country, the government typically allocated blocks of its U.S. import quota to individual factories. "Playing offense" in this context meant working with the factories to secure their quota allocation for NIKE. This was more difficult to coordinate in apparel than in footwear because the apparel factories were relatively less flexible (an individual factory typically worked with only a limited number of the fabrics used by NIKE).

go next. From a company standpoint it really doesn't make too much difference which place he goes. Emotionally, I'd like to say, "Go talk to Woodell or somebody else, and I'm going to figure out quotas."

I have those conflicts. That afternoon there's a meeting with a kind of heavy operating decision coming up, which I should deal with. Then there are some other meetings at the end of the week.

Last month Hayes told me that I was getting too involved in the operating detail of the business: "You ought to be back thinking like you were before, thinking conceptually about where we're going and where we're not going. That's what you're different at from other people."

Historically, I've always reserved enough time to be able to do that; not any time in specific, but enough time to have a pretty good idea of where we were going and to feel comfortable with that. I've done a pretty good job that way. In the operating area my tendency is to wander around. As we get bigger that ultimately leads to problems because I'll wander around in some areas and not in others, and nobody knows where they are. And the operating stuff can absolutely overwhelm you.

Maybe we're getting to the point where we need the traditional chief operating officer and chief executive officer type of thing. Maybe we're kind of getting there, painfully but just out of necessity.

Exhibit 1

Researchers' Summary of Brief Meeting between Knight and Woodell

This late afternoon meeting lasted about 10 minutes. It had been requested by Woodell and took place in Knight's office. During the meeting Woodell referred to a notebook he carried and jotted down several notes in it. The pace was quick. The following topics were discussed:

1. It had recently been decided to send Chang over to head up apparel. Woodell wanted to get his signals straight with Knight on when and how this would be announced. A couple of factors were quickly weighed and an agreement reached.

2. Woodell reported that a young tennis player wanted "a bloody fortune" and that the guy in charge of tennis promotions did not want to sign her. Any problems? Knight: "Do what you want."

3. The marketing and promo people had decided to "cut" several pro basketball players. Woodell wondered if Knight wanted to be involved. Knight: "Show me the list. If I want to get involved, I will."

Exhibit 1 (concluded)

4. Woodell wondered where Knight was in the budget process and said that since he had been very busy, he had asked his people just to send their budgets over to Kurtz directly rather than review them himself. Knight said he had seen a few of the budgets and that this was no problem.

5. A brief discussion ensued about a proposed company newspaper. Several of Woodell's people had put together a concept for a new all-company paper to replace several existing geographical or departmental ones that "nobody hesitated to say were pieces of s——." They had "pitched" Woodell, and he had been persuaded to support the idea. Knight asked Woodell if he had confidence in those people. Woodell said yes. Knight said he was reluctant to proceed but wanted to be "pitched" the following day.

*   *   *   *   *

In commenting on the meeting later, Knight said:

The newspaper was the most controversial thing to me. The other stuff we had discussed before, and it was basically touching base on implementation. With the athletes, people get a little nervous that I might have a favorite player, and they don't want to offend me. With the budget, he was telling me he was pretty well swamped and that was one of the things he has given up a little bit, which is not a particular problem.

With the newspaper, we actually didn't have another face-to-face meeting on the subject, though we probably talked on the phone four times. We finally said we would try it on an experimental basis to see if it is effective in terms of communication. Trying to communicate better with people is a good idea. If it does everything he thinks it will, it'll be good; but if we start it and stop it again, we'll look dumb as hell; and if it generates the feeling that it alone will solve the problem, that's bad. I'm skeptical, but he is sold on it himself. I guess I made him say that. I guess that was about all I did.

NIKE (C1)

In recent months, the cooling of NIKE's domestic shoe sales has pinched profits. On February 24, 1983, NIKE announced that earnings for the third quarter ended February 28 would show the first quarterly decline in the company's history—largely because of "lower than anticipated shoe sales," Gary Kurtz, NIKE's treasurer, said. The surprise statement, which prompted NIKE's over-the-counter per-share bid to drop to $16 a share from $23 a share in one week, followed a second quarter in which earnings were flat despite a 30 percent increase in revenue.[1]

NIKE believed the sales shortfall was due primarily to a pronounced softening in the retail market, as the economic pressures of the recession forced retailers to curtail purchasing and cut inventory levels (see Exhibit 1 for selected financial results). In addition, Treasurer Gary Kurtz noted that a major new product, the *Air Force I* basketball shoe, had been introduced late and thus missed the season. Pressure on earnings had been increased by heavy start-up expenses in the international operation (principally Europe) and by greater overhead spending in anticipation of more rapid growth.

Naturally the announcement of the second- and third-quarter results surprised and concerned the investment community. Analysts, perhaps hypnotized by the company's spectacular past success, rewrote their re-

---

[1] "NIKE Pins Hopes for Growth on Foreign Sales and Apparel," *The New York Times,* March 24, 1983, p. D5.

Copyright © 1984 by the President and Fellows of Harvard College
Harvard Business School case 385–030

ports, replacing phrases such as "one of the great growth situations of the 1980s" with more cautious words such as "outlook uncertain."

Four issues captured the analysts' attention. First, inventory, which had climbed to $280 million at the end of the third quarter from $179 million a year earlier, "seldom increases in value with age," as one said, and would have to be carefully managed. Second, the decline in Futures orders (down 6 percent from the prior year) would probably lead to greater volatility in quarterly results and require the company to learn a different way of doing business. Third, because the company was so large, the growth segments of the business (such as apparel and international) would have to grow very rapidly indeed to maintain the overall growth rate. Fourth, and privately, several analysts noted that they would feel more comfortable if NIKE had more senior managers with extensive business experience.

On balance, however, one analyst concluded:

> There is no question in our minds that NIKE is going to be a better company for having had this experience, and we feel reasonably constructive on the company longer term.

Exhibit 1

Selected Financial Results (Millions of dollars, except earnings per share)

Third Quarter and Nine Months Results, Fiscal 1982–83

	Third Quarter			Nine Months Ending		
	FY 82	*FY 83*	*Change (Percent)*	*FY 82*	*FY 83*	*Change (Percent)*
Sales	$166.8	$199.2	19.4%	$488.5	$644.3	31.9%
Cost of goods sold	115.0	140.8	22.5	332.9	441.2	32.6
Gross profit	51.8	58.4	12.7	155.6	203.1	30.5
Percent of sales	31.1%	29.3%	—	31.9%	31.5%	—
SG&A	23.8	33.6	41.3	65.5	97.0	48.1
Net income	11.1	9.3	(15.5)	36.7	42.1	14.5
Earnings per share	.31	.25	(19.4)	1.03	1.16	12.6

Third Quarter and Nine Months Product Line Sales Increase (Decrease), Fiscal 1982–83

Product Line		
Running	3.4%	21.6%
Court	(22.7)	(5.5)
Cleated	176.5	222.6
Emerging	52.8	41.1
Apparel	36.9	70.5
International	127.2	172.1
Total	19.4%	31.9%

Source: Company records.

NIKE (E)

NIKE's top management group, customarily known as the Friday Club, consisted of 11 senior managers who met every week or two; twice a year they held a large off-site meeting. In the spring of 1983, however, several warning signs motivated Phil Knight to pull together a special group, consisting of himself, Woodell, Strasser, and Hayes, to review the company thoroughly and think through its operating and strategic directions. (See Exhibit 1 for most recent financials.) This group, which became known as the "gang of four," conducted a series of in-depth meetings with managers of each key organizational unit. These meetings were run in NIKE's traditional no-holds-barred fashion.

The four senior managers' comments on this process are presented below.

Phil Knight

Back in January it became clear that shipments and bookings weren't tracking the way we expected. As we dug into that situation, we realized that we weren't going to get the growth we had expected, and it became clear that over the next few years, the company is going to be a little different animal to manage. For example, as demand slows we're going to have to manage the operating expenses more tightly.

I met with Woodell, Strasser, and Hayes in February to talk about some issues before one of our off-site meetings, and we realized that the process

Copyright © 1984 by the President and Fellows of Harvard College
Harvard Business School case 385–033

we had to go through—taking a good hard look at the whole company and sort of confirming or realigning the directions in which we were headed as a company—would just be more efficient with 4 than with 11. There's a communication between us so that, for example, when one person says two words, everybody knows what he's talking about. And with those three guys, we had the major areas of the business pretty much covered. Woodell was sort of the administrator, Hayes the factory guy, and Strasser the creative guy.

Starting in March we went around the company on a series of department audits, which is something we don't do in a normal year. We wanted to review what was going on, trying to check that people were working on the right things, to ask if we were getting the most benefit from major costs such as promo and advertising, to help people focus on some of the immediate problems. For example, in the production area we realized we had too much capacity and that we had to decide which factories to cut. There were some heated arguments about this, because the issues went beyond dollars and cents. [Ultimately, NIKE's Exeter, New Hampshire, plant was closed and five (of 30) Far Eastern factories were cut.]

Bob Woodell

We dug back into operations. The third-quarter earnings figure [see NIKE (C1)] was really the first sign that everything we touched didn't turn to gold. Futures were down, and the product line seemed to be getting a bit stale. At the same time there was a subtle shift in our marketplace. The athletic look wasn't the number one "in" thing anymore; people were starting to dress up a bit more, be a little more conservative.

We also started to see some cracks in the organization. It seemed to take forever to get a shoe to market, with so much coordination required between product management in Beaverton and development in Exeter. And when a product did come through, it sometimes wasn't the right one.

An example is the bicycling shoe. In general we think in terms of a market pyramid; our approach has been to start with the best shoe, at the top of the pyramid, and have that drive the sale of less technical shoes lower in the pyramid. Someone decided that we needed to develop the absolute top-of-the-line bicycling shoe, and we spent over a year doing so. But they didn't develop any basic, simple shoes; nor is it clear that the pyramid concept works in the bicycle shoe market. I don't think bicyclists "look up the pyramid" to see what the pros are wearing.

Yet it would be unfair to say that these things caught us completely by surprise. We knew that growth was covering up a multitude of sins. We made a conscious decision not to try to clean most of them up while we were still riding the rocket straight up but to wait until things started to slow down a bit. And now that's happening.

Del Hayes

Our early years were characterized by no structure—period! This was an incredibly effective approach for a while. We attracted people who weren't necessarily good "managers" but who were excellent team players and good performers. That characterizes Phil as well. There was a lot of emotion here and a tremendous sense of personal involvement and accomplishment.

Then things changed. The business got so large and so complex that it was impossible for Phil, or any of us, to play the same role. We started to lose our hands-on feel for the business. Yet we haven't formalized things. We knew that we were lacking structure and systems, and we knew that we weren't as efficient as we could have been. But we also knew that if we didn't really stretch to seize opportunities, the world would pass us by.

Rob Strasser

I was away in Europe until early 1983. When I came back I noticed that some people seemed to be wandering. In the early days there was so much to do to just keep up with the growth, but we were small and everyone knew everyone else and what they were doing. Now we're in *nine* separate buildings!

Other Perspectives

Several NIKE middle managers spoke with the researchers about the events that led up to this overview process and its subsequent impact—which some labeled recentralization—on the way they operated.

Sales

Through 1982 things were frantic. We made mistakes, but we didn't have time to look over our shoulders—there was too much to do. I think we developed a somewhat arrogant attitude; we thought that if we put a swoosh on anything, it would sell. Maybe, by and large, this was *true*. Then in late 1982 the market changed. Everybody was making athletic footwear, and the market started to tire of the athletic look.

Product Management

We did make some mistakes. For example, we were late with Velcro,[1] and we missed the market for aerobic shoes. But for every wrong move, we made five right ones.

Management didn't give us much real direction in this; it was sort of, "Here's your job, now go do it." And that was often exciting.

This recentralization, however, has really slowed things down. You get the feeling that senior management wants to be involved in lots of decisions. So you go to them and say, "Here's my problem; what do you want me

---

[1] A patented closure system that replaced traditional methods such as laces, buttons, or zippers.

to do?" And they say, "Let me think about it." Then four or five days later when you haven't heard anything, you go back again.

Product Management

We really had no formal communication channels, no bureaucracy, no constraints. It was an incredible stimulus to bust ass. In 22 months my area's sales rose from $32 to $137 million. Of course we made mistakes, but that is the price that you have to pay if you want people to seize the initiative and take risks.

Management hired individuals who had potential and gave them room to run. But now the senior managers are into too many decisions. For instance, we recently had a pricing meeting for a product line. We had done a lot of work and a lot of research. They reviewed it, didn't like it, and five minutes later we had a new pricing scheme. I question whether they are really close enough to the market to make decisions like that. And I *know* that it really affects the motivation of a lot of people when they see that their efforts haven't amounted to much.

The Challenge

A middle manager noted that NIKE faced a major challenge.

There was a real dilemma here. Growth had led us to compartmentalize, to define jobs more narrowly. And this had created a kind of tunnel vision.

For instance, about this time orders came in from our sales force for the summer/fall season. Typically we try to ship these out by June 1. Well it turns out one particular shoe was still in Korea and wasn't going to be in the States until June 10, which means it wouldn't have gotten to the stores until the third week in June. This shoe is a basketball shoe, which dealers usually don't place on the shelves until July 1, anyway.

But because it said "ship June 1" on the order, a clerk decided to have the shoes air-freighted from Korea, which cost us an additional $50,000.

The clerk did check with a supervisor, who was busy and who didn't really know what was going on either. This is what happens when people don't see the big picture. Yet it is this very sense of freedom and autonomy that has made this company what it is. How do we preserve *it* while instituting the structure and systems we need?

Bob Woodell talked about the need for organizational change:

We created a difficult situation; because we were concerned and believed that some things needed to be looked at and changed, it got to the point where very little could happen without one of the four of us being involved. *But* we all perceive the need to decentralize and push some of the authority and responsibility back down the line. We see the need to create smaller units, to let people have the kind of fun that we used to have when this was a small organization. We've gotten so big that it was difficult for people to see that they were having an impact.

There are lots of people in this world who don't want to compete because they are afraid that they will be found lacking. I think NIKE has a bunch of true competitors. Let's organize ourselves so that people can see how good they really are. There is no reason that this challenge can't be as much fun and as exciting as our early challenge of survival was.

Exhibit 1

NIKE
Consolidated Statement of Income
(in thousands, except per share data)

	Fiscal Year Ended May 31		
	1983	*1982*	*1981*
Revenues	$867,212	$693,582	$457,742
Cost and expenses:			
Cost of sales	589,986	473,885	328,133
Selling and administrative	132,400	94,919	60,953
Interest	25,646	24,538	17,859
Other expense	1,057	435	92
Total cost and expenses	749,089	593,777	407,037
Income before provision for income taxes and minority interest	118,123	99,805	50,705
Provision for income taxes	60,922	50,589	24,750
Income before minority interest	57,201	49,216	25,955
Minority interest	197	180	—
Net income	$ 57,004	$ 49,036	$ 25,955
Net income per common share	$1.53	$1.37	$.76
Average number of common and common equivalent shares	37,158	35,708	34,031

Exhibit 1 *(continued)*

NIKE
Consolidated Balance Sheet
(in thousands)

	Fiscal Year Ending May 31	
	1983	*1982*
Assets		
Current assets:		
Cash	$ 13,038	$ 4,913
Accounts receivable, less allowance for doubtful accounts of $3,751 and $3,877, respectively, for year-end figures	151,581	130,438
Inventories	283,788	202,817
Deferred income taxes and purchased tax benefits	10,503	2,145
Prepaid expenses	6,625	5,198
Total current assets	465,535	345,511
Property, plant, and equipment	61,359	41,407
Less accumulated depreciation	21,628	12,485
	39,731	28,922
Other assets	2,762	1,040
Total assets	$508,028	$375,473
Liabilities and Shareholders' Equity		
Current liabilities:		
Current portion of long-term debt	$ 2,347	$ 3,936
Notes payable to banks	132,092	112,673
Accounts payable	91,102	74,064
Accrued liabilities	19,021	22,894
Income taxes payable	11,102	19,774
Total current liabilities	255,664	233,341
Long-term debt	10,503	9,086
Commitments and contingencies	—	—
Minority interest in consolidated subsidiary	948	786
Redeemable preferred stock	300	300
Total liabilities	267,415	243,513
Shareholders' equity:		
Common stock at stated value		
Class A convertible—18,837 and 11,976 shares outstanding	225	166
Class B—18,434 and 5,555 outstanding	2,646	1,414
Capital in excess of stated value	77,457	27,020
Unrealized translation gain (loss)	70	(67)
Retained earnings	160,215	103,427
	240,613	131,960
	$508,028	$375,473

Exhibit 1 *(continued)*

NIKE
Consolidated Statement of Changes in Financial Position
(in thousands)

	1983	*1982*	*1981*
Financial resources were provided by:			
Net income	$ 57,004	$ 49,036	$25,955
Income charges (credits) not affecting working capital:			
Depreciation	9,421	5,135	3,774
Minority interest	197	180	—
Other	(188)	194	131
Working capital provided by operations	66,434	54,545	29,860
Net proceeds from sale of Class B Common Stock in October 1982 and December 1980	51,442	—	27,890
Purchased tax benefits becoming current	14,270	—	—
Additions to long-term debt	4,135	4,477	4,392
Disposal of property, plant, and equipment	584	343	134
Proceeds from exercise of stock options	100	—	450
Minority shareholder contribution	—	648	—
	136,965	60,013	62,726
Financial resources were used for:			
Additions to property, plant, and equipment	21,031	18,228	9,914
Purchase of tax benefits	15,277	—	—
Long-term debt becoming current	2,368	4,002	7,049
Additions to other assets	527	161	670
Unrealized loss from translation of statements of foreign operations, including minority interest	31	109	—
Dividends on redeemable preferred stock	30	30	30
	39,264	22,530	17,663
Increase in working capital	$ 97,701	$ 37,483	$45,063

Analysis of Changes in Working Capital

Increase (decrease) in current assets:			
Cash	$ 8,125	$ 3,121	$ (35)
Accounts receivable	21,143	43,202	23,375
Inventories	80,971	82,588	64,288
Deferred income taxes and purchased tax benefits	8,358	845	1,165
Prepaid expenses	1,427	2,711	336
	120,024	132,467	89,129
Increase (decrease) in current liabilities:			
Current portion of long-term debt	(1,589)	(2,684)	2,753
Notes payable to banks	19,419	51,483	24,690
Accounts payable	17,038	31,572	5,560
Accrued liabilities	(3,873)	7,493	5,102
Income tax payable	(8,672)	7,120	5,961
	22,323	94,984	44,066
Increase in working capital	$ 97,701	$ 37,483	$45,063

Exhibit 1 (concluded)

NIKE Stock Market Performance Summary

Quarter Ending	Price/Share*		P/E†	
	High	Low	High	Low
12/80 offering		$11		13.25
2/28/81	11.62	8.75	18.6	14.2
5/31/81	11.50	8.50	14.0	10.4
8/31/81	12.50	9.25	7.8	5.8
11/30/81	13.88	8.88	10.8	6.9
2/28/82	15.36	13.50	12.4	10.9
5/31/82	15.25	12.36	11.2	9.1
8/31/82	20.12	14.75	8.7	6.4
11/30/82	27.12	20.00	20.5	15.1
2/28/83	28.00	15.75	28.0	15.8
5/31/83	21.37	15.12	13.7	9.7

* Reflects 2:1 split in January of 1983.
† Based on annualized earnings per share for quarterly period stated.

NIKE (E1)

The Announcement

NEWS RELEASE

NIKE, Inc.
3900 S.W. Murray Blvd.
Beaverton, Oregon 97005
Telephone (503) 641–6453

FOR IMMEDIATE RELEASE   FOR FURTHER INFORMATION:
Gary Kurtz (Analyst)
Jay Edwards (Press)

June 10, 1983   (503) 641–6453

Beaverton, Oregon—Robert L. Woodell, 38, has been named president and chief operating officer of NIKE, Inc., the Oregon-based athletic shoe and apparel company. Woodell was previously vice president in charge of worldwide marketing and apparel.

Woodell succeeds Philip H. Knight, founder, who remains chief executive officer and chairman of the board. Knight will devote increased efforts to long-range planning.

"I am delighted with the change," Knight said. "Bob has earned the job. I believe this and other changes we are making will help us maintain our leadership position in the industry and continue our growth."

Copyright © 1984 by the President and Fellows of Harvard College
Harvard Business School case 385–034

Like Knight, Woodell is a native Oregonian. He trained as a long jumper and sprinter at the University of Oregon under Olympic coach and NIKE co-founder Bill Bowerman.

Woodell joined the company in 1968. At various times in his 15-year employment with NIKE, he has been responsible for research and development, international marketing, apparel, production and sales.

Other changes at NIKE include the naming of Ronald E. Nelson, 40, and Richard H. Werschkul, 37, as vice presidents. Nelson will continue as director of production. He has been with the company since 1975. Werschkul, a NIKE employee since 1977, continues as corporate counsel.

George E. Porter, formerly vice president of distribution/administrative services, will assume responsibility for research and development at the NIKE research facility in Exeter, New Hampshire.

David P. C. Chang, vice president, will head the NIKE apparel division and continue his leadership of NIKE's effort in the People's Republic of China.

After two years as managing director of European operations, Rob Strasser, vice president, will resume responsibility for U.S. marketing.

NIKE (E2)

"Board Taps New Members"

NIKE Board Chairman Philip H. Knight has announced that three members have been nominated to the company's board of directors. Robert L. Woodell, Robert T. Davis, and Thomas D. Paine are expected to be elected at the next meeting of the board in September.

Woodell is the new NIKE president.

Davis is the Sebastian S. Kresge professor of marketing and director of the Stanford Executive Program in the Graduate School of Business at Stanford University. Davis also has served on the faculty of St. Lawrence University, Dartmouth College (Tuck School), and Harvard Business School. He has also authored five major texts in the field of business management.

Paine is chairman of Thomas Paine Associates, consultants in high-technology enterprises. He has served as manager of General Electric's Center for Advanced Studies, deputy administrator and administrator of NASA, and president and chief operating officer of Northrop Corporation.

"The expansion of the board from 7 to 10 members," Knight said, "is a response to the increasing complexity of the company and its concerns. We are adding to our depth and expertise."

Excerpts from article in
The NIKE Times, July 22, 1983

Copyright © 1984 by the President and Fellows of Harvard College
Harvard Business School case 385–035

NIKE (E3): Woodell's First Quarter

"Well, I've survived my first quarter," Bob Woodell chuckled, in a typical understatement. "And I still enjoy the job." Woodell had been named president of NIKE on June 10, 1983, succeeding founder Phil Knight, who continued as chairman and chief executive officer. This case describes that transition and Woodell's perspective on his new job and his goals for the coming year. Exhibit 1 presents the most recent financial statements for NIKE.

The Transition

Knight announced the decision to name Woodell president (and to name Ron Nelson and Rich Werschkul vice presidents) in a short Friday Club meeting on June 10. Although it came as a surprise to the senior managers, it was not disruptive. As one said later:

> We knew that Knight would have to pass the baton on at some point, but none of us expected it now. So we were surprised, and I think the wheels were really turning. What does this mean? Is Knight telling us the full scoop? But we weren't on pins and needles either. Woodell is a known quantity, and this is a natural, smooth move. The company really hasn't missed a beat.

And as Woodell explained:

Copyright © 1984 by the President and Fellows of Harvard College
Harvard Business School case 385–036

We all learned the business from, and along with, Knight. So we're not going to start doing things a lot differently. And as he keeps saying, it's the group that does it, not the individual. So I'm not bringing a list of *my* goals or programs to the job.

The announcement was made to the rest of the company and the press that afternoon and to a major sales meeting the next morning. Woodell was on the road the next week and returned on Friday, June 17, to find that Knight had already moved to a vacant suite in the International Building (about two miles from the home office). "We never talked," Woodell smiled. "He said, 'You do short term and I'll do long term.' And that was it. So in typical NIKE fashion, I've had to figure out what the job is."

Woodell and Knight alternated being away from the office much of the summer, and both acknowledged that it would take some time to sort out the boundaries of the two jobs. But neither considered it a big deal. "In many ways," Woodell said, "anything he doesn't want to do, I'll get." He continued:

I think Phil was getting worn down by having his mind constantly torn back and forth between the longer term thinking he's good at and the damn interruptions every five minutes that characterize operating types of things. It is really two very different thought processes, and I think he felt that trying to do both was just resulting in his doing poorly in each area. So one of my jobs is to take care of the short-term operations—day, quarter, year—and let Knight get back to thinking longer term, where we really need him.

Knight quickly pulled out of operating matters and, after some time off, focused his attention on the difficult issue of apparel quotas. He continued his interest in the sourcing from the People's Republic of China and his work as chairman. Woodell reported that he had much less frequent contact with Knight since the transition and that Knight seemed much happier in his new role. Always the storyteller, Woodell summarized his interaction with Knight during the quarter as follows:

> After about a month Phil called up one day to explain something he'd done, and when he finished he said, "Oh, and I had a question for you but I can't remember what it was. . . . Oh, I know, how's it going?"

Woodell's First Quarter

Woodell made few changes during his first few months as president, in part because many wheels were already in motion. He believed, for example, that the company's direction had pretty well been set by the strategic discussions of the past spring (in large part, the "gang of four" meetings described in NIKE (E)). He had already scheduled trips such as his major tour of the European operation in August. And as he noted, "I was doing a lot of things already in my previous job." Woodell's early operating style also reflected his desire to "figure out the job" and provide a low-key transition.

His own work pattern changed very little. He said, "My job is to make sure people focus on what's important. As president, I just have to do that in a broader area." He continued:

> It would have been a real trap to try to copy Phil. I've got to run to my strengths. For example, we've historically had a tendency to go to Knight for decisions. He's been trying to push that back on us, but the old habit was hard to break. My style is to build the organization so people out there make the decisions.

Rob Strasser assumed Woodell's old job as head of worldwide marketing, and an experienced and able middle manager with an administrative bent was assigned to "do the stuff that Strasser hates." "Rob and I work together less," Woodell noted, "and he can't yell at me through the office wall any more, but the transition has been easy."

Early Changes

One of the first changes Woodell made was to redefine the task and reconstitute the membership of the Friday Club. Under Knight this senior management group had been both a reporting session and a decision-making forum on some issues. In August Woodell called the first meeting of his management group, which was immediately dubbed the Wednesday Club. (His initial "ground rules" letter and the distribution list are presented as Exhibit 2.) He explained:

> My purpose is to reinforce the NIKE process of debating the issue, of collaboration, of getting decisions made, of getting counsel from each other. I don't want to put people out on a limb too quickly, but I'm trying to

get people to take more responsibility. For example, if the Policy and Procedures Committee has passed a policy, that should be it—the management group shouldn't have to rediscuss it. If the committee, or an individual, wants counsel, then bring it to the group. By really talking about it, 9 out of 10 times the answer will become clear. And we've gotten some more people involved—not just the organization chart but people who are going to contribute.

Woodell also chose to take a more visible role in the company and with the external constituencies than Knight had done. In his first quarter he visited NIKE's Tennessee and New England facilities and many of the individual departments in the Beaverton area. Activities during these visits ranged from "ceremonial" dinners and scheduled meetings to taking a department out to lunch or wandering around. He also attended several trade shows.

From the researchers' perspective, Woodell's style was to dig into substantive problems (he had a track record of stimulating effective thinking and action) and, while doing so, to reinforce again and again the company's direction and the NIKE way of doing things. Woodell commented:

After this spring I know the direction we're heading for the next year or two or three, and probably 50 other people also feel pretty comfortable with that. One of my jobs is to make sure everyone else hears that message. And you can't say it once or say it in a memo.

In addition this is a period when we're getting some things back in line, making corrections, and that's painful: painful to do the analysis and painful to execute the decisions. I can't solve the problems. The people will have to make the calls, and they'll have to execute them. I can't do that for them. But it helps if I listen. And maybe I can help them figure some things out and maybe help them recover after some inevitable mistakes. I try to make sure that people understand that this is a vote of confidence, not a lecture.

But I'm being visible on particular issues. Things have a way of becoming important if I spend time on them. There are a ton of ways to send signals, but that's one of the most powerful. We've got some real challenges right now—getting the right product in stock and shipped, as we've drawn down the inventory in general and started phasing out some older models in particular, and regaining better control over where our shoes are eventually sold. I'll go to meetings about those issues. I just won't go to other stuff, because then people will think those things are important.

Those of us who've been around for a while—Knight, Strasser, Hayes, Nelly, me, maybe some others—have got to find a way to pass this thing we call NIKE on to the next group so they understand it, can take more of the load, and ultimately can carry it on. So my job—our job—is more and more to teach and not just to do.

On a personal note, Woodell acknowledged the power of the office. While his friendship with people such as Strasser was unaffected by his new position, he did see a subtle change with many others. He found it harder, for example, to play his usual devil's advocate role as freely in many discussions because he sensed that people took his words more literally. And in a typically realistic mood, he noted that he didn't know whether to laugh at or feel bad about the "instant action" that was triggered by his name. Once, for example, he had asked a secretary to get some equipment for a meeting; she was told that it was unavailable— until his name came up. On a sober note, he reflected, "The challenge is to use the power wisely, to save it for really important issues. It gets old real quick."

Looking Ahead

In a final interview with the researchers, Woodell sketched out what he would like to accomplish in his job:

> A lot of it is trying to put the life back into this place, trying to trim it down a little bit, get the attitudes back in sync, get the growth back up, get the profits back to where they should be. People say that our success was due to smart people and luck. But how much of each? I liken us to a rocket. We went for quite a ride on the first stage, and then it kind of burned out. The real test will be if we can ignite the second stage and really get it moving again. I think we can, and I sense that the volcano's starting to rumble again.
>
> Our major problem is in apparel. There's massive demand out there for the products we have now, and we have to figure out how the hell to get them made and delivered, reliably and on time. So I've told Chang that he and I were going to get married for the next six months.
>
> A second problem is to keep the shoes hot. I'll spend some time with leisure shoes to make sure they're tracking the way they ought to be. The regular shoes won't grow as fast as they have in the past, but those shoes set the image, and I'll try to keep the innovation moving.

Exhibit 1

NIKE
Consolidated Statement of Income
(in thousands, except per share data)

	Three Months Ended August 31		
	1983 (1Q 1984)	*1982 (1Q 1983)*	*Fiscal 1983*
Revenues	$270,200	$256,698	$867,212
Cost and expenses:			
Cost of sales	180,003	172,631	589,986
Selling and administrative	39,668	33,367	132,400
Interest	4,981	7,763	25,646
Other expense	232	221	1,057
Total cost and expenses	224,904	213,982	749,089
Income before provision for income taxes and minority interest	45,296	42,716	118,123
Provision for income taxes	22,467	21,785	60,922
Income before minority interest	22,829	20,931	57,201
Minority interest	149	337	197
Net income	$ 22,680	$ 20,594	$ 57,004
Net income per common share	$0.60	$.58	$1.53
Average number of common and common equivalent shares	35,957	35,742	37,158

Note: NIKE's stock price ranged between $15.50 and $20.00 during the first quarter of the 1984 fiscal year—June 1 to August 31, 1983.

Exhibit 1 (concluded)

NIKE
Consolidated Balance Sheet
(in thousands)

	Three Months Ending August 31, 1983 (1Q 1984)	Fiscal Year Ending 1983
Assets		
Current assets:		
Cash	$ 6,998	$ 13,038
Accounts receivable, less allowance for doubtful accounts of $3,751 and $3,877, respectively, for year-end figures	179,062	151,581
Inventories	243,287	283,788
Deferred income taxes and purchased tax benefits	10,593	10,503
Prepaid expenses	6,637	6,625
Total current assets	446,577	465,535
Property, plant, and equipment	62,996	61,359
Less accumulated depreciation	24,108	21,628
	38,888	39,731
Other assets	3,174	2,762
Total assets	$488,639	$508,028
Liabilities and Shareholders' Equity		
Current liabilities:		
Current portion of long-term debt	$ 2,248	$ 2,347
Notes payable to banks	105,922	132,092
Accounts payable	60,587	91,102
Accrued liabilities	20,744	19,021
Income taxes payable	24,118	11,102
Total current liabilities	213,619	255,664
Long-term debt	10,004	10,503
Commitments and contingencies	—	—
Minority interest in consolidated subsidiary	1,103	948
Redeemable preferred stock	300	300
	225,026	267,415
Shareholders' equity:		
Common stock at stated value		
Class A convertible—18,837 and 11,976 shares outstanding		225
Class B—18,434 and 5,555 shares outstanding		2,646
Capital in excess of stated value		77,457
Unrealized translation gain (loss)		70
Retained earnings		160,215
Total shareholders' equity	263,613	240,613
	$488,639	$508,028

Exhibit 2

Meeting Ground Rules

*NOTE NEW TIME!

M E M O R A N D U M

To: R. Strasser   From: Bob Woodell
     J. Manns
     G. Kurtz
     R. Werschkul
     N. Goldschmidt
     D. Chang
     J. Edwards
     N. Lauridsen
     J. Joyce
     D. Wahl
     R. Nelson
     M. Hochhalter

Re: Friday Club Meeting Ground Rules   Date: August 18, 1983

FIRST MEETING: WEDNESDAY, AUGUST 24, 2:30 P.M.—MURRAY
I BOARDROOM

1. Discuss only important issues—no bull s——!
2. *Think,* before you repeat to anyone outside the group something that you heard in the meeting. When you bare your soul on a confidential matter, you don't want to hear it as gossip the next morning around the company.
3. Bring up as subject matter only those issues that you think other members of the group *must* be informed about, or important issues where you need their collective counsel.

Hopefully, at each meeting, one or two important issues facing the company will be fully discussed, and when necessary a collaborative decision will be reached. Don't plan on bringing your grocery shopping list to read, or I am confident you will be blown out of the saddle by the others in the room. Come prepared to mix it up with your friends.

Source: Company records.

Exhibit 3

Researchers' Depiction of the NIKE Organization—September 1983

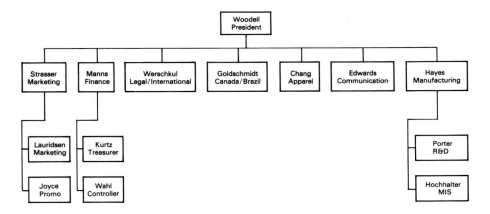

NIKE (E4)

During 1983 NIKE senior management undertook several initiatives to deal with a series of complex problems that were emerging because of a changing market environment and greater organizational size and complexity.

For several years many managers had believed that a more formal salary administration system was needed—yet any action to develop one had always run aground on the shoal of a deep dislike for "systems." In the fall of 1983 a consensus had emerged that *something* had to be done, and a committee was given the assignment of developing a recommendation within 90 days. "We all agree that something needs to be done on this compensation issue," said committee chairman and controller, Dale Wahl. "The question is what?"

Background

As NIKE grew, practices evolved that provided implicit guidelines for most personnel situations, although few were formalized as corporate policies. This informality had worked and had generally been perceived as fair, managers noted, because of the quality of top management. As one manager explained, "They—Knight, Woodell, those guys—are really good guys, they really are. I believe in them. They do some dumb things, sure, but I have faith that their hearts are in the right place."

Copyright © 1984 by the President and Fellows of Harvard College
Harvard Business School case 385–037

Some managers, however, had become concerned about the actual effects of this informal approach. As Vice President George Porter explained:

> The reality is that there are pay inequities down in ranks; that managers sometimes do handle essentially similar situations, such as the granting of sick pay, in upsettingly different ways; and that for some employees, working for NIKE is just a job—but a job that can, nevertheless, be done very well.

The resistance to formal policies reflected NIKE's entrepreneurial roots. Flexibility, thinking, and enthusiasm had been very important to the growing company, and there was a tendency to view policies as a threat to these characteristics. In fact, over the years the establishment of a formal evaluation and compensation system at NIKE had been actively questioned and even opposed. This point of view was expressed in typical NIKE fashion by one senior manager who thought that such plans were "bull——." A middle manager commenting on the same topic asked, "How can you measure performance at NIKE?" Another manager stated his concerns:

> When I see a few people starting to worry about career paths instead of getting the job done; when I see a few people asking for raises because the company is making money rather than because of their own performance, I start to worry. The minute we become eight to five, we're dead.

The Policy and Procedures Committee

Roger Tragesser became NIKE's personnel manager in December 1981. By mid-1982 he was convinced that the personnel department did not have the clout to sponsor corporate personnel policies effectively. In discussions with his then boss, Executive Vice President Del Hayes, he developed the concept of the Policy and Procedures Committee (PPC). "The more people you get involved, the more chance of something flying," an observer commented. Tragesser explained:

> We needed to develop a process to handle the development and ongoing maintenance of our personnel policies, one that would outlive personalities, including mine and, more importantly, that would develop policies the top people will buy into. It can't be my policy. It can't be the personnel department's policy. It has to be NIKE's policy.

Tragesser handpicked the 15 members of the committee that fall. He included both middle managers and senior managers (among them Strasser, Woodell, Nelson, and Chang). George Porter, who became Tragesser's boss in late 1982, chaired the newly formed committee. With substantial experience in two Fortune 500 companies, Porter brought a different perspective to NIKE. He commented:

Everybody has heard stories illustrating the inconsistencies faced by employees. And most managers can recount the dilemmas they've faced in trying to balance a human responsibility to the company. We shouldn't have to fight this battle each time a situation comes up. *There should be a policy that's right for us,* that captures what the company is. It can probably deal with about 90 percent of the cases.

Another committee member stated, "We're trying to preserve the NIKE way, trying to articulate the way we'd like our best employees treated rather than to write rules to protect us from the excesses of a small group."

Under Porter's leadership the PPC quickly broke into six subcommittees to focus on particular policy areas selected by the committee: holidays, sick leave, educational reimbursement, leave of absence, termination, and compensation. Tragesser and the personnel department supported the work of the subcommittees but clearly and carefully tried "not to do it for them."

The first subcommittee recommendation was the holiday policy, which expanded the number of paid holidays from seven to nine. This policy was approved by the Friday Club and Knight in February 1983 after heated discussions. The issue, managers reported, centered on whether NIKE had to (or wanted to) meet external expectations about holidays or could continue to say, "We're special and will do this the way we have in the past." Tragesser noted that "it took a hell of an argument, but the policy was accepted."

In May 1983 subcommittees approved sick leave, leave of absence, and educational reimbursement policies. These were approved by President Bob Woodell in July and communicated to employees in a series of meetings during the early fall.

The Existing Compensation System

While NIKE had a well-established wage system for its hourly production and distribution employees, it had not developed a formal salary administration system for clerical and management personnel. Top management espoused a "pay the person, not the job" philosophy (rooted in Knight's belief that it was ultimately people who constituted the company's competitive edge).

In practice salaried employees were given annual reviews and raises (effective July 1), with occasional adjustments allowed during the year for special cases. Typically, top management approved the magnitude of the salary increase budget (for example, 8 percent of total salary dollars); individual managers were then expected to give particular employees more or less (on a percentage basis) depending on their performance and contribution.

As the company grew, this system became increasingly difficult to administer effectively. Managers believed there were at least three areas of weakness. First, a number of employees, especially in the more visible product development and marketing jobs, received salary offers from other companies that were significantly higher than their NIKE pay. Several people had left, though none who was seen as critical to the company. One senior manager explained, for example:

> I had a product line manager come in and tell me that he had an offer for 250 percent of his NIKE salary. He wasn't threatening to leave but did want me to understand the situation. At some point such offers will draw people, and we probably need to pay more. But we've also got to help some of these people understand that their job here may be quite different from the title that's being offered for big bucks somewhere else.

Second, there was a growing perception that inconsistent practices had led to inequity within the company. Most managers could cite examples of two people who did essentially the same job with the same performance but received very different salaries.

Third, top managers believed that supervisors far too often simply gave their employees increases in a very narrow band around the average rather than rigorously differentiating raises to reflect performance differences.

July 1983 Salary Increases

In establishing guidelines for July 1, 1983 salary increases, top management explicitly asked managers to reward job performance and to recommend adjustments to help correct perceived inequities (see Exhibit 1). Knight formed a salary committee of Woodell, Hayes, Manns, and Kurtz, which spent the better part of several days reviewing the salary recommendations. Woodell described the process:

> We tried to correct many of the internal and external inequities, and frankly I think that we did a pretty good job. But there was a big problem with how the process was perceived. People thought, "These guys don't know me or my job—how can they make a fair decision about my salary?" And it was a nightmare looking at all those recommendations—there was *no way* I wanted to go through this again.

The Committee Begins Its Work

By the fall of 1983 a general agreement had developed among NIKE management that a salary administration program had to be developed. In October the compensation subcommittee of the PPC was asked to make a recommendation to top management within 90 days. Chaired by Controller Dale Wahl, the subcommittee consisted of 12 people, including line managers from footwear, apparel, and international as well as Tragesser.

The committee began its work under significant pressure to avoid a July 1984 repetition of the 1983 difficulties. It called in Bob Doyle, a compensation consultant who had worked with one of the committee members at another company.

The committee quickly identified a series of compensation objectives for NIKE (see Exhibit 2) and began looking at alternative salary administration approaches. Attention soon focused on a job point approach and in particular on the Hay Associates System. Doyle and a couple of committee members had had experience with this system, and the committee held discussions with local companies using it.

The Hay Associates System

The Hay Associates, based in Philadelphia, is one of the most widely known compensation consulting firms, and its system is one of the most widely used in the United States. A major advantage to a company using this approach is the opportunity to compare its compensation practice (on a confidential basis) in a meaningful way with that of the other 4,000 Hay clients.

The Hay guide chart profile method of job evaluation was developed in the 1950s through an inductive process of looking at the factors that made up jobs in real organizations. Four key observations are made:

1. The most significant factors to be considered are the *knowledge* required to do a job, the *kind of thinking* needed to solve the problems commonly faced, and the *responsibilities* assigned.
2. Jobs could be ranked not only in the order of importance within the organization, but the distances between the ranks could also be determined.
3. The factors appear in certain kinds of patterns that seem to be inherent to certain kinds of jobs.
4. Job evaluation must focus on the nature and requirements of the job itself, not on the skills, background, characteristics, or pay of the job holder.

In practice, use of the Hay method typically involves three steps:

1. Each job's responsibilities and duties are described.
2. Each job is rated, using the Hay guide charts. (For a more complete description of the method, see Exhibit 3.)
3. The organization's compensation practice is identified by plotting the points for each job versus the salary of the actual incumbent(s) of the job (see Exhibit 4).

Companies typically use this information to compare their practice with that of other companies; to set a salary policy line (that is, so many dollars for so many job points); to build pay ranges around that salary policy to reflect different performance levels of the job; and to manage salary administration.

The Dilemma

The members of the NIKE compensation subcommittee found themselves in a dilemma. There was a clear need for a more formal, structured system of salary administration, and in many ways the Hay system seemed to fit the bill. Yet there was also an undercurrent of discomfort: Did such a system fit NIKE? Managers and employees voiced several concerns to various committee members:

— The people who work for me and the jobs they fill are unique; they don't fit a pattern determined by the outside world.

— Jobs at NIKE are really defined by the person and built around an individual's competences; they don't fit some mathematical formula.

— I thought the NIKE policy was to pay the person, not the job.

— If we start telling people what to do in their jobs, that's exactly what we'll get—people doing jobs. The strength of this company has always been the willingness of its people to pitch in where they were needed or had an interest.

In spite of these comments there was a genuine sense that managers needed some guidance in this area. One top manager noted:

Deep down, I believe that many managers want some help, some guidance on how to handle the situation. There is a lot of talk about resistance to policies, but I'm not sure whether that really exists or if it's a myth that people have come to believe in.

It was in this environment that the subcommittee had to reach a conclusion and present its recommendation to President Bob Woodell. "We all agree that *something* needs to be done on this compensation issue," said Chairman Dale Wahl. "The question is, *what?*"

Exhibit 1

Excerpts from Knight's Memo

To: List   From: Philip Knight

Re: Fiscal Year 1984 Salary Increases   Date: June 6, 1983

In considering raises for Fiscal Year 1984 we want to be fair and realistic. We want to reward performance and correct inequities if and where they exist. We do not want to reward employees who are not performing acceptably or who are overpaid for their job function. The mere fact that an employee has continued to be employed by the company is not justification alone for a salary adjustment. With this in mind we have developed the following broad guidelines to help in making salary recommendations:

Step 1.   *JOB PERFORMANCE*
           Percentage raise of 7/1/82 Salary

           0%   Below minimal job expectations.
           5%   At job expectations.
           6–9% Above job expectations.

Step 2.   If the job is not being paid appropriately, an additional adjustment may be recommended, taking into consideration:

           a. Comparable job within the company.
           b. Comparable job in the geographical area.
           c. Comparable job within the industry.

Step 3.   You may consider an additional adjustment for an employee who has received an interim promotion or additional responsibilities for which no increase in compensation was received.

Remember: Please take a careful look at your recommendations. Not everyone should or can receive a superior rating or a high raise. Each of you is responsible for involving only the people necessary to complete this task. Please recognize the sensitivity of this issue.

These guidelines have been incorporated into the attached salary form in order to assist you in making your recommendations. We have also attached a copy of the Portland Area Cross-Industry Survey of salaries in which NIKE participated. This will give you a reference for benchmark type positions only.

Although a final decision has not been made, it is possible that we will want to especially recognize a select number of individuals. Please designate any employee(s) who has performed *extraordinarily and has made* a special contribution to the company. Make this designation with a "star" by his/her name on the salary form. You may be contacted for further comment.

Return your recommendations by Monday, *June 13, 1983.*

These recommendations will be reviewed by a salary committee which I shall appoint.

Exhibit 2

Compensation Objectives at NIKE

A. A compensation system should allow NIKE to achieve *internal equity* in salaries—equivalent pay ranges for equivalent jobs.

B. Salaries should be in a *competitive* range with similar jobs in the external labor market.

C. The system should be *flexible* to accommodate the broad and rapid changes in NIKE's organization and personnel placement.

D. The system should allow top management to *control* labor costs:

    1. Set the salary policy line.
    2. Control overall cost (the ability to pay).
    3. Control individual department costs.

E. Pay should be *related to performance* and/or contribution to the success of the organization.

F. The system should be designed to be *consistent* in its application.

G. Employees should be able to perceive the system as being *"fair."*

H. The system should be *easy to administer.*

I. The system should allow for *delegation of individual salary decisions* to the appropriate managerial level.

J. The salary administration system should *work in concert with other forms of compensation* established at NIKE.

Exhibit 3

The Hay Guide Charts

The Hay guide charts are used to assign points to a job. The three charts are built around three significant factors common to all jobs: know-how, problem solving, and accountability. Those factors are described below. An illustrative chart is attached.

Know-How

Know-how is the sum total of every kind of capability or skill, however acquired, needed for acceptable job performance. Its three dimensions are the requirements for:

— Practical procedures, specialized techniques, and knowledge within occupational fields, commercial functions, and professional or scientific disciplines.
— Integrating and harmonizing simultaneous achievement of diversified functions within managerial situations occurring in operating, technical, support, or administrative fields. This involves, in some combination, skills in planning, organizing, executing, controlling, and evaluating and may be exercised consultatively (about management) as well as executively.
— Active, practicing person-to-person skills in work with other people.

Problem Solving

Problem solving is the original self-starting use of know-how required to identify, define, and resolve problems. "You think with what you know in the job." This is true of even the most creative work. The raw material of any thinking is knowledge of facts, principles, and means. For that reason, *problem solving is treated as a percentage of know-how.*

Problem solving has two dimensions:

— The environment in which thinking takes place.
— The challenge presented by the thinking to be done.

Accountability

Accountability is defined as the answerability for action and its consequences. It is the measured effect of the job on end results of the organization. It has three dimensions in the following order of importance:

— Freedom to act—the extent of personal, procedural, or systematic guidance or control of actions in relation to the primary emphasis of the job.
— Job impact on end results—the extent to which the job can directly affect actions necessary to produce results within its primary emphasis.
— Magnitude—the portion of the total organization encompassed by the primary emphasis of the job. This is usually, but not necessarily, reflected by the annual revenue or expense dollars associated with the area in which the job has its primary emphasis.

Exhibit 3 (concluded)   *Illustrative*

GUIDE [HAY] CHART — KNOW-HOW

● ● M A N A G E R I A L   K N O W - H O W

●●● Human Relations Skills

KNOW-HOW		I. None or Minimal			II. Related			III. Diverse			IV. Broad			V. Comprehensive			VI. Overall Corporate Mgmt.		
		1	2	3	1	2	3	1	2	3	1	2	3	1	2	3	1	2	3
A. Primary		50	57	66	66	76	87	87	100	115	115	132	152	152	175	200	200	230	264
		57	66	76	76	87	100	100	115	132	132	152	175	175	200	230	230	264	304
		66	76	87	87	100	115	115	132	152	152	175	200	200	230	264	264	304	350
B. Elementary Vocational		66	76	87	87	100	115	115	132	152	152	175	200	200	230	264	264	304	350
		76	87	100	100	115	132	132	152	175	175	200	230	230	264	304	304	350	400
		87	100	115	115	132	152	152	175	200	200	230	264	264	304	350	350	400	460
C. Vocational		87	100	115	115	132	152	152	175	200	200	230	264	264	304	350	350	400	460
		100	115	132	132	152	175	175	200	230	230	264	304	304	350	400	400	450	528
		115	132	152	152	175	200	200	230	264	264	304	350	350	400	460	460	528	608
D. Advanced Vocational		115	132	152	152	175	200	200	230	264	264	304	350	350	400	460	460	528	608
		132	152	175	175	200	230	230	264	304	304	350	400	400	460	528	528	608	700
		152	175	200	200	230	264	264	304	350	350	400	460	460	528	608	608	700	800
E. Basic Technical Specialized		152	175	200	200	230	264	264	304	350	350	400	460	460	528	608	608	700	800
		175	200	230	230	264	304	304	350	400	400	460	528	528	608	700	700	800	920
		200	230	264	264	304	350	350	400	460	460	528	608	608	700	800	800	920	1056
F. Seasoned Technical, Specialized or Diversed		200	230	264	264	304	350	350	400	460	460	528	608	608	700	800	800	920	1056
		230	264	304	304	350	400	400	460	528	528	608	700	700	800	920	920	1056	1216
		264	304	350	350	400	460	460	528	608	608	700	800	800	920	1056	1056	1216	1400
G. Technical, Specialized or Diversed Mastery		264	304	350	350	400	460	460	528	608	608	700	800	800	920	1056	1056	1216	1400
		304	350	400	400	460	528	528	608	700	700	800	920	920	1056	1216	1216	1400	1600
		350	400	460	460	528	608	608	700	800	800	920	1056	1056	1216	1400	1400	1600	1840
H. Professional Mastery		350	400	460	460	528	608	608	700	800	800	920	1056	1056	1216	1400	1400	1600	1840
		400	460	528	528	608	700	700	800	920	920	1056	1216	1216	1400	1600	1600	1840	2112
		460	528	608	608	700	800	800	920	1056	1056	1216	1400	1400	1600	1840	1840	2112	2432

Row labels (right margin): A, B, C, D, E, F, G, H

Left margin groupings: PRACTICAL PROCEDURES — SPECIALIZED TECHNIQUES — SCIENTIFIC DISCIPLINES

Exhibit 4

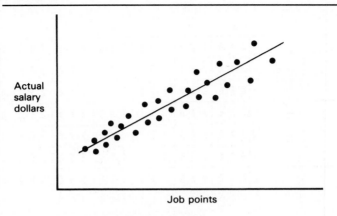

Actual
salary
dollars

Job points

●   Dot represents person.

———   The line, in essence, represents the
organization's salary practice.

Market position

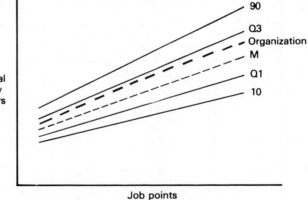

Actual
salary
dollars

Job points

———   Distribution of salary practice lines for
companies using Hay.

– – –   Salary practice of the organization using
this information.

NIKE (F)

The Apparel Division

We don't know the fashion apparel business very well yet, and those guys in New York and San Francisco play that game better than we do. But we've got the athletes. The NIKE name is valid; it's authentic. And that is a feeling that companies like Levi's and LaCoste can't project. It's not that people have to buy the authentic apparel. They just need to identify with it, and then we've won.

Bob Woodell

NIKE's activewear apparel division had developed in the shadow of the much larger footwear operation. But it had grown spectacularly, from $2 million in sales in fiscal 1979 to $107 million in fiscal 1983, and was seen as a major source of growth for the company in the 1980s. A March 1983 article in *The New York Times* quoted NIKE's chairman, Phil Knight, as saying, "There are still opportunities in the United States for further growth in our shoe sales. But the key to our growth beyond the next few years is the performance of our apparel and foreign operations," and noted that some analysts believed the apparel division's revenue potential was around $1 billion annually.[1]

Vice President David Chang, who had joined NIKE in 1981 to manage its China project in footwear manufacturing, was assigned to head

---

[1] "NIKE Pins Hopes for Growth on Foreign Sales and Apparel," *The New York Times,* March 24, 1983, p. D5.

Copyright © 1984 by the President and Fellows of Harvard College
Harvard Business School case 385–039

the apparel division in June 1983. Returning to Beaverton in early October after the fall trade shows in California, Chang reported:

> Market demand for our product is smoking, and some people in the trade say we can be as big as we want to be—if we can deliver. But I'm finding, and I think we're all realizing, that the apparel business is very much more complicated than the footwear side. If we're going to make this thing really go, we have a lot of tough work ahead to build the kind of strong foundation under apparel that we have under our shoe business.

This case describes the competitive arena in which NIKE conducted its apparel business, traces the brief history of the apparel division, describes its strategy and operations, and presents management views on the challenges—operational and strategic—facing the division.

The Activewear Apparel Business

The U.S. apparel industry was characterized by slow overall growth and fierce competition. Sales reached approximately $50 billion (wholesale) in 1982. Some of the approximately 15,000 domestic competitors were fully integrated, but most (such as the many "cut-and-sew" vendors) specialized in one part of the business. And most were small. In this industry a "big" firm might have sales of $100 million. There were a few giants, however, such as Levi Strauss & Co., with 1982 sales of $2.6 billion built on its well-known base in jeans.

The apparel industry was highly labor-intensive—indeed the term *sweatshop* was still used by labor officials to describe many small operations. Imports from low-wage countries (primarily Korea, Taiwan, and Hong Kong) had grown rapidly (to $8 billion in 1982), and the domestic industry had lobbied hard and successfully for the establishment of quotas on imports from those countries (called Multi-Fiber Agreements).

Apparel was a fashion business, traditionally led from the fashion centers of Paris and New York. Companies in the high-fashion business introduced as many as six new lines each year, though the overall industry was keyed to the fall and spring seasons. The business was fast paced, with a few leaders and many followers quick to knock off emerging successful fashions with copies geared to their own price ranges.

Apparel items fell along a continuum from "dresswear" (for dress-up and formal occasions) to "sportswear" (for almost any other occasion). Since the 1960s sportswear had grown at the expense of dresswear, as the American life-style had become more informal. In the late 70s the fitness boom led to disproportionate growth in the activewear segment of sportswear. Although meaningful data on market segments were difficult to obtain, sources estimated that activewear sales were at least $6 billion in 1982 and growing rapidly.

The activewear buyer for a large department store reported:

The dominant action today is at the activewear end of sportswear. We see two segments there. The first is what I'd call authentic activewear— stuff that is functional, can actually be worn for physical activity, though it may be used for street wear too. The customers tend to be young, more active people. There's still some room in this area, but the big opportunity is in nonauthentic activewear, the ath-leisure stuff. These clothes are really an athletic interpretation and are not designed for actual athletic use. They tend to be more fashion oriented and more expensive, and they attract customers who are generally older and more affluent.

Observers acknowledged that clothing inherently had less potential than footwear to improve athletic performance or safety through technical features. Many believed, however, that certain materials, such as the rainproof but breathable Gore-Tex fabric, could contribute to performance, as could some elements of design; properly located seams on a running singlet (running shorts with an underlining sewn in), for example, could avoid chafing in the long distance events.

From the researchers' perspective competitors in the activewear business fell into three groups. At the authentic end of the spectrum a number of small ($3–$30 million) specialty outfits developed and sold high-performance clothing for athletes. These included Frank Shorter Sports Wear (running), CB Sports (skiing), and Fila (tennis). Their products were sold in specialty shops and the better department stores, primarily to serious athletes and secondarily to users attracted by the brand name.

The second group, at the ath-leisure end of the spectrum, comprised the major sportswear houses, such as Levi Strauss, Izod LaCoste, and Merona, and numerous smaller sportswear companies. These companies brought an expertise to the sportswear business and often an established apparel brand name to the game, but they lacked athletic identification.

The third group was the athletic footwear companies. Following the lead of Adidas, almost every major athletic footwear company had introduced sports clothing. Some now saw it as a potentially significant business in itself. For example, it was estimated that Adidas derived 40 percent of its $2 billion sales from its apparel line, which consisted of a full range of authentic and ath-leisure activewear emblazoned with its "three stripes" logo.

Observers agreed that a strong brand awareness was a necessity for a footwear company as it took the plunge into apparel. "Fundamentally," one explained, "the brand name conjures up an authentic, athletic image that appeals to the athlete, for his or her on- and off-the-track wear, and to the consumer who doesn't actively participate but who values a sense of identification with athletes and the active life-style." Apparel was quite a different business, however. "It is much harder to deal with fashion than function," sighed one company president who had successfully made that transition with his consumer product:

> It's hopes and dreams rather than tangible benefits; it's a different perspective about time and money, with shorter product lives and more unpredictability; it's a different kind of research. And the transition we've gone through raises tough questions about managers: do you go with people who know the company or bring in people who know the business?

NIKE's Entry into the Apparel Business

The first NIKE apparel was a logo-imprinted T-shirt, offered to athletes as a form of free advertising. As the company paper reported:

> A big hit at the 1972 Olympic trials was the appearance of custom-printed NIKE logo T-shirts. The Olympic rules at the time prohibited trademarks of any kind from being worn on the track, but NIKE was so new that nobody suspected it was a trademark for anything. So athletes (and even some unsuspecting race officials) paraded around the infield in the new NIKE logo!

In the late 1970s, as it became apparent that the company would eventually "run out of feet," activewear apparel emerged as a major potential growth area, and the company entered the business more seriously with a product line for the 1979 fall season. Knight recalled:

> It was a natural extension—the same accounts, the same customers—and Adidas had already done it. So the question was not whether, but how. At first we tried to do it with insiders, but we just didn't know the business. We thought the hard part was design, for example—until we tried to get the stuff made! We then hired a heavyweight from the industry. He didn't know NIKE, and he sure didn't listen, but he did get us started.

In a departure from NIKE's usual practice the introductory apparel was aimed at the lower middle class market, and it was not a great success. The outside manager left, and Bob Woodell was assigned to the division in early 1980. He recalled:

> The NIKE name stands for sports—for competition and winning and champions. If we could design garments that had enough of that flavor in them, garments that conveyed the NIKE name—of course, they'd have to be styled well enough and made well—then we believed we could drive them through the marketplace.

Woodell's assessment proved accurate. Sales rose rapidly, as shown in Table 1. The apparel business was profitable after the first year, although margins, unreported but said to be increasing, were still less than those in the footwear business.

Table 1

NIKE Apparel Division

Fiscal Year	Sales ($ millions)	Styles	SKUs*
1979	$ 2	N.A.	N.A.
1980	8	45	480
1981	33	115	1,464
1982	70	215	3,272
1983 (est.)	100	270	4,774

* SKU = A stockkeeping unit measures the total number of product variations—not only style but color and size as well.
Source: Company records.

Current Product Line and Strategy

The product line, too, grew rapidly. By 1983 it included a full line of authentic performance clothing (such as running shorts, singlets, warm-ups, and rain suits; soccer shorts and jerseys; and tennis outfits) and comfortable ath-leisure wear (including shirts, sweaters, jackets and pants) for men, women, youths, and children (see Exhibit 1 for pictures of representative items). NIKE apparel was priced in the middle to upper-middle segment: below that of specialty companies such as Fila and roughly on a par with Adidas and the sportswear houses.

Both the design and the manufactured quality of the line improved steadily from season to season, but managers recognized that its enormous market success was due far more to the strength of the NIKE brand name than to the line itself. Woodell emphasized, however, that "we eventually want to put something back into the NIKE name, not just draw it down."

The footwear business had been built on a pyramid model: a high-priced, technically sophisticated product sold through smaller, more specialized dealers at the narrow peak and a lower priced, less sophisticated product sold through larger, more volume-oriented dealers at the far broader base. The apparel business model was much flatter. "Our marketing strategy," one manager commented, "has been keyed to the bigger guys, the department stores, rather than to the smaller guys, the specialty stores. I think there's an increasing awareness that we've perhaps strayed a bit in doing this."

The apparel product line included several performance items, such as running shorts distinguished by their light weight. There was significantly less differentiation, in features and price, between the ath-leisure and performance items in apparel than in footwear. In part this reflected the natural limits on what high-tech apparel could do. "There just aren't many gizmos you can put in a pair of shorts or a singlet," one manager said. But it was also true that NIKE had only recently begun to focus dollars and talent on developing serious high-tech apparel products. Some managers spoke of an eventual "Exeter" for apparel, for example, and noted with excitement current work with new fabrics that held promise for performance applications.

At the other end of the product line the company had introduced several leisure pants models (see Exhibit 1) in 1982, and managers expected to mount a significant effort to develop this market segment. "These pants," one said, "are the equivalent of our $25 shoe. There is a big market out there."

Current Apparel Operations

NIKE's apparel business was housed in a one-story office and warehouse complex in Beaverton, about two miles from the home office (where Woodell was located) and across the road from the international division building (where Knight was located). Apparel had always been physically separate from the rest of the company. "It used to be considered a dungeon," said product design manager Mary Anne White, who had been with the division from the beginning, "but now it's seen as a hot part of the business."

In June 1983 Vice President David Chang was named to head the division, taking over from apparel marketing manager Keith Sparks (who had served on an interim basis since January, when Woodell left to assume responsibility for NIKE's overall worldwide marketing). The division was functionally organized, with four managers reporting to Chang (see Exhibit 2 for a sketch of the organization in September 1983). "It's an intense group," Chang noted, "with relatively limited functional expertise but with a lot of desire and the willingness to work hard." Most of the managerial group had been drawn from NIKE's footwear operation; a few were hired from the outside.

The development of the NIKE apparel product line was a complex process that began with line direction meetings and ended 16 months later with shipment of product to the retailers for the fall or spring season (see Figure 1).[2]

NIKE used a team approach to design rather than relying on a single "guru." The design group for each product category—"youngish people who can relate to the market"—developed and modified items on the basis of factors such as performance requirements, color trends, new materials, and an overriding sense of the "NIKE look"—an elusive

---

[2] Managers noted that each season had its own requirement for colors and materials based on the prevailing weather in addition to changes in design, colors, and materials required by fashion.

Figure 1

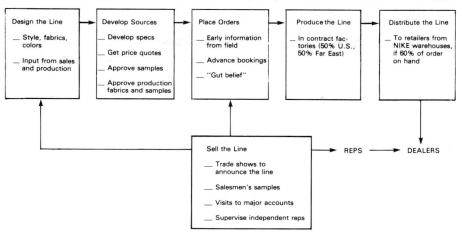

Source: Researchers' interpretation.

yet real sense described by Mary Anne White as "an athletic look, one that an athlete would want to associate him- or herself with." The line was aimed at the young person (aged 14 to 25). Initial line directions were set, and final decisions were made, by the senior management of the apparel division.

The job of translating design samples into products in volume production was aggravatingly complex, often involving many time-consuming cycles of vendor sample submission, NIKE rejection, and further vendor sample submission. One of the most vexing problems was getting commercial quantities of different fabrics dyed by different sources to the exact colors required, but the construction of the garments themselves could also be extremely difficult. Managers acknowledged that the division could alleviate some of this problem by tightening up in-house procedures, such as reducing late design changes.

NIKE had in-house facilities to sew design samples, test fabrics and colors, and assemble the kits sent to vendors to solicit price quotes. Unlike the footwear operation, however, the apparel division owned no manufacturing facilities.

NIKE sourced its apparel line from both domestic and Far East cut-and-sew and integrated vendors. Managers had found domestic sources both expensive and unreliable and were gradually shifting production to factories in the Far East (at the sacrifice of some lead time).[3]

---

[3] Lead time, defined as the elapsed time from the placement of a complete order with the factory to receipt of the goods in the NIKE warehouse, was about 120 days from domestic sources, 135–150 days from Far East sources.

As it had done in footwear, NIKE sent some of its people overseas to work closely with the contract factories.

While less technical than shoe manufacturing, apparel production was far more complicated. "Apparel is typically sold as an outfit—shorts, singlet, and warm-up suit," one manager explained. "But we have to source apparel as individual items because that's the way the factories work. So we'll have pieces of that outfit coming from different factories, often made of different fabrics, that not only have to match in color but have to get to the dealers at roughly the same time." Production was further complicated by apparel quotas. Chang explained:

> Our government sets quotas on imported apparel. One problem here is that the precise definitions of particular classes of items can change or be interpreted differently by Customs, and we have no control over that. Within the foreign country, the governments typically allocate blocks of their quota to the individual factories, which then allocate the quota to their customers. We're relatively new to the business, and the factories tend to give their quota to historical performers; also we find that factories want to use their units of quota on high-priced items like ski jackets rather than on a lower priced warm-up. We just haven't had the chance to build up the credibility and relationships that we have with the footwear factories.

It was particularly difficult to arrange the manufacture of custom orders (including promotional orders), such as team warm-up suits in a college's particular color combination. Factory order minimums were often far larger than NIKE's volume in these custom products.

Whereas footwear managers could be guided by "the knowns of footwear Futures bookings and a long-lived product's track record," apparel managers had to order product from vendors primarily on the basis of "gut belief," as production forecasting manager Dave Dickey said with a sigh.

NIKE developed an apparel Advance Booking program for major customers (over $100,000 per season wholesale), which required that an order be placed four and a half months before the target delivery date. Although it did not guarantee delivery, as footwear Futures did, the program offered better terms than a standard order (an additional 3 percent cash discount and 2 percent advertising allowance) and a "first shot" at the available merchandise; it also allowed the buyer to revise or cancel 10 percent of his order without penalty. In fiscal 1983 about 25 percent of NIKE's apparel orders were placed under this program.

NIKE apparel was sold primarily in department stores (ranging from Filene's to J. C. Penney) and in the large athletic chains (such as Herman's and Footlocker). Significantly smaller amounts were sold in the smaller athletic specialty shops and in some apparel specialty shops. The company offered terms similar to those of competitors such as Adidas but different from those of the sportswear houses (for example, NIKE did not include any "markdown money"—a built-in allowance for product obsolescence). The apparel sales organization worked through the same independent rep agencies that sold NIKE footwear, although the agencies were usually forced to hire salespeople especially for apparel. Reps noted that the apparel sale was quite different, requiring a call on the activewear, rather than footwear, buyer with far bulkier and more extensive product samples.

In addition the company attended the major apparel trade shows around the country, where a highlight was often the NIKE fashion show. "Three years ago," one manager chuckled, "fashion shows were unheard of at NIKE. The company felt that they weren't NIKE and that *fashion* wasn't a word in our vocabulary." An initial, traditional show had been stimulated by an outside proposal, however, and was well received. So the idea stuck, but the format evolved rapidly. As one manager explained, "Models walking down a runway turned into a fast-paced, energetic workout show. We began to feature the clothes in the way they were designed to be worn." (See Exhibit 3 for a description of a NIKE revue at one trade show.)

The apparel division did little promotion and advertising itself, although it was beginning to contract with athletes to promote apparel specifically and to advertise (see Exhibit 4 for an advertisement that appeared in magazines such as *Seventeen* and *Rolling Stone*).

The Delivery Problem

NIKE had a significant apparel delivery problem that concerned many managers, including Knight and Woodell. Although retailers put up with NIKE's delivery performance in its first years in the apparel business (in part because the industry as a whole had a poor record), they were becoming less tolerant. In addition it was estimated that the company's apparel sales would increase by 50–100 percent if the company could simply deliver all orders in a reasonably timely fashion.

The problem was perceived to be very complex. As one apparel manager said, "We've been calling it a production problem and sort of laying it on their shoulders. But as we start to pull it apart, it becomes clear that the problem is deeper and touches all of us." Managers pointed to a range of problems, both within departments (the need for a quicker design process, the challenge of import quotas, the desire for better sales forecasts) and linking departments (adapting the design process to take advantage of available quotas, developing a tighter design-to-sourcing transition, and focusing selling efforts on items being produced).

In anticipation of a lengthy Far Eastern trip, Knight began focusing on the quota issue in the summer and fall of 1983. To get the ball rolling on an operating level, Woodell called a day and a half off-site meeting in early October with Ron Nelson (footwear production and NIKE old-timer), Chang, and about 20 hand-picked middle managers from the several apparel operating groups. Managers reported that this first meeting represented a big step toward developing a broader, more common understanding of the overall problem. Woodell's focus was explicitly on the "big picture," although he expected that operational actions would be identified and implemented along the way. A decision was made after the first meeting, for example, to hire a couple of people to work in the field with the color vendors to speed up the color approval process. The meeting ended in a spirit of "let's do this together." One manager reported:

> I got the guys from my department together after the first half day, and we tried to figure out what Woodell was trying to do. We finally realized that we weren't there to fight for our department. We'd been picked as NIKE middle managers to help solve this problem.

Describing this meeting to the researchers Woodell commented:

> This is a classic example of what Strasser calls "a real life case study." We've got to solve this delivery issue, just got to. And it's going to take time. But we've got to pull some people along, not only to contribute to the solution but to observe the process and to learn it so they can do it on their own. Because that's NIKE.

Looking Ahead

"Apparel is like a big jigsaw puzzle for us," Woodell noted. "We've tried to put the pieces together, but they don't quite fit, so we'll have to do a little scissoring. But if we can solve it, there's no one that has the synergism with footwear, the brand name, the promo clout, and the advertising clout that we do."

"In footwear," Chang reiterated, "we have the dependable, economic sources of supply, and we have the Futures program. We've got to build the basics in apparel, too." Continuing, he said:

> And I think we'll have to broaden our target a bit. We've certainly got to do a little more with high-tech products. We don't like to admit it, but at the other end we're going to be dragged, probably kicking and screaming, into a more fashion-oriented world. But there are opportunities there, too. For example, if we added some product for the 25- to 40-year-old, we'd be in a much higher margin business.

"Innovation is our real niche," Knight concluded. "That's truer in footwear than apparel—there will never be a pair of Air-Shorts, as Strasser keeps reminding me—but there is a lot you can do in apparel." Knight continued:

> The company I really respect in apparel is Descente, a Japanese company. They have worked more with fabrics than anybody. They've made a skintight sprint suit, for example, that they say will help someone run a tenth of a second faster. That is what I'd like our apparel division to be.
>
> Apparel has evolved as a tag-on operation, and now we're wrestling to get it back. We're making good progress but are still miles from where we would like it to be.

Exhibit 1

The Apparel Product Line

A: Performance Products

Source: Company records.

Exhibit 1 (concluded)

B. Ath-Leisure Products

Source: Company records.

Exhibit 2

Apparel Division Organization

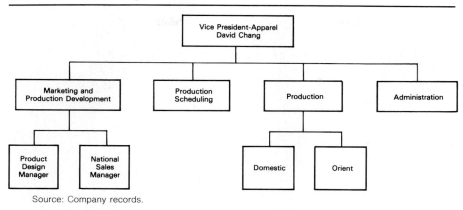

Source: Company records.

Exhibit 3

Researchers' Description of a NIKE Revue

The lights dimmed to signal the start of *The NIKE Revue,* and the 700–800 NIKE dealers, sales reps, and managers in New York for the fall 1983 trade show gathered around the large wooden cabaret dance floor. As the driving disco beat began, the first models—young, energetic men and women clad in NIKE apparel and shoes—jogged out from behind the curtain and began an active, choreographed aerobics routine that flowed into a series of sprint-type warm-ups. This group was followed by a circus of youngsters who tumbled and unicycled out onto the floor. Among them an 8-year-old acrobat performed a series of backward and forward flips. A 6-year-old juggler created a blur of flying rings and bottles.

For 30 minutes a carefully coordinated stream of performers—grouped, one realized later when reflecting upon the show, around product themes such as running apparel or children's apparel—mesmerized the audience, frequently eliciting spontaneous cheers and applause. The triumphant finale featured a New York breakdance team* in bright red NIKE "Wind Runner" suits presenting a stunning display of coordinated movement deeply tied to the pounding beat.

As people slowly relaxed, caught their breath, and turned back to the bar and hors d'oeuvres, one buyer leaned over to another and exclaimed, "That was great!" His friend smiled back, "They've come a long way!"

Down by the floor with a group of NIKE apparel managers, NIKE President Bob Woodell smiled and said, with a shake of his head, "This is a long way from where this company started!" But he was pleased with the show. "We don't just sell rags or shoes," he shouted to the researchers over the din of the continuing party. "We sell magic, excitement, a spirit of winning, of doing your best. The kids in this country know that. We have to put on this kind of show so that these dealers and reps can feel what that means, can catch that excitement."

* Breakdancing is a stylized movement form that developed in New York. It is characterized, in one form, by fast robotic movements and, in another, by synchronized acrobatics.

Exhibit 4

Apparel Advertisement

Source: Company records.

NIKE (F1)

Apparel: The Decision to Grow

During the week following Thanksgiving 1983 NIKE's top managers (Knight, Woodell, Strasser, and Hayes), joined by Nelson and Werschkul, spent several days at a meeting on the Oregon coast grappling with the idea of "igniting" a very aggressive effort to "grow" the company's apparel business. The idea had emerged a week or two earlier as an outgrowth of a discussion on the apparel delivery problem. Immediate action would be required if the effort was to have a meaningful impact upon the fall 1984 selling season (see Exhibit 1). That group concluded their session with the decision that the effort was worth a shot.

On Friday (December 2) several new arrivals (including Lauridsen, Chang, Porter, and Hochhalter) joined the coastal retreat. Woodell outlined the original group's thinking and tentative plan and asked, "What do you think?"

Background

The apparel division's sales had grown rapidly (to $107 million in fiscal 1983), but the division faced a complex delivery problem. Two critical factors emerged during the fall discussions: (1) the relative lack of useful production forecasting information and (2) the relatively weak relationships with a number of NIKE's production sources, due, management

Copyright © 1984 by the President and Fellows of Harvard College
Harvard Business School case 385–040

believed, to the short life of the division and its small size. The contrast to the footwear business, with its strong Futures program and solid, long-term factory relationships, was striking.

And therein lay the motivation for more rapid growth. In outline, senior management's notion was that the division would attempt to grow faster than originally planned (seeking a rousing 100 percent rather than 33 percent annual growth or an additional $100 million in sales over the existing budget figure) in order to reach a size at which it would be a significant factor with the retailing community and with production factories; a "real" Futures program (providing deep discounts—up to 14 percent—for early orders) would be instituted to provide timely and useful production forecasting data.[1] This effort would be supported by an expanded apparel advertising and sales program.

The concept had been reviewed with several apparel division managers and an effort made to develop quick quantitative projections. Management estimated, for instance, that in order to achieve incremental sales of $100 million during the next fiscal year, they would need to invest an additional $15 to $20 million in inventory and that annual expenses would increase as follows:[2]

	Millions of Dollars
Additional sourcing costs	$ 5
Additional sales, advertising, promotion	17
Additional other operating expenses	3
	$25

See the Nike (E3) case for the company's most recent financial statements to put these figures in perspective.

The time frame was exceedingly tight: to affect the fall 1984 selling season, it would be necessary to develop a program within days of the early December meeting, to pull out all the stops in an effort to bring in substantial orders on the new Futures program by February 1, and to locate sources for the additional production. Could it be done? If so, was it the right thing to do? There were many questions. Was the market for the products actually there? (The tentative plans were to expand production of existing items.) Would the program have any retailer credibility given the recent poor delivery performance? Should the

---

[1] The current Advance Booking program accounted for about 25 percent of apparel sales in fiscal 1983. It provided a 5 percent discount for orders placed four to five months ahead of delivery date.

[2] Note that these increased costs are in addition to the normal percent-of-sales figures for these expenses.

program be approached more slowly, perhaps aimed at the spring 1985 season?

But there was an air of excitement, a desire to attack, a feeling that bold moves were needed, and a willingness to incur the necessary increase in short-term marketing and production expenses and to throw several "horses" into the fray (it was expected that Hayes, Nelson, and Joyce would be "loaned" to apparel for at least six months).

Of course, there were major risks in this effort. If the program was not accepted by the major retailers, the financial consequences would be painful. NIKE's reputation would suffer if products were not delivered, and morale would be hurt if people made an all-out effort without success. Furthermore, success in this first stage would be only the first step toward a longer term positioning in the apparel business.

Woodell repeated, "What do you think?"

Exhibit 1

Apparel Season Timeline (Fall 1984)

	Original Plan			*Proposed Aggressive Plan*
3/83	Begin fall 1984 line design	March	–	
		April	–	
		May	–	
		June	–	
		July	–	
		Aug.	–	

Exhibit 1 (concluded)

9/83	Set fall 1984 line	Sept.	–		
		Oct.	–		
		Nov.	–		
12/15/83	First production buy (40% of total)	Dec.	–	12/2/83	Management meetings
				12/4–31	Announce program; find additional production capacity, increase 12/15 buy ($ not %)
1/15/84	12 sample sets complete; present to sales force	Jan.	–	1/1/84	12 sample sets done; introduce to sales force; start meeting with all major accounts
		Feb.	–	2/1/84	First Futures orders due (7/1–8/1 delivery)
2/15/84	Second production buy (30% of total)			2/15/84	Second production buy (based on Futures orders)
		March	–	3/1/84	Second Futures order due (9/1–10/1 delivery)
3/15/84	Advance bookings due (for season)			3/15/84	Third production buy
4/1/84	Final production buy (30% of total)	April	–	4/1/84	Third Futures order done (11/1–12/1 delivery)
				4/15/84	Final production buy
		May	–		
		June	–		
		July	–		
7/1/84	1st delivery			7/1/84	1st delivery
		Aug.	–		

CONCLUSION

In Retrospect: Strategic Management and Corporate Governance

Many of the cases in this book have given you an opportunity to observe the range, unity, and interrelation of the concepts and subconcepts essential to the conscious formulation and implementation of a strategy governing the planned development of a total organization. The idea and its components have now been quite carefully and separately explored. It becomes appropriate at this point, as you reflect on the cases you have studied, to return to the view of corporate strategy not as a concept complete and still but as an organizational process forever in motion, never ending. The merger of the process and substantive content of the concept of strategy takes us to the principal problems of corporate governance and the responsibilities of the board of directors.

Strategy as a Process

For the purposes of analysis, as you have already noted, we have presented strategy formulation as being reasonably complete before implementation begins, as if it made sense to know where we are going before we start. Yet we know that we often move without knowing where we will end; the determination of purpose is in reality in dynamic interrelation with implementation. Implementation is itself a complex process including many subprocesses of thought and organization which introduce into prior resolution tentativeness and doubt and lead us to change direction.

That strategy formulation is itself a *process of organization,* rather than the masterly conception of a single mind, must finally become clear. We introduced you to it when we were considering organization design.

929

Many facts of life conspire to complicate the simple notion that persons or organizations should decide what they can, want, and should do and then do it. The sheer difficulty of recognizing and reconciling uncertain environmental opportunity, unclear corporate capabilities and limited resources, submerged personal values, and emerging aspirations to social responsibility suggests that at least in complicated organizations strategy must be an organizational achievement and may often be unfinished. Important as leadership is, the range of strategic alternatives which must be considered in a decentralized or diversified company exceeds what one person can conceive of. As technology develops, chief executives cannot usually maintain their own technical knowledge at the level necessary for accurate personal critical discriminations. As a firm extends its activities internationally, the senior person in the company cannot learn in detail the cultural and geographical conditions which require local adaptation of both ends and means.

As in all administrative processes managing the process becomes a function distinct from performing it. The principal strategists of technically or otherwise complex organizations therefore manage a strategic decision-making process rather than make strategic decisions. When they "make" a decision approving proposals originating from appraisals of need and opportunity made by others, they are ratifying decisions emerging from lower echelons in which the earliest and most junior participants may have played importantly decisive roles.[1] The structure of the organization, as observed earlier, may predetermine the nature of subsequent changes in strategy. In this sense strategy formulation is an activity widely shared in the hierarchy of management, rather than being concentrated at its highest levels.

Participation in strategy formulation, as we have observed before, may begin with the market manager who sees a new product opportunity or the analyst who first arranges the assumptions that make possible a 30 percent return on investment in a new venture. (A return-on-investment hurdle may in itself contribute to a distortion of strategy by becoming illusory goal rather than achieved result.) Because of the response to reward and punishment systems considered earlier, the strategic alternatives generated in autonomous corporate units may be the product of competition for limited resources or of divisional empire building.

The strategy process, with its evolutionary, structural, analytical, and emotional components, encounters then the real-life challenges for which conscious professional management has been devised. Opportunism remains the principal counterforce; it need not be put down, for it can be turned to use. In the course of an established strategy, changing only imperceptibly in response to changing capabilities and changing

---

[1] See Joseph L. Bower, *Managing the Resource Allocation Process* (Boston: Division of Research, Harvard Business School, 1970).

market environments, sudden opportunity or major tactical decision may intrude to distract attention from distant goals to immediate gain. Thus the opportunity for a computer firm to merge with a large finance company may seem too good to pass up, but the strategy of the company will change with the acquisition or its ability to implement its strategy will be affected. A strategy may suddenly be rationalized to mean something very different from what was originally intended because of the opportunism which at the beginning of this book we declared the conceptual enemy of strategy. The necessity to accommodate unexpected opportunity in the course of continuous strategic decision is a crucial aspect of process. Accepting or refusing specific opportunity will strengthen or weaken the capability of an organization and thus alter what is probably the most crucial determinant of strategy in an organization with already developed market power.

Managing the Process

It is clear then that the strategic process should not be left untended. Study of the cases and ideas of this book usually leads to acceptance of the need for a continuous process of strategic decision as the basis for management action. This process extends from the origin of a discrete decision to its successful completion and incorporation into subsequent decisions. With this need established in an organization the next step is to initiate the process and secure the participation first of those in senior management positions and then of those in intermediate and junior positions. The simplest way for the chief executive of a company to begin is to put corporate objectives on the agenda of appropriate meetings of functional staff, management, or directors.

Consider, for example, a large, long-established, diversified, and increasingly unprofitable company. Its principal division was fully integrated from ownership of sources of raw materials to delivery of manufactured products to the consumer. Its president, after a day's discussion of the concept of strategy, asked his seven vice presidents, who had worked together for years, to submit to him a one-page statement expressing each officer's concept of the company's business, a summary statement of its strategy. He had in mind to go on from there, as users of this book have done in handling these cases. After identifying the strategy deducible from the company's established operations and taking advantage of their participation in resource allocation decisions, the vice presidents would be asked to evaluate apparent current strategy and make suggestions for its change and improvement. This first effort to establish a conscious process of strategic decision came to a sudden halt when the president found that it took weeks to get the statements submitted and that, once collected, they read like descriptions of seven different companies.

When discussion of current strategy resumed, a number of key issues emerged from a study of a central question—why so successful a company was seeing its margins shrink and its profits decline. The communication of similar issues to those assigned responsibility to deal with the function they affect was an obvious next step. The soundness of the company's recent diversification was assigned as a question to the division managers concerned. They found themselves asked to present a strategy for a scheduled achievement of adequate return or of orderly divestment. The alternative uses of the company's enormous resources of raw material were examined for the first time. The record of the research and development department, venerable in the industry for former achievements, was suddenly seen to be of little consequence in the competition that had grown up to take away market share. Decisions long since postponed or ignored began to seem urgent. Two divisions were discontinued, and expectations of improved performance began to alert the attention of division and functional managers throughout the organization to strategic issues.

Getting people who know the business to identify issues needing resolution, communicating these issues to all the managers affected, and programming action leading to resolution usually leads to the articulation of a strategy to which annual operating plans—otherwise merely numerical extrapolations of hope applied to past experience—can be successively related. It is not our purpose here, however, to present a master design for formal planning systems. This is a specialty of its own, which like all such other specialties, needs to be related to corporate strategy but not allowed to smother it.

When formal plans are prepared and submitted as the program to which performance is compared as a basis for evaluation, managers in intermediate position are necessarily involved in initiating projects within a concept of strategy rather than proceeding ad hoc from situation to situation. Senior managers can be guided in their approval of investment decisions by a pattern more rational than their hunches, their instinct for risk, and their faith in the track record of those making proposals, important as all these are. They have a key question to ask: what impact upon present and projected strategy will this decision make?

Sustaining the strategic process requires monitoring resource allocation with awareness of its strategic—as well as operational—consequences and its social and political, as well as financial, characteristics. Seeing to it that the process works right means that the roles of the middle-level general manager be known and appropriately supported.

Middle-level general managers occupy a role quite different from that of the senior general manager, relevant as is their experience as preparation for later advancement. With strategic language and summary corporate goals coming to them from their superiors and the language and problems of everyday operations coming to them from their subordinates, they have the responsibility of translating the operational proposals, improvisations, and piecemeal solutions of their subordinates into the strategic pattern suggested to them by their superiors.

Faced with the need to make reconciliation between short-term and long-term considerations, they must examine proposals and supervise operations with an eye to their effect on long-term development. As they transform general strategic directions into operating plans and programs, they are required to practice the overview of the general manager under the usual circumstance that their responsibility for balanced attention to short- and long-term needs and for bringing diverse everyday activities within the stream of evolving strategy far outruns their authority to require either change in strategy or to alter radically the product line of their division.

General managers at middle level, certainly in a crucial position to implement strategy in such a way as to advance it rather than depart from it, need to be protected against such distractions as performance evaluation systems overemphasizing short-term performance and to be supported continually in their duty of securing results which run beyond their authority to order certain outcomes. They need to learn how to interpret the signals they get as proposals they submit for top-management approval are accepted or turned down. Their superiors will be dependent upon their judgment as their proposals for new investment come in and will often be guided more by past performance or the desire to give them greater responsibility than by the detailed content of their proposals. Their seniors will do well then to realize the complexity of their juniors' positions and the necessity of the juniors being equal to the exigencies of making tactical reality subject to strategic guidance and to directing observation of operations toward appropriate amendment of strategy.

Developing the accuracy of strategic decision in a multiproduct, technically complex company requires ultimately direct attention to organization climate and individual development. The judgment required is to conduct operations against a demanding operating plan and to plan simultaneously for a changing future, to negotiate with superiors and subordinates the level of expected performance, and to see, in short, the strategic implications of what is happening in the company and in its environment. The capacity of the general manager, outlined early in this book, must be consciously cultivated as part of the process of managing the strategy process if the firm is to mature in its capacity to conduct its business and be able to recognize in time the changes in strategy it must effect.

Executive development, viewed from the perspective of the general manager, is essentially the nurturing of the generalist capabilities referred to throughout the text portions of this book. The management of the process of strategic decision must be concerned principally with continuous surveillance of the environment and development of the internal capabilities and distinctive competence of the company. The breadth of vision and the quality of judgment brought to the application of corporate capability to environmental opportunity are crucial. The senior managers who keep their organization involved continuously in appraising its performance against its goals, appraising its goals against the company's concept of its place in its industry and in society, and debating openly and often the continued validity of its strategy will find corporate attention to strategic questions gradually proving effective in letting the organization know what it is, what its activities are about, where it is going, and why its existence and growth are worth the best contributions of its members.

The chief executive of a company has as his or her highest function the management of a continuous process of strategic decision in which a succession of corporate objectives of ever-increasing appropriateness provides the means of economic contribution, the necessary commensurate return, and the opportunity for the men and women of the organization to live and develop through productive and rewarding careers.

The Strategic Function of the Board of Directors

If the highest function of the chief executive is the management of the future-oriented purposeful development of the enterprise, then it is necessarily the responsibility of the board of directors to see that this job is adequately done. Although in the common conception of corporate governance the board is ultimately responsible, its outside directors cannot themselves customarily originate the strategy they must approve. The chief recourse of directors ratifying strategy in highly complex situations is not to substitute their judgment for that of management but to see that the proposals presented to them have been properly prepared and can be defended as strategically consistent and superior to available alternatives. If they are flawed they are usually withdrawn for revision by management. Although the board is usually unable to originate strategy, its detachment from operations equips it to analyze developing strategic decisions with fresh objectivity and breadth of experience. It can be free of the management myopia sometimes produced by operations in places where keeping things going obscures the direction they are taking.

The cases concluding this book gave you at least a partial opportunity to examine the role and function of the board. Under pressure from the public, the Securities and Exchange Commission, and indirectly by the U.S. Senate's Subcommittee on Shareholders' Rights, the board of directors is undergoing revitalization as the only available source of legitimacy for corporate power and assurance of corporate responsibility, given the archaism of corporation law and the dispersed ownership of the large public corporation.

The consensus developing in the current revival of board effectiveness is that working boards will not only actively support, advise, and assist management but also will monitor and evaluate management's performance in the attainment of planned objectives. Boards nowadays are expected to exhibit in decision behavior their responsibility (while representing the economic interest of the shareholders) for the legality, integrity, and ethical quality of the corporation's activities and financial reporting and their sensitivity to the interests of segments of society legitimately concerned about corporate performance.

For our purposes here the central function of a working board is to review the management's formulation and implementation of strategy and to exercise final authority in ratifying with good reason management's adherence to established objectives and policy or in contributing constructively to management's recommendation for change.

It is now widely recognized that boards should be diversely composed, should consist largely of outside directors, and should structure themselves to make their monitoring functions practicable. All firms registered on the New York Stock Exchange, for example, must have audit committees as a condition of membership. Their functions are to recommend to the board and then to shareholders the choice of external auditors, to ensure to the extent possible that the company's control personnel are generating and reporting accurate and complete data fairly representing the financial performance of the company, and to ascertain that internal auditors are examining in detail those situations in which the company is vulnerable to fraud or improper behavior.

Despite the assumptions of some regulatory agency personnel, it is of course not possible for outside directors to detect fraud or identify questionable payments with their own eyes when well-intentioned and competent management auditors have not been able to do so. Their contribution is to inquire into the quality of intention, competence, and process, to observe the capability and command of information of those reporting to the committee, and to raise questions prompted by experience not available in the company. When necessary they recommend to the board replacement of controllers or change of auditors.

Executive compensation committees are expected to oversee the incentive salary programs of the companies and to set the compensation of the most senior managers, evaluating their performance in the course of that activity. A trend is developing toward the establishment of nominating committees to consider executive succession, board composition and performance and to make recommendations to the board of new members. The flow of information to these committees is supposed to economize the time and inform the judgment of the independent directors and to enable them to appraise the caliber of the company's management. The possibility of overwhelming outsiders with information is always imminent. Information useable by the board cannot usually be siphoned off the management information systems. Organization and selection to serve the special functions of the board are required.

In view of the difficulty entailed in enabling independent directors to pass judgment on strategic decisions, it is interesting to note that among the development of other committees (like public responsibility and legal affairs) strategy committees of the board are coming into wider use. It appears likely that as boards become aware of the need to relate approval of specific investment decisions to the purposes of the company, they may wish to focus the attention of some of the directors upon strategic questions now presented without prior detailed consideration to the full board.

Like members of the audit and compensation committees, board members assigned to give additional time to the evaluation of total strategy become familiar not necessarily with the detailed debates shaping specific strategic alternatives but with how the strategic process is managed in the company. You may wish to consider the extent to which familiarity with the strategy of the company and the ability to relate financial performance to it would affect the evaluation by the board of the chief executive officer's performance and to what extent it is available otherwise.

In most boards, at the moment, it is assumed that the independent directors will support the chief executive until it is necessary to remove him. Removal ordinarily comes late after disaster has struck or after early strategic mistakes have produced repeated irretrievable losses. The go/no-go dilemma, which does not apply in any other superior-subordinate relationship in the corporation, could be replaced by discussion and debate at board level of strategic questions presented to the board by the chief executive officer. When interim remediable dissatisfaction with the quality of this discussion appeared, advice to the chief executive officer could be offered in time for it to do some good. Chief executives' longevity is extended in some situations by their securing the participation of the board in crucial strategic decisions. When one of these fails after such participation, responsibility is shared by the board and the chief executive rather than borne by the latter alone. Routine ratification, without real discussion, does not secure the commitment of directors to any major decision. The attainment of proper participation is sometimes complicated by insecurity, unwillingness to share power, and lack of skill in board management on the part of chief executive officers.

The problem of securing competent outside director preparation and participation is compounded by the relationship resulting from the simple fact that independent directors have ordinarily owed their board membership to the chairman or chief executive officer they are supposed to evaluate. The active participation of nominating committees has increased the independence of boards, especially when the chief executive officers participating in the selection process have wanted such a result.

The management of effective boards of directors is a proper research topic in Business Policy and is indeed being studied. The power of strategy as a simplifying concept enabling independent directors to *know* the business (in a sense) without being *in* the business will one day be more widely tested at board level. If strategic management can be made less intuitive and more explicit, it will be possible for management directors and chief executive officers to identify existing strategy, evaluate it against the criteria we suggested at the beginning of this book, consider alternatives for improvement in the presence of the board, and make recommendations to a board equipped to make an intelligent critical response in strategic terms—that is, relating specific proposals to corporate strategy. It is the hope of the authors of this book that your practice in identification, evaluation, and recommendation of strategy in analysis of these cases has introduced you to the possibilities of effectiveness in your own future participation in strategic management at whatever level. The ability to sense the pattern of progress in the welter of operations is essential not only as an economizing analytical concept for outside directors but to junior executives who do not want to get lost among the trees and thickets through which they move.

Strategic management comes to its culmination in the chairmanship of effective boards. For the moment, the Securities and Exchange Commission, the Department of Justice, and the Federal Trade Commission appear to prefer the restructured and revitalized board of directors as the route to a kind of corporate governance sufficiently responsible to meet current concerns about autonomous management power. Most defenders of our mixed economic system prefer this approach to the introduction of new regulation. Voluntary adaptation to public expectations allows the special circumstances of each industry and company situation to be taken into account; regulation does not. On the other hand doing nothing remains a possible though unsatisfactory response to the call for voluntary action.

The mastery of the concept of strategy makes easier the kind of discussion in board rooms that helps managements make better decisions. It performs this function by reducing the world of detail to be considered to those central aspects of external environment and internal resources that affect the company and bear on the definition of its business. The special skill involved in perceiving and communicating the strategic significance of a business decision may be of the highest importance in engaging independent directors in the exercise of their assumed responsibility and in establishing active and effective boards as normal adjuncts to competent professional management. Such a development may reduce the likelihood that corporate governance be judged sufficiently irresponsible that radical legislative checks are imposed upon corporate freedom and initiative.

Index of Cases

This book has been set VideoComp, in 10 and 9 point Times Roman, leaded 2 points. Book section titles are 24 point Helvetica Bold and text titles are 20 point Helvetica Bold. Case titles are 18 point Times Roman Bold italic. The size of the type page is 28 picas by 48 picas.